# Group Dynamics

FIFTH EDITION

# Group Dynamics

FIFTH EDITION

**DONELSON R. FORSYTH**
University of Richmond

Australia • Brazil • Japan • Korea • Mexico • Singapore • Spain • United Kingdom • United States

**Group Dynamics, Fifth Edition**
**Donelson R. Forsyth**

Acquisitions Editor: Jon-David Hague

Assistant Editor: Paige Leeds

Editorial Assistant: Kelly Miller

Technology Project Manager: Rachel Guzman

Marketing Manager: Elisabeth Rhoden

Marketing Assistant: Molly Felz

Marketing Communications Manager: Talia Wise

Production Technology Analyst: Adam Grafa

Project Management, Editorial Production: Pre-Press PMG

Creative Director: Rob Hugel

Art Director: Vernon Boes

Print Buyer: Karen Hunt

Permissions Editor: Mardell Glinski-Schultz

Production Service: Pre-Press PMG

Copy Editor: Pre-Press PMG

Cover Designer: Eric Handel

Cover Image: J. A. Kraulis/Masterfile (700-017079)

Compositor: Pre-Press PMG



Library of Congress Control Number: 2009921212

International Student Edition:

ISBN-13: 978-0-495-80491-8

ISBN-10: 0-495-80491-6

**Wadsworth, Cengage Learning**
10 Davis Drive
Belmont, CA 94002-3098
USA

Cengage Learning products are represented in Canada by Nelson Education, Ltd.

For your course and learning solutions, visit **academic.cengage.com.**

Purchase any of our products at your local college store or at our preferred online store **www.ichapters.com.**

Printed in the United States of America
1 2 3 4 5 6 7 12 11 10 09

# Brief Contents

# Contents

# Preface

This book serves as an introduction to the theories, studies, and empirical findings pertinent to groups. More primer than comprehensive handbook, *Group Dynamics* only samples the results of scientific explorations of the nature of groups, but it strives to integrate, whenever possible, theory and research, basic science and application, classic and contemporary work, and psychological and sociological analyses of groups.

But why study groups? Why learn about the processes that unfold in interacting, dynamic groups? Why study theories that explain these processes? Why extend these theories to explain more and more about groups?

Because groups matter. On a practical level, much of the world's work is done by groups, so by understanding groups we move toward making them more efficient. If we want to improve productivity in a factory, problem solving in a boardroom, or learning in the classroom, we must understand groups. Groups, too, hold the key to solving such societal problems as racism, sexism, and international conflict. Any attempt to change society will succeed only if the groups within that society change.

But groups are also the keys to understanding people—why they think, feel, and act the way they do. Human behavior is so often group behavior that people cannot be studied in isolation, away from their families, friendship cliques, work groups, and so on. All kinds of societies—hunting/gathering, horticultural, pastoral, industrial, and postindustrial—are defined by the characteristics of the small groups that compose them. Societal forces, such as traditions, values, and norms, do not reach directly to individuals, but instead work through the groups to which each individual belongs.

Groups are also important for personal reasons. You will spend your entire life being in groups, getting out of groups, leading groups, and changing groups. Through your membership in groups, you define and confirm your values and beliefs and take on or refine a social identity. When you face uncertain situations, in groups, you gain reassuring information about your problems and security in companionship. In groups, you learn about relations with others, the types of impressions you make on others, and the ways in which you can relate with others more effectively. Groups influence you in consequential ways, so you ignore their influence at your own risk.

## FEATURES

Every attempt has been made to create a textbook that teaches group dynamics rather than one that simply reports basic principles and research findings. The chapters progress from basic issues and processes to the analysis of more specialized topics, but this order is somewhat arbitrary.

### Terms, Glossary, and Names

Key terms are set in boldface type and defined at the bottom of the page where they are first mentioned. Citations are given in the style of the American Psychological Association, and usually include investigators' last names and the date of the publication of the research report or book. A small number of researchers and theorists are mentioned by name in the text rather than in the citations; in such cases their first and last names are included.

### Outlines, Summaries, and Readings

The first page of each chapter asks several questions examined in that chapter, and also outlines the chapter's contents. Each chapter uses three levels of headings. The primary headings are printed in all capitals, the secondary headings are printed in capital and lowercase letters, and the tertiary headings begin individual paragraphs. Each chapter ends with a summary and a list of sources to consult for more information.

### Focuses

Each chapter includes boxed inserts that examine an empirical, theoretical, or practical aspect of groups. These boxes focus on key themes that are woven through the book, such as the impact of computer-mediated communications on group interaction and the differences between men and women when in groups.

### Cases

Chapters 3–17 use case studies to illustrate and integrate the chapter's contents. The chapter on group formation, for example, focuses on the impressionists, and the chapter dealing with leadership highlights the work of an outstanding leader. All the cases are or were real groups rather than hypothetical ones, and the incidents described are documented events that occurred within the group (although some literary license was taken for the Chapter 7 case).

## CHANGES FROM THE FOURTH EDITION

This book's aims have changed over the years. I wrote the first chapters of the first edition of this book in 1979. Following in the footsteps of such scholars as Marvin Shaw (author of *Group Dynamics: The Psychology of Groups*, 1978) and Paul Hare (*Handbook of Small Group Research*, 1976), I sought to write a relatively comprehensive summary of the key principles and findings in group dynamics. Writing now, some 30 years later, I cannot hope for the book to be comprehensive, for groups have been the focus of hundreds of prolific and talented researchers in such fields as communications, computer science, management and organizational behavior, social psychology, and sociology. A comprehensive review would require 17 volumes, rather than the 17 chapters in the current work.

This book's new aim is more circumspect: to encourage the reader to overcome the natural tendency to consider individuals as primary causes and instead begin to consider in more detail complex interpersonal, group-level processes. Each chapter returns to this theme by showing how most forms of human activity—from social identity to influence and power to group performance and productivity—can be best understood when group-level processes are considered.

This book also bears the stamp of my discipline's paradigm. Since I'm a social psychologist, I stress influence and interpersonal processes in general, and tend to view other processes, such as productivity, communication, and mental health, through this lens. The text reviews hundreds of empirical studies of group processes, but most studies extend a social psychological understanding of groups. This emphasis on theory-grounded knowledge sometimes means that less central but nonetheless interesting topics are slighted, but whenever possible the curious reader is referred to other sources for additional information.

Reviewing the work done by my distinguished colleagues in the field of group dynamics has left me in awe of the scope of the field itself. Judging from the quantity and quality of new work on groups, groups remain a central topic of concern in many disciplines, and this revision strives to communicate this excitement to its newest initiates. This assessment of the field's bright future is also based on societal developments that have changed the way people live and work in groups. Societies that were once viewed as mere collections of individuals are gradually being transformed into cultures that embrace a more collectivistic orientation. Corporations continue to evolve into multinational organizations, and with that global perspective comes increased interest in harnessing the power of groups for productive purposes. As society adjusts to a more technological and united world, and as the economic success of countries springs from group decisions and work team efforts, understanding groups and their dynamics will become increasingly relevant, practical, and important.

## ACKNOWLEDGEMENTS

Most things in this world are accomplished by groups rather than by single individuals working alone. This book is no exception. Although I am personally responsible for the ideas presented in this book, many colleagues have provided me with indispensable comments, suggestions, and materials. They include Dom Abrams, Traci Craig, Brent Elwood, Lowell Gaertner, Stan Gully, Verlin Hinsz, Tim Hopthrow, Chuck Huff, Steve Karau, Jared Kenworthy, Norbert Kerr, John Levine, Julian Lichtsteiner, Glenn Littlepage, Susan Losh, Rebecca MacNair-Semands, Richard Moreland, Paul Moxnes, Linda Muldoon, Randolph New, Ernest O'Boyle, Dave Ouellette, Randall Peterson, Anthony Pratkanis, John Robinson, Natalia Sanders, Jim Sidanius, Royce Singleton, Richard Sorrentino, Dennis Stewart, Paul Story, Clifford Stott, Tojo Thatchenkery, Thomas Treadwell, and Will Wattles.

Groups, too, helped me along the way. My social psychological colleagues at the University of Richmond include Jeni Burnette, Al Goethals, Crystal Hoyt, and Scott Allison, and I have benefited from their wise counsel on many topics. My classes at the University of Richmond provided me with the opportunity to refine my presentation of the materials, for my students were all too eager to give me feedback about ambiguities and weaknesses. I particularly appreciate the inputs from my advanced group dynamics class taught in the Fall of 2007. They suffered through a variety of readings and activities associated with such topics as entitativity, team building, and groupthink. The members of the production teams at Wadsworth/Cengage, including Jon-David Hague, Vernon Boes, Trina Tom, and at Pre-PressPMG, including Abigail Greshik, also deserve special thanks for their capable efforts.

My most important group—my family—also deserves special acknowledgement. They provided me with a stream of much-needed respites from the marathon revision sessions, confirming again and again what they say about groups and well-being. So, a special thanks to Claire, David, Rachel, and Carmen (the family dog).

—Donelson R. Forsyth

1

# Introduction to Group Dynamics

## CHAPTER OVERVIEW

The tendency to join with others in groups is perhaps the single most important characteristic of humans, and the processes that unfold within these groups leave an indelible imprint on their members and on society. Group dynamics are the influential processes that take place in groups and also the discipline devoted to the scientific analysis of those dynamics.

- What is a group?
- What are some common characteristics of groups?
- Are there different types of groups?
- What assumptions guide researchers in their studies of groups and their processes?
- What fields and what topics are included in the scientific study of group dynamics?

## CHAPTER OUTLINE

Who can deny the power of groups? Although some may bemoan the growing alienation of individuals from the small social groups that once linked them securely to society-at-large, the single man or woman who has no connection to other men and women is an extraordinarily rare human being. People are in many respects individuals seeking personal, private objectives, yet they are also members of groups that constrain them, guide them, and sustain them. Members of the species *Homo sapiens* are capable of surviving alone, but few choose to, for virtually all human activities—working, learning, worshiping, relaxing, playing, and even sleeping—occur in groups. To understand people, we must understand their groups.

Sages, scholars, and laypersons have been puzzling over **group dynamics**—the actions, processes, and changes that occur within groups and between groups—for centuries. Why, they asked, do humans so frequently join with others in groups? How do members coordinate their efforts and energies? What factors give rise to a sense of cohesion, esprit de corps, and a marked distrust for those outside the group? And how do groups and their leaders hold sway over members? Their inquiries into such questions provide the scientific basis for the field of group dynamics, which is the scientific discipline devoted to studying groups and group process.

This book uses the results of that work to unravel many of the mysteries of groups. It begins with this chapter's two orienting, but essential, questions. First, *what is a group?* What distinguishes a group from a mere collection of people? What features can we expect to find in most groups, and what kinds of processes provide the foundation for their dynamics? Second, *what is this field of study we are calling group dynamics?* What assumptions guide researchers as they describe, analyze, and compare the various groups that populate the planet?

---

**group dynamics** The influential actions, processes, and changes that occur within and between groups over time; also, the scientific study of those processes.

## THE NATURE OF GROUPS

Fish, swimming in synchronized unison, are called a *school.* A pack of foraging baboons is a *troupe.* A threesome of crows cawing their way through a meadow is a *murder.* A *gam* is a group of whales. But what is a collection of human beings called? A *group.*

### What is a Group?

Take a moment and make a mental list of all the groups of which you are a part. Would you include your family? The people you work or study with? How about your neighbors, or people who used to be neighbors but moved away? If you use the Internet, do you consider the people you text message, email, or "friend" in Facebook to be a group? How about people of your same sex, race, and citizenship, and those who share your political beliefs? Are African American men, Canadians, and Republicans groups? Are you in a romantic relationship? Did you include you and your partner on your list of groups? Which collections of humans are groups and which are not?

Theorists are not of one mind when it comes to defining the word *group.* Some stress the importance of communication between members; others highlight the key role played by mutual dependence. Still others suggest that a shared purpose or goal is what turns a mere aggregate of individuals into a bona fide group. Most, however, would agree that a group requires at least two people. With the exception of individuals with extremely rare psychological disturbances, it takes two people to make one group: you cannot be a group until you join with another person. Second, groups connect people to one another. We understand intuitively that three persons seated in separate rooms working on a long list of math problems can hardly be considered a group; they are not linked in any way to each other. If, however, we create a connection among them, then these three individuals can be considered a rudimentary group. Third, in most cases the connection is a socially meaningful one. Members of a group are not linked by surface similarities or their accidental gathering in a specific location but by relatively enduring personal relationships that enfold the members within a collective. A consanguine family is a group because the members are connected, not just by genetic similarities but also by social and emotional bonds that are personally meaningful to each member. People who work together are linked not only by the collaborative tasks that they must complete collectively but also by friendships, alliances, and inevitable antagonisms. Students in a class all recognize that they are members of a smaller subset within the larger educational community and that those who are not in their class are outsiders. Thus, a **group** is *two or more individuals who are connected by and within social relationships.*

**Two or More Individuals** A group can range in size from two members to thousands of members. Very small collectives, such as dyads (two members) and triads (three members) are groups, but so are very large collections of people, such as mobs, crowds, and congregations (Simmel, 1902). On average, however, most groups tend to be relatively small in size, ranging from two to seven members (Mullen, 1987). One researcher who diligently counted the number of people in 7405 informal, spontaneously formed groups discovered that most were small, usually with only two or three members. Deliberately formed groups, such as those created in government or work settings, were also small, with an average of 2.3 members (James, 1951). When observers watched as individuals and groups ate their meals in a cafeteria on a college campus, they noticed that the majority of the groups were dyads, particularly when the cafeteria was crowded (Jorgenson & Dukes, 1976; see Figure 1.1). Although groups come in all shapes and sizes, they tend to "gravitate to the smallest size, two" (Hare, 1976, p. 215).

A group's size influences its nature in many ways, for a group with only two or three members possesses many unique characteristics simply because it includes so few members. The dyad is, by definition, the only group that dissolves when one member leaves and the only group that can never be broken down into subgroups (Levine & Moreland, 1995). The members of dyads are also sometimes linked by a unique and powerful type of relationship—love—that makes their dynamics more intense than those found in other groups. Larger groups also have unique qualities: the members are rarely connected directly to all other members, subgroups are very likely to form, and one or more leaders may be needed to organize and guide the group. By definition, however, all are considered groups.

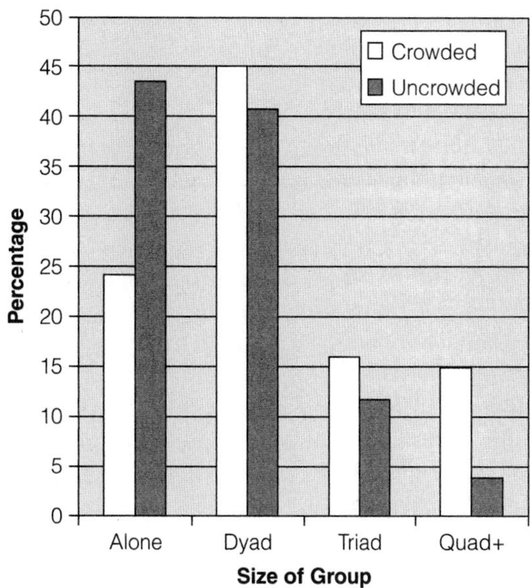


**FIGURE 1.1** The percentage of people who dined alone, in dyads, triads, and larger groups (quads) in a crowded or uncrowded cafeteria.

SOURCE: "Deindividuation as a Function of Density and Group Members," by D. O. Jorgenson and F. O. Dukes, *Journal of Personality and Social Psychology,* 1976, *34*, 24–29. Copyright 1976 by the American Psychological Association.

**Who Are Connected** The members of any given group are networked together like a series of interconnected computers. These connections, or ties, may be based on strong bonds, like the links between the members of a family or a clique of close friends. The links may also be relatively weak ones that are easily broken with the passage of time or the occurrence of relationship-damaging events. Even weak ties, however, can create robust outcomes,

---

**group** Two or more individuals who are connected by and within social relationships.

such as when a group member you hardly know provides you with critical information that is common knowledge in that person's social circles (Granovetter, 1973).

The larger the group, the more ties are needed to join members to each other and to the group. The maximum number of ties within a group in which everyone is linked to everyone else is given by the equation $n(n-1)/2$, where n is the number of people in the group. Only one relationship is needed to create a dyad, but 10 ties would be needed to join each member of a 5-person group to every other member, 45 for a 10-person group, and 190 relationships for a 20-person group. Note, too, that twice as many ties are needed if they are *directed* relations; rather than just A is linked to B, but A links to B and B links to A. Hence, many ties between members within the boundaries of the group are indirect ones. Person A might, for example, talk directly to B but B may talk only to C, so that A is linked to C only through B. But even in large groups, members often feel connected to the majority of the group's members and to the group as a whole (Katz et al., 2005).

**By and Within Social Relationships** Definitions of the word *group* vary, but many stress one key consideration: relationships among the members. Thus, "a group is a collection of individuals who have relations to one another" (Cartwright & Zander, 1968, p. 46); "a group is a social unit which consists of a number of individuals who stand in (more or less) definite status and role relationships to one another" (Sherif & Sherif, 1956, p. 144); and a group is "a bounded set of patterned relations among members" (Arrow, McGrath, & Berdahl, 2000, p. 34). Just as people who are friends are joined in *friendship*, or all the senior members of a law firm are part of a *partnership*, people in a group are said to be linked by their **membership**.

Group relationships link each member to one another and to the group as a whole. They also define who is in the group itself, for groups, unlike **networks**, have boundaries. To become part of a network a person must establish a link with a person who is already in the network. Business professionals say they are *networking* when they are busy establishing ties with other individuals. Groups, in contrast, usually have stable but permeable boundaries—sometimes unstated but also sometimes explicitly defined—that differentiate between those who are within the group and those who are outside of the group. As social psychologist Henri Tajfel (1972) explained, group members share a common identity with one another. They know who is in their group, who is not, and what qualities are typical of insiders and outsiders. This perception of themselves as members of the same group or social category—this **social identity**—creates a sense of *we* and *us*, as well as a sense of *they* (Abrams et al., 2005). Social identity can be thought of as the "sum total of a person's social identifications, where the latter represents socially significant social categorizations internalized as aspects of the self-concept" (Turner, 1985, p. 527).

This definition of a group, two or more individuals who are connected by and within social relationships, although consistent with many theoretical perspectives on groups, is but one definition of many (Greenwood, 2004). The definition is also somewhat hopeful, for it suggests that collections of people can be easily classified into two categories—group and nongroup—when in actuality such classification is rarely so clear-cut. Some groups, such as work teams or families, easily meet the definition's "by and within social relationships" requirement, but others do not. For example, five strangers waiting on a city sidewalk for a bus may not seem to fit the definition of a group, but they may become a group when one passenger asks the others if they can change a dollar bill. And

---

**membership** The state of being a part of, or included within, a social group.

**network** A set of interconnected individuals or groups; more generally, any set of social or nonsocial objects that are linked by relational ties.

**social identity** Aspects of the self-concept that derive from relationships and memberships in groups; in particular, those qualities that are held in common by two or more people who recognize that they are members of the same group or social category.

**Focus 1.1 Are Online Groups Real Groups?**

*Members only may post or reply to messages but everyone is welcome to visit.*
— Message at http://maritimeracers.proboards33.com

When people think of a group they tend to think of a gathering of individuals in some specific location. A family picnicking, a football team practicing, a team of workers assembling a machine, or a clique of friends gossiping about the weekend's events; these are groups. Some groups, however, do not fit people's intuitive conception of the typical group. Consider, for example, 10 people who never see each other face-to-face but only communicate with one another using computers connected to the Internet. Are these people members of a network or a group?

The Internet has transformed people's lives, including their groups. Friendship cliques, support groups, work teams, families, clubs, and even lovers need not meet face-to-face, but may instead congregate via the World Wide Web. This unique, "virtual" environment in which these groups meet undoubtedly influences their dynamics: members of an online group will not interact in precisely the same way as will members of a group that meet together "offline" (face-to-face). Yet, in many cases, their dynamics are similar to those of more traditional, face-to-face groups. Such groups develop norms, admit new members, identify goals, and experience conflict. Members of such groups take the lead, offer suggestions, ask questions, and influence one another. New members must often suffer through a period of initiation; for example, members of many multiplayer game worlds are given the derisive label of *newb* and are ignored until they develop their skills. Members also identify with their online groups and react differently to those who are in their groups and those who are not (McKenna & Seidman, 2005).

Are Internet-based groups true groups? This question is, at core, an empirical one. As researchers explore the dynamics of these groups, they will likely identify aspects of these groups that are consistent with what is known about groups in general: how they form, how members interact with one another, and how they perform over time. But, given their unique setting, researchers will likely also discover these groups are unique in some ways. If their distinctiveness outweighs their similarities to traditional groups, then a case could be made to place Internet groups in their own category. However, until research suggests otherwise, we will cautiously consider online groups to be groups.

what about people playing a MMORPG (Massively Multiplayer Online Role-Playing Game) together on the Internet? As Focus 1.1 asks, are people who are connected to one another by computer-based communication networks a group?

The definition is also limited by its brevity. It defines the barest requirements of a group, and so it leaves unanswered other questions about groups. If we want to understand a group we need to ask many more questions: What do the people do in the group? Does the group have a leader? How unified is the group? How has the group changed over time? Deciding that a collection of people qualifies as a group is only the beginning of understanding that group.

## Describing Groups

Each one of the billions of groups that exist at this moment is a unique configuration of individuals, processes, and relationships. A group of five students in a university library reviewing material for an upcoming test displays tendencies and qualities that are unlike any other study group that has ever existed or ever will exist. The family living at 103 Main Street is different in dozens of ways from the family that lives just next door to them. The team of workers building automobiles in Anytown, U.S.A., is unlike any other team of workers in any other factory in the world.

But all groups, despite their distinctive characteristics, possess common properties and dynamics. When researchers study a group, they must go beyond its unique qualities to consider characteristics that appear with consistency in most groups. Some of these qualities, such as what the group members are doing and the tasks they are attempting, are relatively obvious ones. Other qualities, such as the degree of interdependence among members or the group's overall unity, are harder to discern. Here we start with group's easily detectable qualities before turning to those that are often hidden from view.

**Interaction** Robert F. Bales (1950, 1999) spent his career searching for an answer to the question, "What do people do when they are in groups?" He would find naturally existing groups or create groups in his laboratory and then watch them closely. As he expected, these groups' interactions were quite varied. Group members exchanged information with each other, through both verbal and nonverbal communication; they got into arguments, talked over issues, and made decisions. They upset each other, gave one another help and support, and took advantage of each other's weaknesses. They worked together to accomplish difficult tasks, but they sometimes slacked off when they thought others would not notice. Group members taught each other new things and they touched each other literally and emotionally. Group interaction is as varied as human behavior itself.

Bales, however, eventually concluded that the countless interactions he had witnessed were of two basic types. **Relationship interaction** (or *socioemotional interaction*) pertains to the interpersonal, social side of group life. If group members falter and need support, others will buoy them up with kind words, suggestions, and other forms of help. When group members disagree with the others, they are often roundly criticized and made to feel foolish. When a coworker wears a new suit or outfit, others in his or her work unit notice it and offer compliments or criticisms. Such actions sustain or undermine the emotional bonds linking the members to one another and to the group. **Task interaction**, in contrast, includes all group behavior that is focused principally on the group's work, projects, plans, and goals. In most groups, members must coordinate their various skills, resources, and motivations so that the group can make a decision, generate a product, or achieve a victory. When a jury reviews each bit of testimony, a committee argues over the best course of action to take, or a family plans its summer vacation, the group's interaction is task focused. We will review the method that Bales developed for objectively recording these types of interactions, his *Interaction Process Analysis* (*IPA*), in Chapter 2.

**Goals** Groups usually exist for a reason. A team strives to outperform other teams in competitions. A study group wants to help members get better grades. A jury makes a decision about guilt or innocence. The members of a congregation seek religious and spiritual experiences. In each case, the members of the group are united in their pursuit of common goals. In groups, people solve problems, create products, develop standards, communicate knowledge, have fun, perform arts, create institutions, and even ensure their safety from attacks by other groups. Put simply, groups make it easier to attain our goals. For this reason, much of the world's work is done by groups rather than by individuals.

Just as Bales identified the basic types of interactions that occur within groups, so Joseph E. McGrath's (1984) **circumplex model of group tasks** brings order to the many goal-related activities that groups undertake. McGrath's model distinguishes among four basic group goals: *generating* ideas or plans, *choosing* a solution, *negotiating* a solution to a conflict, or *executing* (performing) a task. As Figure 1.2 indicates, each of these basic categories can be further subdivided, yielding a total of eight basic goal-related activities.

- *Generating*: Groups that concoct the strategies they will use to accomplish their goals (*Type 1: planning tasks*) or to create altogether new ideas and approaches to their problems (*Type 2: creativity tasks*).

---

**relationship interaction** Actions performed by group members that relate to or influence the emotional and interpersonal bonds within the group, including both positive actions (social support, consideration) and negative actions (criticism, conflict).

**task interaction** Actions performed by group members that pertain to the group's projects, tasks, and goals.

**circumplex model of group tasks** A conceptual taxonomy developed by Joseph McGrath that orders group tasks in a circular pattern based on two continua: cooperative–competitive and conceptual–behavioral.

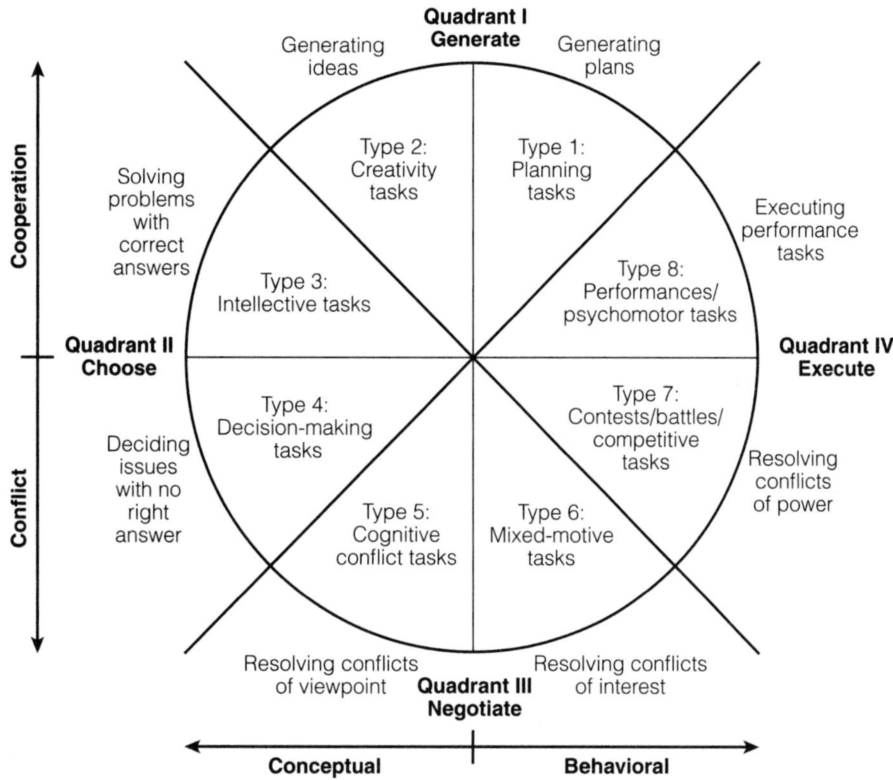


**FIGURE 1.2** McGrath's task circumplex model of group tasks. The theory identifies eight basic activities undertaken by groups—planning, creating, solving problems, making decisions, forming judgments, resolving conflicts, competing, and performing—and arranges them in a circle based on two dimensions: executing–choosing and generating–negotiating. Tasks in the upper four quadrants require cooperation among members, whereas conflict is more likely when groups undertake those tasks in the lower quadrants. Tasks on the right side of the circle are behavioral ones, whereas those on the left side of the circle are more intellectual, conceptual tasks.

SOURCE: McGrath, *Groups: Interaction and Performance,* 1st, © 1984. Reproduced by permission of Pearson Education, Inc., Upper Saddle River, New Jersey.

- *Choosing*: Groups that make decisions about issues that have correct solutions (*Type 3: intellective tasks*) or questions that can be answered in many ways (*Type 4: decision-making tasks*).
- *Negotiating*: Groups that must resolve differences of opinion among members regarding their goals or decisions (*Type 5: cognitive conflict tasks*) or resolve competitive disputes among members (*Type 6: mixed-motive tasks*).
- *Executing*: Groups that do things, including taking part in competitions (*Type 7: contests/battles/competitive tasks)* or working together to create some product or carry out collective actions (*Type 8: Performances/psychomotor tasks).*

McGrath's model also distinguishes between conceptual–behavioral goals and cooperation–conflict goals. Some of the goals that groups pursue require them to take action (Tasks 1, 6, 7, and 8). Others focus on deliberation, for they require a conceptual review (Tasks 2, 3, 4, and 5). Some of the tasks are purely collaborative ones—they require that group members work together to accomplish their goals (Types 1, 2,

3, and 8). Others goals, in contrast, tend to pit individuals and/or groups against each other (Types 4, 5, 6, and 7). Some groups perform tasks from nearly all of McGrath's categories, whereas others concentrate on only one subset of goals (Arrow & McGrath, 1995).

**Interdependence** When people join groups they soon discover that they are no longer masters of their own fate. The acrobat on the trapeze will drop to the net unless her teammate catches her outstretched arms. The assembly line worker is unable to complete his work until he receives the unfinished product from a worker further up the line. The business executive's success and salary is determined by how well her staff completes its work. She can fulfill her personal tasks skillfully, but if her staff fails, then she fails as well. In such situations, members are obligated or responsible to other group members, for they provide each other with support and assistance. This **interdependence** means that members *depend* on one another; their outcomes, actions, thoughts, feelings, and experiences are determined in part by others in the group.

Some groups create only the potential for interdependence among members. The outcomes of people standing in a queue at the checkout counter in a store, audience members in a darkened theater, or the congregation of a large mega-church are hardly intertwined at all. Other groups, such as gangs, families, sports teams, and military squads, create far higher levels of interdependency since members reliably and substantially influence one another's outcomes over a long period of time and in a variety of situations. In such groups the influence of one member on another also tends to be mutual; member A can influence B, but B can also influence A in return (see Figure 1.3). In other groups, in contrast, influence is more unequal and more one-directional. In a business, for example, the boss may determine how employees spend their time, what kind of rewards they experience, and even the duration of their membership in the group. These employees can influence their boss to a degree, but the boss's influence is nearly unilateral: The boss influences them to a greater degree than they influence the boss.

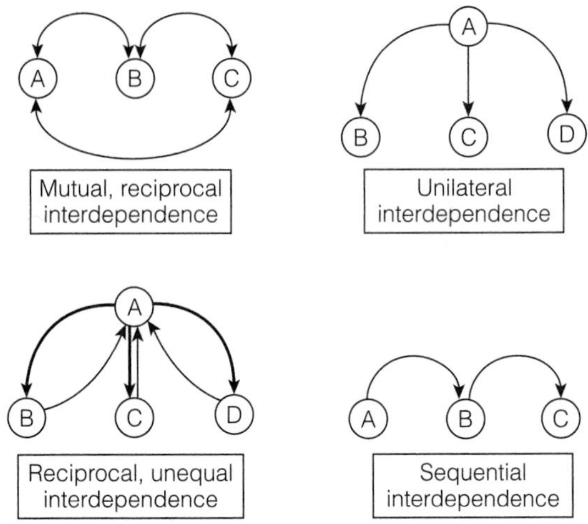


**FIGURE 1.3** Examples of interdependence among group members. Interdependence results when the outcomes of one or more group members are determined, in part, by other group members. Influence is sometimes mutual and reciprocal: all members influence one another. But influence can be unilateral, as when a leader influences others but is not influenced by them. More typically, influence is reciprocal but unequal; a leader's influence over followers is substantially greater than followers' influence on the leader. In some cases influence is sequential, as when A influences B who influences C.

**Structure** Group members are not connected to one another at random, but in organized and predictable patterns. In all but the most ephemeral groups, patterns and regularities emerge that determine the kinds of actions that are permitted or condemned: who talks to whom, who likes whom and who dislikes whom, who can be counted on to perform particular tasks, and whom others look to for guidance and help. These regularities combine to generate

---

**interdependence** The state of being dependent to some degree on other people, as when one's outcomes, actions, thoughts, feelings, and experiences are determined in whole or in part by others.

**group structure**—the complex of roles, norms, and intermember relations that organizes the group. **Roles**, for example, specify the general behaviors expected of people who occupy different positions within the group. The roles of *leader* and *follower* are fundamental ones in many groups, but other roles—information seeker, information giver, elaborator, procedural technician, encourager, compromiser, harmonizer—may emerge in any group (Benne & Sheats, 1948). Group members' actions and interactions are also shaped by their group's **norms**—consensual standards that describe what behaviors should and should not be performed in a given context.

Roles, norms, and other structural aspects of groups, although unseen and often unnoticed, lie at the heart of their most dynamic processes. When people join a group, they initially spend much of their time trying to come to terms with the requirements of their role. If they cannot meet the role's demand, they might not remain a member for long. Norms within a group are defined and renegotiated over time, and conflicts often emerge as members violate norms. In group meetings, the opinions of members with higher status carry more weight than those of the rank-and-file members. When several members form a *subgroup* within the larger group, they exert more influence on the rest of the group than they would individually. When people manage to place themselves at the hub of the group's information exchange patterns, their influence over others also increases. If you had to choose only one aspect of a group to study, you would probably learn the most by studying its structure.

**Unity** Just as a book is not just a set of sequenced pages or a cake just sugar, flour, and other ingredients mixed together and baked, so a group is not just the individuals who compose it. A group, viewed holistically, is a unified whole; an entity formed when interpersonal forces bind the members together in a single unit with boundaries that mark who is in the group and who is outside of it. In consequence, when we speak about groups we refer to them as single objects: for example, a gang *is* menacing or the club *meets* tomorrow.

This quality of "groupness," or solidarity, is determined, in part, by **group cohesion**. In physics, the molecular integrity of matter is known as *cohesiveness*. When matter is cohesive, the particles that constitute it bond together so tightly that they resist any competing attractions. But when matter is not cohesive, it tends to disintegrate over time as the particles drift away or adhere to some other nearby object. Similarly, in human groups, cohesion is the integrity, solidarity, and unity of a group. All groups require a modicum of cohesiveness, else the group would disintegrate and cease to exist as a group (Dion, 2000).

Groupness is also related to **entitativity**. Even though an aggregation of individuals may not be very cohesive, those who observe the group—and even the members themselves—may believe that the group is a single, unified entity. Entitativity, then, is how unified the group appears to be to the perceiver; that is, perceived unity rather than the group's actual unity. Were you to observe six people playing poker or a family of five picnicking in a park you would likely conclude that both were groups; they seem to be cohesive, impermeable units. But what about the audience at the movie theatre? Thousands of spectators at a soccer match? Onlookers may conclude that that they are not groups at all, but just unrelated individuals who happen to be in the same place. Entitativity is cohesiveness perceived, and therefore often is in the eye of the beholder.

What factors determine a group's entitativity? Donald Campbell (1958a), who originally coined the word *entitativity*, suggested that a group's entitativity depends on certain perceptual cues that

---

**group structure** The underlying pattern of roles, norms, and relations among members that organizes groups.
**role** A coherent set of behaviors expected of people who occupy specific positions within a group.
**norm** A consensual and often implicit standard that describes what behaviors should and should not be performed in a given context.

**group cohesion** The strength of the bonds linking individuals to and in the group.
**entitativity** As described by Donald Campbell, the extent to which an assemblage of individuals is perceived to be a group rather than an aggregation of independent, unrelated individuals; the quality of being an entity.

perceivers rely on intuitively to decide if an aggregation of individuals is a true group or just a collection of people. For example, the spectators at a football game may seem to be a disorganized mass of individuals who happen to be in the same place at the same time, but the tendency of the spectators to shout the same cheer, express similar emotions, and move together to create a "wave" gives them entitativity. Entitativity, according to Campbell, is substantially influenced by

- *Common fate*: Do the individuals experience the same or interrelated outcomes?
- *Similarity*: Do the individuals perform similar behaviors or resemble one another?
- *Proximity*: How close together are the individuals in the aggregation?

Consider four people seated at a table in a library. Is this a group? They could be four friends studying together, or just four independent individuals. To answer the question, you must consider their common fate, similarity, and proximity. The principle of common fate predicts that the degree of "groupness" you attribute to the cluster would increase if, for example, all the members began laughing together or moved closer to one another (Castano, Yzerbyt, & Bourguignon, 2002). Your confidence that this cluster was a real group would also be bolstered if you noticed that all four were reading from the same textbook or were wearing the same fraternity shirt. Finally, if the members got up and left the room together, you would become even more certain that you were watching a group (Ip, Chiu, & Wan, 2006). As Focus 1.2 explains, labeling an aggregation a *group* is not just a matter of semantics, since people respond differently to groups than they do to clusters of individuals.

## Types of Groups

The qualities summarized in Table 1.1—interaction, goals, interdependence of members, structure, and unity—are typical of most groups, but even more striking are the many ways groups *differ* from one another. Groups come in a variety of shapes and sizes and perform functions that are vast and varied, so the differences among them are as noteworthy as their similarities. Here we consider four basic types of groups, but admit that these four are only a sample of the many types of groups that have been identified by theorists.

**Primary Groups** In 1860, two young, struggling artists, Claude Monet and Camille Pissarro, met by happenstance and immediately became friends. They spent hours together sharing their ideas about art and politics, and soon other like-minded artists joined with them. The group, challenged by those who criticized their work, became highly unified. They met regularly, each Thursday and Sunday, in a café in Paris to discuss technique, subject matter, and artistic philosophies. They often painted as a group, sharing ideas about style and technique. When one of them fell ill or faced financial crises, the others were there to provide support. In time their approach was recognized by the art community as a new school of painting and the group became famous: they were the impressionists (Farrell, 2001; see Chapter 4).

**Primary groups**, such as family, friends, or tight-knit peer groups, are relatively small, personally meaningful groups that are highly unified. The members are very involved in the group, so much so that they feel a part of something larger than themselves. Because the members interact with one another regularly, and usually face-to-face with many other members present, they know each other very well. Even when the group is not convened, members nonetheless know that they are "in" the group, and they consider the group to be a very important part of their lives.

---

**primary group** A small, long-term group, such as families and friendship cliques, characterized by face-to-face interaction, solidarity, and high levels of member-to-group interdependence and identification; Charles Cooley believed such groups serve as the primary source of socialization for members by shaping their attitudes, values, and social orientation.

**Focus 1.2 When Is Seeing (a group) Believing (in the group)?**

*He stood up, and then others stood up and ranged themselves behind him. They looked like a gang now, with their captain out in front to lead them. Riccio sat where he was, looking up at one face after another.*

—James F. Short (1968, p. 39) *Gang Delinquency and Delinquent Subcultures*

W. I. Thomas once stated that "if men define situations as real, they are real in their consequences" (Thomas & Thomas, 1928, p. 572). This statement, now known as the **Thomas Theorem**, has been called "the single most consequential sentence ever put in print by an American sociologist" (Merton, 1976, p. 174). A corollary, for groups, would be: if people define groups as real, they are real in their consequences. Once people think an aggregate of people is a true group—one with entitativity, as Donald Campbell (1958a) suggested—then the group will have important interpersonal consequences for those in the group and those who are observing it.

People act differently when they are members of a group that they feel is high in entitativity. Group members are much more likely to identify with such groups (Castano, Yzerbyt, & Bourguignon, 2002), and this tendency is particularly strong when people feel uncertain about themselves and the correctness of their beliefs (Hogg et al., 2007). Because proximity influences entitativity, people display more group-level reactions when they meet face-to-face in a single location than when they meet across long distances in telephone conference calls or through computer-mediated discussions (Kiesler & Cummings, 2002). When researchers repeatedly told women working in isolation that they were nonetheless members of a group, the women accepted this label and later rated themselves more negatively after their "group" failed (Zander, Stotland, & Wolfe, 1960). Groups that are high in entitativity also tend to be more cohesive (Zyphur & Islam, 2006) and the members of such groups may also experience enhanced feelings of social well-being (Sani, Bowe, & Herrera, 2008).

People also think differently about entitative groups and the people in them. Entitativity likely plays a role in stereotyping and prejudice, for people are more likely to make sweeping judgments about specific individuals based on their membership in a group provided that entitativity is high rather than low (Rydell et al., 2007). People tend to think members of such groups are basically interchangeable (Crawford, Sherman, & Hamilton, 2002), and they more quickly draw comparisons between them (Pickett, 2001). Observers are more likely to hold the members of such groups collectively responsible for the actions of one of the group members (Denson et al., 2006), and they find the arguments offered by such groups to be more persuasive than those of individual members (Rydell & McConnell, 2005). A sense of **essentialism** tends to permeate perceivers' beliefs about groups that are high in entitativity, for people think that such groups have deep, relatively unchanging essential qualities that give rise to their more surface-level characteristics (Haslam, Rothschild, & Ernst, 2002; Yzerbyt, Judd, & Corneille, 2004).

In sum, all groups "are not created equal in the mind's eye" (Prentice & Miller, 2007, p. 202). Those who proclaim, "We are a group" or say, "They are a group" perceive the world differently than those who see themselves surrounded only by individuals rather than groups.

Sociologist Charles Horton Cooley (1909) referred to these kinds of groups as primary groups because they are typically the first group people join, but also because they fulfill such an important role in people's lives. Cooley thought that primary groups protect members from harm, care for them when they are ill, and provide them with shelter

---

**Thomas Theorem** The theoretical premise, put forward by W. I. Thomas, which maintains that an individual's understanding of a social situation, even if incorrect, will determine how he or she will act in the situation; "If men define situations as real, they are real in their consequences" (Thomas & Thomas, 1928, p. 572).

**essentialism** The belief that all things, including individuals and groups, have a basic nature which makes them what they are and distinguishes them from others; this basic essence, even though hidden, is relatively unchanging and gives rise to surface-level qualities.

**TABLE 1.1 Characteristics of Groups**

| Feature | Description |
|---|---|
| Interaction | Groups create, organize, and sustain relationship and task interactions among members |
| Goals | Groups have instrumental purposes, for they facilitate the achievement of aims or outcomes sought by the members |
| Interdependence | Group members depend on one another, in that each member influences and is influenced by each other member |
| Structure | Groups are organized, with each individual connected to others in a pattern of relationships, roles, and norms |
| Unity | Groups are cohesive social arrangements of individuals that perceivers, in some cases, consider to be unified wholes |

and sustenance. But he believed that their most important function was in creating a bridge between the individual and society at large:

> Primary groups are primary in the sense that they give the individual his earliest and completest experience of social unity, and also in the sense that they do not change in the same degree as more elaborate relations, but form a comparatively permanent source out of which the latter are ever springing. (Cooley, 1909, pp. 26–27)

In many cases, individuals become part of primary groups involuntarily: Most are born into a family, which provides for their well-being until they can join other groups. Other primary groups form when people interact in significant, meaningful ways for a prolonged period of time.

**Social Groups** In 1961, John F. Kennedy and his advisors were considering a plan to help a group of 1400 Cuban exiles invade Cuba at a place called Bahía de Cochinos, the Bay of Pigs. This group's members boasted years of experience in making monumentally important governmental decisions, and various warfare specialists from the CIA and the military attended all the meetings. The group met for many hours, and believed their plan was nearly perfect. Unfortunately, the attack ended in complete disaster, and the members spent the following months wondering at their shortsightedness and cataloging all the blunders they had made (Janis, 1972, 1982, 1983; see Chapter 11).

Cooley (1909) maintained that, in earlier eras, individuals belonged only to small, primary groups. They could live out their entire lives without leaving their small, close-knit families, tribes, or communities. But, as societies became more complex, so did their groups. These groups drew people into the larger community, where they joined with others in **social groups**. These groups are larger and more formally organized than primary groups, and memberships tend to be shorter in duration and less emotionally involving. The boundaries of such groups are more permeable, so members can leave old groups behind and join new ones. These groups are, in general, more instrumental ones: they are likely to stress the performance of tasks rather than enjoying relationships. Various terms have been used to describe this category of groups, such as *secondary groups* (Cooley, 1909), *associations* (MacIver & Page, 1937), *task groups* (Lickel, Hamilton, & Sherman, 2001), and *Gesellschaften* (Toennies, 1887/1963).

**Collectives** At exactly 1:30 in the afternoon on a sunny day outside the student union two students—one dressed in white and another in green—bowed to each other before launching into a barrage of

---

**social group** A relatively small number of individuals who interact with one another over an extended period of time, such as work groups, clubs, and congregations.

mock karate chops punctuated with shouts of "Wha-cha." At that moment, nearly all the people near them—30 to 40 fellow college students—also paired off in make-believe mêlées, which lasted until one of the original combatants fell to the ground. When he collapsed, all the other fighters collapsed as well, leaving but one person standing. As he walked away, the students all stood up, picked up their knapsacks, and went their separate ways. It was a *flash crowd*, or *smart mob*, organized by the use of cell phone technology and instant messaging (Rheingold, 2002; see Chapter 17).

A *collective*, if taken literally, would describe any aggregate of two or more individuals and, hence, would be synonymous with the term *group* (Blumer, 1951). Most theorists, however, reserve the term for larger, more spontaneous and looser forms of associations among people. **Collectives** are larger groups whose members act in similar and sometimes unusual ways. A list of collectives would include a street crowd watching a building burn, an audience at a movie, a line (*queue*) of people waiting to purchase tickets, a mob of college students protesting a government policy, and a panicked group fleeing from danger. But the list would also include mass movements of individuals who, though dispersed over a wide area, display common shifts in opinion or actions.

**Categories** Cuneo was driving a battered Comet and his buddy, Boyle, sat by his side. They were keyed up after working as bouncers at a local bar and were very drunk. On a nearby street Booker and Wilson were in a maroon Buick, headed home after working a shift at the nearby medical center. When the two cars stopped side-by-side at a red light, Boyle began shouting insults at Booker. A savage fight broke out, with the four men using baseball bats, a bottle, a knife, a piece of a picket fence, jumper cables, and even a car to injure each other. Why? Were these old enemies who were settling a grudge? Gang members who had sworn a vow to defend their turf? Drug dealers fighting over territory? No. The two sets of men were strangers to one another. But Cuneo and Boyle were white, Wilson and Booker were black, and these categories created reason enough (Sedgwick, 1982; see Chapter 14).

A **category** is an aggregation of individuals who are similar to one another in some way. For example, people who live in New York City are *New Yorkers*, Americans whose ancestors were from Africa are *African Americans*, and those who routinely wager sums of money on games of chance are *gamblers*. If a category has no social implications, then it only describes individuals who share a feature in common and is not a meaningful group. If, however, these categories set in motion personal or interpersonal processes—if two students in college become friends when they discover they grew up in the same town, if people respond to a person differently when they see he is an African American, or if a person begins to gamble even more of her earnings because her social identity includes the category *gambler*—then a category may be transformed into a highly influential group (Galinsky, Ku, & Wang, 2005). In such cases, categories can be higher in entitativity and essentialism than other types of groups.

**Perceiving Groups: Intuitive Typologies** Theorists are not the only people who divide groups up into coherent clusters like those listed in Table 1.2. When researchers Brian Lickel, David L. Hamilton, Steven J. Sherman, and their colleagues asked laypeople to think about various kinds of groups, most people intuitively drew distinctions between social groups, public groups, collectives, and categories. This study presented people with a list of 40 types of human aggregations: a local street gang, citizens of America, members of a jury, people at a bus stop, Jews, members of a family, students studying for an exam, plumbers, and the like. They then asked people to rate them in terms of their size, duration, permeability, amount of interaction among members, importance to members, and so on. When they examined these data using a statistical procedure

---

**collective** A relatively large aggregation or group of individuals who display similarities in actions and outlook.

**category** An aggregation of people or things that share some common attribute or are related in some way.

**TABLE 1.2 Types of Groups**

| Type of Group | Characteristics | Examples |
|---|---|---|
| **Primary groups** | Small, long-term groups characterized by face-to-face interaction and high levels of cohesiveness, solidarity, and member identification | Close friends, families, gangs, military squads |
| **Social groups** | Small groups of moderate duration and permeability characterized by moderate levels of interaction among the members over an extended period of time, often in goal-focused situations | Coworkers, crews, expeditions, fraternities, sports teams, study groups, task forces |
| **Collectives** | Aggregations of individuals that form spontaneously, last only a brief period of time, and have very permeable boundaries | Audiences, bystanders, crowds, mobs, waiting lines (queues) |
| **Categories** | Aggregations of individuals who are similar to one another in some way, such as gender, ethnicity, religion, or nationality | Asian Americans, New Yorkers, physicians, U.S. citizens, women |

called *cluster analysis*, they identified the basic types of groups listed in Table 1.2 (which they labeled intimacy groups, task groups, loose associations, and social categories). They then asked people to sort the 40 aggregates into stacks. Again, analysis identified the same basic types of groups. They also asked people to list 12 groups that they belong to. When unbiased raters reviewed these lists, once again the four types were in evidence (Lickel et al., 2000).

The research team also asked the perceivers if they considered all these kinds of aggregations of individuals to be true groups. They did not force people to make an either/or decision about each one, however. Recognizing that the boundary between what is and what is not a group is perceptually fuzzy, they instead asked participants to rate the aggregations on a scale from 1 (*not at all a group*) to 9 (*very much a group*). As Figure 1.4 indicates, primary groups and social groups received high average ratings, whereas collectives and categories were rated lower. These findings suggest that people are more likely to consider aggregations marked by strong bonds between members, frequent interactions among members, and clear boundaries to be groups, but that they are less certain that such aggregations as crowds, waiting lines, or categories qualify as groups (Lickel et al., 2000, Study 3).

## THE NATURE OF GROUP DYNAMICS

Group dynamics describes both a subject matter and a scientific field of study. When Kurt Lewin (1951) described the way groups and individuals act and react to changing circumstances, he named these processes *group dynamics*. But Lewin also used the phrase to describe the scientific discipline devoted to the study of these dynamics. Later, Dorwin Cartwright and Alvin Zander supplied a formal definition, calling it a "field of inquiry dedicated to advancing knowledge about the nature of groups, the laws of their development, and their interrelations with individuals, other groups, and larger institutions" (1968, p. 7).

Group dynamics is not even a century old. Although scholars have long pondered the nature of groups, the first scientific studies of groups were not carried out until the 1900s. Cartwright and Zander (1968), in their review of the origins of group dynamics, suggest that its slow development

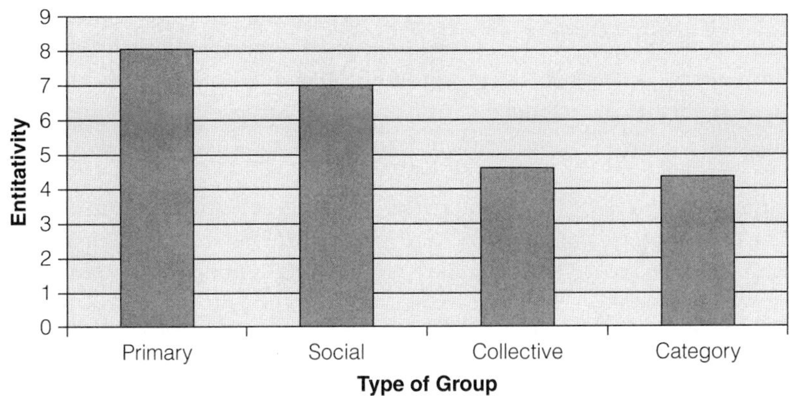


**FIGURE 1.4** The entitativity ratings of four types of groups: Primary groups, social groups, collectives, and categories.

SOURCE: "Varieties of Groups and the Perception of Group Entitativity," by B. Lickel, D. L. Hamilton, G. Wieczorkowska, A. Lewis, S. J. Sherman, and A. N. Uhles, *Journal of Personality and Social Psychology*, 2000, *78*, 223–246. Copyright 2000 by the American Psychological Association.

stemmed in part from several unfounded assumptions about groups. Many felt that the dynamics of groups was a private affair, not something that scientists should lay open to public scrutiny. Others felt that human behavior was too complex to be studied scientifically and that this complexity was magnified enormously when groups of interacting individuals became the objects of interest. Still others believed that the causes of group behavior were so obvious that they were unworthy of scientific attention.

The field also developed slowly because theorists and researchers disagreed among themselves on many basic theoretical and methodological issues. The field was not established by a single theorist or researcher who laid down a set of clear-cut assumptions and principles. Rather, group dynamics resulted from group processes. One theorist would suggest an idea, another might disagree, and the debate would continue until consensus would be reached. Initially, researchers were uncertain how to investigate their ideas empirically, but through collaboration and, more often, spirited competition, researchers developed new methods for studying groups. World events also influenced the study of groups, for the use of groups in manufacturing, warfare, and therapeutic settings stimulated the need to understand and improve such groups.

These group processes shaped the field's **paradigm**. The philosopher of science Thomas S. Kuhn (1970) used that term to describe scientists' shared assumptions about the phenomena they study. Kuhn maintained that when scientists learn their field, they master not only the content of the science—important discoveries, general principles, facts, and so on—but also a way of looking at the world that is passed on from one scientist to another. These shared beliefs and unstated assumptions give them a world view—a way of looking at that part of the world that they find most interesting. The paradigm determines the questions they consider worth studying using the methods that are most appropriate.

What are the core elements of the field's paradigm? What do researchers and theorists notice when they observe a group acting in particular way? What kinds of group processes do they find fascinating, and which ones do they find less interesting? In this chapter, we begin to answer these questions by considering some of the basic assumptions of the field and tracing them back to their source in the work of early sociologists, psychologists, and social psychologists. We then shift from the historical to the contemporary and review current topics and trends in the field. Chapter 2 continues this analysis of the field's paradigm by considering practices and procedures used by researchers when they collect information about groups.

**paradigm** Scientists' shared assumptions about the phenomena they study; also, a set of research procedures.

## Are Groups Real?

When anthropology, psychology, sociology, and the other social sciences emerged as their own unique disciplines in the late 1800s, the dynamics of groups became a topic of critical concern for all of them. Sociologists studying religious, political, economic, and educational social systems highlighted the role groups played in maintaining social order. Anthropologists, as they studied one culture after another, discovered similarities and differences among the world's small tribal groups. Political scientists' studies of political parties, voting, and public engagement led them to the study of small groups of closely networked individuals. In 1895, Gustave Le Bon, who was trained as a physician, published *Psychologie des Foules* (Psychology of Crowds), which describes how individuals are transformed when they join a group. Wilhelm Wundt (1916), recognized as the founder of scientific psychology, also studied groups extensively. His book *Völkerpsychologie* is sometimes translated as "folk psychology," but others suggest that the best translation is "group psychology." It combined elements of anthropology and psychology by examining the conditions and changes displayed by elementary social aggregates, and how group memberships influence virtually all cognitive and perceptual processes.

**Level of Analysis** Almost immediately theorists disagreed about the **level of analysis** to take when studying groups. Some favored an *individual-level analysis* that focused on the person in the group. Researchers who took this approach sought to explain the behavior of each group member, and they ultimately wanted to know if such psychological processes as attitudes, motivations, or personality were the true determinants of social behavior. Others advocated for a *group-level analysis* that assumes each person is "an element in a larger system, a group, organization, or society. And what he does is presumed to reflect the state of the larger system and the events occurring in it" (Steiner, 1974, p. 96; 1983, 1986). Sociological researchers tended to undertake group-level analyses and psychological researchers favored the individual-level analysis.

Researchers working at both levels asked the question, "Are groups real?" but they often settled on very different answers. Group-level researchers believed that groups and the processes that occurred within them were scientifically authentic. Émile Durkheim (1897/1966), for example, argued that individuals who are not members of friendship, family, or religious groups can lose their sense of identity and, as a result, are more likely to commit suicide. Durkheim strongly believed that widely shared beliefs—what he called *collective representations*—are the cornerstone of society, and went so far as to suggest that large groups of people sometimes act with a single mind. He believed that such groups, rather than being mere collections of individuals in a fixed pattern of relationships with one another, were linked by a unifying **collective conscious** (Jahoda, 2007).

Many psychologists who were interested in group phenomena questioned the need to go beyond the individual to explain group behavior. Floyd Allport, the foremost representative of this perspective, argued that group-level phenomena, such as the collective conscious, simply did not exist. In 1924, Allport wrote that "nervous systems are possessed by individuals; but there is no nervous system of the crowd" (p. 5). He added, "Only through social psychology as a science of the individual can we avoid the superficialities of the crowdmind and collective mind theories" (p. 8). Because Allport believed that "the actions of all are nothing more than the sum of the actions of each taken separately" (p. 5), he thought that a full understanding of the behavior of individuals

---

**level of analysis** The specific focus of study chosen from a graded or nested sequence of possible foci. An individual-level analysis examines specific individuals in the group, a group-level analysis focuses on the group as a unit, and an organizational level examines the individual nested in the group, which is, in turn, nested in the organizational context.

**collective conscious (or groupmind)** A hypothetical unifying mental force linking group members together; the fusion of individual consciousness or mind into a transcendent consciousness.

## Focus 1.3 Do Groups Have Minds?

*Under certain circumstances, and only under those circumstances, an agglomeration of men presents new characteristics very different from those of the individuals composing [the group]*

—Gustave Le Bon (1895/1960, p. 23), *Psychologie des Foules*

Groups that undertake extreme actions under the exhortation of exotic, charismatic leaders fascinate both layperson and researcher alike. Although groups are so commonplace that they usually go unnoticed and unscrutinized, atypical groups—cults, violent mobs, terrorist cells, communes—invite wild speculation. Some early commentators on the human condition went so far as to suggest that such groups may develop a group mind that is greater than the sum of the psychological experiences of the members and that it can become so powerful that it can overwhelm the will of the individual.

Very few of these investigators, however, believed that groups literally had minds. They used such concepts such as groupmind and collective conscious as metaphors to suggest that many psychological processes are determined, in part, by interactions with other people, and those interactions are in turn shaped by the mental activities and actions of each individual in the collective. When Durkheim, for example, wrote of the "esprit de group" (groupmind) he was not describing a hive-like mentality that creates a metaphysical bond between members, but only suggesting that individuals and groups are inextricably intertwined:

> "individuals are all that society is made of . . . the mentality of groups is not that of individuals (*particuliers*), precisely because it assumes a plurality of individual minds joined together. A collectivity has its own ways of thinking and feeling to which its members bend but which are different from those they would create if they were left to their own devices" (Durkheim, 1900/1973, pp. 16–17).

Terms such as groupmind and collective conscious are controversial ones, however, and have contributed to a continuing scientific distrust of group-level concepts. Allport, for example, never backed down from his anti-group position. Even though he conducted extensive studies of such group phenomena as rumors and morale during wartime (Allport & Lepkin, 1943) and conformity to standards (the J-curve hypothesis; Allport, 1934, 1961), he continued to question the scientific value of the term *group*. He did, however, eventually conclude that individuals' actions are often bound together in "one inclusive *collective* structure" but he could not bring himself to use the word *group* to describe such collectives (Allport, 1962, p. 17, italics in original).

in groups could be achieved by studying the psychology of the individual group members. Groups, according to Allport, were not real entities. He is reputed to have said, "You can't trip over a group." Allport's reluctance to accept such dubious concepts as group-level mind helped ensure the field's scientific status. His hard-nosed attitude forced researchers to ask some basic questions about groups and their influence on individual members and on society (see Focus 1.3).

**Are Groups More Than the Sum of Their Parts?** The debate between individual-level and group-level approaches waned, in time, as theorists developed stronger models for understanding group-level process. Kurt Lewin's (1951) theoretical analyses of groups were particularly influential. His *field theory* is premised on the principle of *interactionism*, which assumes that the behavior of people in groups is determined by the interaction of the person and the environment. The formula $B = f(P,E)$ summarizes this assumption. In a group context, this formula implies that the behavior ($B$) of group members is a function ($f$) of the interaction of their personal characteristics ($P$) with environmental factors ($E$), which include features of the group, the

---

$B = f(P,E)$ The interactionism formula proposed by Kurt Lewin that assumes each person's behavior ($B$) is a function of his or her personal qualities ($P$), the social environment ($E$), and the interaction of these personal qualities with factors present in the social setting.

group members, and the situation. Lewin believed that, because of interactionism, a group is a Gestalt—a unified system with emergent properties that cannot be fully understood by piecemeal examination. Adopting the dictum, "The whole is greater than the sum of the parts," he maintained that when individuals merged into a group something new was created and that the new product itself had to be the object of study.

**Are Group Processes Real?** Even the earliest researchers doubted the existence of a **groupmind.** However, just because this particular group-level concept has little foundation in fact does not imply that other group-level processes, phenomena, and concepts are equally unreasonable. Consider, for example, the concept of a group norm. As noted earlier, a *norm* is a standard that describes what behaviors should and should not be performed in a group. Norms are not just individual members' personal standards, however, for they are shared among group members. Only when members agree on a particular standard does it function as a norm, so this concept is embedded at the level of the group rather than at the level of the individual.

The idea that a norm is more than just the sum of the individual beliefs of all the members of a group was verified by Muzafer Sherif in 1936. Sherif literally created norms by asking groups of men to state aloud their estimates of the distance that a dot of light had moved. He found that the men gradually accepted a standard estimate in place of their own idiosyncratic judgments. He also found, however, that even when the men were later given the opportunity to make judgments alone, they still based their estimates on the group's norm. Moreover, once the group's norm had developed, Sherif removed members one at a time and replaced them with fresh members. Each new member changed his behavior, in time, until it matched the group's norm. If the individuals in the group are completely replaceable, then where does the group norm "exist"? It exists at the group level rather than the individual level (MacNeil & Sherif, 1976).

### Are Groups Dynamic?

Kurt Lewin (1943, 1948, 1951), who many have argued is the founder of the movement to study groups experimentally, chose the word *dynamic* to describe the activities, processes, operations, and changes that transpire in groups. This word suggests that groups are powerful and influential: they change their members and society-at-large. Dynamic systems are also fluid rather than static, for they develop and evolve over time. Do groups deserve to be called *dynamic*?

**Groups Influence Their Members** As researchers gathered more and more data about groups and group processes they became more firmly convinced that if one wishes to understand individuals, one must understand groups. Groups, they concluded, have a profound impact on individuals; they shape actions, thoughts, and feelings. Some of these changes are subtle ones. Moving from isolation to a group context can reduce our sense of uniqueness, but at the same time it can enhance our ability to perform simple tasks rapidly. In one of the earliest experimental studies in the field, Norman Triplett (1898) verified the discontinuity between people's responses when they are isolated rather than integrated, and this shift has been documented time and again in studies of motivation, emotion, and performance. Groups can also change their members by prompting them to change their attitudes and values as they come to agree with the overall consensus of the group (Newcomb, 1943). As Cooley (1909) explained, people acquire their attitudes, values, identities, skills, and principles in groups, and become practiced at modifying their behavior in response to social norms and others' requirements. As children grow older their peers replace the family as the source of social values (Harris, 1995), and when they become adults, actions and outlooks are

---

**groupmind** A supra-individual level of consciousness that links members in a psychic, telepathic connection.

then shaped by an even larger network of interconnected (Barabási, 2003).

Groups also change people more dramatically. The earliest group psychologists were struck by the apparent madness of people when immersed in crowds, and many concluded that the behavior of a person in a group may have no connection to that person's behavior when alone. Stanley Milgram's (1963) classic studies of obedience offered further confirmation of the dramatic power of groups over their members, for Milgram found that most people placed in a powerful group would obey the orders of a malevolent authority to harm another person. Individuals who join religious or political groups that stress secrecy, obedience to leaders, and dogmatic acceptance of unusual or atypical beliefs (*cults*) often display fundamental and unusual changes in belief and behavior. Groups may just be collections of individuals, but these collections change their members (Richard, Bond, & Stokes-Zoota, 2003).

**Groups Influence Society** At the same time researchers were verifying the dramatic ways in which groups influence individuals, researchers studying societal structures were documenting the role that groups played in maintaining religious, political, economic, and educational systems in society. After the industrial revolution, legal and political systems developed to coordinate actions and make community-level decisions. Organized religions provided answers to questions of values, morality, and meaning. Educational systems took over some of the teaching duties previously assigned to the family. Economic systems developed to regulate production and the attainment of financial goals. All these social systems were based, at their core, on small groups and subgroups of connected individuals. Religious groups provide a prime example. Individuals often endorse a specific religion, such as Christianity or Islam, but their connection to their religion occurs in smaller groups and *congregations*. These groups are formally structured and led by a religious authority, yet they provide members with a sense of belonging, reaffirm the values and norms of the group, and strengthen bonds among members (Krause, N., 2006). At the collective level, communities, organizations, and society itself cannot be understood apart from the groups that sustain these social structures.

**Groups Are Living Systems** A holistic perspective on groups prompted researchers to examine how a group, as a unit, changes over time. Some groups are so stable that their basic processes and structures remain unchanged for days, weeks, or even years, but such groups are rare. Bruce Tuckman's theory of **group development**, for example, assumes that most groups move through the five stages summarized in Figure 1.5 (Tuckman, 1965; Tuckman & Jensen, 1977). In the *forming* phase, the group members become oriented toward one another. In the *storming* phase, conflicts surface in the group as members vie for status and the group sets its goals. These conflicts subside when the group becomes more structured and standards emerge in the *norming* phase. In the *performing* phase, the group moves beyond disagreement and organizational matters to concentrate on the work to be done. The group continues to function at this stage until it reaches the *adjourning* stage, when it disbands. Groups also tend to cycle repeatedly through some of these stages as group members strive to maintain a balance between task-oriented actions and emotionally expressive behaviors (Bales, 1965). A group, in a very real sense, is alive: It acquires energy and resources from its environment, maintains its structure, and grows over time (Arrow et al., 2005).

## The Multilevel Perspective

In time the rift between individual-level and group-level researchers closed as the unique contributions of each perspective were integrated in a **multilevel perspective** on groups. This approach, illustrated in Figure 1.6, suggests that group dynamics are shaped by processes that range along the

---

**group development** Patterns of growth and change that emerge across the group's life span.

**multilevel perspective** Examining group behavior from several different levels of analysis, including individual level (micro), group level (meso), and organizational or societal level (macro).

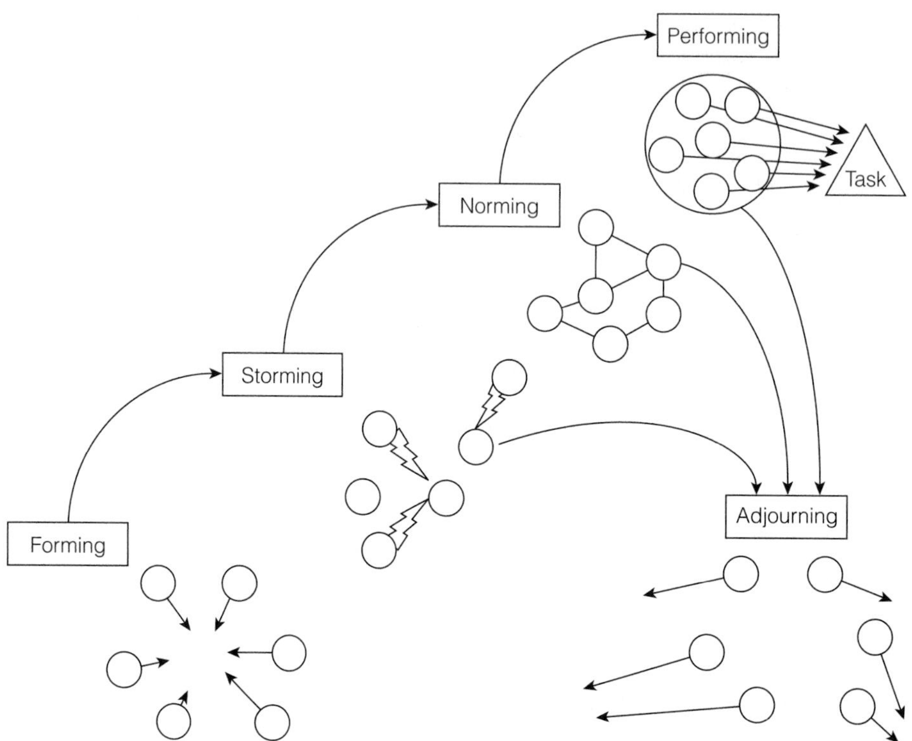


**FIGURE 1.5** Stages of group development. Tuckman's theory of group development suggests that groups typically pass through stages during their development: formation (forming), conflict (storming), structure (norming), productivity (performing), and dissolution (adjourning).

micro-meso-macro continuum. *Micro-level* factors include the qualities, characteristics, and actions of the individual members. *Meso-level* factors are group-level qualities of the groups themselves, such as their cohesiveness, their size, their composition, and their structure. *Macro-level* factors are the qualities and processes of the larger collectives that enfold the groups, such as communities, organizations, or societies. Groups, then, are nested at the meso-level, where the bottom-up micro-level variables meet the top-down macro-level variables.

**Crossing Levels** Hackman and his colleagues' studies of performing orchestras illustrate the value of a multilevel approach (Allmendinger, Hackman, & Lehman, 1996; Hackman, 2003). In their quest to understand why some professional orchestras outperformed others, they measured an array of micro-, meso-, and macro-level variables. At the micro-level they studied the individual musicians: Were they well-trained and highly skilled? Were they satisfied with their work and highly motivated? Did they like each other and feel that they played well together? At the group-level (meso-level) they considered the gender composition of the group (number of men and women players), the quality of the music the orchestra produced, and the financial resources available to the group. They also took note of one key macro-level variable: the location of the orchestras in one of four different countries (U.S., England, East Germany, or West Germany).

Their work uncovered a complex array of interrelations among these three sets of variables. As might be expected, one micro-level variable—the skill of the individual players—substantially influenced the quality of the performance of the group. However,

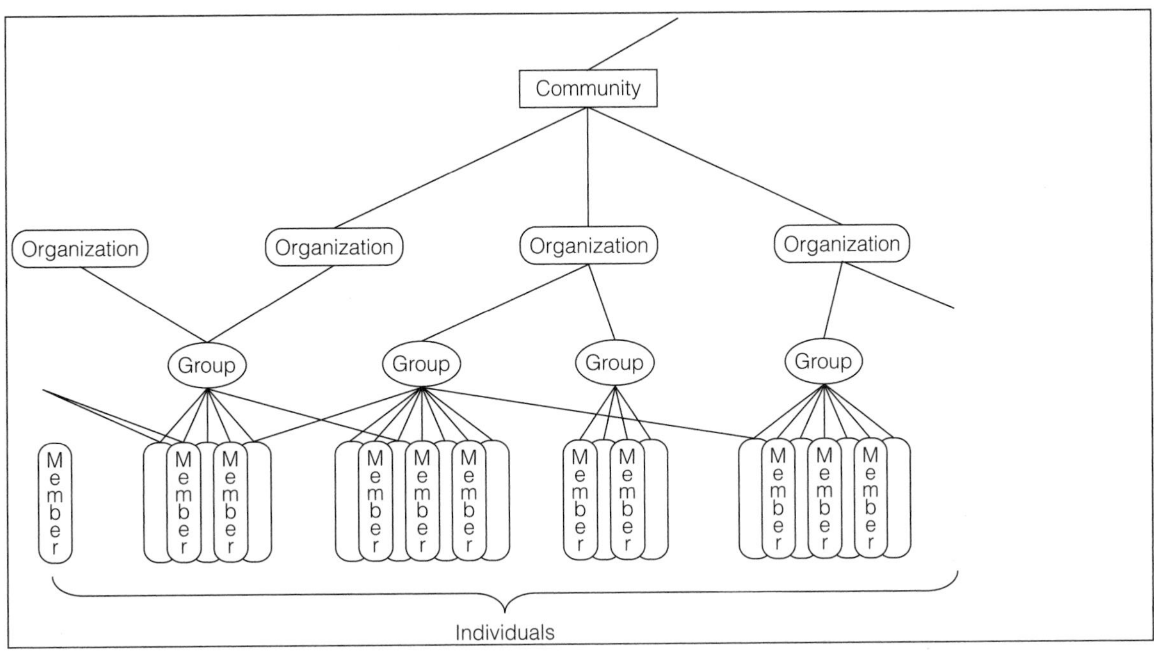


**FIGURE 1.6** A multilevel perspective on groups. Researchers who study groups recognize that individuals are nested in groups, but that these groups are themselves nested in larger social units, such as organizations, communities, tribes, nations, and so on. Researchers may focus on one level in this multilevel system, such as the group itself, but they must be aware that these groups are embedded in a complex of other relationships.

one critical determinant of the talent of individual players was the financial health of the orchestra; better-funded orchestras could afford to hire better performers. Affluent orchestras could also afford music directors who worked more closely with the performers, and orchestras who performed better than expected given the caliber of their individual players were led by the most skilled directors. The country where the orchestra was based was also an important determinant of the group members' satisfaction with their orchestra, but only when one also considered the gender composition of the orchestras. Far fewer women were members of orchestras in West Germany, but as the proportion of women in orchestras increased, members became increasingly negative about their group. In contrast, in the U.S., with its directive employment regulations, more women were included in orchestras, and the proportion of women in the groups was less closely related to attitude toward the group. Given their findings, Hackman and his colleagues concluded that the answer to most of their questions about orchestras was "it depends": on the individuals in the group, on the nature of the orchestra itself, and the social context where the orchestra is located.

**Interdisciplinary Orientation** The multilevel perspective gives group dynamics an interdisciplinary character. For example, researchers who prefer to study individuals may find themselves wondering what impact group participation will have on individuals' cognitions, attitudes, and behavior. Those who study organizations may find that these larger social entities actually depend on the dynamics of small subgroups within the organization. Social scientists examining such global issues as the development and maintenance of culture may find themselves turning their attention toward small groups as the unit of cultural transmission. Political scientists who study national and international leaders may discover that such leaders are centers of a small network of advisors, and that their political actions cannot be understood without taking into account the dynamics of these advisory councils. Although the listing of disciplines that study group dynamics in Table 1.3 is far from comprehensive, it does convey the idea that the study of groups is not limited to any one field. As A. Paul Hare and his colleagues once noted, "This field of research does not 'belong' to any one of the recognized social sciences alone. It is the common property of all" (Hare, Borgatta, & Bales, 1955, p. vi).

### The Practicality of Group Dynamics

A multilevel perspective makes it clear that many of the most important aspects of human existence—including individuals, organizations, communities, and cultures—cannot be fully understood without an understanding of groups. But, practically speaking, why study groups when one can investigate brain structures, cultures, biological diseases, organizations, ancient civilizations, or even other planets? In the grand scheme of things, how important is it to investigate groups?

Groups are relevant to many applied areas, as Table 1.3 shows. Much of the world's work is done by groups, so by understanding groups we move toward making them more efficient. The study of groups in the work setting has long occupied business-oriented researchers, who are concerned with the effective organization of people (Anderson, De Dreu, & Nijstad, 2004; Sanna & Parks, 1997). Social workers have also found themselves dealing

**TABLE 1.3 The Interdisciplinary Nature of Group Dynamics: Examples of Topics Pertaining to Groups in Various Disciplines**

| Discipline | Topics |
|---|---|
| **Anthropology** | Groups in cross-cultural contexts; societal change; social and collective identities; evolutionary approaches to group living |
| **Architecture and Design** | Planning spaces to maximize group-environment fit; design of spaces for groups, including offices, classrooms, venues, arenas, and so on |
| **Business and Industry** | Work motivation; productivity in organizational settings; team building; goal setting; management and leadership |
| **Communication** | Information transmission in groups; discussion; decision making; problems in communication; networks |
| **Criminal Justice** | Organization of law enforcement agencies; gangs and criminal groups; jury deliberations |
| **Education** | Classroom groups; team teaching; class composition and educational outcomes |
| **Engineering** | Design of human systems, including problem-solving teams; group approaches to software design |
| **Mental Health** | Therapeutic change through groups; sensitivity training; training groups; self-help groups; group psychotherapy |
| **Political Science** | Leadership; intergroup and international relations; political influence; power |
| **Psychology** | Personality and group behavior; problem solving; perceptions of other people; motivation; conflict |
| **Social Work** | Team approaches to treatment; community groups; family counseling; groups and adjustment |
| **Sociology** | Self and society; influence of norms on behavior; role relations; deviance |
| **Sports and Recreation** | Team performance; effects of victory and failure; cohesion and performance |

with such groups as social clubs, gangs, neighborhoods, and family clusters, and an awareness of group processes helped crystallize their understanding of group life. Educators were also influenced by group research, as were many of the medical fields that dealt with patients on a group basis. Many methods of helping people to change rely on group principles.

The application of group dynamics to practical problems is consistent with Lewin's call for **action research**. Lewin argued in favor of the intertwining of basic and applied research, for he firmly believed that there "is no hope of creating a better world without a deeper scientific insight into the function of leadership and culture, and of other essentials of group life" (1943, p. 113). To achieve this goal, he assured practitioners that "there is nothing so practical as a good theory" (1951, p. 169) and charged researchers with the task of developing theories that can be applied to important social problems (Bargal, 2008).

Also, on a *personal level*, you spend your entire life surrounded by and embedded in groups. Through membership in groups, you define and confirm your values and beliefs and take on or refine a social identity. When you face uncertain situations, in groups you gain reassuring information about your problems and security in companionship. In groups, you learn about relations with others, the type of impressions you make on others, and the way you can relate with others more effectively. As Focus 1.4 explains, groups influence people in consequential ways, so you ignore their influence at your own risk.

## Topics in Contemporary Group Dynamics

Throughout the history of group dynamics, some approaches that initially seemed promising have been abandoned after they contributed relatively little or failed to stimulate consistent lines of research. The idea of groupmind, for example, was discarded when researchers identified more likely causes of crowd behavior. Similarly, such concepts as syntality (any effects that the group has as a functioning unit; Cattell, 1948), groupality (the personality of the group; Bogardus, 1954), and lifespace (all factors that define an individual's psychological reality; Lewin, 1951) initially attracted considerable interest but stimulated little research.

In contrast, researchers have studied other topics continuously since they were first broached (Berdahl & Henry, 2005; Forsyth & Burnette, 2005). Table 1.4 samples the topics that currently interest group experts and it foreshadows the topics considered in the remainder of this book. Chapters 1 and 2 explore the foundations of the field by reviewing the group dynamics perspective (Chapter 1) and the methods and theories of the field (Chapter 2).

Chapters 3 through 6 focus on group formation and development—how groups come into existence and how they change and evolve over time. Chapters 3 and 4 consider the demands and opportunities of a life in a group rather than alone, including the personal and situational forces that prompt people to join groups or remain apart from them. Chapter 5 focuses more fully on group development by considering the factors that increase the unity of a group and the way those factors wax and wane as the group changes over time. Chapter 6 turns to the topic of group structure—how groups develop systems of roles and intermember relationships—with a particular focus on how structure emerges as groups mature.

A group is a complex social system—a microcosm of powerful interpersonal forces that significantly shape members' actions—and Chapters 7 through 9 examine the flow of influence and interaction in that microcosm. Chapter 7 looks at the way group members sometimes change their opinions, judgments, or actions so that they match the opinions, judgments, or actions of the rest of the

**action research** The term used by Kurt Lewin to describe scientific inquiry that both expands basic theoretical knowledge and identifies solutions to significant social problems.

## Focus 1.4 Are Groups Good or Bad?

*Humans would do better without groups.*
—Christian J. Buys (1978a, p. 123)

For centuries, philosophers and scholars have debated the relative value of groups. Some have pointed out that membership in groups is highly rewarding, for it combines the pleasures of interpersonal relations with goal strivings. Groups create relationships between people, and in many cases these connections are more intimate, more enduring, and more sustaining than connections formed between friends or lovers. Groups provide their members with a sense of identity, support, and guidance, and they are often the means of acquiring knowledge, skills, and abilities. In groups people can reach goals that would elude them if alone.

Groups have a downside, however. They are often the arena for profound interpersonal conflicts that end in violence and aggression. Even though group members may cooperate with one another, they may also engage in competition as they strive to outdo one another. When individuals are members of very large groups, such as crowds, they sometimes engage in behaviors that they would never undertake if they were acting individually. Many of the most misguided decisions have not been made by lone individuals but by groups of people who, despite working together, still managed to make a disastrous decision. Even though people tend to work together in groups, in many cases these groups are far less productive than they should be, given the talents and energies of the individuals in them. Given these problems, psychologist and historian Christian Buys whimsically suggested that all groups be eliminated because "humans would do better without groups" (1978a, p. 123).

Although Buys's suggestion is a satirical one, it does make the point that groups are neither all good nor all bad. Groups are so "beneficial, if not essential, to humans" that "it seems nonsensical to search for alternatives to human groups" (Buys, 1978b, p. 568), but groups can generate negative outcomes for their members. Researchers, however, are more often drawn to studying negative rather than positive processes, with the result that theory and research in the field tend to stress conflict, rejection, dysfunction, and obedience to malevolent authorities and to neglect cooperation, acceptance, well-being, and collaboration. This negative bias, Buys suggested, has led to an unfair underestimation of the positive impact of groups on people.

Buys's comments, by the way, have prompted a number of rejoinders by other group researchers. One group-authored response (Kravitz et al., 1978) suggested that Buys wrongly assigned responsibility for the problems; its authors argued that humans would do better without other humans rather than without any groups. Another proposed that groups would do better without humans (Anderson, 1978), whereas a third simply argued that groups would do better without social psychologists (Green & Mack, 1978).

**TABLE 1.4 Major Topics in the Field of Group Dynamics**

| Chapter and Topic | Issues |
|---|---|
| **Foundations** | |
| 1. Introduction to group dynamics | What are groups and what are their key features? What do we want to know about groups and their dynamics? What assumptions guide researchers in their studies of groups and the processes within groups? |
| 2. Studying groups | How do researchers measure the way groups, and the individuals in those groups, feel, think, and behave? How do researchers search for and test their hypotheses about groups? What are the strengths and weaknesses of the various research strategies used to study groups? What general theoretical perspectives guide researchers' studies of groups and the people in them? |
| **Formation and Development** | |
| 3. Inclusion and identity | Do humans, as a species, prefer inclusion to exclusion and group membership to isolation? What demands does a shift from individuality to collectivity make on |

**TABLE 1.4 (Continued)**

| Chapter and Topic | Issues |
|---|---|
| | people? How do group experiences and memberships influence individuals' identities? |
| 4. Formation | Who joins groups and who remains apart? When and why do people seek out others? Why do people deliberately create groups or join existing groups? What factors influence feelings of liking for others? |
| 5. Cohesion and development | What factors promote the increasing solidarity of a group over time? What is cohesion? As groups become more unified, do they develop a shared climate and culture? How do groups develop over time? What are the positive and negative consequences of cohesion and commitment? |
| 6. Structure | What are norms, and how do they structure interactions in groups? What are roles? Which roles occur most frequently in groups? How and why do status networks develop in groups? What factors influence the group's social structure? What are the interpersonal consequences of relational networks (based on status, attraction, and communication) in groups? |
| **Influence and Interaction** | |
| 7. Influence | When will people conform to a group's standards, and when will they remain independent? How do norms develop, and why do people obey them? Do nonconformists ever succeed in influencing the rest of the group? |
| 8. Power | Why are some members of groups more powerful than others? What types of power tactics are most effective in influencing others? Does power corrupt? Why do people obey authorities? |
| 9. Leadership | What is leadership? If a group without a leader forms, which person will eventually step forward to become the leader? Should a leader be task focused or relationship focused? Is democratic leadership superior to autocratic leadership? Can leaders transform their followers? |
| **Working in Groups** | |
| 10. Group performance | Do people perform tasks more effectively in groups or when they are alone? Why do people sometimes expend so little effort when they are in groups? When does a group outperform an individual? Are groups creative? |
| 11. Decision making | What steps do groups take when making decisions? Why do some highly cohesive groups make disastrous decisions? Why do groups sometimes make riskier decisions than individuals? |
| 12. Teams | What is the difference between a group and a team? What types of teams are currently in use? Does team building improve team work? How can leaders intervene to improve the performance of their teams? |
| **Conflict** | |
| 13. Conflict in groups | What causes disputes between group members? When will a small disagreement escalate into a conflict? Why do groups sometimes splinter into subgroups? How can disputes in groups be resolved? |
| 14. Intergroup relations | What causes disputes between groups? What changes take place as a consequence of intergroup conflict? What factors exacerbate conflict? How can intergroup conflict be resolved? |

**TABLE 1.4 (Continued)**

| Chapter and Topic | Issues |
|---|---|
| **Contexts and Applications** | |
| 15. Groups in context | What impact does the social and physical setting have on an interacting group? Are groups territorial? What happens when groups are overcrowded? How do groups cope with severe environments? |
| 16. Groups and change | How can groups be used to improve personal adjustment and health? What is the difference between a therapy group and a support group? Are group approaches to treatment effective? Why do they work? |
| 17. Crowds and collective behavior | What types of crowds are common? Why do crowds and collectives form? Do people lose their sense of self when they join crowds? When is a crowd likely to become unruly? |

group (*conformity*). Chapter 8 extends this topic by considering how group members make use of social power to influence others and how people respond to such influence. Chapter 9 considers issues of leadership in groups.

Questions of group performance form the focus on Chapters 10 through 12, for people work in groups across a range of contexts and settings. Chapter 10 examines basic questions of group productivity, including brainstorming, whereas Chapter 11 examines groups that share information to make decisions. We study processes and problems in teams in Chapter 12.

Chapters 13 and 14 examine conflict and cooperation in groups. Groups are sources of stability and support for members, but in some cases conflicts erupt within groups (Chapter 13) and between groups (Chapter 14).

The final chapters deal with groups in specific settings. All groups are embedded in a social and environmental context, and Chapter 15 considers how the context in which groups exist affects their dynamics. Chapter 16 reviews groups in therapeutic contexts—helping, supportive, and change-promoting groups. Chapter 17 concludes our analysis by considering groups in public, societal contexts, including such relatively large groups as mobs, crowds, and social movements.

## SUMMARY IN OUTLINE

*What is a group?*

1. No two groups are identical to each other, but a *group*, by definition, is two or more individuals who are connected by and within social relationships.
   - Groups vary in size from dyads and triads to very large aggregations, such as mobs and audiences.
   - Group-based relations are *memberships*.
   - Unlike *networks*, groups usually have boundaries that define who is in the group.
2. *Social identity*, according to Tajfel and his colleagues, is a sense of shared membership in a group or category. People who meet regularly via computers display many of the defining characteristics of a group.

*What are some common characteristics of groups?*

1. People in groups interact with one another. Bales's Interaction Process Analysis (IPA) system distinguishes between *relationship interaction* and *task interaction*.
2. Groups seek goals, such as those specified in McGrath's *circumplex model of group tasks* (generating, choosing, negotiating, and executing).
3. Groups create *interdependence* among the group members (unilateral, reciprocal, etc.).
4. Interaction is patterned by *group structure*, including *roles, norms*, and interpersonal relations.
5. *Group cohesion*, or cohesiveness, determines the unity of the group. *Entitativity* is the extent to which individuals perceive an aggregation to be a unified group.
   - The perception of entitativity, according to Campbell, is substantially influenced by common fate, similarity, and proximity cues within an aggregation.
   - The *Thomas Theorem*, applied to groups, suggests that if individuals think an aggregate is a true group then the group will have important interpersonal consequences for those in the group and for those who are observing it.
   - Groups that are high in entitativity are assumed to have a basic essence that defines the nature of their members (*essentialism*).

*Are there different types of groups?*

1. A number of different types of groups have been identified.
   - *Primary groups* are relatively small, personally meaningful groups that are highly unified. Cooley suggested such groups are primary agents of socialization.
   - Members of *social groups*, such as work groups, clubs, and congregations, interact with one another over an extended period of time.
   - *Collectives* are relatively large aggregations or groups of individuals who display similarities in actions and outlook.
   - Members of a *category* share some common attribute or are related in some way.
2. Research conducted by Lickel, Hamilton, Sherman, and their colleagues suggests that people spontaneously draw distinctions among primary groups, social groups, collectives, and more general social categories.

*What assumptions guide researchers in their studies of groups and the processes within groups?*

1. Lewin first used the phrase *group dynamics* to describe the powerful processes that take place in groups, but group dynamics also refers to the "field of inquiry dedicated to advancing knowledge about the nature of groups" (Cartwright and Zander, 1968, p. 7).
2. Early researchers and theorists who pioneered the study of groups include:
   - Le Bon, a physician best known for his book on the psychology of crowds and mobs, *Psychologie des Foules*.
   - Wundt, a psychologist who wrote *Völkerpsychologie*.
   - Durkheim, a sociologist who argued that society is made possible by the collective representations of individuals.
   - Allport, a psychologist who avoided holistic approaches to groups.
3. A number of assumptions shape the field's conceptual *paradigm*, including the following:
   - *Groups are real.* Early researchers disagreed about the *level of analysis* to take when studying groups. Some, such as Allport, objected to such group-level concepts as the *groupmind* and *collective conscious*.

- *Groups are more than the sum of their parts.* In some cases the characteristics of groups cannot be deduced from the individual members' characteristics. Lewin's field theory maintains that behavior is a function of both the person and the environment, expressed by the formula $B = f(P, E)$.
- *Group processes are real.* Research studies, such as Sherif's study of norm formation, suggest that group-level processes can be created through experimentation.
- *Groups are influential.* Groups alter their members' attitudes, values, and perceptions. Triplett's early study of group performance demonstrated the impact of one person on another, and Milgram's work demonstrated that a group situation can powerfully influence members to cause harm to others.
- *Groups shape society.* Groups mediate the connection between individuals and society-at-large.
- *Groups are living systems.* Tuckman's theory of *group development*, for example, assumes that over time most groups move through the five stages of forming, storming, norming, performing, and adjourning.
- *Groups can be studied on several levels.* Individuals are nested in groups, and these groups are usually nested in larger social aggregations, such as communities and organizations. Hackman's studies of orchestras illustrate the importance of a *multilevel perspective* that cuts across several levels of analysis.
- *The field of group dynamics is an interdisciplinary one.*

*What fields and what topics are included in the scientific study of group dynamics?*

1. Understanding groups is the key to solving a variety of practical problems.
   - Many researchers carry out *action research* by using scientific methods to identify solutions to practical problems.
   - Despite the many problems caused by groups (competition, conflict, poor decisions), Buys notes that humans could not survive without groups.
2. Researchers have examined a wide variety of group processes, including group development, structure, influence, power, performance, and conflict.

## FOR MORE INFORMATION

*Introduction to Groups*

- *Blackwell Handbook of Social Psychology: Group Processes*, edited by Michael A. Hogg and Scott Tindale (2001), includes 26 chapters dealing with all aspects of small group behavior.
- *Group Dynamics: Research and Theory*, edited by Dorwin Cartwright and Alvin Zander (1968), is a classic in the scientific field of groups, with chapters dealing with such topics as group membership, conformity, power, leadership, and motivation.
- "Elements of a Lay Theory of Groups: Types of Groups, Relationship Styles, and the Perception of Group Entitavity," by Brian Lickel, David L. Hamilton, and Steven J. Sherman (2001), describes a programmatic series of investigations into the psychological bases of group typologies.

*Group Dynamics: History and Issues*

- *A History of Social Psychology: From the Eighteenth-Century Enlightenment to the Second World War*, by Gustav Jahoda (2007), is a fascinating history of the early emergence of social psychology in general and, group dynamics in particular.

- *The Disappearance of the Social in American Social Psychology*, by John D. Greenwood (2004), takes a controversial position by arguing that researchers too often overlook truly social processes—particularly individual processes that are influenced by how one thinks other members of a social group would respond.
- *The Psychology of Group Perception: Perceived Variability, Entitativity, and Essentialism*, edited by Vincent Yzerbyt, Charles M. Judd, and Olivier Corneille (2004), draws together the work of expert researchers who are investigating when and why groups are perceived to be real or only ephemeral.

*Contemporary Group Dynamics*

- "Learning More by Crossing Levels: Evidence from Airplanes, Hospitals, and Orchestras," by J. Richard Hackman (2003), provides one lucid example after another of the advantages of a multilevel approach to understanding group behavior.
- "Small-Group Research in Social Psychology: Topics and Trends over Time," by Gwen M. Wittenbaum and Richard L. Moreland (2008), takes a hard look at trends in group research and offers recommendations for areas that need further study.

## Media Resources

Visit the Group Dynamics companion website at www.cengage.com/psychology/forsyth to access online resources for your book, including quizzes, flash cards, web links, and more.

# 2

# Studying Groups

## CHAPTER OVERVIEW

How can we learn more about groups and their complex processes? Just as scientists use exacting procedures to study aspects of the physical and natural environment, so do group researchers use scientific methods to further their understanding of groups. Through research, theorists and researchers separate fact from fiction and truth from myth.

- What are the three critical requirements of a scientific approach to the study of groups?
- How do researchers measure individual and group processes?
- What are the key characteristics of and differences between case, experimental, and correlational studies of group processes?
- What are strengths and weaknesses of case, experimental, and correlational methods?
- What theoretical perspectives guide researchers' studies of groups?

## CHAPTER OUTLINE

Everyone is interested in groups. Aristotle discussed groups in detail, eventually concluding that humans are by nature group-seeking animals. Shakespeare worked groups into his plays, which are all the more interesting for their vivid accounts of the shifting dynamics of group and intergroup relations. Centuries ago, Niccolo Machiavelli considered how one should manage groups, particularly if one aims to increase one's power over the people in them. Ralph Waldo Emerson opined, "There need be but one wise man in a company and all are wise, so a blockhead makes a blockhead of his companions." More recently Bono, lead singer for the group U2, explained why most rock groups break up: "It's hard to keep relationships together" (CNN, 2005).

These historical and contemporary analyses of groups are insightful, but limited in one important way: They are all conjectures based on personal opinion rather than scientific research. Are humans truly social creatures? Is the key to controlling people controlling their groups? What happens when an incompetent person—one "bad apple"—joins a group? Why do groups that are initially unified eventually fall into disarray? Why do groups and their members act, feel, and think the way they do? Without scientific analysis, we cannot be certain.

This chapter reviews three basic activities that science requires: measurement, research, and theorizing. As sociologist George Caspar Homans explained, "When the test of the truth of a relationship lies finally in the data themselves" and "nature, however stretched out on the rack, still has a chance to say 'No!'—then the subject is a science" (1967, p. 4). Homans's definition enjoins researchers to "stretch nature out on the rack" by systematically measuring group phenomena and group processes. Scientists must also test "the truth of the relationship" by conducting research that yields the data they need to understand the phenomenon that interests them. Emerson's belief that "one bad apple can ruin the barrel" may apply to groups, but we cannot be sure until this hypothesis is put to the test empirically. But scientists do not just measure things and collect data through research. They also create conceptual frameworks to organize their findings. Homans recognized that "nothing is more lost than a loose fact" (1950, p. 5) and urged the development of theories that provide a "general form in which the results of observations of many particular groups may be expressed" (p. 21).

## MEASUREMENT IN GROUP DYNAMICS

Science often begins with measurement. Biologists made dozens of discoveries when they perfected the compound microscope, as did astronomers when they peered into the night sky with their telescopes. Researchers' success in studying groups was also tied, in large part, to their progress in measuring group members' interpersonal actions and psychological reactions. Here, we trace the growth and impact of two important measurement methods—observing groups and questioning group members—that gave group dynamics a foothold in the scientific tradition.

### Observation

Researchers who study groups often begin with **observation**. No matter what the group that interests them—temporary gatherings of people in public places, teams in factories, gangs in the inner city, sports teams, families with only one parent, fraternities, classrooms, performing orchestras, gamers on the Internet, and so on—they often watch as the group members interact, perform their tasks, make decisions, confront other groups, seek new members and expel old ones, accept direction from their leaders, and so on. Researchers take various approaches to observation, but the essence of the method remains: watch and record the actions taken by group members.

William Foote Whyte (1943) used observation in his classic ethnography of street corner gangs in

---

**observation** A measurement method that involves watching and recording individual and group actions.

Italian American sections of Boston. These groups were composed of young men who joined together regularly, usually at a particular street corner in their neighborhood. Whyte eventually moved into the neighborhood and joined one of the groups, the Nortons, and also participated in a club known as the Italian Community Club. Whyte observed and recorded these groups for three and a half years, gradually developing a detailed portrait of this community and its groups.

Whyte's study underscored the strong link between the individual members and the group, but it also illustrated some key features of observational measures. He focused on observable actions and avoided making inferences about what group members were thinking or feeling if he had no direct evidence of their inner states. He also focused his observations, for he realized that he could not record every behavior performed by every corner boy. Instead, he concentrated on communication, leadership, and attempts at gaining status. He also sampled across time and settings (McGrath & Altermatt, 2001).

Whyte, like all researchers, made a series of decisions as he planned and conducted his study. He decided he would use observation as his basic assessment tool, but he did not use trained, objective observers as some researchers do; he did the watching himself. He also decided to take part in the group's activities, and he revealed his identity to the group members, who knew they were part of a study. Whyte also decided against quantifying his observations. He did not count, time, or methodically track the Nortons's actions. Instead, he described what he observed in his own words and tried to record, verbatim, the things that the Nortons had said. These decisions shaped his study and its conclusions.

**Covert and Overt Observation** Whyte made no attempt to hide what he was doing from the Nortons. Because he used **overt observation** he let the Nortons know that he was a student of groups and would be studying their behavior for a book he was researching. Other researchers, in contrast, prefer to use **covert observation**, whereby they record the group's activities without the group's knowledge. Researchers interested in how groups organize themselves by race and sex in schools sit quietly in the corner of the lunchroom and watch as students choose their seats. To study gatherings of people in a public park a researcher may set up a surveillance camera and record where people congregate throughout the day. As Focus 2.1 explains, covert observation of behavior in public places raises few ethical issues, so long as it does not violate people's right to privacy.

**Participant Observation** Some researchers observe groups from a vantage point outside the group. A researcher may examine carefully videotapes of therapy groups during a treatment session. Another researcher, seated behind a special one-way mirror, may observe groups discussing issues. But some researchers, like Whyte, use **participant observation:** they watch and record the group's activities and interactions while taking part in the group's social process. Whyte went bowling with the Nortons, gambled with Nortons, and even lent money to some of the members. He worked so closely with the group that Doc, one of the key figures in the Nortons, considered himself to be a collaborator in the research project with Whyte, rather than one of the individuals being studied (Whyte, Greenwood, & Lazes, 1991). A diagram of the Norton's structure, shown in Figure 2.1, includes a member named "Bill"; that would be Bill Whyte himself.

Whyte, as a participant observer, gained access to information that would have been hidden from an external observer. His techniques also gave him a very detailed understanding of the gang. Unfortunately, his presence in the group may have changed the group itself. As Doc remarked, "You've slowed me down plenty since you've been down

---

**overt observation** Openly watching and recording group behavior with no attempt to conceal one's research purposes.

**covert observation** Watching and recording group behavior without the participants' knowledge.

**participant observation** Watching and recording group behavior while taking part in the social process.

### Focus 2.1 Is It Ethical to Study Groups?

*Primum non nocere.* (First, do no harm.)
—Galen, 1st century AD

Group researchers, given their commitment to learning all they can about people in groups, pry into matters that other people might consider private, sensitive, or even controversial. Observers may watch groups—a sports team playing a rival, a class of elementary school children on the playground, a sales team reviewing ways to improve their productivity—without telling the groups that they are being observed. Researchers may deliberately disguise their identities so that they can join a group that might otherwise exclude them. Experimenters often manipulate aspects of the groups they study to determine how these manipulations change the group over time. Do researchers have the moral right to use these types of methods to study groups?

In most cases the methods that group researchers use in their studies—watching groups, interviewing members, changing an aspect of the situation to see how groups respond to these changes—raise few ethical concerns. People are usually only too willing to take part in studies, and investigators prefer to get group members' consent before proceeding. If they do watch a group without the members' knowledge, it is usually a group in a public setting where members have no expectation of privacy or where their identities are concealed. Group researchers strive to treat the subjects in their research with respect and fairness.

In some cases, however, researchers have collected data using methods that raise more complex issues of ethics and human rights. One investigator, for example, used participant observation methods in a study of men having sex with one another in a public restroom. He did not reveal that he was a researcher until later, when he tracked them down at their homes (many of them were married) and asked them follow-up questions (Humphreys, 1975). Other researchers, with the permission of a U.S. district judge, made audio recordings of juries' deliberations without the jurors' knowledge. When the tapes were played in public, an angry U.S. Congress passed legislation forbidding researchers from eavesdropping on juries (see Hans & Vidmar, 1991). In other studies researchers have placed participants in stressful situations, as when researchers studied obedience in groups by arranging for an authority to order participants to give an innocent victim painful electric shocks. The shocks were not real, but some participants were very upset by the experience (Milgram, 1963).

These studies are exceptional ones, and they were conducted before review procedures were developed to protect participants. Present-day researchers must now submit their research plans to a group known as an **Institutional Review Board**, or **IRB**. The IRB, using federal guidelines that define what types of procedures should be used to minimize risk to participants, reviews each study's procedures before permitting researchers to proceed. In most cases researchers are expected to give participants a brief but accurate description of their duties in the research before gaining their agreement to take part. Researchers also use methods that minimize any possibility of harm and they treat participants respectfully and fairly. An investigator might not need to alert people that they are being studied as they go about their ordinary activities in public places, but it is best to let an impartial group—the IRB—make that decision.

---

here. Now, when I do something, I have to think what Bill Whyte would want to know about it and how I can explain it. Before, I used to do things by instinct" (Whyte, 1943, p. 301).

This tendency for individuals to act differently when they know they are being observed is often called the **Hawthorne effect**, after research conducted by Elton Mayo and his associates at the Hawthorne Plant of the Western Electric Company. These researchers studied productivity in the workplace by systematically varying a number of features while measuring the workers' output. They moved one group of women to a separate room and monitored their performance carefully. Next, they manipulated features of the work situation, such as

**Hawthorne effect** A change in behavior that occurs when individuals know they are being studied by researchers.

**Institutional Review Board (IRB)** A group, usually located at a university or other research institution, that is responsible for reviewing research procedures to make certain that they are consistent with ethical guidelines for protecting human participants.

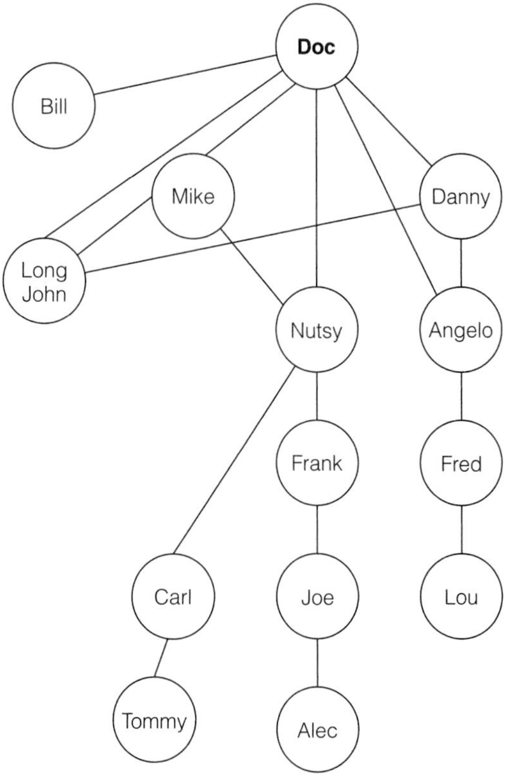


**FIGURE 2.1** The core members of the Nortons, the street corner gang described by William Foote Whyte in his book *Street Corner Society*. Lines between each member indicate interdependence, and members who are placed above others in the chart had more influence than those in the lower positions. Doc was the recognized leader of the group, and Mike and Danny were second in terms of status. Whyte ("Bill" in the diagram), the researcher, was connected to the group through Doc (Whyte, 1955).

SOURCE: From *Street Corner Society* by W. F. Whyte, p. 13. 

the lighting in the room and the duration of rest periods. They were surprised when *all* the changes led to improved worker output. Dim lights, for example, raised efficiency, but so did bright lights. Mayo and his researchers concluded that the group members were working harder because they were being observed and because they felt that the company was taking a special interest in them (Mayo, 1945; Roethlisberger & Dickson, 1939).

Reviews of the Hawthorne studies suggested that other factors besides the scrutiny of the researchers contributed to the increased productivity of the groups. The Hawthorne groups worked in smaller teams, members could talk easily among themselves, and their managers were usually less autocratic than those who worked the main floor of the factory, and all these variables—and not observation alone—may have contributed to the performance gains. Nonetheless, the term *Hawthorne effect* continues to be used to describe any change in behavior that occurs when people feel they are being observed by others (see Bramel & Friend, 1981; Franke & Kaul, 1978; Olson et al., 2004).

**Structuring Observations** Whyte conducted a **qualitative study** of the Nortons. Like a field anthropologist studying a little-known culture, he tried to watch the Nortons without any preconceptions about what to look for, so that he would not unwittingly confirm his prior expectations. Nor did he keep track of the frequencies of any of the behaviors he noted or try explicitly to quantify members' reactions to the events that occurred in the group. Instead he watched, took notes, and reflected on what he saw before drawing general conclusions about the group.

Qualitative methods generate data, but the data describe general qualities and characteristics rather than precise quantities and amounts. Such data are often textual rather than numeric, and may include verbal descriptions of group interactions developed by multiple observers, interviews, responses to open-ended surveys questions, notes from conversations with group members, or in-depth case descriptions of one or more groups. Such qualitative observational methods require an impartial researcher who is a keen observer of groups. If researchers are not careful to remain objective, they may let initial, implicit expectations shape their records (Dollar & Merrigan, 2002; Strauss & Corbin, 1998).

Albert Hastorf and Hadley Cantril's (1954) classic "They Saw a Game" study demonstrated just such a bias by asking college students to watch a film

---

**qualitative study** A research procedure used to collect and analyze nonnumeric, unquantified types of data, such as text, images, or objects.

of two teams playing a football game. They selected a game between Dartmouth and Princeton that featured rough play and many penalties against both teams. When Hastorf and Cantril asked Dartmouth and Princeton students to record the number and severity of the infractions that had been committed by the two teams, the Princeton students were not very accurate. Dartmouth students saw Princeton commit about the same number of infractions as Dartmouth. Princeton students, however, saw the Dartmouth team commit more than twice as many infractions as the Princeton team. Apparently, the Princeton observers' preference for their own team distorted their perceptions.

**Structured observational methods** offer researchers a way to increase the objectivity of their observations. Like biologists who classify living organisms under such categories as phylum, subphylum, class, and order, or psychologists who classify people into various personality types, researchers who use a structured observational method classify each group behavior into an objectively definable category. First, they decide which behaviors to track. Then they develop unambiguous descriptions of each type of behavior they will code. Next, using these behavioral definitions as a guide, they note the occurrence and frequency of these targeted behaviors as they watch the group. This type of research would be a **quantitative study**, because it yields numeric results (Weingart, 1997).

Robert Freed Bales developed two of the best-known structured coding systems for studying groups (Bales, 1950, 1970, 1980). As noted in Chapter 1, Bales spent many years watching group members interact with each other, and for many years he structured his observations using the **Interaction Process Analysis**, or **IPA**. Researchers who use the IPA classify each behavior performed by a group member into one of the 12 categories shown in Figure 2.2. Six of these categories (1–3 and 10–12) pertain to socioemotional, *relationship interaction*. As noted in Chapter 1, these types of actions sustain or weaken interpersonal ties within the group. Complimenting another person is an example of a positive relationship behavior, whereas insulting a group member is a negative relationship behavior. The other six categories (4–9) pertain to instrumental, *task interaction*, such as giving and asking for information, opinions, and suggestions related to the problem the group faces. Observers who use the IPA must be able to listen to a group discussion, break the content down into behavioral units, and then classify each unit into one of the 12 categories in Figure 2.2. If Crystal, for example, begins the group discussion by asking "Should we introduce ourselves?" and Al answers, "Yes," observers write "Crystal–Group" beside Category 8 (Crystal asks for opinion from whole group) and "Al–Crystal" beside Category 5 (Al gives opinion to Crystal). If Rupert later angrily tells the entire group, "This group is a boring waste of time," the coders write "Rupert–Group" beside Category 12 (Rupert shows antagonism towards entire group).

Bales improved the system over the years. His newer version, which generates more global summaries of group behavior, is called the **Systematic Multiple Level Observation of Groups**, or **SYMLOG**. SYMLOG coders use 26 different categories instead of only 12, with these categories signaling members' dominance–submissiveness, friendliness–unfriendliness, and accepting–opposing the task orientation of established authority (Hare, 2005). When a group begins discussing a problem, for example, most behaviors may be concentrated in the dominant, friendly, and accepting authority categories. But if the group argues, then scores in

---

**structured observational method** A research procedure that classifies (codes) group members' actions into defined categories.

**quantitative study** A research procedure used to collect and analyze data in a numeric form, such as frequencies, proportions, or amounts.

**Interaction Process Analysis (IPA)** A structured coding system developed by Robert Bales used to classify group behavior into task-oriented and relationship-oriented categories.

**Systematic Multiple Level Observation of Groups (SYMLOG)** A theoretical and structured coding system developed by Robert Bales which assumes that group activities can be classified along three dimensions: dominance versus submissiveness, friendliness versus unfriendliness, and acceptance of versus opposition to authority.

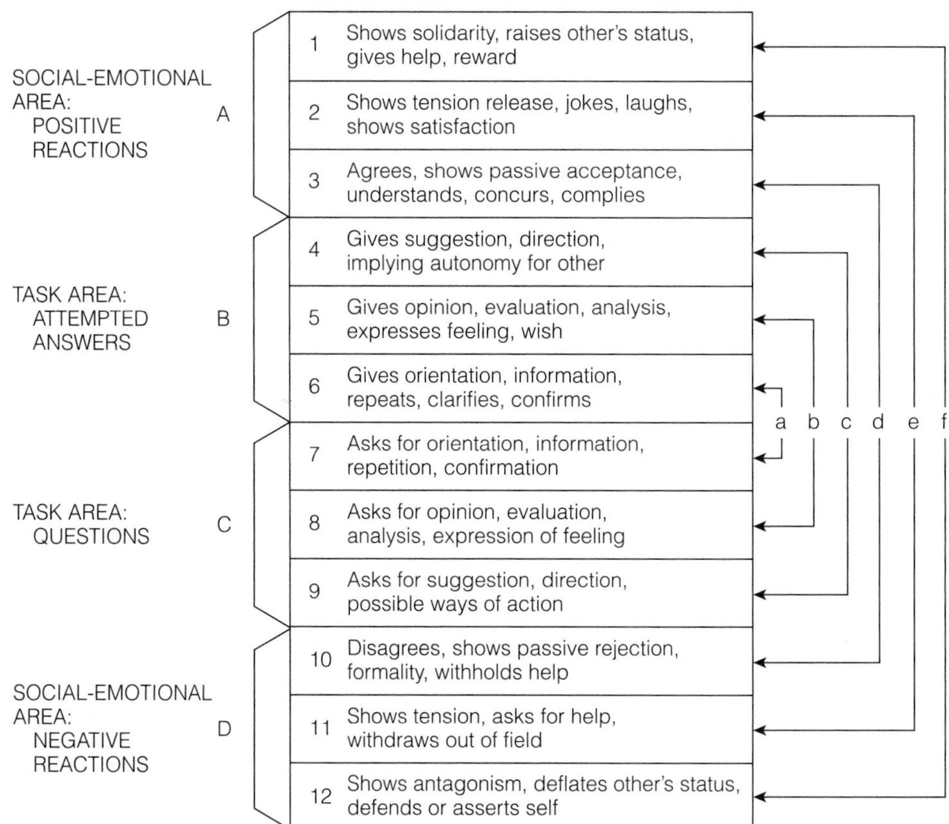


**FIGURE 2.2** Robert F. Bales's original Interaction Process Analysis (IPA) coding system for structuring observations of groups. Areas A (1–3) and D (10–12) are used to code socioemotional, relationship interactions. Areas B (4–6) and C (7–9) are used to code task interaction. The lines to the right (labeled a–f) indicate problems of orientation (a), evaluation (b), control (c), decision (d), tension-management (e), and integration (f).

SOURCE: Adapted from *Personality and Interpersonal Behavior* by Robert Freed Bales. Copyright 1970 by Holt, Rinehart, and Winston, Inc.

the unfriendly, opposing authority categories may begin to climb. Chapter 5 uses SYMLOG to describe changes in relationships among group members that occur over time.

**Reliability and Validity of Observations** Structured observation systems, because they can be used to record the number of times a particular type of behavior has occurred, make possible comparison across categories, group members, and even different groups. Moreover, if observers are carefully trained, structured coding system such as IPA and SYMLOG will yield data that are both reliable and valid. **Reliability** is determined by a measure's consistency across time, components, and raters. If a rater, when she hears the statement, "This group is a boring waste of time," always classifies it as a Category 12 behavior, then the rating is reliable. The measure has

**Reliability** The degree to which a measurement technique consistently yields the same conclusion at different times. For measurement techniques with two or more components, reliablility is also the degree to which these various components all yield similar conclusions.

*interrater reliability* if different raters, working independently, all think that the statement belongs in Category 12. (Researchers once had to arrange for teams of observers to watch the groups they studied, but now they usually videotape the groups for later analysis.) **Validity** describes the extent to which the technique measures what it is supposed to measure. The IPA, for example, is valid only if observers' ratings actually measure the amount of relationship and task interaction in the group. If the observers are incorrect in their coding, or if the categories are not accurate indicators of relationship and task interaction, the scores are not valid (Bakeman, 2000).

Given the greater reliability and validity of structured observations, why did Whyte take a qualitative, unstructured approach? Whyte was more interested in gaining an understanding of the entire community and its citizenry, so a structured coding system's focus on specific behaviors would have yielded an unduly narrow analysis. At the time he conducted his study, Whyte did not know which behaviors he should scrutinize if he wanted to understand the group. Whyte was also unfamiliar with the groups he studied, so he chose to immerse himself in fieldwork. His research was more exploratory, designed to develop theory first and validate hypotheses second, so he used an unstructured observational approach. If he had been testing a hypothesis by measuring specific aspects of a group, then the rigor and objectivity of a structured approach would have been preferable. Qualitative methods, in general, "provide a richer, more varied pool of information" than quantitative ones (King, 2004, p. 175).

### Self-Report Measures

Whyte did not just watch Doc, Mike, Danny, and the others as they interacted with one another and with others in the community. Time and again, Whyte supplemented his observations by questioning the group members. Whenever he was curious about their thoughts, perceptions, and emotions, he would ask them, as indirectly as possible, to describe their reactions: "Now and then, when I was concerned with a particular problem and felt I needed more information from a certain individual . . . I would seek an opportunity to get the man alone and carry on a more formal interview" (Whyte, 1955, pp. 303–304).

**Self-report measures**, despite their variations, are all based on a simple premise: if you want to know what a group member is thinking, feeling, or planning, then just ask him or her to report that information to you directly. In *interviews* the researcher records the respondent's answer to various questions, but *questionnaires* ask respondents to record their answers themselves. Some variables, such as members' beliefs about their group's cohesiveness or their perceptions of the group's leader, may be so complex that researchers need to ask a series of interrelated questions. When the items are selected and pretested for accuracy, a multi-item measure is usually termed a *test* or a *scale*.

**Sociometry** Jacob Moreno (1934), a pioneer in the field of group dynamics, used self-report methods to study the social organization of groups of young women living in adjacent cottages at an institution. The women were neighbors, but they were not very neighborly. Discipline problems were rampant, and disputes continually arose among the groups and among members of the same group who were sharing a cottage. Moreno believed that the tensions would abate if he could regroup the women into more compatible clusters and put the greatest physical distance between hostile groups. So he asked the women to identify five women whom they liked the most on a confidential questionnaire. Moreno then used these responses to construct more harmonious groups, and his efforts were rewarded when the overall level of antagonism in the community declined (Hare & Hare, 1996).

---

**validity** The degree to which a measurement method assesses what it was designed to measure.

**self-report measure** An assessment method, such as a questionnaire, test, or interview, that ask respondents to describe their feelings, attitudes, or beliefs.

Moreno called this technique for measuring the relations between group members **sociometry**. A researcher begins a sociometric study by asking group members one or more questions about the other members. To measure attraction, the researcher might ask, "Whom do you like most in this group?" but such questions as "Whom in the group would you like to work with the most?" or "Whom do you like the least?" can also be used. Researchers often limit the number of choices that participants can make. These choices are then organized in a **sociogram**, which is a diagram of the relationships among group members. As Figure 2.3 illustrates, each group member is represented by a circle, and arrows are used to indicate who likes whom. The researcher can organize the group members' responses into a more meaningful pattern, say, by putting individuals who are frequently chosen by others at the center of the diagram, and the least frequently chosen people could be placed about the periphery. Sociometric data can also be examined using more elaborate statistical methods, such as path diagrams, factor plots, and cluster analysis (Brandes et al., 1999; Wasserman & Faust, 1994). Computer programs such as Netdraw (Borgatti, 2002b), Sociometrics (Walsh, 2003), and KrackPlot (Krackhardt, 2003) can generate mathematically accurate sociograms.

A sociogram yields information about individual members, relationships between pairs of members, and the group's overall structure. Depending on their place in the group's sociogram, and the number of times they are chosen by others, members can be compared and contrasted:

- *populars*, or stars, are well-liked, very popular group members with a high *choice status*: they are picked by many other group members
- *unpopulars*, or rejected members, are identified as disliked by many members and so their choice status is low
- *isolates*, or loners, are infrequently chosen by any group members
- *positives*, or sociables, select many others as their friends
- *negatives* select few others as their friends
- *pairs* are two people who choose each other, and so have reciprocal bonds
- *clusters* are individuals within the group who make up a subgroup, or clique

Sociograms also yield group-level social network information (Borgatti, 2002a). As Chapter 6 explains, highly cohesive groups contain a substantial proportion of mutual pairs and very few isolates. Centralized groups are ones where a relatively small number of people are liked by many others in the group, but decentralized groups have no sociometric stars. Schismatic groups are ones with two or more subgroups with few cross-subgroup ties. Sociograms thus provide the means to identify cliques, schisms, hierarchies, and other relational regularities and oddities.

**Reliability and Validity of Self-Report Measures** Self-report methods, such as sociometry, have both weaknesses and strengths. They depend very much on knowing what questions to ask the group members. A maze of technical questions also confronts researchers designing questionnaires. If respondents do not answer the questions consistently—if, for example, Jos indicates that he likes Gerard the most on Monday but on Tuesday changes his choice to Claire—then the responses will be unreliable. Also, if questions are not worded properly, the instrument will lack validity, because the respondents may misinterpret what is being asked. Validity is also a problem if group members are unwilling to disclose their personal attitudes, feelings, and perceptions or are unaware of these internal processes.

Despite these limitations, self-report methods provide much information about group phenomena, but from the perspective of the participant rather than the observer. When researchers are

---

**sociometry** A research technique developed by Jacob Moreno that graphically and mathematically summarizes patterns of intermember relations.

**sociogram** A graphic representation of the patterns of intermember relations created through sociometry. In most cases each member of the group is depicted by a symbol, such as a lettered circle or square, and the types of relations among members (e.g., communication links, friendship pairings) are depicted with capped lines.

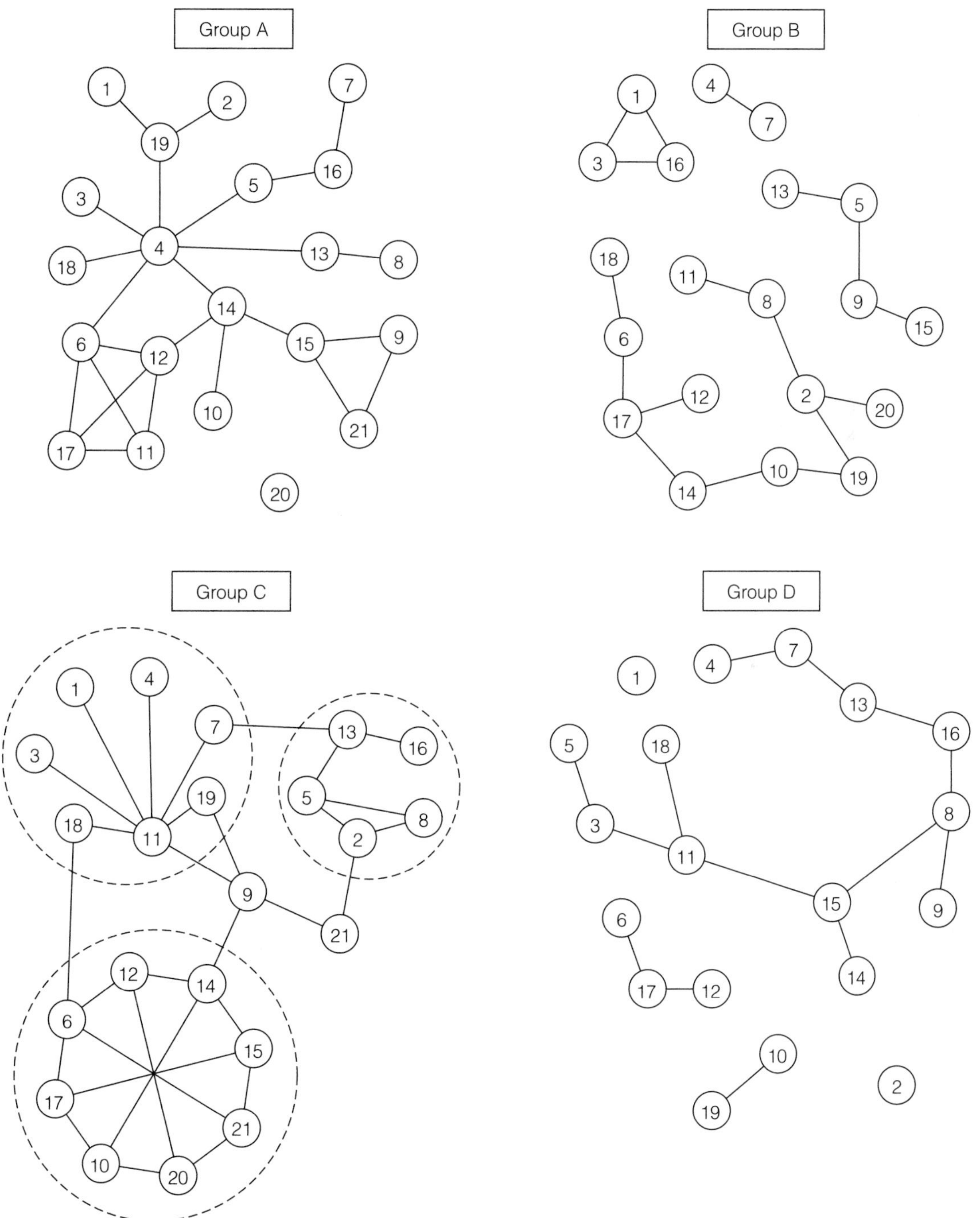


**FIGURE 2.3** Examples of sociograms. Sociograms chart group structure by identifying relationships among the members. Group A is a centralized group, but B is relatively decentralized. Group C has a number of subgroups that are not well-linked, and Group D is relatively disorganized.

primarily interested in personal processes, such as perceptions, feelings, and beliefs, self-report methods may be the only means of assessing these private processes. But if participants are biased, their self-reports may not be as accurate as we would like. Self-reports may also not be accurate indicators of group-level processes, such as cohesiveness or conflict (See Focus 2.2).

## RESEARCH METHODS IN GROUP DYNAMICS

Good measurement alone does not guarantee good science. Researchers who watch groups and ask group members questions can develop a detailed description of a group, but they must go beyond description if they are to *explain* groups. Once researchers have collected their data, they must use that information to test hypotheses about group phenomena. They use many techniques to check the adequacy of their suppositions about groups, but the three most common approaches are (1) *case studies*, (2) *experimental studies* that manipulate one or more aspects of the group situation, and (3) *correlational studies* of the naturally occurring relationships between various aspects of groups.

### Case Studies

Irving Janis (1972) was puzzled. He had studied a wide variety of groups in many contexts, but when his daughter asked him why U.S. President John F. Kennedy's advisors encouraged him to support an invasion of Cuba he had no answer. The members of this group were the top political minds in the country, and they had reviewed their recommendation carefully, yet it was a decidedly mistaken one. What caused this group to perform so far below its potential?

Janis decided to study this group in detail. Relying on historical documents, minutes of meetings, diaries, letters, and group members' memoirs and public statements, he analyzed the group's structure, its communication processes, and its leadership. He also expanded his study to include other groups that made disastrous errors, including the military personnel responsible for the defense of Pearl Harbor before its attack in World War II and advisors who urged greater U.S. involvement in Vietnam. His analyses led him to conclude that these groups suffered from the same problem. Over time they had become so unified that members felt as though they could not disagree with the group's decisions, and so they failed to examine their assumptions carefully. Janis labeled this loss of rationality caused by strong pressures to conform **groupthink**. Chapter 11 examines Janis's theory in more detail.

**Conducting a Case Study** One of the best ways to understand groups in general is to understand one group in particular. This approach has a long and venerable tradition in all the sciences, with some of the greatest advances in thinking coming from the **case study**—an in-depth examination of one or more groups. If the groups have not yet disbanded, the researcher may decide to observe them directly, but in many cases they cull facts about the group from interviews with members, descriptions of the group written by journalists, or members' biographical writings. Researchers then relate this information back to the variables that interest them and thereby estimate the extent to which the examined case supports their hypotheses (Cahill, Fine, & Grant, 1995; Yin, 2009).

Researchers have conducted case studies of all sorts of groups: adolescent peer groups (Adler & Adler, 1995), artist circles (Farrell, 2001), crisis intervention teams in psychiatric hospitals (Murphy & Keating, 1995), cults (Festinger, Riecken, & Schachter, 1956), drug-dealing gangs (Venkatesh, 2008), families coping with an alcoholic member (Carvalho & Brito, 1995), focus groups (Seal,

---

**groupthink** A strong concurrence-seeking tendency that interferes with effective group decision making, identified by Irving Janis.

**case study** A research technique that involves examining, in as much detail as possible, the dynamics of a single group or individual.

## Focus 2.2 Is Drinking a Group-Level Phenomenon?

*Bars and parties are conceptually nested within larger community subsystems and represent the actual drinking situations and environments in which students drink and experience alcohol-related problems.*

—John D. Clapp and colleagues (2007, p. 427)

Most people drink alcohol collectively. College students, for example, sometimes drink alone in their dorms or apartments, but in most cases groups are the context for drinking. In fact, in the course of an evening, students often drink in one group after another. Early in the evening they "pregame" in dyads or other small groups. They then continue drinking in larger groups—in bars, at parties in private homes, or fraternity and sorority organizations located near campus.

Parties are difficult to study. Asking people about the party they attended the night before would likely yield invalid data, as they may not remember the details and they may edit their reports to avoid embarrassment. So when John Clapp decided to study this unique type of group, he assembled a team of observers and interviewers and trained them to enter parties and collect data. Every Thursday, Friday, and Saturday night the teams would patrol the area around campus, looking for parties. Some nights they found only 2 or 3, but on others as many as 20; the average number of parties was 7. The team then chose, at random, four parties to study that evening. If the hosts agreed to take part in the study—and most did—then seven-person crews, carrying notebooks and clip boards and wearing "College Drinking Survey" sweatshirts, entered the party and recorded such variables as number of guests rowdiness, loudness of the music, kind of food available, type of alcohol and drugs being used (e.g., beer, mixed drinks, shots, marijuana), and the distribution of people in the physical location. Clapp's team did not interfere with the natural progression of the party, but they did administer short questionnaires to partygoers and checked their Breath Alcohol Concentrations, or BrAC, as they entered the party and again when they left. They also arranged for rides for drunken partygoers who needed to get home. The team included a security person who remained outside the party in case problems occurred (Clapp et al., 2007, 2008).

Some 224 parties later the researchers concluded that group-level factors played a major role in determining people's BrAC. When alcohol consumption was the party's primary activity, participants had higher BrACs, particularly if they thought that others were drinking excessively. If the party's primary activity was socializing among the guests, then participants drank less. Parties where the students played drinking games also yielded more intoxicated guests, as did parties where people were costumed (e.g., theme parties and Halloween parties). Women, in particular, had higher BrACs levels at theme parties compared to men. Students' intoxication levels dropped as the parties increased in size, disconfirming the idea that the students become more uninhibited in large groups. This effect however, may have been due to the logistics of gaining access to alcohol rather than inhibition. The larger the party, the longer it took students to get a drink.

Clapp and his colleagues, by combining various types of data, succeeded in shedding light on one of the most dynamic of groups—the college party—and their findings suggest ways to minimize the health risks of these groups. Excessive drinking causes thousands of injuries and deaths among students each year. Physical and sexual assault are associated with alcohol, and the tendency for students to binge on weekends may lead, over time, to alcoholism. Curtailing alcohol consumption is therefore a beneficial goal and can be accomplished through relatively simple alterations of group goals and norms. To shift the group's goals to focus on socializing rather than drinking *per se,* hosts should discourage drinking games and avoid theme parties with costumed partygoers. Because people also drink more to keep pace with others' degree of intoxication, hosts should not make it too easy for their guests to drink excessively. Banning shots and kegs, providing food, and encouraging social interaction are a few ways to increase the social value of the event and minimize the harm done by drinking too much alcohol.

Bogart, & Ehrhardt, 1998), government leaders at international summits (Hare & Naveh, 1986), industrialists and inventors (Uglow, 2002), Little League baseball teams (Fine, 1987), mountain climbers (Kayes, 2006), naval personnel living in an undersea habitat (Radloff & Helmreich, 1968), presidential advisors (Goodwin, 2005), religious communes (Stones, 1982), rock-and-roll bands (Bennett, 1980), fans of rock-and-roll bands (Adams, 1998), search-and-rescue squads (Lois, 2003), sororities (Robbins, 2004), sports fans (St. John, 2004), support groups (Turner, 2000), the Supreme Court (Toobin, 2007), and, of course, advisory groups making critically important decisions pertaining to national policy and defense (Allison & Zelikow, 1999; Janis, 1972). Although once considered to be questionable in terms of scientific value, case studies that are carried out with care and objectivity are now widely recognized as indispensible tools for understanding group processes (Yin, 2009).

**Advantages and Disadvantages** All research designs offer both advantages and disadvantages, and case studies are no exception. By focusing on a limited number of cases, researchers often provide richly detailed qualitative descriptions of naturally occurring groups. If the groups have disbanded and researchers are relying on archival data, they need not be concerned that their research will substantially disrupt or alter naturally occurring group processes. Case studies also tend to focus on **bona fide groups** that are found in everyday, natural contexts. Unlike groups that are concocted by researchers in the laboratory for a brief period of time and then disbanded, bona fide groups are embedded in a natural context. Whyte, for example, studied bona fide groups, for the corner gangs existed on the streets of Boston long before he started watching them, and they continued on long after he finished his observations. Families, gangs, work teams, support groups, and cults are just a few of the many naturally occurring groups that researchers have studied by going into the field, locating these groups, and then collecting information about them by observing their members' activities (Frey, 2003).

These advantages are offset by limitations. Researchers who use the case study method must bear in mind that the group studied may be unique, and so its dynamics say little about other groups' dynamics. Also, researchers rarely use quantitative measures of group processes when conducting case studies, so their interpretations can be influenced by their own assumptions and biases. In addition, the essential records and artifacts may be inaccurate or unavailable to the researcher. Janis, for example, was forced to "rely mainly on the contemporary and retrospective accounts by the group members themselves . . . many of which are likely to have been written with an eye to the author's own place in history" (1972, p. v). In the case of the Bay of Pigs, when many key documents were eventually declassified they suggested that the group did not experience groupthink, but instead was misled deliberately by some of the group members (Kramer, 2008). Finally, case studies only imply but rarely establish causal relationships among important variables in the group under study. Janis believed that groupthink was causing the poor decisions in the groups he studied, but actually some other unnoticed factor could have been the prime causal agent.

## Experimental Studies

Kurt Lewin, Ronald Lippitt, and Ralph White started with one basic question: Are people more productive and more satisfied when working for a democratic, group-centered leader rather than an autocratic, self-centered leader? To find an answer they arranged for 10- and 11-year-old boys to meet after school in five-member groups to work on hobbies such as woodworking and painting. An adult led each group by adopting one of three styles of leadership: autocratic, democratic, or laissez-faire. The *autocratic* leader made all the decisions for the group; the *democratic* leader let the boys themselves make their own decisions; and the *laissez-faire* leader gave the group members very little guidance (Lewin, Lippitt, & White, 1939; White, 1990; White & Lippitt, 1968).

The researchers observed the groups as they worked with each type of leader and measured group productivity and aggressiveness. When they reviewed their findings, they discovered that the autocratic groups spent more time working (74%) than the democratic groups (50%), which in turn spent more time working than the laissez-faire groups (33%). Although these results argued in favor of the efficiency of an autocratic leadership

---

**bona fide group** A naturally occurring group (particularly when compared to an ad hoc group created by a researcher in a laboratory study), such as an audience, board of directors, club, or team.

style, the observers also noted that when the leader left the room for any length of time, the democratically led groups kept right on working, whereas the boys in the autocratic groups stopped working. Lewin, Lippitt, and White also noted high rates of hostility in the autocratically led groups, as well as more demands for attention, more destructiveness, and a greater tendency to single out one group member to serve as the target of almost continual verbal abuse. The researchers believed that this target for criticism and hostility, or **scapegoat**, provided members with an outlet for pent-up hostilities that could not be acted out against the powerful group leader.

**Conducting Experiments** Lewin, Lippitt, and White's study of leadership styles possesses the three key features of an **experiment**. First, the researchers identified a variable that they believed caused changes in group processes and then systematically manipulated it. They manipulated this **independent variable** by giving groups different types of leaders (autocratic, democratic, or laissez-faire). Second, the researchers assessed the effects of the independent variable by measuring such factors as productivity and aggressiveness. The variables that researchers measure are called **dependent variables**, because their magnitude depends on the strength and nature of the independent variable. Lewin, Lippitt, and White hypothesized that group leadership style would influence productivity and aggressiveness, so they tested this hypothesis by *manipulating* the independent variable (leadership style) and *measuring* the dependent variables (productivity and aggressiveness).

Third, the experimenters tried to maintain control over other variables. The researchers never assumed that the only determinant of productivity and aggressiveness was leadership style; they knew that other variables, such as the personality characteristics and abilities of the group members, could influence the dependent variables. In the experiment, however, the researchers were not interested in these other variables. They therefore made certain that these other variables were controlled in the experimental situation. For example, they took pains to ensure that the groups they created were "roughly equated on patterns of interpersonal relationships, intellectual, physical, and socioeconomic status, and personality characteristics" (White & Lippitt, 1968, p. 318). Because no two groups were identical, these variations could have resulted in some groups working harder than others. The researchers used *random assignment* of groups to even out these initial inequalities. Thus, they hoped that any differences found on the dependent measure would be due to the independent variable rather than to uncontrolled differences among the participating groups.

In sum, when researchers conduct experiments they manipulate one or more independent variables, assess systematically one or more dependent variables, and control other possible contaminating variables. When the experiment is properly designed and conducted, researchers can assume that any differences among the conditions on the dependent variables are produced by the independent variable that is manipulated, and not by some other variable outside their control.

**Advantages and Disadvantages** Why do researchers so frequently rely on experimentation to test their hypotheses about groups? This preference derives, in part, from the inferential power of experimentation. Researchers who design their experiments carefully can make inferences about the causal relationships linking variables. If the investigators keep all variables constant except for the

---

**scapegoat** An individual or group who is unfairly held responsible for a negative event and outcome; the innocent target of interpersonal hostility.

**experiment** A research design in which the investigator manipulates at least one variable by randomly assigning participants to two or more different conditions and measuring at least one other variable.

**independent variable** Those aspects of the situation manipulated by the researcher in an experimental study; the causal variable in a cause–effect relationship.

**dependent variable** The responses of the participant measured by the researcher; the effect variable in a cause–effect relationship.

independent variable, and the dependent variable changes, then they can cautiously conclude that the independent variable caused the dependent variable to change. Experiments, if properly conducted, can therefore be used to detect causal relationships between variables (Hoyle, 2005).

Experiments offer an excellent means of testing hypotheses about the causes of group behavior, but they are not without their logistical, methodological, and ethical problems. Researchers cannot always control the situation sufficiently to manipulate the independent variable or to keep other variables constant. Moreover, to maintain control over the conditions of an experiment, researchers may end up studying closely monitored but artificial group situations. Experimenters often work in laboratories with ad hoc groups that are created just for the purpose of research, and these groups may differ in important ways from bona fide groups. Although an experimenter can heighten the impact of the situation by withholding information about the study, such deception can be challenged on ethical grounds. Of course, experiments can be conducted in the field using already existing groups, but they will almost necessarily involve the sacrifice of some degree of control and will reduce the strength of the researchers' conclusions. Hence, the major advantage of experimentation—the ability to draw causal inferences—can be offset by the major disadvantage of experimentation—basing conclusions on contrived situations that say little about the behavior of groups in more naturalistic settings. (These issues are discussed in more detail by Anderson & Bushman, 1997 and Driskell & Salas, 1992.)

### Correlational Studies

The students who attended Bennington College in the 1930s were changed by the experience—not just intellectually but politically. When they first entered school most of them were conservative, but by the time they graduated they had shifted to become more liberal. In fact, in 1936 fully 62% of the first-year class preferred the Republican presidential candidate. But only 15% of the juniors and seniors endorsed the Republican candidate, evidence of a profound shift in political beliefs.

Theodore Newcomb (1943), a faculty member at Bennington College in the mid-1930s, believed that the first-year students were changing their group allegiances to match the prevailing politics of Bennington. The younger students were, in effect, accepting seniors as their **reference group**, which is a group that provides individuals with guidelines or standards for evaluating themselves, their attitudes, and their beliefs (Hyman, 1942). Any group that plays a significant role in one's life, such as a family, a friendship clique, colleagues at work, or even a group one admires but is not a member of, can function as a reference group (Singer, 1990). When students first enrolled at Bennington, their families served as their reference group, so their attitudes matched their families' attitudes. The longer students remained at Bennington, however, the more their attitudes changed to match the attitudes of their new reference group—the rest of the college population. Their families had conservative attitudes, but the college community supported mainly liberal attitudes, and Newcomb hypothesized that many Bennington students shifted their attitudes in response to this reference-group pressure.

Newcomb tested this hypothesis by administering questionnaires and interviews to an entire class of Bennington students from their entrance in 1935 to their graduation in 1939. He found a consistent trend toward liberalism in many of the students and reasoned that this change resulted from peer-group pressure because it was more pronounced among the popular students. Those who endorsed liberal attitudes were (1) "both capable and desirous of cordial relations with the fellow community members" (Newcomb, 1943, p. 149), (2) more frequently chosen by others as friendly,

---

**reference group** A group or collective that individuals use as a standard or frame of reference when selecting and appraising their abilities, attitudes, or beliefs; includes groups that individuals identify with and admire and categories of noninteracting individuals.

and (3) a more cohesive subgroup than the conservative students. Individuals who did not become more liberal were less involved in the college's social life, or they were very family-oriented. These reference groups changed the students permanently, for the students who shifted were still liberals when Newcomb measured their political beliefs some 25 years later (Newcomb et al., 1967).

**Conducting Correlational Studies** Newcomb's Bennington study was a nonexperimental, **correlational study**; he examined the naturally occurring relationships among several variables without manipulating any of them. Newcomb believed, for example, that as students came to identify more closely with other students, their attitudes and values changed to match those of their peers. Therefore, he assessed students' popularity, their dependence on their families, and changes in their political attitudes. Then he examined the relationships among these variables by carrying out several statistical tests. At no point did he try to manipulate the group situation.

Correlational studies are so named because, at least initially, researchers indexed the strength and direction of the relationships among the variables they measured by calculating **correlation coefficients**. A correlation coefficient, abbreviated as *r*, can range from −1 to +1, with the distance from zero (0), the neutral point, indicating the strength of the relationship. If Newcomb had found that the correlation between students' popularity and liberal attitudes was close to 0, for example, he would have concluded that the two variables were unrelated to each other. If the correlation was significantly different from 0—in either a positive or a negative direction—his study would have shown that these two variables were related to each other. The sign of the correlation (− or +) indicates the direction of the relationship. If, for example, the correlation between popularity and liberal attitudes was +.68, this positive correlation would indicate that both variables increased or decreased together: the more popular the student, the more liberal her attitude. A negative correlation, such as −.57, would indicate that the variables were inversely related: More popular students would tend to have less liberal attitudes. Thus, a correlation is a handy way of summarizing a great deal of information about the relationship between two variables. Researchers do not always analyze their data by computing correlations, but the term *correlational study* continues to be used to describe studies that measure variables rather than manipulating them.

**Advantages and Disadvantages** Researchers use correlational designs whenever they wish to know more about the relationship between variables. Are group leaders usually older than their followers? Do groups become more centralized as they grow larger? Do people who are more committed to their group tend to express attitudes that match their group's position? These are all questions that researchers might ask concerning the relationship between variables. When coupled with valid measures, correlational studies clearly describe these relationships without disrupting or manipulating any aspect of the group.

Correlational studies, however, yield only limited information about the *causal* relationship between variables, because the researcher does not directly manipulate any variables. Newcomb's data, for example, indicated that the attitude changes he measured were related to reference-group pressures, but he could not rule out other possible causes. Perhaps, unknown to Newcomb, the most popular students on campus all read the same books, which contained arguments that persuaded them to give up their conservative attitudes. Newcomb also could not be certain about the *direction* of the relationship he documented. He believed that individuals who joined the liberal reference group became more liberal themselves, but the causal relationship may have

---

**correlational study** A research design in which the investigator measures (but does not manipulate) at least two variables and then uses statistical procedures to examine the strength and direction of the relationship between these variables.

**correlation coefficient** A statistic that measures the strength and direction of a relationship between two variables. Often symbolized by *r*, correlations can range from −1 to +1.

been just the opposite: People who expressed more liberal attitudes may have been asked to join more liberal reference groups. Although these alternative explanations seem less plausible, they cannot be eliminated, given the methods used by Newcomb.

## Selecting a Research Method

Researchers who study groups rather than individual human beings face some unique logistic and statistical problems. Individuals change over time, but their development tends to be gradual and continuous. Groups, in contrast, can change rapidly and dramatically, so that the group that is studied at one point in time may evolve into a very different group when studied again. The group may also change because its composition changes; if a member joins or leaves a group, the group's structures and processes may change. The interactions that take place within groups are also complex and nuanced, so researchers sometimes encounter more data than they can objectively record and process. "Group process carries literally hundreds of messages," so "even after applying one, two, three, or more content analysis schemes to it, more information remains to be gathered and interpreted" (Mills, 1979, p. 415).

Researchers use a variety of empirical procedures to deal with these complexities. Some observe group processes and then perform a qualitative analysis of their observations, whereas others insist on quantitative measurement methods and elaborate controlled experiments. Some researchers conduct their studies in field situations using bona fide groups, whereas others bring groups into the laboratory or even create groups to study. Some researchers undertake exploratory studies with no clear idea of what results to expect, whereas other research studies are designed to test hypotheses carefully derived from a specific theory. Some study group phenomena by asking volunteers to role-play group members, and others simulate group interaction with computers.

Advances in instrumentation, design, and statistical procedures have also eased some of the labor and time costs of conducting group research. Information technologies provide opportunities to study groups using the Internet, and software can now search out and model the structure of groups. Researchers have even begun developing tools that will allow them to create *virtual reality groups*, where computers are used to immerse individuals in groups that seem to be real but are actually created by virtual environment technologies (Blascovich et al., 2002; Hoyt & Blascovich, 2003).

This diversity of research methods does not reflect researchers' uncertainty about which technique is best. Rather, the diversity stems from the unique advantages and disadvantages offered by each method. Case studies limit the researcher's ability to draw conclusions, to quantify results, and to make objective interpretations. But some topics, such as groupthink, are difficult to study by any other method. As Janis (1982) himself pointed out, it would be difficult to examine groups that make decisions about national policies—including war and civil defense—through traditional quantitative methods such as experimentation. But the real forte of the case study approach is its power to provide grist for the theoretician's mill, enabling the investigator to formulate hypotheses that set the stage for other research methods.

Such stimulation of theory is also frequently a consequence of correlational research. Correlational studies are limited in causal power, but they yield precise estimates of the strength of the relationships between variables. Experimentation provides the firmest test of causal hypotheses by showing that variable $X$ will cause such and such a change in variable $Y$. In a well-designed and -conducted experiment, the researcher can test several hypotheses about groups, making the method both rigorous and efficient. However, when an artificial setting would yield meaningless results, when the independent variable cannot be manipulated, or when too little is known about the topic even to suggest what variables may be causal, some other approach is preferable. The solution, then, is to study groups using multiple methods (see Focus 2.3). As Joseph McGrath explained, "All methods have inherent flaws—though each has certain advantages. These flaws cannot be avoided. But what the researcher can do is to bring

### Focus 2.3 What Is the Unit of Analysis When Studying Groups?

*Should we not assume that just as the eye, the hand, the foot, and in general each part of the body clearly has its own proper function, so man too has some function over and above the function of his parts?*

—Aristotle, *Nicomachean Ethics*

A research team carries out an intriguing study of some aspect of groups, such as group loyalty or absenteeism at meetings. They locate 20 groups, each with five members, and measure things like loyalty, conscientiousness, and duration of membership. But, when it comes time to analyze the data, the researchers face a basic question. How many subjects are in the study: 100 individuals or 20 groups?

The answer depends on the **unit of analysis** in the research. If the researchers choose the individual members as the unit of analysis they may predict that members who have been in a group longer tend to be more loyal to the group, or that members with certain personality characteristics will have fewer absences. But if the group is the unit of analysis the researchers may count how many times the members say the word *we* during a group meeting and use this variable to predict turnover in membership or absenteeism.

Group data are usually multilevel data, since individuals are nested in groups, which are often nested in some larger organization or community. Researchers must therefore exercise special care when designing their measures and examining their data. If they want to examine an individual quality, such as loyalty and absenteeism, they should use questions that focus on the individual: "Are you loyal to this group?" and "How many meetings of this group have you missed in the last year?" But, if they want to know the group's climate of loyalty they might average each member's responses to the "Are you loyal?" question to get an index of group loyalty, but only if most of the members give similar answers to this question. They may also rephrase the question, so that it asks about the group: "Are most members loyal to the group?"

Researchers also exercise special care when examining their data so that they do not attribute effects caused by group-level processes to individual-level processes and vice versa. The investigators may be thrilled, for example, to find that members' individual loyalty scores predict the regularity of their attendance of meetings, until they realize that people who are in the same groups have unusually similar loyalty scores due to some group-level process. It may be that when the groups formed, the members naturally sorted themselves into groups in which members were relatively similar in their loyalty to the group, or a norm of loyalty emerged within a group and most people eventually adopted the group's norm as their own. As a result, most of the variability in loyalty is not between people but between groups, so that when the researchers take into account which group a person belongs to, the effect of individual-level loyalty disappears.

Advances in statistical procedures offer researchers ways to deal with these problems. If data are collected from individual group members, researchers can check for group-level interdependencies by computing intraclass correlations (ICC), average deviation scores (e.g., *rWG* scores), or within-and-between analysis (WABA) statistics. These analyses will indicate if the individual can serve as the unit of analysis or if interdependency among the members' data is so high that their responses should be aggregated at the group level. Some statistical procedures, such as hierarchical linear modeling (HLM), are designed specifically for multilevel data and so are capable of disentangling cause–effect relationships and processes that operate simultaneously at two or more levels (Zyphur, Kaplan, & Christian, 2008). These advances, taken together, highlight the growing methodological sophistication of group researchers as they identify new ways to deal with the challenge of studying individuals nested in groups (Sadler & Judd, 2001).

more than one approach, more than one method, to bear on each aspect of a problem" (1984, p. 30).

**unit of analysis** The focus of empirical and theoretical interest selected when individuals or objects under study are nested in a series of increasingly inclusive or graded clusters; the source of the data the researcher seeks.

## THEORETICAL PERSPECTIVES IN GROUP DYNAMICS

Successful researchers do not just develop ingenious methods for measuring and studying group processes. They also develop compelling theoretical explanations for group phenomena. Science, more than any other approach to gaining knowledge, advocates the long-term goal of increasing and systematizing knowledge about the subject matter. Theories provide the means of organizing known facts about groups and so create orderly knowledge out of discrete bits of information. Theories also yield suggestions for future research. When researchers extend existing theories into new areas, they discover new information about groups, while simultaneously testing the strength of their theories.

Researchers have developed hundreds of theories about groups and their dynamics. Some of these theories are relatively narrow, for they focus on some specific aspect of groups. Others, in contrast, are far broader in scope, for they offer general explanations for groups across a wide variety of times and contexts. These theories, despite their variations, often share certain basic assumptions about what processes are more important than others, the types of outcomes they explain, and the variables that are most influential. This section reviews some of these basic theoretical perspectives on groups, but with the caveat that these approaches are not necessarily mutually exclusive. Most theories embrace assumptions from more than one of the motivational/emotional, behavioral, systems, cognitive, and biological perspectives.

### Motivational and Emotional Perspectives

Why do some people vie for leadership in their groups, whereas others remain content with less prominent roles? Why do some groups struggle against adversity, whereas others give up after the first setback? Why do some people shy away from groups, whereas others join dozens of them? The answers to these "why" questions often lie in people's motivations and emotions. **Motivations** are psychological mechanisms that give purpose and direction to behavior. These inner mechanisms can be called many things—habits, beliefs, feelings, wants, instincts, compulsions, drives—but no matter what their label, they prompt people to take action. **Emotions** often accompany these needs and desires; feelings of happiness, sadness, satisfaction, and sorrow are just a few of the emotions that can influence how people act in group situations. The words *motivation* and *emotion* both come from the Latin word *movere*, meaning "to move."

Motivational approaches offer insight into a wide range of group phenomena. Why, for example, do people take more credit when their group is a successful one, but then downplay their connection to their group when it performs poorly? A motivational explanation of this selectivity might focus on the role groups play in meeting people's basic need for self-esteem. People vary considerably in their appraisal of their own self-worth; the depressed individual feels inferior, discouraged, or even worthless, whereas the narcissist is consumed with self-adoration. Most people, however, are motivated to maintain and enhance their self-esteem, and so they tend to exaggerate the role they played in their group when things go well and avoid responsibility for group failure. In consequence, group members who consider the task to be particularly important or are more invested in their group are more likely to deny blame for group failures and take credit for successes, relative to those who do not think the task, or the group's outcomes, have implications for their self-worth (Savitsky, 2007).

Jennifer George's (1995) theory of **group affective tone** takes a more emotion-focused approach to explaining group behavior. George posits that groups, over time, develop a tendency to display collective mood states. This general affective tone is not tied to any specific aspect of the group's activities or to any one individual, but rather pervades all the group's day-to-day activities. The group's mood may be so taken for granted that members do not realize its influence, but George believes that positive group affect will lead to increases in a number of pro-group actions, including helping out

---

**motivation** Wants, needs, and other psychological processes that energize behavior and thereby determine its form, intensity, and duration.

**emotion** A subjective state of positive or negative affect often accompanied by a degree of arousal or activation.

**group affective tone** The collective emotional mood of a group.

other members, protecting the group, making constructive suggestions, and "spreading goodwill" during interpersonal encounters (George & Brief, 1992, p. 310). Needless to say, a negative affective tone sets the stage for any number of anti-group actions, including absenteeism, low morale, and conflict (Kelly, 2001).

### Behavioral Perspectives

Many theories about groups draw on the seminal work of psychologist B. F. Skinner (1953, 1971). Skinner's **behaviorism** was based on two key assumptions. First, Skinner believed that psychological processes, such as motives and drives, may shape people's reactions in groups, but he also believed that such psychological processes are too difficult to index accurately. He therefore recommended measuring and analyzing how people actually behave in a specific context rather than speculating about the psychological or interpersonal processes that may have instigated their actions. Second, Skinner believed that most behavior was consistent with the *law of effect*—that is, behaviors that are followed by positive consequences, such as rewards, will occur more frequently, whereas behaviors that are followed by negative consequences will become rarer.

John Thibaut and Harold Kelley's (1959) **social exchange theory** extended Skinner's behaviorism to groups. They agreed that individuals hedonistically strive to maximize their rewards and minimize their costs. However, when individuals join groups, they forego exclusive control over their outcomes. Groups create interdependence among members, so that the actions of each member potentially influence the outcomes and actions of every other member. Mara, for example, can spend several days working on a project, struggling to complete it successfully. But what if Mara collaborates with Steven on the project? When Mara works alone, she determines her own success. But when she works with Steven, his actions partially shape her outcomes. Mara may enjoy certain aspects of her interaction with Steven, but she may also find some of the things he does irritating. Social exchange theory predicts that Mara and Steven will negotiate throughout their interaction to secure greater personal rewards while minimizing costs.

### Systems Theory Perspectives

Researchers in a variety of fields, including engineering, biology, and medicine, have repeatedly found that unique results are obtained when a system is formed by creating dependency among formerly independent components. Systems, whether they are bridges, ecological niches, organisms, or groups, synthesize several parts or subsystems into a unified whole.

A **systems theory** approach assumes groups are complex, adaptive, dynamic systems of interacting individuals. The members are the units of the system, who are coupled one to another by relationships. Just as systems can be deliberately designed to function in a particular way, groups are sometimes created for a purpose, with procedures and standards that are designed with the overall goal of the system in mind. Groups can, however, be self-creating and self-organizing systems, for they may develop spontaneously as individuals begin to act in coordinated, synchronized ways. Just as a system receives inputs from the environment, processes this information internally, and then outputs its products, groups gather information, review that information, and generate products. Groups are also responsive to

---

**behaviorism** A theoretical explanation of the way organisms acquire new responses to environmental stimuli through such conditioning processes as stimulus–response associations and reinforcement.

**social exchange theory** An economic model of interpersonal relationships which argues that individuals seek out relationships that offer them many rewards while exacting few costs.

**systems theory** A general theoretical approach which assumes that groups are *systems*—collections of individual units that combine to form an integrated, complex whole.

information concerning the context in which they operate and their impact on that context, and will adapt in response to feedback about the efficacy of their actions. Just as the relaying of information between interdependent units is a key concept in systems theory, so the communication of information between members plays a central role in group systems. Systems theory suggests that parts are, to an extent, interchangeable—specific units can be swapped in and out with no discernable impact on the system—but in some cases because groups are built up of closely entwined parts they can change to an extraordinary degree when one of their constituent components changes.

Systems theory provides a model for understanding a range of group-level processes, including group development, productivity, and interpersonal conflict. **Input–process–output models** of group productivity, or I–P–O models, are systems theories that emphasize *inputs* that feed into the group setting, the *processes* that take place within the group as it works on the task, and the *outputs* generated by the system (see Figure 2.4). Inputs would include any factors that are present in the situation when the group begins its work on the task, such as the characteristics of the individual members (skill, experience, and training) and group-level factors (group structure and cohesiveness). These input factors all influence, through a variety of paths, the processes that take place within the group as members work together to complete the task, including communication, planning, conflict, and leadership. These processes combine to transform inputs into outputs, which include aspects of the group's performance (e.g., products, decisions, errors) and changes in the factors that serve as inputs to the system. If the group performs poorly, for example, it may become less cohesive, or it may seek out new members. Members of successful groups, in contrast, may become more satisfied with their group and take steps to make sure that the group uses the same procedures to solve the next problem (Ilgen et al., 2005; Littlepage et al., 1995).

**input–process–output (I–P–O) model** Any one of a number of general conceptual analyses of groups that assumes group processes mediate the relationship between individual, group, and situational input variables and resulting group outcomes.

## Cognitive Perspectives

A group's dynamics, in many cases, become understandable only by studying the **cognitive processes** that allow members to gather information, make sense of it, and then act on the results of their mental appraisals. When people join a group for the first time, they immediately begin to form an impression of the group. This perceptual work prompts them to search for information about the other group members, rapidly identifying those who are outgoing, shy, and intelligent. Group members also search their memories for stored information about the group and the tasks it must face, and they must retrieve that information before they can use it. A group member must also take note of the actions of others and try to understand what caused the other member to act in this way. Thus, group members are busy perceiving, judging, reasoning, and remembering, and all these mental activities influence their understanding of one another, the group, and themselves (Hinsz, Tindale, Vollrath, 1997; Hodgkinson & Healey, 2008).

John Turner's (1991, 1999) **self-categorization theory**, or SCT, offers a cognitive explanation for a range for group processes, including intergroup perception and stereotyping. This theory explains the cognitive mechanisms that work to align people's self-conceptions with their conception of the groups to which they belong. Turner recognizes that much

**cognitive process** Mental processes that acquire, organize, and integrate information. Cognitive processes include memory systems that store data and the psychological mechanisms that process this information.

**self-categorization theory** A conceptual approach developed by John Turner and his colleagues that explains a range of group behavior, including the development of social identity and intergroup relations, in terms of the social cognitive categorization processes.

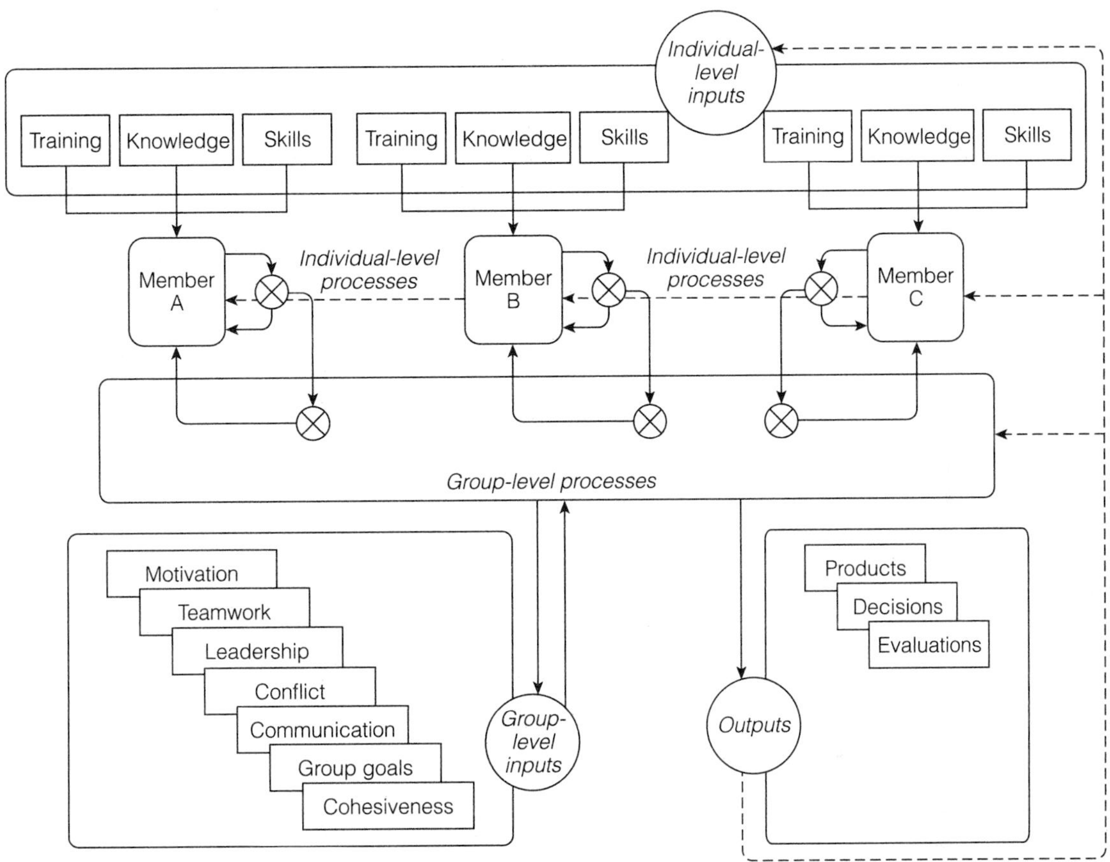


**FIGURE 2.4** An example of an input–process–output model of group productivity. A systems theory approach to some complex aspect of a group, such as its productivity, assumes that group processes mediate the relationship between input factors and outputs. Individual-level inputs (shown at the top of the diagram) include training, knowledge, and skills of each member. Group-level inputs, at the lower left, include motivation, teamwork, leadership, and so on. Individual- and group-level processes are represented by the symbol ⊗. Outputs include products, decisions, and evaluations, and feedback loops are depicted by the dotted lines.

of social perception involves categorizing people into groups based on age, race, nationality, and other categories. Once classified, individuals' perceptions of people are influenced by any stereotypes they may have about the qualities of people in such groups. Turner suggests that people not only categorize others, but they also recognize their own membership in social categories. As Chapter 3 explains, this self-categorization process is what turns the individual-level conception of the self into a group-level conception.

### Biological Perspectives

Group members can solve complex problems, communicate with one another using spoken and written language, build and operate massive machines, and plan their group's future. But group members are also living creatures, whose responses are often shaped by biological, biochemical, and genetic characteristics. When conflict arises in the group, heart rates escalate, and other body changes occur to help members cope with the stress

(Blascovich, Nash, & Ginsburg, 1978). When groups are trapped in confining, cramped spaces, members often become physiologically aroused, and this arousal can interfere with their work (Evans & Cohen, 1987). When people feel that they have been excluded from a group, their neurological reactions betray the distress they are feeling. Their brains display a pattern of activity that is very similar to the brains of people who are experiencing physical pain (Eisenberger, Lieberman, & Williams, 2003).

One biological perspective—**evolutionary psychology**—argues that these processes may be genetically determined, part of the species' biological programming that has evolved through natural selection. This perspective argues that in the last 15 million years, the human species has evolved socially as well as physically. Those individuals who were even slightly genetically predisposed to engage in adaptive social behaviors tended to survive longer, so they were more successful in passing their genes along to future generations (Caporael et al., 2005).

Evolutionary psychology offers insight into a range of group processes, including affiliation, intergroup conflict, and aggression. For example, why do so many groups include the role of leader, even when the group members are fully capable of organizing themselves? Evolutionary psychology suggests that leadership, as a process, likely evolved over time to help relatively small groups of people cope with extremely difficult, life-threatening circumstances. Facing problems of survival, group members needed a way to coordinate their activities and manage the inevitable conflicts that erupt in any group. The person who stepped forward to help the group with this collective task was the leader, and over time individuals adapted to accept the influence of another, more experienced, group member. They also developed the mental apparatus needed to identify those who were most qualified to lead their groups. In the modern world, humans often gather in groups that are not facing danger, yet even in more benign circumstances they often expect someone to lead them because leadership and followership are evolved adaptations. In consequence, group members' preferences for leaders are sometimes influenced by such qualities as strength, sex, and age, even though these qualities were only relevant in prehistoric times (Van Vugt, 2006; Van Vugt, Hogan, & Kaiser, 2008).

## Selecting a Theoretical Perspective

Group dynamics is rich with theory. Some of these theories trace group processes back to psychological processes—the motivations of the individual members, the mental processes that sustain their conception of their social environment, and even their instinctive urges and proclivities. Other theories focus more on the group as a social system that is integrated in the surrounding community and society.

These different theoretical perspectives, however, are not mutually exclusive paradigms, struggling for the distinction as *the* explanation of group behavior. Some researchers test hypotheses derived from only one theory; others draw on several perspectives as they strive to describe, predict, control, and explain groups and their members. Just as the questions, "How should I measure this aspect of the group?" and, "How should I test my hypothesis about groups?" can be answered in more than one way, no one solution can be offered in response to the question, "What theory explains group behavior?" Many of the greatest advances in understanding groups have occurred not when one theory has been pitted against another, but when two or more theories have been synthesized to form a new, more encompassing theoretical perspective. As Homans (1950) wrote: "We have a great deal of fact to work with, [and] we also have a great deal of theory. The elements of a synthesis are on hand" (p. 4).

---

**evolutionary psychology** A biological approach to understanding behavior which assumes that recurring patterns of behavior in animals ultimately stem from evolutionary pressures that increase the likelihood of adaptive social actions and extinguish nonadaptive practices.

## SUMMARY IN OUTLINE

*What are the three critical requirements of a scientific approach to the study of groups (as noted by Homans)?*

1. Researchers must use reliable and valid methods to measure group phenomena.
2. Researchers must design research procedures to test their hypotheses about groups.
3. Researchers must develop theories that organize their findings conceptually and comprehensively.

*How do researchers measure individual and group processes?*

1. *Observation* involves watching and recording events transpiring in groups. Varieties include *overt observation*, *covert observation*, and *participant observation*, which Whyte used in his study of corner gangs.
   - Most group research raises few ethics issues, but researchers are required to have their work approved by an *Institutional Review Board (IRB)*.
   - Covert observation reduces the biasing influences of the *Hawthorne effect*.
2. *Qualitative studies* require the collection of descriptive data about groups, but *quantitative* studies require the enumeration and quantification of the phenomena of interest.
   - *Structured observational measures* require observers to assign each coded activity to a specific category.
   - Bales's *Interaction Process Analysis* (*IPA*), a standard group coding system, classifies behaviors into two categories: relationship and task interaction.
   - Bales's more recent structured coding system is called *SYMLOG* (*Systematic Multiple Level Observation of Groups*).
3. *Reliability* and *validity* are essential qualities of all measures, for they must be consistent and they must measure what they are designed to measure.
4. *Self-report measures* ask group members to describe their own perceptions and experiences.
   - Moreno's *sociometry* method asks members to report whom they like the most. The nominations are used to generate a *sociogram*, or visual image of the interpersonal relations in the group.
   - Clapp used a combination of self-report and observational methods to study alcohol consumption in groups (parties).

*What are the key characteristics of and differences between case, experimental, and correlational studies of group processes?*

1. A *case study* is an in-depth analysis of one or more groups based on interviews with members, observation, and so on.
   - Janis used a case study design in his analysis of *groupthink* in government decision-making groups.
   - By studying naturally occurring, *bona fide groups*, case study researchers can be more certain that the processes they study are not artificial ones influenced by the research process.
2. In an *experiment*, researchers examine cause–effect relationships by manipulating aspects of the group situation (*independent variables*).
   - Lewin, Lippitt, and White studied the impact of autocratic, democratic, and laissez-faire leaders on groups by conducting an experiment. They manipulated the *independent variable* (leadership style), assessed several *dependent variables* (aggressiveness, productivity, etc.), and limited the influence of other possible causal factors by controlling the situation and assigning groups to experimental conditions at random.

- Lewin, Lippitt, and White's study indicated that productivity was high in both democratic and autocratic groups, but that the participants were more aggressive in the autocratic groups. In some cases, one group member (a *scapegoat*) was bullied by the others.

3. In a *correlational study*, the investigator, rather than manipulating aspects of the situation, gauges the strength of the naturally occurring relationships between such variables.
   - Newcomb examined the relationship between members' political attitudes and their popularity in the group in an early study of *reference groups*.
   - Nonexperimental studies are usually called correlational studies because the magnitude of the relationship between variables is often expressed as a *correlation coefficient*.

*What are strengths and weaknesses of case, experimental, and correlational methods?*

1. The conclusions drawn from case studies can be highly subjective, but they stimulate theory and provide detailed information about natural, bona fide groups.
2. Groups studied in experimental settings may not display the dynamics of naturally occurring groups, but experimentation provides the clearest test of cause-and-effect hypotheses.
3. Correlational studies provide only limited information about causality, but they yield precise estimates of the strength of the relationship between two variables and raise fewer questions of ethics for researchers.
4. Researchers also exercise care when selecting the *unit of analysis* and when analyzing their findings so as to not attribute effects caused by group-level processes to individual-level processes and vice versa. Researchers who study multilevel processes must be ever wary of interdependence in their data.

*What theoretical perspectives guide researchers' studies of groups?*

1. Theories that focus on members' *motivations* and *emotions* explain group behavior in terms of members, wants, needs, drives, and feelings. Members' need to maintain self-esteem influences their response to group outcomes, and George's work suggests that groups can develop a collective *group affective tone*.
2. Theories based on Skinner's *behaviorism*, such as Thibaut and Kelley's *social exchange theory*, assume that individuals act to maximize their rewards and minimize their costs.
3. A *systems theory* approach assumes that groups are systems. An *input–process–output model* (I–P–O model) of group performance exemplifies the systems approach.
4. Turner's *self-categorization theory* (SCT) is a *cognitive process* approach, for it assumes that group members' tendency to categorize other people and themselves influences a wide range of group behavior.
5. Biological perspectives, such as *evolutionary theory*, argue that some group behaviors, including leadership, may be rooted in people's biological heritage.

## FOR MORE INFORMATION

*Studying Groups*

- "Methods of Small Group Research," by Norbert L. Kerr, Joel Aronoff, and Lawrence A. Messé (2000), examines the techniques and measures used by investigators in a wide variety of group research.

- *The Handbook of Group Research and Practice*, edited by Susan A. Wheelan (2005), includes chapters by experts who offer their insights into problems and approaches to studying groups.

*Research Methods*

- "Observation and Analysis of Group Interaction over Time: Some Methodological and Strategic Choices," by Joseph E. McGrath and T. William Altermatt (2001), is a complete analysis of structured approaches to group observation.
- *Applications of Case Study Research*, by R. K. Yin (2009), updates and reaffirms the advantages of case study methods.
- *Street Corner Society*, by William Foote Whyte (1943), remains one of the best examples of applying the case study method to understanding a group's dynamics.

*Advances in Group Research Methods*

- "Overcoming Dependent Data: A Guide to the Analysis of Group Data," by Melody S. Sadler and Charles M. Judd (2001), outlines the statistical procedures to use when data are collected from intact groups.
- *Theories of Small Groups: Interdisciplinary Perspectives*, edited by Marshall Scott Poole and Andrea B. Hollingshead (2005), describes, reviews, and synthesizes the full range of theoretical perspectives in groups, including evolutionary approaches, network approaches, and feminist and functionalist perspectives.

## Media Resources

Visit the Group Dynamics companion website at www.cengage.com/psychology/forsyth to access online resources for your book, including quizzes, flash cards, web links, and more.

# 3

# Inclusion and Identity

## CHAPTER OVERVIEW

Most people prefer group membership to isolation, but once they join with others they find they must sometimes do what is best for the group rather than what benefits them personally. Groups blur the boundary between the self and the others, for members retain their personal qualities—their motives, emotions, and outlooks—but add to them a sense of self that incorporates their collective rather than their individual characteristics. Groups transform the *me* into the *we*.

- Do humans, by nature, seek solitude or inclusion in groups?
- When do people embrace collectivism by putting the group's needs before their own?
- What processes transform an individual's sense of self into a collective, social identity?

## CHAPTER OUTLINE

**Palmer and Gorman: From Individualism to Collectivism**

When Brian Palmer was in college his professors wondered if he would ever find success after graduation. Brian himself admits that he did not work all that hard at his studies, for he was more concerned with satisfying his own needs than impressing his professors. But after graduation he got serious about his career, working 60 to 70 hours a week to prove himself. "I'm very competitive. I like to win," he explained in an interview (Bellah et al., 1985, p. 5). He rose through the ranks until he could afford a comfortable lifestyle. He owned a nice car and large home, his sons attended the best schools, and his wife lunched at the country club. But, on the day that he sold his house to move to a larger one she told him that she would not be moving with him: She wanted a divorce. When Brian recovered from the shock he realized that his single-minded devotion to his career had taken all his time and his energy. He had provided well for his family, financially, but he was not involved in their lives. "I got totally swept up in my own progress, in promotions and financial successes" (Bellah et al., 1985, p. 68).

Joe Gorman lives far away from Brian Palmer, both geographically and psychologically. Palmer moved from one community to the next whenever he needed to relocate for work, but Gorman has lived his entire life in his hometown. Gorman works full time, but he spends much of his leisure time with family and friends. A skilled organizer, he frequently ends up in charge of various community fundraisers, parades, and festivals. He was the go-to person, for example, for a series of events celebrating the town's founding, and through his hard work the event was a tremendous success. When asked why he gave so much of his time to this task, he explained that he did it for the community that he loves "being a part of" (Bellah et al., 1985, p. 10). When Gorman's employer offered him a promotion with a higher salary he turned it down because it would require he move to another town: "I was born here . . . We will always stay here. It is my home" (Bellah et al., 1985, p. 11).

Brian Palmer and Joe Gorman illustrate what has been called "the master problem" of social life: What is the connection between the individual and society, including groups, organizations, and communities (Allport, 1962)? Healthy adult human beings can survive apart from other members of the species, yet across individuals, societies, and eras, humans consistently seek inclusion in groups, where they must balance their personal needs and desires against the demands and requirements of their groups. Some, like Palmer, never sink too deeply into their groups; he remained an individualist who was so self-reliant that he refused to rely on others in his rush to personal success. Others, however, respond more like Gorman, who put the group's interests before his own personal needs. He did not just join groups; he identified so strongly with his groups that his sense of self came to be defined by them.

In this chapter, we consider three essential processes that combine to transform the lone individual into a group member: inclusion, collectivism, and identity. Through *inclusion*, the single individual changes from an outsider into an insider by joining a group. Through *collectivism*, group members begin to think about the good of the group as a whole rather than what the group provides them. Through the transformation of *identity*, individuals change their conception of who they are to include their group's qualities as well as their own individual qualities.

## FROM ISOLATION TO INCLUSION

Some species of animals are solitary. The cheetah, giant panda, orangutan, and opossum remain apart from other members of their species and congregate in some cases only to mate or rear offspring. Other animals, such as chimps, hyena, deer, and mice, are social creatures, for they usually forage, feed, sleep, and travel in small groups. What about humans? Do we tend to keep to ourselves, guarding our privacy from the incursions of others, or are we group-oriented animals, who prefer the company of other people to a life alone?

Most theorists, when identifying the fundamental psychological processes that drive humans' actions across a range of situations and settings, include a **need to belong** on their list (Maslow, 1970; Pittman & Zeigler, 2007). All human beings, write Roy Baumeister and Mark Leary (1995, p. 497), "have a pervasive drive to form and maintain at least a minimum quantity of lasting, positive, and impactful interpersonal relationships". They likened the need to belong to other basic needs, such as hunger or thirst. A person who has not eaten will feel hungry, but a person who has little contact with other people will feel unhappy and lonely. In this section we review the evidence that backs up their claim that group membership fulfills a generic need to establish positive, enduring relationships with other people.

## The Need to Belong

Aristotle famously suggested that "Man is by nature a social animal; and an unsocial person who is unsocial naturally and not accidentally is either unsatisfactory or superhuman." Henry David Thoreau disagreed with Aristotle, and to prove his point spent two years relatively secluded at Walden Pond. He deliberately kept his group memberships to a minimum during this period, although he maintained ties to his family and some friends. He explained,

> Society is commonly too cheap. We meet at very short intervals, not having had time to acquire any new value for each other. We meet at three meals a day and give each other a taste of that old musty cheese that we are. Certainly less frequency would suffice for all important and hearty communication. (Thoreau, 1962, p. 206)

Spending time alone, away from others, can be a rejuvenating, pleasurable experience. People, when surveyed about their reactions to isolation, report enjoying the self-discovery, contemplation, and increased spirituality that occurs when one is physically isolated from interactions with and observations by others (Long et al., 2003). When alone, people report they can "discover who I am," "determine what I want to be," "meditate and reflect," "try out some new behaviors," "recover my self-esteem," "protect myself from what others say," and "take refuge from the outside world" (Pedersen, 1999, p. 399). Some philosophers, writers, and artists have reached the apex of their creativity during times of isolation, when they were not distracted by other people (Storr, 1988; Suedfeld, 1997).

But even though people express a desire for privacy, most people spend the majority of their waking hours in the company of other people—only unmarried or widowed adults over the age of 45 reported spending more time alone than with others. The sheer number of groups that exist at any moment in time is also clear evidence of the strength of the need to belong. Voluntary associations, such as churches, farming cooperatives, fraternal clubs, hobby groups, civic service associations, and community councils, are not rare but extremely common (Bonikowski & McPherson, 2006). With groups ranging from the small and distinctive, such as the Pecan Grove Garden Club and the Model T Ford Club of Tulsa, to the large and diverse, such as the American Association of Retired Persons (AARP) and the Assembly of First Nations (AFN), there is a group for anyone who wants to join one, and most people do (see Figure 3.1). Americans are above average in their involvement in voluntary associations, but some countries' citizens—the Dutch, Canadians, Scandinavians—are "groupier" still (Curtis, Baer, & Grabb, 2001).

Even more numerous are the many informal kin-based and social groups, such as family, friends, and acquaintances who meet regularly, that satisfy members' need for inclusion. When surveyed, 87.3% of Americans reported that they lived with other people, including family members, partners, and roommates (Davis & Smith, 2007). The majority, ranging from 50% to 80%, reported doing things in groups of friends and relatives, such as

---

**need to belong** The dispositional tendency to seek out and join with other humans.

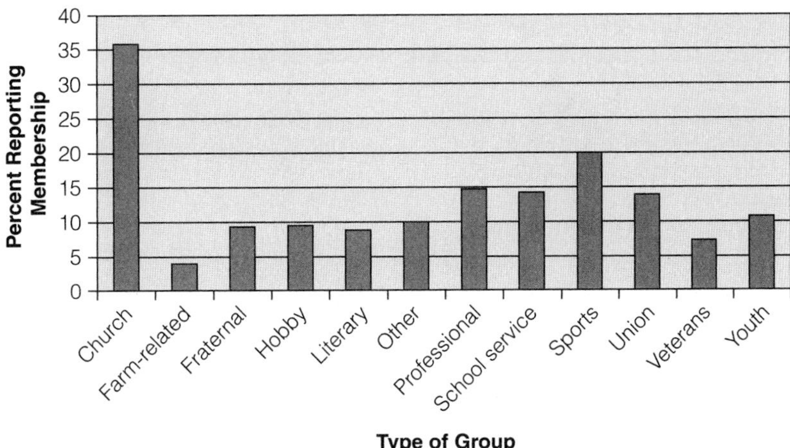


**FIGURE 3.1** Percentage of Americans reporting membership in various types of groups.

SOURCE: General Social Surveys, 1972–2006. [machine-readable data file]. Chicago: National Opinion Research Center. Storrs, CT: The Roper Center for Public Opinion Research. Available at http://www.norc.uchicago.edu.

attending a sports event together, visiting one another for the evening, sharing a meal together, or going out as a group to see a movie (Putnam, 2000). People also satisfy their need to belong, at least temporarily, by joining in larger collectives and categories. People could perform a variety of activities alone—they could learn individually by reading books and studying papers, watch DVDs in the privacy of their homes, and dine each night at their kitchen counters—but most do not: they prefer to perform these activities in groups. Even though people's involvement in certain types of groups has dropped in the last few years—fewer people, for example, belong to bowling leagues now than in the 1960s—joining with others in groups remains a universally observed characteristic of humans across all known societies (see Focus 3.1).

### The Pain of Exclusion

The strength of the need to belong is seen even more clearly when this need is thwarted. Most people, both young and old, find protracted periods of social isolation disturbing (Zubek, 1973). The diaries of individuals who have been isolated from others for long periods of time—stranded explorers, scientists working in seclusion, and prisoners in solitary confinement—often stress the psychological costs of their ordeal rather than physical deprivations. As their isolation wears on, they report fear, insomnia, memory lapses, depression, fatigue, and general confusion. Prolonged periods of isolation are also marked by hallucinations and delusions, as when one solo sailor at sea was startled when he thought he saw a pirate steering his life raft (Burney, 1961).

Jean Twenge, Roy Baumeister, and their colleagues have explored how people react to isolation in a series of "life alone" studies. They first gave participants an extensive personality test to convince them they had knowledge of their basic personality. Then they told some people, at random, that their answers indicated their future would be a solitary one: "You're the type who will end up alone later in life. You may have friends and relationships now, but . . . these are likely to be short-lived and not continue . . . the odds are you'll end up being alone more and more" (Twenge et al., 2007, p. 58). Others were told that they would enjoy meaningful relationships with others throughout

## Focus 3.1 Are Americans Bowling Alone?

*The most whimsical yet discomfiting bit of evidence of social disengagement in contemporary America that I have discovered is this: More Americans are bowling today than ever before, but bowling in organized leagues has plummeted in the last decade or so.*

— Robert Putnam, *Bowling Alone* (1995, p. 69)

The numbers tell the tale. In 1975 people reported playing card games together, like poker and bridge, about 14 times a year. By 2000, that number had been halved. In the 1970s 50% of the people surveyed agreed that their family usually eats dinner together. By the end of the century only about 33% reported regular family meals and the family vacation was also becoming more rare. Today fewer people report visiting with neighbors frequently and they are less likely to join social clubs, such as the Kiwanis and garden clubs. Membership in organized sports leagues is also waning. As Robert Putnam (2000) wrote in his book *Bowling Alone*, in the 1960s 8% of all adult American men belonged to a bowling league, as did nearly 5% of all adult women. However, even though the total number of bowlers in Americans' continues to increase over time, fewer and fewer belong to bowling leagues. Putnam worried that Americans' withdrawal from groups and associations signals an overall decline in **social capital**, which is determined by the strength of "networks, norms, and social trust that facilitate coordination and cooperation for mutual benefit" (Putnam, 1995, p. 66). Just as financial resources determine economic capital, so the scope and strength of connections with others defines one's social capital.

Putnam's findings suggest that the types of groups people join are changing. People are not as interested in joining traditional types of community groups, such as garden clubs, fraternal and professional organizations, or even church-based groups. These social trends likely reflect, however, changes in how people meet their need to belong rather than a basic change in human nature. Some types of groups, such as book groups, support groups, teams at work, and category-based associations (e.g., the AARP) are increasing in size rather than decreasing. Individuals are also more involved in online associations, interactions, and networks, such as MySpace and Facebook. For example, in a recent survey, 91.1% of the individuals who used the Internet regularly reported that at least one of the individuals they interact with regularly via the Internet had become a good friend. It is also difficult to track the extent to which the trends Putnam reported reflect a shift toward more informal associations. Rather than joining formally organized groups, individuals may be spending more time with informal groups, such as friends, coworkers, and acquaintances. These social groups are the ubiquitous "dark matter" of social capital, for they knit people together in social relations but are often overlooked in tallies that track the number and variety of more formal and official groups (Smith D. H., 2000). In fact, even though Putnam's book title suggests that people are bowling alone rather than in groups, Putnam admits that hardly anyone bowls individually. People may not be joining bowling leagues, but bowling remains a group-level activity: people bowl with friends, coworkers, and family members rather than in organized competitive leagues. These groups may be lower in terms of social capital, but they nonetheless are sufficient to meet people's need to belong.

their life, and those in a second control condition were told they would become accident-prone later in life and so experience a series of misfortunes.

Those told that they will likely live out their lives alone displayed a range of negative reactions. They were more critical of others and were more likely to punish others by exposing them to noxious noise levels. They were also more likely to engage in a number of irrational, self-defeating behaviors, such as taking unnecessary risks and procrastinating. They also became less helpful towards others and more competitive overall. In addition, those who were given the prediction of a life alone could not think as clearly as those in the control conditions, for they scored lower on a series of general cognitive aptitude measures. These deleterious effects of the "life alone" prognostication could, however, be undone if people had the chance to reinstate their

---

**social capital** The degree of functional interconnectedness of a group of people thought to promote coordinated action for mutual benefit; analogous to other forms of capital, such as human or economic capital.

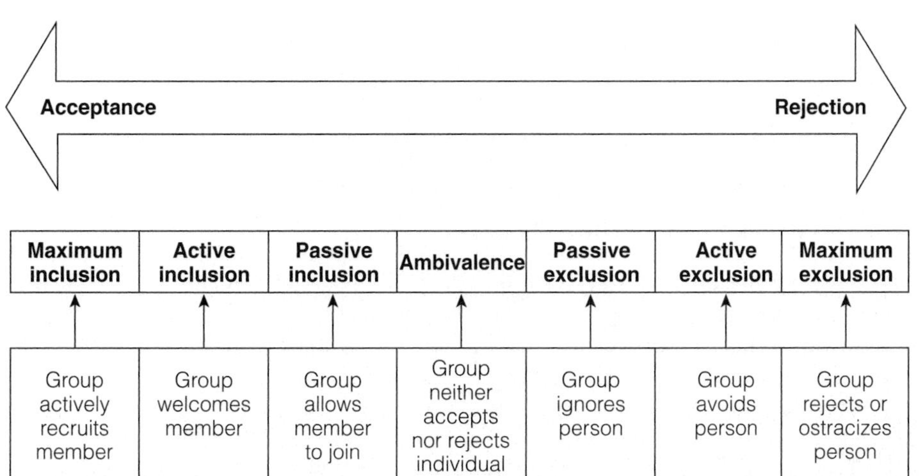


**FIGURE 3.2** The inclusion–exclusion continuum. When individuals are actively sought out by groups they experience maximal inclusion, and when groups actively ostracize them people experience maximal exclusion.
SOURCE: Leary, 1990.

connections to other people—for example, by reflecting on their relationship with a family member or friend (Baumeister et al., 2007; Gardner et al., 2005; Twenge et al., 2001; Twenge et al., 2007; Twenge, Catanese, & Baumeister, 2002).

**Ostracism** People's need to belong is slaked when a group accepts them, but they are most satisfied when a group actively seeks them out. In contrast, people respond negatively when a group ignores or avoids them, and this negative reaction is exacerbated if the group ostracizes, abandons, or banishes them (see Figure 3.2; Leary, 1990). To be isolated from others due to circumstances or accident is one thing, but to be deliberately ignored and excluded by others—**ostracism**—is particularly distressing.

The word *ostracism* dates to the Greeks, who voted to punish a member of the community with banishment using shards of clay called *ostraca* (Williams, 2007). Contemporary forms of ostracism range from formal rejection of a member from a group—as when a church excommunicates a member or a club permanently bans a patron—to more subtle interpersonal tactics, such as the "silent treatment" or the "cold shoulder." Cliques of adolescent girls, for example, use the threat of exclusion and ostracism itself to control the activities of members, with excluded girls finding that they are suddenly outcasts instead of trusted friends. Many religious societies shun members who have broken rules or traditions. People who do not toe the line in work or classroom groups are sometimes ignored by the rest of the group, sometimes for months or even years. Even nonhuman groups practice ostracism, for a variety of social species, including wolves, bees, and primates, sometimes exclude an individual from the group—usually with fatal consequences. The ostracized feel they have been betrayed by the other group members, and they sometimes report frustration, shock, and surprise. Whereas people who are included value their experiences in the group, the excluded sometimes feel as if they are invisible—as if they do not even exist socially.

Ostracism is extremely stressful. When asked, the excluded describe themselves as frustrated,

---

**ostracism** Excluding a person or group of people from a group, usually by ignoring, shunning, or explicitly banishing them.

anxious, nervous, and lonely (Williams, 2007), sometimes using such intensely negative words as heartbroken, depressed, and worthless (Barnett, 2006). Ostracized people evidence physiological signs of stress, including elevated blood pressure and cortisol levels (a stress-related hormone). Brain imaging research even suggests that the pain of exclusion is neurologically similar to pain caused by physical injury. Investigators in one study charted the neurological reactions people have when excluded using a functional magnetic resonance imaging scanner, or fMRI. Such scanners indicate what portions of the brain are more active than others by measuring cranial temperature and blood flow. When people were left out of a group activity, a specific area of the brain—the dorsal anterior cingulate cortex (dACC)—was particularly active. This area of the brain is associated with the experience of physical pain sensations and other negative social experiences (Eisenberger, Lieberman, & Williams, 2003; MacDonald & Leary, 2005).

Kipling Williams (2007) suggests that people's initial, *reflexive* reaction to exclusion is followed by a more deliberative, *reflective* stage during which individuals consider the reasons for their rejection and respond accordingly. Depending on the results of these ruminations, people will display one of five characteristic stress responses: freeze, fight, flight, tend, or befriend. In rare cases, ostracism can lead to a general shutdown in behavioral and emotional reactivity. Such individuals report little change in mood or emotion other than numbness and lethargy; they freeze up (DeWall & Baumeister, 2006). A fight-or-flight or a tend-and-befriend response is more typical, however. The **fight-or-flight response** to stress involves fighting back against the exclusion or escaping the situation. Those who display the fight response become hostile and aggressive when rejected by others. They may confront group members directly, attempt to force their way into the group, insist that the group exclude someone else, and derogate those who have excluded them. In more extreme cases they may respond violently. Others, in contrast, accept their rejection passively and withdraw from the group (Leary, Twenge, & Quinlivan, 2006; see Focus 3.2).

In some cases, however, people display a **tend-and-befriend response** to exclusion (Taylor et al., 2000). Rather than fighting or fleeing the group, they nurture, protect, and support others (tend) or they take steps to strengthen their interpersonal relations (befriending); they express more interest in making new friends, become more cooperative, and treat new acquaintances more positively (Maner et al., 2007). Women are more likely than men to respond to exclusion by tending: they do things to help the group, such as working harder on collective tasks, apologizing for previous behaviors, and making sacrifices for others (Williams & Sommers, 1997).

Williams and his colleagues demonstrated the earnestness of the excluded in three-person groups that included only one real participant and two confederates. When the experimenter left the room, the confederates began to bounce a ball back and forth between them. In some cases, the confederates included the participant in their game, but in other cases, they stopped bouncing the ball to the participant after about a minute. The participants, when later asked how much they liked the other two group members, rated their partners more negatively when they had been ostracized. Women who had been ostracized, however, worked harder on a subsequent collective task, apparently to regain acceptance by the rest of the group. Women were also more likely to blame themselves for their ostracism (e.g., "I have trouble making a good impression with others"). Men, in contrast, did not compensate by working harder,

---

**fight-or-flight response** A physiological response to stressful events characterized by the activation of the sympathetic nervous system (increased heart rate, pupil dilation) that readies the individual to counter the threat (fight) or to escape the threat (flight).

**tend-and-befriend response** An interpersonal response to stressful events characterized by increased nurturing, protective, and supportive behaviors (tending) and by seeking out connections to other people (befriending).

## Focus 3.2 Does Social Rejection Lead to Violence?

*For all of his 23 years of life the most frequent observation made by anyone about him was that Seung Hui Cho had absolutely no social life.*

—*Report of the Virginia Tech Review Panel* (Dupue, 2007, p. N-3)

On December 1, 1997, Michael Carneal walked with his sister Kelly to the main doors of Heath High School in Kentucky. Once there he took a handgun from his bag and began shooting members of Agape, the Christian group that began each day with a communal prayer. Three students died and five were severely injured. In the spring of 1999, Eric Harris and Dylan Klebold, both students at Columbine High School, used semiautomatic weapons, shotguns, and rifles to kill 13 students and teachers in a carefully planned attack. On November 7, 2007, a student at Jokela High School in Finland named Pekka-Eric Auvinen killed six students, the school principal, the school nurse, and then himself after setting fire to the school. On April 16, 2007, Seung Hui Cho, a 23-year-old senior at Virginia Tech, killed 32 people and wounded 17 others before committing suicide (Leary et al., 2003; Newman et al., 2004).

How could these students turn against their fellow classmates and teachers with such monstrous hostility? There is no simple answer to this question, for such horrific actions spring from a complex of interrelated psychological and interpersonal factors. However, when Mark Leary and his colleagues examined 15 cases of post-1995 shootings in schools in the U.S. they found that these terrible acts of violence were tied together by a common thread: rejection. In most cases the aggressors were individuals who did not belong to any groups or take part in common social activities. They were often described as loners, as was Seung Hui Cho, the Virginia Tech gunman:

> Cho lived a life of quiet solitude, extreme quiet and solitude. For all of his 23 years of life the most frequent observation made by anyone about him was that Seung Hui Cho had absolutely no social life. During all of his school years he had no real friends. He had no interest in being with others. In fact, he shied away from other people and seemed to prefer his own company to the company of others. (Dupue, 2007, p. N-3).

Some shooters, such as Cho, were never mistreated by other people, yet they still felt rejected and isolated. In most instances, however, they had been ostracized by others at their schools and were the target of malicious teasing, ridicule, and bullying. These individuals usually chose their targets deliberately, seeking revenge against those who had excluded them. They did not try to blame their behavior on psychological problems, their parents, the media, or the influence of their friends. Nearly all claimed that they had been pushed into violence by a specific group of people who excluded them. Exclusion, by itself, is not associated with behavioral problems in adolescents, but those who are isolated and report "problematic peer encounters" are at risk for a variety of negative outcomes (Kreager, 2004).

Ostracism was not the sole cause of these incidents. In nearly all cases aggressors had a history of psychological problems, although the severity of their troubles was often unrecognized. They were also often preoccupied with violence and death, and were interested in guns and weapons in general. Exclusion, however, was a key social factor in most cases. The harm that these individuals have wrought cannot be undone, but their actions serve as a reminder to curb the sometimes too-human tendency to exclude others from our social lives.

nor did they take the blame for their rejection (Williams & Sommer, 1997).

**Cyberostracism** Groups no longer meet only in face-to-face situations but also in multi-user forums, email discussions, and game sites on the Internet. Just as people sometimes exclude others from group activities in face-to-face activities, online members also sometimes ignore others, effectively excluding them from the interaction. Williams has labeled this form of exclusion **cyberostracism**.

Given that the members of computer-based groups communicate at a distance and are, in some

---

**cyberostracism** The exclusion of one or more individuals from a technologically mediated group interaction, such as a computer-based discussion group.

cases, completely anonymous, one might think that such cyberostracism is relatively inconsequential. The data, however, suggest otherwise. In one study, Williams and his colleagues invited people from 62 different countries to take part in what they thought was an Internet-based study of creative visualization. They thought they would be linked to two other volunteers and that the three would play a game of virtual catch by passing a flying disk from one player to another. In actuality, however, the other two players were simulated, and the participants were randomly assigned to one of four conditions: over-inclusion (thrown the disk 50% of the time), inclusion (33%), partial ostracism (20%), and complete ostracism (they never received a throw after the initial round of tosses). When the game was over and the participants completed a brief survey over the Web, those who had suffered ostracism displayed the same sorts of negative reactions as evidenced by people in face-to-face groups. Even though the game was meaningless and their partners were total strangers, their social self-esteem dropped, their moods turned negative, and they admitted that they felt rejected (Williams, Cheung, & Choi, 2000). Williams reported similar reactions to exclusion in his studies of chat rooms and text-messaging (Williams et al., 2002).

**Sociometer Theory** One of the surest ways to lower individuals' self-esteem is to reject them. Imagine, for example, that you are working with five other people on a joint task. Following the collaborative session you rate each other on a questionnaire, indicating with whom you would most want to work. The researchers, after collecting the questionnaires, then explain that you will be leaving the group because you received the fewest popularity votes.

How would you respond if you were so ostracized? When Mark Leary and his colleagues carried out this procedure they discovered that those who were rejected reported feeling less competent, adequate, useful, smart, and valuable than did the included group members—provided the rejection was an interpersonal one. In half the sessions, the researchers said that the group-versus-individual decision was determined by a random drawing. In such cases individuals would have to leave the group, but it was not because the group rejected them. As Figure 3.3 indicates, isolation caused by bad luck did not sting as much as ostracism caused by a group's deliberate rejection (Bourgeois & Leary, 2001; Leary et al., 1995).

As noted in Chapter 2, across situations individuals act in ways to protect and enhance their self-esteem: many theorists consider the need for

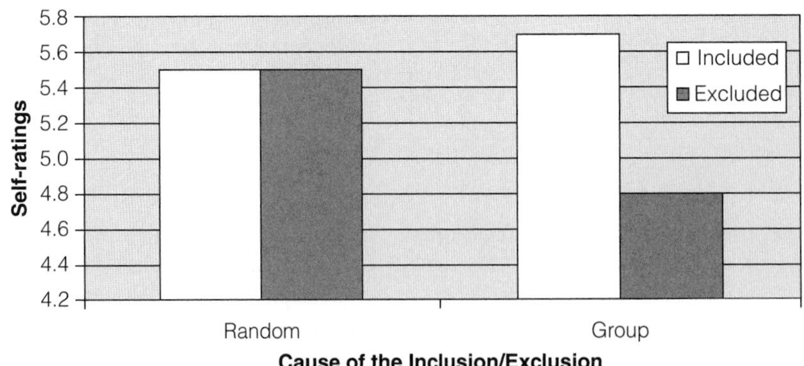


**FIGURE 3.3** Group members' reactions to inclusion and exclusion in two different conditions: When the inclusion/exclusion is determined by random assignment or determined by the preferences of the group.

SOURCE: "Self-Esteem as an Interpersonal Monitor: The Sociometer Hypothesis," by M. R. Leary, E. S. Tambor, S. K. Terdal, and D. L. Downs, *Journal of Personality and Social Psychology*, 1995, *68*, 518–530. Copyright 1996 by the American Psychological Association.

self-esteem to be a master motive. Leary's **sociometer theory**, however, suggests that the need to belong may be the primary motivational force at work rather than a striving for positive self-regard. This theory posits that "self-esteem is part of a sociometer that monitors peoples' relational value in other people's eyes" (Leary, 2007, p. 328). Self-esteem, then, is not an index of one's sense of personal value, but instead an indicator of acceptance into groups. Like a gauge that indicates how much fuel is left in the tank, self-esteem indicates the extent to which a person is included in groups. If the gauge drops, then exclusion is likely. So when we experience a dip in our self-esteem, people search for and correct characteristics and qualities that have put them at risk of social exclusion. The sociometer model concludes that most people have high self-esteem not because they think well of themselves but because they are careful to maintain inclusion in social groups (Leary & Baumeister, 2000). In consequence, self-esteem rises when people feel included in groups and liked by others (Srivastava & Beer, 2005) or when they just think about a time when others included them in a group and made them feel like they belonged (Gailliot & Baumeister, 2007). The model also explains why people who have been excluded are far more attentive to and more likely to remember accurately the details of a group's interaction: They are searching for the cause of their dismissal from the group (Gardner, Pickett, & Brewer, 2000).

## Evolution and Inclusion in Groups

Why do people usually choose membership over isolation? Why do people respond so negatively when others exclude them? Why do groups often deliberately exclude members? Why do people monitor their acceptance in groups, and question their self-worth when others shun them? Evolutionary theory offers a single answer to all these questions: the need to belong to groups is part of human nature.

**The Herd Instinct** The idea that humans are instinctively drawn to gather with other humans is not a new one. Over a century ago, William McDougall (1908) argued that humans are inexorably drawn to "the vast human herd," which "exerts a baneful attraction on those outside it" (p. 303). Advances in evolutionary psychology have revitalized this old idea, however, by specifying both the biological and interpersonal mechanisms that sustain this herd instinct.

Evolutionary psychology uses Charles Darwin's theory of natural selection to explain why contemporary humans act, feel, and think the way they do. Darwin dealt primarily with biological and anatomical adaptations, but evolutionary psychologists assume that recurring patterns of psychological and social tendencies also stem from evolutionary processes that increase adaptive actions and extinguish nonadaptive practices. Nature did not just encourage the development of webbed feet on ducks or a keen sense of smell in dogs, but also certain psychological and social tendencies in humans. Humans' capacity to introspect, to read the emotion in others' faces, to understand the meaning of others' vocal utterances, and even the ability to consider what future event may become more likely if a specific action is undertaken now may all reflect adaptations that were shaped by natural selection. Similarly, humans' preference for living in groups rather than alone may also be sustained by psychological and biological mechanisms that evolved over time to help individuals solve basic problems of survival.

Living in groups yielded both costs and benefits for early humans. Compared to a single individual, a group of humans roaming the ancient forests and plains probably attracted the attention of more predators. Moreover, when with others, those who found a food patch or made a kill could anticipate losing much of their meal to others in the group. They would also be more likely to suffer from communicable diseases and be harmed by more aggressive humans. But the benefits of sociality are far more substantial than these costs. Those who joined with

---

**sociometer theory** A conceptual analysis of self-esteem proposed by Mark Leary that argues self-esteem is not an index of perceived self-worth, but instead is a psychological monitor of one's degree of inclusion and exclusion in social groups.

others in an organized band to hunt large animals or forage for patches of food were likely more successful than individuals who remained alone. Individuals in groups could maintain superior surveillance against predators, they could join forces to ward off predators' attacks, and they could rely on other members of their group to protect them from the aggressive actions of other humans. Human infants cannot survive alone. They must be in a group that cares for them until they can reach an age where they can fend for themselves. Groups, too, bring together men and women who can then form the pair-bonds needed for mating and procreation.

Evolutionary theory assumes that these advantages of group life, over multiple generations, eventually sewed sociality into the DNA of the human race. In the modern world, the advantages of group life over solitude are not so clear. People who buy their food in grocery stores and live in houses with deadbolts on the doors do not need to worry much about effective food-gathering strategies or protection from predation. These modern conditions, however, cannot undo 130,000 years of natural selection. Because those individuals who were genetically predisposed to join groups ("joiners") were much more likely to survive and breed than people who avoided social contacts ("loners"), with each passing generation, the genes that promoted solitude seeking were weeded out of the gene pool, and the genes that encouraged group joining prospered (Marsh & Morris, 1988; see Figure 3.4). In consequence, gregariousness flourished as part of the biological makeup of humans. Your ancestors were, in all likelihood, joiners rather than loners (Kameda & Tindale, 2006).

**Evidence and Issues** Do humans instinctively seek membership in groups? A variety of evidence

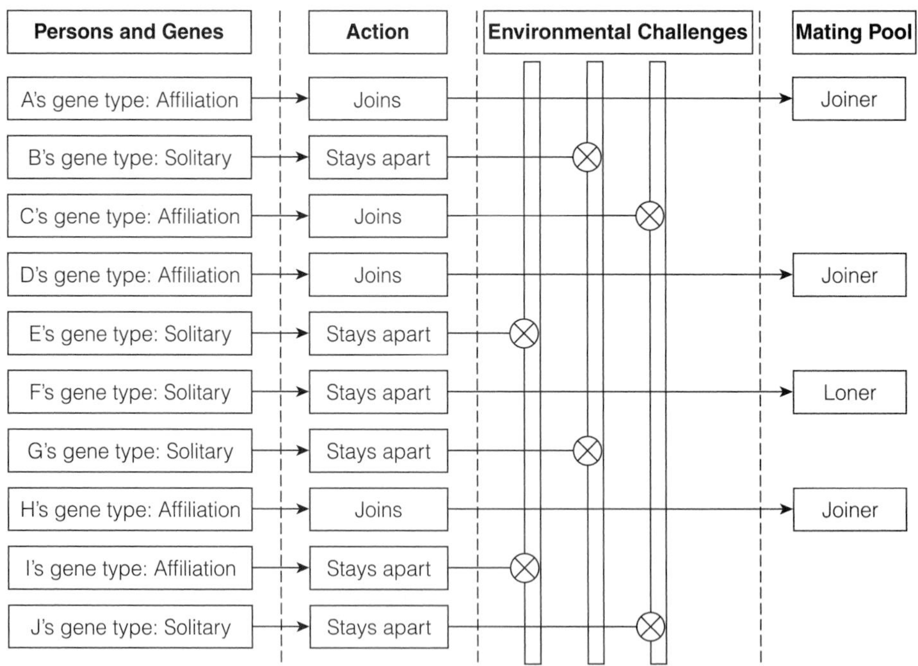


**FIGURE 3.4** A schematic representation of the process of natural selection of group-oriented individuals. If humanity's ancestors lived in an environment that favored those who lived in groups, then over time those who affiliated would gradually outnumber those who were self-reliant loners. Note, too, that one's genetic endowment interacts with the environment, and so not all individuals who are genetically predisposed to affiliate or remain alone will do so (see, for example, person I).

supports the evolutionary argument. Anthropologists have documented the great diversity of human societies, but across all these variations, they have found one constancy: People live in groups rather than alone (Mann, 1988). Careful analysis of the artifacts left behind by prehistoric humans—primarily bones and stone implements—suggest that even ancient humans lived in groups (Caporael, 2007). Other primates, such as chimpanzees and bonobos, also live in small groups with dynamics of inclusion and exclusion that are similar to those seen in human groups (de Waal, 2006). The young of the species instinctively form strong emotional bonds with their caregivers, and babies who are deprived of close human contact have higher mortality rates (Bowlby, 1980). Humans are also consistently cooperative in their dealings with other people, so long as these other people are members of a group to which they belong and not outsiders. As the next section of this chapter notes, cooperative group life is a more stable strategy in evolutionary terms than competition and individualism (Axelrod & Hamilton, 1981).

Evolutionary explanations of social behavior remain controversial, however. Researchers are only now subjecting the theory to close scrutiny, so its assumptions should be considered skeptically. The theory is difficult to test experimentally, and its basic premise—that characteristics that enhance our fitness have a genetic basis—is arguable. Just because groups are useful does not mean that people are instinctively drawn to them (Francis, 2004). The theory also requires an accurate understanding of humanity's evolutionary past, but the fossil record of prehistoric humans is a meager one (Festinger, 1983). Moreover, even if people are gregarious by instinct, other factors also play a role in determining decisions to join or leave a group. Childhood experiences, for example, influence who prefers groups memberships and who does not (Harlow & Harlow, 1966). Nonetheless, the evolutionary approach offers a compelling answer to the question, "Why do people seek out other people?" We instinctively value the contribution that a group can make to our genetic destiny (Caporael, 2007).

## FROM INDIVIDUALISM TO COLLECTIVISM

Brian Palmer and Joe Gorman, like most human beings, were members of many groups. They both had families and in their free time they relaxed with their children and spouses. When working, they spent most of their time with a relatively small group of fellow employees. They also belonged to an assortment of other groups and associations, such as cliques of friends, country clubs, professional associations, church congregations, political parties, and so on. But Palmer and Gorman viewed their memberships very differently. Palmer remained ever mindful of his personal needs and interests. He joined groups, but he never put the group's needs above his own. Gorman, in contrast, was less concerned with his own gains than he was with the group's outcomes. Unlike the self-centered Palmer, he was group-centered.

Palmer and Gorman personify the differences between individualism and collectivism. **Individualism** is based on the independence of each individual. This perspective assumes that people are autonomous and must be free to act and think in ways that they prefer, rather than submit to the demands of the group. Each person is also unique—a true individual—and all people are encouraged to strive to achieve outcomes and goals that will personally benefit them. **Collectivism** recognizes that human groups are not mere aggregations of independent individuals, but complex sets of interdependent actors who must constantly adjust to the actions and reactions of others around them. Each person, if even recognized as an independent entity, is inseparably connected to the group or community. Social existence is centered on group relations, for it is the group

---

**individualism** A tradition, ideology, or personal outlook that emphasizes the primacy of the individual and his or her rights, independence, and relationships with other individuals.

**collectivism** A tradition, ideology, or personal orientation that emphasizes the primacy of the group or community rather than each individual person.

that creates social obligations based on respect, trust, and a sense of community. People are group members first, individuals second (Lukes, 1973).

Individualism and collectivism are complex, multifaceted concepts, with no simple set of qualities that distinguishes one from another. Most treatments of these concepts agree, however, that these two orientations differ in their emphasis on relationships versus independence, on social obligations versus personal freedom, and on how the self is viewed: as independent versus overlapping, in part, with others' selves. The following sections review these three elements, as well as cross-cultural variations in individualism–collectivism. (For more detailed analyses and very differing opinions on the issue of the core dimensions of individualism and collectivism see Brewer & Chen, 2007; Chen & West, 2008; Oyserman & Lee, 2008; Triandis & Suh, 2002.)

## Social Relations

When John Winthrop, the first governor of Massachusetts Bay Colony, spoke to a gathering of the men and women who were about to colonize America in 1630, he urged them to always think first of the group before they thought of themselves:

> We must delight in each other, make others' conditions our own, rejoyce together, mourn together, labor and suffer together, always having before our eyes our community as members of the same body. (Winthrop, 1630/1667, p. 19).

Both individualism and collectivism recognize the human need for belonging and connection, but a collectivistic orientation puts more value on these relationships. Collectivists feel close affinity with one another and, so, are more likely to adopt a communal orientation to their groups (Moemeka, 1998). They value their memberships in their groups more, consider these relationships to be stable and long-lasting, and so are less willing to sever their memberships. Individuals who are collectivists seek jobs that will enhance the quality of their relationships with other people, and their satisfaction with their work depends on the quality of their relationships with their coworkers. Independents choose jobs that are personally fulfilling and that offer them opportunities for advancement (Leary, Wheeler, & Jenkins, 1986). Collectivists, compared to individualists, have a more favorable attitude toward group-level rewards for collective work (Haines & Taggar, 2006), and they are more likely to be corporate citizens who help coworkers rather than compete with them (Leung, 2008). Individualists stress their superiority over others on attributes that pertain to autonomy and independence, but collectivists think of themselves as more relational and self-sacrificing than others (Sedikides, Gaertner, & Toguchi, 2003). Women lean more toward collectivism, at least in Western cultures, where women more often stress connections with other people, whereas men tend to stress independence and autonomy (Cross & Madson, 1997; Gabriel & Gardner, 1999). Collectivists are more firmly rooted to their communities: they report having moved less frequently than individualists (Oishi, Lun, & Sherman, 2007).

**Exchange and Communal Relations** Individualists and collectivists tend to differ in their overall conceptualization of relationships themselves, with individualism associated with the *exchange* of resources and collectivism focusing on sharing *communal* resources. Individuals in **exchange relationships** monitor their inputs into the group, strive to maximize the rewards they personally receive through membership, and will become dissatisfied if their group becomes too costly for them. They expect to receive rewards in exchange for their investment of time, energy, and other personal resources. If individuals cannot identify any personal benefit from helping others in the group or community, then they will not offer any help (Ratner &

---

**exchange relationship** An interpersonal association between individuals based on each person's desire to increase the rewards they receive from others in the relationship.

Miller, 2001). In contrast, people in **communal relationships** are more concerned with what their group receives than with their own personal outcomes. When individuals work in communal groups, they help fellow members more, prefer to think of their work as a joint effort, and feel disappointed if other members insist on reciprocating any help given (Clark et al., 1987). They are also more likely to consider the consequences of their actions for others and are more diligent in making sure that others' needs are met (Mills et al., 2004).

**Reciprocity** This difference between an exchange and communal orientation is particularly clear when the group must allocate resources to members. Individualists think of their relations with others as a "strictly economic exchange" (Fiske, 1992, p. 702). When faced with a common resource pool or a project that requires combined effort individualists favor an evenly balanced, one-for-one exchange. They "often mark their relationship with very concrete operations of balancing, comparing, or counting-out items in one-for-one correspondence" (Fiske, 1992, p. 691). Their interactions also tend to be guided by the **norm of reciprocity**. This norm enjoins members to pay back in kind what others give to them. When this norm guides groups, members they cooperate with others to pay back past favors and to create obligations for future favors (Gouldner, 1960).

Collectivists, in contrast, are not so concerned with equality of allocations or reciprocity. When sharing a resource, group members would be more likely to "take what they need and contribute what they can, without anyone attending to how much each person contributes or receives. A person does not need to give something in order to get something in return—simple membership in the group is sufficient to entitle one to the use of whatever resources the group controls, and long-run imbalance is not a violation of the relationship" (Fiske, 1992, p. 693).

Reciprocity becomes problematic when members of the groups do not share equally in the work, but nonetheless seek an equal share of the rewards (Leung, 1997). Whenever groups earn rewards or cover costs, a fair means must be developed to determine how these rewards and costs are distributed across members. Imagine, for example, that your group has earned a reward by winning a lottery or must pay a fine because one of the group members accidentally broke something. The **equity norm** recommends that group members should receive outcomes in proportion to their inputs. If an individual has invested a good deal of time, energy, money, or other types of inputs in the group, then he or she could expect to receive a good deal of the group payoff. Similarly, individuals who contribute little should not be surprised when they receive little. The **equality norm**, on the other hand, recommends that all group members, irrespective of their inputs, should be given an equal share of the payoff. If your group includes all best friends, and collectivism is high, members would likely favor allocating the winnings on an equal-share basis: All should benefit, even if just one of the group members was the one who picked the winning lottery numbers. However, collectivists may also require that the costs be borne more heavily by the individual member who caused a problem, because the group as a whole must be protected against injury (Utz & Sassenberg, 2002). Individualism, in contrast, would favor an equity norm, because the contributions of each member are recognized and rewarded (or punished).

Members do not, however, share with everyone—in many cases this communal orientation is strictly reserved, for members of one's own group.

---

**communal relationship** An interpersonal association between individuals who are more concerned with what others get rather than what they themselves receive.

**norm of reciprocity** A social standard that enjoins individuals to pay back in kind what they receive from others.

**equity norm** A social standard that encourages distributing rewards and resources to members in proportion to their inputs.

**equality norm** A social standard that encourages distributing rewards and resources equally among all members.

Collectivists are more likely to divide the world up into "us" and "we"—the ingroup—versus "them" and "they"—the outgroup. When individualists think about group membership, they consider it to consist of relatively loose associations that are selected by members and not the groups themselves. Collectivists, in contrast, define belonging as "belonging securely," and they tend to view boundaries between one group and another to be relatively impermeable. Individualists are less likely to restrict their relationships to the ingroup, and they are more trusting of strangers than are collectivists. Collectivists spend more time in group interactions, and they are not as trusting of people who are not members of their groups (Fiske & Yamamoto, 2005).

## Social Obligations

Long ago, the philosopher Jean Jacques Rousseau summed up the problem of collaboration in groups in his story of the Stag Hunt. When a group is hunting a stag everyone realizes that they must work together by staying at their posts in readiness should they flush a deer. But what if a rabbit hops by, wondered Rousseau? Will not the hunter be tempted to head off in pursuit of the rabbit, as it is easy prey to catch, but in doing so let down the group? The hunter who forgoes the rabbit will have made the right choice—to cooperate with the others—only if the others are also cooperative. Should the others abandon their posts and seek rabbits too, then the group-oriented stag hunter will come home with nothing (Skyrms, 2004).

A collectivist orientation requires a willingness to cooperate with others, and a degree of optimism that these others are also committed more to the common good than to their own personal outcomes. Rousseau's term for this assurance is the **social contract**, which he believed individuals intuitively accept when they enter into cooperative arrangements with others, including groups, communities, and societies. Rousseau recognized the tension between collectivism and individualism, for as he explained, "What man loses by the social contract is his natural liberty and the absolute right to anything that tempts him and that he can take; what he gains from the social contract is civil liberty" (1968, p. 65).

If the goals of the group perfectly matched the individual members' goals, then individualists and collectivists would be indistinguishable. By helping the group prosper, the members help themselves prosper. However, if members must choose between maximizing their own personal goals or helping their group reach its goals, then the self-interest of the individualists will prompt them to further their own ends. Individualists tend to be **self-serving**, or *egocentric*—they strive to extract all the resources they can, while minimizing their contribution of personal resources. Collectivists, in contrast, are **group-serving**, or *sociocentric*—they strive to increase the well-being of the community as a whole (see Focus 3.3).

The collectivist is obligated, by the social contract, to have respect for those who hold positions of authority and avoid disagreement or dissent (Schwartz, 1994, 2007). A group, to a collectivist, "binds and mutually obligates" each member (Oyserman et al., 2002, p. 5), and so the individual has no right to create disagreement or to disrupt convened group proceedings. Collectivists prefer, in fact, acquiescence to disagreement and compromise to conflict. They carry out their duties within their groups, and the successful fulfillment of their roles and responsibilities is the primary source of self-satisfaction (Schwartz, 1994). Alan Fiske (1992, p. 701) suggests that groups need a system

---

**social contract** As described by Jean Jacques Rousseau, an agreement, often only implicitly recognized, that obligates the individual to support the "general will" of society as an "indivisible part of the whole."

**self-serving** Emphasizing one's own needs, perspective, and importance, particularly in contrast to those of other individuals or the group (egocentric).

**group-serving** Emphasizing the group's needs, perspectives, and importance, particularly in contrast to those of individual members or oneself (sociocentric).

## Focus 3.3 How Would You Split the "Pie" in the Ultimatum Game?

*Two men who pull at the oars of a boat, do it by an agreement or convention, tho' they have never given promises to each other.*

—David Hume, *A Treatise on Human Nature*

Here is the situation. You are taking part in a simple bargaining simulation called the **Ultimatum Game**. You are paired with another person but you do not know the person's identity except that he or she is a member of your group. You have been allotted \$20 (the "pie") which you must share with your partner. You may offer your partner any portion of the \$20—from 1¢ to \$19.99—but your partner knows the size of the pie. If your partner accepts your offer, the pie will be divided just as you proposed, but if your partner rejects your offer no one gets any money at all. You cannot communicate with your partner and you will not be given a second chance if your partner turns you down.

How much will you offer? If you are motivated solely by profit, then you should offer very little to your partner. Economically speaking, even if you only offer \$1 your partner should take it because \$1, although much less than the \$19 you will receive, is better than \$0. Yet, when people play the Ultimatum Game, they rarely offer or accept so little. People, on average, generally offer between 35% to 50% of the pie; in the example, between \$7 and \$10. People are also quite willing to reject too low an offer, even though it means that they will receive nothing (Henrich et al., 2004). Both the person who offers and

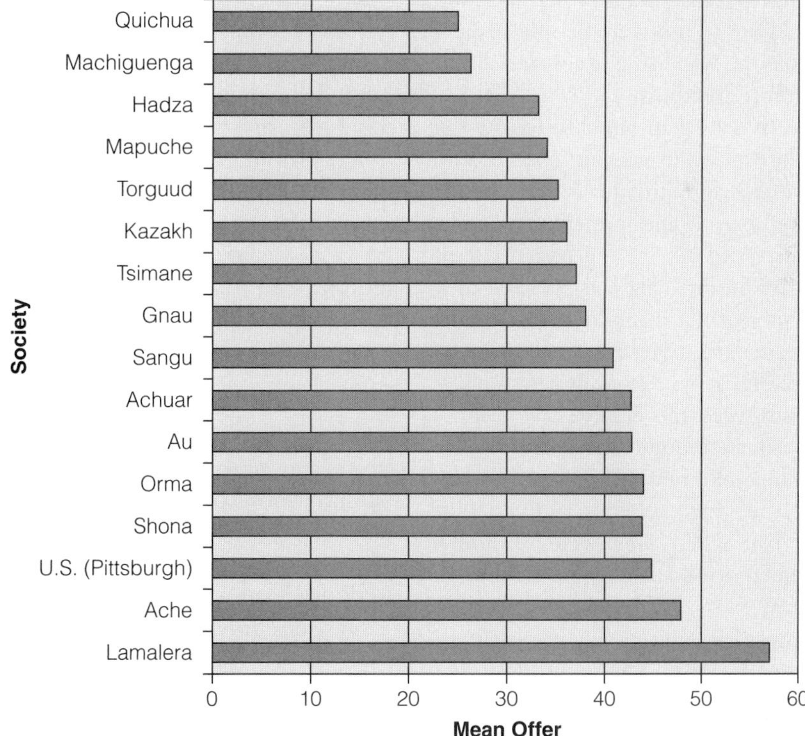


**FIGURE 3.5** The mean distributions in the Ultimatum Game from people living in 16 different indigenous societies and cultures around the world.

SOURCE: "Overview and Synthesis," by J. Henrich, R. Boyd, S. Bowles, C. F. Camerer, E. Fehr, H. Gintis, and R. McElreath, in *Foundations of Human Sociality*, pages 8–54 (Table 2.2, p. 20). Copyright 2004 by J. Henrich, R. Boyd, S. Bowles, C. F. Camerer, E. Fehr, H. Gintis, and R. McElreath. Used by permission.

*(Continued)*

**Focus 3.3 (Continued)**

their partner recognize that a fair distribution is a nearly equal one—selfishness may prompt a person to want to keep as much of the pie as they can, but they realize that their partner is willing to pay to make clear the importance of fairness (Kameda, Takezawa, & Hastie, 2005).

Enterprising researchers have gathered data on responses to the Ultimatum Game in dozens of indigenous societies located around the world. As the results in Figure 3.5 indicate, only one group averaged offers of [According to Figure 3.5, the mean average for the Lamalera was 50%, not "more than 50%"] of the endowment: the Lamalera of East Indonesia. The lowest offer was made by the Quichua of South America. This variability, although pronounced, was related to each group's level of collectivism. Some communities stressed the importance of individuality and the family, whereas in others "one's economic well-being depends on cooperation with non-relatives" (Henrich et al., 2004, p. 29). These more co-operative communities tended to be more generous in their allocations in the game, as were those societies that created more elaborate economic and social connections among various households. As for the Lamalera: their high level of generosity reflects their unique living conditions. The Lamalera are whalers, and traditionally the catch is divided equally among all members of the community—even those who did not participate in the hunt. The Lamalera are quintessential collectivists.

of authority ranking "because stratification and rank distinctions are essential to motivate people to perform arduous duties in leadership roles and other crucial but demanding positions."

Whereas collectivists are enjoined to follow the dictates of social norms when making choices and selecting a course of action, individualists are guided by their personal attitudes and preferences. Individualists are expected to act on the basis of their attitudes, beliefs, and preferences; they believe they have the right to speak their minds and to disagree with others (Triandis, 1996). Researchers illustrated this contrast by asking people to complete a short survey. Collectivists were more likely to comply with the survey takers' request when they were told that many other members of their group had agreed to fill out the form, whereas individualists were more compliant when they were reminded that they had agreed to a similar request before (Cialdini et al., 1999).

Because of these differences in emphasis on duties versus personal rights, collectivistic groups respond more negatively to group members who violate group norms, procedures, and authority. Their operating principle is, "The tall nail gets pounded down." Individualistic groups are more reserved in their reactions to nonconformity *per se,* for they assume that "the squeaky wheel gets the grease." Thus, collectivists hold rule-breakers in contempt, whereas individualists tend to display anger toward those who disregard the group's emphasis on autonomy by seeking to impose their will on others (Rozin et al., 1999).

## Social Self

A communal orientation is not just about relationships and obligations (see Table 3.1). As people adopt a more other-centered orientation they also change the way they think about themselves. Unique, individualistic qualities—traits, beliefs, skills, and so on—constitute the **personal identity**. The **social identity** (or collective identity) includes

---

**Ultimatum Game** An experimental bargaining situation in which one individual, the allocator, must propose a division of a shared resource to other members; if they reject the allocator's proposal, no one receives any of the resource.

**personal identity** The "me" component of the self-concept that derives from individualistic qualities such as traits, beliefs, and skills.

**social identity** (or collective self) The "we" component of the self-concept that includes all those qualities attendant to relationships with other people, groups, and society.

**TABLE 3.1 Common Attributes of Individualism and Collectivism**

| Attribute | Individualism | Collectivism |
|---|---|---|
| **Social relations** | Focus on establishing and maintaining relationships that yield personal rewards with few costs (*exchange orientation*); concern for maintaining equity in relations with others | Focus on fostering nurturing and harmonious relations with others with less emphasis on exchange (*communal orientation*); resources are distributed on the basis of need |
| **Social obligations** | Individuals act to promote their own interests before considering the needs of others; satisfaction comes from personal triumphs in competition with others | Members are obliged to cooperate with others in the pursuit of shared goals; concern for group success; behavior is guided by group norms and roles |
| **Social identity** | The independent self is based on one's personal, idiosyncratic characteristics; each self is autonomous and unique | The interdependent self is based on group-level relationships, roles, and social identities rather than on individual personal qualities |

all those qualities that spring from membership in a vast array of social groups, including families, cliques, work groups, neighborhoods, tribes, cities, regions, and countries. The idea of a self as private and highly personalized is more characteristic of an individualistic outlook; in the collective identity view, some portion of the group becomes represented in each member, so that their individual selves share some qualities in common. The personal identity is the *me* of the self, and the social identity is the *we* (Turner et al., 1987).

If asked to describe the self, an individualist like Brian Palmer would likely mention his physical qualities such as height, weight, and physical appearance; enduring personality traits and beliefs; attitudes and interests; and personal goals and experiences (Kanagawa, Cross, & Markus, 2001). He would be less likely to mention other people or his relations with them, because the self is considered to be independent of others. The self of the collectivist, in contrast, includes all those qualities that spring from his or her relationships with other people and group memberships.

Marilyn Brewer and her colleagues further divide the group-level self into two components: the relational self and the collective self (Brewer, 2007; Brewer & Chen, 2007; Brewer & Gardner, 1996). Joe Gorman's *relational self* is defined by his ties to other people; he is a father, a husband, an employee, and a leader of his community. Gorman's *collective self* is determined by his membership in larger groups and categories; he is a Christian, a man, Irish, and resident of the city where he lives. Few people lack a relational self, for most are members of small groups such as friends and families. Collectivists, however, are more likely to identify themselves in terms of their relational and collective selves, and they also spend more time in activities related to these more group-level selves (Cross, Bacon, & Morris, 2000; Gecas & Burke, 1995; Rhee et al., 1995; Thoits, 1992).

**Independents and Interdependents** Most people's selves are a combination of both personal and collective elements, and so their view of themselves can shift along the continuum from individualistic to collectivistic depending on the situation. People's answers to the question, "Who am I?" will change to include more collectivistic elements if they are first asked to imagine themselves in a group or if they have just read texts that contain many plural pronouns such as *we* or *us*. Asking them to think about how different they are from others, or reading texts with many *I*'s and *me*'s, in contrast, switches on the individualistic self (Oyserman & Lee, 2008).

People however, do vary by disposition in their tendency to respond in an individualistic or a collectivist way. **Independents**, or **idiocentrics**, are emotionally detached from their groups; they put their own personal goals above the goals of the group (Markus, Kitayama, & Heiman, 1996; Triandis, 1995). They value equality, social justice, and self-reliance (Kashima et al., 1995; Triandis et al., 1990). **Interdependents**, or **allocentrics**, in contrast, put their groups' goals and needs above their own (Markus et al., 1996; Triandis, 1995). They are respectful of other members of their groups, and they value their memberships in groups, their friendships, and traditions.

**Individuation in Groups** Individuals who are more independent than interdependent also tend to stress their unique, unusual qualities. One measure of the tendency to set oneself apart from other people—the *Individuation Scale*—asks people to indicate their willingness to engage in attention-getting behaviors, such as self-disclosure and nonconformity (Maslach, Stapp, & Santee, 1985). People who score high on the Individuation Scale report a greater frequency of owning distinctive possessions (such as a special kind of car), having a unique self-expressive symbol (such as a nickname), expressing unique opinions, criticizing someone in front of others, making controversial statements, and looking directly into someone's eyes while talking to him or her. People scoring low on the scale report a greater frequency of wearing the kind of clothes that others wear, owning standard possessions, avoiding distinctive nicknames, avoiding accessories or colors that get attention, controlling distracting gestures, expressing popular opinions, agreeing with other people, not criticizing others, remaining quiet in a group, and avoiding eye contact. They are more likely to engage in conventional behaviors and seek social acceptance. When these scales are used in collectivistic societies, the respondents distinguish between two forms of individuating behaviors: taking the lead and drawing attention to oneself. Taking the lead was considered to be slightly more acceptable than drawing attention to oneself in one study of Japanese students (Kwan et al., 2002).

**Optimal Distinctiveness** Although interdependent types of people are often contrasted with independent types, in all likelihood these two orientations are continuous dimensions of personality that vary in their influence across time and situations. As Marilyn Brewer's **optimal distinctiveness theory** suggested, most people probably have at least three fundamental needs: the need to be assimilated by the group, the need to be connected to friends and loved ones, and the need for autonomy and differentiation. She hypothesized that individuals are most satisfied if they achieve optimal distinctiveness: Their unique personal qualities are noted and appreciated, they are emotionally bonded with intimates, and they feel similar to other group members in many respects (Brewer, Manzi, & Shaw, 1993; Brewer & Pickett, 2002). Achieving a sense of uniqueness is as important as satisfying the need to belong (Snyder & Fromkin, 1980). This theory has implications for how group members think about themselves and others, and we will consider these self-processes in more detail in the final section of this chapter.

## Variations in Collectivism

When the French historian Alexis de Tocqueville visited the United States in the 1830s, he was struck by Americans' self-reliance and independence. He noted they frequently joined together to achieve some collective goal, but even when they were working in groups, they still took inordinate pride in their personal autonomy and self-reliance. It seemed to him that all Americans act as if they "owe no man

---

**independent**(or **idiocentric**) An individual who is dispositionally predisposed to put his or her own personal interests and motivations above the group's interests and goals.

**interdependent**(or **allocentric**) An individual who is dispositionally predisposed to put the group's goals and needs above his or her own.

**optimal distinctiveness theory** A conceptual analysis proposed by Marilyn Brewer that assumes individuals strive to maintain a balance between three basic needs: the need to be assimilated by the group, the need to be connected to friends and loved ones, and the need for autonomy and differentiation.

anything and hardly expect anything from anybody. They form the habit of thinking of themselves in isolation and imagine that their whole destiny is in their own hands" (de Tocqueville, 1831/1969, p. 508). He used the word *individualism* to capture this uniquely American spirit of self-reliance (Lukes, 1973).

**Cultural Differences** The view of people as independent, autonomous creatures may be peculiar to Western society's individualistic leanings. When researchers measured the relative emphasis on the individual and the group in countries all around the world, they found that the United States, other English-speaking countries (e.g., England, Australia), and Western European countries (e.g., Finland, Germany) tended to be more individualistic than Asian, Eastern European, African, and Middle Eastern countries (Hofstede, 1980; Oyserman et al., 2002). Latin and South American countries were more varied, with such countries as Puerto Rico and Chile exhibiting greater individualism than others (e.g., Mexico, Costa Rica).

The Gahuku-Gama of Highland New Guinea, for example, do not recognize individuals apart from their roles as father, mother, chief, and so on. They do not even grasp the concept of friendship, for such a concept requires liking between two individuals (Read, 1986). The Akaramas of Peru paint their bodies so elaborately that individuals are unrecognizable. Tribes sleep in same-sex groups of 10 or 12, and when individuals die, their passing goes unnoticed (Schneebaum, 1969). Students in the United States, more than students in China, assume that people's behaviors are caused by personality traits rather than by factors in the situation (Chiu, Hong, & Dweck, 1997).

People from individualistic and collectivistic cultures even insult one another differently. Personal insults, such as "You are stupid," characterize conflicts in individualistic cultures, whereas remarks about one's family and group typify disputes between two collectivists (Semin & Rubini, 1990). The very idea of self may differ across cultures. In Japan, a relatively collectivistic culture, the word for self, *jibun*, means "one's portion of the shared space" (Hamaguchi, 1985). To the Japanese, "the concept of a self completely independent from the environment is very foreign," as people are not perceived apart from the existing social context (Azuma, 1984, p. 973).

Harry Triandis and his colleagues illustrated this difference by asking people from various countries to describe themselves. As expected, these self-descriptions contained more references to roles and relationships when people were from collectivistic countries (e.g., Japan, China). Some individuals from the People's Republic of China described themselves exclusively in interpersonal terms. And some U.S. residents used only personal descriptors—they reported no elements of a collective self (Triandis, McCusker, & Hui, 1990; cf. Oyserman et al., 2002). Other research has suggested that people from collectivistic countries resist describing their qualities if the social context is not specified. Japanese, for example, described themselves differently when they were with different people and in different social situations. Americans, in contrast, described themselves similarly across different situations (Cousins, 1989).

These observations are only generalities, however, for people within a culture may not adopt their home country's orientation. Triandis and his colleagues (2001) found that about 60% of the people in collectivistic cultures are interdependent types, just as about 60% of the people in individualistic cultures are independent types. They also reported that interdependent individuals in individualistic countries tend to join more groups, but that independent individuals in collectivistic cultures "feel oppressed by their culture and seek to leave it" (Triandis & Suh, 2002, p. 141). Each culture, too, likely expresses its collectivism and individualism in unique ways. Some collectivistic cultures, for example, are much more hierarchically structured (*vertical*) than others, like the culture of India with its caste system, which stresses tradition, duty, and compliance with authority. Other collectivistic cultures, however, stress commonality, and so their society's status and authority structures are relatively flat (*horizontal*). Some collectivistic societies also tolerate considerable conflict within their groups. Members of Israeli kibbutzes, for example, often engage in heated debates, whereas

Koreans strive for harmony and avoid discord. Both cultures are relatively collectivistic, yet their approaches to resolving disputes differ substantially (Triandis, 1995, 1996). In contrast, Scandinavians are extremely individualistic, but they are also noncompetitive (Fiske, 2002). It may be that the dichotomy between individualism and collectivism reflects, in part, the cognitive biases of the Western theorists who first proposed this distinction (Fiske, 2002; Gaines et al., 1997).

**Regional and Ethnic Differences** Classifying entire cultures along a continuum from individualistic to collectivistic also overlooks significant variations across subgroups within a culture and across individuals within a culture (Miller, 2002). In the United States, for example, certain areas are more individualistic, whereas others are more collectivistic (Vandello & Cohen, 2004). Communalism is prominent in the south of the United States, which remains more rural, agricultural, and hierarchically structured than the rest of the country. When polled, its residents were more likely to agree to such statements as, "It is better to fit in with people around you," and "It is more important to be a cooperative person who works well with others." Individuals living in the western portions of the United States, where the frontier, pioneer tradition stresses self-reliance, are more individualistic. Residents of this part of the country felt that "It is better to conduct yourself according to your own standards, even if that makes you stand out," and "It is more important to be a self-reliant person able to take care of oneself" (Vandello & Cohen, 1999, p. 285).

Ethnic groups in the United States also exhibit remarkable variations in individualism and collectivism. When Oyserman and her colleagues (2002) combined the findings obtained across a number of studies they found that Asian Americans tended to be more collectivistic than European Americans, but that Japanese and Koreans are more similar to European Americans than were the more collectivistic Chinese Americans. Hispanic Americans did not differ from European Americans in their level of individualism, but they were more collectivistic. Even though Afrocentric cultural traditions, like those emphasized in the African American celebration of Kwanzaa, stress strong family ties and mutual help, the researchers discovered that African Americans tended to score higher than European Americans on measures of individualism and lower than European Americans on measures of collectivism.

**Generational Differences** Entire generations of individuals living in a given culture may also display overall differences in individualism and collectivism. Robert Putnam (2000) notes that the generation of Americans born during the first portion of the 20th century were so willing to sacrifice for the collective good that they were dubbed the *Greatest Generation*. Their children—the *Baby Boomers* born after the Second World War—displayed a strong work ethic, but their commitment to their employers meant that they had less time to donate to volunteer activities. *Gen-Xers*, born between 1965 and 1980 or so, and the most recent generation, variously labeled *Gen-Y*, the *Millennials*, and the *Me Generation*, are characterized by stronger needs for autonomy, individualism, confirmation, and support. Jean Twenge (2006), in her book *Generation Me*, maintains that the youngest generation to join the workforce is more individualistic than any previous one. Members of this generation are more interested in gratifying their personal needs, less likely to be concerned with the recommendations of authority and less likely to follow social rules.

## FROM PERSONAL IDENTITY TO SOCIAL IDENTITY

Brian Palmer and Joe Gorman would probably have very different answers to the question, "Who are you?" Palmer, the individualist, might answer "I'm Brian Palmer" and then list his accomplishments, his personal qualities, and his goals. Gorman, the collectivist, would talk about his family, his community, and his hometown. But how does a group become a part of one's social identity? What impact does this acceptance of the group into one's identity have on one's self-concept and self-esteem? In this final section we consider one compelling theoretical answer to these questions: social identity theory. (For detailed analyses of groups and identity, see Ashmore, Deaux, & McLaughlin-Volpe, 2004; Hogg, 2005; Roccas et al., 2008).

### Social Identity Theory: The Basics

Henri Tajfel, John Turner, and their colleagues originally developed **social identity theory**, or SIT, in an attempt to understand the causes of conflict between groups. To investigate this process, they created the most minimal of groups—just gatherings of people with no history, no future together, and no real connection to one another. They planned to add elements to this **minimal intergroup situation** to identify when conflict began to erupt between groups. So, they randomly assigned participants to one of two groups, but they told the participants that the division was based on some irrelevant characteristic, such as art preference. Next, the participants were given a series of booklets asking them to decide how a certain amount of money should be allocated to other participants in the experiment. The names of the individuals were not given in the booklets, but the participant could tell which group a person belonged to by looking at his or her code number.

Tajfel and Turner's research revealed a systematic bias even in this minimal intergroup situation. Participants did not know one another, they would not be working together in the future, and their membership in the so-called group had absolutely no personal or interpersonal implications. Yet, they favored the ingroup over the outgroup, and this bias persisted even though (1) members of the same group never interacted face-to-face, (2) the identities of ingroup and outgroup members were unknown, and (3) no one gained personally by granting more or less money to any particular person (Tajfel & Turner, 1979, 1986). How could these "purely cognitive" groups—groups that had no interpersonal meaning whatsoever—nonetheless influence people's perceptions and actions? Social identity theory's answer: Two cognitive processes—*categorization* and *identification*—combine to transform a group membership into an identity (Abrams et al., 2005; Hogg, 2005; Oyserman, 2007).

**Self-Categorization** Social identity theory is based, fundamentally, on the process of **social categorization**. As noted briefly in Chapter 2, people quickly and automatically classify other people into social categories: if we met Joe Gorman on the street we would rapidly slot him into such social groupings as man, middle-aged, American, and white, for example. And once categorized, our perceptions of Gorman would be influenced by our beliefs about the qualities and characteristics of the prototypical American, middle-aged white man. These beliefs, which are termed **prototypes** or **stereotypes**, describe the typical characteristics of people in various social groups. They also include information about how a group is different from other groups (the *metacontrast principle*).

People do not, however, only categorize other people; they also classify themselves into various groups and categories. Joe Gorman would realize that he is a man, an American, white, and middle-aged—that he belongs in these social categories. He might then apply stereotypes about the people in those categories to himself. Gorman might, for example, believe that the prototypical American man his age tends to act as a leader, is involved in business outside the home, is logical and objective in his thinking, and does not get his feelings hurt easily (Broverman, et al.,

---

**social identity theory** A theoretical analysis of group processes and intergroup relations that assumes groups influence their members' self-concepts and self-esteem, particularly when individuals categorize themselves as group members and identify with the group.

**minimal intergroup situation** A research procedure developed by Henri Tajfel and John Turner in their studies of intergroup conflict that involved creating temporary groups of anonymous, unrelated people.

**social categorization** The perceptual classification of people, including the self, into categories.

**prototypes** (or **stereotypes)** A socially shared set of cognitive generalizations (e.g., beliefs, expectations) about the qualities and characteristics of the typical member of a particular group or social category.

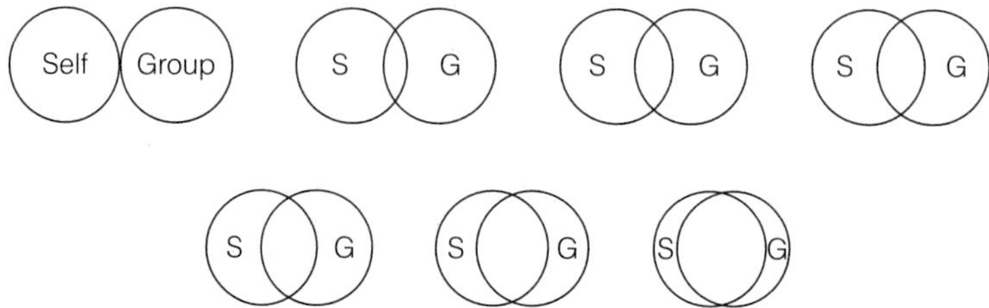


**FIGURE 3.6** The inclusion of the group in the self. If asked to select the set of circles that best indicates the extent to which the group (G) overlaps with the self (S), people who do not identify with their group select circles that don't overlap. Increasing identification is indicated by selecting circles where the self and the group overlap to a greater degree (Tropp & Wright, 2001).

SOURCE: From "Ingroup Identification as the Inclusion of Ingroup in the Self," by Linda R. Tropp & Stephen C. Wright, 2001, *Personality and Social Psychology Bulletin*, 27, pp. 585–600. Reprinted by permission of Sage Publications via Copyright Clearance Center.

1972). Then, through **self-stereotyping**, Gorman would also apply those stereotypes to himself and would come to believe that he, like most American men his age, leads rather than follows, is engaged in his work, bases his decisions on logical analysis, and is emotionally tough (Abrams & Hogg, 2001; Mackie, 1980).

**Identification** Most people belong to many groups and categories, but many of these memberships have no influence on their social identities. Gorman may be a right-hander, a Democrat, and brown-eyed, but he has never given much thought to these categories. Only some of his memberships, such as his involvement with the town council and his team of colleagues at work, are core elements of his sense of self. He *identifies* with these social categories, and so accepts the group as an extension of himself. He also knows that the other group members similarly identify with the group, and so they too possess the qualities that qualify them for membership in the group. As Michael Hogg (2004, p. 136), a leading theorist and researcher in the area of social identity, explains:

> They identify themselves in the same way and have the same definition of who they are, what attributes they have, and how they relate to and differ from specific outgroups or from people who are simply not ingroup members. Group membership is a matter of collective self-construal—*we, us*, and *them*.

As **social identification** increases, individuals come to think that their membership in the group is personally significant. They feel connected and interdependent with other members, are glad they belong to the group, feel good about the group, and experience strong attachment to the group. Their connection to the group also becomes more affectively toned—a "hot" cognitive reaction rather than a "cold" recognition of membership—as individuals incorporate the group into their social identity, "together with the value and emotional significance attached to that membership" (Tajfel, 1981, p. 255). Their self-descriptions also become increasingly *depersonalized* as they include fewer idiosyncratic elements and more characteristics that are common to the group. As indicated by Figure 3.6, the sense of self changes as the group is, literally, included in the self (Wright, Aron, & Tropp, 2002).

**Self and Identity** Research suggests that in some cases, identification with a group is so great that across

---

**self-stereotyping** (or **autostereotyping)** Accepting socially shared generalizations about the prototypical characteristics attributed to members of one's group as accurate descriptions of oneself.

**social identification** Accepting the group as an extension of the self, and therefore basing one's self-definition on the group's qualities and characteristics.

situations people think of themselves as group members first and individuals second, and, within their self concept, their personal idiosyncratic qualities are far outnumbered by their group-level qualities (Phinney & Ong, 2007). More typically, however, the self will shift from *me* to *we* if something in the situation increases the salience of one's membership. Individuals who find that they are the only representative of a particular group—for example, the only man in a group of five women, or the only left-hander in a class of otherwise all right-handers—may suddenly become very aware of that aspect of themselves (McGuire & McGuire, 1988). People who feel that they are being uniquely scrutinized by other people are more likely to think of themselves as individuals than as group members (Mullen, Rozell, & Johnson, 1996).

One of the most important situational triggers of a collective self-representation is the presence of members of the outgroup. As Tajfel and Turner (1986) confirmed in their initial studies of the minimal intergroup situation, categorization and identification become more likely when one group encounters another group. For example, if 10 men are seated in a room, they may not think of themselves as men, but when a group of 10 women enters the room then their sense of membership in the category *man* is activated.

Researchers have also confirmed that individuals sometimes generalize from their stereotypes about their groups to themselves. Children as young as five years of age, when their identity as boys and girls is made salient, are more likely to describe themselves in stereotypical ways (Bennett & Sani, 2008). When women in sororities rated themselves and other women in their sorority on traits often ascribed to sorority women (e.g., popular, well-dressed, conceited, shallow, spoiled), they gave themselves and their group nearly identical ratings—the correlation between self-rating and group rating was .98 (Biernat, Vescio, & Green, 1996). In groups that included both men and women, men's self-descriptions emphasized their masculinity and women's their femininity only when a disagreement had split members along sex lines—men taking one side in the argument and the women the other (Hogg & Turner, 1987).

Another group-level determinant of self-categorization is the relative size of one's group compared to other groups. People in groups with fewer members, such as minority groups based on ethnicity, race, or religion, tend to categorize themselves as members more quickly than do those people who are members of the larger, dominant, majority group. The experience of being in the minority apparently increases the salience of the social identity based on that membership, and so people are more likely to apply the stereotypical features of the minority group to themselves. Researchers informed some participants that a survey they had just completed suggested that they were extraverted and that only 20% of the general population is extraverted. These individuals then gave themselves higher ratings on such traits as *sociable* and *lively* than did people who were told that 80% of the population is extraverted (Simon & Hamilton, 1994).

### Motivation and Social Identity

Social identity theory provides key insights into a host of psychological and interpersonal processes, including collectivism, perceptions of the outgroup, presumptions of ingroup permeability, tolerance of deviance within the group, increased satisfaction with the group, and feelings of solidarity (Kenworthy et al., 2008; Leach et al., 2008). Later chapters will elaborate on the further implications of this theory, but here we conclude this chapter by considering the role social identity processes play in helping individuals protect and maintain their sense of self-worth.

**Evaluating the Self** Michael Hogg (2005) suggests that at least two basic motives influence the way social categorization and identification processes combine to shape one's sense of self. In general, individuals are motivated to think well of themselves, and since their groups comprise a significant portion of their selves, they maintain their self-worth by thinking well of their groups. Second, Hogg suggests that self-understanding is a core motive for most people, and that groups offer people a means of understanding themselves.

When individuals join groups, their self-concept becomes connected to that group, and the value of that group influences their feelings of personal worth. People who belong to prestigious groups tend to have higher self-esteem than those who belong to stigmatized groups (so long as they are not reminded that their group's revered social position is undeserved; Branscombe, 1998). Sports fans' moods swing up and down as their favorite team wins and loses. After a loss, they feel depressed and rate themselves more negatively; but after a win, they feel elated and rate themselves more positively (see Focus 3.4). Adolescent boys and girls are known to seek out membership in a particular peer group, and

## Focus 3.4 Can Social Identity Theory Explain Sports Fans?

*You may glory in a team triumphant, but you fall in love with a team in defeat. Losing after great striving is the story of man, who was born to sorrow, whose sweetest songs tell of the saddest thought.*

–Roger Kahn (1973), *The Boys of Summer*

*Fan* derives from a slightly longer word: fanatic. A *fanatic* is one who engages in extreme, unreasonable devotion to an idea, philosophy, or practice. Similarly, the die-hard sports fan displays great devotion to a team, with emotions rising and falling with the team's accomplishments. Fans are not actually members of the teams they support. They are only watching the games from the sidelines, and no action they take affects the outcome. Yet they often seem to be very closely connected psychologically to their teams. They are happy when their team wins, but after a loss, fans experience a range of negative emotions: anger, depression, sadness, hopelessness, and confusion (Platow et al., 1999; Wann et al., 1994). Moreover, the "agony of defeat" appears to be more psychologically profound than the "thrill of victory." One team of researchers found that fans' moods became more positive after their team won, but the rise in positive affect did not match the drop in mood following failure. The impact of a loss was so great that they concluded the costs of fanship outweigh the benefits (Hirt et al., 1992).

Social identity theory offers insight into this odd but exceedingly common group behavior (Mael & Ashforth, 2001). Sports fans *identify* with their team and so experience the team's outcomes as their own. When the team wins, they can share in that victory. They experience a range of positive emotions, including pride, emotion, happiness, and even joy, and they can gloat over the failure of their rivals. They can, when interacting with other people, **bask in reflected glory**, or **BIRG**, by stressing their association with the successful group, even though they have contributed little to that success (Cialdini et al., 1976; End et al., 2002). They also experience a host of positive interpersonal benefits from supporting a specific team—particularly a local one (Wann, 2006). Fans who support the same team may spend considerable time in enjoyable shared activities and from that group experience gain social support, a sense of belonging, and enhanced overall well-being.

But what if their team should lose? Casual fans can just downplay the loss by switching their allegiance to some other team: **cutting off reflected failure**, or **CORFing** (Snyder, Higgins, & Stucky, 1983). Dedicated fans, whose homes are decorated with team insignia, who wear the team's colors, and who have based much of their sense of self on their loyalty to the team, cannot CORF. Their team's loss will be *their* loss (St. John, 2004). But these die-hard fans can and do rely on a variety of psychological and social tactics to ease the pain of the loss. They may blame their failure on external factors, such as field conditions or the referee. They may spend time talking about past successes, and convince one another that better times lie ahead. They can take solace in their failure collectively, and mourn their group's loss together. They may also take pride in other aspects of their team, such as its sportsmanship or *esprit de corps* (Wann, 2006). They may even vent their frustration by acting violently; fans have been known to attack the supporters of other teams, with fatal outcomes (Doosje, Ellemers, & Spears, 1999).

Fanship, like many social identities, comes with a risk—identifying with a group whose outcomes one cannot control means that one will encounter the joy of victory, but also the agony of a shared defeat. That despair can be profound: Suicide rates tend to rise and fall with the success of the local college sports team—at least in some college towns known for strong fan allegiance (Joiner, Hollar, & Van Orden, 2006). However, victory can bring great elation. Fewer people committed suicide on the day the U.S. Olympic Hockey Team beat the Russian national team (February 22, 1980) than had on that date from 1972 to 1989. Whereas failure may set the stage for collective misery, a team victory may be the "sweetest song of all" (Kahn, 1973).

**TABLE 3.2 Items from the Collective Self-Esteem Inventory**

| Subscale | Issue | Example Item |
|---|---|---|
| **Membership Esteem** | Am I a valuable or an ineffective member of the groups to which I belong? | I am a worthy member of the social groups I belong to. |
| **Private Collective Self-Esteem** | Do I evaluate the groups I belong to positively or negatively? | I feel good about the social groups I belong to. |
| **Public Collective Self-Esteem** | Do other people evaluate the groups I belong to positively or negatively? | In general, others respect the social groups that I am a member of. |
| **Identity** | Are the groups I belong to an important or unimportant part of my identity? | In general, belonging to social groups is an important part of my self-image. |

SOURCE: "A Collective Self-Esteem Scale: Self-Evaluation of One's Social Identity" by R. Luhtanen and J. Crocker, *Personality and Social Psychology Bulletin*, 18, 1992.

these group memberships influence their identity and their self-esteem. One team of researchers, after reviewing over 40 studies of such adolescent peer groups, identified four cliques as the most common, and labeled them the elites, athletes, academics, and deviants (Sussman et al., 2007). Those who are members of the most prestigious groups generally report feeling very satisfied with themselves and their group. Those students who want to be a part of an "in crowd" but are not accepted by this clique are the most dissatisfied (Brown & Lohr, 1987), and this interpersonal failure can lead to long-term negative effects (Barnett, 2007; Wright & Forsyth, 1997).

Jennifer Crocker and her colleagues examined the relationship between people's self-esteem and their feelings about the groups to which they belonged by developing a measure of **collective self-esteem**. Instead of asking people if they felt good or bad about themselves, they asked individuals to evaluate the groups to which they belonged. Drawing on prior work on social identity and self-esteem, the researchers developed items that tapped four basic issues: membership esteem, private collective self-esteem, public collective self-esteem, and importance to identity (see Table 3.2). When they compared scores on the collective self-esteem scale to scores on more traditional measures of self-esteem, they found that people with high membership esteem and public and private collective self-esteem scores had higher personal self-esteem, suggesting that group membership contributes to feelings of self-worth (Crocker & Luhtanen, 1990; Crocker et al., 1994; Luhtanen & Crocker, 1992).

Even membership in a group that others may not admire is generally associated with higher levels of self-esteem (Crocker & Major, 1989). Adolescents with mental retardation do not necessarily have lower self-esteem, even though they know they belong to the negatively stereotyped social category "special education students" (Stager, Chassin, & Young, 1983). African Americans, despite living in a culture where stereotypes about their group tend to be negative, have higher self-esteem than European Americans (Twenge & Crocker, 2002). Members of groups that are criticized often respond by defending their group and reaffirming their commitment to it (Dietz-Uhler & Murrell, 1998). So long as individuals believe that the groups they belong to are valuable, they will experience a heightened sense of personal self-esteem (Crocker et al., 1994).

Sometimes, in fact, members of a group will accept, and apply to themselves and to other members

---

**collective self-esteem** A person's overall assessment of that portion of their self-concept that is based on their relationships with others and membership in social groups.

**basking in reflected glory (BIRGing)** Seeking direct or indirect association with prestigious or successful groups or individuals.

**cutting off reflected failure (CORFing)** Distancing oneself from a group that performs poorly.

of their group, stereotypical qualities that are negative rather than positive. A professor who arrives for class a few minutes late and admits that he left behind all the papers he was to return that day to his class, mumbles something about being an "absent-minded professor." A fair-haired young woman who complains about the amount of statistical information discussed in a class opines, "I'm just a blonde–I don't really like math." Such negative in group stereotyping has been shown to protect individuals' feelings of self-worth. Women who had just discovered they had done poorly on a math test, when reminded of the stereotype of women as weak at math had higher self-esteem than those in a control condition. A second study indicated that it was women with higher self-esteem who embraced the stereotype after failure rather than women with lower self-esteem (Burkley & Blanton, 2008). These studies suggest that a social identity can protect the self, even if the identity is one that includes qualities that are objectively negative ones (Simon, Glässner-Bayerl, & Stratenwerth, 1991).

**Protecting the Collective Self** When individuals identify with their group, they also tend to exaggerate the differences between their group and other groups. Once people begin to think in terms of *we* and *us*, they also begin to recognize *them* and *they*. The tendency to look more favorably on the ingroup is called the **ingroup–outgroup bias**. Gang members view their group more positively than rival gangs. Teammates praise their own players and derogate the other team. If Group A and Group B work side by side, members of A will rate Group A as better than B, but members of B will rate Group B more favorably than A.

The ingroup–outgroup bias often intensifies conflicts between groups (see Chapter 14), but it also contributes to the self-esteem and emotional well-being of group members. Social identity theory posits that people are motivated to maintain or enhance their feelings of self-worth, and because members' self-esteem is linked to their groups, their feelings of self-worth can be enhanced by stressing the relative superiority of their groups to other groups.

Even if the group falters, members can nonetheless find ways to protect the group and, in so doing, protect their own selves. A setback, particularly at the hands of another group, calls for **social creativity:** Group members compare the ingroup to the outgroup on some new dimension. Members of a last-placed ice hockey team (1 win and 21 losses), when asked if their team and their opponents were *aggressive, dirty, skilled,* and *motivated* admitted that their opponents were more skilled, but they also argued that their opponents were more aggressive and that they played dirty (Lalonde, 1992). When emergency medical technicians (EMTs) were told that their group had performed more poorly than another group of EMTs, they later claimed their group members had nicer personalities (Cadinu & Cerchioni, 2001). Hospital employees, when asked to evaluate their hospital and a second hospital that was larger and better equipped, gave the other hospital higher ratings on such variables as community reputation, challenge, and career opportunity, but claimed that their hospital was a better place to work because everyone got along better (Terry & Callan, 1998).

**Protecting the Personal Self** People protect their collective self-esteem just as they protect their personal self-esteem. They deny that their group possesses negative qualities. They consider their group to be superior to alternative groups. They give their group credit for its successes, but blame outside influences when their group fails. Should other, more rewarding groups stand willing and ready to take them in, individuals remain loyal to their original group. Identity is the glue that binds individuals to their groups (Van Vugt & Hart, 2004).

---

**ingroup–outgroup bias** The tendency to view the ingroup, its members, and its products more positively than other groups, their members, and their products. Ingroup favoritism is more common than outgroup rejection.

**social creativity** Restricting comparisons between the ingroup and other groups to tasks and outcomes where the ingroup is more successful than other groups and avoiding areas in which other groups surpass the ingroup.

However, there are limits to what individuals will tolerate. In some cases, individuals strive to resist being seen as a member of a group to which they belong, particularly if they do not wish to have the stereotypes about that group applied to them personally. A college professor may not wish to be labeled absent-minded, a blonde-haired woman may prefer to be recognized for her scientific acumen rather than her sense of fashion, and a man may wish to be considered sensitive and caring rather than sports-oriented. When such individuals enter into situations where they are at risk of being judged on the basis of stereotypes that they wish to resist, they may experience **stereotype threat**. They worry that they might confirm the stereotypes that others may be tempted to apply to them. As a result, they fail to perform as well as they could, and the stereotype becomes a self-fulfilling prophecy (Steele & Aronson, 1995).

In general, people are more disturbed by threats to their personal self-esteem than to their collective self-esteem. They are more likely to deny the accuracy of negative individualized information relative to negative group information, and they more readily claim positive feedback when it focuses on them rather than on their group. For example, an individual, if told "you did very poorly—you must be slow" or "you are excessively moody," will react more negatively than a person who is part of a group told "your group did very poorly—you must be slow" or "people in your group are excessively moody" (Gaertner et al., 2002; Gaertner & Sedikides, 2005). Personal failure is more troubling than collective failure, in most cases.

People will also turn away from a group that continues to threaten their personal self-esteem. When people can choose the groups they belong to or identify with, they often shift their allegiances, leaving groups that are lower in status or prone to failure and seeking membership in prestigious or successful groups (Ellemers, Spears, & Doosje, 2002). The technical term for such a change in allegiance is **individual mobility** (Ellemers, Spears, & Doosje, 1997). More common ways to describe this process include resigning, dropping out, quitting, breaking up, resigning, escaping, bailing, and ditching: the member leaves the group for a more promising one. As the analysis of group formation in Chapter 4 shows, when people's groups are too much trouble, they leave them in search of better ones.

## SUMMARY IN OUTLINE

*Do humans, by nature, seek solitude or inclusion in groups?*

1. Baumeister and Leary suggest that much of human behavior is motivated by a basic *need to belong*. Solitude is sometimes rewarding, but most adults prefer the company of others.
   - Most adults live with others, they spend most of their time with others, and an enormous number of groups exist.
   - Putnam suggests that levels of *social capital* are decreasing due to reductions in involvement in groups, but the shifts he documents may indicate changes in the kinds of associations people seek rather than a reduction *per se*.
2. People react negatively if excluded or isolated from groups.
   - Participants in "life alone" studies conducted by Twenge, Baumeister, and others indicate that the prospect of life alone

---

**stereotype threat** The anxiety-provoking belief that others' perceptions and evaluations will be influenced by their negative stereotypes about one's group which can, in some cases, interfere with one's ability to perform up to one's capabilities.

**individual mobility** Reducing one's connection to a group in order to minimize the threats to individual self-esteem.

triggers a number of negative social and psychological reactions in people.

- *Ostracism*, or deliberate exclusion from groups, is highly stressful, as indicated by self-reports of negative affect as well as analyses of brain activity.

3. Williams maintains that people respond both reflexively and reflectively to ostracism and usually exhibit one of the *freezing, fight-or-flight*, or *tend-and-befriend* responses.
   - Extreme forms of violence, such as mass shootings in schools, have been linked to ostracism by groups.
   - Individuals also react negatively to exclusion from computer-mediated interaction, or *cyberostracism*.
4. The *sociometer theory* of self-esteem developed by Leary explains the relationship between exclusion and self-esteem by hypothesizing that self-esteem provides individuals with feedback about their degree of inclusion in groups.
5. Evolutionary psychology suggests that the need to belong resulted from natural selection as individuals who were affiliated with groups were more likely to survive.

*When do people embrace collectivism by putting the group's needs before their own?*

1. *Individualism* and *collectivism* are distinguishable in their relative emphasis on individuals and groups, with individualism stressing the person and collectivism the group. These two orientations adopting differing orientations with regards to interpersonal relationships, obligations, and self-conceptions.
2. Fiske concludes collectivism's emphasis on relationships is manifested in the emphasis on *communal relationships* over *exchange relationships*. The *norm of reciprocity* and the norm of equity are more consistent with individualism. The *norm of equality* which is associated with collectivism.
3. Social obligations, as described by Rousseau's concept of a *social contract* and illustrated in the *Ultimatum Game*, are more central in collectivism.
   - *Self-serving* tendencies are more likely in individualistic settings, in contrast to the *group-serving* tendencies seen in collectivistic settings.
   - A collectivistic orientation stresses hierarchy and reacts more negatively to nonconformity.
4. Self-concepts differ in individualistic and collectivistic contexts, with greater emphasis on *personal identity* in the former and greater emphasis on *social identity* (or collective identity) in the latter.
   - Brewer distinguishes between two group-level selves: the relational self and the collective self.
   - Individuals differ in the emphasis on the personal and collective selves, with *independents* stressing individualism and *interdependents* putting their groups' goals and needs above their own. Some individuals, too, seek individuation when in groups.
   - Brewer's *optimal distinctiveness theory* suggests that individuals strive to maintain an optimal balance between their personal and collective identities.
5. Cultures and subgroups within countries vary in their relative emphasis on individualism and collectivism.
   - People who live in collectivistic cultures (e.g., Asian, Eastern European, African, and Middle Eastern countries) think of themselves as group members first and individuals second, whereas people who live in individualistic cultures (Western countries) are self-centered rather than group-centered (see research by Triandis).

- Some ethnic groups, such as Asian Americans and Hispanic Americans, are more collectivistic than individualistic, but research conducted by Twenge suggests that individuals may be shifting in a more individualistic direction.

*What processes transform an individual's sense of self into a collective, social identity?*

1. Social identity theory, developed by Tajfel, Turner, Hogg, and their colleagues, traces the development of a collective identity back to two key processes (categorization and identification) that occur even in *minimal intergroup situations.*
2. *Social categorization* involves automatically classifying people into categories.
   - Through self-categorization individuals classify themselves into categories.
   - *Self-stereotyping* occurs when individuals apply the *prototypes* (*stereotypes*) of those categories to themselves.
3. Identification involves bonding with and taking on the characteristics of one's groups.
   - When people identify strongly with a group, their self-descriptions become increasingly depersonalized as they include fewer idiosyncratic elements and more characteristics that are common to the group (see Hogg's research).
   - Identification and categorization become more likely when outgroups are salient and when people are members of smaller groups.
4. Self-esteem is shaped both by individuals' personal qualities and by the perceived value of the groups to which they belong.
   - Those who join prestigious groups often have higher collective self-esteem than those who belong to less positively valued groups.
   - Individuals who identify strongly with a group, such as sports fans, experience the group's outcomes as their own.
   - By *basking in reflected glory* (BIRGing), individuals can stress their association with successful groups. By *cutting off reflected failure* (CORFing), they minimize their connection to stigmatized or unsuccessful group identities.
5. Individuals are motivated to protect both their individual and collective self-esteem.
   - Members of stigmatized groups, failing groups, or groups that are derogated by nonmembers often protect their *collective self-esteem* (as defined by Crocker and her associates) by rejecting negative information about their group, stressing the relative superiority of their group (the *ingroup–outgroup bias*), and selectively focusing on their group's superior qualities (*social creativity*).
   - When *stereotype threat* is high, members become concerned that they will be stereotyped if considered a member of a particular group. Individuals may minimize their association with groups that are performing poorly or resign from the group (*individual mobility*).

## FOR MORE INFORMATION

*Chapter Case: Palmer and Gorman*

- *Habits of the Heart: Individualism and Commitment in American Life*, by Robert N. Bellah, Richard Madsen, William M. Sullivan, Ann Swidler, and Steven M. Tipton (1985), uses detailed cases, including those of Palmer and Gorman, to describe the connection between individuals and their groups.

*Inclusion, Exclusion, and Belonging*

- "Ostracism," by Kipling D. Williams (2007), provides a theoretically driven description of recent empirical investigations into the nature and consequences of exclusion from groups for both those who are excluded and those who do the excluding.
- "Evolutionary Theory for Social and Cultural Psychology," by Linnda R. Caporael (2007), details the implications of an evolutionary perspective for understanding groups and their dynamics.

*Individualism and Collectivism*

- "Rethinking Individualism and Collectivism: Evaluation of Theoretical Assumptions and Meta-Analyses," by Daphna Oyserman, Heather M. Coon, and Markus Kemmelmeier (2002), thoroughly explores the psychological implications of individual and cultural differences in individualism and collectivism, and is followed by a number of fascinating commentaries by experts in this area (Bond, 2002; Fiske, 2002; Kitayama, 2002; Miller, 2002).
- "Where (Who) Are Collectives in Collectivism? Toward Conceptual Clarification of Individualism and Collectivism," by Marilynn B. Brewer and Ya-Ru Chen (2007), reviews cross-cultural work on self-conception, with a focus on how the components of individualism and collectivism are assessed.

*Social Identity*

- "An Organizing Framework for Collective Identity: Articulation and Significance of Multidimensionality," by Richard D. Ashmore, Kay Deaux, and Tracy McLaughlin-Volpe (2004), examines the multiple components of collective identity, concentrating on categorization, evaluation, importance, belonging, embeddedness, involvement, and meaning.
- "The Social Identity Perspective," by Michael A. Hogg (2005), provides a compact but comprehensive review of the basic theoretical assumptions of social identity theory.
- "Understanding the Positive Social Psychological Benefits of Sport Team Identification: The Team Identification–Social Psychological Health Model," by Daniel L. Wann (2006), offers a theoretically grounded analysis of the identification processes that sustain fans' commitment to their teams.

## Media Resources

Visit the Group Dynamics companion website at www.cengage.com/psychology/forsyth to access online resources for your book, including quizzes, flash cards, web links, and more.

# 4

# Formation

## CHAPTER OVERVIEW

Groups form through a combination of personal, situational, and interpersonal processes. Formation depends on the members themselves; some people are more likely than others to join together, and when they do a group is born. Groups also come into existence when the press of environmental circumstances pushes people together rather than keeping them apart. They also spring up, sometimes unexpectedly, when people discover that they like one another, and this attraction provides the foundation for the development of interpersonal bonds.

- Who joins groups?
- When do people seek out others?
- What processes generate bonds of interpersonal attraction between members of groups?

## CHAPTER OUTLINE

**The Impressionists: The Group That Redefined Beauty**

The group formed in Paris, France, in the early 1860s. Some of the group's members—Frederic Bazille, Claude Monet, Auguste Renoir, and Alfred Sisley—were all young art students studying with Charles Gleyre. Others, such as Edouard Manet, had established reputations for being open-minded—if not radical—painters. Separately, they were just a few artists struggling to learn their craft, define their style, and earn enough to pay the bills. But when they joined together to form a group, they transformed themselves and their art, and in time they redefined the world's conception of beauty (Farrell, 1982, 2001).

On the surface, they shared little in common. Some were the sons of relatively wealthy families, but others had working class backgrounds. Some were outgoing and confident, but others were quiet and uncertain. Some had been working at their craft for many years, but others were struggling to learn the basics. But they were united in their belief that the state-supported Academy of Fine Arts was too restrictive and rigid. The Academy alone determined which paintings and sculptures could be displayed at the national gallery, the Salon, and most artists acquiesced to the Academy's guidelines. But this small group of renegade painters shared a different vision. They wanted to capture the beauty of everyday life; outdoor scenes and real people instead of posed portraits and technically precise studio paintings of religious, historical, and mythic scenes.

The young artists developed a new approach to painting, often journeying into the countryside to paint landscapes. They sometimes painted side by side and critiqued one another's work. They also met in cafés in Paris to discuss technique, subject matter, and artistic philosophies. Art critics rejected their approach for years, and the artists scarcely earned enough money to survive. But, in time, they were recognized by the art community as a new school of painting—the *impressionists*—and their paintings are now worth millions.

We can ask many questions about the artists who founded impressionism. How did they settle the many conflicts that threatened their group? Why did Manet become the group's idol, Monet the group's inspirational leader, and Edgar Degas the malcontent? How did the group counter the constraints imposed by the status quo? But one question—perhaps the most basic of all—concerns the group's origin. Why did it come into existence in the first place? In 1858, Manet, Monet, and the others were busy pursuing their careers independently. But by the late-1860s they had joined to form the most influential artists' circle of all time. What were the circumstances that drove these individuals to combine their resources in a group that endured for more than 30 years?

This chapter answers this question in three parts. It begins with the artists themselves, for people's personalities, preferences, and prior experiences influence the extent to which they seek out membership in groups. Some are *joiners* and some are *loners*. Next, it considers the *situation*, for even a collection of highly sociable joiners must affiliate on at least one occasion before a group will form. Some situations push people together; others keep them apart. Affiliation, however, only sets the stage for group formation; if the individuals who find themselves together are not *attracted* to each other, then a long-lasting group like the impressionists likely will not form. Some people like each other; some do not.

## JOINING GROUPS

Monet and Vincent van Gogh were both brilliant artists, but Monet worked with others whenever possible and van Gogh kept to himself. Not everyone who joins a group is a "joiner," and people who prefer independence over association are not necessarily "loners." But due to differences in personality, motivations, and past experiences some people, like Monet, are more likely than others to seek out membership in groups.

### Personality

When Monet learned that Renoir, Bazille, and Sisley were meeting each evening to discuss new

**TABLE 4.1 The Big Five Theory of Personality**

| Dimension | Content |
|---|---|
| **Extraversion** | Outgoing, friendly, gregarious, assertive, emotionally positive, active |
| **Agreeableness** | Sincere, thinks the best of people, frank, concerned with others' welfare, conciliatory, modest, sympathetic |
| **Conscientiousness** | Responsible, organized, achievement-oriented, self-disciplined, planned confident |
| **Neuroticism** | Emotional, anxious, easily angered, self-conscious, prone to feel depressed or sad, impulsive, distressed |
| **Openness** | Intellectually able, appreciative of art and beauty, emotionally expressive, open-minded, imaginative |

SOURCE: Adapted from McCrae & Costa, 1986, p. 1002. McCrae, R. R., & Costa, P. T., Jr. (1986). "A five-factor theory of personality" In L. A. Pervin & O. P. John (Eds.), *Handbook of personality: Theory and research* (2nd ed.). New York: Guilford. Reprinted by permission.

approaches to painting, he was quick to join the group. Why? Part of the answer lies in his basic personality. Monet, like all people, possessed certain traits and dispositional characteristics that, taken together, defined his personality. He was the kind of person who enjoyed being with other people, but he was also very creative and unconventional. Some described him as egotistical, but most thought he was a warm, friendly person. Once he joined the group, he quickly became its leader.

**Extraversion** Researchers have studied hundreds of personality traits, but five of the most central ones are described in the aptly named **Big Five theory** of personality. This theory recognizes that people differ from each other in many ways, but it assumes that the five dimensions summarized in Table 4.1—extraversion, agreeableness, conscientiousness, neuroticism, and openness—describe the most essential ways in which people vary (Costa & McCrae, 1988).

The first of these five dimensions, **extraversion**, is a particularly influential determinant of group behavior (Asendorpf & Wilpers, 1998). First identified by the psychologist Carl Jung (1924), extraversion is the tendency to move toward people or away from people. Those on the introversion end of this personality dimension, the *introverts*, tend to be withdrawn, quiet, reclusive, and shy. Their opposites, the *extraverts*, are sociable, outgoing, gregarious, and talkative. Extraverts are likely to prefer the company of others, particularly in pleasant and enjoyable situations (Lucas & Diener, 2001). Different cultures imbue introversion and extraversion with unique, culture-specific meaning, but people all over the world spontaneously appraise their own and others' social tendencies (Yang & Bond, 1990).

Extraverts may seek out groups because such interactions are stimulating, and extraverts appreciate stimulating experiences more than introverts do (Eysenck, 1990). Extraverts' affinity for being part of a group may also be based on assertiveness, for they tend to be influential group members rather than quiet followers. Groups may also seek out extraverts rather than introverts. Some qualities, like intelligence, morality, and friendliness, are difficult to judge during initial encounters, but observers are particularly good at detecting extraversion in others (Albright, Kenny, & Malloy, 1988). If a group is

---

**Big Five theory** A conceptual model of the primary dimensions that underlie individual differences in personality; the five dimensions are extraversion, agreeableness, conscientiousness, neuroticism, and openness to experience; different theorists sometimes use different labels.

**extraversion** The degree to which an individual tends to seek out social contacts. Introverts are oriented primarily toward inner perceptions and judgments of concepts and ideas, whereas extraverts are oriented primarily toward social experiences.

### Focus 4.1 Are Extraverts Happier than Introverts?

*People who need people are the luckiest people in the world.*

—Jule Styne and Bob Merrill, *Funny Girl*

Extraverts and introverts diverge in their overall level of gregariousness, but they also differ in their level of happiness. Do you enjoy talking to strangers? Enjoy working with others? Like making decisions in groups? Do you like to go to parties? If yes, then you are in all likelihood a happier person than someone who avoids groups and enjoys solitary activities (Lucas et al., 2000, p. 468). This difference appears to know no cultural or national boundaries, for when researchers studied students in 39 countries those who were more extraverted were also the ones who were happiest. Apparently, people who need people are the *happiest* people in the world (Lucas et al., 2000; Lucas & Fujia, 2000).

Why are extraverts so happy? Primarily, because extraverts join more frequently with other people, and strong social relationships are a fundamental determinant of well-being (e.g., Lee, Dean, & Jung, 2008). Extraverts may, however, just be in better moods than introverts, for even when they are alone extraverts report that they are happier than do introverts. They may also be adept at regulating their mood states by dealing with negative events in psychologically healthy ways, and so they keep their mood elevated (Augustine & Hemenover, 2008; Lischetzke & Eid, 2006). Extraverts are more sensitive to rewards than introverts, and so their positivity may be due to their more positive reaction to pleasant experiences (Lucas, 2008). Alternatively, introverts may be more negative in their mood because social demands cause them to associate so frequently with other people, even though they would prefer to be alone.

Extroverts' happiness may also be due to the fact that the kinds of behaviors that define extraversion are more pleasurable than those that characterize introversion. When introverts and extraverts recorded their behavior five times a day for two weeks, researchers discovered that even introverts talking to other people, interacting in groups, and so on reported experiencing more positive emotions. The researchers then went one step further. Reasoning that acting in an extraverted way may directly influence happiness, they asked volunteers taking part in a group discussion to be talkative, energetic, and active (extraverted) or reserved, quiet, and passive (introverted). Those who acted in extraverted ways ended the study in better moods than did people who were told to act as if they were introverted (Fleeson, Malanos, & Achille, 2002; McNiel & Fleeson, 2006). These findings suggest that groups hold the key to happiness, for people are happier when they are connected to other people.

looking for people who will be sociable and connect easily with others, it might recruit extraverts more actively than introverts (Judge & Cable, 1997). Also, as Focus 4.1 explains, extraverts tend to be happier than introverts, and their positivity may make them more desirable members than their less cheerful counterparts.

**Relationality** As noted in Chapter 3, people vary in their attentiveness to their relations with other people. Unlike those who view themselves as lone individuals interacting with other autonomous individuals, people who are higher in **relationality**—that is, their values, attitudes, and outlooks emphasize and facilitate establishing and maintaining connections to others—are more likely to seek out and more highly prize group memberships. Such individuals more frequently play team sports such as volleyball or soccer, and they do so because they prefer exercising with other people rather than alone. They seek jobs that will enhance the quality of their relationships with other people, and their satisfaction with their work depends on the quality of their relationships with their coworkers (Leary, Wheeler, & Jenkins, 1986). In terms of the big five personality traits, relationality is associated with both extraversion and agreeableness (Cross, Bacon, & Morris, 2000).

Social science writer Malcolm Gladwell (2000) uses the term *connector* to describe individuals who are so high in relationality that they have far more ties to other people than most people. Most individuals are

**relationality** The degree to which one's values, attitudes, and outlooks emphasize, and facilitate establishing and maintaining, connections to others.

embedded in a network of friends, family, and acquaintances, but connectors are the hubs of a more vast and far-flung web of relationships. Some of these connections are one-to-one relationships, but connectors are also participants and leaders of dozens of different groups and associations. Partially supporting Gladwell's conjecture, in one study women's relationality did not predict how many relationships and memberships they had, but it did predict their commitment to those relationships. Women interacting briefly in dyads who were high in relationality enjoyed the group interaction more, as did those interacted with someone who was high in relationality (Cross et al., 2000).

### Men, Women, and Groups

Studies of relationality frequently find the sexes differ in their emphasis on connecting interpersonally with other people: women are more relational than men (e.g., Gore & Cross, 2006). Yet, nearly all the impressionists were men; Berthe Morisot and Mary Cassatt were exceptions. Are men or are women the more social sex?

Studies find that men and women differ in their tendency to join groups, but the differences are far from clear. Women tend to be somewhat more extraverted than men, particularly on facets of the trait concerned with interpersonal warmth and gregariousness (Costa, Terracciano, & McCrae, 2001). Women remember more details about their relationships than do men, and they more accurately recount events that occurred in their social networks (Ross & Holmberg, 1992; Taylor et al., 2000). Women report that their relationships are more important to them—that they feel pride, for example, when someone close to them succeeds (Gore & Cross, 2006). When asked to take photographs that describe how they see themselves, women are more likely to include pictures of themselves with other people rather than alone (Dollinger et al., 1996). Overall, women tend to adopt a more collectivistic, interdependent orientation than do men (see Chapter 3).

Other studies, however, have questioned the magnitude and meaning of these differences between the sexes. Even though women may put more value on their relationships, they may not be any more social than men. One survey of 800 adults in the United States found that men belonged to more professional groups, governing boards, political parties, and military organizations than women but women spent more time in their groups than did men (Booth, 1972). The sexes do not differ in the time they spend in solitary activities; their involvement in community groups; or their membership in more unusual types of groups, such as cults and satanic covens (Osgood et al., 1996; Parkum & Parkum, 1980; Pittard-Payne, 1980).

The differences that emerge, although subtle, indicate that women seek membership in smaller, informal, intimate groups, whereas men seek membership in larger, more formal, task-focused groups. These tendencies may reflect women's and men's differing interpersonal orientations, with women more likely to define themselves in terms of their memberships in groups and their relationships with other people. The sexes may also differ in their emphasis on achieving power and establishing connections with others. Both these goals can best be achieved in groups, but they require membership in different types of groups. Men, seeking power and influence, join competitive, goal-oriented groups, where they can vie for status. Women, seeking intimate relationships, would be more likely to join small, supportive groups (Baumeister & Sommer, 1997).

These sex differences are also entangled with role differences and cultural stereotypes. In cultures where men and women tend to enact different roles, the roles may shape opportunities for involvement in groups. If women are primarily responsible for domestic duties and childbearing, their opportunities for membership in groups may be limited (Nielsen, 1990). Hence, as attitudes toward the role of women have changed in contemporary society, differences in social participation have also begun to diminish (Lal Goel, 1980; Smith, 1980). Sexism also works to exclude women and men from certain types of groups. Women, for example, were until recently deliberately excluded from juries in the United States. (The United States Supreme Court ruled that women could not be excused from jury duty because of their sex in 1975.) In Paris, in the 1860s, women modeled for artists, but few could be artists themselves. As sexist attitudes decline, differences in membership in various types of groups may also abate.

## Social Motivation

Why did Monet refuse to follow his father's advice and study with an established teacher of art? Why did Manet refuse to join the group during its first public exhibition? Why did the group try to exclude Paul Cézanne? Such "why" questions can often be answered by considering motivations: psychological processes that energize actions and guide group members in one direction rather than another. These inner mechanisms can be called many things—habits, beliefs, feelings, wants, instincts, compulsions, drives—but no matter what their label they prompt people to take action. Social motivations, unlike the more biologically based motivations such as hunger and thirst, influence people's interpersonal behaviors, and include the need for affiliation, intimacy, and power.

**Need for Affiliation** People who seek out contact with other people often have a high **need for affiliation**. People with a high need for affiliation tend to join groups more frequently, spend more of their time in groups, communicate more with other group members, and accept other group members more readily (McAdams & Constantian, 1983; McClelland, 1985; Smart, 1965). However, they are also more anxious in social situations, perhaps because they are more fearful of rejection by others (Byrne, 1961; McAdams, 1982, 1995). When others treat them badly or reject them, they avoid people rather than seek them out (Hill, 1991).

**Need for Intimacy** Individuals who have a high **need for intimacy**, like those who have a high need for affiliation, prefer to join with others. Such individuals, however, seek close, warm relations and are more likely to express caring and concern for other people (McAdams, 1982, 1995). They do not fear rejection but, instead, are more focused on friendship, camaraderie, reciprocity, and mutual help. In one study, researchers gave people electronic pagers for one week and asked them to write down what they were doing and how they felt each time they were beeped. People who had a high need for intimacy were more frequently interacting with other people when beeped. They were also happier than people with a low need for intimacy if they were with other people when they were beeped (McAdams & Constantian, 1983).

**Need for Power** Because group interactions provide many opportunities to influence others, those with a high **need for power** also tend to seek out groups (McAdams, 1982; Winter, 1973). Researchers studied college students' power needs by asking them to recall 10 recent group interactions that lasted for at least 15 minutes. The students described what had happened in each episode, what had been discussed, and their role in the group. Those with a high power motive took part in relatively fewer dyadic interactions but in more large-group interactions (groups with more than four members). They also reported exercising more control in these groups by organizing and initiating activities, assuming responsibility, and attempting to persuade others. This relationship between the need for power and participation in groups was stronger for men (McAdams, Healy, & Krause, 1984).

**FIRO** William Schutz (1958, 1992) integrated the need for affiliation, intimacy, and power in his **Fundamental Interpersonal Relations Orientation** theory, or **FIRO** (rhymes with "*I* row"). Schutz identified three basic needs that can be satisfied

---

**need for affiliation** The dispositional tendency to seek out others.

**need for intimacy** The dispositional tendency to seek warm, positive relationships with others.

**need for power** The dispositional tendency to seek control over others.

**Fundamental Interpersonal Relations Orientation (FIRO)** A theory of group formation and development proposed by William Schutz that emphasizes compatibility among three basic social motives: inclusion, control, and affection.

by groups. *Inclusion*—the desire to be part of a group and to be accepted by a group—is similar to the need for affiliation. The second motive, *control*, corresponds to the need for power. *Affection*, or openness, is the desire to experience warm, positive relations with others, which is similar to the need for intimacy.

Schutz believed that these needs influence group behavior in two ways: They determine how people treat others and how people want others to treat them. Inclusion refers to people's desire to join with others but also their need to be accepted by those others. Control is the need to dominate others but also the willingness to let others be dominant. Affection is a desire to like others as well as a desire to be liked by them. The FIRO-B scale, which Schutz developed, measures both the need to express and the need to receive inclusion, control, and affection (see Table 4.2).

Groups offer members a way to satisfy these basic needs. If, for example, Angela has a strong need to receive and express inclusion, she will probably prefer to do things in a group rather than to perform tasks individually. If she needs to express control, she may seek membership in a group that she can control. Or if she wishes to receive affection from others, she may seek out other people who seem warm and friendly. In general, then, the greater the intensity of these needs in any given individual, the more likely that person is to take steps to create or seek out membership in a group (Schutz, 1958, 1992).

## Anxiety and Attachment

Just as one's personality and social motives may push people toward groups, other personal qualities may push them away. People who are socially inhibited, or shy, do not join groups as readily as others, and they do not find group activities to be as enjoyable. As early as age 2, some children begin to display fear or inhibition when they encounter a person they do not recognize (Kagan, Snidman, & Arcus, 1992). Some grade school children consistently seek out other people, whereas others show signs of shyness and withdrawal when they are in groups (Asendorpf & Meier, 1993). Shy adults report feeling awkward, uncomfortable, and tense when interacting with people they do not know very well (Cheek & Buss, 1981). Shy people, rather than entering a new group alone, often take a friend with them. This "social surrogate" helps them transition into the group by doing much of the work needed to establish connections with others. In some cases, the surrogate takes the place of the shy members during initial interactions, until they overcome their initial social anxieties (Bradshaw, 1998). Shy people also react differently, neurologically, when they see a stranger's face. Nonshy people's brains show an activation response

**TABLE 4.2 Example Items from the Fundamental Interpersonal Relations Orientation–Behavior (FIRO-B) Scale**

| | Inclusion (I) | Control (C) | Affection (A) |
|---|---|---|---|
| **Expressed toward other people** | • I try to be with other people.<br>• I join social groups. | • I try to take charge of things when I am with people.<br>• I try to have other people do things I want done. | • I try to be friendly to people.<br>• I try to have close relationships with people. |
| **Wanted from other people** | • I like people to invite me to things.<br>• I like people to include me in their activities. | • I let other people decide what to do.<br>• I let other people take charge of things. | • I like people to act friendly toward me.<br>• I like people to act close toward me. |

SOURCE: *FIRO: A Three-Dimensional Theory of Interpersonal Behavior* by W. C. Schutz. Copyright 1958 by Holt, Rinehart, & Winston, Inc.

in the bilateral nucleus accumbens when they see unfamiliar faces, but shy people's brains display heightened bilateral activity in the amygdala; an area of the brain that is responsible for emotional responses, including fear (Beaton et al., 2008).

**Social Anxiety** Most people manage to cope with their shyness. In some cases, however, shyness escalates into **social anxiety** (Vertue, 2003). Historical accounts of the troubled life of van Gogh, for example, comment on his anxiety over his failed relationships. He had some friends, and he tried to join his fellow artists, but he could not sustain these relationships.

Social anxiety sets in when people want to make a good impression, but they do not think that their attempts to establish relationships will succeed (Leary, 2001; Leary & Kowalski, 1995). Because of these pessimistic expectations, when these individuals interact with other people, they suffer troubling emotional, physiological, and behavioral side effects. They feel tense, awkward, uncomfortable, and scrutinized. They become physiologically aroused to the point that their pulse races, they blush and perspire, and they feel "butterflies" in their stomach. This anxiety can cause them to *disaffiliate* by reducing social contact with others (Leary & Kowalski, 1995, p. 157). Socially anxious people, even when they join groups, do not actively participate; they can be identified by their silence, downcast eyes, and low speaking voice. They may also engage in *innocuous sociability* (Leary, 1983): They merge into the group's background by indicating general interest in the group and agreement with the other group members while consistently minimizing their personal involvement in the group interaction.

**Attachment Style** People with certain types of attachment styles are particularly likely to experience anxiety when faced with the prospect of joining a group. *Attachment theory* (e.g., Bowlby, 1980) explains the way people differ in their relationships, or attachments, to others. From an early age, some children seem very secure and comfortable in their relationship to their caregivers, but others seem to be more uncertain of their caregivers' supportiveness and some even seem to ignore other people altogether. These childhood differences emerge in adulthood as variations in **attachment style**—one's basic cognitive, emotional, and behavioral orientation when in a relationship with others (Hazan & Shaver, 1987). Some people enjoy forming close relationships with other people, and they do not worry about being abandoned by their loved ones. Others, however, are uncomfortable relying on other people, they worry that their loved ones will reject them, or they are simply uninterested in relationships altogether. The four basic styles shown in Figure 4.1—secure, preoccupied, fearful, and dismissing—reflect two underlying dimensions: anxiety about relationships and avoidance of closeness and dependency on others (Brennan, Clark, & Shaver, 1998).

Eliot Smith and his colleagues theorized that people also have group-level attachment styles. They suggested that some individuals are anxious about their group experiences, for they question their acceptance by their group and report feeling as if they were unworthy of membership. They tend to agree with such statements as "I often worry my group will not always want me as a member" and "I sometimes worry that my group doesn't value me as much as I value my group" (Smith, Murphy, & Coats, 1999, p. 110). Others, however, are avoidant; they are not interested in getting close to their group, for they agreed with such statements as "I prefer not to depend on my group or to have my group depend on me" and "I am comfortable not being close to my group" (1999, p. 110). Smith's research team discovered that people with anxious group attachment styles spend less time in their groups, engage in fewer collective activities, and

---

**social anxiety** A feeling of apprehension and embarrassment experienced when anticipating or actually interacting with other people.

**attachment style** One's characteristic approach to relationships with other people; the basic styles include secure, preoccupied, fearful, and dismissing, as defined by the dimensions of anxiety and avoidance.

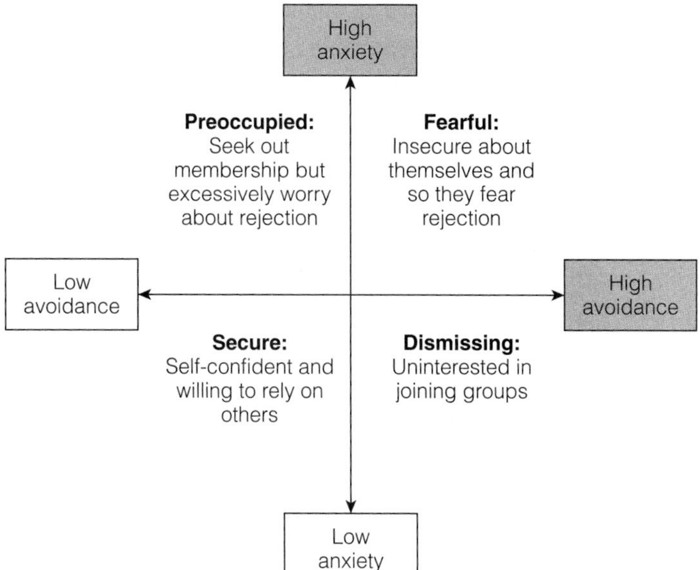


**FIGURE 4.1** Group attachment styles. The four basic styles—secure, preoccupied, fearful, and dismissing—are defined by two dimensions: level of anxiety and degree of avoidance. If, for example, an individual is low in avoidance but high in anxiety, he or she would display a preoccupied attachment style.

are less satisfied with the level of support they received from the group. Those with avoidant group attachment styles felt that the group was less important to them, and they were more likely to claim that they were planning to leave the group. When researchers followed up these ideas by watching people with varying attachment styles interacting in small groups they discovered that people with secure attachment styles contributed to both the instrumental and the relationship activities of the group. Those with more anxious attachment styles, in contrast, contributed less to the group's instrumental work, and those with avoidant attachment styles contributed less to both instrumental and relationship activities (Rom & Mikulincer, 2003). When individuals who were high and low in avoidance and anxiety were given small hand-held computers that tracked their activities throughout the day, researchers discovered that it was the avoidant individuals who spent more of their time alone rather than with others (Brown et al., 2007).

### Experience and Preference

Not everyone is thrilled at the prospect of joining groups. In many situations people have the opportunity to join a new group—a new club, a group of people who socialize together, an amateur sports team, for example—but their prior experiences in groups may make them think twice before joining in. Those with little prior experience may be too uncertain to take part, and those with negative experiences in the past may avoid groups as a general rule. Only those group veterans with many positive prior experiences are likely to seek them out (Bohrnstedt & Fisher, 1986; Corning & Myers, 2002; Ickes & Turner, 1983).

Richard Moreland, John Levine, and their colleagues' studies of college students' decision to join one of the many groups that abound on university campuses underscore the impact of one's past history with groups on one's future in groups. In one study they surveyed more than a thousand first-year students at the University of Pittsburgh, asking them if they took part in groups in high school and if they expected to join groups in college. They identified those students who had positive experiences in their high school groups—they rated their high school groups as both important and enjoyable. These students, when they enrolled in college, actively investigated the groups available to them. These "joiners" tried harder to find a group on campus to join, for they recognized that such memberships would be useful to them in achieving personal goals. They were also more optimistic in their evaluations of potential groups, for they expected that the positive aspects of joining a group would be particularly rewarding. Experience in groups in high school dampened that enthusiasm somewhat, at least for the specific groups that interested them. For example, those who were in student government in high school and were interested in taking part in student politics in college felt that this group would be rewarding, but they also recognized that it would impose costs as well. These students tended to be more deliberate in their review of potential groups, and displayed commitment to a specific group throughout the search process (Brinthaupt, Moreland, & Levine, 1991; Pavelchak, Moreland, & Levine, 1986).

## AFFILIATION

Why do people join together with others in groups? In part, the motivation comes from *within* the members themselves, for people's personalities, preferences, and other personal qualities predispose them to affiliate with others. But the tendency to affiliate with others also comes from *without*—from the situation itself. People often seek the company of others when they need information, social support, or companionship.

### Social Comparison

The young impressionists faced uncertainty each time they stood before a blank canvas. They were convinced that the methods taught by the traditional Parisian art schools were severely limited, but they were not sure how to put their alternative approach into practice. So they often painted together, exchanging ideas about colors and techniques, as they refined their approach to art.

Leon Festinger (1950, 1954) maintained that people often rely on others for information about themselves and the environment. Physical reality is a reliable guide in many cases, but to validate social reality people must compare their interpretations to those of other people. Festinger called this process **social comparison**, and suggested that it begins when people find themselves in ambiguous, confusing situations. Such situations trigger a variety of psychological reactions, most of which are unsettling, and so people affiliate with others to gain the information they need to reduce their confusion. As Figure 4.2 indicates, the final result of social comparison is cognitive clarity, but as the research reviewed in this section suggests, people engage in social comparison for a variety of different reasons—to evaluate their own qualities, to set personal goals, to help other people, or to confirm their belief that they are superior to the people around them (Suls & Wheeler, 2000; Wood, 1996).

**Misery Loves Company** How do people react when they find themselves in an ambiguous, and possibly dangerous, situation? Stanley Schachter (1959) believed that most people, finding themselves in such a predicament, would chose to join with other people to gain the information they need to allay their anxiety. To test his idea he recruited young women college students to meet at his laboratory. There they were greeted by a researcher who introduced himself as Dr. Gregor Zilstein from the Medical School's Departments of Neurology and Psychiatry. In serious tones, he explained that he was studying the effects of electric shock on human beings. In one condition (*low anxiety*), the room contained no electrical devices; the experimenter explained that the shocks would be so mild that they would "resemble more a tickle or a tingle than anything unpleasant" (p. 14). Participants assigned to the *high-anxiety* condition, however, faced a vast collection of electrical equipment and were informed, "These shocks will hurt, they will be painful . . . but, of course, they will do no permanent damage" (p. 13). The researcher then asked the participant if she wanted to wait for her turn alone or with others. Approximately two-thirds of

---

**social comparison** Evaluating the accuracy of personal beliefs and attitudes by comparing oneself to others.

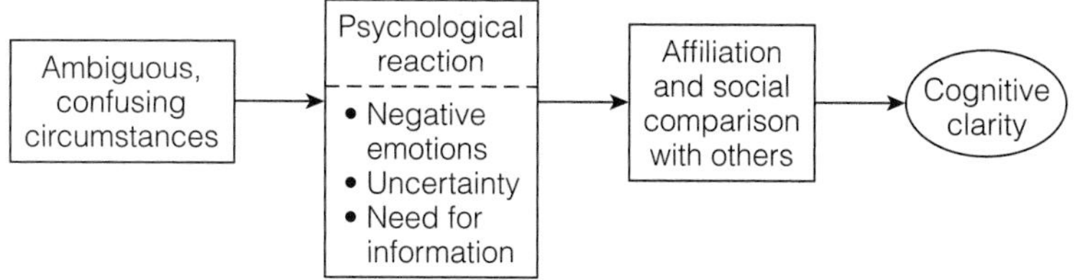


**FIGURE 4.2** Festinger's (1954) theory of social comparison assumes that people, when facing ambiguous situations, seek out others and compare their reactions and interpretations to their own.

the women in the high-anxiety condition (63%) chose to affiliate, whereas only one-third of the women in low-anxiety condition (33%) chose to wait with others. Schachter's conclusion: "misery loves company" (1959, p. 24).

**Misery Loves Miserable Company** The majority of the women Schachter studied chose to affiliate, but what was their primary motivation for joining with others? Did they wish to acquire information through social comparison, or were they just so frightened that they did not want to be alone? Schachter examined this question by replicating the high-anxiety condition of his original experiment, complete with the shock equipment and Dr. Zilstein. He held anxiety at a high level, but manipulated the amount of information that could be gained by affiliating with others. He told half of the women that they could wait with other women who were about to receive shocks; these women were therefore *similar* to the participants. He told the others that they could join women who were waiting for advising by their professors; these women could only wait with people who were *dissimilar.* Schachter hypothesized that if the women believed that the others could not provide them with any social comparison information, there would be no reason to join them. The findings confirmed his analysis: 60% of the women asked to wait with others if they all faced a similar situation, but no one in the dissimilar condition expressed affiliative desires. Schachter's second conclusion: "Misery doesn't love just any kind of company, it loves only miserable company" (Schachter, 1959, p. 24).

Schachter, by suggesting people love "miserable company," meant they seek out those who face the same threat and so are knowledgeable. So how would people respond if offered the chance to wait with someone who had participated in the study the previous day? Such individuals would be ideal sources of clarifying information, for they not only faced the same situation; they had survived it. When given such an alternative, participants preferred to join someone who had already gone through the procedure (Kirkpatrick & Shaver, 1988). A similar preference for someone who had "been there, done that" has been documented in patients who are awaiting surgery. When given a choice, 60% of pre-surgery patients requested a roommate who was recovering from the same type of operation, whereas only 17% wanted "miserable company"—a roommate who was also about to undergo the operation (Kulik & Mahler, 1989). The patients also reported talking with their roommate about the operation more if their roommate had already had the operation and was recovering (Kulik, Mahler, & Moore, 1996). These studies suggest that people are more interested in gaining clarifying information than in sharing the experience with someone, particularly when the situation is a dangerous one and they can converse openly with other group members (Kulik & Mahler, 2000).

**Embarrassed Misery Avoids Company** Even when people need information about a situation, they sometimes refrain from joining others because they do not wish to embarrass themselves. When alone, people might feel foolish if they do something silly, but when they are in a group foolishness turns into embarrassment. In some cases, this fear of embarrassment can be stronger than the need to understand what is happening, resulting in inhibition instead of affiliation.

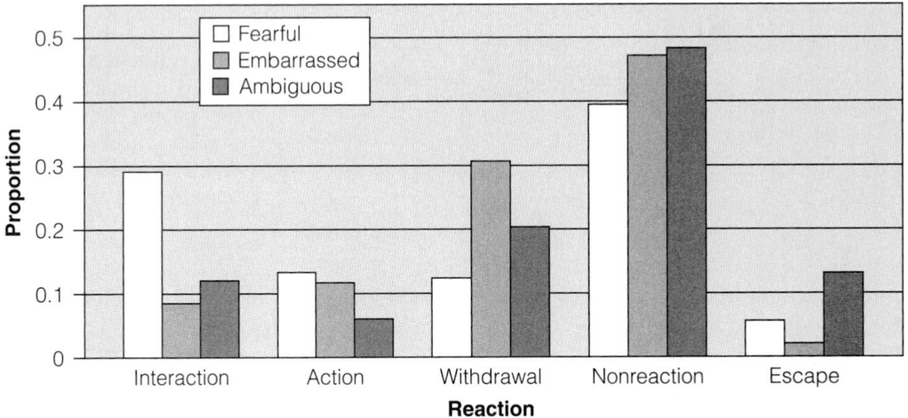


**FIGURE 4.3** Five types of behavioral reactions—interaction, action, withdrawal, nonreaction, and escape—to three different kinds of situations: fear-provoking (fearful), embarrassing (embarrassed), and ambiguous. People who faced an ambiguous situation did not talk among themselves as much as people who were fearful. People who were anxious and embarrassed, in contrast, interacted the least and they often withdrew from the group (Morris et al., 1976).

Researchers examined this process by changing the Schachter-type situation to include an element of public embarrassment. The investigators asked four to six strangers to meet in a room labeled with the sign "Sexual Attitudes: Please Wait Inside." In the *fear* condition, the room contained several electrical devices and information sheets that suggested that the study involved electric shock and sexual stimulation. In the *ambiguous* condition, the participants found only two cardboard boxes filled with computer forms. In the *embarrassment* (anxiety-provoking) condition, the researchers replaced the equipment and boxes with contraceptive devices, books on sexually transmitted diseases, and pictures of naked men and women. Observers behind a two-way mirror watched the group for 20 minutes, recording the five types of behavior shown in Figure 4.3: *interaction* (talking about the situation), *action* (e.g., examining the equipment), *withdrawal* (e.g., reading a book), *controlled nonreaction* (e.g., talking about something other than the experiment), and *escape* (Morris et al., 1976).

The observers discovered that the group members engaged in social comparison the most when they were fearful. As Figure 4.3 indicates, groups who faced the ambiguous situation spent about 12% of the time talking among themselves, but groups sitting in a room with the fear-inducing electrical equipment spent nearly 30% of the time gathering information through communication. Groups who thought that the study involved sexual behavior did very little talking and they showed more withdrawal. Embarrassment blocked affiliation in this situation, but this situation was not a dangerous one. If the need for information or support becomes overwhelming then embarrassment-related anxiety may not keep people away from their groups (Buunk & Hoorens, 1992; Davison, Pennebaker, & Dickerson, 2000).

## Downward (and Upward) Social Comparison

Monet, by joining with the other artists, gained information about art, technique, and ways of dealing with the officials who judged art exhibitions in Paris. This information undoubtedly reduced his confusion, but this cognitive clarity may have come at an emotional cost. Renoir, like Monet, was experimenting with many new methods, but Renoir was prospering; his art sold well in the Parisian market. Compared to Renoir, Monet was a failure. And how did Monet feel when he spoke to his friend Sisley? Sisley's work was never considered to be collectible, and he lived on the brink of poverty for much of his life. When Monet compared himself to Sisley, he must have felt a sense of relief that his own situation was not so bleak, but at the same time, he must have worried that his own career could take a turn for the worst at any moment.

People compare themselves to others when they lack information about the situation they face, but they are not indiscriminate when selecting targets for comparison. When they want information, they select people who are similar to them or are likely to be particularly well-informed. But when self-esteem is on the line, people engage in **downward social comparison** by selecting targets who are worse off than they are (Wills, 1991). Monet, for example, by contrasting himself to the struggling Sisley, could think to himself, "Things are not going so well for me, but at least I'm better off than poor Sisley." Students reviewing their academic progress with other students, spouses discussing their relationships with other husbands and wives, patients talking with other patients about their success in coping with their illness, medical students taking part in a training class, and expectant mothers talking about their pregnancies all show the tendency to seek out, for comparison purposes, people who are doing more poorly than they are (Buunk & Gibbons, 2007).

What if Monet had, instead, compared himself to the more prosperous Renoir? Such a comparison would be an example of **upward social comparison**, which occurs when a person compares himself or herself to others who are better off than he or she is. Renoir may have been an inspiration to Monet—when he started to wonder if he would ever be a success he could perhaps find reassurance in Renoir's accomplishments (Collins, 2000). Monet, by identifying with Renoir, could *bask in the reflected glory* (BIRG) of Renoir's fame, claim that he had a hand in Renoir's success, or elevate his appraisal of his own work since it was connected to that of Renoir's (Zuckerman & Jost, 2001). But upward social comparison can leave people feeling like failures. When students were asked to keep track of the people they compared themselves to over a two-week period, they reported feeling depressed and discouraged when they associated with more competent people (Wheeler & Miyake, 1992). Even if people know they have performed better than average, if they compare themselves to someone who has far outperformed them they feel discouraged (Seta, Seta, & McElroy, 2006).

When will people choose upward comparison over downward comparison? Abraham Tesser's **self-evaluation maintenance (SEM) model** suggests that people often graciously celebrate others' accomplishments—but not when they are bested in a domain that they value greatly. In such cases, others' success will more likely trigger resentment, envy, and shame rather than pride and admiration (Smith, R. H., 2000). The SEM model, using Monet as an example, predicts he would prefer to join with people who (1) performed worse than he did at tasks that were important to him personally, but (2) performed very well on tasks that were not central to his sense of self-worth (Beach & Tesser, 2000; Tesser, 1988, 1991).

Tesser and his colleagues examined this tension between sharing others' successes and highlighting

---

**downward social comparison** Comparing oneself to others who are performing less effectively relative to oneself.

**upward social comparison** Comparing oneself to others who are performing more effectively relative to oneself.

**self-evaluation maintenance (SEM) model** A theory proposed by Abraham Tesser which assumes that individuals maintain and enhance self-esteem by associating with high-achieving individuals who excel in areas that are not relevant to their own sense of self-esteem and avoiding association with high-achieving individuals who excel in areas that are important to their sense of self-esteem.

their failures by asking elementary school students to identify the types of activities (sports, art, music, math) that were personally important to them. The students also identified their most and least preferred classmate. One week later, the students rated their ability, their close classmate's ability, and their distant classmate's ability in one area they felt was important and one area they felt was unimportant. As Figure 4.4 indicates, if the students thought that the task was important, they judged their performance to be superior to that of their close friend. If the task was not important to them personally, they felt that they had performed relatively worse (Tesser, Campbell, & Smith, 1984). Similarly, in a study of married couples, Tesser and his colleagues discovered that happy couples felt that it was more pleasant to be outdone by one's partner in an area that their partner valued but to outperform the partner in an area that he or she did not value. Unhappy couples did not recognize this secret ingredient for marital bliss (Beach et al., 1998).

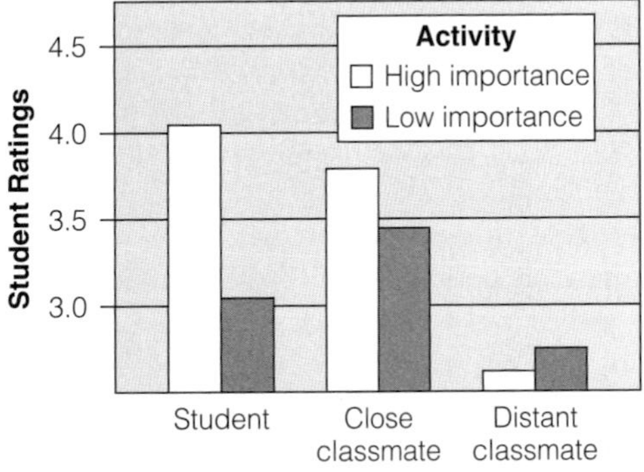


**FIGURE 4.4** Ratings of an individual's own performance and the performance of others on activities that are important or unimportant to the individual doing the rating. When students rated their own performance on a task they felt was important to them, they rated themselves as somewhat better than their close friend and much better than the distant classmate. But students rated their friend more positively than themselves when the task had no implications for their self-worth (Tesser, Campbell, & Smith, 1984).

SOURCE: "Friendship Choice and Performance: Self-evaluation maintenance in children" by Tesser, J. Campbell, and M. Smith, in J. Suls and A.G. Greenwald (Eds.), *Psychological Perspectives on the Self* (vol. 2). Copyright 1983. Reprinted by permission of Abraham Tesser.

Given the negative consequences of outperforming others, people who perform well often keep their success to themselves—particularly when they do well on tasks that are very important to the other group members (Tal-Or, 2008). They may also, however, maintain their superiority over their friends by sabotaging, indirectly, others' performances on tasks that are central to their sense of self-worth. Investigators asked students to keep track of every single one of their interactions with other people for six days. After each interaction, they were to note if the interaction involved academic matters or social matters, what their relationship to the person was (e.g., acquaintance, stranger, close friend), and if they shared information with that person that they thought would help the other to improve. As the SEM model suggests, these students gave helpful information to their friends when the interactions pertained to social matters, but when it came to academics, they helped their friends less than they helped strangers. This tendency was even more pronounced when the students thought that their friend was already performing better than they were (Pemberton & Sedikides, 2001; see Focus 4.2).

## Social Support

Monet initially sought to change the art world single-handedly, but he soon found that he needed help from others. When his work was condemned by the critics, he shared his feelings of rejection with the other artists, who offered him encouragement and advice. Frequently penniless, he sold his work to other artists so he could buy food and pay for his lodging. He could not afford his own studio, so Bazille and Renoir invited him to share one with them. When Monet injured his leg, Bazille cared for him. The group did not just provide him with "cognitive clarity" but with **social support** in times of turbulence and trouble.

---

**social support** A sense of belonging, emotional support, advice, guidance, tangible assistance, and spiritual perspective given to others when they experience stress, daily hassles, and more significant life crises.

## Focus 4.2 Who Is the True Group Animal?

*If you do not compare yourself with another you will be what you are. Through comparison you hope to evolve, to grow, to become more intelligent, more beautiful. But will you?*

—Jiddu Kristnamurti, *Freedom from the Known* (1969, p.64)

One of the members of your study group gets the highest grade on the exam. A member of your work team is singled out by management for a raise. A single player out of 42 is chosen for the all-star team. It isn't you.

Joining together with highly competent people working on shared tasks can be, at the same time, both inspirational and threatening. We can be happy for others when they succeed and strive to emulate their accomplishments ourselves but, then again, when we compare ourselves to our betters our own efforts and accomplishments seem all the more meager. Because upward comparison can be so discouraging, people may deliberately avoid joining groups that include people who will outperform them in spheres they consider to be personally important (Lockwood & Kunda, 1997).

Social comparison researcher Bram Buunk and his colleagues (2007) suggest that some people have found a way to escape this downside to group life; they do not compare themselves to other group members, and they are happier people for it. To test this hypothesis, they first measured people's overall affiliation orientation by asking them if they "like to go to places and settings with lots of people" or "love teamwork" (p. 79). But, they also measured people's **social comparison orientation** (Gibbons & Buunk, 1999). They reasoned that, just as people vary in their affiliative desires, they may also vary in their tendency to compare themselves to other people. So they asked people if they agreed with such statements as "I often compare myself with others with respect to what I have accomplished in life" and "I always pay a lot of attention to how I do things compared with how others do things" (p. 74).

When they used these measures to predict who was most satisfied with their membership in their groups, they discovered affiliation orientation and social comparison orientation combine to determine group satisfaction. The participants were generally satisfied with their groups, but people who were highly affiliative *and* low in their social comparison orientation were particularly happy with membership. Apparently, those who could not resist comparing themselves to others could never completely avoid the negative emotional consequences of upward social comparison. So who is the person who most enjoys being a member of a group? Buunk and his colleagues concluded "that the typical 'group animal' is someone who has a strong preference for affiliation, combined with a low tendency to compare him- or herself with others" (Buunk, Nauta, & Molleman, 2005, p. 69).

**Stress and Affiliation** Schachter (1959) did not just confuse people: he frightened people. The women he studied affiliated with others to acquire clarifying information through social comparison, but they probably also were seeking reassurance. Two people, facing the prospect of receiving electric shocks, simply could review the situation, but also they could talk about their misgivings, calm each other down, and help one another should problems arise. Given a choice between people who are equal in their knowledge of the situation but vary in their emotional reaction to the threat—some are very fearful, but others are calm—people choose to wait with those who are calm (Rabbie, 1963).

Humans are group-seeking animals, but their gregariousness becomes particularly robust under conditions of stress (Rofé, 1984). In times of trouble, such as illness, divorce, catastrophe, natural disaster, or personal loss, people seek out friends and relatives (Dooley & Catalano, 1984). College students who are experiencing problems, academically or socially, spend between 28% and 35% of their time interacting with people they feel are supportive (Harlow & Cantor, 1995). Individuals experiencing work-related stress, such as the threat of layoffs, time pressures, or inadequate supervision, cope by joining with coworkers (Bowling et al., 2004; McGuire, 2007). Individuals who have been reminded of their

---

**social comparison orientation** The dispositional tendency to compare oneself to others.

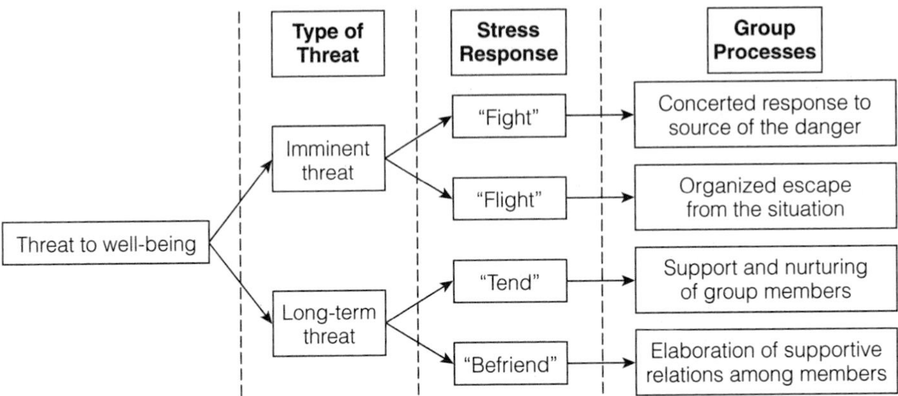


**FIGURE 4.5** Group-level responses to stress. The two basic responses to stress—fight-or-flight and tend-and-befriend—are both enhanced when members rely on resources made available by their groups.

own mortality are more likely to sit closer to other people, even if these other individuals do not share their opinions on important social issues (Wisman & Koole, 2003).

People also react to large-scale traumatic events by joining with others. When U.S. President John F. Kennedy was assassinated, 60% of adult Americans reported seeking solace by talking to others (Sheatsley & Feldman, 1964). In the days following the terrorist attacks on September 11, 2001, 98% of all adult Americans reported talking to others about the attacks, 60% reported taking part in a group activity, and 77% sought to strengthen their connection to their loved ones (Schuster et al., 2001). Many individuals joined virtual groups via the Internet. Internet usage declined overall, but discussion areas, forums, and chat room use surged, as did e-mail rates. Nearly three-quarters of all Internet users (72%) used e-mail to contact family and friends or to share news about the attack (Ranie & Kalsnes, 2001). Individuals who were already heavy users of the Internet tended to be the ones who used this technology to affiliate with others, whereas light users were more likely to rely on more traditional methods (Kim et al., 2004).

As Figure 4.5 suggests, affiliation with others plays a key role in both *fight-or-flight* and *tend-and-befriend* responses to stress. When the group members face an imminent threat, they can work together to fight against it—they can rally against attackers, organize a concerted response to a disaster, and so on. Groups also enhance survival as members escape. If escape routes are not restricted, the dispersion of a group can confuse attackers and increase the chances that all members of the group will escape unharmed. A group can also organize its escape from danger, with stronger members of the group helping less able members to reach safety. If, in contrast, the group faces a long-term threat, then the group may cope by increasing nurturing, protective, and supportive behaviors (*tending*) and by seeking out connections to other people (*befriending*). As the work of Shelley Taylor and her colleagues suggests, women are more likely to respond to stress by affiliating with others. Both men and women, however, show a disproportionate preference to join with women when stressed (Taylor, 2006; Taylor et al., 2000).

**Sources of Support** Table 4.3 lists a number of examples of the ways that groups provide support for their members, beginning with *belonging*: by letting troubled members know that they are valued members, the group reassures them that they are not alone in facing their problems (Krause & Wulff, 2005). Group members provide *emotional support* when they express their caring and concern for one another, often by listening to others' problems without offering criticism or suggestions, encouraging them, and showing general approval (McGuire, 2007). *Informational support* pertains to

**TABLE 4.3 Some Forms of Social Support Provided by Groups**

| Type | Definition | Examples |
|---|---|---|
| **Belonging** | Inclusion in a group | • Expressing acceptance<br>• Reassurance of belonging<br>• Reaffirming membership<br>• Encouraging identification<br>• Group activities |
| **Emotional support** | Expressing caring and concern for one another | • Expressing respect and approval<br>• Encouragement<br>• Listening<br>• Sharing feelings<br>• Responding nonverbally in positive ways (e.g., hugging, nodding) |
| **Informational support** | Providing advice and guidance | • Sharing helpful information<br>• Giving directions, advice, suggestions<br>• Demonstrating a way to perform a task<br>• Problem solving |
| **Instrumental support** | Providing tangible resources | • Doing favors<br>• Lending money or possessions<br>• Assisting with work, duties<br>• Transportation<br>• Providing a place to stay |
| **Spiritual support** | Addressing issues of meaning and purpose | • Explaining challenging events<br>• Allaying existential anxiety, fear of death<br>• Sharing faith<br>• Reconfirming one's world view |

advice and guidance, *instrumental support* provides members with tangible resources, and *spiritual support* helps members deal with existential dilemmas and threats to their worldview (see Uchino, 2004).

Admittedly, some groups fail to deliver on their promise of support. They may even add stressors by stirring up conflicts, increasing responsibilities, and exposing members to criticism (e.g., Newsom et al., 2008). Overall, however, groups are more frequently supportive than burdensome. People who enjoy strong social bonds with other people tend to experience less stress in their lives, are less likely to suffer from depression and other psychological problems, and are physically healthier (Stinson et al., 2008). Social support is particularly valuable when people find themselves in threatening circumstances—a divorce, a job change, a move, or the like. Stressful life circumstances leave people at risk for psychological and physical illness, but groups can serve as protective buffers against these negative consequences (Taylor, 2007). Researchers verified this *buffering effect* in studies of stressors, including health crises, personal tragedies, terrorist attacks, and intergroup conflict. For example, individuals trying to recover from a devastating crisis (e.g., the death of a spouse or child) who were more firmly embedded in a social network of friends, relatives, and neighbors were less depressed than people who were not integrated into groups (Norris & Murrell, 1990). Firefighters who felt they were supported by their peers and their supervisor reported less stress than those who did not feel as closely connected to their group members (Varvel et al., 2007). A survey of New York City residents following the September 11, 2001 terrorist attacks indicated that those who were members of groups or affiliative organizations (e.g., church groups, discussion groups, veterans groups) were more resilient to the stressful effects of the attacks (Bonanno et al., 2007). Participants who played the role of prisoners in a simulation of a prison (in England) provided one another with substantial social support, and in consequence they were relatively unaffected by situational stressors (Haslam & Reicher, 2006). All these studies suggest that a group offers members a safe haven from the storm of stress.

### Companionship

Memberships are not static. At some point in his or her life, an individual may find that he or she belongs to many groups. At other times, however, people may feel that their relationships with others are too few or too superficial. In such situations, people often experience **loneliness**, and to escape it they turn to groups for companionship.

**Types of Loneliness** Loneliness is not the same as being alone, for in some situations people are not troubled by isolation or a relative paucity of relations with others. Loneliness, instead, is an aversive psychological reaction to a lack of personal or social relations with other people. *Emotional loneliness* occurs when the problem is a lack of a long-term, meaningful, intimate relationship with another person; this type of loneliness might be triggered by divorce, a breakup with a lover, or repeated romantic failures. *Social loneliness*, in contrast, occurs when people feel cut off from their network of friends, acquaintances, and group members. People who have moved to a new city, children who are rejected by their peers, and new employees of large companies often experience social loneliness, because they are no longer embedded in a network of friends and acquaintances (Green et al., 2001). Both types of loneliness create feelings of sadness, depression, emptiness, longing, shame, and self-pity.

**Groups Alleviate Loneliness** Groups can provide the antidote to loneliness by (1) organizing and integrating connections with other individuals, and (2) promoting the development of warm, supportive, intimate relationships between members (Shaver & Buhrmester, 1983). College students who belonged to a cohesive, satisfying group reported much less loneliness than students who belonged to poorly integrated groups (Anderson & Martin, 1995; Schmidt & Sermat, 1983). Members of groups with extensive interconnections among all the members were less lonely than members of groups with less dense networks (Kraus et al., 1993; Stokes, 1985). Children with friends—even friends who were considered odd or unusual by their peers—were less lonely than friendless children (Asher & Paquette, 2003). People who belonged to groups (e.g., service organizations, religious or church organizations, business or professional organizations, and social clubs) were healthier and happier than individuals who did not (Harlow & Cantor, 1996). They even lived longer than lonely loners (Stroebe, 1994; Sugisawa, Liang, & Liu, 1994).

All groups are not equally effective in buffering their members from both forms of loneliness. As Table 4.4 suggests, transitory, impersonal collectives do little to ease either social or emotional loneliness. Sitting with other people in a theater or striking up a conversation with a stranger on a bus creates a connection momentarily, but only groups that sustain stable, reliable alliances among members can ward off social loneliness (Jones & Carver, 1991). Likewise, only groups that connect people together in an intimate, meaningful way reduce feelings of emotional loneliness. Having many superficial relationships with others is far less satisfying than having a few high-quality relationships characterized by high levels of social support, mutual caring, and acceptance (Cacioppo, Hawkley, & Berntson, 2003). In consequence, groups that create connections among their members, such as amateur athletic teams, social clubs, or work groups, will reduce members' feelings of social loneliness, but only more intimate, involving types of groups—families, romantic couples, or very close friendship cliques—will meet members' social *and* emotional needs (Stroebe et al., 1996).

---

**loneliness** Feelings of desperation, boredom, self-deprecation, and depression experienced when individuals feel their personal relationships are too few or too unsatisfying.

**TABLE 4.4 The Effectiveness of Different Types of Groups in Ameliorating Loneliness**

| | | Effectiveness in Reducing Emotional Loneliness | |
|---|---|---|---|
| | | **Low** | **High** |
| **Effectiveness in Reducing Social Loneliness** | **Low** | **Collectives** (passengers, queues, audiences) | **Intimate Groups** (couples, long-term close friendship pairs) |
| | **High** | **Social Groups** (congregations, work groups, regulars at a bar, social clubs, amateur athletic teams) | **Primary groups** (families, communes, very close-knit friendship cliques) |

## ATTRACTION

Renoir and Bazille met, quite by happenstance, because both were students of Gleyre. Their desire to learn more about their craft and their enrollment in the same school combined to bring them together. But this chance meeting by itself was not sufficient to spark the formation of the group that would, in time, become the impressionists. Bazille and Renoir would not have chosen to spend more and more time together discussing art, politics, and Parisian society if they had disliked each other. Affiliation may set the stage for a group to form, but *attraction* transforms acquaintances into friends.

### Principles of Attraction

Theodore Newcomb's classic study of the *acquaintance process* anticipated the methods used in many contemporary reality television programs. Those programs arrange for strangers to live together in a mansion, a house, or an island, and then just record the ebb and flow of likes and dislikes among the members. Similarly, Newcomb offered 17 young men starting their studies at the University of Michigan free rent if they answered a detailed survey of their attitudes, likes, and dislikes each week. Then he watched as the 17 students sorted themselves out into friendship pairs and distinct groups (Newcomb, 1960, 1961, 1979, 1981).

Even though attraction is often thought to be a highly capricious and unpredictable social process, Newcomb identified a small number of principles that explain when liking is more likely. As the sections that follow indicate, people are more likely to associate with certain people—those who are nearby, those who express similar attitudes and values, and those who respond positively to them—and such associations often culminate in the creation of a group.

**The Proximity Principle** Group members often assume that their groups result from rational planning or common interests. But the **proximity principle** suggests that in some cases, people join groups that just happen to be close by. Newcomb (1960) assigned the participants roommates at random, but by the study's end most roommates had become close friends. When teachers assign students seats in classrooms, cliques of pupils in adjacent seats develop (Segal, 1974). City dwellers who regularly assemble in the same physical location—commuters at subway stops, patrons at local bars, and frequent picnickers in parks—eventually gel into identifiable groups (see Gieryn, 2000). College students living in dorms send far more emails to those who live near them than they do to those who live in more distant rooms (Sacerdote & Marmaros, 2005).

Leon Festinger and his colleagues tracked the emergence of networks of attraction in a housing residence at the Massachusetts Institute of Technology (MIT). Not only did the majority of best friends live in the same building, they lived next door; 41% of the next-door neighbors were identified as people "seen socially." The numbers then dropped with each increase in distance, so that only 22% of the neighbors two doors down were identified as

---

**proximity principle** The tendency for individuals to form interpersonal relations with those who are close by.

members of the student's social group, 16% of those three doors down, and only 10% of those four doors away. The distances were relatively small ones—22 feet (next door) to 88 feet, but proximity mattered (Festinger, Schachter, & Back, 1950).

We do not form groups with people who happen to be nearby because we are shallow or indiscriminating. First, people show a preference for things—including people—that seem familiar to them (Bornstein, 1989). When people continually encounter other people because their offices, homes, desks, or rooms are located adjacent to theirs, these strangers quickly become acquaintances. So long as this repeated exposure does not reveal that those nearby others have contemptible qualities, then familiarity will breed contentment rather than contempt (Norton, Frost, Ariely, 2007).

Second, proximity increases interaction between people, and interaction cultivates attraction. As Richard Moreland (1987) noted in his *social integration theory* of group formation, groups emerge gradually over time as individuals find themselves interacting with the same subset of other individuals with greater and greater frequency. Repeated interactions may foster a sense of groupness as the people come to think of themselves as a group, and those outside the group begin to treat them as a group (Arkin & Burger, 1980). One investigator watched, for weeks, the interactions of 12 women who worked at separate desks organized in three rows. The individuals' work did not require that they collaborate extensively with one another, but they frequently spoke to each other. Every 15 minutes the observer would note who was interacting with whom, and eventually recorded over 1,500 distinct conversations. The conversations took place primarily between neighbors, or at least between the workers who were seated in the same row, and these interactions accurately predicted the formation of smaller cliques within the larger group of women (Gullahorn, 1952).

Proximity usually promotes interaction, but should it fail to do so, then it could lead to disliking rather than liking. When people were asked to name their friends, most identified people who lived close by and whom they interacted with very frequently. But when they named someone they disliked, they also tended to pick a near neighbor, but someone with whom they rarely interacted. Also, online communities, such as Facebook, Second Life, and multiplayer games, lack propinquity but they stimulate high levels of interaction among members, resulting in the formation of stable groups (Ducheneaut et al., 2006). Perhaps, then, it is interaction rather than propinquity that creates attraction (Ebbesen, Kjos, & Konecni, 1976).

**The Elaboration Principle** Groups, as self-organizing, dynamic systems, tend to increase in complexity over time. A group that begins with only two members tends to grow in size as these individuals become linked to other nearby individuals. According to systems theory, "the basic dynamic of elaboration is the proliferation of elements and ties," which "are linked together to form a functional unit called a group" (Arrow et al., 2000, pp. 91–92; Parks, 2007).

Newcomb's groups, for example, conformed to this **elaboration principle**, for cliques usually evolved from smaller, dyadic pairings. The first friendships were two-person pairs—usually roommates or people living in adjoining rooms who became friends. Over time, these dyads expanded to include other individuals who were attracted to one or both of the original members. This same kind of self-organizing process has been documented in other emerging groups, such as adolescents' peer group associations, leisure groups, and social movements (Benford, 1992). As Focus 4.3 explains, gangs form when three friends refer to themselves with a shared name and recruit other friends to join the group (Tobin, 2008). Friendships are very likely to form between students who were linked to the same individuals (Gibbons & Olk, 2003). Groups form when otherwise unrelated individuals are drawn to a single individual, who becomes the hub for gradually developing bonds among the various members (Redl, 1942). The impressionists

---

**elaboration principle** The tendency for groups to expand as members form dyadic associations with someone who is not in the group and thereby draw the nonmember into the group.

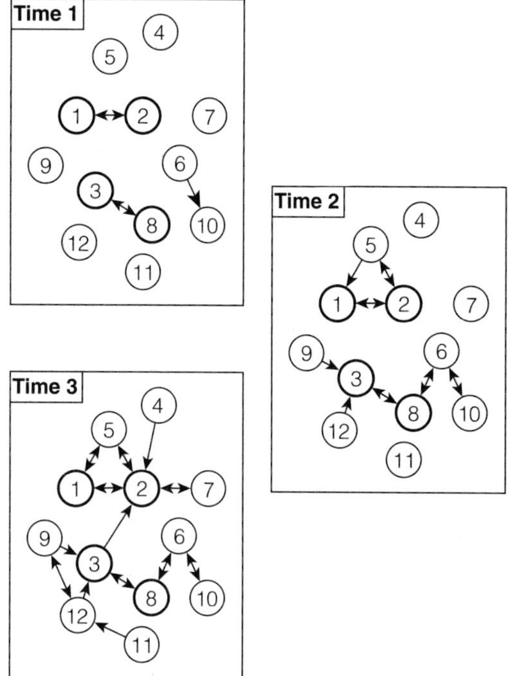


**FIGURE 4.6** The elaboration of groups over time. Groups that begin as simple two-person groups become more complex over time as individuals who are initially linked together only in one-to-one, dyadic relationships (e.g., person 1 and 2, person 3 and 8) expand their networks to include additional elements (members).

developed into a group through such a self-organizing process. Each member of the core group drew in others, until in time the group included artists, sculptors, and writers (see Figure 4.6).

**The Similarity Principle** Newcomb found that the 17 men clustered naturally into two groups containing nine and seven members; one person remained at the fringe of both groups. The seven-man group was particularly unified, for when asked to indicate who they liked out of the total list of 17 they gave relatively high rankings to one another and not to those young men in the other cluster. The members of the other group did not show the same level of mutual attraction as the smaller clique.

When Newcomb (1963) examined these subgroups he noticed that subgroup members' values, beliefs, and interests were similar. One clique, for example, contained men who endorsed liberal political and religious attitudes, were all registered in the arts college, came from the same part of the country, and shared similar aesthetic, social, theoretical, economic, political, and religious values. The members of the second subgroup were all veterans, were majors in engineering, and shared similar religious, economic, and political values. Newcomb had found strong evidence for the **similarity principle**: People are attracted to those who are similar to them in some way.

Similarity is a social magnet that creates all kinds of relationships. People tend to marry people who are similar to them; they join groups composed of others who are like them; and they live in communities where people are more alike than different. Although these similarities often reflect agreements in attitudes, values, and beliefs, they are also based on irrelevant demographic characteristics, such as race, ethnicity, sex, and age (Lazarsfeld & Merton, 1954). As a result, **homophily**—similarity of the members of a group in attitudes, values, demographic characteristics, and so on—is common in groups. The cliques that form in large volunteer organizations tie together people who are similar in some way rather than dissimilar (Feld, 1982). If a group decreases in size, the first individual who is dropped from membership will likely be the one who is the least similar to the other members; ties between similar people are maintained, but ties with dissimilar people dissolve. "Birds of a feather flock together" describes most groups.

Why are people drawn to others who are similar to them in some way? Homophily appears to be sustained by a number of psychological, sociological, and relational factors that combine to promote

---

**similarity principle** The tendency to affiliate with or be attracted to similar others; this tendency causes groups and other interpersonal aggregates to be composed of individuals who are similar to one another rather than dissimilar.

**homophily** The tendency for group members to display certain affinities, such as similarities in demographic background, attitudes, values, or so on; the overall degree of similarity of individuals within the same group.

## Focus 4.3 Why Join a Gang?

*It's like a comfortable feeling, you got someone to back you up and protect you.*

"Billy," 21-year-old North Side Crip
(Decker & Van Winkle, 1996, p. 74)

Gangs are often characterized as disruptive, violent groups of delinquents who commit robberies, hijack cars, distribute drugs, murder, and generally live outside the boundaries of "normal" society. But objective analyses of the characteristics of gangs suggest that violence and social disorganization are rarely the defining features of such groups. Gangs do may contend against legal authorities and members may use violence to establish status and control in the group. Gangs are, however, relatively stable associations within many communities, and their members also connect to their community through more traditional social groups (church congregations, families, schools). Larger gangs also tend to be hierarchically organized, much like a business or formal organization, and the members vary in their commitment to their groups (Vankatesh, 2008). The few core members (called, variously, *ancients, old gangsters, veteranos*) may remain in the group for many years, and for them the gang dominates their social lives. Most members, however, only take part in some gang-related activities (Coughlin & Venkatesh, 2003).

Gangs also emerge for many of the same reasons that any group is formed. One study of gangs in East Los Angeles, for example, traced many of these groups back to a much smaller cluster of friends who lived near one another (Moore, 1991). The founders of the group were very similar to one another in terms of ethnicity and age, and they were committed to increasing the level of safety in their neighborhoods. Over time, more people joined the groups, which gradually became more formally organized, more territorial, and more likely to engage in criminal behavior. Gangs also tend to be relatively task focused (Venkatesh, 2008). When members were asked why they joined the gang, most stressed practical outcomes, such as safety and financial gain (see Figure 4.7). As one member remarked, "There's money in a gang. I want to be in it, you see a lot of money in it, man. That's why I really got in the gang, money and all" (quoted in Decker & Van Winkle, 1996, p. 74). Many gang members also agreed that gang membership increased their status in the community and helped them socially. "One thing I like about gangs it's more people to be around, more partners to go places with . . . social stuff" (quoted in Decker & Van Winkle, 1996, p. 75).

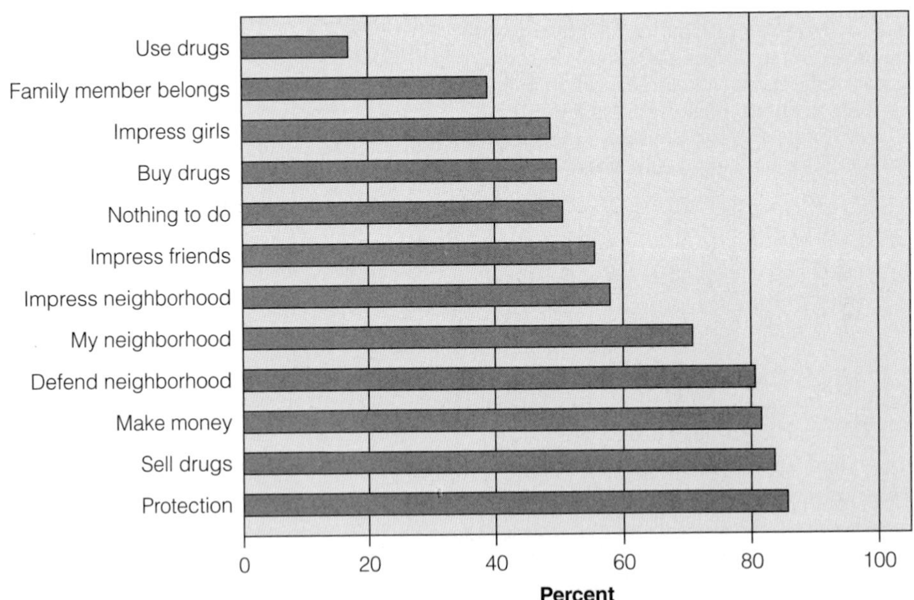

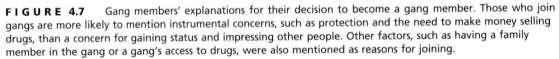

**FIGURE 4.7** Gang members' explanations for their decision to become a gang member. Those who join gangs are more likely to mention instrumental concerns, such as protection and the need to make money selling drugs, than a concern for gaining status and impressing other people. Other factors, such as having a family member in the gang or a gang's access to drugs, were also mentioned as reasons for joining.

contacts between people who share similarities rather than differences (McPherson, Smith-Lovin, & Cook, 2001). Because people who adopt the same values and attitudes that we do reassure us that our beliefs are accurate, we find association with such people very rewarding (Byrne, 1971). People may also assume, with some justification, that future group interactions will be more cooperative and conflict-free when members are all similar to one another (Insko & Schopler, 1972). Similarity may also increase a sense of connectedness to the other person (Arkin & Burger, 1980). Two strangers chatting casually on an airplane, for example, feel united if they find that they share even the smallest similarity, such as the same middle name or favorite television program. Disliking a person who seems similar may also be psychologically distressing. After all, if a person is similar to us, it follows logically that he or she must be attractive (Festinger, 1957; Heider, 1958). Homophily also tends to beget homophily. Because communities, schools, and most workplaces bring people together who are similar in terms of race, attitudes, religion, and ethnicity, people's options for relationships are limited to those who are already similar to them in these ways (McPherson et al., 2001).

**The Complementarity Principle** In most cases similarity trumps dissimilarity when it comes to attraction. People generally associate with similar others, and they are repulsed by those who are dissimilar to them (Rosenbaum, 1986). In one-on-one relations, people are sometimes attracted to individuals who have very desirable personal qualities, but when evaluating groups people base their preferences on the degree of similarity between the group and themselves (Clement & Krueger, 1998).

If, however, people's qualities complement each other—they are dissimilar but they fit well together—then this unique form of dissimilarity may encourage people to associate with one another. If, for example, Claude enjoys leading groups, he will not be attracted to other individuals who also strive to take control of the group. Instead, he will respond more positively to those who accept his guidance (Tiedens, Unzueta & Young, 2007). Similarly, individuals who are forming a group may realize that the members' skills and abilities must complement each other if the group is to be successful (Kristof-Brown, Barrick, & Stevens, 2005). These cases are consistent with the **complementarity principle**, which suggests that people are attracted to those who possess characteristics that complement their own personal characteristics (Winch, 1958).

Which tendency is stronger, similarity or complementarity? Some investigators, working primarily with dyads, have found that similarity is much more common than complementarity (Miller, Perlman & Brehm, 2007). Other researchers, however, have found that the members of close-knit groups tend to possess compatible but somewhat dissimilar needs (Kerckhoff & Davis, 1962; O'Connor & Dyce, 1997). In all likelihood, group members respond positively to both similarity and complementarity. We may, for example, be attracted to people whose qualities complement our own, yet we may also feel that we are very similar to such people (Dryer & Horowitz, 1997). We may also prefer people who are similar to us in some ways, but who complement us in other ways. Studies of interpersonal complementarity indicate that people prefer to interact with others who match their general level of friendliness, warmth, and positivity. Positive behaviors, such as seeming sociable, reassuring, and considerate, tend to elicit similar levels of friendliness in response. However, people generally respond to dominant behaviors by acting submissively and vice versa; so leaders seek out followers, and the strong seek out the weak (e.g., Tracey, Ryan, & Jaschik-Herman, 2001).

Schutz (1958), in his FIRO theory of groups discussed earlier in this chapter, suggested that compatibility can be based on both similarity and on complementarity. **Interchange compatibility** exists when group members have similar expectations

---

**complementarity principle** The tendency for group members to like people who are dissimilar to them in ways that complement their personal qualities.

**interchange compatibility** As described by William Schutz, compatibility between group members based on their similar needs for inclusion, control, and affection.

about the group's intimacy, control, and inclusiveness. Interchange compatibility will be high if all the members expect that their group will be formally organized with minimal expressions of intimacy, but it will be low if some think that they can share their innermost feelings whereas others want a more reserved exchange. **Originator compatibility** exists when people have dissimilar, but complementary, needs with regard to expressing and receiving control, inclusion, and affection. For example, originator compatibility would be high if a person with a high need to control the group joined a group whose members wanted a strong leader.

Schutz tested his theory by constructing groups of varying compatibilities. He created originator compatibility by placing in each group one member with a high need for control, one member with a high need for inclusion, and three members with lower needs for control and inclusion. Moreover, interchange compatibility was established by grouping people with similar needs for affection. All the groups in this set were compatible, but levels of affection were high in half of the groups and low in the other half. A set of incompatible groups was also created by including group members who varied significantly in their need for affection, ranging from high to low. As Schutz predicted, (1) cohesiveness was higher in the compatible groups than in the incompatible groups, and (2) the compatible groups worked on problems far more efficiently than the incompatible groups. He found similar results in studies of groups that formed spontaneously, such as street gangs and friendship circles in fraternities (Schutz, 1958).

**The Reciprocity Principle** When Groucho Marx joked, "I don't want to belong to any club that will accept me as a member," he was denying the power of the **reciprocity principle**—that liking tends to be mutual. When we discover that someone else accepts and approves of us—they give friendly advice, compliment us, or declare their admiration for us—we usually respond by liking them in return. Newcomb (1979) found strong evidence of the reciprocity principle, as did other investigators in a range of different situations (e.g., Kandel, 1978). Some group members, like Groucho Marx, may not like to be liked, but these exceptions to the reciprocity principle are relatively rare. When a person expresses liking for us, it implies that the admirer will treat us with respect, compassion, and benevolence on future occasions (Montoya & Insko, 2008).

Negative reciprocity also occurs in groups: We dislike those who seem to reject us. In one study, college students discussed controversial issues in groups. Unknown to the true participants in the experiment, two of the three group members were confederates of the experimenter, who either accepted or rejected the comments of the participant. During a break between the discussion and the completion of a measure of attraction to the group, the rejecting confederates excluded the participant from their discussion by talking among themselves and giving the participant an occasional dirty look. Naturally, participants were less attracted to their co-members if they had been rejected by them. The rejection also served to lower participants' opinions of themselves (Pepitone & Wilpinski, 1960).

**The Minimax Principle** Social exchange theory offers one final, and particularly important, principle for predicting group formation. The theory assumes that people, as rational creatures, strive to minimize their troubles, their worries, and their losses and instead maximize their positive outcomes, their happiness, and their rewards. Like shoppers searching for a bargain, they are drawn to groups that impose few costs yet offer them the greatest rewards. If a group seems to be a costly one—it will demand much time or will

---

**originator compatibility** As described by William Schutz, compatibility between group members that occurs when individuals who wish to express inclusion, control, or affection within the group are matched with individuals who wish to receive inclusion, control, or affection from others.

**reciprocity principle** The tendency for liking to be met with liking in return; if A likes B then B will tend to like A.

require members to do things that they would rather avoid if possible—then the value of the group will drop and people will be less likely to join. But, if the group offers considerable rewards to its members, such as prestige, desired resources, or pleasant experiences, then they will seek it out. These two basic requirements, taken together, provide the basis for social exchange theory's **minimax principle**: People will join groups and remain in groups that provide them with the maximum number of valued rewards while incurring the minimum number of possible costs (Kelley & Thibaut, 1978; Thibaut & Kelley, 1959).

What kinds of rewards do people seek and what costs do they hope to avoid? When researchers asked prospective group members to identify the rewards and costs they felt a group might create for them, 40% mentioned such social and personal rewards as meeting people, making new friends, developing new interests, or enhancing their self-esteem. They also mentioned such rewards as learning new skills, increased opportunities for networking, and fun. These prospective members also anticipated costs, however. More than 30% expected to lose time and money by joining a group. Other frequently mentioned costs were social pressures, possible injury or illness, and excessive demands made by the group for their time. Nonetheless, the prospective members in this study optimistically felt that the groups they were considering would offer them far more rewards than costs (Brinthaupt, Moreland, & Levine, 1991; Moreland, Levine, Cini, 1993).

The group members themselves are also an important source of rewards and costs. People are usually attracted to groups whose members possess positively valued qualities and avoid groups of people with objectionable characteristics. People prefer to associate with people who are generous, enthusiastic, punctual, dependable, helpful, strong, truthful, and intelligent (Bonney, 1947; Thibaut & Kelley, 1959). People tend to dislike and reject as potential group members those individuals who possess socially unattractive personal qualities—people who seem pushy, rude, self-centered, or boring (Gilchrist, 1952; Iverson, 1964). Those who complain too frequently are also viewed negatively (Kowalski, 1996), as are people who sidetrack the group unnecessarily, show little enthusiasm, and seem preoccupied with themselves (Leary et al., 1986). Many of the impressionists, for example, considered having to interact with Degas a major cost of membership. In a letter to Camille Pissarro, Gustave Caillebotte wrote, "Degas introduced disunity into our midst. It is unfortunate for him that he has such an unsatisfactory character. He spends his time haranguing at the Nouvelle-Athènes or in society. He would do much better to paint a little more" (quoted in Denvir, 1993, p. 181).

### The Economics of Membership

Why did such artists as Manet, Pissarro, and Bazille join with Monet to create an artists' circle? As we have seen, the group offered its members a number of advantages over remaining alone. By joining Monet, the impressionists gained a sounding board for ideas, social support, help with tasks they could not accomplish alone, and friends. But the group also created costs for members, who had to spend time and personal resources before they could enjoy the benefits the group offered. The minimax principle argues that those who joined the group must have felt that the benefits outweighed the costs.

Do we, then, join *any* group that promises us a favorable reward/cost ratio? Howard Kelley and John Thibaut argued that although we may be attracted to such groups, our decision to actually join is based on two factors: our *comparison level* and our *comparison level for alternatives*. **Comparison level (CL)** is the standard by which individuals evaluate the desirability of group

---

**minimax principle** The tendency to prefer relationships and group memberships that provide the maximum number of valued rewards and incur the fewest number of possible costs.

**comparison level (CL)** In John Thibaut and Harold Kelley's social exchange theory, the standard by which the individual evaluates the quality of any social relationship. In most cases, individuals whose prior relationships yielded positive rewards with few costs will have higher CLs than those who experienced fewer rewards and more costs in prior relationships.

**TABLE 4.5 The Impact of Comparison Level (CL) and Comparison Level for Alternatives ($CL_{alt}$) on Satisfaction with Group Membership and the Decision to Join a Group**

| | | Membership in the Group is | |
|---|---|---|---|
| | | **Above CL** | **Below CL** |
| **Membership in the Group is** | Above $CL_{alt}$ | Membership is satisfying, will join group | Membership is dissatisfying, but will join group |
| | Below $CL_{alt}$ | Membership is satisfying, but will not join group | Membership is dissatisfying and will not join group |

SOURCE: Adapted from Thibaut & Kelley, 1959.

membership. The CL derives from the average of all outcomes known to the individual and is usually strongly influenced by previous relationships. If, for example, Degas's prior group memberships yielded very positive rewards with very few costs, his CL should be higher than that of someone who has experienced fewer rewards and more costs through group membership. According to Thibaut and Kelley, groups that "fall above CL would be relatively 'satisfying' and attractive to the member; those entailing outcomes that fall below CL would be relatively 'unsatisfying' and unattractive" (Thibaut & Kelley, 1959, p. 21; see also Kelley & Thibaut, 1978).

Comparison level, however, only predicts when people will be *satisfied* with membership in a group. If we want to predict whether people will join groups or leave them, we must also take into account the value of other, alternative groups. What if Degas could have joined several artists' circles, all of which surpassed his CL? Which one would he then select? According to Thibaut and Kelley (1959), the group with the best reward/cost balance will determine Degas's **comparison level for alternatives (CLalt)**. Thibaut and Kelley argued that "$CL_{alt}$ can be defined informally as the lowest level of outcomes a member will accept in the light of available alternative opportunities" (1959, p. 21).

**comparison level for alternatives (CLalt)** In John Thibaut and Harold Kelley's social exchange theory, the standard by which individuals evaluate the quality of other groups that they may join.

Entering and exiting groups is largely determined by $CL_{alt}$, whereas satisfaction with membership is determined by CL (see Table 4.5). For example, why did Degas initially join the impressionists, but eventually leave the group? According to Thibaut and Kelley, Degas intuitively calculated the positive and negative outcomes that resulted from membership in the group. This index, at least at first, favored the impressionists. If Degas believed that joining the group would surpass his comparison level (CL), then he would likely be satisfied with membership. But over time, the demands of the group became too great and the rewards too small, the group's value dropped below his CL, and he became dissatisfied. If the group's value dropped below Degas's intuitive estimations of the value of other groups (his $CL_{alt}$), then he would likely leave the impressionists and join another, more promising group. In Degas's case, the alternative of remaining alone established the lower level of his $CL_{alt}$.

The rest of the impressionists, however, remained friends. They often exhibited their works individually and spent months in isolation, but they still provided each other with help as necessary. Indeed, for many years, they met regularly at the Café Riche, where they would discuss art, politics, and literature. In time, they reached their goal of fame and fortune. By the turn of the century, most were invited, at last, to present in traditional shows, and collectors paid handsome prices for their work. As individuals, they came to Paris to learn to paint; but as a group they changed the world's definition of fine art.

## SUMMARY IN OUTLINE

*Who joins groups?*

1. The tendency to join groups is partly determined by individuals' personal qualities, including personality traits, sex, social motives, and prior experiences.
2. Personality traits, such as extraversion and relationality, influence who affiliates with others and who does not.
   - *Extraversion* is a primary dimension of personality identified by Jung and the *Big Five theory* of personality. Extraverts are more likely to seek out groups than are introverts.
   - Extraverts tend to be happier than introverts.
   - Individuals who are high in *relationality* are, in Gladwell's terms, *connectors*, for they are more attentive to their relations with others.
3. Women seek membership in smaller, informal, intimate groups, whereas men seek membership in larger, more formal, task-focused groups, but these differences are not substantial ones.
4. The strength of social motives, such as the *need for affiliation*, the *need for intimacy*, and the *need for power* also predict one's group-joining proclivities. Schutz's *Fundamental Interpersonal Relations Orientation (FIRO)* theory explains how people use groups to satisfy their need to receive and express inclusion, control, and affection.
5. Individuals who are socially inhibited, shy, and anxious are less likely to join groups.
   - Individuals who experience *social anxiety* feel threatened in group settings.
   - Smith's analysis of group-level *attachment style* (i.e., secure, preoccupied, fearful, and dismissing) indicates that one's anxiety and avoidance pertaining to relationships influence orientation toward groups.
6. Research Moreland and Levine indicates that individuals who have had prior positive experiences in groups tend to seek out further group memberships.

*When do people seek out others?*

1. Festinger's theory of *social comparison* assumes that people seek the company of others when they find themselves in ambiguous, frightening, and difficult circumstances.
2. Schachter, when putting people into a threatening situation, found that they affiliated with others rather than remain alone ("misery loves company"). However,
   - People prefer to affiliate with individuals who likely have useful information about a situation and others who are in a similar situation ("misery loves miserable company").
   - When people worry that they will be embarrassed when they join a group, they usually do not affiliate with others ("embarrassed misery avoids company").
3. By choosing comparison targets who are performing poorly compared to themselves (*downward social comparison*), individuals bolster their own sense of competence; and by choosing superior targets (*upward social comparison*), individuals can BIRG, as well as refine their expectations of themselves.
   - Tesser's *self-evaluation maintenance (SEM) model* argues that people prefer to associate with individuals who do not outperform them in areas that are very relevant to their self-esteem.
   - Buunk's work suggests that people who have a high affiliative tendency but a low *social comparison orientation* most enjoy being in groups.

4. Groups provide their members with *social support* during times of stress and tension.
   - Group behaviors facilitate "*fight-or-flight*" responses to stress, but also the kinds of "*tend-and-befriend*" responses identified by Taylor and her colleagues.
   - Basic types of support from groups include a sense of belonging and emotional, information, instrumental, and spiritual support.
5. Groups help members avoid two basic forms of *loneliness:* social and emotional.

*What processes generate bonds of interpersonal attraction between members of groups?*

1. Newcomb, in his studies of the acquaintance process, found that people who like one another often bond together to form a group. Attraction patterns are generally consistent with the following principles:
   - *Proximity principle*: People tend to like those who are situated nearby, in part because it increases the likelihood of increased social interaction (Moreland's social integration theory).
   - *Elaboration principle*: From a systems perspective, groups often emerge when additional elements (people) become linked to the original members.
   - *Similarity principle*: People like others who are similar to them in some way. In consequence, most groups tend toward increasing levels of *homophily*.
   - *Complementarity principle*: People like others whose qualities complement their own qualities. Schutz identified two key forms of compatibility: *interchange compatibility* (based on similarity) and *originator compatibility* (based on complementarity).
   - *Reciprocity principle*: Liking tends to be mutual.
   - *Minimax principle*: Individuals are attracted to groups that offer them maximum rewards and minimal costs.
2. Thibaut and Kelley's social exchange theory maintains that satisfaction with group membership is primarily determined by *comparison level* (CL), whereas the *comparison level for alternatives* ($CL_{alt}$) determines whether members will join, stay in, or leave a group.

## FOR MORE INFORMATION

*Chapter Case: The Impressionists*

- *Collaborative Circles*, by Michael P. Farrell (2001), provides a richly detailed analysis of the impressionists and a number of other influential groups, and offers a stage theory that describes how these highly creative groups develop over time.
- *The Chronicle of Impressionism*, by B. Denvir (1993), provides the timeline for the development of the impressionists and includes reproductions of both their art and their personal correspondence.

*Affiliation*

- *The Psychology of Affiliation*, by Stanley Schachter (1959), describes the exacting scientific methods he used to document when and why people seek out others.
- *Handbook of Social Comparison: Theory and Research*, edited by Jerry Suls and Ladd Wheeler (2000), includes chapters on virtually all aspects of social comparison processes.
- "Social comparison: The end of a theory and the emergence of a field," by Abraham P. Buunk and Frederick X. Gibbons (2007), is a

masterful review of the voluminous literature dealing with comparison processes.

*Attraction*

- "The Formation of Small Groups," by Richard L. Moreland (1987), provides an overall framework for understanding group formation by describing four ways individuals become integrated into a group: environmental integration, behavioral integration, affective integration, and cognitive integration.
- *Gangs: An Individual and Group Perspective*, by Kimberly Tobin (2008), is a concise, up-to-date overview of gangs as groups.

## Media Resources

Visit the Group Dynamics companion website at www.cengage.com/psychology/forsyth to access online resources for your book, including quizzes, flash cards, web links, and more!

# 5

# Cohesion and Development

## CHAPTER OVERVIEW

Groups, like all living things, develop over time. The group may begin as a collection of strangers, but uncertainty gives way to cohesion as members become bound to their group by strong social forces. Cohesion, though, is not just group unity or the friendliness of members, but a multifaceted process that influences a wide range of interpersonal and intragroup processes. As cohesion and commitment ebb and flow with time, the group's influence over its members rises and falls.

- What is group cohesion?
- Why do some groups, but not others, become cohesive?
- How does cohesion develop over time?
- What are the positive and negative consequences of cohesion?

## CHAPTER OUTLINE

**The U.S. Olympic Hockey Team: Miracle Makers**

They were underdogs, and they knew it. Their mission: To represent their country, the United States, in the 1980 Winter Olympics. Their goal: To win a bronze, silver, or gold medal in hockey. Their task: To defeat teams from such hockey-rich countries as Sweden and Germany. Their major obstacle: The world-famous U.S.S.R. National Championship Team. The Russian players were practically professionals. They were all members of the Russian army, and they were paid to practice and play their sport. The Russian team had dominated hockey for many years, and were poised to take their fifth consecutive gold medal in the sport. When they played the U.S. team in an exhibition game held just a few days before the start of the Olympic Games, the final score was Russia 10, U.S. 3.

But strange things can happen when groups compete against groups. The U.S. team made its way through the preliminary rounds and faced the Russian team in the medal round. The U.S. team fell behind by two goals, and it looked as though the Russians would take victory with ease. But the plucky U.S. team struggled on, finally taking the lead with eight minutes left to play. During the game's last minutes, the Russians launched shot after shot, but all the while the U.S. coach, Herb Brooks, calmed his players by telling them "Play your game!" As the game's end neared, the announcer counted down the seconds into his microphone before asking his listeners, "Do you believe in miracles?" What else could explain the game's outcome? The U.S. Olympic Hockey Team, expected to win a game or two at most in the entire series, had just beaten an unbeatable team.

The U.S. team was inferior to the Russian team in nearly all respects. The U.S. players were mostly college students or recent graduates. They were smaller, slower, and less experienced. The team was relatively unpracticed, for only six months before, Herb Brooks had recruited each player from schools and jobs across the country. But for all their weaknesses, they had one quality that the Russian team lacked: They were cohesive. They were filled with a sense of purpose, of duty, and esprit de corps. No one player took credit for the victory, but instead spoke only of "we," repeating "we beat those guys" over and over as the bewildered Russian team looked on.

Many believed that the team's cohesiveness was the deciding factor in their victory. But what is group cohesion, after all? Why did the U.S. team have this unique quality, and why did the Russian team lack it? Is cohesiveness such a valuable commodity that it can offset inadequate training and skills and thereby turn a mediocre group into a great group? Is cohesiveness so wondrous that we should strive to make all our groups cohesive ones? This chapter considers the mysteries of cohesiveness by specifying its nature, development over time, and consequences.

## THE NATURE OF COHESION

Cohesion can lay claim to being group dynamics' most theoretically important concept. A uniquely group-level concept, cohesion comes about if, and only if, a group exists. Without at least some degree of cohesion, groups would disintegrate as each member withdraw from the group. Cohesiveness signals, if only indirectly, the health of the group. A cohesive group will be more likely to prosper over time, since it retains its members and allows them to reach goals that would elude a more incoherent aggregate. The group that lacks cohesion is at risk, for if too many members drift away the group may not survive.

The concept of cohesiveness, too, offers insights into some of the most intriguing questions people ask about groups: Why do some groups disintegrate in the face of adversity, whereas others grow even stronger? When do members put the needs of their group above their own personal interests? How does a group, with only meager resources, manage to best another group that is superior in terms of both experience and talent? What is the source of the feeling of confidence and unity that arises in some groups and not in others? If one understands the causes and consequences of cohesion, then one is further along in understanding a host of core processes that occur in groups, including productivity, members' satisfaction and turnover, morale, formation, stability, influence, and conflict.

## Components of Cohesion

What, precisely, is group cohesion? Intuitively, we know the difference between cohesive groups and groups that are not cohesive. Cohesive groups are unified and morale is high. Members enjoy interacting with one another, and they remain in the group for prolonged periods of time. But what about the group where all the members like one another—they are close friends—but they have no commitment to the group as a whole? The group where members no longer feel emotionally connected to one another but still feel proud of their group? The group whose members fit together like parts in a fine watch—so closely conjoined that they function as a single productive unit—yet they do not like one another? Cohesiveness takes so many different forms and fulfills so many functions that some theorists have complained that the concept, ironically, lacks cohesion (e.g., Casey-Campbell & Martens, 2008; McPherson & Smith-Lovin, 2002; Mudrack, 1989; see Table 5.1).

This diversity of meanings and interpretations reflects the complexity inherent in the concept itself. Cohesion is not a simple, unitary process but a *multi-component process* with a variety of indicators. Many cohesive groups are similar to the U.S. Hockey Team—the members worked well together, they

**TABLE 5.1 A Sampling of Definitions of Cohesion**

| Core Concept | Definition and Source |
|---|---|
| **Attraction among the members of a group** | The cohesiveness of small groups is defined in terms of intermember attraction . . . that group property which is inferred from the number and strength of mutual positive attitudes among the members of a group. (Lott & Lott, 1965, p. 259) |
| **Attraction of the members to the group as a whole** | Cohesiveness refers to attraction of members to a group as a whole . . . a kind of synthetic or aggregative property of the sum of the feelings of attraction to the group of each of the individual group members. (Nixon, 1979, p. 76) |
| | Relational cohesion [is] the sense of coming together, of something larger that unifies actors and actions. (Thye, Yoon, & Lawler, 2002, p. 146) |
| **Belonging and morale** | Perceived cohesion encompasses an individual's sense of belonging to a particular group and his or her feelings of morale associated with membership in the group. (Bollen & Hoyle, 1990, p. 482) |
| **Strength of the social forces that keep an individual from leaving a group** | Cohesiveness of a group is here deemed as the result of all the forces acting on the members to remain in the group. These forces may depend on the attractiveness or unattractiveness of either the prestige of the group, members in the group, or the activities in which the group engages. (Festinger, 1950, p. 274) |
| **Tendency to stick together (cohere)** | Social cohesion should also be understood as a state of affairs concerning how well people in a society "cohere" or "stick" to each other. (Chan, To, & Chan, 2006, p. 298) |
| | Cohesion is now generally described as group members' inclinations to forge social bonds, resulting in members sticking together and remaining united. (Casey-Campbell & Martens, 2008, p. 2) |
| **Trust and teamwork** | The essence of strong primary group cohesion, which I believe to be generally agreed on, is trust among group members (e.g., to watch each other's back) together with the capacity for teamwork (e.g., pulling together to get the task or job done). (Siebold, 2007, p. 288) |

became good friends as well as teammates, they were unified, and they played with great emotional intensity—but another cohesive group may not exhibit all of these qualities. As a result, there is no such thing as a typical cohesive group. Nor is there a single theory of cohesion that group experts agree adequately identifies the core components of cohesion. Some, for example, stress the strength of bonds between members, others highlight the group's ability to retain its members, and others emphasize the degree of emotional intensity expressed by members during the group's activities. Recognizing that our review cannot be comprehensive, the following sections examine four interrelated processes—social relations, task relations, perceived unity, and emotions—that serve as the glues that hold groups together (Dion, 2000; Friedkin, 2004; Siebold, 2007).

**Social Cohesion** Kurt Lewin and Leon Festinger and his colleagues conducted some of the earliest studies of cohesion. As early as 1943, Lewin used the term *cohesion* to describe the forces that keep groups intact by pushing members together as well as the countering forces that push them apart. Festinger and his colleagues also stressed social forces that bind individuals to groups, for in their studies they defined *group cohesion* as "the total field of forces which act on members to remain in the group" (Festinger, Schachter, & Back, 1950, p. 164). But when they measured cohesion, they focused on one force more than all others: attraction. They asked the group members to identify all their good friends and calculated the ratio of ingroup choices to outgroup choices. The greater the ratio, the greater was the cohesiveness of the group (Dion, 2000). Attraction between individuals is a basic ingredient for most groups, but when these relations intensify and proliferate throughout a group they can transform a conjoined group into a cohesive one.

Cohesion, however, is a *multi level process* as well as a multi component one, so group members may be bonded to their groups in a number of ways. At the individual level, specific group members are attracted to other group members. Many of the young men on U.S. Hockey Team, for example, were friends from their days playing together in college, and these likes created personal relations among them when they found themselves together once more on the U.S. team. At the group level, members are attracted to the group itself rather than specific individuals in the group. The players on the hockey team, for example, described their team as a "great group of guys" and were proud to be members. Moving further upward in terms of levels of association, the hockey team was just one team in the entire U.S. Olympic Team for 1980—and the members were bonded to that larger group as well as their specific team. The men were also playing for their country, and so their affective bonds not only linked them to each other, to their team, and to their organization but also to their country (Bliese & Halverson, 1996). These various levels of attraction usually covary; for example, friendship among the members of a group tends to generate liking for and pride in the group as a whole (Carless & De Paola, 2000). But forms of attraction need not go hand in hand, particularly if groups focus on work or performance rather than leisure or socializing. When cohesion is based on individual-level attraction and those who are liked leave the group, the remaining members are more likely to quit. When cohesion is based on group-level attraction, people remain members even when specific members leave the group (Ehrhart & Naumann, 2004; Mobley et al., 1979).

Some researchers prefer to reserve the term *cohesion* for group-level attraction only. Michael Hogg and his colleagues, for example, draw on social identity theory in their analysis of cohesion in large aggregates. Hogg noted that although members of cohesive groups usually like one another, this personal attraction is not group cohesion. Rather, group cohesion corresponds to a form of group-level attraction that Hogg labeled *social attraction*—a liking for other group members that is based on their status as typical group members. Unlike personal attraction, which is based on relationships between specific members, social attraction is depersonalized, since it is based on admiration for individuals who possess the kinds of qualities that typify the group. Hogg found that any factor that increases members' tendency to categorize themselves as group members (e.g., conflict with other groups, the presence of an outgroup, activities that focus members' attention on their group identity) will reduce personal attraction but increase depersonalized, social attraction. Hogg's analysis means that cohesiveness is not limited to small groups in which members know one another well but is also a feature of larger collectives and categories (see Hogg, 1992, 2001, for a review).

**Task Cohesion** Each year since 1954, the magazine *Sports Illustrated* has identified one individual from the world of sports for the honor of "Athlete of the Year"—but not in 1980. That year, the Athlete of the Year was a group: the U.S. Hockey Team. The U.S. Women's World Cup Soccer Team was similarly honored in 1999.

Many theorists believe that cohesion has more to do with members' willingness to work together to accomplish their objectives than it does with positive interpersonal relations. Studies of sports teams, for example, find that most players, when asked to describe their team's cohesiveness, stress the quality of their **teamwork** (Carron, 1982; Yukelson, Weinberg, & Jackson, 1984). Task-oriented groups, such as military squads or flight crews, are unified by members' shared drive to accomplish their goals (Siebold, 2007). Much of the unity of the U.S. Hockey Team was based on the members' commitment to their sport and their quest for a gold medal.

A group whose cohesiveness is generated by a shared task focus tends to be high in **collective efficacy**. Unlike general optimism or overall confidence in the group, collective efficacy derives from group members' shared beliefs that they can accomplish all the components of their group's task competently and efficiently. Group members may think, "We are a powerful, successful hockey team," but this overall conception of the group is not collective efficacy. Members of a group with collective efficacy think, "We are fast on the ice," "We can block effectively," and "We have an excellent transition game." These beliefs must also be widely shared by group members. One or two members may doubt the group's potential for success, but overall, the consensus is positive rather than negative. This confidence is also based on the members' belief that the group members will competently coordinate their individual actions in skilled, collective performance, so there is a sense of interdependence and shared resources (Zaccaro et al., 1995). Hence, collective efficacy is "a group's shared belief in its conjoint capabilities to organize and execute the courses of action required to produce given levels of attainment" (Bandura, 1997, p. 476).

**Perceived Cohesion** Cohesion applies to both physical objects as well as social groups. A cohesive object, such as a molecule, a compound, or even a planet, forms a single, unified entity that resists disintegration. It may not, in fact, appear to have any parts at all, as the various components are unified in a single whole. Similarly, cohesive groups are perceived to be highly unified and integrated—individuals fused together to form a whole. At the group level, members and nonmembers alike consider the group to be high in *entitativity*: those who encounter the group will be convinced that it is a unified, tightly bonded group rather than a loose aggregation of individuals (see Chapter 1). At the individual level, members express a sense of belonging to the group by stressing their commitment to the group; they are loyal to the group, identify with the group, and readily classify themselves as members.

Group members often reveal their perceptions of their group's unity in the words that they use to describe their connection to it. When asked, they agree that there is a "a feeling of unity and cohesion in this group" (Moos, Insel, & Humphrey, 1974); that members tend to spend much of their time

---

**teamwork** The combined activities of two or more individuals who coordinate their efforts to make or do something. In many cases, each individual performs a portion of the task, which, when combined with others' work, yields a total group product.

**collective efficacy** The belief, shared among a substantial portion of the group members, that the group is capable of organizing and executing the actions required to attain the group's goals and successfully complete its tasks.

together, even when they do not need to (Chang & Bordia, 2001). When members talk about themselves and their group, they use more plural pronouns than personal pronouns: "We won that game" or "We got the job done" rather than "I got the job done" (Cialdini et al., 1976). They use words like *family*, *community*, or just *we* to describe their group. They may also refuse to differentiate among the members of the group, as when one member refuses to take responsibility for the victory or win and insists that the team as a whole deserves the credit. Members, when asked to comment directly on their sense of belonging to the group, are more likely to say "I feel a sense of belonging to my group" (Bollen & Hoyle, 1990), "I think of this group as a part of who I am" (Henry, Arrow, & Carini, 1999), and "I see myself as a member of the group" (Smith, Seger, & Mackie, 2007).

Was the U.S. Hockey Team cohesive in this sense? Not at first, for many of the players had competed against each other in college, and they remembered their bitter rivalries. But the team coach, Herb Brooks, required each player to pass a series of difficult psychological and physical challenges before earning a spot on the team, and these qualifying trials created a sense of shared adversity. Brooks also stressed the importance of team unity. His goal was to "build a 'we' and 'us' in ourselves as opposed to an 'I,' 'me,' 'myself'" (Warner HBO, 2001). This unity reached its peak in the medal ceremonies after the U.S. team had won its gold medal. Team captain Eruzione waved to the team to join him on the small stage, and somehow the entire team crowded onto the small platform. The captain did not represent the group. The entire group, as a whole, received the medal.

**Emotional Cohesion** Napoleon is said to have proclaimed that the great strength of an army lies not in the skill of its leaders, but in the élan—the emotional intensity—of its members. Durkheim, in discussing the nature of ritualized interactions in cohesive groups, stressed how they develop intense emotional experiences, for when all "come together, a sort of electricity is formed by their collecting which quickly transports them to an extraordinary degree of exaltation" (1912/1965, p. 262). Durkheim was describing the large gatherings of local communities in New Guinea, but he believed that *collective effervescence* resulted from the sharing of emotional reactions within a group. As the positive and elevated mood of one person is picked up by the next, the group members eventually display a shared emotional experience (see Focus 5.1).

A variety of terms is used to describe group-level emotional states, including élan, morale, esprit de corps, and positive affective tone, but no matter what its label, this shared positive emotion is one of the most obvious features of many cohesive groups. The Russian and U.S. teams were equal in confidence and collective efficacy, for both groups had the talent needed to win at hockey. But they differed dramatically in their level of emotionality. The Russian team was confident but unenthusiastic. The U.S. team was not so confident, but the team was brimming with energy, enthusiasm, and team spirit. A group with high levels of collective efficacy may expect to succeed, but a group with esprit de corps has emotional vitality, passion, vim, and vigor. **Esprit de corps**, or *positive affective tone*, predicts a number of positive behaviors in the group, including helping teammates, protecting the organization, making constructive suggestions, improving one's personal performance, spreading goodwill, and even enhancing survival (Spoor & Kelly, 2004; Zhou & George, 2001). It was this emotionality that Coach Brooks whipped up to its peak intensity before the U.S. team's game with the Russians. He told them that the Russians were taking their victory for granted, but "we can beat them." He told his team, "you were born to be a player," you were "destined to be here today," and this is "our time." When he told them to "spit in the eye of the tiger," they did.

Emotional cohesion, like the other components of cohesion, is a multi level process. Emotions, although traditionally thought to be personal reactions rather an interpersonal ones, can be collective. In

---

**esprit de corps** A feeling of unity, commitment, confidence, and enthusiasm for the group shared by most or all of the members.

**Focus 5.1 Does Collective Movement Build Cohesion?**

*Drill, dance, and battle belong together. All three create and sustain group cohesion.*

—William McNeill, *Keeping Together in Time* (1995, p. 10).

Some rituals and practices, such as collective singing, chanting, praying, and marching, result in the development of a shared emotional elevation among group members. Historian William McNeill (1995), in his book *Keeping Together in Time*, describes this feeling by drawing on his personal experience as a new recruit during basic training in the U.S. Army.

> Marching aimlessly about on the drill field, swaggering in conformity with prescribed military postures, conscious only of keeping in step so as to make the next move correctly and in time somehow felt good. Words are inadequate to describe the emotion aroused by the prolonged movement in unison that drilling involved. A sense of pervasive well-being is what I recalled; more specifically, a strange sense of personal enlargement; a sort of swelling out, becoming bigger than life, thanks to participation in collective ritual (p. 2).

McNeill suggests that much of the history of modern forms of warfare can be traced to the cohesion-building effects of close-group training. His collective-movement hypothesis offers, for example, a solution to one of military history's great mysteries: How did the Greek forces of Athens and Sparta, in the period from 600 B.C. to 300 B.C., manage to overwhelm vastly superior forces? McNeill's proposal: The Greeks relied on highly cohesive groups of ground forces that moved forward as a synchronized unit. This formation is known as a *phalanx*, from the Greek word for fingers. These units varied in size, but were typically at least eight rows deep and stretched wide enough across a field of battle to prevent flanking. In some cases, each man's shield was designed so that it covered the soldier beside him as well, thereby further increasing the unity of the group. The men of these phalanxes trained together over long periods of time, and they became synchronized to the point that they acted as a single unit that could inflict great damage against even the best-trained individual soldiers. These phalanxes eventually gave way to other means of organizing men in battle, given their vulnerability to cavalry and more maneuverable adversaries.

some cases, individuals experience emotions even if they personally have not experienced the emotion-provoking event (e.g., all the members become angry when they learn one of their own has been mistreated). Collective emotions are also socially shared, in the sense that all the group members experience the same emotional reaction, as if they had reached consensus on the feelings they should be experiencing. These group-level emotions also become more intense when individuals strongly identify with their group—although this tendency is stronger for positive emotions than for negative ones (Smith, Seger, & Mackie, 2007).

## Antecedents of Cohesion

Table 5.2 suggests that the strength of the bonds linking members to one another and their group depends on a number of components, including attraction relations (social cohesion), the degree to which the group members coordinate their efforts to achieve goals (task cohesion), the sense of belonging and unity in group (perceived cohesion), and the intensity of the members' communal emotions (emotional cohesion). These qualities, in part, define the nature of cohesion, but they also suggest the antecedents of cohesiveness as well. Consider social cohesion, as an example. Because one of the key components of cohesion is degree of attraction among members, any variable that influences liking among the members will contribute to the development of cohesion within a group, and any factor that discourages the development of attraction will limit cohesion. In this section we review, briefly, some of the factors that set the stage for the emergence of cohesion in groups, with the caveat that our review is more illustrative than comprehensive.

**Interpersonal Attraction** As Chapter 4 explained, groups often form when individuals develop feelings of attraction for one another. But just as such factors as proximity, frequency of interaction,

**TABLE 5.2 A Multicomponent Conception of Cohesion in Groups**

| Component | Description | Examples |
|---|---|---|
| **Social cohesion** | Attraction of members to one another and to the group as a whole | I have many friends in this group.<br>I love this group.<br>This group is the best. |
| **Task cohesion** | Capacity to perform successfully as a coordinated unit and as part of the group | This group is effective.<br>This group is the best at what it does.<br>I do my best for this group. |
| **Perceived cohesion** | The construed coherence of the group; sense of belonging to the group; unity | United we stand.<br>This is a unified group.<br>I am one with this group. |
| **Emotional cohesion** | Emotional intensity of the group and individuals when in the group | This group has tremendous energy.<br>This group has team spirit.<br>I get excited just being in this group. |

similarity, complementarity, reciprocity, and rewarding exchanges can prompt a group to form, so too can they turn the rudimentary group into a highly cohesive one (Lott & Lott, 1965).

Muzafer and Carolyn Sherif documented many of these processes and their impact on cohesiveness in a series of unique field studies conducted in 1949, 1953, and 1954. During the summers of those years the Sherifs would run a camp for 11- and 12-year-old boys that was, for the most part, just a typical summer camp experience—with canoeing, campfires, crafts, hikes, athletics, and so on. But, unbeknownst to the campers, the Sherifs also recorded the behavior of the boys as they reacted to one another and to situations introduced by the investigators. In the 1949 study, conducted in a remote location in northern Connecticut, the 24 campers all bunked in one cabin for three days. During this period, friendships developed quickly based on proximity of bunks, similarities in interests, and maturity. The Sherifs then intervened, and broke the large group into two smaller ones: the Bulldogs and the Red Devils. In creating these groups they deliberately split up any friendship pairs that had formed by assigning one best friend to the Bulldogs and the other to the Red Devils. They equated the members with respect to "size, strength, ability in games, intelligence, and ratings on personality tests" (Sherif & Sherif, 1956, p. 197).

Even under these conditions—with the factors that produced attraction between the boys minimized—new attractions formed quickly and resulted in high levels of cohesion within both groups. The Sherifs made certain that the boys' first few days in their new groups were spent in a variety of positive experiences (hiking, cookouts, games), and before long the boys, when asked to name their friends, chose members of their new groups rather than the boys that they had liked when camp first began. When first split up, 65% of the boys picked as friends those in the other group. But when the groups became cohesive, fewer than 10% named boys as friends who were in the other group. Another of the Sherifs' studies, the well-known Robbers Cave experiment, which is discussed in more detail in Chapter 14's analysis of conflict between groups, yielded similar findings.

**Stability of Membership** During an exhibition game just prior to the Olympics, defensive player Jack O'Callahan was so badly injured that he could not play in the tournament. But rather than send him home and replace him with a new player, Coach Brooks kept him on the roster—he did not want to alter the chemistry of the team he had been developing for so long.

As Brooks surmised, cohesiveness tends to increase the longer members remain in the group. Consider, for example, the findings from a year-long study of 138 women living in one of 13 apartment-like dormitories at the University of Minnesota. These dorms were relatively small—the largest housed only 16 women—but they nonetheless varied substantially in membership stability. In some dorms as many as 90% of the students were new residents, but in others residents were returning for a second or third year in the same dorm. The dorms varied, too, in turnover during the year itself, with some seeing more students move out to take up residence elsewhere. As expected, the more stable dorms were also the more cohesive ones. These dorms often had a core of faithful members, and each year new members would enter into the group to replace those who graduated. The members usually remained in their group for the entire year, and were not lured away by some other living arrangement. Those groups with more unstable membership faced influxes of new members each year and during the year itself (Darley, Gross, & Martin, 1951).

These findings are consistent with Robert Ziller's (1965) distinction between **open groups** and **closed groups**. Ziller maintained that groups differ in the extent to which their boundaries and membership rosters are open and fluctuating versus closed and fixed. In open groups, members are voted out of the group, quit the group for personal reasons, or join other groups. Regardless of the reasons for these changes in membership, open groups are especially unlikely to reach a state of equilibrium, since members recognize that they may lose or relinquish their place within the group at any time. In contrast, closed groups are often more cohesive, because competition for membership is irrelevant and group members anticipate future collaborations. Thus, in closed groups, individuals tend to focus on the collective nature of the group and are more likely to identify with their group as they work together to accomplish a collective goal. Ziller's theory suggests that open groups, by their very nature, are less cohesive (Burnette & Forsyth, 2008).

**Group Size** The dorms in the Minnesota study were all relatively small, ranging in size from 7 to 16 women, but the smaller dorms tended to be more cohesive nonetheless. They had member turnover at the end of each year when residents graduated from college, but they had less turnover during the academic year, confirming other research that finds smaller groups tend to be more unified than larger ones. Studies of classes, for example, find that students learn more in small classes, in part because these groups are higher in social engagement as well as academic engagement (Finn, Pannozzo, & Achilles, 2003). Investigations of neighborhoods indicate that size determines sense of community (Vela-McConnell, 1999). As groups increase in size, a larger proportion of the members no longer takes part in all the group activities (Bales & Borgatta, 1955). In small juries, for example, most jurors take part in the discussions, but in larger juries deliberation is dominated by a small subset of members.

The impact of group size on cohesion is, in part, a consequence of the sheer number of interpersonal demands that larger networks make of their members. As a group increases in size the number of possible relations among individuals increases so rapidly that members can no longer maintain strong, positive ties with all group members. In a five-person group, for example, only 10 ties are needed to join every single member to every other member. But, if the group is relatively large—say, 20 members—then 190 relationships would be needed to create a completely connected group. Maintaining such relationships becomes burdensome as groups increase in size, and in consequence "the common features that fuse its members into a social unit become ever

---

**open group** A group whose boundaries are so permeable that membership varies considerably as members enter and leave the group.

**closed group** A group whose boundaries are closed and fixed; as a result, membership is relatively unvarying.

fewer . . . . The variety of persons, interests, events becomes too large to be regulated by the center" (Simmel, 1950, pp. 397–398).

**Structural Features** Cohesion is related to group structure in two basic ways. First, cohesive groups tend to be relatively more structured ones. The U.S. Hockey Team, for example, was a well-structured one in that each player had a position on the ice that he played; off the ice each individual was joined in specific ways to others; the group had a leader, whose authority was well-established; and the group had clear rules about how it operated and what kinds of behaviors were acceptable. As groups become more and more structured—in the socially organized sense rather than the bureaucratic sense—they tend to become more cohesive as well.

Second, certain types of group structures are associated with higher levels of cohesion than are others. The members of one group, for example, may be linked primarily to other group members, rather than to outsiders. If asked to name their best friends, the people they respect, or those they communicate with most frequently, they identify other group members. The members of another group, in contrast, may name people outside of the group when asked these questions. The higher the proportion of ties to nongroup members relative to ties to group members, the lower the overall cohesiveness of the group (McPherson & Smith-Loving, 2002).

The patterning of relations within the group itself may also be more or less conducive for the development of cohesion. When the U.S. Hockey Team began practicing, for example, a number of subgroups, or cliques, formed within the group as a whole. Some of the young men had played for Boston University whereas others were from the Midwest—many had graduated from Minnesota. These two cliques created a schism within the group, and tensions between the groups sometimes surfaced during practices. Coach Brooks broke these cliques down in various ways, reaching success when the men stopped referring to their colleges in their self-descriptions (e.g., "I played for Minnesota") and instead shifted to a team-based identity (e.g., "I am a U.S. hockey player").

Other structural patterns, besides cliques, that influence cohesion include the centrality, density, and the number of isolates within the group. Both of the groups studied by the Sherif and Sherif (1953, 1956), for example, included 12 young boys, but different structures developed within the two groups. As Figure 5.1 indicates, the Red Devils team was more stratified than the Bulldogs. When the boys were asked to name as many as 5 friends at the camp, 9 of the 12 Bulldogs named each other in a tightly knit pattern of reciprocal and overlapping choices. The remaining 3 individuals received no friendship nominations, but they picked others who were part of the main cluster as friends and were not rejected. In the Red Devils, liking was more concentrated: the two most-liked individuals in the group garnered 50% of all friendship choices. The Red Devils also included several cliques, as well as one member who was rejected by the other group members. The Red Devils lost the tournament between the two groups.

**Initiations** Many groups require prospective members to pass an initiation test before they join the group. Initiates in biker gangs, for example, must earn the right to wear the letters and emblems of their gang—their "colors"—by performing a variety of distasteful behaviors (Davis, 1982). Pledges to fraternities at some universities are ritually beaten, subjected to ridicule and embarrassment, and required to drink unhealthy amounts of alcohol (Nuwer, 1999). Sports teams often test new players in various ways, both physically and mentally, as do military units. Many religious groups require new members to pass through a period of review before they gain acceptance as full members.

Initiations—formal and informal requirements that must be met before an individual can gain membership in a group—contribute to a group's cohesion by strengthening the bond between the individual and the group. Groups with initiation policies may also be more attractive to members, since their exclusiveness may make them seem more prestigious. Since membership must be earned, people who join do so more intentionally, and therefore will more likely be active,

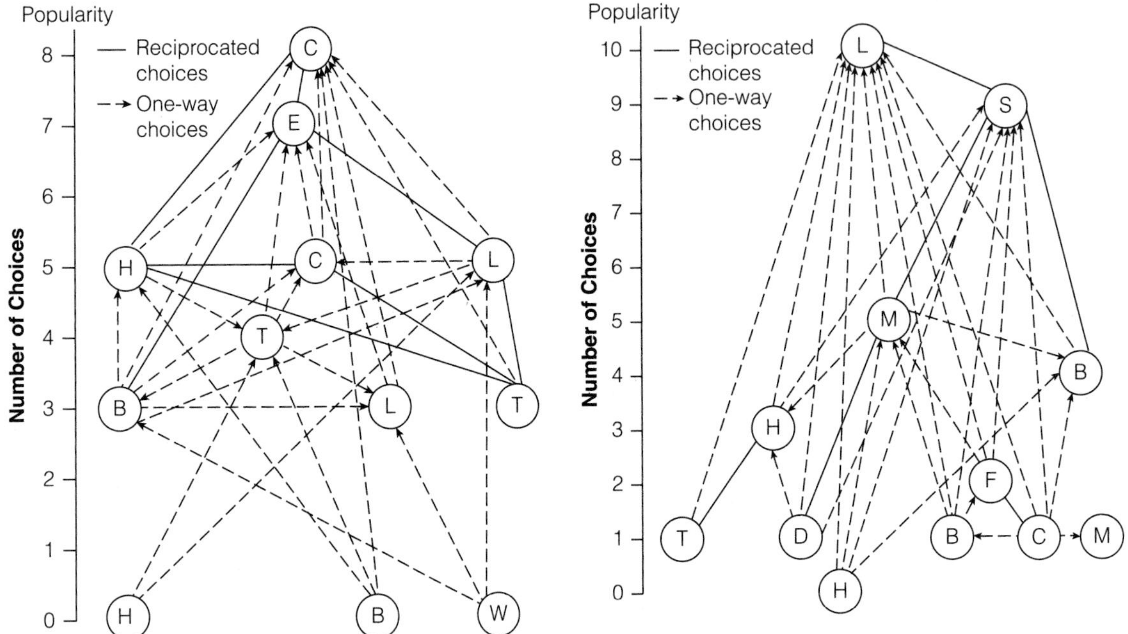


**FIGURE 5.1** The attraction relations among the Bulldogs (on the left) and the Red Devils (on the right), as documented by Sherif and Sherif (1956) in their field studies of group processes.

contributing members. Groups with less stringent requirements are hampered by the unevenness of the contributions of members: some may contribute a great deal to the group, but others may actually draw out more resources than they contribute. Groups with strict membership policies, including initiations, avoid this problem by screening and monitoring members closely and dismissing those individuals who do not demonstrate their worth (Iannaccone, 1994).

People who join emotionally involving groups such as fraternities, social movements, or cults may also become more committed to the group as a result of **cognitive dissonance**. This psychological process, first proposed by Leon Festinger (1957), suggests that initiations force the prospective members to invest in the group, and that these investments will increase

---

**cognitive dissonance** An adverse psychological state that occurs when an individual simultaneously holds two conflicting cognitions.

their commitment. Because the two cognitions, "I have invested in the group" and "The group is loathsome" are dissonant, these beliefs cause the members psychological discomfort. Although people can reduce cognitive dissonance in many ways, one frequent method is to emphasize the rewarding features of the group while minimizing its costly characteristics.

Festinger and his colleagues (1956) investigated this process in their study of an atypical group that formed around a psychic, Marion Keech. Keech convinced her followers that the world was coming to an end, but that the inhabitants of a planet named Clarion would rescue the group before the apocalypse. Many members of the group committed all their personal resources to the group or gave away their possessions in the weeks before the scheduled departure from the planet. Yet the group did not disband even when the rescuers never arrived. Keech claimed that the dedication of the group had so impressed God that the Earth had been spared, and many of the members responded by becoming even more committed to their group. Membership was costly, but each investment tied them more strongly to the group.

Other researchers have tested the impact of costs and commitment using more traditional research procedures (Aronson & Mills, 1959; Axsom, 1989; Gerard & Mathewson, 1966). Elliot Aronson and Judson Mills, for example, manipulated the investments that individuals made before joining a group discussing topics related to sexual behavior. They randomly assigned female college students to one of three experimental conditions: a severe initiation condition, a mild initiation condition, and a control condition. Participants assigned to the *severe initiation* condition had to read aloud to the male experimenter a series of obscene words and two "vivid descriptions of sexual activity from contemporary novels." In the *mild initiation* condition, participants read five sex-related but nonobscene words. In the *control* condition, participants were not put through any kind of initiation whatsoever.

After the initiation the researchers told the women that the group they would be joining was already meeting, but that they could listen in using an intercom system. But instead of listening to an actual group, the researchers played a recording of a discussion that was contrived deliberately to be exceedingly boring and dull. After listening for a time the participants rated the group they had listened to on a number of dimensions. As predicted, women who experienced the severe initiation rated the group more positively than those who had experienced a mild initiation or no initiation at all.

Aronson and Mills concluded that the initiation increased cohesion by creating cognitive dissonance; but other factors may also account for the initiation–cohesion relationship. Individuals may find strict, demanding groups attractive because the group's stringent standards ensure that other members will be highly involved in the group, so all members will likely contribute equally and at high rates to the group (Iannaccone, 1994). Their public expressions of liking for such groups may also stem more from a desire to save face after making a faulty decision than from the psychic discomfort of cognitive dissonance (Schlenker, 1975). Initiations also fail to heighten attraction if they frustrate new members or make them angry (Lodewijkx & Syroit, 1997). As Focus 5.2 explains, extreme initiations may harm new members rather than binding them to the group.

### Indicators of Cohesion

Cohesion is the strength of the bonds linking individuals to and in the group, but a variety of factors influence the group's social, task, perceptual, and emotional unity. These components have multiple causes, and they also cut across levels of analysis, with some pertaining to relations among individuals and others connecting individuals to the group itself. Given the complexity of this process, what unifies the members of a work group may not unify the members of a religious congregation, a classroom, or a military squad (Ridgeway, 1983).

Just as theorists have debated the precise meaning of the concept of cohesiveness, so have researchers proposed a variety methods for measuring cohesion. Some researchers use social network methods, indexing the unity of a group by considering sociometric choices and group structure. Others rely on observational strategies, monitoring interpersonal relations among members, noting instances of conflict or tension, and judging how smoothly the group works together as a unit (e.g., Fine & Holyfield, 1996). In many cases, too, investigators hope that group members are accurate observers of their group's cohesiveness and, if asked, will share these perceptions. Investigators have used a variety of questions to tap into cohesion, including, "Do you want to remain a member of this group?" and "How strong a sense of belonging do you feel you have to the people you work with?" (Schachter, 1951; Indik, 1965, respectively). Researchers also use multi-item scales that include many questions that can be combined to yield a single index of cohesiveness, such as the *Group Environment Scale* (Moos et al., 1974), *Group Attitude Scale* (Evans & Jarvis, 1986), *Group Environment Questionnaire* (Widmeyer, Brawley, & Carron, 1992), *Perceived Cohesion Scale* (Bollen & Hoyle, 1990), *Group Identification Scale* (Henry et al., 1999), *Sports Cohesiveness Questionnaire* (Martens, Landers, & Loy, 1972), *Gross Cohesion Questionnaire* (Stokes, 1983),

## Focus 5.2 Why Do Groups Haze Their Members?

*You don't understand that everything we have done has a meaning and a purpose . . . . When you are sisters, you will understand.*

—Sorority member to a pledge class (in Nuwer, 1999, p. 147)

Most groups have banned severe initiations, known as **hazing**, yet this practice continues unofficially. Some mild rites and rituals—as when new members must take a public oath of loyalty, endure teasing, or carry a distinctive object about—cause little harm, but in other cases, new members must endure physical and psychological abuse before they are accepted into the group. Many university fraternities, for example, haze new members because they believe that hazing has many positive benefits, including building group unity, instilling humility in new members, and perpetuating group traditions (Nuwer, 1999). Each year, however, many students are killed or seriously injured in hazing incidents (Goldstein, 2002).

Many members of groups defend their right to haze, citing the benefits of initiation for increasing the cohesion of the group. However, research does not offer very much support for this position. One team of investigators asked the members of a number of groups and teams to differentiate between appropriate and inappropriate activities on a list of 24 practices commonly used in initiations and hazing. Appropriate activities included requirements to take part in group activities, swearing an oath, taking part in skits and team functions, doing community service, and maintaining a specific grade point average. Inappropriate activities, in contrast, included kidnapping and abandonment, verbal abuse, physical punishment (spankings, whippings, and beatings), degradation and humiliation (such as eating disgusting things or drinking alcohol in excessive amounts), sleep deprivation, running errands, and exclusion. Somewhat unexpectedly, a number of the behaviors that the researchers felt belonged on the list of inappropriate hazing behaviors, such as wearing inappropriate clothing, head shaving, and sexual activities, were viewed as relatively innocuous by participants (Van Raatle et al., 2007).

Did these experiences work to build a cohesive group? Some of these practices were rarely used by groups, but groups that did use inappropriate hazing methods were judged to be less cohesive rather than more cohesive. Hazing, and illicit hazing in particular, backfired, for it did not contribute to increased cohesion, whereas more positive forms of team-building did (Van Raatle et al., 2007). Given that hazing is illegal in a number of states, is aggressive in character, yields unhealthy consequences, and does not even work to increase cohesion, groups should consider other methods to increase new members' commitment to the group and the group's overall cohesiveness.

the *Group Cohesion Scale-Revised* (Treadwell et al., 2001), and the *Questionnaire sur l'Ambiance du Groupe* (Buton et al., 2007).

Cohesion, as a multilevel concept, can also be measured at multiple levels. Those who consider cohesion to be a psychological quality that is rooted in members' feelings of attraction for others, the group, and a sense of unity measure cohesion at the individual level. They might ask members of a group to only describe their own attraction to and commitment to the group through such questions as, "Are you attracted to the group?" or "Do you feel a strong sense of belonging to the group?" Other researchers, in contrast, may feel that only a group can be cohesive, and so cohesion should be located at the group level (Mason & Griffin, 2002). These investigators may ask group members to estimate the group's cohesion directly through such questions as, "Are members attracted to this group?" and "Is this group a cohesive one?" They might also decide to have the group answer these types of questions as a group (see Paskevich et al., 1999).

This plethora of operational definitions can create challenges for researchers. When they measure cohesiveness in different ways, they often report different conclusions. A study using a self-report measure of cohesion might find that cohesive groups outproduce groups that are not cohesive, but other investigators may not replicate this finding when they use observational measurement

**hazing** An initiation into a group that subjects the new member to mental or physical discomfort, harassment, embarrassment, ridicule, or humiliation.

methods (Mullen et al., 1994). Moreover, some operational definitions of cohesion may correspond more closely to the theoretical definition than others. A measure that focuses only on group members' perceptions of their group's cohesiveness, for example, may be assessing something very different than a measure that focuses on the actual strength of the relationships linking individuals to their group.

## COHESION AND COMMITMENT OVER TIME

The U.S. Olympic Hockey Team that faced the Russian team in February of 1980 was, without question, cohesive. The team was extraordinarily unified—most of the members liked one another, and they worked diligently to achieve their goals. But the group did not become cohesive all at once. When Coach Brooks first invited the best amateur hockey players to a training camp in Colorado Springs in July 1979, the players showed few signs of camaraderie, fellowship, or cohesion. Coach Brooks was tough on them; many had played against one another in college and still held grudges, and some were so temperamental that no one would befriend them. But the hockey team changed over time. Initial uncertainties gave way to stable patterns of interaction; tensions between members waned; many players were cut from the team and replaced by new ones; and members abandoned old roles to take on new ones. Over time, the team grew from a collection of talented individuals into a cohesive team.

The U.S. Hockey Team's evolution over time followed a predictable course. Few groups become cohesive, efficient teams from the moment their members first meet. Instead, they experience *group development*—a pattern of growth and change beginning with initial formation and ending, in most cases, with dissolution.

### Stages of Group Development

The group dynamicist William Fawcett Hill was at one time so intrigued by developmental processes in groups that he diligently filed away each theory that he found on that subject. Over the years, his collection grew and grew, until finally the number of theories reached 100. At that moment, Hill noted, the "collecting bug was exterminated, as the object of the quest had lost its rarity" (Hill & Gruner, 1973, p. 355; see also Hare, 1982; Lacoursiere, 1980).

The morass of theoretical models dealing with group development, though daunting, is not altogether irremediable. Theoreticians are at variance on many points, but most agree that groups pass through several phases, or *stages*, as they develop. Just as humans mature from infancy to childhood, adolescence, adulthood, and old age, stage models of group development theorize that groups move from one stage to the next in a predictable, sequential fashion. The U.S. Hockey Team, for example, became unified, but only after progressing through earlier stages marked by confusion, conflict, and growing group structure.

What stages typify the developmental progression of groups? The number and names of the stages vary among theorists. Many models, however, highlight certain interpersonal outcomes that must be achieved in any group that exists for a prolonged period. Members of most groups must, for example, discover who the other members are, achieve a degree of interdependence, and deal with conflict (Hare, 1982; Lacoursiere, 1980; Wheelan, 1994). Therefore, most models include the basic stages shown in Table 5.3 and illustrated earlier in Chapter 1's Figure 1.4. First, the group members must become oriented toward one another. Second, they often find themselves in conflict, and some solution is sought to improve the group environment. In the third phase, norms and roles develop that regulate behavior, and the group achieves greater unity. In the fourth phase, the group can perform as a unit to achieve desired goals. The final stage ends the sequence of development with the group's adjournment. Bruce Tuckman (Tuckman, 1965; Tuckman & Jensen, 1977) labeled these five stages *forming* (orientation), *storming* (conflict), *norming* (structure development), *performing* (work), and *adjourning* (dissolution).

**TABLE 5.3 Stages of Group Development**

| Stage | Major Processes | Characteristics |
|---|---|---|
| Orientation: *Forming* | Members become familiar with each other and the group; dependency and inclusion issues; acceptance of leader and group consensus | Communications are tentative, polite; concern for ambiguity, group's goals; leader is active; members are compliant |
| Conflict: *Storming* | Disagreement over procedures; expression of dissatisfaction; tension among members; antagonism toward leader | Criticism of ideas; poor attendance; hostility; polarization and coalition formation |
| Structure: *Norming* | Growth of cohesiveness and unity; establishment of roles, standards, and relationships; increased trust, communication | Agreement on procedures; reduction in role ambiguity; increased "we-feeling" |
| Work: *Performing* | Goal achievement; high task-orientation; emphasis on performance and production | Decision making; problem solving; mutual cooperation |
| Dissolution: *Adjourning* | Termination of roles; completion of tasks; reduction of dependency | Disintegration and withdrawal; increased independence and emotionality; regret |

**Forming: The Orientation Stage** The first few minutes, hours, days, or even weeks of a newly formed group's life are often marked by tension, guarded interchanges, and relatively low levels of interaction. During this initial *forming stage*, members monitor their behavior to avoid any embarrassing lapses of social poise and are tentative when expressing their personal opinions. Because the group's structure has not had time to develop, the members are often uncertain about their role in the group, what they should be doing to help the group reach its goals, or even who is leading the group.

With time, tension is dispelled as the ice is broken and group members become better acquainted. After the initial inhibitions subside, group members typically begin exchanging information about themselves and their goals. To better understand and relate to the group, individual members gather information about their leaders' and comembers' personality characteristics, interests, and attitudes. In most cases, too, members recognize that the others in the group are forming an impression of each other, and so they facilitate this process by revealing some private, personal information during conversations and Internet-based exchanges. This gradual, and in some cases tactical, communication of personal information is termed *self-disclosure*, and it serves the important function of helping members to get to know one another (Jourard, 1971). Eventually, the group members feel familiar enough with one another that their interactions become more open and spontaneous.

**Storming: The Conflict Stage** As the relatively mild tension caused by the newness of a group wanes, tension over goals, procedures, and authority often waxes. On the U.S. Hockey Team, for example, the players from the schools in the eastern part of the United States often excluded the players from the Midwest. Several players were considered hotshots more interested in their personal performance than in team success. And nearly all the players rebelled against the hard-driving coaching style of Herb Brooks. He would yell, insult, swear, and curse the players whenever they failed to perform up to his standards, and he often threatened to cut players from the team.

The *storming stage* is marked by personal conflicts between individual members who discover that they just do not get along, procedural conflict over the group's goals and procedures, and competition between individual members for authority, leadership, and more prestigious roles. In groups that have an official leader, like the U.S. Hockey

Team, the conflict often centers on relationships between the leader and the rest of the group. In the orientation stage, members accept the leader's guidance with few questions, but as the group matures, leader–member conflicts disrupt the group's functioning. Members may oscillate between fight and flight. Some may openly challenge the leader's policies and decisions (*fight*), whereas others may respond by minimizing contact with the leader (*flight*). In groups that have no formally appointed leader, conflicts erupt as members vie for status and roles within the group. Once stable patterns of authority, attraction, and communication have developed, conflicts subside, but until then, group members jockey for authority and power (Bennis & Shepard, 1956; Wheelan & McKeage, 1993).

Many group members are discouraged by this outbreak of conflict in their young groups, but conflict is as common as harmony in groups. As Chapter 13's analysis of the roots of conflict suggests, the dynamic nature of the group ensures continual change, but along with this change come stresses and strains that surface in the form of conflict. In rare instances, group members may avoid all conflict because their actions are perfectly coordinated; but in most groups, the push and pull of interpersonal forces inevitably exerts its influence. Low levels of conflict in a group can be an indication of remarkably positive interpersonal relations, but it is more likely that the group members are simply uninvolved, unmotivated, and bored (Fisher, 1980).

Conflict is not just unavoidable, however; it may be a key ingredient for creating group cohesion. If conflict escalates out of control, it can destroy a group. But in some cases, conflict settles matters of structure, direction, and performance expectations. Members of cohesive groups must understand one another's perspectives, and such understanding sometimes deepens when hostility has surfaced, been confronted, and been resolved (Bennis & Shepard, 1956; Deutsch, 1969). Conflicts may "serve to 'sew the social system together' by canceling each other out, thus preventing disintegration along one primary line of cleavage" (Coser, 1956, p. 801). However, as Chapter 13's analysis of conflict concludes, mild conflict over issues that are relevant to the group's task might improve performance, but other types of conflict likely cause more loss than gain (De Dreu & Weingart, 2003). Most groups that survive resolve conflicts quickly, before the disagreement causes permanent damage to members' relationships.

**Norming: The Structure Stage** With each crisis overcome, the U.S. Hockey Team became more stable, more organized, and more cohesive. Eruzione emerged as the group's leader and was selected to be captain. The players revised their initial impressions of each other and reached more benevolent conclusions about their teammates. The players still complained about the team rules, the practice schedules, and the coach's constant criticisms, but they became fiercely loyal to the team, their teammates, and their coach.

Groups in the third stage of group development, the *norming stage*, become both unified and organized. Whereas groups in the orientation and conflict stages are characterized by low levels of intimacy, friendship, and unity, the group becomes a unified whole when it reaches the structure-development stage. Mutual trust and support increase, members cooperate more with each other, and members try to reach decisions through consensus. The group becomes cohesive (Wheelan, 1994).

As the group becomes more organized it resolves the problems that caused earlier conflicts—uncertainty about goals, roles, and authority—and prepares to get down to the work at hand. Norms—those taken-for-granted rules that dictate how members should behave—emerge more clearly and guide the group members as they interact with one another. Differences of opinion still arise, but now they are dealt with through constructive discussion and negotiation. Members communicate openly with one another about personal and group concerns, in part because members know one another better. On the U.S. Hockey Team, the players did not always agree with the coach, but they changed the way they dealt with disagreement. Instead of grumbling about their treatment, several players started compiling a book of *Brooksisms*—the odd expressions Coach Brooks used during practice to motivate his players. Nearly every player, interviewed 20 years after they played for

Brooks, remembered such Brooksisms as "You are playing worse every day and now you are playing like the middle of next week" and "Gentlemen, you don't have enough talent to win on talent alone."

**Performing: The Work Stage** The U.S. Hockey Team played 41 games against other teams in preparation for the Olympics and won 30 of those matches. They reached their peak of performance when they beat the Russian team to qualify for the final, gold-medal game against Finland. Before that game, Coach Brooks did not give them a pep talk, as he had before the Russian game. Instead, he only said, "You lose this game and you will take it to your . . . graves" (Warner HBO, 2001). They won.

Few groups are productive immediately; instead, productivity must usually wait until the group matures. Various types of groups, such as conferences, factory workers assembling relay units, workshop participants, and the members of expeditions, become more efficient and productive later in their group's life cycle (Hare, 1967, 1982; Hare & Naveh, 1984). The more "mature" a group, the more likely the group will spend the bulk of its time working rather than socializing, seeking direction, or arguing. When researchers coded the content of group members' verbal interactions they discovered task-focused remarks are found to occur later rather than sooner in the group's life (Bales & Strodtbeck, 1951; Borgatta & Bales, 1953; Heinicke & Bales, 1953). Conflict and uncertainty also decrease over time as work-focused comments increase. Groups that have been together longer talk more about work-related matters, whereas younger groups are more likely to express conflict or uncertainty and make requests for guidance (Wheelan, Davidson, & Tilin, 2003). Once the group reaches the *performing stage* "members shift their attention from what the group is to what the group needs to do" (Bushe & Coetzer, 2007, p. 193).

Not all groups, however, reach this productive work stage. If you have never been a member of a group that failed to produce, you are a rare individual indeed. In a study of neighborhood action committees, only 1 of 12 groups reached the productivity stage; all the others were bogged down at the forming or storming stages (Zurcher, 1969). An early investigation of combat units found that out of 63 squads, only 13 could be clearly classified as effective performance units (Goodacre, 1953). An analysis of 18 personal growth groups concluded that only 5 managed to reach the task performance stage (Kuypers, Davies, & Glaser, 1986). These studies and others suggest that time is needed to develop a working relationship, but time alone is no guarantee that the group will be productive (Gabarro, 1987). Chapter 12 examines issues pertaining to team performance in detail.

**Adjourning: The Dissolution Stage** Susan Wheelan's (1994) *Group Development Questionnaire*, summarized in Table 5.4, measures the group's stage of development by asking members to describe their group's success in dealing with issues of orientation, conflict, structure, and productivity. Some groups, however, move through these four basic stages to a fifth one: the *adjourning stage*. The U.S. Hockey Team, for example, was invited to the White House to meet the President of the United States after their victory. That ceremony marked the end of the group's existence, for the team never reconvened or played again. After meeting the President, the teammates clapped one another on the back one last time, and then the group disbanded.

A group's entry into the dissolution stage can be either planned or spontaneous. *Planned dissolution* takes place when the group accomplishes its goals or exhausts its time and resources. The U.S. Hockey Team meeting the President, a wilderness expedition at the end of its journey, a jury delivering its verdict, and an ad hoc committee filing its final report are all ending as scheduled. *Spontaneous dissolution*, in contrast, occurs when the group's end is not scheduled. In some cases, an unanticipated problem may arise that makes continued group interaction impossible. When groups fail repeatedly to achieve their goals, their members or some outside power may decide that maintaining the group is a waste of time and resources. In other cases, the group members may no longer find the group and its goals sufficiently satisfying to warrant their continued membership. As social exchange theory

## Focus 5.3 Why Do Soldiers Fight?

*From this day to the ending of the world,*
*But we in it shall be remembered.*
*We few, we happy few, we band of brothers;*
*For he today that sheds his blood with me*
*Shall be my brother;*

—William Shakespeare,
*Henry V*, Saint Crispin's Day Speech

The military unit is the epitome of the cohesive group. Combat units must develop bonds of trust and commitment, for they face situations where a lack of cohesiveness may threaten their survival. These groups, too, are formed deliberately and their development is a guided one; each step along the way is designed to maximize their cohesiveness using methods that—based on experience and commonsense—are consistent with research findings about cohesiveness (Siebold, 2007).

Basic training, where recruits are transformed into a cohesive group, is a study in accelerated group development. Recruits are deliberately clustered into subunits of 10 or less, all under the watchful eye of a highly involved leader. When forming details, every attempt is made to assign duties to intact groups rather than rotating individuals from one task to another. Basic training is a form of severe initiation, for recruits experience harsh conditions that they must endure to be accepted into the group. The environments' demands are arranged so that virtually all activities—eating, sleeping, marching, working—are performed within the same basic group, and the groups are kept segregated from other groups. If time is given for the soldiers to leave camp, they are encouraged to remain together when off-duty. The military provides strong leadership, but of a more social, inspirational style rather than a bureaucratic, managerial style. When possible, rewards the soldiers receive are meted out by their immediate superior, rather than high-level leaders. The norms of the group encourage unity, mutual support, and respect for the values of the nation (Henderson, 1985). Cohesiveness reaches its peak during deployment, since the squads are no longer in contact with family or friends, and members can devote their full attention to the group and its needs. As the group approaches the end of its tour, then cohesion sometimes decreases, as the group readies for the adjourning stage (Bartone & Adler, 1999).

The cohesiveness created through these experiences is robust, and is only tempered further by combat. In one study, it was found that World War II veterans' combat units were still cohesive some 40 years after the war, particularly in those groups that saw substantial action in the war. Units that had been in combat and had casualties were the most cohesive, those that had been in combat but had suffered no casualties were less cohesive, and those that had not been in combat were the least cohesive (Elder & Clipp, 1988).

**TABLE 5.4 A Sampling of Items from the Group Development Questionnaire (GDQ)**

| Stage | Sample Items |
|---|---|
| **Orientation (forming)** | Members tend to go along with whatever the leader suggests. |
| | There is very little conflict expressed in the group. |
| **Conflict (storming)** | People seem to have very different views about how things should be done in this group. |
| | Members challenge the leader's ideas. |
| **Structure (norming)** | The group is spending its time planning how it will get its work done. |
| | Members can rely on each other. They work as a team. |
| **Work (performing)** | The group gets, gives, and uses feedback about its effectiveness and productivity. |
| | The group encourages high performance and quality work. |

SOURCE: "Validation Studies of the Group Development Questionnaire" by S. A. Wheelan and J. M. Hochberger, *Small Group Research*, 27, February 1996. 

maintains, when the number of rewards provided by group membership decreases and the costly aspects of membership escalate, group members become dissatisfied. If the members feel that they have no alternatives or that they have put too much into the group to abandon it, they may remain in the group even though they are dissatisfied. If, however, group members feel that other groups are available or that nonparticipation is preferable to participation in such a costly group, they will be more likely to let their current group die (Rusbult & Van Lange, 2003).

The dissolution stage can be stressful for members (Birnbaum & Cicchetti, 2005). When dissolution is unplanned, the final group sessions may be filled with conflict-laden exchanges among members, growing apathy and animosity, or repeated failures at the group's task. Even when dissolution is planned, the members may feel distressed. Their work in the group may be over, but they still mourn for the group and suffer from a lack of personal support. Members of disbanding partnerships sometimes blame one another for the end of the group (Kushnir, 1984).

## Cycles of Group Development

Tuckman's model, which can be operationalized using measures like the ones in Table 5.4, is a *successive-stage theory*: It specifies the usual order of the phases of group development. Sometimes, however, group development takes a different course.

Although interpersonal exploration is often a prerequisite for group solidarity, and cohesion and conflict often precede effective performance, this pattern is not universal. Some groups manage to avoid particular stages; others move through the stages in a unique order; still others seem to develop in ways that cannot be described by Tuckman's five stages (McMorris, Gottlieb, & Sneden, 2005). Also, the demarcation between stages is not clear-cut. When group conflict is waning, for example, feelings of cohesion may be increasing, but these time-dependent changes do not occur in a discontinuous, stepwise sequence (Arrow, 1997).

Many theorists believe that groups repeatedly cycle through stages during their lifetime, rather than just moving through each stage once (e.g., Arrow, 1997). These *cyclical models* agree that certain issues tend to dominate group interaction during the various phases of a group's development, but they add that these issues can recur later in the life of the group. Very long-term groups, such as teams of software engineers who work on products for many years, show signs of shifting from task-focused stages back to conflict (*re-storming*) and norming (*re-norming*) stages (McGrew, Bilotta, & Deeney, 1999). Robert Bales's **equilibrium model** of group development therefore assumes that group members strive to maintain a balance between accomplishing the task and enhancing the quality of the interpersonal relationships within the group. In consequence, groups cycle back and forth between what Tuckman called the norming and performing stages: A period of prolonged group effort must be followed by a period of cohesion-creating, interpersonal activity (Bales & Cohen, 1979). The discussion groups that Bales studied followed this general pattern of oscillation between the two types of group activity.

**Punctuated equilibrium models** agree with Bales's view, but they add that groups often go through periods of relatively rapid change. These changes may be precipitated by some internal crisis, such as the loss of a leader, or by changes in the type of task the group is attempting (Eldredge & Gould, 1972). The halfway point in the group's life, too, can trigger dramatic changes in the group, as members realize that the time they have available to them is dwindling (Arrow, 1997; Gersick, 1989).

The U.S. Hockey Team's development, although stage-like in many respects, also changed more rapidly following specific, critical events. Perhaps the most

---

**equilibrium model** A conceptual analysis of group development, proposed by Robert Bales, that assumes the focus of a group shifts back and forth between the group's tasks and the interpersonal relationships among group members.

**punctuated equilibrium model** A group development theory that assumes groups change gradually over time but that the periods of slow growth are punctuated by brief periods of relatively rapid change.

dramatic turning point in the group's life occurred when the team lost an exhibition game to a weak team. Coach Brooks believed the team played without any heart or energy, and after the game he kept them on the ice rather than letting them shower and change. He made the players skate back and forth between the goals (the players called these drills "Herbies") for what seemed like hours. Even when the arena manager turned off the lights and went home, Brooks kept the team skating back and forth in the dark. The experience created a feeling of unity in the group, and this cohesiveness carried them through the remainder of their games and on to victory. Such turning points may, however, be relatively rare in groups. More typically, the shift from an initial orientation focus to a task focus occurs gradually as groups and their members pace their progress toward the completion of their final goal (Seers & Woodruff, 1997).

## CONSEQUENCES OF COHESION

Cohesion is something of a "purr word." Most of us, if asked to choose between two groups—one that is cohesive and another that is not—would likely pick the cohesive group. But cohesiveness has its drawbacks. A cohesive group is an *intense* group, and this intensity affects the members, the group's dynamics, and the group's performance in both positive and negative ways. Cohesion leads to a range of consequences—not all of them desirable.

### Member Satisfaction and Adjustment

Many of the men of the U.S. Hockey Team, years later, said that their six months together in 1980 was a special time in their lives. People are usually much more satisfied with their groups when the group is cohesive rather than noncohesive. Across a range of groups in industrial, athletic, and educational settings, people who are members of highly compatible, cohesive groups report more satisfaction and enjoyment than members of noncohesive groups (Hackman, 1992; Hare, 1976; Hogg, 1992). One investigator studied teams of masons and carpenters working on a housing development. For the first five months, the men worked at various assignments in groups formed by the supervisor. This period gave the men a chance to get to know virtually everyone working on the project and natural likes and dislikes soon surfaced. The researcher then established cohesive groups by making certain that the teams only contained people who liked each other. As anticipated, the masons and carpenters were much more satisfied when they worked in cohesive groups. As one of them explained, "Seems as though everything flows a lot smoother . . . . The work is more interesting when you've got a buddy working with you. You certainly like it a lot better anyway" (Van Zelst, 1952, p. 183).

A cohesive group creates a healthier workplace, at least at the psychological level. Because people in cohesive groups respond to one another in a more positive fashion than the members of noncohesive groups, people experience less anxiety and tension in such groups (Myers, 1962; Shaw & Shaw, 1962). In studies conducted in industrial work groups, for example, employees reported less anxiety and nervousness when they worked in cohesive groups (Seashore, 1954). Investigations of therapeutic groups routinely find that the members improve their overall level of adjustment when their group is cohesive (Yalom with Leszcz, 2005). People also cope more effectively with stress when they are in cohesive groups (Bowers, Weaver, & Morgan, 1996; Zaccaro, Gualtieri, & Minionis, 1995).

Cohesive groups can, however, be emotionally demanding (Forsyth & Elliott, 1999). The **old sergeant syndrome**, for example, is more common in cohesive military squads. Although the cohesiveness of the unit initially provides psychological support for the individual, the loss of comrades during battle

---

**old sergeant syndrome** Symptoms of psychological disturbance, including depression, anxiety, and guilt, exhibited by noncommissioned officers in cohesive units that suffer heavy casualities. Strongly loyal to their unit and its members, these leaders feel so responsible for their unit's losses that they withdraw psychologically from the group.

### Focus 5.4 Can Cohesion Make a Bad Job Good?

*My account of how one group of machine operators kept from "going nuts" in a situation of monotonous work activity attempts to lay bare the tissues of interaction which made up the content of their adjustment.*

—Donald F. Roy, on "Banana Time" (1960, p. 158)

Cohesiveness increases with interaction, for the more people do things together as a group—talking, working, eating, relaxing, socializing, traveling, and so on—then the more cohesive the group will become. This generalization, however, comes with qualifications, for any number of situational factors can turn interaction into a negative rather than a positive. If the interactions take place in a hostile environment; if a substantial number of group members are interpersonally irritating in some way; if the group interactions are uncoordinated and boring; if many of the members feel that they are unfairly excluded from the group's activities, the interaction–cohesion relationship will not hold.

This relationship, however, is a surprisingly resilient one, as Donald Roy's (1960/1973) "banana time" case study reveals. Roy worked, for two months, in 12-hour shifts lasting from 8 AM to 8:30 PM, with three other men in an isolated room in a garment factory operating a press machine. The work was not just tedious, but menial, repetitive, and tiring, since he stood the entire day feeding material to the press. He felt he could not last more than a week, but that was before he was drawn into the interaction of the small group. The group filled its days with jokes, teasing, kidding around, and horseplay that gave structure and meaning to their work. To break up the day into smaller segments, the men stopped from time to time for various refreshments and breaks. There was, of course, lunch time, but the men added many others, such as coffee time, peach time, fish time, and banana time. These rituals and social activities, collectively called "banana time" by Roy, turned a bad job into a good one.

All cohesive groups have their *banana times*—interaction rituals that elevate the degree of social connection among the members. Like traditional rituals, such as grace said before meals or singing the national anthem, such interaction rituals provide structure and meaning for the group and its members. Reading the minutes of the last meeting, introducing new members, joking about the member who is always late, or commenting on someone's appearance, are all simple rituals that ensure that the group's activities will unfold in a predictable and orderly way. Rituals have been linked to increases in a shared focus among members, increased emotional energy, and increased overall cohesiveness (Collins, 2004).

causes severe distress. When the unit is reinforced with replacements, the original group members are reluctant to establish emotional ties with the newcomers, partly in fear of the pain produced by separation. Hence, they begin restricting their interactions, and these "old sergeants" can eventually become completely isolated within the group. Some highly cohesive groups may also purposefully sequester members from other groups in an attempt to seal members off from competing interests. Individuals who leave high-demand religious groups due to changes in beliefs or social mobility may experience loneliness, chronic guilt and isolation, a lingering distrust of other people and groups, and anxiety about intimate relationships (Yao, 1987).

Individuals who are members of cohesive groups—with *cohesion* defined as a strong sense of belonging to an integrated community—are more actively involved in their groups, are more enthusiastic about their groups, and even suffer from fewer social and interpersonal problems (Hoyle & Crawford, 1994). Members are also more committed to their groups, where commitment is indicated by the degree of attachment to the group, a long-term orientation to the group, and intentions to remain within the group (Arriaga & Agnew, 2001; Wech et al., 1998). They will even sacrifice their own individual desires for the good of the group (Prapavessis & Carron, 1997).

## Group Dynamics and Influence

As cohesion increases, the internal dynamics of the group intensify. In consequence, the pressure to conform is greater in cohesive groups, and individuals' resistance to these pressures is weaker. When members of cohesive groups discovered that some others in their group disagreed with their interpretations of three ambiguous stimuli, they tried to exert greater influence over their partners than did members of noncohesive groups. Partners also conformed more in cohesive dyads, perhaps because they wanted to avoid confrontation (Back, 1951). When the group norms emphasize the value of cooperation and agreement members of highly cohesive groups avoid disagreement more than members of noncohesive groups. Irving Janis's (1982) theory of *groupthink* suggests that these pressures undermine a group's willingness to critically analyze its decisions. As Chapter 11 explains, in some cases, this breakdown in decision-making effectiveness can be disastrous.

Anecdotal accounts of highly cohesive groups—military squads, adolescent peer groups, sports teams, fraternities and sororities, and cults—often describe the strong pressures that these groups put on their members (Goldhammer, 1996). Drug use and illegal activities are often traced back to conformity pressures of adolescents' peer groups (Giordano, 2003). Cohesive gangs exert strong pressure on members (Coughlin & Venkatesh, 2003). Cults may demand extreme sacrifices from members, including suicide. Even sports teams, if highly cohesive, may extract both compliance and sacrifice from members (Prapavessis & Carron, 1997). Cohesion can also increase negative group processes, including hostility and scapegoating (French, 1941; Pepitone & Reichling, 1955). In one study, cohesive and noncohesive groups worked on a series of unsolvable problems. Although all the groups seemed frustrated, coalitions tended to form in noncohesive groups, whereas cohesive groups vented their frustrations through interpersonal aggression: overt hostility, joking hostility, scapegoating, and domination of subordinate members. The level of hostility became so intense in one group that observers lost track of how many offensive remarks were made; they estimated that the number surpassed 600 comments during the 45-minute work period (French, 1941).

## Group Productivity

Most people consider cohesion to be a key ingredient for group success. The cohesive, unified group has, throughout history, been lauded as the most productive, the most likely to win in battle, and the most creative. The Spartans who held the pass at Thermopylae were a model of unity, courage, and strength. The explorers on the ship *Endurance*, which was crushed by ice floes during a voyage to the Antarctic, survived by working together under the able leadership of Ernest Shackleton. The engineers at the Palo Alto Research Center (PARC) invented the personal computer and other assorted technologies, including the mouse, a graphical interface (clickable icons), e-mail, and laser printers. When the U.S. Hockey Team won, most sports commentators explained the victory by pointing to the U.S. team's cohesiveness, even suggesting that a unified team could work "miracles." But is this folk wisdom consistent with the scientific evidence? Are cohesive groups really more productive?

**Do Cohesive Groups Outperform Less Unified Groups?** Studies of all kinds of groups—sports teams, work groups in business settings, expeditions, military squads, and laboratory groups—generally confirm the cohesion–performance relationship: Cohesive groups tend to outperform less unified groups. But a series of meta-analytic studies, in which researchers combined the results of all available research, statistically, suggests that the relationship does not emerge in all studies and in all groups (Beal et al., 2003; Carron et al., 2002; Gully, Devine, & Whitney, 1995; Mullen & Copper, 1994; Oliver et al., 1999). One analysis of 49 studies of 8702 members of a variety of groups reported that 92% of these studies supported cohesive groups over noncohesive ones. However, this cohesion–performance relationship was stronger (1) in bona fide groups than in ad hoc laboratory groups, (2) in correlational studies than in experimental studies, and (3) in smaller groups than in larger groups (Mullen & Copper, 1994). The relationship between cohesion and performance was also strongest in studies of sports teams, somewhat weaker in military squads, weaker still in nonmilitary bona fide groups, and weakest overall in ad hoc, artificial groups (Carron et al., 2002).

**Are Cohesion and Performance Causally Connected?** Prior studies of groups that work on tasks have found that "nothing succeeds likes success" when it comes to cohesion. When a group performs well at its identified task, the level of cohesion in the group increases, but should it fail, disharmony, disappointment, and a loss of esprit de corps are typically observed. These effects of performance on cohesion occur even when groups are identical in all respects except one—when some are arbitrarily told they performed well, but others are told they did not do well. Even under these highly controlled circumstances, groups given positive feedback became more cohesive than groups that are told they performed poorly. These studies suggest that cohesion is related to performance, not because cohesion causes groups to perform better, but because groups that perform better become more cohesive (e.g., Forsyth, Zyzniewski, & Giammanco, 2001).

Brian Mullen and Carolyn Copper (1994) examined the flow of causality in the cohesion–performance relationship by comparing experimental studies that manipulated cohesion with studies that used correlational designs. Because the cohesion–performance relationship emerged in both types of studies, they concluded that cohesion causes improved performance. However, the relationship between cohesion and performance is stronger in correlational studies. This disparity suggests that cohesion aids performance, but that performance also causes changes in cohesiveness. Mullen and Copper closely examined seven correlational studies that measured cohesion and performance twice rather than once. These studies suggested that a group's cohesiveness at Time 1 predicted its performance at Time 1 and at Time 2. But in these studies, group performance at Time 1 was a particularly powerful predictor of *cohesiveness* at Time 2! These findings prompted Mullen and Copper to conclude that the cohesion–performance relationship is bidirectional: Cohesion makes groups more successful, but groups that succeed also become more cohesive (see Figure 5.2).

**What Is It About Cohesive Groups That Makes Them More Effective?** Cohesive groups do outperform less cohesive groups. But what is it about a cohesive group that makes it more successful? Does the high level of attraction among members reduce conflict, making it easier for the group to concentrate on its work? Or perhaps group members are more dedicated to their group if it is cohesive, and this sense of dedication and group pride prompts them to expend more effort on behalf of their group.

The success of cohesive groups lies, in part, in the enhanced coordination of their members. In noncohesive groups, members' activities are uncoordinated and disjointed, but in cohesive groups, each member's contributions mesh with those of the other group members. Cohesion thus acts as a "lubricant" that "minimizes the friction due to the human 'grit' in the system" (Mullen & Copper, 1994, p. 213). Members of cohesive groups all share the same "mental model" of the group's task and its demands, and this shared prescription for how the task is to be accomplished facilitates their performance. Hence, cohesive groups are particularly likely to outperform noncohesive

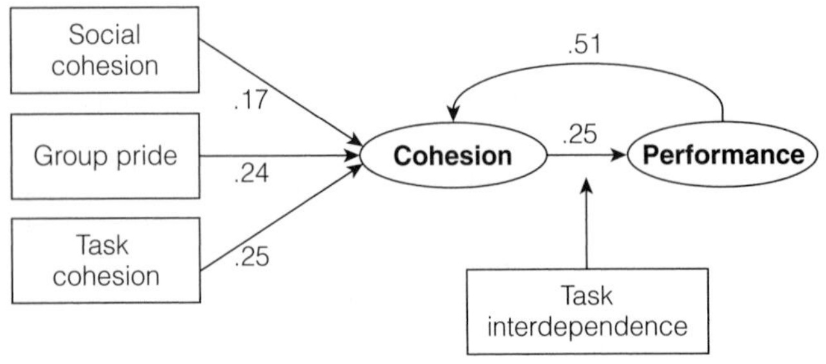


**FIGURE 5.2** The relationship between three components of cohesion (social and task cohesion, and group pride), cohesion, and performance. Meta-analyses suggest that cohesion influences performance (and task cohesion is strongest predictor of cohesion), but that the impact of performance on cohesion is stronger than the impact of cohesion on performance.

groups when the group's task requires high levels of interaction and interdependence. The degree of interdependency required by the type of tasks the group is working on also determines the size of the cohesion–performance relationship; the more group members must coordinate their activities with one another, the more likely a cohesive group will outperform a less cohesive one (Beal et al., 2003; Gully et al., 1995).

These meta-analytic studies also show support for the value of a multicomponent conceptualization of cohesion, for they suggest that even when cohesion is operationalized in different ways, the cohesion–performance relationship still holds true. In their analysis, Mullen and Copper (1994) gave the edge to task cohesion, particularly in studies involving bona fide groups rather than artificial ones. Subsequent analyses, however, found evidence that all three components—social, task, and perceptual ("group pride") cohesion—were related to performance when one looked only at group-level studies (Beal et al., 2003). Figure 5.2 synthesizes the findings from these meta-analytic reviews.

These analyses confirm the relative performance gains achieved by cohesive groups, but they suggest that attraction and pride are not always enough: without task cohesion and commitment to the group's goals, a cohesive group may be surprisingly *unproductive*. In a field study of this process, researchers surveyed 5871 factory workers who worked in 228 groups. They discovered that the more cohesive groups were not necessarily more productive, but their productivity level from one member to the next was less variable. The individuals working in cohesive groups produced nearly equivalent amounts, but individuals in noncohesive groups varied considerably from one member to the next in their productivity. Furthermore, fairly low standards of performance had developed in some of the highly cohesive groups; thus, productivity was uniformly low in these groups. In contrast, in cohesive groups with relatively high performance goals, members were extremely productive (Seashore, 1954; Langfred, 1998). As Figure 5.3 indicates, so long as group norms encourage high productivity, cohesiveness and productivity are positively related: The more cohesive the group, the greater its productivity. If group norms encourage low productivity, however, the relationship is negative.

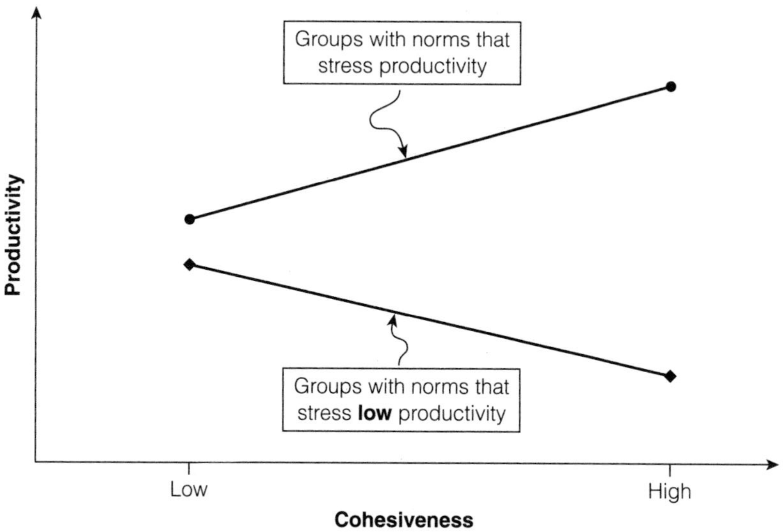


**FIGURE 5.3** The relationship between cohesion and productivity when norms stress high and low productivity. If the group's norms encourage productivity, cohesiveness and productivity will be positively correlated. If the group standards for performance are low, however, cohesiveness will actually undermine productivity.

This tendency for the group's norms about productivity to moderate the strength of the cohesion–performance relationship was also confirmed experimentally by manipulating both cohesion and production norms (Berkowitz, 1954; Gammage, Carron, & Estabrooks, 2001). In one illustrative study, cohesive and noncohesive groups worked on a simple assembly-line type task. Then, during the task, messages were ostensibly sent from one worker to another to establish performance norms. In some instances, the messages called for increased production (*positive messages*), but in other instances, the messages requested a slowdown (*negative messages*). As expected, the impact of the messages was significantly greater in the cohesive groups than in the noncohesive groups. Furthermore, the decreases in productivity brought about by the negative messages were greater than the increases brought about by the positive messages (Schachter et al., 1951).

The take-home lesson from these studies—that creating social cohesiveness may make members happy but not productive—does not apply to the U.S. team. Every one of the team members was committed to the goal of winning the Olympics, so there was no worry that the performance norm would be set too low. In addition, because of the intervention of a thoughtful coach who skillfully built the group's unity, their cohesion developed over time until its peak during the Olympics. The team's triumph was called a miracle by some; but in retrospect, it was due to effective group dynamics.

## SUMMARY IN OUTLINE

*What is group cohesion?*

1. Group cohesion is the strength of the bonds linking members to a group. Cohesiveness is an indication of the health of the group and is related to a variety of other group processes.
2. Theorists have debated the nature of this construct, but a multicomponent, multilevel approach assumes cohesion has a variety of indicators, including:
   - Social cohesion: Lewin and Festinger, taking a social psychological approach to cohesion, emphasized the impact of attraction (in both individuals and groups) on cohesion. Hogg's concept of social attraction stresses a specific form of group-level attraction based on social identity processes.
   - Task cohesion: The strength of the group's focus on a task, and the degree of (a) *teamwork* displayed by group members as they coordinate their efforts and (b) the group's level of *collective efficacy*.
   - Perceived cohesion: The extent to which the group members feel as though they belong in the group (individual-level) and the overall entitativity of the group (group-level).
   - Emotional cohesion: The affective intensity of the group, often described as élan, morale, *esprit de corps*, or positive affective tone. Group-level, consensual emotions are distinct from an individual-level emotions.

*Why do some groups, but not others, become cohesive?*

1. A number of factors combine to determine a group's level of cohesiveness, including:
   - Attraction: Sherif and Sherif, using a unique field-study method in a boys' summer camp, found that the same sorts of variables that influence liking and group formation also influence the cohesiveness of the group that is formed.
   - Stability, size, and structure: As defined by Ziller, *open groups* display less cohesion than *closed groups*. Smaller groups tend to be more cohesive than larger groups, as do groups with particular structural features

(such as the absence of subgroups, less hierarchy, etc.).

- Initiations: Festinger's theory of *cognitive dissonance* explains why initiations can increase commitment to a group, and Aronson and Mills confirmed that people who go through some kind of initiation to join a group tend to like that group more. However, when an initiation is severe, such as some extreme *hazing* practices, it does not increase cohesiveness.

2. Researchers have developed a number of operational definitions of cohesion, using observation, structured observation, and self-report methods. Cohesion, as a multilevel concept, can also be measured at multiple levels.

*How does cohesion develop over time?*

1. Cohesion is, in most cases, the consequence of a period of group development—a pattern of growth and change beginning with initial formation and ending, in most cases, with dissolution.
2. As Hill notes, many theories have been developed to explain group development. Most, however, are consistent with Tuckman's five-stage model:
   - Orientation (forming) stage: Members experience tentative interactions, tension, concern over ambiguity, growing interdependence, and attempts to identify the nature of the situation.
   - Conflict (storming) stage: Members express dissatisfaction with the group, respond emotionally, criticize one another, and form coalitions.
   - Structure (norming) stage: Unity increases, membership stabilizes, members report increased satisfaction, and the group's internal dynamics intensify.
   - Work (performing) stage: The group's focus shifts to the performance of tasks and goal attainment. Not all groups reach this stage, for even highly cohesive groups are not necessarily productive.
   - Dissolution (adjourning) stage: The group disbands. A group's entry into the dissolution stage can be either planned or spontaneous, but even planned dissolution can create problems for members as they work to reduce their dependence on the group.
3. Wheelan's Group Development Questionnaire measures group development.
4. Tuckman's model is a successive-stage theory—it specifies the usual order of the phases of group development. Cyclical models, such as Bales's *equilibrium model*, maintain that groups cycle through various stages repeatedly. *Punctuated equilibrium models* suggest that groups sometimes move through periods of accelerated change.

*What are the positive and negative consequences of cohesion?*

1. In most instances, cohesion is associated with increases in member satisfaction and decreases in turnover and stress. Roy's analysis of "banana time" in work groups illustrates how groups maintain cohesiveness through ritual and social interaction.
2. Cohesion intensifies group processes. Cohesive groups can be so psychologically demanding that they cause emotional problems for members (e.g., the *old sergeant's syndrome*). Dependence, pressure to conform, and acceptance of influence are greater in cohesive groups, and can result in the mistaken decisions identified by Janis in his theory of groupthink.
3. Cohesion and performance are linked, both because success increases a group's cohesion and because cohesive groups tend to outperform less cohesive groups. Meta-analytic studies by Mullen, Copper, and other researchers suggest that each component of cohesion contributes to task proficiency.

- Even though cohesive groups tend to outperform less cohesive groups, this relationship is strongest when members are committed to the group's tasks. If group norms do not encourage high productivity, then cohesiveness and productivity are negatively related.

## FOR MORE INFORMATION

*Chapter Case: U.S. Olympic Hockey Team*

- *Do You Believe in Miracles? The Story of the 1980 U.S. Hockey Team*, a videotape produced by Warner HBO (2001), provides details about the team and the coach.

*Defining and Measuring Cohesion*

- "Group Cohesion: From 'Field of Forces' to Multidimensional Construct," by Kenneth L. Dion (2000), reviews key issues in the study of cohesion, with a focus on definitional debates and problems in measurement.
- *The Social Psychology of Group Cohesiveness: From Attraction to Social Identity*, by Michael A. Hogg (1992), thoroughly reviews conceptual analyses of the concept of cohesion and bases its integrative theoretical reinterpretation on social identity theory.

*Group Development*

- *Group Process: A Developmental Perspective*, by Susan A. Wheelan (1994), provides an extensive analysis of each stage that marks the maturation of most groups.
- "Traces, Trajectories, and Timing," by Holly Arrow, Kelly B. Henry, Marshall S. Poole, Susan Wheelan, and Richard Moreland (2005), provides a conceptually sophisticated review of research and theory that considers group dynamics from a temporal perspective.

*Consequences of Cohesion*

- "Cohesion and Performance in Groups: A Meta-Analytic Clarification of Construct Relations," by Daniel Beal, Robin Cohen, Michael Burke, and Christy McLendon (2003), carefully considers the methodological issues involved in examining the cohesion–performance relationship and then provides clear documentation of that relationship.
- "The Essence of Military Group Cohesion," by Guy L. Siebold (2007), provides a clear introduction to the standard model of cohesion that guides experts' analyses of cohesion in combat groups.

## Media Resources

Visit the Group Dynamics companion website at www.cengage.com/psychology/forsyth to access online resources for your book, including quizzes, flash cards, web links, and more!

# 6

# Structure

## CHAPTER OVERVIEW

Group processes are shaped by unobservable, but influential, group structures. All but the most ephemeral groups develop written and unwritten norms that dictate conduct in the group, expectations about members' roles, and networks of connections among the members.

- What is group structure?
- Why do norms, both formal and informal, develop to regulate group behavior?
- What kinds of roles are common in groups and how do they influence members?
- How can the social structure of a group be measured?
- What are status, attraction, and communication networks?

## CHAPTER OUTLINE

### Andes Survivors: One Group's Triumph over Extraordinary Adversity

The group chartered the Fairchild F-227 to travel from Uruguay to Chile. Most of the passengers on the flight were either members of the Old Christians amateur rugby team or their family and friends. But they never reached their destination. The pilot and copilot misjudged their course and began their descent far too soon. The plane clipped the peak of Mt. Tinguiririca and crashed deep in the snow-covered Andes of South America.

Author Piers Paul Read (1974) recounts the challenges facing those who survived the crash. They were lost, without food or water, in the harsh, subzero temperatures of the barren Andes. During the first days of the ordeal they argued intensely over the likelihood of a rescue. Some insisted that searchers would soon find them. Others wanted to climb down from the mountain. Some became so apathetic that they didn't care. At night the cries of the injured were often answered with anger rather than pity, for the cramped sleeping arrangements created continual conflict. But the search planes never spotted them and then a second tragedy struck the group: Early one morning, an avalanche filled the wrecked fuselage where they slept with snow and many died before they could dig their way out.

A lone individual would have certainly perished in the harsh climate, but the group managed to survive by pooling their resources and skills. They organized their work, with some cleaning their sleeping quarters, some tending the injured, and others melting snow into drinking water. When their food ran out, they made the difficult decision to eat the frozen bodies of those who had died in the crash. And when starvation seemed imminent, they sent two men, Fernando Parrado and Roberto Canessa, down the mountain to seek help. After hiking for 14 days the two explorers, running low on food and supplies, stumbled into a farmer tending his cattle. Parrado himself guided the rescue helicopters back to the crash site. All of them, when asked how they survived, credited the "unity" of the group (Read, 1974, p. 310). And when they read Read's book about their ordeal, they complained of only one inaccuracy: They felt that Piers Paul Read failed to capture the "faith and friendship which inspired them" for 70 days.

The group that came down from the Andes was not the same group that began the chartered flight. Many members were lost to the group forever, and the trauma changed each one of the survivors permanently. But its *group structure*—the underlying pattern of roles, norms, and networks of relations among members that define and organize the group—also changed. The group of survivors had new *norms* that defined and regulated members' actions. The group began the flight with one set of *roles* and positions—a captain, a coach, parents, supporters, and friends—but ended with an entirely different set of roles, including commanders, lieutenants, and explorers. The *network* of relationships linking members one to another, in terms of status, liking, and communication, also changed. Men who were at first afforded little respect or courtesy eventually earned considerable status within the group. Some who were well-liked before the crash became outcasts. Some who had hardly spoken to the others before became active communicators within the group.

Any group, whether stranded in the Andes, sitting at a conference table, or working to manufacture some product, can be better understood by examining its structure. Such an analysis assumes that despite widespread differences among groups, all share a common structural core. In a sense, examining group structures is like studying an individual's personality. An acquaintance's personality cannot be observed directly, but people assume that his or her behavior is the external manifestation of basic traits and dispositions. Similarly, a structural analysis assumes that interaction among members follows a predictable, organized pattern because it is regulated by influential interpersonal structures. In this chapter, we examine three of the most commonly noted aspects of a group's "personality": norms, roles, and intermember relations (see Biddle, 2001; Hechter & Op, 2001 for reviews).

## NORMS

The survivors of the crash needed to coordinate their actions if they were to stay alive. With food, water, and shelter severely limited, they were forced to interact with and rely on each other continually, and any errant action on the part of one person would disturb and even endanger several other people. So members soon began to follow a shared set of rules that defined how the group would sleep at night, what types of duties each healthy individual was expected to perform, and how food and water were to be apportioned.

*Norms* are the emergent, consensual standards that regulate group members' behaviors. They are *emergent*, in that they develop gradually during the course of interaction among members—in some cases through deliberation and choice but often only gradually as members' actions align. They are also *consensual* because norms are shared rules of action; norms are social standards that are accepted by a substantial proportion of the group.

A group's norms regulate the group's activities by identifying what is normal and what is not. Just as a physician's prescription recommends a medicine, so **prescriptive norms** define the socially appropriate way to respond in a social situation. **Proscriptive norms**, in contrast, are prohibitions; they define the types of actions that should be avoided if at all possible (Sorrels & Kelley, 1984). For example, some of the prescriptive norms of the Andes group were "Food should be shared equally," "Those who are not injured should work to help those who are injured," and "Follow the orders of the leader," whereas some proscriptive norms were "Do not urinate inside the airplane" and "Do not take more than your share of food and water." **Descriptive norms** describe what most people *usually* do, feel, or think in a particular situation. In a business group, for example, most people arrive for the meeting on time. Very few people fall asleep during the meeting. Most people clap when the speaker finishes. **Injunctive norms** are more evaluative—they describe the sorts of behaviors that people *ought* to perform. People who do not comply with descriptive norms may be viewed as unusual, but people who violate injunctive norms are negatively evaluated and are open to sanction by the other group members. In the Andes group, for example, those who failed to do their fair share of work were criticized by the others, given distasteful chores, and sometimes even denied food and water (Cialdini, Reno, & Kallgren, 1990; Miller & Prentice, 1996).

Some norms are specific to a given group, but others are accepted across groups. When one group meets it may be appropriate to interrupt others when they are talking, to arrive late and to leave early, and to dress informally. In another group, however, such behaviors would be considered inappropriate violations of group norms of dress and decorum. Some social norms, in contrast, are so widely adopted within a given context and culture that they structure behavior across groups.

Norms are a fundamental element of a group's structure, for they provide direction and motivation, organize social interactions, and make other people's responses predictable and meaningful. Simple behaviors such as choice of clothing ("Wear shoes in public"), manners ("Do not interrupt others"), and conventions of address ("Call the professor 'Dr.'") reflect norms, but so do general societal principles of fairness ("Help others when they are in need"), morality ("Do not lie to members of the group"), and value ("Work hard for the group"). Each group member is restrained to a degree by norms, but each member also benefits from the order that norms provide.

---

**prescriptive norm** A consensual standard that identifies preferable, positively sanctioned behaviors.

**proscriptive norm** A consensual standard that identifies prohibited, negatively sanctioned behaviors.

**descriptive norm** A consensual standard that describes how people typically act, feel, and think in a given situation.

**injunctive norm** An evaluative consensual standard that describes how people should act, feel, and think in a given situation rather than how people do act, feel, and think in that situation.

## The Development of Norms

Groups sometimes discuss and formally adopt norms as their group's rules, but more frequently norms are implicit standards rather than explicit ones. Because members gradually align their behaviors until they match certain standards, they are often not even aware that their behavior is dictated by the norms of the situation. People do not, for example, spend a great deal of time wondering, "Should I be quiet in the library?" "Should I nap during the group meeting?" or "Should I stop when the light turns red?" They take these norms for granted so fully that they comply with them automatically (Aarts, Dijksterhuis, & Custers, 2003).

The Andes survivors, for example, grew up in a culture that condemned cannibalism, but this taboo was largely unstated. But when the group grew weak from starvation one member casually remarked that the only source of nourishment was the frozen bodies of the crash victims. The others took the remark to be a joke until the tenth day, when "the discussion spread as these boys cautiously mentioned it to their friends or those they thought would be sympathetic" (Read, 1974, p. 76). When the topic was discussed by the entire group, two cliques emerged; one favored eating the corpses, but a second group claimed that they could not bring themselves to think of their dead friends as food. The next day, however, they learned by radio that the air force had given up the search. Most of the members then ate a few pieces of meat and, in the end, cannibalism became the norm (Parrado, 2006).

Muzafer Sherif, as noted briefly in Chapter 1, studied this norm emergence process by taking advantage of the *autokinetic* (self-motion) *effect*. This visual illusion occurs when a person stares at a pinpoint of light in an otherwise dark room. Ordinarily the visual system compensates for naturally occurring motions of the eye, but when only a single light is visible with no frame of reference, the light appears to wander in unpredictable directions and at variable speeds. Sherif found that when individuals judged the dot's movement repeatedly, they usually established their own idiosyncratic average estimates, which varied from 1 to 10 inches. But when people made their judgments in groups, their personal estimates blended with those of other group members. One group, for example, included three people who had already been tested individually. During these initial tests, Person A thought the light moved very little—about 1 inch. Person B estimated the movement at 2 inches, but C's estimates were higher, averaging about 7 inches. When these three people made their estimates of the movement aloud when seated together, their judgments converged. It took three meetings, but by the third session, a norm had emerged: All the members felt the light was moving about 3 inches. Figure 6.1 graphs this convergence process: Over time, individuals with the highest and lowest estimates revise their judgments to match the group average.

## The Transmission of Norms

Sherif confirmed that norms emerge, gradually, as group members' behaviors, judgments, and beliefs align over time. But Sherif also arranged for people to make their judgments alone after taking part in the group sessions where a norm emerged. Did these individuals revert back to their original estimates of movement, or did they continue to base their estimates on the norm that emerged within their group? Sherif discovered that, even though the other group members were no longer present, the individuals retained the group norm (Sherif, 1966). They had *internalized* the norm.

Norms, because they are both consensual (accepted by many group members) and internalized (personally accepted by each individual member), are social facts—taken-for-granted elements of the group's stable structure. Even if the individuals who originally fostered the norms are no longer present, their normative innovations remain a part of the organization's traditions, and newcomers must change to adopt that tradition. Researchers have studied this norm transmission experimentally using a *generational* paradigm: They create a group, and then add newcomers to it and retire old-timers until the entire membership of the group has turned over. Do these succeeding generations of members remain true to the group's original norms, even if these norms are arbitrary or cause the group to

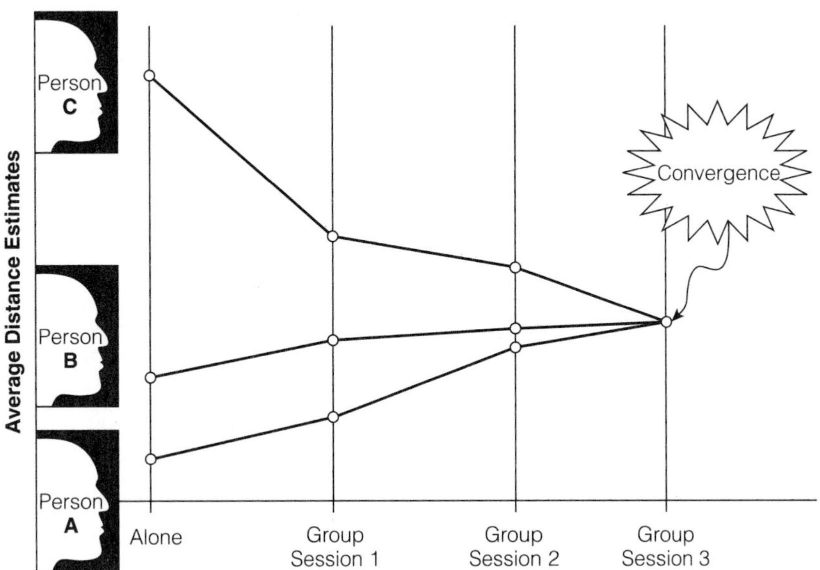


**FIGURE 6.1** Sherif's experimental creation of group norms. Individuals' private, pre-group judgments differed markedly, but when they joined with others their judgments converged.

SOURCE: Data from M. Sherif, *The Psychology of Social Norms*, 1936, Harper & Row.

make errors and mistakes (Focus 6.1)? In one autokinetic effect study, researchers established an extreme norm by planting a confederate in each three-member group. The confederate steadfastly maintained that the dot of light was moving about 15 inches—an excessive estimate given that most estimates averaged about 3 to 4 inches. Once the confederate deflected the group's distance norm upward, he was removed from the group and replaced by a naive participant. The remaining group members, however, still retained the large distance norm, and the newest addition to the group gradually adapted to the higher standard. The researchers continued to replace group members with new participants, but new members continued to shift their estimates in the direction of the group norm. This arbitrary group norm gradually disappeared as judgments of distance came back down to an average of 3.5 inches, but in most cases, the more reasonable norm did not develop until group membership had changed five or six times (Jacobs & Campbell, 1961; MacNeil & Sherif, 1976). In another generational study, researchers gave groups feedback that suggested that their norm about how decisions should be made was causing them to make errors, but this negative feedback did not reduce the norm's longevity across generations (Nielsen & Miller, 1997).

Because norms tend to resist revision, some group's norms may seem pointless and arbitrary rather than reasonable and functional (Rimal & Real, 2005). They are, however, aspects of the group's structure, and even odd or unusual norms organize interactions, increase predictability, and enhance solidarity (Collins, 2004). The traditional group that moves at seemingly glacial speed through a formal agenda of roll call, approving the minutes, old business, new business, and adjournment, is moving along at a pace and through a process that is defined by its norms. Adults who want to take part in an ongoing game of "pickup" basketball learn to ask the question "Who has next?" to inform the other players that they wish to play and that they will complain if they are passed over for a player who arrived after they did (Jimerson, 1999). When a Little League baseball team takes to calling an opposing team "the string

## Focus 6.1 Are Groups Bad for Your Health?

*Everyone on the [cheerleading] squad binges and vomits. That's how I learned.*

—Laura (quoted in Squire, 1983, p. 48)

Theodore Newcomb, in his 1943 study of political attitudes discussed in Chapter 2, discovered that students changed their attitudes until their political preferences matched the attitudes of their classmates and professors. Some 40 years later, Christian Crandall (1988) documented similar shifts in a study of *bulimia*—a pernicious cycle of binge eating followed by self-induced vomiting or other forms of purging. Certain social groups, such as cheerleading squads, dance troupes, sports teams, and sororities, tend to have strikingly high rates of eating disorders (Petrie & Greenleaf, 2007). In explanation, Crandall noted that such groups adopt norms that encourage binging and purging. Rather than viewing these actions as abnormal and a threat to health, the sororities that Crandall studied accepted purging as a normal means of controlling one's weight. The women who were popular in such groups were the ones who binged at the rate established by the group's norms. Even worse, women who did not binge when they first joined the group were more likely to take up the practice the longer they remained in the group. Other studies suggest that unhealthy eating patterns increase with the perceived strength of peer pressure within the sorority and the longer the woman lives in the sorority house itself (e.g., Basow, Foran, & Bookwala, 2007).

Similar results have been obtained in studies of other sorts of socially undesirable or unhealthy behaviors (Smith & Christakis, 2008). Entire college campuses can develop unique, and risky, norms pertaining to the need to take precautions, such as the use of condoms (Fisher & Fisher, 1993). Interventions designed to help at-risk adolescents by placing them in special programs may actually contribute to increased violence, drug use, and other antisocial behaviors when these groups develop negative rather than positive norms (Dishion & Dodge, 2005). On some college campuses students abuse alcohol because the norms of that subculture encourage excessive alcohol consumption and discourage moderation (Kuntsche et al., 2005). Obesity tends to spread among individuals who are linked together in a social network, in part because norms encourage lifestyle choices that promote weight gain rather than fitness (Christakis & Fowler, 2007).

**Pluralistic ignorance** can also contribute to unhealthy behaviors. Pluralistic ignorance occurs when the majority of the individuals in a group privately disagree with the group's norm but feel that they are alone in their misgivings (Prentice, 2007). So, the norm continues to regulate behavior, due to misperception rather than shared consensus. College students, for example, often misperceive the extent to which other students drink excessive amounts of alcohol. Most of the students who participated in one study were personally opposed to overindulgence, but they believed that their campus's norms encouraged heavy alcohol consumption. The men responded to this norm by gradually internalizing the misperceived norm. They began to drink more the longer they stayed at the school. The women, in contrast, responded by distancing themselves from their university and its norms about drinking (Prentice & Miller, 1993).

Norms may, however, promote healthy actions as well as unhealthy ones. Individuals who wish to reduce their negative indulgences often find success by joining a group and accepting that group's norms as their own. Many fitness, weight-loss, and anti-addiction programs, as noted in more detail in Chapter 16, take a group approach to change. Alcoholics Anonymous, for example, has clear norms about the types of behaviors members must enact in order to stay sober, and those individuals who become highly involved members are less likely to continue to drink heavily (Bond, Kaskautas, & Weisner, 2003). Groups have also been found to be effective in preventing the onset of eating disorders, such as bulimia, in young women. The investigators in one clinical trial identified 481 women, averaging 17 years old, who were already experiencing dissatisfaction with their bodies. They then arranged for some of these women to meet in small groups to learn more about nutrition and ways to manage their weight in healthy ways. In some situations, these women also developed, as a group, arguments against the thin-body norm typical in American society. When the investigators assessed their health three years later, they discovered that, compared to those in the control condition, the women who took part in these groups were significantly less likely to have developed eating disorders (Stice et al., 2008). Groups, then, can either promote or threaten members' health, depending on their norms. Some groups may put members at risk by encouraging unhealthy actions, whereas others are the path to good health and wellness.

---

**pluralistic ignorance** When members of a group privately vary in outlook and expectations, but publicly they all act similarly because they believe that they are the only ones whose personal views are different from the rest of the group.

**TABLE 6.1 Characteristics and Varieties of Norms**

| Common Features | Description |
|---|---|
| **Descriptive** | Describe how most members act, feel, and think |
| **Consensual** | Shared among group members, rather than personal, individual-level beliefs |
| **Injunctive** | Define which behaviors are considered "bad" or wrong and which are "good" or acceptable |
| **Prescriptive** | Set the standards for expected behavior; what should be done |
| **Proscriptive** | Identify behaviors that should not be performed |
| **Informal** | Describe the unwritten rules of conduct in the group |
| **Implicit** | Often so taken for granted that members follow them automatically |
| **Self-generating** | Emerge as members reach a consensus through reciprocal influence |
| **Stable** | Once they develop, resistant to change and passed from current members to new members |

beans" because of the greenish color of their uniform, the players share a sense of collusion and secrecy when their shortstop calls out "bean the bean" to the pitcher (Fine, 1979). Norms do not just maintain order in the group; they also maintain the group itself (Youngreen & Moore, 2008; see Table 6.1).

## ROLES

On the day after the Andes crash, Marcelo, the captain of the rugby team, organized the efforts of those who could work. Two young men and one of the women administered first aid to the injured. One subgroup of boys melted snow for drinking water, and another team cleaned the cabin of the airplane. These various positions in the group—leader, doctor, snow melter, cabin cleaner—are all examples of *roles*: coherent sets of behaviors expected of people in specific positions within a group or social setting.

Roles in a group are similar in some respects to roles in a play. A play's roles describe the characters that the actors portray before the audience. To become Juliet in Shakespeare's *Romeo and Juliet*, for example, an actor must perform certain actions and recite her dialogue accordingly. Similarly, roles in groups structure behavior by dictating the part that members take as they interact. Once cast in a role such as leader, outcast, or questioner, group members perform certain actions and interact with other group members in a particular way—but this consistency reflects the requirements of their role rather than their personal predilections or inclinations. But in many cases members can negotiate within the group as they move in and out of different roles. For example, group members who want to influence others may seek the role of leader, and those who wish to maintain a low profile may seek out the role of follower (Hare, 2003; Moxnes, 1999).

Just as some variability is permitted in theatrical roles, group roles do not structure group members' actions completely. An actor playing the role of Juliet must perform certain behaviors as part of her role—she would not be Shakespeare's Juliet if she did not fall in love with Romeo. She can, however, recite her lines in an original way, change her stage behaviors, and even ad-lib. In social groups, too, people can fulfill the same role in somewhat different ways, and so long as they do not stray too far from the role's basic requirements, the group tolerates this variation. However, like the stage director who replaces an actor who presents an unsatisfactory Juliet, the group can replace members who repeatedly fail to play their part within the group. The role often supersedes any particular group member. When the role occupant departs, the role itself remains and is filled by a new member (Stryker & Burke, 2000).

## Role Differentiation

As with norms, groups sometimes deliberately create roles to organize the group and thereby facilitate the attainment of the group's goals. A group may decide that its efficiency would be augmented if someone takes charge of the meetings and different tasks are assigned to subcommittees. In some cases, too, someone outside the group, such as the group's supervisor, may mandate roles within the group (Stempfle, Hübner, & Badke-Schaub, 2001). But even without a deliberate attempt at creating a formal group structure, the group will probably develop an informal role structure. Members may initially consider themselves to be just members, basically similar to each other. But in time, some group members will begin to perform specific types of actions and interact with other group members in a particular way. As this **role differentiation** process unfolds, the number of roles in the group increases, whereas the roles themselves gradually become more narrowly defined and specialized. In the Andes survivors, for example, the roles of *leader, doctor*, and *cleaner* emerged first, soon followed by the *inventor*, who created makeshift snowshoes, hammocks, and water-melting devices; *explorer*, who was determined to hike down from the mountain; and *complainer, pessimist, optimist*, and *encourager*. This rapid proliferation of roles is typical of groups facing difficult problems or emergencies (Bales, 1958).

**Types of Roles** What roles tend to emerge as a group becomes organized? Certainly, the role of *leader* is a fundamental one in many groups, but other roles should not be overlooked. Many of these roles, such as *expert, secretary*, and *organizer*, are similar in that they revolve around the task the group is tackling. People who fulfill a **task role** focus on the group's goals and on the members' attempts to support one another as they work. Marcelo, in the Andes group, was a task-oriented leader, for he organized work squads and controlled the rationing of the group's food supplies, and the rest of the members obeyed his orders. He did not, however, satisfy the group members' interpersonal and emotional needs. As if to offset Marcelo's inability to cheer up the survivors, several group members became more positive and friendly, actively trying to reduce conflicts and to keep morale high. Liliana Methol, in particular, provided a "unique source of solace" (Read, 1974, p. 74) to the young men. She came to fill a **relationship role** (also frequently termed *socioemotional role*) in the Andes group. A group may need to accomplish its tasks, but it must also ensure that the interpersonal and emotional needs of the members are met. Whereas the *coordinator* and *energizer* structure the group's work, such roles as *supporter, clown*, and even *critic* help satisfy the emotional needs of the group members.

The tendency for groups to develop both task roles and relationship roles is consistent with Kenneth Benne and Paul Sheats's (1948) classic study conducted at the National Training Laboratories (NTL), an organization devoted to the improvement of groups. Benne and Sheats concluded that a group, to survive, must meet two basic demands: The group must accomplish its tasks, and the relationships among members must be maintained. Their extensive list of roles, shown in Table 6.2, includes task roles, relationship roles, and

---

**role differentiation** An increase in the number of roles in a group, accompanied by the gradual decrease in the scope of these roles as each one becomes more narrowly defined and specialized.

**task role** Any position in a group occupied by a member who performs behaviors that promote completion of tasks and activities, such as initiating structure, providing task-related feedback, and setting goals.

**relationship role** Any position in a group occupied by a member who performs behaviors that improve the nature and quality of interpersonal relations among members, such as showing concern for the feelings of others, reducing conflict, and enhancing feelings of satisfaction and trust in the group.

**TABLE 6.2 Benne and Sheats' Typology of Roles in Groups**

| Category | Types |
|---|---|
| **Task Roles** | **Initiator/contributor**: Recommends novel ideas about the problem at hand, new ways to approach the problem, or possible solutions not yet considered |
| | **Information seeker**: Emphasizes getting the facts by calling for background information from others |
| | **Opinion seeker**: Asks for more qualitative types of data, such as attitudes, values, and feelings |
| | **Information giver**: Provides data for forming decisions, including facts that derive from expertise |
| | **Opinion giver**: Provides opinions, values, and feelings |
| | **Elaborator**: Gives additional information, examples, rephrasings, implications about points made by others |
| | **Coordinator**: Shows the relevance of each idea and its relationship to the overall problem |
| | **Orienter**: Refocuses discussion on the topic whenever necessary |
| | **Evaluator/critic**: Appraises the quality of the group's methods, logic, and results |
| | **Energizer**: Stimulates the group to continue working when discussion flags |
| | **Procedural technician**: Cares for operational details, such as materials, machinery, and so on |
| | **Recorder**: Takes notes and maintains records |
| **Relationship Roles** | **Encourager**: Rewards others through agreement, warmth, and praise |
| | **Harmonizer**: Mediates conflicts among group members |
| | **Compromiser**: Shifts his or her own position on an issue in order to reduce conflict in the group |
| | **Gatekeeper/expediter**: Smooths communication by setting up procedures and ensuring equal participation from members |
| | **Standard setter**: Expresses or calls for discussion of standards for evaluating the quality of the group process |
| | **Group observer/commentator**: Points out the positive and negative aspects of the group's dynamics and calls for change if necessary |
| | **Follower**: Accepts the ideas offered by others and serves as an audience for the group |
| **Individual Roles** | **Aggressor**: Expresses disapproval of acts, ideas, and feelings of others; attacks the group |
| | **Blocker**: Negativistic; resists the group's influence; opposes the group unnecessarily |
| | **Dominator**: Asserts authority or superiority; manipulative |
| | **Evader/self-confessor**: Expresses personal interests, feelings, and opinions unrelated to group goals |
| | **Help seeker**: Expresses insecurity, confusion, and self-deprecation |
| | **Recognition seeker:** Calls attention to him- or herself; self-aggrandizing |
| | **Playboy/girl**: Uninvolved in the group; cynical, nonchalant |
| | **Special-interest pleader**: Remains apart from the group by acting as representative of another social group or category |

SOURCE: Adapted from "Functional Roles of Group Members" by K. D. Benne and P. Sheats, *Journal of Social Issues,* 1948, 4(2), 41–49. 

individualistic roles—roles in which members emphasize their own needs over the group's needs.

**Why Differentiation?** Why do task roles and relationship roles emerge in so many different groups? One answer, proposed by Robert Bales and his colleagues, suggests that very few individuals can simultaneously fulfill both the task and the relationship needs of the group (Bales, 1955, 1958; Parsons et al., 1953). When group members are task-oriented, they must direct others to act in certain ways, restrict others' options, criticize other members, and prompt them into action. These actions may be necessary to reach the goal, but others may react negatively to these task-oriented activities—so they then look to others in the group for socioemotional, relational support. The peacekeeper who intercedes and tries to maintain harmony is the relationship specialist. Task and relationship roles, then, are a natural consequence of these two partly conflicting demands.

Bales's research team identified these tendencies by tracking role differentiation in decision-making groups across four sessions. Bales used his *Interaction Process Analysis* (IPA) system to identify certain specific types of behavior within the groups. As noted in Chapter 2 (see Figure 2.2), half of the categories in IPA focus on task-oriented behaviors—either attempts to solve specific problems in the group or attempts to exchange information via questioning. The remaining six categories are reserved for positive relationship behaviors (*shows solidarity, tension release, agreement*) or negative relationship behaviors (*disagrees, shows tension, shows antagonism*). Bales found that individuals rarely performed both task and relationship behaviors: Most people gravitated toward either a task role or a relationship role. Those who took on a task role (labeled the "idea man") offered mostly suggestions and expressed opinions. Those who gravitated to the relationship roles (labeled the "best-liked man") showed solidarity, more tension release, and greater agreement with other group members. The task roles elicit more questions, displays of tension, antagonism, and disagreement, whereas the relationship roles received more demonstrations of solidarity, tension reduction, and solutions to problems. Moreover, this differentiation became more pronounced over time. During the first session, the same leader occupied both the task and the relationship roles in 56.5% of the groups. By the fourth session, only 8.5% of the leaders occupied both roles. In most cases, individuals dropped their role as task leader in favor of the relationship role (Bales, 1953, 1958; Bales & Slater, 1955).

Subsequent work suggests that this division of task and relationship roles is more likely when a group is experiencing conflict about its goals (Burke, 1967). But role differentiation is not an inevitable occurrence in all groups (Turner & Colomy, 1988). Some individuals are the small-group equivalent of master leaders, for they are both well-liked and they focus on the work to be done (Borgatta, Couch, & Bales, 1954). When players on football teams were asked to identify the best players on the team and those who contributed most to the group's harmony, many named the same person—usually a senior or first-string player—to both roles (Rees & Segal, 1984). When students in classroom groups rated each other on Benne and Sheats's (1948) roles listed in Table 6.2, many slotted the same person into both task and relationship roles. Groups with members who filled both roles were also more cohesive and performed more effectively (Mudrack & Farrell, 1995). Differentiation of these two types of roles is more common than their combination, however, perhaps because few people have the interpersonal and cognitive skills needed to enact both roles successfully.

## Group Socialization

An actor answering a casting call may hope to land the lead role of Juliet, but the director may instead offer her only a smaller part, such as the role of the nurse or Lady Capulet. She may decide that the role is too insubstantial for her talents and not accept it, or she may decide that any role in the production is better than no role at all. Similarly, individuals often seek particular roles in groups, but the group may not permit them to occupy these roles. In the Andes group, for example, many sought to be one of the

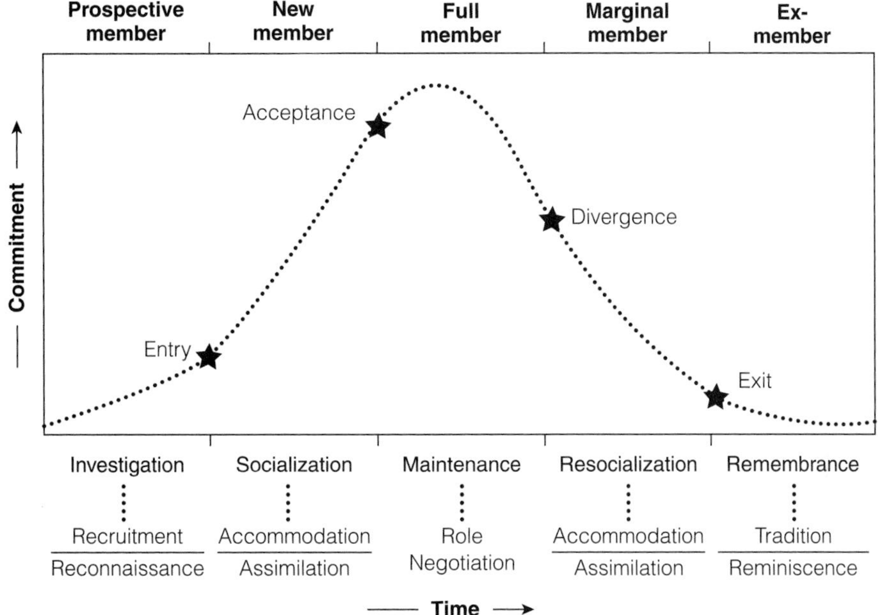


**FIGURE 6.2** The Moreland and Levine theory of group socialization. The model identifies five types of roles (top of the figure), five stages and processes of socialization (bottom of the figure), and four transition points (identified as stars on the curve). The curved line represents the gradual increase (and eventual decrease) of a hypothetical member's commitment to the group. Commitment increases as the member moves from prospective member to new member to full member, but then declines as the member moves to the role of marginal member and finally to ex-member.

"expeditionaries"—explorers who were selected to hike away from the crash site and seek help. But only three were chosen. The group also selected some group members to perform certain tasks, and although some members openly complained about their roles, the group insisted that they take on the role despite their protestations.

Richard Moreland and John Levine (1982) described this negotiation of roles between the individual and the group in their theory of **group socialization**. This theory, which is summarized in Figure 6.2, recognizes that individuals are often asked to take on roles that they would prefer to avoid. Newcomers must "learn their place" in the group and acquire the behaviors required by the roles to which they have been assigned. Veteran group members must, in some cases, be ready to take on new roles within the group that force them to learn new skills and seek new challenges. But group members also feel that their groups should be flexible enough to change to meet their particular needs. So individuals attempt to influence the group. Hence, group socialization is a mutual process; through assimilation, the individual accepts the group's norms, values, and perspectives, and through accommodation, the group adapts to fit the newcomer's needs.

Moreland and Levine's theory distinguishes between five classes of roles—*prospective member, new member, full member, marginal member*, and *ex-member*. Prior to actually joining a group, individuals may study the group and the resources it offers, and part of this reconnaissance involves identifying the type

---

**group socialization** A pattern of change in the relationship between an individual and a group that begins when an individual first considers joining the group and ends when he or she leaves it.

of role they will be given should they join. The group, in contrast, seeks to recruit new members; often by promising them roles and responsibilities that once they are in the group they will not actually be given (Kramer, 1998). Should the individuals choose to enter the group (*entry*), their commitment to the group increases, and their socialization by the full members begins in earnest. To the full members, the newcomers are inexperienced and cannot be completely trusted until they accept the group's norms and role allocations.

The role of newcomer can be a stressful one (Moreland & Levine, 2002). New to the group and its procedures, newcomers lack basic information about their place in the group and their responsibilities. Although the passage of time will eventually transform them into rank-and-file members, newcomers often prolong their assimilation into the group by remaining cautiously aloof or by misinterpreting other members' reactions. Moreland (1985), to study this process, led some members of a newly formed group to think that they were newcomers surrounded by more senior members. He arranged for groups of five unacquainted individuals to meet for several weeks to discuss various topics. He told two of the five that the group had been meeting for some time and that they were the only newcomers. Although the role of newcomer existed only in the minds of these two participants, the people who thought themselves newcomers behaved differently from the others. They interacted more frequently and more positively with each other, they were less satisfied with the group discussion, and their descriptions of the group made reference to members' seniority. Thus, the belief that one is a newcomer who will be treated differently by the old-timers can act as a self-fulfilling prophecy: Just thinking of oneself as a newcomer caused people to act in ways that isolated them from the rest of group (Major et al., 1995). This "mistreatment," which they themselves partially cause, may undermine their loyalty to the group (Levine, Moreland, & Choi, 2001).

The socialization process does not end when individuals become full-fledged group members. Even seasoned group members must adjust as the group adds new members, adopts new goals in place of its old objectives, or modifies status and role relationships. Much of this maintenance phase is devoted to role negotiation. The group may, for example, require the services of a leader who can organize the group's activities and motivate members. The individual, in contrast, may wish instead to remain a follower who is responsible for relatively routine matters. During this phase, the group and the individual negotiate the nature and quantity of the member's expected contribution to the group.

Many group members remain in the maintenance period until their membership in the group reaches a scheduled conclusion. An employee who retires, a student who graduates from college, or an elected official whose term in office expires all leave the group after months or years of successful maintenance. In some cases, however, the maintenance process builds to a transition point that Moreland and Levine labeled *divergence*. The group may, for example, force individuals to take on roles that they do not find personally rewarding. Individuals, too, may fail to meet the group's expectations concerning appropriate behavior, and role negotiation may reach an impasse.

When the divergence point is reached, the socialization process enters a new phase—*resocialization*. During resocialization, the former full member takes on the role of a marginal member, whose future in the group is uncertain. The individual sometimes precipitates this crisis point, often in response to increased costs and dwindling rewards, waning commitment to the group, and dissatisfaction with responsibilities and duties. The group, too, can be the instigator, reacting to a group member who is not contributing or is working against the group's explicit and implicit purposes (see Focus 6.2). Moreland and Levine identified two possible outcomes of resocialization. The group and the individual, through accommodation and assimilation, can resolve their differences. In this instance, *convergence* occurs, and the individual once more becomes a full member of the group. Alternatively, resocialization efforts can fail (see Figure 6.2). The group may conclude that the individual is no longer acceptable as a member and move to expel him or her. Similarly, the individual may reevaluate his or her commitment to

### Focus 6.2 Are Professors Immune from Socialization?

*If professors "speak truth to power," as they must if they are to serve the public good, they are with some regularity bound to disturb or offend those in power—and therefore to require the protection of tenure from their righteous anger or retribution.*

—James Axtell, *The Pleasures of Academe*, 1998, p. 227.

Group socialization achieves two purposes. First, it provides the means for group members to change their group, so that it better suits their conception of its purpose and procedures. Second, and more frequently, group socialization is the mechanism by which a group will influence the member to change to meet the group's requirements. Groups, inevitably, attempt to keep their members focused on group goals and, when they stray too far, they apply pressure to bring them back into the fold—they *resocialize* them, as Moreland and Levine (1982) explain.

Some groups try to limit the impact of the group on the individual by creating safeguards that will protect errant members from threats, punishment, and exclusion. The group's norms may stress openness and freedom of expression, for example, and champion the value of diversity for creativity and productivity. Some groups, too, increase members' freedom to act without fear of recrimination by granting them tenure, which is a guarantee that their position or employment is permanent.

Tenure is particularly common in educational settings, and is designed to ensure academic freedom. For example, in many countries professors in colleges and universities are recruited into their departments through a careful search process. Once in the department, they then undergo a prolonged period of probation, during which time their work is monitored closely. In some departments their membership can be terminated at any point during this probationary period, so professors are careful not to stray too far from the requirements of their role. Eventually, however, if they have fulfilled their role adequately (as defined by the senior members of the group), new members transition from untenured professors into the role of tenured professors.

Tenure does not terminate the group socialization process, however. Professors who take positions on issues that are unpopular with their colleagues, the administration, or students often find that they are the targets of pressures to conform to the social norms of the group (Hunt, 1999). Tenure can also be "broken" if the professor violates a core group norm; for example, an individual can be fired for incompetence, criminal behavior, or moral turpitude. In most cases, too, professors themselves do not feel free to violate the group's norms until they have been promoted to the role of senior, or full, professor. Researchers examined these normative pressures by asking university professors what a hypothetical professor, Dr. X, should do if Dr. X discovers that his or her colleagues might "frown on" the content of a course Dr. X was thinking of teaching. All these professors, regardless of their own tenure status, felt that Dr. X should modify the contents of the course to make it match the group's norms rather than teach it as planned. Many, too, recommended just forgetting about teaching it altogether. The only exception to this cautiousness occurred when Dr. X was described as both tenured and a senior, full professor. Only in this case did the professors recommend teaching the course as planned (Ceci, Williams, & Mueller-Johnson, 2006). Seniority, then, was a stronger protection against influence than was tenure, suggesting that "tenure is fine, but rank is sublime" (Peters, 2006, p. 583).

the group and decide to leave. As a result, the divergence between the group and the individual becomes so great that a final role transition is reached: *exit.*

## Role Stress

Roles influence group members' happiness and well-being in significant ways. By taking on a role in a group, individuals secure their connection to their fellow members, building the interdependence that is essential for group cohesion and productivity. But roles also permit group members to express themselves, for even though roles constrain individuals, they are not so rigid that they undermine the role occupants' sense of control and autonomy (Bettencourt & Sheldon, 2001).

But some roles are more satisfying than others. People prefer to occupy roles that are prestigious and significant rather than roles that are menial and unimportant, but they also like roles that require specialized skills and talents more than unchallenging, uninvolving roles (Rentach & Steel,

1998). The demands of a role can also be stressful for the occupants of that role. One of the young men in the Andes group, for example, was told to act as a doctor and tend the sick, but he did not have any medical training and was worried that he was doing more harm than good. When a role is ambiguously defined, internally inconsistent, or fits the occupant poorly, roles can be great challenges for group members (Kahn et al., 1964).

**Role Ambiguity** The responsibilities and activities that are required of a person who occupies a role are not always clear either to the occupant of the role (the *role taker*) or to the rest of the group (the *role senders*). Even when a role has a long history in the group (e.g., many groups have always had a leader, a secretary, and a treasurer) or the group deliberately creates the role for some specific purpose (e.g., a note taker is appointed) the responsibilities of the role may be ill-defined. In such cases, role takers will likely experience **role ambiguity**—they wonder if they are acting appropriately, they perform behaviors that others in the group should be carrying out, and they question their ability to fulfill their responsibilities.

**Role Conflict** In some instances, group members may find themselves occupying several roles at the same time, with the requirements of each role making demands on their time and abilities. If the multiple activities required by one role mesh with those required by the other, role takers experience few problems. If, however, the expectations that define the appropriate activities associated with these roles are incompatible, **role conflict** may occur (Brief, Schuler, & Van Sell, 1981).

**Interrole conflict** develops when role takers discover that the behaviors associated with one of their roles are incompatible with those associated with another of their roles. When assembly line workers are promoted to managerial positions, for example, they often feel torn between the demands of their new supervisory role and their former roles as friend and workmate. Similarly, college students often find that their student role conflicts with other roles they occupy, such as spouse, parent, or employee. If the student role requires spending every free moment in the library studying for exams, other roles will be neglected.

**Intrarole conflict** results from contradictory demands within a single role. A supervisor in a factory, for example, may be held responsible for overseeing the quality of production, training new personnel, and providing feedback or goal-orienting information. At another level, however, supervisors become the supervised, because they take directions from a higher level of management. Thus, the members of the team expect the manager to keep their secrets and support them in any disputes with the management, but the upper echelon expects obedience and loyalty (Katz & Kahn, 1978).

Role conflict also arises when role takers and role senders have different expectations. The newly appointed supervisor may assume that leadership means giving orders, maintaining strict supervision, and criticizing incompetence. The work group, however, may feel that leadership entails eliciting cooperation in the group, providing support and guidance, and delivering rewards.

---

**role ambiguity** Unclear expectations about the behaviors to be performed by an individual occupying a particular position within the group, caused by a lack of clarity in the role itself, a lack of consensus within the group regarding the behaviors associated with the role, or the individual role taker's uncertainty with regard to the types of behaviors expected by others.

**role conflict** A state of tension, distress, or uncertainty caused by inconsistent or discordant expectations associated with one's role in the group.

**interrole conflict** A form of role conflict that occurs when individuals occupy multiple roles within a group and the expectations and behaviors associated with one of their roles are not consistent with the expectations and behaviors associated with another of their roles.

**intrarole conflict** A form of role conflict that occurs when the behaviors that make up a single role are incongruous, often resulting from inconsistent expectations on the part of the person who occupies the role and other members of the group.

**Person–Role Conflict** Sometimes, the behaviors associated with a particular role are completely congruent with the basic values, attitudes, personality, needs, or preferences of the person who must enact the role: A stickler for organization is asked to be in charge of organizing the group's records; a relationship expert must take on a role that requires sensitivity and warmth. In other cases, though, **role fit** is poor. An easygoing, warm person must give performance appraisals to the unit's employees. An individual with high ethical standards is asked to look the other way when the company uses illegal accounting practices.

When role fit is low, people do not feel that they can "be themselves" in their roles. College students who held roles in campus groups were asked if they felt that their role "reflected their authentic self and how much they felt free and choiceful as they fulfilled their role" (Bettencourt & Sheldon, 2001, p. 1136). Those who felt more authentic when enacting their role reported more positive mood, less negative mood, and a higher level of satisfaction with life overall. Feeling competent when enacting one's role was also a powerful predictor of well-being. In another study, students first rated themselves on 20 different traits (e.g., cooperative, outgoing, imaginative). Later in the semester, they were given a list of five discussion roles (idea person, devil's advocate, moderator, secretary, and announcer) and then asked to indicate how valuable these 20 traits were for enacting each role. For example, how important is it for the idea person to be cooperative? Outgoing? Imaginative? Then they were assigned to one of these roles in a class discussion. As the concept of role fit suggests, individuals assigned to roles that required the kinds of characteristics that they believed they possessed felt more authentic, and their moods were more positive (Bettencourt & Sheldon, 2001).

**Role and Well-Being** Uncertainty about one's role, including role ambiguity, role conflict, and poor role fit, results in stress and tension, and the results are rarely positive for the group member or for the group itself. In one study, accountants and hospital employees who reported experiencing role stress also displayed high levels of tension, decreased job satisfaction, and increased employee turnover (Kemery et al., 1985). In another study, athletes who complained of role ambiguity felt less confident in their ability to fill their roles adequately, and they also played more poorly (Beauchamp et al., 2002). Although the impact of role ambiguity varies depending on the type of position in the group, meta-analytic reviews suggest that increases in role ambiguity are associated with increases in depersonalization, emotional exhaustion, and tension, and decreases in organizational commitment and performance (Örtqvist & Wincent, 2006; Tubre & Collins, 2000). Role conflict is most strongly associated with decreased job satisfaction and increased tension but is also linked to organizational commitment and propensity to quit (Gilboa et al., 2008; Örtqvist & Wincent, 2006).

What can groups and organizations do to help their employees cope with role stress? One solution involves making role requirements explicit: Managers should write job descriptions for each role within the organization and provide employees with feedback about the behaviors expected of them (Pritchard et al., 2008). The workplace can also be designed so that potentially incompatible roles are performed in different locations and at different times. In such cases, however, the individual must be careful to engage in behaviors appropriate to the specific role, because slipping into the wrong role at the wrong time can lead to both embarrassment and a loss of coordination within the group (Goffman, 1959). Some companies, too, develop explicit guidelines regarding when one role should be sacrificed so that another can be enacted, or they may prevent employees from occupying positions that can create role conflict (Sarbin & Allen, 1968). Managers and the leaders of groups should also be mindful of the characteristics of the members of their groups and be careful to maximize role fit when selecting members for particular tasks.

---

**role fit** The degree of congruence between the demands of a specific role and the attitudes, values, skills, and other characteristics of the individual who occupies the role.

## INTERMEMBER RELATIONS

On the 17th day of their ordeal, an avalanche swept down on the Andes survivors as they slept, filling their makeshift shelter with snow. Many were killed, and soon a new order emerged in the group. Three young men stepped forward to take over control of the group. They were cousins, and their kinship bonds connected them to one another securely, but they also were friends with many of the remaining group members.

Connections among the members of a group provide the basis for the third component of group structure—the network of intermember relations. The Andes survivors were a group, but they were also many individuals who were connected to one another in different ways. Which one of the three cousins had the most authority? Who in a group is most liked by others, and who is an isolate? How does information flow through a group from one person to the next? The answers depend on social networks.

### Social Network Analysis

The study of relations among individuals in groups, organizations, and even larger collectives is termed **social network analysis**, or **SNA**. This approach dates back to some of the earliest work in sociology and psychology, for these fields' founders explored various ways to create "maps" of human relationships. These efforts, which included sociometric studies of attraction in groups (e.g., Moreno, 1934) and experimental studies of communication channels in groups (e.g., Bavelas, 1948; Leavitt, 1951), culminated in the 1990s in a set of analysis procedures defined by (a) a focus on the structures of social groups and on linkages among group members in particular; (b) the systematic measurement of these structures; (c) the use of graphics to represent these structures; and (d) the application of statistical and mathematic procedures to quantify these structures (Freeman, 2004).

**Groups as Networks** Figure 6.3 illustrates an application of SNA to groups. Each network member, or node, is represented as a point or circle, and the lines connecting nodes indicate who is linked to whom—say, by a line of communication or by friendship. The arrows indicate the direction of the relationship. A line with a single arrow indicates the relationship is an asymmetric, directed one. For example, the links between person 2 and persons 3, 4, 5, and 6 go out from 2 and are received by 3, 4, 5, and 6. A line with arrows at both ends indicates a symmetric, reciprocal relationship (for example, 1 and 20). Relations that have no directional flow, such as a conversation in an Internet discussion area or a face-to-face conversation, are graphed using undirected links without arrows at all. Distance, in social networks, is defined by relationships rather than physical distance. Two people who are directly linked to one another, such as persons 2 and 3, are separated by a distance of 1. But persons 2 and 15 are separated by a distance of 3, because they are linked by two intermediaries.

Group-level, or network, indexes describe aspects of the group's pattern of relationships. The **density** of a group, for example, is determined by how many people are linked to one another out of the total possible number of links. Consider, for example, the subgroup formed by persons 1, 2, and 7 in Figure 6.3. Since the relationships are directed ones in this example (e.g., 1 sends to 2, and 2 sends back to 1), six relationships are needed to link fully the three individuals. Since only four of six links are present, its density is 4/6, or .66. Thus, a density of 1.0 means that all members are linked to one another, whereas a density of 0.0 means that no one is linked to anyone else (and therefore the group is probably not a group). Looking at the group as a

---

**social network analysis (SNA)** A set of analysis procedures used to describe the structure through graphic representations and through mathematical procedures that quantify these structures.

**density** The degree of connectedness of group's members, as indexed by the number of actual ties linking members divided by the number of possible ties.

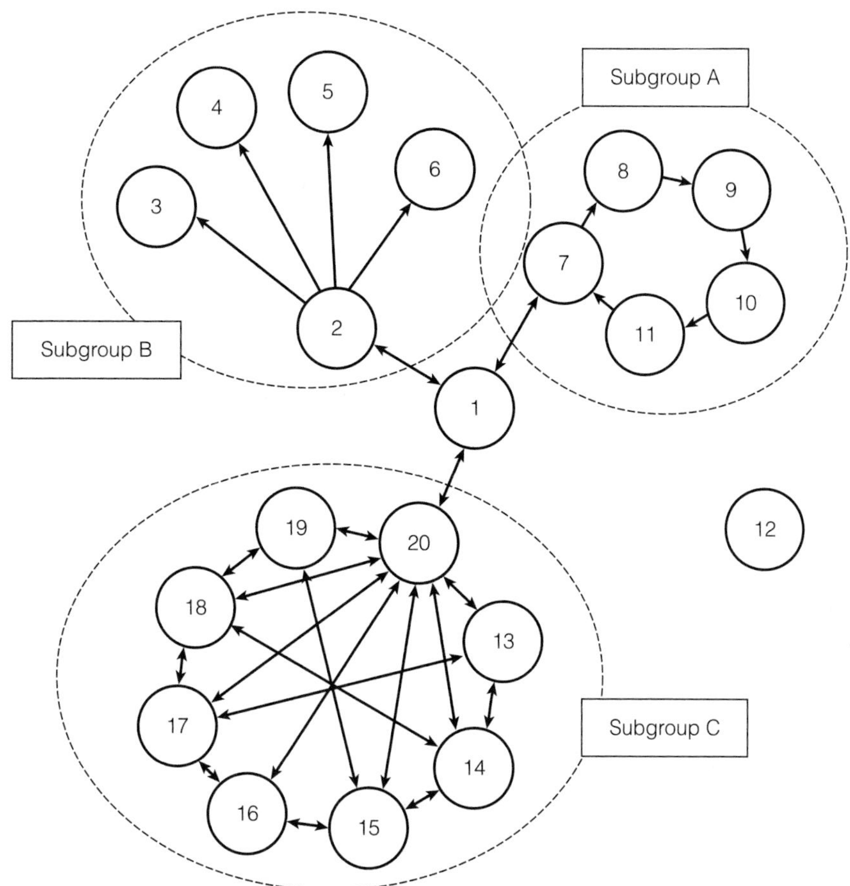


**FIGURE 6.3** An example of a social network. Person 20 is highest in indegree centrality, outdegree centrality, and closeness, whereas Person 1 is the highest in betweenness. The density of the group itself is .12.

whole, density is much lower than 1.0 because many group members are only linked to one or two others and not to all the 19 other members. A 20-person group would require 380 directed ties to link all the members to one another, but only 47 ties are present in this group. The density of the group is therefore .12 (47/380).

**Individuals in Networks** Individual-level, or egocentric, indexes yield information about each member's location in the network relative to the others. Unlike sociocentric indexes, which yield a single value for the entire network (or a portion of the network), egocentric indexes have a value for each actor. Centrality, for example, depends on how many connections a person has and where he or she is positioned within the network itself. In the terminology of SNA, a member with high **degree centrality** is connected to many other actors. Person 20, for example, has the highest degree centrality (linked to eight others), whereas person

**degree centrality** The number of ties between group members; the group's degree centrality is the average of the direct connections among group members.

12, who is not linked to anyone, has the lowest. When relationships are directed ones, a distinction can be made between how many relationships extend out from a person and how many he or she receives from others. **Outdegree** is the number of links to others, whereas **indegree** is the number of links from others. Person 2's outdegree centrality, for example, is five, since she is linked to 1, 3, 4, 5, and 6 through out-directed relationships. Person 2's indegree centrality is only 1, however, because only person 1 directs a relationship to person 2. Out- and indegree centrality are equivalent when the relationships linking members are reciprocal or undirected (Wasserman & Faust, 1994; see Borgatti, 2005, for more information about centrality indexes).

Degree is a local index of centrality—it depends on direct, first-order ties to others in the group. **Betweenness** and **closeness** are also indexes of centrality, but they take into account ties to more distant actors in the network (Freeman, 1979). A position with a high degree of betweenness is one that is located between many of the other individuals in the network. Person 1, for example, has a much lower degree centrality than person 20, but far higher betweenness since he or she joins together the three subgroups that make up the entire group. An individual in such a position often acts as the "go-between" or "gate-keeper," linking people in the network who could otherwise not contact one another. Closeness, on the other hand, is determined by distance to all other members of the group. Person 1, for example, can reach all other members through relatively short paths, whereas other group members (such as 4 or 9) are separated from others by greater distances. Essentially, closeness centrality involves summing the distances between the actor in question and every other actor, and then taking the inverse of that sum so that the term "closeness" makes sense (otherwise it would be an index of "distance").

**Groups in Networks** Social network analysis can reveal aspects of a group's structure that often go unnoticed even by members of the group themselves. Researchers Pamela Paxton and James Moody (2003), for example, used SNA to examine the structure of a specific type of group—a sorority in a university located in the southern United States that they gave the fictitious name of Alpha Beta Chi, or ABX. ABX appeared to be a highly cohesive group with strong relations among all members, but SNA revealed the existence of four cliques within the overall group, which Paxton and Moody labeled the Separatists, the Middles, the Random Chapter Members, and the Small Clique. The Separatists were noteworthy in that they were relatively isolated from the other members of the sorority, and their density was much higher than the other groups. The Middles, in contrast, were more likely to have ties to people outside of their clique. The group also included several women who had high levels of betweenness, labeled as "liaisons" by the researchers and women who were linked to the group by only a single tie ("hangers-on").

As expected, women's locations within this network predicted their commitment to their sorority and their involvement in its various activities. Those in the Middles, for example, had a stronger sense of belonging to the group, particularly in comparison to the Separatists. Paxton and Moody also used a specialized method of calculating overall degree centrality. To index an individual's connection to other well-connected members, they weighted each person's centrality by the centrality of those to whom she was tied (Bonacich, 1987). This index was a strong predictor of satisfaction with the group, as well as sense of belonging. Overall popularity—as indexed by how many times a woman was picked as a friend by others (indegree)—was not, however. Also, within any particular clique, those

---

**outdegree** For nonsymmetric data, the number of ties initiated by the individual.

**indegree** For nonsymmetric data, the number of ties received by the individual.

**betweenness** The degree to which a group member's position in a network is located along a path between other pairs of individuals in the network.

**closeness** The distance, in terms of ties, of an individual from all others in the network.

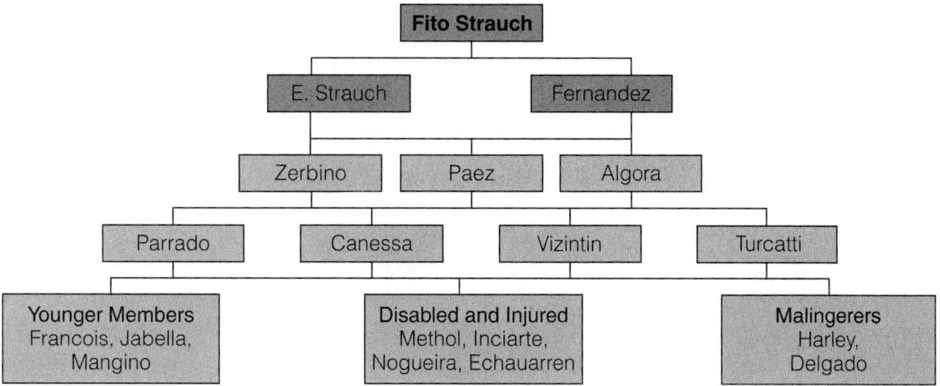


**FIGURE 6.4** The chain of command in the Andes group. Before the avalanche killed the team captain, the survivors' authority structure was based on the rugby team's structure and seniority. But after the avalanche, the group became organized in a hierarchical, centralized authority structure based on kinship.

women with more central locations within the clique tended to be less committed to their sorority as a whole. Devoting one's relational energies to a small subset of the group may leave little time for the interpersonal work required to maintain good relations with the entire group.

Paxton and Moody based their analysis of ABX's social network on one particular type of relationship: social attraction. They asked the women to describe who they spent time with socially and to identify a best friend. Yet, networks can also be based on other types of relationships and processes. Some describe patterns of influence, status, and prestige within the group. Still others define the channels of information that flow from one member to the next. The sections that follow examine these three types of networks—status, attraction, and communication—and their influence on the Andes survivors.

### Status Networks

Rare is the group where all members enjoy equal amounts of authority. In the Andes group, for example, some members became more influential as time passed, whereas others found that they could do little to persuade others to accept their lead. After the avalanche, Fito Strauch was more influential than the other group members; when he gave orders, most of the others obeyed. Also, the group's explorers were afforded more authority than the rank-and-file members. These stable variations in members' relative dominance and authority have such names as *authority, power, status network, pecking orders, chain of command, or prestige ranking.*

Initially, group members may start off on an equal footing, but over time, **status differentiation** takes place: Certain individuals acquire authority by laying claim to a position of greater status and by having their claim accepted by the other members of the group. In the Andes group, for example, Fito Strauch, E. Strauch, and Fernandez formed a coalition that controlled most of the group's activities (see Figure 6.4). Below this top level was a second stratum of members who had less power than the leaders but more prestige than the occupants of lower echelons. These "lieutenants" had less status than Fito Strauch, but they still commanded a fair amount of respect. The explorers ("expeditionaries") occupied a niche just below the lieutenants. These individuals had been chosen to hike down the mountain in search of help.

---

**status differentiation** The gradual rise of some group members to positions of greater authority, accompanied by decreases in the authority exercised by other members.

In preparing for their journey, they were given special privileges, including better sleeping arrangements and more clothing, food, and water. The rank-and-file members included the youngest men in the group, the injured, and those thought to be malingering. Hence, the lines of group authority became hierarchical and centralized, rather like the pyramid-shaped organizational charts of formally organized groups such as businesses and military organizations (Dale, 1952).

**Claiming Status** All social animals know how to communicate the message, "I am in charge." Dominant chimpanzees chatter loudly at potential rivals, the leader of the wolf pack growls and bares his teeth at low-ranking wolves, and the ranking lioness in the pride swats another with her paw. Members of these social groups compete for status, for the individual at the top of the hierarchy—the so-called *alpha* male or female—enjoys greater access to the group's resources. These high-ranking members maintain their position by threatening or attacking low-ranking members, who in turn manage to avoid these attacks by performing behaviors that signal deference and submissiveness. This system of dominance and submission is often called a **pecking order** because (at least in chickens) it determines who will do the pecking and who will be pecked. Biologists argue that pecking orders limit conflict in groups and increase individual and group survival (Bergman et al., 2003; Mazur, 2005).

Humans, too, compete for status in their groups. Humans rarely snarl at one another to signal their status, but they do use such nonverbal cues as a firm handshake, an unwavering gaze, a relaxed but poised posture, or an unsmiling countenance to let others know that they should be respected (Chaplin et al., 2000; Leffler, Gillespie, & Conaty, 1982). People also seek status by speaking clearly and loudly, whereas those who speak softly and pepper their comments with nervous giggles are afforded less authority (Lee & Ofshe, 1981; Patterson, 1991). Displays of emotion also signal differences in status. Group members who seem angry are thought to be more influential and accorded higher status, whereas those who seem sad are thought to be lower in status (Tiedens, 2001; Tiedens, Ellsworth, & Mesquita, 2000).

People also signal their authority through their verbal communications. Those seeking status often initiate conversations and shift the discussion to their own areas of competence (Godfrey, Jones, & Lord, 1986). A person seeking high status would be more likely to (1) tell other people what they should do, (2) interpret other people's statements, (3) confirm or dispute other people's viewpoints, and (4) summarize or reflect on the discussion (Stiles et al., 1997). In a study group, for example, a high-status member may say, "I've studied this theory before," "I know this stuff backward and forward," or "I think it's more important to study the lecture notes than the text." A low-status individual, in contrast, may lament that "I always have trouble with this subject" or "I'm not sure I understand the material." Status seekers use strong rather than weak influence tactics and are more likely to voice their opinions (Bonito & Hollingshead, 1997; Dovidio et al., 1988; Islam & Zyphur, 2005). Group members also assert their authority over the group by interrupting other speakers frequently (Schmid Mast, 2002).

**Perceiving Status** People's status-seeking efforts will be for naught if the group rejects them. In the Andes group, one young man, to attain the high-status role of explorer, tried to impress others by undertaking risky physical adventures. The other group members, however, wanted explorers to be cautious rather than risk takers, and so they selected someone else for the role. The young man displayed characteristics and actions that he felt would earn him status, but because these claims did not match the group members' intuitive beliefs about who deserved status, his bid for authority failed (Driskell & Salas, 2005).

---

**pecking order** A stable, ordered pattern of individual variations in prestige, status, and authority among group members.

**Expectation-states theory**, developed by Joseph Berger and his colleagues, provides a detailed analysis of the impact of group members' expectations on the status-organizing process. This theory assumes that status differences are most likely to develop when members are working collectively on a task that they feel is important. Because the group hopes that it can successfully complete the project, group members intuitively take note of one another's *status characteristics*—personal qualities that they think are indicative of ability or prestige. Those who possess numerous status characteristics are implicitly identified and permitted to perform more numerous and varied group actions, to provide greater input and guidance for the group, to influence others by evaluating their ideas, and to reject the influence attempts of others (Berger, Ridgeway, & Zelditch, 2002; Ridgeway, 2001; Wagner & Berger, 2002).

Expectation-states theorists believe that group members generally take two types of cues into consideration when formulating expectations about themselves and other group members. **Specific status characteristics** are qualities that attest to each individual's level of ability at the task to be performed in the given situation. On a basketball team, for example, height may be a specific status characteristic, whereas prior jury duty may determine status in a jury (Strodtbeck & Lipinski, 1985). In the Andes group, the higher status explorers were chosen on the basis of several specific status qualities: strength, determination, health, and maturity.

**Diffuse status characteristics** are more general qualities that the members assume are relevant to ability and evaluation. Sex, age, wealth, ethnicity, status in other groups, or cultural background can serve as diffuse status characteristics if people associate these qualities with certain skills, as did the members of the Andes group. Among the survivors, age was considered an important diffuse status characteristic, with older members gaining great status. In other groups—ones that value youth—the opposite might hold true (Oldmeadow, 2007).

Researchers have largely confirmed expectation-states theory's prediction that individuals with positively evaluated specific status and diffuse status characteristics usually command more authority than those who lack status-linked qualities (Wilke, 1996). In police teams, officers with more work experience exercised more authority than their less experienced partners (Gerber, 1996). Members of dyads working on a perceptual task deferred to their partner if he or she seemed more skilled at the task (Foddy & Smithson, 1996). People who are paid more are permitted to exert more influence over people who are paid less (Harrod, 1980; Stewart & Moore, 1992). When air force bomber crews work on nonmilitary tasks, rank predicts influence (Torrance, 1954). Juries allocate more status to jurors who have previously served on juries or who have more prestigious occupations (Strodtbeck, James, & Hawkins, 1957). The bulk of the research also confirms the following causal sequence in status allocation: (1) group member X displays specific and diffuse status characteristics, (2) group members form higher expectations about X's capabilities, and (3) group members allow X to influence them (Driskell & Mullen, 1990).

**Status Generalization** Groups do not always allocate status fairly (Schneider & Cook, 1995). Imagine, for example, a jury that includes these three individuals:

- Dr. Prof, a 40-year-old European American woman who teaches in the School of Business and who has written several books on management.

---

**expectation-states theory** An explanation of status differentiation in groups which assumes that group members allocate status to group members judged to be competent at the task at hand and to group members who have qualities that the members think are indicators of competence and potential.

**specific status characteristic** In status characteristics theory, task-specific behavioral and personal characteristics that people consider when estimating the relative competency, ability, and social value of themselves and others.

**diffuse status characteristic** In status characteristics theory, general personal qualities such as age, race, and ethnicity that people consider when estimating the relative competency, ability, and social value of themselves and others.

- Mr. Black, a 35-year-old African American high school principal.
- Dr. White, a 58-year-old European American male physician who has an active practice.

Considerable evidence suggests that a jury of middle-class European Americans, when selecting a foreman, would be biased against Dr. Prof and Mr. Black and in favor of Dr. White. Dr. Prof and Mr. Black, despite their specific status credentials, may be disqualified from positions of status in the group by their (completely irrelevant) diffuse status characteristics. In contrast, Dr. White poses little incongruency for the group if the group members unfairly consider advanced age, pale skin, an M.D. degree, and upper-class social status to be positive features (York & Cornwell, 2006). This phenomenon is known as **status generalization:** Group members let general status (i.e., diffuse status) characteristics influence their expectations, even though these characteristics may be irrelevant in the given situation (Molm, 1986; Ridgeway & Balkwell, 1997).

Status generalization explains why women and African Americans are given less status and authority in groups than European Americans and men. Despite changes in sexist and racist attitudes in society, stereotypical biases still make gaining status in small groups a difficult task for women, African Americans, and other minorities (Nielsen, 1990). Women and racial minorities report more dissatisfaction about how status is allocated in groups (Hembroff, 1982). Women are less likely to be selected as leaders of their groups, and they are more likely to be assigned to lower status roles (Eagly & Carli, 2007). Women and minorities must put extra effort into their groups and reach higher performance standards just to reach the same level of respect and authority granted to less productive European American men (Biernat & Kobrynowicz, 1997; Foschi, 1996). Groups, failing to recognize women's expertise, tend to underperform when women, rather than men, have the expertise a task demands (Thomas-Hunt & Phillips, 2004).

These unfair status allocation processes are magnified when individuals who are members of stereotyped minority societal groups are also underrepresented in the group itself. Women, for example, react more negatively than do men to **solo status**—being the only representative of their social category (in this case, the only woman) in the group. Solo status causes minority members to feel that the other group members are categorizing them in terms of their social group rather than as a comember. In consequence, they are less likely to identify with the group, will not be as loyal to the group, and will not contribute as much to the group's activities—especially when they do not feel they will be able to influence prestige allocations (Branscombe et al., 2002; Jetten et al., 2003). They may experience a decline in self-confidence when they work in the group, and their performance may also suffer (Biernat et al., 1998; Sekaquaptewa & Thompson, 2002, 2003). In one study, women preferred reassignment to a different group if they were going to be a solo member, whereas men showed no aversion to being the only man in the group (Cohen & Swim, 1995). Solo members are also rarely allocated high status in groups (Carli, 2001).

These negative status effects often fade over time as group members gain experience in working together. Groups that initially allocate status unfairly revise their hierarchies as they recognize the skills and abilities of previously slighted members (Watson, Kumar, & Michaelsen, 1993). Given enough time, women and minorities find that they no longer need to continually prove themselves to the others (Hembroff & Myers, 1984; Markovsky, Smith, & Berger, 1984). Women and minorities

---

**status generalization** The tendency for individuals known to have achieved or been ascribed authority, respect, and prestige in one context to enjoy relatively higher status in other, unrelated, contexts (e.g., a celebrity who exercises influence in a group even though this diffuse status characteristic is not relevant in the current group context).

**solo status** The state of being the only group member who is a representative of a specific social category in an otherwise homogenous group (e.g., a man in an otherwise all female group).

who communicate their involvement in the group to the other members also tend to gain status more rapidly, as do those who act in a group-oriented rather than a self-oriented way (Carli et al., 1995; Ridgeway, 1982). If a solo woman in an otherwise all-male group remains actively involved in the group by asking questions, the negative effects of her solo status are eliminated (Fuegen & Biernat, 2002). When men who deliberately adopted either a cooperative, friendly interaction style or an emotionally distant, self-absorbed style joined otherwise all-female groups, they achieved high status no matter what style they exhibited. Women solo members in male groups, in contrast, achieved high status only if they displayed a group-oriented motivation. External authorities can also undo unfair status generalizations by explicitly stressing the qualifications of women and minorities or by training group members to recognize their biases (Ridgeway, 1989). Moreover, groups may reduce biases in the allocation of status to their members by making use of computer-based technology to make decisions and exchange information (see Focus 6.3).

### Attraction Networks

Some of the 19 Andes survivors rose to positions of authority, whereas others remained relatively powerless. Yet to describe the group in just these terms would miss a vital part of the group's structure. The individuals were not just leaders and followers, powerful and powerless; they were also friends and enemies. This network of likes and dislikes among group members is called by many names, including **attraction network**, *social status*, or *sociometric structure*.

**Sociometric Differentiation** Jacob Moreno, the developer of sociometry, maintained that the tendency to react to one another on a spontaneous, affective level imparts a unique quality to human groups (Moreno, 1934). Consider, for example, the relationships among the rank-and-file group members and the four designated explorers in the Andes group, Turcatti, Parrado, Vizintin, and Canessa. Nearly everyone admired Turcatti and Parrado; their warmth, optimism, and physical strength buoyed the sagging spirits of the others. Vizintin and Canessa, in contrast, "did not inspire the same affection" (Read, 1974, p. 141). They liked each other but had few other friends within the group. Mangino, one of the younger men, was an exception; he liked them both. Most of the others, however, quarreled with them constantly.

Attraction patterns like those in the Andes group are not a disorganized jumble of likes and dislikes but a network of stable social relationships (Doreian, 1986). Just as status differentiation results in variations in status, so, too, **sociometric differentiation** results in a stable ordering of members from least liked to most liked (Maassen, Akkermans, & van der Linden, 1996). Some members are liked by many, some are rejected by most; some have few friends in the group, others are liked by several others within a small subset of the group. The Andes survivors, for example, showed signs of reciprocity, transitivity, and clustering.

*Reciprocity*, or mutual liking, is a powerful tendency in most settings; as noted in Chapter 4, it has been documented repeatedly in a variety of groups, including football teams, police squads, psychotherapy groups, and classroom groups. Vizintin liked Canessa, and Canessa liked Vizintin in return.

*Transitivity* is the passing of a relationship from one element to the next: If person A likes person B, and B likes C, then the structure is transitive if A likes C as well. In the Andes group, for example, Canessa liked Mangino, Mangino liked Vizintin, and, in confirmation of transitivity, Canessa liked Vizintin.

*Clusters*, or *cliques*, also existed in the Andes group, for Vizintin, Canessa, and Mangino formed a unified coalition within the larger group. Others

---

**attraction network** Patterns of liking/disliking, acceptance/rejection, and inclusion/exclusion among members of a group.

**sociometric differentiation** The development of stronger and more positive interpersonal ties between some members of the group, accompanied by decreases in the quality of relations between other members of the group.

## Focus 6.3 Do Online Groups Allocate Status More Fairly Than Face-to-Face Groups?

*Somewhere in desolate wind-swept space*
*In Twilight land, in No-man's land*
*Two hurrying Shapes met face to face*
—Thomas Bailey Aldrich

When people meet offline—in face-to-face, collocated groups—to make decisions or solve problems, their impact on the final outcome is often a function of their status in the group. Those who have risen to the top of the group's hierarchy speak as much as 40 to 50% of the time (Stephan & Mischler, 1952), even when the meeting is supposed to be a discussion. The remainder of the speaking will be done by two or three other group members, but these people will have higher status than the rank-and-file members (Gibson, 2003). Those at the bottom of the "speaking order" may say nothing at all during the course of a meeting. Contributions to the discussion also tend to be clustered. Once individuals enter the discussion stream, they tend to concentrate their comments during periods of high vocality, or *megaturns* (Dabbs & Ruback, 1987; Parker, 1988). This pattern occurs, in part, because some individuals are too slow to speak when the previous speaker concludes, so they never manage to capture the floor. Moreover, as expectation-states theory suggests, individuals who are more influential are given more latitude in speaking than are those who are low in status (Bonito & Hollingshead, 1997).

What happens when groups meet online, via the Internet, rather than face to face? In many online groups, the effects of status on participation are muted, resulting in a *participation equalization effect* (Hollingshead, 2001). One early investigation of participants who varied in status tracked their involvement in discussions conducted via e-mail or in face-to-face meetings. E-mail reduced the participation differences between group members, with the result that low-status members participated more and high-status members participated relatively less (Dubrovsky, Kiesler, & Sethna, 1991). Studies of online discussions in college classes also indicated that students participate more equally than they do in face-to-face discussions and that differences in participation due to the cultural background (Kim & Bonk, 2002) or the sex of the student (Davidson-Shivers, Morris, & Sriwongko, 2003) are reduced. Students who eventually earn better grades are more active in such online discussions, but these differences in contribution likely reflect motivational differences rather than status differences (Wang, Newlin, & Tucker, 2001).

Other studies, however, have suggested that people in online groups behave, in most respects, like those in offline groups. Many of the cues that people implicitly use to allocate status to others are minimized when people interact via computers—a group member's height, age, sex, and race can be kept private in online groups, and the computer-mediated format prevents the exchange of nonverbal signs of dominance and authority. There can be no raised voice, no long stare, and no rolling of the eyes when members are connected only by a computer. Online groups, however, still exhibit signs of structural differentiation. Participants, through the content of their messages, level of involvement, and style of communication (e.g., punctuation; capitalization such as I AGREE TOTALLY!!!!; slang; humor; and emoticons—text-based faces created with periods, commas, parentheses, semicolons, and so on) lay claim to characteristics that define their place within the group. In some cases, group members may even be *more* influenced by irrelevant diffuse status characteristics in online groups, because they have no other information to use to guide their perceptions of the other members. If all Ed knows about his partner in a discussion is that his or her name is Jolina, then he may inevitably draw conclusions about her personality and interests from her name alone (Spears, Lea, & Postmes, 2007).

In consequence, in most studies, the format of the group has little impact on status and attraction differentiation. Those who possess qualities that would likely earn them high status in face-to-face groups tend to participate more in computer-based groups as well (Driskell, Radtke, Salas, 2003). The goal of creating online groups that escape the implicit biases introduced by a group's tendency to favor the powerful—the utopian vision of a group where all members are created equally—remains elusive (McKenna, 2008; McKenna & Green, 2002).

rarely hesitated to show their disdain for the members of this subgroup, but these three were joined by strong bonds of attraction. As Paxton and Moody's (2003) analysis of a southern sorority suggests, members of cliques tend to be more similar to each other than to the rest of the group, so as a result cliques are higher in homophily. Members of the same racial category, for example, may join to form a coalition, or the group may separate naturally into all-male and all-female cliques (Hallinan, 1981; Schofield & Whitley, 1983; Thorne, 1993). Group members also often deliberately form and manipulate cliques within larger groups by systematically including some individuals and excluding others (Adler & Adler, 1995).

**Maintaining Structural Balance** Why do most groups tend toward reciprocity, transitivity, and clusters? According to Fritz Heider's **balance theory**, some patterns of relationships in groups are more structurally sound, or balanced, than others, and so groups naturally tend to gravitate toward these rather than toward unbalanced states (Cartwright & Harary, 1956, 1970; Heider, 1958; Newcomb, 1963). Consider, for example, the triad of Vizintin, Canessa, and Mangino. This triad was *balanced* because everyone in it liked one another; all bonds were positive. What would happen, however, if Mangino came to dislike Canessa? According to Heider, this group would be *unbalanced*. Such a group pattern is considered so unstable that it has been given the ominous name "the forbidden triad" (Granovetter, 1973). In general, a group is balanced if (1) all the relationships are positive, or (2) an even number of negative relationships occurs in the group. Conversely, groups are unbalanced if they contain an odd number of negative relations.

Because unbalanced sociometric structures generate tension among group members, people are motivated to correct the imbalance and restore the group's equilibrium. Heider noted that this restoration of balance can be achieved either through psychological changes in the individual members or through interpersonal changes in the group (Gawronski, Walther, & Blank, 2005). If Mangino initially likes only Vizintin and not Canessa, he may change his attitude toward Canessa when he recognizes the strong bond between Vizintin and Canessa. Alternatively, group members who are disliked by the other group members may be ostracized, as in the case of Delgado (Taylor, 1970). Finally, because the occurrence of a single negative relationship within a group can cause the entire group to become unbalanced, large groups tend to include a number of smaller, better balanced cliques (Newcomb, 1981). The Andes group, for example, was somewhat unbalanced overall, but its subgroups tended to be very harmonious. As a result, the group was high in cohesiveness.

**Determinants of Attraction Structure** Why did Parrado gain social standing in the group, and why was Delgado held in disregard? One's popularity, in large part, is determined by the interpersonal factors reviewed in Chapter 4—similarity, complementarity, reciprocity, personal qualities, and even physical attractiveness can influence one's sociometric ranking in a group. Parrado was similar to the others in age and background, and he possessed qualities that the others admired: He was optimistic, handsome, dependable, helpful, and strong. Delgado, unfortunately, did not possess such attributes. Interaction with Delgado incurred considerable costs and yielded very few interpersonal rewards (Thibaut & Kelley, 1959).

Popularity cannot be predicted solely on the basis of the group members' personal qualities, for different groups value different attributes. The qualities that earn a person popularity in a boardroom differ from those that predict sociometric standing on a baseball team or in a biker gang. Thus, predictions of social standing must take into account the *person–group fit*: the degree to which individuals' attributes match the qualities valued by the group to which they belong. In another group, Delgado might have been well-liked, for he was quite articulate and socially skilled. In the Andes group, however, the fit between his personal qualities and the group was poor (Anderson et al., 2001; Bukowski, Newcomb, & Hartup, 1996; Hubbard et al., 2001).

---

**balance theory** A conceptualization advanced by Fritz Heider which assumes that interpersonal relationships can be either balanced (integrated units with elements that fit together without stress) or unbalanced (inconsistent units with elements that conflict with one another). Heider believed that unbalanced relationships create an unpleasant tension that must be relieved by changing some element of the system.

## Communication Networks

In the Andes group, the three leaders stayed in close communication, discussing any problems among themselves before relaying their interpretations to the other group members. The other members usually routed all information to the threesome, who then informed the rest of the group. In contrast, the injured members were virtually cut off from communication with the others during the day, and they occasionally complained that they were the last to know of any significant developments. These regular patterns of information exchange among members of a group are called **communication networks**.

**Centrality Effects** Patterns of communication among group members, like other structural features of groups, are sometimes deliberately set in place when the group is organized. Many companies, for example, adopt a centralized, hierarchical communication network that prescribes how information is passed up to superiors, down to subordinates, and horizontally to one's equals. Even when no formal attempt is made to organize communication, an informal communication network will usually take shape over time. Moreover, this network tends to parallel status and attraction patterns. Take the Andes group as a case in point: Individuals who occupied high-status roles—the explorers, the food preparers, and the lieutenants—communicated at much higher rates and with more individuals than individuals who occupied the malingerer and injured roles (Shelly et al., 1999).

Communication networks become more complex and varied as groups increase in size, but some of their basic forms are graphed in Figure 6.5. In a *wheel* network, for example, most group members communicate with just one person. In a *comcon*, all members can and do communicate with all other members. In a *chain*, communication flows from one person to the next in a line. A *circle* is a closed chain, and a *pinwheel* is a circle where information flows in only one direction (Shaw, 1964).

---

**communication network** Patterns of information transmission and exchange that describe who communicates most frequently and to what extent with whom.

Centrality is a particularly important feature of communication networks. With centralized networks, one of the positions in the group has a very high degree of centrality—it is located at the crossroads (the *hub*) of communications—relative to the other positions in the group (e.g., the wheel, the kite, or the Y in Figure 6.5). Groups with this type of structure tend to use the hub position as the data-processing center, and its occupant typically collects information, synthesizes it, and then sends it back to others. In decentralized structures, like the circle or comcon, the number of channels at each position is roughly equal, so no one position is more "central" than another. These groups tend to use a variety of organizational structures when solving their problems, including the so-called *each to all* pattern, in which everyone sends messages in all directions until someone gets the correct answer (Shaw, 1964, 1978).

Early studies of communication networks suggested that groups with centralized networks outperformed decentralized networks (Bavelas, 1948, 1950; Bavelas & Barrett, 1951; Leavitt, 1951). A group with a wheel structure, for example, took less time to solve problems, sent fewer messages, detected and corrected more errors, and improved more with practice than a group with a decentralized structure, such as a circle or comcon (Shaw, 1964, 1978). The only exceptions occurred when the groups were working on complicated tasks such as arithmetic, sentence construction, problem solving, and discussions. When the task was more complex, the decentralized networks outperformed the centralized ones.

These results led Marvin E. Shaw to propose that network efficiency is related to *information saturation*. When a group is working on a problem, exchanging information, and making a decision, the central position in the network can best manage the inputs and interactions of the group. As work progresses and the number of communications being routed through the central member increases, however, a saturation point can be reached at which the individual can no longer efficiently monitor, collate, or route incoming and outgoing messages. Shaw noted that saturation can occur in a decentralized network, but it becomes more likely when a group with a centralized structure is working on complex problems. Because the

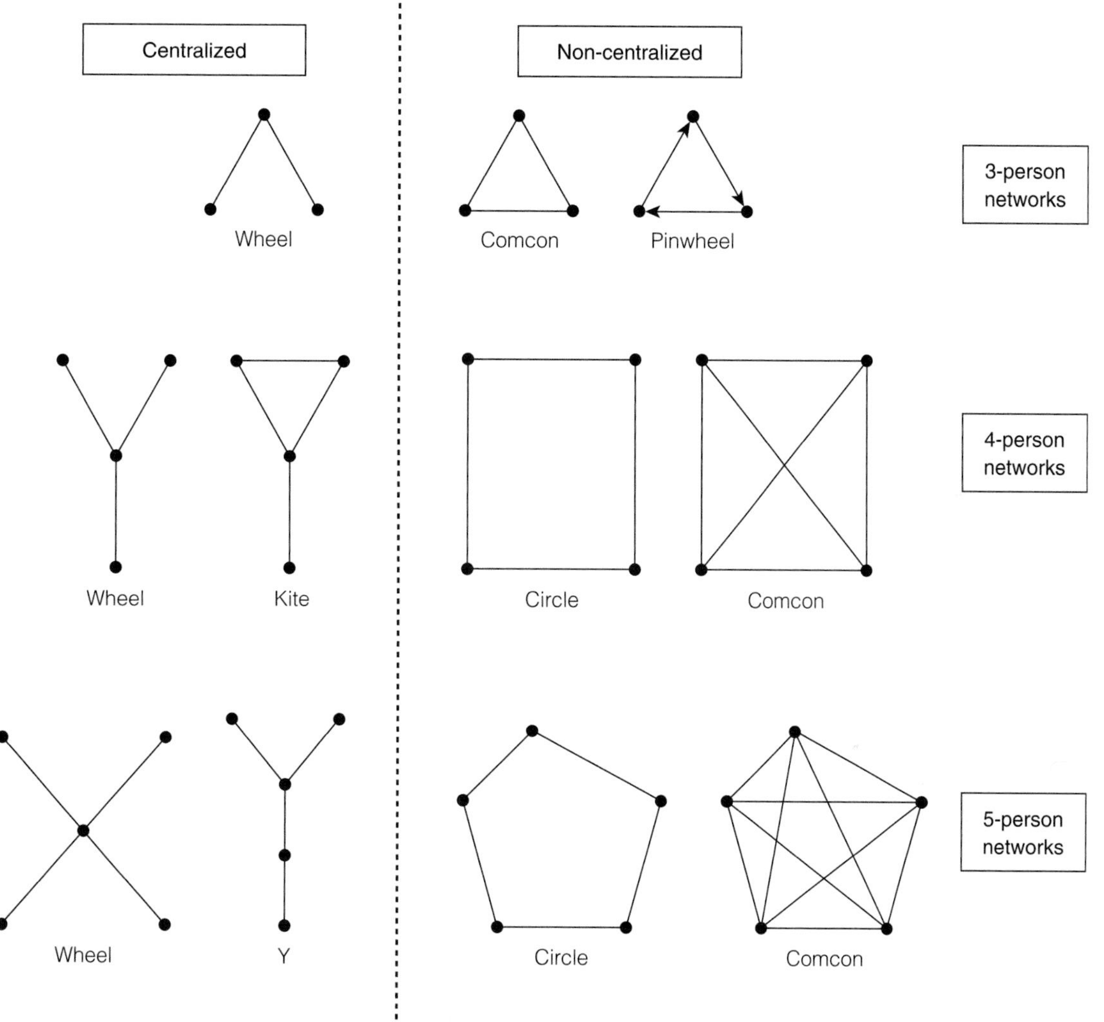


**FIGURE 6.5** Examples of common communication networks in small groups. These networks are a sample of the various kinds of communication networks that can be created by opening and closing lines of communication among members. In most of these examples the lines are undirected ones, with information flowing back and forth between members. Only the pinwheel has directed, one-way communication links.

SOURCE: Adapted from "Communication Networks," by M.E. Shaw. In L. Berkowitz (ed.), *Advances in Experimental Social Psychology* (Vol. 1). Copyright © 1964 by Academic Press. Reprinted by permission.

"greater the saturation the less efficient the group's performance" (Shaw, 1964, p. 126), when the task is simple, centralized networks are more efficient than decentralized networks; when the task is complex, decentralized networks are superior. In consequence, groups tend to gravitate naturally to more decentralized network structures when the tasks they must accomplish become more complex and multifaceted (Brown & Miller, 2000).

These different types of centrality also influence role allocations, overall commitment, and satisfaction with membership in the group (Krackhardt & Porter, 1986; Lovaglia & Houser, 1996). Individuals who occupy positions of high betweenness in centralized communication networks, such as a wheel or a Y (see Figure 6.5), are nearly always thought to be the leader of their group, even when they are randomly assigned to this position (Leavitt, 1951). In studies of employees in work groups, those who are more central in their network are less likely to quit than are employees at the periphery of the company's communication network (Feeley, 2000). Peripheral members are also more likely to quit in clumps. Because individuals in decentralized positions are connected to very few of the other members, when one peripheral member leaves the group, the individuals located near that person in the network also tend to leave the group (Krackhardt & Porter, 1986). Finally, centralized networks, by definition, have fewer centralized positions than decentralized positions. In consequence, the overall level of satisfaction in a centralized group is almost always lower than the level of satisfaction in a decentralized group (Shaw, 1964).

**Directional (Up–Down) Effects** Only small groups with decentralized communication networks outperform groups with centralized networks. Once the group becomes too large, members can no longer keep up with the high rate and quantity of information they are receiving. Therefore, most larger groups and organizations manage information flow by adopting hierarchical communication networks (Goetsch & McFarland, 1980). In such networks, information can pass either horizontally between members on the same rung of the communication ladder or vertically up and down from followers to leaders and back (Jablin, 1979).

Upward communications tend to be very different from downward communications (Sias, Krone, & Jablin, 2002). Downward-flowing information moves from the leaders to the followers of the group, and so generally includes explanations of actions to be taken, the reasons for actions, suggestions to act in a certain manner, and feedback concerning performance. In some cases, too, up-down messages are urgent ones, sent using more immediate channels of communication such as e-mail rather than face-to-face meetings (Byrne & LeMay, 2006). Upward communications from subordinates to superiors, in contrast, include information on performance, insinuations about a peer's performance, requests for information, expressions of distrust, factual information, or grievances concerning the group's policies. These upward communications, moreover, tend to be fewer in number, briefer, and more guarded than downward communications. In larger organizations, the upward flow of information may be much impeded by the mechanics of the transferral process and by the low-status members' reluctance to send information that might reflect unfavorably on their performance, abilities, and skills (Bradley, 1978; Browning, 1978; Manis, Cornell, & Moore, 1974). This reticence of low-status members means that good news travels quickly up the hierarchy, whereas the top of the ladder will be the last to learn bad news.

## Social Structures and Interactions: SYMLOG

Robert Freed Bales's theory of group structure and process, **Systematic Multiple Level Observation of Groups**, or **SYMLOG**, provides a fitting conclusion to the structural analysis of the Andes group. As noted in Chapter 2, Bales and his associates have spent years searching for regularities in group interaction (Bales, 1950, 1970, 1980, 1999; Bales, Cohen, & Williamson, 1979). Initially, they assumed that most of the variation in group behavior revolved around role structures. Hence, their initial system, Interaction Process Analysis (IPA), underscored the differences between task-oriented and socioemotional behavior. In time, however, Bales expanded his model to include two additional structural dimensions—status (dominance/ submission) and attraction (friendly/unfriendly).

The 26 basic roles identified by SYMLOG are listed in Table 6.3. Each role is labeled (e.g., U, DNF,

---

**Systematic Multiple Level Observation of Groups (SYMLOG)** Robert Bales's theory and observational system which assumes that group activities can be classified along three dimensions (dominance versus submissiveness, friendliness versus unfriendliness, and acceptance versus nonacceptance of authority) and that groups are more effective when these three aspects of the group align.

**TABLE 6.3 The SYMLOG Model of Group Structure**

| Label | Behavior | Description |
|---|---|---|
| U | Active, dominant, talks a lot | Material success and power |
| UP | Extrovert, outgoing, positive | Popularity and social success |
| UPF | A purposeful, democratic task leader | Social solidarity and progress |
| UF | An assertive, businesslike manager | Strong effective management |
| UNF | Authoritarian, controlling, disapproving | A powerful authority, law and order |
| UN | Domineering, tough-minded, powerful | Tough-minded assertiveness |
| UNB | Provocative, egocentric, shows off | Rugged individualism, self-gratification |
| UB | Jokes around, expressive, dramatic | Having a good time, self-expression |
| UPB | Entertaining, sociable, smiling, warm | Making others feel happy |
| P | Friendly, egalitarian | Egalitarianism, democratic participation |
| PF | Works cooperatively with others | Altruism, idealism, cooperation |
| F | Analytical, task-oriented, problem-solving | Established social beliefs and values |
| NF | Legalistic, has to be right | Value-determined restraint of desires |
| N | Unfriendly, negativistic | Individual dissent, self-sufficiency |
| NB | Irritable, cynical, won't cooperate | Social nonconformity |
| B | Shows feelings and emotions | Unconventional beliefs and values |
| PB | Affectionate, likable, fun to be with | Friendship, liberalism, sharing |
| DP | Looks up to others, appreciative, trustful | Trust in the goodness of others |
| DPF | Gentle, willing to accept responsibility | Love, faithfulness, loyalty |
| DF | Obedient, works submissively | Hard work, self-knowledge, subjectivity |
| DNF | Self-punishing, works too hard | Suffering |
| DN | Depressed, sad, resentful, rejecting | Rejection of popularity |
| DNB | Alienated, quits, withdraws | Admission of failure, withdrawal |
| DB | Afraid to try, doubts own ability | Noncooperation with authority |
| DPB | Quietly happy just to be with others | Quiet contentment, taking it easy |
| D | Passive, introverted, says little | Giving up all selfish desires |

SOURCE: Adapted with permission of The Free Press, a Division of Simon & Schuster Adult Publishing Group, from *SYMLOG: A System for Multiple Level Observation of Groups*, by Robert F. Bales and Stephen P. Cohen with Stephen A. Williamson. 

UPB) depending on its location along SYMLOG's three basic dimensions of group structure:

- **U**p versus **D**own, or dominance/submissiveness: Is this member active, outgoing, and talkative, or passive, quiet, and introverted?
- **P**ositive versus **N**egative, or friendliness/unfriendliness: Is this member warm, open, and positive or negative and irritable?
- **F**orward versus **B**ackward, or acceptance of the task-orientation of the established authority/non-acceptance of authority: Is this member analytic and task-oriented or emotional, untraditional, and (in some cases) resentful?

Observers, or the group members themselves, can rate each individual in the group using the 26 categories shown in the table. The group leader's behaviors, for example, might be concentrated in the "active, dominant, talks a lot" category rather than the "passive, introverted, says little" category. A disillusioned group member, in contrast, might get high scores for "irritable, cynical, won't cooperate." These ratings can be used to chart the flow of a group's interaction over time. When a group first begins to discuss a problem, most of the behaviors may be concentrated in the dominant, friendly, and accepting authority categories. But if the group is wracked by disagreement, then scores in the unfriendly, non-accepting authority categories may begin to climb. SYMLOG can also be used to create a graph of the group profile of each member's location on the dominance, friendliness, and authority dimensions (Hare, 1985, 2005; Hare & Hare, 2005; Isenberg & Ennis, 1981; Polley, 1989).

Although SYMLOG ratings were never completed for the Andes group, Figure 6.6 presents a hypothetical map of the group's structure based on Bales's model. The vertical axis corresponds to the role-related behavior in the group. People like Fito Strauch and Fernandez rank near the task-oriented, accepting of authority end of this dimension, whereas Harley and Mangino are located near the opposing authority end of this dimension because they tended to resist group pressures and to express their feelings and emotions within the group. The

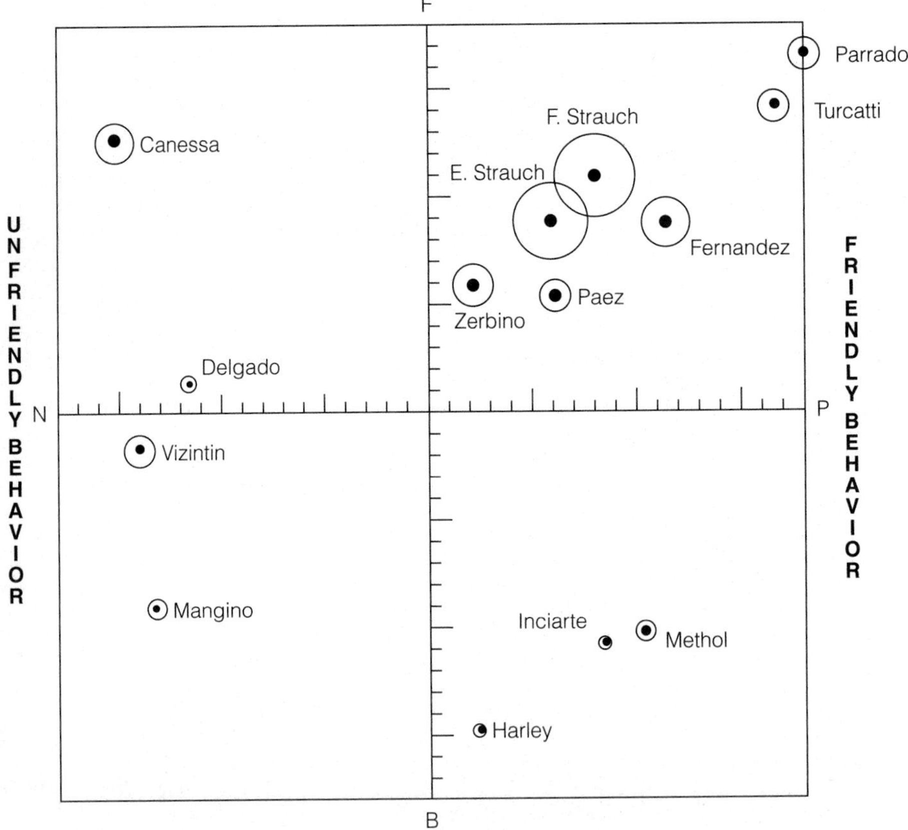


**FIGURE 6.6** Possible locations of a subset of the Andes group members in the three-dimensional space described by the SYMLOG rating system.

horizontal axis pertains to attraction relations among the members. Parrado and Turcatti, for example, occupy positions at the friendly end of this dimension because they were both very popular within the group, whereas Delgado's and Canessa's low social standing places them at the unfriendly end. Bales uses circles of varying size to illustrate the third structural dimension: dominance/submission. The larger the circle, the greater the group member's status in the group; hence, Fito Strauch is represented by a very large circle, whereas Harley (one of the malingerers) is represented by a very small circle.

SYMLOG, by taking into account role, status, and attraction, yields an integrative and in-depth picture of the organization of groups (Hare et al., 2005). The task-oriented acceptance of authority/non-acceptance of authority dimension focuses on role structure, the dominant/submissive dimension parallels status structure, and the friendly/unfriendly dimension pertains to attraction structure. Also, although communication structure is not considered explicitly, studies of task-performance groups indicate that individuals who are task-oriented and friendly communicate more frequently with others, whereas those who are dominant tend to receive more communications from others. Thus, SYMLOG is a powerful conceptual and methodological tool that provides a clearer understanding of the unseen group structures that underlie recurring patterns of interpersonal behaviors in groups.

## SUMMARY IN OUTLINE

*What is group structure?*

1. Groups are not unorganized, haphazard collections of individuals, but organized systems of interactions and relationships regulated by group structure.
2. Three important elements of group structure are norms, roles, and networks of connections among the members.

*Why do norms, both formal and informal, develop to regulate group behavior?*

1. Norms are implicit, self-generating, and stable standards for group behavior.
   - *Prescriptive norms* set the standards for expected group behavior.
   - *Proscriptive norms* identify behaviors that should not be performed.
   - *Descriptive norms* define what most people do, feel, or think in the group.
   - *Injunctive norms* differentiate between desirable and undesirable actions.
2. Norms develop gradually over time as members align their actions with those displayed by others, but Sherif's work using the autokinetic effect indicates that group members do not merely imitate others; rather, they often internalize these consensual standards.
3. Because norms are transmitted to other group members, they tend to be consensual, implicit, self-generating, and stable.
4. In some cases, individuals may engage in unhealthy behavior as a result of normative pressures, as documented by Crandall in his study of eating disorders in groups, and due to *pluralistic ignorance.*

*What kinds of roles are common in groups and how do they influence members?*

1. Roles specify the types of behaviors expected of individuals who occupy particular positions within the group.
2. As members interact with one another, their role-related activities become patterned (*role differentiation*) with
   - *Task roles* pertaining to the work of the group, and
   - *Relationship roles* pertaining to maintaining relations among members.

3. The same person rarely holds both the task role and the relationship role in the group.
4. Moreland and Levine's theory of *group socialization* describes the ways roles are allocated to individuals and the ways in which members transition through the roles of prospective member, new member, full member, marginal member, and former member.
5. The role differentiation and socialization processes often create stress and tension for groups and group members.
   - *Role ambiguity* occurs when the behaviors associated with a role are poorly defined.
   - *Role conflict* occurs when group members occupy two or more roles that call for incompatible behaviors (*interrole conflict*) or when the demands of a single role are contradictory (*intrarole conflict*).
   - When *role fit* is low, members do not feel that they match the demands of their roles.

*How can the social structure of a group be measured?*

1. *Social network analysis*, or *SNA*, offers researchers the means to describe a group's structure both visually and quantitatively. Common indexes used in SNA include *density, degree centrality, indegree, outdegree, betweenness*, and *closeness*.
2. Paxton and Moody's study of a southern sorority suggested that those members with high centrality indexes for a clique within the overall group were less committed to the sorority as a whole.

*What are status networks?*

1. Most groups develop a stable pattern of variations in authority and power (e.g., status networks, chains of command) through a *status differentiation* process.
2. In some instances, people compete with one another for status in groups; the resulting *pecking order* determines who is dominant and who is submissive.
3. Group members' perceptions of one another also determine status. Berger's *expectation-states theory* argues that group members allocate status by considering *specific status characteristics* and *diffuse status characteristics*.
4. When *status generalization* occurs, group members unfairly allow irrelevant characteristics such as race, age, or ethnic background to influence the allocation of prestige.
   - Status allocations are particularly unfair when individuals who are members of stereotyped minority societal groups are also underrepresented in the group itself, with the most extreme case being *solo status* (being the only individual of that category in the group).
   - In many online groups the effects of status on participation are muted, resulting in a participation equalization effect.

*What are attraction networks?*

1. A group's *attraction network*, or, in Moreno's terms, *sociometric structure*, develops through a *sociometric differentiation* process that orders group members from least liked to most liked.
2. Attraction relations tend to be reciprocal and transitive, and clusters or coalitions often exist within the group that are higher in homophily than the group as a whole.
3. As Heider's *balance theory* suggests, sociometric structures also tend to reach a state of equilibrium in which likes and dislikes are balanced within the group.
4. Sociometric differentiation generally favors individuals who possess socially attractive qualities, such as cooperativeness or physical appeal, but social standing also depends on the degree to which the individual's attributes match the qualities valued by the group (person–group fit).

*What are communication networks?*

1. A group's *communication network* may parallel formally established paths, but most groups also have an informal network that defines who speaks to whom most frequently.
2. Centralized networks are most efficient, but as Shaw's concept of information saturation suggests, not if tasks are too complex and require high levels of information exchange.
3. A group's network, in addition to structuring communication, influences a variety of group and individual outcomes, including performance, effectiveness, and members' level of satisfaction. Individuals who occupy more central positions in communication networks are often more influential than those located at the periphery. Because centralized networks have lower levels of closeness, the overall level of member satisfaction in such groups tends to be lower.
4. More information generally flows downward in hierarchical networks than flows upward, and the information that is sent upward is often unrealistically positive.
5. Bales's *Systematic Multiple Level Observation of Groups*, or *SYMLOG*, model of interaction and structure assumes that structure is based on three dimensions: dominance/submissiveness (Up/Down), friendliness/unfriendliness (Positive/Negative) and acceptance of task-orientation of authority/non-acceptance of task-orientation of authority (Forward/Backward).

## FOR MORE INFORMATION

*Chapter Case: The Andes Survivors*

- *Alive*, by Piers Paul Read (1974), is the best-selling account of the young men who crashed in the Andes and survived by creating a potent group.
- *Miracle in the Andes*, by Nando Parrado (2006), with Vince Rause, is a first-person account of the collective spirit of the rugby team. Parrado, the author, was one of the men who hiked down from the mountain to bring back help.

*Norms and Roles*

- "Role theory," by Bruce J. Biddle (2001), provides a concise summary of the history of role theory in the social sciences, as well as a review of current applications and trends.
- *Social Norms*, edited by Michael Hechter and Karl-Dieter Op (2001), is a collection of outstanding theoretical and empirical reviews of the nature of norms and their influence in groups.
- "A meta-analysis of work demand stressors and job performance: Examining main and moderating effects," by Simona Gilboa, Arie Shirom, Yitzhak Fried, and Cary Cooper (2008), synthesizes the results of 169 studies of 35,265 employees and their experiences with role-related stress.

*Intermember Relations*

- *The Development of Social Network Analysis: A Study in the Sociology of Science*, by Linton C. Freeman (2004), traces the roots of SNA back to some of the earliest work in the social sciences, and then attempts to explain why the methods grew relatively slowly until the explosion of interest in this method that occurred in the 1990s.
- "Social Status and Group Structure," by Cecilia L. Ridgeway (2001), offers a brief overview of the voluminous research and theory dealing with expectation states and status allocations in groups.

- *Analysis of Social Interaction Systems*, edited by A. Paul Hare, Endre Sjøvold, Herbert G. Baker, and Joseph Powers (2005), includes 26 chapters dealing with a variety of aspects of the SYMLOG method of group analysis, with sections pertaining to leadership, organizational development, cross-cultural implications, and methodology.

## Media Resources

Visit the Group Dynamics companion website at www.cengage.com/psychology/forsyth to access online resources for your book, including quizzes, flash cards, web links, and more!

# 7

# Influence

## CHAPTER OVERVIEW

An interpersonal undercurrent flows beneath the surface of most groups that pushes group members together, toward greater consensus, uniformity, homogeneity, and conformity. But other forces push members in divergent directions, promoting dissension, uniqueness, heterogeneity, and independence. Groups require both conformity and rebellion if they are to endure.

- When do people conform in groups?
- When do people resist the group's influence and, instead, change the group?
- Why do people conform?
- Do social influence processes shape juries' verdicts?

## CHAPTER OUTLINE

### Twelve Angry Men: Social Influence in Juries

On the sixth day of the trial, the judge faced the jury and explained:

> Murder in the first degree . . . premeditated homicide . . . is the most serious charge tried in our criminal courts. You have heard a long and complex case, gentlemen, and it is now your duty to sit down and try and separate the facts from the fancy. One man is dead. The life of another is at stake. If there is a reasonable doubt in your minds as to the guilt of the accused—then you must declare him not guilty. If—however—there is no reasonable doubt, then he must be found guilty. Whichever way you decide, the verdict must be unanimous (Rose & Sergel, 1958, p. 9).

The jurors file out and make their way to the Jury Room. There, the men find their seats as the foreman reminds them of their task and its seriousness; a son is accused of attacking, stabbing, and killing his own father. Yet, without discussing any of the evidence or the judge's instructions, the jury immediately pushes to take a straw vote to discover where it stands. The foreman asks who favors a guilty verdict; four jurors immediately raise their hands, and then another five join in. When Jurors #9 and #11 slowly raise their hands as well, all eyes turn to look at Juror #8, who looks down at the table in front of him. "Eleven to one," announces the foreman.

The jurors, from that moment onward, begin the task of bending Juror #8 to the will of the group. Juror #3 leans across the table and mutters to #8, "You are in left field." Juror #4 urges Juror #8 to be reasonable—it is far more likely that the eleven who agree on guilt are correct and that the lone individual is wrong. Juror #3 tries to bully the holdout, exclaiming, "You sat right in the court and heard the same things I did. The man's a dangerous killer. You could see it!" (Rose & Sergel, 1958, p. 14). Juror #7, who wants to end the discussion quickly since he has plans for the evening, tells #8 that it is hopeless to resist the group's decision: "I think the guy's guilty. You couldn't change my mind if you talked for a hundred years" (Rose & Sergel, 1958, p. 15). Juror #8 answers back, "I want to talk for a while."

And, talk they do. As Juror #8 explains the source of his doubts, suggests alternative interpretations of the evidence, and questions the accuracy of some of the witnesses, the jurors become uncertain. They vote time and time again, and with each vote the numbers favoring guilt and innocence shift; from 11 against 1 to 10 against 2 to 9 against 3 until, in time, the tables are turned. Juror #3, who was so sure that the son was guilty, finds that he is now the lone holdout. The group then pressures him to change, and grudgingly, angrily, he admits he was wrong, and the shift of opinion is complete. The jury's verdict: not guilty.

This jury's deliberations were described by Reginald Rose in his play *Twelve Angry Men* (Rose & Sergel, 1955). Although a dramatization, the play is based on Rose's experiences when he was summoned to jury duty. Like the jurors in the play, Rose found himself in the midst of an angry group of argumentative jurors who struggled to find common ground. As Rose explained: "I was overwhelmed. I was on a jury for a manslaughter case, and we got into this terrific, furious, eight-hour argument in the jury room" (Internet Movie Database, 2008).

How did the jury reach its verdict? The answer lies in **social influence**—interpersonal processes that produce, sometimes directly but often very subtly and indirectly, changes in other people. A jury member changing his vote, clique members mimicking the mannerisms of the group's leader, children endorsing the political views of their parents, and the uncertain restaurant patron using her small fork for her salad because everyone else at the table used that fork are all influenced by other people rather than by their own private ideation.

Much of this influence flows from the group to the individual, as Figure 7.1 suggests. When the majority of the group's members champion a particular view, they may pressure the few dissenting group members to change for the sake of the group's unity. However, social influence also flows

---

**social influence** Interpersonal processes that change the thoughts, feelings, or behaviors of another person.

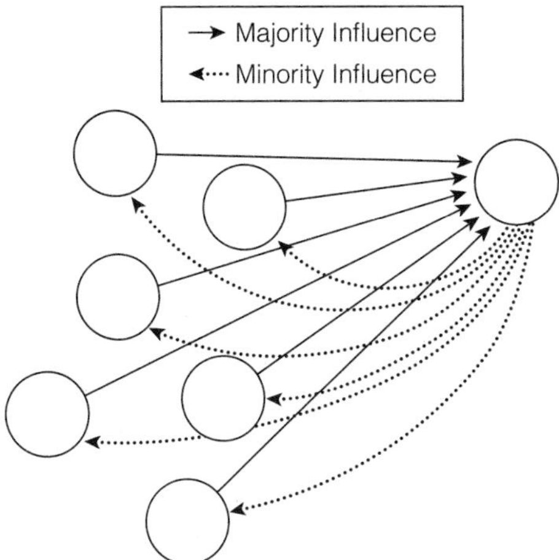


**FIGURE 7.1** Majority and minority influence in groups. In many cases, group members change as a result of direct group pressure by the majority (*majority influence*), but in other cases, one or more group members succeed in changing the entire group. This *minority influence* is indicated by the curved lines of influence from the lone minority back to the majority group members.

from the individual to the group. If the group is to meet new challenges and improve over time, it must recognize and accept ideas that conflict with the status quo. In the jury described in *Twelve Angry Men*, for example, the lone minority prevailed. He held his ground, offered reasons for his views, and in time the currents shifted and he prevailed. Whereas **majority influence** increases the consensus within the group, **minority influence** sustains individuality and innovation. In this chapter, we consider the nature of this give-and-take between majorities and minorities and the implications of this influence process for understanding how juries make their decisions.

---

**majority influence** Social pressure exerted by the larger portion of a group on individual members and smaller factions within the group.

**minority influence** Social pressure exerted by a lone individual or smaller faction of a group on members of the majority faction.

## MAJORITY INFLUENCE: THE POWER OF THE MANY

Lone individuals are free to think and act as they choose, but group members must abandon some of their independence. Once they walked into the jury room, the 12 jurors had to coordinate their actions with the activities of the other group members. Each one strove to change the group to suit his personal inclinations, but at the same time, the group influenced its members: It swayed their judgments, favored one interpretation of reality over another, and encouraged certain behaviors while discouraging others. When the group first polled the members, several members were uncertain that the young man was guilty. But when they saw so many others voting that way, they quickly agreed with them. They displayed **conformity**.

How strong is the urge to conform? Muzafer Sherif (1936; see Chapter 6) verified that group members modify their judgments so that they match those of others in their groups. Theodore Newcomb, in his 1943 study of Bennington students (see Chapter 2), showed that members of a group will gradually take as their own the group's position on political and social issues. But it was Solomon Asch who most clearly demonstrated the power of the many to influence the few (Asch, 1952, 1955, 1957).

### Influence in the Asch Situation

If you were a participant in Asch's experiment, you would have entered the test room thinking you were taking part in a simple study of visual acuity. After you and the rest of the participants sat down around the table, the experimenter would explain that he wanted the group to make a series of judgments about the length of some test lines. On each trial (or round), he would show you two cards. One card had a single line that was to serve as the

---

**conformity** A change in opinion, judgment, or action to match the opinions, judgments, or actions of other group members or the group's normative standards.

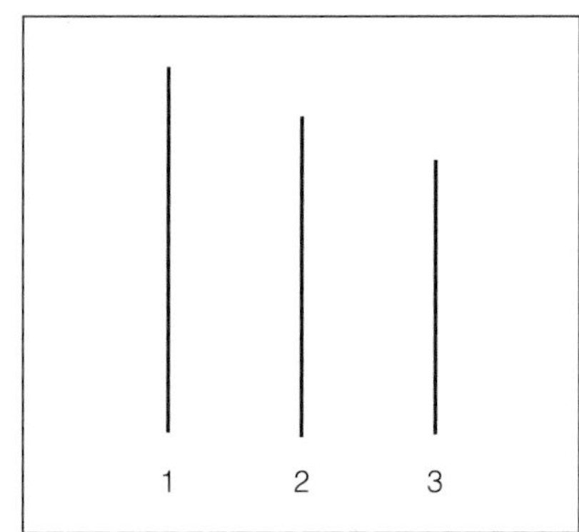

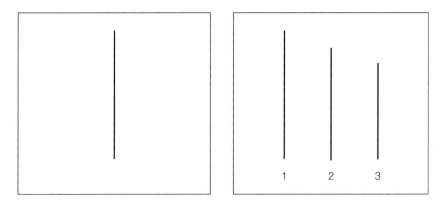


**FIGURE 7.2** An example of the problems given to participants in the Asch study. Subjects were told to look at the standard line (on the card on the left) and then match it to one of the three lines on the card at the right. The task was an easy one, but all of the group members save the one true subject were Asch's confederates who deliberately made many mistakes. For example, of the lines shown here the standard line was 8 inches long, and comparison Line 1 was the correct answer. However, the group chose Line 2, which was actually 7 inches long.

SOURCE: Asch, 1952.

standard. Three lines, numbered 1, 2, and 3, were displayed on the second card (see Figure 7.2). Your job? Just pick the line that matched the standard line in length. As one test line was always the same length as the standard line, the correct answer was fairly obvious. Few people made mistakes when making such judgments alone.

On each trial, the experimenter displayed two cards and asked the participants to state their answers aloud, starting at the left side of the table. The first few trials passed uneventfully, with everyone in the group picking the correct answer. But on the third trial, the first participant picked Line 2, even though Line 1 was a closer match to the standard stimulus. To your surprise, each of the other group members followed the first participant's lead by selecting Line 2 as the correct answer. When your turn came to answer, would you go along with the group and select Line 2, or would you stand your ground and select Line 1?

The majority's mistaken choice was no accident, for only one group member was an actual participant; all others were trained confederates who deliberately made errors on 12 of the 18 trials to see if the real participant would conform to a unanimous majority's judgments. When the participant arrived, he was seated so that he would answer only after most of the other participants did. He would study the lines, identify the correct answer, but hear everyone else make a different selection. When they heard the first person name the incorrect line as the best match, they probably thought little of it. But when the second person agreed with the first, they must have started to wonder. Then a third, a fourth, and a fifth person—all agreeing with one another, all selecting the wrong answer. What should they do?

Many conformed when placed in the **Asch situation**, showing a "marked movement toward the majority" (Asch, 1963/2003, p. 297). In fact, across several studies, Asch discovered that people conformed on about one third of the trials. Some participants, as Table 7.1 indicates, never conformed, but most did so at least once, and a few did on every single trial of the experiment. Between 75% and 80% of the participants agreed with the erroneous group at least once.

---

**Asch situation** An experimental procedure developed by Solomon Asch in his studies of conformity to group opinion. Participants believed they were making perceptual judgments as part of a group, but the other members were confederates who made deliberate errors on certain trials.

**TABLE 7.1 Results of Asch's Study of Conformity**

| Measure | Result (%) |
|---|---|
| How many members made at least one error? | 76.4 |
| How many times did the average member conform? | 36.8 |
| How many group members never conformed? | 24.0 |
| How many group members conformed 10 times or more? | 11.0 |
| How many individuals made at least one error when tested alone? | 5.0 |

SOURCE: Data from Asch, 1952, 1957.

Asch himself was surprised by his findings (Gleitman, Rozin, & Sabini, 1997). He had expected that his participants would resist the pressure to conform and speak out against the incorrect majority's view. Some did, but each time the group made its judgment many of the participants sided with the incorrect majority (Leyens & Corneille, 1999). Had the group been making important decisions—deliberating over a verdict in a murder trial, forging a plan to deal with an emergency, or crafting a solution to a difficult problem—then the participants would have let the group make a mistake at least one out of every three times.

In search of an explanation, Asch and other researchers tested a series of hypotheses about conformity. First, did it matter that the participants faced the others alone—just one voice disagreeing with an entire group? Second, what about group size? Did people conform so much because the group was so large that it overwhelmed them? Finally, did the people in Asch's study really accept the others' estimates as more accurate than their own, or were they just acquiescing? In other words, did they publicly agree, but privately disagree?

**All Against One** Juror #8 in *Twelve Angry Men* faced 11 other men who disagreed with him. Asch's participants faced a similar situation, for they were the only ones in the group who favored the correct line; all of the other group members chose a different line as the correct one. Did some of the force of the Asch situation derive from the unanimity of the majority?

Asch examined this possibility by running his study again, but this time he provided each subject with a partner; either another subject or a confederate who gave the correct answer on certain trials. This second individual sat in the fourth seat, and the participant sat in the eighth seat. As predicted, when participants had an ally, their conformity rates were cut to one fourth their previous levels. In yet another variation, Asch arranged for some confederates to disagree with the majority but still give an incorrect answer. Participants did not agree with the erroneous nonconformist, but his dissent made it easier for them to express their own viewpoint (Asch, 1955).

Why is a unanimous majority so influential? First, individuals who face the majority alone, without a single ally, bear 100% of the group's pressure. Psychologically, being completely alone is very different from having another person join with you against the others (Allen, 1975). Gaining a partner, however, helps one withstand the pressure to conform only as long as the partner remains supportive. Asch discovered that if the partner reverts back to the majority position, then subjects do as well. Second, the larger the size of the minority coalition, the smaller the majority's coalition—each time a member of the majority shifts to the minority the minority grows stronger and the majority weaker (Clark, 1990). Third, a partner makes a very embarrassing situation less so. The kinds of judgments that Asch studied were simple ones, so most participants probably realized that if they dissented, they would make an odd impression on others. After all, "the correct judgment appeared so obvious that only perceptual incompetents, fools, or madmen could err" (Ross, Bierbraurer, & Hoffman, 1976, p. 149). But if two members of the group disagree, then the situation's potential to lead to great embarrassment is lessened. A partner—and particularly one who is the first to dissent—takes much of the risk for going against the group (Sabini, Garvey, & Hall, 2001).

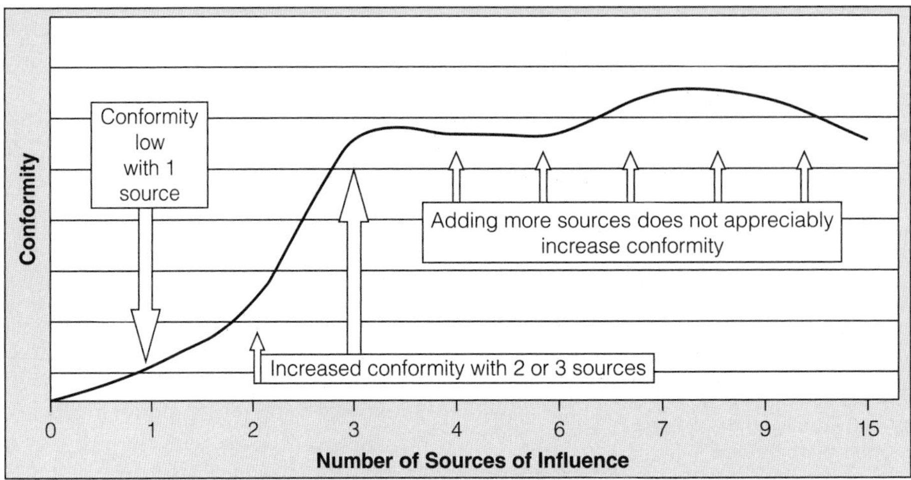


**FIGURE 7.3** The relationship between conformity and group size. Studies conducted in a number of settings suggest that few people conform when they face just one other person who disagrees with them, but that conformity rises rapidly when a lone individual faces a group of two or three. Adding more people to the majority beyond three does not appreciably increase conformity.

**Strength in Numbers (Up to a Point)** How many people does it take to create maximum conformity? Is two against one enough? Are smaller groups less influential? Is 11 to 1 too many, since individuals feel so anonymous in large groups they can resist group forces? Asch explored these questions by studying groups with 2 to 16 members. His findings, summarized in Figure 7.3, confirm that larger majorities are more influential—but only up to a point. People in two-person groups conformed very little; most were unsettled by the erroneous choices of their partner, but they did not go along with him or her (3.6% error rate). But the error rate climbed to 13.6% when participants faced two opponents, and when a single individual was pitted against three others, conformity jumped to 31.8%. Asch studied even larger groups, but he found that with more than three opponents, conformity increased only slightly (reaching its peak of 37.1% in the seven-person groups); even 16 against 1 did not raise conformity appreciably above the level achieved with three against one (Asch, 1952, 1955). As Focus 7.1 explains, "there is a marginally decreasing effect of increased supplies of people" (Latané, 1981, p. 344).

Rod Bond (2005), in a meta-analytic review of subsequent studies that used Asch's line-length judgment task, concluded that most studies confirm the pattern shown in Figure 7.3, but that the precise shape of the relationship between size and influence depends on a number of situational factors. When, for example, individuals in larger groups state their opinions publicly, the findings tend to match the Asch pattern. But when they keep their opinions to themselves, people are more likely to dissent. A large group can also lose some of its influence when its members do not reach their decisions independently of one another. If individuals learn that a six-person group disagrees with them, but they believe that the group members worked together as a group to make their decision, then the size of the dissenting group matters little. But when individuals believe that the other group members reached their conclusions independently of one another, then their influence increases as the number of sources increases. In fact, two 2-person groups (two separate entities) are more influential than one 4-person group whose members worked together (Wilder, 1977, Experiment 2; see also Jackson, 1987; Latané, 1981; Mullen, 1987; Wolf, 1987).

### Focus 7.1 When Is a Group's Impact Strongest?

During a staff meeting, discussion focuses on whether or not your company should purchase Windows computers or Apple computers. You strongly favor Apples, but everyone else favors computers that run Windows. Will you go along with the group's position, or continue to hold out for Apples?

Bibb Latané's **social impact theory** offers a compelling answer. This theory's *Principle of Social Impact* suggests that social influence is a function of the strength (S), the immediacy (I), and number (N) of sources present, or Impact = "*f*(SIN)". Imagine, for example, what happens when you turn on a single lamp in an otherwise dark room. The room is illuminated, but the amount of light in the room depends on, for example, the strength of the lightbulb in the lamp—a 25-watt bulb gives just enough light to see by, while a floodlight might reach every corner. And where is the lamp located? A lamp in the corner may leave the opposite corner of the room in shadows, but if you want more light, you can always turn to more lamps. However, if you continue to add light from whatever source, eventually the room will become so bright that turning on more lights will not make much difference. In an analogous fashion, your reaction to the Windows contingent depends upon the relative strength of the other group members. If you have just joined the company, then they have more strength than you do. You are a 25-watt bulb surrounded by 100-watt bulbs and you will likely chose to conform (Jetten, Hornsey, & Yorno, 2006).

Social impact theory also assumes that immediacy is correlated with influence, for people who are physically present in the room will have more of an impact than people who are absent. For example, the company's tech consultant may have been unable to attend the meeting, so she might have sent a message saying she preferred Apples; therefore, her immediacy is low, since she is not part of the face-to-face group meetings.

Sheer numbers are also critical. How many people oppose you? Four? Eight? Twelve? As with light bulbs, the more people, the more impact they will have on you—up to a point. The first light you turn on in a dark room has more of an impact than the hundredth. Similarly, the first person who disagrees with you has more impact than the hundredth person added to a majority that disagrees with you. Thus, conformity pressures do not increase at a constant rate as more people join the majority (Latané, 1981, 1996, 1997; Latané & Bourgeois, 2001; Latané & Wolf, 1981).

Social impact theory explains people's reactions across a range of influence settings, including Asch's conformity studies, reactions to emergencies, attitude change among dormitory residents, the formation of spontaneous crowds on street corners, donations to charities, and even a society's cultural practices (Harton & Bullock, 2007; Latané, 1997). One study, for example, asked college students to imagine themselves singing the "Star Spangled Banner" alone or with others in front of audiences of one, three, or nine listeners who were either music experts or students who were partially tone deaf. As the theory suggests, performers were more nervous when the audience was high rather than low in strength (experts vs. students) and nervousness increased at a decreasing rate as the audience grew larger. Performers also felt less anxiety when they imagined themselves performing, or actually performed, in front of audiences when they themselves were part of a group. Size, however, still mattered. People's anxiety declined when their groups increased from two, to three, to four, but once they reached four members, adding members did not appreciably reduce anxiety (Jackson & Latané, 1981). For these performers there was "safety in numbers," and the number was four.

**Forms of Social Reponse** Juror #2 in *Twelve Angry Men* sided initially with the majority, voting in favor of guilt. Was he just going along with the group? Or did he truly believe the defendant was guilty, and was just voting his conscience when he cast his ballot?

When a group member goes along with the decisions favored by others they may be displaying one of three different kinds of social responses to group

---

**social impact theory** An analysis of social influence developed by Bibb Latané which proposes that the impact of any source of influence depends upon the strength, the immediacy, and number of people (sources) present.

**compliance** Change that occurs when the targets of social influence publicly accept the influencer's position but privately maintain their original beliefs.

pressure. If showing **compliance** (or *acquiescence*), they privately disagree with the group but publicly express an opinion that matches the opinion expressed by the majority of the group. If **conversion** (or *private acceptance*), their agreement indicates a true change of opinion; they personally accept the influencer's position as their own. If **congruence**, they agree with the group, but in a strict sense they are not conforming. Their opinion matches the group's from the outset, so they do not need to shift their opinion in the direction advocated by the group.

Nonconformity can involve at least two different processes. People who refuse to bend to the will of the majority may be displaying **independence** (or *dissent*)—the public expression of ideas, beliefs, and judgments that are consistent with their personal standards. On ballot after ballot, Juror #8 refused to vote "guilty"; he remained independent. Second, nonconformity can reflect **anticonformity** (or *counterconformity*)—the expression of ideas or the taking of actions that are the opposite of whatever the group recommends. In some cases, anticonformity is motivated by rebelliousness or obstinacy rather than by the need to accurately express oneself. In other cases, however, members will play the "devil's advocate" to make sure that the group considers alternatives carefully. Juror #8 in *Twelve Angry Men*, for example, initially voted "not guilty," even though he believed the defendant was guilty. He explained, however, that he had voted "not guilty" to ensure that the jury would review all the evidence thoroughly. Figure 7.4 summarizes these five types of social responses. (Nail, MacDonald, & Levy, 2000, provided a detailed analysis of these and other forms of social response.)

Asch's subjects displayed two predominant forms of social response to the group pressure: compliance and independence. Of those who conformed, some questioned their own accuracy and ended up believing that the others were right. Most, however, thought the majority was wrong, but they went along with the group's choice. As Asch explained, they "suspected that the majority were 'sheep' following the first responder, or that the majority were victims of an optical illusion; nevertheless, these suspicions failed to free them at the moment of decision" (1955, p. 33).

Nearly all of the subjects, however, disagreed with the majority more frequently than they agreed. People conformed, on average, 3 of 12 times, but that means they *disagreed* 9 out of 12 times. Asch's study is often used to suggest that people are, by nature, conformists who tend to go along unthinkingly with whatever the majority favors. The data, however, suggest otherwise. Participants did not comply on all the trials; instead, their more frequent social response was to remain independent. They spoke their minds even when confronted with a unanimous majority, and agreed with the others only occasionally—when their error was a slight one or by choosing an answer that was intermediate between the correct answer and the majority's mistaken one (Hodges & Geyer, 2006).

## Predicting Majority Influence

Asch studied young men (mostly) making public judgments about relatively inconsequential matters. All lived in the United States at a time when their culture was politically conservative. Would his findings hold with other kinds of people, from other cultures, and in other groups facing different issues?

---

**conversion** Change that occurs when group members personally accept the influencer's position; also, the movement of all members of a group to a single, mutually shared position, as when individuals who initially offer diverse opinions on a subject eventually come to share the same position.

**congruence** Unprompted, natural agreement between the individual and the group.

**independence** Expressing opinions, making judgments, or acting in ways that are consistent with one's personal beliefs but inconsistent with the opinions, judgments, or actions of other group members or the group's norms.

**anticonformity** (or **counterconformity**) Deliberately expressing opinions, making judgments, or acting in ways that are different from those of the other group members or the group's norms in order to challenge the group and its standards rather than simply for the purpose of expressing one's personal preferences.

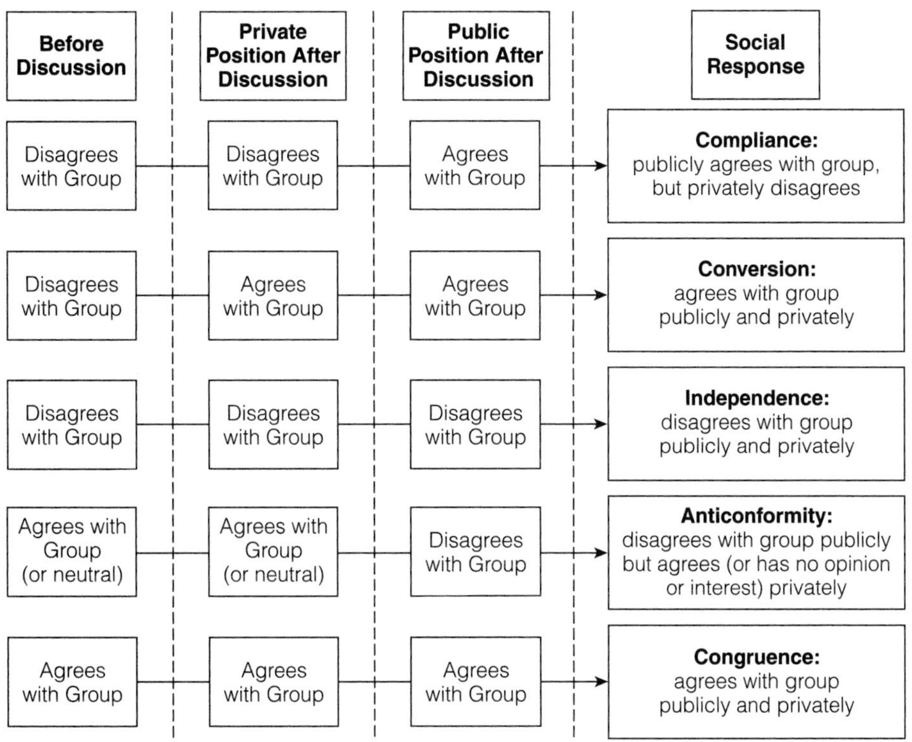


**FIGURE 7.4** Forms of social response. When people react to group pressures, conformity can be labeled *compliance*, and nonconformity can be thought of as *anticonformity*. In the opposite situation, when the response is prompted by one's personal standards, conformity becomes *conversion*, and nonconformity, *independence*. People who agree with the group from the outset are not technically conformists, because they do not shift their opinion in the direction advocated by the group; they already hold that position. They display *congruence* with their groups.

**Conformity Across People** Asch discovered that people differed, to an extraordinary degree, in their reaction to the conformity situation. Those who conformed often became increasingly disoriented as the study progressed, hesitating before they disagreed and apologizing to the others for their temerity. Others, in contrast, remained confident and self-assured throughout the experiment, never wavering from their convictions as they disagreed time and time again with the others. As one participant remarked, "The answers of the others didn't change my mind—an honest answer was expected. I did not change my answer once." When asked about the others in the group, he simply said "They were wrong" (Asch, 1952, p. 467).

Table 7.2 summarizes some of the differences between those who yield and those who remain resolute in the face of social pressure. Conformists tend to be more rigid in their thinking; their conventionality, conservative values, and unwillingness to confront authority increase their willingness to accept the majority's opinion. They let the situation and other people influence their perceptions, opinions, and outlooks. People who rely on situational cues when making perceptual judgments, self-conscious individuals, and those who are continually checking to see how well they are fitting into the group or situation (high self-monitors) are more likely to make certain that their actions match the group's standards. People who conform show a greater

**TABLE 7.2 A Sampling of Personality Characteristics That Are Reliably Associated with Conformity and Nonconformity**

| Characteristic | Reaction to Influence |
|---|---|
| **Age** | Conformity increases until adolescence, and then decreases into adulthood (Costanzo & Shaw, 1966). |
| **Authenticity** | Individuals who are higher in dispositional authenticity tend to resist external influences (Wood et al., 2008). |
| **Authoritarianism** | Authoritarians respect and obey authorities and social conventions (Altemeyer, 1988; Feldman, 2003). |
| **Big Five personality factors** | Introverts experience more discomfort when disagreeing with a group, and so conform more (Matz, Hofstedt, & Wood, 2008). Agreeableness, conscientiousness, and stability are associated with greater conformity (DeYoung, Peterson, & Higgins, 2002), but openness with less conformity (McCrae, 1996). |
| **Birth order** | First-born children tend to conform more than later-born children, who tend to be more rebellious and creative (Sulloway, 1996). |
| **Dependency** | People who are high in dependency (a strong motivation to please other people) display heightened compliance, conformity, and suggestibility (Bornstein, 1992). |
| **Gender identity** | Masculine individuals and androgynous individuals conform less on gender-neutral tasks than feminine individuals (Bem, 1982). |
| **Individualism–collectivism** | People from collectivistic cultures (e.g., Asians) value conformity as a means of achieving harmony with others, whereas those from individualistic cultures (e.g., European Americans) value uniqueness (Kim & Markus, 1999). |
| **Individuation** | People with a high desire to publicly differentiate themselves from others (*high individuators*) are more willing to express dissenting opinions and contribute more to group discussions (Whitney, Sagrestano, & Maslach, 1994). |
| **Intelligence** | Less intelligent people and individuals who are uncertain of their abilities conform more (Crutchfield, 1955). |
| **Need for closure** | Conformity pressures are stronger in groups with a preponderance of members with a high need for closure (De Grada et al., 1999). |
| **Need for uniqueness** | Individuals with a high need for uniqueness (NFU) are more likely to make unusual choices and prefer the unconventional to the conventional (Simonson & Nowlis, 2000). |
| **Self-blame** | Adolescents who tend to blame themselves for negative outcomes conform more than individuals low in self-blame (Costanzo, 1970). |
| **Self-esteem** | Individuals with low self-esteem conform more than individuals with moderate and high-self esteem (Berkowitz & Lundy, 1957); however, adolescents with high self-esteem conform more than those with low self-esteem (Francis, 1998). |
| **Self-monitoring** | High self-monitors, because of their higher self-presentational tendencies, conform more when striving to make a positive impression (Chen, Shechter, & Chaiken, 1996). |
| **Yea-saying** | Yea-sayers, particularly when working under a cognitive load, say "yes" faster and more frequently than individuals who thoughtfully consider their position (Knowles & Condon, 1999). |

interest, overall, in other people. They have a higher need for social approval, are more interpersonally oriented, and are more fearful of social rejection. Factors that undermine self-confidence—low self-esteem, incompetence, low intelligence—also increase conformity.

**Conformity across the Sexes** Did Asch underestimate the urge to conform by studying mostly men? Is it not true, "at least in our culture, that females supply greater amounts of conformity under almost all conditions than males" (Nord, 1969, p. 198)? That "women have been found to yield more to a bogus group norm than men" (Hare, 1976, p. 27)? Meta-analytic reviews suggest women conform more than men, but only to a small degree and in specific kinds of situations—when, for example, in face-to-face groups discussing nonpersonal issues or stating opinions aloud. In more anonymous, low surveillance situations, differences between men and women are almost nonexistent (Bond & Smith, 1996; Cooper, 1979; Eagly & Carli, 1981; Leaper & Ayres, 2007).

Why do women only conform more than men in face-to-face groups? The difference may reflect women's relatively greater concern for maintaining positive relationships with others. Whereas men tend to use disagreement to dominate others or even to separate themselves from the group, women may use agreement to create consensus and cohesion (Leaper & Ayres, 2007; Maslach, Santee, & Wade, 1987). These differences may also reflect continuing biases in the allocation of status to women. Despite changes in stereotypes about women and men, groups traditionally reward men for acting in dominant, nonconforming ways and women for acting in cooperative, communal ways. If women feel that they should behave in a traditional way, they may conform more than men (Eagly, Wood, & Fishbaugh, 1981). Women who do not accept the traditional role of women, however, do not conform more than men (Bem, 1985). Sexism in groups and in society at large may also prevent women from expressing their dissent in groups. The studies of status allocation reviewed in Chapter 6, for example, have indicated that groups only grudgingly allocate status to qualified women. This sexist bias against women undermines their resistance to influence and weakens their power to influence others (Eagly, 1987). As women have become more successful in work and educational settings, their social status has risen, along with their independence and assertiveness (Twenge, 2001).

**Conformity across Cultures and Eras** In the years since Asch first published his findings, other researchers have replicated his basic procedure in dozens of countries, including the United States, Britain, Belgium, Fiji, Holland, Kuwait, Portugal, and Zimbabwe. When Rod Bond and Peter Smith (1996) surveyed these studies, they concluded that Asch may actually have underestimated conformity by studying people living in a relatively individualistic culture. As noted in Chapter 3, the individualistic cultures typical of Western societies tend to place the individual above the collective. Collectivistic societies, which are more prevalent in Asia, Africa, and South America, stress shared goals and interdependence. As a result, people tend to conform more in collectivistic cultures, especially when the source of influence is family members or friends (Frager, 1970).

Bond and Smith also checked for changes in conformity during the period from 1952 to 1994 to determine if conformity rates fluctuated as society's tolerance of dissent waxed and waned. When Asch carried out his work in the 1950s, social norms stressed respect for authority and traditional values, whereas the late 1960s were marked by student activism and social disobedience. This period of rebelliousness was followed by a prolonged period of social stability. Do entire generations of people become more or less conforming, depending on the sociopolitical climate of the times in which they live? Bond and Smith discovered that conformity rates have dropped since the 1950s, but they found no support for the idea that conformity is a "child of its time." Conformity is decreasing, but this decline was not sharper in the 1960s or more gradual in the relatively placid 1970s and 1980s (Larsen, 1982; Perrin & Spencer, 1980, 1981).

**Conformity across Contexts** Asch studied conformity in newly formed groups working on a very simple task that was not particularly consequential. The members did not know each other; they sat together in a well-lit room, and they made their decisions by announcing their choice aloud. The members of juries, in contrast, first meet when the

**TABLE 7.3 A Sampling of Group and Situational Characteristics That Reliably Increase and Decrease Conformity**

| Factor | Conformity Increases If | Conformity Decreases If |
|---|---|---|
| **Accountability** (Quinn & Schlenker, 2002) | Individuals are striving for acceptance by others whose preferences are known | Individuals are accountable for their actions and are striving for accuracy |
| **Accuracy** (Mausner, 1954) | Majority's position is reasonable or accurate | Majority position is unreasonable or mistaken |
| **Ambiguity** (Spencer & Huston, 1993) | Issues are simple and unambiguous | Issues are complex and difficult to evaluate |
| **Anonymity** (Deutsch & Gerard, 1955) | Responses are made publicly in face-to-face groups | Responses are anonymous and members cannot see each other |
| **Attraction** (Kiesler & Corbin, 1965) | Members are attracted to the group or its members | Members dislike each other |
| **Availability of mating partners** (Griskevicius et al., 2006) | Individuals are motivated to stand out from the crowd | Nonconformists could be revealed as incorrect |
| **Awareness** (Krueger & Clement, 1997) | Individuals are aware they disagree with the majority | Individuals do not realize their position is unusual |
| **Cohesion** (Lott & Lott, 1961) | Group is close-knit and cohesive | Group lacks cohesion |
| **Commitment to position** (Gerard, 1964) | Individuals are publicly committed to their position from the outset | Members' responses are not known to the other group members |
| **Commitment to membership** (Kiesler, Zanna, & DeSalvo, 1966) | Individuals are committed to remaining in the group | Groups or membership are temporary |
| **Existential threat** (Renkema et al., 2008) | Aspects of the situation trigger existential anxieties | Situation buffers individual from existential threat |
| **Priming** (Epley & Gilovich, 1999) | Unnoticed cues in the setting prime conformity | Situational cues prime independence |
| **Size** (Asch, 1955) | Majority is large | Majority is small |
| **Task** (Baron, Vandello, & Brunsman, 1996) | Task is important but very difficult | Task is important and easy, or task is trivial |
| **Unanimity** (Asch, 1955) | Majority is unanimous | Several members disagree with the majority |

trial begins, and sometimes spend days, weeks, or even months together. Juries have a leader charged with keeping order, and the members vote by secret ballot—unless they decide otherwise. Juries are also making extremely important decisions: some juries make life-and-death decisions.

Just as some individuals lean toward conformity rather than independence, so some group situations create more pressure to conform than do others (see Table 7.3). Groups that are cohesive, larger in size, unanimous, and more highly structured increase members' conformity, but ones with internal dissention, norms that encourage creativity, or a history of poor decision making are easier to resist. Similarly, such factors as anonymity, allies, and high status bolster the individual's position within the group, and therefore reduce the pressure to conform. Other situational factors, however, undercut group members' capacity to resist the group—for example, accountability, commitment to the group, and the difficulty of the task. These aspects of the situation are therefore associated with increased conformity.

Consider, for example, the difference between the Asch situation and the so-called **Crutchfield situation**. Participants in Asch's studies stated their choices aloud under the watchful eyes of all the other members, and this procedure likely increased their feelings of embarrassment and of being evaluated. His procedure was also inefficient, for many confederates were required to study just one participant. Richard Crutchfield (1955) solved this latter problem by eliminating the confederates. In Crutchfield's laboratory, the participants made their judgments while seated in individual cubicles (see Figure 7.5). They flipped a small switch on a response panel to report their judgments to the researcher, and their answers would supposedly light up on the other group members' panels as well. Crutchfield told each person in the group that he or she was to answer last, and he himself simulated the majority's judgments from a master control box. Thus, during the critical trials, Crutchfield could lead participants to think that all the other participants were giving erroneous answers.

The Crutchfield situation sacrifices face-to-face interaction between the participant and confederates, but was efficient: Crutchfield could study five or more people in a single session, and he did not need to recruit confederates. Because group members' responses were private, however, fewer people conformed in the Crutchfield situation relative to the Asch situation (Bond & Smith, 1996). Indeed, the change that takes place in such groups may reflect conversion rather than a temporary compliance that disappears when the individual is separated from the group and its influence.

**Conformity across the Internet** Crutchfield's studies of individuals making decisions as a group but connected only electronically anticipated the use of computer-based networks to facilitate group interaction. In his day, most groups met in face-to-face settings, but today's groups often interact in computer-mediated meetings. Freed from the constraints of public evaluation and the immediate scrutiny of others, individuals might be expected to conform less and dissent more when their interactions take place via e-mail, in chat rooms, or through instant messaging (Kraut et al., 1998). Yet, research suggests that online groups' dynamics tend to be similar to face-to-face, offline groups (Bargh & McKenna, 2004). Through discussion, consensus emerges within the group, and members move in the direction of agreement rather than continually debating issues. Online groups develop norms that structure interactions and status, and new members are socialized to follow these rules. Members sometimes act in ways that violate the group's norms of etiquette ("netiquette") by expressing hostility and exchanging insults, but such deviations are usually sanctioned, and offenders who do not conform are eventually ostracized from the group (Straus, 1997).

Conformity may actually be more prevalent in online groups rather than offline groups, and the *Social Identity Model of Deindividuation Effects*—or SIDE for short—explains why (Spears, Lea, & Postmes, 2007). SIDE suggests that in the relatively anonymous online world, individuals tend to define themselves in terms of their collective, social identities rather than their individualistic, personal identities. Online interactions are depersonalized ones, but only in the sense that individual motivations, qualities, and beliefs become less salient. One's collective, shared attributes, in contrast, become more salient, and so the social component of the self comes to the fore. Some people, faced with increased depersonalization, may strive to reassert their individuality by acting in unusual, distinctive ways, but if their group identity is salient they will

---

**Crutchfield situation** An experimental procedure developed by Richard Crutchfield to study conformity. Participants who signaled their responses using an electronic response console believed that they were making judgments as part of a group, but the responses of the other members that appeared on their console's display were simulated.

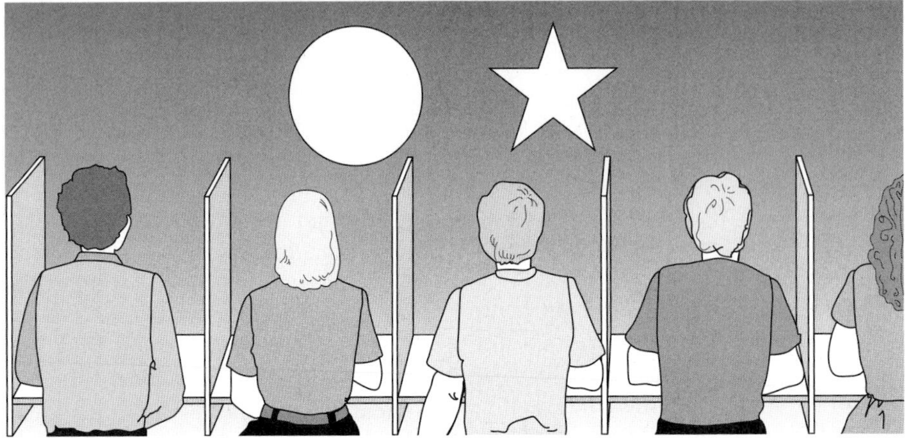

**FIGURE 7.5** Conformity in the Crutchfield situation. Crutchfield studied conformity by seating subjects in individual booths and gathering their responses electronically. When asked a question such as "Which one of the figures has a greater area, the star or the circle?" subjects answered by flipping the appropriate switch in their booth. They thought that their answers were being transmitted to the experimenter and the other subjects, but in actuality the experimenter was simulating the majority's judgment from a master control panel.

SOURCE: Wrightsman, 1977.

more likely conform to the group's norms (Spears et al., 2002). Because of these "SIDE effects," when individuals receive electronic messages from other individuals—even people they do not know and will not communicate with in the future—they frequently change their decisions to match the recommendations of these anonymous strangers (Lee & Nass, 2002). When small groups of students use e-mail in classes, each group develops idiosyncratic norms that regulate the group's interactions, and conformity to these norms increases through the semester (Postmes, Spears, & Lea, 2000). People comply with norms of reciprocity and cooperation in online groups even when completely anonymous, provided they identify with the group (Cress, 2005). Members of groups will also trust each other to fairly share financial resources, provided these others are members of the same online group (Tanis & Postmes, 2005). Apparently, the urge to conform, which Asch found so powerful in face-to-face settings, is no less powerful when people who are separated by space and time are united by an Internet connection.

## MINORITY INFLUENCE: THE POWER OF THE FEW

The other 11 members of the *Twelve Angry Men* jury relentlessly pressured Juror #8 to change his verdict to guilty, but he refused to yield. Despite pressure from religious authorities, Galileo insisted that the planets revolve around the Sun rather than the Earth. Many in the civil rights movement of the 1960s favored using violence, if necessary, to overcome discrimination and racism, but Dr. Martin Luther King Jr. ensured that the movement succeeded through the application of nonviolent methods. Sigmund Freud actively rebuked critics of his theory of the unconscious mind until it was grudgingly accepted by many psychologists. The composer Igor Stravinsky was denounced as a musical heretic when *The Rite of Spring* was first performed, but he refused to change a note.

These historical examples demonstrate that the majority does not always overwhelm the dissenter, for sometimes it is the minority that is the influencer and the majority that is influenced. Asch found that the majority can bring powerful and potentially overwhelming pressure to bear upon the minority, but other studies have shown that minorities can fight back with pressure of their own.

## Conversion Theory of Minority Influence

Just as Asch's studies highlighted the power of the majority, so the work of Serge Moscovici and his colleagues underscored the power of the minority. Moscovici, in an insightful analysis of conformity in science itself, suggested that for too long theorists and researchers assumed that change comes from within existing social systems rather than from external revolutionary sources; that the victory of the majority is more democratic than the victory of the minority; and that innovation occurs as a result of direct rather than indirect interaction between the majority and minority. In contrast to this majority-rules model of social influence, Moscovici's **conversion theory** maintains that disagreement within the group results in conflict, and that the group members are motivated to reduce that conflict—sometimes by getting others to change but also by changing their own opinions (Moscovici, 1976, 1980, 1985).

Conversion theory suggests that minorities influence in a different way than majorities do. Minorities, Moscovici theorized, influence through a *validation process*. When someone in the group breaks the group's unanimity—such as Juror #8 arguing "not guilty"—members take notice of this surprising turn of events. The minority captures their attention, and though most do not believe that the minority is correct, they nonetheless consider the arguments closely. The majority's message, in contrast, is less intriguing to members. When people discover where most of the group stands on a position, through a *comparison process* they check to see if they can join the majority. Because being in the majority is, in most cases, more rewarding than membership in the minority—those in the majority usually find that they control the group's resources whereas those in the minority may have little say in the group's decisions—people usually change to comply with the group's consensus. This compliance reflects a desire to be included within the group, however, rather than any kind of in-depth review of the majority's reasons for their position. In consequence, the change is relatively superficial and may evaporate once the individual leaves the group.

Moscovici maintained that the validation processes instigated by a minority are more long-lasting than those triggered by the comparison processes of majority influence. Comparison results in direct influence as members public comply. Validation, in contrast, leads to private acceptance, making minorities a source of innovation in groups. They shake the confidence of the majority and force the group to seek out new information about the situation. This conversion process takes longer, however, than the compliance process, and so the effects of a minority on the majority sometimes do not emerge until some time has passed. In some cases, the influence of minorities becomes evident only when the group has completed its initial deliberations and moved on to another task (Moscovici, 1994; see also Maass, West, & Cialdini, 1987; Nemeth, 1986).

Moscovici and his colleagues, in one of the first tests of the theory, reversed the usual Asch situation by planting two confederates in six-person groups and then arranging for the confederates to systematically disagree with the majority's decision. Instead of judging lines, Moscovici's subjects judged, aloud, the color and brightness of a series of color slides. All of the 36 slides were shades of blue, varying only in luminosity. But when it was their turn to name the color of the slides the confederates consistently said "green" rather than "blue." In some cases, the confederates answered first and second, but in other groups one answered first and the other answered fourth (Moscovici, Lage, & Naffrechoux, 1969).

Moscovici and his colleagues confirmed the power of the minority. When tested alone, one person said two of the slides were green: a 0.25%

---

**conversion theory** Serge Moscovici's conceptual analysis of the cognitive and interpersonal processes that mediate the direct and indirect impact of a consistent minority on the majority.

error rate. When in the presence of the green-saying confederates, this error rated jumped to 8.4%—not as much influence as that found by Asch in his studies of majority influence, but a significant amount considering the obviousness of the correct answer. Moscovici also found evidence of the delayed effects of the minority on the majority. After the public judgment task, a second experimenter entered the room and explained that he was also doing a study of vision. Participants were then shown another set of colors that included 3 blue slides, 3 green slides, and 10 slides in the blue-green range, and they privately labeled each one either blue or green. Those who had been previously exposed to a minority-group opinion were more likely to label the ambiguous slides as green rather than blue, and this bias was more marked among those members who *did not* change their public choices when they first encountered the minority. This delayed, indirect impact of minorities on the majority has been documented in a wide variety of laboratory and field studies, which indicate that "minorities tend to produce profound and lasting changes in attitudes and perceptions that generalize to new settings and over time . . . whereas majorities are more likely to elicit compliance that is confined to the original influence setting" (Maass et al., 1987, pp. 56–57).

## Predicting Minority Influence

Moscovici's conversion theory began as a minority opinion that many researchers rejected, but it eventually won over even the most stubborn members of the opposition—confirming the theory's own predictions. The question changed, over time, from "Are minorities influential?" to "When are minorities influential?" Answers to that question, which are reviewed briefly in the next sections, suggest that minorities who argue consistently for their positions but all the while manage to remain members in good-standing in the group given time, will shift the group's consensus away from the majority's position toward the one they favor (see Crano & Seyranian, 2007; Martin & Hewstone, 2008, for reviews).

**Consistency and Influence** In *Twelve Angry Men*, Juror #8 always voted in favor of "not guilty." He did not waver, for a moment, as the majority pressured him to change his vote. He did not always have compelling arguments to back up his position, but he was always consistent in the defense of his view.

A consistent minority is an influential one. Moscovici verified the importance of maintaining consistency in his original blue–green study by also including a condition in which the confederates labeled the blue slides green on two-thirds of the trials instead of all of the trials. The error rate dropped down to 1.25%—hardly any influence at all (Moscovici et al., 1969; Moscovici & Personnaz, 1980).

Subsequent studies have confirmed the importance of behavioral consistency on the part of the minority, but also suggest that minorities must walk the line between appearing self-assured and unreasonable. Minorities are particularly influential when the majority interprets the consistency positively (Wood et al., 1994) and if minorities offer coherent, compelling arguments that contradict the majority's position (Clark, 1990). They are also more influential if they signal their confidence in their opinion by sitting at the head of the table (Nemeth & Wachtler, 1974) or by reminding the group of their experience (Shackelford, Wood, & Worchel, 1996). Successful minorities grant minor concessions to the majority (Pérez & Mungy, 1996), or engage in small talk about unrelated matters prior to revealing their position (Dolinski, Nawrat, & Rudak, 2001). In general, minorities are more influential when they are perceived to be team players who are committed, competent, and group centered (Levine & Russo, 1987).

An influential minority also avoids threatening the integrity of the group itself. Many groups will tolerate debate and disagreement, but if the dissent creates deep divisions in the group, the majority may take steps to quash the minority or exclude its members from the group. If a group is just a loose conglomeration of individuals with no clear sense of identity, then the members of this "group" do not feel threatened by disagreement. But if the group members identify strongly with their group, and they feel that the dissenter is undermining its collective identity, they are more likely to feel a sense of loss when members begin to take a minority's arguments seriously (Prislin, Brewer, & Wilson, 2002). In such cases, an individual who is not even a member of the group may be more influential than an ingroup member (Phillips, 2003).

**Idiosyncrasy Credits** In *Twelve Angry Men*, Juror #8 was influential, but so was Juror #11. That juror voted guilty on the first ballot, as did the other 10 jurors. But, when Juror #8 noted several conflicting aspects of the evidence, Juror #11 changed his mind and shifted his vote. Did prefacing his dissent with conformity increase or decrease his influence?

Edwin Hollander (1971) developed the concept of **idiosyncrasy credits** to explain the group's positive reaction to a minority who prefaces dissent with conformity. According to Hollander, idiosyncrasy credits are "the positive impressions of a person held by others, whether defined in the narrower terms of a small face-to-face group or a larger social entity such as an organization or even a total society" (1971, p. 573). These credits accumulate as members interact—typically as the member contributes to the progress of the group toward desired goals. Because high-status members have usually contributed more in the past and possess more valued personal characteristics, they have more idiosyncrasy credits. Therefore, if they do not conform, their actions are more tolerable to the other members. The low-status members' balance of credits is, in comparison, very low; hence, they are permitted a smaller latitude for nonconformity. The idiosyncrasy model, which has been supported experimentally, suggests that influence levels in a group are increased by careful conformity to group norms during the early phases of group formation, followed by dissent when a sufficient balance of idiosyncrasy credit has been established (Hollander, 2006).

Hollander's advice about early conformity contrasts to some extent with Moscovici's recommendations concerning consistent nonconformity. Hollander warned that dissenters who challenge the majority without first earning high status in the group will probably be overruled by the majority, but Moscovici argued that consistent nonconformity will lead to innovation and change. Both tactics, however, may prove effective. Researchers compared the two in group discussions of three issues. One minority built up idiosyncrasy credits by agreeing on the first two issues that the group discussed, but then disagreeing on the third. The second minority built up consistency by disagreeing with the group on all three issues. Both minorities were influential, but the minority who built up idiosyncrasy credits was more influential in all-male groups (Bray, Johnson, & Chilstrom, 1982).

**The Diligence of Dissenters** Part of the secret of the unique influence of minorities lies in the quality of their argumentation. Those who know that they are members of the majority position on an issue feel less pressure to articulate their points clearly, for they expect that, with numbers on their side, they are likely to carry the day. But the individual who holds the minority position feels more intently the need to craft persuasive messages. Disagreeing with others is not a situation most people find enjoyable, and so few enter into this predicament without considering the strength of their own arguments and their reasonableness. Minorities are likely to have put more thought into the issue, and as a result they are able to ready a stronger defense of their position (Guinote, Brown, & Fiske, 2006).

Researchers tested the augmented argumentative skill of minorities by asking individuals to read about a controversial medical case and then decide if they supported the physicians' decision in the matter. Before being given the opportunity to meet with others to discuss the case, the participants were told that they agreed either with the majority

---

**idiosyncrasy credit** In Edwin Hollander's explanation for the leniency groups sometimes display toward high status members who violate group norms, the hypothetical interpersonal credit or bonus that is earned each time the individual makes a contribution to the group but is decreased each time the individual influences others, makes errors, or deviates from the group's norms.

or the minority of the group. Those assigned to the majority condition were told that 78% of the others agreed with them, and those in the minority condition were led to believe that only 22% shared their view. Participants then were asked to provide their arguments and reasons in support of their position in writing. The researchers then gave these written arguments to raters who evaluated the messages for creativity and strength. As expected, the "minorities" crafted better arguments than those in the "majority" (Kenworthy et al., 2008). In a related study, researchers found that individuals who knew they would be arguing against the views of the majority prepared more diligently for their meetings (Van Hiel & Franssen, 2003).

**Decision Rules and Dissent** Juror #8 faced a difficult situation—he alone disagreed with all the others in the group—but one aspect of the group situation helped him cope: the group's decision rule. The law required the group to operate under the rule of unanimity, meaning that all group members had to agree on the decision before the case was closed. If a group operates under a unanimity rule, then the lone minority has far more power over the others. But if the group adopts a majority-rules procedure, then the majority can reach its decision without having to even consider the validity of the minority's position (Thompson, Mannix, & Bazerman, 1988). A unanimity rule helps the minority, and the majority-rules procedure benefits the majority.

Investigators examined the impact of the group's decision rule on the relative influence of majorities and minorities by asking three-person groups to role play owners of three small businesses negotiating to rent a shared marketplace. Two of the members agreed with one another on several of the key issues, but the third member was the lone minority. Some of the groups worked under a unanimity rule, which stipulated that all three parties must agree to the terms of the final decision, but others were bound by the majority-rules stipulation. As expected, the group working under the unanimity rule reached a decision that was fairer to all three of the parties than did the groups that operated under the majority-rules order, but when the group based its decision on majority-rules, the majority formed a coalition that blocked the minority. Group members' personal motivations, however, moderated this tendency in a significant way, for the pernicious effects of the groups' decision rule only occurred when members were motivated to maximize their own personal rewards rather than the rewards for the entire group (Ten Velden, Beersma & De Dreu, 2007).

## Dynamic Social Impact Theory

Why did the members of the *Twelve Angry Men* jury initially vote, 11 to 1, in favor of a guilty verdict? And why did they, over time, change their votes? From the majority's perspective, change takes place when group members recognize the wisdom of the collective and conform to its choices. From the minority's perspective, change takes place when the majority reexamines and possibly revises its position. But change in groups is actually a mutual process—the majority influences the minority, and the minority influences the majority.

**Dynamic social impact theory**, as proposed by Bibb Latané and his colleagues, describes the processes underlying this give-and-take between the majority and the minority. As noted in Focus 7.1, social impact theory suggests that influence is determined by the strength, immediacy, and number of sources present. *Dynamic* social impact theory extends this basic principle by describing how groups, as complex systems, change over time. Groups are not static, but constantly organizing and reorganizing in four basic patterns: consolidation, clustering, correlation, and continuing diversity (Harton & Bullock, 2007; Latané, 1996, 1997; Latané & Bourgeois, 1996, 2001; Vallacher & Nowak, 2007).

---

**dynamic social impact theory** Bibb Latané's extension of his social impact theory, which assumes that influence is a function of the strength, the immediacy, and the number of sources present, and that this influence results in consolidation, clustering, correlation, and continuing diversity in groups that are spatially distributed and interacting repeatedly over time.

1. *Consolidation.* As individuals interact with one another regularly, their actions, attitudes, and opinions become more uniform. For example, even when individuals are assigned at random to rooms in college dormitories, over the course of the academic year their attitudes on a variety of topics become more and more similar (Cullum & Harton, 2007). The opinions held by a majority of the group tend to spread throughout the group, and the minority dwindles in size.
2. *Clustering.* As the law of social impact suggests, people are more influenced by their closest neighbors, so clusters of group members with similar opinions emerge in groups. Clustering is more likely when group members communicate more frequently with members who are close by and less frequently with more distant group members, and if members change locations to join similar others.
3. *Correlation.* Over time, the group members' opinions on a variety of issues—even ones that are not discussed openly in the group—converge, so that their opinions become correlated. Students living on the same floor of a dorm, for example, find that they agree on topics that they have discussed during the year—such as the value of certain majors or the best times to work out in the fitness center—but that they also agree on topics they have never discussed or even considered discussing: the value of labor unions, the benefits of the Greek system, and human cloning (Cullum & Harton, 2007).
4. *Continuing diversity.* Because of clustering, members of minorities are often shielded from the influence attempts of the majority, and their beliefs continue within the group. Diversity drops if the majority is very large and if the members of the minority are physically isolated from one another, but diversity continues when the minority members who communicate with the majority resist the majority's influence attempts.

Helen Harton and her colleagues identified all four patterns in a study of classroom groups (Harton et al., 1998). They asked students to answer several multiple-choice questions twice—once on their own, and once after talking about the questions with the two people sitting on either side of them. *Consolidation* occurred on several of the questions. On one question, 17 of the 30 students favored an incorrect alternative before discussion. After discussion, 5 more students changed their answers and sided with the incorrect majority—including 3 students who had initially answered the question correctly. The majority increased from 57% to 73%. *Clustering* was also apparent; 11 students disagreed with both of their neighbors initially, but after discussion, only 5 students disagreed with both neighbors—indeed, two large clusters of 6 and 13 students who all agreed with one another emerged. Students within clusters also tended to give the same answers on other items (*correlation*), and some individuals refused to change their answers, even though no one else agreed with them (*continuing diversity*).

These four patterns vary depending on the number of times the group holds its discussion, the dispersion of the group members, the group's communication network, the status of particular individuals, the group members' desire to reach agreement, and other aspects of the situation (Kameda, 1996; Kameda & Sugimori, 1995; Latané, 1997). The four tendencies are robust, however, and answer some key questions about influence in groups. Do most groups eventually converge on a single opinion that represents the average across all members? Dynamic social impact theory says no—groups tend to become polarized on issues as clusters form within the group. Does social pressure eventually force all those who disagree with the majority to conform? Again, dynamic social impact theory suggests that minorities, particularly in spatially distributed groups, are protected from influence. So long as minorities can cluster together, diversity in groups is ensured (Nowak, Vallacher, & Miller, 2003).

## SOURCES OF GROUP INFLUENCE

Many people think of conformity in a negative way. They assume that people who change to agree with others are so weak-willed that they lack the independence to stand up for their personal beliefs. This pejorative view, unfortunately, underestimates the complexity of social influence, for individuals in any group change their behavior for a variety of reasons. First, conformity is often the most reasonable response in a situation: when others are well-informed but we ourselves are ignorant, it's wise to use them as an informational resource. Second, people often conform because they implicitly accept the legitimacy of the group and it's norms. Last, conformity is often interpersonally rewarding: Groups tend to be aggregations of like-minded individuals and so those who do not go along with the majority find that they are pressured to change. These three causes of conformity—the informational, the normative, and the interpersonal—are examined in the next section (Deutsch & Gerard, 1955; Kelley, 1952).

### Informational Influence

In the *Twelve Angry Men* trial, Juror #11 changed his verdict from guilty to not guilty, but he did not mindlessly go along. Rather, when #11 learned that #8 had a "reasonable doubt," he wondered, "Why did #8 draw different conclusions about the case than I did?" and "Am I correct in my interpretation of the evidence?" He reconsidered his position because another group member provided him with clarifying information.

**Informational influence** occurs when group members use the responses of others in the group as reference points and informational resources. If a group member learns that 99 other people favor Plan A over Plan B, that individual will likely adopt Plan A simply because "everyone else does." If one group member smiles or laughs, soon after, other group members will begin smiling (Semin, 2007). Frowns, too, are contagious, and will spread from one group member to another (Bourgeois & Hess, 2008). If a sufficiently large number of people begin to adopt a new fashion, hairstyle, or attitude, the rest of the group and community may adopt the craze as well (Gladwell, 2000). As Robert Cialdini's (2009) *principle of social proof* suggests, people assume that a behavior is the correct one when they see others performing it.

**Social Comparison** Social comparison theory assumes that group members, as active information processors, evaluate the accuracy of their beliefs and gauge the quality of their personal attributes by comparing themselves to other individuals. If individuals facing questions with no clear solution—"Is the defendant guilty?" "Is Plan A better than Plan B?" "Is majority influence stronger than minority influence?"—cannot reduce this uncertainty by consulting objective sources of information, they turn to the views endorsed by others in the group (see Chapter 4). In some cases, groups deliberately gather information about their members' opinions. Many deliberating groups, including juries, stop their discussions periodically to take a so-called *straw poll* to see which way the group, as a whole, is leaning (picture the wind blowing across a field of straw). In most cases, however, information about others' views is gathered during routine interactions (Gerard & Orive, 1987). Like pollsters who gauge public opinion by sampling opinions in surveys of communities, people informally take note of their fellow group members' actions and beliefs and revise their own positions accordingly. Festinger and his colleagues put it this way:

> The "social reality" upon which an opinion or attitude rests for its justification is the degree to which the individual perceives that this opinion or attitude is shared by others. An opinion or attitude that is

---

**informational influence** Interpersonal processes that promote change by challenging the correctness of group members' beliefs or the appropriateness of their behavior directly (e.g., though communication and persuasion) or indirectly (e.g., through social comparison processes).

> not reinforced by others of the same opinion will become unstable generally. (Festinger et al., 1950, p. 168)

Members' sampling of others' opinions is not, however, systematic or objective. They oversample, for example, the opinions of those in their own group compared to those of people outside of their group (Denrell & Le Mens, 2007). If people happen to interact more frequently with some group members than with others, in time the opinions of those more frequent contacts will come to define their inferences about the group's overall position on issues—even if the frequent contacts are only a small sample of the group. Those on the group's periphery may endorse positions that are not fully consistent with the group, but not because the group ostracized them. Their isolation prevents them from accessing the social information they need to hone their opinions and also prevents the other group members from gaining their unique insights. As a result, both members of the majority and the minority display a **false consensus effect**: they assume that there is more support for their position than there actually is (Krueger, 2000; Krueger & Clement, 1997; see, too, McGregor et al., 2005).

**Dual Process Approaches** Judging from the number of models proposed by theorists, those who study majority and minority influence must be nonconformists themselves. Robin Martin and Miles Hewstone (2008) examined no fewer than eight distinct theories that seek to explain when group members change their opinions and judgments and when they hold fast to their original positions. Most of these theories, despite their differences in emphases, are **dual process theories of influence**. They agree that both majority and minority influence, like persuasion and other types of influence processes, result from direct and indirect cognitive processes. *Direct processes* (or central, systematic processes) entail a thoughtful analysis, or elaboration, of the issues at hand. Group members, confronted with an opinion that is different from their own, review the arguments, look for weaknesses, reexamine their own ideas on the topic, and revise their position if revision is warranted. *Indirect processes* (or peripheral, heuristic processes), in contrast, do not require very much mental effort or elaboration. During a group discussion members may not pay much attention, they do not really understand the arguments completely, and they forget what other people have suggested. Yet they still change their minds (Maio & Haddock, 2007).

Diane Mackie (1987), for example, traced much of the impact of a majority on a minority back to direct informational influence. She led her participants to believe that they were part of a small minority that disagreed with a majority on such matters as foreign policy and juvenile justice. After they listened to members of both the minority and the majority argue their positions, Mackie asked them to record their thoughts and reactions. When Mackie examined these cognitive reactions, she found that participants recalled more of the arguments offered by the majority, and they had more positive reactions to the majority's view after the discussion. Mackie also found that people who more extensively processed the majority's message changed their opinions more than those who did not process the message. Exposure to others' positions—in addition to providing further information and prompting a more thorough analysis of that information—can also cause group members to reinterpret or cognitively restructure key aspects of the issue (see Martin & Hewstone, 2008, for a review).

Minorities' viewpoints, too, can stimulate cognitive elaboration of decision-relevant information. As Moscovici argued, minorities influence majorities by creating cognitive conflicts that challenge the status quo of the group and call for a reevaluation of issues at hand. Minority dissent can

---

**false consensus effect** Perceivers' tendency to assume that their personal qualities and characteristics are common in the general population.

**dual process theories of influence** In general, a conceptual analysis arguing that individuals change in response to direct forms of influence (such as persuasion) and indirect forms of influence (such as mimicking another's response).

undermine the majority's certainty and force the group to seek out new information about the situation. When minority opinion is present, groups take longer to reach their conclusions and are more likely to consider multiple perspectives when drawing conclusions (Peterson & Nemeth, 1996). If the majority considers the minority to be part of the ingroup, it will think positively rather than negatively about the minority position (Crano & Seyranian, 2007). Minorities also prompt group members to use more varied strategies in solving problems and to devise more creative solutions (Nemeth, 1986). In some cases, group members recall information presented by the minority more clearly than information presented by the majority (Nemeth et al., 1990; cf. Walther et al., 2002).

These direct informational influence processes are complemented by more indirect, less rational processes (Moskowitz & Chaiken, 2001). Particularly when members' cognitive resources are limited or when group members are not motivated to do the cognitive work necessary to weigh the information available to them, they will use simplifying inferential principles, termed **heuristics**, to reach decisions quickly. They might, for example, base their decision on their general mood rather than the quality of others' arguments—people in good moods tend to conform more than those in bad ones (Tong et al., 2008). If someone in the group speaks eloquently using very general, abstract terms rather than specifics, the group may assume that person knows what he or she is talking about and gravitate toward their position (Sigall, Mucchi-Faina, & Mosso, 2006). And, as the principle of social proof suggests, people tend to have faith in the collective wisdom (Cialdini, 2009). Is a restaurant a good place to eat? Is this a good book? People tend to assume that a restaurant is a good one if many people dine there, and that best-selling books are better than unranked ones. Behavioral economists call this preference for popular choices *herding*, and underscore its rational basis: there is information revealed in the choices other people make (Venkatesh & Goyal, 1998).

A minority's influence also depends, in part, on these kinds of cognitive shortcuts. Because group members are also sensitive to shifts in the group's general opinion, if members notice that the minority position is gaining ground on the majority, then they may shift sides as well—creating a cascade of opinion shift (Chamley, 2004). Russell Clark (1999, 2001) examined this process by measuring observers' verdicts after each round of balloting in a jury trial. He first provided observers with a detailed description of a hypothetical trial and jury deliberation patterned after the one described in *Twelve Angry Men*. He then asked the observers to rate the guilt of the defendant after learning that on the first ballot, the vote was 11 against 1, with the majority favoring a guilty verdict. Nearly all the observers agreed with the majority, but as the deliberations progressed, the observers learned that the minority position was growing from 9 to 3, to 6 to 6, to 3 to 9, and eventually 0 to 12. With each progressive vote, the observers shifted their own ratings from guilty to not guilty. Other research has suggested that individuals are particularly likely to join an expanding minority when the minority offers cogent arguments supporting its position and when other defectors are thought to have been swayed by the logic of the minority's arguments rather than by self-interest (Gordijn, De Vries, & De Dreu, 2002).

## Normative Influence

Informational influence occurs because others' responses convey information concerning the nature of the social setting and how most people are responding to that setting. **Normative influence**,

---

**heuristic** An inferential principle or rule of thumb that people use to reach conclusions when the amount of available information is limited, ambiguous, or contradictory.

**normative influence** Personal and interpersonal processes that cause individuals to feel, think, and act in ways that are consistent with social norms, standards, and convention. Because individuals internalize their group's norms, they strive to act in ways that are consistent with those norms.

in contrast, occurs when members tailor their actions and attitudes to match the norms of the group situation. The members of the majority in the *Twelve Angry Men* jury, for example, did more than just think, "Most everyone in the group agrees with me." They also recognized that their position was the normative one: "This group has decided the defendant is guilty and anyone who believes differently is going against the norms of this group."

Normative influence causes members to feel, think, and act in ways that are consistent with the group's norms. At an interpersonal level, people feel compelled to act in accordance with norms because a variety of negative consequences could result from nonconformity. People who consistently violate their group's norms are often reminded of their duty and told to mend their ways. Normative influence has, however, a personal, psychological foundation. Norms are not simply external constraints but internalized standards. When people identify with their groups, they feel duty-bound to adhere to the group's norms; they accept the legitimacy of the established norms and they recognize the importance of supporting these norms. Thus, people obey norms not only because they fear the negative interpersonal consequences—ostracism, ridicule, punishment—that their nonconformity may produce, but also because they feel personally compelled to live up to their own expectations.

Normative influence generates conformity in a range of everyday situations. Even in relatively fleeting social encounters, individuals are loath to violate the implicit rules that specify the "normal" way to act. Milgram (1992) examined this process, informally, by asking people to deliberately violate social norms and then describe how they felt afterwards. His student researchers broke the "first-come, first-served" norm of subway seating by asking subway riders in New York City to give up their seats. Many people turned over their seats to the students, but Milgram was more interested in how the students felt. The students were volunteers who knew they were breaking an inconsequential norm in the name of research, but all "felt anxious, tense, and embarrassed. Frequently, they were unable to vocalize the request for a seat and had to withdraw" (Milgram, 1992, p. 42). Milgram, who also performed the norm violation task himself, described the experience as wrenching and concluded that there is an "enormous inhibitory anxiety that ordinarily prevents us from breaching social norms" (p. xxiv).

This negative psychological reaction to discovering one has managed to wander outside of the group's norms generates a negative reaction that is akin to *cognitive dissonance*. As noted in Chapter 5, Festinger (1957) suggested that cognitive dissonance is such an unpleasant state that people are motivated to take steps to reduce dissonance whenever it occurs. Dissonance theory originally focused on how people respond when they hold two inconsistent cognitions, but researchers have confirmed that people also experience dissonance when they discover that they do not agree with other group members. In one study, individuals with extreme opinions on issues were led to believe they were going to discuss these issues with four or five other people who had directly opposing opinions. Before the discussion, the participants described their emotions, and as expected they were not positive: participants reported feeling more uneasy, uncomfortable, tense, bothered, and concerned—all indications of cognitive dissonance (Matz & Wood, 2005).

The discomfort of disagreeing with others can be so great that it even triggers activity in portions of the brain associated with pain, fear, and stress. To examine brain activity during conformity and independence, investigators used a functional magnetic resonance imaging (fMRI) scanner to monitor participants' neuronal activity. Volunteers were told that the study would examine their spatial-relations abilities by asking them to decide if two rotated 3-dimensional objects were identical. To create social influence during the mental rotation task, as participants made their judgments, they were presented with the responses of four peers who, on half of the trials, chose the wrong answer. The researchers discovered that when participants agreed with the group (even when the group was incorrect) portions of their brain associated with processing visual information were most active—they assumed the others' responses were valid and adopted their solution as their own. But when they disagreed with the group, portions of the brain that are responsible for strong emotional responses (the amygdala) showed evidence of high neuronal activity (Berns et al., 2005).

Given its emotional impact, normative influence often leads to more potent and longer lasting influence than informational influence (see Focus 7.2). Robert Cialdini and his colleagues contrasted these two forms of influence in their studies of pro-environment actions (Cialdini, Kallgren, & Reno, 1991; Cialdini, Reno, & Kallgren, 1990). Cialdini's research team put handbills under the windshield wipers of cars in a parking lot, and then they watched to see if people threw these scraps of paper on the ground when they returned to their cars. They then manipulated the salience of norms about littering across three conditions. To create information influence, some participants, while walking toward their car, passed by a confederate who carefully dropped a bag of trash into a garbage can. This condition suggested, "Most people do not litter." In a second condition, participants saw a confederate actually pick up a piece of litter (the same bag of trash) and dispose of it in the garbage can. Cialdini and his colleagues believed that this confederate made salient the injunctive norm, "It is wrong to litter!" In the control condition, the confederate merely walked by the participant. Participants encountered the confederate either in the lot where the participant's car was parked or on the path leading to the parking lot.

These researchers discovered that the informational influence worked only for a short period of time. Participants who saw the confederate throw away his trash just before they got to their car were less likely to litter than those who saw him or her on the path leading to their car. In contrast, the injunctive norm became more powerful over time. No one who saw the confederate pick up litter on the path leading to the parking lot littered (Reno, Cialdini, & Kallgren, 1993, Study 3).

## Interpersonal Influence

Western societies claim to value nonconformity and independence, but in most situations dissent is not rewarded. In fact, it is met with **interpersonal influence**: social responses that encourage, or even force, group members to conform. In the *Twelve Angry Men* jury the men did not dispassionately discuss their perceptions of the evidence calmly and carefully. Instead, they complained, demanded, threatened, pleaded, negotiated, pressured, manipulated, insulted, and shouted—even threatening one another with physical harm—in an attempt to change one another's opinions so the group could reach a unanimous decision. When informational influence ("But we all believe he is guilty") and normative influence ("This jury has decided that the defendant is guilty, and as a member of this group you should accept this decision") failed, then the group tried to force its members to conform.

Stanley Schachter (1951) documented interpersonal influence by planting three kinds of confederates in a number of all-male discussion "clubs." The *deviant* always disagreed with the majority. The *slider* disagreed initially, but conformed over the course of the discussion. The *mode* served as a control; he consistently agreed with the majority. Schachter also manipulated the groups' cohesiveness by putting some of the participants in clubs that interested them and others in clubs that did not interest them. He assumed that people with common interests would be more cohesive than those with disparate interests. He also had the groups discuss a topic that was either relevant or irrelevant to the group's stated purpose.

Schachter was interested in how group members would pressure the deviant during the course of the discussion, so he kept track of each comment directed to the deviant, slider, and mode by the other group members. He predicted that the group would initially communicate with the mode, deviant, and slider at equal rates. But once the group became aware of the deviant's and slider's disagreement, group members would concentrate on these two participants. Schachter believed that communication

**interpersonal influence** Social influence that results from other group members selectively encouraging conformity and discouraging or even punishing nonconformity.

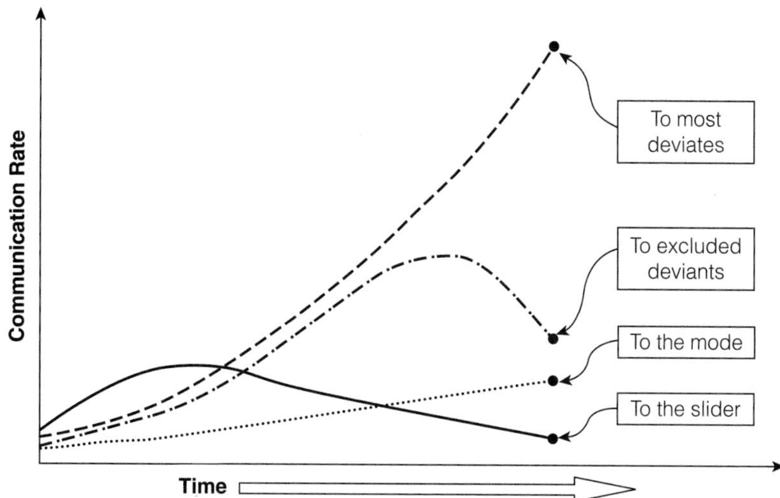


**FIGURE 7.6** Communication rates with a *mode*, a *slider*, a *deviant* who is excluded, and a *deviant* who is included. Schachter's (1951) study of communication found that the person who disagreed with the others (the deviant) usually received the most communication throughout the discussion period. The only exception occurred in cohesive groups working on a relevant task whose members disliked the deviant. In this case, communications tapered off. The average number of communications addressed to the mode increased slightly over the session, while communication with the slider decreased.

would continue at a high rate until the dissenter capitulated to the majority opinion (as in the case of the slider) or until the majority concluded that the deviant would not budge from his position (as in the case of the persistent deviant), but that this reaction would be exacerbated by the group's cohesiveness and the relevance of the task.

**Influence and Ostracism** Figure 7.6 summarizes Schachter's findings. In most cases, the group communicated with the slider and the mode at a relatively low rate throughout the session, whereas communications with the deviant increased during the first 35 minutes of discussion. At the 35-minute mark, however, some groups seemed to have rejected the deviant. These groups were cohesive ones working on a task that was relevant to the group's goals and whose members developed a negative attitude toward the deviant. Schachter discovered that not all groups disliked the deviant, and that this level of liking played a key role in how the deviant was treated. If the group developed more positive feelings for the deviant, communication increased all the way up to the final minute. If the group disliked the deviant, communication dropped precipitously.

Schachter's findings highlight the difference between inclusive and exclusive reactions to minorities (see Levine & Kerr, 2007, for a review). Most of the groups displayed an *inclusive* reaction to the deviant: Communication between the majority and the minority was intensive and hostile, but the minority was still perceived to be a member of the ingroup. If an *exclusive* reaction occurred, however, communication with the deviant dwindled along with overt hostility, and the deviant was perceptually removed from the group by the majority members. An exclusive reaction becomes more likely when group members think that their group is very heterogeneous (Festinger, Pepitone, & Newcomb, 1952; Festinger & Thibaut, 1951). Highly cohesive groups, too, will sometimes "redefine the group's boundary" if the dissenter is inflexible and the issue is important (Gerard, 1953). So-called *double minorities*—individuals who disagree with the group and also possess one or more other unique qualities that distinguish them from the rest of the group—are also more likely to face exclusion (Sampson & Brandon, 1964).

**Interpersonal Rejection** The group members did not just argue with the deviant—they also rejected the deviant. When Schachter's participants rated each other on likability, the deviant was the sociometric outcast, whereas the mode was liked the most. The deviant was also saddled with the secretarial chores of the group; the mode and slider were assigned more desirable positions. This rejection was more pronounced in the more cohesive groups.

The group's dislike of dissenters even extended to the slider. Sliders, it could be argued, do little to provoke rejection. They begin the discussion by taking a position that few favor, but after a time they listen to reason and shift. What's not to like about such a reasonable person? Yet, Schachter's findings show that the slider was not as well-liked as someone who sided with the majority all along (the mode). Indeed, any disagreement with a group is enough to lower one's interpersonal acceptance. John Levine and his associates, across a series of studies, have examined reactions to all types of deviants: ones who start off neutral and then conform, others who begin as extreme deviants and then shift over to the majority, and even those who start off with the majority and then slide toward dissent (see Levine, 1980; Levine & Kerr, 2007). Levine like Schachter, found that nonconformists and those who were initially neutral but eventually disagreed were liked the least. Moreover, even the individual who abandons his or her initial position to agree with the group is liked less than a conformist. These reactions to the dissenter likely reflect group members' sensitivity to the size of shifting majorities and minorities. Majority members are gratified when a member of the minority converts, but they are particularly troubled when a member of the majority "goes over to the other side" (Prislin, Limbert, & Bauer, 2000).

Subsequent studies have replicated this relationship between rejection and nonconformity, although these studies also identify certain situational factors that increase the magnitude of this relationship. Task relevance, cohesiveness, group consensus, interdependence, behavior extremity, and the degree of threat posed by the dissenter all work to increase rejection. The deviant's contribution to the task, apologies for deviation, and history of previous conformity reduce the likelihood of rejection, as do norms that encourage deviation and innovation (Levine & Kerr, 2007; Tata et al., 1996).

Social identity processes play a particularly critical role in determining members' reactions to deviants and conformists. Social identity theory, as discussed in Chapter 3, suggests that members share a common identity that defines the prototypical qualities of a member and encourages a distinction between members and nonmembers. Group members find deviants within their midst to be distressing because they call into question the group's positive identity and make hazy the distinctiveness of the ingroup relative to outgroups. These psychological processes, which are referred to as **subjective group dynamics**, will cause individuals to react negatively to dissenters with whom they share only category memberships. A fan of the Arsenal soccer team, for example, will react negatively to another Arsenal fan who expresses admiration for the play of the Manchester United forward—even though the two fans might never actually meet. One intriguing consequence of subjective group dynamics: ingroup members are sometimes judged more harshly than outgroup members when they perform identical behaviors. A statement that Manchester United played brilliantly will be tolerated when spoken by a Man U fan, but if an Arsenal fan expresses such a belief he or she would be roundly criticized by other Arsenal fans. This tendency is termed the **black-sheep effect** (Abrams, Hogg, & Marques, 2005).

---

**subjective group dynamics** Psychological and interpersonal processes that result from social categorization and identification processes, including members' desire to sustain the positive distinctiveness of the ingroup and the validity of its shared beliefs.

**black-sheep effect** The tendency for group members to evaluate a group member who performs an offensive behavior more harshly than an outgroup member who performs the same offense.

## Focus 7.2 Are Groups Apathetic?

*We are discreet sheep; we wait to see how the drove is going, and then go with the drove.*

—Mark Twain

In the early morning of March 13, 1964, a young woman named Catherine Genovese ("Kitty" to her friends) was attacked and killed in Queens, New York. Thirty-eight people witnessed the murder, but none of them helped. Only one person even called the police (Seeman & Hellman, 1975).

Many blamed this failure on the bystanders, suggesting that the urbanites were cruel, apathetic, or lacking the moral compunction needed to compel them to act. But when Bibb Latané and John Darley (1970) read about the murder of Kitty Genovese, they were struck by the large number of witnesses. Could social pressures, they wondered, have interfered with people's capacity to respond in a helpful way to the emergency? Latané and Darley investigated this possibility by creating a false emergency in their laboratory. While male college students completed some bogus questionnaires, Latané and Darley pumped white smoke through an air vent into the test room. Some participants were alone in the room, but others worked in three-person groups consisting of one participant and two confederates. The confederates pretended to be participants, but they ignored the emergency. As the room filled with smoke, they nonchalantly glanced at the vent, shrugged, and went back to their questionnaires. If the participant mentioned the smoke to them, they said merely "I dunno." In a third condition, all three members of the group were actual participants.

When tested alone, participants usually left the room to report the smoke within two minutes; 75% reported the emergency within the six-minute time limit. Participants tested in groups behaved very differently. Only 10% of the participants tested with the passive confederates ever reported the smoke, and the reporting percentage reached no higher than 15% even when all three group members were actual participants. By the time the six-minute period was up, the room was so smoky that participants could not see the far wall. They coughed and rubbed their eyes, but they stayed at their tables, fanning the fumes away from their papers so they could finish their questionnaires.

Latané and Darley's work demonstrated the **bystander effect**—people are less likely to help when in groups rather than alone—and soon other investigators confirmed these results. A statistical review of approximately four dozen studies of nearly 6000 people who faced various apparent emergencies alone or in a group indicated that groups impede helping. Across these various studies, about 75% of the participants tested alone intervened, but only 53% of the participants in groups helped (Latané & Nida, 1981).

But why do people in groups not help as much as single individuals? First, informational influence prompts individuals to rely on the actions of the other bystanders to guide their interpretation of the situation. Unfortunately, because emergencies are sometimes ambiguous, each nonresponding bystander sends the same inaccurate message to every other nonresponding bystander: "It's OK; no help is needed." In situations that are obviously emergencies, the bystander effect disappears (Clark & Word, 1972, 1974).

Second, normative influence does not enjoin bystanders to help. In most everyday situations "common law" (the natural norms that dictate proper conduct) does not require one act as a Good Samaritan (Feigenson, 2000). What bystanders do worry about, however, is breaking norms of civil inattention. Most people prefer to appear poised and normal in social settings, and actively avoid doing anything that may lead to embarrassment. In an ambiguous emergency, people fear that they will look foolish if they offer assistance to someone who does not need it, so they look the other way rather than get involved (Schwartz & Gottlieb, 1976).

Third, people feel less responsible when in groups compared to alone, and this **diffusion of responsibility** leaves bystanders feeling that it is not their

*(Continued)*

---

**bystander effect** The tendency for people to help less when they know others are present and capable of helping. The effect was initially thought to be the result of apathy and a selfish unwillingness to get involved, but research suggests a number of cognitive and social processes, including diffusion of responsibility and misinterpretation that help is not needed, contribute to the effect.

**diffusion of responsibility** A reduction of personal responsibility experienced by individuals in groups and social collectives identified by John Darley and Bibb Latané in their studies of bystanders' failures to help someone in need.

**Focus 7.2 (Continued)**

responsibility to help. "The pressures to intervene do not focus on any one of the observers; instead, the responsibility for intervention is shared among all the onlookers and is not unique to any one" (Darley & Latané, 1968, p. 378). Simply imagining that one will be with others in a group is sufficient to reduce feelings of accountability and helpfulness (Garcia et al., 2002).

These factors, although relatively mundane social processes in most contexts, combine to cause bystanders to overlook the suffering of others. The bystander effect is not caused by apathy or a loss of humanity that overtakes people when they become part of a collective. The effect is, instead, the predictable result of group-level social influence processes that leave members confused, uncertain of the proper course of action, and unable to take action.

## APPLICATION: UNDERSTANDING JURIES

Groups have served as the final arbiter of guilt and innocence for centuries. As far back as the 11th century, the neighbors of those accused of wrongdoing were asked both to provide information about the actions of the accused and to weigh the evidence. Witnesses and experts now provide the evidence, but the jury remains responsible for weighing the testimony of each person before rendering a verdict. More than 300,000 juries convene each year in American courtrooms alone (Hyman & Tarrant, 1975).

### Jury Dynamics

The jury situation is designed to foster careful decision making and tolerance for all viewpoints, but at its core, a jury is a group. The jury's final decision depends not only on the evidence presented at the trial, the attorneys' arguments, and the judge's instructions, but also on social influence.

**Stories, Evidence, and Verdicts** The Chicago Jury Project, conducted in the 1950s, was one of the first attempts to study, systematically, the ways juries carry out their responsibilities and render their verdicts. Using a variety of methods, including jury simulations, recording actual deliberations, and post-trial interviews, the investigators discovered that most juries follow the same basic procedures during deliberation. Juries usually begin by electing a leader and deciding if balloting will be secret or public. Most juries take a straw poll of their initial preferences, and more than 30% reach complete consensus on that first ballot (Kalven & Zeisel, 1966). But when members disagree, they initiate a consensus-seeking process. During this phase of the deliberation, the group may ask the judge for instructions and request additional information concerning the evidence. The group spends most of its time, however, discussing points related to the verdict (Hans & Vidmar, 1991).

The jury's approach to the deliberations depends, in part, on how it structures the task. Jury researchers Reid Hastie, Steven Penrod, and Nancy Pennington (1983), in their **story model** of jury deliberation, noted that jurors generally approach the decision in one of two ways. Some jurors appear to be *verdict driven*. They reach a decision about the verdict before deliberation and cognitively organize the evidence into two categories: evidence that favors a verdict of guilty and evidence that favors a verdict of not guilty. *Evidence-driven* jurors, in contrast, resist making a final decision on the verdict until they have reviewed all the available evidence; then they generate a story that weaves together the evidence of trial and their own expectations and assumptions about people and similar situations in a coherent narrative (Pennington & Hastie, 1986, 1992). Should the jurors find, during deliberations, that their stories are relatively similar,

---

**story model** A theory of cognitive processing of trial information that suggests jurors mentally organize evidence in coherent, credible narratives.

then the group will be able to reach a verdict quickly. If, however, their stories are different then they spend time discussing alternative stories until a consensus can be reached.

When juries contain both verdict-driven and evidence-driven jurors, the approach preferred by the majority of the jurors is generally used to structure the deliberations. When researchers created mock three-person juries containing two members who shared the same type of cognitive orientation, this cognitive majority dominated the deliberations, and in most cases, the individual with the alternative viewpoint restructured his or her approach so that it matched the majority's approach (Kameda, 1994).

**Minority Influence in Juries** Most of the *Twelve Angry Men* jury, as they listened to the evidence presented during the trial, made sense of it all with a simple story: the ungrateful, disrespectful son fought with his father and, in a fit of anger, killed him. Juror #8, in contrast, developed a different story: the father, who had many enemies in the neighborhood, was attacked by one of them, who stabbed him with a knife identical to one owned by the man's son. These two stories lead in very different directions in terms of the verdict, but over the course of the deliberations Juror #8 managed to convince all the others that his story was more credible than theirs.

The success of Juror #8 was a rarity. As Figure 7.7 indicates, the verdict favored by the majority of the jurors—7 to 11 jurors in a regular 12-person jury—on the first ballot becomes the jury's final decision in 90% of all jury trials

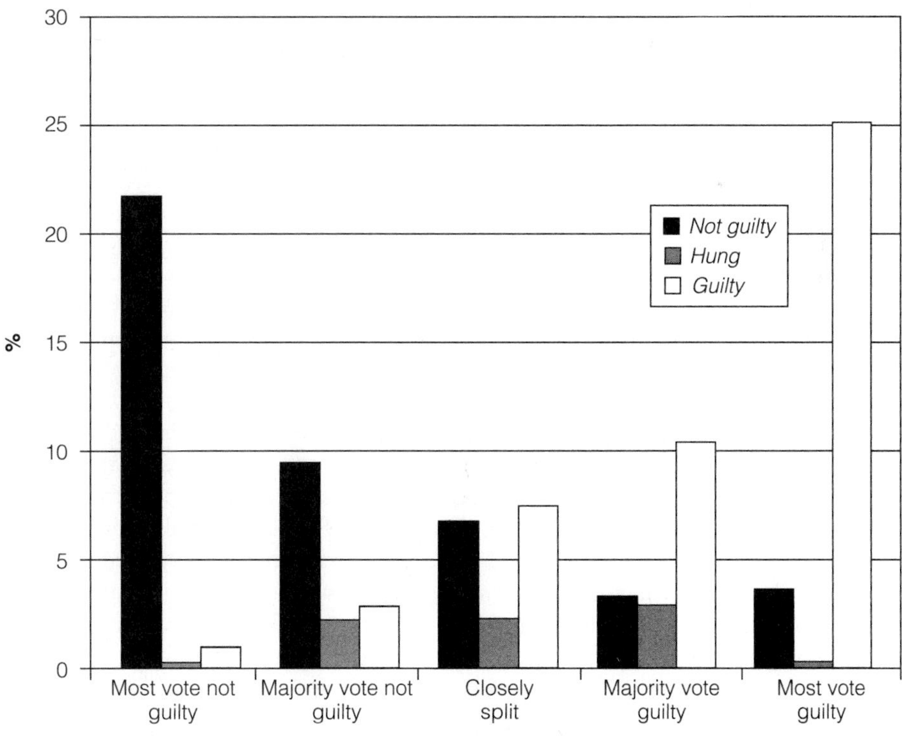


**FIGURE 7.7** The percentage of different types of outcomes in jury trials by initial distribution of votes. In most cases, the decision favored by the majority of the jurors when deliberations first begin is the verdict returned by that jury. Minority influence, although rare, occurred in about 10% of the cases when the majority favored acquittal and 15% of the cases when the majority favored conviction.

(Devine et al., 2001). Most jurors implicitly adopt a majority-rules decision norm: If a significant majority of the members (say, two-thirds) favor a verdict, then everyone in the group should agree with that verdict. In fact, a computer model that simulates jury deliberations (DICE) assumes that a 3-person coalition in a standard 12-person jury will be relatively weak, but a 4- or 5-person coalition will be fairly influential (Hastie et al., 1983).

Minorities are not powerless, however. Even though the majority tends to prevail in juries, as Figure 7.7 suggests, the minority convinces the majority to change in about 1 trial out of every 10. For example, in the trial of the second defendant in the Oklahoma City Bombing, Terry Nichols, the first vote was 10 to 2 for acquittal (Bartels, 2001). But the two lone jurors who favored a guilty verdict dug in to their position and carefully reviewed the evidence for six long days. One of the jurors, a geophysicist, used his skill, logic, and persuasive talents to craft a compromise verdict of guilty of conspiracy but not guilty of first-degree murder. He was successful, in part, because of his recognized expertise and the rapid change in votes by four of the other jurors. These findings confirm the importance of encouraging juries to take the time they need to deliberate before rendering a final decision (Hans et al. 2003).

Minorities can also deadlock the jury by refusing to conform to the majority's verdict, resulting in a *hung jury* if a unanimous verdict is required. The origin of the term "hung jury" is not certain, but it was apparently first used to describe American juries that could not reach a verdict. It matches "most closely to the meaning of the word hung as caught, stuck, or delayed" (Hans et al., 2003, p. 33). Hung juries generally occur when the evidence does not clearly favor one verdict, and even then occur only in approximately 10% of such cases. When a hung jury does occur, it is often just one or two jurors holding out against the majority (Hans et al., 2003).

**Status and Influence** Some members of the *Twelve Angry Men* jury had higher status within the group than the other rank-and-file members: Juror #4, for example, was a stockbroker, whereas Juror #6 worked in construction. Is it a coincidence that the jury paid far more attention to the ideas and suggestions of Juror #4 rather than #6?

Fairly or unfairly, people who have high prestige or status are more influential than low-status members. Researchers in the Chicago Jury Project carefully replicated all aspects of an actual trial. They selected sets of 12 individuals from a pool of eligible jurors, simulated the pretrial interview process designed to eliminate biased jurors (*voir dire*), and assembled the group in the courtroom. A bailiff then played a recording of a trial and asked the group to retire to a jury room to decide on a verdict. Except for the use of a recording, the groups were treated just like actual juries (Strodtbeck & Hook, 1961; Strodtbeck et al., 1957; Strodtbeck & Mann, 1956).

Consistent with Chapter 6's analysis of expectation-states theory, juries favored people of higher socioeconomic status (proprietors and clerical workers) over those of lower socioeconomic status (blue-collar workers) when choosing a foreman, even though no mention of occupation was made (Strodtbeck & Lipinski, 1985). High-status members also participated more frequently in the jury's discussions, often by offering more suggestions and providing more orientation to the task. High-status members were also more successful in convincing the others that their judgments on the case were the most accurate. The correlation between private predeliberation opinion and the jury's final decision was .50 for proprietors, but it dropped all the way down to .02 for laborers (Strodtbeck et al., 1957).

In these studies, conducted in the 1950s, sex and race differences were also apparent in juries. Women and racial minorities joined in the discussion less frequently than men (James, 1959; Strodtbeck et al., 1957). Furthermore, women's comments were more often relational in nature, showing solidarity and agreement, whereas men's comments were more task-focused (Strodtbeck & Mann, 1956; see also Nemeth, Endicott, & Wachtler, 1976). These inequities, however, have faded over time. Recent analyses suggest that race and sex no longer determine influence in juries, but that social status remains a potent factor; those jurors who are more affluent or well-educated continue to be more influential than others (York & Cornwell, 2006).

### How Effective Are Juries?

Given what we know about conformity and nonconformity in groups, should the jury system be modified? Asch's studies tell us that people often conform and that even a correct minority often loses to an incorrect majority. As we have seen, normative, informational, and interpersonal influence are powerful forces in groups, and they can quash individuals' freedom to speak their minds. Juries are a time-honored tradition, but are they effective?

Determining the effectiveness of juries as deciders of guilt or innocence is a complicated task, for we can never know when the jury has been correct or incorrect in condemning or freeing a defendant. If a clear criterion for determining guilt existed, juries would not be necessary in the first place. Several bits of evidence, however, provide partial support for the effectiveness of juries as decision makers. First, jurors seem to take their role very seriously. One jury expert, after studying the responses of more than 2000 jurors participating in the Chicago Jury Project, concluded,

> The most consistent theme that emerged from listening to the deliberations was the seriousness with which the jurors approached their job and the extent to which they were concerned that the verdict they reached was consistent with the spirit of the law and with the facts of the case. (Simon, 1980, p. 521)

Second, juries do well when compared with judges' decisions. In a survey of nearly 8000 actual criminal and civil trials, judges and juries disagreed on only 20% of the cases; for criminal trials, the jury was somewhat more lenient than the judge, but for civil trials, the disagreements were evenly split for and against the defendant. Furthermore, 80% of these disagreements occurred when the weight of the evidence was so close that the judge admitted that the verdict could have gone either way. This match between verdicts may explain why 77% of the judges surveyed felt that the jury system was satisfactory, 20% felt that it had disadvantages that should be corrected, but only 3% felt the system to be so unsatisfactory that its use should be curtailed (Kalven & Zeisel, 1966).

Third, jurors are hardly unbiased, rational weighers of evidence; the defendant's physical appearance, the lawyer's style of questioning, and the sequencing of evidence are just a few of the factors that bias jurors' decisions (Dane & Wrightsman, 1982; Hastie et al., 1983; Kaplan, 1982; Wrightsman, Nietzel, & Fortune, 1998). These biases are largely controlled, however, by relying on group decisions rather than individual decisions. Simulations of juries suggest that the lone juror's initial biases and preferences have very little impact on the group's final decision, no matter what the size of the jury (Kerr & Huang, 1986).

Each of these pro-jury arguments, however, can also be countered by other, more disquieting data about juries and their capabilities. In recent years, a number of very high-profile juries have made decisions that in retrospect appear to have been based on emotion and prejudice rather than on the thoughtful analysis of the evidence. Studies of their deliberation processes indicate that a handful of group members dominated the group discussion, and these individuals succeeded, in most cases, in determining the final verdict. When investigators have asked jurors about their understanding of the legalities of the case, they discovered that many understood less than half of the judges' instructions to the jury (Ellsworth & Reifman, 2000). Jury members also have a particularly difficult time following the arguments and evidence introduced in complex, time-consuming trials (Cecil, Hans, & Wiggins, 1991). These findings have prompted some to suggest that the jury system should be abolished, but others favor a more moderate solution—improving juries by modifying their structure and dynamics.

### Improving Juries

The judicial system is long on tradition, but in recent years, several innovations have been suggested and even implemented (Vidmar & Hans, 2007). Some of these reforms, such as reducing the size and the decision rules of juries, are designed to improve the general efficiency of juries and the fairness of their procedures. Others, such as note taking, help jurors to process the evidence and testimony that they must consider when reaching their decision.

**Jury Size** In 1970, the U.S. Supreme Court returned a landmark ruling in the case of *Williams v. Florida* (National Center for State Courts, 1976). Williams sought to have his conviction overturned on the grounds that the deciding jury had included only six persons. The Supreme Court, however, found in favor of Florida, ruling that a six-person jury is large enough to promote group deliberation, protect members from intimidation, fairly represent the community, and weigh the facts in the case (*Williams v. Florida*, 1970). Psychology and law expert Michael J. Saks, however, has suggested that the Supreme Court should have taken group dynamics research into consideration before making its decision. As he noted, modifying jury size could influence:

- *Group structure*. Members of smaller juries participate at more equal rates; smaller juries are more cohesive; and members of larger juries exchange more information.
- *Representativeness*. Smaller groups are not as representative of the community as larger ones. For example, if a community was 10% Latino and 90% Anglo, in all probability, about 80% of the 12-person juries selected from that community would include at least one Latino, but only 40% of the 6-person juries would contain Latinos.
- *Majority influence*. The majority's influence may be greater in smaller juries, because the likelihood of finding a partner for one's minority coalition becomes smaller.

Further, Saks contended that the Court erred in assuming that a 5 to 1 vote in a 6-person jury was the same as a 10 to 2 split in a 12-person group. With the 10 to 2 vote, one is joined by a dissenting partner, whereas in the 5 to 1 vote, one faces the majority alone. As a result, the likelihood of a hung jury is greater in larger juries (Kerr & MacCoun, 1985). Saks also noted, however, that despite size-related changes in group dynamics, small juries and large juries do not appear to differ significantly in the types of verdicts reached—except in certain civil cases, where smaller juries tend to return larger damages (Saks, 1977; Saks & Hastie, 1978; Saks & Marti, 1997).

**Unanimity** In 1972, three men were convicted, in separate trials, of assault, grand larceny, and burglary by the court system of Oregon. They appealed to the U.S. Supreme Court on the grounds that their right to a fair trial had been violated because the votes of the juries had not been unanimous. To the defendants' dismay, the Supreme Court ruled in favor of Oregon (*Apodoca v. Oregon*, 1972), concluding that the Sixth Amendment to the U.S. Constitution guarantees only that a "substantial majority of the jury" must be convinced of the defendant's guilt. Later in the ruling, the Supreme Court suggested that a 75% agreement constitutes an acceptable minimum for most juries.

The Court's conclusion is, for the most part, justified by the empirical evidence. The verdict preferred by the majority of the jurors on their first vote usually becomes the final verdict in a large percentage of the cases, with or without a unanimity rule. The minority's opinion sometimes prevails, but in such cases, the minority is usually so substantial that a 9 out of 12 majority would not have been reached anyway. Most juries implicitly operate according to either a basic two-thirds or a 10 out of 12 rule (Davis, Bray, & Holt, 1977; Davis et al., 1975; Stasser, Kerr, & Bray, 1982).

Relaxing the requirement for unanimity, however, changes the decision-making process in juries. Juries that do not have to reach a unanimous decision render their judgments twice as quickly and are far less likely to come to a stalemate (Foss, 1981; Kerr et al., 1976). Saks and Hastie (1978) feared that juries that do not deliberate to unanimity do not deliberate sufficiently and make more mistakes—"convictions when the correct decision is acquittal; acquittals when the correct decision is conviction" (pp. 84–85).

**Procedural Innovations** Whereas jurors were once forbidden from taking notes or discussing the case prior to deliberations, in a series of modifications, courts have experimented with various types of procedural changes to determine if notes help jurors to remember and process the volumes of information they receive during the trial. For example, the courts have worked to try to clarify information about the legal terms used in the case under consideration. The revised wording of such concepts as "reasonable doubt" and "preponderance of evidence," for example, has triggered changes in how long juries deliberate and in their eventual verdicts (Horowitz & Kirkpatrick, 1996). Courts have studied ways to make the instructions given to the jurors prior to deliberation clearer and more understandable (Ellsworth & Reifman, 2000). Some courts also permit jurors to (1) take notes during the presentation of evidence and use these notes during deliberation; (2) submit questions to the court that, after review by judge and legal counsel, can be considered in summary statements during the trial or in the presentation of additional evidence; and (3) discuss the trial among themselves while the trial is ongoing (Vidmar & Hans, 2007). These innovations are generally associated with increased involvement of jurors in the deliberation process, but their impact on decision outcomes appears to be modest (Devine et al., 2001).

**Voir Dire** The selection of jury members from a pool of potential participants occurs through a process known as **voir dire**. Voir dire—an alteration of the French phrase *vrai dire*, which means "to speak truly"—calls for verbal or written questioning of prospective jurors to uncover any biases or prejudices that may stand in the way of fairness and impartiality (Hans & Vidmar, 1982).

Until the 1970s, voir dire was left primarily to the judge's discretion; defense lawyers could submit questions, but judges were free to disregard them if they desired. However, when convictions were overturned on appeal because trial judges had disallowed defense participation in voir dire (e.g., *Ham v. S. Carolina*, 1973), trial courts began opening up the jury selection procedure to attorneys. Systematic jury selection, where lawyers carefully study the prospective jurors in the pool and use voir dire to identify sympathetic and antagonistic jurors, is now a common practice in major trials. Voir dire is regularly used, for example, in cases in which the defendant, if convicted, faces the death penalty. By rejecting from the jury anyone who objects to the death penalty, the prosecution can assemble what is termed a *death-qualified jury*.

Systematic jury selection is controversial. Proponents argue that in many political and criminal trials, biases produced by unfair publicity, regional prejudices, and unrepresentative jury rosters must be controlled if the defendant is to receive just treatment. Critics feel that systematic jury selection is tantamount to jury rigging, as it produces biased rather than fair juries and works to exclude certain types of people from juries. Death-qualified juries, for example, are not just willing to impose a death sentence, but they are also more conviction prone than non–death-qualified juries (Filkins, Smith, & Tindale, 1998).

Lawrence Wrightsman, an expert on psychology and the law, has argued that judges should limit the number of jurors that lawyers can challenge during voir dire. He also recommended stricter guidelines for lawyers, who sometimes use the voir dire process to influence the jurors in their favor. Wrightsman suggested that voir dire questioning be carried out carefully, so that jurors will respond honestly, and that judges supervise the process more closely. Voir dire is a useful way of identifying highly biased individuals, but it should not be a means of manipulating the composition of the jury (Wrightsman et al., 1998).

---

**voir dire** The oral or written questioning of prospective jurors by counsel or the judge.

## SUMMARY IN OUTLINE

*When do people conform in groups?*

1. *Social influence* in groups occurs when the majority of the members influence smaller subgroups within the group to change (*majority influence*) and when the minority members succeed in converting the majority of group members to their position (*minority influence*).

2. Asch studied *conformity* by measuring people's decisions when the majority of their group's members made errors judging line lengths (the *Asch situation*).
   - Approximately one-third of the people that Asch studied conformed.
   - Conformity increased when the majority was large and unanimous, but increasing the majority beyond four did not significantly increase conformity. This decreasing impact of increased numbers of sources of influence is consistent with Bond's meta-analytic review and Latané's *social impact theory* (the principle of social impact suggests Impact = *f* SIN).
   - When group members change their position, their conformity may result from temporary *compliance* to the group's pressure rather than true *conversion* (private acceptance). Those who do not comply may be displaying *independence* or deliberate defiance of the group (*anticonformity*). When *congruence* occurs, members were in agreement from the outset.

3. Conformity rates vary across time, cultures, sexes, and group settings.
   - Certain personality traits are related to conformity. People who conform consistently in groups tend to be more authoritarian but seek social approval. Nonconformists are more self-confident.
   - Women conform slightly more than men, primarily in face-to-face groups. Women may use conformity to increase group harmony, whereas men use nonconformity to create the impression of independence.
   - Bond and Smith's review suggests group members in collectivistic societies yield to majority influence more often than those in individualistic societies.
   - Conformity rates have dropped slightly in the last half of the 20th century.
   - Majority influence varies in strength depending on the size, structure, cohesiveness, and goals of the group and the nature of its tasks. For example, fewer group members conform when they can respond anonymously via secret ballot or from a distance (the *Crutchfield situation*).
   - Individuals in groups engaged in computer-mediated interactions conform at rates equal to and sometimes greater than face-to-face groups (*Social Identity Model of Deindividuation Effects*—or SIDE effects).

*When do people resist the group's influence and instead change the group?*

1. Moscovici's *conversion theory* suggests that consistent minorities will be influential, although that influence may in some cases be indirect and delayed. Minorities, therefore, create more conversion and innovation, whereas majorities tend to create compliance.
   - Moscovici found that a minority, particularly if behaviorally consistent, can influence the majority.
   - Hollander suggests that minorities that are accorded high status in the group can also influence the majority, for their *idiosyncrasy credits* protect them from sanctions when they display nonconformity.

- Minorities exert more effort in their attempts to influence than do majorities, and the decision rule the group adopts will differentially influence the success of majorities (majority-rules) and minorities (unanimity).

2. Latané's *dynamic social impact theory* uses the processes of consolidation, clustering, correlation, and continuing diversity to explain majority and minority influence in spatially distributed groups that interact repeatedly over time.

*Why do people conform?*

1. *Informational influence* takes place whenever group members base their reaction on Cialdini's principle of social proof: they look to others for information.
   - As social comparison theory notes, people are a valuable source of information, although individuals often misjudge the extent to which others agree with their viewpoint (the *false consensus effect*).
   - *Dual process theories*, as reviewed by Martin and Hewstone, recognize that social influence occurs when group members systematically process available information (*direct process*) or base their choices on nonrational processes, such as *heuristics* and emotional responses (*indirect process*).
2. *Normative influence* prompts group members to feel, think, and act in ways that are consistent with their group's social standards.
   - Milgram documented the negative emotions associated with violating norms in his study of seat requests on the subway.
   - Cialdini's work suggests that, in some cases, normative influence is a more potent and longer lasting form of influence than informational influence.
3. Latané and Darley's analysis of the Kitty Genovese incident concludes that individuals sometimes take others' inaction in emergencies (the *bystander effect*) to be a sign that no help is needed. Informational and normative influence contributes to the bystander effect, as does *diffusion of responsibility*.
4. *Interpersonal influence* includes verbal and nonverbal tactics—complaining, demanding, threatening, pleading, negotiating, pressuring, manipulating, rejecting, and so on—designed to induce change.
   - Schachter's analysis of group rejection indicates that a nonconformist is generally less liked by others in the group.
   - Communication with a disliked deviant eventually diminishes, at least when cohesive groups are working on relevant tasks. Schachter's findings, as well as those by Levine and his colleagues, indicates that any dissent from the group mode will reduce likability.
   - Reaction to deviants results, in part, from *subjective group dynamics* triggered by social identity processes. Group members who violate norms can trigger the *black-sheep effect*—they will be evaluated more negatively than an individual who is not a group member who performs the same type of action.

*Do social influence processes shape juries' verdicts?*

1. The magnitude of social influence suggests that the decisions reached by groups, including juries, are shaped by social processes rather than by an unbiased weighing of evidence.
   - The Chicago Jury Project and work by Hastie, Penrod, and Pennington suggests that jurors, through deliberation, develop narratives to account for evidence (*story model*).
   - Juries tend to use either *verdict-driven* or *evidence-driven* deliberation strategies. In most cases, they choose the method of deliberation favored by the majority of the members.

- The verdict favored by the majority of the members prior to deliberation (or on the first straw poll) is usually the jury's final verdict.
- Jurors who have higher status occupations tend to dominate the group's discussion.

2. Available evidence suggests that juries are satisfactory vehicles for making legal decisions.

- Despite size-related changes in group dynamics, small and large juries do not appear to differ significantly in the types of verdicts reached.
- Juries that do not have to reach a unanimous decision render their judgments twice as quickly and are far less likely to be hung juries.
- Several alterations of procedure have been developed to help jurors remember and process trial information, but their impact is not yet known.
- *Voir dire* procedures are often used to select jury members, but Wrightman maintains this process can undermine the representativeness of the jury.

## FOR MORE INFORMATION

*Chapter Case: Twelve Angry Men*

- *Twelve Angry Men: A Play in Three Acts*, by Reginald Rose and Sherman L. Sergel (1958), is a play based on Rose's experience while serving on a jury. Although a fictional dramatization, the play demonstrates the pressures to conform present in groups. Both movie versions of the play, one made in 1957 and starring Henry Fonda as Juror #8, and a 1997 version with Jack Lemon taking the role, are illustrative depictions of group processes.

*Majority and Minority Influence*

- "Majority and Minority Influence," by William D. Crano and Viviane Seyranian (2007), is a concise summary of the last 30 years of research investigating minority and majority influence in groups.
- "Dynamic Social Impact: A Theory of the Origins and Evolution of Culture," by Helen C. Harton and Melinda Bullock (2007), reviews recent studies of dynamic social impact theory and applies the theory to explain the origins of consistencies in human culture.

*Social Influence*

- "Majority Versus Minority Influence, Message Processes, and Attitude Change: The Source–Context–Elaboration Model," by Robin Martin and Miles Hewstone (2008), is a detailed review of a number of theories of influence in groups, including conversion theory, convergent–divergent theory, objective consensus theory, source-based congruity theory, conflict elaboration theory, context/categorization theory (or "leniency contract theory"), dual role theory, and the authors' own source–context–elaboration theory.
- "Social Influence: Compliance and Conformity," by Robert B. Cialdini and Noah J. Goldstein (2004), reviews the recent research and literature on social influence.
- "Inclusion and Exclusion: Implications for Group Processes," by John M. Levine and Norbert L. Kerr (2007), integrates a number of literatures pertaining to motives for remaining in groups, including how groups respond to members who consistently disagree with the majority.

*Juries*

- *Inside the Jury*, by Reid Hastie, Steven D. Penrod, and Nancy Pennington (1983), presents a masterful analysis of communication, influence, and decision-making in juries.
- *American Juries*, by Neil Vidmar and Valerie P. Hans (2007), is a carefully researched analysis of the strengths and possible weaknesses of the jury system.

## Media Resources

Visit the Group Dynamics companion website at www.cengage.com/psychology/forsyth to access online resources for your book, including quizzes, flash cards, web links, and more!

# 8

# Power

## CHAPTER OVERVIEW

Power is essential to group life. Authorities coordinate activities of members and guide them toward their goals, but members exert influence in return by forming cooperative alliances. Power, however, can be used against the group, for authorities sometimes demand actions that members would otherwise never consider. We would not be social beings if we were immune to the impact of power, but power can corrupt.

- What are the limits of an authority's power over group members?
- What are the sources of power in groups?
- Who seeks power and what group processes limit their success?
- How do people react when they use their power to influence others?
- How do those without power react when power is used to influence them?

## CHAPTER OUTLINE

**The People's Temple: The Metamorphic Effects of Power**

Jim Jones was the founder and minister of the People's Temple Full Gospel Church of San Francisco. Jones was a visionary, inspiring leader, who decried the racism, inequality, and spiritual emptiness of American society. Under his charismatic leadership the congregation grew to 8000 members, and Jones was recognized by many for his good works and moral fortitude—until rumors of improprieties and unusual practices began to circulate within the community. Former members reported that at some services, people were beaten before the whole congregation, with microphones used to amplify their screams. Jones, some said, insisted on being called Father, and he demanded absolute dedication and obedience from his followers. He asked members to donate their property to the church, and he even forced one family to give him their six-year-old son.

Jones, to transform his church into a collective society free from the interference of outsiders, moved his entire congregation to Guyana, in South America. He called the isolated settlement Jonestown, and claimed that it would be the model for a new way of living where all would find love, happiness, and well-being. But the men, women, and children of Jonestown did not find contentment. They found, instead, a group that exercised incredible power over their destiny. Jones asked members to make great personal sacrifices for the group, and time and again they obeyed. They worked long hours in the fields. They were given little to eat. They were forbidden to communicate with their loved ones back in the United States. Then disaster struck when church members attacked and killed visitors who were part of a congressional delegation from the United States. Jones, fearing the dismantling of his empire, ordered his followers to take their own lives.

Authorities who first reached the settlement were met by a scene of unbelievable ghastliness. On Jones's orders, more than 900 men, women, and children had either killed themselves or been killed by other followers. Jones's body lay near his chair, where he sat beneath the motto "Those who do not remember the past are condemned to repeat it" (Krause, 1978; Reston, 2000).

Why did the group members obey Jones's order? What force is great enough to make parents give poison to their children? Many blamed Jim Jones—his persuasiveness, his charisma, his depravity. Others emphasized the kind of people who join such groups—their psychological instability, their willingness to identify with causes, and their religious fervor. Still others suggested more fantastic explanations—mass hypnosis, government plots, and even divine intervention.

Such explanations underestimate the power of groups and their leaders—their capacity to influence members, even when members try to resist this influence (Cartwright, 1959). As Chapter 7 noted, groups influence the way their members feel, think, and act. But in some cases this influence can be extraordinarily strong. Rather than subtly shaping members' opinions and choices, powerful people and groups can compel obedience among members who would otherwise resist the group's wishes. Here we consider the sources of that power and the consequences of power for those who wield it as well as those who are subjected to it.

## OBEDIENCE TO AUTHORITY

Bertrand Russell concluded many years ago that "the fundamental concept in social science is Power, in the same sense in which Energy is the fundamental concept in physics" (1938, p. 10). Few interactions advance very far before elements of power and influence come into play. The coach demanding obedience from a player, the police officer asking the driver for the car's registration, the teacher scowling at the errant student, and the boss telling an employee to get back to work are all exerting their social power over others. Power, although notoriously difficult to define, suggests influence, the potential to influence, and control over outcomes (Fiske & Berdahl, 2007; Lukes, 2005). Powerful people can influence other people in significant ways: "A has power over B to the extent that he can get B to do something that B would not otherwise do" (Dahl, 1957, p. 202). In some cases, power is a potential to influence that is not actually put into practice, and it is often rooted in inequalities in control over resources, outcomes, or activities. Power is, fundamentally, a group-level process, for it involves some members of a group conforming to the requirements of others in situations that range from the purely cooperative and collaborative to those rife with conflict, tension, and animosity.

But can **social power**—a commonplace process that shapes nearly all group interactions—generate such a dramatic and disastrous outcome as the Jonestown mass suicide? Can group members be so bent to the will of an authority that they would follow any order, no matter how noxious? Stanley Milgram's (1974) laboratory studies of obedience to authority suggest that the answer to these questions is *yes*.

### The Milgram Experiments

Milgram analyzed power by creating small groups in his laboratory at Yale University. In most cases, he studied three-man groups: One member was a volunteer who had answered an advertisement; one member was the experimenter who was in charge of the session; and one member appeared to be another participant recruited from the community but was in actuality a confederate, who was part of the research team. The confederate looked to be in his late 40s, and he seemed friendly and a little nervous. The experimenter, in contrast, acted self-assured as he set the group's agenda, assigned tasks to the group members, and issued orders. He assigned the participants to one of two roles—teacher or learner. Those given the "teacher" role read a series of paired words (*blue box*, *nice day*, *wild day*, etc.) to the "learner," who was supposed to memorize the pairings. The teacher would later check the learner's ability to recall the pairs by reading the first word in the pair and several possible answers (e.g., *blue*: *sky*, *ink*, *box*, *lamp*). Failures would be punished by an electric shock. What the volunteer did not know, however, was that the confederate was always assigned to the learner role and that the learner did not actually receive shocks.

After assigning the participants to their roles, the experimenter took both group members into the next room. The teacher then watched as the experimenter strapped the learner into a chair that was designed "to prevent excessive movement during the shock." The learner sat quietly while an electrode was attached to his wrist. When he asked if the shocks were dangerous, the experimenter replied, "Oh, no. Although the shocks can be extremely painful, they cause no permanent tissue damage" (Milgram, 1974, p. 19).

The experimenter then led the participant back to the other room and seated him at the shock generator. This bogus machine, which Milgram himself fabricated, featured a row of 30 electrical switches. Each switch, when depressed, would supposedly send a shock to the learner. The shock level of the first switch on the left was 15 volts (*v*) the next switch was 30, the next was 45, and so on, all the way up to 450 *v*. Milgram also labeled the voltage levels, from left to right, *Slight Shock*, *Moderate Shock*, *Strong Shock*, *Very Strong Shock*, *Intense Shock*, *Extreme Intensity Shock*, and *Danger: Severe Shock*. The final two switches were marked *XXX*. The rest of the face of the shock generator was taken up by dials, lights, and meters that flickered whenever a switch was pressed.

The experimenter administered a sample shock of 45 *v* to the participant, supposedly to give him an idea of the punishment magnitude. The study then began in earnest. Using a microphone to communicate with the learner, the teacher read the list of word pairs and then began "testing" the learner's memory. Each time the teacher read a word and the response alternatives, the learner indicated his response by pushing one of four numbered switches that were just within reach of his bound hand. His response lit up on the participant's control panel. Participants were to deliver one shock for each mistake and increase the voltage one step for each mistake.

---

**social power** The capacity to influence others, even when these others try to resist influence.

Milgram set the stage for the order-giving phase by having the learner make mistakes deliberately. Although participants punished that first mistake with just a 15-*v* jolt, each subsequent failure was followed by a stronger shock. At the 300-*v* level, the learner also began to protest the shocks by pounding on the wall, and after the next shock of 315 *v*, he stopped responding altogether. Most participants assumed that the session was over at this point, but the experimenter told them to treat a failure to respond as a wrong answer and to continue delivering the shocks. When the participants balked, the experimenter, who was seated at a separate desk near the teacher's, would use a sequence of prods to goad them into action (Milgram, 1974, p. 21):

- *Prod 1*: "Please continue," or "Please go on."
- *Prod 2*: "The experiment requires that you continue."
- *Prod 3*: "It is absolutely essential that you continue."
- *Prod 4*: "You have no other choice; you must go on."

The situation was extremely realistic and served as a laboratory analog to real-world groups where authorities give orders to subordinates. The experimenter acted with self-assurance and poise. He gave orders crisply, as if he never questioned the correctness of his own actions, and he seemed surprised that the teacher would try to terminate the shock sequence. Yet from the participants' point of view, this authority was requiring them to act in a way that was harmful to another person. When they accepted the $4.50 payment, they implicitly agreed to carry out the experimenter's instructions, but they were torn between this duty and their desire to protect the learner from possible harm. Milgram designed his experiment to determine which side would win in this conflict.

### Milgram's Findings

Milgram was certain that very few of his participants would carry out the experimenter's orders. He went so far as to purchase special equipment that would let him record precisely the duration of each shock administered, expecting that few participants would give more than four or five shocks (Elms, 1995). He also polled a number of psychological researchers and psychiatrists on the subject, asking them to predict how people would react in his study. None believed that participants would shock to the 450-*v* level; they predicted that most would quit by the 150-*v* level.

Milgram and the other experts, however, underestimated the power of the group situation. Of the 40 individuals who served as teachers in the initial experiment, 26 (65%) administered the full 450 *v* to the presumably helpless learner (see Figure 8.1). None broke off before the 300-*v* level, and several of the eventually disobedient participants gave one or two additional shocks before finally refusing to yield to the experimenter's prods. The comments made by the participants during the shock procedure and their obvious psychological distress revealed that they were reluctant to go on but felt unable to resist the experimenter's demands for obedience.

Milgram studied nearly 1000 people in a series of replications and extensions of his original study. In these later studies, some of which are discussed here, different aspects of the setting were systematically manipulated, allowing Milgram to assess their influence on obedience rates. Although he continued to search for the limits of obedience, again and again his participants buckled under the pressure of the experimenter's power.

**Harm versus Rights** Surprised that so few people disobeyed authority, Milgram wondered if the participants fully realized what was happening to the learner in the next room. All they heard was an ambiguous pounding on the wall, which the experimenter told them to ignore. So Milgram, in subsequent studies, added additional cues that signaled the learner's suffering and his unwillingness to continue in the study.

To make it clear that the learner did not wish to continue participation, Milgram added an explicit declaration of refusal. In the *voice-feedback condition* the learner's shouts and pleas (carefully rehearsed and tape-recorded) could be heard through the wall.

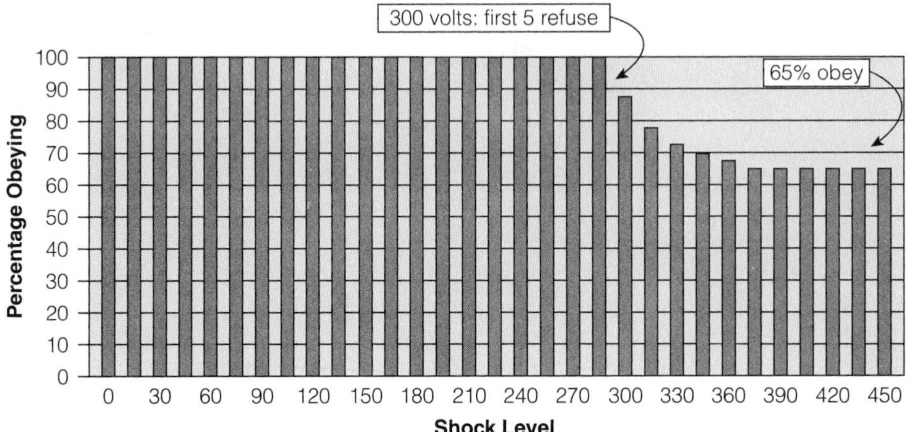


**FIGURE 8.1** Level of obedience in the original condition of the Milgram experiment, with limited feedback between the teacher and the learner. Milgram (1974) found that all participants obeyed the authority's orders up to the 300-volt level. More people resisted the authority's order as the shocks became more powerful, but a full 26 of the 40 participants (65%) were completely obedient up to the end of the study.



The learner grunted when shocked at levels below 120 *v* and complained about the pain. At 150 *v*, he cried out, "Experimenter, get me out of here! I won't be in the experiment any more! I refuse to go on!" (Milgram, 1974, p. 23). He continued screaming and demanding release until the 300-*v* level, when he refused to answer any more questions.

These cues did not substantially reduce the level of obedience seen in the initial study, for fully 62.5% of the participants still obeyed to the 450-*v* level. Moreover, those who did disobey seemed to be responding more to the learner's demand to be released than to his suffering. If participants were going to disobey, they usually did it when the learner retracted his consent to continue—at the 150-*v* mark. Those who passed that milestone usually continued to 450 *v*, even though the learner screamed in pain until he eventually lapsed into silence (Packer, 2008). Faced with the orders of the authority to continue and the learner's demand to be released, the majority sided with the authority.

To test whether participants would respond explicitly to the learner's signs of suffering, Milgram increased the possibility of significant harm befalling the learner in the *heart problem condition*. When the experimenter connected the wires to his arm, the learner mentioned that he had a heart condition and asked about complications. The experimenter said that the shocks would cause no permanent damage. When shocked the learner's groans and shouts of protest could be heard through the wall, and he also repeatedly complained that his heart was bothering him. Even when the learner stopped responding after 330 *v*, 65% of the participants continued to administer shocks to the 450-*v* level.

**Proximity and Surveillance Effects** In earlier pilot studies the teacher and learner were separated only by a glass observation window. Milgram noticed that, even though teachers could see the learner react to the shocks, most averted their eyes and expressed discomfort at having to watch. So, to make the consequences of their actions even clearer to subjects, Milgram moved the learner into the same room as the teacher. In the *proximity condition*, the learner sat in the same room as the teacher, voicing the same complaints used in the voice-feedback condition and writhing with pain at each shock. Obedience dropped to 40%. In the most extreme of all the variations, the *touch-proximity condition*, the learner sat next to the teacher and received his shock when he put his hand on a shock plate. At the 150-*v* level, he refused to put his hand down on the plate, so the experimenter gave the participant an insulated glove and told him to press the learner's hand down onto the plate as he depressed the shock switch. Still, 30% obeyed.

Milgram also examined the impact of increased distance between the experimenter and the teacher on rates of obedience by having the experimenter leave the room after he reviewed the procedures with the participant. He continued giving orders to the participant by telephone, but he lost his ability to monitor the subject's actions. In this *low surveillance condition*, 25% of the participants stopped as soon as the learner insisted on release (the 150-*v* level). Only 20% of the participants were obedient to the 450-*v* level, and many participants disobeyed by deceiving the authority—they assured the experimenter that they were administering increasingly large shocks with each mistake, when they were actually only delivering 15 *v*.

**Prestige and Legitimacy** Milgram conducted his initial studies on the campus of Yale University, which most people recognize as a prestigious center of learning and science. Milgram was concerned that people obeyed the experimenter because he was perceived to be a "Yale scientist" and could therefore be trusted to act appropriately. So, in the *office-building condition*, Milgram moved the study away from prestigious Yale University. He set up the study in an office building located in a shopping area. "The laboratory was sparsely furnished, though clean, and marginally respectable in appearance. When subjects inquired about professional affiliations, they were informed only that we were a private firm conducting research for industry" (Milgram, 1974, pp. 68–69). Obedience dropped to 48%—still a surprisingly large figure given the unknown credentials of the staff.

Milgram next lowered the legitimacy of the experimenter, who was trained to exude confidence and scientific expertise; he seemed to know exactly what he was doing throughout the shock process. Milgram therefore arranged, in some conditions, for the orders to come from someone other than the expert experimenter. In the *ordinary-man variation*, he added a fourth member to the group, who was given the task of recording the shock levels used. The experimenter explained the study, as in the other conditions, but gave no instructions about shock levels before he was called away. The new participant, who was actually a confederate, filled the role of the authority; he suggested that shocks be given in increasingly strong doses and ordered the participant to continue giving shocks when the learner started to complain. Obedience dropped to 20%. But when the participants refused to continue, the confederate left the experimenter's desk and began administering the shocks. In this case, most of the participants (68.75%) stood by and watched without stopping the confederate—although one "large man, lifted the zealous shocker from his chair, threw him to a corner of the laboratory, and did not allow him to move until he had promised not to administer further shocks" (1974, p. 97).

Milgram further explored the legitimacy of the authority in the *authority-as-victim condition*. Here the experimenter agreed to take the role of the learner, supposedly to convince a reluctant learner that the shocks were not harmful. The experimenter tolerated the shocks up to 150 *v*, but then he shouted, "That's enough, gentlemen!" The confederate, who had been watching the procedure, then insisted, "Oh, no, let's go on. Oh, no, come on, I'm going to have to go through the whole thing. Let's go. Come on, let's keep going" (Milgram, 1974, p. 102). In all cases, the participant released the experimenter; obedience to the ordinary person's command to harm the authority was nil.

**Group Effects** Milgram (1974) studied obedience rather than conformity, since the authority did not himself engage in the action he demanded of the teacher, and the teacher faced the power of the authority alone. Milgram considered, however, the possibility that in most cases other group members are present, and the group may be a second source of power in the situation—either in standing against the authority or taking sides with him.

Milgram verified that a compliant group only makes people more obedient. In the *peer administers shock* condition, the subjects did not have to administer the shock: a confederate, who was fully compliant, did so. In this variation, 92.5% obediently fulfilled their tasks without intervening. Membership in a defiant group, however, did contribute to disobedience. To examine the relative power of conformity versus obedience, in the *two peers rebel condition* Milgram added two more confederates to the situation. They posed as peers of the real participant and the three worked together to deliver the shocks to the learner. One read the list of words, one gave the verbal feedback to the learner, and the participant pushed the shock button. As shown in Figure 8.2, the subject sat before the shock machine, and the other group members sat on either side.

The confederates played out their roles until the learner cried out in pain at 150 *v*. Then, one of the confederates refused to continue, and left the table. The experimenter could not convince him to return, and so ordered the remaining two to continue. However, at the 210-*v* mark the second confederate quit as well, explaining, "I'm not going to shock that man against his will" (1974, p. 118). Only the real subject was left to give the shocks, and in most cases he sided with the group and refused to obey. Only 10% of the participants were fully obedient—although these individuals had to administer the shocks as the disobedient confederates looked on. Membership in a group helped participants defy the authority.

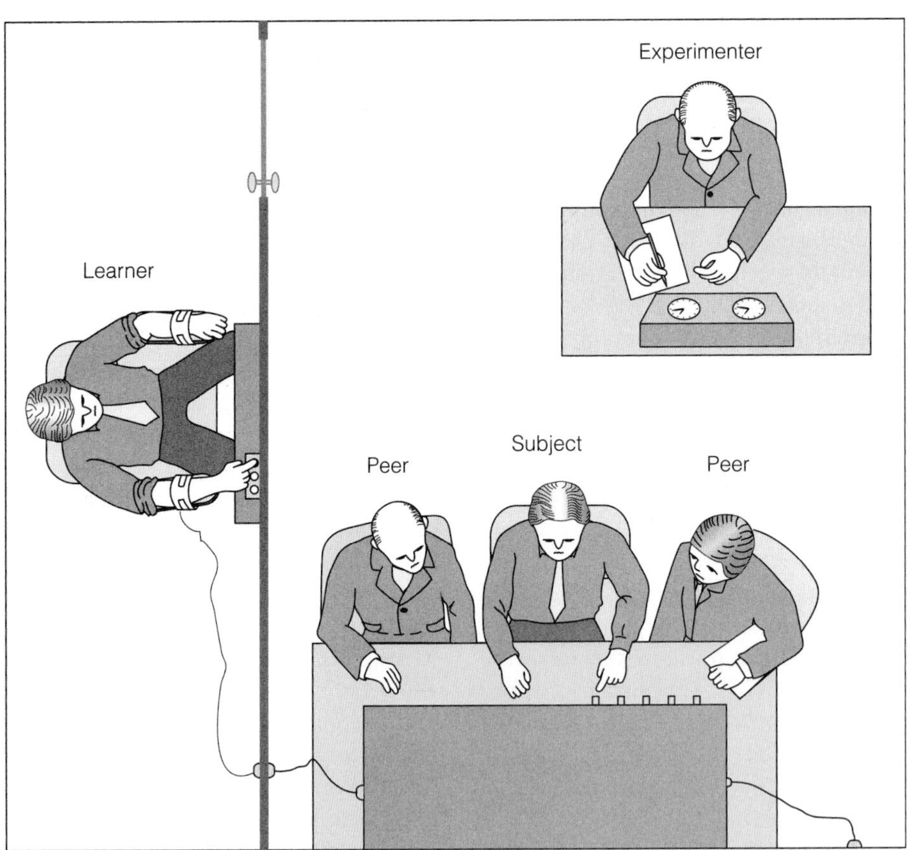


**FIGURE 8.2** Layout of the experimental situation in which Milgram tested the obedience of groups. When the subject worked with others who obeyed the experimenter's orders, very few disobeyed. But if the others refused to continue to shock the learner, most of the subjects also refused to obey the experimenter.

SOURCE: Adapted from *Obedience to Authority: An Experimental View*, by Stanley Milgram. Copyright © 1974 by Stanley Milgram. Reprinted by permission of HarperCollins Publishers, Inc.

### The Power of the Milgram Situation

Milgram's results sparked controversies that are unresolved even today (Blass, 2000b; Miller, 2004). Some researchers believe that the participants were not taken in by Milgram's subterfuge. They suggested that the participants knew that no shocks were being administered, but they played along so as not to ruin the study (Mixon, 1977; Orne & Holland, 1968). Milgram's research team, however, carefully interviewed all the participants, and fewer than 20% challenged the reality of the situation (Elms, 1995). Moreover, if participants saw through the elaborate duplicity, then why did they become so upset? According to Milgram,

> Many subjects showed signs of nervousness in the experimental situation, and especially upon administering the more powerful shocks. In a large number of cases the degree of tension reached extremes that are rarely seen in sociopsychological laboratory studies. Subjects were observed to sweat, tremble, stutter, bite their lips, groan, and dig their fingernails into their flesh. (1963, p. 375)

The distress of the participants was so great that the publication of the study sparked a controversy over the ethics of social–psychological research (Blass, 2004). Even a museum exhibit that featured the Milgram experiment sparked public debate over its ethics when it toured U.S. science museums (Marsh, 2000).

Other experts, when trying to explain why so many people obeyed in the study, have pointed to the participants themselves—their personalities, their temperaments, their society's views of obedience. Just as many people, when first hearing of the Guyana tragedy, wondered, "What strange people they must have been to be willing to kill themselves," when people are told about Milgram's findings, they react with the question, "What kind of evil, sadistic men did he recruit for his study?" Yet by all accounts, Milgram's participants were normal and well-adjusted, and subsequent attempts to link obedience to personality traits have been relatively fruitless (see Blass, 1991, for an analysis). Also, even though Milgram's participants were mostly men, they were paid for their time, and they lived at a time when people trusted authorities more than they do now, his findings appear to be highly reliable over time and across situations. Replications of the study using different procedures and participants have generally confirmed Milgram's initial findings (see Blass, 2000a). Many believe that the level of obedience that Milgram documented in his laboratory matches levels found in military, organizational, and educational settings (Fiske, Harris, & Cuddy, 2004; Hinrichs, 2007; Pace & Hemmings, 2007; see Focus 8.1).

## SOURCES OF POWER

More than 4000 members of the Unification Church married each other in a mass ceremony because their leader, Reverend Sun Myung Moon, told them to do so. The Branch Davidians remained barricaded in their compound until their leader, David Koresh, ordered them to set it on fire. Thirty-seven members of the religious group Heaven's Gate took their own lives because their leader convinced them that they were leaving their bodies to join extraterrestrials in a nearby spaceship. Members of the People's Temple drank cyanide-laced punch and died. Sixty-five percent of Milgram's participants administered painful electric shocks to an innocent person as he begged them to stop.

Reverend Moon, Jim Jones, Milgram's experimenter, coaches, police officers, and teachers exact obedience from others. But where does this remarkable power come from? Here we seek answers by considering the bases of power in groups, as well as the tactics members often use to influence others.

### Bases of Power

John R. P. French and Bertram Raven (1959), in a brilliant analysis of the roots of power in groups and

## Focus 8.1 How Strong Are Pressures to Obey in the Cockpit?

*The pilot in command of an aircraft is directly responsible for, and is the final authority as to, the operation of that aircraft.*

—Federal Aviation Agency, Code of Federal Regulation, Paragraph 91.3

Commercial jetliners are not piloted by individuals, but by groups. No one individual could carry out the many and varied actions needed when taxiing, at takeoff, when aloft, in final approach, and when landing, so the captain and crew work together to pilot the plane safely to its destination. In some cases, however, the smooth teamwork of the crew is disrupted by power dynamics. Flight personnel are organized along quasi-military lines of authority, with rank defining power and responsibility. Most larger aircraft require the services of a pilot, a copilot, and a flight engineer but, as a signal of the authority of each position, these roles are also labeled *captain*, *first officer*, and *second officer*. Captains are, by law, the final authority on board, and in many cases, they exert their power over the rest of the crew in both subtle and unsubtle ways (Sexton & Helmreich, 2000). The flight deck of the craft is often called the *cockpit*, which is also the name of the pen where contests between fighting roosters (cocks) are held (Foushee, 1984).

Investigations conducted by the National Transportation Safety Board (NTSB) traced several fatal crashes back to two group-level sources: (1) a captain's refusal to comply with the suggestions of other crew members, and (2) the crew's excessive obedience to the captain's authority (NTSB, 1994). When a DC-8 ran out of fuel and crashed in Portland, analysis of the flight recorder indicated that the flight engineer repeatedly reminded the pilot of their dwindling fuel, but the pilot ignored him (Milanovich et al., 1998). The pilot of Northwest Express Flight 5719 spent much of the flight issuing orders to the first officer, many of which were considered unnecessary. The copilot eventually failed to correct the pilot's error on the approach, and the plane crashed (Tarnow, 2000). A copilot on a flight involved in a *near miss*—two aircraft almost colliding in midair—claimed that he warned the captain to reduce airspeed, but that the captain ignored him (Foushee, 1984, p. 888):

> After several attempts to convey the information, the captain responded by saying, "I'll do what I want." Air traffic control inquired as to why the aircraft had not been slowed, advised the crew that they had almost collided with another aircraft, and issued a new clearance that was also disregarded by the captain despite repeated clarification by the copilot. Following the last advisory from the copilot, the captain responded by telling the copilot to "just look out the damn window."

Aviation and group experts, recognizing the destructive impact of excessive obedience by flight crews and the abuse of power by pilots, have instituted changes in personnel training. Rather than attempt to change the long-standing norms of hierarchy, control, and deference in the cockpit, these programs instead seek to improve communications between all members of the flight crew. Through workshops, structured group activities, and simulations, copilots learn how to challenge errors made by the pilot, and pilots are encouraged to accept warnings from crew members rather than ignore them. Many airlines carry out team-based training using advanced flight simulators (Line-Oriented Flight Training, or LOFT) and deliberately simulate emergencies that can only be solved if the crew members communicate clearly and decisively with the captain (Ginnett, 1993; Helmreich & Foushee, 1993; Merritt & Helmreich, 1996).

organizations, identified the six key **power bases** shown in Table 8.1. Group members who control these bases are more influential than those who fail to secure a base of power.

**Reward Power** In many cases, power is closely tied to the control of valued resources. The members of the People's Temple, for example, thought that Jim Jones possessed the things that they needed—security, economic support, companionship, political reform, and spirituality. His ability to control,

---

**power bases** Sources of social power in a group, including one's degree of control over rewards and punishment, authority in the group, attractiveness, expertise, and access to and control over information needed by group members.

**TABLE 8.1 French and Raven's Six Bases of Power**

| Power Base | Sample Indicators |
|---|---|
| **Reward:** The capability of controlling the distribution of rewards given or offered to the target. | determines pay level<br>gives desirable job assignments<br>can promote<br>compliments and praises |
| **Coercive:** The capacity to threaten and punish those who do not comply with requests or demands. | can terminate employment (fire)<br>controls who is given undesirable assignments<br>can suspend without pay<br>verbal reprimands and warnings |
| **Legitimate:** Authority that derives from the legitimate right to require and demand obedience. | duly appointed supervisor, manager, etc.<br>representative of the group or organization<br>role is sanctioned by the group or organization<br>has the right to make demands of others |
| **Referent:** Influence based on the identification with, attraction to, and respect of others. | is a person meriting respect<br>is someone who is admired by others<br>someone with whom others identify<br>is a nice person |
| **Expert:** Influence based on others' belief that the powerholder possesses superior skills and abilities. | can devise clever solutions to problems<br>can provide sound task-related advice<br>source of needed technical knowledge<br>shares considerable experience/training |
| **Informational:** Influence based on the potential use of informational resources, including rational argument, persuasion, or factual data. | explains the basis for request<br>gives good reasons for exactions<br>uses reason to handle problems<br>promotes understanding of procedures and changes |

SOURCE: Adapted from French & Raven, 1959; Raven, Schwarzwald, & Koslowsky, 1998; Schriesheim, Hinkin, & Podsakoff, 1991.

exclusively and completely, the distribution of material and symbolic rewards, secured his **reward power** within the group.

Raven (1992) draws a distinction between impersonal and personal rewards. Impersonal rewards are material resources, such as food, shelter, protection, promotions, wages, and awards. Personal rewards are positive interpersonal reinforcements, such as verbal approbation, compliments, smiles, and promises of liking or acceptance. As social exchange theory suggests, both types of rewards are potent sources of power, particularly during times of scarcity. Money and food, for example, are valued resources, but they become a source of power when the rest of the group is penniless and starving. Rewards that one controls exclusively are also more likely to augment one's power, for group members who depend on someone for a reward will likely comply with that individual's requests.

---

**reward power** Power based on one's control over the distribution of rewards (both personal and impersonal) given or offered to group members.

Once Jones moved the church to Jonestown he became the sole source of rewards that members once acquired from non-church sources (Cook, Cheshire, & Gerbasi, 2006; Emerson, 1962).

Ironically, the tendency for the "rich to get richer" also applies to reward power, because group members often implicitly assume that the rewards given them by powerful people are more valuable than the rewards given them by those without power. When members of groups were given the opportunity to trade goods of equal monetary value with other group members, most were willing to pay more for goods they received from a high-status group member, and they considered those resources to be more valuable, important, and worth having. Because powerful individuals' rewards were overvalued by others, they did not need to expend as many of their resources to achieve the same level of success in the exchange as did those members with low power, so their resources tended to grow rather than diminish (Thye, 2000).

**Coercive Power** Accounts of the People's Temple describe Jones's reliance on physical and psychological punishment as a means of exacting obedience from his followers. When members broke the rules or disobeyed his orders, he was quick to punish them with beatings, solitary confinement, denials of food and water, and long hours of labor in the fields.

**Coercive power** derives from one's capacity to dispense punishments, both impersonal and personal, to others (Raven, 1992). Terrorists attacking other countries, employers threatening employees with the loss of pay or dismissal, and teachers punishing mischievous students with extra assignments are relying on impersonal coercive bases of power. Disagreeing friends insulting and humiliating one another, the boss shouting angrily at his secretary, and religious leaders threatening members with loss of grace or ostracism derive their power from personal sources (Raven, 1992; Raven, Schwarzwald, & Koslowsky, 1998).

Certain people consistently rely on coercion to influence others (Kramer, 2006; see Focus 8.2). Most people, however, only turn to coercive power when they feel it is the only means they have to influence others. In consequence, and ironically, individuals in positions of authority who feel relatively powerless are more likely to use coercion than more powerful individuals. Some parents and teachers, for example, feel that their children and students are controlling them even though they occupy a position of greater authority in the home or school. These individuals feel relatively powerless, and so, in contentious situations, they tend to use coercive threats, punishments, and abuse more than do empowered authorities (Bugental & Lewis, 1999). In contrast, when individuals who are equal in coercive power interact, they often learn over time to avoid the use of their power (Lawler, Ford, & Blegen, 1988; Lawler & Yoon, 1996). Group members also prefer to use reward power rather than coercive power if both are available and they fear reprisals from others in the group should they act in a coercive way (Molm, 1997).

**Legitimate Power** Individuals who have **legitimate power** have the socially sanctioned right to ask others to obey their orders. The security personnel at the airport telling a passenger to remove her shoes, the drill sergeant ordering the squad to attention, the professor waiting for the class to become quiet before a lecture, and the minister interpreting the Gospel for the congregation are powerful because they have the right to command others, and others are obligated to obey. Jones, for example, was the legitimate head of the People's Temple. He was an ordained minister; his work had been commended by many political and religious leaders, and he had received such honors as the Martin Luther King Jr.,

---

**coercive power** Power based on one's ability to punish or threaten others who do not comply with requests or demands.

**legitimate power** Power based on an individual's socially sanctioned claim to a position or role that gives the occupant the right to require and demand compliance with his or her directives.

## Focus 8.2 Bullying: A Harmless Phase or Coercive Abuse?

*Courage is fire, and bullying is smoke.*
—Benjamin Disraeli

Each day, as Erick boards the bus, Jonathan berates him, making fun of his hair and clothes. No one will sit with Erick for fear of being drawn into the abuse. Donzella and her friends deliberately circulate nasty rumors about Carol, who was once part of the Donzella clique but who is now considered an outcast. Each day at recess, Greg finds Albert on the playground and, after teasing him, pushes him up against the school wall and punches him. At Columbine High School, a clique of athletes made loud, negative remarks about a group of outcasts who did not fit into any of the school's other cliques.

**Bullying** is a form of coercive interpersonal influence. It involves deliberately inflicting injury or discomfort on another person repeatedly through physical contact, verbal abuse, exclusion, or other negative actions. Both males and females bully, but they tend to do so in different ways: girls are relationally aggressive, for they use gossip, criticism, and exclusion against their victims. Boys tend to be physically aggressive. Bullying, as Dan Olweus (1997) noted, signals a marked imbalance in the power relationship between the bully and his or her victim. The victim of abuse "has difficulty in defending himself or herself and is somewhat helpless against" the bully (p. 216). Bullying, then, is not retaliation between parties in a dispute or conflict, but the mistreatment of a less powerful person by someone with power. Bullying was once considered a phase that children pass through on their way to adulthood, but instances of bullying escalating into violence and catastrophic reactions of victims to bullying have caused a shift in this view. Bullying is not "child's play" but aggression—a form of peer abuse. Bullying is common in school settings, but it also occurs in military, business, and professional organizations (Geffner et al., 2004).

Bullying is also a group behavior. Victims are sometimes isolated and friendless children abandoned to their fate by the rest of the school, but in many cases, groups of children are abused by groups of bullies. Similarly, although bullies are often thought to be poorly adjusted children who are expressing anger by picking on those who cannot defend themselves, bullies are often relatively popular members of the school. They often are involved in sports, for example (for the boys) and considered attractive and more mature (for the girls), and are known as school leaders and trend setters (Vaillancourt, Hymel, & McDougall, 2003). Yet, they tend to be disliked, as most condemn the way they treat other people of lower status in the group. Bullying also involves more than just the bully and the victim, as other children are drawn into the harmful bully–victim exchange. Some children take the role of henchmen or facilitators; they do not initiate the abuse, but they take an active part once the bullying event has begun. Others encourage bullies or signal support by smiling and laughing. Others impassively watch the interaction without speaking, and a few members of the bystander group may intercede on behalf of the victim, either directly or by seeking help from officials or authorities (O'Connell, Pepler, & Craig, 1999; Olweus, 2000).

Because bullying is rooted in both power dynamics and group dynamics, experts recommend school- and group-level interventions for preventing peer abuse. Olweus's (1997) pioneering program stressed restructuring the role of teachers in schools to increase their control over social behavior as well as instruction. Olweus recommended creating a school atmosphere that is warm and supportive, but also closely monitored by authorities who consistently enforce anti-bullying norms. These norms must be supported through the dissemination of information about bully–victim problems and by discussing expectations with students in classes and schoolwide assemblies. Victims of bullying can also be supported through the development of buddy systems, cooperative learning activities, and the use of peer-conflict mediation programs. Families, too, can be involved in reducing bullying by monitoring children's behavior closely and by setting standards for appropriate conduct (Giannetti & Sagarese, 2001; Horne, Stoddard, & Bell, 2007).

---

**Bullying** Repetitively teasing, ridiculing, provoking, or tormenting others through various types of irritating, harassing, or aggressive actions, such as name-calling, threats, insults, and physical injury.

Humanitarian Award. When individuals joined the People's Temple, they tacitly agreed to follow Jones's orders. Thus, "legitimacy empowers authority. Normative regulation is the price that power pays for legitimacy" (Zelditch, 2001, p. 8).

Those who rely on reward or coercive power often find that their authority dwindles when their control over the resources diminishes. In contrast, those who achieve a position of authority through methods that the group considers fair or proper generally find that their decisions are accepted, without resistance, by others in the group (Tyler 2005). Members obey these legitimate authorities because they personally accept the norms of the group. Their obedience is not coerced but voluntary, for it springs from an internalized sense of loyalty to the group rather than the desire to gain resources or avoid harm. Even duly appointed or selected authorities will lose their legitimate power, however, if they violate principles of fairness, social responsibility, and reciprocity (Lammers et al., 2008). Those who engage in unethical behavior, for example, or do not show proper respect for their subordinates run the risk of losing the members' loyalty—and once loyalty is gone so is willingness to obey (Tyler & Blader, 2003).

**Referent Power** Who is the best-liked member of the group? Who is the most respected? Is there someone in the group whom everyone wants to please? The individual with **referent power** lies at the interpersonal center of the group. Just as group members seek out membership in selective, desirable groups, so they identify with and seek close association with respected, attractive group members. The members of the People's Temple were devoted to Jones—to the point where they loved, admired, and identified with him. Many made financial and emotional sacrifices in the hope of pleasing him. As one of his followers explained, Jones "was the God I could touch" (quoted in Reston, 2000, p. 25).

The concept of referent power explains how charismatic leaders manage to exert so much control over their groups. It was sociologist Max Weber who first used the term **charisma** to account for the almost irrational devotion that some followers exhibit for their leaders. People often refer to a charming leader as charismatic, but Weber reserved the term to describe the tremendous referent and legitimate power of the "savior–leader." Charisma originally described a special power given by God to certain individuals. These individuals were capable of performing extraordinary, miraculous feats, and they were regarded as God's representatives on Earth (Weber, 1921/1946). Weber argued that charismatic leaders do not have unique, wondrous powers, but they succeed because their followers *think* they have unique, wondrous powers. Weber himself was struck by the charismatic leader's power to demand actions that contradict established social norms: "Every charismatic authority . . . preaches, creates, or demands new obligations" (1921/1946, p. 243). Charismatic leaders such as Jones usually appear on the scene when a large group of people is dissatisfied or faces a stressful situation. The leader offers these people a way to escape their problems, and the masses react with intense loyalty.

**Expert Power** Group members often defer to and take the advice of those who seem to possess superior skills and abilities. A physician interpreting a patient's symptoms, a local resident giving directions to an out-of-towner, a teacher spelling a word for a student, and a computer technician advising a user all transform their special knowledge into **expert power**.

As with most of the power bases identified by French and Raven, a person does not actually need to be an expert to acquire expert power; the person must only be *perceived* by others to be an expert (Kaplowitz, 1978; Littlepage & Mueller, 1997). Researchers demonstrated the impact of perceived expertise on influence by arranging for dyads to work on a series of problems. Half of the participants were led to believe that their partner's ability on the task was superior to their own, and the rest

---

**referent power** Power based on group members' identification with, attraction to, or respect for the powerholder.

**charisma** Derived by Max Weber from the Greek *xarisma* (a divine gift of grace), the ascription of extraordinary or supernatural acumen, ability, and value to a leader by his or her followers.

**expert power** Power that derives from subordinates' assumption that the powerholder possesses superior skills and abilities.

were told that their partner possessed inferior ability. As the concept of expert power suggests, individuals who thought that their partners were experts accepted their recommendations an average of 68% of the time, whereas participants paired with partners perceived as inferior accepted their recommendations only 42% of the time (Foschi, Warriner, & Hart, 1985).

**Informational Power** In 1965, Raven separated out **informational power** from expert power: Group members can turn information into power by providing it to others who need it, by keeping it from others, by organizing it, increasing it, or even falsifying it. Some individuals achieve informational power by deliberately manipulating or obscuring information, or at least making certain that the information remains a secret shared by only a few group members (Messick, 1999). Other individuals are recognized as the keepers of the group's truths or secrets, and these individuals must be consulted before the group makes a decision (Fine & Holyfield, 1996). People who share information with others can achieve informational power, even by passing unverified and, in some cases, private information through the group's "grapevine" (Kurland & Pelled, 2000).

## Bases and Obedience

French and Raven's power base theory explains why so many people obeyed Jim Jones, but it also offers insights into participants' reactions in the Milgram experiments. Even though the experimenter was not an authority in a traditional sense—he was not formally identified as the group's leader and given an impressive title such as *captain*, *president*, *director*, or *doctor*—he did draw power from all six of the bases identified by French and Raven (1959). His power to reward was high, because he gave out the payment, and also because he was an important source of positive evaluations; participants wanted to win a favorable appraisal from this figure of authority. He also used coercive prods: "The experiment requires that you continue," and, "You have no other choice, you must go on" warn of possible negative consequences of disobedience. Many participants also assumed that the experimenter had a legitimate right to control their actions and that the learner had no right to quit the study. The participants also respected Yale University and recognized the importance of scientific research, so the experimenter had referent power. Very few participants knew much about electricity, either, so they considered the experimenter an expert. He also persuaded them to continue by telling them that the study was important and that its findings would answer questions about how people learn.

Thomas Blass (2000a) confirmed the power of the experimenter in the Milgram study by asking a group of unbiased observers to review a 12-minute videotape of Milgram's procedures. The observers then reviewed six possible reasons why the participant obeyed the experimenter's orders. The reasons were derived from French and Raven's power base model. The coercive power explanation, for example, asked if people obeyed because the experimenter insisted they continue and seemed to "warn of negative consequences" (Blass, 2000a, p. 42) The expert power explanation, in contrast, suggested that the participants assumed that the experimenter was an expert and that his explanation of the procedure reassured them. These observers ranked the experimenter as higher on expert, legitimate, coercive, and informational power, but lower on reward power, and lower still on referent power. The experimenter adopted a very brusque manner during the study, so he did not seem particularly likable; hence his low referent power. His stern, no-nonsense manner, however, apparently made him seem like a duly appointed expert whose orders could not be disobeyed.

## Power Tactics

People do not use only promises, rewards, threats, punishment, expertise, and information to influence

---

**informational power** Power based on the potential use of informational resources, including rational argument, persuasion, or factual data.

people—they have far more **power tactics** at their disposal when they need to poke, prod, or prompt others into action. Table 8.2 gives examples of some of these tactics, which differ in terms of their softness, rationality, and laterality (Falbo & Peplau, 1980; Raven et al., 1998).

- *Soft and hard.* Soft tactics exploit the relationship between the influencer and the target to extract compliance. When individuals use such methods as collaboration, socializing, friendships, personal rewards, and ingratiation they influence more indirectly and interpersonally. Hard tactics, in contrast, are often described as *harsh, forcing,* or *direct* because they rely on economic, tangible outcomes, such as impersonal rewards or threats to well-being. Hard tactics are not, however, necessarily more powerful than soft ones; threatening people with exclusion from a group or public embarrassment may lead to substantially greater change than the threat of some deprivation or corporal punishment (Fiske & Berdahl, 2007).
- *Rational and nonrational.* Tactics that emphasize reasoning, logic, and good judgment are *rational* tactics; bargaining and persuasion are examples. Tactics such as ingratiation and evasion are nonrational tactics of influence, because they rely on emotionality and misinformation.
- *Unilateral and bilateral.* Some tactics are interactive, involving give-and-take on the part of both the influencer and the target of the influence. Such *bilateral* tactics include persuasion, discussion, and negotiation. *Unilateral* tactics, in contrast, can be enacted without the cooperation of the target of influence. Such tactics include demands, faits accomplis, evasion, and disengagement.

People vary in their habitual use of one type of power tactic over another. When asked the question, "How do you get your way?" more interpersonally oriented people—those more concerned with being liked and accepted—showed a preference for soft, indirect, and rational power tactics (Falbo, 1997). Those who espoused a Machiavellian, manipulative philosophy when dealing with others tended to use indirect/nonrational tactics, as did those who scored lower in terms of agreeableness and emotional stability (Butkovic & Bratko, 2007). Extraverts use a greater variety of tactics than introverts (Caldwell & Burger, 1997). Men and women also differ somewhat in their choice of power tactics (Keshet et al., 2006). Men and women who supervised an ineffective employee used both rewards and criticism, but women intervened less frequently with a more limited range of tactics. They promised fewer pay raises and threatened more pay deductions than men, and they were more likely to criticize subordinates (Instone, Major, & Bunker, 1983). The sexes also differ in their use of power in more intimate relationships, for men tend to use bilateral and direct tactics, whereas women report using unilateral and indirect methods (Falbo & Peplau, 1980).

People also choose different power tactics depending on the nature of the group situation (Yukl & Michel, 2006). A person who has high status in a group that is already rife with conflict will use different tactics than an individual who is low in status and wants to minimize conflict. In a corporate setting, authorities rely on referent and expert power, but in an educational setting teachers may turn to reward and punishment power (Krause & Kearney, 2006). Who one is attempting to influence can also dictate choice of power tactic; for example, people report using a variety of soft and hard methods to influence subordinates but, when dealing with superiors, they rely heavily on rational methods such as persuasion and discussion (Kipnis et al., 1984). People also shift from soft to hard tactics when they encounter resistance (Carson, Carson, & Roe, 1993; Teppner, 2006). The interpersonal consequences of the use of these various types of influence methods will be considered later in this chapter.

## POWER PROCESSES

The micro-society of the group is not, in most cases, egalitarian. The members of a newly formed

---

**power tactics** Specific strategies used to influence others, usually to gain a particular objective or advantage.

**TABLE 8.2 A Sampling of the Many Power Tactics People Use to Influence Other People in Everyday Situations**

| Tactic | Examples |
|---|---|
| **Apprise** | I point out what she will gain.<br>I note the personal benefits he'll receive. |
| **Bully** | I yell at him.<br>I push him around. |
| **Collaboration** | I offer to help.<br>I provide assistance as needed. |
| **Complain** | I gripe about all the work I have to do.<br>I grumble about having to study. |
| **Consulting** | I ask him to help me with the project.<br>I get her involved in the work. |
| **Criticism** | I point out her limitations.<br>I find fault with their work. |
| **Demand** | I demand that the problem be solved.<br>I order her to continue. |
| **Discuss** | I give him supporting reasons.<br>We talk about it. |
| **Disengage** | I give him the cold shoulder.<br>I stop talking to her. |
| **Evade** | I change the subject when it comes up.<br>I skip the meeting. |
| **Expertise** | I let her know I'm an expert.<br>I rely on my experience. |
| **Fait accompli** | I just do it.<br>I don't get anyone's permission. |
| **Humor** | I try to make a joke out of it.<br>I tell a funny story. |
| **Ingratiate** | I flatter her.<br>I compliment him on the way he looks. |
| **Inspire** | I appeal to her sense of fair play.<br>I cheer him on. |
| **Instruct** | I teach him how to do it.<br>I set an example. |

*(continued)*

**TABLE 8.2 (Continued)**

| Tactic | Examples |
|---|---|
| **Join forces** | I get the boss to agree with me.<br>I turn the group against her. |
| **Manipulate** | I lie.<br>I leave out important details. |
| **Negotiate** | I offer her a bargain.<br>I wheel and deal. |
| **Persist** | I don't take no for an answer.<br>I reiterate my point. |
| **Persuade** | I coax her into it.<br>I convert him to my side. |
| **Promise** | I promise to never do it again.<br>I offer to do some of his work for him. |
| **Punish** | I fire her.<br>I slap him. |
| **Put Down** | I insult him.<br>I say something like, "You are an idiot." |
| **Request** | I ask him to do me a favor.<br>I tell her what I expect. |
| **Reward** | I increase his pay.<br>I give her a present. |
| **Socialize** | I make small talk for a while.<br>I ask about the family. |
| **Supplicate** | I plead.<br>I beg humbly for permission. |
| **Threaten** | I threaten legal action.<br>I tell him that he might get fired. |

SOURCE: Drawn from various studies of influence, including Caldwell & Burger, 1997; Dillard & Fitzpatrick, 1985; Emans, Munduate, Klaver, & Van de Vliert, 2003; Falbo, 1977; Falbo & Peplau, 1980; Fu, Peng, Kennedy, & Yukl, 1997; Howard, Blumstein, & Schwartz, 1986; Instone, Major, & Bunker, 1983; Kipnis, 1984; Littlepage, Nixon, & Gibson, 1992; Stets, 1997; Wiseman & Schenck-Hamlin, 1981; Yukl & Michel, 2006.

group begin as equals, but before long, some members gain greater influence over others. Influence often settles on the shoulders of those who most seek it, for some wish to not only control their own outcomes, but others' outcomes as well. Power, however, is a group-level process, and so the rise to a position of authority also depends on the group itself: its status hierarchies, systems of roles and duties, and reciprocal networks of influence among members (Stolte, Fine, & Cook, 2001).

## Who Seeks Power?

Not everyone seeks power over others. Some members are content to be rank-and-file members, equal in responsibilities and influence to most of the others in the group, and so do not desire to rise upward in the group's hierarchy. Other individuals seek only *personal power*: They wish to control their own individual outcomes and experiences, but they are not concerned about controlling other's outcomes (Van Dijke & Poppe, 2006). Some, however, lust for the power to control other people, and they pursue it across time, groups, and situations.

People who are high in their need or hope for power, for example, tend to pursue status and prestige more vigorously than others. They describe themselves as hoping to have power in the future: "I want to have power in every aspect of my life" (Harms, Roberts, & Wood, 2007). Need for power, measured when people are first hired for a large company, predicts their rise to positions of authority in the corporation's management hierarchy some 8 to 16 years later (McClelland & Boyatzis, 1982). They are more likely to hold offices in groups and organizations. They report *feeling* more powerful when they interact with others (Fodor & Riordan, 1995), but if they are not able to act on this need, they tend to have high blood pressure and other health problems (McClelland, 1975). When individuals who were high in need for power watched a videotape of someone acting very assertively rather than submissively they reported experiencing negative emotions and exhibited physiological signs of tension, such as muscle activity in the corrugator supercilli of the brow (Fodor, Wick, & Hartsen, 2006).

Individuals who seek and use power also tend to view the world—and the individuals and groups within it—as ordered in terms of relative dominance. This **social dominance orientation (SDO)** is, at its core, a general predisposition toward anti-egalitarianism within and between groups, manifested by a preference for "group-based hierarchy and the domination of 'inferior' groups by 'superior' groups" (Sidanius & Pratto, 1999, p. 48). Individuals who are high in SDO strive to protect and even increase the differences between group members, and they prefer membership in hierarchical groups. They are dominant and assertive rather than submissive and passive, and match the prototype of the driven, tough, and relatively uncaring seeker of power who views the world as a "dog-eat-dog" jungle where only the strong survive (Cozzolino & Snyder, 2008; Duckitt, 2006). Men tend to be higher in SDO than women (Wilson & Liu, 2003).

SDO also predicts reactions to outgroups. Just as individuals who are high in SDO believe that a pecking order of individuals structures groups, so they feel that a group-level pecking order ranks all societies. They would tend to agree with such statements as, "Some groups of people are simply inferior to other groups" and "It's probably a good thing that certain groups are at the top and other groups are at the bottom" (Sidanius & Pratto, 1999, p. 67). In consequence, SDO is a powerful predictor of stereotyping and prejudice (Whitley, 1999).

---

**social dominance orientation (SDO)** A dispositional tendency to accept and even prefer circumstances that sustain social inequalities, combined with a general preference for hierarchical social structures.

## Hierarchies of Dominance

Jack Washington, a participant in Milgram's experiment, administered all the shocks up to 450 *v* with barely a hesitation. The experimenter never prodded Jack to continue, but throughout he seemed subdued—almost sad. When later asked why he followed orders, he said, "I merely went on. Because I was following orders. I was told to go on. And I did not get a cue to stop" (Milgram, 1974, p. 50).

Humans, like many social species, live in groups with organized systems of power relations. Field studies of many primates, such as chimpanzees, baboons, and bonobos, reveal complex patterns of power relations that determine various privileges and responsibilities. As an evolutionary account of human gregariousness would suggest, group members accept influence from others because such behavioral responses are adaptive. So long as the authority is motivated to advance the interests of the group, then those lower in the status hierarchy—the low men or women on the totem pole—tend to do as they are told by those with higher status (Kessler & Cohrs, 2008). "Each member's acknowledgement of his place in the hierarchy stabilizes the pack" (Milgram, 1974, p. 124). Those with lower status are not powerless, however. When observers looked closer they noted that, along with the classic dominance of the alpha male or female, there was a complex pattern of control exercised by subordinates (de Waal, 2006). By forming coalitions with others, selectively disobeying unreasonable demands, and by directly challenging selfish authorities they redressed any abuses of power by those at the top of the status hierarchy. Power in social species, then, is a dynamic, negotiated process rather than a top-down chain of influence (Keltner et al., 2008).

**Interpersonal Complementarity** The **interpersonal complementarity hypothesis** suggests that obedience and authority are reciprocal, complementary processes. This hypothesis assumes that each group member's action tends to evoke, or "pull," a predictable set of actions from the other group members (Carson, 1969). If, for example, an individual seems agreeable, pleasant, and cooperative, the other group members would tend to react in kind: they would behave in positive, friendly ways. Friendly behaviors are reciprocated by friendly behaviors. But what if group members act in dominant, firm, directive ways—issuing orders, taking charge, giving advice? Such behaviors would tend to evoke submissive responses from the other group members. People also report feeling more comfortable when interacting with someone who displays complementary rather than similar reactions. Group members who display signs of submissiveness when talking to someone who seems powerful are better liked, as are those who take charge when interacting with docile, submissive individuals (Tiedens & Fragale, 2003). The interpersonal complementary hypothesis thus predicts that (1) positive behaviors evoke positive behaviors and negative behaviors evoke negative behaviors, and (2) dominant behaviors evoke submissive behaviors and submissive behaviors evoke dominant behaviors (Sadler & Woody, 2003).

Researchers put this hypothesis to the test by arranging for young women to work, for a short period of time, with a partner who was trained to enact a particular behavioral style. When she enacted a dominant, leading style she exuded confidence and authority. In some cases, she added a degree of friendliness to her dominance, frequently intervening to keep the group working. In others, she was dominant, but less friendly; she stressed her superiority and autonomy, and her self-confidence bordered on self-absorption and conceit. In other conditions, she acted in more submissive, self-effacing ways. Rather than take charge, she would seem timid, uncertain, passive, and inhibited (Strong et al., 1988).

The videotapes of the sessions revealed clear evidence of complementarity. Participants who were paired with a dominant confederate acted submissively; they acquiesced, behaved passively, and showed respect for their partner. Only rarely did a participant respond in a dominant manner when faced with a dominant interaction partner. Conversely, if the confederate behaved in a docile manner, then the participants tended to take charge by acting in a dominant fashion—strong evidence of the power of complementarity.

**Power of Roles** When participants arrived for the Milgram experiment, they were carefully cast into the role of teacher. The duties of that role were made clear to them, and it was not until the shock sequence progressed that they realized the demands that their role would put on them. Their role required their actions.

Phillip Zimbardo and his colleagues examined the power of roles in their Stanford Prison Experiment. Zimbardo selected two dozen healthy, intelligent, and psychologically normal men from a large group of student volunteers to serve as either

---

**interpersonal complementarity hypothesis** The predicted tendency for certain behaviors to evoke behaviors from others that are congruous with the initial behavior, with positive behaviors evoking positive behaviors, negative behaviors evoking negative behaviors, dominant behaviors evoking submissive behaviors, and submissive behaviors evoking dominant behaviors.

guards or prisoners in a simulated prison. The students randomly assigned to the role of prison guard were issued khaki uniforms, billy clubs, whistles, and reflective sunglasses. They were then put in charge of a mock prison that Zimbardo and his colleagues had constructed in the basement of the psychology building at Stanford University. The students assigned to the role of prisoner were "arrested" by uniformed police, booked, and transported to the prison. There they were sprayed with a deodorant, searched, issued an identification number, and outfitted in a dresslike shirt, heavy ankle chain, and stocking cap.

The study was scheduled to run for two weeks, but was terminated after only six days. Why? According to Zimbardo (2007), the participants became too immersed in their roles. The prisoners seemed literally to become prisoners; although some rebelled, the majority became withdrawn and depressed. The guards also changed as the study progressed; many became increasingly tyrannical and arbitrary in their control of the prisoners. They woke the prisoners in the middle of the night and forced them to stand at attention for hours, locked them in a closet, strictly enforced pointless rules, and censored prisoners' mail. Some of their actions crossed the line between intimidation and abuse. They threatened the prisoners with physical injury, ran hooded prisoners into walls as they walked them to the bathrooms at night, and forced them to engage in feigned sexual activities ("floor-humping" and mock anal intercourse). Zimbardo confessed that even he found himself sinking too deeply into the role of superintendent, worrying over possible "prison breaks" and autocratically controlling visiting procedures (Haney, Banks, & Zimbardo, 1973; Zimbardo, Maslach, & Haney, 2000; Zimbardo, 2004, 2007).

Why did the prisoners respond so obediently and the guards so autocratically? Zimbardo believed that the participants felt compelled to act consistently with their roles. All of the participants had a general idea of what it meant to act like a prisoner or like a guard. As the study progressed, they became more and more comfortable in their roles. Eventually, to be a guard meant controlling all aspects of the prison and protecting this control with force if necessary. Prisoners, on the other hand, were supposed to accept this control and try to get through the experience as easily as possible by obeying all the prison's rules. Participants who refused to obey these norms were pressured by the other participants to bring their behavior back in line; nonconformity was not tolerated. Zimbardo concluded that the "Stanford Prison Experiment made it evident that initially our guards were 'good apples,' some of whom became soured over time by powerful situational forces" (2007, p. 329). Zimbardo calls the tendency for people to be corrupted by negative group environments the **Lucifer effect**.

**Responsibility and the Agentic State** One's power in a group and one's responsibility for what happens in the group tend to covary. Those who occupy positions of authority—leaders, executives, managers, and bosses—are generally viewed as more accountable than those who occupy such low-status positions as subordinate or employee (Blass, 1995, 1996; Hamilton & Sanders, 1995). Because responsibility is thought to be concentrated in the role of the superior, however, subordinates in hierarchically organized groups sometimes no longer feel personally responsible for their own actions. They enter what Milgram called the **agentic state**—they become agents of a higher authority (Milgram, 1974). They feel "responsibility to the authority" but "no responsibility for the content of the actions that the authority prescribes" (Milgram 1974, pp. 145–146). Like Jack Washington, who was just "following orders" when he shocked the screaming learner, many individuals who have little power in the group assume that they are supposed to carry out

---

**Lucifer effect** The transformation of benign individuals into morally corrupt ones by powerful, but malevolent, social situations; named for the biblical character Lucifer, an angel who fell from grace and was transformed into Satan.

**agentic state** A psychological state described by Stanley Milgram that occurs when subordinates in an organized status hierarchy experience such a marked reduction in autonomy that they are unable to resist authorities' orders.

the orders of the authority without questioning those orders. They no longer feel that they are in control of their own actions, and so they become willing cogs in the group machine, carrying out authorities' orders without considering their implications or questioning their effects (Hamilton & Sanders, 1999; Kelman & Hamilton, 1989).

Researchers examined this loss of responsibility in chains of command by adding a second layer to the hierarchy in the usual obedience situation (Kilham & Mann, 1974). They modified the basic Milgram experiment to include a *transmitter*, who relayed orders, and an *executant*, who actually delivered the shocks. As predicted, transmitters were more obedient than executants (54% versus 28%). In this study, men were more obedient than women, but other studies found either no difference between men and women (Milgram, 1974) or heightened obedience among women (Sheridan & King, 1972).

Milgram himself documented the relationship between a feeling of responsibility and obedience by asking his participants to allocate responsibility for the situation among the three participants—the experimenter, the teacher, and the learner. Obedient participants gave more responsibility to the experimenter than they gave to themselves. They also gave twice as much responsibility to the victim as did disobedient participants. These disobedient participants, in contrast, took more responsibility than they attributed to the experimenter (Mantell & Panzarella, 1976; Meeus & Raaijmakers, 1995; West, Gunn, & Chernicky, 1975). Milgram's analysis of responsibility is also consistent with studies of diffusion of responsibility: People feel less personally responsible when they are in groups than when they are alone. Other negative group behaviors, such as reductions in collective effort, conflict, mob behaviors, and vandalism have all been attributed to the diffusion of responsibility that occurs in groups (see Focus 7.2).

### The Power of Commitment

Jim Jones's order to commit suicide did not surprise his followers. Jones had talked about mass suicide even before the People's Temple moved to Guyana. On more than one occasion, Jones had told the congregation that he had poisoned the sacramental wine and that all would be dead within the hour. He went so far as to plant confederates in the audience who feigned convulsions and death. He repeated this ceremony in Jonestown, calling it the White Night. After enough repetitions, the thought of suicide, so alien to most people, became commonplace in the group.

Jones's White Night tactic illustrates the power of *behavioral commitment*. Jones did not suddenly order his followers to commit suicide. Instead, he prefaced his request with months of demands that increased in their intensity. Similarly, Milgram did not ask participants to push a lever that would deliver 450 *v* to the learner at the outset of the study. Instead, he asked them only to give the learner a mild shock if he answered incorrectly. No one refused. Over time, however, the demands escalated, and participants were unable to extricate themselves from the situation. Once they began, they could not stop (Gilbert, 1981; Modigliani & Rochat, 1995).

Studies of the influence tactics used by panhandlers, salespeople, fundraisers, and authorities confirm the power of gradually escalating demands (Cialdini, 2009). The **foot-in-the-door technique**, for example, works by prefacing a major request with a minor one that is so inconsequential that few people would refuse to comply. Investigators demonstrated the strength of this technique by asking home owners to post a large, unattractive sign in their yards. Nearly all refused—unless this major request had been preceded by a smaller request (Freedman & Fraser, 1966). Similar studies have also found that the two requests called for by the foot-in-the-door technique are superior to a single request for many types of behaviors, although such factors as the sex of the influencer and the amount of time that elapses between the two requests moderate the power of the foot-in-the-door method (Beaman et al., 1983; Dillard, 1991).

---

**foot-in-the-door technique** A method of influence in which the influencer first makes a very small request that the target will probably agree to; once the target agrees to the minor request, he or she is more likely to agree to the influencer's more important request.

Interrogators often use behavioral commitment to extract compliance from detainees. Chinese military personnel, for example, used the foot-in-the-door tactic in the so-called "brainwashing" methods during the Korean War. They began by subjecting U.S. prisoners of war to physical hardships and stressful psychological pressures. The men were often fatigued from forced marches, and their sleep was disrupted. Their captors broke down the chain of command in these units by promoting nonranking soldiers to positions of authority, and friendships among the men were systematically discouraged.

Although the Chinese relied heavily on traditional methods of influence, such as persuasion, indirect techniques proved more effective. The prisoners were initially asked to perform inconsequential actions, such as copying an essay out of a notebook or answering some questions about life in the United States. Once the men agreed to a minor request, a more significant request followed. They might be asked to write their own essays about communism or discuss the problems of capitalism. Each small concession led to a slightly larger one, until the men found themselves collaborating with the Chinese. The Chinese rarely succeeded in permanently changing the men's attitudes and values, but they did extract obedience to their authority: Morale within the prison was poor, and the men rarely tried to escape (Schein, 1961; Segal, 1954).

### Power and the Fundamental Attribution Error

A church member obediently swallowing poison. A soldier executing innocent civilians. A worker installing substandard building materials. A participant in an experiment giving an innocent victim painful shocks. On first hearing about such events, people often fall prey to the **fundamental attribution error (FAE)**: They blame the personalities of the individuals rather than the powerful group processes at work that forced them to obey. In extreme instances, when a powerholder inflicts tremendous suffering and misfortune on people, the group members blame themselves for their misery. The members of the People's Temple may have felt so deserving of their fate that they chose to suffer rather than escape suffering. These feelings of self-condemnation may account for their willingness to take their own lives (Clark, 1971; Fanon, 1963).

Yet obedience is not a reflection of the nature of the individuals in the group, but an indication of the power of the group itself. By controlling key bases of power, using power tactics, exploiting the nature of the subordinate–authority relationship, and prefacing large demands with minor ones, authorities exert great influence on group members. As John Darley explained, "Many evil actions are not the volitional products of individual evil-doers. Instead, they are in some sense societal products, in which a complex series of social forces interact to cause individuals to commit multiple acts of stunning evil" (Darley, 1992, p. 204).

---

**fundamental attribution error (FAE)** The tendency to overestimate the causal influence of dispositional factors and underemphasize the causal influence of situational factors.

## THE METAMORPHIC EFFECTS OF POWER

The metamorphic effects of power have long fascinated observers of the human condition (Kipnis, 1974). In their tragedies, the Greeks dramatized the fall of heroes who, swollen by past accomplishments, conceitedly compared themselves to the gods. Myth and folklore are replete with tales of the consequences of too much power, as in the case of Icarus, whose elation at the power of flight caused his own death. As Lord Acton warned, "Power tends to corrupt, and absolute power corrupts absolutely." But what of those without power? The ancients also pitied those who were powerless to control their own destinies, for they were doomed to "a dark and meaningless existence" (Griffin, 1983, p. 143). No one, Nietzsche believed, could survive if they lose the will to power. In the next sections, we consider the metaphoric effects of power: how power changes both those in positions of power and those who are the targets of that influence.

## Changes in the Powerholder

**Approach/inhibition theory**, developed by Dacher Keltner and his colleagues (2003, 2008), agrees with the wisdom of the ancients, for its assumes that power—having power, using power, even thinking about power—transforms individuals' psychological states. The theory notes that most organisms display one of two basic types of reactions to environmental events. One reaction, *approach*, is associated with action, self-promotion, seeking rewards and opportunities, increased energy, and movement. The second reaction, *inhibition*, is associated with reaction, self-protection, avoiding threats and danger, vigilance, loss of motivation, and an overall reduction in activity. Significantly, the approach/inhibition model suggests that power increases approach tendencies, whereas reductions in power trigger inhibition. Power activates people—it causes them to experience increases in drive, energy, motivation, and emotion—and so often leads to positive consequences. The powerful can bring their heightened energy, clearer insights, and positive emotions to bear on the issues facing the group, and so help the group overcome difficulties and reach its goals. But power, and the activation it brings, also has a dark side, for it can create a Jim Jones or an Adolph Hitler as often as a Mahatma Gandhi or an Abraham Lincoln.

**The Positive Effects of Power** Power prompts people to take action rather than remain passive. Powerful individuals are usually the busiest people in the group and organization, for they are engaged with the group and responsive to changes within the group and its environment (Keltner et al., 2008). They are proactive; they would rather speak first during a debate, make the first move in a competition, or make the first offer during a negotiation (Magee, Galinsky, & Gruenfeld, 2007). Their actions also tend to be more focused on the goals appropriate to the given situation. If in a leisure setting, powerful people plan to enact more relaxing activities than less powerful people. In a work setting, they plan more task-related activities (Guinote, 2008). These effects of power more often occur in individuals who occupy positions that are more prestigious or influential (leaders, bosses, managers), but as Focus 8.3 explains, they also occur when power is primed by subtle features of the situation.

Powerful people also tend to experience, and express, more positive emotions than those who are lower in power. High-power individuals usually feel good about things—their moods are elevated, they report higher levels of such positive emotions as happiness and satisfaction, and they even smile more than low-power group members (Berdahl & Martorana, 2006; Watson & Clark, 1997). In a study of dyads, those with more power than their partner reported feeling such positive emotions as more happiness, pride, and amusement. Their partners, unfortunately, reported more anger, fear, tension, and sadness (Langner & Keltner, 2008). Power is also associated with optimism about the future, apparently because more powerful individuals tend to focus their attention on more positive aspects of the environment (Anderson & Galinsky, 2006).

One's level of power also influences what one notices in others and in any given situation. Individuals with power seek out rewards and are more likely to realize when desirable resources can be acquired. Those without power, in contrast, are more likely to be watching out for threats and punishments and, therefore, are more likely to interpret ambiguous situations as threatening ones (Keltner et al., 2003). Those with power also tend to think more globally—they focus on the forest rather than the trees (Guinote, 2007; Smith & Trope, 2006). Those with power seem to carry out executive cognitive functions more rapidly and successfully, including general internal control mechanisms that coordinate attention, decision-making, planning, and goal-selection (Smith et al., 2008).

---

**approach/inhibition theory** An integrative conceptual analysis of the transformative effects of power that finds power to be psychologically and behaviorally activating but the lack of power inhibiting.

## Focus 8.3 Is Power a State of Mind?

*On the first day, he said "I felt a king, like I rule them brown-eyes. Like I was better than them. Happy." The second day, he said, "I felt down, unhappy, like I couldn't do anything, like I was tied up and couldn't get loose."*

—Raymond Hansen, quoted in *A Class Divided* (Peters, 1987, p. 88).

Are you a powerful person? Do you have the capacity to influence others, even if they resist you? Some people, across time and settings, feel more interpersonally powerful than others. When they describe themselves they are apt to say, "I can get people to listen to what I say" or "If I want to, I get to make decisions," and "I think I have a great deal of power" (Anderson & Galinsky, 2006). Yet, a sense of power also depends on the situation; if you win an election, are appointed to a position of influence in an organization, or are granted membership in a high-status group, in all likelihood you will experience a feeling of heightened power that comes from the circumstances (Keltner et al., 2008).

The subjective feeling of power was vividly demonstrated by Jane Elliott's well-known classroom demonstration of prejudice. On one day, she told her blue-eyed third graders that they were superior to brown-eyed children, and gave them special privileges appropriate for their elevated status. Then, on the next day, she reversed the favoritism. The shift in the emotions, actions, and moods of the two groups of children from one day to the next was clear evidence of the psychological effects of power (Peters, 1987).

A sense of power can also be triggered in more subtle ways. Environmental or cognitive cues can prime a sense of power, by activating pre-existing beliefs, concepts, or memories of experiences relevant to power. The researchers in one study primed power by asking people to complete a task that involved looking for words embedded in a table of letters. Those who searched for power-related words, such as *authority* and *boss* rather than *house* or *clock*, were more likely to act on the basis of their personal preferences. A similar result occurred when power was primed by seating people in a "power chair" in a professor's office. Those students who were seated in the professor's chair, behind the desk, acted in more powerful ways than those who sat in the chair reserved for visitors (Chen, Lee-Chai, & Bargh, 2001).

Individuals' own thoughts about their experiences with power can also "empower" them. In one study, researchers first asked some people to think back to a time when they had power over other individuals. Others thought of a time when they had little power. They were then left to wait for the next phase of the study at a table positioned too close to an annoying fan blowing directly on them. Some of the participants just put up with this irritation, but others took steps to solve the problem: they moved the fan or turned it off. As predicted, 69% of the individuals who recalled a time they were powerful removed the bothersome fan, compared to only 42% of less powerful participants (Galinsky, Gruenfeld, & Magee, 2003).

These studies all suggest that power is, to some extent, a subjective experience. Some individuals who occupy positions of authority and influence report that they feel powerless and without any control over events that transpire in their lives. Yet, other individuals, who face situations that seem to be ones that they cannot in any way influence and control, report feeling very powerful and in charge. They may not have power, yet they feel powerful. Power, then, is in part a state of mind—a feeling of authority rather than authority per se. Feeling powerful may well be the first step to being powerful.

**Does Power Corrupt?** The positive consequences of power, in terms of action orientation, emotions, and judgmental tendencies, can also be liabilities. Powerful people are proactive, but in some cases their actions are risky, inappropriate, or unethical ones (Emler & Cook, 2001). Just as their moods tend to be positive, they tend to generate negative emotional reactions in their subordinates, particularly when there is disagreement and conflict in the group (Fodor & Riordan, 1995). Some individuals, driven by their need for power, overstep the boundaries of their authority or engage in inappropriate actions. When individuals gain power, their self-evaluations grow more favorable, whereas their evaluations of others grow more negative (Georgesen & Harris, 1998). If they feel that they have a mandate from their group or organization to get things done, they may do things they are not empowered to do (Clark & Sechrest, 1976). When individuals feel powerful, they sometimes treat others unfairly, particularly if they are more self-centered rather than focused on the overall good of the group (Chen, Lee-Chai, & Bargh, 2001). Some individuals (primarily men) associate power with sexuality, and so when they are empowered, they engage in inappropriate sexual behaviors, including sexual harassment (MacKinnon, 2003).

Powerful people often misjudge, misunderstand, and even derogate their subordinates. Powerholders can be discerning judges of those who work for them, but often only when their personal success depends on recognizing the strengths and weaknesses of subordinates (Overbeck and Park, 2001). Power tends to weaken one's social attentiveness, with the result that powerful people have a more difficult time understanding other people's point of view (Galinsky et al., 2006). Powerful individuals also spend less time gathering and processing information about their subordinates and, as a result, may perceive them in a stereotypical fashion (Fiske, 1993a)—particularly if their primary loyalty is to the organization rather than to the individuals who are subordinate to them (Overbeck & Park, 2001).

Powerful people tend to be more behaviorally oriented, but in some cases that means they use their power unnecessarily. David Kipnis (1974) examined this tendency by arranging for advanced business students to participate as managers in a simulated manufacturing company. Some had considerable power, in that they could award bonuses, cut pay, threaten and actually carry out transfers to other jobs, give additional instructions, and even fire a worker, but others could not. Kipnis controlled the level of productivity of the fictitious workers (all performed adequately), but powerful managers nonetheless initiated roughly twice as many attempts at influence as the less powerful managers. Moreover, power determined the power tactics managers used—the powerless ones relied on persuasion, whereas the powerful ones coerced or rewarded their workers. Other studies have yielded similar support for the idea that people with power tend to make use of it, but the magnitude of this effect depends on many other factors (Fiske & Berdahl, 2008).

Once power has been used to influence others, changes in powerholders' perceptions of themselves and of the target of influence may take place. In many instances, the successful use of power as a means of controlling others leads to self-satisfaction, unrealistically positive self-evaluations, and overestimations of interpersonal power (Galinsky, Jordan, & Sivanathan, 2008). When Kipnis (1974) asked participants if their subordinates were performing well because of (1) the workers' high self-motivation levels, (2) their manager's comments and suggestions, or (3) their desire for money, the high-power managers believed that their workers were only in it for the money (which the manager could control). The low-power managers believed that the workers were "highly motivated." Other studies have also revealed this tendency for powerful individuals to assume that they themselves are the prime cause of other people's behavior (Kipnis et al., 1976). Powerholders tend to (1) increase the social distance between themselves and nonpowerful individuals, (2) believe that nonpowerful individuals are untrustworthy and in need of close supervision, and (3) devalue the work and ability of less powerful individuals (Kipnis, 1974; Strickland, Barefoot, & Hockenstein, 1976).

**The Iron Law of Oligarchy** Some people are power hungry. They seek power, not because they can use it to achieve their goals, but because they value power per se. Hence, once such people attain power, they take steps to protect their sources of influence. This protective aspect of power translates into a small-group version of Robert Michels's (1915/1959) **iron law of oligarchy**—individuals in power tend to remain in power. Eventually, too, powerholders may become preoccupied with seeking power, driven by a strong motivation to acquire greater and greater levels of interpersonal influence (McClelland, 1975, 1985; Winter, 1973).

---

**iron law of oligarchy** Robert Michels's principle of political and social control which predicts that in any group where power is concentrated in the hands of a few individuals (an oligarchy), these individuals will tend to act in ways that protect and enhance their power.

This need for power, as noted earlier in the chapter, is a prominent personality characteristic in individuals who rise to positions of authority in organizations and politics. Evidence also indicates, however, that when those with a high power motivation cannot exercise that power, they experience increased tension and stress (McClelland, 1985). Under such conditions, they also exaggerate the amount of conflict that exists in the group and overlook group members' efforts at cooperation (Fodor, 1984, 1985).

## Reactions to the Use of Power

Power, by its very nature, suggests tension, conflict, and turmoil. In many cases, power does not just include power *with* people and *over* people, but also power *against* people. Powerholders can influence, sometimes dramatically, the outcomes of those who have little power, prompting them to do things they would rather not. How do people respond—behaviorally, cognitively, and emotionally—when the directives of authorities conflict with the goals they have set for themselves?

**Reactions to Power Tactics** Approach/inhibition theory suggests that individuals who find themselves without power, relative to others, avoid rather than approach. They not only lack resources, but they are dependent on others for the resources that they need. They therefore tend to display more negative affect, they are sensitive to threats and punishments, and they tend to follow closely the dictates of the norms of the group (Keltner et al., 2003).

These negative effects of power differentials are more or less pronounced, however, depending on the type of power tactic used by powerholders. Studies conducted in a range of settings, including schools, military organizations, prisons, and families, suggest that harsh influence tactics—such as punishment (both personal and impersonal), legitimate authority (such as rule-based sanctions), and nonpersonal rewards—are less effective than soft influence methods—expert power, referent power, and personal rewards (Fiske & Berdahl, 2007; Pierro, Cicero, & Raven, 2008). Harsh tactics generate a range of negative emotions, including hostility, depression, fear, and anger, whereas those influenced by softer methods tend to reciprocate with cooperation (Krause, D. E., 2006). Moreover, even when mildly coercive methods, such as threats, are used, people often overreact and respond with even stronger counterthreats, setting in motion an upward spiral of conflict (Youngs, 1986). Hence, although coercive powerholders may be successful in initial encounters, influence becomes more difficult in successive meetings as the target's anger and resistance to pressure grow. Coercive and reward power can also cause group members to lose interest in their work. Supervisors who create feelings of autonomy sustain their subordinates' intrinsic interest in their work, whereas those who use coercive or rewarding methods find that productivity dwindles when they are not monitoring the group (Deci, Nezlek, & Sheinman, 1981; Pelletier & Vallerand, 1996). Organizational experts advocate sharing power with subordinates by delegating responsibilities, empowering workers, and making use of self-directed work teams (Hollander & Offermann, 1990).

The conflict created by coercive influence can disrupt the entire group's functioning. Studies of classrooms, for example, indicate that many teachers rely heavily on coercion, but that these methods cause rather than solve disciplinary problems (Kounin, 1970). Coercive tactics, such as physical punishment, displays of anger, and shouting, not only fail to change the target student's behavior but also lead to negative changes in the classroom's atmosphere (Kounin & Gump, 1958). When misbehaving students are severely reprimanded, other students often become more disruptive and uninterested in their schoolwork, and negative, inappropriate social activity spreads from the trouble spot throughout the classroom. This *disruptive contagion*, or *ripple effect*, is especially strong when the reprimanded students are powerful members of the classroom status structure or when commands by teachers are vague and ambiguous. On the basis of these findings, researchers have suggested that teachers avoid the ripple effect by relying on other influence bases, including reward power, referent power, and expert power.

**Resistance to Coercive Influence** Group members do not always rebel against a "benevolent despot." A powerholder who uses coercive influence tactics, such as threats and punishments, is often tolerated by group members when the group is successful (Michener & Lawler, 1975), the leader is trusted (Friedland, 1976), and the use of such tactics is justified by the group's norms (Michener & Burt, 1975). Coercive methods are also more effective when they are applied frequently and consistently to punish prohibited actions (Molm, 1994).

In some cases, however, group members resist the authority's influence. They may escape the powerholder's region of control or apply influence in return. Members contend against those in power individually—particularly when they feel that others in the group have more power than they do. But when members feel a sense of shared identity with the other low-power members of the group, they are more likely to join with them in a **revolutionary coalition** that opposes the powerholder (Dijke & Poppe, 2004; Lawler, 1975). In one study of group rebellion, group members worked under the direction of a leader who was appointed to that post because he or she had outscored them on a bogus test of ability. The leader then proceeded to keep more than half of the money earned by the group, giving each participant less than one fourth. If the leader had personally decided how to apportion payment, 58% of the participants rebelled by forming a coalition with the other low-status participants. If the leader was not responsible for the payment scheme, only 25% revolted (Lawler & Thompson, 1978, 1979).

Group members are also more likely to resist an authority who lacks referent power, uses coercive influence methods, and asks the group members to carry out unpleasant assignments (Yukl, Kim, & Falbe, 1996). Such conditions can generate *reactance* in group members. When **reactance** occurs, individuals strive to reassert their sense of freedom by affirming their autonomy (Brehm, 1976). In one study, in which teammates had to make a choice between two alternatives marked 1-A and 1-B, 73% chose 1-A if their partner said, "I prefer 1-A," but only 40% chose 1-A if the partner demanded, "I think we should both do 1-A" (Brehm & Sensenig, 1966). In another study, 83% of the group members refused to go along with a group participant who said, "I think it's pretty obvious all of us are going to work on Task A" (Worchel & Brehm, 1971, p. 299).

**Compliance and Conversion** Both Milgram's participants and the People's Temple members did as they were told, but the two groups differed in one crucial respect: Most of Milgram's participants struggled to withstand the authority's pressure, for they believed that the learner should not be held against his will. Many of Jones's followers, in contrast, zealously followed his orders. They did not strain against his authority; they had converted to his way of thinking (Darley, 1995; Lutsky, 1995; Staub, 1989, 2004).

Herbert Kelman (1958, 1961, 2006) identified three basic reactions that people display in response to coercive influence (see Table 8.3). In some cases, the powerholder only produces *compliance*—the group members do what they are told to do, but only because the powerholder demands it. Privately, they do not agree with the powerholder, but publicly they yield to the pressure. Like Milgram's participants, they obey only when the powerholder maintains surveillance. *Identification* occurs when the target of the influence admires and therefore imitates the powerholder. When group members identify with the powerholder, their self-image changes as they take on the behaviors and characteristics of the person with power. Many members of the People's Temple admired Jones and wanted to achieve his level of spirituality. They obeyed his orders because they identified with him.

---

**revolutionary coalition** A subgroup formed within the larger group that seeks to disrupt or change the group's authority structure.

**reactance** A complex emotional and cognitive reaction that occurs when individuals feel that their freedom to make choices has been threatened or eliminated.

**TABLE 8.3 Kelman's Compliance-Identification-Internalization Theory of Conversion**

| Stage | Description |
|---|---|
| Compliance | Group members comply with the powerholder's demands, but they do not personally agree with them. If the powerholder does not monitor the members, they will likely not obey. |
| Identification | Group members' compliance with the actual or anticipated demands of the powerholder are motivated by a desire to imitate and please the authority. The members mimic the powerholder's actions, values, characteristics, and so on. |
| Internalization | Group members follow the orders and advice of the powerholder because those demands are congruent with their own personal beliefs, goals, and values. They will perform the required actions even if not monitored by the powerholder. |

SOURCE: Kelman, 1958.

Identification, if prolonged and unrelenting, can lead to the final stage—internalization. When *internalization* occurs, the individual "adopts the induced behavior because it is congruent with his value system" (Kelman, 1958, p. 53). The group members are no longer merely carrying out the powerholder's orders; instead, their actions reflect their own personal beliefs, opinions, and goals. Even if the powerholder is not present, the group members will still undertake the required actions. Extreme obedience—such as occurred with Jonestown, the murder of millions of Jews by the Nazis during World War II, the My Lai massacre, and the Heaven's Gate group—often requires internalization. The group members' actions reflect their private acceptance of the authority's value system (Hamilton & Sanders, 1995, 1999; Kelman & Hamilton, 1989).

Kelman's three-step model of conversion explains how groups convert recruits into fervent members over time. Cults, for example, insist that the members adopt the group's ideology, but in the early stages of membership, they only require compliance. New recruits are invited to pleasant group functions, where they are treated in a warm, positive way. Once they agree to join the group for a longer visit, the veteran members disorient them by depriving them of sleep, altering their diet, and persuading them to join in physically exhilarating activities. The recruits are usually isolated from friends and family to prevent any lapses in influence, subjected to lectures, and asked to take part in group discussions. Compliance with these small requests is followed by greater demands, as with the U.S. prisoners of war in Korea. Eventually, the recruits freely agree to make personal sacrifices for the group, and these sacrifices prompt a further consolidation of their attitudes (Baron, 2000; Baron, Kerr, & Miller, 1992). Once recruits reach the consolidation stage, they have fully internalized the group's ideology and goals.

## Questioning Authority

In 1976, Jim Jones fought for the improvement of housing and for progressive political change in the San Francisco area, and his followers worked diligently toward the goals outlined by their leader. In 1978, he was accused of human rights violations, physical assault, and illicit sexual practices. Power changed all the members of the People's Temple, including Jones himself.

Authority is essential to group life. Without its organizing guidance, group members could not coordinate their efforts and achieve their goals. Yet authorities that overstep their boundaries can undermine members' motivations, create conflict, and break the bonds between members. Authorities, too, must be wary of their own power, for power is easily misused. Who should question authority? Those who have it and those who are controlled by it.

## SUMMARY IN OUTLINE

*What are the limits of an authority's power over group members?*

1. *Social power* is the capacity to influence others, even when these others try to resist this influence.
2. Milgram tested people's ability to resist a powerful authority who ordered them to give painful and potentially harmful electric shocks to a confederate.
   - A majority (65%) of Milgram's participants obeyed, apparently because they felt powerless to refuse the orders of the authority.
   - Obedience rose and fell systematically as Milgram manipulated various aspects of the setting, including the risk of the procedure to the victim, the proximity of the victim to the group member, the prestige of the research location, surveillance by the experimenter, the legitimacy of the authority, and the presence of groups.
   - Critics noted methodological flaws of the procedures and suggested that the personal characteristics of Milgram's participants prompted them to obey, but Milgram argued that his studies substantiated the power of authorities.
3. Milgram's studies suggest that obedience is common in hierarchically organized groups, such as those found in military, educational, and organizational settings. Studies of flight crews, for example, suggest that aircraft accidents are in some cases due to excessive obedience to the pilot's authority.

*What are the sources of power in groups?*

1. French and Raven's theory of *power bases* emphasizes six sources of power—*reward power*, *coercive power*, *legitimate power*, *referent power*, *expert power*, and *informational power*. Blass confirmed empirically that the experimenter in the Milgram experiments derived power from all six bases.
2. *Bullying* is the use of coercive influence against another, less powerful person. It can involve physical contact, verbal abuse, exclusion, or other negative actions. Bullying can and should be prevented by restructuring the group situation.
3. Group members' influence over others depends on their control of these six power bases. Weber's concept of *charisma* suggests that certain charismatic leaders, for example, exert their influence by relying on legitimate power and referent power.
4. *Power tactics* are specific methods, such as persuasion, bargaining, and evasion, that people use to attain the goal of influencing others. These methods vary in a number of ways (hard–soft, rational–irrational, lateral–bilateral), with individuals selecting particular tactics depending on their personal characteristics and the nature of the group setting.

*Who seeks power and what group processes limit their success?*

1. Personal characteristics, such as need for power and *social dominance orientation*, predict those individuals who are more likely to strive for power over others.
2. A number of group and structural processes sustain variations in power in groups.
   - Individuals tend to obey orders in groups with clear superior–subordinate hierarchies.
   - Individuals tend to respond submissively when they confront authority, and they tend to behave assertively when they encounter someone who is submissive (the *interpersonal complementarity hypothesis*).

- Individuals feel compelled to comply with the requirements of the role they occupy within the group, as Zimbardo's simulated prison study confirms. The *Lucifer effect* suggests that, in extremely powerful groups, even benign individuals can be induced to perform extremely negative, immoral actions.
- Milgram's theory of the *agentic state* traces obedience back to the nature of the authority–subordinate relationship. When individuals become part of an organized hierarchy, they tacitly agree to follow the leader's orders. They also experience a reduction of responsibility.
- Powerholders extract obedience from group members by taking advantage of the *foot-in-the-door technique*, prefacing major demands with minor, inconsequential ones. This method played a role in the so-called "brainwashing" methods used by Chinese military personnel during the Korean War.
- People who blame obedience on the individuals in the situation may be displaying the *fundamental attribution error (FAE)*, which underestimates the power of group-level processes.

*How do people react when they use their power to influence others?*

1. The idea that "power corrupts, and absolute power corrupts absolutely" is consistent with Keltner's approach/inhibition theory, which suggests that power activates the approach response system whereas the loss of power inhibits actions.
2. The positive effects of power include increased responsiveness, more positive emotions, a narrowing of attention, and increased executive functioning.
3. The negative effects of power include excessive self-regard, an increased tendency to act in a risky or inappropriate way, loss of perspective-taking, and the tendency to misjudge others.
   - Kipnis's studies of the metamorphic effects of power found that people who are given coercive power will use this power, and that once it is used, the powerholders tend to overestimate their control over others and devalue their targets.
   - Powerholders may become so enamored of power that they are preoccupied with gaining it and using it to the exclusion of all other goals (Michels's *iron law of oligarchy*).

*How do those without power react when power is used to influence them?*

1. Coercive methods have been linked to a number of dysfunctional group processes, including *revolutionary coalitions, reactance*, increases in conflict as more group members rebel against authority (the *ripple effect*), and disrupted interpersonal relations.
2. People also react more negatively to direct, irrational power tactics than to power tactics that are more indirect, rational, and bilateral.
3. Kelman's compliance–identification–internalization model predicts that targets of influence may begin by merely complying with the authority's request, but over time, they may experience *identification* and *internalization*. When group members identify with the authority or internalize the authority's demands, their obedience reflects their personal beliefs rather than the constraints of the situation.

## FOR MORE INFORMATION

*Chapter Case: The People's Temple*

- *Our Father Who Art in Hell: The Life and Death of Jim Jones*, by James Reston, Jr. (2000), relies on the analysis of over 800 hours of tape recordings, as well as personal interviews with Jonestown survivors, to develop a full analysis of the People's Temple.
- *Guyana Massacre: The Eyewitness Account*, by Charles A. Krause (1978), provides a factual analysis of the demise of the People's Temple, as well as commentaries on cults in general.

*Obedience to Authority*

- *Obedience to Authority: Current Perspectives on the Milgram Paradigm*, edited by Thomas Blass (2000b), provides both a personal and an objective analysis of the study that some feel is "one of the best carried out in this generation" (Etzioni, 1968, pp. 278–280).
- *Obedience to Authority*, by Stanley Milgram (1974), describes his classic obedience studies in graphic detail.

*Source of Power in Groups*

- "Social Power," by Susan T. Fiske and Jennifer Berdahl (2007) provides is a concise analysis of the nature of power, with sections dealing with definitional issues, bases of power, and antecedents.
- *Influence: Science and Practice*, by Robert B. Cialdini (2009), presents an engaging discussion of the techniques that "compliance professionals"—salespeople, advertisers, charity workers, and panhandlers—use to influence others.
- *The Lucifer Effect: Understanding How Good People Turn Evil*, by Philip Zimbardo (2007), describes in detail the methods and results of the Stanford Prison Experiment, and applies the insights gained to suggest ways to resist situational influences.

*Metamorphic Effects of Power*

- "Power, Approach, and Inhibition," by Dacher Keltner, Deborah H. Gruenfeld, and Cameron Anderson (2003), offers a sophisticated theoretical analysis of how power influences behavior based on the idea that power activates approach but that loss of power leads to inhibition.
- "A Reciprocal Influence Model of Social Power: Emerging Principles and Lines of Inquiry," by Dacher Keltner, Gerben A. Van Kleef, Serena Chen, and Michael W. Kraus (2008), discusses power as an interactional outcome, possibly rooted in evolutionary mechanisms.

### Media Resources

Visit the Group Dynamics companion website at www.cengage.com/psychology/forsyth to access online resources for your book, including quizzes, flash cards, web links, and more!

# 9

# Leadership

## CHAPTER OVERVIEW

Groups generally require guidance as they strive to reach their goals, and the individual who coordinates and motivates the group can fundamentally shape the group's future. If asked, "What one thing would you change to turn an inept group into a productive one?" most people would answer, "The leader."

- What is leadership?
- Who will lead?
- Why do some leaders succeed and others fail?

## CHAPTER OUTLINE

### Wendy Kopp: Transforming Groups through Leadership

Wendy Kopp kept putting off writing her senior thesis until she finally found a topic that she truly cared about: the uneven quality of public education in America. How, she wondered, could injustices and discrimination in American society be eliminated if the quality of schooling depends so much on the wealth of the community where one was raised? For her thesis, she proposed the creation of a national teacher corps, similar to the Peace Corps, whose members would be recent college graduates who were willing to spend two years teaching before starting their corporate careers or graduate studies.

After graduation she decided to follow through on her idea. That first summer she worked alone in donated office space in New York City, sending out an endless stream of letters seeking donations of the funds she needed to get the program started. She called her corps Teach For America (TFA) and worked tirelessly talking to potential corporate sponsors. Many of those who met her told her to start small to see if the approach would work before shifting to a larger scale. But she held fast to her original vision, explaining that "this was not going to be a little non-profit organization or model teacher-training program. This was going to be a *movement*" (Kopp, 2003, p. 23).

By late fall, she had appointed boards of directors and advisors and hired a staff. They worked tirelessly in a hive-like office space deep in Manhattan, but they also traveled out across the nation to recruit potential students on college campuses. By the spring they had attracted thousands of applicants from across the county, and Kopp had succeeded in gaining commitments from funders for the 2.5 million dollars needed to run TFA for a single year. So, in the spring of 1990, 500 new corps members attended a summer institute in Los Angeles in preparation for two years of teaching in schools located in low-income areas of the U.S. Asked how she managed to succeed at such a monumental task so quickly, Kopp explained, "There was nothing magical about it. I simply developed a plan and moved forward step by step" (2003, p. 47).

Over the years since Kopp first founded the organization, Teach for America has placed thousands of teachers in schools, many of whom decided to stay in the schools and become permanent teachers once their two-year term ended. The board, the staff, and the teachers of TFA deserve much of the credit for the success of the organization, but it was Wendy Kopp's **leadership** that made the difference. Her success, and the successes of others like her, raise many questions about the complicated and intricate interpersonal process called leadership. First, what is leadership? What did Kopp do as she led her staff in the pursuit of its challenging goals? Second, why did Kopp take on the role of leader? Third, Kopp was not just a leader, but a successful leader: TFA faced one difficulty after another and nearly collapsed under the pressure of criticism, funding limitations, and internal restructuring. Yet Kopp managed to guide her organization successfully through each new quagmire, and each year TFA attracted applications from the best colleges and universities. Why did she succeed where others might have failed?

---

**leadership** Guidance of others in their pursuits, often by organizing, directing, coordinating, supporting, and motivating their efforts; also, the ability to lead others.

## THE NATURE OF LEADERSHIP

People have probably been puzzling over leadership since the first hominid cave dweller told the rest of the group, "We're doing this all wrong. Let's get organized." Egyptian hieroglyphics written 5000 years ago include the terms *leader* and *leadership* (Bass, 1990). The great epics, such as *Beowulf*, the *Song of Roland*, and the *Odyssey*, are filled with the exploits of leaders of small bands of adventurers. Leaders, like sex, language, and groups, make the anthropologist's list of universals that have been identified as common to all cultures and all civilizations, without exception (Brown, 1991). But what is leadership?

**TABLE 9.1 Political Leaders' Comments on the Nature of Leadership**

| Source | Conception of Leadership |
|---|---|
| Napoleon Bonaparte | "A leader is a dealer in hope." |
| George W. Bush | "Leadership to me means duty, honor, country. It means character, and it means listening from time to time." |
| Benjamin Disraeli | "I must follow the people. Am I not their leader?" |
| Dwight D. Eisenhower | "Leadership is the ability to decide what is to be done, and then to get others to want to do it." |
| Adolf Hitler | "To be a leader means to be able to move masses." |
| Jesse Jackson | "Time is neutral and does not change things. With courage and initiative, leaders change things." |
| Ho Chi Minh | "To use people is like using wood. A skilled worker can make use of all kinds of wood, whether it is big or small, straight or curved." |
| Theodore Roosevelt | "The best executive is the one who has the sense enough to pick good men to do what he wants done, and self-restraint enough to keep from meddling with them while they do it." |
| Margaret Thatcher | "If you want something said, ask a man; if you want something done, ask a woman." |
| Harry S. Truman | "A leader is a man who has the ability to get other people to do what they don't want to do, and like it." |
| Lao Tzu | "A leader is best when people barely know that he exists, not so good when people acclaim him, worst when they despise him." |

## Leadership Myths

The political scientist James McGregor Burns (1978) has asserted that leadership is "one of the most observed and least understood phenomena on earth" (p. 2). Other experts have expressed dismay at the prevalence of misunderstanding about leadership, complaining that most people "don't have the faintest concept of what leadership is all about" (Bennis, 1975, p. 1) and that "the nature of leadership in our society is very imperfectly understood" (Gardner, 1965, p. 3). Many prescriptive suggestions are offered to leaders, but they are too often based on some questionable assumptions about leadership.

**Is Leadership Power?** Many people, including some prominent political leaders, assume that good leaders are those capable of manipulating, controlling, and forcing their followers into obedience. Adolf Hitler, for example, defined leadership as the ability to move the masses, whether through persuasion or violence, and Ho Chi Minh once said that a good leader must learn to mold, shape, and change people just as a woodworker must learn to use wood (see Table 9.1). But people who use domination and coercion to influence others—whether they are kings, presidents, bosses, or managers—are not necessarily leaders. Constructive leaders act in the best interests of a group with the consent of that group. Leadership is a form of power, but power *with* people rather than *over* people—a reciprocal relationship between the leader and the led.

**Are Leaders Born or Made?** Aristotle believed that leadership was an innate talent: "Men are marked out from the moment of birth to rule or be ruled." Some people, he believed, are born leaders, for their unique dispositional qualities predestine them for the role of leader, just as others are born to be followers. But studies of leadership development and effectiveness suggest that nurture, as well as nature, plays a role in determining who will lead and who will follow. Some people, by nature, possess certain highly stable personal qualities—such as particular temperaments, intelligence, or skill in dealing with people—that predispose them to be selected as leaders and to be successful in that role. But most people—through diligent effort and careful mentoring—can acquire the skills needed to become an effective leader.

**Do All Groups Have Leaders?** Groups can function without a leader, but this role is usually the first to emerge in a newly formed group (see Chapter 6). In groups that exist only briefly, all members may share leadership responsibilities, but groups working for an extended duration on more complex tasks require coordinated action, as do those experiencing conflict. The size of the group is also critical: members of larger groups are more likely to rely on one of their members to make rules clear, keep members informed, and make group decisions. In general, leaders appear in groups when (1) members feel that success on the group task is within their reach, (2) the rewards of success are valued, (3) the task requires group effort rather than individual effort, and (4) an individual with previous experience in the leadership role is present in the group. A group that is facing a stressful situation—such as a potential failure or danger—is also likely to embrace a leader's guidance (Guastello, 2007; Hemphill, 1950).

Some evidence suggests that a group of men will be more likely to include a leader than will a group of women (Schmid Mast, 2002). Investigators tested for this sex difference by arranging for three- to five-person groups to meet over three weeks. Some of the groups were all male, some were all female, and some included two men and two women. At the end of each day's session, the group members rated one another on leadership, and the researchers used these ratings to determine if control over the group's activities was concentrated, by consensus, on one group member. Centralization decreased, over time, in all the groups, but it remained higher across the three weeks in the all male-groups. The investigators concluded that men, in general, are more tolerant of inequality than women, so they favor social hierarchy and centralization (Berdahl & Anderson, 2005).

**Do Followers Resist Leaders?** Some laypersons and experts have suggested that groups function best without leaders—that reliance on a central authority figure weakens the group and robs members of their self-reliance. Some, too, have noted that groups chafe under the control of a leader, for they begrudge the authority and power of the leader (Gemmill, 1986). Yet most people prefer to be led rather than be leaderless. Group members are usually more satisfied and productive when their groups have leaders (Berkowitz, 1953). Group members often complain about the quality of their leaders—surveys that ask employees to identify the worst thing about their job find these complaints tend to converge on the leader—but they seek out better leaders rather than avoiding them altogether (Hogan & Kaiser, 2005). Most people do not just accept the need for a leader but appreciate the contribution that the leader makes to the group and its outcomes (Friedman & Saul, 1991; Stewart & Manz, 1995).

This "need for a leader" becomes particularly strong in groups that are experiencing interpersonal turmoil and can sometimes cause members to see leadership potential in people where none exists. Members of troubled groups, compared to more tranquil groups, exaggerate the potential of possible leaders. They even misremember crucial details, tending to recall their prospective leader as having performed any number of leader-consistent behaviors and forgetting any past behaviors that conflict with their image of the person as a suitable leader. Thus, members do not resist having a leader; instead, they conspire to create leaders both interpersonally and psychologically (Emrich, 1999).

**Do Leaders Make a Difference?** In 1991, Kopp got a job offer. An entrepreneur was starting up a new company devoted to educational reform, and he wanted Kopp to join his staff. What would have happened if Kopp had taken that job? Would TFA be as successful today? Would it even exist at all?

Leaders influence their groups in significant ways. Studies of leaders in all kinds of group situations—flight crews, politics, schools, military units, and religious groups—all suggest that groups prosper when guided by good leaders. Groups of individuals, when they face an emergency, often fail to respond; but if a leader is present in the group this bystander effect is less likely to occur (Baumeister et al., 1988). Groups, when discussing solutions to problems, tend to spend too much time discussing information shared by many members—unless a leader is present in the group who controls the group's tendency to focus on shared information (Larson et al., 1996). When a company gets a new CEO, its performance tends to climb (Jung, Wu, & Chow, 2008). Newly appointed leaders who inspire and excite members with fresh ideas and strategies can spur the group on to great achievements and successes (Zaccaro & Banks, 2001).

Unfortunately, the difference leaders make is not always a positive one. Leaders sometimes take their group in directions it should not go. They act to promote their own personal outcomes and overlook the good of the group. Leaders manipulate followers, persuading them to make sacrifices, while the leaders enjoy the rewards of their power and influence. They push their agendas too hard, their groups obey their demands, and only later do all realize their mistakes (Lipman-Blumen, 2005). Such leaders are influential—but in a negative way.

**Do Leaders Make *All* the Difference?** Leaders significantly influence their group's dynamics, but sometimes people think that leaders do *everything*. In Western cultures, in particular, people assume that leaders are so influential that they, and they alone, determine their group's outcomes. This romanticized view of leaders as rescuers and heroes has been aptly termed the **romance of leadership** (Meindl, Ehrlich, & Dukerich 1985).

This romance of leadership ignores both the limited influence wielded by most leaders and the many other factors that influence a group and its dynamics. When a team fails, those in charge often replace the group's leaders, for they assume that a different leader could have rescued the failing team. When people give all the credit for a group's success to the leader, or blame him or her for a failure, they overlook the contributions of the other group members. Leaders like Wendy Kopp are influential, but few leaders deserve all the blame for their group's failures, and fewer still are heroes who can fairly claim the lion's share of credit for their group's achievements (Meindl, Pastor, & Mayo, 2004).

## What Is Leadership?

Leadership is not the power to coerce others, an inborn trait, a necessity of group life, or a mysterious capacity to heal sick groups. Instead, leadership is the process by which an individual guides others in their collective pursuits, often by organizing, directing, coordinating, supporting, and motivating their efforts. Leadership, then, is not a static characteristic of an individual or a group, but a complex of interpersonal processes whereby cooperating individuals are permitted to influence and motivate others to promote the attainment of group and individual goals. These processes are reciprocal, transactional, transformational, cooperative, and adaptive.

- Leadership is a *reciprocal* process, involving the leader, the followers, and the group situation. The leader does not just influence the group members; rather, the leader–follower relationship is mutual. An interactional view assumes that leadership cannot be understood independently of ***followership***—the skills and qualities displayed by nonleaders (Hollander, 2006; Messick, 2005; see Focus 9.1.
- Leadership is a *transactional* process, in which leaders and followers work together,

---

**romance of leadership** The tendency to overestimate the amount of influence and control leaders exert on their groups and their groups' outcomes.

**followership** Working effectively with a leader and other group members.

## Focus 9.1 What Is a Leader Without Followers?

*Unhappy the land that has no heroes. No, unhappy the land that is in need of heroes.*

—Bertolt Brecht

Many cultures emphasize the role of the leader in determining the group's outcome, but this leader-centric view overlooks the equally important role played by nonleaders—often described with words that lack the potency of the word *leader*, for they are *followers*, *subordinates*, *assistants*, or merely *reports*. Leadership and followership are reciprocal social processes, and the group depends as much on the actions of those who accept others' influence as it does on those who provide guidance and direction. Followers are the yin to the leader's yang.

But just as bad leaders are mixed with the good ones, so followers vary in their effectiveness. Robert Kelley (1988, 2004), who has examined the nature of followership closely, asks two basic questions about followers: Are they active or passive and are they independent or dependent? First, the best followers are committed to the group and their role within it; they are actively engaged in their work rather than passive and withdrawn. Second, effective followers can be self-reliant, when necessary. By definition, they follow the leader, but they must also be able to exercise their independence and monitor themselves and their progress. Ineffective followers are overly dependent on the leader, and they are unable to think for themselves. Kelley, by considering these two aspects of followers—degree of active engagement and independence—identifies the five basic types shown in Figure 9.1.

- *Conformist followers* (yes people) are active and energized, but they are devoted to the leader; they do not think to question the leader's directions and will defend him or her vigorously.
- *Passive followers* (sheep) follow the lead of others, but without great enthusiasm or commitment. They put time into the group and will eventually finish their assignments, but they must be continually monitored or they will simply stop contributing.
- *Pragmatic followers* are the rank-and-file members of the group; they are neither active nor passive, conforming or independent, but likely to remain in the background and contribute what they can.

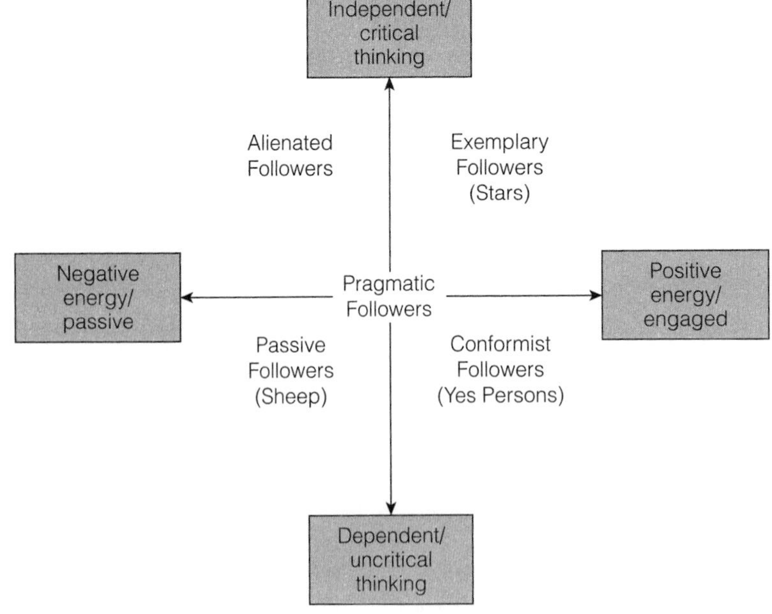


**FIGURE 9.1** Kelley's theory of followers.

SOURCE: "Kelley's Follower Gride" reprinted by permission of Harvard Business Review. From "In Praise of Followers", 1988. Copyright © 1988 by the Harvard Business School Publishing Corporation. All rights reserved. Also in Kelley, Robert E. "Followership." Encyclopedia of Leadership. Vol. 2. Thousand Oaks, CA: Sage Reference, 2004. 504–513. Reprinted by permission of Sage Publications.

**Focus 9.1 (Continued)**

- *Alienated followers* are not committed to the group or its goals, in part because they steadfastly maintain their independence from others' influence. They are often sullenly silent, but when they speak they are critical of their fellow members for remaining true to the group, and they question the leader's choices. They often think of themselves as the rightful leader of the group, and refuse to invest in the group or its activities until they are accorded their rightful position.
- *Exemplary followers* (stars) are actively engaged in the group, but they do not simply do what they are told. If they have issues with the leader's position, they express their dissent openly, but constructively. The leader can delegate responsibilities to them, and they can be trusted to complete the task with an enthusiasm that springs from their concern for the group's interests.

The leader's task, suggests Kelley (1988, 2004), is to transform the followers into exemplary followers, using any means possible. Groups with "many leaders," he concludes, "can be chaos. Groups with none can be quite productive" (1988, p. 148)—so long as these followers are exemplary ones who are actively engaged in their work, treat one another as colleagues, and engage in constructive debate with their leaders.

exchanging their time, energies, and skills to increase their joint rewards (Avolio, 2004).

- Leadership is a *transformational* process, for leaders heighten group members' motivation, confidence, and satisfaction by uniting members and changing their beliefs, values, and needs (Burns, 2003).
- Leadership is a *cooperative* process of legitimate influence rather than sheer power. The right to lead is, in most instances, voluntarily conferred on the leader by some or all members of the group, with the expectation that the leader is motivated by the group's collective needs rather than his or her own interests (Avolio & Locke, 2002).
- Leadership is an *adaptive, goal-seeking* process, for it organizes and motivates group members' attempts to attain personal and group goals (Parks, 2005).

A distinction is often drawn between leadership and other forms of influence in groups and organizations, such as management and supervision. Leaders often hold supervisory positions in groups, but holding a position does not always translate into leadership; there are many bosses, supervisors, and managers who are not leaders. Conversely, many individuals in groups and organizations who do not hold formal positions of authority are leaders, for they influence others as they pool their efforts in the pursuit of shared goals (Bedeian & Hunt, 2006; Kotter, 1990; see Rost, 2008, for a discussion of issues involved in defining leadership).

## What Do Leaders Do?

Wendy Kopp, as the leader of TFA, hired personnel and supervised them closely, providing them with feedback about their strengths and weaknesses. She spent much of her time planning and organizing the organization, focusing on both day-to-day operations as well as long-range goals years in the future. She made minor and major decisions everyday, from picking furnishings for the offices to the difficult choice of who to let go when the organization could no longer afford to pay the salaries of all the staff members. Kopp also represented TFA in dealings with funding agencies and school systems, coordinated the meetings held regularly among the staff, and delivered motivational speeches to the corps members before they began their workshops on teaching skills. Leading, for Kopp, involved a number of interrelated activities, including analyzing, consulting, controlling, coordinating, deciding, monitoring, negotiating, organizing, planning, representing, and supervising (Mintzberg, 1973).

**TABLE 9.2 Task and Relationship Leadership: Definitions, Related Terms, and Sample Behaviors**

| Factor | Terms | Sample Behaviors |
|---|---|---|
| ***Task leadership*** promoting task completion; regulating behavior, monitoring communication, and reducing goal ambiguity | Task-oriented, agentic, goal oriented, work facilitative, production centered, administratively skilled, goal achievement | • Assigns tasks to members<br>• Makes attitudes clear to the group<br>• Critical of poor work<br>• Sees to it that the group is working to capacity<br>• Coordinates activity |
| ***Relationship leadership*** maintaining and enhancing positive interpersonal relations in the group; friendliness, mutual trust, openness, recognizing performance | Relationship oriented, communal, socioemotional supportive, employee centered, relations skilled, group maintenance | • Listens to group members<br>• Easy to understand<br>• Friendly and approachable<br>• Treats group members as equals<br>• Willing to make changes |

**The Task-Relationship Model** Wendy Kopp carried out a staggering array of diverse activities as the Chief Executive Officer (CEO) of TFA, but the **task-relationship model** of leadership assumes that these many and varied behaviors cluster into one of two basic categories described in Table 9.2.

- *Task leadership* focuses on the group's work and its goals. To facilitate the achievement of group goals, the leader initiates structure, sets standards and objectives, identifies roles and positions members in those roles, develops standard operating procedures, defines responsibilities, establishes communication networks, gives evaluative feedback, plans activities, coordinates activities, proposes solutions, monitors compliance with procedures, and stresses the need for efficiency and productivity (Lord, 1977; Yukl, 2006).
- *Relationship leadership* focuses on the interpersonal relations within the group. To increase socioemotional satisfaction and teamwork in the group, the leader boosts morale, gives support and encouragement, reduces interpersonal conflict, helps members to release negative tensions, establishes rapport, and shows concern and consideration for the group and its members (Lord, 1977; Yukl, 2006).

Different situations require different skills of leaders, but researchers have identified these two dimensions of leadership in study after study of what leaders actually do when they are in groups. For example, in the Ohio State University Leadership Studies conducted in the 1950s, investigators first developed a list of hundreds of types of behaviors observed in military and organizational leaders—behaviors that included initiating new practices, providing praise, interacting informally with subordinates, delegating responsibilities, representing the group, and coordinating group action. They then refined the list by asking members of various groups to indicate how many of these behaviors their leaders displayed. Using factor analysis, a statistical technique that identifies clusters of interrelated variables, they discovered that 80% of the variability in followers' ratings could be explained by the two basic factors: *task leadership* (initiation of structure) and *relationship leadership* (consideration for group members; Fleishman, 1953; Halpin & Winer, 1952).

---

**task-relationship model** A descriptive model of leadership which maintains that most leadership behaviors can be classified as either performance maintenance or relationship maintenance.

The Ohio State researchers built these two dimensions into their *Leader Behavior Description Questionnaire* (LBDQ; Kerr et al., 1974; Schriesheim & Eisenbach, 1995). Group members complete the LBDQ by rating their leader on items such as those presented in the right-hand column of Table 9.2. The totals from the two separate sets of behaviors index the two dimensions of leadership specified in the task-relationship model.

Researchers in many countries who have studied many different types of groups have repeatedly confirmed this two-dimensional model of leadership behaviors. Although the labels vary—*work-facilitative* versus *supportive* (Bowers & Seashore, 1966), *production-centered* versus *employee-centered* (Likert, 1967), *administratively skilled* versus *relations-skilled* (Mann, 1965), *goal achievement* versus *group maintenance* (Cartwright & Zander, 1968), and *performance* versus *maintenance* (Misumi, 1995)—the two basic clusters emerge with great regularity (Shipper & Davy, 2002).

**Leadership Substitutes** The task-relationship model assumes that leaders, despite their widely varying methods and styles, tend to do two basic things when they lead others—they coordinate the work that the group must accomplish and they attend to the group's interpersonal needs. But these two forms of leadership, though commonplace, are not needed in every leadership situation. Kopp, for example, spent much of her time initiating structure: planning, strategizing, organizing, and soliciting funding. She did not need to spend very much time attending to the interpersonal needs of the group members because the young staff of TFA was such a highly cohesive group and so committed to the work that Kopp did not need to monitor their interpersonal needs.

The TFA case is consistent with **leadership substitutes theory**, which maintains that substitutes for leadership sometimes "negate the leader's ability to either improve or impair subordinate satisfaction and performance" (Kerr & Jermier, 1978, p. 377). As Table 9.3 indicates, aspects of the group (e.g., members' indifference to rewards), the task (e.g., the level of intrinsic reward), and the group or organization (e.g., the cohesiveness of the group) can make leadership unnecessary and unlikely. In TFA, for example, the staff members were chosen for their commitment to equality in education, and this shared vision served as a substitute for relationship leadership. TFA was not, however, a formally organized group with specified staff functions. Thus the group responded well to, and very much needed, Kopp's task-oriented approach to leadership (Dionne et al., 2005).

**Sex Differences in Leadership Behavior** Leadership has two sides—the task side and the relationship side—and humans come in two varieties—man and woman. Do these variations in leadership correspond to sex differences in leadership? Are men task-oriented, whereas women are more relationship-oriented?

Despite changes in the role of men and women in contemporary society, when men and women gather in groups, the men tend to be *agentic*—task oriented, active, decision focused, independent, goal oriented—whereas women are more *communal*—helpful to others, warm in relation to others, understanding, aware of others' feelings (Abele, 2003). Women, to speak in generalities, when asked to describe themselves to others in just-formed groups, stress their communal qualities with such adjectives as open, fair, responsible, and pleasant. Men describe themselves as influential, powerful, and skilled at the task to be done (Forsyth et al., 1985). Women, more so than men, engage in relationship maintenance, including giving advice, offering assurances, and managing conflict (Leaper & Ayres, 2007). In day-to-day activities with same-sex friends, women tend to be more agreeable than men (Suh et al., 2004). Women connect more positively to other group members by smiling more, maintaining eye contact, and responding more tactfully to others' comments (Hall, 2006). These differences can be seen in groups of children, with boys

---

**leadership substitutes theory** A conceptual analysis of the factors that combine to reduce or eliminate the need for a leader.

**TABLE 9.3 Characteristics That Can Substitute for and Neutralize Relationship and Task Leadership**

| | Substitutes for or Neutralizes | |
|---|---|---|
| **Characteristic** | **Relationship Leadership** | **Task Leadership** |
| **Of the group member** | | |
| 1. Has ability, experience, training, knowledge | | X |
| 2. Has a need for independence | | X |
| 3. Has a "professional" orientation | X | X |
| 4. Is indifferent to group rewards | X | X |
| **Of the task** | | |
| 5. Is unambiguous and routine | | X |
| 6. Is methodologically invariant | | X |
| 7. Provides its own feedback concerning accomplishment | | X |
| 8. Is intrinsically satisfying | X | |
| **Of the organization** | | |
| 9. Is formalized (has explicit plans, etc.) | | X |
| 10. Is inflexible (rigid, unbending rules, etc.) | | X |
| 11. Has specified staff functions | | X |
| 12. Has cohesive work groups | X | X |
| 13. Has organized rewards not controlled by leader | X | X |
| 14. Has physical distance between leader and members | X | X |

SOURCE: "Substitutes for leadership: Their meaning and measurement" by S. Kerr & J.M. Jermier, *Organizational Behavior and Human Performance*, 22, 1978. 

undertaking physical activities, competing with one another, and playing in rough ways, and girls carrying out coordinated activities with a minimum of conflict (Maccoby, 2002). These differences may even reflect evolutionary pressures that encouraged the development of communal tendencies in women and task-focused activity in men (Van Vugt, Hogan, & Kaiser, 2008; compare with Eagly & Karau, 2002).

This sex difference is only a tendency, and it does not manifest itself across all groups and situations. Kopp, for example, remains a task-focused leader: she is not the type of leader who likes to "walk around, rally the troops, and make sure that everyone was feeling good" (2003, p. 66). Nor does it determine how men and women respond when they become a group's leader. When Alice Eagly and Blair Johnson (1990) reviewed more than 150 studies that compared the leadership styles adopted by men and women, they discovered that as the agentic–communal tendency suggests, women performed more relationship-oriented actions in laboratory groups and also described themselves as more relationship-oriented on questionnaires. The sexes did not differ, however, in studies conducted in organizational settings (Dobbins & Platz, 1986). Indeed, as leaders, women tended to be both task- and relationship-oriented, whereas men were primarily task-oriented (Stratham, 1987). Women and men often adopted different styles of leadership, but they did not differ in their agentic and communal tendencies.

## LEADERSHIP EMERGENCE

Manet was the leader of the impressionist painters. Fito Strauch took control of the day-to-day activities of the Andes survivors. Jim Jones was the charismatic leader of the People's Temple. John F. Kennedy was elected president of the United States. Wendy Kopp is the CEO of TFA. But why Manet and not Degas? Why Strauch and not Canessa? Why Kennedy and not Nixon? Why did Kopp, armed with just her senior thesis written in her last semester in college, emerge as the CEO of an internationally successful nonprofit organization and remain the leader of that group for all these years? What determines who will lead their groups, organizations, and countries? What determines **leadership emergence**?

Scholars have debated this question for centuries. In the 19th century, for example, the historian Thomas Carlyle offered up his **great leader theory** of history (Carlyle called it the "great man" theory). He asserted that leaders do not achieve their positions by accident or twist of fate. Rather, these individuals possess certain characteristics that mark them for greatness. Carlyle (1841) believed that leaders are different from followers, so history could be best studied by considering the contributions of the few great men and women. The Russian novelist Leo Tolstoy disagreed. To Tolstoy, such leaders as Alexander the Great and Napoleon came to prominence because the spirit of the times—the *zeitgeist*—was propitious for the dominance of a single individual, and the qualities of the person were largely irrelevant to this rise to power. Tolstoy's **zeitgeist theory** posited that the conquests and losses of military leaders such as Napoleon were caused not by their decisions and skills but by uncontrollable aspects of the historical situation (Tolstoy, 1869/1952).

These two perspectives—Carlyle's great leader theory and Tolstoy's zeitgeist approach—continue to shape theoretical analyses of leadership emergence. The great leader theory is consistent with a *trait approach* to leadership, which assumes that leaders possess certain personality traits and characteristics and that these characteristics are responsible for their rise in the leadership ranks. Tolstoy's zeitgeist view, in contrast, is consistent with *situationism*, which suggests that leadership is determined by a host of variables operating in the leadership situation, including the size of the group, its cohesion, the quality of leader-member relations, and the type of task to be performed.

An *interactional* approach to leadership, however, reconciles these two models by asserting that traits and situations interact to determine who will lead and who will not. If a group is about to disintegrate because of heated conflicts among the members, for example, the effective leader will be someone who can improve the group's interpersonal relations (Katz, 1977). Similarly, if individuals possess skills that facilitate performance on intellectual tasks but undermine performance on artistic tasks, then they are likely to emerge as effective leaders only if the group is working on intellectual tasks (Stogdill, 1974). Lewin's $B = f(P, E)$ formula for interactionism, applied to leadership, suggests that a leader's behavior is a function both of the characteristics of the person and the characteristics of the group situation (see Chapter 1).

### Personal Qualities of Leaders

Kopp was fresh out of college when she started TFA, and so she lacked the skills of a seasoned

---

**leadership emergence** The process by which an individual becomes formally or informally, perceptually or behaviorally, and implicitly or explicitly recognized as the leader of a formerly leaderless group.

**great leader theory** A view of leadership, attributed to historian Thomas Carlyle, which states that successful leaders possess certain characteristics that mark them for greatness, and that such great leaders shape the course of history.

**zeitgeist theory** A view of leadership, attributed to Leo Tolstoy, which states that history is determined primarily by the "spirit of the times" rather than by the actions and choices of great leaders.

leader with years of experience. Yet, she knew how to organize people to work together on tasks, and in college she was the manager of a staff of 60 working for a nonprofit called Foundation for Student Communications. She was not trained to lead, yet she had a natural talent for it.

**Personality Traits** Early leadership researchers believed that leaders possessed certain personality traits that set them apart from others. This trait approach, which in its strongest form assumed that some people were natural-born leaders, faded in popularity as researchers reported a series of failures to find any consistent impact of personality on leadership behavior across a wide variety of situations. After conducting hundreds of studies, researchers began to wonder if personality made much of a difference when trying to predict who would emerge as a leader and who would not (Mann, 1959; Stogdill, 1948).

In retrospect, this rejection of the trait approach was premature. When researchers used more precise measures of personality—and ones that theoretically should have been related to leadership—stronger relationships were identified. They also discovered that single traits sometimes said little about emergence, but when they looked at personality profiles that took into account several traits then clearer patterns emerged (e.g., Smith & Foti, 1998). More sophisticated research procedures also yielded stronger evidence of the power of personality as a predictor of leadership emergence. For example, longitudinal designs that involved tracking people over a long period of time indicated that personality measured as long as 20 years before successfully predicted promotion to positions of leadership in business settings (Miner, 1978). Rotational designs, as noted in Focus 9.2, suggested that leadership might be rooted in the person (e.g., Foti &

### Focus 9.2 Does the Great Leader Theory Apply to Groups?

*An oak boasted to the reed of his strength, but in a strong wind the reed bent, but did not break. The oak, standing firm, was torn out by the roots.*

—Aesop (620–560 BC)

During World War II, Germany, America, and England all experimented with various methods for identifying natural leaders to serve in the military. In many cases they used the so-called leaderless-group tests, in which a group of individuals, strangers to one another, were given a task to complete. For example, a group might be assembled on one side of a ravine and told to use the available boards, ropes, and beams to build a temporary bridge to the other side (Eaton, 1947).

These creative methods of measuring leadership left one significant question unanswered: would the individuals who emerged as leaders be chosen, again, by another group of men or women? Their unique personal qualities may have destined them to be leader in that group and others as well, but it may be that their rise to leadership was context specific: the result of the group's zeitgeist, and not their personalities. To solve this problem, researchers turned to rotational designs. Individuals worked in leaderless groups on a task, but once that work was done the groups were broken up and reformed. If an individual emerges as the leader again and again despite the changes in group composition, then this pattern suggests something about the person, and not the group, is responsible (Borgatta, Couch, & Bales, 1954).

Stephen Zaccaro and his colleagues used a rotational design in their analysis of personality and leadership, but with yet another twist. They not only rotated individuals through new groups but they also changed the types of tasks the groups performed. Some of the tasks, such as group discussions of controversial topics, called for a leader who was good with people. Other tasks, in contrast, called for a leader who was task-oriented. Even with this new challenge, leadership tended to follow individuals. If the group was working on a task that required good "people skills," natural leaders became more interpersonally oriented. But when the group needed a directive, task-oriented leader, these individuals shifted their style to address the task. These findings suggest that *flexibility* may be one of the most important qualities to look for in an effective leader. Skilled leaders will respond to the demands of the situations they face, but some leaders "may be better than others at perceiving these requirements and responding accordingly" (Zaccaro, Foti, & Kenny, 1991, p. 312).

Hauenstein, 2007). Statistical advances also provided better tools for testing the strength of relationship, allowing researchers to distinguish between group-level determinants of leadership emergence and personality factors. Meta-analysis also helped researchers sift through all the findings, for this type of review catalogs the findings from multiple studies more precisely by using statistics rather than subjective interpretation (Zaccaro, 2007; Zaccaro, Gulick, & Khare, 2008).

Table 9.4 samples the results of just a few of the hundreds of studies of leadership emergence and such personality qualities as assertiveness, authenticity, strength of character, dominance, narcissism, self-efficacy, self-monitoring, and social motivation. These studies examine a wide range of personality

**TABLE 9.4 A Sampling of Personality Characteristics That Are Reliably Associated with Leadership Emergence**

| Characteristic | Relationship to Leadership Emergence |
|---|---|
| Assertiveness | The relationship between assertiveness and leadership emergence is curvilinear; individuals who are either low in assertiveness or very high in assertiveness are less likely to be identified as leaders (Ames & Flynn, 2007). |
| Authenticity | Individuals who are more aware of their personality qualities, including their values and beliefs, and are less biased when processing self-relevant information, are more likely to be accepted as leaders (Ilies, Morgeson, & Nahragang, 2005). |
| Big Five personality factors | Those who emerge as leaders tend to be more extraverted, conscientious, emotionally stable, and open to experience, although these tendencies are stronger in laboratory studies of leaderless groups (Judge, Bono, Ilies, & Gerhardt, 2002). |
| Birth order | Those born first in their families and only children are hypothesized to be more driven to seek leadership and control in social settings. Middle-born children tend to accept follower roles in groups, and later-borns are thought be rebellious and creative (Grose, 2003). |
| Character strengths | Those seeking leadership positions in a military organization had elevated scores on a number of indicators of strength of character, including honesty, hope, bravery, industry, and teamwork (Matthews et al., 2006). |
| Dominance | Individuals with dominant personalities—they describe themselves as high in the desire to control their environment and influence other people, and are likely to express their opinions in a forceful way—are more likely to act as leaders in small-group situations (Smith & Foti, 1998). |
| Gender identity | Masculine individuals are more likely to emerge as leaders than are feminine individuals (Lord, De Vader, & Alliger, 1986). |
| Narcissism | Individuals who take on leadership roles in turbulent situations, such as groups facing a threat or ones in which status is determined by intense competition among rivals within the group, tend to be narcissistic: arrogant, self-absorbed, hostile, and very self-confident (Rosenthal & Pittinsky, 2006). |
| Self-efficacy for leadership | Confidence in one's ability to lead is associated with increases in willingness to accept a leadership role and success in that role (Hoyt & Blascovich, 2007). |
| Self-monitoring | High self-monitors are more likely to emerge as the leader of a group than are low self-monitors, since they are more concerned with status-enhancement and are more likely to adapt their actions to fit the demands of the situation (Bedeian & Day, 2004). |
| Social motivation | Individuals who are both success-oriented and affiliation-oriented, as assessed by projective measures, are more active in group problem-solving settings and are more likely to be elected to positions of leadership in such groups (Sorrentino & Field, 1986). |

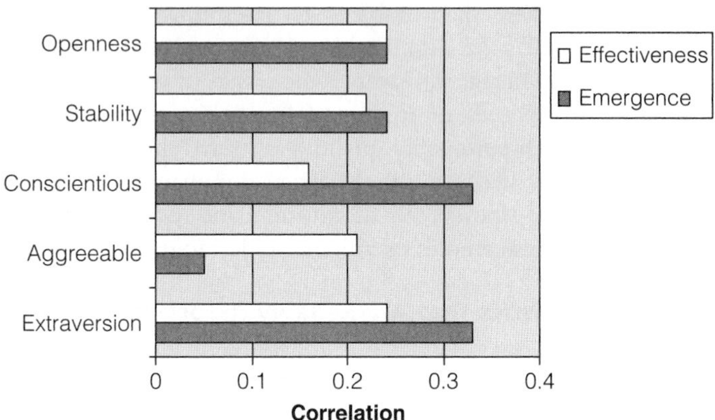


**FIGURE 9.2** The relationship between the personality factors identified in the Big Five model of personality and leadership emergence and effectiveness. When researchers used meta-analysis to combined the results of 222 correlational findings generated in 73 samples of the personality-leadership relationship, they found that extraversion is the strongest predictor of emergence and agreeableness is the weakest (Judge, Bono, Ilies, & Gerhardt, 2002).

SOURCE: "Personality and leadership: A qualitative and quantitative review" by T.A. Judge, J.E. Bono, R. Ilies, & M.W. Gerhardt, *Journal of Applied Psychology*, 87, 2002. Reprinted by permission.

traits, but the results are generally consistent with the Big Five model of personality discussed in Chapter 4 (see Table 4.1 and Figure 9.2). One of the most influential determinants of leadership is the quality that observers judge most easily in others: introversion–extraversion. When researchers ask five strangers to talk for 30 minutes about any topic, by the session's end the person who is higher in extraversion—dominance, gregariousness, power motivation, and so on—is generally named by the others as the leader. Conscientiousness (dependability, self-regulation, drive, and need to achieve) comes in second in its predictive power, followed by openness and emotional stability. The only Big Five personality factor that is not reliably associated with leadership emergence is agreeableness; leaders, apparently, need not be warm and kind (Hogan, 2005). Note, though, these two caveats. First, studies involving students generally found stronger relationships between personality and leadership emergence than studies of leaders in military, government, and business settings. Second, as Figure 9.2 indicates, agreeableness did not predict leadership emergence, but it did predict effectiveness—even more so than conscientiousness (Judge et al., 2002).

**Intelligence** Wendy Kopp has many qualities, but when people describe her they often start with one word: smart. Intelligence and leadership emergence and effectiveness go hand in hand. The average correlation is small, between .25 and .30, but is consistent across studies, populations, and settings (Stogdill, 1948, 1974). Leaders tend to score higher than average on standard intelligence tests and they make superior judgments with greater decisiveness. They tend to be knowledgeable both generally and about their particular field, and their verbal skills—both written and oral—are superior relative to nonleaders.

Leaders, however, typically do not exceed their followers' intellectual prowess by a wide margin (Simonton, 1985). Groups generally prefer leaders who are more intelligent than the average group member, but too great a discrepancy introduces problems in communication, trust, and social sensitivity. Although highly intelligent individuals may be extremely capable and efficient leaders, their groups may feel that large differences in intellectual abilities translate into large differences in interests, attitudes, and values. Hence, although high intelligence may mean skilled leadership, a group prefers to be "ill-governed by people it can understand" (Gibb, 1969, p. 218).

**Emotional Intelligence** When people think of intelligence, they often stress cognitive abilities such as mathematics, verbal skill, and intellectual problem solving. But some people are also interpersonally intelligent: They have the ability to understand and relate to people, for they deal with others wisely and effectively. They have elevated

**emotional intelligence:** "the ability to perceive emotions in self and others; to understand how emotions blend, unfold, and influence cognition and behavior; to use emotions to facilitate thinking; and to manage emotions in self and others" (Lopes & Salovey, 2008, p. 81; Mayer, Salovey, & Caruso, 2008).

Skill in communicating and decoding emotions is essential for an effective leader. The emotionally intelligent leader can see problems coming, for such problems are often conveyed indirectly by others' moods and emotions. Better able to read the politics of the situation, such leaders can detect shifting alliances and recognize where to put their energies and when to bide their time. They can also communicate their ideas to others in more robust ways, for they can use their own emotional energy to influence others. They are also less likely to lose control of their emotions—they are not inappropriately angry, critical, or histrionic. In consequence, emotional intelligence is associated with various aspects of leadership, including emergence as a leader, willingness to cooperate with others, empathy for others, the tendency to take others' perspectives, and the emotional intensity of one's interpersonal relations (Goleman, Boyatizis, & McKee, 2002).

**Skills and Experience** When groups work collectively on tasks, individuals with more expertise usually rise higher in the group's leadership hierarchy. One review of 52 studies of characteristics typically ascribed to the leader discovered that technical, task-relevant skills were mentioned in 35% of the studies (Stogdill, 1974). Groups are more accepting of leaders who have previously demonstrated task ability and are more willing to follow the directions of a task-competent person than those of an incompetent person (Goldman & Fraas, 1965; Hollander, 1965). Furthermore, although high task ability facilitates leadership, low task ability seems to be an even more powerful factor in disqualifying individuals from consideration as leaders (Palmer, 1962). Initially, if group members do not know one another well, then they may rely on diffuse status characteristics such as rank, age, and tenure with the group to infer expertise, but over time they will shift to specific, behavioral cues to determine who is competent and who is not (Bunderson, 2003). Given enough experience in working together, most group members can distinguish between the skilled and the unskilled (Littlepage, Robison, & Reddington, 1997; Littlepage & Silbiger, 1992).

Field studies of leadership in organizational and military settings suggest that individuals who possess valued skills are more often recognized as leaders. The successful head of the accounting department, for example, is usually recognized as a better accountant than his or her subordinates or other, less highly regarded managers (Tsui, 1984). Studies of ratings of military leadership ability have also found that physical ability and task performance skills are highly correlated with leadership emergence (Rice, Instone, & Adams, 1984). Particular, task-specific skills are more important in determining leadership emergence in performance-oriented, service–delivery-oriented groups, whereas interpersonal and conceptual skills are more important in upper-echelon leadership positions (Yukl, 2006).

**Participation** Individuals with much to offer the group—those who are intelligent, emotionally adept, and highly skilled at the tasks the group must complete—may nonetheless not emerge as a leader if they are disengaged from the group and its activities. Leaders are active within their groups rather than aloof; they show up for meetings, they ask questions, they offer comments and suggestions, they talk to other members on the phone, and they send out emails. The correlation between leadership emergence and most personal characteristics usually averages in the low .20s, but the correlation between participation rate and leadership ranges from .61 to .72 (Littlepage & Mueller, 1997; Malloy & Janowski, 1992; Stein & Heller, 1979).

---

**emotional intelligence** The component of social intelligence that relates to one's capacity to accurately perceive emotions, to use information about emotions when making decisions, and to monitor and control one's own and others' emotional reactions.

Group members take note of participant rate in part because it tells them who is interested in the group and is willing to take responsibility for its performance. One of the surest ways to escape serving as the leader of a group is to not say much during meetings. But which matters more: quality or quantity of participation? Do people who talk a lot at meetings but add little of substance rise to positions of leadership, or does quality count more: the value of the ideas expressed rather than the volume of one's words?

Some studies support the so-called *babble effect*: quantity of participation is more important than quality of contribution. One study, for example, examined this effect by manipulating both the quantity and quality of the statements of a trained confederate in a problem-solving group. The researchers created four-person groups and set them to work, but one of the group members was a confederate who systematically offered either many comments or few comments that were either high in quality (they promoted success on the tasks) or low in quality (they promoted failure on the tasks). When the participants later rated the confederate's confidence, influence, and contributions, both quantity and quality counted, but the effects due to quantity were still stronger (Sorrentino & Boutillier, 1975).

Other work, however, calls into question the generality of the babble effect. Eric Jones and Janice Kelly (2007) noted that comparing quality to quantity is like comparing apples to oranges. Since they are two different variables that can range in intensity from high to low, comparing their relative impact on leadership requires that they be matched in terms of strength. They therefore conducted a series of studies where they pitted quantity against quality, but they first calibrated the strength of these two variables so that each one had a fair chance of overpowering the other one. As in prior research, they created low- and high-quality arguments and low- and high-quantity messages, but they also made sure the high conditions were twice the level of the low conditions for both variables. The high-quality arguments were viewed as twice as good as the low-quality arguments, and they used twice as many messages in the high-quantity condition than the low-quantity condition. In this way they made sure that low and high were proportional to one another. What they discovered was that quantity did matter; but only if the comments offered were of high quality. As Figure 9.3 indicates, people who made low-quality comments during the group discussion received relatively low ratings on leadership potential, even when they offered a substantial number of these comments. Quantity did boost one's leadership ratings, but only if the comments were of high quality. Rationality (quality) trumped babble (quantity), at least in this case.

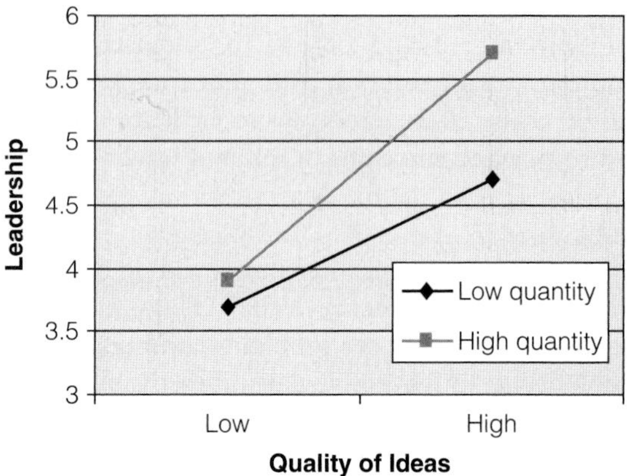


**FIGURE 9.3** The impact of quantity and quality of participation on leadership emergence in small groups.

SOURCE: Copyright © 2007 by the American Psychological Association. Reproduced with permission. The official citation that should be used in referencing this material is Contributions to a group discussion and perceptions of leadership: Does quantity always count more than quality? by Jones Eric E.; Kelly, Janice R, from Group Dynamics: Theory, Research, and Practice, March 1, 2007. The use of APA information does not imply endorsement by APA.

## The Look of Leaders

When Kopp, fresh out of college, first met with funders and other experts in education they often expressed their incredulity, for they did not think that a young woman in her twenties could lead the organization successfully. One executive asked her, point blank, "Who is going to run this?" When Kopp answered that she was, the executive said,

"That's just not going to work" (quoted in Kopp, 2003, p. 19). Kopp's qualities were not those that these people expected in a leader, for leadership emergence depends not only on personal qualifications and achievements but also on general demographic characteristics, such as age, race, and sex.

**Physical Appearances** Leaders tend to differ physically from their subordinates. They are often older, taller, and heavier than the average group member. Ralph Stogdill (1948, 1974), after thoroughly reviewing the relationship between height and leadership, noted that correlations varied from –0.13 to +0.71, but the average was about +0.30. Group members seem to associate height with power, but the relationship is not so strong that height is a prerequisite for leadership. Leaders also tend to be more physically fit. The smaller a man's waist-to-hip ratio (an indicator of fitness, because those with larger ratios tend to be out of shape), the more others rated him as leader-like when working in leaderless groups that were observed by others (Campbell et al., 2002).

Stogdill found that the link between age and leadership emergence is more complicated. Leaders in informal discussion groups vary in age, whereas political and business leaders are often older than their subordinates. Stogdill suggested that in organizations and political settings, the climb up the ladder of leadership takes time. Fewer than 1% of the corporate executives for the top Fortune 700 companies are under 40 years of age, and 81% are 50 or older (Spencer Stuart, 2004). As Stogdill noted, "Organizations tend to rely upon administrative knowledge and demonstration of success that comes with experience and age" (1974, p. 76). Furthermore, if group members assume that age is an indicator of wisdom, experience, and sagacity, they are likely to prefer a leader who is older rather than younger.

Even hair color predicts who will lead and who will follow. A study of the 500 top CEOs in England discovered fewer blonds and more redheads than might be expected given the distribution of these hair colors in the overall population of the country. The authors suggest that stereotypes about blondes—that they are less cognitively swift—and red heads—that they are mean but competent—may be sufficient to cause their under- and overrepresentation in leadership positions. However, of these 500 CEOs, only two were women, and they both had brown hair (Takeda, Helms, & Romanova, 2006).

**Diversity** The CEO of TFA (Wendy Kopp) is white, and the majority (61%) of the corps members are white as well. The president of the student government association of Florida A&M University, which is a traditionally African American university, is a black woman. The executive director of the Organization of Chinese Americans is a Chinese American. The director of the Mexican American Community Services Agency is a Latino woman. In 2007, how many African Americans were leaders (CEOs) of a Fortune 500 company in the United States? Only nine.

Leadership is not limited to any particular cultural, ethnic, or racial group, for the role of leader is firmly embedded in the traditions of African, European, Latino, Asian, and Native American groups (Smith & Bond, 1993; Zamarripa & Krueger, 1983). But how do the members of a subculture fare in groups where they are outnumbered by members of another ethnic group?

First, minorities tend to be less influential in heterogeneous small groups and, as a result, are less likely to emerge as leaders (Bass, 1990; Mai-Dalton, 1993). For example, when Mexican American and European American women interacted in groups, the Mexican American women exerted less influence than the European American women (Roll, McClelland, & Abel, 1996). In a study conducted in Australia that paired Chinese students with Australian students, the Chinese students were less influential than the Australian students (Jones et al., 1995).

Second, minorities tend to be underrepresented in leadership roles in business and organizational settings (Bass, 1990). African Americans in U.S. organizations and military groups, for example, are typically denied leadership positions in racially diverse groups, even if their experience qualifies them for these roles (Molm, 1986; Webster & Driskell,

1983). When senior managers review the leadership potential of lower-level managers, they give higher marks to European Americans than to African Americans and Asian Americans (Landau, 1995). Asian Americans, despite their success in scientific and technical fields, are less likely than European Americans and African Americans to achieve positions of leadership in their fields (Tang, 1997). Ethnic and racial minorities are underrepresented in the leadership world (Hooijberg & DiTomaso, 1996; Scandura & Lankau, 1996).

**Sex** Kopp, as both a woman and a leader, is something of an exception. Although the gender gap in leadership has narrowed in recent years, it has not closed. Both men and women, when surveyed, express a preference for a male rather than a female boss (Eagly & Carli, 2007). Women receive lower evaluations and fewer promotions than men, even when actual performance data or behaviors are held constant (Heilman, Block, & Martell, 1995). A recent survey of over 40 countries, including Austria, Israel, and Singapore, indicated that women hold 20–30% of the governmental, legislative, and managerial positions in those countries (Schein, 2007). The percentage has risen steadily over the years, but men still hold a near monopoly on high-level leadership positions (Eagly & Carli, 2007). In 2008, only 12 women were the CEOs of Fortune 500 companies. Female managers are more likely to feel excluded from career-related and informal interactions with senior managers than are male managers (Cianni & Romberger, 1995), and some have also expressed less confidence in their leadership abilities (Watson & Hoffman, 1996). The term *glass ceiling* is often used to represent many of the barriers that block women's rise into top management positions.

This gender difference also shapes men's and women's actions in small-group settings. Men are five times more likely to enact leadership behaviors than women in small, mixed-sex, leaderless groups and so are more likely to emerge as leaders (Walker et al., 1996). Both leaders and subordinates perceive female leaders to be less dominant than male leaders (Carli, 2001). The lone man in an otherwise all-female group often becomes the leader, whereas the lone woman in an otherwise all-male group has little influence (Crocker & McGraw, 1984). When a woman exerts influence in a group, members tend to frown and tighten their facial muscles; but when a man takes charge, members are more likely to nod in agreement (Butler & Geis, 1990). The tendency for men to dominate women in informal discussion groups was observed even when the men and women were all deemed to be androgynous (Porter et al., 1985), when group members were personally committed to equality for men and women (Sapp, Harrod, & Zhao, 1996), when the women in the group were dispositionally more dominant than the men (Megargee, 1969; Nyquist & Spence, 1986), and when the men and women were equally extraverted (Campbell et al., 2002). When researchers paired together a person who tended to be interpersonally powerful with one who was more submissive, the dispositionally dominant person emerged as the leader in 73% of same-sex dyads. But in mixed-sex dyads, the dominant man became the leader 90% of the time, and the dominant woman became the leader only 35% of the time (Nyquist & Spence, 1986).

This tendency for men to emerge as leaders more frequently than women is particularly ironic because studies of sex differences in the qualities that have been shown to predict leadership effectiveness—extraversion, conscientiousness, skill in working with others, acknowledging the good work of subordinates, communicating clearly, and facilitating others' development—all suggest that women are superior in these qualities to men. Hence, although women are more qualified to be leaders, they are less likely to become leaders (Eagly, Johannesen-Schmidt, & Engen, 2003).

## Who Will Lead?

The individual who emerges as the group's leader is often the one who is the most conscientious, experienced, socially intelligent, flexible, and capable. But not always, for some groups let themselves be led by people who are outgoing, talkative, older, and male. Why?

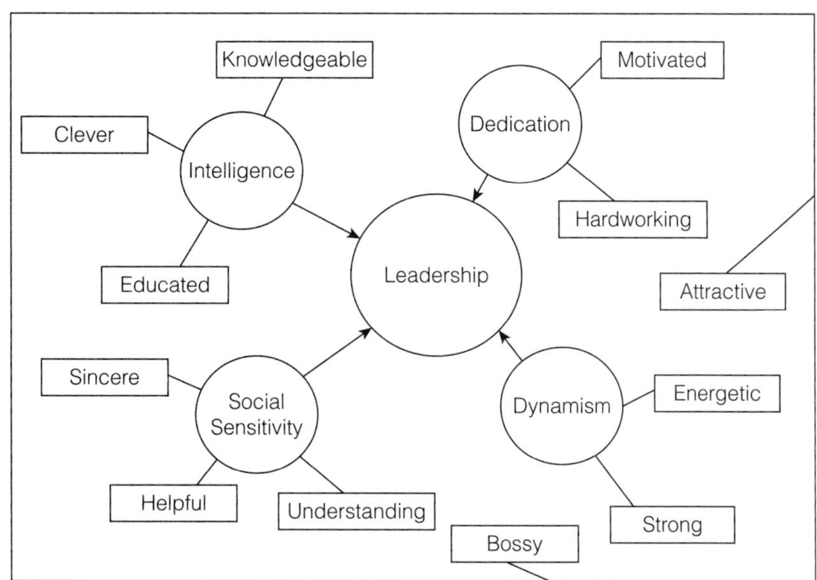


**FIGURE 9.4** A representation of the associations that make up an implicit leadership theory.

**Implicit Leadership Theory** **Implicit leadership theory (ILT)** offers a cognitive explanation for these partially conflicting tendencies. This theory, developed by Robert Lord and his colleagues, assumes that each group member comes to the group equipped with a set of expectations, beliefs, and assumptions about leaders and leadership. These cognitive structures are termed *implicit leadership theories* or *leader prototypes*. These structures are described as *implicit* because they are not overtly stated and are called *theories* because, like formal theories, they include generalities about leadership and hypotheses about the qualities that characterize most leaders (Lord, Foti, & De Vader, 1984; Lord & Maher, 1991).

Consider the hypothetical ILT shown in Figure 9.4. A follower who adopted this ILT would believe that social skill, intelligence, dedication, and dynamism are closely associated with leadership, but that dedication and dynamism are somewhat more closely associated with leadership than social skill and intelligence. This ILT also indicates how such specific traits as sincerity and strength are linked to more general traits, which are in turn associated with leadership itself. Sincerity is linked to sensitivity, for example, but not to dedication; hardworking is associated with dedication, but not intelligence. Also, certain qualities, such as bossiness and attractiveness, are not associated with leadership but are linked to other qualities outside the ILT (Epitropaki & Martin, 2004). Although each group member may have a unique conception of leadership, most people's ILTs include task skills—the leader should be active, determined, influential, and in command—and relationship skills—the leader should be caring, interested, truthful, and open to others' ideas (Kenney et al., 1996).

Members rely on their ILTs to sort group members into one of two categories—leader or follower. They intuitively note the actions and characteristics of the individuals in their group, compare them to their ILTs, and favor as leader the individual who matches that prototype of a leader. ILTs also guide subordinates' evaluations of their leaders.

---

**implicit leadership theories (ILTs)** Group members' taken-for-granted assumptions about the traits, characteristics, and qualities that distinguish leaders from the people they lead.

If members believe that leaders should be dominant, for example, they may only remember their leader acting dominantly and forget the times when their leader engaged in submissive behavior. Lord and his colleagues illustrated the biasing effects of ILTs in one study by arranging for raters to watch a videotape of a group interaction. After the tape, they asked the observers to identify behaviors that the leader had or had not performed. Lord found that the raters were less accurate, less confident, and slower to respond when trying to judge behaviors that were part of their ILTs but had not been performed by the leader they had watched (Foti & Lord, 1987).

If ILTs were like actual scientific theories, then group members would discard them when they fail to explain who is and who is not an effective leader. But ILTs, because they are *implicit* theories, are rarely recognized or revised. In consequence, if individuals' ILTs are biased in favor of individuals who are white, masculine, tall, or just highly vocal, then members with these qualities will rise to positions of authority in the group, even if they are not qualified for these positions. Lord (1985) concluded that when subordinates describe their leaders, these ratings reflect the subordinates' ILTs more than their leaders' actions (see Forsyth & Nye, 2008, for a review).

**Social Identity Theory** Michael Hogg and his colleagues believe that social identity processes, which were discussed in Chapter 3, influence a wide range of leadership processes, including who the group selects to be their leader. They theorize that individuals who identify with their group include in their self-definition—their social identity—qualities that they share in common with other group members. They also develop an idealized image of the prototypical member of the group, similar to an ILT, and over time consensus will emerge on these characteristics. Applied to leadership, social identity theory maintains that individuals who most closely match the qualities of the shared prototype will be more likely to emerge as leaders. For example, groups that prize cooperation and sensitive communication among members should favor relationship-oriented leaders, whereas groups of individuals who pride themselves on their action and productivity will support task-oriented leaders (Hogg, 2007, 2008; Reicher, Haslam, & Hopkins, 2005).

As Hogg notes, social identity theory best applies to choices of leaders in groups where members strongly identify with their groups. In a test of this hypothesis, Hogg and his colleagues formed ad hoc groups in the laboratory, and then appointed one member as leader of each group. They manipulated the psychological salience of the groups by telling some members that everyone in the group shared certain qualities, whereas others were told the groups were just loose aggregations with no commonalities. They also circulated some background information about the leader among the members to indicate that he or she matched the fictitious group prototype or did not match it. As predicted, group members who identified with the group were more positive about the prototypical leader (Hains, Hogg, and Duck, 1997).

**Social Role Theory** Alice Eagly's **social role theory**, like ILT and social identity theory, suggests that group members have definite expectations about what kind of qualities are needed in a person who will fill the role of leader. These expectations tend to emphasis the agentic, task-oriented side of leadership rather than the communal and interpersonal. When group members are asked to describe the qualities needed in a leader, they stress the importance of competition with peers, high energy, dominance, forcefulness, and skill at taking command and controlling a situation (Eagly & Karau, 2002).

These expectations, however, favor men relative to women as leaders. Although gender stereotypes vary across time and place, people in virtually all cultures, when asked to describe women, speak of their expressive qualities, including nurturance,

---

**social role theory** A conceptual analysis of sex differences developed by Alice Eagly recognizing that men and women take on different types of roles in many societies, and that these role expectations generate gender stereotypes and differences in the behavior of women and men.

emotionality, and warmth. They expect a "she" to be sentimental, affectionate, sympathetic, soft hearted, talkative, gentle, and feminine. When describing men, they stress their instrumental qualities, including productivity, energy, and strength (Williams & Best, 1990). In consequence, the expectations associated with leadership mesh with the male gender role stereotype, but the leadership role is inconsistent with widely held stereotypes about women (Forsyth, Heiney, & Wright, 1997). When people think "leader," they think "male" (Schein, 2007).

This *role incongruity* not only disqualifies women from taking the lead in groups, but it also creates a double standard for women once they achieve a position of leadership. Women, to be evaluated as positively as men, must outperform men. When Eagly and her colleagues reviewed 61 different studies that asked people to evaluate the performance of male and female leaders, they found that the behaviors and outcomes achieved by men were viewed more positively than the exact same outcomes achieved by women (Eagly, Makhijani, & Klonsky, 1992). Ironically, this bias reaches its peak when a female leader adopts a more task-oriented approach to leadership. In a classic example of a "Catch-22," women are urged to act more like male leaders, but when they do, they are denigrated for not being "ladylike" (Hoyt, 2007; Rudman & Glick, 2001). Caught in this double-bind, women respond by avoiding taking the role of leader, by underperforming as leaders due to the pressure of the negative stereotypes, or by actively resisting the stereotypes and doing what they can to invalidate members' negative expectations (Hoyt & Chemers, 2008).

**Terror Management Theory** Many theorists have suggested that humans have a fundamental need for leaders. Sigmund Freud (1922), for example, is best known for his insightful analyses of personality and adjustment, but he also undertook an analysis of group behavior. Freud suggested that, for psychological reasons, humans have a "thirst for obedience": people, used to life in the primal horde, willingly accept guidance from parental figures who are forceful, directive, and charismatic leaders (Goethals, 2005; Moxnes, 1999).

The idea that people are drawn to powerful leaders for less than rational reasons is consistent with **terror management theory (TMT)**. This theory assumes that humans, perhaps uniquely, are aware that someday their earthly existence will come to an end. This awareness of one's inevitable demise, if cognitively inescapable, would be the source of continuous existential anguish, so the human mind has developed defenses against thoughts of death. TMT suggests, for example, that culture diminishes this psychological terror by providing meaning, organization, and a coherent world view. Self-esteem and pride, too, function to elevate one's sense of worth, and serve as a defense against the intrusive thoughts of death (Greenberg, Solomon, & Pyszczynski, 1997).

TMT explains why the popularity of a leader often grows, exponentially, during times of tumult and crisis. The theory, as an explanation of leadership emergence and endorsement, suggests that followers will show a marked preference for strong, iconic leaders when their mortality is made salient to them. After the terrorist attacks on the U.S. in 2001, for example, U.S. citizen's approval ratings of then-president George W. Bush jumped from 40–50% to 90%. TMT suggests that the attack made citizens aware of their mortality, and also threatened their world view. Bush, by promising to find the terrorists responsible for this horrible action and bring them to justice swiftly, provided an antidote to their existential concerns.

Researchers have put TMT to the test by reminding some people of their motality and then assessing their preferences for different types of leaders (Cohen et al., 2004, 2005; Landau et al., 2004). One study, for example, compared preferences for three candidates for political office. The *task-oriented leader* stressed setting difficult but achievable goals, strategic planning, and initiating structure. The *relationship-oriented leader* communicated

---

**terror management theory (TMT)** A conceptual analysis of the implicit psychological processes thought to defend individuals from the emotionally terrifying knowledge that they are mortal and will someday die.

compassion, respect, trust, and confidence in others. The *charismatic leader* spoke of long-term goals, the unique value of the nation, and working together. Before evaluating these candidates, participants in the mortality-salience condition were reminded of their eventual demise in a not-so-subtle way: they were asked to describe the emotions that the thought of their own death aroused in them, and to write down what will happen to them, physically, when they die. Those in the control condition were asked parallel questions, but about their next exam rather than their death. The results indicated that in the control condition people were more positive towards the task- and relationship-oriented leaders relative to the charismatic one. Conversely, in the mortality-salience condition, ratings of the charismatic leader climbed and ratings of the relationship-oriented leader dropped. The task-oriented leader was the most favorably rated in both conditions (Cohen et al., 2004). Other research finds that, as social role theory might suggest, individuals reminded of their mortality prefer as their leaders (a) members of their own group, or (b) men rather than women (Hoyt, Simon, & Reid, in press).

**Evolutionary Theory** Evolutionary psychology also offers an answer to the question, "Who will lead?" As noted briefly in Chapter 2, evolutionary psychology suggests that leadership is an adaptation: a heritable characteristic that developed in a population over a long period of time. Adaptations, in the language of Darwin, increase individuals' fitness, for they increase the chances of their genetic material being represented in future generations of the species. Leadership, as an adaptation, evolved because it contributed so substantially to the survival of human beings in the *environment of evolutionary adaptation* (EEA). For much of their evolutionary past, humans likely lived in relatively small groups, or tribes, of genetically related individuals. These groups moved constantly, in search of water and food, often in response to seasonal and climate changes. Hence, someone often took the role of the leader of the group, with a quite literal meaning: this individual guided the group from one place to the next, and as their facilitative impact was an improvement over more diffuse, unorganized movement, over time individuals learned to follow. Humans also developed the mental apparatus needed to identify those who were most qualified to lead their groups. The acceptance of a leader, and one with particular qualities, is therefore based on instincts that evolved during a time when humans lived in much harsher settings (Van Vugt, 2006; Van Vugt, Hogan, & Kaiser, 2008).

Little is known about the EEA, and so evolutionary psychology can only speculate about the nature of the environmental pressures that shaped the evolution of leadership. If, however, the EEA was similar to the situations faced by many indigenous people—competition with other adjoining tribes for scarce food resources, high rates of infant mortality, subsistence living from hunting and gathering rather than agriculture, and high stability in group membership and cohesion—then it is no wonder that people prefer leaders who can help their group reach its goals and solve disputes that occur within the group, but who do not take unfair advantage of others once they are installed in their position of authority.

## LEADER EFFECTIVENESS

Alexander the Great controlled a huge empire without any modern means of transportation or communication. General George S. Patton inspired those under his command by displaying high levels of personal confidence, sureness, and an immense strength of character. Wendy Kopp built TFA from the ground up and steered the company through a period of organizational and funding nightmares. Alexander, Patton, and Kopp are not simply leaders. They are *effective* leaders. But what is the key to their effectiveness?

### Fiedler's Contingency Model

Fred Fiedler spent years studying groups that worked to achieve collective goals under the direction of an appointed, elected, or emergent leader.

He focused his attention on groups that generated products and performances that could be evaluated, and he measured aspects of the groups' settings and their leaders to see what combinations consistently led to good results. His basic conclusion was that a leader's effectiveness cannot be predicted just by considering the leader's qualities. Nor can it be predicted on the basis of the situation. Rather, Fiedler's **contingency theory** assumes that leadership effectiveness is contingent on both the leaders' motivational style and the leader's capacity to control the group situation (Fiedler, 1964, 1967, 1971, 1978, 1981, 1993, 1996).

**Motivational Style** Consistent with the task-relationship model of leadership, Fiedler suggests that leaders naturally tend to adopt one of two leadership styles, which he measured using the **Least Preferred Co-Worker Scale (LPC)**. Respondents first think of the one individual with whom they have had the most difficulty working at some time. They then rate this person, dubbed the *least preferred coworker*, on bipolar adjective scales such as "pleasant–unpleasant," "friendly–unfriendly," and "tense–relaxed." People with high scores on the LPC are assumed to be relationship-oriented; after all, they even rate the person they do not like to work with positively. Low LPC scorers are assumed to be task-oriented.

**Situational Control** Just as leadership style is the key *personal* variable in contingency theory, control is the key *situational* factor in the model. If leaders can control the situation, they can be certain that decisions, actions, and suggestions will be carried out by the group members. Leaders who have trouble gaining control, in contrast, cannot be certain that the group members will carry out their assigned duties. What factors determine control? Fiedler highlighted leader–member relations, task structure, and position power.

- *Leader–member relations*. What is the quality of the relationship between the leader and the group? If the group is highly cohesive and relatively conflict-free, the leader will be less concerned with peacekeeping and monitoring behavior.
- *Task structure*. Do group members clearly understand what is expected of them? When task structure is high, the group's tasks are straightforward and have only one right solution, whose correctness is easily verified. Tasks that are unstructured, in contrast, are ambiguous, admit many correct solutions, and offer no one correct way of reaching the goal.
- *Position power*. How much authority does the leader possess? Leaders with high position power can control rewards, punishments, salaries, hiring, evaluation, and task assignment. In some groups, on the other hand, the leader may have relatively little power.

Figure 9.5 summarizes the relationship between these three variables and the favorability of the leadership situations. Octant I in the chart is the most favorable setting—leader–member relations are good, the task is structured, and the leader's power is strong. Octant VIII is the least favorable situation, for all three variables combine in a group that is difficult for the leader to control.

**Predicting Leadership Effectiveness** Fiedler did not believe that either type of leader—task-motivated or relationship-motivated—is better overall. Instead, he predicted that task-oriented leaders (low LPC score) would be most effective in situations that are either highly favorable or highly unfavorable, whereas relationship-oriented leaders (high LPC score) would be most effective in

---

**contingency theory** Fred Fiedler's conceptual analysis of leadership which posits that a leader's success is determined by his or her leadership style and the favorability of the group situation; more generally, any analysis of leadership that suggests that the effectiveness of leaders depends on the interaction of their personal characteristics and the group situation.

**Least Preferred Co-Worker Scale (LPC)** An indirect measure, developed by Fred Fiedler, of the tendency to lead by stressing the task (low LPC) or relationships (high LPC).

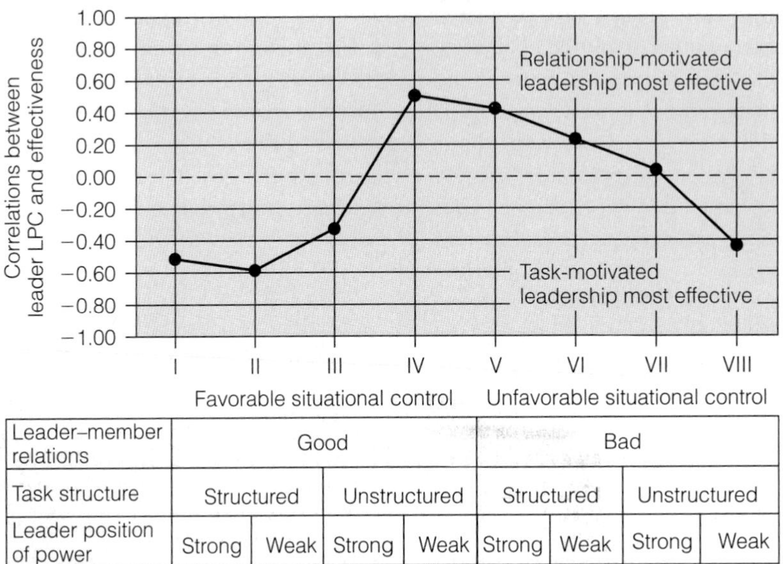


| Leader–member relations | Good | | | | Bad | | | |
|---|---|---|---|---|---|---|---|---|
| Task structure | Structured | | Unstructured | | Structured | | Unstructured | |
| Leader position of power | Strong | Weak | Strong | Weak | Strong | Weak | Strong | Weak |

**FIGURE 9.5** Fiedler's contingency model of leadership. The theory assumes that effectiveness depends on three aspects of the group situation: leader/member relations, task structure, and leader's position of power. Octant I corresponds to the most controllable and favorable situation, and Octant VIII corresponds to the least controllable and least favorable setting. The vertical axis indicates the predicted relationship between LPC scores and task performance. If the correlation is greater than 0 (positive), effectiveness is positively related to LPC; that is, relationship-motivated leaders are more effective. If the correlation is smaller than 0 (negative), effectiveness is negatively related to LPC; task-motivated leaders are more effective. The graph suggests that a task-oriented leader is more effective when the situation is favorable (Octants I, II, and II) or unfavorable (Octant VIII) for the leader.

SOURCE: The Contingency Model and the Dynamics of the Leadership Process. Advances in Experimental Social Psychology, Volume 11, 1978, Pages 59-112, by Fred E. Fiedler. Reprinted by permission of Elsevier.

middle-range situations. If, for example, Kopp is a low-LPC leader (task-motivated), then she will get the most out of groups in Octants I, II, and III, where situational favorability is high, as well as in Octant VIII, the least favorable situation. Were she a high-LPC leader, her groups would perform best in the middle-range situations—Octants IV to VII. Why? Fiedler suggested that in difficult groups (Octant VIII), task-motivated leaders drive the group toward its goals, but relationship-motivated leaders spend too much time repairing relations. In highly favorable (Octants I through III) situations, in contrast, task-oriented leaders become more considerate, yielding a more satisfied workgroup.

Studies of a variety of working groups support the complex predictions charted in Figure 9.5 (Ayman, Chemers, & Fiedler, 2007). For example, when Fiedler (1964) studied anti-aircraft artillery crews, he measured both the commander's leadership style (high or low LPC) and the favorability of the situation. In most crews, the leaders enjoyed a strong position of power because their authority was determined by rank. Moreover, task structure was high because the same sequence of decisions had to be made for each target. In some crews, however, the commander was well liked—placing the crew in the most favorable situation (Octant I), whereas in other crews, the commander was disliked (Octant V). Thus, a low-LPC leader should be more effective for Octant I crews, but groups in Octant V should perform better with a high-LPC leader. Supporting this prediction, Fiedler (1955) found that LPC scores were negatively correlated with effectiveness for artillery squads in Octant I

($r = -0.34$), but positively correlated with effectiveness in Octant V ($r = 0.49$).

The effectiveness of a unique leadership training program, called *Leader Match*, also supports the validity of contingency theory. Although many different programs and techniques have been developed to train leaders, the results of these procedures are typically disappointing (Stogdill, 1974). Fiedler, however, suggested that these programs fail because they place too much emphasis on changing the leaders—making them more supportive, more decisive, more democratic, and so on. He suggested instead that the situation should be engineered to fit the leader's particular motivational style. He called his training program *LeaderMatch* because he taught trainees to modify their group situation until it matched their personal motivational style (Fiedler, Chemers, & Mahar, 1976). Studies of the effectiveness of this innovative training program suggest that trained leaders outperform untrained leaders (Burke & Day, 1986; Csoka & Bons, 1978; Fiedler, 1978).

**Questions and Conclusions** Contingency theory, like all theories, has both weaknesses and strengths. Despite years of research, experts are divided on the model's validity, with some arguing that evidence supports the model and others arguing against it (see Chemers, 1997, for a review). Investigators have challenged not only the strength of the relationships that provide the basis of the predictions in the eight octants in Figure 9.5, but they have also questioned the methods that Fiedler used to measure leaders' motivational style. In defense of contingency theory, however, the contingency model was one of the first theories of leadership effectiveness that fully considered both personal factors (LPC score) and situational factors (situational control). Few would dispute its key take-home message—that the effectiveness of a leader cannot be predicted without taking into account both the leader's perceptions of his or her followers and the leader's degree of control in the situation (Chemers, 2000; Rice, 1979). The work also led Fiedler to examine how leaders respond to stressful leadership settings (Fiedler, 1986).

## Style Theories

Fiedler's contingency model assumes that leaders have a preferred "style" of leading: Some tend to be relationship-oriented leaders, and others are task-oriented leaders. Many other leadership theories accept this basic premise, but add that some leaders integrate both task and relationship elements in their approach to leadership. These style theories argue that effective leaders balance these two basic ingredients in the groups they lead (see Northouse, 2007, for a review).

**The Leadership Grid** Robert Blake and Jane Mouton hypothesized that leadership style depends on how one answers two basic questions: (1) How important is the production of results by the group? (2) How important are the feelings of group members? To some leaders, the key goal is achieving results. For others, positive feelings in the group are so important that they emphasize teamwork and personal satisfaction. Others may feel that both these goals are important (Blake & McCanse, 1991; Blake & Mouton, 1964, 1982, 1985).

Blake and Mouton summarized these differences in their **Leadership Grid** (formerly called the *Managerial Grid*), which is presented in Figure 9.6. Both dimensions—concern for people and concern for results—are represented as 9-point scales ranging from *low concern* to *high concern*. Although a person's orientation could fall at any of 81 possible positions on the grid, Blake and Mouton emphasized the five located at the four corner positions and the center. An apathetic, impoverished 1,1 leader is hardly a leader, for he or she is not interested in either subordinates' feelings or the production of results. The 9,1 individual (high on concern for production, but low on concern for people, located in the lower right corner of the grid) is a taskmaster, who seeks productivity at any cost. The 1,9 leader, in contrast,

---

**Leadership Grid** A theory of management and leadership, proposed by Robert Blake and Jane Mouton, assuming that people vary in their concern for results and their concern for people, and that individuals who are high on both dimensions (9,9) are the best leaders.

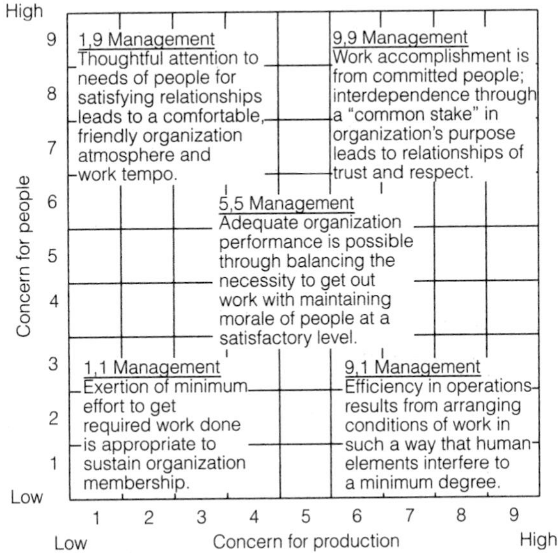
High
9
8
7
6
5
4
3
2
1
Low
Concern for people
1,9 Management
Thoughtful attention to needs of people for satisfying relationships leads to a comfortable, friendly organization atmosphere and work tempo.
9,9 Management
Work accomplishment is from committed people; interdependence through a "common stake" in organization's purpose leads to relationships of trust and respect.
5,5 Management
Adequate organization performance is possible through balancing the necessity to get out work with maintaining morale of people at a satisfactory level.
1,1 Management
Exertion of minimum effort to get required work done is appropriate to sustain organization membership.
9,1 Management
Efficiency in operations results from arranging conditions of work in such a way that human elements interfere to a minimum degree.
1 2 3 4 5 6 7 8 9
Low
Concern for production
High

**FIGURE 9.6** The *Leadership Grid* (formerly, the *Managerial Grid*). This model distinguishes between five basic leadership styles, and recommends the 9,9 style above all others.

SOURCE: Adapted from *Leadership Dilemmas - Grid Solutions*, p. 29, p. Robert R. Blake and Anne Adams McCanse. Copyright © 1991 by Robert R. Blake and the Estate of Jane S. Mouton. Used with permission. All rights reserved.

adopts a "country club" approach that makes subordinates feel comfortable and relaxed in the group. The "middle-of-the-roader," located at 5,5, tries to balance both performance and morale but sometimes sacrifices both when results and individuals' feelings come into conflict. Finally, the 9,9 leader values both people and products highly and therefore tackles organizational goals through teamwork—"a high degree of shared responsibility, coupled with high participation, involvement, and commitment" (Blake & Mouton, 1982, p. 41).

Blake and Mouton (1982) were not contingency theorists; they felt that the 9,9 leadership style was the most effective style overall. In their initial studies, they found that managers who adopted the 9,9 style were far more successful in their careers than managers who adopted other methods. They also noted that studies conducted in educational, industrial, and medical organizations supported the utility of the 9,9 leadership style, as did the favorable results of their management training system. These results are impressive, but many experts still question their strong claim that the 9,9 style works in *all* situations.

**Situational Leadership Theory** Paul Hersey and Kenneth Blanchard also described leadership in terms of the relationship and task dimensions. Unlike Blake and Mouton's grid, however, their **situational leadership theory** suggests that effective leaders combine supportive behaviors with directive behaviors depending on the developmental level, or *maturity*, of the group or subordinate. Mature individuals or groups are ones who are committed to the group and its task, and they are usually confident, self-assured, and highly motivated. Maturity is also related to competence, for mature members possess the skills and knowledge needed to perform their assigned tasks, perhaps because they have been trained, or because they have experience (Hersey & Blanchard, 1976, 1982; Hersey, Blanchard, & Johnson, 2001).

The theory recommends leaders start with a task-focused, directive style. When group members are low in both commitment and competence, they work most effectively with a *directing* leader who is not supportive (S1). As the group develops and gains experience on the task and commitment to the group's goals, the leader can increase relationship behavior and adopt a *coaching* style (S2; high direction and support). Still later in the group's development, the leader can ease off on both types of leadership, starting first with direction. In moderately mature groups, the *supporting* leader is most effective (S3), and in fully mature groups, a *delegating* leadership style is best (S4). Thus, an effective leader must display four different leadership styles as the group moves through its life cycle—directing, coaching, supporting, and delegating (Hersey et al., 2001).

Some critics have argued that situational leadership theory puts too much emphasis on matching the maturity of the members; these experts

---

**situational leadership theory** A theory of leadership, proposed by Paul Hersey and Kenneth Blanchard, suggesting that groups benefit from leadership that meshes with a group's stage of development.

call for a careful balancing of task and relationship orientation at all developmental levels (Nicholls, 1985). But the basic premise on which the model rests—that different groups need varying amounts of task and relationship leadership—is consistent with research findings. For example, newly hired employees needed and appreciated greater task structuring from their manager than did veteran employees (Vecchio, 1987). Conversely, members with higher levels of education and greater levels of job tenure preferred a leader who provided less task structure (Vecchio & Boatwright, 2002). Moreover, measures of leadership flexibility based on the theory, such as the *Leader Behavior Analysis II*®, are useful tools for assessing rigidity in leadership style (Hersey, 1985; cf. Graeff, 1997; Lueder, 1985). The theory's training methods are also very popular among business professionals. Situational leadership theory forms the basis for the "one-minute management" approach to leadership in organizational settings (Blanchard & Johnson, 1981; Blanchard, Zigarmi, & Nelson, 1993; Carew, Parisi-Carew, & Blanchard, 1986).

### Leader–Member Exchange Theory

Most theories of leadership, such as Fiedler's (1978) contingency theory and Blake and Mouton's (1980) *Leadership Grid*, focus on the leader's style or strategy and how the group responds as a whole to various interventions. But such a "one size fits all" approach does not always match the needs of specific group members. Whereas one group member may work well with a task-oriented leader, others may prefer a leader who provides them with support.

**Leader–member exchange theory** (LMX theory) uniquely stresses the quality of the one-to-one relationship between a leader and a subordinate. LMX theory (and its predecessor, *vertical dyad linkage theory*) notes that leaders have dyadic relationships with each group member and that these dyadic relationships may be substantially different within the total group. Some leaders may work well with only a subset of the group members who are more engaged in the group and its tasks. Other group members, however, may not respond as positively to the leader, so their responses are defined by their role and their fixed responsibilities (Dansereau, Graen, & Haga, 1975; Graen & Uhl-Bien, 1995).

LMX theory suggests that group members tend to cleave into subgroups within the overall group. One group, the *ingroup*, or *inner group*, includes those individuals with positive linkages to the leader. Leaders spend more time working with these members, value their inputs more, and also provide them with more resources. These group members respond by working harder for the group, taking on additional role responsibilities, and declaring their loyalty to the leader and the group. They are less likely to leave the group and more likely to earn higher performance evaluations, get promoted more rapidly, express more commitment to the organization, voice more positive attitudes about their work and the group, and garner more attention and support from their leader. They often view their relationship with their boss as a *partnership*. The second group, the *outgroup*, or *outer group*, includes individuals with less satisfying linkages to the leader. These individuals do their work, but do not contribute as much to the group. They also express less loyalty and support for the leader (Dienesch & Liden, 1986).

LMX theory's basic assumptions have been verified empirically (Gerstner & Day, 1997; cf. Schriesheim, Castro, & Cogliser, 1999). Researchers have documented the natural tendency for subgroups to develop within groups, and for disparities in performance to exist between these two cliques (Bass, 1990). Those who enjoy a positive LMX are more likely to do things that benefit their group and organization. These *organizational citizenship behaviors* include helping other group members, common courtesy, job dedication, civic virtue, supporting organizational changes, and so on (Ilies,

---

**leader–member exchange theory (LMX)** A dyadic, relational approach to leadership assuming that leaders develop exchange relationships with each of their subordinates, and that the quality of these leader–member exchange (LMX) relationships influences subordinates' responsibility, decision influence, access to resources, and performance.

Nahrgang, & Moregeson, 2007). Individuals who are not satisfied with their LMX tend to perform more poorly, but the strength of this relationship depends, in part, on the degree of differentiation within the group. In undifferentiated groups there is little variation in LMX—no ingroup and outgroup at all. In highly differentiated groups, in contrast, the LMX relation varies substantially from one member to the next; there are those who work well with the leader, and those who do not. Such variation can lead to dissatisfaction, overall, since it is inconsistent with principles of fairness and equal treatment (Hooper & Martin, 2008). Therefore, leaders who recognize this tendency can improve their overall relations with their group by minimizing the number of people in the outer group (Graen & Uhl-Bien, 1991). However, some research suggests that differentiation can be motivating. In such groups, low LMX members recognize that they may, through hard work, meet the leader's standards, for they view the leader as a discriminating judge of group members (Liden et al., 2006).

LMX theory's dyadic approach—stressing the relationship between each member and the leader—also provides an additional way of looking at leadership in general. Researchers have returned to other leadership theories, such as Fiedler's contingency model, and have begun to explore the type of leadership style that leaders use with each group member. These dyadic-level approaches add a second layer of information about leadership to the more common group-level analysis (Yammarino & Dansereau, 2008; Yammarino et al., 2005).

### Participation Theories

Some leaders do all the leading—they, and they alone, make decisions, dole out assignments, supervise work quality, communicate with other groups, set goals, and so on. Such leaders adopt a *command-and-control* leadership style; they give the orders and subordinates carry them out. Other leaders, however, share their leadership duties with others in the group (Burns, 2003). Kopp, for example, set the general goals for TFA, but she expected the other staff members and recruiters to make choices, create structures, and recommend changes in procedures. She adopted a *participatory leadership style.*

**The Lewin–Lippitt–White Study** As noted in Chapter 2, Kurt Lewin, Ronald Lippitt, and Ralph White conducted one of the earliest laboratory studies of interacting groups to determine the relative effectiveness of shared and unshared approaches to leadership. They arranged for groups of 10- and 11-year-old boys to meet after school to work on various hobbies. In addition to the boys, each group included a man who adopted one of three leadership styles (Lewin, Lippitt, & White, 1939; White & Lippitt, 1960, 1968):

- The *authoritarian*, or *autocratic*, leader took no input from the members in making decisions about group activities, did not discuss the long-range goals of the group, emphasized his authority, dictated who would work on specific projects, and arbitrarily paired the boys with their work partners.
- The *democratic* leader made certain that all activities were first discussed by the entire group. He allowed the group members to make their own decisions about work projects or partners and encouraged the development of an egalitarian atmosphere.
- The *laissez-faire* leader rarely intervened in the group activities. Groups with this type of atmosphere made all decisions on their own without any supervision, and their so-called leader functioned primarily as a source of technical information.

In some cases, the boys were rotated to a different experimental condition, so that they could experience all three types of participation.

The three types of leadership resulted in differences in efficiency, satisfaction, and aggressiveness. The autocratic groups spent as much time working on their hobbies as the democratic groups, but the laissez-faire groups worked considerably less (see Figure 9.7). When the leader left the room, however, work dropped off dramatically in the

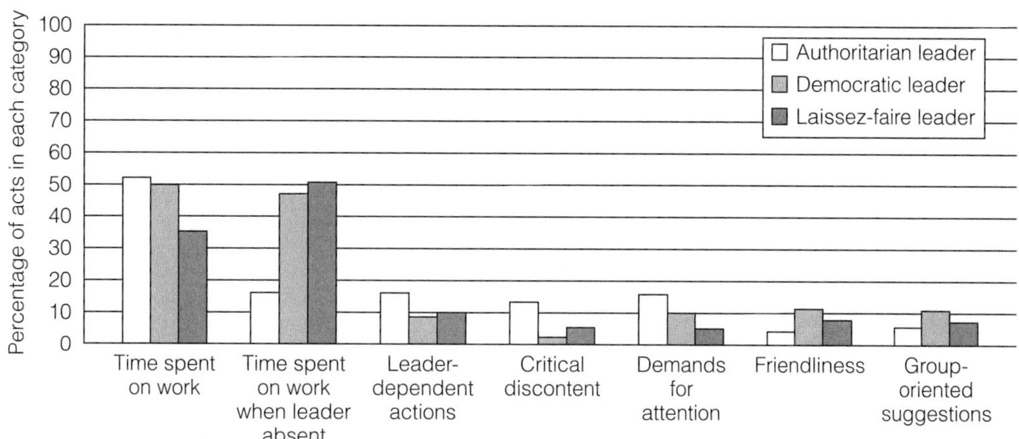


**FIGURE 9.7** The results of Lewin, Lippitt, and White's 1939 study of authoritarian, democratic, and laissez-faire leaders. Groups with either the authoritarian and democratic leaders were more productive than the laissez-faire groups, but the autocratic groups were less productive when the leader left the room. Other findings suggest the democratic groups were more cohesive.

SOURCE: Adapted from *Autocracy and Democracy* by R.K. White and R. Lippitt. Copyright © 1960 by the authors. Reprinted by permission of HarperCollins Publishers, Inc.

autocratically led groups, remained unchanged in the democratic groups, and actually increased in the laissez-faire groups. Furthermore, members of groups with an autocratic leader displayed greater reliance on the leader, expressed more critical discontent, and made more aggressive demands for attention. Democratic groups tended to be friendlier and more group oriented. Overall, the boys preferred democratic leaders to the other two varieties.

Although these findings seem to recommend democratic leadership over the two alternatives, the findings of Lewin, Lippitt, and White were not as clear-cut as Figure 9.7 implies. Several of the groups reacted to the autocratic leader with hostility, negativity, and scapegoating, but others responded very passively to their authoritarian leaders. In these latter groups, productivity was quite high (74%) when the leader was present, but it dropped to 29% when he left the room. Aggression—very apparent in some of the autocratically led groups—was replaced in these passive groups by apathy and acceptance of the situation. Although the group became aggressive if the autocratic leader was replaced with a more permissive one, when he was present, the group members worked hard, demanded little attention, only rarely engaged in horseplay, and closely followed his recommendations. As a methodological aside, the findings should also be interpreted with caution because the laissez-faire condition was not originally included when Lewin and his team designed the study. But when one of the experimenters was unable to enact an autocratic style correctly and instead just distanced himself from the groups, the investigators relabeled the leadership style he used as laissez-faire leadership (White, 1990).

**Shared Leadership** Lewin, Lippitt, and White's (1939) findings, although far from definitive evidence of the superiority of democratic leadership, offer some support for sharing leadership responsibility across the entire group. Such decentered leadership models go by many names—co-leadership, collective leadership, democratic leadership, delegated leadership, empowerment, peer leadership, self-leadership, shared leadership, team leadership, and participatory leadership—but underlying these various models is a common emphasis on breaking the leader's monopoly on power, influence, and authority in the group and distributing responsibility for core leadership functions to all the group members (Pearce & Conger, 2003).

When people think about leadership, they generally think of it as concentrated in a single position, rather than distributed across a group (Seers, Keller, & Wilkerson, 2003). In consequence, groups sometimes move away from shared leadership to more vertical forms of leadership—with an up-down form of organization rather than side-to-side *and* up-and-down (Pearce, Conger, & Locke, 2008). However, if the members' reactions to their work are a key factor in maintaining and evaluating success, a participatory approach will be superior to a more leader-centered method (Levin, 2006; Miller & Monge, 1986). As Stogdill (1974) noted after reviewing more than 40 studies of various leadership methods that ranged along the participation continuum, satisfaction with the group seems to be highest in democratic groups, as opposed to autocratic and laissez-faire groups. Shared methods of leadership are also more effective in smaller rather than in larger groups, and so are well-suited to organizations that rely on small, self-directed teams or networks of distributed, relatively independent employees (Vroom & Mann, 1960). Groups often share leadership when making decisions and when organized to function as a team, so we will reexamine issues related to participatory leadership in Chapters 11 (Decision Making) and 12 (Teams).

## Transformational Leadership

Wendy Kopp is no ordinary CEO. She does not just set goals and plan future initiatives, but she inspires, excites, and captures the imaginations of those who work for her. When she spoke to the first group of future teachers at the start of their summer training, she inspired them with her vision of their work and their future. TFA's mission: "One day, all children in this nation will have the opportunity to attain an excellent education" (Kopp, 2003, p. 185).

Kopp is a transformational leader. She is not content with the status quo or with merely making certain TFA functions smoothly; she seeks to change the people who work in TFA, the teachers who join her corps, the school systems where the teachers are placed, and America itself. She focuses on change or, more precisely, transformation: she seeks to elevate herself, her followers, her organization, and even society.

Early theory pertaining to transformational leaders focused on their charismatic qualities. Such leaders, like Kopp, through the force of their personality, their spoken word, and their dynamic presentational style, profoundly affect others. Max Weber (1921/1946), as noted in Chapter 8, used the word *charisma* to describe such leaders, for they seem to possess a "divinely inspired gift" that sets them apart from other, more commonplace leaders. Charismatic leaders inspire others, often by expressing ideas that are both appealing and easily understood. They tend to act in ways that provide their group members with a model that they can emulate (Gardner, 1995; House & Baetz, 1979).

But it was James McGregor Burns (1978) who set forth the basic assumptions of the transformational approach to leadership in his book *Leadership*. Burns argued that most leaders engage primarily in what he called **transactional leadership**. The follower and the leader cooperate with one another in the pursuit of a shared goal, but their relationship is based on the exchange of resources, which can include time, money, help, and instruction. Transactional leadership "occurs when one person takes the initiative in making contact with others for the purpose of an exchange of valued things" (Burns, 1978, p. 19). It is "pursuit of change in measured and often reluctant doses" (Burns, 2003, p. 24). The only thing that unites the leader and follower are the resources that are exchanged. In contrast, **transformational leadership** "occurs

---

**transactional leadership** A traditional form of leadership that involves contributing time, effort, and other resources in the pursuit of collaborative goals in exchange for desired outcomes.

**transformational leadership** An inspiring method of leading others that involves elevating one's followers' motivation, confidence, and satisfaction, by uniting them in the pursuit of shared, challenging goals and changing their beliefs, values, and needs.

when one or more persons *engage* with others in such a way that leaders and followers raise one another to high levels of motivation and morality" (1978, p. 20, italics in original). Burns believed that transformational leaders not only change their groups, organizations, and societies, but they also transform themselves and their followers.

Bernard Bass (1997), drawing on Burns's work, identified the components of both transactional and transformational leadership and contrasted these two methods with laissez-faire leadership. Most leaders, Bass suggests, are transactional: They define expectations, offer rewards, "formulate mutually satisfactory agreements, negotiate for resources, exchange assistance for effort, and provide commendations for successful follower performance" (Bass, 1997, p. 134). Transformational leaders, however, go beyond rewards and punishments. These leaders tend to be self-confident and determined, and their communications with their followers are usually eloquent and enthusiastic (Yammarino & Bass, 1990). In contrast to both transactional and transformational leadership, some leaders adopt a passive/avoidant, or laissez-faire, style. They point out members' failings or ignore problems until they become dire.

Bruce Avolio and Bass (1995) developed the *Multifactor Leadership Questionnaire* to measure the key components of transformational, transactional, and passive/avoidant leadership. Transformational leadership's four components, the so-called 4Is, include (paraphrased from Bass, 1997, p. 133):

- *Idealized influence*: Leaders who express their conviction clearly and emphasize the importance of trust; they take stands on difficult issues and urge members to adopt their values; they emphasize the importance of purpose, commitment, and the ethical consequences of decisions.
- *Inspirational motivation*: Leaders who articulate an appealing vision of the future; they challenge followers with high standards, talk optimistically with enthusiasm, and provide encouragement and meaning for what needs to be done.
- *Intellectual stimulation*: Leaders who question old assumptions, traditions, and beliefs; they stimulate in others new perspectives and ways of doing things, and they encourage the expression of ideas and reasons.
- *Individualized consideration*: Leaders who deal with others as individuals; they consider individual needs, abilities, and aspirations; they listen attentively and further individual members' development; they advise, teach, and coach.

Transactional leadership's two key components are (paraphrased from Bass, 1997, p. 134):

- *Contingent reward*: Leaders who provide rewards to followers contingent on performance, recognize achievements, and provide direction and positive feedback; they define expectations, arrange mutually satisfactory agreements, and negotiate for resources.
- *Management by exception (active)*: Leaders who supervise followers' performances and intervene if they detect failures to reach goals or maintain standards.

Passive/avoidant forms of leadership (and nonleadership) include (paraphrased from Bass, 1997, p. 134):

- *Passive management by exception*: Leaders who are uninvolved in the group activity until a serious problem occurs; they do not take action until mistakes are brought to their attention.
- *Laissez-faire*: These individuals are not, according to Bass, leaders, for they do not accept the responsibility of the role; they are often absent when needed, ignore their followers' requests for help, and do not make their views and values known to others.

Both transactional and transformational leaders are more effective than passive leaders, but groups working with transformational leaders often achieve the best results of all. A meta-analytic review, of 87 studies concluded that transformational leadership

## Focus 9.3 What Do People Look for in an Effective Leader?

*Leaders must invoke an alchemy of great vision.*
—Henry A. Kissinger

Leadership is not recognized as a positive force in all countries and cultures, but nearly all societies consider transformational leaders who maintain high moral standards to be superior to less virtuous authorities. To explore leadership around the world, researchers in the Global Leadership and Organizational Behavior Effectiveness (GLOBE) Program asked 15,022 managers in 62 countries to describe desirable and undesirable characteristics of a leader. They then identified those qualities that nearly all of the individuals agreed were critical by calculating indexes of agreement for each country. As Table 9.5 suggests, many of the qualities identified as desirable in an outstanding leader were transformational ones such as visionary, inspirational, and high in integrity. Those qualities that were considered to be most undesirable in a leader were those associated with a lack of integrity, self-centeredness, and asocial tendencies (House & Javidan, 2004).

Some countries, however, had relatively unique conceptions of their ideal leaders. Whereas most people surveyed expected effective leaders to be charismatic and team-focused, some cultures stressed these qualities more than in others. Highly collectivistic societies, for example, favored charismatic leaders more so than more individualistic cultures. Cultures that displayed higher levels of gender egalitarianism stressed participative, team-focused leadership. Those individuals who lived in cultures marked by hierarchical power structures and greater levels of elitism were more tolerant of self-centered leaders who were status conscious and formalistic. The GLOBE researchers also discovered that certain specific traits were highly valued in some cultures but seen as harmful to leadership in others. Even such questionable qualities as risk-taking, cunning, elitism, micromanagement, and willfulness were viewed as positive qualities in some cultures, suggesting that some aspects of leadership are dependent on local norms (Dorfman, Hanges, & Brodbeck, 2004).

**TABLE 9.5 Cross-cultural, Universal Qualities That Are Considered Desirable and Undesirable in a Leader**

| Type | General Dimension | Specific Examples |
|---|---|---|
| **Desirable qualities** | Visionary, inspirational, integrity, group focused, diplomatic, administratively competent, decisive, performance-oriented | Has foresight, plans ahead, dynamic, positive, encouraging, confidence builder, motivational, trustworthy, just, honest, informed, communicative, coordinator, team builder, win–win problem solver, effective bargainer |
| **Undesirable qualities** | Self-centered, malevolent, ruthless, egocentric, face-saver | Asocial, loner, irritable, noncooperative, nonexplicit |

SOURCE: Data from Den Hartog, House, Hanges, Ruiz-Quintanilla, Dorfman et. al., 1999.

was more strongly associated with followers' job satisfaction, satisfaction with the leader, motivational levels, performance quality, and ratings of the leader's effectiveness than transactional leadership—although transactional leadership predicted these positive outcomes as well. Passive forms of leadership were unrelated to these outcomes or were negatively related (Judge & Piccolo, 2004). Meta-analysis also suggests that women tend to be more likely to use transformational styles of leadership, whereas men are more likely to enact laissez-faire and transactional styles (Eagly, Johannesen-Schmidt, & van Engen, 2003; Eagly & Johnson, 1990; van Engen, 2001). Cross-cultural research, as discussed in Focus 9.3, supports Bass's (1997) belief that the transactional–transformational distinction applies across all world cultures. Last, confirming the idea that "there is nothing so practical as a good theory" (Lewin, 1951, p. 169), leadership training programs based on the model have also proven to be a relatively effective means of improving performance in businesses and other organizations (e.g., Dvir et al., 2002).

## The Future of Leadership

The future promises many changes in the nature and application of leadership principles. As organizations continue to become more decentralized—flatter rather than hierarchically organized—leadership methods will likely shift from leader-centered approaches to group-centered ones. Also, the increase in the use of information technologies likely will also change the way leaders interact with their followers, as traditional forms of leadership give way to new forms of *e-leadership* (Avolio, Walumbwa, & Weber, 2009; Coovert & Burke, 2005). Increases in diversity across groups will also create challenges for leaders, particularly if they must adapt their methods and style to match the varied needs of heterogeneous work groups (Hooijberg & DiTomaso, 1996).

The future may see increased numbers of women rising to positions of leadership in groups and organizations. As noted earlier, male and female leaders differ to a degree in their basic approaches to leadership, but the sexes are equivalent when it comes to providing members with task-orientation and relational support (Eagly, Karau, & Makhijani, 1995). However, given that women tend to be participative and transformational leaders rather than autocratic, laissez-faire, and transactional ones, and given that these styles are more effective methods of leadership, as prejudicial biases give way to fairer promotional practices, the Wendy Kopps of the world will become the standard rather than the exception.

# SUMMARY IN OUTLINE

*What is leadership?*

1. Contrary to common myths pertaining to leadership, leadership is neither power over group members nor resisted by them.
   - Certain personality variables are associated with effective leadership, but leadership is not an inborn trait.
   - Not all groups have leaders, but as groups increase in size and complexity, most select someone to lead. The power in all-male groups is more likely to be centralized.
   - Most people prefer to be led rather than be leaderless.
   - Leaders make a difference, for groups prosper when guided by good leaders.
   - People sometimes assume that leaders are so influential that they, and they alone, determine their group's outcomes (the *romance of leadership*).
2. *Leadership* is the process by which an individual guides others in their pursuits, often by organizing, directing, coordinating, supporting, and motivating their efforts. This process can be characterized as reciprocal, transactional, transformational, cooperative, and adaptive.
3. Kelly's theory of *followership* suggests that followers vary along two dimensions: active/passive and independent/dependent. He identifies five types of followers: conformist, passive, pragmatic, alienated, and exemplary.
4. The *task-relationship model* identifies two basic sets, or clusters, of leadership behavior:
   - Task leadership focuses on the group's work and its goals.
   - Relationship leadership focuses on the interpersonal relations within the group.
   - The Ohio State University Leadership Studies identified these clusters, and the *Leader Behavior Description Questionnaire* (LBDQ) assesses both task and relationship leadership.

5. *Leadership substitutes theory* suggests that certain features of the situation can fulfill critical interpersonal and task functions and so reduce the need for a leader.
6. Men tend to be more agentic and task oriented in groups, whereas women are more communal and relationship oriented. The sexes differ only negligibly, however, in their emphasis on task versus relationship leadership when they occupy positions of leadership.

*Who will lead?*

1. Paralleling Carlyle's *great leader theory* and Tolstoy's *zeitgeist theory*, early analyses of *leadership emergence* adopted either a trait model or a situational model. Most modern theories are *interactional* models that base predictions on the reciprocal relationships among the leader, the followers, and the nature of the group situation.
2. Certain personal qualities (traits) are associated with the rise to a position of leadership, including:
   - personality traits, such as extraversion, conscientiousness, and openness. Studies using rotational designs, such as those conducted by Zacarro, suggest that leadership is partly based on personal skills and qualities.
   - intelligence (with groups preferring leaders who are somewhat more intelligent than the average group member) and *emotional intelligence* (degree of social skill).
   - expertise, skill, and experience.
   - level of participation in discussion, for people who speak more in groups are likely to emerge as leaders (the babble effect), although work by Jones and Kelly suggests that quality of comments is more influential than sheer quantity.
3. Leadership is also associated with demographic variables:
   - Leaders tend to be older, taller, and heavier than the average group member.
   - Ethnic minorities and women are less likely to be selected as leaders in groups.
   - The bias against women is ironic because, in general, women possess more of the skills needed to be a successful leader.
4. A number of theories offer an explanation for leadership emergence processes.
   - Lord's *implicit leadership theory* suggests that individuals who act in ways that match the group members' leader prototypes are likely to emerge as leaders.
   - Hogg's *social identity theory* predicts that leaders will closely match the group members' shared prototype of a member.
   - Eagly and her colleagues' *social role theory* maintains that stereotypes of sex roles and leadership roles can create negative expectations for women leaders.
   - *Terror management theory*, like Freud, suggests that individuals may have a deep-seated need for leaders, particularly in times of crisis, when mortality is salient.
   - Evolutionary theory suggests that leadership is an evolutionary adaptation that improves the fitness of both leaders and followers.

*Why do some leaders succeed and others fail?*

1. Fiedler's *contingency theory* suggests that leadership effectiveness is determined by the leader's motivational style and the favorability of the situation.
   - The leader's motivational style can be either task motivated or relationship motivated, as measured by the *Least Preferred Co-Worker Scale (LPC)*.
   - Situational favorability is determined by leader–member relations, the task structure, and the leader's power.
   - Fiedler's theory predicts that task-motivated (low-LPC) leaders will be most effective in situations that are either extremely unfavorable or extremely favorable, whereas

relationship-motivated leaders are most effective in intermediate situations.

2. Leadership style theorists assume that effectiveness depends on the leader's task and relationship behaviors.
   - The *Leadership Grid*, proposed by Blake and Mouton, assumes that people vary in their concern for results and in their concern for people, and that individuals who are high on both dimensions (9,9) are the best leaders.
   - The *situational leadership theory*, proposed by Hersey and Blanchard, suggests that groups benefit from leadership that meshes with the developmental stage of the group.
3. *Leader–member exchange theory (LMX)* focuses on the dyadic relationship linking the leader to each member of the group and notes that in many cases, two subgroups of linkages exist (the inner group and the outer group). Groups with more inner-group members are more productive.
4. Participation theories of leadership extend the early findings of Lewin, Lippitt, and White regarding the effects of autocratic, democratic, and laissez-faire leaders. This approach provides the theoretical and empirical basis for shared leadership models, such as co-leadership, collective leadership, and peer leadership.
5. Transformational theories of leadership examine how charismatic leaders promote change.
   - Burns distinguished between *transactional leaders* and *transformational leaders*, and suggested that the latter are able to elevate both themselves and their followers.
   - Bass identified four components of transformational (rather than transactional) leadership: idealized influence (or charisma), inspirational motivation, intellectual stimulation, and individualized consideration, and they are measured by Bass and Avolio's *Multifactor Leadership Questionnaire.*
   - The GLOBE study has identified transformational leadership as common in cultures across the world.
6. Women tend to adopt participative and transformational styles of leadership, whereas men are more likely to enact autocratic, laissez-faire, and transactional styles. Women's skills are particularly well suited for organizations of the future, which will be less hierarchical and require a collaborative, shared approach to leadership.

## FOR MORE INFORMATION

*Chapter Case: Wendy Kopp*

- *One Day, All Children . . .*, by Wendy Kopp (2003), provides a first-person account of the founder of Teach For America, a highly successful educationally focused nonprofit corporation.

*The Nature of Leadership*

- *Encyclopedia of Leadership*, edited by George R. Goethals, Georgia J. Sorenson, and James McGregor Burns (2004), is a massive compilation of scholarship dealing with all aspects of leaders and leadership: 1927 pages filled with 1.2 million words written by 311 scholars.
- *Leadership in Organizations*, by Gary Yukl (2006), is a masterful integration of theory, research, and application of leadership studies in business and organizations.
- "Leadership: Current Theories, Research, and Future Directions," by Bruce J. Avolio, Fred O. Walumbwa, and Todd J. Weber (2009) is a concise summary of the leading

edge of leadership research, with sections dealing with authentic leadership, implicit leader theory, and e-leadership.

*Theoretical Perspectives*

- *Leadership and Psychology*, edited by Crystal L. Hoyt, George R. Goethals, and Donelson R. Forsyth (2008), collects together in a single volume a variety of papers that examine the relationship between a range of social psychological processes—such as motivation, personality, and social cognition—and leadership.
- *Leadership and the Fate of Organizations*, by Robert B. Kaiser, Robert Hogan, and S. Bartholomew Craig (2008), makes a strong case for examining leadership at the group level.

*Women and Leadership*

- "Women and Leadership," by Crystal L. Hoyt (2007), is a concise review of research examining sex differences in leadership style and effectiveness, with a focus on the impact of sex stereotypes on biases against women as leaders.
- *Through the Labyrinth*, by Alice Eagly and Linda L. Carli (2007), examines closely the findings from hundreds of studies of women and leadership, including trends in biases against women as leaders and differences between men and women in their leadership styles.

## Media Resources

Visit the Group Dynamics companion website at www.cengage.com/psychology/forsyth to access online resources for your book, including quizzes, flash cards, web links, and more!

# 10

# Performance

## CHAPTER OVERVIEW

People join with others in groups to get things done. Groups are the world's workers, protectors, builders, decision makers, and problem solvers. When individuals combine their talents and energies in groups, they accomplish goals that would overwhelm individuals. People working collectively inevitably encounter problems coordinating their efforts and maximizing effort, but groups are the crucible for creativity.

- Do people work better alone or with others?
- Do people work as hard when in groups as they do when working by themselves?
- Why are groups more successful when working on some tasks and not on others?
- What steps can be taken to encourage creativity in groups?

## CHAPTER OUTLINE

**Saturday Night Live: Working with Others in Groups**

Their production schedule was a nightmare. They spent most of Monday thinking up new ideas for Saturday's shows and by the night's end they settled on their favorites. They wrote from that point on until Wednesday, at 3 in the afternoon, when they had the first reading of each sketch. After selecting the ones they would put on the show and scrapping the others, they moved on to production—the blocking of the actors in the shots, the camera angle choices, the lighting, set-design, costuming, rewriting, and rehearsals. By Saturday night, at 11:30 PM, ready or not, the show broadcast live with a "cold open": a skit delivered with no warm-up or explanation, ending with the now stock phrase, "Live from New York: it's Saturday night!"

The show was the product of a ferociously productive and creative group of talents. Lorne Michaels, the producer, was given very little direction by NBC executives other than to develop a show to fill a gap on Saturday night after the news. Michaels set about finding and recruiting a group of writers who would develop the jokes and skits for the show. He also tracked down and put on contract young comics from various improvisational and comedy troupes in the U.S. and Canada. These two groups melded into one as they worked on the show, with writers sometimes taking the stage playing roles in the skits, and the actors developing characters and working on their dialogue.

The result, *Saturday Night Live*, or *SNL*, was an immediate sensation. The first few shows lurched somewhat as the writers and cast found their rhythm and their style, but by the fifth telecast, as Michaels explained, "we sort of hit our stride" (quoted in Shales & Miller, 2002, p. 59). The on-air time for the musical acts and celebrity hosts shrank, and instead the program showcased the talents of the repertory company, who included such future stars as Chevy Chase, John Belushi, Jane Curtin, Gilda Radner, Dan Aykroyd, and Bill Murray. All these group members left the program within its first five years, but *SNL* continues to thrive as each group member is replaced by yet another talented new comic—a group that continues to exist even though its original members have moved on.

Most of the billions of groups in the world exist to get a particular job done. People use groups to discuss problems, concoct plans, forge products, and make decisions. When a task would overwhelm a single person's time, energy, and resources, individuals turn to groups. Even when tasks can be accomplished by people working alone (such as studying group dynamics), people often prefer to work in the company of others. Table 10.1 offers a sampling of various tasks accomplished by groups.

The world relies on groups to achieve its goals, but people sometimes challenge the wisdom of this custom. Although groups sometimes turn out excellent products, they often fall short of expectations. One task force may formulate an effective plan for dealing with a problem, whereas another may create a plan that ends in disaster. A team may practice diligently, yet still play miserably during the big game. A group of talented but untried comedic talents may come together in a moment of great syncopation and create great humor, but over time their productivity may dwindle as personal problems and interpersonal conflicts sap the energy of the group. Why do some groups perform impressively whereas others disappoint? Chapters 11 and 12 examine groups making decisions and working as teams, respectively. This chapter explores productivity and performance in all types of groups, beginning with the simplest type of group situation—two people working side by side on separate tasks—and then progressing to more complex forms of group performance in which members are highly interdependent.

## SOCIAL FACILITATION

Many of the tasks that people must perform each day—cooking, cleaning, dining, studying, writing, reading, watching television, and virtually all forms of work—could be performed in isolation, but rarely do we attempt such tasks sequestered away

**TABLE 10.1 Some of the Many Goals Accomplished by Groups**

| Purpose of the Group | Typical Groups |
|---|---|
| Accomplish heavy, arduous tasks | Construction crew, assembly line, expeditionary team |
| Administer a company or organization | Executive committee, trustees, regents, administrators |
| Advise others | Consulting group |
| Build and repair | Roofers, team of carpenters, auto shop |
| Discover new information | Research team, professional society |
| Effect social change | Citizens action group, political party |
| Entertainment–fine arts | Orchestra, dance company, drama troupe |
| Entertainment–informal | Parties, dinners, cook-outs |
| Entertainment–leisure | Hobby club, discussion group, book club |
| Entertainment–sports | Baseball team, soccer club, intramural team |
| Heal members and nonmembers | Surgery team, emergency room staff |
| Home life and care of relatives | Families, communes, kibbutzim |
| Maintain and enforce the law | Police, citizen security groups, judicial groups |
| Make resources available | Bank, rental agency |
| Observe and celebrate | Patriotic society, veterans' groups |
| Plan strategy, direct others, lead | Executives, board of directors |
| Production | Factory, production line |
| Protect members from harm | Neighborhood watch association, gangs, platoons, police units, army |
| Reduce costs for members | Buyers' cooperative, trade association |
| Reduce monotony | Quilting groups, cohesive work teams |
| Render decisions on guilt | Jury, hearing panel |
| Respond to problems | Firefighters, paramedic squad |
| Set standards for others to follow | Legislative body, ethics review board |
| Solve problems | Committee, commission, task force, research staff |
| Teach and learn | School, class, study group |
| Transport | Airplane crew, ship captain and crew |
| Worship | Religious body, congregation, cult, sangha, ashram |

SOURCE: Adapted from Arrow, McGrath, & Berdahl, 2000; Devine, 2002; Zander, 1985.

from other people. The writers for *Saturday Night Live* (*SNL*) could have worked at their tasks in seclusion, undistracted by others, developing each episode's dialog and sketches. But they chose, instead, to work in a crowded, noisy, endlessly messy office on the 17th floor of the NBC headquarters at Rockefeller Center. Most of them congregated in that space, for they preferred to be collocated rather than separated. Did the presence of other people help them as they developed their creative ideas or were the others a hindrance?

## Studies of Social Facilitation

Norman Triplett (1898) decided to conduct his experiment, one of the first in the field of group dynamics, after watching a series of bicycle races. In some events cyclists raced alone and their performance was timed. Other events were competitions, with cyclists racing each other. In a third type of race a rider was paced by a motor-driven cycle. Invariably, riders achieved their best times when they competed or they were paced, and they were slowest when racing alone.

Many observers at the time thought the differences were caused by drafting: the lead cyclist creates a partial vacuum that pulls followers along while also breaking down wind resistance. Triplett, however, was more interested in "dynamogenic factors":

> The bodily presence of another rider is a stimulus to the racer in arousing the competitive instinct; that another can thus be the means of releasing or freeing nervous energy for him that he cannot of himself release; and, further, that the sight of movement in that other by perhaps suggesting a higher rate of speed, is also an inspiration to greater effort. (p. 516)

To eliminate the possibility of drafting, he arranged for 40 children to perform a simple reel-turning task. When the children turned the reels faster in pairs than when they were alone, Triplett had succeeded in experimentally documenting what is now known as **social facilitation**: the enhancement of an individual's performance when working with other people rather than when working alone. (A reanalysis of Triplett's data using modern statistics confirmed Triplett's conclusions, but the differences between the conditions he studied were not very substantial. In all likelihood, had he performed his study today instead of in 1898 his fellow researchers would have sent him back to his laboratory to find more convincing evidence of those mysterious dynamogenic factors; see Strube, 2005).

**Coaction, Audiences, and Inconsistencies** Triplett studied **coaction**: people working in the presence of other people, but not necessarily interacting with one another. People digging separate holes in a field, taking a test in a classroom, or riding bicycles with friends are common coaction situations that could trigger social facilitation. But researchers soon discovered that social facilitation also occurs when individuals perform for an *audience*. One investigator discovered that audiences can trigger social facilitation when he watched people exercising in a weight room. He noted that people who were watched when working out suddenly could lift heavier weights (Meumann, 1904).

Other studies, however, did not confirm the "presence of people improves performance" effect. Floyd Allport (1920), for example, arranged for participants to complete tasks twice—once while alone in a small testing cubicle, and once with others at a table. To reduce competition, Allport cautioned participants not to compare their scores with one another, and he also told them that he himself would not be making comparisons. He found that people in groups produced more than isolated individuals, but that their products were often lower in quality. Likewise, other researchers sometimes reported gains in performance through coaction or when an audience was watching, but they also documented performance decrements (Aiello & Douthitt, 2001).

**Zajonc's Resolution** Confusion reigned until Robert Zajonc (1965) explained why different studies yielded such divergent results. Some behaviors, he noted, are easier to learn and perform than others. These *dominant responses* are located at the top of the organism's response hierarchy, so they dominate all other potential responses. Behaviors that are part of the organism's behavioral repertoire but are less likely to be performed are *nondominant responses*. Zajonc observed that studies documenting social facilitation focused on well-learned or instinctual responses, such as lifting weights, bicycling, or

---

**social facilitation** Improvement in task performance that occurs when people work in the presence of other people.

**coaction** Performing a task or other type of goal-oriented activity in the presence of one or more other individuals who are performing a similar type of activity.

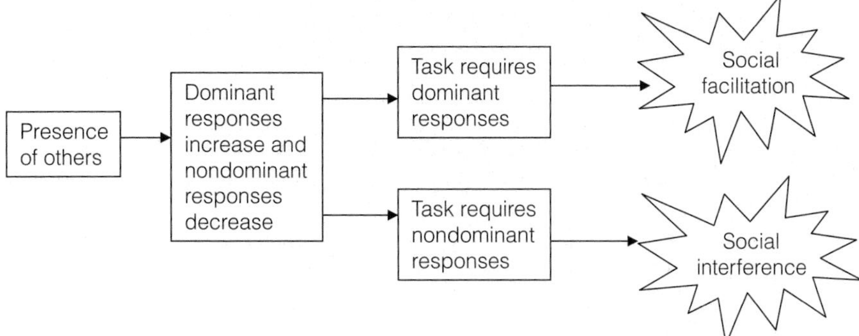


**FIGURE 10.1** Zajonc's theory of social facilitation. Zajonc (1965) integrated previous research by noting that people display more dominant responses, and perform such behaviors more rapidly, when others are present. If the dominant response is appropriate in the situation, the presence of others is facilitating. If, however, the situation calls for a nondominant response, the presence of others will interfere with performance.

eating rapidly. Studies involving novel, complicated, or unpracticed actions, such as solving difficult math problems or writing poetry, usually found little evidence of social facilitation.

Zajonc's insight was that the presence of others increases the tendency to perform dominant responses and decreases the tendency to perform nondominant responses. If the dominant response is the correct or most appropriate response in a particular situation, then social facilitation occurs; people will perform better when others are present than when they are alone. If the task calls for nondominant responses, however, then the presence of other people interferes with performance (see Figure 10.1). Imagine that you must memorize some pairs of words. If the pairs are common associations, such as *blue–sky* or *clean–dirty*, then the task is an easy one, for which the dominant response is correct. Hence, your performance will be better if other people are present. If, however, you are trying to learn some uncommon associations—such as *blue–dynamogenic* or *clean–nondominant*—then you are required to make a nondominant response and an audience will hurt more than help.

Zajonc's analysis has been supported by a number of studies, including those sampled in Table 10.2 and discussed in Focus 10.1. Consistent with the distinction between dominant and nondominant responses, the effect is strongest when speed and quantity count more than correctness and quality. One meta-analysis of 241 different studies of nearly 24,000 human subjects verified that people work faster and produce more when others are present and they work at simple tasks. Rarely, though, did the presence of others enhance the quality of performance even on simple tasks, and the presence of others decreased both the quantity and quality of work on complex tasks. Overall, the gains that occurred when people worked together on simple tasks were not as great as the losses that occurred when people worked on complex tasks (Bond & Titus, 1983).

### Why Does Social Facilitation Occur?

The situations studied by Triplett and Zajonc barely qualify as groups, for they involved strangers working on individualized tasks without any interaction, influence, shared identity, or common goals. Yet, even in these circumstances the mere presence of others was sufficient to improve performance when tasks were simple and interfere with performance when tasks were difficult. Zajonc's analysis explained *when* social facilitation occurs, but the *why* is less certain (see Aiello & Douthitt, 2001; Strauss, 2002; Uziel, 2007).

**Drive Processes** Zajonc coined the word *compresence* to describe the state of responding in the presence of others. Compresence, he hypothesized, touches off a basic arousal response in most social species "simply

**TABLE 10.2 A Sampling of Empirical Demonstrations of Social Facilitation and Inhibition**

| Situation | Findings |
|---|---|
| Making speeches | When asked to write out as many words as they could in response to a word, most people (93%) produced more words when another person was present than when they were alone (Allport, 1920). When this study was replicated with individuals who stuttered when they spoke, 80% of the subjects produced more words when alone rather than with another person (Travis, 1928). |
| Handwriting | College students were told to copy a list of words as quickly as they could. For one list they wrote with their dominant hand (easy task), but for the other list they used their nondominant hand (hard task). They completed the task in the presence of an image of their favorite television personality (displayed on a computer screen) or an image of another character from the same program. When the task was easy they wrote more words in the presence of their favorite character; when the task was difficult, the favorite character inhibited their performance (Gardner & Knowles, 2008). |
| Getting dressed | People were asked to perform a familiar task (taking off their own shoes and socks) and a less familiar task (putting on a robe that tied in the back) when alone and when with another person. People removed their shoes and socks three seconds faster if another person was in the room. They were even faster—by two seconds on average—when the observer watched as they removed their footwear. In contrast, they donned the unfamiliar clothes more slowly when the observer was present and watchful (Markus, 1978). |
| Shooting pool | People playing pool were surreptitiously watched to identify skilled and unskilled players. Skilled players made at least two-thirds of their shots, and unskilled players missed at least two-thirds. The observer then moved near the pool table and watched their play. Skilled players' performance improved 14% when they were observed, but unskilled players' performance dropped by more than 30% (Michaels et al., 1982) |
| Driver's test | Individuals seeking their license to drive an automobile took their driving test with only the tester in the car or with another test-taker in the car, seated in the rear seat. Forty-nine percent of the applicants passed the test when alone, but only 34% passed when an audience was present (Rosenbloom et al., 2007). |
| Jogging | Solitary women jogging along a footpath encountered, when they rounded a bend, a woman who either watched them as they ran or sat facing away from them. Joggers accelerated when they encountered the watchful observer (Worringham & Messick, 1983). |

because one never knows, so to speak, what sorts of responses—perhaps even novel and unique—may be required in the next few seconds" when others are nearby (Zajonc, 1980, p. 50). Zajonc believed that compresence in and of itself elevated drive levels, and these elevated drives triggered social facilitation when tasks were so easy that only dominant responses are needed to perform them.

Zajonc's **drive theory** uniquely predicts that social facilitation will occur even when all forms of social interaction, communication, and evaluation between the individual and the observer are blocked. Investigators tested this hypothesis by asking people to work on simple or complex tasks in the presence of an "observer" who was blindfolded and wore earplugs. Even though the observer could not interact with participants in any way, his mere presence still enhanced their performance when they worked on simple tasks and slowed their performance on complex ones (Schmitt et al., 1986).

But do people actually show signs of physiological changes whenever they are joined by other

**drive theory** In general, an analysis of human motivation that stresses the impact of psychological or physiological needs or desires on individuals' thoughts, feelings, and actions; also an explanation of social facilitation proposed by Robert Zajonc, which maintains that the presence of others evokes a generalized drive state characterized by increased readiness and arousal.

**Focus 10.1 Is Social Facilitation a Uniquely Human Phenomenon?**

Social facilitation is not limited to *Homo sapiens*: horses, puppies, chickens, mice, rats, monkeys, armadillos, ants, beetles, and opossums are on the list of animals that show signs of increased performance in the presence of other members of their species (Clayton, 1978). Even the lowly cockroach will work harder when surrounded by other cockroaches. As anyone who has surprised a roach in the kitchen late at night knows, cockroaches run from bright lights. So Zajonc and his colleagues (1969) designed two mazes with a start box near a light and a goal box hidden from the light. One maze was easy, even for a roach—just a straight runway from start to the goal. The second maze was more complex: the roaches had to turn to the right to reach their goal. Zajonc then timed how quickly 72 roaches (*Blatta orientalis*) completed the mazes when alone, when with another roach, or when watched by other cockroaches—although we cannot be sure the spectator roaches actually watched. They were sealed in small plastic boxes adjacent to the mazes, with holes allowing air to circulate between spectator and subject.

Zajonc's findings were consistent with the findings from studies of humans. In the simple maze, single roaches reached home base in an average of 40.6 seconds. Coacting roaches trimmed 7.6 seconds off this time, returning in just 33 seconds flat. This tendency reversed when the maze was complex: Single roaches crawled to the finish line 19.6 seconds faster than did coacting roaches. Roaches watched by an audience were the slowest contestants of all, but they were particularly slow when the maze was complex—taking nearly two minutes longer than single roaches.

humans? Researchers have found evidence of increased heart rate and blood pressure, with the impact of physiological effects dependent on the type of situation and on who is watching. James Blascovich and his colleagues (1999), for example, verified that an audience triggers increases in cardiac and vascular reactivity. Blascovich's team also discovered, however, that this arousal was physiologically very different when people worked on an easy task rather than on a hard one. When the task was easy, people displayed a *challenge response*. At the physiological level, they appeared to be ready to respond to the challenge that they faced (elevated heart rate and sympathetic nervous system activation). But when the task was difficult, people displayed a *threat response*; they appeared to be stressed rather than ready for effective action. Other studies found that the presence of certain people—such as close friends—can have a calming rather than an arousing influence. When women performed a difficult math test with a friend who was merely present—the friend could touch the participant's wrist but was preoccupied with another task and was wearing a headset that blocked all sound—the participant's cardiovascular responses were lowered (Kamarck, Manuck, & Jennings, 1990).

Psychoneurologists have also offered suggestive evidence of the basic neurological reactivity of the human brain to the presence of other humans. A team of researchers used a functional magnetic resonance imaging (fMRI) scanner to image volunteers' brains while they were looking at 36 video clips of a single individual followed by a short segment of that individual interacting with another person. While watching these clips, areas of the volunteers' brains that are thought to be dedicated to monitoring social information (the medial parietal and dorsomedial prefrontal cortices) showed signs of increased activity, suggesting that simply seeing other human beings triggers a cortical reaction. The scans showed that these areas of the brain were more active when people watched the clip of the interaction, but they also responded when people watched a clip of just a single person. The investigators concluded that "thinking about social relationships is apparently part of the brain's default state circuitry" (Iacoboni et al., 2004, p. 1171).

**Motivational Processes** Many of the writers of *SNL* had worked for years writing material that they sold to other comics and shows. If the joke was a dud, the only consequence was that no one bought it. But working in a group was different. When they offered up an idea to the others during a late-night session on the 17th floor they could face ridicule and embarrassment. The group was a tough audience.

Nickolas Cottrell (1972) suggested that this evaluative pressure is one of the reasons why people tend to be more productive in the presence of others. His **evaluation apprehension theory** assumes that individuals have learned through experience that other people are the source of most of the rewards and punishments they receive. Thus, individuals learn to associate social situations with evaluation, so they feel apprehensive whenever other people are nearby. This evaluation apprehension enhances performance on simple tasks, but it becomes debilitating when people attempt more difficult projects. Cottrell thus believed that apprehension, and not the arousal response identified by Zajonc, is the source of social facilitation effects.

**Self-presentation theory** also underscores the motivational impact of evaluation apprehension (Goffman, 1959). Self-presentation theory assumes that group members actively control others' impressions of themselves by displaying social behaviors that establish and maintain a particular social image, or *face*. Group members do not want the others to think that they possess negative, shameful qualities and characteristics, so they strive to make a good impression. Performance situations create self-presentational challenges for members, particularly when they feel they might fail. To avoid that embarrassment, group members redouble their efforts when self-presentational pressures are strong—as they were in the *SNL* group (Bond, Atoum, & VanLeeuwen, 1996).

The primary hypothesis that derives uniquely from such motivational models—that any stimulus increasing the organism's apprehension over future rewards or punishments should increase drive levels—has received some support. When people find themselves in evaluative situations, they tend to perform dominant rather than nondominant responses (Seta et al., 1989). When, for example, individuals who were watched by an observer were told that the observer was evaluating them, their performance improved, but only when they were working on a simple task (Bartis, Szymanski, & Harkins, 1988). When people who had already failed once tried the task a second time, they performed worse when others were present (Seta & Seta, 1995). Also, situational factors that decrease evaluation apprehension, such as allowing for private responses, unevaluative audiences, and the absence of a definable task that can be evaluated, often eliminate social facilitation effects (Henchy & Glass, 1968). Finally, individuals who are highly confident perform better when evaluated by others, whereas those who doubt their ability perform better when alone (Sanna, 1992).

The presence of other people—even friends—also increases physiological reactivity if these friends are evaluative. As noted earlier, people were more relaxed when working on a task with a friend nearby. Their friend, however, was wearing earphones and could not evaluate the participant's performance (Kamarck et al., 1990). What would happen if the friend was a potential source of evaluation? When people are watched closely by a friend, they tend to show signs of physiological arousal rather than relaxation. In fact, people are more relaxed when they are with their pets rather than with other people. Pets are an ideal source of social support, for they provide reassurance through their presence but they do not (we assume) evaluate their owner's performance (Allen et al., 1991; Allen, Blascovich, & Mendes, 2002).

Other findings, though, do not support this emphasis on evaluation. Even when the companion refrains from attending to the individual in any way, social facilitation still occurs (Berger, 1981; Platania & Moran, 2001). As Focus 10.1 notes, animals that likely lack the capacity to feel nervous or embarrassed—rats, armadillos, and roaches, for

---

**evaluation apprehension theory** An analysis of performance gains in groups arguing that individuals working in the presence of others experience a general concern for how these others are evaluating them, and that this apprehension facilitates their performance on simple, well-learned tasks.

**self-presentation theory** An analysis of performance gains in groups assuming that social facilitation is caused by individuals striving to make a good impression when they work in the presence of others.

example—perform simple tasks better when other members of their species are present. Moreover, activities that involve little threat of evaluation, such as eating, drinking, or getting dressed, still show social facilitation effects.

**Cognitive Processes** Zajonc stressed drive levels, Cottrell underscored the importance of evaluation, but several cognitive theories have suggested that the presence of others changes people's capacity to process information adequately. When people work in the presence of other people, they must split their attention between the task they are completing and the other person (Guerin & Innes, 1982). The presence of an audience may also increase individuals' self-awareness, and as a result, they may focus their attention on themselves and fail to pay sufficient attention to the task (Mullen & Baumeister, 1987).

Distractions, however, do not inevitably undermine performance. **Distraction-conflict theory** suggests that distraction interferes with the attention given to the task, but that these distractions can be overcome with effort. Therefore, on simple tasks that require dominant responses, the interference effects are inconsequential compared with the improvement that results from concentrating on the task, so performance is facilitated. On more complex tasks, the increase in drive is insufficient to offset the effects of distraction, and performance is therefore impaired (Baron, 1986; Sanders, Baron, & Moore, 1978).

Clearly, people are a distraction—the stories of the interpersonal dramas, the sexual intrigue, the drug abuse, and the playful shenanigans of the *SNL* group as they worked and played together make one wonder how they managed to get anything accomplished. But, oddly enough, if people are working in the presence of other people and those people are not at all distracting, then social facilitation does not occur even when tasks are simple ones (Bond et al., 1996; Sanders et al., 1978). Distractions have also been shown to improve performance on certain tasks, such as the *Stroop Task*. In the Stroop task, participants are shown a color name (e.g., *Red*, *Blue*) printed in a primary color (such as red or blue) and asked to name the color of the *ink*. For example, if the word *Red* is printed in blue ink, the participant should answer *blue*. When the ink and the color word match, people have no problems. But when the ink and the color word are incongruent, reaction time and errors increase. These errors, however, decrease when individuals complete the task with others. The presence of others may work by helping people narrow their focus of attention, and thereby filter out the distracting color name cue (Huguet et al., 1999). The effect may also be due to the (a) extra cognitive demands imposed on participants by the presence of the observer and the need to evaluate the task itself (Klauer, Herfordt, Voss, 2008), or (b) increased attentional focusing on the task that is triggered by a threat of self-evaluation (Muller & Butera, 2007).

**Personality Processes** Alan Zwiebel, one of the *SNL* writers, talks of how he was so intimidated by the pressure of the talented group that he hid behind a potted plant during the first writing session until Gilda Radner coaxed him out. In contrast, Chevy Chase and writer Michael O'Donoghue thrived under the pressure; they accepted the challenge of the evaluation and it motivated them to work even harder.

**Social orientation theory** suggests that people differ in their overall orientation towards social situations, and these individual differences in social orientation predict who will show facilitation in the presence of others and who will show impairment.

---

**distraction-conflict theory** An analysis of performance gains in groups assuming that when others are present, attention is divided between the other people and the task; this attentional conflict increases motivation, and so it facilitates performance on simple, well-learned tasks.

**social orientation theory** An analysis of performance gains in groups suggesting individual differences in social orientation (the tendency to approach social situations apprehensively or with enthusiasm) predict when social facilitation will occur.

According to this theory, individuals who display a *positive orientation* are so self-confident that they react positively to the challenge the group may throw their way; for them, there is "safety in numbers." Others, in contrast, display a *negative orientation*. They approach social situations apprehensively, for they feel inhibited and threatened by other people. People may be capable of adopting either orientation in a given situation, but people tend to be dispositionally either positive or negative in their orientations. Some people, like Chase, are naturally positive in their orientation toward tasks. Others, like Zwiebel, possess personality traits that prompt them to be more negative, such as low self-esteem, self-consciousness, and anxiety. A meta-analysis of previous studies of social facilitation, focusing on only those studies that included measures that might be indicators of participants' degree of positive or negative orientation, supported the theory. Individuals with qualities that suggested their social orientation was positive usually showed social facilitation effects, whereas those with a negative orientation showed a social interference effect (Uziel, 2007).

### Conclusions and Applications

Social facilitation occurs because humans, as social beings, respond in predictable ways when joined by other members of their species (see Table 10.3). Some of these reactions, as Zajonc suggested, are very basic ones, for the mere presence of other people elevates drive levels. But arousal becomes more substantial when group members realize that the people around them are evaluating them and might form a negative impression of them if they perform badly. Cognitive and personality

**TABLE 10.3 Four General Explanations of Social Facilitation**

| Theory | Mediating Process | Evidence |
|---|---|---|
| Drive theory (Zajonc, 1965) | *Unlearned drive*: The mere presence of others elevates drive levels; this drive triggers social facilitation when tasks are so easy that only dominant responses are needed to perform them. | ■ People show signs of physiological arousal when others are present<br>■ Many species perform basic tasks more efficiently in the presence of other species members<br>■ Facilitative arousal occurs primarily for simple tasks |
| Evaluation apprehension theory (Cottrell, 1972) | *Motivational process*: Through experience, people learn to associate the presence of others with evaluation; this concern for evaluation facilitates performance on well-learned tasks. | ■ The presence of others is facilitative only when the observers can evaluate the quality of the performance<br>■ Facilitative effects are strongest when individuals are striving to make a good impression |
| Distraction-conflict theory (Baron, 1986; Sanders, 1981) | *Cognitive process*: When others are present, attention is divided between the other people and the task; attentional conflict increases motivation, which facilitates performance so long as the task is a simple one. | ■ Recall is poorer when stimulus is presented in presence of others, suggesting others are distracting<br>■ Facilitation is reduced if the others in the situation are not noticed<br>■ Presence of others improves performance on interference tasks (e.g., the *Stroop Task*) |
| Social orientation theory (Uziel, 2007) | *Personality process*: Individuals who display a positive interpersonal orientation are more likely to display social facilitation effects. | ■ Presence of others improves performance among individuals with high self-esteem and low anxiety<br>■ Those with an attention-seeking tendency (exhibitionism) perform better than self-conscious individuals in coaction settings |

## Focus 10.2 Are Groups Good for the Appetite?

*A good meal tastes better if we eat it in the company of friends.*

—Harry F. Harlow (1932, p. 211)

One of the most ubiquitous of all groups is the one that eats. At breakfast, lunch, dinner, feasts, fêtes, and snack time, people gather to consume nutrition as a group. Most people report that they prefer to eat with others rather than dine alone (Clendenen et al., 1994). A shared meal, however, is a complex interpersonal event that sets the stage for social facilitation. When researchers ask people to keep track of how much they eat and whom they eat with, they usually find that people eat more—sometimes 40% to 50% more—when they dine in groups (e.g., de Castro et al., 1997; Patel & Schlundt, 2001). As meals eaten by groups are longer in duration than the ones eaten by solo individuals, people have more opportunity to keep eating when in groups than alone. Watching someone else eat also increases social imitation of the eating response. When the participants in one study witnessed another person eating 20 soda crackers, they ate far more crackers themselves than did participants who saw someone eat only one (Nisbett & Storms, 1974). People even seem to prepare relatively larger portions for meals to be eaten in groups than individually, as if they anticipate that the group members will be able to consume more than they would if alone. So long as the group does not include a substantial portion of dieters, the group may continue to eat until all the available food is consumed. Solitary eaters are more likely to eat only until they are sated (Herman, Roth, & Polivy, 2003). In general, larger groups trigger greater increases in eating, although at a decreasing rate, similar to response patterns suggested by social impact theory (Latané, 1981).

Groups do not always facilitate eating, however. Women who are introverted and anxious are less likely to be motivated to eat in groups; in fact, they are more likely to display symptoms of eating disorders, such as bulimia (Miller et al., 2006). The social facilitation of eating is weak when co-eaters are strangers or disliked, and strongest when people dine with families and friends. Social facilitation of eating is also limited to coaction rather than audience situations. People eat more when others with them are eating, but they tend to eat less when the other people who are present are observing them. One explanation for the inhibiting impact of others on eating suggests that the observers may trigger excessive evaluation apprehension, so individuals may reduce their consumption because they expect that observers will not think well of them if they eat too much. Diners may also engage in social comparison as they eat, for only by comparing their own consumption amounts to those of others at the table can they determine if they are eating too much or too little (Herman et al., 2003).

mechanisms that govern how individuals process information and monitor the environment also come into play when people work in the presence of others. As the following examples and Focus 10.2 illustrate, these physiological, motivational, cognitive, and personality processes influence group members' reactions across a wide range of performance settings.

**Prejudice and Social Facilitation** *Prejudices* are deeply ingrained negative attitudes about the members of other groups. Such prejudices as racism and sexism are increasingly recognized as unfair and socially inappropriate, so individuals who are prejudiced often try to keep their prejudices to themselves to avoid being labeled a racist or sexist (Kleinpenning & Hagendoorn, 1993). But prejudice is often a well-learned, *dominant* response; so, ironically, the presence of other people may lead individuals to express even more biased opinions when they are in public rather than in private. The presence of others may work to facilitate prejudice, rather than keep it in check (Lambert et al., 1996; Lambert et al., 2003).

**Electronic Performance Monitoring (EPM)** Social facilitation is not limited to face-to-face, or collocated, group settings. The *presence* of others in a virtual sense—made possible when people join with others via computers, telephones, or other communication systems—can also enhance performance on simple tasks but undermine performance on complicated ones. John Aiello, for example, drew on studies of social facilitation in his analyses of **electronic performance monitoring**, or **EPM**. Many businesses can now track the performance of their employees throughout the workday with computer information networks. When workers use their computer to enter data, communicate with one another, or search databases for stored information, their activity can be monitored automatically. Does EPM enhance performance, or does it create so much evaluation anxiety that performance suffers? Aiello found that EPM may enhance employees' productivity, but in ways that are consistent with social facilitation effects. He studied people working on a data entry task. Some were alone, some were working with others, and some were members of a cohesive group. Aiello discovered that EPM enhanced the performance of highly skilled workers, but interfered with the performance of less skilled participants. Monitoring also increased workers' feeling of stress, except among those who were part of a cohesive work group (Aiello & Kolb, 1995). Individuals responded more positively to monitoring when they believed that they could turn off the monitoring and that only their job-related activities were being monitored, as well as when they had the opportunity to participate in decisions about the use of the monitoring system (Alge, 2001; Douthitt & Aiello, 2001).

**Social Facilitation in Educational Settings** Groups are used in a variety of ways in educational settings (small seminars, group discussions, problem-based learning teams, etc.), but perhaps the most common of all educational collectives is the **study group**. Unlike groups created and monitored by the instructor, study groups are self-organized and self-directive, for they are formed by students themselves for the purpose of studying course material.

"Join a study group" is the advice often given to college students who are struggling in their classes, but do study groups fulfill their promise? Study groups offer members some advantages over studying alone. Some groups enhance members' motivation and help students stay focused on their academic goals (Gillies, 2007). Moreover, if students receive useful instruction from other group members, then students who are members of study groups outperform students who do not study in groups (Webb, Troper, & Fall, 1995). Students who are committed to their groups and value the learning experiences they provide generally outperform students who react negatively to such groups (Freeman, 1996).

Study group, however, may inhibit the acquisition of new concepts and skills. The presence of others can be distracting, and during the early phases of learning, this distraction can interfere with learning. The presence of other people also interferes with overt and covert practicing. When the participants in one project needed to learn a list of words, they were too embarrassed to rehearse the material by saying it aloud, and their performance suffered (Berger et al., 1981). Studies of athletes acquiring new skills, of students learning a second language, and of clinicians developing their therapeutic skills have indicated that learning proceeds more rapidly, at least initially, when learners work alone (Berger et al., 1982; Ferris & Rowland, 1983; MacCracken & Stadulis, 1985; Schauer, Seymour, & Geen, 1985). Once they have learned their skills, however, people should perform with others present if possible (Utman, 1997). Zajonc suggested the student

> study all alone, preferably in an isolated cubicle, and arrange to take his examinations in the company of many other students, on stage, and in the presence of a large audience. The results of his examination would be beyond his wildest expectations, provided, of course, he had learned his material quite thoroughly. (Zajonc, 1965, p. 274)

---

**electronic performance monitoring (EPM)** The use of information technologies, such as computer networks, to track, analyze, and report information about workers' performance.

**study group** A self-organized, self-directive group formed by students for the purpose of studying course material.

## PROCESS LOSSES IN GROUPS

The *SNL* writers and actors were very productive, but given their level of talent and comedic genius, did they reach their full potential? Some of the group members, when asked about their experiences, recalled that some of the writers and actors did not pull their weight. One writer, for example, felt that he and a few others were "coming up with the show almost every week," while the others "were hopeless. They did nothing." Another admitted that he did not do all that much writing for the show because he was more interested in the music: "I spent a lot of time with the *SNL* band" instead of working, he explained (Shales & Miller, 2002, p. 214, 215).

Why might people working on group tasks fail to be as productive as they could be? Ivan Steiner (1972), in his classic work *Group Process and Productivity*, drew on the concept of **process losses** to provide an answer. Steiner recognized that groups have great potential, for their resources, expertise, and abilities outstrip those of any single individual. But Steiner also realized that groups rarely reach their full potential because a variety of interpersonal processes detracts from their overall proficiency. His "law" of group productivity predicts that

*Actual productivity* = *Potential productivity*
− *Losses owing to faulty processes*

Thus, even when a group includes skilled members who possess all the resources they need to accomplish their tasks, faulty group processes may prevent them from succeeding. When process losses proliferate, the group's chance to become greater than the sum of its parts dwindles.

### The Ringelmann Effect

Max Ringelmann (1913), a 19th-century French agricultural engineer, was one of the first researchers to study the relationship between process loss and group productivity. Ringelmann's questions were practical ones: How many oxen should be yoked in one team? Should you plow a field with two horses or three? Can five men turn a mill crank faster than four? But Ringelmann, instead of speculating about the answers to these questions, set up teams of varying sizes and measured their collective power.

Ringelmann's most startling discovery was that workers—and that includes horses, oxen, and men—all become less productive in groups. A group of five writers developing funny skits can easily outperform a single person, just as a team pulling a rope is stronger than a single opponent or an audience applauding makes more noise than an individual. But even though a group outperforms an individual, the group does not usually work at maximum efficiency. When Ringelmann had individuals and groups pull on a rope attached to a pressure gauge, groups performed below their theoretical capabilities (Steiner, 1972). If person A and person B could each pull 100 units when they worked alone, could they pull 200 units when they pooled their efforts? No, their output reached only 186. A three-person group did not produce 300 units, but only 255. An eight-person group managed only 392, not 800. Groups certainly outperformed individuals—but as more and more people were added, the group became increasingly inefficient (see Figure 10.2). To honor its discoverer, this tendency for groups to become less productive as group size increases is now known as the **Ringelmann effect** (Kravitz & Martin, 1986, present an excellent summary and interpretation of Ringelmann's work.)

Ringelmann identified two key sources of process losses when people worked together. First, Ringelmann believed some of the decline in

---

**process loss** Reduction in performance effectiveness or efficiency caused by actions, operations, or dynamics that prevent the group from reaching its full potential, including reduced effort, faulty group processes, coordination problems, and ineffective leadership.

**Ringelmann effect** The tendency, first documented by Max Ringelmann, for people to become less productive when they work with others; this loss of efficiency increases as group size increases, but at a gradually decreasing rate.

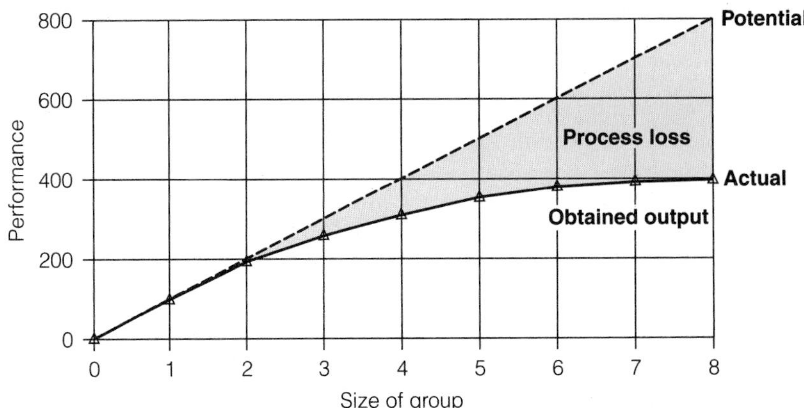


**FIGURE 10.2** The Ringelmann effect. Ringelmann (1913) recorded how much work single individuals did as well as the output of groups ranging in size from two to eight members. If a group's performance was based strictly on members' individual efforts, then a two-person group could produce 200 units, a three-person group could produce 300 units, and so on. Ringelmann found much less productivity. The means for his groups were 186, 255, 308, 350, 378, 392, and 392.

SOURCE: Based on data presented in Group Processes and Productivity by I.D. Steiner. © 1972 by Academic Press

productivity was caused by *motivation losses*: people may not work so hard when they are in groups. Second, *coordination losses*, caused by "the lack of simultaneity of their efforts" (Ringelmann, 1913, p. 9), also interfere with performance. Even on a simple task, such as rope pulling, people tend to pull and pause at different times, resulting in a failure to reach their full productive potential. In the next section, we consider the role these two processes—loss of motivation and coordination problems—play in preventing groups from reaching their full potential.

### Motivation Loss: Social Loafing

Ringelmann documented what others had noticed: People sometimes do not work as hard as they could when they are part of a group. After watching a group of prisoners turning the crank of a flour mill, for example, he noted that their performance was "mediocre because after only a little while, each man, trusting in his neighbor to furnish the desired effort, contented himself by merely following the movement of the crank, and sometimes even let himself be carried along by it" (p. 10; translation from Kravitz & Martin, 1986, p. 938). This reduction of effort by individuals working in groups is known as **social loafing** (Williams, Harkins, & Latané, 1981).

People carrying out all sorts of physical and mental tasks—including brainstorming, evaluating employees, monitoring equipment, interpreting instructions, and formulating causal judgments—have been shown to exert less effort when they combine their efforts in a group situation. Even worse, loafing seems to go unrecognized by group members. When people in groups are asked if they are working as hard as they can, they generally claim that they are doing their best, even though the objective evidence indicates that they are loafing. Evidently, people are not aware that they are loafing, or they are simply unwilling to admit it (Karau & Williams, 1993).

Bibb Latané, Kipling Williams, and Stephen Harkins examined social loafing by studying groups performing an extremely easy task: making noise. They told the men who participated that they

---

**social loafing** The reduction of individual effort exerted when people work in groups compared to when they work alone.

were researching "the effects of sensory feedback on the production of sound in social groups," and that all they needed to do was to cheer as loudly as they could. They asked the participants to wear blindfolds and headsets, so their performance would not be influenced by "the effects of sensory feedback" (1979, p. 824). They then asked participants to shout as loudly as they could while the headsets played a stream of loud noise. Consistent with the Ringelmann effect, groups of participants made more noise than individuals, but groups failed to reach their potential. When the participants were tested alone, they averaged a rousing 9.22 dynes/cm$^2$ (about as loud as a pneumatic drill). In dyads, each participant shouted at only 66% of capacity, and in six-person groups, at 36%. This drop in productivity is charted in Figure 10.3 (Latané, Williams, & Harkins, 1979, Experiment 2, p. 826; see also Harkins, Latané, & Williams, 1980; Williams et al., 1981).

But how much was this drop in productivity due to social loafing and how much due to coordination problems? Latané and his colleagues separated out these sources of process loss by testing noise production in "pseudogroups." In these conditions, participants were led to believe that either one other participant or five other participants were shouting with them, but in actuality, they were working alone. (The blindfolds and headsets made this deception possible.) Thus, any loss of production obtained in these pseudogroup conditions could not be due to coordination problems, because there were no other group members shouting. Instead, any decline in production could only be blamed on the reduced effort brought about by social loafing. As Figure 10.3 indicates, when participants thought that one other person was working with them, they shouted only 82% as intensely, and if they thought that five other persons were shouting, they reached only 74% of their capacity. These findings suggest that even if work groups are so well organized that virtually all losses due to faulty coordination are eliminated, individual productivity might still be below par because of social loafing.

## Causes of and Cures for Social Loafing

Many of the members of *SNL* never loafed. Dan Aykroyd, Lorne Michaels, and Rosie Shuster, for example, worked very long days and took on a variety of tasks to make certain that the group's

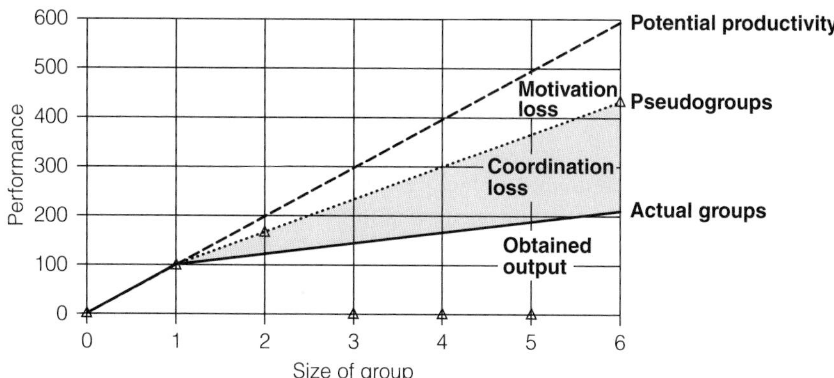


**FIGURE 10.3** Social loafing and coordination losses in groups. Latané and his colleagues disentangled the two major causes of productivity losses in groups working on additive tasks by leading people to think they were working in groups when they actually were not. The people in these "groups" (labeled the "pseudogroups") suffered from motivation loss, but not from coordination loss since they were actually working alone. The unshaded portion represents motivation loss (social loafing), and the lightly shaded portion represents coordination loss. They combine to create the Ringelmann effect.

SOURCE: Adapted from "Many hands make light the work: The causes and consequences of social loafing: by B. Latané, K. Williams, & S. Harkins, Journal of Personality and Social Psychology, 37, 1979.

performances would be successful. For every slack group member—workers leaning on their shovels instead of digging with them, meetings that degenerate into gabfests, task forces that perform no tasks—there are those who strive to reach new levels of efficiency and productivity. So what can be done to reduce the level of social loafing in a group?

**Increase Identifiability** Studies of social loafing suggest that people are *less* productive when they work with others. But studies of social facilitation, discussed earlier in this chapter, find that people are *more* productive when others are present (at least when the task is easy). Which is it?

Both. When people feel as though their level of effort cannot be ascertained because the task is a collective one, then social loafing becomes likely. But when people feel that they are being evaluated, they tend to exert more effort, and their productivity increases. If the task is an individualistic one, and is easy, the presence of other people increases evaluation apprehension, so social facilitation occurs. But when group members are anonymous, and their contributions are unidentifiable, the presence of others reduces evaluation apprehension, and social loafing becomes more likely (Arterberry, Cain, & Chopko, 2007; Harkins & Szymanski, 1987, 1988; Jackson & Latané, 1981).

Researchers illustrated the importance of evaluation by asking the members of a four-person group to generate as many ideas as possible for a common object. The participants did not discuss their ideas out loud but simply wrote them on slips of paper. Some of the participants thought that their ideas were individually identifiable, whereas others thought that their ideas were being collected in a common pool. Moreover, some participants believed that everyone was devising uses for the same object, but others thought that each group member was working with a different object. In this study, loafing occurred not only when ideas were pooled, but also when the participants believed that their individual outputs were not comparable or could not be evaluated (Harkins & Jackson, 1985). When each individual member's output was identifiable, on the other hand, loafing was virtually eliminated (Hardy & Latané, 1986; Kerr & Bruun, 1981; Sanna, 1992; Williams et al., 1981).

**Minimize Free Riding** Thousands of people listen to public radio without making a contribution when the radio asks for donations. Some audience members do not clap during the call for an encore because they know their applause will not be missed. Many students avoid group projects where the entire group receives the same grade, because inevitably one or more members of the group will not do their share of the work (Hoffman & Rogelberg, 2001).

All these situations invite **free riding**—members doing less than their share of the work because others will make up for their slack. Although norms of fairness warn members to do their part, if they feel that the group does not need them or their contribution, they will be tempted to free-ride. When group members think that they are an indispensable part of the group—perhaps because their contribution is unique or essential for the group's success—they work harder (Kerr & Bruun, 1983). They also free-ride less in smaller groups, because each person plays a larger role in determining the group's outcomes (Kameda et al., 1992). But free riding sometimes increases when members become suspicious of the level of effort being invested by the other group members. Rather than looking like a "sucker" by working harder than the others, group members reduce their efforts to match the level that they think other group members are expending. This **sucker effect** is strongest when they feel that their fellow group members are competent but lazy (Hart, Bridgett, & Karau, 2001).

---

**free riding** Contributing less to a collective task when one believes that other group members will compensate for this lack of effort.

**sucker effect** The tendency for individuals to contribute less to a group endeavor when they expect that others will think negatively of someone who works too hard or contributes too much (considering them to be a "sucker").

**Set Goals** Groups that set clear, challenging goals outperform groups whose members have lost sight of their objectives. When truck drivers who hauled logs from the woods to the mill were initially told to do their best when loading the logs, the men only carried about 60% of what they could legally haul (Latham & Baldes, 1975). When the drivers were later encouraged to reach a goal of 94% of the legal limit, they increased their efficiency and met this specific goal. In a study of groups generating ideas, members were more productive when they had a clear standard by which to evaluate the quality of their own work and the group's work (Harkins & Szymanski, 1989). Other research has suggested that clear goals stimulate a number of production-enhancing processes, including increases in effort, better planning, more accurate monitoring of the quality of the group's work, and increased commitment to the group (Weldon, Jehn, & Pradhan, 1991). The group's goals should also be challenging rather than too easily attained. The advantages of working in a group are lost if the task is so easy that it can be accomplished even if the group loafs, so care should be taken to set the standards high—but not so high that they are unattainable (Hinsz, 1995; Latham & Locke, 2007; Weldon & Weingart, 1993).

**Increase Involvement** Loafing is less likely when people are involved in their work. Those who enjoy working with other people in groups, because they value both the group experience and the results they achieve, are less likely to loaf compared to less group- and achievement-oriented individuals (Stark, Shaw, & Duffy, 2007). So long as the competition remains "friendly," group members may persevere with much greater intensity when they are vying with others in the group for the best score (Hinsz, 2005). Challenging, difficult tasks reduce loafing, but so do ones that will determine group members' personal outcomes—either by reward or by punishment (Brickner, Harkins, & Ostrom, 1986; Shepperd, 1993, 1995; Shepperd & Wright, 1989). Social loafing is also reduced when rewards for successful performance are group-based rather than individually based—so long as the group is not too large in size (DeMatteo, Eby, & Sundstrom, 1998) and the reward is divided nearly equally among all the group members (Honeywell-Johnson & Dickinson, 1999; Liden et al., 2004).

Involvement may even prompt group members to compensate for the expected failures or incompetencies of their fellow group members by expending extra effort. Kipling Williams and Steven Karau (1991) documented **social compensation** by convincing individuals that their group's task was a meaningful one, but that the motivation of other group members was in doubt (apparently because one of the other experimenters considered the research topic to be boring). Participants were also led to expect that their partners were either skilled or unskilled at the task. Williams and Karau discovered that group members worked hardest when the task was meaningful and the members believed that their coworkers' ability was minimal. A field study of loafing in a classroom setting even suggests that a high level of involvement may trump the sucker effect. If students' grades were on the line, when they discovered that one of their group members was a loafer they tended to work harder themselves, rather than reducing their own effort to look less like a sucker (Liden et al., 2004).

**Increase Identification with the Group** Social identity theory also suggests a way to reduce loafing: increase the extent to which group members identify with their group (Haslam, 2004). Many of the writers and actors in the *SNL* team had grave doubts about the project, because American television was known more for conformity than for creative innovation. However, as their misgivings were answered by the show's popularity, they came to take considerable pride in their membership in this very elite group of entertainers.

---

**social compensation** The tendency for group members to expend greater effort on important collective tasks to offset the anticipated insufficiencies in the efforts and abilities of their co-members.

Social identity theory suggests that the difference between a hard-working group and a loafing group is the match between the group's tasks and its members' self-definitions. If people are working together, but the group and its tasks have no meaning to them, they care very little if their group succeeds or fails. But when individuals derive their sense of self and identity from their membership in the group, then *social loafing* is replaced by *social laboring* as members expend extra effort for their group. Individuals sometimes work hard when they think, "This task is important to me," but they are likely to work even harder when they think, "This task is important to *us*" (Haslam, 2004; cf. Gockel et al., 2008).

**The Collective Effort Model** Karau and Williams's (1993, 2001) **collective effort model (CEM)** provides a comprehensive theoretical framework for understanding the causes and cures of social loafing. Drawing on classic expectancy-value theories of motivation, they suggested that two factors determine group members' level of motivation: their expectations about reaching a goal and the value of that goal. Motivation is greatest when people think that the goal is within their reach (expectations are high) and they consider the goal to be valuable. Motivation diminishes if expectations are low or individuals do not value the goal. Working in a group, unfortunately, can diminish both expectations about reaching a goal and the value that is placed on that goal. In groups, the link between our effort and the chance of success is ambiguous. Even if we work hard, others may not, and the group may fail. Moreover, even if the group does succeed, we personally may not benefit much from the group's good performance. Earning a good grade on a project completed by a group may not be as satisfying as earning a good grade on a project that we complet working on our own.

**collective effort model (CEM)** A theoretical explanation of group productivity developed by Steven Karau and Kipling Williams that traces losses of productivity in groups to diminished expectations about successful goal attainment and the diminished value of group goals.

Karau and Williams tested the CEM's basic predictions in a meta-analysis. Their review of 78 studies supported their basic theoretical contention that loafing is reduced if individuals' expectations for success are high and they feel that the goal they are seeking is a valuable one. They also identified a number of other consistencies that emerged across studies. For example, loafing was greater among men than women, in Western countries compared to Eastern ones, and for simple tasks rather than complex ones.

## Coordination Problems in Groups

Groups, even though they tend to lose some of their productivity due to social loafing, usually outperform individuals. A lone individual in a tug-of-war with a group will lose. Individuals racing each other will run faster than they would if racing against the clock. A group taking a multiple-choice test will probably get a higher score than an individual taking the same test. A single person will not write a sketch that is as funny as one cooked up by a dozen writers. Two heads are better than one.

But how well do groups perform on more complex tasks that require high levels of member coordination and collaboration? Companies and businesses must monitor, regulate, and organize the activities of hundreds of employees. The members of sports teams must synchronize their actions if they are to win the game. Work crews must plan each action as raw construction materials are transformed into a finished building. Members of orchestras must learn their parts, but they must also learn how to perform their part in harmony with the other orchestra members. Mountaineers can climb alone, but most must work with others to reach the summit.

When individuals work by themselves their performance depends strictly on their personal resources, including their talents, skills, and effort. But when individuals join together to work in groups their performance depends on each individual's resources *plus* the interpersonal processes that determine how these resources are combined. A group may have all the resources it needs to reach its objectives, but if it fails to coordinate its efforts and activities it may perform poorly. Two heads may be better than one, but sometimes too many cooks spoil the broth.

**TABLE 10.4 A Summary of Steiner's Taxonomy of Tasks**

| Question | Task Type | Qualities | Examples |
|---|---|---|---|
| **Component**: Can the task be broken down into subtasks? | Divisible | The task has subcomponents that can be identified and assigned to specific members | Playing a football game<br>Preparing a six-course meal |
| | Unitary | The task does not have subcomponents | Pulling on a rope<br>Reading a book |
| **Quantity versus quality**: Is quantity produced more important than quality of performance? | Maximizing | *Quantity*: The more produced the better the performance | Generating many ideas<br>Lifting a great weight<br>Scoring the most goals |
| | Optimizing | *Quality*: A correct or optimal solution is needed | Developing the best answer<br>Solving a math problem |
| **Interdependence**: How are individual inputs combined to yield a group product? | Additive | Individual inputs are added together | Pulling a rope<br>Shoveling snow |
| | Compensatory | A decision is made by averaging together individual decisions | Estimating a pig's weight by asking three people to guess and averaging their guesses<br>Averaging ratings of job applicants |
| | Disjunctive | The group selects one solution or product from a pool of members' solutions or products | Picking one person's answer to a math problem to be the group's answer<br>Letting one art project represent the entire school |
| | Conjunctive | All group members must contribute to the product for it to be completed | Climbing a mountain<br>Eating a meal as a group |
| | Discretionary | The group decides how individual inputs relate to group product | Deciding to shovel snow together<br>Choosing to vote on the best answer to a problem |

SOURCE: Adapted from *Group Processes and Productivity* by I. D. Steiner. Copyright © 1972 by Academic Press.

Steiner (1972) traced problems in coordination back to one key source: the type of task the group is performing. Some tasks, Steiner explained, require high levels of coordinated activity on the part of groups and can only be completed when each group member provides his or her part of the puzzle. Other tasks, in contrast, do not require very much in the way of coordinated action on the part of the group members; even if group members make little or no attempt to adapt their actions to match those of others the group will still succeed. A group working on an assembly line, for example, must combine members' products in ways that differ from the combination process used by a team playing baseball or writers trying to create a comedy sketch for broadcast in three days.

Steiner called the combination processes dictated by the problem or group activity the **task demands** and suggested that they vary depending on the divisibility of the task, the type of output desired, and the combination rules required to complete the task (see Table 10.4).

---

**task demands** The effect that a problem or task's features, including its divisibility and difficulty, have on the procedures the group can use to complete the task.

First, some tasks are *divisible*—they can be broken down into subtasks that can be assigned to different members—whereas other tasks are *unitary*. Building a house, planting a large garden, or working a series of math problems by assigning one to each group member are all **divisible tasks**, because the entire task can be split into parts. **Unitary tasks**, however, cannot be divided: Only one painter is needed for a small closet in a house, only one gardener can plant a single seed, and only one person is needed to solve a simple math problem.

Second, some tasks call for a high rate of production (*maximization*), whereas others require a high-quality, correct outcome (*optimization*). With **maximizing tasks**, quantity is what counts. In a relay race, tug-of-war, or block-stacking problem, performance depends on sheer quantity; the emphasis is on maximal production. For **optimizing tasks**, a good performance is the one that most closely matches a predetermined criterion. Examples of optimizing tasks include estimating the number of beans in a jar or coming up with the best solution to a problem.

Third, members' contributions to the group task can be *combined* in different ways. On an assembly line, for example, the members perform a specific task repeatedly, and the product is finished when each member has made his or her contribution. The members of a rock band, in contrast, all play and sing together, so each member's contribution must mesh with the other members' contributions. Steiner (1972) describes five basic combinatorial strategies: *additive*, *compensatory*, *disjunctive*, *conjunctive*, and *discretionary*.

**divisible task** A task that can be broken down into subcomponents that can then be assigned to individuals or to subgroups within the group.
**unitary task** A task that cannot be performed piecemeal because it does not break down into any subcomponents.
**maximizing task** A task or project that calls for a high rate of production.
**optimizing task** A task or project that has a best solution and outcome, thus the quality of the group's performance can be judged by comparing the product to a quality-defining standard.

**Additive Tasks** **Additive tasks** are divisible and maximizing, for they require the summing together of individual group members' inputs to maximize the group product. In consequence, so long as each group member can perform the simple, individualistic task required—such as pulling on a rope, cheering at a football game, clapping after a concert, or raking leaves in a yard—the productivity of the group will probably exceed the productivity of the single individual. However, as studies of social loafing have suggested, people in groups do not always as work hard at additive tasks; as the saying goes, "many hands make light the work."

**Compensatory Tasks** When groups attempt **compensatory tasks**, the members must average their individual judgments or solutions together to yield the group's outcome. A group may not want to meet in a face-to-face meeting, for example, so members submit their votes to the chair, who tallies them up to reach a conclusion (Lorge et al., 1958).

Legendary 19th-century polymath Francis Galton was surprised by the accuracy of groups when making compensatory decisions. Known for his studies of intelligence, Galton questioned whether a group could possibly make more accurate judgments than an expert. He had the opportunity to test his hypothesis when came across a "Guess the weight of an Ox" contest at a local fair. Each contestant estimated the ox's weight, and the person who came closest to the ox's actual weight won a prize. Galton took the estimates home and examined them, expecting that the crowd would be far off the mark. Yet, the weight of the ox was 1,198 pounds, and the average of the judgments of the 800 contestants was 1,197, confirming the "wisdom of the crowd" (Surowiecki, 2004). Some people overestimated the ox's weight,

**additive task** A task or project that a group can complete by cumulatively combining individual members' inputs.
**compensatory task** A task or project that a group can complete by literally averaging together (mathematically combining) individual members' solutions or recommendations.

but others underestimated, so the "group" judgment, which was an average of all the estimates offered, was more accurate than the judgments made by experts and by most of the individuals (Shaw, 1981).

The compensatory method owes its advantages to its relative immunity to group process loss. In face-to-face groups, those who are well-respected by the group—but not necessarily any better informed—often sway the group's decision. They do not when groups work on compensatory tasks. Because the group members make their judgments independently of others, conformity pressures do not influence their responses. The method does not work so well, however, if members are uninterested in the issue and they have so little information that they are merely guessing. The increased accuracy of compensatory methods springs more from the use of multiple judgments than from the greater accuracy of groups per se. When single individuals make multiple estimates, and their estimates are averaged, their judgments are also more accurate (Stoop, 1932). The method also requires a large enough number of judgments to compensate for the extreme judgments.

**Disjunctive Tasks** When groups work at **disjunctive tasks**, they must generate a single solution that will stand as the group's outcome. Juries making decisions about guilt or innocence, computer technicians deciding which program bug to fix first, or the coaching staff setting the lineup for the day's game, are all performing disjunctive tasks. These types of tasks tend to be both unitary and optimizing, for they cannot be broken down into subtasks, and they require a high-quality or correct solution rather than a large quantity of product.

Disjunctive tasks often require discussion and decision, and Chapter 11 provides a more detailed analysis of how groups tackle such tasks. In general, however, groups perform disjunctive tasks better than most of the individual members. For example, if four students complete a quiz as a group, the group will likely outscore most of the individual students, because more heads means more information and better detection of errors. If the students would have gotten 70%, 80%, 80%, and 90% when tested as individuals, the group will likely score at least 80%.

The group may even score 90% if it accepts the recommendations of its highest scoring member. In some cases, once someone in the group mentions the correct answer, the group adopts it as the group solution—a *truth-wins rule*. Sometimes, however, the group rejects the correct answer. Rosa may be certain that the answer to the question, "Who first documented the reduction of individual productivity when in groups?" is "Ringelmann," but her group may not accept her solution, because they doubt her skills or because someone of higher status may propose a different solution. Ringelmann is the correct answer, but this truth will not win out over error unless someone in the group supports Rosa and her answer—a *truth-supported-wins rule*.

The truth-wins rule usually holds for groups working on *Eureka problems*, whereas the truth-supported-wins rule holds for groups working on *non-Eureka problems*. When we are told the answer to a *Eureka problem*, we are very certain that the answer offered is correct. It fits so well, we react with an "Aha!" or "Eureka!" The answers to *non-Eureka problems*, in contrast, are not so satisfying. Even after arguing about them, we often wonder if the recommended answer is the correct one. Consider, for example, the famous horse-trading problem:

> A man bought a horse for $60 and sold it for $70. Then he bought it back for $80 and again sold it for $90. How much money did he make in the horse-trading business? (Maier & Solem, 1952, p. 281)

When 67 groups discussed this problem, many included a member who knew the correct answer, but many of these groups nonetheless adopted the wrong solution. In this case, truth lost because knowledgeable members had a difficult time persuading the other members to adopt their solutions. In fact, some people later changed their answers to

---

**disjunctive task** A task or project that is completed when a single solution, decision, or recommendation is adopted by the group.

match the incorrect solution advocated by their groups (Maier & Solem, 1952; the answer, by the way, is $20). Thus, groups perform at the level of the best member of the group only if (1) the member who knows the answer shares his or her answer with the others and (2) the group adopts this answer as the group's solution (Davis, 1973; Littlepage, 1991; Steiner, 1972).

Patrick Laughlin (1980) draws a similar distinction between intellective and judgmental tasks. **Intellective tasks**, like some Eureka tasks, yield solutions that can be objectively reviewed and judged as right or wrong. They have a demonstrably correct solution. **Judgmental tasks**, in contrast, require evaluative judgments for which no correct answer can be authoritatively determined. Logic and math problems are intellective tasks, whereas a jury's decision in a trial or the question "Is a sketch about people with cone-shaped heads very funny?" would be judgmental tasks. As tasks move along the continuum from clearly intellective to clearly judgmental, the superiority of groups relative to individual also changes: Groups are more clearly superior when performing intellective tasks than when performing judgmental tasks (Bonner & Baumann, 2008; Laughlin, Bonner, & Miner, 2002; Laughlin et al., 2003).

These studies suggest that groups perform very well on intellective tasks, but can a group outperform even the best member of the group? If students score 70%, 80%, 80%, and 90% individually, can they, through discussion, manage to score a perfect 100% when tested as a group? As Focus 10.3 notes, such *synergistic* effects are very rare in groups.

**Conjunctive Tasks** On most tasks the group's performance results from some combination of all the group members' efforts. For **conjunctive tasks**, however, the group's overall performance is determined by the most inferior group member (the IGM): the proverbial "weakest link," who determines the strength of the entire group.

The hosts on *SNL* were often the show's weakest link. From its inception, *SNL* featured a guest host who worked with the cast and writers throughout the week, learning an opening monologue, rehearsing their part in the skits, and even joining in the writing. Some of these hosts were comics themselves, and so were experienced in the fluid creativity the show required of its performers. Others, though, never adapted to the demands of the program, and when that happened, they dragged down the show with their awkward (or sloppy, incompetent, drunken, or drug-addled) performances. Portions of the performance might succeed, but sketches with the host were always risky.

Because such conjunctive tasks are not finished until all members of the group complete their portion of the job, the speed and quality of the work depends on the group's least skilled member. The speed of a group of mountain climbers moving up the slope is determined by its slowest member. The trucks in a convoy can move no faster than the slowest vehicle. Because of this coordination problem, groups often take steps to improve their proficiency on conjunctive tasks. If the conjunctive tasks are divisible, then the group can assign group members to the subcomponents that best match their skill levels. If the least competent member is matched with the easiest task, a more satisfying level of performance may be obtainable. If the least competent member is matched with a difficult subtask, group performance will, of course, decline still further (see Steiner, 1972, Chapter 3, for a detailed review of group performance on divisible tasks).

Few group members relish the role of the group's IGM so they often respond to this indignity by expending more effort than they would if they were working alone—a rare group motivation gain rather than loss. This tendency is known as the

---

**intellective task** A project, problem, or other type of task with results that can be evaluated objectively using some normative criterion, such as a mathematics problem with a known solution or the spelling of a word.

**judgmental task** A project, problem, or other type of task with results that cannot be evaluated objectively because there are no clear criteria to judge them against.

**conjunctive task** A task that can be completed successfully only if all group members contribute.

## Focus 10.3 Does Synergy Occur in Groups?

*Let's form proactive synergy restructuring teams.*
—Dogbert, organizational consultant in Scott Adams's cartoon *Dilbert*

Synergy is a critical concept in a number of theoretical analyses of biological, physiological, chemical, and physical systems. **Synergy** occurs whenever the combined effect of two or more discrete systems is greater than the effect of these systems when they operate independently. Two drugs, for example, combine synergistically if their effects are greater when they are taken together rather than separately. In groups, if synergy occurs, the group as a whole is greater than the sum of its parts. For example, four students taking a test may score 70%, 80%, 80%, and 90%, but when they work together—if synergy occurs—they should be able to score better than 90%. Synergy is sometimes called an **assembly bonus effect** because "the group is able to achieve collectively something which could not have been achieved by any member working alone or by a combination of individual efforts" (Collins & Guetzkow, 1964, p. 58).

Synergy in groups is relatively rare, however. When individuals work on a collective task, the whole is often much less than the sum of the parts, as members exert less effort (*social loafing*) or let others do their share of the work (*free riding*). Groups often outperform the most incompetent group member (the "better than the worst" effect), and they may perform as well as the most competent member (the "equal to the best" effect), but the "better than the best" effect occurs only rarely. Patrick Laughlin and his colleagues, for example, found evidence of synergy when groups worked on extremely complex logic problems, but only when group members who did not know the right answer could recognize the correct solution when it was proposed, and group members who knew the right answer could convince the others they were correct (Laughlin, Bonner, & Miner, 2002; Laughlin et al., 2003).

Synergy also becomes more likely when the group members are highly motivated to find the correct solution—when grades, jobs, or lives depend on finding the best solution, synergy becomes more likely. In one study, 222 classroom groups took multiple-choice tests that were counted toward their course grades. These groups often outperformed their best members, suggesting that the groups could identify new and better solutions when they worked together in collaborative groups (Michaelsen, Watson, & Black, 1989). Other investigators replicated these findings, although they concluded that the synergistic effects occurred primarily because someone in the group other than the best member knew the right answer and could correct the best member. Thus, synergistic gains in groups are not due to mystical processes whereby groups generate new knowledge, ideas, and energies; instead, they result when the group abandons incorrect answers when better ideas are proposed by someone in the group.

**Köhler effect**, after Otto Kohler, the researcher who first documented the performance gains of weaker individuals striving to keep up with the accomplishments of others in the group (Köhler, 1926; Witte, 1989).

Norbert Kerr and his colleagues (2007) studied the Köhler effect by arranging for women to complete a simple weight-lifting task. They were told to hold a three-pound dumbbell horizontally for as long as they could. When they lowered the weight it would break a trip wire monitored by a laboratory computer, and the trial would end. The longer they held the weight, the more money they could possibly earn at the end of the study. They completed this task four times, with both their dominant and nondominant arm. Women assigned to the control condition completed the task without any partner; they thought they were alone. Others, however, were led

---

**synergy** The combining of two or more independent systems that yields an effect that is greater than the sum of the individual effects.

**assembly bonus effect** Producing an outcome as a group that is superior to the results that could have been achieved by a simple aggregation or accumulation of group members' individual efforts; a gain in performance that is caused by the way the members fit together to form the work group.

**Köhler effect** An increase in performance by groups working on conjunctive tasks that require persistence but little coordination of effort and is likely due to the increased effort expended by the less capable members.

**TABLE 10.5 A Summary of the Potential Productivity of Groups Working on Various Tasks**

| Type of Task | Productivity Effect |
|---|---|
| Additive | *Better than the best*: The group exceeds the performance of even the best individual member. |
| Compensatory | *Better than most*: The group exceeds the performance of a substantial number of the individual members. |
| Disjunctive | *Better than average and sometimes equal to the best:* The group performs best if it accepts the most capable member's input as the group solution; groups rarely perform *better than the best* member (synergy, or assembly bonus effect). |
| Conjunctive: Unitary | *Equal to the worst*: The group equals the performance of its least capable member. |
| Conjunctive: Divisible | *Better than the worst*: Performance will be superior if subtasks are matched to members' capabilities. |
| Discretionary | *Variable*: Performance depends on the combination rules adopted by the group. |

to believe that an "Anne Roberts" was in the next room, and that she was also performing the task. In both the coaction and conjunctive conditions, participants could monitor Anne's performance on Trials 3 and 4 via computer as they themselves struggled to hold up their weight. But in the conjunctive condition, participants were also told that whoever lowered her weight first would determine the group's score. Since Anne did not actually exist and therefore never tired, subjects were always the IGM. But reluctant IGMs, judging by how much longer they managed to hold up the weight when paired with Anne. They achieved a 20-second gain in the coaction condition and a 33-second gain in the conjunctive condition.

A recent meta-analysis of 22 studies of group performance confirms these findings. Individuals who find that their work is inferior to someone else's show improvement relative to others deprived of this comparison information, but this performance gain is particularly dramatic when they are part of a group working on a conjunctive task. IGMs are much more likely to improve when in face-to-face groups and when information about the quality of other people's performance is readily available. The Köhler effect is also stronger in women than men (Weber & Hertel, 2007).

**Discretionary Tasks** Steiner noted that a group can complete some of the tasks it faces by using a variety of combination procedures. How, for example, would a group estimate the temperature of the room in which it is working? One simple method would involve averaging individual judgments. Alternatively, members can determine whether anyone in the group is particularly good at such judgments and then use this person's answer as the group solution. Judging the temperature of the room is a **discretionary task**, because the members themselves can choose the method for combining individual inputs.

## PROCESS GAINS IN GROUPS

Is a group more or less capable than a single individual? Steiner's theory argued that a group's success depends, ultimately, on the resources that the group members contribute and the processes that determine how their inputs are combined and coordinated. In general, as indicated in Table 10.5, groups outperform the most skilled individual when the task is an additive one, and they perform

---

**discretionary task** A relatively unstructured task that can be completed by using a variety of social-combination procedures, thus leaving the methods used in its completion to the discretion of the group or group leader.

better than the average group member on many other kinds of tasks (compensatory, disjunctive, divisible conjunctive with matching, and discretionary).

But can groups actually exceed their potential? Steiner's (1972) law of productivity pessimistically predicted that productivity in groups is equal to potential productivity minus losses owing to such negative processes as conflict, tension, and loss of motivation. However, when people work in groups, they sometimes gain new solutions, energy, and insights into old problems that they would never have achieved as individuals. If good group processes can yield benefits for groups, then the revised law of productivity states

*Actual productivity* = *Potential productivity*
− *Losses owing to faulty processes*
+ *Gains owing to good processes*

This final section of this chapter examines process gains: ways to push groups to the limits of their creative potential.

## Brainstorming

The *SNL* group developed ideas for their show collectively. On Mondays they would meet, sometimes for hours, throwing out ideas for the week's sketches. Each idea was toyed with, elaborated upon and refined, and then added to the list of "possibles." After the meeting, the writers developed at least two of these ideas into full-fledged bits, complete with scripts. By Wednesday, the group had dozens of scripts to choose from for the show, and so had the luxury of picking only a few to broadcast.

*SNL's* approach is a form of group **brainstorming**, which is a technique for using groups to increase creativity. The method was developed by Alex Osborn (1957), an advertising executive, to help his colleagues identify novel, unusual, and imaginative solutions. The technique requires an open discussion of ideas, and is guided by the four basic rules:

- *Be expressive.* Express any idea that comes to mind, no matter how strange, wild, or fanciful. Do not be constrained or timid; freewheel whenever possible.
- *Postpone evaluation.* Do not evaluate any of the ideas in any way during the idea-generation phase. All ideas are valuable.
- *Seek quantity.* The more ideas, the better. Quantity is desired, for it increases the possibility of finding an excellent solution.
- *Piggyback ideas.* Because all ideas belong to the group, members should try to modify and extend others' ideas whenever possible. Brainstorming is conducted in a group, so that participants can draw from one another.

### Does Brainstorming Work?

When groups need to think of new ideas the call to "brainstorm" is often raised, but their faith in this method may be misplaced. Researchers began testing this method by comparing brainstorming groups to individuals and to so-called *nominal groups*: groups created by having individuals work alone and then pooling their ideas (a group "in name" only). These studies offered support to brainstorming. A four-person brainstorming group, for example, would not only outperform any single individual but also a nominal group of four individuals. However, these investigations stacked the deck against the nominal groups; brainstorming groups were told to follow the four basic brainstorming rules, whereas the individuals composing the nominal group were not given any special rules concerning creativity. When individuals working

---

**brainstorming** A method for enhancing creativity in groups that calls for heightened expressiveness, postponed evaluation, quantity rather than quality, and deliberate attempts to build on earlier ideas.

**nominal group** A collection of individuals that meets only the most minimal of requirements to be considered a group, and so is a group in name only; in studies of performance, a control or baseline group created by having individuals work alone and then pooling their products.

alone were better informed about the purposes of the study and the need for highly creative responses, they often offered more solutions than individuals working in groups. In one study, for example, four-person groups came up with an average of 28 ideas in their session, whereas four individuals working alone suggested an average of 74.5 ideas when their ideas were pooled. The quality of ideas was also lower in groups—when the researchers rated each idea on creativity, they found that individuals had 79.2% of the good ideas. Groups also performed more poorly even when given more time to complete the task (Diehl & Stroebe, 1987; Mullen, Johnson, & Salas, 1991; see Paulus & Brown, 2007, for a review).

Brainstorming groups, like many performing groups, must struggle to overcome process losses as they strive to generate ideas. Even though members strive to expend maximum effort, social loafing detracts from their performance unless such safeguards as high identifiability, clear goals, and involvement prevent the undercutting of individual effort (Wegge & Haslam, 2005). But brainstorming groups also suffer coordination and cognitive losses. The originators of brainstorming thought that hearing others' ideas would stimulate the flow of ideas, but the clamor of creative voices instead resulted in **production blocking**. In brainstorming groups, members must wait their turn to get the floor and express their ideas, and during that wait, they forget their ideas or decide not to express them. Hearing others is also distracting and can interfere with one's ability to do the cognitive work needed to generate ideas. Even when researchers tried to undo this blocking effect by giving brainstormers notepads and organizing their speaking turns, the groups still did not perform as well as individuals who were generating ideas alone (Diehl & Stroebe, 1987, 1991; Nijstad & Stroebe, 2006).

Evaluation apprehension can also limit the effectiveness of brainstorming groups, even though the "no evaluation" rule was designed to free members from such concerns (Diehl & Stroebe, 1987). Groups become even less effective when an authority watches them work. Apparently, members worry that the authority may view their ideas negatively (Mullen et al., 1991). Individuals with high social anxiety are particularly unproductive brainstormers and report feeling more nervous, anxious, and worried than group members who are less anxiety prone (Camacho & Paulus, 1995).

Social comparison processes also conspire to create a **social matching effect**. Although undercontributors are challenged to reach the pace established by others, overcontributors tend to reduce their contributions to match the group's mediocre standards. Since overcontribution is more effortful than undercontribution, over time the high performers tend to adjust their rate downward to match the group's lower norm (Brown & Paulus, 1996; Seta, Seta, & Donaldson, 1991).

Brainstorming groups are also unproductive because they often overestimate their productivity. In many cases, a group has no standard to determine how well it is performing, so individual members can only guess at the quantity and quality of their group's product and their personal contributions to the endeavor. These estimates, however, are often unrealistically positive, resulting in a robust **illusion of group productivity**(Stroebe, Diehl, & Abakoumkin, 1992). Members of groups working on collective tasks generally think that their group is more productive than most (Polzer, Kramer, & Neale, 1997). Nor do group members feel that they are doing less than their fair share. When members of a group trying to generate solutions

---

**production blocking** A loss of productivity that occurs when group and procedural factors obstruct the group's progress toward its goals, particularly when individuals in a brainstorming session are delayed in stating their ideas until they can gain the floor and when group members are distracted by others' ideas and so generate fewer of their own.

**social matching effect** The tendency for individuals in brainstorming groups to match the level of productivity displayed by others in the group.

**illusion of group productivity** The tendency for members to believe that their groups are performing effectively.

to a problem were asked to estimate how many ideas they provided, each group member claimed an average of 36% of the ideas, when in reality they generated about 25% of the ideas (Paulus et al., 1993).

Several processes appear to combine to sustain this error in performance appraisal. Group members may intuitively mistake others' ideas for their own, and so when they think about their own performance they cognitively claim a few ideas that others actually suggested (Stroebe et al., 1992). When they brainstorm in groups, they can also compare themselves to others who generate relatively few ideas, reassuring them that they are one of the high performers (Paulus et al., 1993). Group brainstorming may also "feel" more successful since the communal process means that participants rarely experience failure. When alone and trying to think creatively, people repeatedly find that they are unable to come up with a new idea. In groups, because others' ideas are being discussed, people are less likely to experience this failure in their search for new ideas (Nijstad, Stroebe, & Lodewijkx, 2006).

### Improving Brainstorming Sessions

Studies of brainstorming offer a clear recommendation: Do not use face-to-face deliberative groups to generate ideas unless special precautions are taken to minimize production blocking, evaluation apprehension, social matching, and social loafing. Groups can be creative, but Osborn's original suggestions should be augmented with additional requirements (see Paulus & Brown, 2007; Paulus et al., 2006), such as:

- Stick to the rules: Members should be trained to follow brainstorming rules and be given feedback if they violate any of the basic principles. Groups that have not practiced brainstorming methods usually generate only mediocre ideas.
- Pay attention to everyone's ideas: The key to brainstorming is exposure to other's ideas, but people tend to focus on their own suggestions and pay little attention to other people's. Many techniques can be used to force members' attention onto others' ideas, including listing the ideas on a board or asking members to repeat others' ideas.
- Mix individual and group approaches: Members should be given the opportunity to record their ideas individually during and after the session. One technique, called **brainwriting**, involves asking members to write down ideas on paper and then pass the paper along to others, who add their ideas to the list. A post-group session during which members generate ideas by themselves enhances idea generation (Dugosh et al., 2000).
- Take breaks: Members should deliberately stop talking periodically to think in silence (Ruback, Dabbs, & Hopper, 1984).
- Do not rush: Members should have plenty of time to complete the task. Groups that work under time pressure often produce more solutions initially, but the quality of those solutions is lower than if they had spent more time on the task (Kelly, Futoran, & McGrath, 1990; Kelly & Karau, 1993).
- Persist: Members should stay focused on the task and avoid telling stories, talking in pairs, or monopolizing the session; they must continue to persist at the task even through periods of low productivity.
- Facilitate the session: Members' efforts should be coordinated by a skilled discussion leader. A skilled leader can motivate members by urging them on ("We can do this!"), correcting mistakes in the process ("Remember, the rules of brainstorming forbid criticism"), and providing them with a clear standard ("Let's reach 100 solutions!"). A facilitator can also record all ideas in full view of the participants, as exposure to others' ideas is critical for successful brainstorming.

---

**brainwriting** Brainstorming sessions that involve generating new ideas in writing rather than orally, usually by asking members to add their own ideas to a circulating list.

**Alternatives to Brainstorming** Many individuals often feel that creativity is a rare quality, and that only some people—and some groups—are capable of generating fresh ideas and new insights into old problems. Yet nearly all groups can expand their creativity by using creativity-building techniques (Sunwolf, 2002). When stumped for new ideas, members can break up into *buzz groups*, which are small subgroups that generate ideas that can later be discussed by the entire group. Members can jot down a *bug list* of small irritations pertaining to the problem under discussion, and the group can then discuss solutions for each bug. Groups can use the *stepladder technique*, which requires asking each new member of the group to state his or her ideas before listening to the group's position (Rogelberg & O'Connor, 1998). Groups can even use elaborate systems of idea generation with such exotic-sounding names as *synectics* and *TRIZ*. In synectics, a trained leader guides the group through a discussion of members' goals, wishes, and frustrations using analogies, metaphors, and fantasy (Bouchard, 1972). TRIZ is used primarily in science and engineering, and involves following a specific sequence of problem analysis, resource review, goal setting, and review of prior approaches to the problem (Moehrle, 2005).

Several alternative methods, recognizing both the drawbacks of interacting in face-to-face groups and the surprising "wisdom" of groups working on compensatory tasks, integrate individual idea-generating sessions with group-level methods. The **nominal group technique (NGT)** minimizes blocking and loafing by reducing interdependence among members; it achieves this by starting with a nominal group phase before turning to a group session (Delbecq & Van de Ven, 1971).

*Step 1.* The group discussion leader introduces the problem or issue in a short statement that is written on a blackboard or flip chart. Once members understand the statement, they silently write ideas concerning the issue, usually working for 10 to 15 minutes.

*Step 2.* The members share their ideas with one another in a round-robin; each person states an idea, which is given an identification letter and written beneath the issue statement, and the next individual then adds his or her contribution.

*Step 3.* The group discusses each item, focusing primarily on clarification.

*Step 4.* The members rank the five solutions they most prefer, writing their choices on an index card.

The leader then collects the cards, averages the rankings to yield a group decision, and informs the group of the outcome. The group may wish to add two steps to further improve the procedure: a short discussion of the vote (optional Step 5) and a revoting (optional Step 6). These methods are particularly useful when groups discuss issues that tend to elicit highly emotional arguments. NGT groups produce more ideas and also report feeling more satisfied with the process than unstructured groups. The ranking and voting procedures also provide for an explicit mathematical solution that fairly weights all members' inputs and provides a balance between task concerns and interpersonal forces (Delbecq & Van de Ven, 1971; Gustafson et al., 1973).

The **Delphi technique** eliminates the group-level discussion altogether. This method, named for the legendary Delphic oracle, involves surveying members repeatedly, with the results of each round of surveys informing the framing of the questions for subsequent rounds. The Delphi coordinator begins the process by developing a short list of questions on the topic, and then gathering the answers of a carefully selected group of respondents. Their answers are then pooled and communicated

---

**nominal group technique (NGT)** A group performance method wherein a face-to-face group session is prefaced by a nominal-group phase during which individuals work alone to generate ideas.

**Delphi technique** A group performance method that involves repeated assessment of members' opinions via surveys and questionnaires as opposed to face-to-face meetings.

back to the entire group, and members are asked to restate their responses to the original items, comment on others' responses, or respond to new questions that emerged in the first round of surveying. This process is repeated until a solution is reached. The method is particularly well-suited for problems that cannot be solved by a systematic review of the available data (Rowe & Wright, 1999).

**Electronic Brainstorming (EBS)** Computer technology offers yet another alternative to face-to-face brainstorming. **Electronic brainstorming (EBS)** allows members to communicate via the Internet rather than meeting face-to-face. Using software designed specifically for groups (called *group decision support systems* or *groupware*), group members seated at individual computers can share information rapidly and more completely. One program, *GroupSystems*, opens up several windows on each group member's computer—one window is for entering ideas, another displays all the ideas, and another shows a counter that tracks how many ideas the group has generated.

EBS offers practical advantages over more traditional face-to-face sessions, such as reduced travel, time, and cost. But EBS may also be more effective than face-to-face brainstorming, since the format may reduce factors that lead to creative mediocrity. Members do not need to wait their turn, so EBS reduces production blocking. Working from a distance, participants may also feel less evaluation apprehension and nervousness about contributing, and they may be able to persist longer at the task. EBS also enhances one of the key features of brainstorming—idea building—for online exposure to others' ideas tends to stimulate the production of additional novel ideas (DeRosa, Smith, & Hantula, 2007).

Groups using EBS, although they are freed from some of the constraints created by face-to-face meetings, still display problems of social coordination and motivation. Computer-mediated discussions can overwhelm group members with a flood of information to process (Nagasundaram & Dennis, 1993). Social matching can also occur in groups if members know how many ideas each group member has contributed (Roy et al., 1996). EBS sessions are also not particularly productive if the group members become so focused on generating ideas that they ignore the ideas generated by other members. When researchers arranged for groups and individuals to use *GroupSystems* to generate solutions to a problem, they discovered that EBS groups reached high levels of creativity only when members were told that their memory of the ideas expressed by others would be tested later (Dugosh et al., 2000).

More research is needed to explore fully the gains and losses associated with EBS methods, but preliminary results are positive. In a meta-analysis, investigators compared EBS to (a) traditional face-to-face groups, (b) nominal groups, and (c) *e-nominal groups*; individuals who generated ideas in isolation using a computer. They discovered that EBS was clearly superior to traditional brainstorming groups, both in terms of productivity and also members' satisfaction: they liked the EBS approach better. EBS was generally equal to nominal and e-nominal groups, unless the size of the group was large (greater than eight); in this case EBS was superior even to nominal groups. Osborn, the inventor of brainstorming, surely never could have imagined the possibility that people in locations widely dispersed around the world could work together creatively using an adaptation of his brainstorming methods (DeRosa, Smith, & Hantula, 2007).

---

**electronic brainstorming (EBS)** Generating ideas and solving problems using computer-based communication methods such as online discussions and real-time e-mail rather than face-to-face sessions.

## SUMMARY IN OUTLINE

*Do people work better alone or with others?*

1. Triplett's 1898 study of *social facilitation* confirmed that people work more efficiently when other people are present. Social facilitation occurs for both *coaction* tasks and audience tasks.
2. As Zajonc noted, social facilitation usually occurs only for simple tasks that require dominant responses, whereas social interference or impairment occurs for complex tasks that require nondominant responses. Studies conducted in a variety of settings, such as classrooms and jogging trails, have confirmed the effect, which also holds for a variety of species—including cockroaches.
3. Researchers have linked social facilitation to several personal and interpersonal processes, including arousal, evaluation apprehension, distraction, and personality differences (see Table 10.3).
   - Zajonc's *drive theory* argues that the mere presence of a member of the same species raises the performer's arousal level by touching off a basic alertness response; Blascovich's studies of the challenge-threat response and brain imaging work have confirmed that people respond physiologically to the presence of others.
   - Cottrell's *evaluation apprehension theory* proposes that the presence of others increases arousal only when individuals feel that they are being evaluated. *Self-presentation theory* suggests that this apprehension is greatest when performance may threaten the group member's public image.
   - *Distraction-conflict theory* emphasizes the mediational role played by distraction, attentional conflict, and increased motivation. Distractions due to the presence of other people have been shown to improve performance on certain tasks, such as the *Stroop Task.*
   - *Social orientation theory* suggests that individuals who display a positive interpersonal orientation (extraverted and low anxiety) are more likely to display social facilitation effects.
4. Eating in groups, some forms of prejudice, reactions to *electronic performance monitoring*, and the performance of *study groups* can all be explained as forms of social facilitation.

*Do people work as hard when in groups as they do when working by themselves?*

1. Steiner, in his analysis of group productivity, suggests that few groups reach their potential, because negative group processes (*process losses*) place limits on their performance. He believed that *Actual productivity* = *Potential productivity* − *Losses owing to faulty processes.*
2. Groups become less productive as they increase in size. This *Ringelmann effect* is caused by coordination losses and by *social loafing*—the reduction of individual effort when people work in a group.
3. Latané, Williams, and Harkins identified the relative contributions of coordination losses and social loafing to the Ringelmann effect by studying groups and pseudogroups producing noise.
4. Social loafing depends on a number of group-level factors, including,
   - Identifiability: When people feel as though their level of effort cannot be ascertained because the task is a collective one, then social loafing becomes likely. But when people feel that they are being evaluated, they tend to exert more effort, and their productivity increases (leading to social facilitation if the task is easy).

- *Free riding*: Individuals in collective work sometimes work less, knowing that others will compensate for their lack of productivity. They also work less to avoid being the "sucker" who works too hard (the *sucker effect*).
- Goals: Groups that set clear, challenging goals outperform groups whose members have no clear standard to evaluate their performance.
- Involvement: Loafing is less likely when people work at exciting, challenging, and involving tasks. Williams and Karau confirmed that such tasks reduce loafing and even trigger *social compensation* (highly involved group members work harder to compensate for the poor performance of others in the group).
- Identity: According to social identity theory, when individuals derive their identity from their membership in a group, social loafing is replaced by social laboring as members expend extra effort for their groups.

5. Karau and Williams's collective effort model draws on expectancy-value theories of motivation to provide a comprehensive theoretical framework for understanding social loafing.

*Why are groups more successful when working on some tasks and not on others?*

1. Steiner's typology of group tasks argued that group effectiveness depends on the task the group is attempting. *Task demands* are defined by the task's divisibility (*divisible tasks* versus *unitary tasks*), the type of output desired (*maximizing tasks* versus *optimizing tasks*), and the social combination rule used to combine individual members' inputs.
   - Groups outperform individuals on *additive tasks* and *compensatory tasks*. Galton confirmed the "wisdom of the crowd" by finding that independent individuals' judgments, when averaged together, tend to be highly accurate.
   - Groups perform well on *disjunctive tasks* if the group includes at least one individual who knows the correct solution. The truth-wins rule usually holds for groups working on Eureka problems, whereas the *truth-supported-wins* rule holds for groups working on non-Eureka problems.
   - Groups are more effective decision makers than individuals, particularly when dealing with problems that have a known solution (*intellective tasks*) rather than problems that have no clear right or wrong answer (*judgmental tasks*).
   - Groups perform poorly on *conjunctive tasks*, unless the task can be subdivided, with subtasks matched to members' abilities. In some cases the *Köhler effect* occurs: the poorest-performing members increase their productivity due to competitive strivings and the recognition that their poor performance is holding the group back from success.
   - The effectiveness of groups working on *discretionary tasks* covaries with the method chosen to combine individuals' inputs (see Table 10.4).
2. Groups rarely perform better than the best member (synergy, or assembly bonus effect).

*What steps can be taken to encourage creativity in groups?*

1. *Brainstorming* groups strive to find creative solutions to problems by following four basic rules that encourage the flow of ideas among members: "Be expressive," "Postpone evaluation," "Seek quantity," and "Piggyback ideas."
2. Brainstorming groups rarely generate as many ideas as individuals in *nominal groups*. Their

less than expected performance has been linked to social loafing, *production blocking*, social matching, and the *illusion of productivity*.

3. Other methods, including *brainwriting*, *synectics*, the *nominal group technique (NGT)*, the *Delphi technique*, and *electronic brainstorming* (*EBS*), offer advantages over traditional brainstorming.

## FOR MORE INFORMATION

*Chapter Case: Saturday Night Live*

- *Live from New York*, by Tom Shales and James Andrew Miller (2002), provides details about the inner workings of the writers, performers, musicians, production staff, and executives who launched one of the most innovative programs in the history of television.

*Social Facilitation and Loafing*

- "Social Facilitation from Triplett to Electronic Performance Monitoring," by John R. Aiello and Elizabeth A. Douthitt (2001), reviews the literature on social facilitation before offering an integrative model of performance processes in groups.
- "Group Performance and Decision Making," a chapter in the *Annual Review of Psychology*, by Norbert L. Kerr and R. Scott Tindale (2004), reviews much of the recent work on performance in both simple and complex groups.
- "Understanding Individual Motivation in Groups: The Collective Effort Model," by Steven J. Karau and Kipling D. Williams (2001), is an updated review of work examining the factors that contribute to motivation loss in groups. This chapter is one of many excellent papers in *Groups at Work*, edited by Marlene E. Turner (2001).

*Coordination, Independence, and Performance*

- *Group Process and Productivity*, by Ivan D. Steiner (1972), is a timeless analysis of groups that includes entire chapters examining the relationship between group composition, motivation, size, and performance.
- "Group Idea Generation: A Cognitive-Social-Motivational Perspective of Brainstorming," by Paul B. Paulus and Vincent R. Brown (2007), organizes much of the research on brainstorming within a cognitive-social-motivational model.
- *Group Genius*, by Keith Sawyer (2007), examines in fine detail the collaborative nature of most creative innovations.

## Media Resources

Visit the Group Dynamics companion website at www.cengage.com/psychology/forsyth to access online resources for your book, including quizzes, flash cards, web links, and more!

# 11

# Decision Making

## CHAPTER OVERVIEW

People turn to groups when they must solve problems and make decisions. Groups often make better decisions than individuals, for groups can process more information more thoroughly. But groups, like individuals, sometimes make mistakes. When a group sacrifices rationality in its pursuit of unity, the decisions it makes can yield calamitous consequences.

- Why make decisions in groups?
- What problems undermine the effectiveness of decision making in groups?
- Why do groups make riskier decisions than individuals?
- What is groupthink, and how can it be prevented?

## CHAPTER OUTLINE

### The Bay of Pigs Planners: Disastrous Decisions and Groupthink

The U.S. presidential election of 1960 pitted John F. Kennedy against then vice president Richard M. Nixon. Kennedy, searching for a major issue to stress in his campaign, picked Fidel Castro and Cuba. He promised that, if elected, he would do something to stem the spread of communism in the world, and would start close to home: at that small island located just south of Miami, Florida. So, once he reached office he faced a basic problem: What should the U.S. do about Cuba?

The Central Intelligence Agency (CIA) had an answer: Use a covert operation to topple Castro's government. Their plan assumed that a squad of well-trained troops could capture and defend a strip of land in the Bahía de Cochinos (Bay of Pigs) on the southern coast of Cuba. The men would then launch raids and encourage civilian revolt in Havana. Kennedy shared the CIA plan with the executive committee (ExCom) of the National Security Council (NSC). This committee, as diagrammed in Figure 11.1, included White House senior advisors and staff members, cabinet members, the CIA and their consultants, and the Joint Chiefs of Staff (leaders of the branches of the military)—all highly skilled individuals well-trained in making critically important policy and military decisions. This group, after thorough review, advised the president to give the CIA the go-ahead.

The Bay of Pigs invasion took place on April 17. The assault that was so carefully planned was a disaster. The entire attacking force was killed or captured within days, and the U.S. government had to send food and supplies to Cuba to ransom them back. Group expert Irving Janis described the decision as one of the "worst fiascoes ever perpetrated by a responsible government" (1972, p. 14), and President Kennedy lamented, "How could I have been so stupid?" (quoted in Wyden, 1979, p. 8).

ExCom was not unique. Like many other groups, the committee faced a problem needing a solution. Through discussion, the members pooled their expertise and information. They sought out information from available sources, and they thoroughly weighed alternatives and considered the ramifications of their actions. When their alternatives were narrowed down to two—to invade or not to invade—they made a decision as a group. But the committee was typical in another way. Like so many other groups, it made the wrong decision.

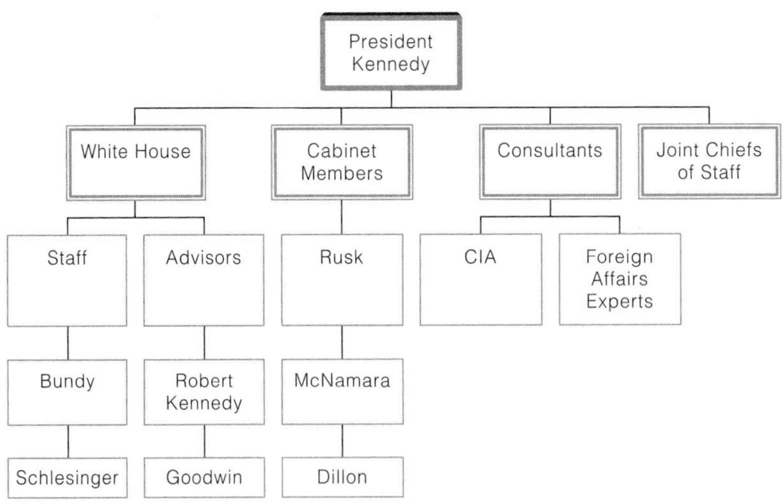


**FIGURE 11.1** The members of ExCom, the advisory committee who planned the Bay of Pigs invasion.

We owe much to groups. Groups put humans on the moon, built the Empire State Building, performed the first symphony, and invented the personal computer. But groups also killed innocent civilians at My Lai, marketed thalidomide, doomed the space shuttles *Challenger* and *Columbia*, and decided that the best way to deal with terrorism was to invade Iraq. Groups have great strengths, but their limitations can only be ignored at great risk.

## GROUPS AND DECISIONS: THE FUNCTIONAL PERSPECTIVE

In office buildings, executives hold conferences to solve problems of management and production; at the dinner table, families talk over moving to a new neighborhood; in courthouses, juries weigh evidence to determine guilt and innocence; on the battlefield, a combat squad identifies a target and plans an attack. In these and thousands of other similar settings, interdependent individuals make decisions in groups.

Why this reliance on groups? People turn to groups because, in most cases, groups are better at choosing, judging, estimating, and problem solving than are individuals (Stasser & Dietz-Uhler, 2001). Groups form more accurate perceptions of people than do individuals (Ruscher & Hammer, 2006). Groups using Google can find the information they need faster than single individuals can (Lazonder, 2005). Teams of physicians making a diagnosis are more accurate than single physicians (Glick & Staley, 2007). Students permitted to take a test in groups get better grades than individual students (Zimbardo, Butler, & Wolfe, 2003). Burglars who work in groups are less likely to be caught than are thieves who work alone (Warr, 2002). Even very powerful leaders—presidents of the United States, for example—rarely make decisions without consulting others. Instead, they rely on groups, for they assume that the weighty problems that they must handle on a daily basis would overwhelm a lone individual. Apparently "none of us alone is as smart as all of us together" (Myers, 2002, p. 317).

Marjorie Shaw (1932) examined the sagacity of groups by putting 21 individuals and 5 four-person groups to work on several intellective tasks, including the famous (at least to people who study groups) missionary–cannibal dilemma:

> Three missionaries and three cannibals are on one side of the river and want to cross to the other side by means of a boat that can only hold two persons at a time. All the missionaries can row, but two cannibals cannot. For obvious reasons, the missionaries must never be outnumbered by the cannibals, under any circumstances or at any time, except where no missionaries are present at all. How many crossings will be necessary to transport the six people across the river?

When the groups and individuals finished the first set of problems, Shaw reorganized them, so that those who worked alone initially solved several new problems in groups and those who initially worked in groups solved several new problems individually.

Shaw's findings attested to the wisdom of groups. Compared to individuals, groups generated more correct solutions, and they were also better at checking for errors in calculations and faulty inferences about the problems. If a group member recommended a solution that was inaccurate, groups were more likely to reject that solution. Groups, when they did make mistakes, also erred later in the decision process than did individuals, in part because groups were more proficient at noticing and correcting errors than were individuals. Groups, however, took longer to complete the task than did individuals. (The answer to the missionary–cannibal problem, by the way, is 13 crossings! Note, too, that this study was conducted by Marjorie E. Shaw—no relation to Marvin E. Shaw, who also studied groups and whose classic 1981 text, *Group Dynamics*, is this book's intellectual progenitor.)

What is the secret to groups' superiority in making decisions? A **functional theory of group decision making** suggests that skilled decision-making groups are more likely to make use of group procedures that enhance the way they gather, analyze, and weigh information. Although no two groups reach their decisions in precisely the same way (and no two theorists agree on *the* definitive list of decision functions), the stages shown in Figure 11.2 and examined in this section are often in evidence when groups make decisions. The group defines the problem, sets goals, and develops a strategy in the *orientation phase.* Next, during the *discussion phase,* the group gathers information about the situation and, if a decision must be made, identifies and considers options. In the *decision phase,* the group chooses its solution by reaching consensus, voting, or using some other social decision process. In the *implementation phase,* the decision must be put into action and the impact of the decision assessed. Groups that follow these four stages are more likely to make better decisions than those who sidestep or mishandle information at any particular stage (Hollingshead et al., 2005; Wittenbaum et al., 2004).

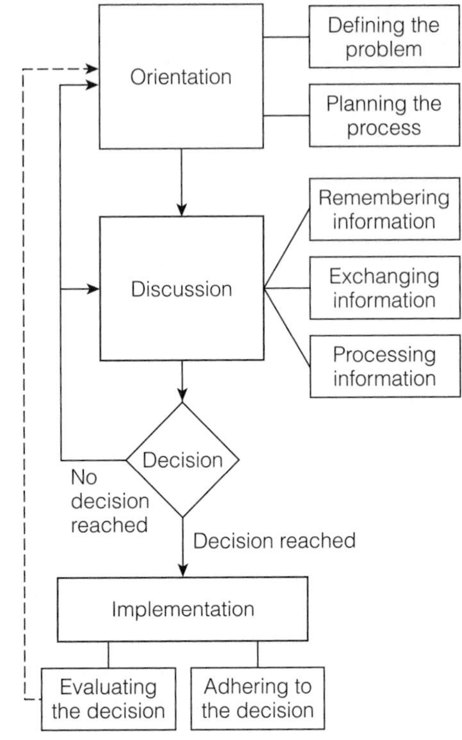


**FIGURE 11.2** A functional model of group decision making.

## Orientation

Decisions begin with a problem that needs a solution. A group of concerned college students wonders what can be done about the lack of recycling in their community and its effect on the environment. The president of the United States is briefed by the CIA on the invasion of Cuba. The combat unit is under attack and suffering substantial casualties. Such situations trigger a decision-making process that often begins with recognition of the unsatisfactory state of the current situation and the search for a solution. But groups also meet, more routinely, to check progress, review feedback, identify any possible issues, and to identify new goals.

In the first stage of problem solving the group must organize the procedures it will use in its work. Members clarify the group's goals, identify the resources needed to make the decision, enumerate obstacles that must be overcome or avoided, specify the procedures to be followed in gathering information and making the decision, and agree on procedures to follow during the meeting (paraphrased from Gouran & Hirokawa, 1996, p. 76–77). All this planning provides the blueprint for "the order in which a sequence of operations is to be performed" (Miller, Galanter, & Pribram, 1960, p. 16), so that actions are structured effectively.

The group should, by the end of the orientation phase, understand its purpose, its procedures, and the tasks that it will undertake. Armed with a shared plan, groups no longer simply react to situations; rather, they proactively influence events so that their expectations are affirmed.

---

**functional theory of group decision making** A conceptual analysis of the steps or processes that groups generally follow when making a decision, with a focus on the intended purpose of each step or process in the overall decision-making sequence.

## Focus 11.1 Do Groups Waste Time?

*Groups take minutes but waste hours.*

—Unknown

Making decisions in groups requires, in many cases, a trade-off between efficiency and accuracy. Groups' decisions are often superior to those of individuals, but groups require more time to draw conclusions and to reach agreement. The humorist C. Northcote Parkinson (1957) has identified two fundamental "laws" that groups all too frequently obey. Parkinson's first law, which he modestly named **Parkinson's law**, states that a task will expand so as to fill the time available for its completion. Hence, if a group gathers at 1 PM for a one-hour meeting to discuss five items of business, the group will likely adjourn at 2 PM no matter how simple or routine the issues.

Parkinson's second law, the **law of triviality**, states that the time a group spends on discussing any issue will be in inverse proportion to the consequentiality of the issue (Parkinson, 1957, paraphrased from p. 24). Parkinson described a hypothetical finance committee dealing with Item 9 on a long agenda, a $10-million allocation to build a nuclear reactor. Discussion is terse, lasting about 2½ minutes, and the committee unanimously approves the item. However, when the group turns to Item 10, the allocation of $2350 to build a bicycle shed to be used by the office staff, everyone on the committee has something to say. As Parkinson explained,

> A sum of $2350 is well within everybody's comprehension. Everybody can visualize a bicycle shed. Discussion goes on, therefore, for forty-five minutes, with the possible result of saving some $300. Members at length sit back with a feeling of achievement. (1957, p. 301)

**Defining the Problem** One particularly valuable outcome of this period of orientation is the development of a **shared mental model**—a cognitive schema that organizes declarative and procedural information pertaining to the problem and the group that is held in common by the group members (Klimoski & Mohammed, 1994). Because of differences in prior experiences, knowledge, expectations, and so on, each individual may have a differing view of the history of the issue, the current situation, and even the methods that will be used to reach a decision. Some of these differences may lead to misunderstandings and inefficiencies as the group does its work, so the emergence of agreement—the shared mental model—will facilitate the group's functioning. When group members adopt the same general conceptualization of their tasks, goals, and procedures, their final choices reflect the group's preferences rather than the group members' personal biases (Tindale et al., 2001).

**Planning Process** In a time-urgent world, groups sometimes rush through the orientation stage; they want to get on with the work, and not waste time with preliminaries (Varela, 1971). However, research clearly favors delaying the discussion of the issue at hand until the group reviews and, if needed, clarifies its goals, procedures, and time constraints (Weingart, 1992; Weldon, Jehn, & Pradhan, 1991). The importance of planning is so great that in some cases it is the only thing that differentiates successful groups from unsuccessful ones (Hirokawa, 1980). In a study of six conferences in which panels of experts evaluated new medical technologies, participants were more satisfied when the decisional procedures had been discussed in advance (Vinokur et al., 1985). Similarly, in a project that experimentally manipulated the use of process planning, groups were more productive when they were encouraged to discuss

---

**shared mental model** Knowledge, expectations, conceptualizations, and other cognitive representations that members of a group have in common pertaining to the group and its members, tasks, procedures, and resources.

**Parkinson's law** A task will expand to fill the time available for its completion.

**law of triviality** The amount of time a group spends on discussing any issue will be in inverse proportion to the consequentiality of the issue.

their performance strategies before working on a task requiring intermember coordination (Hackman, Brousseau, & Weiss, 1976). Planning that addresses deadlines and time constraints also enhances performance (see Focus 11.1). Groups are notorious for the injudicious use of time, but groups that recognize that their time is limited plan out their work better than groups that assume their time is unlimited (Sanna et al., 2005). In one survey of 48 self-managing teams, those who spent time during their initial stages with temporal planning developed strong norms about time, and these norms helped these groups to perform better than groups that did not put enough time into planning (Janicik & Bartel, 2003).

Given the clear benefits of spending time planning process, it is unfortunate that few groups show much interest in planning their procedures (Tindale et al., 2001). When a group member raises the issue of planning, very rarely do any of the other group members respond positively (Hackman & Morris, 1975). When groups are given a task, their first tendency is to begin their task rather than consider process-related issues. Even when enjoined to plan, groups believe that planning activities are less important than actual task activities (Shure et al., 1962). This anti-planning bias stems, in part, from the tendency of groups to apply whatever method they used in the past to current and future projects (Hackman & Morris, 1975). Even Kennedy's group moved through the orientation stage too hastily. Kennedy had just taken over the office of president, and his advisors had not worked together before, so the members should have spent several meetings talking about the problem and the strategy they would take in solving it. Instead, the planners immediately began to discuss logistics and operations (Stern, 1997).

## Discussion

If information is the lifeblood of decision making, then the discussion phase must be the heart of that process (Kowert, 2002). During the discussion stage, group members gather and process the information needed to make a decision. As Robert Freed Bales (1955) and his colleagues discovered when they watched and recorded groups at work, more than 50% of all comments made by members are suggestions, expressions of opinion, and attempts at orientation (see Figure 11.3). Group members also share information about the problem, express agreement or disagreement, and ask for more information and clarification. The levels of these actions shown in Figure 11.3 will vary depending on the nature of the group discussion and its level of intensity, but in most groups communication peaks during this phase.

What is the value of all this discussion and debate? An *information processing approach* to decisions assumes that people strive, in most cases, to make good decisions by acquiring the information that is relevant to the issue and processing that information thoroughly, so that its implications are clearly understood. A ***collective* information processing approach** to decision making also assumes that people seek out and process relevant information, but that they do this cognitive work during the group discussion. Three information processing gains that result from discussion are noted in Figure 11.2 —improved memory for information, increased information exchange, and more thorough processing of information (Hinsz, Tindale, & Vollrath, 1997; Larson & Christensen, 1993; Propp, 1999).

**Collective Memory** Two heads are better than one because groups have superior memories for information relative to individuals. Arthur Schlesinger, for example, knew a great deal about international relations, but he could not compete with the combined informational resources of all the Bay of Pigs planners. ExCom's members' memories, when combined, contained a vast assortment of information about Cuba, Castro, weaponry, and even the terrain of the beach where the troops would

---

**collective information processing model** A general theoretical explanation of group decision making assuming that groups use communication and discussion among members to gather and process the information needed to formulate decisions, choices, and judgments.

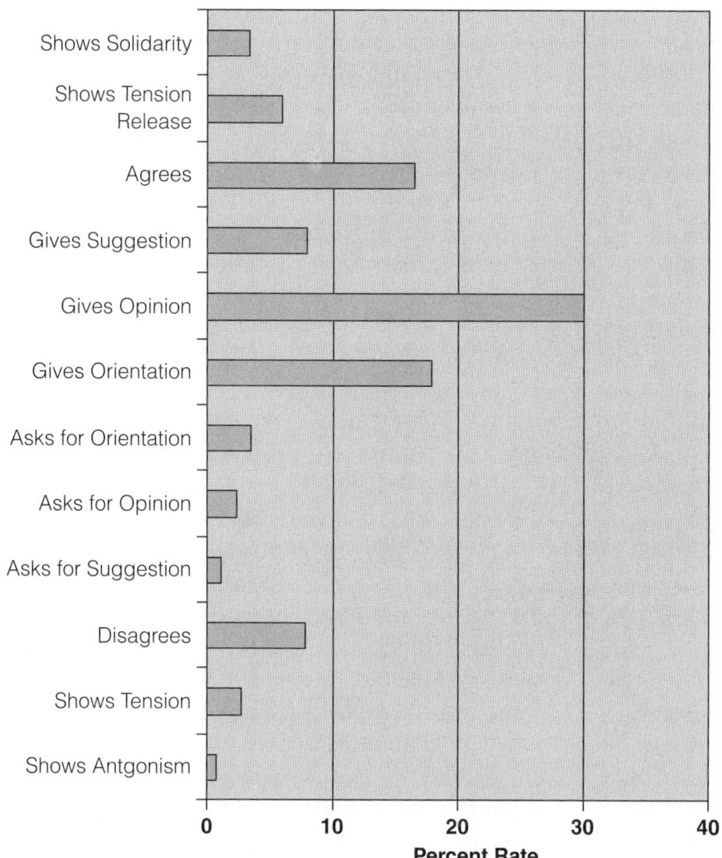


**FIGURE 11.3** Average interaction profile for discussion groups (Bales, 1999).

SOURCE: *Social Interaction Systems: Theory and Measurement,* by Robert Freed Bales, Transaction Publishers, 1999, p. 240.

land (Clark, Stephenson, & Kniveton, 1990; Harris, Paterson, & Kemp, 2008; Hirst & Manier, 2008).

A groups' **collective memory** is the shared reservoir of information held in the memories of two or more members of a group. Groups remember more than individuals, because groups draw on more memories that contain different types of information. The CIA operatives who met with the Bay of Pigs planners knew all about the weapons, tactics, and the morale of Castro's troops, but Dean Rusk was an expert on the relationship between Cuba and the Soviet Union. When they joined together, they could pool their individual expertise to form the group's decisions. (Unfortunately, no one in the group knew that the Bay of Pigs was Castro's favorite fishing spot, so he was thoroughly familiar with every path, road, and hill in the area.) Similarly, when students are permitted to take examinations as a group, they usually outperform individuals, for the student who is stumped by the question, "Name four common phases of group decision making," may be saved by a group member who remembers the mnemonic acronym ODD-I: Orientation, Discussion, Decision, and Implementation (Michaelsen, Watson, & Black, 1989; Stasson & Bradshaw, 1995). Groups can also *get* more information than individuals can. In many cases, decision-making groups are staffed by individuals who have widely differing experiences, backgrounds, and associations, so each one can acquire a unique set of information that he or she can contribute to the discussion (Henningsen & Henningsen, 2007).

---

**collective memory**A group's combined memories, including each member's memories, the group's shared mental models, and transactive memory systems.

But groups are not mnemonic marvels (Van Swol, 2008). When researchers compared the memories of collaborative groups, nominal groups (groups of noninteracting individuals), and individuals, collaborative groups outperformed both the average single individual and the best single individual. Collaborative groups did not, however, perform as well as nominal groups, and the groups displayed many of the characteristics typically seen in individual memory. Individuals, for example, generally have better memory for information that they process more deeply and better memory for pictures than for words. Groups displayed these same tendencies when their memories were tested (Weldon & Bellinger, 1997). Groups also reported words that were not on the original list, and their memories were also less well structured (Finlay, Hitch, & Meudell, 2000).

Groups do not remember as much as they could because members free-ride and loaf. As noted in Chapter 10, when members know that others will be on hand should they forget any details, they put less effort into processing and storing the information. But even when factors that produce loafing are eliminated—members are made identifiable, each individual is promised a substantial reward for performing well, and group cohesion is high—three-person groups who worked together at a memory task still remembered less information than three individuals whose memories were tested when alone (Weldon, Blair, & Huebsch, 2000). Apparently, the complexity of the group setting disrupts group members' ability to organize information in memory and then retrieve that information. In consequence, collaborating groups perform particularly poorly when trying to remember badly organized information, but perform the same as noninteracting (nominal) groups when trying to remember organized information (Basden et al., 1997). These inadequacies in collective memory may be so substantial that groups cannot remember their decisions unless they keep a written record of them (minutes). Although few group members relish the role of recorder, without minutes, details of the group's actions may be forgotten.

**Information Exchange** Groups do not merely draw on a larger pool of information than individuals. They can also exchange information among the members of the group, thereby further strengthening their access to information as well as their recall of that information. A group, then, is a "multiagent connectionist" informational network "that consists of a collection of individual recurrent networks that communicate with each other and, as such, is a network of networks" (Van Overwalle & Heylighen, 2006, p. 606).

When group members exchange information, they may give each other cues that help them remember things that they would not recall if working alone. This process is known as **cross-cueing**. For example, President Kennedy may not remember where the force will land, but perhaps he will say, "I think it's a bay." This cue may trigger someone else's memories, so that the name "Bay of Pigs" is retrieved by the group, even though none of the members could generate this name individually (Meudell, Hitch, & Kirby, 1992). Unfortunately, if a group member offers up a misleading cue—instead of saying, "I think it's a bay," the ExCom member said, "I think it's near a lagoon"—then such cueing can inhibit memory retrieval rather than facilitate it (Andersson, Hitch, Meudell, 2006).

**Transactive memory** (TM) also enhances the groups' capacity to store and quickly access information by dividing data among the members. Members working in the same group often specialize, to a degree, in different areas. These individuals not only have more information on a given topic, but they are also the ones who should be more responsible for storing any new information that is relevant to their area of expertise. In the committee, for example, the CIA was recognized as the source of all

---

**cross-cueing** The enhancement of recall that occurs during group discussion when the statements made by group members serve as cues for the retrieval of information from the memories of other group members.

**transactive memory system** A process by which information to be remembered is distributed to various members of the group who can then be relied upon to provide that information when it is needed.

information about the invasion force, so other group members spent little effort deliberately storing information on that topic. When anyone needed to check a fact pertaining to the commandos, they turned to the CIA and their memory stores (Hollingshead, 2001a; Wegner, Giuliano, & Hertel, 1985). It was unfortunate for the ExCom that the CIA was so committed to the plan that they deliberately misled the group about conditions in Cuba and the possibility of success (Kramer, 2008). As discussed in more detail in Chapter 12, TM is enriched through practice working as a group and by trust among members.

**Processing Information** Groups not only recall and exchange information more effectively than individuals, they also process that information more thoroughly through discussion. Members ask questions, and others offer answers. Alternative options are discussed, and the strengths and weaknesses of each option are considered. Group members analyze each others' ideas and offer corrections when they note errors. Members dialogue with one another, sharing viewpoints and seeking a shared meaning. Ideas are debated, with some group members seeking to convince others that their position is better. The group members also monitor their work and intervene as necessary to bring the group back on task. Most group discussions also include an interpersonal element that complements the focus on the work to be done (Barge, 2002). Decision-making groups not only share and evaluate information; they also encourage each other, express commitment to the group, and help each other (Jehn & Shah, 1997; Weingart & Weldon, 1991).

Just as the orientation period is essential to effective decision making, so the time spent in active discussion increases the quality of the group's decision (Katz & Tushman, 1979). When researchers monitored group members' communications while working on a problem that could be solved only by properly sequencing individuals' responses, they found that the group's use of essential information through discussion proved to be the best predictor of success (Lanzetta & Roby, 1960). Groups working on *collective induction problems*—tasks that require a cycle of hypothesis generation and testing—performed best when members discussed the problems actively and focused their analysis on evidence rather than on hypotheses (Laughlin & Hollingshead, 1995). Flight crews that confront sudden emergencies often overcome the problem if they share information with one another; but those crews that do not take advantage of group discussion often make errors in judgment that are not corrected by the group (Paris, Salas, & Cannon-Bowers, 1999; see Focus 8.1). Studies of online groups have found that the online format substantially hampers the group's ability to make an informed decision if the rate of information exchange is too low and too slow (Baltes et al., 2002). When researchers watched groups make decisions, they found that information sharing (talking a great deal, free expression of ideas, thoughts, and feelings) and critical evaluation of ideas (critically evaluating each other's ideas or works, differences of opinion, disagreement among group members, disagreements on who should do what or how something should be done) were correlated with judgmental accuracy (Jehn & Shah, 1997).

## Decision

By early April, the Bay of Pigs committee was ready to make its decision. The members had spent days examining the CIA's plan, and even though many questions remained unanswered, the group could delay no longer. Word of the plan had leaked to the press, and the group was worried that Castro might begin to shore up his defenses. They needed to make up their minds.

**Social Decision Schemes** A **social decision scheme** is a group's method for combining individual

---

**social decision scheme** A strategy or rule used in a group to select a single alternative from among various alternatives proposed and discussed during the group's deliberations, including explicitly acknowledged decision rules (e.g., the group accepts the alternative favored by the majority) and implicit decisional procedures (e.g., the group accepts the alternative favored by the most powerful members).

members' inputs in a single group decision. Some groups have clearly defined ways of making a decision—their bylaws may state, for example, that they will follow a particular rule of order (such as *Robert's Rules*). In many cases, though, the social decision scheme is an implicit one that is taken for granted by group. Not until someone says, "Let's take a vote" does the group realize that a decision must be made about how to make decisions (Ladbury & Hinsz, 2005). Some common social decision schemes are *delegation, averaging, voting, consensus* (discussion to unanimity), and *random choice* (Hastie & Kameda, 2005).

- *Delegating decisions*: An individual, subgroup, or external party makes the decision for the group. Under an *authority scheme*, the leader, president, or other individual makes the final decision with or without input from the group members. When an *oligarchy* operates in the group, a coalition speaks for the entire group. Other forms of delegation include asking an expert to answer (the best-informed member) or forming a subcommittee made up of a few members to study the issue and reach a conclusion.
- *Averaging decisions*: Each group member makes his or her decision individually (either before or after a group discussion) and these private recommendations are averaged together to yield a nominal group decision. As with compensatory tasks discussed in Chapter 10, such decisions do not necessarily require any interaction among members. For example, to choose among five possible candidates for a job opening each member could rank the candidates from 1 to 5 and the group could then average these rankings.
- *Plurality decisions*: Members express their individual preferences by voting, either publicly or by secret ballot. In most cases, the group selects the alternative favored by the majority of the members (the very common *majority-rules scheme*), but in some cases, a more substantial plurality (such as a *two-thirds majority scheme*) is needed before a decision becomes final. Some groups also use ranking methods, with more points awarded to alternatives that are ranked higher than others (the *Borda count method*).
- *Unanimous decisions (consensus)*: The group discusses the issue until it reaches unanimous agreement without voting. As noted in Chapter 7, this decision rule is imposed on many juries in the United States.
- *Random decisions*: The group leaves the final decision to chance by, say, flipping a coin.

Each decision scheme has strengths as well as weaknesses. Delegation saves the group time and is appropriate for less important issues. Mandates from authorities can, however, leave members feeling disenfranchised and ignored. As noted in Chapter 10, when groups average individual members' inputs, all the group members' opinions are considered, and this procedure often cancels out errors or extreme opinions. But a group that just averages without discussion may make an arbitrary decision that fails to satisfy any of the group members, all of whom may end up feeling little responsibility for implementing the decision.

Most groups, at least in Western cultures, rely on some type of voting procedure to make final decisions (Mann, 1986). Voting is a way of making a clear-cut decision, even on issues that deeply divide the group. When researchers compared these decision rules, plurality was the most consistent in yielding a superior decision, and it involved the least amount of effort from individual group members (Hastie & Kameda, 2005). But plurality, despite its overall effectiveness, has limitations. When the vote is close, some members of the group may feel alienated and defeated. In consequence, they become dissatisfied with membership and are less likely to lend support to the decision (Castore & Murnighan, 1978). Voting can also lead to internal politics, as members get together before meetings to apply pressure, form coalitions, and trade favors to ensure the passage of proposals that they favor. Also, if the vote is taken publicly, individuals may conform to previously stated opinions rather than expressing their personal views (Davis et al., 1988).

Some groups avoid these drawbacks by relying on *consensus* to make decisions. Consensus decision schemes are involving and often lead to high levels of commitment to the decision and to the group. Unfortunately, groups may not be able to reach consensus on all issues. Consensus building takes a good deal of time, and if rushed, the strategy can misfire. In many cases, too, groups explicitly claim to be using the unanimity scheme, but the implicit goal may be something less than unanimity. When nine people on a jury all favor a verdict of guilty, for example, the three remaining jurors may hold back information that they believe would cause dissent within the group (Kameda et al., 2002). Groups often prefer to reach consensus on questions that require sensitive judgments, such as issues of morality, but they favor a majority-rules voting scheme on problem-solving tasks (Kaplan & Miller, 1987).

### Implementation

When the die is cast and the decision made, two significant pieces of work remain to be done. First, the decision must be *implemented.* If a union decides to strike, it must put its strike plan into effect. If a city planning commission decides that a new highway bypass is needed, it must take the steps necessary to begin construction. If an advisory committee approves an invasion, its members must mobilize the necessary military forces. Second, the quality of the decision must be *evaluated.* Was the strike necessary? Did we put the highway where it was needed the most? Was it really such a good idea to invade Cuba?

**Procedural Justice** Implementation is affected by **procedural justice**: group members' evaluation of the fairness in the processes that the group used to make its decisions. Willingness to endorse and support a group's decisions depends on such factors as members' sense of control over the process, involvement in it, and evaluation of the outcome itself; if the group members believe that the procedures that the group used to make its decision were fair ones, then they will be more likely to act in supportive, pro-group ways. For example, many of the members of the ExCom group were against the Bay of Pigs plan, but they believed that the group had examined the issue in a fair, impartial way, and so when the decision was made they went to work implementing it. People are more likely to regard a decision as a fair one if the decisional procedures are implemented "(a) consistently, (b) without self-interest, (c) on the basis of accurate information, (d) with opportunities to correct the decision, (e) with the interests of all concerned parties represented, and (f) following moral and ethical standards" (Brockner & Wiesenfeld, 1996, p. 189). The group that uses procedurally just methods for making decisions will be more successful during the implementation stage (Colquitt & Greenberg, 2003; Skitka, Winquist, & Hutchinson, 2003).

**Participation and Voice** Many factors influence perceptions of procedural fairness, but when people believe that they had a voice in the matter—that they could have expressed any concerns they had and others would have listened and responded—then they tend to be far more engaged in the implementation of the final decision. This *voice effect* was examined in an early study by Lester Coch and John French (1948). The management of a clothing mill asked Coch and French to identify a way to improve employees' commitment to new production methods. Coch and French suspected that employees would respond more positively if they were involved in planning changes, so they devised three different training programs. Employees in the *no-participation* program were just given an explanation for the innovations. Those in the *participation-through-representation* program attended group meetings where the need for change was discussed openly and an informal decision was reached. A subgroup was then chosen to become the "special" operators, who

---

**procedural justice** Perception of the fairness and legitimacy of the methods used to make decisions, resolve disputes, and allocate resources; also, in judicial contexts, the use of fair and impartial procedures.

would serve as the first training group. Employees in the third program—*total participation*—followed much the same procedures as those in the second program, but here *all* the employees, not a select group, took part in the training system.

Confirming the voice effect, hostility, turnover, and inefficiency was highest in the no-participation group; 17% quit rather than learn the new procedures, and those who remained never reached the goals set by management. Those in the two participation conditions, in contrast, learned their new tasks quickly, and their productivity soon surpassed prechange levels and management goals. Morale was high, only one hostile action was recorded, and none of the employees quit in the 40 days following the change. Furthermore, when the members of the no-participation control condition were run through a program of increased voice and involvement several months later they, too, reached appropriate production levels (cf. Bartlem & Locke, 1981).

*Autonomous work groups* and *self-directed teams* are the modern-day counterparts to Coch and French's total-participation groups (Cascio, 1995). These groups vary considerably in composition and goals, but in most cases, they are charged with identifying problems that are undermining productivity, efficiency, quality, or job satisfaction. These groups spend considerable time discussing the causes of the problems and suggesting possible solutions, either with or without a formal leader or supervisor. Once decisions are made about changes (usually by consensus), these changes are implemented and evaluated. If the changes do not have the desired effect, the process is repeated. These groups are considered in more detail in Chapter 12.

### Who Decides—Individuals or Groups?

President Kennedy was given the secret document JCSM-57-61, "Military Evaluation of the CIA Paramilitary Plan—Cuba," early in February (Wyden, 1979, p. 90). It suggested that the United States should arm and train a group of Cuban exiles, who would then return to their homeland and lead a revolt against that country's current leader. Kennedy could have studied the report and made a decision at that moment. Instead, he turned the decision over to a group rather than make the choice alone.

Making a decision in a group offers a number of advantages over making a decision alone. Groups, with their greater informational resources and capacity to process that information, may be able to identify better solutions and to detect errors in reasoning. Members may also find a group's decision more satisfying than that of a single individual, particularly if the group uses a consensus-building decision process. Group decisions, however, can take more time than people wish to give to them, and so groups too often sacrifice quality for timeliness. Some issues, too, are so trivial, so convoluted, or so contentious that a group approach may end in failure.

Given this mix of benefits and liabilities, Victor Vroom's **normative model of decision making** suggests that different types of situations call for different types of decision-making methods (Vroom, 2003; Vroom & Jago, 1988, 2007; Vroom & Yetton, 1973). In some cases, the decision maker should not even consult with others before he or she makes a choice. In other cases, however, the leader should seek input from the group or even turn the decision over to the group entirely. Although procedures can fall anywhere along the continuum from leader-centered, authoritarian to group-centered, democratic decision making, Vroom's (2003) most recent model identifies these five basic types of decision-making process:

- *Decide*: The leader solves the problem or makes the decision and announces it to the group. The leader may rely on information available to him or her at that time, but may also obtain information from group members. The members only provide information to the leader and

---

**normative model of decision making** A theory of decision making and leadership developed by Victor Vroom that predicts the effectiveness of group-centered, consultative, and autocratic decisional procedures across a number of group settings.

the leader may not tell the group members why the information is needed.

- *Consult (Individual)*: The leader shares the problem with the group members individually, getting their ideas and suggestions one-on-one without meeting as a full group. The leader then makes the decision, which may not reflect the group members' influence.
- *Consult (Group)*: The leader discusses the problem with the members as a group, collectively obtaining their input. Then the leader makes the decision, which may not reflect the group members' influence.
- *Facilitate*: The leader coordinates a collaborative analysis of the problem, helping the group reach consensus on the issue. The leader is active in the processes, but does not try to influence the group to adopt a particular solution. The leader accepts the will of the group and implements any decision that is supported by the entire group.
- *Delegate*: If the group already functions independently of the leader, then he or she can turn the problem over to the group. The group reaches a decision without the leader's direct involvement, but the leader provides support, direction, clarification, and resources as the group deliberates.

Vroom's normative model does not advocate one decision-making method as superior to another. Rather, the situation must be considered and an approach selected that is most suited to the given context. One of the most important of all factors to consider is the significance of the decision itself—if the problem is not very important then it can be solved using a method that involves the least amount of time and the fewest individuals. But when the problem becomes increasingly important, other situational factors must also be considered: Does the leader have substantial knowledge about the issue? Does the group know even more about the problem? Will the group be committed to the solution and its implementation if it does not get involved in the decision-making process, and does that even matter? How well do the group members work together? Is conflict so high in the group that members may not be able to work together on the problem? In general, when problems are simple ones, the leader is well-informed, and the consequences for a poor decision are relatively minor, then in the interest of time the leader should decide. A group-focused approach, in contrast, is best whenever a high quality solution is needed, along with support from the group to implement it. However, choosing between an individual and a group approach is so complex that Vroom and his colleagues have developed a computer program that guides the choice between deciding, consulting, facilitating, and delegating (Vroom, 2003).

The normative model synthesizes studies of leadership, group decision making, and procedural fairness to predict when a choice should be made by an authority and when it should be handled by the group. Although the model may oversimplify this complex process, it translates theoretical ideas into concrete suggestions, and thus is a practical approach to group decision making. Existing research also supports the basic assumptions underlying the model. For example, Vroom and his colleagues reported that when expert managers read a case study of a leadership decision and then made a recommendation about an appropriate leadership method, their suggestions coincided with the predictions of the normative model (Vroom, 2003).

## GROUPS AS IMPERFECT DECISION MAKERS

People often have harsh words to say about the decisions made by groups. Members complain about time wasted in groups and swap jokes such as "An elephant is a mouse designed by a committee," "Trying to solve a problem through group discussion is like trying to clear up a traffic jam by honking your horn," and "Committees consist of the unfit appointed by the unwilling to do the unnecessary." Although groups, with their vastly greater informational and motivational resources, have the *potential* to outperform individuals, they

**TABLE 11.1 Group Members' Descriptions of Problems Experienced When Trying to Make a Group Decision**

| Problem | Frequency | Description |
|---|---|---|
| Communication skills | 10% | Poor listening skills, ineffective voice, poor nonverbal communication, lack of effective visual aids, misunderstands or does not clearly identify topic, is repetitive, uses jargon |
| Egocentric behavior | 8% | Dominates conversation and group; behaviors are loud, overbearing; one-upmanship, show of power, manipulation, intimidation, filibustering; talks to hear self talk; followers or brown-nosers; clowns and goof-offs |
| Nonparticipation | 7% | Not all participate, do not speak up, do not volunteer, are passive, lack discussion, silent starts |
| Sidetracking | 6.5% | Leaves main topic |
| Interruptions | 6% | Members interrupt speaker; talk over others; socialize; allow phone calls, messages from customers/clients |
| Negative leader behavior | 6% | Unorganized and unfocused, not prepared, late, has no control, gets sidetracked, makes no decisions |
| Attitudes and emotions | 5% | Poor attitude, defensive or evasive, argumentative, personal accusations, no courtesy or respect, complain or gripe, lack of control of emotions |

SOURCE: Adapted from Di Salvo, Nikkel, & Monroe, 1989.

do not always reach that potential. When and why do groups make poor decisions?

## Group Discussion Pitfalls

Most experts on group communication agree that misunderstanding seems to be the rule in groups, with accurate understanding being the exception. On the sender side, many group members lack the skills needed to express themselves clearly. They fail to make certain that their verbal and nonverbal messages are easily decipherable and so unintentionally mislead, confuse, or even insult other members. One study of college students reported that 33% could not give accurate directions, 49% could not summarize the points made by a person who disagreed with them, and 35% could neither state their point of view clearly nor defend it (Rubin, 1985). On the receiver side, inaccuracies also arise from the information-processing limitations and faulty listening habits of human beings. Listeners tend to *level* (simplify and shorten), *sharpen* (embellish distinctions made by the speaker), and *assimilate* (interpret messages so that they match personal expectations and beliefs) information offered by others during a discussion (Campbell, 1958b; Collins & Guetzkow, 1964).

Nor do all group members have the interpersonal skills that a discussion demands (Spitzberg & Cupach, 2002). When researchers asked 569 full-time employees who worked at jobs ranging from clerical positions to upper-level management to describe "in their own words what happens during a meeting that limits its effectiveness," they received nearly 2500 answers. The problems reported, which are summarized in Table 11.1, fell into seven basic categories—communication skills, egocentric behavior, nonparticipation, failure to stay focused (tendency to become sidetracked), interruptions, negative leader behaviors, and negative attitudes and emotions. The participants in this research, and the research discussed in Focus 11.2, suggested that the groups failed more frequently than they succeeded (Di Salvo, Nikkel, & Monroe, 1989).

Sometimes groups use discussion to *avoid* rather than make a decision. People tend to be "reluctant decision makers" who will do anything to avoid making a hard choice (Janis & Mann, 1977). Avoidance tactics include the following:

**Focus 11.2 Are Meetings Interruptions?**

*The most painful problem in business: Death by meeting.*

—Patrick M. Lencioni (2004)

People in organizational settings attend many meetings, and relatively lengthy ones at that. Usually scheduled by someone in authority, meetings serve a variety of purposes, including solving problems, sharing information, making decisions, identifying goals, establishing procedures, increasing coordination, and providing feedback. One source estimates the number of meetings held in the United States in a year's period to be about three billion (Nunamaker et al., 1997).

People, however, are not particularly enthusiastic about meetings. They may be essential tools for organizing productivity, but those who attend often consider them to be boring, uninteresting, and inefficient. They can also, in some cases, be filled with conflict, so that they are not just boring but also threatening. They can also be viewed as interruptions of the work that must be done, particularly by those who do not need to coordinate their activities with others.

Steve Rogelberg and his colleagues explored the downside of meetings by asking workers in England, Australia, and the United States about their involvement in meetings and to rate them on a scale from 1 (extremely ineffective) to 5 (extremely effective). The researchers also measured such variables as job satisfaction, stress (e.g., tension, anxiety, worry, gloom, depression, and misery), and the degree of interdependence required by their job. People who thought their meetings were effective felt more enthusiastic about their work, more satisfied, and more productive. But if they rated their meetings as ineffective, then they were more depressed, more anxious, and more likely to be thinking about quitting—particularly if they did not feel that they needed to work closely with other people to accomplish their work-related tasks. Many saw meetings as interruptions—not as ways to get more work done, but as obstacles to productivity (Luong & Rogelberg, 2005; Rogelberg et al., 2006).

These findings suggest that most people would appreciate two things: a reduction in the number of meetings and an improvement in the quality of those that take place. Meetings need not be tedious wastes of time, but to avoid this fate both leaders and followers should structure their groups so that they are efficient, productive, and interpersonally enjoyable (Lencioni, 2004).

- *Procrastination.* The group postpones the decision rather than studying alternatives and arguing their relative merits.
- *Bolstering.* The group quickly but arbitrarily formulates a decision without thinking things through completely, and then bolsters the preferred solution by exaggerating the favorable consequences and minimizing the importance and likelihood of unfavorable consequences.
- *Denying responsibility.* The group avoids taking responsibility by delegating the decision to a subcommittee or by diffusing accountability throughout the entire assembly.
- *Muddling through.* The group muddles through the issue (Lindblom, 1965) by considering "only a very narrow range of policy alternatives that differ to only a small degree from the existing policy" (Janis & Mann, 1977, p. 33).
- "*Satisficing*" (what "satisfies" will "suffice"). Members accept a low-risk, easy solution instead of searching for the best solution.
- *Trivializing the discussion.* As noted in Focus 11.1, the group avoids dealing with larger issues by focusing on minor issues.

### The Shared Information Bias

The Bay of Pigs planners spent much time talking about the incompetence of Castro's forces and how U.S. citizens would react to the invasion. They did not spend as much time talking about the weapons that the troops would carry, the political climate in Cuba, the terrain of the area where the invasion would take place, or the type of communication system used by Cuban military forces. Only the CIA representatives knew that the morale of the invasion force was very low, but they never mentioned that information during the discussion. President

Kennedy had information from many sources that would have forced the group to reappraise its decision, but Kennedy kept this information to himself during the group discussions (Kramer, 2008).

The good news is that groups can pool their individual resources to make a decision that takes into account far more information than any one individual can consider. The bad news is that groups spend too much of their discussion time examining *shared information*—details that two or more group members know in common—rather than unshared information (Stasser, 1992; Wittenbaum, Hollingshead, & Botero, 2004). If all the members of a group discussing an invasion plan know that the majority of U.S. citizens oppose communism, then this topic will be discussed at length. But if only the CIA representative knows that the invading troops are poorly trained or only Kennedy knows that Cuban citizens support Castro, these important—but unshared—pieces of information might never be discussed.

The harmful consequences of this **shared information bias** are substantial when the group must have access to the unshared information to make a good decision. If a group is working on a problem where the shared information suggests that Alternative A is correct, but the unshared information favors Alternative B, then the group will only discover this so-called *hidden profile* if it discusses the unshared information. Garold Stasser and William Titus (1985) studied this problem by giving the members of four-person groups 16 pieces of information about three candidates for student body president. Candidate A was the best choice for the post, for he possessed eight positive qualities, four neutral qualities, and four negative qualities. The other two candidates had four positive qualities, eight neutral qualities, and four negative qualities. When the group members were given all the available information about the candidates, 83% of the groups favored Candidate A—an improvement over the 67% rate reported by the participants before they joined their group. But groups did not fare so well when Stasser and Titus manipulated the distribution of the positive and negative information among the members to create a hidden profile. Candidate A still had eight positive qualities, but Stasser and Titus made certain that each group member received information about only two of these qualities. Person 1, for example, knew that Candidate A had positive qualities P1 and P2; Person 2 knew that he had positive qualities P3 and P4; Person 3 knew that he had positive qualities P5 and P6; and Person 4 knew that he had positive qualities P7 and P8. But they all knew that Candidate A had negative qualities N1, N2, N3, and N4. Had they pooled their information carefully, they would have discovered that Candidate A had positive qualities P1 to P8, and only four negative qualities. But they oversampled the shared negative qualities and chose the less qualified candidate 76% of the time (Stasser & Titus, 1985, 1987).

**What Causes the Shared Information Bias?** The shared information bias reflects the dual purposes of discussion. As a form of *informational influence*, discussions help individuals marshal the evidence and information they need to make good decisions. But as a form of *normative influence*, discussions give members the chance to influence each other's opinions on the issue. Discussing unshared information may be enlightening, but discussing shared information helps the group reach consensus. Hence, when group members are motivated more by a desire get closure or to convince the group to back their initial preferences, biases are stronger; but if members are striving to make the best decision, the shared information bias becomes less pronounced (Postmes, Spears, & Cihangir, 2001; Scholten et al., 2007). The bias is strongest when groups work on judgmental tasks that do not have a demonstrably correct solution, as the goal of the group is to reach agreement rather than to find the right answer (Stewart & Stasser, 1998). Groups are also more biased when their members think that they do not have enough information to make a fully informed decision (Stasser & Stewart, 1992).

---

**shared information bias** The tendency for groups to spend more time discussing information that all members know (shared information) and less time examining information that only a few members know (unshared).

The shared information bias also reflects the psychological and interpersonal needs of group members. If group members enter into the group discussion with a clear preference, they will argue in favor of their preference and resist changing their minds. If the shared information all points in one direction—as it did in Stasser and Titus's (1985) study of hidden profiles—then all the group members begin the discussion with a negative opinion of Candidate A. The group's final choice reflects these initial preferences (Brodbeck et al., 2002; Gigone & Hastie, 1997; Greitemeyer & Schulz-Hardt, 2003; Henningsen & Henningsen, 2003).

The shared information bias also reflects the nature of group discussion. Members are striving to reach the best decision possible, but they have other motivations as well: they are trying to establish reputations for themselves, secure tighter bonds of attraction with others, and possibly compete with and succeed against other group members (Wittenbaum et al., 2004). Therefore, they are selective regarding when they disclose information and to whom they disclose it, often emphasizing shared information to express their agreement with others in the group. Ironically, people consider shared information to be highly diagnostic, so they mistakenly believe that people who discuss shared information are more knowledgeable, competent, and credible than are group members who contribute unshared information to the discussion (Wittenbaum, Hubbell, & Zuckerman, 1999). Members, to make a good impression with the group, dwell on what everyone knows rather than on the points that only they understand. Group members who anticipate a group discussion implicitly focus on information that they know others also possess, instead of concentrating on information that only they possess (Wittenbaum, Stasser, & Merry, 1996).

**Can the Shared Information Bias Be Avoided?** Even though groups prefer to spend their time discussing shared information, experienced members avoid this tendency, and they often intervene to focus the group's attention on unshared data (Wittenbaum, 1998). When researchers studied medical teams making decisions, they noted that the more senior group members repeated more shared information, but they also repeated more unshared information than the other group members. Moreover, as the discussion progressed, they were more likely to repeat unshared information that was mentioned during the session—evidence of their attempt to bring unshared information out through the discussion (Larson et al., 1996). Groups can also avoid the shared information bias if they spend more time actively discussing their decisions. Because group members tend to discuss shared information first, groups are more likely to review unshared information in longer meetings (Larson, Foster-Fishman, & Keys, 1994; Winquist & Larson, 1998). Other methods of avoiding the bias include increasing the diversity of opinions within the group (Smith, 2008), using an advocacy approach rather than general discussion (Greitemeyer et al., 2006), emphasizing the importance of dissent (Klocke, 2007), and introducing the discussion as a new topic (new business) rather than a return to a previously discussed item (Reimer, Reimer, & Hinsz, 2008).

Technology also offers a solution to the bias. **Group decision support systems** (GDSS) offer members a way to catalog, more comprehensively, the group's total stock of information and then share that information collectively. Depending on the GDSS, the group would have access to an array of decision-making tools, such as databases, search engines for locating information, communication tools for sending messages to specific individuals and to the entire group, shared writing and drawing areas where members can collaborate on projects, and computational tools that will poll members automatically and help them to estimate costs, risks, probabilities, and so on (Hollingshead, 2001b). The value of a GDSS—even a simple one that only automated communication among members but did not structure voting or information search—was

---

**group decision support systems** A set of integrated tools groups use to structure and facilitate their decision making, including computer programs that expedite data acquisition, communication among group members, document sharing, and the systematic review of alternative actions and outcomes.

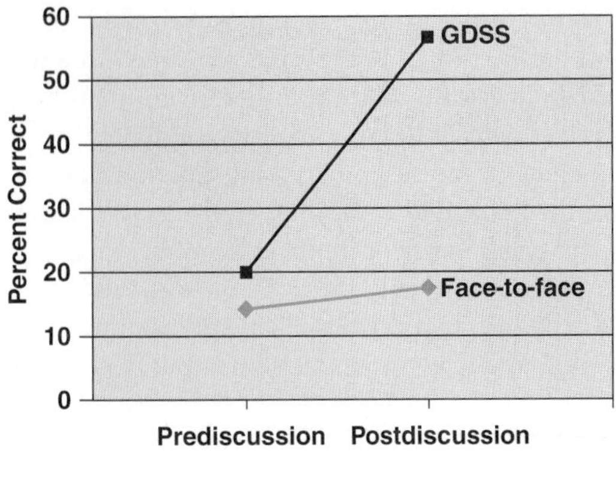


**FIGURE 11.4** The improvement in performance when groups use a decision support system (GDSS). Groups that met in a traditional face-to-face group session fell prey to the shared information bias, for very few of them solved a hidden-profile problem correctly. But groups that met via computer, and could access a shared list of discussion items, were more likely to select the best solution to the problem.

SOURCE: Lam & Schaubroeck, 2000.

confirmed by researchers who asked group members to select between three applicants for a job. As in previous hidden-profile studies, in some cases the information about the candidate was distributed to group members so that the shared information favored Candidate B, but if all the information was considered, Candidate A would be selected. Participants worked either in face-to-face groups or used the GDSS, and they also made their choices before any discussion and after the discussion. As Figure 11.4 indicates, groups that used the GDSS were more likely to select the best candidate after their discussion (Lam & Schaubroeck, 2000).

## Cognitive Limitations

Groups generate decisions through processes that are both active and complex. Members formulate initial preferences, gather and share information about those preferences, and then combine their views in a single group choice. Although these tasks are relatively ordinary ones, they sometimes demand too much cognitive work from members. The president's committee, for example, wanted to weigh all the relevant factors carefully before making its choice, but the complexity of the problem outstripped the members' relatively meager cognitive capacity. People's judgments in such demanding situations are often systematically distorted by cognitive and motivational biases. People use the information they have available to them inappropriately, putting too much emphasis on interesting information and ignoring statistical information. People sometimes form conclusions very quickly and then do not sufficiently revise those conclusions once they acquire additional information. When people cannot easily imagine an outcome, they assume that such an outcome is less likely to occur than one that springs easily to mind. People overestimate their judgmental accuracy because they remember all the times their decisions were confirmed and forget the times when their predictions were disconfirmed. People make mistakes (Arkes, 1993; Brownstein, 2003; Plous, 1993).

Groups, unfortunately, are not immune from these judgmental biases. When Norbert Kerr, Robert MacCoun, and Geoffrey Kramer (1996a, 1996b) reviewed the research literature looking for studies of these mental glitches in decision making, they identified the three general categories of potential bias summarized in Table 11.2:

- *sins of commission*: the misuse of information
- *sins of omission*: overlooking useful information
- *sins of imprecision*: relying inappropriately on mental rules of thumb, or heuristics, that oversimplify the decision

After reviewing studies that compared individuals' and groups' resistance to these types of biases, Kerr and his colleagues cautiously ruled against groups: Groups amplify rather than suppress these biases. For example, they use information that has already been discredited or they have been told to ignore; they overlook statistical information about general tendencies; they overemphasize personality as a cause of behaviors that are due, in part, to pressures of the situation; and they base decisions on information that is readily available rather than actually diagnostic. More so even than individuals, groups know decisional sin.

**TABLE 11.2 Types of Errors Made by Individuals and by Groups When Making Decisions**

| Type of Error | Examples |
|---|---|
| Sins of Commission | *Belief perseverance*: reliance on information that has already been reviewed and found to be inaccurate |
| | *Sunk cost bias*: reluctance to abandon a course of action once an investment has been made in that action |
| | *Extra-evidentiary bias*: the use of information that one has been told explicitly to ignore |
| | *Hindsight bias*: the tendency to overestimate the accuracy of one's prior knowledge of an outcome |
| Sins of Omission | *Base rate bias*: failure to pay attention to information about general tendencies |
| | *Fundamental attribution error*: stressing dispositional causes when making attributions about the cause of people's behaviors |
| Sins of Imprecision | *Availability heuristic*: basing decisions on information that is readily available |
| | *Conjunctive bias*: failing to recognize that the probability of two events occurring together will always be less than the probability of just one of the events occurring |
| | *Representativeness heuristic*: excessive reliance on salient but misleading aspects of a problem |

Groups must exercise care to keep these biases in check (Härtel & Härtel, 1997; Littlepage & Karau, 1997). Consider, for example, individuals' and groups' resistance to the **confirmation bias**. In decision-making situations, people often start off with an initial preference and then seek out additional information to test the accuracy of their initial inclinations. Unfortunately, this review is biased in many cases, for people usually seek out information that confirms their preferences, and they avoid disconfirming evidence. Groups, too, seek out information that supports the prediscussion preferences of most members, but they can minimize this bias if they deliberately ban any public statements of initial preferences (Dawes, 1988).

Groups also avoid the confirmation bias when they include individuals who adopt divergent minority positions on the issue. Researchers studied this possibility by giving individuals some background information about a company that was considering relocating its production facilities. Participants indicated their initial preference on the matter, and the experimenters then used those choices to create three kinds of groups: (1) unanimous groups, composed of individuals who shared the same initial preference; (2) groups with one member who took a minority position on the issue; and (3) groups with two minority members. Participants in these three conditions were given the opportunity to select and review 10 additional background readings, which were summarized by short thesis statements that indicated they either supported or opposed relocation. A fourth set of participants made these choices as individuals. As Figure 11.5 indicates, the confirmation bias was robust—particularly in the homogeneous group. The inclusion of one dissenter lowered the tendency somewhat, such that the bias was equal to that shown by lone individuals. Including two dissenters, however, tended to subdue the bias. These results confirm the value of including people with a range of experiences and opinions as members of groups that must make critical decisions (Schulz-Hardt et al., 2000; see also Schulz-Hardt, Jochims, & Frey, 2002).

---

**confirmation bias** The tendency to seek out information that confirms one's inferences rather than disconfirms them.

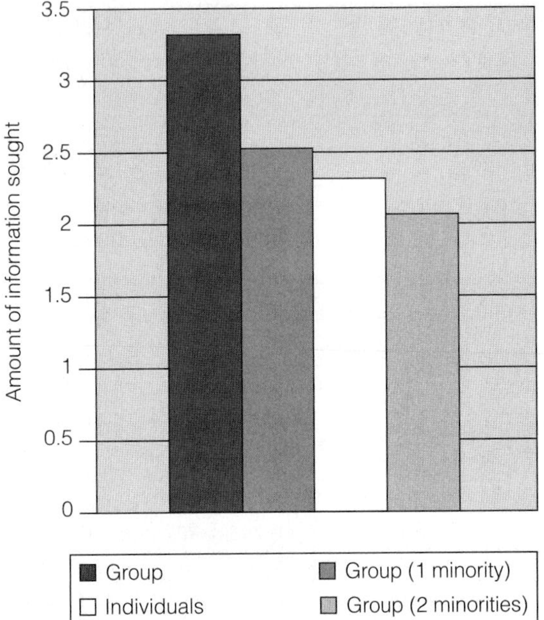


**FIGURE 11.5** The magnitude of the confirmation bias in groups and individuals. Individuals, when they must make a decision, tend to seek out information that supports their initial preferences. This tendency is even stronger in groups, for groups showed a stronger preference for confirming information. Groups that include two members who initially disagree with the position taken by the majority of the members, however, are somewhat *less* biased than individuals.

## GROUP POLARIZATION

Historians cannot say why President Kennedy decided to create a committee to help him review the invasion plan, but he may have acted on the intuitively appealing notion that groups have a moderating impact on individuals. He may have assumed that a group, if faced with a choice between a risky alternative, such as "Invade Cuba," and a more moderate alternative, such as "Use diplomatic means to influence Cuba," would prefer the moderate route. Unfortunately for Kennedy, for his advisers, and for the members of the attack force, groups' decisions are often more extreme than individuals' decisions. Groups do not urge restraint; instead, they *polarize*.

### The Risky-Shift Phenomenon

At about the time that Kennedy's committee was grappling with the problems inherent in the invasion plan, group experts were initiating studies of the effects of group discussion on decision making. Although some researchers discovered that groups preferred more conservative solutions than individuals, others found a surprising shift in the direction of greater risk (Stoner, 1961, 1968).

This shift was often measured using the **Choice-Dilemmas Questionnaire**, which asked individuals or groups to consider questions such as:

> Mr. A, an electrical engineer, who is married and has one child, has been working for a large electronics corporation since graduating from college five years ago. He is assured of a lifetime job with a modest, though adequate, salary and liberal pension benefits upon retirement. On the other hand, it is very unlikely that his salary will increase much before he retires. While attending a convention, Mr. A is offered a job with a small, newly founded company which has a highly uncertain future. The new job would pay more to start and would offer the possibility of a share in the ownership if the company survived the competition of the larger firms.
>
> Imagine that you are advising Mr. A. Listed below are several probabilities or odds of the new company proving financially sound. Please check the lowest probability that you would consider acceptable to make it worthwhile for Mr. A to take the new job.

---

**Choice-Dilemmas Questionnaire** A self-report measure of willingness to make risky decisions that asks respondents to read a series of scenarios involving a course of action that may or may not yield financial, interpersonal, or educational benefits, then indicate what the odds of success would have to be before they would recommend the course of action.

____The chances are 1 in 10 that the company will prove financially sound.
____The chances are 3 in 10 that the company will prove financially sound.
____The chances are 5 in 10 that the company will prove financially sound.
____The chances are 7 in 10 that the company will prove financially sound.
____The chances are 9 in 10 that the company will prove financially sound.
____Place a check here if you think Mr. A should not take the new job no matter what the probabilities. (Pruitt, 1971, p. 359)

When individuals were asked to make decisions individually and then they convened in a group to revisit their choices, the group decisions were somewhat riskier than those favored by individuals. For example, in one study that used the *Choice Dilemmas Questionnaire* the mean of prediscussion individual decisions was 5.5 on the scale from 1 (most risky) to 9 (least risky). The mean of the group's consensual decision, however, was 4.8—a shift of 0.7 in the direction of greater risk. This shift also occurred when individual judgments were collected after the group discussion and when the individual postdiscussion measures were delayed two to six weeks (the delayed post-tests were collected from male participants only). Participants in a control condition shifted very little (Wallach, Kogan, & Bem, 1962).

The finding that groups seem to make riskier decisions than individuals was dubbed the **risky-shift phenomenon**. Shifts were reliably demonstrated in countries around the world, including Canada, the United States, England, France, Germany, and New Zealand, and with many kinds of group participants (Pruitt, 1971). Although commentators sometimes wondered about the generality and significance of the phenomenon (Smith, 1972), laboratory findings were eventually corroborated by field studies (Lamm & Myers, 1978).

---

**risky-shift phenomenon** The tendency for groups to make riskier decisions than individuals.

### Polarization Processes in Groups

During this research period, some investigators hinted at the possibility of the opposite process—a *cautious shift*. For example, when the early risky-shift researchers examined the amount of postdiscussion change revealed on each item of the *Choice-Dilemmas Questionnaire*, they frequently found that group members consistently advocated a less risky course of action than did individuals on one particular item (Wallach et al., 1962). Intrigued by this anomalous finding, subsequent researchers wrote additional choice dilemmas, and they, too, occasionally found evidence of a cautious shift. Then, in 1969, researchers reported evidence of individuals moving in both directions after a group discussion, suggesting that both cautious and risky shifts were possible (Doise, 1969).

Researchers also discovered that group discussions not only amplify choices between risky and cautious alternatives, but also group members' attitudes, beliefs, values, judgments, and perceptions (Myers, 1982). In France, for example, where people generally like their government but dislike Americans, group discussion improved their attitude toward their government but exacerbated their negative opinions of Americans (Moscovici & Zavalloni, 1969). Similarly, strongly prejudiced people who discussed racial issues with other prejudiced individuals became even more prejudiced. However, when mildly prejudiced persons discussed racial issues with other mildly prejudiced individuals, they became less prejudiced (Myers & Bishop, 1970).

Somewhat belatedly, researchers realized that risky shifts after group discussions were a part of a more general process. When people discuss issues in groups, they sometimes draw a more extreme conclusion than would be suggested by the average of their individual judgments. The direction of this shift depends on their average initial preferences. A group of liberal people who gather to discuss gun control will likely become even more enthusiastic about regulating handguns after the discussion. When supporters gather to discuss a candidate's strengths and weaknesses, by the meeting's end their opinions will likely become even more

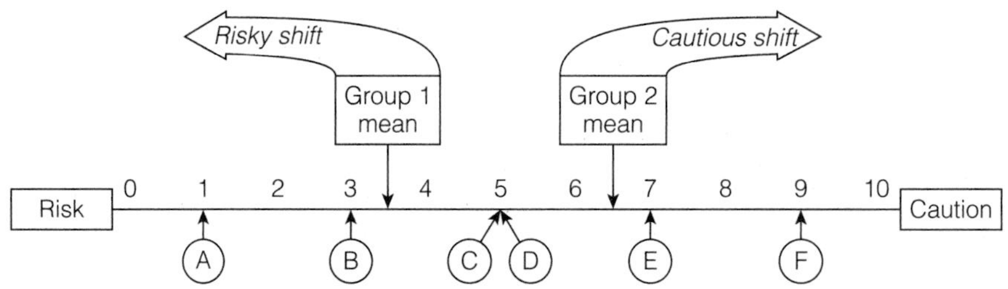


**FIGURE 11.6** A schematic representation of polarization in groups. Imagine that Group 1 includes Person A (who chose 1), Person B (who chose 3), and Persons C and D (who both chose 5); the average of pregroup choices would be (1 + 3 + 5 + 5)/4, or 3.5. Because this mean is less than 5, a risky shift would probably occur in Group 1. If, in contrast, Group 2 contained Persons C, D, E, and F, their pregroup average would be (5 + 5 + 7 + 9)/4, or 6.5. Because this mean is closer to the caution pole, a cautious shift would probably occur in the group.

favorable toward the candidate. A gathering of students who are moderately negative about a professor's teaching methods will become openly hostile after a discussion. David Myers and Helmut Lamm called this process **group polarization** because the "average postgroup response will tend to be more extreme in the same direction as the average of the pregroup responses" (Myers & Lamm, 1976, p. 603; see also Lamm & Myers, 1978).

Imagine two groups of four individuals whose opinions vary in terms of preference for risk. As Figure 11.6 indicates, when the average choice of the group members before discussion is closer to the risky pole of the continuum than to the cautious pole (as would be the case in a group composed of Persons A, B, C, and D), a risky shift will occur. If, in contrast, the group is composed of Persons C, D, E, and F, a cautious shift will take place, because the pregroup mean of 6.5 falls closer to the cautious pole. This example is, of course, something of an oversimplification, because the shift depends on the distance from the psychological rather than the mathematical midpoint of the scale. As Myers and Lamm (1976) noted, on choice dilemmas, an initial pregroup mean of 6 or smaller is usually sufficient to produce a risky shift, whereas a mean of 7 or greater is necessary to produce a cautious shift. If the pregroup mean falls between 6 and 7, a shift is unlikely.

**group polarization** The tendency for members of a deliberating group to move to a more extreme position, with the direction of the shift determined by the majority or average of the members' predeliberation preferences.

### What Causes Group Polarization?

How do groups intensify individuals' reactions? Early explanations suggested that groups feel less responsible for their decisions and are overly influenced by risk-prone leaders, but in time, investigators recognized that polarization results from social influence processes that operate routinely in groups, including *social comparison*, *persuasion*, and *social identity* (Friedkin, 1999; Liu & Latané, 1998).

**Social Comparison** When people make decisions individually, they have no way to determine whether they are risk-averse or risk-takers; whether they are responding as most people do or are overreacting; whether the position they are defending is reasonable or whether they are arguing for an idea that most people think is bizarre. But when group members make choices together, they use others as reference points to evaluate their own preferences and positions (Goethals & Zanna, 1979; Myers, 1978). As social comparison theory suggests, individuals spontaneously compare themselves to others, and if they find a difference between their view and the group's, they may move toward the group's view (Sanders & Baron, 1977). Polarization occurs because group members, through discussion, discover the group's norm on the issue, and then they stake a claim to a position that exceeds that norm in whatever direction the majority of the members endorse. If the group discussion indicates that the majority of the group likes Plan A, then a desire to create a positive impression in the group may prompt members to claim that they *really* like Plan A (Weigold & Schlenker, 1991): "To be virtuous . . . is to be different from the mean—in the right direction and to the right degree" (Brown, 1974, p. 469).

**Persuasive Arguments** Group members also change their opinions in response to others' arguments and ideas. If, for example, the discussion reveals several strong arguments that favor Plan A rather than Plan B, members will shift in that direction. But as **persuasive-arguments theory** notes, groups usually generate more arguments that support the position endorsed by the majority of the group, or the position that is most consistent with dominant social values—in part because members may be more willing to express arguments that are consistent with social norms. As a result, the group persuades itself, as more arguments favoring the dominant viewpoint are brought up during the discussion (Burnstein & Vinokur, 1973, 1977; Vinokur & Burnstein, 1974, 1978). If discussants are asked to repeat the arguments raised in the discussion, polarization increases because members are more likely to be persuaded by the content of the pool of available arguments (Brauer, Judd, & Gliner, 1995). The group's social decision scheme may also favor a more extreme position rather than a moderate one. If, for example, a group adopts a "risk-supported-wins" rule, and two members of the group express a willingness to tolerate extreme risk, then the group may shift in that direction (Davis, Kameda, & Stasson, 1992; Zuber, Crott, & Werner, 1992).

**Social Identity** Curiously, at least for persuasive-arguments theory, group members sometimes shift their opinions when they discover others' positions but not their arguments (Blascovich, Ginsburg, & Howe, 1975, 1976). Why? Social identity theory suggests that people are not persuaded by the content of other's arguments, but by consensus of opinion. If, through discussion, members come to believe that the prototypical group member holds a relatively extreme attitude on the issue, those who identify with the group will shift in that direction (Haslam, 2004). This shift causes the diversity of opinions in the group to decrease, as members converge on what they hold to be the opinion of the prototypical group member. This conception of the prototype may also shift towards more extreme positions to differentiate the ingroup from other groups. When, for example, group members learned another group had taken a risky position on an issue, the group members differentiated themselves from that group by becoming more cautious. When the group learned the other group was cautious, then the group shifted in the direction of risk (Hogg, Turner, & David, 1990). Polarization may also result because people are far more likely to respond positively to the arguments offered by ingroup members than outgroup members, and so those who hold a shared social identity may end up persuading each other to take increasingly more extreme positions (Mackie & Queller, 2000).

---

**persuasive-arguments theory** An explanation of polarization in groups assuming that group members change their opinions during group discussion, generally adopting the position favored by the majority of the members, because the group can generate more arguments favoring that position.

## The Consequences of Polarization

Would people who believe that environmental pollution is a serious problem be more likely, after discussion, to insist on severe measures to prevent pollution? Would bringing together two sides in a community conflict and allowing them to meet separately for an hour before a joint meeting create even more tensions between the two groups? Would a group of government experts who slightly favored an invasion plan enthusiastically endorse the plan after they discussed it? Do groups amplify group members' shared tendencies? Studies of polarization say *yes* (Sunstein, 2002).

Polarization may, in some cases, yield positive effects. Groups, when viewed from an evolutionary perspective, were designed to monitor risk—hence

## Focus 11.3 Alcohol and Risk: Groupdrink?

*It is also their general practice to deliberate upon affairs of weight when they are drunk. . . . Sometimes, however, they are sober at their first deliberation, but in this case they always reconsider the matter under the influence of wine.*

—Herodotus (480–425 BC), *Histories* (p. 63)

People have been brewing and consuming alcoholic beverages for centuries. Ethanol, the active ingredient in beers, wines, and liquors, is a depressant, yet it tends to disinhibit many forms of behavior, particularly when ingested in larger quantities. But drinking is usually group drinking, or **groupdrink**. Most people who drink alcohol do so in social settings with other people, rather than alone. In such groups people become more interpersonally active, less task-focused, and more emotionally labile. Alcohol is also associated with cognitive changes, including slowed reaction time and impaired information processing, and group drinking may exacerbate these effects.

Anecdotal accounts of intoxicated groups confirm the idea that drunken groups behave differently than sober ones; they tend to be more socially dynamic and emotionally intense, and they are also more likely to engage in risky, ill-considered actions (Schweitzer & Kerr, 2000). Laboratory studies of such groups also suggest that intoxicated groups take more risks and are more competitive, although some exceptions have been noted. For example, in one investigation, researchers provided group members either with alcohol or with a placebo before asking them to make a choice between two alternatives that varied in risk. The low-risk choice involved answering a questionnaire that would take about 30 minutes to finish. The high-risk choice involved flipping a coin to make the decision: if heads they could complete an hour-long questionnaire but if tails they could skip the questionnaire altogether. Only one of the sober groups asked to flip the coin, but six of the nine drunken groups chose the more risky option (Sayette et al., 2004). Other investigators, turning their attention to cooperation, found that inebriated groups were less cooperative than sober ones (Hopthrow et al., 2007).

Other studies suggest, however, that alcohol may improve group functioning by increasing social monitoring. In one study, investigators provided group members with alcohol or with placebos, and then asked them to make a series of wagers that varied in level of risk. Individuals who were inebriated made more risky decisions, but the drunken groups did not—these groups made their decisions more slowly than the sober groups, and this slower pace may have helped the groups recalibrate the riskiness of their choices (Abrams et al., 2006). These findings suggest that, at least in some circumstances, drunken groups realize that they might be making errors in judgment, and so are more careful to check for mistakes and misinterpretations. When the group is only slightly intoxicated, members' diligence results in a process gain, and so reduces the likelihood of risk taking and decisional errors (Frings et al., 2008). Additional research is needed, however, to determine if these gains associated with alcohol occur in groups outside of the laboratory and in groups that have ingested higher levels of alcohol.

they are sensitive to threats and urge caution when alarmed (Kameda & Tamura, 2007). A group's collective efficacy may rise as individually optimistic members join together and discuss their chances for success. The members of a support group may become far more hopeful of their chances for recovery when they gather together with others who are moderately optimistic. Innovations and new ideas may be adopted by large numbers of people as polarization amplifies enthusiasm for the new products, methods, or outlooks. Polarization may also encourage the strengthening of positions within the group that might go unexpressed or even be suppressed. Thus, polarization, though sometimes a source of error and bias, can in some cases have a beneficial impact on the group and its members (see Focus 11.3).

## VICTIMS OF GROUPTHINK

Irving Janis was intrigued by President Kennedy's ExCom group. The committee, like so many others, failed to make the best decision it could.

---

**groupdrink** Imbibing alcoholic drinks in a group context; also, the psychological and group-level changes that occur when groups become inebriated.

Its failure, though, was so spectacular that Janis wondered if something more than such common group difficulties as faulty communication and judgmental biases were to blame.

Janis pursued this insight by searching for other groups that made similar errors in judgment. And he found many that qualified: Senior naval officers who ignored repeated warnings of Japan's aggressive intentions regarding Pearl Harbor and took few steps to defend it; President Truman's policy-making staff who recommended that U.S. troops cross the 38th parallel during the Korean War, prompting China to ally with North Korea against the United States; President Nixon's staff who decided to cover up involvement in the break-in at Watergate. After studying these groups and their gross errors of judgment, he concluded that they suffered from *groupthink*—"a mode of thinking that people engage in when they are deeply involved in a cohesive ingroup, when the members' strivings for unanimity override their motivation to realistically appraise alternative courses of actions" (Janis, 1982, p. 9). During groupthink, members try so hard to agree with one another that they make mistakes and commit errors that could easily be avoided.

Janis sought to identify both the causes of groupthink, as well as the symptoms that signal that a group may be experiencing this malady. As Figure 11.7 indicates, Janis identified three key sets of antecedent conditions that set the stage for groupthink, including cohesion, structural faults of the group or organization, and provocative situational contexts. These conditions cause members to seek out agreement with others (concurrence-seeking tendency), which in turn leads to two classes of observable consequences: symptoms of groupthink and symptoms of defective decision-making. In this section, we will work backwards through the model shown in Figure 11.7: We will start with the warning signs of groupthink and then consider the antecedent conditions.

### Symptoms of Groupthink

Like a physician who searches for symptoms that signal the onset of the illness, Janis identified a number of recurring patterns that occur in groupthink situations. He organized these symptoms into three categories: *overestimation of the group*, *closed-mindedness*, and *pressures toward uniformity* (Janis, 1972, 1982, 1983, 1985, 1989; Janis & Mann, 1977; Longley & Pruitt, 1980; Wheeler & Janis, 1980).

**Overestimation of the Group** Groups that have fallen into the trap of groupthink are actually planning fiascoes and making all the wrong choices. Yet the members usually assume that everything is working perfectly. They even express enthusiasm in their public statements about their wrong-headed decisions (Tetlock, 1979). Janis traced this unwarranted optimism to illusions of invulnerability and illusions of morality.

The Bay of Pigs planners, like many groups, overestimated their group's decisional savvy. Members felt that they were performing well, even though they were not. This illusory thinking, though commonplace, becomes so extreme during groupthink that Janis called it an *illusion of invulnerability*. Feelings of assurance and confidence engulfed the group. The members felt that their plan was virtually infallible and that their committee could not make major errors in judgment. Such feelings of confidence and power may help athletic teams or combat units reach their objectives, but the feeling that all obstacles can be easily overcome through power and good luck can cut short clear, analytic thinking in decision-making groups (Silver & Bufanio, 1996).

The planners also believed in the inherent morality of their group and its decisions. Yet the plan to invade Cuba could unsympathetically be described as an unprovoked sneak attack by a major world power on a virtually defenseless country. But the decision makers, suffering from *illusions of morality*, seemed to lose their principles in the group's desire to bravely end Castro's regime. Although groups are capable of reaching admirable levels of moral thought, this capability is unrealized during groupthink (McGraw & Bloomfield, 1987).

**Closed-mindedness** Groups that are overtaken by groupthink are not open-minded groups,

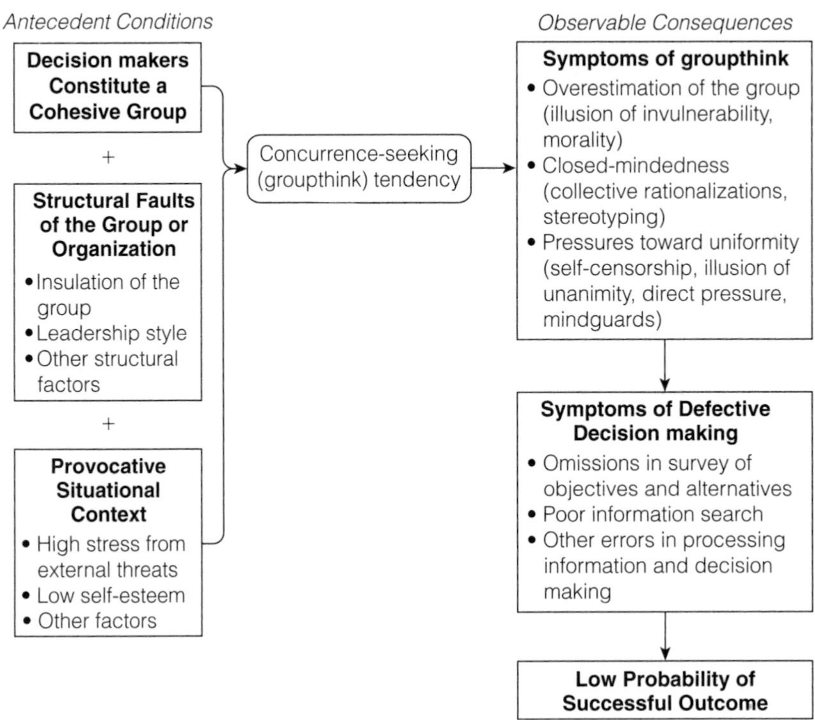


**FIGURE 11.7** Irving Janis's (1982) original theory of *groupthink*.

searching for new ideas and perspectives. Rather, they are *closed-minded*—rigidly shut off from alternatives, merely seeking to bolster their initial decision through *rationalization*. One key element of this closure is the tendency to view other groups in biased, simplistic ways. For example, the members of the planning group shared an inaccurate and negative opinion of Castro and his political ideology, and they often expressed these *stereotypes about the outgroup* during group discussions. Castro was depicted as a weak leader, an evil communist, and a man too stupid to realize that his country was about to be attacked. His ability to maintain an air force was discredited, as was his control over his troops and the citizenry. The group participants' underestimation of their enemy was so pronounced that they sent a force of 1400 men to fight a force of 200,000 and expected an easy success. The group wanted to believe that Castro was an ineffectual leader and military commander, but this oversimplified picture of the dictator turned out to be merely wishful thinking.

**Pressures toward Uniformity** The struggle for consensus is an essential and unavoidable aspect of life in groups, but in groupthink situations, interpersonal pressures make agreeing too easy and disagreeing too difficult. Tolerance for any sort of dissent seems virtually nil, and groups may use harsh measures to bring those who disagree into line. In the president's committee, criticism was taboo, and members who broke this norm were pressured to conform. Janis highlighted four indicators of this pressure: self-censorship, the illusion of unanimity, direct pressure on dissenters, and self-appointed mindguards.

*Self-censorship* is Janis's term for a personal ban on expressing disagreements about the group's decisions. In the planning group, many of the members of the group privately felt uncertain about the plan, but they kept their doubts to themselves. Some even sent private memorandums to the president before or after a meeting; but when the group convened, the doubting Thomases sat in silence. As Schlesinger (1965) later wrote,

> In the months after the Bay of Pigs I bitterly reproached myself for having kept so silent during those crucial discussions in the Cabinet Room, though my feelings of guilt were tempered by the knowledge that a course of objection would have accomplished little save to gain me a name as a nuisance. I can only explain my failure to do more than raise a few timid questions by reporting that one's impulse to blow the whistle on this nonsense was simply undone by the circumstances of the discussion. (p. 225)

This self-imposed gag order created an *illusion of unanimity* in the group. The members seemed to agree that the basic plan presented by the CIA was the only solution to the problem. In later discussions, they appeared to just be "going through the motions" of debate. Retrospective accounts reveal that many of the group's members objected to the plan, but these objections never surfaced during the meetings. Instead, a "curious atmosphere of assumed consensus" (Schlesinger, 1965, p. 250) characterized the discussion, as each person wrongly concluded that everyone else liked the plan. As Janis (1972) explained, the group members played up "areas of convergence in their thinking, at the expense of fully exploring divergences that might disrupt the apparent unity of the group" (p. 39). The Bay of Pigs planners, like the group discussed in Focus 11.4, apparently felt that it would be "better to share a pleasant, balmy group atmosphere than be battered in a storm" (p. 39).

This easygoing, supportive atmosphere did not extend to those who disagreed with the group, however. *Direct pressure* was applied to dissenters, often by self-appointed vigilantes, or **mindguards**, who shielded the group from information that would shake the members' confidence in themselves or their leader. The mindguard diverts controversial information away from the group by losing it, forgetting to mention it, or deeming it irrelevant and thus unworthy of the group's attention. Alternatively, the mindguard may take dissenting members aside and pressure them to keep silent. The mindguard may use a variety of strategies to achieve this pressure: requesting the change as a personal favor, pointing out the damage that might be done to the group, or informing the dissenter that in the long run, disagreement would damage his or her position in the group (Uris, 1978). But whatever the method, the overall goal is the same—to contain dissent before it reaches the level of group awareness.

President Kennedy, Rusk, and the president's brother, Robert Kennedy, all acted as mindguards. Kennedy, for example, withheld memorandums condemning the plan from both Schlesinger and Fulbright. Rusk suppressed information that his own staff had given him. One extreme example of this mindguarding occurred when Rusk, unable to attend a meeting, sent Undersecretary of State Chester Bowles. Although Bowles was said to be horrified by the plan under discussion, President Kennedy never gave him the opportunity to speak during the meeting. Bowles followed bureaucratic channels to voice his critical misgivings, but his superior, Rusk, did not transmit those concerns to the committee, and he told Bowles that the plan had been revised. Bowles was fired several weeks after the Bay of Pigs defeat—partly because a scapegoat was needed, but also because President Kennedy disliked him intensely (Kramer, 2008).

### Defective Decision Making

If luck had been on the side of the Bay of Pigs planners—if, for example, one of Castro's generals had decided to take over the military on the same day as the invasion—then the attack might have

---

**mindguard** A group member who shields the group from negative or controversial information by gatekeeping and suppressing dissent.

## Focus 11.4 When Is Agreement Difficult to Manage?

*We'd just done the opposite of what we wanted to do.*
—Jerry Harvey (1988, p. 14)

The day was hot and dusty, as was often the case in July in the small town of Coleman, Texas. Jerry Harvey, his wife, and his wife's parents were fanning themselves on the back porch, playing dominoes and drinking lemonade. Suddenly, Jerry's father-in-law suggested, "Let's get in the car and go to Abilene and have dinner at the cafeteria" (Harvey, 1988, p. 13). Abilene was 53 miles away, it was 104 degrees in the shade, and the only available means of transportation was an unairconditioned 1958 Buick. But the rest of the family chimed in with "Sounds great," and "Sure, I haven't been to Abilene in a while." They traveled all the way to Abilene, had a miserable time, and only when they were back on the porch did they realize that none of them had wanted to go in the first place. After blaming each other for the bad decision,

> we all sat back in silence. Here we were, four reasonably sensible people who—of our own volition—had just taken a 106-mile trip across a godforsaken desert in furnace-like heat and dust storm to eat unpalatable food in a hole-in-the-wall cafeteria in Abilene, when none of us had really wanted to go. To be concise, we'd just done the opposite of what we wanted to do. (Harvey, 1988, p. 14)

Groups sometimes make decisions that veer far from the plans, desires, and preferences of their individual members. Organizational expert Jerry Harvey's **Abilene paradox** aptly illustrates this tendency, highlighting two factors that can cause members to mismanage their group's agreement.

First, the Abilene group suffered from a severe case of **pluralistic ignorance**. The group members mistakenly believed that their private opinion about the Abilene outing was discrepant from the other group members' opinions. Therefore, each group member, wishing to be seen as a cooperative member of the family, publicly conformed to what they thought was the group's norm, each one erroneously assuming that he or she was the only one with misgivings. Jerry went to Abilene because that is what everyone else wanted to do—or so he thought. Unfortunately, everyone else was thinking the same thing, so the group mismanaged its consensus (Miller & McFarland, 1991). Pluralistic ignorance prompts people to conform to norms that do not actually exist—except in their minds.

Second, the group committed to its decision quickly, and did not reconsider its choice when negative consequences—the heat, the cost, the discomfort—mounted. This process is sometimes termed **entrapment**—a special form of escalation that occurs when the group expends "more of its time, energy, money, or other resources than seems justifiable by external standards" (Pruitt & Kim, 2004, p. 165). Entrapment occurs when groups become so invested in a course of action that they refuse to reverse their decisions (Brockner, 1995; Brockner & Rubin, 1985). Such situations often lure in groups by raising concerns over investments the group has already made in the choice (Arkes & Blumer, 1985). If a group discovers that the costs for a project are escalating, then the members will rarely consider canceling the project altogether. Instead, they will continue to fund the project, because the initial investment, or **sunk cost**, must be honored. Unfortunately, the money and time invested in a plan of action is already spent and should no longer be considered in weighing the ultimate value of the project. Sunk costs, however, can cause groups to continue to expend resources on projects that will ultimately fail. Analyses of truly massive, much-criticized projects that cost millions of dollars—such as the Millennium Dome in London, EuroDisney, and the Denver International Airport—can often be traced to entrapment (Nutt, 2002).

---

**Abilene paradox** The counterintuitive tendency for a group to decide on a course of action that none of the members of the group individually endorses, resulting from the group's failure to recognize and manage its agreement on key issues.

**pluralistic ignorance** When members of a group hold a wide range of opinions, beliefs, or judgments but express similar opinions, beliefs, or judgments publicly because each member believes that his or her personal view is different from that of the others in the group.

**entrapment** A form of escalating investment in which individuals expend more of their resources in pursuing a chosen course of action than seems appropriate or justifiable by external standards.

**sunk cost** An investment or loss of resources that cannot be recouped by current or future actions.

succeeded. But the Bay of Pigs planners would still have been a groupthink group. Janis did not consider the group to be one overtaken by groupthink only because it made a bad decision, but because it displayed symptoms of groupthink *and* symptoms of defective decision making. The committee, for example, discussed two extreme alternatives—either endorse the Bay of Pigs invasion or abandon Cuba to communism—while ignoring all other potential alternatives. Moreover, the group lost sight of its overall objectives as it became caught up in the minor details of the invasion plan, and it failed to develop contingency plans. The group actively avoided any information that pointed to limitations in its plans, while seeking out facts and opinions that buttressed its initial preferences. The group members did not just make a few small errors. They committed dozens of blunders. The invasion was a fiasco, but it was the faulty decisional strategies of the group that indicated that the group suffered from groupthink.

### Causes of Groupthink

To Janis, groupthink is like a disease that infects healthy groups, rendering them inefficient and unproductive. The symptoms of this disease, such as conformity pressures, illusions, misperceptions, and faulty decision-making strategies, all signal the group's decline, but they are not the root causes of groupthink. These processes undoubtedly contribute to poor judgments, but Janis (1989) distinguished between symptoms of groupthink and its *causes*: *cohesiveness*, *structural faults* of the group or organization, and *provocative situational factors* (see Figure 11.7).

**Cohesiveness** The members of the president's committee felt fortunate to belong to a group that boasted such high morale and esprit de corps. Problems could be handled without too much internal bickering, personality clashes were rare, the atmosphere of each meeting was congenial, and replacements were never needed, because no one ever left the group. However, these benefits of cohesiveness did not offset one fatal consequence of a close-knit group—group pressures so strong that critical thinking degenerates into groupthink.

Of the many factors that contribute to the rise of groupthink, Janis emphasized cohesiveness above all others. He agreed that groups that lack cohesion can also make terrible decisions—"especially if the members are engaging in internal warfare"—but they cannot experience groupthink (Janis, 1982, p. 176). In a cohesive group, members refrain from speaking out against decisions, avoid arguing with others, and strive to maintain friendly, cordial relations at all costs. If cohesiveness reaches such a level that internal disagreements disappear, then the group is ripe for groupthink.

Measures of cohesiveness were, of course, never collected for the president's committee. But many signs point to the group's unity. The committee members were all men, and they were in many cases close personal friends. These men, when describing the group in their memoirs, lauded the group, suggesting that their attitudes toward the group were exceptionally positive. The members also identified with the group and its goals; all proudly proclaimed their membership in such an elite body. Robert Kennedy's remarks, peppered with frequent use of the words *we* and *us*, betrayed the magnitude of this identification:

> It seemed that with John Kennedy leading *us* and with all the talent he had assembled, nothing could stop *us*. *We* believed that if *we* faced up to the nation's problems and applied bold, new ideas with common sense and hard work, *we* would overcome whatever challenged *us*. (quoted in Guthman, 1971, p. 88; italics added)

Other evidence, however, suggests that the ExCom group was not as unified as Janis believed. The membership of the group was not stable, so different people were present at different meetings, and therefore it is likely that no strong sense of identity actually developed. Also, like many groups composed of influential, successful individuals, personalities and differences in style and strategy caused tension within the group. To a large extent, group members were not motivated by group-centered motives, but by their own political ambitions (Kramer, 2008).

**Structural Faults of the Group or Organization** Cohesion is a necessary condition for groupthink, but the syndrome is more likely to emerge when the group is organized in ways that inhibit the flow of information and promote carelessness in the application of decision-making procedures. *Insulation* of the group from other groups, for example, can promote the development of unique, potentially inaccurate perspectives on issues and their solution. The Bay of Pigs planners worked in secret, so very few outsiders ever came into the group to participate in the discussion. The committee was insulated from criticism. Many experts on military questions and Cuban affairs were available and, if contacted, could have warned the group about the limitations of the plan, but the committee closed itself off from these valuable resources.

President Kennedy's *leadership style* also shaped the way the Bay of Pigs planners worked and may have contributed to groupthink. By tradition, the committee meetings, like cabinet meetings, were very formal affairs that followed a rigid protocol. The president could completely control the group discussion by setting the agenda, permitting only certain questions to be asked, and asking for input only from particular conferees (Stasson, Kameda, & Davis, 1997). He often stated his opinion at the outset of each meeting; his procedures for requiring a voice vote by individuals without prior group discussion paralleled quite closely the methods used by Asch (1952) to heighten conformity pressures in discussion groups. Ironically, Kennedy did not give his advisors opportunities to advise him (Kowert, 2002).

**Provocative Situational Context** A number of provocative situational factors may push the group in the direction of error rather than accuracy. As humans tend to be reluctant decision makers in the best of circumstances, they can unravel when they must make important, high-stakes decisions. Such decisions trigger greater tension and anxiety, so group members cope with this provocative *decisional stress* in less than logical ways. Through collective discussion, the group members may rationalize their choice by exaggerating the positive consequences, minimizing the possibility of negative outcomes, concentrating on minor details, and overlooking larger issues. Because the insecurity of each individual can be minimized if the group quickly chooses a plan of action with little argument or dissension, the group may rush to reach closure by making a decision as quickly as possible (Callaway, Marriott, & Esser, 1985). Janis also suggested that any factors that work to lower members' self-esteem, such as a history of mistakes or prior lapses of morality, may further increase the possibility of groupthink.

## The Emergence of Groupthink

Because of the complexity of the groupthink model, few tests of the entire model have been conducted. Researchers have, however, attempted to replicate Janis's findings through archival case studies of other historical and political groups. They have also examined specific aspects of the theory—such as the impact of cohesion and stress on decision-making groups—to determine if its key assumptions hold up under empirical scrutiny. These studies, which are reviewed briefly hereafter, sometimes support, sometimes challenge, and sometimes clarify Janis's theory.

**Archival Case Studies** Janis, using an archival method, compared groups that made very poor decisions to groups that made excellent choices to determine if error-prone groups exhibited more of the symptoms of groupthink. In later work, he enlarged his pool of cases to a total of 19 decision-making groups and had external raters who worked from the same historical texts rate the groups' symptoms. As predicted, the higher the number of groupthink symptoms, the more unfavorable the outcome of the group's deliberations ($r = .62$; Herek, Janis, & Huth, 1987, 1989; Welch, 1989).

Other archival studies have yielded checkered support for the groupthink model (Esser, 1998;

Turner & Pratkanis, 1998b). Philip E. Tetlock (1979), for example, analyzed the content of leaders' public speeches when in groupthink and vigilant decision-making situations. He discovered that leaders in the groupthink situations showed signs of reduced complexity and they were more likely to make positive statements about the ingroup. Tetlock and his colleagues (1992; Peterson et al., 1998) extended these findings in several studies by applying a sophisticated rating system (a *Q-sort*) to several successful and unsuccessful groups in political and organizational contexts. They found that structural faults were related to groupthink, but cohesiveness and provocative situational context factors were not. Studies of other disasters and mistake-prone groups, such as the launch of the *Challenger* and the Iran-Contra affair, also provided partial support for Janis's model (see Baron, 2005, for a review). It may be, however, that members' retrospective descriptions of their experiences in groups are so distorted that they are too biased to use as evidence of groupthink. Particularly when their groups performed poorly, members, accounts may reflect their attempts to make sense of the experience and hence correspond very little to what actually happened (Henningsen et al., 2006).

**Cohesion and Groupthink** Janis maintained that groupthink was a characteristic of cohesive groups only. If a group lacked cohesion, it might make poor decisions, but those decisions would be due to processes other than groupthink. His basic prediction was that cohesion, combined with one or more of the other potential causes of groupthink (e.g., structural faults, provocative situational context), would trigger groupthink. He admitted that cohesive groups are not necessarily doomed to be victims of groupthink, but "a high degree of group cohesiveness is conducive to a high frequency of symptoms of groupthink, which, in turn, are conducive to a high frequency of defects in decision-making" (Janis, 1972, p. 199).

A meta-analytic review of the results of seven different studies involving more than 1300 participants provided some support for this prediction (Mullen et al, 1994). High cohesiveness impaired decision making, provided that one or more of the other triggering conditions for groupthink were present in the situation. If the other causes of groupthink were absent, then cohesiveness increased the quality of a group's decision-making processes. The cohesion–groupthink relationship may also depend on the source of the group's cohesion. Groups that derived their cohesiveness from their members' commitment to the task, for example, displayed significantly fewer symptoms of groupthink, whereas groups that were interpersonally cohesive displayed more symptoms of groupthink (Bernthal & Insko, 1993).

**Structural Faults and Groupthink** Janis identified several structural features of groups that can contribute to groupthink, but researchers have concentrated most of their attention on the group leader (Chen et al., 1996; Flowers, 1977). In one project, group members discussed evidence pertaining to a civil trial. Researchers told some of the groups' assigned leaders to adopt a *closed style* of leadership: They were to announce their opinions on the case prior to discussion. *Open-style* leaders were told to withhold their own opinions until later in the discussion. Groups with a leader who adopted a closed style were more biased in their judgments, particularly when many of the group members had a high need for certainty (Hodson & Sorrentino, 1997). Groups with leaders with a strong need for power also performed less effectively, irrespective of the group's level of cohesion (Fodor & Smith, 1982). Other evidence, however, suggests that leaders who are highly directive improve their group's decisions, provided that they limit their control to the group's decisional processes rather than the group's decisional outcomes (Peterson, 1997).

**Provocative Situational Context** Studies of groups under stress suggest that they are more likely to make errors, lose their focus on the primary goals, and make use of procedures that members know have not been effective in the past. Janis Kelly and her colleagues, for example, have documented the negative impact of time pressures on both group performance and process (Kelly & Loving, 2004; Kelly & Karau, 1999). They find that when groups work under time pressure, members focus much of their attention on the task, but doing so leaves them at risk of overlooking important contextual information. They also tend to concentrate on getting the task completed as quickly as possible, and so become more concerned with efficiency and quick results rather than accuracy and quality. As a result, time pressures cause groups to "produce a less creative, less adequate, and less carefully reasoned decision. However, when a decision is routine or straightforward, these strategies can lead to adequate or even good decision making" (Kelly & Loving, 2004, p. 186).

## Alternative Models

Groupthink is not an obscure idea known only to those who study groups. A mere three years after the publication of Janis's 1972 analysis, the term *groupthink* appeared in *Webster's New Collegiate Dictionary* (Turner & Pratkanis, 1998b). The theory offers insight into very puzzling groups—those that make wrong-headed decisions—and has been applied to political decision makers, cults, businesses, and communities. In 2004, for example, the U.S. Senate Select Committee on Intelligence concluded that the intelligence community of the U.S. government had displayed a number of the symptoms of groupthink when it erroneously concluded that the country of Iraq was assembling weapons of mass destruction (U.S. Senate Select Committee on Intelligence, 2004). The theory serves as a reminder that if we are to understand political events that change the lives of people the world over, we must understand groups.

Researchers, however, continue to debate the validity of the model itself (Baron, 2005). Some, noting the theory's limited support, suggest that it should be drastically revised. Others feel that the jury is still out and encourage more research. Others have proposed alternative models.

**Group-centrism Theory** Arie Kruglanski and his colleagues (2006), like Janis, have identified a syndrome that characterizes groups and often causes them to make faulty decisions. They term this syndrome **group-centrism**, because it springs primarily from the group members' striving to maintain and support their group's unity. Group-centric groups tend to rush to make judgments on the basis of insufficient information, particularly if they face situations that interfere with their capacity to process information—time pressures, severe ambiguity, noise, or fatigue. They are more likely to reject a member who disagrees with the group, and they express a strong desire for agreement with other members. Stereotyped thought and tendencies to favor the ingroup over the outgroup increase, and willingness to compromise in order to reach integrative solutions during bargaining decreases. The group also strives for **cognitive closure**—"a desire for a definite answer to a question, any firm answer, rather than uncertainty, confusion, or ambiguity" (Kruglanski et al., 2002, p. 649)—and so adopts a more centralized structure with autocratic leaders. These groups' discussions are dominated by high-status group members who have a much greater impact on the group's communications and decisions than the rank-and-file members. These consequences of group-centrism are consistent with the symptoms of groupthink identified by Janis (De Dreu, 2003).

**Social Identity and the Ubiquity Model** Robert Baron (2005), after reviewing much of the existing research on Janis's theory, agrees with Janis that members of groups often strive for consensus, and that in doing so they tend to limit dissent, denigrate the outgroup, and misjudge their own group's competence. Baron's *ubiquity model* of groupthink, however, suggests that these qualities are ubiquitous

---

**group-centrism** A group-level syndrome caused by members' excessive strivings to maintain and support their group's unity that results in perturbations in a group's decision-making capability and intergroup relations.

**cognitive closure** The psychological desire to reach a final decision swiftly and completely; also, the relative strength of this tendency, as indicated by a preference for order, predictability, decisiveness, and closed-mindedness.

features of groups, rather than rare ones. They only lead to problems, Baron suggests, when three conditions are met. First, it is not group unity per se that increases groupthink symptoms, but rather a threat to a shared social identity that may result should the group fail (Haslam et al., 2006; Turner & Pratkanis, 1998a). Second, the group must be one that has developed a set of norms that constrains members' opinions with regard to the topic under discussion. Third, groupthink is more likely if group members lack self-confidence. In such cases they are likely to rely on others' judgments, with the result that the group does not adequately consider its alternatives (Sniezek, 1992).

### Preventing Groupthink

Kennedy did not take his Bay of Pigs failure lightly. In the months following the defeat, he explored the causes of his group's poor decision making. He fired those he felt had misled him, put in place improved procedures for handling information, and learned how to decipher messages from his military staff. These changes prepared him for the next great issue to face his administration—the Cuban Missile Crisis of 1962. When Kennedy learned that the Soviet Union was constructing a missile base in Cuba, he assembled ExCom again. This time, Kennedy and his advisors made the right decision. Essentially the same people meeting in the same room and guided by the same leader worked equally hard under similar pressures. Both crises occurred in the same area of the world, involved the same foreign powers, and could have led to equally serious consequences. Why did the Missile Crisis advisors succeed where the Bay of Pigs committee had failed?

**Limiting Premature Seeking of Concurrence** If conformity was the norm in the Bay of Pigs group, dissent was championed by the group during the Missile Crisis. Kennedy deliberately suspended the rules of discussion that guided such meetings; agendas were avoided, and new ideas were welcomed. Although pressures to conform surfaced from time to time during the discussion, the members felt so comfortable in their role as skeptical, critical thinkers that they were able to resist the temptation to go along with the consensus. In fact, the group never did reach 100% agreement on the decision to turn back Soviet ships.

The atmosphere of open inquiry can be credited to changes designed and implemented by Kennedy. He dropped his closed style of leadership to become an open leader as he (1) carefully refused to state his personal beliefs at the beginning of the session, waiting instead until others had let their views be known; (2) required a full, unbiased discussion of the pros and cons of each possible course of action; (3) convinced his subordinates that he would welcome healthy criticism and condemn "yea-saying"; (4) arranged for the group to meet without him on several occasions; and (5) encouraged specific members of the group to take the role of dissenter, or *devil's advocate*, during the group discussions.

Kennedy also arranged for this committee to meet separately in two subgroups. The committee members had practiced this approach on other policy issue decisions, and they were satisfied that it yielded many benefits: Arbitrary agreement with the views of the other subgroup was impossible; the lower-level staff members felt more at ease expressing their viewpoints in the smaller meetings; and the presence of two coalitions in the subsequent combined meetings virtually guaranteed a spirited debate (Wheeler & Janis, 1980).

**Correcting Misperceptions and Biases** Janis's image of people as reluctant decision makers does not quite match the executive committee members. The participants fully realized that some course of action had to be taken, and they resigned themselves to their difficult task. Their decisional conflict was fanned by doubts and worries over questions that they could not answer, and at times, they must have been tempted to ease their discomfort by overestimating American superiority, belittling the Russians, and denying the magnitude of the dangers. Yet through vigilant information processing, they succeeded in avoiding these misperceptions, illusions, and errors.

According to the official version of this incident, no trace of the illusion of superiority that had permeated the planning sessions of the Bay of Pigs invasion was in evidence during the executive committee meetings. The men knew that they and their decision were imperfect and that wishful thinking would not improve the situation. President Kennedy repeatedly told the group that there was no room for error, miscalculation, or oversight in their plans, and at every meeting, the members openly admitted the tremendous risks and dangers involved in taking coercive steps against the Russians. Each solution was assumed to be flawed, and even when the blockade had been painstakingly arranged, the members developed contingency plans in case it failed.

As members admitted their personal inadequacies and ignorance, they willingly consulted experts who were not members of the group. No group member's statements were taken as fact until independently verified, and the ideas of younger, low-level staff members were solicited at each discussion. Participants also discussed the group's activities with their own staffs and entered each meeting armed with the misgivings and criticisms of these unbiased outsiders.

The committee discussed the ethics of the situation and the proposed solutions. For example, although some members felt that the Russians had left themselves open to any violent response the Americans deemed appropriate, the majority argued that a final course of action had to be consistent with "America's humanitarian heritage and ideals" (Janis, 1972, p. 157). Illusions of morality and invulnerability were supposedly minimized along with biased perceptions of the outgroup (see, for an alternative interpretation of this incident, Alterman, 2004).

**Using Effective Decision-Making Techniques** The executive committee is not an example of an effective decision-making body simply because its solution to the missile crisis worked. Rather, just as the decision-making methods used by the Bay of Pigs committee ensured its failure, the executive committee's use of effective decision-making techniques increased its chances of success ('t Hart, 1998). Members analyzed a wide range of alternative courses of action, deliberately considered and then reconsidered the potential effects of their actions, consulted experts, and made detailed contingency plans in case the blockade failed to stop the Russians. Many initially favored military intervention, but the majority of the group's members insisted that other alternatives be explored. This demand led to an expanded search for alternatives, and soon the following list emerged:

1. Do nothing.
2. Exert pressure on the Soviet Union through the United Nations.
3. Arrange a summit meeting between the two nations' leaders.
4. Secretly negotiate with Castro.
5. Initiate a low-level naval action involving a blockade of Cuban ports.
6. Bombard the sites with small pellets, rendering the missiles inoperable.
7. Launch an air strike against the sites with advance warning to reduce loss of life.
8. Launch an air strike without advance warning.
9. Carry out a series of air attacks against all Cuban military installations.
10. Invade Cuba.

Once this list was complete, the men focused on each course of action before moving on to the next option. They considered the pros and cons, fleshed out unanticipated drawbacks, and estimated the likelihood of success. During this process, outside experts were consulted to give the members a better handle on the problem, and contingency plans were briefly explored. Even those alternatives that had initially been rejected were resurrected and discussed, and the group invested considerable effort in trying to find any overlooked detail. When a consensus on the blockade plan finally developed, the group went back over this alternative, reconsidered its problematic aspects, and meticulously reviewed the steps required to implement it. Messages were sent to the Russians, military strategies were worked out to prevent any slipups that would escalate the conflict, and a graded series of actions was developed to be undertaken should the blockade fail. Allies were contacted and told of the U.S. intentions, the legal basis of the intervention was established by arranging for a hemisphere blockade sanctioned by the Organization of American States, and African countries with airports that could have been used by Russia to circumvent the naval blockade were warned not to cooperate. To quote Robert Kennedy, "Nothing, whether a weighty matter or a small detail, was overlooked" (1969, p. 60).

## SUMMARY IN OUTLINE

*Why make decisions in groups?*

1. Groups working on a variety of problems prove to be more effective decision makers than individuals; Shaw's study of groups working on intellective tasks confirmed the superiority of group decisions in certain situations.
2. A *functional theory of group decision making* identifies four stages that appear consistently in many groups: orientation, discussion, decision, and implementation (see Figure 11.2).
3. During the orientation stage the group identifies the problem to be solved and plans the process to be used in reaching the decision.
   - Many groups bypass this stage, but time spent in orientation predicts effectiveness.
   - Groups develop a *shared mental model* at this stage, and they may also take steps to improve their time focus, thereby avoiding confirmation of *Parkinson's law* and his *law of triviality*.
4. As Bales's work suggests, during the *discussion stage* the group gathers information about the situation, identifies and weighs options, and tests its assumptions.
   - A *collective information processing model* assumes that groups gather information and process that information to generate decisions and judgments.
   - Three information processing gains that result from discussion are improved memory for information, increased exchange of information, and more thorough processing of information.
   - A group's *collective memory* includes the combined memories of all individual members, and *cross-cueing* and *transactive memory systems* work to enhance group memory.
   - Group memory is weakened by social loafing, free riding, and by the complexity of the group setting, which disrupts group members' ability to organize information in memory and subsequently retrieve that information.
5. During the decision stage the group relies on an implicit or explicit *social decision scheme* to combine individual preferences into a collective decision.
   - Common schemes include delegating decisions, averaging decisions, plurality decisions, unanimous decisions (consensus), and random decisions.
   - Groups generally use consensus when dealing with sensitive issues, but they tend to use a plurality voting scheme when making simple choices.
6. During the implementation stage the group carries out the decision and assesses its impact.
   - Implementation is related to *procedural justice*; as Coch and French's classic study of motivation in the workplace suggests, members were more satisfied and more likely to implement decisions when they

were actively involved in the decision-making process (the *voice effect*).

- Contemporary group-management methods are based on increasing productivity by increasing participation in the decision-making process.

7. Vroom's *normative model of decision making* suggests that different types of situations call for either autocratic (decide), consultative (individual and group), facilitating, or delegating group decision-making methods.

*What problems undermine the effectiveness of decision-making groups?*

1. The usefulness of group discussion is limited, in part, by members' inability to express themselves clearly and by their limited listening skills. Janis and Mann suggest that groups sometimes use discussion to avoid making decisions, and they often spend more time discussing minor matters than important ones. Research conducted by Rogelberg suggests that meetings are often viewed by group members as interruptions of their workflow rather than as means to increase productivity.
2. Groups are prone to the *shared information bias*—they spend more of their discussion time examining details that two or more of the group members know in common than discussing unshared information. Work by Stasser and Titus confirms that this oversampling of shared information leads to poorer decisions when a hidden profile would be revealed by considering the unshared information more closely.
   - The shared information bias increases when tasks have no demonstrably correct solution and when group leaders do not actively draw out unshared information.
   - Groups can avoid the shared information bias if they spend more time actively discussing their decisions or if they make use of *group decision support systems* (GDSS).
3. Judgment errors that cause people to overlook important information and overuse unimportant information are often exacerbated in groups.
   - Kerr, MacCoun, and Kramer describe three types of errors—*sins of commission*, *sins of omission*, and *sins of imprecision*—and research suggests that groups exacerbate these errors.
   - Groups, more so than individuals, fall prey to the *confirmation bias*—they start off with an initial preference and then seek out additional information to confirm the accuracy of their initial inclinations.

*Why do groups make riskier decisions than individuals?*

1. Common sense suggests that groups would be more cautious than individuals, but early studies carried out using the *Choice-Dilemmas Questionnaire* found that group discussion generates a shift in the direction of a more risky alternative (the *risky-shift* phenomenon).
2. When researchers such as Myers and Lamm later found evidence of cautious shifts as well as risky shifts, and a tendency for various types of attitudes to become more extreme in groups, they realized that the risky shift was a specific case of *group polarization*: a shift in the direction of greater extremity in individuals' responses (e.g., choices, judgments, expressions of opinions) when in groups.
3. Group polarization is sustained by the desire to evaluate one's own opinions by comparing them to those of others (social comparison theory), by exposure to other members' pro-risk or pro-caution arguments (*persuasive-arguments theory*), and by social identity processes.

4. Studies of groups whose members have consumed alcohol (*groupdrink*) suggest that such groups make riskier choices than do sober groups.

*What is groupthink, and how can it be prevented?*

1. Janis argued that fiascoes and blunders such as the decision to invade Cuba at the Bay of Pigs occur when group members strive for solidarity and cohesiveness to such an extent that any questions or topics that could lead to disputes are avoided. Janis called this process *groupthink*.
2. Groupthink has multiple symptoms, which Janis organized into three categories:
   - Overestimation of the group: illusion of invulnerability and illusion of morality
   - Closed-mindedness: rationalizations, stereotypes about the outgroup
   - Pressures toward uniformity: self-censorship, the illusion of unanimity, direct pressure on dissenters, and self-appointed *mindguards*.
3. The *Abilene paradox*, as described by Harvey, occurs when groups mismanage agreement. Studies of *pluralistic ignorance* have verified the tendency for group members to erroneously assume that their private opinion is discrepant from the other group members' opinions. Groups also experience *entrapment* when they become committed too quickly to a decision and continue to invest in it despite high *sunk costs*.
4. Groupthink groups also display defective decision-making processes.
5. Janis identified three sets of causes of groupthink: cohesiveness, structural faults of the group or organization (such as isolation and a closed leadership style), and provocative situational factors (including decisional stress).
6. Research has yielded partial—but not robust—support for many of Janis's hypotheses regarding decision making in groups:
   - Archival studies conducted by Janis, Tetlock, and other investigators have found mixed support for the theory's most basic prediction—that groups that display more of the symptoms of groupthink tend to make poorer decisions.
   - Studies have suggested that cohesive groups sometimes display groupthink tendencies, provided that one or more of the other triggering conditions for groupthink are present.
7. Given these limitations, researchers have proposed alternative models, including:
   - Kruglanski's *group-centrism* theory suggests that groups whose members have a high *need for cognitive closure* are more likely to make poorer decisions.
   - Baron's ubiquity model suggests that many groups display the negative decisional features identified by Janis, but that these factors combined with a shared social identity, restrictive norms, and lack of confidence will trigger groupthink-like decisions.
8. Janis noted that groups need not sacrifice cohesiveness to avoid the pitfall of groupthink. Rather, he recommended limiting premature seeking of concurrence, correcting misperceptions and errors, and improving the group's decisional methods.

## FOR MORE INFORMATION

*Chapter Case: The Bay of Pigs Planners*

- *Bay of Pigs: The Untold Story*, by Peter Wyden (1979), offers a wealth of detail about the group that planned the invasion, and draws on personal interviews with many of the original group members.

*Making Decisions in Groups*

- "A Look at Groups from a Functional Perspective," by Andrea A. Hollingshead, Gwen M. Wittenbaum, Paul B. Paulus, Randy Y. Hirokawa, Deborah G. Ancona, Randall S. Peterson, Karen A. Jehn, and Kay Yoon (2005), examines "how group composition, projects, structures, and ecology affect group interactions and outcomes" (p. 21).
- "The Emerging Conceptualization of Groups as Information Processors," by Verlin B. Hinsz, R. Scott Tindale, and David A. Vollrath (1997), is a wide-ranging synthesis of how such cognitive mechanisms as attention, encoding, storage, retrieval, processing, and learning shape group decisions.
- "Group Performance and Decision Making," by Norbert L. Kerr and R. Scott Tindale (2004), reviews recent studies of group decision making.

*Faulty Decision Making in Groups*

- "Presidential Leadership and Group Folly: Reappraising the Role of Groupthink in the Bay of Pigs Decisions," by Roderick M. Kramer (2008), uses declassified documents and historical records not available to Janis before concluding that many aspects of the Bay of Pigs decision are inconsistent with the groupthink theory.
- "So Right It's Wrong: Groupthink and the Ubiquitous Nature of Polarized Group Decision Making," by Robert S. Baron (2005), reviews the basic evidence supporting Janis's theory of groupthink before offering a novel interpretation that identifies a new set of critical causes of groupthink.
- *Why Decisions Fail: Avoiding the Blunders and Traps that Lead to Debacles*, by Paul C. Nutt (2002), reviews a series of terrible mistakes made by corporate leaders in the United States, including the construction of EuroDisney and the failure to recall dangerous automobiles with known risks.

## Media Resources

Visit the Group Dynamics companion website at www.cengage.com/psychology/forsyth to access online resources for your book, including quizzes, flash cards, web links, and more!

# 12

# Teams

## CHAPTER OVERVIEW

When the goals people want to accomplish are so complex that they would overwhelm any individual's capabilities—such as building a bridge, flying a spacecraft to the moon, or performing Bach's Brandenburg concerto—people turn to teams. Teams, when successful, transform groups into complex, adaptive, dynamic task-performing systems. Teams are groups, but not all groups are teams.

- What are teams and when should they be used?
- How does the team's composition influence effectiveness?
- What group processes mediate the input-output relationship?
- How effective are teams, and how can they be improved?

## CHAPTER OUTLINE

### Mountain Medical's Cardiac Surgery Team

The members of the Mountain Medical Center's cardiac surgery team were excited, but also a bit nervous. They were about to use a new method for performing the most technically challenging of all surgeries: the repair of the heart. Only last week they had been using the traditional, open-heart procedure that requires splitting the patient's chest at the breastbone, stopping the heart and transferring its duties to a heart-lung bypass machine, clamping off arteries and values as necessary, isolating and repairing the damaged portions of the heart, and then closing the 8-inch long wound in the chest. But they would not be using those methods today. Instead, the team would be carrying out a minimally invasive surgical procedure. The surgeon would make a small incision between the patient's ribs and snake high-tech instruments to the heart, guided by feedback from a network of computers, cameras, and ultrasound scanners.

These new procedures would make entirely new demands of the surgical team. Traditional surgical teammates work closely with one another, but they are not continually interdependent. The anesthesiologist sedates the patient and monitors his or her breathing. The perfusionist is the technician who operates the heart-lung machine. The surgeon makes the incision, splits the chest, repairs the heart, and then closes the incisions. The scrub nurse or technician prepares the sterile field, suctions blood from the site, and passes instruments to the surgeon as needed. The new procedure is not so modularized. The surgeon can no longer see the heart, but must rely on the computer-enhanced images provided by the perfusionist and anesthesiologist. Because the surgeon cannot apply clamps directly to the heart to stop the flow of blood, that work is done by the anesthesiologist, who threads a catheter into the aorta through the femoral vein. The scrub nurse monitors and maintains pressures and vital signs and attaches, when needed, forceps, scissors, scalpels, and other surgical tools to the surgeon's operating mechanicals.

The new procedures require an unprecedented degree of teamwork, but the Mountain Medical team was ready for the challenge. They had practiced for months to learn the new method, and their diligence showed in their level of coordination and communication in the operating room. The operation took somewhat longer than they had expected it would, but there were no surprises: Their first patient recovered fully, but also more quickly because of their use of the minimally invasive, and team-intensive, technique (Healey, Undre, & Vincent, 2006; Pisano, Bohmer, & Edmondson, 2001).

One hundred years ago most **teams** were either pulling plows or playing games. Groups assembled for work that required many hands and much muscle, but less physically demanding labor was given over to skilled individuals. Over time, however, the complexity of the tasks that humans undertook grew, and so did their need to work in teams in order to achieve their ends. A single person could, in theory, perform coronary surgery, design a new telecommunication device, create an online database of all knowledge, or pilot a spacecraft to the moon, but such tasks are now done by groups of people working in teams.

Those who understand groups are well on their way to understanding teams, since teams are groups. Like all groups, teams include multiple members, who are interdependent and share a collective goal. But teams, unlike many groups, require more from the members in the way of collaboration and coordination. This chapter considers how these demands determine the nature of teams by examining issues of team composition, process, and outcomes. This chapter also reviews the overall effectiveness of teams as performance tools and examines ways to improve them. After all, teams are groups, so their success is not always assured.

## WORKING TOGETHER IN TEAMS

Teams are often spawned when one or more individuals confront an obstacle, a problem, or a task they wish to overcome, solve, or complete, but

---

**team** An organized, task-focused group.

they recognize that the solution is beyond the reach of a single person. Such situations require collaboration among individuals, who combine their personal energies and resources in joint activities aimed at reaching both individual and team goals (Zander, 1985).

## What Is a Team?

The word *team* is used to describe a wide assortment of human aggregations. For example, in business settings, work units are sometimes referred to as production teams or management teams. At a university, professors and graduate students may form a research team to conduct experiments cooperatively. In the military, a small squad of soldiers train as a special operations team. In schools, a teaching team may be responsible for the education of 500 students. In multiplayer games, people use computers to join carefully composed teams to attempt challenges ("instances") that require the skills of many types of characters.

Despite this diversity in terms of focus, composition, and design, teams are fundamentally groups, and so they possess the basic characteristics of any group: interaction, goals, interdependence, structure, and unity. But what sets teams apart from other groups is the intensity of each these attributes within teams. The level of *interaction* in teams is concentrated and continuous, and it includes both task-oriented action as well as relationship-sustaining interactions (e.g., social support, self-disclosure, mutual aid). The sine qua non of teams is their pursuit of *goals*, and collective ones at that. With a team, success and failure occurs at the group level, with all members sharing in the outcome irrespective of their own personal performances. Teams stress outcomes to such an extent that their very existence is threatened should they fail to achieve their agreed-upon goals. All group members are *interdependent* to a degree, but members of teams are so tightly coupled that each member's outcomes are inextricably tied to each other member's outcomes. Each member is assumed to have specialized knowledge, skill, and ability that he or she contributes to the team and the team's success depends on combining these individual inputs effectively. Teams are also relatively well-*structured* groups. The members of an athletic team, such as soccer or baseball, all know what their role is within the group because of the specific position they occupy on the team. Similarly, in work teams each member's role in the group is defined, as are norms, status, and communication relations. The membership of teams also tends to be clearly defined, as does its duration. Last, the close coupling of the members of teams means that they have a high degree of *unity*; teams are typically cohesive, particularly in the sense that their members are united in their efforts to pursue a common goal. External pressures may magnify this unity, for teams usually work under some kind of pressure, such as a heavy workload, limited time, or competition with other groups. Teams, then, are hypergroups: They possess all the basic qualities of any group, but to a more extreme degree.

## Types of Teams

Teams come in a wide variety of forms, and they fulfill many different functions in military, educational, industrial, corporate, research, and leisure settings. A general distinction, however, can be made between teams that process information and teams that plan, practice, and perform activities (Devine, 2002). Table 12.1 offers an even more fine-grained analysis of teams within these two general categories, distinguishing between management, project, and advisory teams within the information cluster and service, production, and action teams within the performance cluster.

- *Executive teams* and *command teams* such as administrative units, review panels, boards of directors, and corporate executive teams, are *management teams*. They identify and solve problems, make decisions about day-to-day operations and production, and set the goals for the organization's future.
- *Project teams*, or *cross-functional teams*, include individuals with different backgrounds and areas of expertise who join together to develop

**TABLE 12.1 Types of Teams**

| Type and Subtypes | Function | Examples |
|---|---|---|
| **Management** | | |
| Executive | Plan, direct | Board of directors, city council |
| Command | Integrate, coordinate | Control tower, combat center |
| **Project** | | |
| Negotiation | Deal, persuade | Labor management, international treaty |
| Commission | Choose, investigate | Search committee, jury |
| Design | Create, develop | Research and development team, marketing group |
| **Advisory** | Diagnose, suggest | Quality circle, steering committee |
| **Service** | Provide, repair | Fast food, auto service team |
| **Production** | Build, assemble | Home construction, automotive assembly |
| **Action** | | |
| Medical | Treat, heal | Surgery, emergency room |
| Response | Protect, rescue | Fire station, paramedics |
| Military | Neutralize, protect | Infantry squad, tank crew |
| Transportation | Convey, haul | Airline cockpit, train crew |
| Sports | Compete, win | Baseball, soccer |

SOURCE: Adapted from D. J. Devine, 2002

innovative products and identify new solutions to existing problems. These teams are extremely common in organizational settings, for they often are composed of individuals from a variety of departments and are deliberately organized to reduce the lack of communication that isolates units within the overall organization. *Negotiation* teams represent their constituencies; *commissions* are special task forces that make judgments, in some cases about sensitive matters; and *design* teams are charged with developing plans and strategies.

- *Advisory teams*, such as review panels, quality circles, and steering committees are sometimes called *parallel teams* because they work outside the usual supervisory structures of the company.
- *Work teams*, such as assembly lines, manufacturing teams, and maintenance crews, are responsible for the organization's tangible output; they create products (*production teams*) or deliver services (*service teams*). Some of these teams can also be considered *action teams*.
- *Action teams* include sports teams, surgery teams, police squads, military units, and orchestras. All are specialized teams that generate a product or a service through highly coordinated actions (Devine, 2002; Sundstrom et al., 2000).

**Task Forces and Crews** Distinctions can also be drawn between teams and other task-focused groups, such as crews and task forces. These three work groups differ in longevity and the scope of their tasks. *Task forces* have a specific, well-defined purpose, and they exist for only as long as the project. *Crews* are teams that use specialized tools or equipment to accomplish their appointed tasks. The staff of an emergency room and the men and women piloting a jumbo jet would be crews (Arrow & McGrath, 1995; McGrath, 1984).

Teams also differ in terms of their source or origin. Some teams, such as the young engineers building a prototype of a computer in a garage, a highly organized study team, or an expedition would all be *member-founded teams*. Other teams, in contrast, are begun by individuals or authorities outside the team. The team that pulls the tarp over the baseball field when the rains starts and the teams that play on that field during the game would be *mandated teams* (or *concocted* teams), because those who created them are not actually members of the team (Arrow, McGrath, & Berdahl, 2000). Complex organizations, such as large corporations, usually include both types of teams.

**Appropriate Autonomy** One of the key aspects of teams—one that sets teams apart from many other groups—is their degree of autonomy. Some teams are semi-autonomous or supervisor-led, for they have a formally recognized leader who is responsible for organizing the members and reviewing their performance. Other teams, in contrast, are more autonomous, for these teams can manage their own work-related activities, including their own operating procedures and structures (Stewart, 2006; Sundstrom et al., 2000).

Hackman's (1986) model of team autonomy is shown in Figure 12.1. The model describes, along the left side of the figure, four different levels of control: execution of the task itself, managing the work process, designing the team itself within the organization context, and leading the team by setting its overall mission and objectives. Each step up this hierarchy increases the team's autonomy. The model also identifies, along the bottom of the chart, four types of teams that differ in their degree of responsibility and autonomy. In a manager-led team, members do the work of the team, but

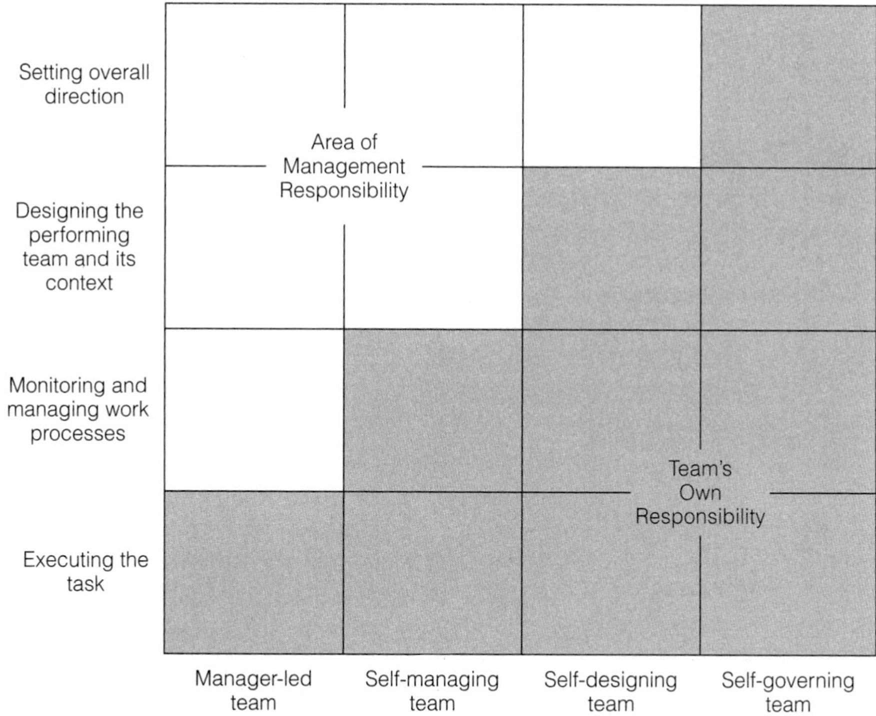


**FIGURE 12.1** The authority matrix: Four levels of team self-management.

SOURCE: Hackman, J. R. (1986). "The psychology of self-management in organizations." In Michael S. Pallak and Robert O. Perloff (Eds.), *Psychology and work: Productivity, change, and employment*. (pp. 89–136). Washington, DC, US: American Psychological Association. doi: 10.1037/10055-003 p. 92

someone external to the group—their manager, for example—carries out all executive functions for the team. Members of self-managing teams have more autonomy, for they are charged with both executing the task and monitoring and managing the team's work. Self-designing teams enjoy more discretion in terms of control over their team's design, for they have the authority to change the team itself. The team's leader sets the direction, but the team members have full responsibility for doing what needs to be done to get the work accomplished. Finally, members of self-governing teams have responsibility for all four of the major functions listed in Figure 12.1. They decide what is to be done, structure the team and its context, manage their own performance, and actually carry out the work. The Mountain Medical cardiac surgery team was such a self-governing team. The surgeon who founded the team was the one who lobbied the hospital to try the new procedure, and he worked closely with staff to design the team. The team, as it worked, closely monitored its processes and the team members themselves completed the work.

### When to Team?

Not all tasks require the skills, attentions, and resources of a group of people working in close collaboration. Teams, with their greater resources, goal-focus, and vast potential, are becoming the default choice in a variety of performance settings, but some caution is needed before rushing to form a team to solve a problem. Studies of group performance and decision making (see Chapters 10 and 11, respectively) suggest that groups are not all gain without loss. A team may be the best choice in a given situation, but that choice should be shaped by an analysis of the task at hand rather than the popularity of the method.

In general, as tasks become more difficult, complex, and consequential, the more likely people will prefer to complete them through coordinated activity rather than individual action (Karau & Williams, 1993; Zander, 1985).

- *How difficult is the task?* In some circumstances, people are faced with tasks that are well beyond the skills and resources of a single individual. No one person, no matter how talented, can compile a dictionary of all the words in the English language, construct a nuclear power plant, or overthrow a political dictator. Other tasks are difficult ones because they require enormous amounts of time or strength. One talented individual could build a car or dig a 100-yard-long trench, but a crew of workers will accomplish these tasks far more quickly and with better results. The duration of the task also influences its difficulty. Projects that take months or years to complete are best attempted by multiple individuals, so that the work continues even when specific individuals leave the team.
- *How complex is the task?* A single person cannot perform Beethoven's Fifth Symphony or compete against the New York Yankees. Individuals may be able to carry out specific assignments with great skill, but some tasks involve multiple interdependent subtasks that must each be completed in a specific sequence before the goal is reached.
- *How important is the task?* Problems are not equal in their overall significance. A flat tire or a bad head cold pale in importance when compared to inequalities in the criminal justice system, uncontrolled pollution, and heart disease. When the effects of succeeding or failing at a task are consequential for many people for a long period of time, individuals are more likely to collaborate with others.

Other, more psychological and interpersonal, factors also influence people's interest in collaborating with others. Many people prefer to carry out their work in the company of other people, and so even when others are more of a distraction than a help, they prefer to work in teams rather than alone. When individuals fear that they will be blamed for a bad decision or outcome, they might form a team to make the decision to avoid full responsibility for the negative outcome (Leary & Forsyth, 1987). People may even found a team or join an existing team so that they can enjoy the

## Focus 12.1 When Were Teams Invented?

*The word "team" derives from the old English, Frisian and Norse word for a bridle and thence to a set of draught animals harnessed together and, by analogy, to a number of persons involved in a joint action.*

—Annett and Stanton (2001, p. 1045)

Teams are everywhere today, but for centuries humans did not work in teams—the word was reserved for harnessed animals. Apparently groups of humans working collectively were not called a *team* until the 1600s, when Ben Jonson wrote in *Bartholomew Fayre*, "Twere like falling into a whole Shire of butter: they had need be a teeme of Dutchmen, should draw him out" (OED Online, 1989).

Even then, teams were not the first choice for organizing individuals in work-related settings. For many years, experts assumed that people do not like to work and must be prodded into action by the promise of financial incentives, close supervision, and clear goals that they can attain with little effort. The experts considered workers to be mere "adjuncts to machines," and they designed workplaces in which employees did not waste time talking to one another (Taylor, 1923). There were notable exceptions to this tendency—including the famous Hawthorne studies of productivity that suggested that gains in performance could be achieved if individuals worked in collaborative, cohesive groups under favorable conditions—but it was not until the second half of the 20th century that teams began their ascension to prominence.

Eric Sundstrom and his associates (2000), in their brief history of teams, observe that teams were rarely used outside of sports and military settings even into the 1950s. It was not until the 1960s that complaints about the authoritarian nature of most organizations prompted a search for alternatives (Likert, 1967; McGregor, 1960). Heeding the call for worker autonomy and participation in decision making, a number of companies began experimenting with true teams: General Motors used teams rather than an assembly line in one of its truck factories; General Foods set up autonomous work teams at its Topeka, Kansas plant; the Banner Company, a large manufacturer, set up work groups with varying levels of authority and organizational overlap; and Volvo and Saab both began using teams in their production plants.

From these initial beginnings organizations began relying on teams for production, management, distribution, and general decision making. Half the workers in the United States now belong to at least one team at work. Almost all Fortune 500 companies use project teams, and the majority charge long-term teams with responsibility for a variety of tasks. Teams are used by a majority of all larger organizations in the United States, and in countries like Sweden and Japan, the use of teams approaches 100% (Devine et al., 1999). Nonprofit organizations, such as health care organizations and public service corporations, are particularly heavy adopters of team approaches to work (81%), followed by such blue collar industries as construction, manufacturing, and retail sales (50%), and white collar industries like banking, real estate, and insurance (34%). The modern organization is no longer a network of individuals, but rather a network of interconnected teams (Kozlowski & Bell, 2003).

fruits of the team's labors without having to invest very much of their own personal time. As shown in Chapter 10, when people's individual contributions to a group's goal are not easily identified, they often do less than their fair share.

Teams are also sometimes used because they are popular, rather than effective or appropriate. Just as the "romance of leadership" describes people's tendency to put too much faith in their leaders as saviors who will rescue them when they face difficult circumstances, the **romance of teams** is a "faith in the effectiveness of team-based work that is not supported by, or is even inconsistent with, relevant empirical evidence" (Allen & Hecht, 2004, p. 440). As Edwin Locke and his colleagues (2001, p. 501) put it: "the emphasis on groups and teams has gone far beyond any rational assessment of their practical usefulness. We are in the age of groupomania." They suggest a careful consideration of the demands of the task before committing to using a team to perform it (see Focus 12.1).

---

**romance of teams** The intuitive appeal of teams as effective means of improving performance in business and organizational settings, despite the relative lack of definitive evidence supporting their utility.

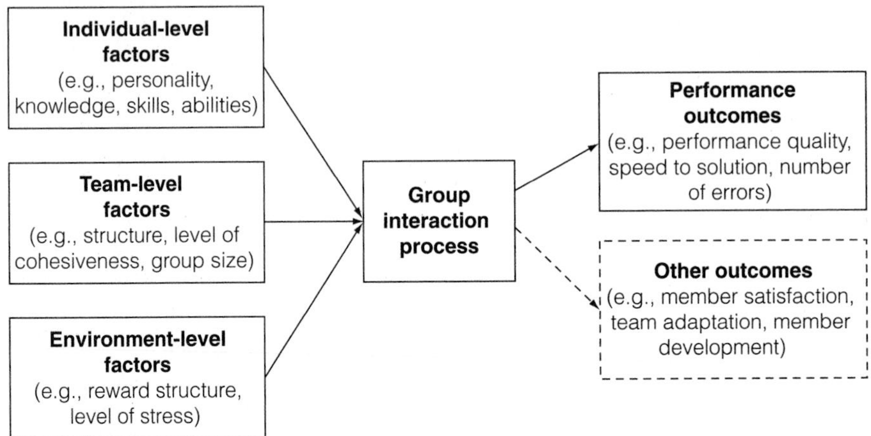


**FIGURE 12.2** The traditional Input–Process–Output (I-P-O) model of team performance.

SOURCE: Adapted from: Hackman, J. R., & Morris, C. G. (1975). "Group tasks, group interaction process, and group performance effectiveness: A review and proposed integration." *Advances in Experimental Social Psychology, 8*, 47–99. Reprinted by permission of J. Richard Hackman.

## The I-P-O Model of Teams

Teams are often conceptualized as complex performance systems. They emerge from and in turn sustain patterns of coordinated interdependences among individual members (see Chapter 2). Teams, because of their great emphasis on achievement of desired goals, are more likely than most groups to plan, prior to action, a strategy to enact over a given time period, seek feedback about the effectiveness of the plan and implementation, and make adjustments to procedures and operations on the basis of that analysis (Arrow et al., 2000; Kozlowski et al., 1999). Rather than assuming that variables in the system are linked to one another in simple, one-to-one relationships, systems theory recognizes factors that set the stage for teamwork (inputs), that facilitate or inhibit the nature of the teamwork (processes), and a variety of consequences that result from the team's activities (outputs). This assumption is the basis of the well-known *input– process–output model* of teams shown in Figure 12.2.

- *Inputs* include any antecedent factors that may influence, directly or indirectly, the team members and the team itself. These antecedents include individual-level factors (e.g., who is on the team and what are their strengths and weakness), team- level factors (e.g., how large is the team and what resources does it control), and environmental-level factors (e.g., how does this team work with other units within the organization).
- *Processes* are operations and activities that mediate the relationship between the input factors and the team's outcomes. These processes include steps taken to plan the team's activities; initiating actions and monitoring processes; and processes that focus on interpersonal aspects of the team's system, such as dealing with conflict and increasing members' sense of commitment to the team (Marks, Mathieu, & Zaccaro, 2001).
- *Outputs* are the consequences of the team's activities. The team's emphasis on outcome means that the tangible results of the team effort draw the most attention—did the team win or lose, is the team's product high in quality or inadequate, did the team successfully complete the operation or did it kill the patient—but other outcomes are also important, including changes in the team's cohesiveness or the degree to which it changed so that it will be able to deal with similar tasks more efficiently in the future.

The I-P-O model, despite years of steady service to researchers studying teams, is a relatively simplistic model of a highly complex interpersonal system, and three specific limitations are worth noting. First, the model, with its categorization of factors as inputs, processes, or outputs, understates the complex interdependencies among the variables that influence team performance. Second, some of the so-called "processes" within the process category are not actually processes at all, but rather characteristics of the team that emerge over time as members interact with one another. These emergent states certainly influence the team's outcomes, but it would be more accurate to call them mediators of the relationship between inputs and output rather than processes. Third, given that the I-P-O model is a systems theory, it is essential to always consider feedback processes that occur over time. The model is often interpreted as a sequential one, with inputs leading to processes/mediators and these leading to outcomes; but the reverse causal sequences are also a part of the complete model. In consequence, some suggest that the I-P-O model should be reconfigured into an Input–Mediator–Output–Input model (the I-M-O-I) to indicate the diversity of elements in the process stage and the fact that the outputs feed back to become inputs (Ilgen et al., 2005; Marks et al., 2001).

These limitations not withstanding, the I-P-O model provides a heuristic framework for this chapter's examination of teams. The next section considers team composition, with a focus on who is recruited to the team and how their personal qualities shape the team's interaction. The chapter then turns to issues of process, including teamwork and cognitive work, before considering ways to evaluate the effectiveness of teams.

## BUILDING THE TEAM

In 1996, hospitals around the United States began considering adopting noninvasive surgical methods for cardiac surgeries. Technological developments ensured that the procedure was a safe one, but each hospital needed to determine how to change from the traditional method to the newer procedure (Pisano et al., 2001).

Nearly all hospitals settled on a team approach: They would create teams of physicians, nurses, and technicians who would study the method and implement it locally once they had mastered its demands. One hospital, given here the fictitious name of Chelsea Hospital, put the chief of cardiac surgery in charge of building the team. He was an extremely skilled surgeon, but he did not view the new surgery as much of a challenge. He was also very busy, and did not get involved in selecting the members of his team. The composition of the Chelsea team was determined by seniority and who was available to attend the three-day offsite training session.

Mountain Medical did things a little differently from Chelsea. The young surgeon, who was new to the hospital, volunteered to get the team started. He talked with the staff in all the departments, and he picked people for the team "based on their experience working together" rather than their seniority (Edmondson et al., 2001, p. 128). He was part of the team during the training sessions, and held meetings with physicians in other departments to share information about the procedure and to identify the best patients for referrals. The members of the team met regularly, prior to the procedure, to walk through the basic steps and to share information about what each of them would be doing and how their actions fit with what the other members of the team were doing.

Gary Pisano, Richard Bohmer, and Amy Edmondson (2001), who studied 16 hospitals that used the new method, discovered that things worked out differently for Chelsea Hospital and Mountain Medical. The Chelsea team did not lose patients, but the operations took longer than they should have, even after they gained experience with the procedure. Mountain Medical, in contrast, performed the first few operations slowly, but then became one of the fastest and most effective surgical teams in the group of 16 studied—despite being led by the one of the least experienced surgeons.

Mountain Medical, like most teams, owes much of its success to its composition: the individuals who were selected to make up the team. All teams are composites formed by the joining together of multiple, relatively independent individuals. Each member of the group brings to the team a set of unique personal experiences, interests, skills, abilities, and motivations, which merge together with the personal qualities of all the other individual members to form the team as a whole (Moreland, Levine, & Wingert, 1996).

### The Team Player

Mountain Medical deliberately sought out "team players" for their surgical team. Such people are often identified on the basis of their personalities, for people assume that some people, by temperament, make better teammates than others. Is a cold, emotionally unstable, narrow-minded person someone to recruit for a team that is attempting a challenging task where lives are at stake? Or, would the team be more likely to prosper if composed of people who are outgoing, stable, and conscientious?

As with other group processes, including affiliation (Chapter 4) and leadership (Chapter 9), the qualities identified in the big five theory of personality have been linked, reliably, to team performance (Bell, 2007; see Table 4.1). The big five theory recognizes that people differ from each other in many ways, but it assumes that extraversion, agreeableness, conscientiousness, emotional stability (low neuroticism), and openness are all qualities that facilitate working on teams. As Figure 12.3 suggests, extraversion is consistent with a number of desirable qualities in a teammate: affiliativeness, social perceptiveness, expressivity, and, to a lesser extent, leadership (dominance). Similarly, agreeableness, which connotes trust and cooperation, and conscientiousness's suggestion of dependability, dutifulness, and achievement are also likely team-promoting qualities. Even emotional stability and openness are likely associated with success working with others, since they are indicators of adjustment, confidence (self-esteem), and flexibility.

A recent meta-analysis confirmed these predictions, with some qualifications (Bell, 2007; Peeters et al., 2006). Studies of teams working in laboratory settings showed little association between personality and performance. The studies

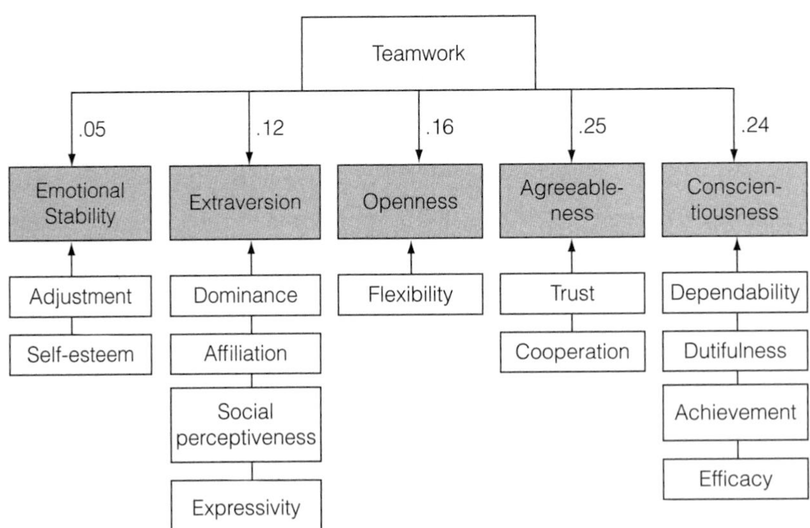


**FIGURE 12.3** Hierarchical model of personality characteristics and facets related to teamwork.

SOURCE: Adapted from Driskell, J. E., Goodwin, G. F., Salas, E., & O'Shea, P. G. (2006). "What makes a good team player? Personality and team effectiveness." *Group Dynamics: Theory, Research, and Practice, 10*, 249–271. doi: 10.1037/1089-2699.10.4.249

of teams in organizational settings, in contrast, revealed the small, but consistent, correlations shown in Figure 12.3. All were significant, except for the emotional stability–performance relationship; this personality trait did not predict how well the team member performed once on the team (Driskell et al., 2006).

Researchers have also examined other personality variables, in addition to those emphasized by the big five, including assertiveness (Pearsall & Ellis, 2006), Type A tendency (Keinan & Koren, 2002), locus of control (Boone et al., 2004), and achievement motivation (LePine, 2003). In many cases, the effects of these variables depend, in part, on the entire team's composition and the situational context. In one investigation, for example, researchers distinguished between people who were Type As or Type Bs. Type A individuals tend to be aggressive, competitive, and excessively time oriented, but they are also high in their achievement orientation. Type B individuals, in contrast, are more relaxed and slow-going. Researchers then created teams, being careful to control the number of Type As and Bs in each. They made some teams all Type A, others all Type B, and some teams with a mixture of both types. After they worked together for a time, the members of these teams were asked to indicate level of satisfaction with their team and its members. In general, people were more satisfied when their teammates were similar in terms of personality. Teams composed of all Type As or all Type Bs were rated as more satisfying by their members than were teams where Type As and Bs were mixed together. Teams of only Type As did, however, get a lot more done (Keinan & Koren, 2002).

### Knowledge, Skill, and Ability (KSA)

Some teams fail because they simply do not include people with the qualities and characteristics needed for success at the task. A team struggling to generate solutions to math puzzles may not have any mathematicians at the table. A soccer team made up of slow-moving defensive fullbacks but no offensive goal scorers will likely lose. A team's performance depends, in part, on its members' *knowledge, skills, and abilities*, or **KSAs**.

What KSAs are important to teams? On the task side, teams whose members are more skilled at the work to be done outperform teams composed of less-skilled members. A team of mediocre individuals can, with enough practice, good leadership, and determination, reach lofty goals, but it is difficult to make a silk purse out of a bunch of sow's ears (Devine & Philips, 2001; Ellis et al., 2003). Teams that succeed in creating new products and solutions to long-standing problems are generally staffed by individuals of high intelligence, motivation, and energy (see Focus 12.2). Studies of sport teams indicate that "the best individuals make the best team" (Gill, 1984, p. 325). In many sports, the players' offensive and defensive performances can be tracked so that their skill levels can be identified accurately. These qualities can then be used to calculate the statistical aggregation of the talent level of the team, which can be compared to the team's outcomes. Such analyses indicate that the correlation between the aggregation of individual members' ability and team performance is very strong: .91 in football, .94 in baseball, and .60 in basketball (Jones, 1974; Widmeyer, 1990). The relationship is somewhat reduced in basketball because this sport requires more coordination among members and the teams are smaller in size. Hence, the team members' ability to play together may have a larger impact on the outcome of a basketball game, whereas the sheer level of ability of players has a greater impact on a football or baseball game's outcome.

On the social side, members must be able to work well with others on joint tasks (Cannon-Bowers, Tannenbaum, Salas, & Volpe, 1995; Stevens & Campion, 1994). Although different teams require different skills of their members, many performance settings reward individuals who are skilled

---

**KSAs** Acronym for knowledge, skills, abilities, and other characteristics that are needed to complete a job or task successfully.

## Focus 12.2 What Makes a Team Great?

*Great groups are inevitably forged by people unafraid of hiring people better than themselves.*

—Warren Bennis and Patricia Ward Biederman (1997, p. 12)

There are good teams, but there are also great teams. Many work crews can build houses and put out fires, but only a handful are capable of building a 40-story skyscraper or capping a burning wellhead on an oil derrick. Many sports teams play excellent soccer and baseball, but there is only one Manchester United; only one Boston Red Sox. There are excellent-performing orchestras, but only one Berlin Philharmonic. Many space crews have flown into orbit around the Earth, but only a few have traveled to the Moon and back.

What are the ingredients for a work group that makes remarkable advances in science, technology, art, and education? Warren Bennis and Patricia Ward Biederman (1997) studied seven such groups, including the Walt Disney Studios of the 1930s, which created the first full-length animated film; the members of Lockheed's Skunk Works, who designed the first supersonic jets and stealth fighters; and the Palo Alto Research Center (PARC), which invented, among other things, laser printers, the ethernet and e-mail, the mouse, and a graphical user interface for personal computers. Although each group was unique in many ways, Bennis and Biederman traced much of their success back to their composition. Walt Disney, the founder and leader of the Disney Studios, recruited the finest animators in the world to work together to create his films. The members of PARC were creative engineers who knew more about computing than anyone else on the planet. Those at Skunk Works were recruited from every unit in Lockheed and charged to work in secret to build planes that could fly faster than the speed of sound.

Many of the members of these groups were relatively young men and women who lacked experience, but they had no fear of failure. Many were "fueled by an invigorating, completely unrealistic view of what they can accomplish" (Bennis & Biederman, 1997, p. 15). But their most essential characteristic was their talent and expertise. If a team is assembled from relatively mediocre individuals who are good, but not great, at what they do, then that team will likely be a mediocre one. People naively assume that synergistic effects are common in teams, but they rarely outperform the level of their most effective member. As influential as teams are in terms of organizing and motivating members, even they can rarely work the transformational magic needed to turn the adequate into the excellent. Careful design and leadership cannot take a team beyond the limits set by the skills and capabilities of the individual members.

Bennis and Biederman did find that skilled leadership was critical in all the teams they studied, but these leaders' primary contribution to the team was their effectiveness in recruiting and retaining gifted individual members. Leaders must not be afraid to hire people who are far more talented than they are, for "recruiting the right genius for the job is the first step in building many great collaborations. Great groups are inevitably forged by people unafraid of hiring people better than themselves" (p. 12).

in conflict resolution, can collaborate with others to solve problems, and are good communicators (Morgeson, Reider, & Campion, 2005). Conflict resolution KSAs include the ability to distinguish between harmful and constructive conflicts and an emphasis on integrative dispute resolution skills rather than a confrontational orientation. Collaborative problem-solving KSAs involve skill in using group approaches to decision making. Communication KSAs require a range of finely tuned listening and messaging skills, including the capacity to engage in small talk: "to engage in ritual greetings and small talk, and a recognition of their importance" (Stevens & Campion, 1994, p. 505).

How, for example, would you respond if you found yourself in the following situation: You and your coworkers do not agree about "who should do a very disagreeable, but routine task" (Stevens & Campion, 1999, p. 225). Should you:

A. have your supervisor decide, because this would avoid any personal bias?

B. arrange for a rotating schedule so everyone shares the chore?

C. let the workers who show up earliest choose on a first-come, first-served basis?

D. randomly assign a person to do the task and not change it?

Or what if you wanted to improve the quality and flow of conversations among the members of the teams. Should you:

A. use comments that build upon and connect to what others have already said?

B. set up a specific order for everyone to speak and then follow it?

C. let team members with more to say determine the direction and topic of conversation?

D. do all of the above?

According to the Teamwork-KSA Test (Stevens & Campion, 1999), the best choice, in the situation in which you were arguing with others about who must do the unpleasant chore, is option B. In contrast, the best choice in terms of KSAs for interpersonal skill for the second question is option A. An individual who scores well on the Teamwork-KSA test is more likely to cooperate "with others in the team," "help other team members accomplish their work," and talk "to other team members before taking actions that might affect them" (Morgeson, Reider, & Campion, 2005, p. 611).

## Diversity

The Mountain Medical team was, in some ways, a relatively homogeneous team. Members were similar in terms of ethnicity, skill level, age, motivation, background, and experience with the new procedure. They were, however, heterogeneous with regard to sex, status in the hospital, and training. Would these differences make a difference when they pulled together to form a team?

The diversity of a team is determined by the extent to which members are different from one another. A sample of the many ways that people do, in fact, differ from each other is shown in Table 12.2, which identifies six general clusters of differences: social categories, knowledge and skills, values and beliefs, personality, status, and social connections (Mannix & Neale, 2005). Some of these differences pertain to demographic qualities of people, such as race and sex. Others are based on differences in knowledge and skill, and are better considered to be informational or functional variations.

**Diversity and Team Performance** From a strictly informational perspective, diverse teams should win out against less diverse ones. Diversity brings variety to the team, and with that variety should come a broader range of expertise, knowledge, insight, and ideas. A team like Mountain Medical

**TABLE 12.2 Categories and Types of Diversity**

| Categories | Types of Diversity |
|---|---|
| Social-category differences | Race, ethnicity, gender, age, religion, sexual orientation, physical abilities |
| Differences in knowledge or skills | Education, functional knowledge, information, expertise, training, experience, abilities |
| Differences in values or beliefs | Cultural background, ideological beliefs, political orientation |
| Personality differences | Cognitive style, affective disposition, motivational factors |
| Organizational- or community-status differences | Tenure or length of service, title |
| Differences in social and network ties | Work-related ties, friendship ties, community ties, in-group membership |

SOURCE: E. Mannix and M. A. Neale, "What Differences Make a Difference? The Promise and Reality of Diverse Teams in Organizations." *Psychological Science in the Public Interest, 6*, 31–55. Copyright 2005 by the American Psychological Society.

faces a stressful, difficult situation, and it needs all the data it can find to help it identify ways to succeed in such a trying situation. If a team is composed of highly similar individuals, then they bring the same information and insights to the team, so they are less able to identify new strategies and solutions. A diverse team, in contrast, should maximize performance, particularly in situations where success is not determined by the capacity to apply traditional solutions.

But diversity has a possible downside. Diversity can also separate members of the team from one another (Harrison & Klein, 2007). As social categorization theory suggests (Chapters 2 and 3), individuals are quick to categorize other people based on their membership in social groups. Although the members of a team should think of each other as "we" or "us," when members belong to a variety of social categories some members of the team may be viewed as "they" and "them" (van Knippenberg, De Dreu, & Homan, 2004). Diversity may therefore create *faultlines* within the team, and when the team experiences tension, it may break apart along these divisions (Lau & Murnighan, 1998). As Chapter 5 noted, because people are attracted to those who are similar to them, homogeneous teams tend to be cohesive teams, and so members may be more willing to perform the supportive, cooperative actions that are so essential for team success.

Given these advantages and disadvantages associated with diversity, it is no wonder that the research literature does not provide a definitive answer to the question "Do diverse teams outperform less diverse, homogenous teams?" (Horwitz & Horwitz, 2007; Stewart, 2006). Diversity, when based on information and expertise, tends to improve team outcomes, particularly on difficult tasks (Bowers, Pharmer, & Salas, 2000). When members vary in ability, then by definition the team will include at least one individual with high ability. Some homogeneous teams will be uniformly unskilled, so these teams will perform particularly badly at their task. As studies of social compensation discussed in Chapter 10 suggest, heterogeneous teams may also become more productive because the low-performing members are motivated by the high standards set by the others in the team, and the others in the team may also be a source of help and assistance as the low performers work to increase their performance.

But other types of diversity, such as variations in ethnicity, race, age, and sex, influence performance less reliably. Teams of researchers were more productive when they joined with researchers from other disciplines (Pelz, 1956, 1967), but top management teams and work groups were less productive and experienced more turnover when their members varied noticeably in age and tenure (Pelled, Eisenhardt, & Xin, 1999). Management teams in banks that were diverse in terms of their educational histories and backgrounds were more innovative than teams that were homogeneous (Jackson, 1992), but diversity in affective levels—substantial and continuing variations in positive and negative mood—within top management teams was associated with declines in the firm's financial performance (Barsade et al., 2000). Teams that included Asian, African, Hispanic, and European Americans outperformed teams that only included European Americans (McLeod, Lobel, & Cox, 1996), but a study of 151 teams in three large organizations indicated that those individuals who were more unlike the other members of their teams felt the least psychologically connected to them and had higher rates of absenteeism (Tsui, Egan, & O'Reiley, 1992).

**Designing for Diversity** These conflicting findings attest to the mixed benefits and limitations offered by diversity in teams. Diverse teams may be better at coping with changing work conditions, because their wider range of talents and traits enhances their flexibility. Diverse teams, however, may lack cohesion, because members may perceive one another as dissimilar. Heterogeneity may increase conflict within the team (Mannix & Neale, 2005; van Knippenberg & Schippers, 2007; Williams & O'Reilly, 1998).

Steps can, however, be taken to minimize the negative side-effects of diversity and maximize diversity's gains. First, diverse teams will need time to work through the initial period in which differences between people based on their *surface-level qualities*—race, sex, age—lower the team's overall level of cohesiveness. Intervention may also be required when, after time, members have discovered that these surface-level differences are unimportant, but that their *deep-level differences* in values and principles are causing unexpected turbulence in the team (Harrison et al., 2002). Second, because teams exist in an organizational context, the nature of that organization's culture will influence how teammates respond to diversity. If the organization's culture encourages collectivistic values and minimizes distinctions based on tenure and status, then diverse teammates tend to behave more cooperatively than they would in more traditional organizations (Chatman & Spataro, 2005). Third, to minimize conflict between team members from different social categories, steps should be taken to minimize any tendency to draw distinctions between people based on their category memberships (see Chapter 14). Team leaders should remind members of the importance of involving all members of the team in the process, and make certain that individuals in the minority do not become isolated from the rest of the team (see Chapter 7's analysis of minority influence).

## Men, Women, and Teams

Same-sex teams are becoming increasingly anachronistic. Whereas women were once barred from many types of teams in business and organizational settings, changes in social climate—and in employment law—have increased sex-based diversity in the workforce.

These changes are not welcomed as progress in all quarters of society, or recognized as adaptive by all theories of collective action. Some evolutionary anthropologists, for example, argue that the presence of women in previously all-male teams may disrupt the functioning of such teams in substantial ways. This perspective suggests that it was males, and not females, who affiliated in same-sex groups for adaptive reasons, so that over time male bonding became a stronger psychological force than female bonding. In consequence, heterogeneously gendered teams may be less productive than same-sex teams, since all-male teams would be more cohesive than mixed-sex teams. Bonding theorists also suggest "the difficulty females experience in male work groups is not that males dislike females but rather that the force of their enthusiasm for females can disrupt the work and endanger the integrity of groups of men" (Tiger & Fox, 1998, p. 145).

The data do not support either the idea that males bond more cohesively in all-male groups than females bond in all-female groups, or that in consequence male teams outperform female teams. Wendy Wood (1987), after reviewing 52 studies of sex differences in group performance, noted that two factors covaried with sex differences in group performance—task content and interaction style. First, in the studies that favored men, the content of the task was more consistent with the typical skills, interests, and abilities of men than of women. Groups of men were better at tasks that required math or physical strength, whereas groups of women excelled on verbal tasks. Second, Wood suggested that sex differences in performance are influenced by the different interaction styles that men and women often adopt in groups. Men more frequently enact a task-oriented interaction style, whereas women tend to enact an interpersonally oriented interaction style. Thus, men outperform women (to a small extent) when success is predicated on a high rate of task activity, and women outperform men when success depends on a high level of social activity (Wood, Polek, & Aiken, 1985).

But what of mixed-gender teams—teams that include both men and women? Studies of men and women working together in teams suggest that such teams, because of their diversity, have greater informational resources than same-sex teams, and so excel at tasks that require a broad range of expertise, experience, and information. However, sexism, sexual harassment, and stereotyping continue to dog such teams. As with other forms of diversity, sex-based diversity can create subgroups within the team and increase levels of conflict. Diverse teams must also deal with problems of proportion, particularly when very few men are entering into groups that were traditionally staffed by women and vice versa. Teams that achieve diversity by adding only one or two members of a social category, such as a team with one woman and many men, tend to encounter more problems than homogeneous teams. When work groups include a single token or "solo," woman, for example, coworkers are more likely to categorize each other in terms of their sex (see Chapter 6). Solo members are also scrutinized more than other group members, and this unwanted attention may make them so apprehensive that their performance suffers (Kanter, 1977). Token members are more often targets of sexism and prejudice (Fiske, 1993) and must, in many cases, work harder and express higher levels of commitment to the group to overcome other members' biases (Eagly & Johnson, 1990; Ridgeway, 1982).

In some cases, teams with token members will outperform homogeneous teams, even when the teams attempt tasks that are traditionally reserved for homogeneous teams. For example, one team of researchers watched groups working on a wilderness survival exercise—an activity that favors people who have a knowledge of the outdoors. Groups of men generally outperformed women, but groups of men that included one woman performed best of all. The researchers speculated that the addition of a woman to the otherwise all-male groups may have tempered the men's tendency to compete with one another and, thus, helped them to function as a team (Rogelberg & Rumery, 1996).

Hackman and his colleagues have explored the complex relationships among gender diversity, the proportion of men and women, and the organizational context in their studies of a particular type of team: the concert orchestra (Allmendinger, Hackman, & Lehman, 1996; Hackman, 2003). Many of the orchestras they studied were in the midst of a transition from all-male groups to groups that included both men and women. Some orchestras were only beginning this transition, for they included very few women (2% was the lowest), whereas others were more heterogeneous (up to 59% women). When they measured members' work motivation and overall satisfaction with their orchestras, they discovered that orchestras with a larger proportion of female members were viewed more negatively. This tendency was more pronounced among the men in the group, and also in countries with traditional conceptions of the role of men and women in society. Hackman wrote:

> Life in a homogeneously male orchestra surely is not much affected by the presence of one or two women, especially if they play a gendered instrument such as a harp. Larger numbers of women, however, can become a worrisome presence on high-status turf that previously had been an exclusively male province, engendering intergroup conflicts that stress all players and disrupt the social dynamics of the orchestra. (2003, p. 908)

## WORKING IN TEAMS

Chelsea Hospital and Mountain Medical both faced the same problem, and they both decided to solve the problem by forming a team. But they designed their teams differently. Both teams included a scrub nurse, a perfusionist, an anesthesiologist, and a cardiac surgeon, and each trained so carefully that they were skilled at the tasks they needed to perform. But the leaders of the two teams had different views about how they should work together. The young surgeon who headed the team at Mountain Medical insisted that everyone's ideas would be considered, and during the operation itself he asked that everyone communicate with everyone else and not focus on only their own duties. Chelsea's head surgeon, in contrast, believed that most of the staff were so well-trained that they were interchangeable. He did not stress the importance of teamwork, and explained, "Once I get the team set up, I never look up [from the operating field]. It's they who have to make sure that everything is flowing" (Edmondson, Bohmer, & Pisano, 2001, p. 128).

### Teamwork

Before Mountain Medical carried out its first surgery the members of the team had already worked, for weeks, as a team. They met regularly to discuss the procedure, and all had trained together for three days offsite in a simulated operation procedure. They had discussed the sequence of steps that would begin with an anesthetized patient and end with a repaired heart, so that when it was time to work together, they functioned as a team.

**Teamwork** is the psychological, behavioral, and mental work that members of the team carry out as they collaborate with one another on the various tasks and subtasks that they must complete to reach their desired goal. A team may include many talented individuals, but they must learn how to pool their individual abilities and energies to maximize the team's performance. Team goals must be set, work patterns structured, and a sense of group identity developed. Individual members must learn how to coordinate their actions, and any strains and stresses in interpersonal relations need to be identified and resolved (Cannon-Bowers et al., 1995; Cohen & Bailey, 1997).

A functional approach to teamwork begins with a simple question: What does an effective team look like as it carries out its work? Such an analysis recognizes that teams are complex systems, but examines closely the tendencies and patterns of teams' interactions, searching for the core processes that sustain that complexity. What, for example, did the Mountain Medical team do as it prepared for, conducted, and completed each of its operations? And how did Mountain Medical differ from less effective teams—ones that were more dysfunctional rather than effective?

Table 12.3 presents one such functional analysis, developed by Michelle Marks, John Mathieu, and Stephen Zaccaro (2001). Their taxonomy of teamwork functions stresses three key processes: transitioning, acting, and managing interpersonal relations among members. Marks and her associates point out that teams, unlike some performance groups, act episodically. During the initial phase of their work, teams plan out what they will do in later stages, set their goals, and plan strategy. The group then transitions to the actual action stage, where it carries out its assigned tasks through coordinated activity. Once this action phase is completed, the team re-enters the transition phase and begins preparing for subsequent tasks. Across all phases, the members are also managing the interpersonal aspects of the team in order to minimize conflict and maximize motivation. Thus, as Table 12.3 indicates, Marks and her associates break teamwork down into three fundamental components: transition processes, action processes, and interpersonal processes.

**Transition Processes** Often, teams attempt tasks that are so complex that they cannot be completed, at least with any degree of success, without advance planning. The first type of transition process, *mission analysis*, focuses on the current situation: the tasks and subtasks that must be completed, the resources available to the team, and any environmental conditions that may influence the team's work. Teams also engage in *goal specification* and *strategy formulation* between action episodes, since experience working together will provide the members with a clearer idea of the team's potential and limitations. Strategy formulation is particularly essential if the team is unable to reach the goals it has set for itself, for by reviewing the causes of failure team members may find ways to improve their efficiency and outcomes (Cannon & Edmondson, 2005).

**Action Processes** When teams are at work, their task-related actions are so perceptually vivid that the action processes that make up the teamwork portion of their activities often go undetected. When, for example, the Mountain Medical team began to repair the patient's heart, an observer watching the team would see a physician incising and suturing, a nurse monitoring the patient's vital signs, and an anesthesiologist sedating the patient. But Marks, Mathieu, and Zaccaro suggest that four other, teamwork-related actions are also taking place during the action period. First, the group is *monitoring progress* towards its goals,

---

**teamwork** The process by which members of the team combine their knowledge, skills, abilities, and other resources, through a coordinated series of actions, to produce an outcome.

**TABLE 12.3 Taxonomy of Team Processes**

| Process Dimension | Definition |
|---|---|
| | **Transition processes** |
| Mission analysis | Interpretation and evaluation of the team's mission, including identification of its main tasks as well as the operative environmental conditions and team resources available for mission execution |
| Goal specification | Identification and prioritization of goals and subgoals for mission accomplishment |
| Strategy formulation | Development of alternative courses of action for mission accomplishment and identification of the sequence in which subtasks will be completed |
| | **Action processes** |
| Monitoring progress toward goals | Tracking task and progress toward mission accomplishment, interpreting system information in terms of what needs to be accomplished for goal attainment, and transmitting progress to team members |
| Systems monitoring | Tracking team resources and environmental conditions as they relate to mission accomplishment, which involves (1) internal systems monitoring (tracking team resources such as personnel, equipment, and other information that is generated or contained within the team), and (2) environmental monitoring (tracking the environmental conditions relevant to the team) |
| Team monitoring and backup behavior | Assisting team members to perform their tasks. Assistance may occur by (1) providing a teammate verbal feedback behavior or coaching, (2) helping a teammate behaviorally in carrying out actions, or (3) assuming and completing a task for a teammate |
| Coordination | Orchestrating the sequence and timing of interdependent action |
| | **Interpersonal processes** |
| Conflict management | Preemptive conflict management involves establishing conditions to prevent, control, or guide team conflict before it occurs. Reactive conflict management involves working through task and interpersonal disagreements among team members |
| Motivation and confidence building | Generating and preserving a sense of collective confidence, motivation, and task-based cohesion with regard to mission accomplishment |
| Affect management | Regulating member emotions during mission accomplishment, including (but not limited to) social cohesion, frustration, and excitement |

SOURCE: "A Temporally Based Framework and Taxonomy of Team Processes," by Michelle A. Marks, John E. Mathieu, and Stephen J. Zaccaro. *Academy of Management Review, 2001, 26*, 356–376. Reprinted by permission of Academy of Management via Copyright Clearance Center.

as members implicitly check their own actions as well as those performed by others. Second, *systems monitoring* involves keeping track of the resources the team needs, whether they be physical resources, time, or even energy. Third, *team monitoring and backup behavior*, considered by some to be a key difference between teams and task groups, occurs when one member of the team delivers assistance to another member, simply because that team member needs help. Finally, *coordination* of action involves a change in the behaviors of the team members so that each one's actions mesh with other's actions, resulting in synchrony.

**Interpersonal Processes** Consistent with studies of work groups in general, during both the transition and action periods teammates must spend some of their time tending to the relational side of their team. To reach a high level of effectiveness, teams require a degree of unity; yet the pressures often encountered by groups as they strive to reach their goals can produce tension within the group.

Members of effective teams tend to reduce the threat of such conflict to the group's cohesion through *conflict management*. Other types of interpersonal work required of the group members include *motivation and confidence building* and *affect management*.

A recent meta-analytic review lends empirical support to this three-level functional model of teamwork (LePine et al., 2008). A team of researchers identified over 150 studies that had examined team effectiveness and had measured, in some way, one or more of the processes in Table 12.3 and also measured team performance. When they used structural equations modeling to test the proposed three-category model, they discovered that it provided a good fit for the data—the 10 second-order indicators of teamwork were organized, as predicted, into three superordinate clusters. They also discovered that each of the 10 factors was significantly correlated with performance, ranging from a low of .12 for systems monitoring to a high of .30 for both strategy formulation and motivation. The average correlation was .24. These findings are encouraging; but even so, the list in Table 12.3 may not be complete. Such factors as communication (Kozlowski & Ilgen, 2006), pacing (Nieva, Fleishman, & Rieck, 1978), role clarification (Ross, Jones, & Adams, 2008), and creativity (Gibson et al., 2005) have also been suggested as necessary conditions for effective teamwork.

## Team Cognition

Teams need to spend time working together before they jell into an effective working unit. However, time alone is not what enhances the team's expertise but also what happens during the passage of that time. As noted in the last chapter, teams improve their performance over time as they develop a shared understanding of the team and the tasks they are attempting. Some semblance of this *mental model* is present nearly from its inception, but as the team practices, differences among the members in terms of their understanding of their situation and their team diminish as a consensus becomes implicitly accepted (Tindale, Stawiski, & Jacobs, 2008).

The team mental model includes shared representations of the task—how it is to be performed, the type of results sought, the kinds of behaviors that are recognized as useful by the team, and so on—as well as shared representations of the team. Although team members, initially, are often poor judges of members' abilities, given time they become more proficient at recognizing, and taking advantage of, the strengths of each team member. In one study of this process, members of groups completed two geography quizzes about U.S. cities, with such questions as "What city is known as the Crescent City?" and "Through what city does the Trinity River run?" Unbeknownst to the group, one of their members was a confederate who had been prepped with the answers, and he answered seven of the eight questions correctly on the first test. The group used some of his answers (60.3%) on the first test, but when they were given feedback and a chance to do a second quiz, they used his answers almost exclusively (84.7%) (Littlepage, Robison, & Reddington, 1997; see, too, Littlepage et al., 2008; Littlepage & Silbiger, 1992). They learned to rely on his expertise.

**Transactive Memory** Teams also need time to develop *transactive memory systems* (Wegner, 1987). In the complex world of the operating room during heart surgery, there is too much information about the equipment, the proper settings, the instruments, the heart-lung machine, and so on, for a single individual to retain it all with any degree of accuracy. The surgical team therefore distributes the information it needs to each member of the team, depending on his or her role in the team and general expertise. Then, when the information is required, the team consults with the team member known to be the "expert" on that particular matter, who supplies the necessary information, to the best of his or her ability. (see Chapter 11).

Richard Moreland and his colleagues (Moreland, Argote, & Krishnan, 1996) examined the development of transactive memory systems by training volunteers to build radios from hobby kits. Each kit included a circuit board and dozens of components that had to be put in the correct locations and connected before the radio would function. All the participants received the same training in the first session, but some of them worked alone practicing building the radio whereas others practiced in three-person teams. One week later, the participants returned and assembled a radio, this time with an offer of a cash prize if they performed well. All the subjects worked in teams, but only some of them were assigned to the same team they had worked with originally. These individuals outperformed the subjects who were trained individually, apparently because they were able to form a collaborative, transactive memory for the procedures in the first session. Moreland and his colleagues discovered that teams that performed the best showed signs of (a) memory differentiation—some of the team members were better at remembering certain parts of the assembly procedures than others; (b) task coordination—the team-trained teams worked with less confusion; and (c) task credibility—the teams with stronger transactive memories trusted one another's claims about the assembly process.

**Team Learning** Because these cognitive foundations of teamwork develop as the teammates experience working together, teams require group rather than individual practice. Although in years past organizations often sent their personnel offsite to individually receive training in team skills at institutes and workshops, team members need to be trained together—as a unit—rather than separately. Only by confronting the learning situation as a group can the team engage in team learning, which is a "process in which a group takes action, obtains and reflects upon feedback, and makes changes to adapt or improve" (Sessa & London, 2008, p. 5).

The success of the Mountain Medical Center's cardiac surgery team illustrates the importance of learning as a team. The 16 hospitals that Pisano, Bohmer, and Edmondson (2001) studied all used the same equipment, and the operating room staff were all trained by the equipment's manufacturer. These highly trained surgical teams performed their work well, and nearly all of the patients fully recovered after their surgery. Some, however, recovered more rapidly and with fewer complications than others, and this gain was indicated by the speed of the operation. None of the teams operated too quickly, but some were relatively slow. With each patient, the teams improved—minimizing the amount of time that the patient was on the heart-lung machine is an indicator of recovery time—but some teams learned more quickly than others. Surprisingly, the educational backgrounds and surgical experience of the teams did not predict learning rates, nor did the overall support for the new procedure by the hospital's administrative staff. The status of the head surgeon on the team was also unrelated to learning rate, as was the amount of time the teams spent in formal debriefing sessions after each case.

What did predict learning rates? The way the teams were designed and trained. In the slow-to-learn teams, the surgeons assigned to the team happened to be the ones who were available to attend the training session. They showed little interest in who was on their surgical team—in fact, the members of the team varied from case to case, violating a basic rule of good team design (Hackman, 2002). These teams did not fully realize how intense the new surgical methods would be in terms of coordination demands, and the surgeons did not explicitly discuss the need for greater attention to teamwork.

At places like Mountain Medical, in contrast, the team surgeon was usually an advocate for the procedure, and he or she was actively involved in selecting all the other members of the team. These individuals worked together during the training sessions as a team, and they remained together longer during the first cases using the new methods. The surgeons in these teams also stressed the importance of working together as a team rather than the acquisition of new individual skills: "They made it clear that this reinvention of working relationships would require the contribution of every team member" (Edmondson, Bohmer, & Pisano, 2001, p. 130). These fast learners also continued to increase their efficiency, as they developed an open pattern of communication where all felt free to make suggestions for improving the work.

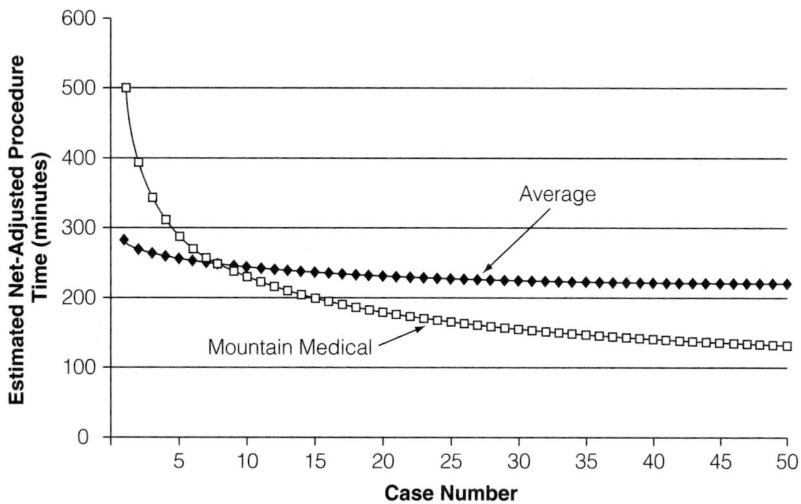


**FIGURE 12.4** Estimated net-adjusted procedure times for Mountain Medical and the average of all other hospitals.

SOURCE: "Organizational Differences in Rates of Learning: Evidence from the Adoption of Minimally Invasive Cardiac Surgery," by Gary P. Pisano, Richard M. J. Bohmer, and Amy C. Edmondson (2001). *Management Science, 47*, 752–768. Copyright 2001 INFORMS. Reprinted by permission.

Figure 12.4 provides a partial summary of the findings for one of the fast-learning teams. This team began slowly, taking much longer to finish the procedure than most other teams. By the fifth case, however, this team was performing at the same speed as most other teams, and they continued to improve their rate with each new case until they were able to conduct the operation faster than all the other teams.

## Maintaining Cohesion

Teams owe part of their success to the strength of the bonds linking group members one to another. As noted in Chapter 5, teams need not be interpersonally cohesive, but given the need for honest communication, strong commitment to the shared task, and willingness to put the needs of the team before individual interests, cohesiveness is in most cases associated with performance gains in teams (Kozlowski & Ilgen, 2006).

Building cohesion requires augmenting its components: social cohesion (attraction of the members to one another and to the group as a whole), task cohesion (capacity to perform successfully as a coordinated unit and as part of the group), perceived cohesion (the construed coherence of the group), and emotional cohesion (the affective intensity of the group and individuals when in the group). Any factor that promotes *attraction*, such as proximity, similarity in attitudes, and the absence of negative personal qualities, will prompt team members to become friends, and thereby the team to become more cohesive. Organizations can also communicate a *communal perspective* to the team through rhetoric that stresses unity, by not singling out individual members, and by providing financial incentives for good team work rather than for individual work. Organizations may also place their teams in challenging environments, so that the members will learn teamwork skills but also develop a sense of unity as a result of surviving the ordeal. Team-building adventures, such as backpacking together in the wilderness, spending the day in a ropes course, or playing a paintball game against a rival team, continue to be popular methods of increasing cohesion. Some organizations also rely on technology to create psychologically closer, albeit physically distant, relations between team members (Gajendran & Harrison, 2007; see Focus 12.3).

## Focus 12.3 What Will the Team of the Future Look Like?

*There is no reason anyone would want a computer in their home.*

—Ken Olson, founder of Digital Equipment Company (see Maney, 2005)

The executive leadership team of Donross Industries is examining the proposed initiative T231. Most members of the team are willing to endorse it, but Diana is still uncertain. As the corporate financial officer, she monitors all monetary outlays, and the initiative will be a costly one with an uncertain promise of payoff. She asks James to run the five-year payout simulation one more time, increasing the risk level and changing several of the cost parameters to provide a more pessimistic forecast. When the chart is displayed it provokes an animated discussion, and in 10 minutes' time everyone on the team has waded in with ideas and suggestions. Except for Giora and Travis. They are whispering back and forth about how to deal with the unexpected resignation of one of their most talented young executives. Sensing that all issues have been raised, Eduardo asks James to run the summary of the discussion, and the group reviews the word count and theme statistics for a few minutes. After several clarifying comments James then displays the ballot box, and the initiative is approved. The team moves along on its agenda.

A common enough segment in the life of a senior leadership team, except that this group is a virtual one. Members are interacting via electronic devices and are distributed in workplaces across the globe. Diana is at the company headquarters in New York. Eduardo is using a handheld device and is in the back seat of a cab somewhere in Tokyo. Giora is still in her pajamas in her den and she "whispers" to Travis using a private channel on their teamware program. And, since this fictitious team is meeting in the future, some of the group members are not even humans. James, in this example, is a program that runs the meeting and acts as a simulated secretary. This notion is not that far-fetched. Researchers are already exploring how people work with teammates who are computers rather than humans (Fogg, 2003).

**Virtual teams** (VTs), like any other type of team, are task-focused groups characterized by high levels of interaction, goal-focus, interdependence, structure, and unity. These teams, however, work from distributed locations, and so are online groups rather than offline groups. They meet in cyberspace rather than in conference rooms, and rely on computer-based information technologies to create channels of communication that may include voice, text, and visual information. These differences in their context (see Focus 15.2) significantly influence how members interact with one another, and as a result VTs are not identical to offline teams (for an excellent summary see Martins, Gilson, & Maynard, 2004). Virtual teams take somewhat longer to make decisions, and in some cases members communicate less when they use technology rather than oral exchanges. VTs sometimes encounter difficulties when planning and strategizing relative to offline groups, but they tend to equalize participation rates among members. In some VTs members communicate only formally, but in others members actually disclose more intimate types of information than they do in face-to-face situations. And the findings with regard to the most crucial question—do VTs generate better products than face-to-face groups?—are mixed. Some studies support VTs, but others side with offline groups.

These differences are not insignificant ones, but they suggest that VTs are not qualitatively different from teams in other contexts. Studies find that cultural differences influence actions in VT, with people from individualistic cultures conforming less. Women feel that VTs are more inclusive and supportive than do men. People form coalitions in online groups, often to increase their control over the team's deliberations. Members of VTs identify with their teams, particularly if the teams meet for an extended period of time. These same things happen in face-to-face teams, for the group-level processes that create uniformities in the behavior of people in groups are more powerful than the situational effects of how members are linked to one another. Individuals who are interacting via computers are, psychologically, members of groups, and all the team-level processes that one can expect to occur in teams will occur in online groups as well.

Besides, even if VTs are not exactly the same as face-to-face teams, they are close enough in design, process, and performance, so there is little to prevent their proliferation. Technology will continue to change virtually all aspects of people's lives, and teams will not escape untouched. Teams will meet more and more frequently online rather than offline, until in time the face-to-face meeting of the team may possibly be considered not just atypical, but bizarre.

---

**virtual teams** (VTs) Task-focused groups that work and communicate by using information technologies, such as email and video conferencing.

## TEAM PERFORMANCE: EVALUATING EFFECTIVENESS

Organizational experts recommend using teams to achieve excellence. No matter what system the experts propose—job enrichment, balanced scorecard management, business process reengineering, activity-based management, or an updated version of management by objectives—most will tout the benefits of using teams to get work done. But do teams offer the best means to maximize human potential? This section examines the final segment of the input–process–output model of teams: What do teams generate by way of direct and indirect outcomes? The analysis raises the question of evaluation—how effective are teams?—and also considers ways to improve teams.

### Defining Team Effectiveness

Teams are task-focused groups, and so the major criterion for determining their success is their performance: Do they reach the goals they, and others, set for them? By this standard, Mountain Medical was a success. The team learned to perform the new surgery quickly and safely, and this efficiency meant a better recovery for the patients *and* substantial savings for the hospital. The team needed less time in the operating room, and its efficiency was so high that it could do more operations than other teams. At a price of approximately $36,000 per case, the team proved to be both medically and economically profitable.

A team's productivity, however, is only one of the outputs that should be considered when determining its effectiveness. Mountain Medical may have become a crack surgical team, but what if the demands of the task were too great, so that members felt so pressured they left the group? What if the team was productive, but over time members grew to dislike working with each other? What if the Mountain Medical group became stagnant—repeating the motions required for the operation with each case, but losing the capacity to adapt and change that made them a high-performance team in the first place?

Hackman (2002) suggests three key factors that should be considered when evaluating the success of a team. Task performance is the first and foremost criterion. Teams are created for the purpose of generating results, and a successful group is one that meets or exceeds agreed-upon "standards of quantity, quality, and timeliness" (Hackman, 2002, p. 23). But Hackman adds to this criterion two other, more indirect, outcomes: adaptive growth of the team as a whole and individual development of the members. Many teams can perform their basic work effectively, but over time they fail to profit from their experiences of working together. A truly successful team is one that grows stronger over time, so that it can undertake even more challenging tasks in the future. Hackman (2002, p. 28) also feels that a high-performing team should contribute, in positive ways, "to the learning and personal well-being of individual team members":

> If the group prevents members from doing what they want and need to do, if it compromises their personal learning, or if members' main reactions to having been in the group are frustration and disillusionment, then the costs of generating the group product were too high. (Hackman, 2002, p. 29).

### The Success of Teams

Viewed from an evolutionary perspective, teams are highly successful social organisms. As noted in Focus 12.1, from relatively humble beginnings in athletics, farming, and agriculture teams have spread out to populate much of the world. Teams are gaining popularity as preferred approaches to management, and "how to" books on team methods continue to make the bestseller lists. Teams have also taken the place of some traditional groups as people's source of social connection, for more people report belonging to teams than they do to hobby, community, and social groups. Teams now have only one group to overtake in terms of popularity: religious groups (see Figure 3.1).

But do teams live up to their promise as systems for increasing productivity and members' well-being? Anecdotal evidence and research findings converge on a verdict that favors teams, but with reservations. Case study approaches are generally, but not uniformly, positive (Applebaum & Blatt, 1994). Texas Instruments, for example, increased productivity when it organized its employees into small groups whenever possible, took steps to build up team cohesiveness, and went to great lengths to establish clear goals based on realistic levels of aspiration (Bass & Ryterband, 1979). When a manufacturer in the United States shifted to teams, supportive supervision, participant leadership, organizational overlap among groups, and intensity of group interaction, employee satisfaction increased and turnover decreased (Seashore & Bowers, 1970). Case studies have, however, uncovered examples of spectacularly ineffective teams. For example, Hackman (1990), after examining the effectiveness of 33 teams, had to revise the proposed title of the book he had planned: *Groups That Work* was given the subtitle *(and Those That Don't)* because he found considerable variation in performance quality across the teams he studied.

Field studies of the use of groups and team development generally support the wisdom of relying on teams (Sundstrom et al., 2000). The Harley-Davidson Motor Company, for example, dramatically transformed their production methods by shifting from a traditional command-and-control culture to one based on self-managing work teams, and the positive results of this conversion appear to depend in large part on the high level of cohesiveness maintained by these groups (Chansler, Swamidass, & Cammann, 2003). When researchers, through meta-analysis, examined the link between organizational change and performance, they found that companies that made multiple changes usually improved their performance and that group-level interventions were more closely linked to productivity than individual-level interventions (Macy & Izumi, 1993). A recent survey of people's satisfaction with their team memberships, however, suggests that members themselves are not so happy with their teams. Only 13% of the 23,000 managers, workers, and executives in one survey agreed that their "teams work smoothly across functions" (Covey, 2004, p. 371).

## Suggestions for Using Teams

Even the most optimistic appraisal of the available data on team effectiveness would suggest that there is room for improvement in the use of teams in performance settings. Teams are a group with extraordinary promise, but to fulfill that promise they must be implemented correctly, and members must be given assistance to use them to their full advantage (Cordery, 2004; Kozlowski & Ilgen, 2006).

**Fidelity of Team Innovations** The popularity of team approaches has brought with it a significant drawback—in the rush to claim that they are using team methods, individuals sometimes call work groups "teams" even though they lack the defining features of real teams. More than 80% of the executives, managers, and team members surveyed in one study reported that their teams lacked clear goals; that their members did not engage in creative discussion; that team members did not hold each other accountable for their assigned tasks; and that members of their team rarely initiated actions to solve problems (Covey, 2004). These are basic, essential qualities of teams, and if they are lacking, then these work groups likely are not actually teams.

These responses may indicate that the very concept of a team—individuals working collaboratively to achieve shared goals—is unworkable, but it may also be that team-based methods have not been properly implemented. Researchers and theorists have identified a number of other characteristics that are conditions for highly-effective teams. Some suggest, for example, that to qualify as a team a group must have shared leadership, control its methods and purposes, and solve problems through open-ended discussion (Katzenbach & Smith, 2001). Others suggest that to be called a team, a group must work at a task that cannot be accomplished without collaboration and that membership must be clearly defined and stable (Hackman, 2002). If a team fails, but it lacked these key ingredients, then the blame most likely rests with those who built the team rather than the team itself.

**Training in Teamwork** Too many organizations create teams but then do little to help team members develop the skills they need to work in those teams. Only 29% of the organizations in one survey gave their teams any kind of training in teamwork or interpersonal relations, and only 26% based compensation (salary, bonuses) on team performance (Devine et al., 1999). Given the complexity of interpersonal and cognitive demands that teams require, members will likely need assistance in learning how to work effectively in them.

Fortunately, when implemented team training has robust effects on team effectiveness (Kozlowski & Ilgen, 2006). Team expert Eduardo Salas and his colleagues, for example, examined the effectiveness of several types of training interventions in a meta-analysis before concluding that (a) most methods work, but (b) the best ones focus on improving member coordination rather than communication strategies (Salas, Nichols, & Driskell, 2007). Cross-training, which involves rotating members throughout the various positions within the group, was particularly helpful, in that it provided members with a clearer understanding of the demands associated with each role and the interconnections among members' responsibilities. Other studies suggest that interventions that increase team members' control over and involvement in work, for example, are more powerful than interventions that focus on morale boosting or envisioning goals (Cotton, 1993; Levine & D'Andrea Tyson, 1990).

**Situational Support** A final condition for implementing teams is the degree of organizational support available to the teams. Organizations may, in the rush to implement teams, create them but then fail to provide them with the support they need to flourish. Features of the organizational context, such as support for technologically based group support systems, development of group-level reward systems to supplement or complement individual rewards, degree of collectivism in the organizational culture, and the availability of external coaches who can assist the team to navigate trouble spots, will increase the probability that team-based approaches will be successful (Mathieu et al., 2008). Other organizational features, such as traditional leadership styles, hierarchical patterns of organization, and individually based compensation systems, will increase the likelihood that team approaches will not prosper.

The case of **quality circles** (QCs) provides a lesson in the importance of providing support for group-level innovations. QCs were popular in the 1980s. These small, self-regulated decision-making groups usually included 5 to 10 employees who performed similar jobs within the organization. The groups were often led by a supervisor who had been trained for the role, but participation in the circle was often voluntary and no monetary incentives were offered to those involved. These groups were thought to be excellent ways to increase workers' participation in the management of the organization, and to increase productivity, efficiency, quality, and job satisfaction. Yet, by the 1990s, most of these groups were gone—the failure rate was between 60 and 70% (Tang & Butler, 1997). What happened?

QCs were not teams, and they had their own unique limitations—participants volunteered and were not compensated, and in many cases conflicts developed between participants and nonparticipants. Worse, however, was the lack of support provided the QCs. They were originally viewed as an easy means of increasing involvement and satisfaction, but the suggestions of QCs were rarely heeded by management. They were essentially powerless, and members soon realized they were an ineffective means of achieving valued outcomes. A few transformed from QCs into true self-managing teams, but most were just abandoned (Lawler & Mohrman, 1985).

The lesson of QCs should not be ignored. As many as 90% of Fortune 500 companies implemented

---

**quality circles** (QCs) Small self-regulated groups of employees charged with identifying ways to improve product quality.

such methods in their plants, factories, and meeting rooms at the peak of their popularity, but the method did not take. Without institutional support or proper design, QCs rapidly disappeared. It would be unfortunate if teams went the way of quality circles, due to failures to implement them correctly, failures to train individuals to work effectively in them, and failures to support them.

## SUMMARY IN OUTLINE

*What are teams and when should they be used?*

1. *Teams* are specialized types of performance groups. Teams, like any group, promote interaction and interdependence among members, pursue goals, and are structured and unified, but teams exhibit these qualities with greater intensity than do groups in general.
2. Teams tend to focus on intellective, informational tasks or performance, action-oriented tasks.
    - Informational teams include management (executive, command), project (negotiation, commission, design), and advisory teams.
    - Performance-focused teams include service, production, and action (medical, response, military, transportation, sports) teams.
    - More specific types of teams include task forces, crews, member-founded teams, and mandated (or concocted) teams.
3. Hackman's model of team autonomy distinguishes between four types of groups on the basis of their control over their processes and goals: manager-led, self-managing, self-designing, and self-governing.
4. Teams are more likely to be implemented when tasks are difficult, complex, and important. In some cases, however, people use teams because they are popular management tools (the *romance of teams*) rather than effective ones. Locke describes the excessive use of teams in performance settings as "groupomania."
5. The input–process–output (I-P-O) model guides much of the theoretical and empirical study of teams.

*How does the team's composition influence effectiveness?*

1. Pisano, Bohmer, and Edmondson examined the performance of medical teams and related their effectiveness to composition and design.
2. Extraversion, conscientiousness, agreeableness, and openness, all key personality qualities described by the big five model, are associated with team effectiveness; emotional stability is not.
3. Members' knowledge, skills, and abilities, or *KSAs*, predict team effectiveness. Highly effective groups tend to be staffed by highly effective individuals, both in terms of specific task skills and general social skills.
4. There are advantages and disadvantages associated with team diversity.
    - Diversity increases the team's resources, providing more perspectives and sources of information.
    - Diverse groups may lack cohesion, because their members may perceive each other as dissimilar. If cohesion is essential for the group to succeed, a diverse group will be disadvantaged.
    - Teams can minimize the negative side-effects of diversity and maximize diversity's gains.
5. Wood's meta-analysis of sex differences found that men and women do not differ in their effectiveness as team members.

- Groups that include a lone representative of a particular social category (tokens, or solos) may encounter problems of fairness, influence, and so on.
- Hackman's studies of performing orchestras indicate that the group's history and the larger social context in which the group is embedded influence the impact of a group's gender heterogeneity on performance.

*What group processes mediate the input–output relationship?*

1. The three key components of working in teams are teamwork, team cognition, and interpersonal engagement.
2. *Teamwork* is the psychological, behavioral, and mental work that members of the team carry out as they collaborate with one another on the various tasks and subtasks that they must complete to reach their desired goal.
3. Marks, Mathieu, and Zaccaro's taxonomy of teamwork functions stresses three key processes: transitioning, acting, and managing interpersonal relations among members.
4. Cognitive processes sustain team processes, including mental models, transactive memory, and learning.
   - Members develop a collective understanding of the group and its task over time (mental model).
   - Moreland and his associates examined the development of transactive memory by training individuals either in groups or individually, and then examining how much of that training transferred to a subsequent group situation.
   - The Pisano, Bohmer, and Edmondson study of surgical teams identified the factors that promoted learning in some groups and reduced the learning capacity of others.
5. As teams work together they spend time maintaining the quality of social bonds between individual members. Cohesiveness promotes the exchange of information and trust required for effectiveness. Teams that meet online rather than offline—*virtual teams*—display levels of cohesiveness that are comparable to face-to-face teams.

*How effective are teams, and how can they be improved?*

1. Hackman identified three factors that define the success of a team: task performance, adaptive growth of the team, and individual development of the members.
2. Team approaches do not ensure success, but they are reliably associated with increases in effectiveness and member satisfaction.
3. Experience with past group-level methods, such as quality circles, suggests that fidelity, training, and support are required to maximize effectiveness.

## FOR MORE INFORMATION

*Chapter Case: Mountain Medical's Cardiac Surgery Team*

- "Organizational Differences in Rates of Learning: Evidence from the Adoption of Minimally Invasive Cardiac Surgery," by Gary P. Pisano, Richard M. J. Bohmer, and Amy C. Edmondson (2001), examined how the surgery teams at 16 different medical centers adjusted to a new surgical procedure that required a higher degree of teamwork (see, too, Edmondson et al., 2001).

*Teams*

- "Work Groups and Teams in Organizations," by Steve W. J. Kozlowski and Bradford Bell (2003), provides a balanced analysis of the use of teams in organizational settings.

- "Team Effectiveness 1997–2007: A Review of Recent Advancements and a Glimpse into the Future," by John Mathieu, M. Travis Maynard, Tammy Rapp, and Lucy Gilson (2008), carefully examines the ever-expanding research literature dealing with teams in organizations by offering, for each primary topic, a set of exemplars that illustrate core concerns and conclusions.
- "Work Group Diversity," by Daan van Knippenberg and Michaela C. Schippers (2007), reviews theory and research pertaining to diversity within work groups and teams.

*Improving Teams*

- *Leading Teams*, by J. Richard Hackman (2002), combines years of experience working with teams with extensive research to offer a useful model of ways to help groups reach their maximum effectiveness.
- "Enhancing the Effectiveness of Work Groups and Teams," by Steve W. J. Kozlowski and Daniel R. Ilgen (2006), reviews the current state of knowledge with regard to teams, with particularly detailed sections pertaining to cognitive processes in teams; cohesion, emotions, and productivity; and team design and development.
- "The 'Romance of Teams': Toward an Understanding of Its Psychological Underpinnings and Implications," by Natalie J. Allen and Tracy D. Hecht (2004), explores some of the practical and psychological factors that may be sustaining business and industry's current fascination for group-level approaches to productivity, before reviewing research that suggests the use of teams may not be appropriate in many contexts.

## Media Resources

Visit the Group Dynamics companion website at www.cengage.com/psychology/forsyth to access online resources for your book, including quizzes, flash cards, web links, and more!

# 13

# Conflict

## CHAPTER OVERVIEW

Group members do not always get along well with one another. Even in the most serene circumstances the group's atmosphere may shift rapidly, so that once close collaborators become hostile adversaries. Because conflict is a ubiquitous aspect of group life, it must be managed to minimize its negative effects.

- What is conflict?
- What are the sources of conflict in groups?
- Why does conflict escalate?
- How can group members manage their conflict?
- Is conflict an unavoidable evil or a necessary good?

## CHAPTER OUTLINE

### iConflict: When Group Members Turn Against Each Other

It was a time before the iPod, iPhone, and iMac. Apple Computers had started strong under the leadership of co-founder Steve Jobs, but now was struggling to hold its own during a downturn in sales of technology and software. Jobs and the executive board decided they needed a chief executive officer (CEO) with a more traditional background in business. They picked John Sculley, of Pepsi, hoping that he would stabilize Apple, improve efficiency, and increase sales.

All worked well, for a time. Jobs and Sculley admired each other's strengths as leaders and visionaries, and they conferred constantly on all matters of production and policy. But they did not see eye-to-eye on key issues of corporate goals. Their working relationship dissolved into a series of disagreements, each one more problematic than the last. Both men played central roles as leaders in the company, but their differences in direction, vision, and style were disruptive. As the conflict over Jobs's pet project, the Macintosh (predecessor of the iMac), reached a peak, Sculley asked the executive board to strip Jobs of much of his authority. The group did so, reluctantly (Linzmayer, 2004).

Jobs did not go quietly into the night. He met individually with the board members, seeking to reverse the decision and to win approval for his plan to fire Sculley in a corporate coup. He waited to spring his plan when Sculley was traveling in China, but Sculley was tipped off by one of the board members. Sculley canceled his trip, called a board meeting, and confronted Jobs:

"It's come to my attention that you'd like to throw me out of the company, and I'd like to ask if that's true."

Jobs's answer: "I think you're bad for Apple and I think you're the wrong person to run this company. . . . You really should leave this company. . . . You don't know how manufacturing works. You're not close to the company. The middle managers don't respect you."

Sculley, voice rising in anger, replied, "I made a mistake in treating you with high esteem. . . . I don't trust you, and I won't tolerate a lack of trust."

Sculley then polled the board members. Did they support Sculley or Jobs? All of them declared great admiration for Jobs, but they felt that the company needed Sculley's experience and leadership. Jobs then rose from the table and said, "I guess I know where things stand," before bolting from the room (Sculley, 1987, pp. 251–252). Jobs later resigned from the company he had founded. He would return, eventually, but not until Sculley had resigned.

*Jobs versus Sculley* was one of corporate America's most spectacular conflicts, but it was no anomaly. Groups of all kinds experience periods of disagreement, discord, and friction. Good friends disagree about their weekend plans and end up exchanging harsh words. Families argue over finances, rules, and responsibilities. Struggling work teams search for a person who can be blamed for their inefficiency. College classes, angered by their professors' methods of teaching, lodge formal complaints with the dean. Rock bands split up when artistic tensions between members become unacceptable. When **conflict** occurs in a group, the actions or beliefs of one or more members of the group are unacceptable to and resisted by one or more of the other group members. Members stand against each other rather than in support of each other (Levine & Thompson, 1996; Pruitt & Kim, 2004; Wilmot & Hocker, 2007).

Why do allies in a group sometimes turn into adversaries? This chapter answers that question by tracing the course of conflict in groups. As Figure 13.1 suggests, the process begins when the routine course of events in a group is disrupted by an *initial conflict*—differences of opinion, disagreements over who should lead the group, individuals competing with each other for scarce resources, and the like. Whatever the cause of the initial disunity, the conflict grows as persuasion gives way to arguing, emotions take the place of logic, and the once unified group splits into factions and coalitions. This

---

**conflict** Disagreement, discord, and friction that occur when the actions or beliefs of one or more members of the group are unacceptable to and resisted by one or more of the other group members.

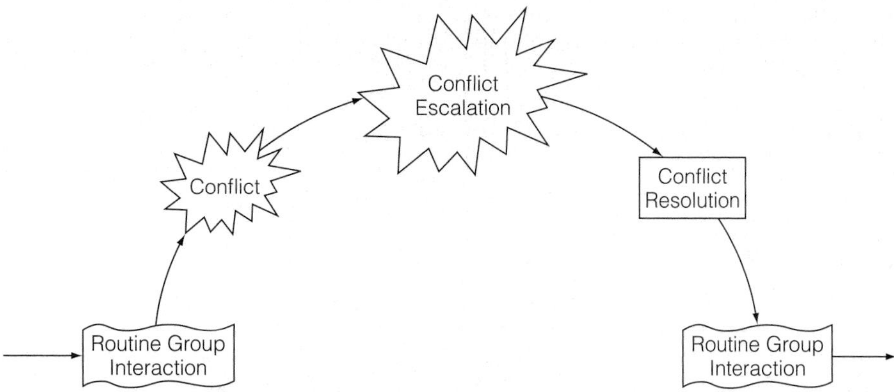


**FIGURE 13.1** The course of conflict in groups.

period of *conflict escalation* is, in most cases, followed by a reduction in conflict through *conflict resolution*. The board of directors at Apple, for example, managed their conflict by backing Sculley and demoting Jobs—a rather severe means of dealing with the dispute. This chapter, then, focuses on conflict inside a group—between two or more members—or **intragroup conflict**. A second form of conflict—conflict between groups, or **intergroup conflict**—is examined in the next chapter.

## THE ROOTS OF CONFLICT

Conflict is everywhere. When the members of 71 groups were asked, "Did your group experience any conflict?" they identified 424 instances of interpersonal irritation (Wall & Nolan, 1987). When Robert Freed Bales and his colleagues used *Interaction Process Analysis* (IPA) to record group interactions, some of the groups they observed spent as much as 20% of their time making hostile or negative comments (Bales & Hare, 1965). Researchers who asked group members to work together on a frustrating, impossible-to-solve task were startled by the intensity of the conflict that overtook the groups. In one particularly hostile group, members averaged 13.5 antagonistic comments *per minute* (French, 1941).

Most people, if given the choice, avoid situations that are rife with conflict (Witteman, 1991). Yet conflict seems to be an unavoidable consequence of life in groups. When individuals are sequestered away from other people, their ambitions, goals, and perspectives are their own concern. But a group, by its very nature, brings individuals into contact with other people—people who have their own idiosyncratic interests, motivations, outlooks, and preferences. As these individuals interact with one another, their diverse interests and preferences can pull them in different directions. Instead of working together, they compete against one another. Instead of sharing resources and power, members selfishly claim more than their fair share. Instead of accepting each other for who they are, members treat those they like better than those they dislike.

### Winning: Conflict and Competition

Before Sculley joined Apple, Scully was *independent* of Jobs. Sculley's success or failure in manufacturing and marketing Pepsi did nothing to influence Jobs's outcomes and vice versa. When they both worked at Apple, that changed. At first, the two worked

---

**intragroup conflict** Disagreement or confrontation between members of the same group.

**intergroup conflict** A disagreement or confrontation between two or more groups and their members that can include physical violence, interpersonal discord, and psychological tension.

together cooperatively, for each one's success helped the other succeed. Their relationship changed yet again when they ran headlong into a dispute over the Mac. The two men refused to change their minds, and so their once *cooperative* relationship turned into a *competitive* one. For Sculley to succeed, Jobs would have to fail. For Jobs to succeed, Sculley would have to fail.

When people are independent of each other, their pursuit of their aims and objectives influences no one else. The lone artist and craftsperson struggle alone in the pursuit of their goals, but their **independence** from others means that should they succeed or fail only they are influenced. But people in groups are, by definition, interdependent, so their outcomes are often linked together. Many such situations promote **cooperation** between members, for the success of any one member of the group will improve the chances of success for the other members. Morton Deutsch called this form of interaction *promotive interdependence* (Deutsch, 1949b). But situations can also pit individuals against one another. When two people play backgammon, one must win and the other must lose. When two coworkers both want to be promoted to office manager, if one succeeds the other will fail. In a footrace, only one runner will end up in first place. As Deutsch explained, such situations involve **competition**: The success of any one person means that someone else must fail. Deutsch (1949b) called this form of interaction *contrient interdependence.*

Competition is a powerful motivator of behavior. When individuals compete against one another, they typically expend greater effort, express more interest and satisfaction in their work, and set their personal goals higher (Tjosvold et al., 2006). But competition can also promote conflict between individuals. When people compete, they must look out for their own interests, even at the cost to others. They cannot take pride in other group members' accomplishments, for each time someone else in the group excels, their own outcomes shrink. In cooperative groups, members enhance their outcomes by helping other members achieve success, but in competitive groups, members profit from others' errors. Because competing group members succeed if others fail, they have two options open to them. First, they can improve their own work in the hopes that they rise above the others. Second, they can undermine, sabotage, disrupt, or interfere with others' work so that their own becomes better by comparison (Amegashie & Runkel, 2007).

Deutsch studied the dark side of competition by creating two different grading systems in his college classes. In competitive classes, students' grades were relative: The individual who did the best in the group would get the highest grade, whereas the individual who did the worst would get the lowest grade. Deutsch created cooperative groups as well. These students worked together in groups to learn the material, and everyone in the group received the same grade. As Deutsch predicted, conflict was much more pronounced in the competitive groups. Members reported less dependency on others, less desire to win the respect of others, and greater interpersonal animosity. Members of cooperative groups, in contrast, acted friendlier during the meetings, were more encouraging and supportive, and communicated more frequently (Deutsch, 1949a, 1949b, 1980).

Other researchers, too, have found that cooperative situations tend to be friendly, intimate, and involving, whereas competitive situations are viewed as unfriendly, nonintimate, and uninvolving (Graziano, Hair, & Finch, 1997; King & Sorrentino, 1983). Work units with high levels of cooperation have fewer latent tensions, personality conflicts, and verbal confrontations (Tjosvold, 1995). Sports teams tend to be more cohesive and—depending on the

---

**independence** A performance situation that is structured in such a way that the success of any one member is unrelated to the chance of other members' succeeding.

**cooperation** A performance situation that is structured in such a way that the success of any one member of the group improves the chances of other members' succeeding.

**competition** A performance situation that is structured in such a way that success depends on performing better than others.

demands of the particular sport—more successful when coaches instill a desire for team success rather than individual success (Schmitt, 1981). Students in classrooms that stress cooperation rather than individualism or competition work harder, show greater academic gains, and display better psychological adjustment. They also foster stronger and more emotionally satisfying student-to-student relations (Roseth, Johnson, & Johnson, 2008).

**Mixed-Motive Conflict** Few situations involve pure cooperation or pure competition; the motive to compete is often mixed with the motive to cooperate. Sculley wanted to gain control over the Mac division, but he needed Jobs's help with product development. Jobs valued Sculley's organizational expertise, but he felt that Sculley misunderstood the company's goals. The men found themselves in a **mixed-motive situation**—they were tempted to compete and cooperate at the same time.

Researchers use a specialized technique, known as the **prisoner's dilemma game (PDG)**, to study conflict in mixed-motive situations (Poundstone, 1992). This procedure takes its name from an anecdote about two prisoners. The criminals, when interrogated by police detectives in separate rooms, are both offered a deal. They are told they can retain their right to remain silent, or they can confess and implicate their accomplice. If both remain silent, then they will be set free. If both confess, both will receive a moderate sentence. But if one confesses and the other does not, then the one who confesses will receive a minimal sentence, and his partner will receive the maximum sentence. The prisoners, as partners in crime, want to cooperate with each other and resist the demands of the police. However, by defecting—competing with each other by confessing—then they may end up with a lighter sentence (Luce & Raiffa, 1957).

When researchers use the prisoner's dilemma to study conflict, the participants play for points or money (see Figure 13.2). The two participants must individually pick one of two options, labeled C and D. Option C is the cooperative choice. If both players pick C, then both will earn money. Option D is the defecting, *competitive choice*. If only one of the two players defects by picking D, that player will make money, and the other will lose money. But if both pick D, both will lose money. Figure 13.2 shows the payoff matrix that summarizes how much money the two will win or lose in each of the four possible situations:

1. If John chooses C and Steve chooses C, both earn 25¢.
2. If John chooses C and Steve chooses D, John loses 25¢ and Steve wins 50¢.

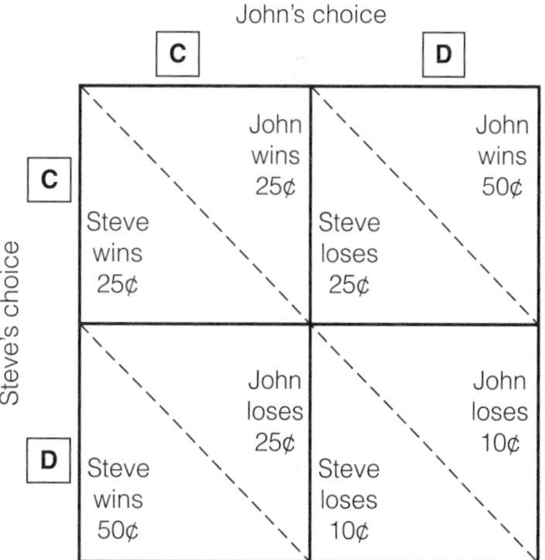


**FIGURE 13.2** The prisoner's dilemma game. Two players, John and Steve, must select either option C (cooperation) or option D (defection). These choices are shown along the sides of the matrix. The payoffs for these joint choices are shown within each cell of the matrix. In each cell, John's outcomes are shown above the diagonal line, and Steve's outcomes are shown below. For example, if Steve picks C and John picks C, they each earn 25¢. But if Steve picks C and John picks D, then Steve loses 25¢ and John wins 50¢.

---

**mixed-motive situation** A performance setting in which the interdependence among interactants involves both competitive and cooperative goal structures.

**prisoner's dilemma game (PDG)** A simulation of social interaction in which players must make either cooperative or competitive choices in order to win; used in the study of cooperation, competition, and the development of mutual trust.

3. If John chooses D and Steve chooses C, John wins 50¢ and Steve loses 25¢.
4. If John chooses D and Steve chooses D, both lose 10¢.

The PDG captures the essence of a mixed-motive situation. Players want to maximize their own earnings, so they are tempted to defect (Option D). But most people realize that their partner also wants to maximize his or her profit—and if both defect, then they will both lose money. So they are drawn to cooperate (Option C), but are wary that their partner may defect. Players usually cannot communicate with each other, and they cannot wait to pick until after they learn their partner's choice. In most cases, players also make their choices several times. Each pair of choices is termed a *trial* or *round*.

How do people react when asked to make a choice in the prisoner's dilemma game? Some cooperate and some compete, but the proportion of cooperators to competitors varies depending on the relationships between members, their expectations and personalities, and a variety of other factors (Weber & Messick, 2004; see Focus 13.1). If, for example, the gains for competing relative to cooperating are increased, people compete more. When people are told they are playing the "Wall Street Game" they compete more than if the simulation is called the "Community Game" (Ross & Ward 1995). If the instructions refer to the other person as the "opponent" then competition increases, but the label "partner" shrinks competitiveness (Burnham, McCabe, & Smith, 2000). And, if people know they will be playing multiple trials against the same person, then cooperation increases. In one study, for example, people played the PDG in large groups of 30 to 50 other people. The game randomly paired people together on each trial, but the odds of being paired with the same person repeatedly were varied experimentally from low to high. The greater the chances of playing with a person in the future, the more cooperative players became (Bó, 2005).

When played for several rounds, people's actions in the PDG are also profoundly influenced by their partner's choices. When playing with someone who consistently makes cooperative choices, people tend to cooperate themselves. Those who encounter competitors, however, soon adopt this strategy, and they, too, begin to compete. Gradually, then, **behavioral assimilation** occurs as group members' choices become synchronized over time.

This behavioral assimilation is an outward expression of a strong regulatory social norm: **reciprocity**. Reciprocity suggests that when people who help you later need help, you are obligated to return their favor. However, reciprocity also implies that people who harm you are also deserving of harm themselves. The converse of "You scratch my back and I'll scratch yours" is "An eye for an eye, a tooth for a tooth" (Falk & Fischbacher, 2006). If one group member criticizes the ideas, opinions, or characteristics of another, the victim of the attack will feel justified in counterattacking unless some situational factor legitimizes the aggression of the former. Unfortunately, negative reciprocity tends to be stronger than positive reciprocity. A cooperative person who runs into a competitive partner is more likely to begin to compete before the competitive person begins to cooperate (Kelley & Stahelski, 1970a, 1970b, 1970c). Negative reciprocity is kept in check if cooperatively oriented individuals have the opportunity to withdraw from the interaction or can communicate their "good" intentions to their partners, but in most situations, a partner turns into an opponent faster than an opponent turns into an ally (Kollock, 1998; Miller & Holmes, 1975).

**SVO: Social Values Orientation** Both Jobs and Sculley were successful, tough-minded business professionals. As they strategized and schemed, their choices were shaped by their most basic of motivations. Should they act in ways that will maximize

---

**behavioral assimilation** The eventual matching of the behaviors displayed by cooperating or competing group members.

**reciprocity** The tendency for individuals to pay back in kind what they receive from others.

## Focus 13.1 Are You a Friend or Foe?

*Ah, who is nigh? Come to me, friend or foe, and tell me who is victor.*

—Shakespeare, *Henry VI, Part 3*

Television game shows, such as *Jeopardy, Weakest Link, Wheel of Fortune*, and *Survivor*, allow the audience to watch competition trigger conflict in groups. On *Survivor*, for example, only one contestant can win the grand prize, and members must vote a person out of the group each time their team loses. On *Weakest Link*, members cooperate by answering strings of questions, but after each round they vote to identify and eliminate the weakest player from their teams. The competition among players invariably introduces tension, conflict, and hostility, dividing the players one against the other.

One game show, *Friend or Foe*, is so similar to the prisoner's dilemma game that researchers have studied it to learn about people's choices in high-stakes competitions. The six players pair up into three teams who compete to build up winnings. After each round, the team with the lowest score drops out, until only one team is left. But all the teams, as they leave, must decide how they will split their earnings. Each player has a button, which no one else can see, and they can press the button if they wish to compete instead of cooperate. The possible outcomes are: *Friend-Friend*: Neither player presses the button and they split their earnings; *Friend-Foe*: The player who presses the button keeps all the earnings; and (c) *Foe-Foe*: Both players press the button and they lose all their earnings.

The situation has some unique features. The groups work together to make their money, and their choices are public ones—everyone watching knows if they pick friend or foe. They are also playing for real money, and substantial amounts in some cases. The average amount that the group plays for is $3,705, although some teams try for much more—as much as $16,400 in one case. Will people cooperate or compete in such a context?

When behavioral economists examined the choices of over 100 teams making their choice in the game, they discovered that players defected, trying to take all the money, 50% of the time. Men tended to compete more than women (55% vs. 46%), and younger players were much more competitive than older ones (59% vs. 37%). Hence, competitive men who were paired with older women tended to take home much more money than all other players. Money, however, did not make people either more or less cooperative. Even when people where playing for substantial amounts, they were as likely to cooperate as they were to compete. This competitive urge ended up saving the game show producers a considerable amount of money. Contestants left nearly $100,000 behind as a result of two players making the fatal foe-foe choice (List, 2005; Oberholzer-Gee, Waldfogel, & White, 2003).

their outcomes and minimize their costs; does the self come first? Or, should they seek first to benefit others and, if necessary, sacrifice their own interests for the greater good?

Degree of concern for other people's outcomes relative to one's own determines a person's **social values orientation (SVO)**. Many people seek to maximize their gains; when they play the PDG they want to earn as many points as they can; they are said to be *proself.* But some people are also concerned with other's gains and losses. These *prosocials* wish to maximize everyone's outcomes (Van Lange et al., 2007). Individualistic and competitive SVOs are proself, and cooperative and altruistic SVOs are prosocial:

- *Individualistic orientation*: Proself individualists are concerned only with their own outcomes. They make decisions based on what they think they personally will achieve, without concern for others' outcomes. They neither interfere with nor assist other group members, for they focus only on their own outcomes. Their actions may indirectly impact other group members, but such influence is not their goal.
- *Competitive orientation*: Competitors are proself individuals who strive to maximize their own

---

**social values orientation (SVO)** The dispositional tendency to respond to conflict settings in a particular way; cooperators, for example, tend to make choices that benefit both parties in a conflict, whereas competitors act to maximize their own outcomes.

outcomes, but they also seek to minimize others' outcomes. They view disagreements as *win–lose situations* and find satisfaction in forcing their ideas on others. Concessions and compromise, they believe, are only for losers. A competitor believes that "each person should get the most he can" and plays to win even when playing a game with a child (Brenner & Vinacke, 1979, p. 291).

- *Cooperative orientation*: Prosocial cooperators strive to maximize their own outcomes and others' outcomes as well. They value accommodative interpersonal strategies that generate *win–win situations*. A cooperator would argue that "when people deal with each other, it's better when everyone comes out even." If they play a game with a child they would be more likely to make sure "no one really wins or loses" (Brenner & Vinacke, 1979, p. 291).
- *Altruistic orientation*: Altruists are motivated to help others who are in need. They are low in self-interest and highly prosocial. They willingly sacrifice their own outcomes in the hopes of helping others achieve some gain.

Individuals with competitive SVOs are more likely to find themselves in conflicts. The competitor's style is abrasive, spurring cooperative members to react with criticism and requests for fairer treatment. Competitors, however, rarely modify their behavior in response to these complaints, because they are relatively unconcerned with maintaining smooth interpersonal relations (De Dreu, Weingart, & Kwon, 2000). Hence, competitors try to overwhelm cooperators, who sometimes respond by becoming competitive themselves. For cooperators, the perception of others' cooperativeness is *positively* correlated with their own cooperativeness. If they think that others will cooperate, they cooperate. For competitors, perceptions of others' cooperativeness is *negatively* correlated with their own cooperativeness. If they think that others will cooperate, they compete (Smeesters et al., 2003). When two competitors meet, the result is an intense conflict like that seen at Apple, and when competitors lose, they often withdraw from the group altogether (Shure & Meeker, 1967).

These differences in SVOs have been linked to other personal qualities, including agreeableness, achievement orientation, interpersonal orientation, and trust in others (Van Lange et al. 2007). SVOs also vary systematically across cultures. Many Western societies, for example, openly value competition. Their economic systems are based on competition, their schools teach children the importance of surpassing others' achievements, and popular games and sports have winners and losers. More cooperative—and more peaceful—societies, in contrast, condemn competition, devalue individual achievement, and avoid any kind of competitive games (Van Lange et al., 1997).

**Men, Women, and Competition** What if John Sculley were Joanna Sculley—a woman rather than a man? Would she and Jobs have battled as fiercely? Or would Joanna have used other, less competitive methods for settling the dispute?

Common gender role stereotypes generally assume that men are more competitive than women. Stories of executives conjure up images of individuals who are driven, ruthless, self-seeking, and male. Yet experimental studies of cooperation and competition suggest that women are just as competitive as men (Sell, 1997). One review of previous work found that in 21 experiments, women were more competitive, but 27 other studies suggested that women were less competitive (Rubin & Brown, 1975). Both men and women use more contentious influence methods when they are paired with a man than with a woman, perhaps because they anticipate more conflict (Carli, 1989, 1999). When sex differences do emerge, they suggest that men are somewhat more competitive than women, particularly when competition is a riskier alternative or will yield a greater payoff (Simpson, 2003). Women are also more likely to endorse prosocial SVOs, relative to men (Knight & Dubro, 1984). Women's reactions during conflicts are also more nuanced than men's. If, for example, their partner is attractive, women make more cooperative choices. If they do not like their partner, they are more likely to compete. Men, on the other hand, simply compete (Kahn, Hottes, & Davis, 1971).

## Sharing: Conflict over Resources

Steve Jobs faced a dilemma. The board of directors of Apple had hired John Sculley to be CEO, and they expected all the company's employees to support Sculley's initiatives. But Sculley called for sacrifices, for he wanted to shift personnel and financial resources away from Jobs's division. Jobs could have accepted this decision and gone along with the group's decision, but instead he chose his own path.

Group life, by its very nature, creates **social dilemmas** for group members. As noted in Chapter 3, the members, as individuals, are motivated to maximize their own rewards and minimize their costs. They strive to extract all they can from the group, while minimizing the amount of time and energy the group takes from them. Yet, as group members, they also wish to contribute to the group, for they realize that their selfishness can destroy the group. Conflicts arise when individualistic motives trump group-oriented motives, and the collective intervenes to redress the imbalance.

**Commons Dilemmas** Consider the "tragedy of the commons." Shepherds with adjoining farms all share a common grazing field. The large pastures can support many sheep, so the shepherds grow prosperous. Then, one or two shepherds decide to add a few sheep to their flock, so that they can make more profit. Others notice the extra sheep, so they, too, add to their flocks. Soon, the commons is overgrazed, and all the sheep die of starvation (Hardin, 1968).

This **social trap,** or **commons dilemma**, occurs when members share a common resource that they want to maintain for their group, but individual members are tempted to take more than their fair share (Pruitt, 1998). But if everyone acts selfishly, the common resource will be destroyed. Members are tempted by the short-term gains that will bring about long-term losses to the collective (Komorita & Parks, 1994; Shepperd, 1993).

Researchers have studied when people choose self-interest over group interest by giving groups of four or five people the chance to draw as many tokens as they want from a pool of available tokens. The pool is a renewable resource, for after each round of harvesting, it regenerates in direct proportion to the number of tokens remaining in the pool. If members quickly draw out all the tokens, the pool is permanently exhausted; cautious removal of only a small number of tokens ensures replenishment of the resource. Nonetheless, group members tend to act in their own self-interest by drawing out all the tokens, even when they realize that the pool is quite small (Brewer & Kramer, 1986; Yamagishi, 1994).

How can groups escape this dilemma? Both experience with the situation and communication among members appear to be critical factors (Allison & Messick, 1985a; Bischoff, 2007). In one study, triads harvested from either a large or a small token pool. The members of half of the groups could communicate with one another, but the rest could not. The differences between these groups were striking. More than 80% of the groups that could not communicate bankrupted their pool within a minute. Even when the pool was large, the noncommunicating groups still had problems with overharvesting. Many of these groups realized the long-term negative consequences of overharvesting, but they did not manage their resources as well as the communicating groups. These results suggest that groups can avoid traps if their members can plan a strategy for dealing with the situation through communication (Brechner, 1977).

**Public Goods Dilemmas** In a commons dilemma, group members take more than their fair share. In a **public goods dilemma**, they fail to

---

**social dilemma** An interpersonal situation where individuals must choose between maximizing their personal outcomes or maximizing their group's outcomes.

**social trap** (or **commons dilemma)** A social dilemma where individuals can maximize their outcome by seeking personal goals rather than the collective goals, but if too many individuals act selfishly then all members of the collective will experience substantial long-term losses.

**public goods dilemma** A social dilemma where one may not contribute any resources in support of a public good (such as a park or a highway system) but also cannot be excluded for failing to contribute.

give as much as they should (Komorita & Parks, 1994). At the community level, individuals may be able to use public parks, enjoy the protection of the police, and send their children to public school, even though they do not contribute to the community by paying taxes. At the group level, members who have not contributed their time, energy, or resources to the group effort—free riders—may nonetheless benefit from group activities and experiences. When students work on class projects as teams, one member may miss meetings and leave assignments undone, but still get a good grade because the group scores well on the final project. When everyone is asked to bring a covered dish to a reception, a few attendees will show up empty-handed.

Free riding can spark group conflict. When group members in a college class described the sources of conflicts in their project groups, more than 35% of their comments targeted disputes over work load. People had much to say about the dedication of their comembers to the group's goals, for some did not put in as much time, effort, and resources as the others expected (Wall & Nolan, 1987). Some groups respond to free riding by extracting promises of satisfactory contributions from members and by imposing costs on the free riders—criticism, public humiliation, physical punishment, and fines are all ways to punish free riders. People are even willing to impose costs on themselves if it means that free riders can be punished in some way (Kiyonari & Barclay, 2008). But some individual group members, to counter the inequity of working in a group with free riders, may reduce their own contributions or withdraw from the group altogether (the "sucker effect"; see Komorita & Parks, 1994, for a review).

**Fairness Dilemmas** Groups must often make decisions about how their resources will be apportioned among and made available to members. A company issues wages to workers. More personnel must be assigned to more important work units. Office space must be allocated to executives, along with company cars, staff support, and budgets. Because resources are limited, groups must develop a fair means of doling them out to members.

Fairness judgments are determined by two forms of social justice: procedural and distributive. As discussed in Chapter 11, *procedural justice* is concerned with the methods used to make decisions about the allocation of resources. Questions of procedural justice arise when groups do not use consistent, open, and agreed-upon methods for allocating their resources. Procedural justice asks, "Did we make the decision in a fair way?" (van den Bos, Wilke, & Lind, 1998). **Distributive justice**, in contrast, concerns how rewards and costs are shared by (distributed across) the group members. When one's piece of cake seems smaller than it should be, when others get the best seats right up near the front of the bus, when workers who do the same job are paid different salaries, or when group leaders give all their attention to one or two favorite members and ignore the others, group members feel that distributive justice has not been done. Distributive justice asks, "Did I get my fair share?" and the answer often depends on distributive norms:

- *Equity:* Base members' outcomes on their inputs: An individual who has invested a good deal of time, energy, money, or other type of input in the group should receive more from the group than individuals who have contributed little.
- *Equality:* All group members, irrespective of their inputs, should be given an equal share of the payoff. For example, even though a person contributes only 20% of the group's resources, he or she should receive as much as the person who contributes 40%.
- *Power:* Those with more authority, status, or control over the group should receive more than those in lower-level positions ("to the victor go the spoils").
- *Need:* Those with the greatest needs should be provided with the resources they need to meet those needs.

---

**distributive justice** Perceived fairness of the distribution of rights and resources.

## Focus 13.2 Are Humans the Only Species That Can Judge What Is Fair?

*Conflict is best understood as an integral part of the social network. It operates within a set of constraints as old as the evolution of cooperation in the animal kingdom.*

—Frans de Waal (2000, p. 590)

Humans are not the only species with a highly evolved sense of distributive justice, at least according to research conducted by Frans de Waal and his colleagues. They trained capuchin monkeys to work for food rewards. The monkeys, when given a token, would be rewarded with a small portion of food when they handed the token back. These monkeys would work for bit of cucumber (low-value reward), but they preferred a grape above all else (high-value reward).

Once trained, de Waal set up several different payment conditions to see how the worker monkeys would respond. In the equity condition, two monkeys worked side-by-side for the same low-value reward; and work they did, diligently exchanging a coin for food. In the inequity condition, the monkeys did the same amount of work, but one of them received the high-value reward and the other was only given the low-value reward. The latter monkeys were none too pleased. In addition to vocalized complaints and gestures of defiance, they refused to continue exchanging the tokens for food, and when given their food reward they would indicate their displeasure by returning it—aiming for the researchers. These reactions were worse still in a third, "free food," condition. Conflict reached its peak when the one monkey was given grapes without even having to trade coins back and forth (Brosnan & de Waal, 2003; de Waal, 2006).

De Waal concludes that these monkeys' reactions were guided by their instinctive sense of fairness, for they appeared to recognize the inequity of the situation. He adds, however, that not all primate species react so negatively to such inequities. Rhesus monkeys, for example, do not seem to be sensitive to distributive justice, perhaps because they live in small groups with very differentiated chains of authority that create great inequalities in the distribution of rewards. De Waal also notes that the monkeys that prospered under the inequitable arrangement showed no sign of concern over getting more than their fair share. They were not so altruistic that they shared their ill-gotten gains with their unrewarded partner. But would *Homo sapiens* have acted any more generously?

- *Responsibility:* Those who have the most should share with those who have less.

Money (and other resources) may not be the root of all evil, but its distribution often causes conflicts within groups (Allison & Messick, 1990; Samuelson & Allison, 1994; Samuelson & Messick, 1995). Members who contribute less to the group often argue in favor of the equality norm, whereas those who contribute more tend to favor the equity norm. Women prefer equality over equity even when they outperform their coworkers (Wagner, 1995). Members of larger groups prefer to base allocations on equity, whereas members of smaller groups stress equality (Allison, McQueen, & Schaerfl, 1992). Some countries stress equality and need more than equity, as do different organizations and groups within each country (Fischer et al., 2007). Members of groups working on tasks where one individual's contributions are critically important for success prefer equitable distributions over egalitarian ones.

Group members who feel that they are receiving too little for what they are giving—*negative inequity*—sometimes withdraw from the group, reduce their effort, or turn in work of lower quality. Receiving too much for what one has given—*positive inequity*—sometimes causes people to increase their efforts so they deserve what they get, but it is negative inequity that causes conflict (Fortin & Fellenz 2008; Rivera & Tedeschi, 1976). Even monkeys, as Focus 13.2 explains, respond with hostility when they are the victims of negative inequity.

These reactions are driven, in part, by self-interest. Group members strive to maximize their personal rewards, so they react negatively when they are denied what they feel they deserve. But group members are also concerned with the issues of fairness and justice, because these are indications of their status and inclusion in groups. When group members feel that their group has acted with integrity while allocating rewards, they feel a sense of pride in their group. They also feel that the rewards they receive from the group are an indication of their prestige and respect within the group. These reactions are shaped more by the group's procedural justice than by its distributive justice (Blader & Tyler, 2003; Tyler & Blader, 2003).

**Responsibility Dilemmas** When a group completes its work, members often dispute who deserves credit and who deserves blame. The board of directors at Apple blamed Jobs's devotion to the Mac for the company's economic misfortunes. Sculley credited his skilled marketing interventions for Apple's prosperity in the years following Jobs's dismissal. Jobs blamed Sculley for ruining the company.

Just as individuals carry out extensive appraisals of their own successes and failures, so do group members devote significant cognitive resources to the analysis and comprehension of their collective endeavors. This appraisal, however, is complicated by the collaborative nature of group activities. Group members must identify the factors that contributed to each member's performance, assign credit and blame, and make decisions regarding rewards, power, and status. Each group member, however, generally sees himself or herself as somewhat more worthy of credit than others in the group. This tendency, termed **egocentrism**, can be easily documented just by asking people to indicate how responsible they feel they are for any group activity, where 0% means they are not responsible at all and 100% that they alone are responsible for what the group has achieved. These scores, when summed across group members, invariably exceed 100% (Ross & Sicoly, 1979; Savitsky, 2007).

This bias occurs, in part, because people are far more aware of their own contributions than those of others—they literally see themselves busily contributing to the group effort and overlook the work of others. Thus, egocentrism can be reduced by asking group members to think about their collaborators' contributions; a process termed *unpacking*. When, for example, the authors of multi-authored research articles were asked to estimate their responsibility for the joint project, they were less egocentric if they were also asked to estimate how much the other co-authors had contributed (Caruso et al., 2006; Savitsky et al., 2005).

Group members' claims of responsibility can be either group-serving (*sociocentric*) or self-serving (*egocentric*). After success, members may praise the entire group for its good work with such comments as "We all did well," or "Our hard work really paid off." Likewise, after failure, members may join together in blaming outside forces and absolving one another of blame. Because these types of responsibility claims protect and enhance the group, they lower levels of relationship conflict within the group (Peterson & Behfar, 2003). Frequently, however, self-serving members blame one another for the group's misfortunes or take the lion's share of the credit after a success (Forsyth, Zyzniewski, & Giammanco, 2002; Rantilla, 2000).

These self-serving attributions result in conflict and a loss of cohesion (Leary & Forsyth, 1987). In one study, members of successful and unsuccessful groups were asked to complete a confidential report of their responsibility and others' responsibilities for the outcome. Then, to their surprise, this report was shared with other group members. Unbeknownst to the group members, the actual reports were switched with standard ones indicating that another group member either took high, moderate, or low responsibility for the outcome. Group members who blamed others for failure or tried to claim the lion's share of responsibility after success were not well-liked (Forsyth, Berger, & Mitchell, 1981). Other studies confirmed that those who engage in self-serving attributions in groups are often viewed as braggarts, narcissists, or even untrustworthy liars, but that those who share responsibility appropriately are

---

**egocentrism** Giving oneself more responsibility for an outcome or event than is warranted; often indexed by comparing one's own judgments of personal responsibility to judgments of responsibility allocated by others.

considered trustworthy teammates (Greenberg, 1996; Schlenker, Pontari, & Christopher, 2001).

### Controlling: Conflict over Power

The conflict between Sculley and Jobs was rooted in each man's desire to control the company. Jobs thought that he would be content to allow another person to make key decisions about Apple's future, but when those decisions did not mesh with his own vision, he sought to regain control. Sculley believed that Jobs was undermining his authority. Both Jobs and Sculley sought the power they needed to control the company, and their power struggle caused turmoil within the group.

As noted in earlier chapters, the differentiation of members in terms of status, prestige, and power is a ubiquitous feature of groups. As the group strives to coordinate its members' task-directed activities, some individuals will begin to assert more authority over the others. Those who occupy positions of authority have the right to issue orders to others, who are expected to follow those directives. Once individuals gain power over others, they tend to defend their sources of power through manipulation, the formation of coalitions, information control, and favoritism. These power processes occur with great regularity in groups, but they nonetheless cause waves of tension, conflict, and anger to ripple through the group (Coleman, 2000; Sell et al., 2004).

Infighting, power struggles, and disputes are particularly common in business and corporate settings. Calvin Morrill (1995) spent several years collecting ethnographic data on the sources and consequences of conflict between executives in corporations. His analysis confirmed the image of companies as arenas for power struggles, where group members compete with each other for power, promotions, and prominence, often by using manipulative, illicit tactics. Contests of authority and power were so commonplace in one company that the executives developed an elaborate set of terms and expressions pertaining to company politics, which Morrill recorded much like an anthropologist would record the rituals and incantations of the members of an isolated tribe. An *ambush* was a "covert action to inconvenience an adversary" (synonyms: *bushwhack* and *cheap shot*); *blindsiding* was "an intentional and surprising public embarrassment by one executive at another's expense"; an *outlaw* was "an executive who handles conflict in unpredictable ways but who is regarded as especially task competent." In some cases, this maneuvering would result in a *meltdown*—a "physical fight between executives" (1995, pp. 263–265).

### Working: Task and Process Conflict

As the group goes about its work on shared tasks and activities, members sometimes disagree with one another. This type of conflict is termed **task conflict** or *substantive conflict* because it stems from disagreements about issues that are relevant to the group's goals and outcomes. No group of people is so well-coordinated that its members' actions mesh perfectly, so conflicts over the group tasks are inevitable. Groups and organizations use such conflicts to make plans, increase creativity, solve problems, decide issues, and resolve misunderstandings. Sculley and Jobs, as the leaders of Apple, were supposed to argue and debate over substantive issues having to do with making and selling computers.

Although task conflicts help groups reach their goals, these disagreements can spill over into more personal conflicts. People who disagree with the group, even when their position is a reasonable one, often provoke considerable animosity within the group. The dissenter who refuses to accept others' views is liked less, assigned low-status tasks, and sometimes ostracized. As the group struggles to reach consensus on the substantive issues at hand, it responds negatively to those group members who slow down this process (Kruglanski & Webster, 1991). Researchers studied this process by planting a confederate in discussion groups. The confederate deliberately slowed down the group with such

---

**task conflict** (or substantive conflict) Disagreements over issues that are relevant to the group's recognized goals and procedures.

interruptions as "What do you mean?" "Do you think that's important?" or "I don't understand." In some groups, the confederate had an excuse: He told the group that his hearing aid was not working that day. Other groups, in contrast, received no exculpating explanation. At the end of the session members were asked to identify one person to exclude from the group. Everyone (100%) picked the disruptive confederate if there was no excuse for his actions (Burstein & Worchel, 1962).

Task conflict occurs when ideas, opinions, and interpretations clash. **Process conflict**, or procedural conflict, occurs when strategies, policies, and methods clash. Group members may find themselves uncertain about how to resolve a problem, with some championing continued discussion and others favoring a vote. The leader of the group may make decisions and initiate actions without consulting the group; but the group may become irritated if denied an opportunity to participate in decision making (Smoke & Zajonc, 1962). During procedural conflicts, groups do not just disagree—they disagree on *how* to disagree.

Many groups minimize procedural ambiguities by adopting formal rules—bylaws, constitutions, statements of policies, or mission and procedure statements—that specify goals, decisional processes, and responsibilities (Houle, 1989). Many decision-making groups also rely on specific rules to regulate their discussions. The best-known set of rules was developed by Henry M. Robert, an engineer who was irritated by the conflict that characterized many of the meetings he attended. *Robert's Rules of Order*, first published in 1876, explicated not only "methods of organizing and conducting the business of societies, conventions, and other deliberative assemblies," but also such technicalities as how motions should be stated, amended, debated, postponed, voted on, and passed (Robert, 1915/ 1971, p. i). No less than seven pages were used to describe how the group member "obtains the floor," including suggestions for proper phrasings of the request, appropriate posture, and timing. More complex issues, such as the intricacies of voting, required as many as 20 pages of discussion. Robert purposely designed his rules to "restrain the individual somewhat," for he assumed that "the right of any individual, in any community, to do what he pleases, is incompatible with the interests of the whole" (1915/1971, p. 13). As a result, his rules promote a formal, technically precise form of interaction, sometimes at the expense of openness, vivacity, and directness. Additionally, the rules emphasize the use of voting procedures, rather than discussion to consensus, to resolve differences.

## Liking and Disliking: Personal Conflicts

Beth Doll and her colleagues (2003) studied conflict at recess—the period of relatively unsupervised interaction that many schoolchildren consider to be an oasis of play in the otherwise work-filled school day. They discovered that many conflicts stemmed from disagreements and power struggles, as children argued about the rules of games, what is fair and what is not, and who gets to make decisions. But the most intense conflicts were personal. Children who disliked each other got into fights. Children who had irritating personal habits were routinely excluded by others. Children in one clique were mean to children in other cliques and to those who were excluded from all cliques. When children who said they had a rotten time at recess were asked why, in most cases they explained, "I had to play alone" and, "Other kids would not let me join in" (Doll, Murphy, & Song, 2003).

Adults do not always play well together either. **Personal conflicts**, also called *affective conflicts* (Guetzkow & Gyr, 1954), *personality conflicts* (Wall & Nolan, 1987), *emotional conflicts* (Jehn, 1995), or

---

**process conflict** (or procedural conflict) Disagreement over the methods the group should use to complete its basic tasks.

**personal conflict** Interpersonal discord that occurs when group members dislike one another.

*relationship conflicts* (De Dreu & Weingart, 2003), are rooted in individuals' antipathies for other group members. Personal likes and dislikes do not always translate into group conflict, but people often mention their disaffection for another group member when they air their complaints about their groups (Alicke et al., 1992). Morrill's (1995) study of high-level corporate executives, for example, revealed both task and power conflicts, but more than 40% of their disputes were rooted in "individual enmity between the principals without specific reference to other issues." Disputants questioned each others' moral values, the way they treated their spouses, and their politics. They complained about the way their adversaries acted at meetings, the way they dressed at work and at social gatherings, their hobbies and recreational pursuits, and their personality traits. They just did not like each other very much (Morrill, 1995, p. 69).

Just as any factor that creates a positive bond between people can increase a group's cohesion, so any factor that creates disaffection can increase conflict. In many cases, people explain their conflicts by blaming the other person's negative personal qualities, such as moodiness, compulsivity, incompetence, communication difficulties, and sloppiness (Kelley, 1979). People usually dislike others who evaluate them negatively, so criticism—even when deserved—can generate conflict (Ilgen, Mitchell, & Fredrickson, 1981). Group members who treat others unfairly or impolitely engender more conflict than those who behave politely (Ohbuchi, Chiba, & Fukushima, 1996). People who have agreeable personalities are usually better liked by others, and they also exert a calming influence on their groups. In a study of dyads that included people who were either high or low in agreeableness, dyads with two highly agreeable individuals displayed the least conflict, whereas dyads that contained two individuals with low agreeableness displayed the most conflict (Graziano, Jensen-Campbell, & Hair, 1996). Agreeable people also responded more negatively to conflict overall. When people described their day-to-day activities and their daily moods, they reported feeling unhappy, tense, irritated, and anxious on days when they experienced conflicts—especially if they were by nature agreeable people (Suls, Martin, & David, 1998). Because, as Chapter 4 explained, similarity usually triggers attraction and dissimilarity disliking, diverse groups must deal with conflict more frequently than more homogenous ones (see Focus 13.3).

## CONFRONTATION AND ESCALATION

Early in 1985, Sculley and Jobs began moving toward a showdown, pushed into conflict by their incompatibilities, their marked differences of opinion about the company, the competitive nature of their interdependence, and their refusal to take less than they felt was their due. They tried to quell the tension, but by spring, the men were trapped in an escalating conflict.

Conflicts *escalate*. Although the parties to the conflict may hope to reach a solution to their dispute quickly, a host of psychological and interpersonal factors can frustrate their attempts to control the conflict. As Sculley continued to argue with Jobs, he became more committed to his own position, and his view of Jobs and his position became biased. Sculley used stronger influence tactics, and soon other members of Apple were drawn into the fray. All these factors fed the conflict, changing it from a disagreement to a full-fledged corporate war.

### Uncertainty → Commitment

As conflicts escalate, group members' doubts and uncertainties are replaced by a firm commitment to their position. Sculley, for example, became more certain that his insights were correct, and his disagreement with Jobs only increased his commitment to them (Staw & Ross, 1987). When people try to persuade others, they search out supporting arguments. If this elaboration process yields further consistent information, they become even more committed to their initial position. People

## Focus 13.3 Which Is Worse: Conflict with a Friend or with a Foe?

*Secrets are divulged when friends fight.*
—Hindu proverb

People prefer to work in cohesive groups that are free from conflict: where members are not only linked by their communal tasks but also strong relational bonds of friendship. But what happens when conflict erupts in these more personally unified groups? To disagree with a colleague whom you respect but do not think of as a friend is one thing, but this same disagreement with a friend may be far more disruptive. Was the intensity of the dispute between Jobs and Sculley due, in part, to their friendship as much as their substantive disagreement?

Such a possibility is suggested by Heider's balance theory. As noted in Chapter 6's analysis of the stability of group structures, balance theory suggests that arguing and fighting with a friend is particularly jarring. Whereas disagreeing with someone you dislike is cognitively "harmonious"—the elements of the situation all "fit together without stress" (Heider, 1958, p. 180) —disagreeing with someone who is liked is an imbalanced state that will create psychological discomfort.

Could arguing with a friend be worse than arguing with someone who is less well liked? Sociologist Howard Taylor examined this question by arranging for male college students to discuss an issue with another student whom they liked or disliked. This student was Taylor's confederate, who unbeknownst to the group members was trained to deliberately agree or disagree on key issues. Taylor then watched the groups for evidence of conflict, including tension (nervousness, stammering, blushing, expressions of frustration, and withdrawal), tension release (giggling, joking, cheerfulness, silliness), and antagonism (anger, hostility, taunting, and defensiveness).

Figure 13.3 partly summarizes the findings. As balance theory suggests, tension was highest in the unbalanced pairs—when disagreeing people liked each other or when people who disliked each other agreed. People did not like disagreeing with friends, or agreeing with their foes. The greatest amount of antagonism, however, occurred when discussants both disagreed and disliked each other. So, the predictions of balance theory were only partially confirmed. The most harmonious groups were ones whose members liked each other and found themselves in agreement. However, the least harmonious groups were balanced, but by negative rather than positive forces: members disliked each other *and* they disagreed. Taylor (1970) concluded that such groups would likely not long endure outside the confines of the laboratory.

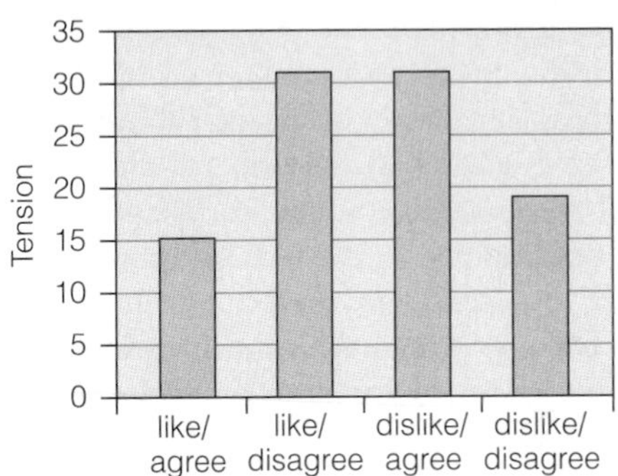


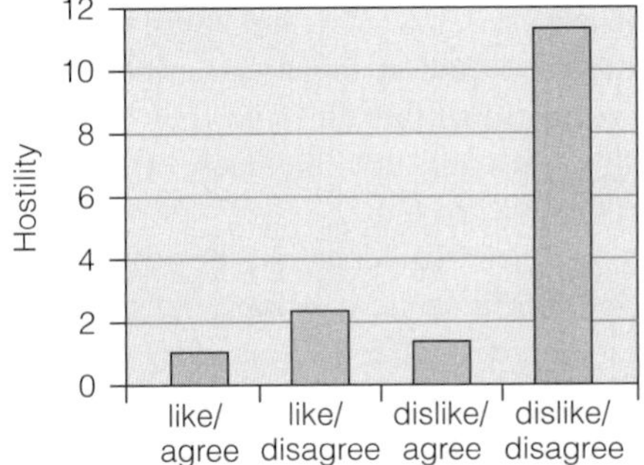


**FIGURE 13.3** Levels of tension and hostility when people who disagreed or agreed on an issue and either liked or disliked each other talked for 30 minutes.

SOURCE: Taylor, 1970.

rationalize their choices once they have made them: They seek out information that supports their views, they reject information that conflicts with their stance, and they become entrenched in their original position (Ross & Ward, 1995). Moreover, people feel that once they commit to a position publicly, they must stick with it. They may realize that they are wrong, but to save face, they continue to argue against their opponents (Wilson, 1992). Finally, if other group members argue too strongly, *reactance* may set in. As noted in Chapter 8, when reactance occurs, group members become even more committed to their position (Brehm & Brehm, 1981; Curhan, Neale, & Ross, 2004).

The *dollar auction* illustrates the impact of commitment on conflict. Members bid for $1, but one special rule is added. The highest bidder gets to keep the dollar bill, but the second highest bidder gets no money *and* must pay the amount he or she bid. Bids flow slowly at first, but soon the offers climb over 50 cents toward the $1 mark. As the stakes increase, however, quitting becomes costly. If a bidder who offers 50 cents for the $1 is bested by someone offering 60 cents, the 50-cent bidder will lose 50 cents. So he or she is tempted to beat the 60-cent bid. This cycle continues upward—well beyond the value of the dollar bill in some cases. On occasion, players have spent as much as $20 for the $1 (Teger, 1980).

### Perception → Misperception

Individuals' reactions during conflict are shaped in fundamental ways by their perception of the situation and the people in that situation. Group members' inferences about each others' strengths, attitudes, values, and other personal qualities provide the basis for mutual understanding, but during conflict these perceptions tend to be so distorted that they inflame rather than smooth conflict (Thompson & Nadler, 2000).

**Misattribution** Sometimes group members settle on explanations that sustain and enhance members' interpersonal relations. Jobs, in trying to explain Sculley's actions, may have assumed Sculley was under pressure from the board, he was unaccustomed to the demands of running a high-tech firm, or that he was dealing with the stress of his relocation. But frequently, people explain their conflicts in ways that make the problem worse. In that case, Jobs would think that Sculley's actions were caused by his personal qualities, such as incompetence, belligerence, argumentativeness, greed, or selfishness. Jobs might also believe that Sculley was deliberately trying to harm him, and that Sculley therefore deserved to be blamed and punished (Fincham & Bradbury, 1992, 1993). In short, Jobs would fall prey to the *fundamental attribution error* (FAE) and assume that Sculley's behavior was caused by personal (dispositional) rather than situational (environmental) factors (Ross, 1977). If the conflict continued, he may have eventually decided it was an intractable one. People expect intractable conflicts to be prolonged, intense, and very hard to resolve (Bar-Tal, 2007).

**Misperceiving Motivations** When conflict occurs in a group, members begin to wonder about one another's motivations. "Why," Steve Jobs may have wondered, "is Sculley not supporting my work with the Mac? He must know how important this project is to the company, so why is he not giving it the attention it deserves?"

During conflict members often become distrustful of one another, wondering if their once cooperative motivations have been replaced by competitive ones. This loss of trust is one of the primary reasons why people, when they begin to compete with one another, have difficulty returning to a cooperative relationship. Researchers examined just this process by pairing people playing a PDG-like game with partners who used one of four possible strategies described earlier: competition, cooperation, individualism, and altruism. When later asked to describe their partners' motives, the players recognized when they were playing with an individualist or a competitor, but they had more trouble accurately perceiving cooperation and altruism (Maki, Thorngate, & McClintock, 1979).

People with competitive SVOs are the most inaccurate in their perceptions of cooperation. When cooperators play the PDG with other cooperators, their perceptions of their partner's strategy are inaccurate only 6% of the time. When competitors play the PDG with cooperators, however, they misinterpret their partner's strategy 47% of the time, mistakenly believing that the cooperators are competing (Kelley & Stahelski, 1970a, 1970b, 1970c; Sattler & Kerr, 1991). Competitors are also biased in their search for information, for they are more likely to seek out information that confirms their suspicions—"I am dealing with a competitive person"—rather than information that might indicate the others are attempting to cooperate (Van Kleef & De Dreu, 2002). Competitors also tend to deliberately misrepresent their intentions, sometimes claiming to be more cooperatively intentioned than they actually are (Steinel & De Dreu, 2004).

### Soft Tactics → Hard Tactics

People can influence other people in dozens of different ways; they can promise, reward, threaten, punish, bully, discuss, instruct, negotiate, manipulate, supplicate, ingratiate, and so on. Some of these tactics are harsher than others. Threats, punishment, and bullying are all hard, contentious tactics because they are direct, nonrational, and unilateral. People use softer tactics at the outset of a conflict, but as the conflict escalates, they shift to stronger and stronger tactics. Sculley gradually shifted from relatively mild methods of influence (discussion, negotiation) to stronger tactics (threats). Eventually, he demoted Jobs (Carnevale & Pruitt, 1992).

One team of researchers studied this escalation process by creating a simulated birthday card factory where people were paid a small amount for each card they manufactured using paper, colored markers, and ribbons. The work went well until one of the group members, a confederate of the researchers, began acting selfishly by hoarding materials that the other members needed. As the hour wore on, it became clear that this person was going to make far more money than everyone else, and the group became more and more frustrated. It responded by using stronger and more contentious influence tactics. As Table 13.1 indicates, the group tried to solve the problem initially with statements and requests. When those methods failed, they shifted to demands and complaints. When those methods failed, they tried problem solving and appeals to a third party (the experimenter). In the most extreme cases, they used threats, abuse, and anger to try to influence the irritating confederate (Mikolic, Parker, & Pruitt, 1997).

People who use harder tactics often overwhelm their antagonists, and such methods intensify conflicts. Morton Deutsch and Robert Krauss (1960)

**TABLE 13.1 Influence Methods Used in Groups Sharing Scarce Resources**

| Behavior | Example | Percentage Using |
|---|---|---|
| **Requests** | May I use the glue? | 100.0 |
| **Statements** | We need the glue. | 100.0 |
| **Demands** | Give me the glue, now! | 88.9 |
| **Complaints** | What's wrong with you? Why don't you share? | 79.2 |
| **Problem solving** | You can use our stapler if you share the glue. | 73.6 |
| **Third party** | Make them share! | 45.8 |
| **Angry** | I'm mad now. | 41.7 |
| **Threat** | Give me the glue or else. | 22.2 |
| **Harassment** | I'm not giving you any more ribbon until you return the glue. | 16.7 |
| **Abuse** | You are a selfish swine. | 0.7 |

SOURCE: Mikolic, Parker, & Pruitt, 1997.

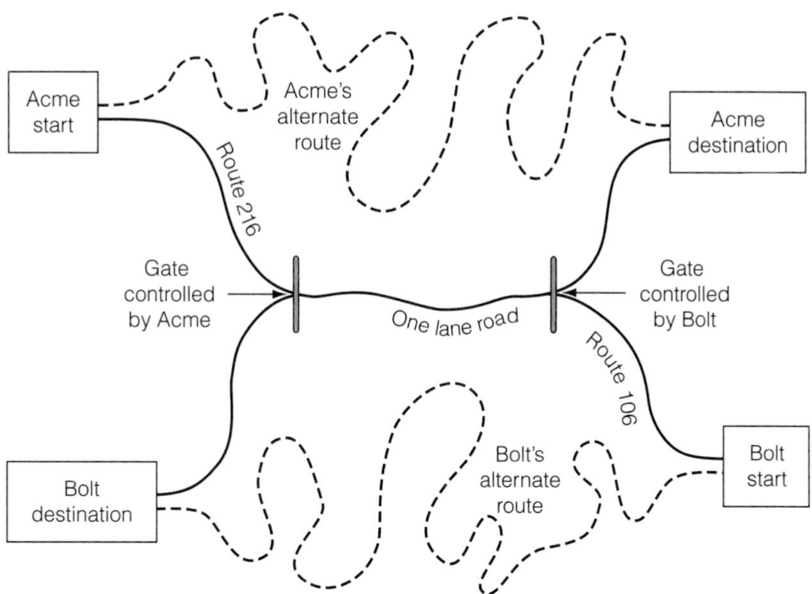


**FIGURE 13.4** The Deutsch and Krauss trucking game simulation. Players took the role of either Acme or Bolt, and maneuvered their trucks along Route 216, Route 106, or the longer, alternate routes. In some cases one or both of the players were given gates that they could close to bar access by their opponent.

SOURCE: *The Resolution of Conflict: Constructive and Destructive Processes,* by M. Deutsch. Copyright 1973 by Yale University Press. Reprinted by permission.

examined this intensification process in their classic **trucking game experiment**. They asked pairs of women to role-play the owners of a trucking company. The two companies, Acme and Bolt, carried merchandise over the roads mapped in Figure 13.4. Acme and Bolt each earned 60 cents after each complete run, minus 1 cent for each second taken up by the trip.

The truck route set the stage for competition and conflict between Acme and Bolt. The shortest path from start to finish for Acme was Route 216 and for Bolt was Route 106, but these routes merged into a one-lane highway. When trucks encountered each other along this route, one player had to back up to her starting position to let the other through. Acme and Bolt could avoid this confrontation by taking the winding alternate route, but this path took longer.

All the pairs played the same basic game, but some were provided with the power to threaten their opponents, and others were not. In the *unilateral threat* condition, Acme was told that a gate, which only she could open and close, was located at the fork in Route 216. When the gate was closed, neither truck could pass this point in the road, making control of the gate a considerable benefit to Acme. If Bolt attempted to use the main route, all Acme had to do was close the gate, forcing Bolt to back up and enabling Acme to reopen the gate and proceed quickly to her destination. Thus, when only Acme possessed the gate, Bolt's profits were greatly threatened. In the *bilateral threat* condition, both sides had the use of gates located at the ends of the one-lane section of Route 216, and in the *control* condition, no gates were given to the players.

Deutsch and Krauss's control participants soon learned to resolve the conflict over the one-lane road. Most of these pairs took turns using the

---

**trucking game experiment** A research procedure developed by Morton Deutsch and Robert Krauss in their studies of conflict between individuals who differ in their capacity to threaten and punish others.

main route, and on the average, each participant made a $1 profit. Winnings dwindled, however, when one of the players was given a gate. Participants in the unilateral threat condition lost an average of $2.03. Bolt's losses were twice as great as Acme's, but even Acme lost more than $1 at the game. Conflict was even worse when both Acme and Bolt had gates. In the bilateral threat condition, both players usually took the longer route because the gates on the main route were kept closed, and their losses in this condition averaged $4.38.

These findings convinced Deutsch and Krauss that the capacity to threaten others intensifies conflict. They also noted that establishing a communication link between adversaries does not necessarily help them to solve their dispute (Krauss & Morsella, 2000). If one party can or does threaten the other party, the threatened party will fare best if he or she cannot respond with a counterthreat (Borah, 1963; Deutsch & Lewicki, 1970; Froman & Cohen, 1969; Gallo, 1966). Equally powerful opponents, however, learn to avoid the use of their power if the fear of retaliation is high (Lawler, Ford, & Blegen, 1988).

### Reciprocity → Upward Conflict Spiral

Conflict-ridden groups may seem normless, with hostility and dissatisfaction spinning out of control. Yet upward conflict spirals are in many cases sustained by the norm of reciprocity. If one group member criticizes the ideas, opinions, or characteristics of another, the victim of the attack will feel justified in counterattacking unless some situational factor legitimizes the hostility of the former (Eisenberger, et al., 2004).

If interactants followed the norm of reciprocity exactly, a mild threat would elicit a mild threat in return, and an attack would lead to a counterattack. But interactants tend to follow the norm of *rough* reciprocity—they give too much (*overmatching*) or too little (*undermatching*) in return. In one study, women playing a PDG-like game against a confederate could send notes to their opponent and penalize her by taking points from her winnings. Reciprocity guided the player's actions, for the more often the confederate sent threats, the more often the participant sent threats; when the confederate's threats were large, the participant's threats were large; and confederates who exacted large fines triggered large fines from the participant. This reciprocity, however, was rough rather than exact. At low levels of conflict, the participants overmatched threats and punishments, and at high levels of conflict, they undermatched their threats. The overmatching that occurs initially may serve as a strong warning, whereas the undermatching at high levels of conflict may be used to send a conciliatory message (Youngs, 1986).

### Few → Many

During the Jobs–Sculley conflict, Jobs tried to persuade each member of the board to side with him in the dispute. His goal was to form a powerful coalition that would block Sculley's plans and swing the vote of the board in his favor.

Coalitions exist in most groups, but when conflict erupts, group members use coalitions to shift the balance of power in their favor. The initial disagreement may involve only two group members, but as conflicts intensify, previously neutral members often join with one faction. Similarly, even when members initially express many different views, with time, these multiparty conflicts are reduced to two-party blocs through coalition formation. Coalitions can even link rivals who decide to join forces temporarily to achieve a specific outcome (a mixed-motive situation). Although allies may wish to compete with one another, no single individual has enough power to succeed alone. Hence, while the coalition exists, the competitive motive must be stifled (Komorita & Parks, 1994).

Coalitions contribute to conflicts because they draw more members of the group into the fray. Coalitions are often viewed as contentious, heavy-handed influence tactics because individuals in the coalition work not only to ensure their own outcomes but also to worsen the outcomes of non-coalition members. Coalitions form *with* people and *against* other people. In business settings, for example, the dominant coalition can control the organization, yet it works outside the bounds of the formal group structure. Those who are excluded from a coalition react with hostility to the coalition members and seek to regain power by forming their own coalitions. Thus, coalitions must be constantly maintained through strategic bargaining and negotiation (Mannix, 1993; Murnighan, 1986; Stevenson, Pearce, & Porter, 1985).

### Irritation → Anger

Few people can remain calm and collected in a conflict. When disputes arise, tempers flare, and this increase in negative emotions exacerbates the initial conflict. Most people, when asked to talk about a time when they became angry, said that they usually lost their temper when arguing with people they knew rather than with strangers. Many admitted that their anger increased the negativity of the conflict; 49% became verbally abusive when they were angry, and 10% said they became physically aggressive (Averill, 1983). Participants in another study reported physically attacking someone or something, losing emotional control, or imagining violence against someone else when they were angry (Shaver et al., 1987). Even when group members began by discussing their points calmly and dispassionately, as they became locked into their positions, emotional expression begins to replace logical discussion (De Dreu et al., 2007). Unfortunately, all manner of negative behaviors, including the rejection of concessions, the tendering of unworkable initial offers, and the use of contentious influence strategies, increase as members' affect becomes more negative (Pillutla & Murnighan, 1996; Van Kleef, De Dreu, & Manstead, 2004). Anger is also a contagious emotion in groups (Kelly, 2001). Group members, when negotiating with someone who has become angry, tend to become angry themselves (Van Kleef et al., 2004).

## CONFLICT RESOLUTION

In one way or another, conflicts subside. Even when members are committed to their own viewpoints, high levels of tension cannot be maintained indefinitely. Disputants may regain control of their tempers and break the upward conflict spiral. The group may fissure, splitting into two or more subgroups whose members are more compatible. One member may leave the group, as was the result in the Jobs–Sculley dispute. In time, group hostility abates.

### Commitment → Negotiation

Just as conflicts escalate when group members become firmly committed to a position and will not budge, conflicts de-escalate when group members are willing to negotiate with others to reach a solution that benefits all parties. **Negotiation** is a reciprocal communication process whereby two or more parties to a dispute examine specific issues, explain their positions, and exchange offers and counteroffers. Negotiation sometimes amounts to little more than simple bargaining or mutual compromise. In such *distributive negotiations*, both parties retain their competitive orientation and take turns making small concessions until some equally dissatisfying middle ground is reached. Haggling and bartering ("I'll give you $20 for it, and not a penny more!") illustrate this form of negotiation (Lewicki, Saunders, & Barry, 2006).

*Integrative negotiation*, in contrast, is a collaborative conflict resolution method (Rubin, 1994). Such negotiators are principled rather than competitive, to use the terminology of the Harvard Negotiation Project. Harvard researchers, after studying how people solve problems through negotiation, identified three basic kinds of negotiators—soft, hard, and principled (see Table 13.2). *Soft bargainers* see negotiation as too close to competition, so they choose a gentle style of negotiation. They make offers that are not in their best interests, they yield to others' demands, they avoid any

---

**Negotiation** A reciprocal communication process whereby two or more parties to a dispute examine specific issues, explain their positions, and exchange offers and counteroffers to reach agreement or achieve mutually beneficial outcomes.

**TABLE 13.2 Comparisons between the Three Approaches to Negotiation**

| Element | Soft Negotiation | Hard Negotiation | Principled Negotiation |
|---|---|---|---|
| **Perception of others** | Friends | Adversaries | Problem solvers |
| **Goals** | Agreement | Victory | A wise outcome reached efficiently and amicably |
| **Concessions** | Make concessions to cultivate the relationship | Demand concessions as a condition of the relationship | Separate the people from the problem |
| **People vs. problems** | Be soft on the people and the problem | Be hard on the problem and the people | Be soft on the people, hard on the problem |
| **Trust** | Trust others | Distrust others | Proceed independently of trust |
| **Positions** | Change your position easily | Dig into your position | Focus on interests, not positions |
| **Negotiation** | Make offers | Make threats | Explore interests |
| **Bottom line** | Disclose your bottom line | Mislead as to your bottom line | Avoid having a bottom line |
| **Losses and gains** | Accept one-sided losses to reach agreement | Demand one-sided gains as a price of agreement | Invent options for mutual gains |
| **Search** | Search for a single answer—the one they will accept | Search for a single answer—the one you will accept | Develop multiple options to choose from; decide later |
| **Criteria** | Insist on agreement | Insist on your position | Insist on using objective criteria |
| **Contest of will** | Avoid a contest of wills | Win the contest of wills | Reach a result based on standards, independent of will |
| **Pressure** | Yield to pressure | Apply pressure | Reason and be open to reason; yield to principle, not pressure |

SOURCE: Adapted from Fisher & Ury, 1981.

confrontation, and they maintain good relations with fellow negotiators. *Hard bargainers*, in contrast, use tough, competitive tactics during negotiations. They begin by taking an extreme position on the issue, and then they make small concessions only grudgingly. The hard bargainer uses contentious strategies of influence and says such things as "Take it or leave it," "This is my final offer," "This point is not open to negotiation," "My hands are tied," and "I'll see you in court" (Fisher, 1983).

*Principled negotiators*, meanwhile, seek integrative solutions by sidestepping commitment to specific positions. Instead of risking entrapment, principled negotiators focus on the problem rather than the intentions, motives, and needs of the people involved. Positional bargaining, they conclude, is too dangerous:

> When negotiators bargain over positions, they tend to lock themselves into those positions. The more you clarify your position and defend it against attack, the more committed you become to it. The more you try to convince the other side of the impossibility of changing your opening position, the more difficult it becomes to do so. Your ego becomes identified with your position. (Fisher & Ury, 1981, p. 5)

The Harvard Negotiation Project recommends that negotiators explore a number of alternatives to the problems they face. During this phase, the negotiation is transformed into a group problem-solving session, with the different parties working together in search of creative solutions and new information that the group can use to evaluate these alternatives. Principled negotiators base their choice on objective criteria rather than on power, pressure, self-interest, or an arbitrary decisional procedure. Such criteria can be drawn from moral standards, principles of fairness, objective indexes of market value, professional standards, tradition, and so on, but they should be recognized as fair by all parties (Kolb & Williams, 2003).

### Misperception → Understanding

Many conflicts are based on misperceptions. Group members often assume that others are competing with them, when in fact those other people only wish to cooperate. Members think that people who criticize their ideas are criticizing them personally. Members do not trust other people because they are convinced that others' motives are selfish ones. Group members assume that they have incompatible goals when they do not (Simpson, 2007).

Group members must undo these perceptual misunderstandings by actively communicating information about their motives and goals through discussion. In one study, group members were given the opportunity to exchange information about their interests and goals, yet only about 20% did. Those who did, however, were more likely to discover shared goals and were able to reach solutions that benefited both parties to the conflict (Thompson, 1991). Other studies have suggested that conflict declines when group members communicate their intentions in specific terms, make explicit references to trust, cooperation, and fairness, and build a shared ingroup identity (Harinck, 2004; Weingart & Olekalns, 2004).

Communication is no cure-all for conflict, however. Group members can exchange information by communicating, but they can also create gross misunderstandings and deceptions. Communication offers group members the means to establish trust and commitment, but it can also exacerbate conflict if members verbalize feelings of hatred, disgust, or annoyance. For example, when Deutsch and Krauss (1960) let participants in their trucking game experiment communicate with each other, messages typically emphasized threats and did little to reduce conflict (Deutsch, 1973). Communication is detrimental if these initial messages are inconsistent, hostile, and contentious (McClintock, Stech, & Keil, 1983). Communication can be beneficial, however, if interactants use it to create cooperative norms, if it increases trust among participants, and if it generates increased cohesion and unity in the group (Messick & Brewer, 1983).

### Hard Tactics → Cooperative Tactics

Group members cope with conflict in different ways. Some ignore the problem. Others discuss the problem, sometimes dispassionately and rationally, sometimes angrily and loudly. Still others to push their solution onto others, no matter what the others may want. Some actually resort to physical violence (Sternberg & Dobson, 1987). Some of these tactics escalate conflicts, but others are reliably associated with reduced hostility.

**Dual Concerns** As with social values orientations, variations in methods of dealing with conflict can be organized in terms of two essential themes: concern for self and concern for the other person. According to the **dual concern model** of conflict resolution, some strategies aim to maximize one's own outcomes; others—such as overlooking a problem until it subsides—de-emphasize proself goals. Some conflict resolution strategies are also more other-focused. Yielding, for example, is prosocial, whereas contending and forcing are less prosocial (Pruitt, 1983; Sheppard, 1983; Thomas, 1992; van de Vliert & Janssen, 2001).

---

**dual concern model** A conceptual perspective on methods of dealing with conflict that assumes avoiding, yielding, fighting, and cooperating differ along two basic dimensions: concern for self and concern for other.

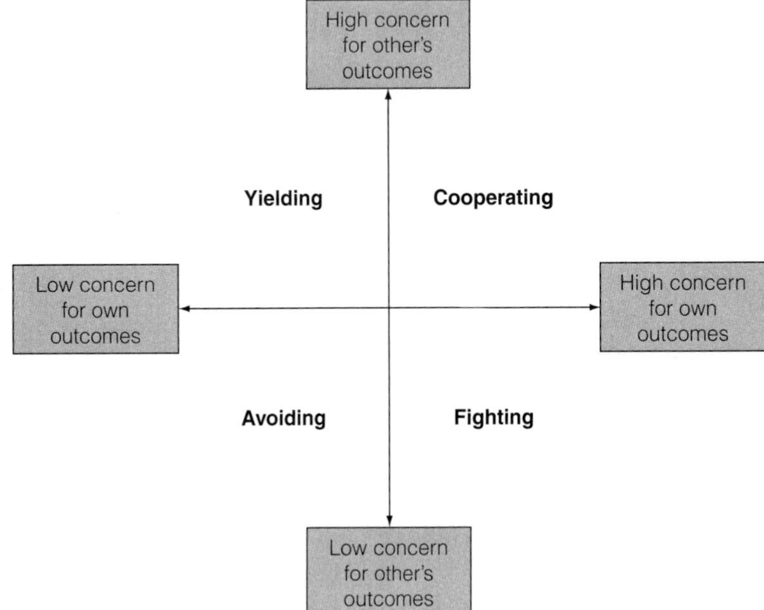


**FIGURE 13.5** The dual concern model of conflict resolution. Avoiding, yielding, cooperating, and fighting, as means of dealing with conflict, differ in the degree to which they are based on concern for oneself and concern for the other person.

When both concern for self and concern for other are taken into account, the dual concern model identifies the four core conflict resolution modes shown in Figure 13.5.

- *Avoiding*: Inaction is a passive means of dealing with disputes. Those who avoid conflicts adopt a "wait and see" attitude, hoping that problems will solve themselves. Avoiders often tolerate conflicts, allowing them to simmer without doing anything to minimize them. Rather than openly discussing disagreements, people who rely on avoidance change the subject, skip meetings, or even leave the group altogether (Bayazit & Mannix, 2003). Sometimes they simply agree to disagree (a modus vivendi).
- *Yielding*: Accommodation is a passive but prosocial approach to conflict. People solve both large and small conflicts by giving in to the demands of others. Sometimes, they yield because they realize that their position is in error, so they agree with the viewpoint adopted by others. In other cases, however, they may withdraw their demands without really being convinced that the other side is correct, but—for the sake of group unity or in the interest of time—they withdraw all complaints. Thus, yielding can reflect either genuine conversion or superficial compliance.
- *Fighting*: Contending is an active, proself means of dealing with conflict that involves forcing others to accept one's view. Those who use this strategy tend to see conflict as a win–lose situation and so use competitive, powerful tactics to intimidate others. Fighting (*forcing*, *dominating*, or *contending*) can take many forms, including authoritative mandate, challenges, arguing, insults, accusations, complaining, vengeance, and even physical violence (Morrill, 1995). These conflict resolution methods are all contentious ones because they involve imposing one's solution on the other party.
- *Cooperating*: Cooperation is an active, prosocial, and proself approach to conflict resolution. Cooperating people identify the issues underlying the dispute and then work together to identify a solution that is satisfying to both

sides. This orientation, which is also described as collaboration, problem solving, or a win–win orientation, entreats both sides in the dispute to consider their opponent's outcomes as well as their own.

Some theorists consider *conciliation* to be a fifth distinct way to resolve conflicts, but trying to win over others by accepting some of their demands can also be thought of as either yielding or cooperating (van de Vliert & Euwema, 1994).

**Cooperation and Conflict** When conflict erupts, group members can use any or all of the basic modes of conflict resolution shown in Figure 13.5, but most conflict-management experts recommend cooperation above all others: "work things out," "put your cards on the table," and "air out differences," they suggest. This advice assumes that avoidance, fighting, and yielding are only temporary solutions, for they quell conflicts at the surface without considering the source. Avoiding and fighting are generally considered to be negative methods, for they tend to intensify conflicts (Sternberg & Dobson, 1987) and they are viewed as more disagreeable (Jarboe & Witteman, 1996; van de Vliert & Euwema, 1994). The more positive, prosocial methods, yielding and cooperation, mitigate conflict and are viewed as more agreeable. They are more likely to involve more of the members in the solution, and hence they tend to increase unity.

Groups may respond well to cooperation when it is used to deal with task conflicts, but what if the problems stem from personal conflicts—differences in personality, values, lifestyles, likes, and dislikes? Research conducted by Carsten De Dreu and his colleagues suggests that, in such cases, collaborative approaches may aggravate the group conflict more than they mollify it (e.g., De Dreu, 1997; De Dreu & Van Vianne, 2001; De Dreu & Weingart, 2003). In one field study, members of semi-autonomous teams working on complex, nonroutine tasks were asked about the ways they handled conflicts in their teams. All these teams included both men and women, and they ranged in size from 4 to 13 members. Members of these teams typically interacted with each other in face-to-face settings at least once a week in planning sessions, and they reported interacting with each other informally nearly every day. As expected, negative methods of dealing with conflicts, such as arguing and forcing one's views onto others, were associated with negative team functioning. In these groups, however, collaborative methods of conflict resolution (e.g., "discussing the issues," "cooperating to better understand others' views," "settling problems through give and take") were also negatively correlated with team functioning. Only avoiding responses, such as "avoiding the issues," "acting as if nothing has happened," and "hushing up the quarrel" were associated with increases in group adjustment to the conflict. Apparently, the consistent use of collaboration to deal with intractable differences or petty disagreements distracted the groups from the achievement of their task-related goals (De Dreu & Van Vianne, 2001).

These findings suggest that groups may wish to heed the advice of one member of a successful musical quartet who, when asked how his group managed conflicts, explained, "We have a little saying in quartets—either we play or we fight" (Murnighan & Conlon, 1991, pp. 177–178). As Focus 13.4 suggests, cooperative, prosocial solutions work in many cases, but sometimes groups must ignore the conflict and focus, instead, on the work to be done.

### Upward → Downward Conflict Spirals

Consistent cooperation among people over a long period generally increases mutual trust. But when group members continually compete with each other, mutual trust becomes much more elusive (Haas & Deseran, 1981). When people cannot trust one another, they compete simply to defend their own best interests (Lindskold, 1978).

How can the upward spiral of competition and distrust, once initiated, be reversed? Robert Axelrod (1984) explored this question by comparing a number of strategies in simulated competitions. After studying dozens of different strategies, ranging from always competing with a competitor to always cooperating with one, the most effective competition

## Focus 13.4 Is Conflict Managed or Resolved?

*Every aspect of organizational life that creates order and coordination of effort must overcome other tendencies to action, and in that fact lies the potentiality for conflict.*

—Daniel Katz and Robert Kahn (1978, p. 617).

Conflict is rooted in some basic problems that people face when they must join together in groups. Although people may hope that conflicts can be *resolved* completely so that the group need never face unpleasant disagreements or disruptions, in reality, conflict can only be *managed*: controlled by the group and its members so that its harmful effects are minimized and its beneficial consequences are maximized.

Just as individuals develop certain styles of dealing with conflict—some people are competitive in their orientation, whereas others are more likely to avoid conflicts—groups also develop their own set of typical practices for managing conflict (Gelfand, Leslie, & Keller, 2008). Kristin Behfar and her colleagues (2008) examined the development of these group-level styles of conflict management—these "conflict cultures"—in a detailed quantitative analysis of 57 autonomous work teams. These groups all worked with the same resources, on the same types of projects, and with the same time constraints. Over time, some of the groups became more capable in the task realm, but others did not. Some, too, enjoyed increasingly positive relations among members, whereas others exhibited declines in the quality of their cohesion.

Behfar's group discovered that these changes in task success and interpersonal bonds were related to the group's methods of dealing with conflict. All of the groups experienced conflicts as their work progressed, but they dealt with these problems in different ways. The 21 best teams proactively forecasted possible problems before they happened. They developed schedules and assigned responsibilities carefully, in unemotional, fact-driven discussions, to reach consensus. They did not report dealing with relationship conflict, because they did not have any. A second set of 11 high-performance groups had little cohesiveness, but these groups all expressly discussed their lukewarm interpersonal relations and dismissed the importance of social connections. These groups resolved task and process conflicts by voting. The 14 worst teams, who exhibited both declining performance and interpersonal dysfunction, also used discussion, but the discussion never resolved their problems. These groups reported trying to deal with their problems openly, but members would just give in to more dominant members because they grew tired of arguing. They dealt with their performance problems by rotating duties from one member to another, but they never analyzed the effectiveness of this technique.

These findings suggest that the impact of conflict on a group cannot be predicted until the group's conflict culture is known. Groups that take proactive steps to prevent conflict from arising in the first place tend to be more satisfying to members than those that only respond—and respond poorly at that—to conflicts when they arise. Successful groups also tended to adopt pluralistic strategies for dealing with conflict, rather than particularistic ones. They resolved conflicts using methods that applied to the group as a whole, such as developing rules, standardizing procedures, and assigning tasks to members based on skill and expertise rather than status. Less successful groups, in contrast, used strategies that focused on specific individuals' complaints or the group's concerns about one or two members. In these groups, the "squeaky wheel would get the grease," but the repair was not sufficient to restore the group to health.

reverser to emerge was a strategy called **tit for tat** (TFT). TFT begins with cooperation. If the other party cooperates, too, then cooperation continues. But if the other party competes, then TFT competes as well. Each action by the other person is countered with the matching response—cooperation for cooperation, competition for competition.

The TFT, strategem, is said to be nice, provocable, clear, and forgiving. It is *nice* because it begins with cooperation and only defects following competition. It is *provocable* in the sense that it immediately retaliates against individuals who compete, and it is *clear* because people playing against someone using this strategy quickly recognize its

**tit for tat** (TFT) A bargaining strategy that begins with cooperation, but then imitates the other person's choice so that cooperation is met with cooperation and competition with competition.

contingencies. It is *forgiving*, however, in that it immediately reciprocates cooperation should the competitor respond cooperatively.

TFT is also a *reciprocal* strategy, for it fights fire with fire and rewards kindness in kind. Individuals who follow a tit-for-tat strategy are viewed as "tough but fair"; those who cooperate with a competitor are viewed as weak, and those who consistently compete are considered unfair (McGillicuddy, Pruitt, & Syna, 1984). Because the effectiveness of TFT as a conflict reduction method is based on its provocability; any delay in responding to cooperation reduces the effectiveness of TFT. If a group member competes, and this defection is not countered quickly with competition, TFT is less effective (Komorita, Hilty, & Parks, 1991). TFT also loses some of its strength in "noisy" interactions, when behaviors cannot be clearly classified as either competitive or cooperative (Van Lange, Ouwerkerk, & Tazelaar, 2002; Wu & Axelrod, 1995). It is less effective in larger groups, although this decline is minimized if individual members believe that a substantial subgroup within the total group is basing its choices on the TFT strategy (Komorita, Parks, & Hulbert, 1992; Parks & Komorita, 1997).

### Many → Few

Conflicts intensify when others take sides, but they shrink when third-party **mediators** help group members reach a mutually agreeable solution to their dispute (Kressel, 2000). Although uninvolved group members may wish to stand back and let the disputants "battle it out," impasses, unflagging conflict escalation, or the combatants' entreaties may cause other group members or outside parties to help by:

- creating opportunities for both sides to express themselves while controlling contentiousness
- improving communication between the disputants by summarizing points, asking for clarification, and so on
- helping disputants save face by framing the acceptance of concessions in positive ways and by taking the blame for these concessions
- formulating and offering proposals for alternative solutions that both parties find acceptable
- manipulating aspects of the meeting, including its location, seating, formality of communication, time constraints, attendees, and agenda
- guiding the disputants through a process of integrative problem solving

However, if the disputants want to resolve the conflict on their own terms, third-party interventions are considered an unwanted intrusion (Carnevale, 1986a, 1986b; Pruitt & Rubin, 1986; Raiffa, 1983; Rubin, 1980, 1986).

Go-betweens, facilitators, diplomats, advisers, judges, and other kinds of mediators vary considerably in terms of their power to control others' outcomes (LaTour, 1978; LaTour et al., 1976). In an *inquisitorial procedure*, the mediator questions the two parties and then hands down a verdict that the two parties must accept. In *arbitration*, the disputants present their arguments to the mediator, who then bases his or her decision on the information they provide. In a *moot*, the disputants and the mediator openly and informally discuss problems and solutions, but the mediator can make no binding decisions. Satisfaction with a mediator depends on how well the intermediary fulfills these functions and also on the intensity of the conflict. Mediational techniques such as arbitration are effective when the conflict is subdued, but they may not work when conflict intensity is high. Overall, most people prefer arbitration, followed by moot, mediation, and inquisitorial procedures (LaTour et al., 1976; Ross, Brantmeier, & Ciriacks, 2002; Ross & Conlon, 2000).

### Anger → Composure

Just as negative emotions encourage conflicts, positive affective responses increase concession making, creative problem solving, cooperation, and the use of noncontentious bargaining strategies (Forgas, 1998; Van Kleef et al., 2004). Hence, when tempers flare, the group should encourage members to regain

---

**mediator** One who intervenes between two persons who are experiencing conflict, with a view to reconciling them.

control over their emotions. "Count to ten," calling a "time-out," or expressing concerns in a written, carefully edited, letter or e-mail are simple but effective recommendations for controlling conflict, as is the introduction of humor into the group discussion (Mischel & DeSmet, 2000). Apologies, too, are effective means of reducing anger. When people are informed about mitigating causes—background factors that indicate that the insult is unintentional or unimportant—conflict is reduced (Betancourt & Blair, 1992; Ferguson & Rule, 1983). Groups can also control anger by developing norms that explicitly or implicitly prohibit shows of strong, negative emotion or by holding meetings on controversial topics online (Yang & Mossholder, 2004).

### Conflict versus Conflict Management

Conflict is a natural consequence of joining a group. Groups bind their members and their members' outcomes together, and this interdependence can lead to conflict when members' qualities, ideas, goals, motivations, and outlooks clash. Conflict is also an undeniably powerful process in groups. In the case of Apple, the dispute between Jobs and Sculley was resolved, but not without a considerable investment of time, resources, and energy. Two men who were once friends parted as enemies. A company that once profited from the leadership of two visionary thinkers lost one of them to competitors. Before the conflict, Apple was an unconventional, risk-taking trendsetter. After the conflict, the company focused on costs, increasing sales, and turning a profit. Conflict stimulates change–both positive and negative.

Did Apple gain from the conflict, or did it suffer a setback as its top executives fought for power and control? Conflict, many cases, brings with it dissent, discord, disagreement, tension, hostility, and abuse. It undermines satisfactions, engenders negative emotions, disrupts performance, and can even trigger violence. When Carsten De Dreu and Laurie Weingart (2003) conducted a meta-analysis of dozens of studies of conflict in groups, they discovered that, in study after study, conflict undermined satisfaction and lowered performance. Nor did it matter if the difficulties stemmed from personal conflicts (disruptions of interpersonal bonds between members) or from substantive, task conflicts. Conflict undermined performance and satisfaction.

Is conflict always harmful—a pernicious process that should be avoided? This question remains open to debate, but it may be that the problem is not conflict, per se, but mismanaged conflict. As noted in Chapter 5 many groups pass through a period of conflict as they mature. This conflict phase, so long as it is managed well, expands the range of options, generates new alternatives, and enhances the group's unity by making explicit any latent hostilities and tensions. Conflict can make a group's goals more explicit and help members understand their role in the group. It may force the members to examine, more carefully, their assumptions and expectations, and may help the group focus on its strengths and diagnose its weaknesses. A group without conflict may be working so perfectly that no one can identify any improvements, but more likely it is a group that is boring and uninvolving for its members. Conflict, then, is not the culprit. It is poor management of the conflicts that inevitably arise in groups that leads to problems (Bormann, 1975; Jehn, 1997; Jehn & Bendersky, 2003).

## SUMMARY IN OUTLINE

*What is conflict?*

1. When *conflict* occurs in a group, the actions or beliefs of one or more members of the group are unacceptable to and resisted by one or more of the other members.
2. *Intergroup conflict* involves two or more groups, and *intragroup conflict* occurs within a group.
3. Conflict follows a cycle from conflict escalation to resolution.

*What are the sources of conflict in groups?*

1. Many group and individual factors conspire to create conflict in a group, but the most common sources are competition, conflicts over the distribution of resources, power struggles, decisional conflicts, and personal conflicts.
2. Deutsch's early theorizing suggests that *independence* and *cooperation* lower the likelihood of conflict, whereas competition tends to increase conflict by pitting members against one another.
   - *Mixed-motive situations*, like the *prisoner's dilemma game* (PDG), stimulate conflict because they tempt individuals to compete rather than cooperate. Individuals tend to compete less in the PDG if they play repeatedly against the same partner.
   - *Behavioral assimilation* is caused by *reciprocity*; competition sparks competition and cooperation (to a lesser extent) provokes cooperation.
   - Individuals differ in their basic orientation towards conflict. Those with a competitive *social values orientation* (SVO) are more likely to compete than are those with cooperative, individualistic, or altruistic orientations, even if they think that others will be acting in a cooperative fashion.
   - Men and women are equally competitive, although both sexes use more contentious influence methods when they are paired with a man rather than with a woman, perhaps because they anticipate more conflict.
3. *Social dilemmas* stimulate conflict by tempting members to act in their own self-interest to the detriment of the group and its goals. Disputes arise when members:
   - exploit a shared resource (a *commons dilemma* or *social trap*)
   - do not contribute their share (a *public goods dilemma*, free riding)
   - disagree on how to divide up resources (*distributive justice*) or on the procedures to follow in dividing the resources (procedural justice)
   - do not agree on the norms to follow when apportioning resources (e.g., equality, equity, power, responsibility, and need)
   - take more than their fair share of responsibility for an outcome (*egocentrism*), avoid blame for group failure, or take too much personal responsibility for group successes (self-serving attributions of responsibility)
4. These reactions are driven, in part, by self-interest, but group members respond negatively to perceived mistreatment because it calls into question their status and inclusion. Work by de Waal suggests that other species are sensitive to unfair distributions of resources.
5. Power struggles are common in groups as members vie for control over leadership, status, and position.
6. *Task conflict* stems from disagreements about issues that are relevant to the group's goals and outcomes. Even though such substantive conflicts help groups reach their goals, these disagreements can turn into personal, unpleasant conflicts.
7. *Process conflicts* occur when members do not agree on group strategies, policies, and methods. Groups avoid such conflicts by clarifying procedures.
8. *Personal conflict* occurs when individual members do not like one another. Doll's work finds that such conflicts are prevalent in children's groups.
   - Any factor that causes disaffection between group members (e.g., differences in attitudes, objectionable personal qualities) can increase personal conflict.
   - Balance theory predicts that group members will respond negatively when they disagree with those they like or agree with those they dislike, but as Taylor's work

confirmed, conflict is greatest when group members both disagree with and dislike each other.

*Why does conflict escalate?*

1. Once conflict begins, it often intensifies before it begins to abate.
2. When individuals defend their viewpoints in groups, they become more committed to their positions; doubts and uncertainties are replaced by firm commitment.
3. Conflict is exacerbated by members' tendency to misperceive others and to assume that the other party's behavior is caused by personal (dispositional) rather than situational (environmental) factors (*fundamental attribution error*).
4. As conflicts worsen, members shift from soft to hard tactics. Deutsch and Krauss studied this process in their *trucking game experiment*. Conflict between individuals escalated when each side could threaten the other.
5. Other factors that contribute to the escalation of conflict in groups include:
   - negative reciprocity, as when negative actions provoke negative reactions in others
   - the formation of coalitions that embroil formerly neutral members in the conflict
   - angry emotions that trigger expressions of anger among members.

*How can group members manage their conflict?*

1. In many cases, members use *negotiation* (including integrative negotiation) to identify the issues underlying the dispute and then work together to identify a solution that is satisfying to both sides.
2. The Harvard Negotiation Project maintains that principled, integrative negotiation is more effective than either soft or hard bargaining.
3. Because many conflicts are rooted in misunderstandings and misperceptions, group members can reduce conflict by actively communicating information about their motives and goals through discussion.
4. The *dual concern model* identifies four means of dealing with conflicts—avoiding, yielding, fighting, and cooperating—that differ along two dimensions: concern for self and concern for others.
   - In some cases, cooperation is more likely to promote group unity.
   - Personal conflicts—ones that are rooted in basic differences in attitude, outlook, and so on—may not yield to cooperative negotiations. De Dreu and his colleagues suggest that the avoiding method may be the best way to cope with such conflicts.
5. Behfar and her colleagues suggest that groups develop their own approaches to dealing with conflict, and some of the so-called conflict cultures are more effective than others.
6. If a group member continues to compete, the *tit-for-tat* (TFT) strategy has been proven by Axelrod and others to be useful as a conflict resolution strategy.
7. Third-party interventions—*mediators*—can reduce conflict by imposing solutions (inquisitorial procedures and arbitration) or guiding disputants to a compromise (moot and mediation procedures).
8. Just as negative emotions encourage conflict, positive affective responses reduce conflict.

*Is conflict an unavoidable evil or a necessary good?*

1. Conflict is a natural consequence of joining a group and cannot be avoided completely.
2. Some evidence suggests that conflicts, when resolved successfully, promote positive group functioning, but a meta-analysis by De Dreu and Weingart suggests that conflict causes more harm than good—particularly if it is not adequately managed.

## FOR MORE INFORMATION

*Chapter Case: iConflict*

- *Apple Confidential 2.0: The Definitive History of the World's Most Colorful Company*, by Owen W. Linzmayer (2004), provides a well-researched history of the many conflict-laden episodes in the life of Apple, Inc.

*Causes of Conflict*

- "Conflict in Groups," by John M. Levine and Leigh Thompson (1996), is a relatively high-level analysis of the causes, benefits, and liabilities of conflict in small groups.
- *Social Conflict: Escalation, Stalemate, and Settlement* (3rd ed.), by Dean G. Pruitt and Sung Hee Kim (2004), provides a thorough analysis of the causes and consequences of interpersonal conflict.
- *The Executive Way*, by Calvin Morrill (1995), is a compelling analysis of the causes and consequences of conflict in the upper echelons of large corporations.

*Conflict Resolution*

- *Getting to YES: Negotiating Agreement Without Giving In* (2nd ed.), by Roger Fisher, William Ury, and Bruce Patton (1991), describes a step-by-step strategy for resolving conflicts to the mutual benefit of both parties.
- *The Handbook of Conflict Resolution*, edited by Morton Deutsch and Peter T. Coleman (2000), is the definitive sourcebook for general analyses of conflict resolution but also provides practical recommendations for resolving conflicts.
- *Negotiation*, by Roy J. Lewicki, David M. Saunders, and Bruce Barry (2006), is a comprehensive text dealing with all aspects of negotiation, including power, bargaining, and interpersonal and intergroup conflict resolution.

### Media Resources

Visit the Group Dynamics companion website at www.cengage.com/psychology/forsyth to access online resources for your book, including quizzes, flash cards, web links, and more!

# 14

# Intergroup Relations

## CHAPTER OVERVIEW

As a social species, humans strive to establish close ties with one another. Yet the same species that seeks out connections with others also metes out enmity when it confronts members of another group. Intergroup relations are more often contentious than harmonious.

- What interpersonal factors disrupt relations between groups?
- What are the psychological foundations of conflict between groups?
- How can intergroup relations be improved?

## CHAPTER OUTLINE

**The Rattlers and the Eagles: Group against Group**

On two midsummer days in 1954, twenty-two 11-year-old boys from Oklahoma City boarded buses for their trip to summer camp. They were "normal, well-adjusted boys of the same age, educational level, from similar sociocultural backgrounds and with no unusual features in their personal backgrounds" (Sherif et al., 1961, p. 59). Their parents had paid a $25 fee, signed some consent forms, and packed them off to a camp situated in Robbers Cave State Park, located in the San Bois Mountains of southeast Oklahoma.

Robbers Cave was not your everyday summer camp. All the boys had been handpicked by a research team that included Muzafer Sherif, O. J. Harvey, Jack White, William Hood, and Carolyn Sherif. The team had spent more than 300 hours interviewing the boys' teachers, studying their academic records, reviewing their family backgrounds, and unobtrusively recording their behavior in school and on the playground. The parents knew that the camp was actually part of a group dynamics research project, but the boys had no idea that they were participants in an experiment. The staff randomly assigned the boys to one of two groups and brought them to camp in two separate trips. Each group spent a week hiking, swimming, and playing sports in their area of the camp, and both groups developed norms, roles, and structure. Some boys emerged as leaders, others became followers, and both groups established territories within the park (see Figure 14.1). The boys named their groups the Rattlers and the Eagles and stenciled these names on their shirts and painted them onto flags. The staff members, who were also collecting data, noted clear increases in group-oriented behaviors, cohesiveness, and positive group attitudes.

When the groups discovered another group was nearby, they expressed wariness about these outsiders. After some guarded encounters between members, they asked the staff to set up a competition to determine which group was better than the other. Since a series of competitions between the two groups was exactly what the staff had in mind, they held a series of baseball games, tugs-of-war, tent-pitching competitions, cabin inspections, and a (rigged) treasure hunt.

As the competition wore on, tempers flared. When the Eagles lost a game, they retaliated by stealing the Rattlers' flag and burning it. The Rattlers raided the Eagles' cabin during the night, tearing out mosquito netting, overturning beds, and carrying off personal belongings. When the Eagles won the overall tournament, the Rattlers absconded with the prizes. When fistfights broke out between the groups, the staff had to intervene to prevent the boys from seriously injuring one another. They moved the two groups to different parts of the camp, amid shouts of "poor losers," "bums," "sissies," "cowards," and "little babies."

Groups are everywhere, and so are conflicts between them. *Intergroup conflict* occurs at all levels of social organization—rivalries between gangs, organized disputes in industrial settings, race riots, and international warfare. Groups provide the means to achieve humanity's most lofty goals, but when groups oppose each other, they are sources of hostility, abuse, and aggression. Although conflict between groups is one of the most complicated phenomena studied by social scientists, the goal of greater understanding and the promise of reduced tension remain enticing. This chapter considers the nature of intergroup relations, with a focus on the sources of intergroup conflict and the ways such conflicts can be resolved (for reviews, see Bornstein, 2003; Brewer, 2007; Dovidio et al., 2003).

## INTERGROUP CONFLICT: US VERSUS THEM

The researchers' plans for the Robbers Cave study worked all too well. In just two weeks they created a full-fledged war-in-miniature between the Rattlers and the Eagles, complete with violent schemes, weapons of destruction, hostility, and mistreatment of each side by the other. The Sherifs, by starting with two newly formed groups with no history of

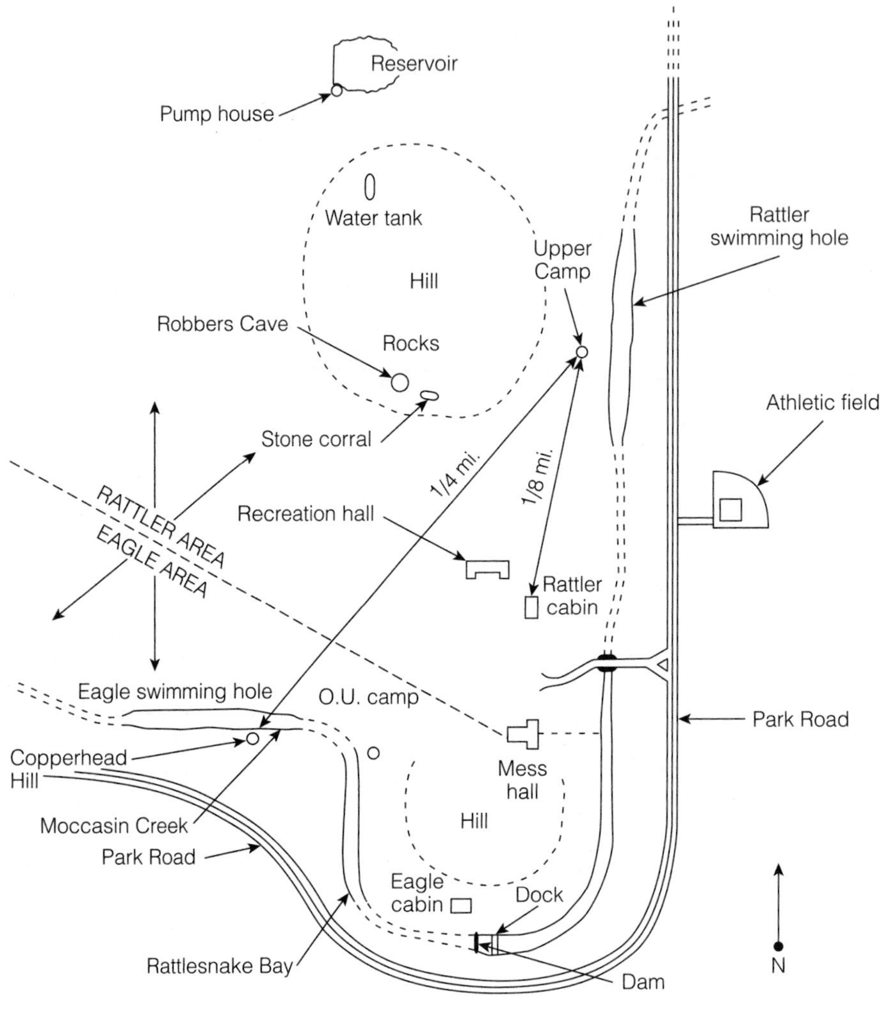


**FIGURE 14.1** The layout of the campgrounds in the Robbers Cave Experiment.

rivalry, succeeded in documenting the social and psychological factors that combined to push these two groups into an escalating conflict. Each group at the Robbers Cave viewed the other as a rival to be bested, and these perceptions were soon joined by other antecedents of conflict: norms, struggles for status, and ever-strengthening negative emotional reactions. This section examines these causes of conflict, focusing on the Robbers Cave study but suggesting implications for other intergroup situations as well.

## Competition and Conflict

On the ninth day of the **Robbers Cave Experiment**, the Rattlers and the Eagles saw the tournament prizes for the first time: the shining trophy,

---

**Robbers Cave Experiment** A field study performed by Muzafer and Carolyn Sherif and their colleagues that examined the causes and consequences of conflict between two groups of boys at Robbers Cave State Park in Oklahoma.

medals for each boy, and—best of all—four-blade camping knives. The boys wanted these prizes, and nothing was going to stand in their way. From then on, all group activities revolved around the ultimate goal of winning the tournament. Unfortunately, although both groups aspired to win the prizes, success for one group meant failure for the other. When groups are pitted against each other in a contest for resources, intergroup relations that were once amicable often become antagonistic.

Many of the things that people want and need are available in limited supply. Should one group acquire and control a scarce commodity—whether it be food, territory, wealth, power, natural resources, energy, or the prizes so desperately desired by the Rattlers and the Eagles—other groups must do without that resource. According to **realistic group conflict theory**, this struggle between groups to acquire resources inevitably leads to conflict (Campbell, 1965; Esses et al., 2005). All groups would prefer to be "haves" rather than "have-nots," so they take steps to achieve two interrelated outcomes—attaining the desired resources and preventing the other group from reaching its goals. Theorists have traced many negative intergroup dynamics—including struggles between the classes of a society (Marx & Engels, 1947), rebellions (Gurr, 1970), international warfare (Streufert & Streufert, 1986), racism (Gaines & Reed, 1995), religious persecutions (Clark, 1998), tribal rivalries in East Africa (Brewer & Campbell, 1976), police use of lethal force against citizens (Jacobs & O'Brien, 1998), interorganizational conflicts (Jehn & Mannix, 2001), and even the development of culture and social structure (Simmel, 1955)—to competition over scarce resources.

Robert Blake and Jane Mouton discovered competition's capacity to create conflict in their work with business executives. They assigned participants in a two-week management training program to small groups charged with solving a series of problems. Blake and Mouton never explicitly mentioned competition, but the participants knew that a group of experts would decide which group had produced the best solution. Many viewed the project as a contest to see who was best, and they wholeheartedly accepted the importance of winning. Leaders who helped the group beat the opponent became influential, whereas leaders of losing groups were replaced. The groups bonded tightly during work and coffee breaks, and only rarely did any participant show liking for a member of another group. In some cases, hostility between the two groups became so intense that the "experiment had to be discontinued" and special steps taken to restore order, tempers, and "some basis of mutual respect" (Blake & Mouton, 1984, 1986, p. 72). These findings and others suggest that *competition*—even competition that is only anticipated—can spark intergroup hostility (Bornstein, Budescu, & Zamir, 1997; Polzer, 1996; van Oostrum & Rabbie, 1995).

### The Discontinuity Effect

Chapter 13 traced conflict between two or more people—intragroup or interindividual—to competition. Correspondingly, when two or more groups compete, intergroup conflict becomes more likely. In fact, the competition–conflict relationship is even more powerful at the group level than at the individual level, resulting in the **discontinuity effect**: the competitiveness of groups is out of proportion to the competitiveness displayed by individuals when interacting with other individuals. Even though individuals in the group may prefer to cooperate, when they join groups, this cooperative orientation tends to be replaced by a competitive one (see Wildschut et al., 2003, for a theoretically rigorous review of this area).

---

**realistic group conflict theory** A conceptual framework arguing that conflict between groups stems from competition for scarce resources, including food, territory, wealth, power, natural resources, and energy.

**discontinuity effect** The markedly greater competitiveness of groups when interacting with other groups, relative to the competitiveness of individuals interacting with other individuals.

**Studies of Discontinuity** Chet Insko, John Schopler, and their colleagues documented this discontinuity between interindividual conflict and intergroup conflict by asking individuals and groups to play the *prisoner's dilemma game* (PDG). As noted in Chapter 13, this mixed-motive game offers the two participating parties a choice between cooperative responding and competitive responding, and competition yields the highest rewards only if one of the two parties cooperates. The sample PDG matrix in Figure 14.2 illustrates the group's dilemma. Option C is the cooperative choice, and D is the competitive, defecting-from-cooperation, choice. Cooperation (option C) will yield the best outcomes for both groups if they both select C, but if one picks C and the other picks D, then the cooperative group's payoff will be small (20 points) compared to the competitive group's payoff (60 points). If both groups select Option D, then their rewards will be cut in half.

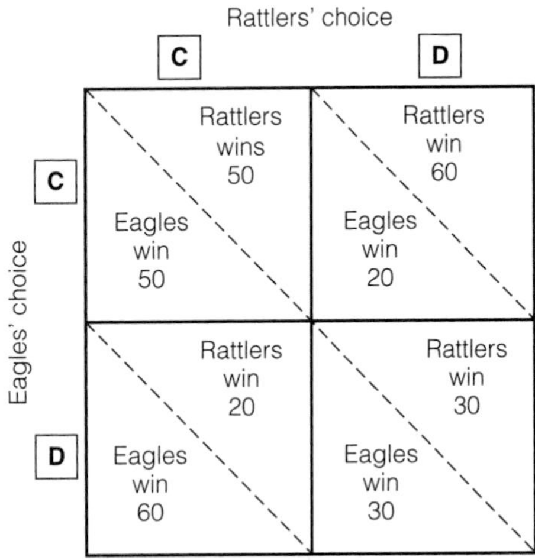


**FIGURE 14.2** The *prisoner's dilemma game* payoff matrix used to study competition and intergroup conflict. Two groups, the Rattlers and the Eagles, must select either option C (cooperation) or option D (defection). These choices are shown along the sides of the matrix. The payoffs for these joint choices are shown within each cell of the matrix. In each cell, Rattlers' outcomes are shown above the diagonal line, and Eagles' outcomes are shown below it. Groups tend to select option D much more frequently than option C.

When two individuals played, they averaged only 6.6% competitive responses over the course of the game. Competition was also rare when three independent, noninteracting individuals played three other independent individuals (7.5%). But when an interacting triad played another interacting triad, 36.2% of their choices were competitive ones, and when triads played triads but communicated their choices through representatives selected from within the group, competition rose to 53.5% (Insko et al., 1987). These findings are remarkably consistent—a meta-analysis of 48 separate studies conducted in 11 different group dynamics laboratories confirmed that groups are disproportionately more competitive than individuals (Wildschut et al., 2003).

This discontinuity between individuals and groups is not confined to laboratory groups playing a structured conflict game. When researchers examined everyday social interactions, they found that group activities were marked by more competition than one-on-one activities. Participants diligently recorded their interpersonal activities for an entire week, classifying them into one of five categories:

- *One-on-one interactions*: playing chess, walking to class with another person, and so on.
- *Within-group interactions*: interactions with members of the same group, such as a club meeting or a classroom discussion.
- *One-on-group interactions*: the individual participant interacting with a group, such as a student meeting with a panel of faculty for career information.
- *Group-on-one interactions*: the individual is part of a group that interacts with a single individual.
- *Group-on-group interactions*: a soccer game, a joint session of two classes, and the like.

As Figure 14.3 indicates, the proportion of competitive interactions within each type of interaction climbed steadily as people moved from one-on-one interactions to group interactions. These effects also emerged when sports activities, which could have exacerbated the competitiveness of groups, were eliminated from the analysis (Pemberton, Insko, & Schopler, 1996).

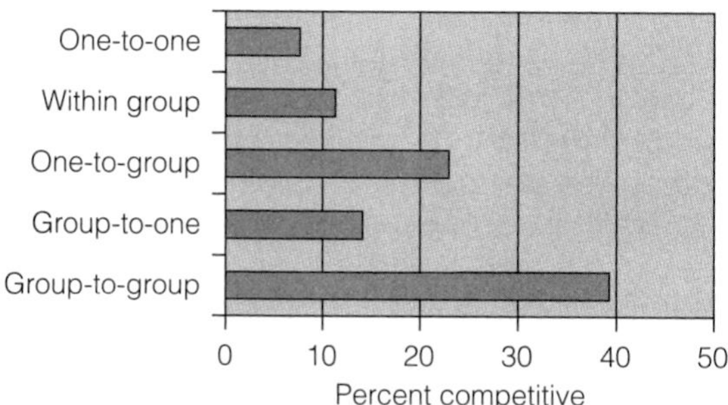


**FIGURE 14.3** The level of competitiveness of five everyday situations ranging from one-to-one interactions to group-to-group interactions.

The discontinuity between groups and individuals is also apparently when members plan and strategize. When they expect to bargain with a group they worry more about exploitation and fair play. They often convey their distrust by saying such things as "We don't trust you" and "You better not cheat us" to their opponents, so communication between groups does little to quell tensions. People are more likely to withdraw from a competitive interaction with a group than an individual (Insko et al., 1990, 1993, 1994; Schopler et al., 1995; Schopler & Insko, 1992).

**Causes of Discontinuity** The consistency of the discontinuity effect suggests that it springs from a number of causes that combine to exacerbate conflicts between groups, including greed, anonymity, fear, ingroup favoritism, and diffusion of responsibility (Pinter et al., 2007). First, individuals are greedy, but greed is even greater in groups. When people discover that others in the group are also leaning in the direction of maximizing gains by exploiting others, this social support spurs the group members on to greater levels of greed. When researchers changed the PDG matrix payoff so that greed was no longer so lucrative, groups learned how to cooperate with each other to maximize joint gains (Wolf et al., 2008).

Second, people fear groups more than they fear individuals. They describe groups as more abrasive (competitive, aggressive, proud) and less agreeable (cooperative, trustworthy, helpful) than individuals. This pessimistic outlook also colors their expectations about specific group interactions, for people who were about to play the PDG against a group felt that the experience would be more abrasive than did individuals about to play the game as individuals (Hoyle, Pinkley, & Insko, 1989). This generalized distrust, in the extreme, has been termed *intergroup paranoia*: the belief held by the members of one group that they will be mistreated in some way by the members of a malevolent outgroup (Kramer, 2004).

Third, group members may feel that, as part of a group, they should do what they can to maximize the group's collective outcomes—that part of being good group members or leaders is to do what they can to increase the team's achievements, even if that comes at a cost to those outside of the group (Pinter et al., 2007). This sense of group duty may also trigger a stronger desire to outdo the other group as well as generate the best possible outcome for the ingroup. Groups playing a game where cooperation would have favored both groups equally seemed to transform, psychologically, the payoff matrix from a cooperation-favoring game into the more competitive PDG game (Wolf et al., 2008).

Fourth, diffusion of responsibility may also contribute to the discontinuity effect (Meier & Hinsz, 2004). In one experiment investigators told individuals and groups they were studying people's reactions to different foods, but that for the purposes of experimental control the subjects themselves would be selecting the amount of food given to others. All the subjects were led to believe that they had been assigned to the hot sauce condition, which involved giving helpings of painfully hot spiced sauce to others to eat. They were also told that they were paired with either a group or an individual, and that their partner had measured out a substantial portion of hot sauce for them to consume. They were then given the opportunity to select the amount of sauce to send back to their partner in the nearby room.

The study's results confirmed the discontinuity effect. Groups allocated, and received, more grams of hot sauce than individuals, with the result that group-to-group aggression was substantially higher than the individual-to-group and group-to-individual pairs. The individual-to-individual pairs yielded the least amount of aggression relative to the group-to-group pairings, replicating the discontinuity effect. The greater aggressiveness did not appear to be due to the more aggressive group members convincing the others to dispense more punishment to their partners. Even though the researchers measured each group member's personal level of aggressiveness, they did not find that groups with more aggressive individuals acted more aggressively as a group. They did find that those in groups reported feeling less responsible for their actions, suggesting that diffusion of responsibility may play a role in producing the shift towards greater hostility.

What can be done to reduce the exaggerated competitiveness of groups relative to individuals? Insko and his associates find that communication does little to reduce the effect, since in many cases the two factions communicate negative information or misinformation. Communication did lower the magnitude of the discontinuity, but not by lowering the level of conflict between groups. Instead, it tended to increase the level of conflict between individuals, to the point that they were as competitive as groups. This unexpected effect of communication was more likely to occur when communication was restricted in some way, as when interactants could only send written messages (Wildschut et al., 2003).

A tolerant, pacifistic appeasement approach to conflict also proved ineffective in reducing discontinuity. As with studies conducted with individuals, when groups respond cooperatively even when the other party competes—hoping to signal their good intentions and inviting a reduction in conflict—the other group responds by exploiting the pacifistic group. A reciprocal strategy, such as *tit for tat* (TFT), was a more effective strategy to counter discontinuity. As noted in Chapter 13, TFT matches competition with competition and cooperation with cooperation. This strategy, Insko suggests, allays groups' fears that they will be exploited, for it reassures them that they can trust the other group. Other methods for reducing the discontinuity effect include decreasing the rewards of competition (by changing the values in the PDG matrix) and increasing individual identifiability (Wildschut et al., 2003).

## Power and Domination

Intergroup conflicts, though initially rooted in competition for scarce resources, can escalate into *intergroup exploitation* as one group tries to dominate the other. Not only do groups wish to monopolize and control scarce resources but they also wish to gain control over the other group's land, resources, peoples, and identity (Rouhana & Bar-Tal, 1998). As Herbert Spencer wrote in 1897, the first priority of most governments is the identification of "enemies and prey" (p. 547).

Just as groups seek to subdue and exploit other groups, the targets of these attacks struggle to resist this exploitation. In some cases, this competition is purely economic. By manufacturing desirable goods or performing valuable services, one group can come to dominate others in the intergroup trade system (Service, 1975). But domination can also occur through force and coercion (Carneiro, 1970). European countries, during their period of colonialism, established colonies throughout the world and exploited the original inhabitants of these areas both economically and through military force. Europeans seized the lands of Native Americans and used captured Africans as slaves in their workforce. Both Napoleon and Hitler sought to expand their empires through the conquest of other nations. In Russia, the ruling class exploited workers until the workers rose up in revolution and established a communist nation.

**Social dominance theory**, developed by Jim Sidanius, Felicia Pratto, and their colleagues,

---

**social dominance theory** An approach to oppression and domination, developed by Jim Sidanius, Felicia Pratto, and their colleagues, assuming that conflict between groups results from dynamic tensions between hierarchically ranked groups within society.

maintains that these conflict-laden relationships among social groups result from the natural tendency for people to form subgroups within the larger society, and then for these subgroups to vie with one another for power and resources. Some groups come to control more of the resources of the society, including wealth, property, status, and protection. Other groups, in contrast, occupy positions subordinate to these higher status groups, and may even be oppressed by them. They are unable to secure the resources they need, and so experience a range of negative outcomes, including poorer health, inadequate education, higher mortality rates, poverty, and crime. Sidanius and Pratto further suggest that members of the dominant groups tend to believe that this inequitable apportioning of resources is justified by precedent, by custom, or even by law. They may deny that the distribution of resources is actually unfair or claim that the dominance of one group over another is consistent with the natural order (Sidanius et al., 2007; Sidanius & Pratto, 1999).

This cycle of domination and resistance occurs between nations, classes, ethnic groups, the sexes, and even small groups in controlled experimental situations (Focus 14.1). Chet Insko and his colleagues examined exploitation and conflict by creating a simulated social system in the laboratory. Insko's *microsocieties* included three interdependent groups, multiple generations of members, a communication network, products, and a trading system (Insko et al., 1980, 1983). Insko assigned the microsocieties to one of two experimental conditions. In the *economic power condition*, one group could produce more varied products, so it quickly became the center of all bargaining and trading. In the *coercive power condition*, the group whose members were supposedly better problem solvers was given the right to confiscate any products it desired from the other groups. (Insko referred to these conditions as the *Service condition* and the *Carneiro condition*, respectively.)

These differences in power had a dramatic effect on productivity and intergroup relations. In the economic power condition, all three groups reached very high levels of productivity, with the advantaged group slightly outperforming the others. In contrast, none of the groups in the coercive power condition were very productive. As the "idle rich" hypothesis suggests, the members of the powerful group spent less time working when they could confiscate others' work. But the other groups reacted very negatively to this exploitation, and as the powerful group continued to steal their work, the members of the other groups held strikes and work slowdowns and sabotaged their products. (Men, in particular, were more likely to strike back against the oppressive group.) Eventually, the groups worked so little that the dominant group could not confiscate enough products to make much profit. These results suggest that as with intragroup conflict, one sure way to create conflict is to give one party more coercive power than the other (Deutsch & Krauss, 1960). Apparently, when it comes to power, more is not always better.

## Norms of Engagement

Conflicts between groups—protests between rioters and police, war between nations, gang fights, or even the conflict between the Rattlers and the Eagles—are not out-of-control, atypical interpersonal actions that occur when the social order breaks down. Normatively, competition and hostility between groups are often completely consistent with the standards of conduct in that situation.

**Reciprocity** Groups, like individuals, tend to obey the norm of *reciprocity*. They answer threats with threats, insults with insults, and aggression with aggression. Consider, for example, the infamous Hatfield–McCoy feud, which involved a dispute between two large families in a rural area of the United States in the late 19th century (Rice, 1978). The conflict originated with the theft of some hogs by Floyd Hatfield. The McCoys countered by stealing hogs from another member of the Hatfield clan, and soon members of the two families began taking potshots at one another. Between 1878 and 1890, more than 10 men and women lost their lives as a direct result of interfamily violence. Likewise, studies of gangs indicate that many street fights stem from some initial negative action that in reality may pose little threat

### Focus 14.1 Do You Believe Your Group Should Dominate Other Groups?

*One day God came down to Vladimir, a poor peasant, and said: "Vladimir, I will grant you one wish. Anything you want will be yours." However, God added: "There is one condition. Anything I give to you will be granted to your neighbor, Ivan, twice over." Vladimir immediately answered, saying: "OK, take out one of my eyes."*
—Eastern European fable (Sidanius et al., 2007, p. 257)

Social dominance theory assumes that all "human societies tend to be structured as systems of *group-based social hierarchies*" (Sidanius & Pratto, 1999, p. 31). The theory also suggests, however, that individuals within a society vary in the extent to which they recognize, and even support, the idea that some groups should be dominant and others oppressed. Do you, for example, agree with these statements?

- If certain groups of people stayed in their place, we would have fewer problems.
- Inferior groups should stay in their place.
- Sometimes other groups must be kept in their place.

Or, are these statements more consistent with your beliefs about groups?

- We should do what we can to equalize conditions for groups.
- Group equality should be our ideal.
- [We should] increase social equality.

These items are drawn from the Social Dominance Orientation (SDO) questionnaire. As noted in Chapter 8, individuals who are high in social dominance tend to be more interested in gaining and using power, whereas those who are low in social dominance are more likely to seek cooperative ways to handle conflicts. But individuals who are high in SDO are also strongly motivated to maximize their gains relative to other groups. Like Vladimir in the fable who will bear a cost so that his rival will suffer even more, someone who adopts a social dominance orientation will forfeit gross gain in order to maximize relative gain.

Sidanius, Pratto, and their colleagues confirmed this curious tendency by having individuals who varied in SDO play an experimental simulation they called Vladimir's Choice. White college students were led to believe that they were being consulted by the school's administration regarding how student activity funds should be spent. They were given a list of seven options that split the funds between White student interests and minority student interests. These options were contrived so that in order to receive the maximum allocation for their group—19 million dollars—it would mean that minority groups would receive 25 million. In order to lower the amount given to the outgroup, they had to choose an option that yielded less money for their group.

The majority of the students, 56%, chose the option that split the funds equally between the two groups (13 million to each). Many also favored allocations that would raise the amount given to both Whites and minorities, for they apparently were not concerned with getting more than the outgroup. Some, however, preferred receiving less money to ensure that their group received more than the minority group. And who was most likely to base their choice on the ingroup's gain over the outgroup's? Those who were high in social dominance orientation (Sidanius et al., 2007).

to the offended group. The target of the negative action, however, responds to the threat with a counter-threat, and the conflict spirals. Battles resulting in the death of gang members have begun over an ethnic insult, the intrusion of one group into an area controlled by another group, or the theft of one gang's property by another gang (Gannon, 1966; Yablonsky, 1959). Large-scale intergroup conflicts, such as race riots and warfare between countries, have also been caused by gradually escalating hostile exchanges (Myers, 1997; Reicher, 2001).

A *spiral model of conflict intensification* accurately describes the unfolding of violence at Robbers Cave. The conflict began with minor irritations and annoyances but built in intensity. *Exclusion*, a mild form of rejection, occurred as soon as the boys realized that another group was sharing the camp. This antipathy escalated into *verbal abuse* when the groups met for the tournament. Insults were exchanged, members of the opposing team were given demeaning names, and verbal abuse ran high. Next, *intergroup discrimination* developed. The groups isolated themselves from each other at meals, and the boys expressed the belief that it was wrong for the other team to use the camp facilities or to be given an equal amount of food. Last came the acts of *physical violence*—the raids, thefts, and fistfights. Thus, the conflict at Robbers Cave built in a series of progressively more dangerous stages from exclusion to verbal abuse to discrimination and, finally, to physical assault (Streufert & Streufert, 1986).

**Cultural Norms** The extent to which groups respond in hostile ways to other groups varies from culture to culture. The Mbuti Pygmies of Africa, !Kung, and many Native American tribes (e.g., the Blackfoot and Zuñi) traditionally avoid conflict by making concessions. The members of these societies live in small groups and, rather than defend their territories when others intrude, they withdraw to more isolated areas. Men are not regarded as brave or strong if they are aggressive, and war with other groups is nonexistent (Bonta, 1997). In contrast, the Yanomanö of South America and the Mundugumor of New Guinea linked aggression to status within the group (Chagnon, 1997; Mead, 1935). The anthropologist Napoleon Chagnon called the Yanomanö the "fierce people," for during the time he studied them they seemed to choose conflict over peace at every opportunity. Among the Yanomanö, prestige was accorded to those who were most aggressive, with bravery in battle being the most revered personal quality one can have. Villages routinely attacked other villages, and personal conflicts were usually settled through violence. Even among the Yanomanö, however, conflicts were regulated by a relatively stable set of social norms that prevented excessive causalities on either side (Chirot & McCauley, 2006).

Somewhat closer to home, Dov Cohen, Richard Nisbett, and their colleagues have examined the impact of norms pertaining to honor on conflict in the southern region of the United States. Murder, they note, is a tradition down South; nearly three times as many men are murdered each year in the southern states as in other parts of the country. In explanation, they suggest that when Europeans first occupied this area they forcefully defended their crops and herds against others because they could not rely on the authorities to provide them with protection. Over time, they developed a strong "culture of honor" that rewarded men who responded violently to defend their homes, their property, and their reputations. Southerners are not more positive about aggression in general, but they are more likely to recommend aggressive responses for self-defense and in response to insults (Nisbett & Cohen, 1996; Vandello & Cohen, 2003).

These norms of the culture of honor are now anachronistic, but they are sustained by misperceptions about the commonness of aggressive behavior. Just as students who drink excessively on college campuses tend to think that many other students drink heavily (see Focus 6.1), so southern men—relative to those in the north—believe that a man is likely to act aggressively when his honor has been threatened. They also judge the neutral actions of others in conflict situations as more threatening than northerners do (Vandello, Cohen, & Ransom, 2008). These group norms leave them ready to respond aggressively when others provoke them.

**Group Norms** Some groups within the larger society adopt unique norms and values pertaining to intergroup conflict. In the United States, the Mennonites and the Amish avoid interpersonal conflict and strive instead for cooperative, peaceful living. Other types of groups, such as urban youth gangs, sports fans, and cliques in schools, accept norms that emphasize dominance over other groups. Soccer fans show high levels of ingroup loyalty, but equally intense forms of aggression against fans of rival clubs (Foer, 2004). Groups of young girls develop intricate patterns of ingroup favoritism and outgroup rejection (Wiseman, 2002). Even though they rarely engage in physical aggression, their relational aggression can be so pointed and unrelenting that it leads to long-term negative consequences for those they target. Studies of gangs living in urban areas suggest that these groups, although violent, use aggression in instrumental ways to maintain group structures and patterns of authority. Much of the most intense violence is intergroup conflict, when one gang must defend its area from another, or when the gang decides that it must inflict harm on someone who has acted in ways that undermine the local gang's authority (Venkatesh, 2008).

### Anger and Scapegoating

When intergroup competitions end, one side is often branded the *winner* and one the *loser*. Like the victorious Eagles, winners experience a range of positive emotions, including pride, pleasure, happiness, and satisfaction. Losers, in contrast, experience the "agony of defeat"—humiliation, anger, embarrassment, and frustration (Brown & Dutton, 1995). These emotions can contribute to continuing conflict between groups, for negative emotional experiences such as frustration and anger can provoke aggression and retaliation. The Rattlers, for example, were very angry when they lost, and they responded by vandalizing the Eagles' cabin and stealing the prizes (Meier, Hinsz, & Heimerdinger, 2008).

In most cases, if a group interferes with another group, the injured party retaliates against the pe rpetrator. If, however, the aggressor is extremely powerful, too distant, or difficult to locate, then the injured party may respond by turning its aggression onto another group. This third group, although not involved in the conflict in any way, would nonetheless be blamed and thereby become the target of aggressive actions. The third group, in this case, would be the *scapegoat*—a label derived from the biblical ritual of guilt transference. Anger originally aroused by one group becomes displaced on another, more defenseless group. Attacking the guiltless group provides an outlet for pent-up anger and frustration, and the aggressive group may then feel satisfied that justice has been done. At the Robbers Cave, for example, the cause of the Rattlers' failure was not the Eagles—who beat them in a fair contest. Rather, it was the experimenters, who rigged the contest so that the Rattlers would fail.

The **scapegoat theory** of intergroup conflict explains why frustrating economic conditions often stimulate increases in prejudice and violence (Poppe, 2001). Studies of anti-Black violence in southern areas of the United States between 1882 and 1930 have indicated that outbreaks of violence tend to occur whenever the economy of that region worsened (Hovland & Sears, 1940). The correlation between the price of cotton (the main product of that area at the time) and the number of lynchings of Black men by Whites ranged from −.63 to −.72, suggesting that when Whites were frustrated by the economy, they took out these frustrations by attacking Blacks (see also Hepworth & West, 1988, for a more sophisticated analysis of the Hovland-Sears data).

Scapegoating, as a possible cause of intergroup rather than interindividual conflict, requires a degree of consensus among group members. Individuals often blame others for their troubles and take out their frustrations on them, but group-level scapegoating occurs when the group, as a whole, has settled on a specific target group to blame for their problems (Glick, 2005). Scapegoating is also more likely when a group has experienced difficult, prolonged negative experiences—not just petty annoyances or a brief economic downturn, but negative conditions that frustrate their success in meeting their most essential needs (Staub, 2004). In such cases the group may develop a compelling, widely shared ideology that, combined with political and social pressures, leads to the most extreme form of scapegoating: genocide. Scapegoating can also prompt oppressed groups to lash out at other oppressed groups. Even though the minority group is victimized by the majority group, minorities sometimes turn against other minority groups rather than confront the more powerful majority (Harding et al., 1969; Rothgerber & Worchel, 1997).

### Evolutionary Perspectives

Evolutionary psychology offers a final set of causes, somewhat more distal than proximate, for conflict

---

**scapegoat theory** An explanation of intergroup conflict arguing that hostility caused by frustrating environmental circumstances is released by taking hostile actions against members of other social groups.

between groups. The tendency for conflict to emerge between groups is so pervasive, and so difficult to keep within nonlethal limits, that some experts believe that it may have a genetic basis. As noted in Chapter 3, evolutionary psychologists suggest that, during the longest period of human evolution, individuals lived in small bands of between 50 and 150. These groups provided such an advantage to their members in terms of survival that, over time, humans became a social species—ready to cooperate with other humans in the pursuit of shared goals.

These same evolutionary pressures, however, also left humans ready to respond negatively to any human who was not a member of his or her group or tribe. Each group competed, forcefully, against all other groups to the point that each group plundered the resources of neighboring groups and harmed the members of those groups (the males, in particular). These groups were likely territorial, staking a claim to exclusive use of a geographic area, but if a member strayed too far from the safety of the group then the greatest danger was not from wild animals but from humans who were outsiders. Because the outgroups were a substantial threat, the human mind developed the capacity to recognize others and determine, with unerring accuracy, the other persons' tribal allegiance. Those who failed to distinguish between insiders and outsiders were less likely to survive.

Intergroup conflict was also instrumental in fostering the conditions needed to promote ingroup cooperation. Few experts believe that humans, as a species, could have survived had they not developed the means to cooperate with one another in the pursuit of joint outcomes. The development of this remarkable human capacity required a stable community of members, with care focused first on genetically related individuals and secondarily on group members who would be present on future occasions when the helping could be reciprocated. These conditions, so essential to the survival of these fragile groups, could be maintained only if group members were well-known to one another and normatively bound to reciprocate exchanges without undue levels of selfishness. This capacity for intragroup cooperation may have been further enhanced by the presence of outgroups. Facing a threat from an outgroup, the ingroup became more unified, producing a level of solidarity that increased each members' likelihood of surviving by linking him or her to the survival of the group as a whole (Van Vugt, De Cremer, & Janssen, 2007).

These aspects of the evolutionary environment, over time, resulted in adaptations that increased the fitness of the individual, but at the price of creating a generalized hostility for members of other groups. The human species developed an extraordinary capacity for altruism, cooperation, and selflessness, but these prosocial behaviors are usually reserved for members of the ingroup and sustained by hostility toward the outgroup.

## INTERGROUP BIAS: PERCEIVING US AND THEM

The boys at Robbers Cave displayed antipathy toward the other group even before the idea of a competitive tournament was mentioned. The Rattlers and Eagles had not even seen each other when they began to refer to "those guys" in a derogatory way:

> When the ingroup began to be clearly delineated, there was a tendency to consider all others as outgroup.... The Rattlers didn't know another group existed in the camp until they heard the Eagles on the ball diamond; but from that time on the outgroup figured prominently in their lives. Hill (Rattler) said "They better not be in our swimming hole." The next day Simpson heard tourists on the trail just outside of camp and was convinced that "those guys" were down at "our diamond" again. (Sherif et al., 1961, p. 94)

The conflict at the Robbers Cave was fueled by the competitive setting, situational norms, the struggle for power, and the frustrations that followed each loss, but these factors cannot fully account for the almost automatic rejection of members of the other group. Group members reject members of other groups not because they fear them or because they must compete with them, but simply because they belong to a different group.

## Conflict and Categorization

When Mills, a Rattler, met Craig, an Eagle, on the path to the dining hall, he spontaneously classified him as an Eagle rather than a Rattler. This *social categorization* process, although adaptive in the long run, nonetheless provides a cognitive foundation for intergroup conflict. Once Mills realized the boy approaching him was an Eagle and not a Rattler, he considered him to be one of *them*—an outsider who was different from the Rattlers. As Sherif (1966, p. 12) explained, "Whenever individuals belonging to one group interact, collectively or individually, with another group or its members in terms of their group identification, we have an instance of intergroup behavior."

Does social categorization, in and of itself, cause conflict? Does the mere existence of identifiable groups within society, and the cognitive biases generated by this differentiation, inevitably push groups into conflict? Research by Henri Tajfel, John Turner, and their colleagues, as discussed in Chapter 3, demonstrated the pervasiveness of the intergroup bias in their studies of the minimal group situation. Like the Sherifs, they examined groups that had no prior group history. But, unlike the Sherifs, they took this minimalism to its limit, by creating groups that were hardly groups at all. Formed on the basis of some trivial similarity or situational factor, the group members did not talk to each other, were anonymous throughout the study, and could not personally gain in any way from advantaging one person in the study over another. These were minimal groups, yet participants showed favoritism toward members of their own group. When given the opportunity to award money, they gave more money to members of their own group when they could and withheld money from the outgroup. Tajfel and Turner concluded that the "mere perception of belonging to two distinct groups—that is, social categorization per se—is sufficient to trigger intergroup discrimination favoring the ingroup" (Tajfel & Turner, 1986, p. 13; see also Hogg & Abrams, 1999).

Categorization sets in motion a number of affective, cognitive, emotional, and interpersonal processes that combine to sustain and encourage conflict between groups. People do not simply segment people into the categories "member of my group" and "member of another group" and then stop. Once people have categorized others according to group, they feel differently about those who are in the ingroup and those who are in the outgroup, and these evaluative biases are further sustained by cognitive and emotional biases that justify the evaluative ones—stereotypic thinking, misjudgment, and intensification of emotions. This section reviews these processes, beginning with the most basic: the tendency to favor one's own group.

### The Ingroup–Outgroup Bias

The sociologist William Graham Sumner (1906) maintained that humans are, by nature, a species that joins together in groups. But he also noted a second, equally powerful, human tendency: favoring one's own group over all others. "Each group nourishes its own pride and vanity, boasts itself superior, exalts its own divinities, and looks with contempt on outsiders" (p. 13). At the group level, this tendency is called the *ingroup–outgroup bias*. This bias, among such larger groups as tribes, ethnic groups, or nations, is termed **ethnocentrism** (Sumner, 1906).

The magnitude of the bias depends on a host of situational factors, including the group's outcomes, the way perceptions are measured, ambiguity about each group's characteristics, and members' identification with the group. Overall, however, the ingroup–outgroup bias is robust. A rock band knows its music is very good and that a rival band's music is inferior. One

---

**ethnocentrism** The belief that one's own tribe, region, or country is superior to other tribes, regions, or countries.

ethnic group prides itself on its traditions and also views other groups' traditions with disdain. One team of researchers thinks that its theory explains intergroup conflict and criticizes other researchers' theories as inadequate. After a bean-collecting game, the Rattlers overestimated the number of beans collected by Rattlers and slightly underestimated the number of beans supposedly collected by Eagles. Across a range of group and organizational settings, members rate their own group as superior to other groups (Hewstone, Rubin, & Willis, 2002; Hinkle & Schopler, 1986).

**Ingroup Positivity and Outgroup Negativity** The ingroup–outgroup bias is really two biases combined: (1) the selective favoring of the ingroup, its members, and its products, and (2) the derogation of the outgroup, its members, and its products. But at Robbers Cave, the pro-ingroup tendency went hand in hand with the anti-outgroup tendency. When they were asked to name their friends, 92.5% of the Eagles' choices were Eagles, and 93.6% of the Rattlers' choices were fellow Rattlers. When asked to pick the one person they disliked the most, 95% of the Eagles selected a Rattler, and 75% of the Rattlers identified an Eagle. In many intergroup conflicts, however, ingroup favoritism is stronger than outgroup rejection. For example, during a conflict between the United States and Iraq, U.S. citizens may feel very positive about the United States and its people, but they may not condemn Iraqis. Marilyn Brewer, after surveying a number of studies of intergroup conflict, concluded that the expression of hostility against the outgroup depends on the similarity of ingroup and outgroup members, anticipated future interactions, the type of evaluation being made, and the competitive or cooperative nature of the intergroup situation (see Brewer, 1979; Brewer & Brown, 1998; Hewstone et al., 2002).

**Implicit Intergroup Biases** Group members often express their preferences openly. Sports fans cheer on their own team and boo their opponents. The Rattlers expressed pride in their own group's accomplishments and ridiculed the Eagles. Racists express support for members of their own group and speak harshly of people with racial backgrounds different from their own.

But in many cases, the ingroup–outgroup bias is an implicit one—subtle, unintentional, and even unconscious, operating below the level of awareness (Fiske, 2004). Even though people may, when asked, claim that they are not biased against outgroup members and do not favor their own group, their biases emerge when their implicit attitudes are measured. One such measure, the Implicit Association Test (IAT) developed by Anthony Greenwald and his colleagues, assesses the extent to which people associate one concept—such as the ingroup—with another concept—such as goodness. When individuals are shown pairs of words or images that match their intuitive associations of these two concepts, such as ingroup/kind, outgroup/evil, they respond more quickly and without error. When, however, they respond to pairings of concepts that they do not associate with one another, such as ingroup/bad and outgroup/friendly, then they respond more slowly (Greenwald, McGhee, & Schwartz, 2008).

The IAT has revealed robust ingroup–outgroup biases in dozens of studies using all types of social categories, including race, ethnicity, religion, nationality, age, and sex. These biases occur even when people are striving to suppress their biases or when they claim that they are free of such tendencies (Nosek, Greenwald, & Banaji, 2007). The IAT has also revealed biases in the most minimal of intergroup situations. In one study, participants were categorized on the basis of their supposed preference for one of two artists; one named Quan and the second Xanthie (Ashburn-Nardo, Voils, & Monteith, 2001). The participants then completed the IAT, which asked them to classify people into one of two categories, fan of Quan or fan of Xanthie. To help them, they were told that if a person's name included a letter Q somewhere in the name they preferred Quan, whereas those who preferred Xanthie would be indicated by an X in their name. The time it took them to classify people into the Quan and Xanthie categories was recorded by the computer, which paired various Q and X names with positive adjectives (e.g., joyous, loving, glorious, happy) or negative adjectives (e.g., terrible, horrible, nasty, evil). As expected, people responded more quickly when the name they were shown was from their ingroup and it was associated with a positive adjective. If, for example, they had been told they preferred Xanthie, when shown a name with an X paired with a positive adjective (e.g., Merxes/glorious) they classified that person as a lover of Xanthie more quickly than if the X name had been paired with a negative word (e.g., Merxes/evil).

**Double-Standard Thinking** The ingroup–outgroup bias often fuels **double-standard thinking**. Members rationalize their own group's actions as fair and just and condemn the actions of the outgroup as unfair and unjust. Our warnings are *requests*, but the other side calls them *threats*. We are *courageous*, though they consider us *stubborn*. Pride in our own group is *nationalism*, but the other group takes it as evidence of *ethnocentrism*. We offer them *concessions*, but they interpret them as *ploys* (De Dreu, Nauta, & Van de Vliert, 1995).

Ralph White found that both sides in the major Middle East wars of 1948, 1956, 1967, and 1973 believed the other side to have been the aggressor in all four wars. In two of these wars (1956, 1967), the Palestinians believed that Israel had simply attacked without provocation. In the remaining two (1948, 1973), the Palestinians admitted that they had initiated hostilities, but believed that they had been forced to do so by the expansionistic policies of Israel. Conversely, the Israelis felt that the 1948 and 1973 wars were examples of blatant, unmitigated Palestinian aggression and that the 1956 and 1967 wars had been indirectly caused by the threats and malevolent intentions of the Palestinians (White, 1965, 1966, 1969, 1977, 1998). Similar biases have been found when students in the United States are asked to evaluate actions performed by their country and by the Soviet Union (Oskamp & Hartry, 1968) and when Whites' and Blacks' judgments of ambiguously aggressive actions committed by either a Black or a White person are compared (Sagar & Schofield, 1980). People judge actions that their own group performs positively, but they negatively evaluate these same actions when they are performed by outsiders. People also attribute other nations' hostile actions to internal factors—things about that country—but their nation's actions to external factors (Doosje & Branscombe, 2003).

**double-standard thinking** The tendency to consider the actions and attributes of one's own group as positive, fair, and appropriate, but to consider these very same behaviors or displays to be negative, unfair, and inappropriate when the outgroup performs them.

## Cognitive Bias

When Hill saw Craig he did not merely judge him more negatively than he would one of his fellow Rattlers (the ingroup–outgroup bias). He probably made inferences about Craig—his physical strength, his athletic skill, even his morality—solely on the basis of one piece of information: Craig was an Eagle. When people categorize others, their perceptions of these individuals are influenced more by their category-based expectations than by the evidence of their senses.

**Outgroup Homogeneity Bias** Most group members are quick to point out the many characteristics that distinguish them from the other members of their own group ("Why, I'm not like them at all!"), but when they evaluate members of outgroups, they underestimate their variability ("They all look the same to me"). If you were an Eagle, for example, you would describe the Rattlers as poor sports who cheated whenever possible. When describing the Eagles, in contrast, you might admit that a few of the members were sissies and that maybe one Eagle liked to bend the rules, but you would probably argue that the Eagles were so heterogeneous that sweeping statements about their typical qualities could not be formulated. Studies of a variety of ingroups and outgroups—women versus men, physics majors versus dance majors, Sorority A versus Sorority B, Princeton students versus Rutgers students, Canadians versus Native Americans, and

Blacks versus Whites—have documented this **outgroup homogeneity bias**. Group members' conceptualizations of other groups are simplistic and undifferentiated, but when they turn their eye to their own group, they note its diversity and complexity (see Boldry, Gaertner, & Quinn, 2007, and Linville & Fischer, 1998, for reviews).

The outgroup homogeneity bias does not emerge across all intergroup settings. The group that is disadvantaged in some way is usually viewed as more homogeneous, whereas the more powerful group is viewed as more variable (Guinote, Judd, & Brauer, 2002). The bias can also reverse entirely, resulting in *ingroup homogeneity bias* (Haslam & Oakes, 1995; Simon, Pantaleo, & Mummendey, 1995). Under conditions of extreme conflict, both tendencies may emerge, prompting group members to assume that "none of us deserve this treatment," and "they have harmed us; they must all be punished" (Rothgerber, 1997).

**Group Attribution Error** Group members tend to make sweeping statements about the entire outgroup after observing one or two of the outgroup's members. If an African American employee is victimized by a European American boss, the victim may assume that all European Americans are racists. Similarly, a visitor to another country who is treated rudely by a passerby may leap to the conclusion that everyone who lives in that country is discourteous. Individuals in intergroup situations tend to fall prey to the **law of small numbers**: They assume that the behavior of a large number of people can be accurately inferred from the behavior of a few people (Quattrone & Jones, 1980).

The opposite process—assuming that the characteristics of a single individual in a group can be inferred from the general characteristics of the whole group—can also bias perceptions. If we know our group's position on an issue, we are reluctant to assume that any one of us agrees with that position. When we know another group's position, however, we are much more willing to assume that each and every person in that group agrees with that position. Researchers studied this **group attribution error** by telling students that an election had recently been held either at their college or at another college to determine how much funding should be given to the college's athletics programs. They then told the students the results of the vote and asked them to estimate the opinion of the "typical student" at the college where the vote was taken. When the students thought that the vote had been taken at their own college, they did not want to assume that the individual's opinion would match the group's opinion. But when they thought that the vote was taken at another college, they were much more confident that the individual's opinions would match the group's opinions (Allison & Messick, 1985b; Allison, Worth, & King, 1990).

**Ultimate Attribution Error** When individuals form impressions of other individuals, the *fundamental attribution error* (FAE) prompts them to attribute the actions of others to their personal qualities rather than to the constraints of the situation. But when group members form impressions of outgroup members, the **ultimate attribution error** (UAE) prompts them to attribute only negative actions to outgroup members' dispositional qualities

---

**outgroup homogeneity bias** The perceptual tendency to assume that the members of other groups are very similar to each other, whereas the membership of one's own group is more heterogeneous.

**law of small numbers** The tendency for people to base sweeping generalizations about an entire group on observations of a small number of individuals from that group.

**group attribution error** The tendency for perceivers to assume that specific group members' personal characteristics and preferences, including their beliefs, attitudes, and decisions, are similar to the preferences of the group to which they belong; for example, observers may assume that each member of a group that votes to reelect the president supports the president, even though the group's decision was not a unanimous one.

**ultimate attribution error** The tendency for perceivers to attribute negative actions performed by members of the outgroup to dispositional qualities and positive actions to situational, fluctuating circumstances.

(Hewstone, 1990; Pettigrew, 2001). If outgroup members rob a bank or cheat on a test, then their actions are explained by reference to their personality, genetics, or fundamental lack of morality. But should an outgroup member perform a positive behavior, that action is attributed to a situational factor—perhaps good luck or a special advantage afforded the outgroup member. In any case, the perceiver will conclude that the good act, and the outgroup member who performed it, is just a special case. Because of the UAE, the perceiver concludes that there is no need to reappraise the group because the outgroup member is not responsible for the positive act.

The **linguistic intergroup bias** is a more subtle form of the UAE. Instead of attributing the behavior to dispositional factors or to the situation, group members describe the action differently depending on who performs it. If an ingroup member engages in a negative behavior, such as crying during a game, then members would describe that behavior very concretely—Elliott "shed some tears." If an outgroup member performed the same behavior, they would describe the action more abstractly—Elliott "acted like a baby." Positive behaviors, in contrast, are described in abstract terms when attributed to an ingroup member but in very concrete terms when performed by an outgroup member (Carnaghi et al., 2008; Maass, 1999).

**Stereotypes** When an Eagle met another Eagle on the trail, he probably expected the boy to be friendly, helpful, and brave. But if he encountered a Rattler, he expected the boy to be unfriendly, aggressive, and deceitful. These expectations are based on **stereotypes**—cognitive generalizations about the qualities and characteristics of the members of a particular group or social category. In many ways, stereotypes function as cognitive labor-saving devices by helping perceivers make rapid judgments about people based on their category memberships (Schneider, 2004). Because they are widely adopted by most of the ingroup, stereotypes are group-level perceptions; shared social beliefs rather than individualistic expectations (Bar-Tal, 2000). But stereotypes tend to be exaggerated rather than accurate, negative rather than positive, and resistant to revision even when directly disconfirmed. People tend to cling to stereotypes so resolutely that they become unreasonable beliefs rather than honest misconceptions. As Gordon Allport (1954) wrote, "Prejudgments become prejudices only if they are not reversible when exposed to new knowledge" (p. 8).

If stereotypes have all these perceptual and cognitive limitations, why do they persist? Walter Lippmann (1922), who first used the word *stereotype* to describe mental images of people, argued that the stereotype resists disconfirmation because "it stamps itself upon the evidence in the very act of securing the evidence." When group members see through eyes clouded by stereotypes, they misperceive and misremember people and events. Because individuals tend to interpret ambiguous information so that it confirms their expectations, stereotypes can act as self-fulfilling prophecies (Allport & Postman, 1947). Stereotypes also influence memory, so that recall of information that is consistent with stereotypes is superior to recall of stereotype-inconsistent information (Howard & Rothbart, 1980; Rothbart, Sriram, & Davis-Stitt, 1996). Because members expect outgroup members to engage in negative behavior and can more easily remember the times that they acted negatively rather than positively, they feel vindicated in thinking that membership in the outgroup and negative behaviors are correlated (Hamilton & Sherman, 1989).

The stereotypes about any given group include unique information pertaining to that group, but

---

**linguistic intergroup bias** The tendency to describe positive ingroup and negative outgroup behaviors more abstractly and negative ingroup and positive outgroup behaviors more concretely.

**stereotype** A socially shared set of cognitive generalizations (e.g., beliefs, expectations) about the qualities and characteristics of the members of a particular group or social category.

the **stereotype content model** suggests that most stereotypes are based on two general qualities: warmth and competence. Some groups (including the ingroup, in most cases) are viewed as warm, nice, friendly, and sincere, whereas other groups are considered to be filled with unpleasant, unfriendly, and even immoral people. The second dimension is competence: Some groups are thought to include competent, confident, skillful, able individuals, whereas others are viewed as incompetent or unintelligent. The Rattlers, for example, may have adopted a stereotypic view of the Eagles that rated them as neutral on the warm dimension but more negatively on the competence dimension (Cuddy, Fiske, & Glick, 2007, 2008; see Figure 14.4).

### Intergroup Emotions

People do not just categorize and judge the outgroup. They also respond emotionally to the outgroup, usually leaning in a negative direction. This negativity may be relatively mild, amounting to little more than mild discomfort when interacting with outgroup members or a general preference to be with someone from the ingroup rather than the outgroup, but this negativity bias can reach the emotional extreme of hatred and loathing. In some cases, people may not even admit their negativity towards members of the other group, yet they display it through their nonverbal actions, social awkwardness, and nervousness when in the presence of the outgroup (Dovidio et al., 2004).

In addition to these more general negative and positive reactions to the outgroup and ingroup, respectively, people may also display specific emotions, depending on the nature of the intergroup context. Intergroup emotions theory suggests that when individuals are members of a group that has lower social status than other groups, its members will experience a different set of intergroup emotions than will members of higher status groups (Smith & Mackie, 2005). Fear and jealousy, for example, are more common emotions in members of the lower status groups, whereas contempt or anger are characteristic of those who are members of higher status groups. Similarly, as Figure 14.4 indicates, the stereotype content model links intergroup emotions to expectations about the warmth and competence of the outgroup.

- *Envy* is most likely when the outgroup, although judged negatively, is nonetheless higher in status than the ingroup and this status difference is thought to be due to the competence of the outgroup. The Eagles, when they lost a game to the Rattlers, were likely to be envious of the Rattlers' athleticism. They did not trust the Rattlers, however, and may have suspected that they gained their advantage unfairly. Groups who are envious of other groups covet what the outgroup has achieved and view the outgroup as a competitor.
- *Contempt* is one of the most common of intergroup emotions, occuring when the outgroup is the most negatively stereotyped, that is, viewed as low in terms of both competence and warmth. The members of such an outgroup are viewed as responsible for their failings, and there is little consideration given to the idea that the division between the two groups can ever be lessened.
- *Pity*, as an intergroup emotion, is directed at outgroups that are viewed negatively in terms of competence, but are thought to also have positive, endearing qualities. Pity is usually directed downward, to outgroups that are low in the overall status ranking. Outgroups that evoke pity are not blamed for their plight, unlike outgroups that are held in contempt.
- *Admiration* is rare in intergroup contexts, for it is experienced when the outgroup is perceived as being both high in warmth and high in competence, an unusual occurrence. Intergroup admiration occurs when the

---

**stereotype content model** A theory of group perception positing that people's stereotyped views about social groups reflect their beliefs about the warmth and competence of the stereotyped group.

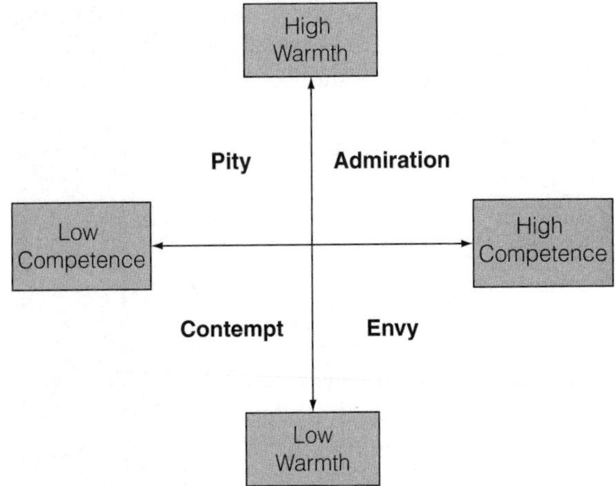

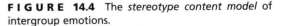

**FIGURE 14.4** The *stereotype content model* of intergroup emotions.

SOURCE: *The BIAS Map: Behaviors from intergroup affect and stereotypes*, by Cuddy, Amy J.C.; Fiske, Susan T.; Glick, Peter from JOURNAL OF PERSONALITY AND SOCIAL PSYCHOLOGY, April 1, 2007. The use of APA information does not imply endorsement by APA.

outgroup is thought to be completely deserving of its accomplishments, when the outgroup's gains do not come at a cost to the ingroup, and when the outgroup members are generally judged positively. Such an emotion is most likely when individuals can take some pride in association with the outgroup, even though they are not an actual member of the group.

**Group Hate** Hatred, as Allport (1954) explained in *The Nature of Prejudice*, is usually a group-level emotion. Drawing on ideas discussed by Aristotle, Allport observed that "anger is customarily felt toward individuals only, whereas hatred may be felt toward whole classes of people" (1954, p. 363). And while individuals often regret giving way to anger directed at another person, they feel no such remorse about their group-level hatred. "Hatred is more deep-rooted, and constantly desires the extinction of the object of hate" (1954, p. 363).

Hate causes a more violently negative reaction to the outgroup than such emotions as fear or anger. Often, group members fear the other group, for example, when outgroup members are viewed as competitors who may take harmful action towards the ingroup. Anger is also a dominant emotion in intergroup conflict settings, when previous negative exchanges between groups are a cause for irritation, annoyance, and hostility. Hate, however, is the feeling associated with many of the most negative consequences of intergroup conflict. Hate is expressed primarily when group members believe that previously harmful acts done by members of the outgroup were intentional ones that purposely harmed the ingroup, and that the actions were caused by the intrinsically evil nature of the outgroup. In one study of people's reactions to terrorist attacks, fear was associated with avoiding the outgroup and anger with support for improved education to improve intergroup relations. Those who felt hatred for the other group, in contrast, advocated their destruction, expressed a desire to do evil against them, and called for physical violence against them (Halperin, 2008; Sternberg, 2003).

**Moral Exclusion and Dehumanization** Throughout history, the members of one group have done great harm to the members of other groups. When intergroup conflict reaches extreme levels, with members of one group attacking, harming, and killing members of other groups, the ingroup–outgroup bias becomes equally extreme. During extreme intergroup conflicts, group members view their own group as morally superior and members of the outgroup as less than human (Bandura, 1999; Leyens et al., 2003; Reicher, Haslam, & Rath, 2008).

Such **moral exclusion** is more likely to occur in cases of extreme violence perpetrated by one group against another—European Americans enslaving Africans; Nazi Germany's attempted genocide of Jews; "ethnic cleansing" in Croatia and Serbia; and the continuing warfare between Israelis and Palestinians (Staub, 2004). Those who subjugate others tend to rationalize their violence by attributing it to the actions, intentions, or character of their victims. As their aggression intensifies, however, their rationalizations prompt them to increasingly devalue their victims. Eventually, the aggressors denigrate the outgroup so completely that the outsiders are excluded from moral concern, for it is difficult to savagely harm people whom one evaluates positively or strongly identifies with (Staub, 1990, p. 53). Groups that have a history of devaluing segments of their society are more likely to engage in moral exclusion, as are groups whose norms stress respect for authority and obedience. These groups, when they anticipate conflict with other groups, rapidly revise their opinions of their opponents so that they can take hostile actions against them (Opotow, 2000).

Moral exclusion places the outgroup outside the *moral* realm. **Dehumanization** moves the outgroup outside the *human* realm. Dehumanization occurs when the ingroup denies the outgroup those qualities thought to define the essence of human nature. Some of these qualities may be ones thought to be uniquely human: culture, refinement, high moral standards, and the capacity to think rationally. Others are qualities that the ingroup associates with humanity's strengths, such as emotional responsiveness, warmth, openness, self-control, and depth (Haslam, 2006). The ingroup may also come to believe that the outgroup experiences raw, primary emotions such as anger or happiness, but not the more refined emotions that make humans truly human: affection, admiration, pride, conceit, remorse, guilt, and envy (Leyens et al., 2003). People describe dehumanized outgroup members as disgusting or revolting because they are thought to be sources of contamination and impurity (Chirot & McCauley, 2006; Maoz & McCauley, 2008).

This concept of dehumanization is no hyperbole. When researchers used an fMRI scanner to track perceivers' reactions to images of people from various groups, their results suggested that dehumanized outgroup members are no longer perceived to be humans. When individuals viewed general images of people, the areas of the brain that typically respond when people process social information (the medial prefrontal cortices) showed increased activity. However, when they were shown images of people from an extreme outgroup—homeless individuals and drug addicts—those same areas did not rise above their resting state of neuronal activity. The insula and amygdala were activated, however; these portions of the brain are most active when people are experiencing strong emotions, such as disgust and contempt (Harris & Fiske, 2006).

Dehumanization also increases the likelihood that the ingroup will aggress against the outgroup. Albert Bandura and his associates tested this possibility experimentally by giving groups the opportunity to deliver painful electric shocks to a second group each time it performed poorly. In reality, there was no other group, but participants nonetheless believed that they could control both the intensity and duration of the shocks they gave the group. In one condition, the experimenter mentioned that the outgroup members—who were similar to one another in background but different from the subjects—seemed like nice people. But in the other condition the experimenter mentioned, in an offhand remark, that they were an "animalistic, rotten bunch." As expected, when dehumanized by the experimenter the groups increased their hostility and aggression, delivering more intense shocks (Bandura, Underwood, & Fromson, 1975).

---

**moral exclusion** A psychological process whereby opponents in a conflict come to view each other as undeserving of morally mandated rights and protections.

**dehumanization** Believing that other individuals or entire groups of individuals lack the qualities thought to distinguish human beings from other animals; such dehumanization serves to rationalize the extremely negative treatment often afforded to members of other groups.

### Categorization and Identity

Social identity theory offers a compelling explanation for the robust relationship between categorization and conflict. This theory, as noted in Chapter 3, assumes that membership in groups can substantially influence members' sense of self. When the boys joined the Robbers Cave Experiment and became firmly embedded in their groups, their identities changed. They came to think of themselves as Rattlers or Eagles, and they accepted the group's characteristics as their own. The theory also suggests that as the boys came to identify with their group, their own self-worth became more closely tied to the worth of the group. If a Rattler dedicated himself to the group and the Rattlers failed, the boy would likely experience a distressing reduction in his own self-esteem. Group members, therefore, stress the value of their own groups relative to other groups as a means of indirectly enhancing their own personal worth (Tajfel & Turner, 1986).

The basic premise of social identity theory is supported by evidence that people favor their group, even in minimal group conditions, and by the fact that the biasing effects of group membership are even more substantial when (a) individuals identify with their group rather than simply belong to it and (b) the relative status of existing groups is salient (Kenworthy et al., 2008). Black Africans' attitudes toward an outgroup (Afrikaans Whites) were negatively associated with the strength of their ingroup identification (Duckitt & Mphuthing, 1998). British people's attitudes toward the French were negatively correlated with the strength of their British identities (Brown et al., 2001). When individuals feel that the value of their group is being questioned, they respond by underscoring the distinctiveness of their own group and by derogating others (Brown & Hewstone, 2005; Dietz-Uhler & Murrell, 1998).

Social identity theory's suggestion that ingroup favoritism is in the service of ingroup members' self-esteem is also consistent with findings that individuals who most need reassurance of their worth tend to be the most negative towards other groups. Individuals who experience a threat to their self-esteem tend to discriminate more against outgroups, and low-status, peripheral members of the group are often the most zealous in their defense of their group and in the rejection of the outgroup (Noel, Wann, & Branscombe, 1995). Individuals are also more likely to draw comparisons between their group and other groups in areas where the comparison favors the ingroup. The Rattlers, for example, lost the tournament, so they admitted that the Eagles were better than the Rattlers at sports. But the Rattlers could stress their superiority in other spheres unrelated to the games, such as toughness or endurance (Reichl, 1997). Group members also display group-level *schadenfreude*. They take pleasure when other groups fail, particularly when the failure is in a domain that is self-relevant and when the ingroup's superiority in this domain is uncertain (Leach et al., 2003).

But does condemning other groups raise one's self-esteem? The effectiveness of this technique for sustaining self-esteem has not been confirmed consistently by researchers. In some cases, derogating outgroup members raises certain forms of self-esteem, but praising the ingroup tends to bolster self-esteem more than condemning the outgroup (Brown & Zagefka, 2005). Also, though people are quick to praise their ingroup, they still think that they are superior to most people—including all the members of their own group (Lindeman, 1997).

## INTERGROUP CONFLICT RESOLUTION: UNITING US AND THEM

The Robbers Cave researchers were left with a problem. The manipulations of the first two phases of the experiment had worked very well, for the Rattlers–Eagles war yielded a gold mine of data about intergroup conflict. Unfortunately, the situation had degenerated into a summer camp version of William Golding's (1954) *Lord of the Flies*. The two groups now despised each other. As conscientious social scientists, the Sherifs and their colleagues felt compelled to try to undo some of the negative effects of the study—to seek a method through which harmony and friendship could be restored at the Robbers Cave campsite.

### Intergroup Contact

The Robbers Cave researchers first tried to reduce the conflict by uniting the groups in shared activities. They based their intervention on the **contact hypothesis**, which assumes that ingroup–outgroup biases will fade if people interact regularly with members of the outgroup. So the Sherifs arranged for the Rattlers and the Eagles to join in seven pleasant activities, such as eating, playing games, viewing films, and shooting off firecrackers. Unfortunately, this contact had little impact on the hostilities. During all these events, the lines between the two groups never broke, and antilocution, discrimination, and physical assault continued unabated. When contact occurred during meals, "food fights" were particularly prevalent:

> After eating for a while, someone threw something, and the fight was on. The fight consisted of throwing rolls, napkins rolled in a ball, mashed potatoes, etc. accompanied by yelling the standardized, unflattering words at each other. The throwing continued for about 8–10 minutes, then the cook announced that cake and ice cream were ready for them. Some members of each group went after their dessert, but most of them continued throwing things a while longer. As soon as each gobbled his dessert, he resumed throwing. (Sherif et al., 1961, p. 158)

**Creating Positive Contact** *Contact* lies at the heart of such social policies as school integration, foreign student exchange programs, and the Olympics, but simply throwing two groups together in an unregulated situation is a risky way to reduce intergroup tensions. Contact between racial groups at desegregated schools does not consistently lower levels of prejudice (Gerard, 1983; Schofield, 1978). When units of an organization that clash on a regular basis are relocated in neighboring offices, the conflicts remain (Brown et al., 1986). In some cases students experience so much tumult during their semesters spent studying abroad that they become more negative toward their host countries rather than more positive (Stangor et al., 1996). Competing groups in laboratory studies remain adversaries if the only step taken to unite them is mere contact (Stephan, 1987). Even before they initiated the contact, the Sherifs predicted that a "contact phase in itself will not produce marked decreases in the existing state of tension between groups" (Sherif et al., 1961, p. 51).

Why does contact sometimes fail to cure conflict? Contact situations can create anxiety for those who take part, so the contact must be of sufficient duration to allow this anxiety to decrease and for individuals to feel comfortable interacting with one another (Kenworthy et al., 2005). Moreover, if members of the two groups use the contact situation as one more opportunity to insult, argue with, physically attack, or discriminate against one another, then certainly such contact should not be expected to yield beneficial effects (Riordan & Riggiero, 1980). The setting must, instead, create *positive contact* between groups by including such ingredients as:

- *Equal status.* The members of the groups should have the same background, qualities, and characteristics that define status levels in the situation. Differences in academic backgrounds, wealth, skill, or experiences should be minimized if these qualities will influence perceptions of prestige and rank in the group (Schwarzwald, Amir, & Crain, 1992).
- *Personal interaction.* The contact should involve informal, personal interaction with outgroup members rather than superficial, role-based

---

**contact hypothesis** The prediction that contact between the members of different groups will reduce intergroup conflict.

contacts. If the members of the groups do not mingle with one another, they learn very little about the other group, and cross-group friendships do not develop (Cook, 1985; Schofield, 1978).

- *Supportive norms.* The contact should encourage friendly, helpful, egalitarian attitudes and condemn ingroup–outgroup comparisons. These norms must be endorsed explicitly by authorities and by the groups themselves (Stephan & Rosenfield, 1982).
- *Cooperation.* Groups should work together in the pursuit of common goals (Gaertner, Dovidio, Rust, et al., 1999).

These ingredients were identified by a team of researchers led by Kenneth Clark and including Isidor Chein, Gerhart Saenger, and Stuart Cook. This group developed the social science statement filed in the U.S. Supreme Court case of *Brown vs. Board of Education*, which ruled that segregation of schools was unconstitutional (Benjamin & Crouse, 2002).

**The Effects of Contact** Does contact, across various types of situations and between various kinds of groups, stimulate conflict reduction? Thomas Pettigrew and Linda Tropp (2000, 2006) examined this question in a meta-analysis of 515 separate studies of contact and conflict. This massive pool of studies examined the responses of nearly a half a million people from around the world. It included studies with tightly controlled methods as well as those with less stringent controls. Some studies measured contact directly, whereas others based measures of contact on participants' own self-reports. Some studies were experimental, with treatment and control conditions, but others were correlational or quasi-experimental. The studies examined a variety of intergroup conflicts, including those based on race, sexual orientation, age, and ethnicity.

Their careful meta-analysis (which took the researchers eight years to complete) confirmed the utility of the contact method in reducing conflict. They found that face-to-face contact between group members reduced prejudice in 94% of these studies, and that the basic correlation between contact and conflict was −.21; the more contact, the less prejudice between groups. They also noted, however, that contact had a stronger impact on conflict when researchers studied high-quality contact situations that included equal status, cooperation between groups, and so on. In such studies, the correlation between contact and conflict climbed to −.29.

The effects of contact also varied across situations. Contact in recreational and work settings had the strongest impact on conflict, whereas contact that occurred when group members visited another group's country (i.e., as tourists) had the least impact (see Figure 14.5). The impact of contact on conflict also varied across countries. For example, it was greatest in Australia and New Zealand, followed by the United States and Europe. Contact worked to reduce conflict in all other countries, but its strength was less in some parts of the world (e.g., Africa, Asia, Israel). Some types of intergroup conflicts were also more resistant to the curative power of contact than others. Heterosexuals' attitudes toward gay men and lesbians improved the most after contact, followed by attitudes related to race and ethnicity. Contact lost some of its strength in studies of contact between people of different ages. Also, contact had less effect on the attitudes of members of minority groups relative to

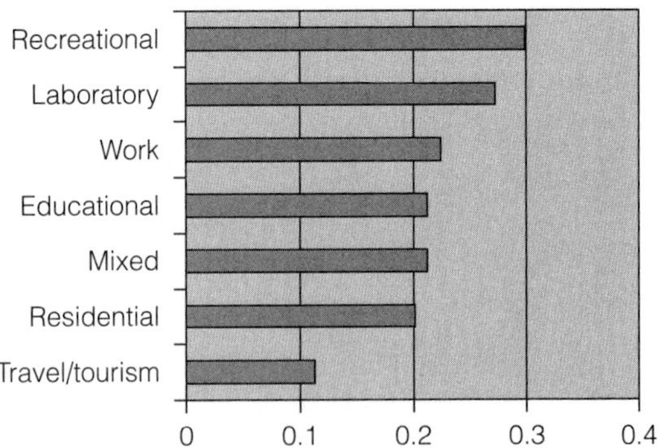


**FIGURE 14.5** Degree of conflict reduction between groups across seven contact situations.

SOURCE: Pettigrew & Tropp, 2006.

members of majority groups (Pettigrew & Tropp, 2000).

Pettigrew and Tropp conclude that contact works best in situations that conform to researchers' recommendations for positive contact, but they were also heartened by the positive effects obtained in less-than-ideal situations. Drawing on both their findings and social identity theory, they suggest that contact works most effectively when it helps reduce the anxiety associated with conflict between the groups and when membership in the two groups is salient to their members. They suspect that contact fails when members feel threatened by the outgroup, and that the level of contact is not enough to assuage that anxiety (Brown & Hewstone, 2005). This suggestion is also consistent with research that finds that stress, as measured by levels of cortisol reactivity, decreases with each additional contact between people in a situation that encourages the formation of friendships (Page-Gould, Mendoza-Denton, & Tropp, 2008).

**Contact and Superordinate Goals** Contact also reduced the conflict at the Robbers Cave site once the Sherifs improved the quality of the contact between the Rattlers and Eagles. Following the failure of simple contact, they arranged for the groups to work together in the pursuit of **superordinate goals**—that is, goals that can be achieved only if two groups work together. The staff created these superordinate goals by staging a series of crises. They secretly sabotaged the water supply and then asked the boys to find the source of the problem by tracing the water pipe from the camp back to the main water tank, located about three-quarters of a mile away. The boys became quite thirsty during their search and worked together to try to correct the problem. Eventually, they discovered that the main water valve had been turned off by "vandals," and they cheered when the problem was repaired. Later in this stage, the boys pooled their monetary resources to rent a movie that they all wanted to see, worked together to pull a broken-down truck, prepared meals together, exchanged tent materials, and took a rather hot and dusty truck ride together. Like feuding neighbors who unite when a severe thunderstorm threatens to flood their homes, or warring nations that pool their technological skills (in a recurring science fiction theme) to prevent the imagined collision of Earth with an asteroid, the Rattlers and the Eagles were reunited when they sought goals that could not be achieved by a single group working alone.

Other factors that enhance the impact of contact are friendship, success, and time. Stephen Wright and his colleagues, for example, have tested what they called the *extended contact hypothesis*: When group members learn that one or more members of their group have a friend in the outgroup, they express more positive intergroup attitudes (Wright et al., 1997; See Focus 14.2). Intergroup experiences that lead to successes, too, are more effective than intergroup experiences that lead to negative outcomes (Worchel, 1986). A disastrous performance during cooperation will only serve to further alienate groups (Blanchard, Adelman, & Cook, 1975). Contact is also more effective when groups share a common fate and when cues that signal status differences between the groups are minimized (Gaertner, Dovidio, Rust, et al., 1999; Gardham & Brown, 2001).

Contact also takes *time* to work its cure. In the Robbers Cave research, a whole series of superordinate goals was required to reduce animosity. Similarly, when students from two different colleges worked together on problems, students who worked with the outgroup just once or not at all rated the members of the outgroup more negatively than students who worked with the outgroup twice (Wilder & Thompson, 1980). Similar findings have been obtained in studies of desegregated schools. A long period of favorable intergroup contact may reduce prejudice, but if this favorable contact is followed by an equally long period in which contact is not encouraged, the groups inevitably drift apart once again (Schofield & Sagar, 1977).

---

**superordinate goal** A goal that can only be attained if the members of two or more groups work together by pooling their efforts and resources.

## Focus 14.2 Is Friendship Stronger Than Hate?

*Tis but thy name that is my enemy:*
*Thou art thyself, though not a Montague.*
*What's Montague? It is nor hand nor foot*
*Nor arm nor face nor any other part*
*Belonging to a man. O be some other name.*
*What's in a name? That which we call a rose*
*By any other word would smell as sweet.*
—Shakespeare, *Romeo and Juliet*, Act 2, Scene 2

The Robbers Cave Experiment was Sherif's third field study of intergroup conflict. One of the earlier studies, in which the Panthers battled the Pythons, had to be aborted when the two groups realized that the camp administration was creating the intergroup friction (Sherif, White, & Harvey, 1955). The other, conducted in 1949 in a camp in northern Connecticut, pitted friendship against intergroup bias (Sherif & Sherif, 1953). As noted in Chapter 5, these boys were not separated into groups until a full week of campwide activities had been held. During that time, strong patterns of friendship developed between the boys, but the researchers deliberately separated friends when they segregated the two groups during the second week. Many of the Red Devils had friends on the Bull Dogs team and many Bull Dogs had Red Devil friends.

Categorization, however, virtually obliterated these original friendships. Boys who continued to interact with members of the outgroup were branded traitors and threatened with bodily harm unless they broke off their friendships. One member of the Bull Dogs who did not completely identify with the group was partially ostracized, and eventually his parents had to remove him from the camp. A Red Devil who suggested that the two groups get together for a party was punished by the Red Devil's leader. This observational evidence was buttressed by the sociometric choice data collected before and after the groups were formed. Before the intergroup conflict, more than 60% of the boys reported that their best friends were members of what would eventually become the outgroup. Later, after the groups were separated, cross-group friendships dwindled down to 10%.

Other studies, however, have suggested that friendship can sometimes cure intergroup conflict. Thomas Pettigrew (1997), in a study of 3,806 people living in four countries in Europe, discovered that people who reported having friends who were members of an outgroup (another race, nationality, culture, religion, or social class) were less prejudiced than those who had no outgroup friends. Other investigations have confirmed this tendency (Pettigrew & Tropp, 2000). For example, Stephen Wright and his colleagues conceptually replicated the Robbers Cave Experiment with college students who spent an entire day working in one of two groups on a variety of tasks. Groups first developed a sense of cohesiveness by designing a logo for their team and sharing personal information. The groups then competed against each other, and during lunch, they watched as each group was given prizes and awards for defeating the other group. Later in the day, the groups worked on solitary tasks, except for two individuals who met together—supposedly to take part in an unrelated study. This meeting, however, was designed to create a friendly relationship between these two individuals, who then returned to their groups just before a final competition.

Wright discovered that the two group members who were turned into friends were more positive toward the outgroup. More importantly, however, this positivity generalized throughout the rest of the group. Even though the other group members had not themselves developed friendships with members of the outgroup, the knowledge that someone in their group considered an outgroup member to be likable moderated the ingroup–outgroup bias. Wright concluded that intergroup conflict sometimes prevents friendships from forming, but that friendships that cut across groups can undo some of the pernicious effects of the ingroup–outgroup bias (Wright et al., 1997).

### Cognitive Cures for Conflict

Intergroup contact does more than just promote positive interactions between people who were once antagonists. When individuals cooperate with the outgroup, their "us versus them" thinking fades, along with ingroup favoritism, outgroup rejection, and stereotyping (Brewer & Brown, 1998; Brewer & Miller, 1984; Crisp & Hewstone, 2007).

**Decategorization** During the waning days at the Robbers Cave, the boys began to abandon their collective identities. Some boys became less likely to think of themselves as Rattlers, but instead viewed themselves as individuals with specific interests, skills, and abilities. This **decategorization**, or *personalization*, of group members reduces intergroup conflict by reminding group members to think of outgroup members as individuals rather than as typical group members (Brewer, 2007). In one study, researchers personalized the outgroup by merging two distinct groups and giving them problems to solve. Some of the groups were urged to focus on the task, but others were encouraged to get to know one another. This latter manipulation decreased the magnitude of the ingroup–outgroup bias, although it did not eliminate it completely (Bettencourt et al., 1992). Individuation can also be increased by reducing the perceived homogeneity of the outgroup. When group members were told that one member of the outgroup strongly disagreed with his or her own group during an episode of intergroup conflict, ingroup–outgroup biases were muted (Wilder, 1986b). The participants looked at the outgroup and saw a collection of individuals rather than a unified group (Wilder, Simon, & Faith, 1996).

**Recategorization** The **common ingroup identity model**, developed by Samuel Gaertner, John Dovidio, and their colleagues, recommends reducing bias by shifting group members' representations of themselves away from two separate groups into one common ingroup category. This **recategorization** will undo the conflict-exacerbating cognitive factors that are rooted in the ingroup–outgroup bias, but will also permit members to retain their original identities (so long as they do not conflict with the recategorized groups). Because people belong to multiple groups, they may be able to conceive of themselves as members of different groups who are currently members of one, more superordinate group. Recategorization can also be achieved by systematically manipulating the perceptual cues that people use to define "groupness." When the members of competing groups were urged to adopt a single name, space was minimized between the members, and their outcomes were linked, these cues increased the perceived unity *(entitativity)* of the group members, and ingroup–outgroup biases diminished (Gaertner & Dovidio, 2000; Gaertner, Dovidio, Nier, et al., 1999; Gaertner, Dovidio, Rust, et al., 1999; Gaertner et al., 2000).

Jason Nier and his colleagues (2001) confirmed this shifting of identities at a football game between the University of Delaware and Westchester State University. They arranged for European and African American interviewers to approach European American fans and ask them if they would answer a few questions about their food preferences. The interviewers manipulated shared social identity by wearing different hats. For example, when interviewers approached a Delaware fan, they wore a Delaware hat to signal their shared identity, but a Westchester hat to indicate they were members of the outgroup. Ingroup–outgroup identity did not influence European Americans' compliance with a European American interviewer's request. However, the participants were more likely to agree to be interviewed by an African American if the interviewer and interviewee apparently shared a common university affiliation.

The Sherifs made use of recategorization in their 1949 study by pitting a softball team made up of members from both groups against an outside camp (Sherif & Sherif, 1953). This *common-enemy approach* was partially successful. During the game, the boys cheered one another on and, when the home team won, congratulated themselves without paying heed to group loyalties. By introducing the third party, the common-enemy approach forced the boys to redefine themselves in terms of a single

---

**decategorization** Reducing social categorization tendencies by minimizing the salience of group memberships and stressing the individuality of each person in the group.
**common ingroup identity model** An analysis of recategorization processes and conflict, developed by Samuel Gaertner, John Dovidio, and their colleagues, predicting that intergroup conflict can be reduced by emphasizing membership in inclusive social categories and the interdependence of the individuals in the groups.
**recategorization** A reduction of social categorization tendencies by collapsing groups in conflict into a single group or category.

shared group identity. The Sherifs pointed out, however, that combining groups in opposition to a common enemy "enlarges" the conflict as new factions are drawn into the fray (Kessler & Mummendey, 2001). The old conflicts can also return once the common enemy is dispatched.

**Cross-Categorization** Ingroup–outgroup biases are also minimized when group members' other classifications—in addition to their group identity that is the focus of the conflict—are made salient to them (Crisp & Hewstone, 2007). **Cross-categorization**, or multiple social categorization, instead of uniting all individuals in a single group or breaking down groups altogether, decreases the power of the problematic group identity by shifting attention to alternative memberships that are less likely to provoke ingroup–outgroup tensions. The Sherifs, if they had implemented this strategy at the Robbers Cave, would have introduced at least one other category and split the Rattlers and the Eagles into two new groups. The boys, for example, were drawn from both the north and the south side of Oklahoma City, so the Sherifs could have separated them into these two groups and introduced activities that would have made these identities salient.

When others are viewed as belonging to multiple categories rather than just one, intergroup differentiation decreases, and with it goes intergroup bias. Cross-categorization also prompts individuals to develop a more complex conceptualization of the outgroup, which leads in some cases to decategorization. The effectiveness of cross-categorization depends, however, on individuals' willingness to do the cognitive work needed to rethink their conceptualization of the outgroup and their mood. If pressured by time constraints that placed demands on their ability to process information or a mood-souring situation, the boys at Robbers Cave may have fallen back on the older, better-known Eagles–Rattlers distinction (Brewer, 2000; Crisp & Hewstone, 2007; Urban & Miller, 1998).

**Controlling Stereotyped Thinking** Rather than attacking the categorization process, Patricia Devine (1989, 2005) recommended controlling the impact of stereotypes on perceptions. Although people may not be able to avoid the activation of stereotypes, they can control their subsequent thoughts to inhibit ingroup–outgroup biases. Devine found that the European Americans she studied could easily list the contents of their culture's stereotype about African Americans. She also found that European Americans who were low in prejudice could describe the stereotype as accurately as those who were high in prejudice. The unprejudiced European Americans, however, could control their thoughts after the stereotypes were activated. When asked to list their thoughts about African Americans, the unprejudiced participants wrote such things as "Blacks and Whites are equal" and "It's unfair to judge people by their color—they are individuals." Prejudiced people, in contrast, listed negative, stereotypical thoughts. Devine and her colleagues have also found that unprejudiced European Americans feel guilty when they respond to African Americans in stereotypical ways, whereas prejudiced European Americans do not (see Devine, 2005, for a review).

## Conflict Management

Many practical approaches to dealing with conflict build on both the contact and cognitive approaches while adding elements designed to fit the given situation. These approaches include cultural awareness training, self-esteem workshops, roundtable discussions with peers, structured training programs, and cooperative learning interventions (for a comprehensive review see Paluck & Green, 2009). These programs, when applied with diligence, often yield substantial reductions in conflict, although their success depends on their duration, their design, and their fidelity to the intervention strategy (Stephan & Stephan, 2005).

---

**cross-categorization** A reduction of the impact of social categorization on individuals' perceptions by making salient their memberships in two or more social groups or categories that are not related to the categories that are generating ingroup–outgroup tensions.

**Jigsaw Learning Groups** Studies of public schools in the United States suggest that desegregation often fails to eliminate racial and ethnic prejudices. Although integrated schools bring students from various groups into contact, they do not always promote cooperation between these groups. Instead of including the necessary ingredients for positive intergroup interaction, many school systems fail to encourage interaction among the members of various subgroups, and staff openly express hostile attitudes toward outgroup members. Some schools, too, group students on the basis of prior academic experiences; as a result, educationally deprived students are segregated from students with stronger academic backgrounds (Amir, 1969; Brewer & Miller, 1984; Cook, 1985; Schofield, 1978).

Desegregation will reduce prejudice only when supplemented by educational programs that encourage cooperation among members of different racial and ethnic groups. One technique that has yielded promising results involves forming racially mixed teams within the classroom. In the **jigsaw method**, for example, students from different racial or ethnic groups are assigned to a single learning group. These groups are then given an assignment that can be completed only if each individual member contributes his or her share. Study units are broken down into various subareas, and each member of a group must become an expert on one subject and teach that subject to other members of the group. In a class studying government, for example, the teacher might separate the pupils into three-person groups, with each member of the group being assigned one of the following topics: the judiciary system (the Supreme Court of the United States), the duties and powers of the executive branch (the office of the President), and the functions of the legislative branch (Congress). Students can, however, leave their three-person groups and meet with their counterparts from other groups. Thus, everyone assigned to study one particular topic, such as the Supreme Court, would meet to discuss it, answer questions, and decide how to teach the material to others. Once they have learned their material, these students rejoin their original groups and teach the other members of their group what they had learned. Thus, the jigsaw class uses both group learning and student teaching techniques (Aronson, 2000; Aronson & Patnoe, 1997; Aronson et al., 1978).

**Learning to Cooperate** Intergroup conflicts resist resolution, despite the best intentions of those involved to settle the problem amicably. In one of the Sherifs' studies, for example, an informal attempt by one of the Bull Dogs' leaders to negotiate with the Red Devils ended in increased antagonism:

> Hall ... was chosen to make a peace mission. He joined into the spirit, shouting to the Bull Dogs, "Keep your big mouths shut. I'm going to see if we can make peace. We want peace." Hall went to the Red Devil cabin. The door was shut in his face. He called up that the Bull Dogs had only taken their own [belongings] ... and they wanted peace. His explanation was rejected, and his peaceful intentions were derided. He ran from the bunkhouse in a hail of green apples. (Sherif & Sherif, 1953, p. 283)

Conflict experts, such as Herbert Kelman (1992), recommend training people to be more effective managers of intergroup conflict. Kelman and his colleagues have met repeatedly with high-ranking representatives from countries in the Middle East to solve problems in that region of the world. Kelman has carefully structured the workshops so that participants can speak freely, and he intervenes only as necessary to facilitate the communication process. The workshops are completely confidential, discussion is open but focused on the conflict, and expectations are realistic. The workshops are not designed to resolve the conflict, but to give participants the behavioral skills needed to solve conflicts themselves (Rouhana & Kelman, 1994).

---

**jigsaw method** A team-learning technique developed by Elliot Aronson and his colleagues that involves assigning topics to each student, allowing students with the same topics to study together, and then requiring these students to teach their topics to the other members of their groups.

David and Roger Johnson have applied these principles in their school-based cooperative learning program. They designed their program to achieve three major goals: to decrease the amount of tension between groups in schools and colleges; to increase students' ability to solve problems without turning to authorities; and to give students skills they can use when they become adults. The program teaches students a five-step approach to resolving conflicts: (1) define the conflict; (2) exchange information about the nature of the conflict; (3) view the situation from multiple perspectives; (4) generate solutions to the conflict; (5) select a solution that benefits all parties.

Johnson and Johnson, in evaluations of the program, reported substantial reductions in discipline problems after training, as well as increases in academic achievement (Roseth, Johnson, & Johnson, 2008). These programs can be made even more effective by structuring the task so that each group member makes a contribution, randomly assigning students to roles within the group, and making certain that all groups contain an equal number of representatives from the groups being merged. Too much of an emphasis on individual performance—created by assigning grades based on relative performance or degree of preparation—can undermine the effectiveness of the program, but research suggests that the intervention yields positive gains even in less-than-ideal settings (Miller & Davidson-Podgorny, 1987).

### Resolving Conflict: Conclusions

In his classic treatise *The Nature of Prejudice*, Allport (1954) wrote that "conflict is like a note on an organ. It sets all prejudices that are attuned to it into simultaneous vibration. The listener can scarcely distinguish the pure note from the surrounding jangle" (p. 996).

The Sherifs and their colleagues created just such a "jangle" at the Robbers Cave. The Rattlers and the Eagles were only young boys camping, but their conflict followed patterns seen in disputes between races, between regions, and between countries. But just as the Robbers Cave Experiment is a sobering commentary on the pervasiveness of conflict, so the resolution of that conflict is cause for optimism. The Sherifs created conflict, but they also resolved it. When it came time to return to Oklahoma City, several of the group members asked if everyone could go in the same bus:

> When they asked if this might be done and received an affirmative answer from the staff, some of them actually cheered. When the bus pulled out, the seating arrangement did not follow group lines. Many boys looked back at the camp, and Wilson (E) cried because camp was over. (Sherif et al., 1961, p. 182)

If the Robbers Cave conflict can end peacefully, perhaps others can as well.

## SUMMARY IN OUTLINE

*What interpersonal factors disrupt relations between groups?*

1. Muzafer and Carolyn Sherif and their colleagues' carried out the *Robbers Cave Experiment* to identify the causes of intergroup conflict.
2. *Realistic group conflict theory* assumes conflict occurs because groups must compete with one another for scarce resources.

- The heightened competitiveness of groups is known as the *discontinuity effect*.
- Research by Insko and his colleagues suggests the effect is due to individuals' desire to maximize profit (greed), distrust of groups (fear), group loyalty, and the lack of identifiability. Limiting these tendencies can work to reduce the aggressiveness of groups.

3. Conflict increases when one group attempts to dominate and exploit another group, and the target group resists exploitation.
   - *Social dominance theory*, developed by Sidanius and Pratto, examines tensions between hierarchically ranked groups in society. Individuals who are high in social dominance orientation are more likely to prefer allocations that benefit their group relative to other groups.
   - Groups exploit other groups both economically and coercively, but Insko's generational studies suggest that coercive influence is associated with greater increases in conflict.
4. Normative processes instigate and sustain conflict.
   - Intergroup conflict, like intragroup conflict, tends to escalate over time. Both the norm of reciprocity and the use of contentious influence tactics stimulate conflict spirals.
   - The extent to which groups respond in hostile ways to other groups varies from culture to culture, with some cultures eschewing intergroup conflict and others (such as the "fierce" Yanomanö studied by Chagnon) accepting it routinely.
   - Subgroups within the large cultural context may adopt unique norms pertaining to violence. Work by Nisbett, Cohen, and their colleagues suggests that in the South of the United States men tend to respond more aggressively to threat.
5. Negative emotional reactions can trigger anti-outgroup reactions. *Scapegoat theory* explains why groups that experience setbacks sometimes fight other, more defenseless groups.
6. Intergroup conflict may be instinctive—the result of evolutionary pressures that favored individuals who preferred ingroup members over outgroup members.

*What are the psychological foundations of conflict between groups?*

1. Social categorization leads perceivers to classify people into two mutually exclusive groups—the ingroup and the outgroup. Individuals in Tajfel and Turner's minimal intergroup situation displayed the ingroup–outgroup bias, leading them to conclude that social categorization may be sufficient to create conflict.
2. Members tend to favor the ingroup over the outgroup (the ingroup–outgroup bias). This bias, when applied to larger groups such as tribes or nations, was labeled *ethnocentrism* by Sumner.
   - Ingroup favoritism tends to be stronger than outgroup rejection, but both forms of ingroup–outgroup bias emerged at Robbers Cave.
   - Implicit measures of bias, such as the Implicit Association Test (IAT) developed by Greenwald and his colleagues, can detect subtle, unconscious forms of bias.
   - *Double-standard thinking*, as described by White, occurs when group members frame the behaviors and characteristics of the ingroup in more positively than these same behaviors and characteristics displayed by the outgroup.
3. During intergroup conflict, group members' judgments are often distorted by a number of cognitive biases:
   - *Outgroup homogeneity bias*: The outgroup is assumed to be much more homogeneous than the ingroup. Members assume that their own group is diverse and heterogeneous, although when the group is threatened, members may exaggerate the similarity of everyone in their group.
   - *Law of small numbers*: The behaviors and characteristics exhibited by a small number of outgroup members are generalized to all members of the outgroup.

- *Group attribution error*: Group decisions are assumed to reflect individual group members' attitudes, irrespective of the particular procedures used in making the decisions.
- *Ultimate attribution error*: Group members attribute the negative behaviors performed by outgroup members to internal dispositions, but their positive behaviors are explained away as situationally caused aberrations.
- *Linguistic intergroup bias*: Actions performed by the ingroup are described differently than actions performed by the outgroup.
- *Stereotypes*: Lippmann coined the word stereotypes to describe cognitive generalizations about the qualities and characteristics of the members of a particular group or social category. The *stereotype content model* suggests that the contents of most stereotypes reflect judgments of the outgroup's competence and warmth.

4. When conflicts become more intense, members may display more extreme emotional reactions to outgroups.
   - In addition to a generalized negative reaction to the outgroup, individuals may also experience specific emotions, such as envy, contempt, pity, and admiration, depending on their stereotypes about the outgroup.
   - As Allport observed, hatred tends to be directed at groups rather than individuals.
   - Extreme conflict can result in both *moral exclusion* and *dehumanization* of members of the outgroup. Dehumanized individuals evoke a different reaction, at the neurological level, than those who are not dehumanized, and Bandura's research indicates that a group is likely to be treated more negatively when described as "animalistic."
5. Social identity theory suggests that individuals, by championing the ingroup, maintain and even raise their self-esteem.

*How can intergroup relations be improved?*

1. The Sherifs' first, relatively unsuccessful attempt to reduce conflict was based on the *contact hypothesis*.
2. Pettigrew and Tropp, using meta-analysis, concluded that contact is an effective means of reducing conflict.
   - The effectiveness of contact increases in more positive contexts; ones that include the elements identified by Clark and his colleagues. Contact is more effective when it creates cooperation between the groups, when participants are equal in status, when interaction is intimate enough to sustain the development of friendships across the groups, and when norms encourage cooperation.
   - Contact is more effective when it creates extensive opportunities for interaction, as in sports and work settings rather than tourist settings.
   - The Sherifs successfully reduced conflict in the Robbers Cave camp by prompting the boys to work toward *superordinate goals*.
   - Studies of the *extended contact hypothesis* posited by Wright and others suggest that encouraging the development of cross-group friendship relations reduces prejudice.
3. Cognitive approaches to conflict reduction seek to reverse the negative biases that follow from parsing individuals into ingroups and outgroups.
   - *Decategorization* encourages members to recognize the individuality of the outgroup members.
   - The *common ingroup identity model* developed by Gaertner and Dovidio suggests

that *recategorization*—collapsing the boundaries between groups—reduces conflict yet can promote the retention of identities. The common-enemy approach is an example of recategorization.

- *Cross-categorization* involves making salient multiple group memberships.
- Devine's studies of stereotypic thinking indicate that even though individuals may be aware of the contents of stereotypes pertaining to outgroups, they can learn to control the impact of this biased cognitive response on their judgments.

4. Conflict experts such as Kelman suggest managing conflict by teaching group members the skills they need to resolve interpersonal disputes.
   - Aronson's *jigsaw method* is an educational intervention that reduces prejudice by assigning students from different racial or ethnic groups to a single learning group.
   - School-based conflict management programs liked those developed by Johnson and Johnson are designed to reduce conflict between groups by teaching students to recognize conflict, communicate about the source of the conflict, and identify mutually acceptable solutions.

## FOR MORE INFORMATION

*Chapter Case: The Robbers Cave Experiment*

- *Intergroup Conflict and Cooperation: The Robbers Cave Experiment*, by Muzafer Sherif, O. J. Harvey, B. Jack White, William R. Hood, and Carolyn W. Sherif (1961), describes in detail the well-known study of conflict between two groups of boys at a summer camp.

*Causes of Intergroup Conflict*

- "Intergroup Relations," by Marilyn B. Brewer and Rupert J. Brown (1998), is a theoretically sophisticated review of the theory and research pertaining to intergroup processes.
- "Beyond the Group Mind: A Quantitative Review of the Interindividual–Intergroup Discontinuity Effect," by Tim Wildschut, Brad Pinter, Jack L. Vevea, Chester A. Insko, and John Schopler (2003), examines prior scholarly analyses of the transformation that occurs when conflict erupts between groups rather than individuals and provides a summary of work on the discontinuity effect.

*Intergroup Relations*

- "The Social Psychology of Intergroup Relations," by Marilyn B. Brewer (2007), provides a comprehensive but efficient review of research dealing with cognitive factors that cause and sustain intergroup bias.
- *On the Nature of Prejudice: Fifty Years after Allport*, edited by John F. Dovidio, Peter Glick, and Laurie A. Rudman (2005), draws together papers on Allport's insights into the nature of intergroup conflict, with sections pertaining to preferential thinking, sociocultural factors, and prejudice reduction.
- *The Psychology of Stereotyping*, by David J. Schneider (2004), examines issues of stereotype and bias, as well as a wide variety of cognitive processes that pertain to groups, including perceptions of entitativity, categorization, and ingroup–outgroup bias.

*Resolving Intergroup Conflict*

- "Prejudice Reduction: What Works? A Review and Assessment of Research and Practice," by Elizabeth Levy Paluck and Donald P. Green (2009), reviews a wide variety of methods used to reduce conflict between groups, with a focus on the rigor of the methods used to evaluate their efficacy.

- "An Integrative Theory of Intergroup Contact," by Rupert Brown and Miles Hewstone (2005), is a detailed review of theory and research on intergroup contact, with a focus on the mediating role of group salience and anxiety.

## Media Resources

Visit the Group Dynamics companion website at www.cengage.com/psychology/forsyth to access online resources for your book, including quizzes, flash cards, web links, and more!

# 15

# Groups in Context

## CHAPTER OVERVIEW

Just as individuals are embedded in groups, so groups are embedded in physical and social environments. Groups alter their environments substantially, but in many cases, it's the place that shapes the group. As Kurt Lewin's (1951) formula, $B = f(P, E)$, states, group behavior ($B$) is a function of the persons ($P$) who are in the group and the environment ($E$) where the group is located.

- How does the social and physical environment influence groups and their dynamics?
- What is the ecology of a group?
- What are the causes and consequences of a group's tendency to establish territories?

## CHAPTER OUTLINE

### Apollo 13: The Group That Lost the Moon

In 1961, President John F. Kennedy set the goal: to send Americans to the surface of the moon by the end of the decade. His plan initiated the largest engineering project in modern history, with as many as 400,000 individuals eventually working together to solve the endless technical, psychological, and medical problems posed by such an unprecedented undertaking. On July 20, 1969, Apollo 11 commander Neil Armstrong made history when he stepped on the moon's surface.

One year later, Apollo 13 commander James Lovell also made history, but in his case by *not* stepping on the moon. On April 11, 1970, Lovell, John Swigert, and Fred Haise piloted the National Aeronautics and Space Administration (NASA) Apollo 13 into space without any sign of a problem. Lovell and his crew were to spend four days crowded together in their command module, named the *Odyssey*, before reaching the moon. The team members had trained for years for the mission, and throughout the trip they would remain in constant communication with ground control teams in Houston, Texas. Once in orbit around the moon, Lovell and Haise would descend to the surface of the moon in the Lunar Excursion Module (LEM), the *Aquarius*.

But 56 hours into the mission, Swigert initiated a procedure designed to stir the cryogenic oxygen tanks. One of the tanks exploded. With oxygen escaping from their ship and battery power dwindling, Lovell coolly radioed NASA his famous understatement, "Houston, we have a problem." (Actually, he said "Houston, we've had a problem.") During the next three days, the crew and the teams on the ground identified and responded to one life-threatening challenge after another, including near-freezing temperatures and a buildup of carbon dioxide in the cabin. The group managed to return to Earth, and splashed down safely in the Pacific Ocean on April 17, 1970.

Groups exist in any number of distinct physical locations: from classrooms, museums, factories, and boardrooms to coal mines, battlefields, and even space capsules. The impressionists thrived in Paris in the 1860s in the midst of its countless galleries, art schools, restaurants, bistros, and parks. The 1980 U.S. Olympic Hockey Team trained and played for hours and hours on hockey rinks across the world. The Bay of Pigs planners met in an elegantly appointed conference room, speaking to each other in subdued voices across an imposing mahogany table. The Rattlers and the Eagles met, fought, and befriended each other at the cabins and on the fields of the Robbers Cave State Park. Each one of these groups slept, worked, played, interacted, argued, and fought in a specific environmental context, and these places substantially influenced their dynamics. This chapter examines the nature of this environment–group relationship, focusing on places, spaces, and territorial locations.

## PLACES: GROUP SETTINGS

Groups can be found in both natural and built environments. At a post office, workers sort mail in noisy rooms bathed in fluorescent light. Hikers trek through the woods, taking care to leave no evidence of their passing. Rows of college students sit in a classroom listening to a lecturer drone. Shoppers crowd into a store to take advantage of special holiday prices. In a corporate conference room, executives sit in leather chairs and stare impassively at reports projected on a computer screen. The crew of Apollo 13 lived in a high-tech environment filled with multiple controls and few comforts.

Many disciplines, including sociology, environmental psychology, ethology, human ecology, demography, and ecological psychology, affirm the important impact of environmental variables on human behavior (Bell et al., 2001; Gieryn, 2000; Sundstrom, et al., 1996; Werner, Brown, & Altman,

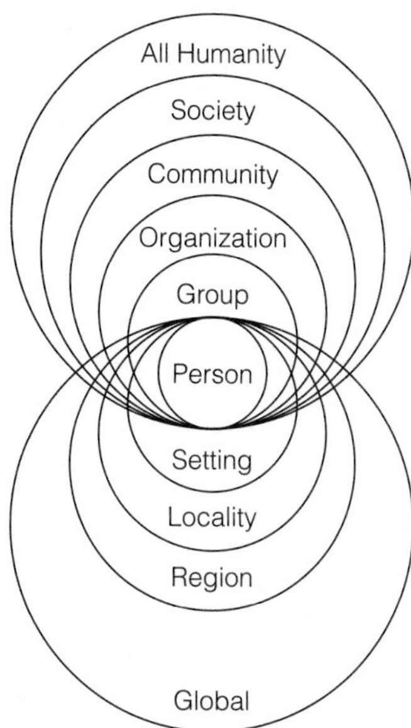


**FIGURE 15.1** A multi-level model of the embeddedness of individuals in both social aggregates (e.g., groups, organizations, communities) and in geographic domains (e.g., settings, localities, regions).

2002). All share a concern for the *setting* or *context* in which behavior occurs. Just as a group-level orientation assumes that individuals' actions are shaped by the groups to which they belong, an environmental orientation assumes that groups are shaped by their environments. As Figure 15.1 suggests, a multilevel analysis of human behavior recognizes that individuals are nested in a hierarchy of increasingly inclusive social aggregates, such as groups, organizations, and communities. But individuals and their groups also exist in a physical setting located in a particular geographic locality in a specific region of the world, and that place will eventually influence the group's dynamics and outcomes.

## Comfort in Contexts

Sometimes groups and the setting fit comfortably together. The place suits the group, leaving members free to focus on interpersonal and task dynamics. Other environments, in contrast, are less comfortable ones for the occupants. Humans' comfort zone is a relatively narrow one, and when groups must live and work on the edges of that zone changes in their dynamics are inevitable.

Physical settings are often said to have **ambience**, or *atmosphere*, for they can create a distinctive cognitive and emotional reaction in people who occupy these spaces (Schroeder, 2007).

> We have strong feelings in and about places. Some places make us feel good: glad to be there, relaxed, excited, warm all over. We are drawn to these places and return to them as often as we can. Other places make us feel bad: uncomfortable, insignificant, unhappy, out of place. We avoid these places and suffer if we have to be in them (Farbstein & Kantrowitz, 1978, p. 14)

Although people's evaluations of places vary depending on their culture, experiences, and personal preferences, most are based on two dimensions: How *pleasant* is the place (positive versus negative), and how *intense* is the place (arousing versus relaxing)? First, a group environment that is orderly, tastefully decorated, clean, and spacious usually prompts a more favorable reaction than one that is poorly designed, shabby, unkempt, and odorous (see Figure 15.2). Second, whereas some places are restful, others are so stimulating that they arouse their occupants rather than relax them. The astronauts and engineers working in the control room at Houston all responded positively to their highly arousing habitat, and so they considered it an exhilarating place. Visitors to the control room, in contrast, often reacted negatively to its harsh lights, countless monitors, displays, and cacophony of voices issuing orders, relaying information, and asking questions. Few considered it boring or tranquil (Russell, 2003; Russell & Snodgrass, 1987).

Groups generally respond best, in terms of performance and satisfaction, in affectively pleasant situations. Studies of manufacturing teams in factories, students in classrooms, and workers in offices, for

---

**ambience** The psychological reaction (mood, feelings, emotions) evoked by a setting.

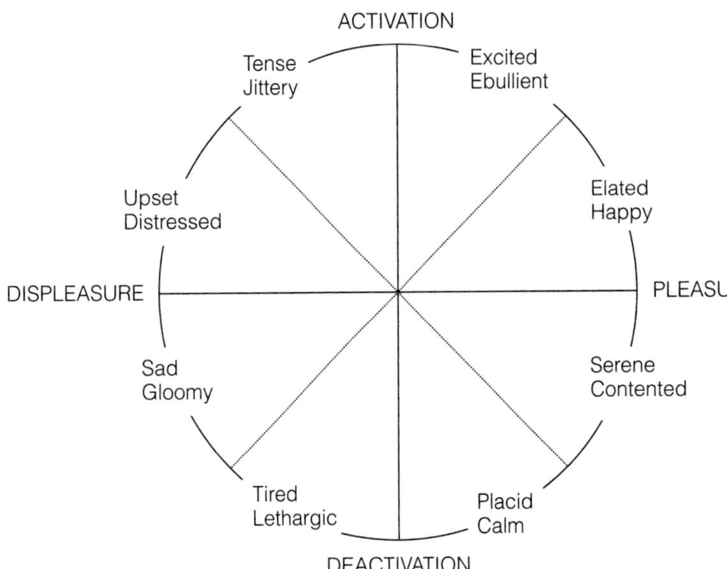


**FIGURE 15.2** Core affect experienced by people in various types of group environments.

SOURCE: Russell, J. A. 2003. "Core affect and the psychological construction of emotion." *Psychological Review, 110,* 145–172. doi: 10.1037/0033-295X.110.1.145.

example, have found that they respond better when working in attractive spaces that are visually interesting rather than drab (Sundstrom et al., 1996). Physical features that stimulate or provoke positive emotions—including music, furnishings, art, decor, decorations, color, and lighting—tend to be associated with a range of positive group dynamics, including increased cohesion, improved communication, productivity, and reduced absenteeism (Brief & Weiss, 2002). An attractive environment is not, however, a requirement for group effectiveness. Many successful groups work, without problems, in relatively shabby settings. A too-pleasant environment may distract the group from the task at hand, providing counterproductive levels of comfort. Highly effective groups may also be so focused on the task that they can work anywhere, since what matters is the quality of their tools and their personnel rather than the setting (Bennis & Biederman, 1997).

Groups also thrive in stimulating, but not in excessively stimulating, spaces. Studies of groups living in harsh circumstances, such as teams stationed in Antarctica and explorers living for months on end in a confined space, complain more about the monotony of the environment than about the danger, discomfort, or isolation (Stuster, 1996). As one officer aboard a research ship wintering in the Arctic wrote, "Monotony was our enemy, and to kill time our endeavor; hardship there was none. . . . Monotony, as I again repeat, was the only disagreeable part of our wintering" (quoted in Mowat, 1977, p. 272). Such groups strive to make their environments more interesting, often by decorating common areas extensively. But too much stimulation can contribute to **overload** when complex, stimulating environments overwhelm group members (Greenberg & Firestone, 1977). In everyday situations, people cope with overload by reducing their contact with others, limiting the amount of information they notice and process, or ignoring aspects of the situation. In Apollo 13, the only way astronauts could control the overload was to sleep—which they rarely did.

These coping strategies are often effective. Individuals living in high-density settings who used screening strategies to limit their contact with other

---

**overload** A psychological reaction to situations and experiences that are so cognitively, perceptually, or emotionally stimulating that they tax or even exceed the individual's capacity to process incoming information.

people, for example, tended to be better adjusted than those who did not (Baum et al., 1982; Evans, Lepore, & Allen, 2000). In other cases, though, these strategies did not reduce members' stress. Men who coped with environmental stress by withdrawing from the very people who could have helped them cope with the situation (friends and loved ones), for example, were more maladjusted than men who did not withdraw (Evans et al., 1989; Lepore, Evans, & Schneider, 1991).

### Stressful Group Settings

People often report feeling rejuvenated and energized by the places that their groups occupy. They feel more at ease and content when they can spend time in places they feel attached to, including their homes, their rooms, or even cubicles in an office (Altman & Churchman, 1994; Carlopio, 1996). However, some aspects of the environment can be sources of **stress**—strain caused by environmental circumstances that threaten one's sense of well-being and safety. Groups do not exist in neutral, passive voids, but in fluctuating environments that are sometimes too hot, too cold, too impersonal, too intimate, too big, too little, too noisy, too quiet, too restrictive, or too open—but rarely just right (Evans & Stecker, 2004; Veitch et al., 2007).

**Temperature** One of the minor miseries of life occurs when people must work in a room that is either too hot or too cold. Although people generally rate temperatures from the mid-60s to the mid-80s Fahrenheit as "comfortable," temperatures that fall outside this range cause discomfort, irritability, and reduced productivity (Bell, 1992). When groups were assigned to work either in a room at normal temperature (72.4° F) or in a hot room (93.5° F), the overheated group members reported feelings of fatigue, sadness, and discomfort, whereas participants in the normal-temperature room reported feeling more elated, vigorous, and comfortable (Griffitt & Veitch, 1971). Studies have also suggested that extremes in temperature can reduce interpersonal attraction (Griffitt, 1970) and interfere with successful task performance (Parsons, 1976). One of the concomitants of high temperatures in groups is exposure to others' body odors—a sensation that most people find objectionable (McBurney, Levine, & Cavanaugh, 1977). The odor of men's sweat is perceived as particularly repugnant (Stevenson & Repacholi, 2003).

Groups tend to be more aggressive when they are hot, as colloquialisms like "hot under the collar" and "flaring tempers" suggest. Collective violence is seasonal, with more riots occurring in the summer than the winter (Anderson & Bushman, 1997; Rotton & Cohn, 2002). Groups may also disband when the environment they occupy becomes unpleasantly hot. In one study, researchers measured people's aggressiveness in a comfortable room versus a hot room. Instead of acting more aggressively in the hot room, the participants responded as rapidly as possible, so that they could escape the noxious environmental setting. The heat-stressed participants were angry, but they were so uncomfortable that their primary concern was to finish the experiment as quickly as possible (Baron & Bell, 1975, 1976; Bell, 1992).

Extreme temperatures are also physically harmful (Folk, 1974). When temperatures are high, people are more likely to suffer from exhaustion, stroke, and heart attacks. Extreme cold can lead to hypothermia and death. The Apollo 13 astronauts, for example, struggled to maintain their body heat at healthy levels when the loss of power forced them to turn off the cabin heaters. It was, as Lovell characteristically understated, "very uncomfortable. Basically, the cold made it uncomfortable" (quoted in Godwin, 2000, p. 109). Accounts of groups struggling in extremely cold natural environments, such as teams wintering over in Antarctica or mountain climbers, document the lethal effects of exposure to extremely cold temperatures.

---

**stress** Negative physiological, emotional, cognitive, and behavioral responses to circumstances that threaten—or are thought to threaten—one's sense of well-being and safety.

**Noise** The crew of the Apollo 13 lived with noise constantly during their five days in space. The Saturn V rockets were deafening, burning 3400 gallons of fuel per second. Once in orbit, the cabin was filled with the humming of computers, the whirring of fans and pumps circulating air and liquids, and the crackling of transmissions between the crew and COMCON, the flight controller back in Houston. There was also the one sound that signaled to the crew that something was wrong; Lovell described it as a "bang-whump-shudder" that was felt more than heard (Lovell & Kluger, 1994, p. 94).

*Noise* is any sound that is unwanted. Sounds in the range of 0 to 50 decibels (dB) are very soft and generally produce little irritation for the listener. Sounds of more than 80 dB, in contrast, may be bothersome enough to be called noise. In general, the louder the noise, the more likely it will produce distraction, irritation, and psychological stress (Cohen & Weinstein, 1981). Group communication becomes impossible in such environments, so members have problems coordinating their efforts. Coping with chronic noise also exacts a psychological toll. Groups in noisy places—people who work in noisy offices, families living in homes near airports, and children on playgrounds located near major highways—generally find that the noise has a disruptive impact on their social behaviors. People are less likely to interact with other people in noisy places, and they also tend to be less helpful (Edelstein, 2002; Mathews, Canon, & Alexander, 1974; Veitch, 1990).

Much of the unwanted sound in a group originates within the group itself. Depending on the qualities of the room, 15 people talking informally with one another will create so much noise that conversation between adjoining pairs is inhibited. When a conversing group passes by an individual who is attempting to perform a difficult task, the noise of the group can be distracting. People can often ignore ambient sounds, but speech is another matter. Neurological evidence indicates that even when people strive to deliberately ignore speech by refocusing attention on the task at hand some of their cognitive resources are being used to monitor the overheard conversation (Campbell, 2005).

People can cope with noise for short periods of time. When researchers bombarded people working on both simple and complex tasks with tape-recorded noise, the participants became so inured to the stimulus that it had no effect on their performance (Glass, Singer, & Pennebaker, 1977). Groups cannot, however, cope for long periods of time with noise. As "individuals expend 'psychic energy' in the course of the adaptive process," they become "less able to cope with subsequent environmental demands and frustrations" (Glass et al., 1977, p. 134). One investigation found that exposure to low levels of ambient noise in an office setting did not cause increases in stress, but people had trouble coping with other stressful events—an irritating boss or coworker, role ambiguities, or time pressures—when they worked in a noisy place (Leather, Beale, & Sullivan, 2003). Over time, exposure to loud noise is associated with substantial threats to health, including physical illnesses (headaches, heart disease, allergies, and digestive disorders), infant and adult mortality rates, mental illness, interpersonal conflict, and even impotence (Bronzaft, 2002; Wallenius, 2004).

**Dangerous Places** The astronauts sat atop millions of pounds of rocket fuel at launch, traveled though space in a thin-shelled spacecraft at speeds of nearly 25,000 miles an hour, and during reentry relied on a heat shield to deflect the heat away from the command module and parachutes that would slow the craft's descent. All the dangers were minimized through planning, design, and training, but one danger that all crews faced but could not protect themselves against was always present—a collision with a meteor.

Of all the possible disaster scenarios that astronauts and controllers consider in planning a mission, few are more ghastly—or more capricious, or more sudden, or more total, or more feared—than a surprise hit by a rogue meteor. At speeds encountered in Earth orbit, a cosmic sand grain no more than a tenth of an inch across would strike a spacecraft with an energetic wallop equivalent to a bowling ball traveling at 60 miles per hour on Earth (Lovell & Kluger, 1994, p. 94)

Groups sometimes live and work in places filled with dangers, both recognized and unknown. Some natural calamity, such as a flood, earthquake, or blizzard, may overtake a group. Some groups, too, work at jobs that are riskier than most: Miners, ship crews, police officers, and military units often live and work in circumstances that can be life threatening. The group, too, may occupy an inhospitable environment. Some people live in neighborhoods where violence and aggression are so commonplace that their lives are often at risk (Herzog & Chernick, 2000).

Groups generally cope with danger by taking precautions designed to make the situation safer. Astronauts, military combat squads, and explorers all minimize the possibility of exposure to danger by training, stressing cooperation among members, and monitoring each individual's connection to the group (Harrison & Connors, 1984; Suedfeld, 1987). In consequence, dangerous circumstances often promote an increased level of teamwork. During routine flights, astronauts and the mission specialists on the ground tend to adopt an "us versus them" orientation against each other (Bechtel, 2002). Disagreements and disputes are common, with both sides viewing the other side as stubborn and misinformed. These tensions dissolve, however, during the crucial moments of each mission, and they were nearly nonexistent during the flight of the Apollo 13—the crew and mission control worked together seamlessly to solve each problem as it arose. Groups that face dangerous circumstances but do not manage to work as a team to overcome their problems place themselves at risk (see Focus 15.1).

### Behavior Settings

The Apollo 13 was more than a metal spacecraft filled with expensive instrumentation and equipment. It was also a **behavior setting**—a physical location where people's actions are prescribed by the features and functions of the situation. The counter at a fast food restaurant, the waiting area in a doctor's office, a computer lab on a college campus, a conference room in a business office, and a bench in a park are all behavior settings, for once people enter these spaces, their behavior is shaped more by the space than by their personal characteristics. For example, when people enter a fast food restaurant, they join a line, place their order, pay for their food, and then find a table where they eat their meal. A group in a conference room sits in chairs, exchanges information, and eventually decides to adjourn. The astronauts, once they entered the Apollo 13, acted in ways that the situation required.

The concept of a behavior setting was developed by ecological psychologist Roger Barker and his colleagues in their studies of common interpersonal situations. Barker, after studying offices, homes, schools, neighborhoods, communities, and entire towns, concluded that most behavior—at least, most routine, ordinary behavior—is determined by the environmental settings in which it occurs. These behavior settings tend to be specific spatial areas—actual places where group members interact with one another. These places often have *boundaries*—such as walls, doors, or fences—that identify the edge of one behavior setting and possibly the beginning of the next. Some boundaries can also be temporal, as when a group is present only during a certain time (e.g., a group may occupy a classroom only on Mondays and Wednesdays from 9 to 10:30). Most settings also include both people (group members) and things (equipment, chairs, etc.); Barker called them both *components* of the setting. Barker noted that individuals and settings are often inseparable, for the meaning of actions often depends on the physical features of the situation, just as a situation takes its meaning from the individuals in the setting. Barker believed that people routinely follow a *program* that sequences their actions and reactions in behavior settings. They may, for example, make use of the settings' objects in very predictable, routine ways, as when people who enter a room with chairs in it tend to sit on them (Barker, 1968, 1987, 1990; Barker et al., 1978).

---

**behavior setting** As defined by Roger Barker in his theory of ecological psychology, a physically and temporally bounded social situation that determines the actions of the individuals in the setting.

### Focus 15.1 Why Is Mount Everest So Deadly to Groups?

*I felt disconnected from the climbers around me—emotionally, spiritually, physically—to a degree I hadn't experienced on any previous expedition. We were a team in name only, I'd sadly come to realize.*
—Jon Krakauer (1997, p. 163)

On May 10, 1996, two groups led by experts set off to scale Mount Everest, the highest peak in the world. One group, Adventure Consultants Guided Expedition, was led by Rob Hall, who had reached the summit of Mount Everest four times between 1990 and 1995. Scott Fischer was the leader of Mountain Madness Guided Expedition. Fischer was also an expert guide and climber.

Both teams met with disaster, caused in part by the dangerous environment of Mount Everest. Everest is subject to high winds, bitter temperatures, and icy conditions. Climbers prepare for the summit attempt at a camp high on the mountain, but they must reach the peak and return to that camp in a single day, because the chances of surviving a night on the summit of Everest are slim. But the teams were overtaken by an unexpectedly powerful storm as they descended and they could not reach the shelter of their camp. Several members of the team also suffered from a lack of oxygen, for the air is thin at that altitude. Everest climbers usually carry tanks of oxygen, but even these supplements cannot counteract the negative effects of climbing treacherous terrain 29,000 feet above sea level.

These negative environmental events interacted with negative group dynamics in both teams. Jon Krakauer (1997), a member of Hall's group, suggested that an inattention to teamwork may have contributed to the failure. Even though the climb is extremely dangerous and many who attempt it are killed, the groups did not practice together, did not establish routines for dealing with supplies (including oxygen), and did not set up contingency plans. A hierarchy of authority was not established, despite the possibility that one of the leaders could be injured. Hall and Fischer did not share their plans for the summit with the group, and they did not remain in contact with the other guides during the climb. The leaders of both teams also made errors in judgment, possibly due to inexperience, the ill effects of too little oxygen (hypoxia), and the desire to outdo the other team. Even though the climbers, before attempting the summit, agreed on a turnaround time—the time during the day when they must turn back from the summit if they were to reach their base safely before nightfall—Hall and Fischer ignored that deadline and continued on. The other guides recognized the danger in not returning at the turnaround time, but they did not feel that they had the authority to intervene. As a result, several climbers managed to reach the summit, but they were overtaken by the snowstorm during the descent and perished.

As Krakauer later described, a sense of isolation pervaded the camp on the night before the summit attempt:

> The roar of the wind made it impossible to communicate from one tent to the next. In this godforsaken place, I felt disconnected from the climbers around me—emotionally, spiritually, physically—to a degree I hadn't experienced on any previous expedition. We were a team in name only, I'd sadly come to realize. Although in a few hours we would leave camp as a group, we would ascend as individuals, linked to one another by neither rope nor any deep sense of loyalty. (Krakauer, 1997, p. 163)

Krakauer's foreboding proved prophetic. Everest claimed the lives of eight members of the two teams, including Rob Hall and Scott Fischer.

Not every physical setting is a behavior setting. Some situations are novel ones, which group members have never before encountered, so they have no expectations about how they should act. Some individuals, too, may enter a behavior setting, but they are not aware of the norms of the situation, or they simply do not accept them as guides for their own action. But in most cases, group members act in predictable, routine ways in such situations. Libraries, for example, are behavior settings because they create a readiness for certain types of action: One should be subdued, quiet, and calm when in a library. These normative expectations guide behavior directly, and in many cases, group members are not even aware of how the situation automatically channels their actions. To demonstrate this automatic, unconscious impact of place on people, researchers first showed people a picture of either a library or a railroad station. Later, their reaction times to various words, including words relevant to libraries (e.g., *quiet, still, whisper*), were measured. As expected, people recognized library-related words more quickly after seeing the picture of a library, suggesting that the picture activated norms pertaining to the situation (Aarts & Dijksterhuis, 2003).

**Synomorphy and Staffing** Barker and his colleagues noted that in some behavior settings, people are seamlessly embedded in the place itself. The cockpit of the Apollo 13, for example, was designed so that the astronauts could monitor all their instruments and reach all their controls. A fast food restaurant may use a system of guide chains and multiple cash registers to handle large numbers of customers efficiently. A classroom may contain areas where students can work on individual projects, a reading circle where the teacher can lead small groups, and an art area where students can easily access the supplies they need. In other behavior settings, however, the people do not fit the place. A classroom may have chairs bolted to the floors in rows, so the teacher can never have students work in small groups. An office may have windows that provide workers with a view of the city, but the light from the windows prevents them from reading their computer screens. A concert hall may have so few doors that concertgoers clog the exits. Barker used the word **synomorphy** to describe the degree of fit between the setting and its human occupants. When settings are high in synomorphy, the people fit into the physical setting and use its objects appropriately. The people and the place are unified. Settings that are low in synomorphy lack this unity, for the people do not mesh well with the physical features and objects in the place.

Allan Wicker's **staffing theory** draws on the concept of synomorphy to explain group performance (Wicker, 1979, 1987, 2002). Consider office workers in a small business, university, or government agency who are responsible for typing papers and reports, answering the telephone, duplicating materials, and preparing paperwork on budgets, schedules, appointments, and so on. If the number of people working in the office is sufficient to handle all these activities, then the setting is *optimally staffed*. But if, for example, telephones are ringing unanswered, reports are days late, and the photocopier is broken and no one knows how to fix it, then the office lacks "enough people to carry out smoothly the essential program and maintenance tasks" and is *understaffed* (Wicker, 1979, p. 71). On the other hand, if the number of group members exceeds that needed in the situation, the group is *overstaffed* (Sundstrom, 1987).

Table 15.1 summarizes staffing theory's predictions about the relationship between staffing and performance. Overstaffed groups may perform adequately—after all, so many extra people are available to carry out the basic functions—but overstaffing can lead to dissatisfaction with task-related activities and heightened rejection among group members. Understaffed groups, in contrast, often respond positively to the challenging workload. Instead of complaining about the situation, understaffed groups sometimes display increased involvement in their work and contribute more to the group's goals (Arnold & Greenberg, 1980; Wicker & August, 1995). Four-man groups, for example, when placed in an overstaffed situation (too few tasks to keep all members active), reported feeling less important, less involved in their work, less concerned with performance, and less needed. These effects were reversed in understaffed groups (Wicker et al., 1976). In another study, the increased

---

**synomorphy** In ecological psychology, the quality of the fit between the human occupants and the physical situation.

**staffing theory** An ecological analysis of behavior settings arguing that both understaffing (not enough people) and overstaffing (too many people) can be detrimental.

**TABLE 15.1 Group Members' Reactions to Understaffed and Overstaffed Work Settings**

| Reaction | Understaffed groups | Overstaffed groups |
|---|---|---|
| **Task performance** | Members engage in diligent, consistent, goal-related actions | Members are perfunctory, inconsistent, and sloppy |
| **Performance monitoring** | Members provide one another with corrective, critical feedback as needed | Members exhibit little concern for the quality of the group's performance |
| **Perceptions** | Members are viewed in terms of the jobs they do rather than their individual qualities | Members focus on the personalities and uniqueness of members rather than on the group |
| **Self-perceptions** | Members feel important, responsible, and capable | Members feel lowered self-esteem, with little sense of competence |
| **Attitude toward the group** | Members express concern over the continuation of the group | Members are cynical about the group and its functions |
| **Supportiveness** | Members are reluctant to reject those who are performing poorly | Members are less willing to help other members of the group |

SOURCE: Adapted from Barker, 1968; Wicker, 1979.

workload brought on by understaffing increased professionals' and long-term employees' involvement in their work, but understaffing also led to decreased commitment among new employees and blue-collar workers. Understaffing was also associated with more negative attitudes toward the group (Wicker & August, 1995). Staffing theory also explains why individuals who are part of smaller groups and organizations get more involved in their groups; for example, even though a large school offers more opportunities for involvement in small-group activities, the proportion of students who join school-based groups is higher in smaller schools (Gump, 1990).

How do groups cope with staffing problems? When researchers asked leaders of student groups this question, nearly 75% recommended recruiting more members or reorganizing the group as the best ways to deal with understaffing. Other solutions included working with other groups and adopting more modest group goals (see Figure 15.3). These leaders offered a wider range of solutions for overstaffing, including encouraging members to remain active in the group (often by assigning them specific duties), enforcing rules about participation, dividing

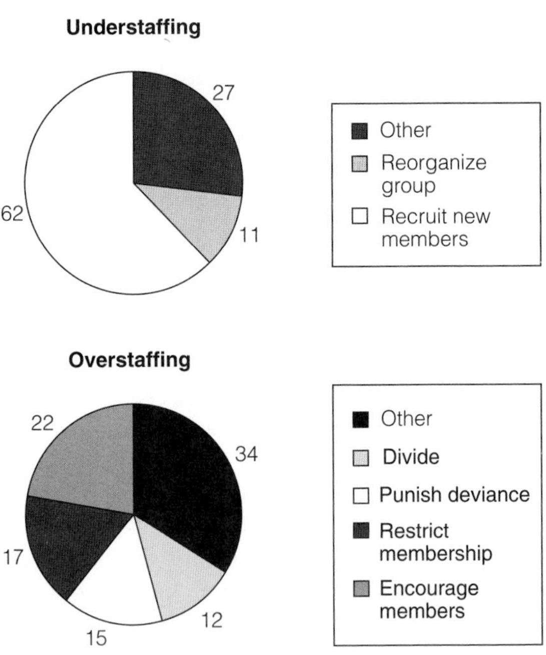


**FIGURE 15.3** Leaders' recommendations for dealing with understaffed groups and overstaffed groups.

SOURCE: "Group Staffing Levels and Responses to Prospective and New Group Members" by M. A. Cini, R. L. Moreland, & J. M. Levine, *Journal of Personality and Social Psychology*, 65. 1993 American Psychological Association. Reprinted by permission.

the group, taking in fewer members, changing the group's structure to include more positions, and adopting more ambitious goals (Cini, Moreland, & Levine, 1993).

**Designing Group Spaces** In many cases, people fail to recognize the close connection between individuals, groups, and their environment. They may realize that they are part of nature, but they do not as easily recognize their connection to an artificial, built environment (Mowday & Sutton, 1993; Schultz et al., 2004). Unfortunately, not all physical settings are designed so carefully as the Apollo 13, and as a result, many groups may not even realize that they are working and playing in areas that lack synomorphy.

Studies of all types of behavior settings—classrooms, factories, offices, playgrounds, highways, theaters, and so on—frequently find that these areas need to be redesigned to maximize the fit between the people and the place. Groups in workplace settings, for example, will increase their productivity if their work areas promote interaction, communication, task completion, and adaptation. The group members should have access to common spaces, where members can interact on a regular basis without interruption and interference. This *shared group space* should encourage the development of a group identity through decorative styles, boundaries, the use of signs and labels, and so on. The setting should also encourage communication among members. In many cases, buildings are designed around formally recognized locations for communication—such as conference rooms—but groups also meet informally and spontaneously, and these locations should be incorporated into the building's design. Many high-performance organizations go so far as to integrate work areas with other areas to promote additional interaction among group members, as when shared eating facilities and fitness facilities are included in the building's design. The setting should, however, promote rather than inhibit task performance. The materials and equipment needed for the group members to do their work should be readily available and in good working order (Becker, 2004; McCoy, 2002).

The kind of space needed by a group will also depend on the type of tasks the group must accomplish. A group that is working on tasks that require high levels of collaboration and interaction among members will need a very different space than a group working on divisible tasks that are best solved by individuals who can concentrate on them for long periods of time without interruption. Francis Duffy (1997), by examining a number of groups working in large corporations, identified four types of groups that needed four types of spaces—hives, cells, dens, and clubs.

- *Hives.* Members who function as "worker bees" by performing divisible, highly structured tasks require little interaction with other group members. Such groups function well in open, cubicle-type offices where each individual has a defined, relatively small workspace.
- *Cells.* Members working on complex, long-term, relatively individualized projects need private spaces to carry out their work. They may also be able to work by telecommuting from a home office.
- *Dens.* When members who are similar in terms of skills and responsibilities work together on collective tasks and projects, they need an open space that all members share. So long as the task is highly structured and is facilitated by a high rate of collaboration and interaction, such groups do not need individualized areas.
- *Clubs.* Members who are talented, well trained, or possess very specialized skills often work on diverse tasks and projects that vary greatly in their collaborative demands. Their work space must be flexible, permitting them to collaborate as needed but also to secure privacy.

Duffy found that club offices tend to be the most productive, but he added that nearly all group spaces must be changed to increase the fit between the group and its tasks. Even the most carefully designed and implemented setting may fail, as the group and its tasks change, to meet members' needs and so require revision.

## SPACES: THE ECOLOGY OF GROUPS

*Ecology* is the science of the interrelationship of organisms and their habitats (Lawrence, 2002). Ecologists examine how organisms—whether they are plant, animal, or microbe—interact with and adapt to other organisms in their environment and to the environment itself. Similarly, those who study the ecology of small groups explore how individuals interact with and adapt to the group habitat. Just as frogs issue their croaks from their favorite places in the stream, and birds neatly space themselves along a telephone wire, so humans display consistent patterns of spacing and seating when immersed in a group habitat.

### Personal Space

Anthropologist Edward T. Hall (1966) argued that much of our behavior is shaped by a "hidden dimension." In Apollo 13, this dimension determined where each astronaut sat as he carried out scheduled tasks; how crew members moved through the tunnel between the command module and the service module; where they positioned themselves when they looked out the windows of their ship as it passed over the surface of the moon. What is this hidden dimension? *Space.*

People prefer to keep some space between themselves and others. This **personal space** provides a boundary that limits the amount of physical contact between people. This boundary extends farther in the front of the person than behind, but the individual is always near the center of this invisible buffer zone. Personal space is portable, but it is actively maintained and defended. When someone violates our personal space, we tend to take steps to correct this problem (Aiello, 1987). The term *personal space* is something of a misnomer, as the process actually refers to distances that people maintain between one another. Hence, it is an *interpersonal space* (Patterson, 1975). Some people seem to require more space than others. Spatial processes operate across a broad range of people and situations.

**Interpersonal Zones** Different group activities require different amounts of personal space. Hall, in describing these variations, proposed four types of interpersonal zones (see Table 15.2). The *intimate zone* is appropriate only for the most involving and personal behaviors, such as arm wrestling and whispering. The *personal zone*, in contrast, is reserved for a wide range of small-group experiences, such as discussions with friends, interaction with acquaintances, and conversation. More routine transactions are conducted in the *social zone*. Meetings held over large desks, formal dining, and professional presentations to small groups generally take place in this zone. The *public zone* is reserved for even more formal meetings, such as stage presentations, lectures, or addresses.

Table 15.2 also adds a fifth zone to those described by Hall. In the years since Hall proposed his taxonomy of interpersonal zones, groups have begun to meet more frequently in the *remote zone*. Many groups now exist, in whole or in part, in a virtual environment. Instead of interacting face-to-face or even via voice communication, these groups use computer-based tools such as email, chat rooms, social networking sites, and other multi-user support interfaces. The members of these groups are not physically present with each other, making online groups considerably different—at least spatially—than face-to-face groups. The astronauts, for example, communicated with COMCON from a distance—a great distance, in fact. They used voice messages, in some cases, but they were also in touch using communication technologies that allowed them to send and receive information via computers (see Focus 15.2).

Closer, smaller spaces are generally reserved for friendlier, more intimate interpersonal activities. As a result, cohesive groups tend to occupy smaller spaces than noncohesive gatherings (Evans & Howard, 1973); extraverted people maintain smaller

---

**personal space** The area that individuals maintain around themselves into which others cannot intrude without arousing discomfort.

**TABLE 15.2 Types of Social Activities That Occur in Each Interpersonal Zone**

| Zone | Distance | Characteristics | Typical Activities |
|---|---|---|---|
| **Intimate** | Touching to 18 inches | Sensory information concerning the other is detailed and diverse; stimulus person dominates perceptual field | Sex, hugging, massage, comforting, jostling, handshakes, slow dancing |
| **Personal** | 18 inches to 4 feet | Other person can be touched if desired; gaze can be directed away from the other person with ease | Conversations, discussion, car travel, viewing performances, watching television |
| **Social** | 4 feet to 12 feet | Visual inputs begin to dominate other senses; voice levels are normal; appropriate distance for many informal social gatherings | Dining, meeting with business colleagues, interacting with a receptionist |
| **Public** | 12 feet or more | All sensory inputs are beginning to become less effective; voices may require amplification; facial expressions unclear | Lectures, addresses, plays, dance recitals |
| **Remote** | Different locations | Primarily verbal inputs; facial and other behavioral and nonverbal cues unavailable | Electronic discussions, conference calls, telephone voice mail, e-mail, online gaming communities |

SOURCE: Adapted from E. T. Hall, 1966.

distances from others than do introverted ones (Patterson & Sechrest, 1970); people who wish to create a friendly, positive impression usually choose smaller distances than do less friendly people (Evans & Howard, 1973); and groups of friends tend to stand closer to one another than do groups of strangers (Edney & Grundmann, 1979). Physical distance has little impact on remote groups, although individuals communicating via computer respond differently when their interface becomes informationally richer by including voice and video information (Thurlow, Lengel, & Tomic, 2004).

Why does distance influence so many group processes? One explanation, based on an **equilibrium model of communication**, suggests that personal space, body orientation, and eye contact define the level of intimacy of any interaction. If group members feel that a low level of intimacy is appropriate, they may sit far apart, make little eye contact, and assume a relatively formal posture. If, in contrast, the members are relaxing and discussing personal topics, they may move close together, make more eye contact, and adopt more relaxed postures (Argyle & Dean, 1965; Patterson, 1996). By continually adjusting their nonverbal and verbal behavior, group members can keep the intimacy of their interactions at the level they desire (Giles Wadleigh, 1999).

**Men, Women, and Distance** Would the amount of personal space maintained by the astronauts in Apollo 13 have differed if they had been women? Probably, for studies suggest that women's personal spaces tend to be smaller than men's (Hayduk, 1983). Relative to men, women allow others to get closer to them, and they approach other people more closely. Men also tend to approach women more closely than other men. Women tend to take up less space by sitting with their arms close to their sides and by crossing their legs, whereas men claim more space by assuming expansive, open positions

---

**equilibrium model of communication** An explanation of distancing behavior in interpersonal settings arguing that the amount of eye contact, the intimacy of the topic influence the amount of personal space required by interactants.

## Focus 15.2 Is Cyberspace a Behavior Setting?

*I have gotten to know my guildmates in our chat channel so much better, to the point where I feel have made new friends among people I barely knew before.*

—Kwill, a player on EverQuest, a massively multiplayer online fantasy game

Times have changed since Roger Barker studied groups interacting in behavior settings and Edward Hall offered up his theory of interpersonal distances. Neither researcher examined one particular type of setting for the simple reason that it did not exist in their era: cyberspace. The groups they studied interacted in physical, geographical spaces where group members encountered one another in the same location. **Online groups**, in contrast to **offline groups**, meet in cyberspace; they rely on computer-based information technologies to create channels of communication among individuals who do not occupy the same physical location.

When groups began to meet via computer, experts predicted one of two possible outcomes for these groups. Some suggested that such groups would be relatively uninvolving for members and their unique locale would prevent these gatherings from even remotely resembling "real" groups. The Internet provided a way to exchange ideas, opinions, and information, but online meetings were lower in **social presence** than face-to-face meetings; members did not "perceive (sense) the actual presence of the communication participants and the consequent appreciation of an interpersonal relationship" (Lowry et al., 2006, p. 633). When group members interacted via computers, their nonverbal reactions, their personal characteristics, and even their identities remained unknown to others. The members of online groups could not touch one another, see what they were wearing, mingle together informally, display nonverbal signs of boredom or mirth, or any of the other forms of connection that were possible when collocated.

Other experts, in contrast, expected online groups would be unstructured, chaotic encounters, with many individuals using the anonymity of the online environment to escape the usual constraints that govern more traditional forms of interaction. Shielded from scrutiny, people would display more openly their emotions—which would likely be hostile ones in most cases, as people who disagreed with each other would "flame" one another.

Experience, however, proved both of these perspectives wrong. Online groups, like any group, include multiple individuals who are connected to one another by and within social relationships, so they meet the basic criteria for any group. Members often become very involved in such groups, and react negatively when they are denied membership in such groups (*cyberostracism*, see Chapter 3). Individuals, even when they interact only via a computer network, come to develop strong affective bonds with one another (Chapter 4)—although in some cases relationships that start online move offline. Online groups are structured groups, complete with norms, roles, and intermember relations (Chapter 6). Members of online groups are as likely to conform as members of offline groups—indeed, they are more conforming in some cases (Chapter 7). Online individuals react with heightened productivity when joined by others, and they usually brainstorm in much the same way offline groups do (Chapter 10). Distributed teams (Chapter 12) are, in some cases, more productive than are teams that meet frequently in face-to-face settings, and the same kinds of social identity processes seen in offline groups influence actions of the members of online ones (Chapter 17). Groups on the web also lean to the unselfish side, for they collaborate in open markets such as e-Bay, play together in online multiplayer games, and share knowledge and information as contributors to blogs and wikis.

Members of an online group do not interact in precisely the same way as do members of a group that meet together face-to-face, but then again neither do groups that occupy widely different physical environments—a group in an office building will act differently than this same group walking on a golf course or sitting in a darkened movie theater. Cyberspace, it turns out, is just another behavior setting where group members come together for interaction, influence, and action.

---

**online group** A group whose members communicate with one another solely or primarily through computer-based information technologies that create a virtual group experience regardless of the members' geographic locations.

**offline group** A group whose members interact with one another in face-to-face, collocated settings.

**social presence** The degree to which individuals feel that they are in the presence of another person.

(Henley, 1995). The interactions between the men of Apollo 13 occurred almost exclusively in the personal zone, except when Lovell hugged the shivering Haise, who had become increasingly ill during the mission.

**Status** The type of relationship linking group members plays a particularly significant role in determining personal space (Hall, Coats, & LeBeau, 2005). A study of U.S. Naval personnel, for example, found that subordinates needed more space when conversing with superiors than when conversing with peers (Dean, Willis, & Hewitt, 1975). Furthermore, many studies suggest that when people are with friends rather than with strangers or mere acquaintances, their personal space needs become relatively small. This effect occurs in both same-sex and mixed-sex dyads, although the effect is more pronounced when women interact (Hayduk, 1983).

**Culture** Hall (1966) argued that cultures differ in their use of space. People socialized in the *contact cultures* of the Mediterranean, the Middle East, and Latin America prefer strong sensory involvement with others, and so they seek direct social contact whenever possible. In contrast, residents in such *noncontact cultures* as the United States, England, and Germany try to limit their spatial openness with others. Given that the crew of Apollo 13 included only Americans, they shared similar norms about how much distance should be maintained. Crews on space stations, such as Mir or Salyut, involve astronauts from different cultural backgrounds, so misunderstandings caused by spatial confusions may be more common (Remland, Jones, & Brinkman, 1995). Culture also influences how people interact in the remote zone, for people with different cultural backgrounds vary in how much emotion, personal information, and responsiveness to others they express when communicating via the Internet (Reeder et al., 2004).

### Reactions to Spatial Invasion

Individuals cannot always protect their personal space from intrusion by others. In some cases, group members may find themselves in places where the available space is so limited that people cannot maintain appropriate distances between one another. In other instances, the group may have sufficient space, but for some reason, a member approaches so closely that he or she seems "too close for comfort."

How do group members react to such intrusions? High density does not always lead to feelings of crowding and other negative interpersonal outcomes. **Density** refers to a characteristic of the environment—literally, the number of people per unit of space. **Crowding**, in contrast, refers to a psychological, experiential state that occurs when people *feel* that they do not have enough space (Stokols, 1972, 1978). Although the density of a given situation, such as a party, a rock concert, or Apollo 13, may be very high, the interactants may not feel crowded at all. Yet two people sitting in a large room may still report that they feel crowded if they expected to be alone, are engaged in some private activity, or dislike each other intensely. Passengers on a train when density was low—there were plenty of empty seats in the car—displayed the negative effects of crowding (e.g., more negative mood, evidence of stress, loss of motivation) if others were seated near them in their row (Evans & Wener, 2007).

**Arousal and Stress** Physiologically speaking, what happens to people when they find themselves in high-density situations? In many cases, they become *aroused*—their heart rate and blood pressure increase, they breathe faster, and they sometimes perspire more (Evans, 1979). This link between personal space violations and arousal was confirmed in a study of men using a public restroom (Middlemist, Knowles, & Matter, 1976). Reasoning that arousal would lead to a general muscular contraction that would delay urination onset and reduce its duration, the researchers set up a situation in which men using wall-mounted urinals were joined by a confederate

---

**density** The number of individuals per unit of space.
**crowding** A psychological reaction that occurs when individuals feel that the amount of space available to them is insufficient for their needs.

who used either the next receptacle (*near condition*) or one located farther down the wall (*far condition*). When onset times and duration for men in the near and far condition were compared with those same times for men in a no-confederate control condition, the researchers found that personal space invasion significantly increased general arousal.

This arousal is not always stressful, however. If the intruder is a close friend, a relative, or an extremely attractive stranger, closeness can be a plus (Willis, 1966). Similarly, if we believe that the other person needs help or is attempting to initiate a friendly relationship, we tend to react positively rather than negatively (Murphy-Berman & Berman, 1978). These findings suggest that the label that individuals use to interpret their arousal determines the consequences of crowding. If people attribute the arousal to others' standing too close, then they will conclude, "I feel crowded." If, in contrast, they explain the arousal in some other way—"I drank too much coffee," "I'm in love," "I'm afraid our ship will burn up in the atmosphere," and so on—they will not feel crowded.

Researchers tested this attributional model of crowding by seating five-person groups in chairs placed either 20 inches apart or touching at the legs. These researchers told the groups that an inaudible noise would be played in the room as they worked on several tasks. They told some groups that the noise was detectable at the unconscious level and would lead to stressful, discomforting effects. They told other groups that the noise would have relaxing and calming effects, or they gave no explanation for the noise at all. The groups were not actually exposed to any noise, but, crowded groups who thought that the noise would arouse them felt less crowded. Why? Because they attributed the arousal caused by crowding to the supposed noise rather than to the proximity of other people (Worchel & Yohai, 1979; see also Worchel & Teddlie, 1976).

**Intensity** Jonathan Freedman also argued that high-density situations are not always aversive situations. His **density–intensity hypothesis** suggested that high density merely intensifies whatever is already occurring in the group situation (Freedman, 1975, 1979). If something in the situation makes the group interaction unpleasant, high density will make the situation seem even more unpleasant. If the situation is a very pleasant one, however, high density will make the good situation even better. Freedman tested this notion by placing groups of people in large or small rooms and then manipulating some aspect of the group interaction to create either unpleasantness or pleasantness. In one investigation, groups of 6 to 10 high school students sat on the floor of either a large room or a small room. Each delivered a speech and then received feedback from the other group members. Freedman made certain that in some groups, the feedback was always positive, whereas in other groups, the feedback was always negative. When the participants later rated the room and their group, Freedman discovered that crowding *intensified* the effects of the feedback: People liked their group the most when they received positive feedback under high-density conditions, and they liked their group the least when they got negative feedback when crowded. Furthermore, Freedman found that these effects were clearest for all-female groups as opposed to all-male or mixed-sex groups (see also Storms & Thomas, 1977).

**Controllability** Crowded situations are unsettling because they undermine group members' control over their experiences. Crowded situations bring people into contact with others they would prefer to avoid, and if working groups cannot cope with the constraints of their environment, they may fail at their tasks. Group members can therefore cope with crowding by increasing their sense of control over the situation. Just as a sense of high personal control helps people cope with a range of negative life events, including failure, divorce, illness, and accidents, people are less stressed by environmental threats when they feel they can

---

**density–intensity hypothesis** An explanation of crowding proposed by Jonathan Freedman, predicting that high density makes unpleasant situations more unpleasant but pleasant situations more pleasant.

control their circumstances (Evans & Lepore, 1992; Rodin & Baum, 1978; Schmidt & Keating, 1979; Sherrod & Cohen, 1979).

Researchers tested the benefits of controllability by asking groups of six men to work on tasks in either a small room or a large one. One task required participating in a 15-minute discussion of censorship, and the second involved blindfolding a member and letting him wander about within a circle formed by the rest of the group. To manipulate control, one of the participants was designated the *coordinator*; he was responsible for organizing the group, dealing with questions concerning procedures, and blindfolding members for the second task. A second participant, the *terminator*, was given control over ending the discussion and regulating each member's turn in the center of the circle. Significantly, the two group members who could control the group tasks through coordination or termination were not as bothered by the high-density situation as the four group members who were given no control (Rodin, Solomon, & Metcalf, 1978).

**Interference** Crowding is particularly troublesome when it interferes with the group's work. The Apollo 13 crew, for example, did not react negatively to their high-density living conditions so long as the crowding did not undermine their group's effectiveness. Difficulties only occurred when they needed to fix a problem—such as a hatch that would not secure properly, where there was only enough room for one person to reach it. Similarly, studies that find no ill effects of crowding generally study groups working on coaction problems that require little interaction. Studies that require the participants to complete interactive tasks, in contrast, tend to find negative effects of crowding (e.g., Heller, Groff, & Solomon, 1977; Paulus et al., 1976).

Researchers demonstrated the importance of interference by deliberately manipulating both density and interaction. All-male groups worked in either a small laboratory room or in a large one collating eight-page booklets. The order of the pages was not constant, however, but was determined by first selecting a card that had the order of pages listed in a random sequence. In the *low-interaction condition*, each person had all eight stacks of pages and a set of sequence cards. In the *high-interaction condition*, the stacks were located at points around the room, so participants had to walk around the room in unpredictable patterns. In fact, the participants often bumped into one another while trying to move from one stack to another. The interference created in the high-interaction condition led to decrements in task performance—provided that density was high (Heller et al., 1977).

## Seating Arrangements

At launch and during most key maneuvers, the three Apollo 13 astronauts were seated side-by-side in front of the control panel, and the seat on the left was reserved for the mission commander, or the officer who was piloting the ship. As Robert Sommer (1967) noted, seating arrangements play a large role in creating a group's ecology. Although often unrecognized, or simply taken for granted, seating patterns influence interaction, communication, and leadership in groups.

**Seating Patterns and Social Interaction** Groups behave very differently if their seating pattern is sociopetal rather than sociofugal. **Sociopetal spaces** promote interaction among group members by heightening eye contact, encouraging verbal communication, and facilitating the development of intimacy. **Sociofugal spaces**, in contrast, discourage interaction among group members and can even drive participants out of the situation altogether. A secluded booth in a quiet restaurant, a park bench, or five chairs placed in a tight circle are sociopetal environments, whereas classrooms organized in rows, movie theaters, waiting rooms, and airport waiting areas are sociofugal. Sommer concluded that airport seating was deliberately designed to disrupt

---

**sociopetal spaces** Environmental settings that promote interaction among group members, including seating arrangements that facilitate conversation.

**sociofugal spaces** Environmental settings that discourage or prevent interaction among group members.

interaction. He noted that even people seated side by side on airport chairs cannot converse comfortably:

> The chairs are either bolted together and arranged in rows theater-style facing the ticket counters, or arranged back-to-back, and even if they face one another they are at such distances that comfortable conversation is impossible. The motive for the sociofugal arrangement appears the same as that in hotels and other commercial places—to drive people out of the waiting areas into cafés, bars, and shops where they will spend money (Sommer, 1969, pp. 121–122).

Group members generally prefer sociopetal arrangements (Batchelor & Goethals, 1972; Giesen & McClaren, 1976). This preference, however, depends in part on the type of task undertaken in the situation (Ryen & Kahn, 1975; Sommer, 1969). As Figure 15.4 shows, Sommer found that corner-to-corner and face-to-face arrangements were preferred for conversation, and side-by-side seating was selected for cooperation. Competing pairs either took a direct, face-to-face orientation (apparently to stimulate competition) or tried to increase interpersonal distance, whereas coacting pairs preferred arrangements that involved a visual separation. As one student stated, such an arrangement "allows staring into space and not into my neighbor's face" (Sommer, 1969, p. 63). Similar choices were found with round tables.

Groups in sociopetal environments act differently than groups in sociofugal spaces. In one study, dyads whose members sat facing each other seemed more relaxed, but dyads whose members sat at a 90-degree angle to each other were more affiliative (Mehrabian & Diamond, 1971). When researchers compared circle seating with L-shaped seating, the circle was associated with feelings of confinement but fostered greater interpersonal attraction (Patterson et al., 1979; Patterson, Roth, & Schenk, 1979). People seated in the L-shaped groups, on the other hand, engaged in more self-manipulative behaviors and fidgeting, and they paused more during group discussions. Overall, the positive effects of the circle arrangement relative to the L-shaped arrangement were stronger in female groups than in male groups.

**Men, Women, and Seating Preferences** Women and men diverge, to a degree, in their preferences for seating arrangements. Men prefer to position themselves across from those they like, and women

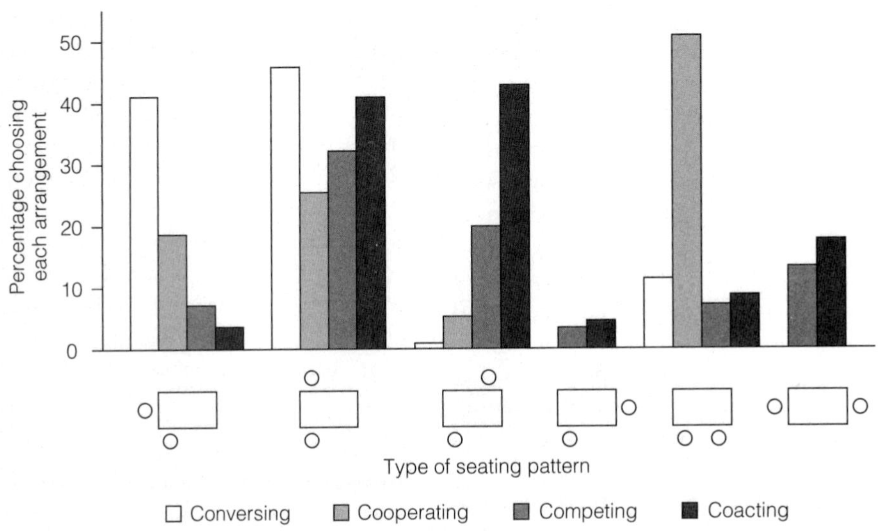


**FIGURE 15.4** Preference for various types of seating arrangements when individuals expected to converse, cooperate, compete, or coact.

SOURCE: Sommer, 1969.

prefer adjacent seating positions (Sommer, 1959). Conversely, men prefer that strangers sit by their side, whereas women feel that strangers should sit across from them. Researchers studied the confusion that this difference can cause by sending confederates to sit at the same table as solitary women and men working in a library. After a brief and uneventful period, the confederate left. When a second researcher then asked the participant some questions about the confederate and the library, the researchers discovered that men were the least favorably disposed toward the stranger who sat across from them but that women reacted more negatively to the stranger who sat next to them (Fisher & Byrne, 1975). Clearly, group members should be sensitive to the possibility that their spatial behaviors will be misinterpreted by others and should be willing to make certain that any possible misunderstandings will be short-lived.

**Communication Patterns** Bernard Steinzor's early studies of face-to-face discussion groups indicated that spatial patterns also influence communication rates in groups. Although at first he could find few significant relationships between seat location and participation in the discussion, one day, while watching a group, he noticed a participant change his seat to sit opposite someone he had argued with during the previous meeting. Inspired by this chance observation, Steinzor (1950) reanalyzed his findings and discovered that individuals tended to speak after the person seated opposite them spoke. He reasoned that we have an easier time observing and listening to the statements of people who are seated in a position central to our visual field, so that their remarks serve as stronger stimuli for our own ideas and statements. The tendency for members of a group to comment immediately after the person sitting opposite them is now termed the **Steinzor effect**. The phenomenon appears to occur primarily in leaderless discussion groups, for later research has suggested that when a leader is present group members direct more comments to their closest neighbor (Hearne, 1957).

**Head-of-the-Table Effect** Where should the leader sit—at the head of the table or in one of the side chairs? With great consistency, leaders seek out the head of the table. Sommer (1969), for example, found that people appointed to lead small discussion groups tended to select seats at the head of the table. Those who move to this position of authority also tend to possess more dominant personalities (Hare & Bales, 1963), talk more frequently, and often exercise greater amounts of interpersonal influence (Strodtbeck & Hook, 1961). When people are shown pictures of groups with members seated around a rectangular table, when asked to identify the likely leader they tend to settle on the person sitting at the head of the table (Jackson, Engstrom, & Emmers-Sommer, 2007).

Sommer suggested two basic explanations for this intriguing **head-of-the-table effect**—*perceptual prominence* and the *social meaning* associated with sitting at the head of the table. Looking first at prominence, Sommer suggested that in many groups, the chair at the end of the table is the most salient position in the group and that the occupant of this space can therefore easily maintain greater amounts of eye contact with more of the group members, can move to the center of the communication network, and (as the Steinzor effect suggests) can comment more frequently. Moreover, in Western cultures, where most studies of leadership have been conducted, the chair at the head of the table is implicitly defined to be the most appropriate place for the leader to sit. Sommer was careful to note that this norm may not hold in other societies, but in most Western cultures, leadership and the head of the table go together.

Both factors play a role in the head-of-the-table effect. Investigators manipulated salience by having

**Steinzor effect** The tendency for members of a group to comment immediately after the person sitting opposite them.

**head-of-the-table effect** The tendency for group members to associate the leadership role and its responsibilities with the seat located at the head of the table; as a result, individuals who occupy such positions tend to emerge as leaders in groups without designated leaders.

two persons sit on one side of the table and three on the other side. Although no one sat in the end seat, those seated on the two-person side of the table could maintain eye contact with three of the group members, but those on the three-person side could focus their attention on only two members. Therefore, group members on the two-person side should be able to influence others more and hence be the more likely leaders. As predicted, 70% of the leaders came from the two-person side, and only 30% came from the three-person side (Howells & Becker, 1962).

In another study, the tendency for people to automatically associate the head of the table with leadership was examined by arranging for confederates to voluntarily choose or be assigned to the end position or to some other position around a table (Nemeth & Wachtler, 1974). These confederates then went about systematically disagreeing with the majority of the group members on the topic under discussion, and the extent to which the participants altered their opinions to agree with the deviant was assessed. Interestingly, the deviants succeeded in influencing the others only when they had freely chosen to sit in the head chair. Apparently, disagreeing group members sitting at the "side" locations around the table were viewed as "deviants," whereas those who had the confidence to select the end chair were viewed more as "leaders" (Riess, 1982; Riess & Rosenfeld, 1980).

## LOCATIONS: GROUP TERRITORIALITY

When Lovell, Swigert, and Haise entered the Apollo 13 spaceship for their mission, they entered a cylinder filled with computers, controls, equipment, and supplies. But within days, this physical space was transformed into the group's territory. The men stowed personal gear in their lockers. The controls over which they had primary responsibility became "their controls," and they were wary when any of the other crew members would carry out procedures in their area. Haise, more so than either Lovell and Swigert, became attached to *Aquarius*, the lunar excursion module. When the time came to jettison the module prior to their descent, Haise collected small objects as momentos, and mission control remarked, "Farewell, *Aquarius*, and we thank you" (Lovell & Kluger, 1994, p. 329).

Like so many animals—birds, wolves, lions, seals, geese, and even seahorses—human beings develop proprietary orientations toward certain geographical locations and defend these areas against intrusion by others. A person's home, a preferred seat in a classroom, a clubhouse, a football field, and *Aquarius* are all **territories**—specific areas that an individual or group claims, marks, and defends against intrusion by others.

When people establish a territory, they generally try to control who is permitted access. As Irwin Altman noted, however, the degree of control depends on the type of territory (see Table 15.3). Control is highest for *primary territories*—areas that are maintained and "used exclusively by individuals or groups . . . on a relatively permanent basis" (Altman, 1975, p. 112). People develop strong *place attachments* to these areas, for they feel safe, secure, and comfortable when in them (Hernández et al., 2007). Individuals maintain only a moderate amount of control over their *secondary territories*. These areas are not owned by the group members, but because the members use such an area regularly, they come to consider it "theirs." College students, for example, often become very territorial about their seats in a class (Haber, 1980, 1982). Control over *public territories* is even more limited. Occupants can prevent intrusion while they are physically present, but they relinquish all claims when they leave. A bathroom stall or a spot on the beach can be claimed when occupied, but when the occupant leaves, another person can step in and claim the space. (Brown, 1987, thoroughly reviewed much of the work on human territoriality.)

---

**territory** A specific geographic area that individuals or groups of individuals claim, mark, and defend against intrusion by others.

**TABLE 15.3 Three Types of Territories Established and Protected by Individuals and Groups**

| Type | Degree of Control | Duration of Claim | Examples |
|---|---|---|---|
| **Primary** | *High*: Occupants control access and are very likely to actively defend this space. | *Long-term*: Individuals maintain control over the space on a relatively permanent basis; owner ship is often involved. | A family's house, a bedroom, a clubhouse, a dorm room, a study |
| **Secondary** | *Moderate*: Individuals who habitually use a space come to consider it "theirs." Reaction to intrusions is milder. | *Temporary but recurrent*: Others may use the space, but must vacate the area if the usual occupant requests. | A table in a bar, a seat in a classroom, a regularly used parking space, the sidewalk in front of your home |
| **Public** | *Low*: Although the occupant may prevent intrusion while present, no expectation of future use exists. | *None*: The individual or group uses the space only on the most temporary basis and leaves behind no markers. | Elevator, beach, public telephone, playground, park, bathroom stall, restaurant counter |

SOURCE: *The Environment and Social Behavior* by Irving Altman, Brooks/Cole Publishing Company, 1976.

## Group Territories

Territoriality is, in many cases, a group-level process. Instead of an individual claiming an area and defending it against other individuals, a group will lay claim to its turf and prevent other groups from using it. South American howler monkeys, for example, live together in bands of up to 20 individuals, and these groups forage within a fairly well-defined region. The bands themselves are cohesive and free of internal strife, but when another group of howlers is encountered during the day's wandering, a fight begins. Among howlers, this territorial defense takes the form of a "shouting match," in which the members of the two bands simply howl at the opposing group until one band—usually the invading band—retreats. Boundaries are rarely violated, because each morning and night, the monkeys raise their voices in a communal and far-carrying howling session (Carpenter, 1958).

Human groups have also been known to territorialize areas. Classic sociological analyses of gangs, for example, often highlighted the tendency for young men to join forces in defense of a few city blocks that they considered to be their turf (Thrasher, 1927; Whyte, 1943; Yablonsky, 1962). Many gangs took their names from a street or park located at the very core of their claimed sphere of influence and sought to control areas around this base. Contemporary gangs, despite changes in size, violence, and involvement in crime, continue to be rooted to specific locations. Gangs in San Diego, California, for example, can be traced to specific geographical origins: the Red Steps and the Crips to Logan Heights and the Sidros to San Ysidro (Sanders, 1994).

Gangs mark their territories through the placement of graffiti, or "tags," and also attack intruders. Philadelphia researchers found that the number of graffiti mentioning the local gang's name increased as one moved closer and closer to the gang's home base, suggesting that the graffiti served as *territorial markers*, warning intruders of the dangers of encroachment. This marking, however, was not entirely successful, for neighboring gangs would occasionally invade a rival's territory to spray-paint their own names over the territorial markers of the home gang or, at least, to append a choice obscenity. In fact, the frequency of graffiti attributable to outside groups provided an index of group power and prestige, for the more graffiti written by opposing gangs in one's territory, the weaker was the home gang (Ley & Cybriwsky, 1974).

Human groups also maintain secondary and public territories. People at the beach, for example, generally stake out their claim by using beach towels, coolers, chairs, and other personal objects (Edney &

Jordan-Edney, 1974). These temporary territories tend to be circular, and larger groups command bigger territories than smaller groups. Groups also create territories when they interact in public places, for in most cases, nonmembers are reluctant to break through group boundaries. Just as individuals are protected from unwanted social contact by their invisible bubble of personal space, so groups seem to be surrounded by a sort of "shell" or "membrane" that forms an invisible boundary for group interaction. Various labels have been used to describe this public territory, including **group space** (Edney & Grundmann, 1979; Minami & Tanaka, 1995), *interactional territory* (Lyman & Scott, 1967), *temporary group territory* (Edney & Jordan-Edney, 1974), *jurisdiction* (Roos, 1968), and *group personal space* (Altman, 1975). No matter what this boundary is called, the evidence indicates that it often effectively serves to repel intruders.

Eric Knowles examined the impermeability of groups by placing two or four confederates in a hallway (Knowles, 1973). Participants who wished to move through this space were forced either to walk between the interactants or to squeeze through the approximately two-foot space between the group and the hallway wall. Knowles found that 75% of the passersby chose to avoid walking through the group, but this figure dropped to about 25% in a control condition in which the interacting individuals were replaced by waste barrels. Knowles and his colleagues (Knowles et al., 1976) also discovered that when passing by an alcove that was occupied by a group, people would shift their path to increase the distance between themselves and the group. People begin invading a group's public territory only if the distance between interactants becomes large (Cheyne & Efran, 1972) or if the group is perceived as a crowd rather than as a single entity (Knowles & Bassett, 1976). Furthermore, mixed-sex groups whose members are conversing with one another seem to have stronger boundaries (Cheyne & Efran, 1972), as do groups whose members are exhibiting strong emotions (Lindskold et al., 1976).

**group space** A temporary spatial boundary that forms around interacting groups and serves as a barrier to unwanted intrusion by nonmembers.

**Benefits of Territories** Studies of territoriality in prisons (Glaser, 1964), naval ships (Heffron, 1972; Roos, 1968), neighborhoods (Newman, 1972), and dormitories (Baum & Valins, 1977) have suggested that people feel far more comfortable when their groups can territorialize their living areas. For example, Andrew Baum, Stuart Valins, and their associates confirmed the benefits of territories in their studies of college students who were randomly assigned to one of two types of dormitories. Some students lived in a traditionally designed, corridor-style dorm, which featured 17 double-occupancy rooms per floor. These residents could only claim the bedrooms they shared with their roommates as their territories. In contrast, students who lived in suite-style dorms controlled a fairly well-defined territory that included a private space shared with a roommate as well as a bathroom and lounge shared with several suitemates (Baum & Davis, 1980; Baum, Davis, & Valins, 1979; Baum, Harpin, & Valins, 1975).

Even though nearly equal numbers of individuals lived on any floor in the two types of designs, students in the corridor-style dormitories reported feeling more crowded, complained of their inability to control their social interactions with others, and emphasized their unfulfilled needs for privacy. Suite-style dorm residents, on the other hand, developed deeper friendships with their suitemates, worked with one another more effectively, and even seemed more sociable when interacting with people outside the dormitory. Baum and Valins concluded that these differences stemmed from the corridor-style dorm residents' inability to territorialize areas that they had to use repeatedly.

**Territories and Intergroup Conflict** Territories tend to reduce conflict between groups, since they organize and regulate intergroup contact by isolating one group from another. Even in the absence of open conflict between groups, members tend to remain within their group's territories and avoid trespassing into other areas. Consider, for example, the distribution of people in a cafeteria of a public university in the United Kingdom. When researchers studied, over the course of two weeks, where students sat for their meals they discovered that White students tended to sit in one area of the cafeteria, but that Asian students tended to sit in a different area. As Figure 15.5 indicates, some members of one racial group moved across territorial lines, but for the most part students in this desegregated school tended to resegregate themselves by forming territories based on their race (Clack, Dixon, & Tredoux, 2005).

Group members often feel more comfortable when they can establish a territory for their group, but territoriality can cause conflict if the groups do not agree on their borders. All kinds of intergroup conflicts—from disputes between neighbors, to drive-by gang shootings, to civil wars, to wars between nations—are rooted in disputes over territories (Ardry, 1970). Such conflicts may be based on ancient group traditions. Because most human cultures harvest the animals and plants from the land around them, they establish control over certain geographical areas (Altman & Chemers, 1980). Territories also are defended for symbolic reasons. A group's power is often defined by the quality and size of the space it controls, so groups protect their

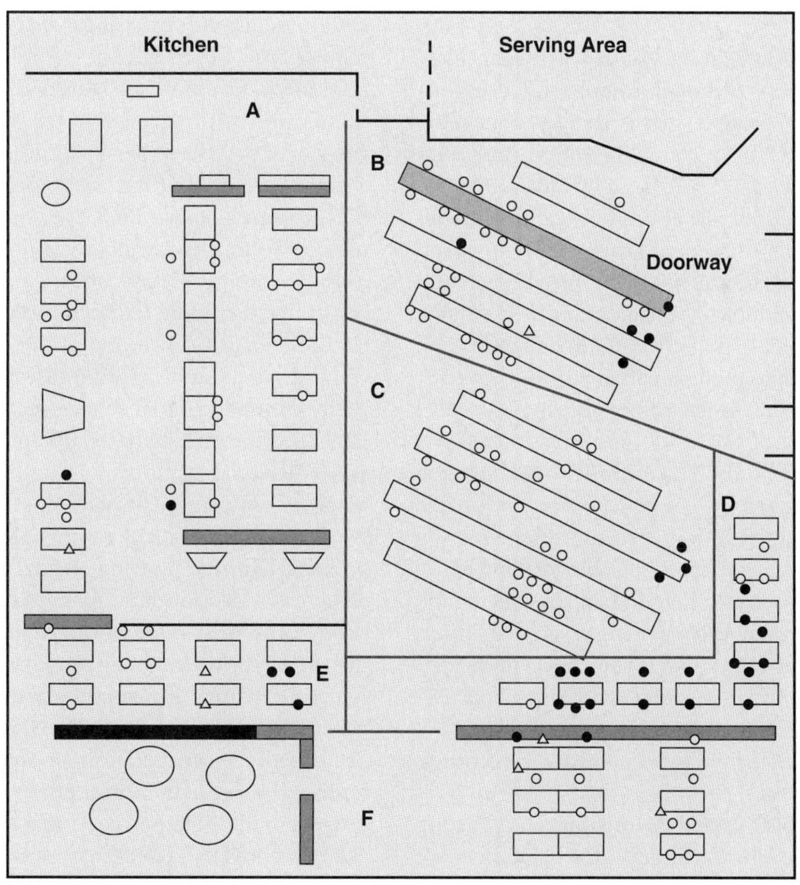


**FIGURE 15.5** Group territories based on race differences in a cafeteria. The white dots indicate White students, the dark dots Asian students, and the triangles students from other racial categories.

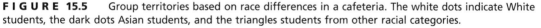

SOURCE: B. Clack, J. Dixon, & C. Tredoux, 2005. "Eating together apart: Patterns of segregation in a multi-ethnic cafeteria." *Journal of Community and Applied Social Psychology*, 15, 1–16. Copyright 2004 John Wiley and Sons.

turf as a means of protecting their reputations. An urban gang, for example, must be ready to attack intruding gangs because "a gang cannot lay any legitimate claim to public areas otherwise" (Sanders, 1994, p. 18). Most drive-by shootings are territorial disputes, occurring when the members of one gang deliberately enter an area controlled by a rival gang and shoot a member of that gang. Disputes over territories are often one-sided, however, for groups that are defending their territory usually triumph over groups that are invading territories (see Focus 15.3).

## Territoriality Within Groups

Territoriality also operates at the level of each individual in the group. Although members develop attachment to the group's space, they also develop spatial attachments to specific areas within the group space (Moser & Uzzell, 2003). Such *individual territories*—a bedroom, a cubicle at work, a park bench no one else knows about, or one's car—can help group members maintain their privacy by providing them with a means of reducing contact with others (Fraine et al., 2007). As Altman (1975) noted, depending on the situation, people prefer a certain amount of contact with others, and interaction in excess of this level produces feelings of crowding and invasion of privacy. The student in the classroom who is distracted by a jabbering neighbor, employees who are unable to concentrate on their jobs because of their noisy officemates' antics, and the wife who cannot enjoy reading a novel because her husband is playing his music too loudly are all receiving excessive inputs from another group member. If they moderated their accessibility by successfully establishing and regulating a territorial boundary, they could achieve a more satisfying balance between contact with others and solitude.

Territories also work as organizers of group members' relationships (Edney, 1976). Once we know the location of others' territories, we can find or avoid them with greater success. Furthermore, because we often grow to like people we interact with on a regular basis, people with contiguous territories tend to like one another (Moreland, 1987). Territories also work to regularize certain group activities. Students must return to a classroom regularly, but they do not spend time searching for an available seat each class session because they tend to return to the same seat over and over again. Finally, territories define what belongs to whom; without a sense of territory, the concept of stealing would be difficult to define, because one could not be certain that the objects carried off actually belonged to someone else.

Territories also help individual group members define and express a sense of personal identity. Office walls often display posters, diplomas, crude drawings produced by small children, pictures of loved ones, or little signs with trite slogans, even when company regulations specifically forbid such personalizing markings. Although such decorations may seem insignificant to the chance visitor, to the occupant of the space, they have personal meaning and help turn a drab, barren environment into home.

Researchers studied personal territories by photographing the walls over the beds of students living in campus dormitories. As an incidental finding, they discovered that most of the decorations on these walls fit into one of the categories listed in Table 15.4. They also found that students who eventually dropped out of school seemed to mark their walls more extensively—particularly in the categories of personal relations and music and theater—than students who stayed in school. Although "stay-ins" used fewer markers, their decorations revealed greater diversity, cutting across several categories. Whereas a dropout's wall would feature dozens of skiing posters or high school memorabilia, the stay-in's decorations might include syllabi, posters, wall hangings, plants, and family photos. The researchers concluded that the wall decorations of dropouts "reflected less imagination or diversity of interests and an absence of commitment to the new university environment" (Hansen & Altman, 1976; Vinsel et al., 1980, p. 1114).

**Territory and Status** The size and quality of individuals' territories within a group often indicates their social status within the group. In undifferentiated

## Focus 15.3 The Home Advantage: Real or Myth?

*We didn't rally them there. We never went looking for trouble. We only rallied on our own street, but we always won there.*

—Doc, leader of the Nortons (quoted in Whyte, 1943, p. 51)

When individuals and groups establish a proprietary claim to a place, they usually strive to control who is allowed to enter. Nations patrol their borders to make certain that people from neighboring countries cannot enter the country easily. Neighborhood associations erect fences and gates to keep others out. When families move into a new home or apartment, they often install locks and elaborate burglar alarms to prevent intrusions by nonmembers. Students who find someone sitting in their usual chair will ask the intruder to leave (Haber, 1980).

These territorial disputes, curiously enough, most often end with the defender of the territory vanquishing the intruder—the **home advantage**. Case studies of street gangs, for example, find that defending groups usually succeed in repelling invading groups, apparently because they are more familiar with the physical layout of the area and have access to necessary resources (W. F. Whyte, 1943). One member of the Nortons, a street gang discussed in Chapter 2, explained that his group never lost a fight ("rally") so long as it took place on the group's turf:

> Once a couple of fellows in our gang tried to make a couple of girls on Main Street. The boyfriends of these girls chased our fellows back to Norton Street. Then we got together and chased the boyfriends back to where they came from. They turned around and got all Garden Street, Swift Street, and Main Street to go after us. . . . It usually started this way. Some kid would get beaten up by one of our boys. Then he would go back to his street and get his gang. They would come over to our street, and we would rally them. . . . I don't remember that we ever really lost a rally. Don't get the idea that we never ran away. We ran sometimes. We ran like hell. They would come over to our street and charge us. We might scatter, up roofs, down cellars, anywhere. We'd get ammunition there. . . . Then we would charge them—we had a good charge. They might break up, and then we would go back to our end of the street and wait for them to get together again. . . . It always ended up by us chasing them back to their street. We didn't rally them there. We never went looking for trouble. We only rallied on our own street, but we always won there. (Whyte, 1943, p. 51)

Individuals, too, are often more assertive when they are within their own territorial confines rather than encroaching on others' turf. College students working with another student on a cooperative task spent more time talking, felt more "resistant to control," and were more likely to express their own opinions when they were in their own room rather than in their partner's room (Conroy & Sundstrom, 1977; Edney, 1975; Taylor & Lanni, 1981). Individuals and groups seem to gain strength and resolve when the dispute takes place on their home territory, even if they are encountering an opponent who is physically stronger or more socially dominant.

This home advantage also influences the outcome of sporting events, for the home team is more frequently the victor than the loser (Schlenker et al., 1995a). When a basketball team must travel to the rival team's home court to play, they often make more errors, score fewer points, and end up the losers rather than the winners of the contest (Schwartz & Barsky, 1977). This advantage becomes even greater when the visiting team must travel longer distances and when the fans watching the game support the home team and jeer the opponent (Courneya & Carron, 1991; Greer, 1983). Playing at home, however, can become something of a disadvantage in rare circumstances. When athletes play must-win games on their home field and they fear that they will fail, the pressure to win may become too great. And when a team is playing a series of games and it loses an early game at home, it may lose its home advantage to the emboldened adversary. Overall, however, groups tend to win at home (for more details, see Baumeister, 1984, 1985, 1995; Baumeister & Showers, 1986; Schlenker et al., 1995a, 1995b).

---

**home advantage** The tendency for individuals and groups to gain an advantage over others when interacting in their home territory.

**TABLE 15.4 Displays and Decorations Used by Students to Mark Personal Territories in Dorm Rooms**

| Category | Examples of Markers and Identifiers |
|---|---|
| **Entertainment or equipment** | Bicycles, skis, radios, stereos, climbing gear, tennis rackets, computers, phones |
| **Personal relations** | Pictures of friends and family, flowers, photographs of vacations, letters, drawings by siblings |
| **Values** | Religious or political posters, bumper stickers, ecology signs, flags, sorority signs |
| **Abstract** | Prints or posters of flowers, landscapes, art reproductions, cartoons |
| **Reference items** | Schedules, syllabi, calendars, maps |
| **Music or theater** | Posters of ballet, pictures of rock groups, theater posters |
| **Sports** | Ski posters, pictures of athletes, motorcycle races, magazine covers, hiking posters |
| **Idiosyncratic** | Handmade items (wall hangings, paintings), plants, unique items (e.g., stolen road signs), animal skins, stuffed animals |

SOURCE: "Privacy Regulation, Territorial Displays, and Effectiveness of Individual Functioning" by A. Vinsel, B. B. Brown, I. Altman, and C. Foss, *Journal of Personality and Social Psychology*, 1980, 1104–1115. Copyright 1980 by the American Psychological Association.

societies, people rarely divide up space into "yours," "mine," and "ours." The Basarawa of Africa, for example, do not make distinctions between people on the basis of age, sex, or prestige. Nor do they establish primary territories or build permanent structures (Kent, 1991). But stratified societies with leaders, status hierarchies, and classes are territorial. Moreover, the size and quality of the territories held by individuals tend to correspond to their status within society. The political and social elite in the community live in large, fine homes rather than small, run-down shacks (Cherulnik & Wilderman, 1986). Executives with large offices hold a higher, more prestigious position in the company than executives with small offices (Durand, 1977). Prison inmates who control the most desirable portions of the exercise yard enjoy higher status than individuals who cannot establish a territory (Esser, 1973). As one informal observer has noted, in many large corporations, the entire top floor of a company's headquarters is reserved for the offices of the upper echelon executives and can only be reached by a private elevator (Korda, 1975). Furthermore, within this executive area, offices swell in size and become more lavishly decorated as the occupant's position in the company increases. Substantiating these informal observations, a study of a large chemical company headquarters, a university, and a government agency found a clear link between office size and status (Durand, 1977). The correlation between size of territory and position in each group's organization chart was .81 for the company, .79 for the government agency, and .29 for the university.

The link between territory and dominance in small groups tends to be more variable. Several studies have suggested that territory size increases as status increases (Sundstrom & Altman, 1974). Other studies, however, indicated that territory size seems to decrease as status in the group increases (Esser, 1968; Esser et al., 1965). Eric Sundstrom and Irwin Altman (1974) suggested that these contradictory results occur because territorial boundaries are more fluid in small groups. In one study that they conducted at a boys' rehabilitation center, they asked each participant to rank the other boys in terms of ability to influence others. Also, an observer regularly passed through the residence bedrooms, lounge, TV area, and bathrooms and recorded territorial behaviors. The boys evaluated each area to determine which territories were more desirable than others.

Sundstrom and Altman found evidence of the territory–dominance relation, but the strength of this relation varied over time. During the first phase of the project, the high-status boys maintained clear control over more desirable areas, but when two of the most dominant boys were removed from the group, the remaining boys competed with one another for both status and space. In time the group had quieted back down, although certain highly dominant members continued to be disruptive. When formal observations ended the group's territorial structures were once more beginning to stabilize with higher status members controlling the more desirable areas.

These findings suggest that dominance–territory relations, like most group processes, are dynamic. In many small groups, the higher-status members possess larger and more aesthetically pleasing territories, but chaotic intermember relations or abrupt changes in membership can create discontinuities in territorial behavior. Moreover, the hostility that surfaced in the group when spatial claims were disputed suggests that territories can work as tension reducers by clarifying the nature of the social situation and increasing opportunities for maintaining privacy.

**Territory and Stress in Extreme and Unusual Environments** Groups often find themselves in an *EUE*—an *Extreme and Unusual Environment* (Suedfeld & Steel, 2000). During the International Geophysical Year (1957–1958), for example, several countries sent small groups of military and civilian personnel to outposts in Antarctica. These groups were responsible for collecting various data concerning that largely unknown continent, but the violent weather forced the staff to remain indoors most of the time. Equipment malfunctioned regularly, radio contact was limited, and water rationing restricted bathing and laundering. As months went by and these conditions continued, interpersonal friction frequently surfaced, and the group members found themselves arguing over trivial issues. The members summarized their group malaise with the term *antarcticitis*—lethargy, low morale, grouchiness, and boredom brought on by their unique living conditions (Gunderson, 1973; see also Carrere & Evans, 1994; Stuster, 1996).

These Antarctic groups are by no means unique, for accounts of sailors confined in submarines (Weybrew, 1963), divers living in SEALAB (Helmreich, 1974; Radloff & Helmreich, 1968), astronauts in a spacecraft (Sandal et al., 1996), work teams on large naval ships (Luria, 1990), and crews on space stations (Stuster, 1996) have reported evidence of stress produced by EUEs. Although technological innovations make survival in even the most hostile environments possible, groups living in these space-age settings must learn to cope with age-old problems of interpersonal adjustment. Leaders must make certain that group members remain active and busy, and conflicts must be handled quickly and decisively. Groups that achieve high levels of teamwork tend to be more successful than ones with rigid, traditional hierarchies. Attention to spatial concerns, however, is critical also, for groups that develop individual and group territories tend to prosper, whereas those that fail to territorialize their spaces founder (Harrison, Clearwater, & McKay, 1991; Harrison & Connors, 1984; Leon, 1991; Palinkas, 1991).

Irwin Altman and his colleagues at the Naval Medical Research Institute in Bethesda, Maryland, studied territoriality in EUEs by confining pairs of volunteers to a 12-by-12-foot room equipped with beds, a toilet cabinet, and a table and chairs (see Altman, 1973, 1977). The groups worked for several hours each day at various tasks, but were left to amuse themselves with card games and reading the rest of the time. The men in the isolation condition never left their room during the 10 days of the experiment; matched pairs in a control condition were permitted to eat their meals at the base mess and sleep in their regular barracks.

The members of isolated groups quickly claimed particular bunks as theirs. Furthermore, this territorial behavior increased as the experiment progressed, with the isolated pairs extending their territories to include specific chairs and certain positions around the table. Not all of the groups, however, benefited by establishing territories. In some of the groups, territories structured the group dynamics and eased the stress of the situation, but in other dyads, these territories worked as barricades to social interaction and exacerbated the strain of isolation. Overall, withdrawal and time spent sleeping increased across the 10 days of the study, whereas time spent in social interaction decreased. Other measures revealed worsened task performance and heightened interpersonal conflicts, anxiety, and emotionality for isolates who drew a "psychological and spatial 'cocoon' around themselves, gradually doing more things alone and in their own part of the room" (Altman & Haythorn, 1967, p. 174).

Altman and his colleagues followed up these provocative findings in a second experiment by manipulating three aspects of the group environment: (1) availability of privacy (half of the groups lived and worked in a single room; the remaining groups had small adjoining rooms for sleeping, napping, reading, etc.); (2) expected duration of the isolation (pairs expected the study to last either 4 days or 20 days); and (3) amount of communication with the outside world. Although the study was to last for eight days for all the pairs, more than half terminated their participation early. Altman explained this high attrition rate by suggesting that the aborting groups tended to "misread the demands of the situation and did not undertake effective group formation processes necessary to cope with the situation" (1973, p. 249). On the first day of the study, these men tended to keep to themselves, never bothering to work out any plans for coping with what would become a stressful situation. Then, as the study wore on, they reacted to increased stress by significantly strengthening their territorial behavior, laying increased claim to particular areas of the room. They also began spending more time in their beds, but they seemed simultaneously to be increasingly restless. Access to a private room and an expectation of prolonged isolation only added to the stress of the situation and created additional withdrawal, maladaptation, and eventual termination (Altman, Taylor, & Wheeler, 1971).

Groups that lasted the entire eight days seemed to use territoriality to their advantage in structuring their isolation. On the first day, they defined their territories, set up schedules of activities, and agreed on their plan of action for getting through the study. Furthermore, the successful groups tended to relax territorial restraints in the later stages of the project, thereby displaying a greater degree of positive interaction. As Altman (1977) described,

> The epitome of a successful group was one in which the members, on the first or second day, laid out an eating, exercise, and recreation schedule; constructed a deck of playing cards, a chess set, and a Monopoly game out of paper. (p. 310)

The men who adapted "decided how they would structure their lives over the expected lengthy period of isolation" (Altman, 1977, p. 310). Although territorial behavior worked to the benefit of some of the groups, the last-minute attempts of some of the faltering groups to organize their spatial relations failed to improve their inadequate adaptation to the isolation.

### Groups in Context: Beyond Apollo 13

The Apollo 13 astronauts were not the first group to face difficult environmental circumstances. For centuries, explorers have hiked, sailed, flown, and ridden from their homes to distant lands and places, and many of these groups have endured very long periods of isolation in harsh climates. Sir Ernest Shackleton and the crew of *Endurance* survived the destruction of their ship on an ice floe in the Antarctic. Fridtjof Nansen and Hjalmar Johansen spent nine months in a hut in the Arctic. Teams of divers have lived for weeks on end in SEALAB, 200 feet beneath the ocean's surface. NASA's crews have endured months in space, and plans are being made for a three-year voyage to Mars (Bechtel, 2002; Stuster, 1996).

These groups survived and achieved their goals because they did not underestimate the impact of the environment. Whereas harsh environments and circumstances overwhelm lone individuals, groups are capable of overcoming the limiting conditions created by these environmental stressors. Some groups may not survive in a hostile environment, but others respond to stress by becoming better groups—more organized, more cohesive, and more efficient.

Certainly these groups experience conflicts, and some degenerate as members continually squabble over insignificant matters. But many groups not only persevere in these adverse circumstances; they find the experience to be exhilarating. Groups like Apollo 13 and the Shackleton explorers have faced disaster, death, and ruin at each turn, yet their autobiographical accounts of their experiences speak eloquently about their adventures—which they do not regret, but instead describe as "a cherished and important part of their life, perceived as an impetus to growing, strengthening, and deepening, to be remembered with pride and enjoyment" (Suedfeld & Steel, 2000, p. 229).

## SUMMARY IN OUTLINE

*How does the social and physical environment influence groups and their dynamics?*

1. An environmental approach recognizes that individuals and their groups are embedded in a physical and social setting, and that the characteristics of that setting can substantially influence group dynamics.
2. Physical settings (*ambience*) are often said to create a distinctive cognitive and emotional reaction in people.
   - Affective reactions to environments range along two dimensions: pleasure–displeasure and activation-deactivation.
   - People generally prefer positive, stimulating environments, but excessive stimulation can lead to *overload*.
3. Features of the environment, such as extremes in temperature and noise, information overload, and dangerousness, can engender *stress* in groups and undermine performance.
   - High temperatures are linked to loss of attention as well as a number of other unpleasant consequences, including discomfort, aggression, and reduced productivity. Extremes in heat and cold are also physically hazardous.
   - Group members can cope with exposure to noise for a short duration, but prolonged exposure is associated with psychological and physical difficulties.
   - Groups that must live or work in dangerous settings adapt by improving communication and teamwork. Groups that do not emphasize a team approach in such environments, such as the 1996 expeditions to Mount Everest, are less likely to escape such situations unharmed.
4. Barker, after studying many groups in their natural locations, concluded that most behavior is determined by the *behavior setting* in which it occurs.
   - The boundaries, components, and programs of such settings define the functions of the situation and the type of behaviors performed in it.
   - Behavior settings that lack *synomorphy* are inefficient and distressing.
   - *Staffing theory*, developed by Wicker, describes the causes and consequences of understaffing and overstaffing.
5. Some groups work and interact in spaces that need to be redesigned to maximize the fit between the people and the place. Duffy suggests that the kind of space needed by a group will depend on the type of task the group must accomplish.

*What is the ecology of a group?*

1. Researchers who study the ecology of small groups explore how individuals interact with and adapt to the group habitat.

2. Studies of *personal space* suggest that group members prefer to keep a certain distance between themselves and others.
   - Closer distances are associated with greater intimacy, so space requirements tend to increase as the situation becomes less intimate. The four zones described by Hall are the intimate, personal, social, and public.
   - Online groups meet in the remote zone. Despite their unusual features—particularly their lower level of *social presence*—members of online groups display dynamics that are similar to those of *offline groups*.
   - The *equilibrium model of communication* predicts that individuals will moderate their distances to achieve the desired level of intimacy, but researchers have also found that variations in space are linked to the gender, status, and cultural background of the interactants.
3. *Density* describes the number of people per unit of space, whereas *crowding* is a psychological reaction to high physical density.
4. Crowding is exacerbated by a number of factors, including cognitive processes that prompt individuals to make attributions about the causes of their arousal, group members' overall evaluation of the high-density setting (Freedman's *density–intensity hypothesis*), perceptions of control, and the degree to which others interfere with task performance.
5. Sommer found that seating arrangements make up an important part of the ecology of small groups. *Sociopetal* spaces tend to encourage interaction, whereas *sociofugal* patterns discourage interaction. People generally prefer interaction-promoting, sociopetal patterns, but these preferences vary with the type of task being attempted and the gender of the interactants.
6. Seating arrangements significantly influence patterns of attraction, communication, and leadership. For example, in many groups, individuals tend to speak immediately after the person seated opposite them (the *Steinzor effect*), and leadership is closely associated with sitting at the end of the table (the *head-of-the-table effect*).

*What are the causes and consequences of a group's tendency to establish territories?*

1. Like many other animals, humans establish *territories*—geographical locations that an individual or group defends against intrusion by others.
2. Altman distinguished between primary territories, secondary territories, and public territories.
   - Various groups, including gangs, territorialize areas; they prevent nongroup members from entering them and they mark them in various ways.
   - Studies of *group space* suggest that, like individuals and their personal space, groups are surrounded by an interaction boundary that prevents nongroup members from approaching too closely.
   - Individuals feel more comfortable when their groups can territorialize their living areas. Territories promote adjustment and reduce stress, but they also promote intergroup conflict, as in the case of gang-related territoriality.
   - Groups with a *home advantage* tend to outperform groups that are outside their territories.
3. Individual members of the group establish their own personal territories within the group's territory.
   - Personal territories fulfill privacy, organizing, and identity functions for individual members. Territorial markings, for example, are associated with membership stability.
   - Higher-status individuals generally control larger and more desirable territories;

changes in status hierarchies can disrupt the allocation of territory.

4. A group's capacity to adapt and even thrive in extreme and unusual environments (EUEs) depends on its members' judicious management of the environment, including territories.

## FOR MORE INFORMATION

*Chapter Case: Apollo 13*

- *Apollo 13: The NASA Mission Reports*, edited by Robert Godwin (2000), provides complete documentation of the mission, including press releases, transcripts of the crew debriefing, the text of the committee investigations of the cause of the accident, and recordings of the crew transmissions during the flight.
- *Lost Moon: The Perilous Journey of Apollo 13*, by Jim Lovell and Jeffrey Kluger (1994), is a forthright summary of the Apollo 13 mission, with details about the group's dynamics and relations with ground control teams and family members.

*Groups in Context*

- *Handbook of Environmental Psychology*, edited by Daniel Stokols and Irwin Altman (1987), contains chapters written by leading researchers and theorists in the field of person–environment relations. The 22 chapters in Volume One focus on basic processes, and the 21 chapters in Volume Two consider applications and cross-cultural implications. The updated *Handbook of Environmental Psychology*, edited by Robert B. Bechtel and Arzah Churchman (2002), supplements the 1987 edition with expanded coverage of topics dealing with environmental preservation.
- *Environmental Psychology*, by Paul A. Bell, Thomas C. Greene, Jeffery D. Fisher, and Andrew Baum (2001), is a comprehensive text dealing with environmental psychology in general, but with key chapters focusing on topics of interest to group researchers, including ecological perspectives, personal space, crowding, and territoriality.

*Small-Group Ecology and Territoriality*

- *The Environment and Social Behavior*, by Irwin Altman (1975), remains the definitive analysis of privacy, personal space, territoriality, and crowding in groups.
- *Personal Space*, by Robert Sommer (1969), takes an entertaining look at interpersonal distancing processes.
- *The Social Net: Human Behavior in Cyberspace*, edited by Yair Amichai-Hamburger (2005), includes research-based reviews of group and individual behavior in online settings.

*Groups in Extreme and Unusual Environments*

- *Bold Endeavors: Lessons from Polar and Space Exploration*, by Jack Stuster (1996), draws on interviews, historical documentation, and empirical research to develop a comprehensive, detailed analysis of the dynamics of groups that live and work in atypical environments, such as bases in Antarctica and space stations.
- "The Environmental Psychology of Capsule Habitats," by Peter Suedfeld and G. Daniel Steel (2000), examines the social and psychological consequences of prolonged stays in secluded and dangerous environments.

## Media Resources

Visit the Group Dynamics companion website at www.cengage.com/psychology/forsyth to access online resources for your book, including quizzes, flash cards, web links, and more!

# 16

# Groups and Change

## CHAPTER OVERVIEW

The usefulness of groups is nowhere more apparent than when groups are used to help their members change. Groups, by their very nature, provide their members with information, support, and guidance, and so many personal and interpersonal problems can be resolved more readily when confronted in a group rather than alone.

- What are some of the ways that groups are used to help members change?
- How do groups promote change?
- How effective are groups in bringing about change?

## CHAPTER OUTLINE

**The Bus Group: Groups as Interpersonal Resources**

The group had visited the Taj Mahal and was returning to the ship when the accident happened. They were teachers and students taking part in Semester-at-Sea: an educational program that combined classes on a floating university with tours to historic sites in countries throughout the world. Their bus fishtailed, flipped twice, and came to rest in a ravine by the roadside. Of the 25 students on the bus, 4 were killed in the tragedy, along with 3 staff members.

The physicians in area clinics and on the Semester-at-Sea ship dealt with the survivors' physical injuries, and counselors and therapists sought to help them with their psychological ones. In the days immediately after the accident, the members of the "bus group," as they came to call themselves, met to deal with their emotions, pain, and uncertainties. The ship continued on its way, and the group met regularly in therapy sessions designed to help members cope with their grief and attempt to stave off the long-term negative consequences of such a horrific experience. With great sensitivity, the therapists helped each survivor deal with the painful memories of that night, the recurrent nightmares most reported, and the inability to concentrate on normal activities. The group also examined ways to remain connected to the other students on the ship who were not involved in the accident, and explored existential issues related to their survival and the loss of the lives of their friends and classmates. Some had more difficulty than others in dealing with the tragedy, and they worked with therapists in individual sessions as well as in group sessions. The bus group met for a dozen times on the ship, in sessions lasting approximately 90 minutes.

When the ship docked at Seattle, Washington, the members went their separate ways. They left behind the bus group, but it had served its purpose. A year after the tragedy, most "appeared to be coping well and getting on with their lives" (Turner, 2000, p. 147).

The idea that a group can be used for therapeutic purposes is not a new one. For centuries, people have sought help from groups in religious rites, community ceremonies, and tribal sessions intended to help those suffering from both physical and psychological problems. These palliative and therapeutic effects of groups were rediscovered by practitioners in the early years of the 20th century when physicians began to use them to help their patients better manage their illnesses (Pratt, 1922). At first, they used groups to increase efficiency, but practitioners soon realized that their patients were benefiting from the groups themselves. Members supported each other, shared nontechnical information about their illnesses and treatment, and seemed to appreciate the opportunity to express themselves to attentive and sympathetic listeners. In time the veracity of Kurt **Lewin's law of change** became widely recognized: "It is usually easier to change individuals formed into a group than to change any one of them separately" (1951, p. 228).

This chapter asks three questions about groups as agents of treatment and change. First, what are some of the ways that groups are used to achieve change in their members? Second, how do groups and group processes promote change? Third, are groups effective means of bringing about change? Did the bus group actually help the members, or did it do more harm than good?

## GROUP APPROACHES TO CHANGE

People join groups to solve many different kinds of problems. Some want to get rid of something—weight, sadness, irrational thoughts, or overwhelming feelings of worthlessness and despair. Others are seeking something—new skills and outlooks, insight into their own characteristics, or a new repertoire of behaviors they can use to improve their relationships with others. Still others seek the strength they need to resist an addiction or obsession—the temptation to drink alcohol, use drugs, or batter their spouses.

---

**Lewin's law of change** Basic principle of attitude and behavioral change, proposed by Kurt Lewin, stating that individuals are more easily changed when they are part of a group.

**TABLE 16.1 Ways Groups Are Used as Agents of Personal and Interpersonal Change**

| Type | Basic Goal | Leader | Examples |
|---|---|---|---|
| Psychotherapy group | Improve psychological functioning and adjustment of individual members | Mental health professional: psychologist, psychiatrist, clinical social worker | Psychoanalytic and Gestalt groups, psychodrama, interpersonal, cognitive–behavioral group therapy |
| Interpersonal learning group | Help members gain self-understanding and improve their interpersonal skills | Varies from trained and licensed professionals to untrained laypersons | T-groups, encounter groups, seminars and workshops |
| Support group | Help members cope with or overcome specific problems or life crises | Usually a volunteer layperson; many groups do not include a leadership position | Alcoholics Anonymous, Grow (a group for ex-mental patients), support groups for caregivers |

The variety of change-promoting groups reflects the variety of individuals' goals. The group formats devised by early psychologists and physicians have evolved into today's jogging and fitness clubs; consciousness-raising groups; support groups for parents, children, grandparents, and ex-spouses; workshops and leadership seminars; marriage and family counseling groups; religious retreats; self-help groups; psychotherapy groups; and so on. These groups, despite their many varieties, all help individuals to achieve goals that they cannot reach on their own (DeLucia-Waack & Kalodner, 2005). **Psychotherapy groups**, for example, help people overcome troublesome psychological problems. **Interpersonal learning groups** help individuals gain self-understanding and improve their relationships with others. **Support groups**, or *self-help groups*, are voluntarily formed groups of people who help one another cope with or overcome a common problem. But not all change-promoting groups fall neatly into one and only one of the three categories shown in Table 16.1. Many support groups, for example, are formed and organized by health care professionals, but they nonetheless have many of the other properties of member-led groups (Schubert & Borkman, 1991).

**psychotherapy group** (or **group psychotherapy**) Individuals seeking treatment for a psychological problem who meet as a group with a trained mental health professional.

**interpersonal learning group** A group formed to help individuals extend their self-understanding and improve their relationships with others (e.g., experiential group, growth group).

**support group** (or self-help group) A group of people who meet regularly to help one another cope with or overcome a problem they hold in common.

## Group Psychotherapy

The therapists who worked with the bus group from Semester-at-Sea were trained to help people overcome psychological and personal problems. They frequently worked with clients in one-on-one psychotherapy sessions, but they also treated some of their clients "in groups, with the group itself constituting an important element in the therapeutic process" (Slavson, 1950, p. 42). When such groups were initially proposed, skeptics questioned the wisdom of putting people who were suffering from psychological problems together in one group. How, they asked, could troubled individuals be expected to cope in a group when they had failed individually? How could the therapist guide the therapeutic process in a group? History, however, has proved the skeptics wrong. Group psychotherapy is currently used to treat all types of psychiatric problems, including addictions, thought disorders, depression, eating disorders, post-traumatic stress disorder, and personality disorders (Barlow, Burlingame, & Fuhriman, 2000; Kanas, 1999).

Group therapists vary widely in theoretical orientation. Some, for example, are primarily psychoanalytic in orientation, for their basic approach is based on Sigmund Freud's therapeutic principles. Others, in contrast, adopt a more interpersonal perspective that stresses the exploration of the social processes that unfold in the group. But most group therapists are eclectic—they draw on any number of perspectives as they work with the group (Ettin, 1992).

**Group Psychoanalysis** For many people the psychoanalytic interview—complete with a note-taking therapist and a free-associating client reclining on a comfortable couch—is the prototypical psychotherapy session. In multiple sessions the client talks in detail about such concerns as early life experiences, current problems and difficulties, dreams, worries, and hopes, and the therapist provides interpretations and directions that help the client recognize the meaning of these materials. As the relationship between the therapist and client becomes more intense, the client unconsciously transfers feelings for and thoughts about others to the therapist, and the therapist can use this *transference* to help the client understand their relations with others. With time, the client develops healthy insight into unresolved conflicts that had been repressed in the unconscious mind (Langs, 1973).

But Sigmund Freud's psychoanalysis also generated the first group therapy: **group psychoanalysis**. Psychoanalysis, by tradition, was used with one patient and one therapist who, through directives, free association, interpretation, and transference, helped the patient gain insight into unresolved unconscious conflicts. But in *Group Psychology and the Analysis of Ego*, Freud (1922) recognized that groups, in many cases, become an unconscious means of regaining the security of the family. Some have suggested that Freud himself practiced group psychoanalysis when he and his students met to discuss his theories and cases (Kanzer, 1983; Roth, 1993). In such groups, the therapist is very much the leader, for he or she directs the group's discussion during the session, offers interpretations, and summarizes the group's efforts. Just as the goal of individual therapy is the gradual unfolding of repressed conflicts, in group therapy, as members talk about their memories, fantasies, dreams, and fears, they will gain insight into their unconscious motivations.

Freud believed that therapy stimulates **transference**—patients transfer wishes, fantasies, and feelings associated with the significant people in their lives to the therapist. Group psychoanalysis also stimulates transference, but in a group, the therapist and the other group members are included in the process. Members may find themselves reacting to one another inappropriately, but their actions, when examined more closely, may parallel the way they respond to people they know in their everyday lives. In the therapy group, for example, clients are demonstrating transference when they accidentally call their male therapist Dad, display anger at another member who seems to challenge them, or confess that they want to be mothered by one of the older female group members. Some therapists are more fully Freudian in their orientation than others, but rare is the therapist who does not deal with transference processes, the interpretation of fantasies or dreams, familial tensions, and other latent conflicts during a group session (see Focus 16.1).

**Gestalt Groups and Psychodrama** Fritz Perls, the founder of Gestalt therapy, frequently conducted his therapeutic sessions in groups rather than with single individuals. Perls drew his theoretical

---

**group psychoanalysis** An approach to group therapy that is grounded in Sigmund Freud's method of treatment, and so includes a directive therapist who makes use of free association, interpretation, and transference processes.

**transference** The displacement of emotions from one person to another during the treatment, as when feelings for a parent are transferred to the analyst or feelings about siblings are transferred to fellow group members.

## Focus 16.1 Can Groups Interpret the Meaning of Dreams?

*The interpretation of dreams is the royal road to a knowledge of the unconscious activities of the mind.*
—Sigmund Freud

Psychoanalytic group therapy involves helping the group members identify the sources of dissatisfaction in their lives that clients themselves do not recognize. One means to explore these conflicts is to interpret dreams, which Freud believed symbolize wishes, expectations, and concerns that can only be expressed indirectly.

Dream interpretation is a mainstay of individual psychoanalytic therapy, but it can also be used in groups. Members of therapeutic groups are striving to enhance self-development and adjustment by collaborating with their peers and the therapist in a personally involving and private setting, but as in any group, members may be unable to surmount unrecognized barriers that block their success in reaching therapeutic goals. Dreams offer the means of bypassing such blockages, for they can be informative, formative, and transformative (Friedman, 2008). When informative, they reveal something about the person who tells the dream to the group, but very often the dream yields information about the group itself. When formative, the dream helps the group and its members achieve some therapeutically positive outcome particularly when the dream's meaning helps the group move past issues that it has been denying or deliberately ignoring. When transformative, the dream may galvanize the group into action, changing it in some fundamental and possibly unexpected way.

For example, in one session a group member recounted his dream of the entire therapy group biking together on a mountain road. The member explained that the leader was in the front of the bikers at first, but that eventually the group member passed the leader to scout the way. The rest of the group could not keep up, so the dreamer had to circle back frequently to make sure that everything was okay (Friedman, 2008).

This highly symbolic dream provided the client and the group with the opportunity to examine his relationship with the group—which was not very secure, despite his long-term tenure in the group. A highly reserved individual, the dream he told was viewed by others as one of the most personally revealing pieces of information he had ever shared in the group. It redefined many members' impressions of the dreamer, and also revealed to him his feelings of instability within the group. The dream proved to be a turning point in the self-development of the dreamer, and changed substantially the course of the group's progress.

principles from Gestalt psychologists, who argued that perception requires the active integration of perceptual information. The word *Gestalt*, which means both "whole" and "shape," suggests that we perceive the world as unified, continuous, and organized. Like Freud, Perls assumed that people often repress their emotions to the point that unresolved interpersonal conflicts turn into "unfinished business." Perls, however, believed that people are capable of self-regulation and great emotional awareness, and he used therapy to help patients reach their potential (Perls, 1969; Perls, Hefferline, & Goodman, 1951).

In some cases, **Gestalt group therapy** is one-to-one Gestalt therapy conducted in a group setting: Group members observe one another's "work," but they do not interact with each other. More frequently, however, interaction takes place among group members, with the therapist actively orchestrating the events. Many group therapists make use of unstructured interpersonal activities, such as the "hot seat" or the "empty chair," to stimulate members' emotional understanding. When using the *hot seat*, one person in the group sits in the center of the room and publicly works through his or her emotional experiences. The *empty chair* method involves imagining that another person or a part of oneself is sitting in an empty chair and then carrying on a dialogue with that person. These techniques,

**Gestalt group therapy** An approach to group therapy in which clients are taught to understand the unity of their emotions and cognitions through a leader-guided exploration of their behavior in the group situation.

when properly applied, often elicit strong emotional reactions among members, but Gestalt therapists resist offering interpretations to their patients (Goulding & Goulding, 1979; Greve, 1993).

**Psychodrama**, developed by Jacob Moreno (1934), also makes use of exercises to stimulate emotional experiences in group members. Moreno conducted therapeutic groups perhaps as early as 1910, and he used the term *group therapy* in print in 1932. Moreno believed that the interpersonal relations that developed in groups provided the therapist with unique insights into members' personalities and proclivities, and that by taking on roles, the members become more flexible in their behavioral orientations. He made his sessions more experientially powerful by developing psychodrama techniques. When *role playing*, for example, members take on the identity of someone else and then act as he or she would in a simulated social situation. *Role reversal* involves playing a role for a period of time before changing roles with another group member. *Doubling* is the assignment of two group members to a single role, often with one member of the pair playing him- or herself. Moreno believed that psychodrama's emphasis on physical action was more involving than passive discussion, and that the drama itself helped members overcome their reluctance to discuss critical issues (Kipper, 2006; Kipper & Ritchie, 2003; Rawlinson, 2000).

**Interpersonal Group Psychotherapy** An interpersonal approach to psychological disturbances assumes that many psychological problems, such as depression, anxiety, and personality disorders, can be traced back to *social* sources—particularly, interactions with friends, relatives, and acquaintances. Rather than searching for psychodynamic causes, interpersonal theorists assume that maladaptive behavior results from "an individual's failure to attend to and correct the self-defeating, interpersonally unsuccessful aspects of his or her interpersonal acts" (Kiesler, 1991, pp. 442–443).

Many group therapists, recognizing the social basis of psychological problems, use the group setting to help members examine their interpersonal behavior. Irvin Yalom's **interpersonal group psychotherapy** (also called *interactive group psychotherapy* or *process groups*), for example, uses the group as a "social microcosm," where members respond to one another in ways that are characteristic of their interpersonal tendencies outside of the group. Therapy groups, as groups, display a full array of group dynamics, including social influence, structure, conflict, and development. The therapist takes advantage of the group's dynamics to help members learn about how they influence others and how others influence them. Members do not discuss problems they are facing at home or at work, but instead focus on interpersonal experiences within the group—the *here and now* rather than the *then and there*. Yalom's process approach assumes that, during the course of the group sessions, each member's unique interpersonal pathologies will begin to express themselves, providing an opportunity to review these limiting tendencies and offer suggestions for ameliorating them. When, for example, two members begin criticizing each other, someone uses powerful or bizarre influence tactics, or another refuses to get involved in the group's meetings, therapists prompt group members to examine and explain the members' interactions (Yalom, with Leszcz, 2005).

**Cognitive–Behavioral Therapy Groups** Some therapists, rather than searching for the cause of the problematic behavior in unseen, unconscious conflicts or interpersonal transactions, take a behavioral approach to mental health. This approach assumes that problematic thoughts and behaviors are acquired

---

**psychodrama** A therapeutic tool developed by Jacob Moreno that stimulates active involvement in the group session through role playing.

**interpersonal group psychotherapy** An approach to the treatment of psychological, behavioral, and emotional problems that emphasizes the therapeutic influence of interpersonal learning.

through experience, so behavior theory teaches people to exhibit desirable cognitions and behaviors but seeks to extinguish undesirable cognitions and behaviors. **Cognitive–behavioral therapy groups** use these principles with two or more individuals (Emmelkamp, 2004). A cognitive-behavioral approach to the Semester-at-Sea bus group, for example, may ask members to identify the thoughts that are triggered by their memory of their experiences and then provide them with the cognitive and behavioral skills they need to control those reactions. The therapist may ask the group members to focus their attention on the accident, and then to share their reaction with the others in the group. When members report experiencing dysfunctional ideation—such as "I wonder why I survived and others didn't?" or "I wonder if I deserve to live"—then the leader guides the group through the disputation of such thoughts. The leader might also model, with the group members assisting, methods of emotional and cognitive self-regulation such as mood monitoring, relaxation, and thought-stopping (Hollon & Beck, 2004).

A group format interfaces seamlessly with the process-structuring methods used in behavioral treatments. In many cases therapists follow a series of standard procedures before, during, and after the group intervention. Prior to treatment, they can observe the reactions of each member to the group to index the degree of functioning prior to any intervention. Pretherapy reviews, in which the therapist reviews the theories and procedures that sustain the intervention, can be carried out in a psychoeducational group setting, and through discussion the members can clarify their expectations and goals. Therapists can also use public commitment to these goals to enhance the binding strengths of a *behavioral contract* that describes in objective terms the goals the group members are trying to achieve. During the therapeutic sessions themselves, the cognitive-behavioral group therapist can capitalize on the presence of multiple actors to magnify the effects of modeling, rehearsal, and feedback. Members of the group can be asked to demonstrate particular behaviors while the group members observe, providing members with the opportunity to practice particular skills themselves. These practice sessions can be videotaped and played back to the group so that the participants can see precisely what they are doing correctly and what aspects of their behavior need improvement. During this feedback phase the leader offers reassurance and praise, and members add their support and encouragement (e.g., Franklin, Jaycox, & Foa, 1999; Whittal & McLean, 2002).

**cognitive–behavioral therapy group** The treatment of interpersonal and psychological problems through the application of behavioral principles in a group setting.

### Interpersonal Learning Groups

Many psychologists are united in their belief that the human race too frequently fails to reach its full potential. Although human relationships should be rich and satisfying, they are more often than not superficial and limiting. People are capable of profound self-understanding and acceptance, yet most people are strangers to themselves. These limitations are not so severe that the help of a psychotherapist is needed, but people's lives would be richer if they could overcome these restraints.

Lewin was one of the first to suggest using small groups to teach people interpersonal skills and self-insight. Lewin believed that groups and organizations often fail because their members are not trained in human relations. He therefore recommended close examination of group experiences to give people a deeper understanding of themselves and their groups' dynamics. Other theorists expanded on this basic idea, and by 1965, the human potential movement was in high gear (Back, 1973; Gazda & Brooks, 1985; Lakin, 1972).

**Training Groups (T-Groups)** How can people learn about group dynamics? Members could learn the facts about effective interpersonal relations by attending lectures or by reading books about group dynamics (as you are doing now), but Lewin argued that good group skills are most easily acquired by directly experiencing human relations. Hence, he developed specialized **training groups,** or **T-groups**. Lewin discovered the utility of such groups when running educational classes dealing with leadership and group dynamics. At the end of each day, he arranged for observers to discuss the dynamics of the groups with the group leaders who conducted the training sessions. These discussions were usually held in private, until one evening, a few of the group members asked if they could listen to the observers' and leaders' interpretations. Lewin agreed to their request, and sure enough, the participants confirmed Lewin's expectations by sometimes vehemently disagreeing with the observers. However, the animated discussion that followed proved to be highly educational, and Lewin realized that everyone in the group was benefiting enormously from the analysis of the group's processes and dynamics (Highhouse, 2002).

One of the most noteworthy aspects of T-groups is their lack of structure. Although, from time to time, the trainees might meet in large groups to hear lectures or presentations, most of the learning takes place in small groups. Even though the group includes a designated leader, often called a *facilitator* or *trainer*, this individual acts primarily as a catalyst for discussion rather than as a director of the group. Indeed, during the first few days of a T-group's existence, group members usually complain about the lack of structure and the ambiguity, blaming the trainer for their discomfort. This ambiguity is intentional, however, for it shifts responsibility for structuring, understanding, and controlling the group's activities to the participants themselves. As the group grapples with problems of organization, agenda, goals, and structure, the members reveal their preferred interaction styles to others. They also learn to disclose their feelings honestly, gain conflict reduction skills, and find enjoyment from working in collaborative relationships.

After Lewin's death in 1947, his colleagues organized the National Training Laboratory (NTL). The laboratory was jointly sponsored by the National Education Association, the Research Center for Group Dynamics, and the Office of Naval Research (ONR). Researchers and teachers at the center refined their training methods in special workshops, or *laboratories*. Although the long-term effectiveness of T-groups is still being debated, training groups continue to play a key role in many organization development interventions (Bednar & Kaul, 1979; Burke & Day, 1986; Kaplan, 1979; see Moreno, 1953, for a completely different historical perspective on the development of interpersonal skill training).

**Growth Groups** The T-group was a precursor of group techniques designed to enhance spontaneity, increase personal growth, and maximize members' sensitivity to others. As the purpose of the group experience shifted from training in group dynamics to increasing sensitivity, the name changed from T-group to **sensitivity training group**, or **encounter group** (Johnson, 1988; Lieberman, 1994).

The humanistic therapist Carl Rogers (1970) was a leader in the development of encounter groups. Rogers believed that most people come to experience a loss of self-regard because their needs for approval and love are rarely satisfied. Rogers believed that the encounter group helps people restore their trust in their own feelings, their acceptance of their most personal qualities, and their openness when interacting with others. "Rogerian" therapists focus on emotions and encourage members to "open up" to one another by displaying their inner emotions, thoughts, and worries. Recognizing that

---

**training group** or **T-group** A skill development training intervention in which individuals interact in unstructured group settings and then analyze the dynamics of that interaction.

**sensitivity training group** An unstructured group designed to enhance spontaneity, increase personal awareness, and maximize members' sensitivity to others.

**encounter group** A form of sensitivity training that provides individuals with the opportunity to gain deep interpersonal intimacy with other group members.

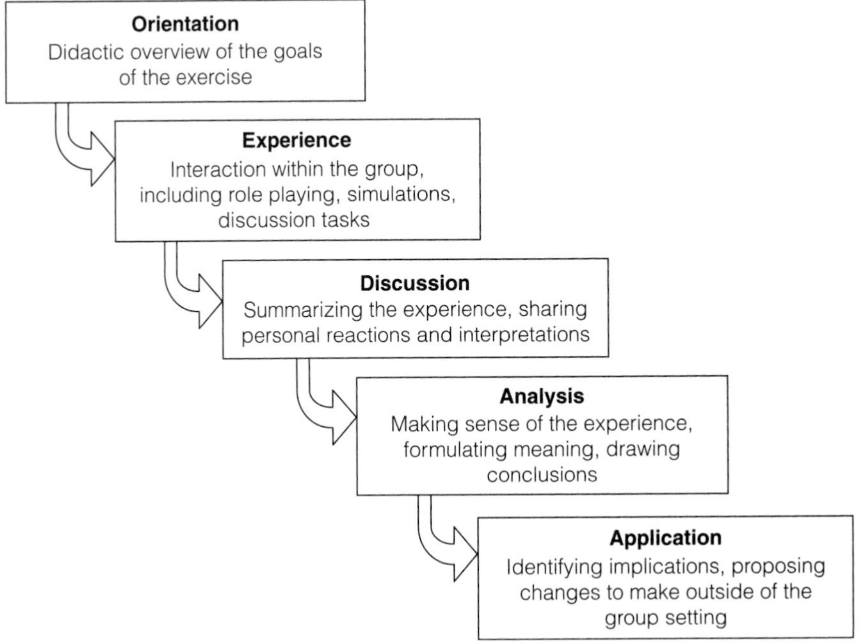


**FIGURE 16.1** The experiential learning cycle.

the group members probably feel insecure about their social competencies, therapists are sources of unconditional positive regard—meaning that they avoid criticizing group members if possible. Rogers believed that group members, in the security of the group, would drop their defenses and facades and encounter each other "authentically" (Page, Weiss, & Lietaer, 2002).

**Structured Learning Groups** Both T-groups and encounter groups are open-ended, unstructured approaches to interpersonal learning. Members of such groups follow no agenda; they examine events that unfold spontaneously within the confines of the group itself, and give one another feedback about their interpersonal effectiveness when appropriate. **Structured learning groups**, in contrast, are planned interventions that focus on a specific interpersonal problem or skill. Integrating behavioral therapies with experiential learning, the group leaders identify specific learning outcomes before the sessions. They then develop behaviorally focused exercises that will help members practice these targeted skills. In a session on nonverbal communication, for instance, group members may be assigned a partner and then be asked to communicate a series of feelings without using spoken language. During assertiveness training, group members might practice saying no to one another's requests. In a leadership training seminar, group members may be asked to role-play various leadership styles in a small group. These exercises are similar in that they actively involve the group members in the learning process.

Thousands of local and national institutes use structured learning groups in their seminars and workshops. Although the formats of these structured experiences differ substantially, most include the components summarized in Figure 16.1. The leader begins with a brief *orientation* session, in which he or

---

**structured learning group** A planned intervention, such as a workshop, seminar, or retreat, focusing on a specific interpersonal problem or skill.

she reviews the critical issues and focuses members on the exercise's goals. Next, the group members *experience* the event or situation by carrying out a structured group exercise. When they have completed the exercise, the members engage in a general *discussion* of their experiences within the group. This phase can be open-ended, focusing on feelings and subjective interpretations, or it, too, can be structured through the use of questioning, information exchange procedures, or videotape recording. This discussion phase should blend into a period of *analysis*, during which the consultant helps group members to identify consistencies in their behavior and the behaviors of others. In many cases, the consultant guides the group's analysis of underlying group dynamics and offers a conceptual analysis that gives meaning to the event. The interpersonal learning cycle ends with *application*, as the group members use their new-found knowledge to enhance their relationships at work and at home.

### Support Groups

Instead of seeking help from a mental health professional, the men and women in the bus group could also have joined a support group—a voluntary group whose members share a common problem and meet for the purpose of exchanging social support. Support groups, also known as *self-help groups* or *mutual aid groups*, exist for nearly every major medical, psychological, or stress-related problem. There are groups for sufferers of heart disease, cancer, liver disease, and AIDS; groups for people who provide care for those suffering from chronic disease, illness, and disability; groups to help people overcome addictions to alcohol and other substances; groups for children of parents overcome by addictions to alcohol and other substances; and groups for a wide variety of life problems, including groups to help people manage money or time (see Table 16.2). The groups meet at a wide variety of locations in the community, including churches, schools, universities, and private homes. They also meet, in some cases, via computer connections to the Internet. As Focus 16.2 notes, *Internet support groups* provide individuals with advice, support, and information 24 hours a day, 7 days a week (Goodman & Jacobs, 1994; Katz, 1993; Levy, 2000).

**TABLE 16.2 Varieties of Self-Help Groups**

| Type of Group | Examples |
|---|---|
| Addictions | Alcoholics Anonymous, Gamblers Anonymous, TOPS (Take Off Pounds Sensibly), Weight Watchers |
| Family and life transitions | In Touch (for parents of children with mental handicaps), Adult Children of Alcoholics, Al-Anon |
| Mental and physical health | The Bell's Palsy Network, CARE (Cancer Aftercare and Rehabilitation Society), Recovery, Inc. (for recovering psychotherapy patients), Reach to Recovery (for breast cancer patients) |
| Advocacy | Campaign for Homosexual Equality, Mothers Against Drunk Driving (MADD), the Gay Activists' Alliance |

**Characteristics of Support Groups** No two support groups adopt identical procedures and structures, but most focus on a specific problem, encourage members to form personal relations with one another, and stress mutuality in helping. Some qualities of support groups are as follows:

- Problem-specific: Unlike general therapeutic groups or social groups, support groups usually deal with one specific type of medical, psychological, stress-related, or social problem. The members face a common predicament, so they are "psychologically bonded by the compelling similarity of member concerns" (Jacobs & Goodman, 1989, p. 537).
- Interpersonal: Support groups tend to be personally and interpersonally involving. Even though individuals' identities are often masked within such groups (e.g., Alcoholics Anonymous), members nonetheless establish personal relationships with one another that might continue outside of the confines of the group (unlike in psychotherapy groups). Members are expected to be honest and open,

## Focus 16.2 Can Groups Give Support Online?

*No one should have to face cancer alone.*

—Online Cancer Care Support Group (http://supportgroups.cancercare.org)

Just as information technology has changed the way groups solve problems, collaborate on projects, and make decisions, so too has it altered many self-help groups. Such groups, by tradition, meet regularly at designated locations where members share information and support. Information technology, however, has made it possible for these groups to "meet" across great distances and at any time. Members, instead of leaving their homes and traveling to a meeting, can now take part in a range of group activities using a computer and a connection to the Internet (Tate & Zabinski, 2004). No matter what problem an individual faces—a serious physical illness, stress caused by providing care for an ill family member, a negative life event such as divorce or the death of a loved one, addiction and drug dependency, social rejection, prejudice, or problems of adjustment and mental health—an online group likely exists somewhere on the Internet that can provide self-care information, support, and referral services. Some of these sites are primarily repositories of information about the problem or issue, and may be sponsored by professionals who treat these problems. Others, however, are true self-help groups, for they were created by individuals who all face the same difficulty and are designed to help fellow sufferers connect to and support each other.

Some support groups create *synchronous* communication among members using instant messaging, discussion boards, and chats. Members log into a chat room at a preset time, and then all in attendance can send and receive messages during the session. In many cases, the software identifies all those who are logged into the group by their user name, and members are asked to announce their presence and departure from the group. Other support groups are *asynchronous*, with members using e-mail and electronic bulletin boards to read messages from others and to post messages and responses to others' postings. Both synchronous and asynchronous groups can be moderated by a group leader who facilitates the discussion (and intervenes to remove content as necessary).

How helpful can these online support groups be, given that they meet in a relatively sterile online world? Studies of online groups for problems ranging from cancer to sexual abuse to psychological disorders suggest that these groups are surprisingly effective, and may even rival face-to-face groups in terms of functionality. Participants report that they feel supported and valued by their group and, after taking part in an online session, feel more hopeful about their situation. Members stress the quality and quantity of the information they receive from others in the online community, and instances of inappropriate commentary or hostile postings are rare and inconsequential (Miller & Gergen, 1998).

Some aspects of the online format may even enhance aspects of a self-help approach to coping with negative events (Tanis, 2007). Because members are not identifiable, they report being able to reveal more intimate information about their experiences and to respond more emotionally to others than they would if interacting face to face. Members of online sessions also tend to exchange more practical advice and factual information than they do in face-to-face sessions, and members value this aspect of online groups as well. They report that the information is useful to them in understanding their condition and in dealing more effectively with their health care providers (Houston, Cooper, & Ford, 2002). Internet support groups are also particularly valuable for individuals whose illness restricts their mobility and for those who are suffering from a stigmatized illness, such as prostate cancer or AIDS. Individuals may feel self-conscious about their condition, but the comfort they experience by joining with others who are "in the same boat" overwhelms this concern about embarrassment (Davison, Pennebaker, & Dickerson, 2000).

---

so that they learn to trust and rely on one another. Members are also expected to be respectful of one another and one another's needs, and to treat people fairly.

- Communal: Most support groups develop a strong sense of community and sharing within the group. Members of the group draw support and encouragement from the group, but they are also expected to provide support and encouragement to others within the group. Each person, then, is both a provider and a recipient of help and support. The primary determinant of status in such groups is experience with the problem. Most support groups include veteran individuals who have more knowledge and experience with both the problem and with the means of dealing with the problem, and these individuals serve as role models for others.

- Autonomous: Self-help groups usually charge little in the way of fees, for in most cases they are not operated by health care professionals. In fact, they often stand in contrast to more traditional forms of treatment, for they arise spontaneously because their members' needs are not being satisfied by existing educational, social, or health agencies. Local groups may be aligned to national organizations that mandate specific procedures for all their chapters, but even this standardization does not eliminate the emphasis on the local group's control of its methods.
- Perspective-based: Support groups' independence from more traditional approaches is also manifested in their adoption of a novel perspective with regard to their problem domain. A grief group may adopt fervently a particular model of the stages of grieving, and base its interventions and recommendations on that perspective. A support group for alcoholics may maintain that recovery is never permanent, and so one must abstain from all forms of alcohol to overcome the addiction. These perspectives may not be complex, nor are they always explicitly recognized by members, but in many cases the group's perspective on its affliction may become the centerpiece of the group's discussions, with new members urged to adopt the group's worldview as a means of coping effectively with the problem.

**Alcoholics Anonymous (AA)** Alcoholics Anonymous (AA) is an example of a support group. AA was founded by Bill Wilson in 1935. Wilson had tried to quit drinking for years, but no matter what he tried, he always returned to his addiction. After a fourth hospital stay for acute alcoholism, Wilson experienced a profound, almost mystical experience that convinced him that he could overcome his drinking problem. To explain the experience, he examined the writings of psychologists William James and Carl Jung and eventually concluded that such experiences could be triggered by periods of negativity, depression, and helplessness. Wilson then connected with a small spiritual group, the Oxford Group Movement, and with his physician friend William D. Silkworth developed a support system that included self-examination, admitting past wrongs, rebuilding relationships and making amends, and reliance on and helping others.

Wilson's program formed the basis of Alcoholics Anonymous, which grew to be an international organization with millions of members. Despite AA's size, change is still achieved through local chapters of alcoholics who meet regularly to review their success in maintaining their sobriety. AA meetings emphasize testimonials, mutual self-help, and adherence to the 12-stage program (the "12 steps") described by the AA doctrine. These steps recommend admitting one's powerlessness over alcohol; surrendering one's fate to a greater power; taking an inventory of personal strengths, weaknesses, and moral failings; and helping others fight their addiction (Flores, 1997).

AA is a multipronged approach to addiction. It stresses the goal of total abstinence and the need to remain ever vigilant against the pressure to resume drinking. It asks members to take specific actions to prevent relapse, and assigns veteran members to newcomers to help strengthen their resilience. Much of the success of the approach also rests on changing members' social networks. By participating actively in AA, members associate with people who are no longer drinking heavily, and the longer this positive association continues the more they can resist the "negative pull of 'wet' social circles that support drinking" (Bond, Kaskutas, & Weisner, 2003, p. 580). One team of researchers studied people one and three years after they first entered an AA-based treatment program. Those who remained abstinent after one year had attended far more AA meetings

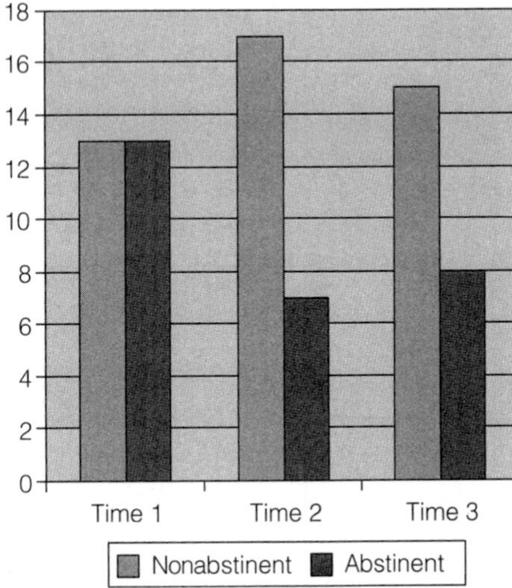


**FIGURE 16.2** The percentage of abstinent and nonabstinent participants in AA who indicated they regularly interacted with a friend who was a heavy drinker when they began the program (Time 1), after one year (Time 2), and after three years (Time 3).

than those who were still drinking: an average of 93 meetings compared to only 25. They also reported having fewer heavy drinkers in their social network (7% vs. 17%) and more people who encouraged them to remain sober (see Figure 16.2; Bond et al., 2003; Kaskutas et al., 2005).

## SOURCES OF CHANGE IN GROUPS

Group approaches to change, despite their wide variations in method, structure, and procedure, have certain key elements in common (Ingram, Hayes, & Scott, 2000). Some of these common **therapeutic factors** are equivalent to the change-promoting forces that operate in individualistic, one-on-one therapies, but others are unique to group approaches to change. All therapies, for example, help clients gain self-insight, but only group approaches stimulate interpersonal comparisons and provide members with a forum for practicing their interpersonal skills. All therapies provide clients with support and help, but in groups, members are also sources of help rather than only recipients.

Although no one list of therapeutic factors has been verified by researchers and accepted by practitioners, Table 16.3 summarizes some of the most frequently identified change-promoting factors. Some of these factors, such as giving hope to group members, are more influential during the early stages of the group's history, whereas others become more potent with time (e.g., self-insight). Some focus on cognitive processes, whereas others promote changes in behavior directly. But all these processes combine to generate changes in group members' adjustment and well-being (see Yalom with Leszcz, 2005, for a thorough review of empirical studies of these therapeutic factors).

### Universality and Hope

In the aftermath of the bus accident, the survivors coped with their physical injuries, their fears, and their grief. In unguarded moments, they may have flashed back to the accident and psychologically relived their loss—so vividly that they may have questioned their own sanity. As they found that they could not concentrate on their work even months after the accident, they may have started to feel that they would never get over the anguish. They may also have found that their moods would take unexpected turns—they may have become inexplicably angry for little reason or unexpectedly disinterested in things that once fascinated them.

When suffering alone, individuals may not realize that their feelings and experiences are relatively common ones. But when surrounded by other people who are suffering similarly, members recognize the *universality* of the problems they face. When all the members of the bus group compared their stress-related symptoms, they could recognize that they

---

**therapeutic factor** An aspect of group settings that aids and promotes personal growth and adjustment; includes such factors as the installation of hope, universality, providing information, altruism, and interpersonal learning.

**TABLE 16.3 Factors That Promote Change in Groups**

| Factor | Definition | Meaning to Member |
|---|---|---|
| Universality | Recognition of shared problems, reduced sense of uniqueness | We all have problems. |
| Hope | Increased sense of optimism from seeing others improve | If other members can change, so can I. |
| Vicarious learning | Developing social skills by watching others | Seeing others talk about their problems inspired me to talk, too. |
| Interpersonal learning | Developing social skills by interacting with others | I'm learning to get along better with other people. |
| Guidance | Offering and accepting advice and suggestions to and from the group | People in the group give me good suggestions. |
| Cohesion and support | Comfort, confirmation of feelings; acceptance | The group accepts, understands, and comforts me. |
| Self-disclosure | Revealing personal information to others | I feel better for sharing things I've kept secret for too long. |
| Catharsis | Releasing pent-up emotions | It feels good to get things off my chest. |
| Altruism | Increased sense of efficacy from helping others | Helping other people has given me more self-respect. |
| Insight | Gaining a deeper understanding of oneself | I've learned a lot about myself. |

were all in the same boat (literally, in this case). Research confirms that when people are with others who face similar problems or troubling events, they feel better, in terms of self-esteem and mood, than when they are with dissimilar people (Frable, Platt, & Hoey, 1998). This collective sharing is best illustrated by the AA "hello" ritual: Everyone at an AA meeting publicly states, "I am an alcoholic," and this public declaration reassures all the other participants that their problem is shared by others.

Yalom (with Leszcz, 2005) believes that this collective process results in the "installation of hope" in members, and research confirms that group-derived hope contributes to well-being, life satisfaction, and inspiration (Cheavens et al., 2006). Groups that are designed so that they elevate members' sense of hope tend to be more powerful agents of change than groups that use other procedures (e.g.,Worthington et al., 1997).

These therapeutic gains may be due, in part, to group members' tendencies to compare themselves to other members—the process of social comparison, as described in Chapter 4. Even when the group includes individuals who are experiencing particularly negative outcomes, these individuals can serve as targets for *downward social comparison*. Such comparisons reduce group members' own sense of victimization and can raise their overall sense of self-esteem (Wills & Filer, 2000). The group may also include individuals who are coping well with many difficulties, and these *upward social comparison* targets can encourage members by symbolizing the possibility of progress (Buunk, Oldersma, & De Dreu, 2001; Taylor & Lobel, 1989). Although successful group members—the fellow cancer survivor who is in complete remission, the AA member who has stayed sober for three years, or the caregiver who is managing to care for her elderly mother and still attend college—may make some group members feel like failures, they also provide a standard for future gains (Tennen, McKee, & Affleck, 2000).

## Social Learning

When an individual who is striving to change meets with one other person—whether a trained therapist, counselor, friend, or relative—he or she can discuss problems, identify solutions, and receive support and encouragement. But even in the most therapeutic of dyads, the individual shares perspectives, feedback, guidance, acceptance, and comfort with only one other person. A larger group, with its multiple members, is richer in terms of its interpersonal and therapeutic resources. Within the social microcosm of the small group, individuals experience a fuller range of interpersonal processes, including feedback about their strengths and weaknesses, pressure to change behaviors that other members find objectionable, role models whose actions they can emulate, and opportunities to practice the very behaviors they are seeking to refine. Of the 10 therapeutic factors in Table 16.3, vicarious learning, interpersonal learning, and guidance are most closely related to social learning processes that help members explore themselves, their problems, and their social relationships with others.

**Vicarious Learning** **Social learning theory**, developed by Albert Bandura (1977, 1986), maintains that people can acquire new attitudes and behaviors *vicariously*—by observing and imitating others' actions. This theory, which explains how infants learn their native language, why adolescents adopt the unhealthy habits of their peers, and how viewers of televised violence mimic the aggressive actions they watch, suggests that group members can learn by observing other group members, provided they: (1) are motivated to learn from their peers; (2) attend closely to the behavior being modeled by the other group member; (3) are able to remember and reenact the behavior they observed; and (4) are aware that the consequences of the model's behavior are positive rather than negative (Shebilske et al., 1998).

Groups provide members with multiple models to emulate, including the leader or leaders. When, for example, group members who are skilled in expressing their feelings deftly describe their emotional reactions, the less verbally skilled members may learn how they, too, can put their feelings into words. When two members who regularly disagree with each other reach an accord, other group members who watch this reconciliation unfold learn how they can resolve interpersonal conflicts. Group leaders can also model desirable behaviors by treating the group members in positive ways and avoiding behaviors that are undesirable (Dies, 1994). In one study, the coleaders of therapy groups modeled social interactions that the group members considered difficult or anxiety provoking. The leaders then helped the group members perform these same behaviors through role playing. Groups that used explicit modeling methods showed greater improvement than groups that only discussed the problematic behaviors (Falloon et al., 1977).

**Interpersonal Learning** Although people tend to believe that they can come to know themselves through self-reflection, in reality people learn who they are—their strengths, their weaknesses, their tendencies, and their satisfactions—by watching how other people react to them. In groups, members implicitly monitor their impact on the other people in their group and draw conclusions about their own qualities from others' reactions to them. The other group members become, metaphorically, a "mirror" that members use to understand themselves (Cooley, 1902). A group member may begin to think that she has good social skills if the group always responds positively each time she contributes to the group discussion. Another member may decide that he is irritating if his comments are always met with anger and hostility. This indirect feedback helps members perceive themselves more accurately. Individuals who are socially withdrawn, for example, tend to evaluate their social skills negatively even though the other group members view them positively (Christensen & Kashy, 1998). Individuals

---

**social learning theory** A conceptualization of learning developed by Albert Bandura that describes the processes by which new behaviors are acquired by observing and imitating the actions displayed by models, such as parents and peers.

also tend to rate themselves as more anxious than others tend to perceive them as being (Marcus, 1998; Marcus & Wilson, 1996). Extended contact with others in a group setting should repair these negative, inaccurate perceptions.

Groups are also very willing to give direct, unambiguous feedback to members when they engage in objectionable or praiseworthy actions (Kivlighan, 1985). Kurt Lewin was one of the first theorists to borrow the term *feedback* from engineering and use it to describe how others' responses to group members served as corrective guides for subsequent actions (Claiborn, Goodyear, & Horner, 2001). The individual who is lonely because he alienates everyone by acting rudely may be told, "You should try to be more sensitive," or "You are always so judgmental, it makes me sick." Some groups exchange so much evaluative information that members withdraw from the group rather than face the barrage of negative feedback (Scheuble et al., 1987). Most group leaders, however, are careful to monitor the exchange of information between members so that individuals receive the information they need in positive, supportive ways (Morran et al., 1998).

**Guidance** When group members discuss issues, concerns, problems, and crises, other group members frequently help by providing advice, guidance, and direction. Members of support groups, for example, exchange considerable factual and personal information about their disorder or concern, as well as suggestions for problem management (e.g., LaBarge, Von Dras, & Wingbermuehle, 1998). Group leaders, in addition to guiding the flow of the session through questioning, summarizing, and rephrasing members' statements, also provide information, suggest solutions, confront the members' interpretations of problems, and offer their own interpretation of the causes of the members' problems (Hill et al., 1988). This guidance ranges from explicit suggestions and directions to suggestions of minor adjustments to deepen an emotional process or cognitive interpretation (Heppner et al., 1994).

Therapists and facilitators, like all group leaders, vary considerably along the directive–nondirective dimension. Those who adopt a leader-centered approach—typical of psychoanalytic, Gestalt, and behavioral groups—are more directive. They guide the course of the interaction, assign various tasks to the group members, and occupy the center of the centralized communication network. In some instances, the group members may not even communicate with one another, but only with the group leader. Other facilitators, however, advocate a nondirective style of leadership, in which all group members communicate with one another. These group-oriented methods, which are typified by interpersonal approaches, encourage the analysis of the group's processes, with the therapist/leader sometimes facilitating the process but at other times providing no direction whatsoever.

Both directive and nondirective approaches are effective, so long as the leaders are perceived to be caring, help members interpret the cause of their problems, keep the group on course, and meet the members' relationship needs (Lieberman & Golant, 2002; Lieberman, Yalom, & Miles, 1973). Moreover, just as effective leaders in organizational settings sometimes vary their interventions to fit the situation, so effective leaders in therapeutic settings shift their methods over time. During the early stages of treatment, members may respond better to a task-oriented leader, whereas in the later stages, a relationship-oriented leader may be more helpful (Kivlighan, 1997).

Several studies have suggested that groups with two leaders are more effective than groups with only one leader. **Coleadership** eases the burdens put on the group's leader (Dugo & Beck, 1997). The two leaders can lend support to each other, and they can also offer the group members their combined knowledge, insight, and experience. Also, male–female teams may be particularly beneficial, as they offer a fuller perspective on gender issues and serve as models of positive, nonromantic heterosexual relationships. The advantages of

---

**coleadership** Two or more individuals sharing the organizational, directive, and motivational duties of the leadership role.

coleadership, however, are lost if the leaders are unequal in status or engage in power struggles during group sessions (Arnardottir, 2002).

## Group Cohesion

Just as cohesion is a key ingredient for effective sports, production, and management teams, so cohesion is a critical ingredient for effective change-promoting groups. If groups are to be used as change agents, the members should have a strong sense of group identity and belonging; otherwise, the group will not exert sufficient influence over its members (Cartwright, 1951). Without cohesion, feedback is not accepted, norms do not develop, and groups can not retain their members. Most importantly, however, cohesion creates the climate for acceptance that is so critical for therapeutic success. As Yalom (with Leszcz, 2005, p. 56) explains, "It is the affective sharing of one's inner world and then the acceptance by others that seem of paramount importance."

**Acceptance and Support** Cohesive groups are superior sources of emotional and social support for their members (Burlingame, Fuhriman, & Johnson, 2001). When a group is cohesive, the members are more engaged in the group and its change-promoting processes. Members rarely miss meetings, they take part in the planning of the group's topics and activities, and they express a sense of closeness with the other members. Avoidance and conflict, in contrast, are clear indicators of a lack of cohesiveness (Kivlighan & Tarrant, 2001; Ogrodniczuk & Piper, 2003). In many cases, members who are hostile and socially inhibited attend sessions infrequently, and as a result, are not sufficiently engaged in the group change process (MacNair-Semands, 2002).

Because group members are more likely to identify with a cohesive group, members are more likely to experience gains in collective self-esteem when members of such groups (Cameron, 1999; Marmarosh, Holtz, & Schottenbauer, 2005). In one study of this process researchers reinforced members' identification with the group by giving them a group identification card. They were told to carry their card with them, to serve as a symbol of their membership in the group, and a reminder that their group was with them all the time. Those group members given an identity card reported greater collective self-esteem and displayed more positive treatment gains than members in a no-card control condition (Marmarosh & Corazzini, 1997).

**Cohesion over Time** A group's cohesiveness fluctuates over time, depending on its longevity and stage of development. Even when the group's task is a therapeutic one, time is needed to achieve cohesiveness. In one study, investigators observed and coded the behaviors displayed by adolescents in a program of behavioral change. These groups did not immediately start to work on self-development issues, nor did the group members try to help one another. Rather, the groups first moved through orientation, conflict, and cohesion-building stages before they began to make therapeutic progress (Hill & Gruner, 1973).

Other studies have also suggested that the success of the group depends to a large extent on its movement through several stages of development. Although these stages receive various labels from various theorists, many accept the five emphasized by Bruce Tuckman (1965)—forming, storming, norming, performing, and adjourning (see Chapter 1, Figure 1.5). During the *forming* stage, individual members are seeking to understand their relationship to the newly formed group and strive to establish clear intermember relations. During the *storming* stage, group members often find themselves in conflict over status and group goals; consequently, hostility, disruption, and uncertainty dominate group discussions. During the next phase (*norming*), the group strives to develop a group structure that increases cohesiveness and harmony. The *performing* stage is typified by a focus on group productivity and decision making. Finally, when the group fulfills its goals, it reaches its last stage of development—*adjourning*. If a group does not move through these stages, its members will not be able to benefit from the experience (MacKenzie, 1994, 1997; Yalom with Leszcz, 2005).

Dennis Kivlighan and his colleagues illustrated the important impact of group development on therapeutic outcomes by matching interventions to the developmental "maturity" of the group. Group members were given structured help in expressing either anger or intimacy before either the fourth or the ninth group session of their therapy. The information dealing with anger clarified the value of anger as a natural part of group participation and provided suggestions for communicating it. The information dealing with intimacy clarified the value of intimacy in groups and provided suggestions for its appropriate expression toward others. As anticipated, when the interventions were matched to the most appropriate developmental stage—for example, when group members received the information on anger during the storming phase (Session 4) and the information on intimacy during the norming phase (Session 9)—the participants displayed more comfort in dealing with intimacy, more appropriate expressions of intimacy and anger, fewer inappropriate expressions of intimacy, and more congruence between self-ratings and other ratings of interpersonal style (Kivlighan, McGovern, & Corazzini, 1984).

## Disclosure and Catharsis

Groups become more unified the more the members engage in **self-disclosure**—the sharing of personal, intimate information with others (Corey & Corey, 1992; Leichtentritt & Shechtman, 1998). When groups first convene, members usually focus on superficial topics and avoid saying anything too personal or provocative. In this *orientation stage*, members try to form a general impression of each other and also make a good impression themselves. In the *exploratory affective stage*, members discuss their personal attitudes and opinions, but they avoid intimate topics. This stage is often followed by the *affective stage*, when a few topics still remain taboo. When the group reaches the final stage, *stable exchange*, all personal feelings are shared (Altman & Taylor, 1973).

Self-disclosure can be something of a challenge for some individuals. Individuals experiencing personality or psychological disturbances, for example, often disclose the wrong sorts of information at the wrong time (McGuire & Leak, 1980). Men and boys, too, are generally more reserved in their self-disclosure (Brooks, 1996; Kilmartin, 1994; Shechtman, 1994). Thus, therapists must sometimes take special steps to induce the male members of therapy groups to share personal information about themselves, including modeling disclosure and incorporating disclosure rituals in the group (Horne, Jolliff, & Roth, 1996). Men's reluctance to disclose can even undermine the quality of the group experience for all participants: The more men in the therapeutic group, the fewer benefits are reported by participants (Hurley, 1997).

Self-disclosure and cohesion are reciprocally related. Each new self-disclosure deepens the group's intimacy, and this increased closeness then makes further self-disclosures possible (Agazarian, 2001). In sharing information about themselves, members are expressing their trust in the group and signaling their commitment to the therapeutic process (Rempel, Holmes, & Zanna, 1985). Disclosing troubling, worrisome thoughts also reduces the discloser's level of tension and stress. Individuals who keep their problems secret but continually ruminate about them display signs of physiological and psychological distress, whereas individuals who have the opportunity to disclose these troubling thoughts are healthier and happier (Pennebaker, 1997).

Members can also vent strong emotions in groups, although the value of such emotional venting continues to be debated by researchers. Some side with Freud's initial analysis of emotions and tension. Freud believed that strong emotions can build up, like steam in a boiler. If this psychological steam is not vented from time to time, the strain on the system can cause psychological disorders. Therefore, healthy people discharge these emotions in a process Freud called **catharsis**. Others, however, have suggested that "blowing off steam" is rarely helpful, for in the extreme, venting heightens members' psychological distress and upset (Ormont, 1984).

---

**self-disclosure** The process of revealing personal, intimate information about oneself to others.

**catharsis** The release of emotional tensions.

## Altruism

The group's leader is not the only source of help available to group members. Other group members can sometimes draw on their own experiences to offer insights and advice to one another. This mutual assistance provides benefits for both parties. Even though the group's leader is the official expert in the group, people are often more willing to accept help from people who are similar to themselves (Wills & DePaulo, 1991). The helper, too, "feels a sense of being needed and helpful; can forget self in favor of another group member; and recognizes the desire to do something for another group member" (Crouch et al., 1994, p. 285). Mutual assistance teaches group members the social skills that are essential to psychological well-being (Ferencik, 1992).

Mutual assistance is particularly important in self-help groups. Mended Hearts—a support group that deals with the psychological consequences of open-heart surgery—tells its members that "you are not completely mended until you help mend others" (Lieberman, 1993, p. 297). AA groups formalize and structure helping in their 12-step procedures. Newcomers to the group are paired with sponsors, who meet regularly with the new member outside of the regular group meetings. As Focus 16.3 notes, collective helping is also an essential component of group-level approaches to dealing with traumatic events.

## Insight

Individuals' perceptions of their own personal qualities are generally accurate. Individuals who think of themselves as assertive tend to be viewed that way by others, just as warm, outgoing individuals tend to be viewed as friendly and approachable (Kenny et al., 1996; Levesque, 1997). In some cases, however, individuals' self-perceptions are inaccurate (Andersen, 1984). An individual may believe that he is attractive, socially skilled, and friendly, when in fact he is unattractive, interpersonally incompetent, and hostile.

Groups promote self-understanding by exposing us to the unknown areas of ourselves. Although we are not particularly open to feedback about our own attributes, when several individuals provide us with the same feedback, we are more likely to internalize this information (Jacobs, 1974; Kivlighan, 1985). Also, when the feedback is given in the context of a long-term, reciprocal relationship, it cannot be so easily dismissed as biased or subjective. Group leaders, too, often reward members for accepting rather than rejecting feedback, and the setting itself works to intensify self-awareness. In a supportive, accepting group, we can reveal hidden aspects of ourselves, and we therefore feel more open and honest in our relationships.

Even qualities that are unknown to others and to ourselves can emerge and be recognized during group interactions (Luft, 1984). As self-perception theory suggests, people often "come to 'know' their own attitudes, emotions, and other internal states partially by inferring them from observations of their own overt behavior and/or the circumstances in which this behavior occurs" (Bem, 1972, p. 2). If individuals observe themselves acting in ways that suggest that they are socially skilled—for example, disclosing information about themselves appropriately and maintaining a conversation—then they may infer that they are socially skilled (Robak, 2001).

Studies of group members' evaluations of the therapeutic experience attest to the importance of insight. When participants in therapeutic groups were asked to identify the events that took place in their groups that helped them the most, they stressed universality, interpersonal learning, cohesion (belonging), and insight (see Figure 16.3). During later sessions, they stressed interpersonal learning even more, but universality became less important (Kivlighan & Mullison, 1988; Kivlighan, Multon, & Brossart, 1996). In other studies that asked group members to rank or rate the importance of these therapeutic factors, the group members emphasized self-understanding, interpersonal learning, and catharsis (MacNair-Semands & Lese, 2000; Yalom with Leszcz, 2005). In general, individuals who stress the value of self-understanding tend to benefit the most from participation in a therapeutic group (Butler & Fuhriman, 1983).

## Focus 16.3 How Can We Cope with Disasters and Trauma?

*Each time I tell my story, I remove one small bit of hurt from inside me. I ease my wound.*

—Carol Staudacher, *Time to Grieve* (1994, p. 61).

In rural India, a bus carrying 25 college students and their guides crashes, killing 7 and injuring all the other passengers. A series of tornadoes crisscrosses North Carolina, leaving a path of devastation and death. In Columbine High School, Eric Harris and Dylan Klebold kill 13 people and wound dozens of others before killing themselves. When a cloud of gas from a leak at a petrochemical plant in Texas ignites, 23 workers are killed and hundreds injured. Millions of Americans grieve the loss of thousands of fellow citizens killed by terrorist attacks on September 11, 2001.

People the world over experience catastrophes, crises, and disasters. Some of these stressful events—such as volcanoes, floods, hurricanes, blizzards, and tornadoes—can be blamed on naturally occurring disruptions in the planet's meteorological and geological systems. Others, however, are man-made—wars, terrorist attacks, violence, nuclear accidents, transportation accidents, building fires, industrial accidents, and so on.

These events take their toll on human adjustment and well-being. One comprehensive review of dozens of published studies of psychological reactions to disasters concluded that people who survive a stressful event are more likely to suffer from anxiety, sleeplessness, and fearfulness. Such stressors also lead to small increases in drug use and depression among people exposed to a hazard. Between 7% and 40% of the survivors of disasters will exhibit some sign of psychopathology (Rubonis & Bickman, 1991). Many victims of disasters, such as Americans who lived and worked near the sites of the 2001 terrorist attacks, civilians in Bosnia, and victims of sarin attack in Japan, show evidence of *post-traumatic stress disorder*, even if not directly harmed.

These negative mental health consequences (anxiety, depression, sleeplessness, compulsions, intrusive thoughts) can be reduced through stress management crisis interventions. These interventions—usually designed and implemented by community health professionals—often make use of group-level therapeutic coping processes, including social comparison, social support, and social learning (Davies, Burlingame, & Layne, 2006; Layne et al., 2001). The students who survived the bus crash in India met with counselors for six weeks to deal with issues of trauma, coping, and grief (Turner, 2000). In the aftermath of the devastating tornadoes, North Carolina residents met at the local community college to share worries and anxieties, recount their stories of surviving the storm, and exchange information about resources, insurance claim procedures, and cleanup efforts (McCammon & Long, 1993). Following the explosion at a petrochemical plant, a response team provided a constant flow of information to the community, conducted group sessions for individuals who lost family members in the accident, and organized *critical incident stress debriefing* (CISD) sessions for workers who were part of the emergency team that sought, in vain, to fight the blaze (Mitchell & Everly, 2006).

The effectiveness of such interventions depends, in part, on timing, procedures, and the characteristics of the individuals involved. Ideally, the intervention occurs immediately following the event, and provides continuing treatment as group members progress through the cumulative stages of the coping process. Interventions should also be planned carefully in advance, and in some cases, methods used in traditional therapeutic circumstances must be replaced by methods that will work in the chaos and confusion of a disaster or community trauma (Raphael & Wooding, 2006). Interventions must also take into account the characteristics of the individuals involved. Children and elderly people, for example, require a different set of group experiences than do adults, family members, and emergency personnel. Interventions must also be sensitive to each individual's reaction to the event. Some may appreciate the opportunity to interact with others who are coping with a disaster, but others may not respond well to the evocative demands of the group (Foy & Schrock, 2006). Not everyone can share their grief with others, and the continued discussion of the event may only exacerbate their anxieties and emotional reprocessing (Melamed & Wills, 2000). A group approach to treatment works for many people, but some will require individual assistance rather than group help (McNally, Bryant, & Ehlers, 2003).

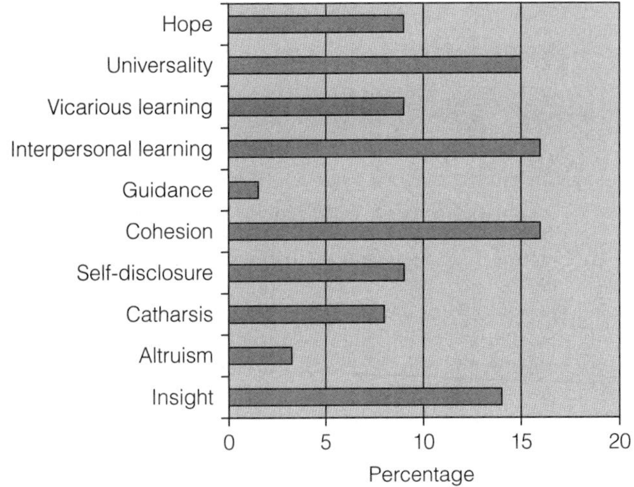

**FIGURE 16.3** Group members' ratings of the value of therapeutic factors in groups.

SOURCE: Kivlighan & Mullison, 1988, Participants' perception of therapeutic factors in group counseling: The role of interpersonal style and stage of group development. Small Group Behavior, 19, 1988. Copyright 1988 by Sage Publications, Inc. Reprinted by permission of Sage Publications, Inc.

## THE EFFECTIVENESS OF GROUPS

What would you do if you were bothered by some personal problem? Perhaps you have trouble making friends. Maybe you are having problems adjusting to a new job or wish that you could be more productive when you are at work. Perhaps you have finally resolved to stop smoking or drinking, or you just cannot seem to get over the depression that has enveloped you since your mother passed away last year. Whatever the problem, you have not succeeded in changing on your own. So you decide to join a change-promoting group.

Would this group really help you achieve the changes you desire? Researchers and therapists have been debating this question for many years. Reviewers, after sifting through hundreds of studies evaluating the effectiveness of group interventions, rejected many studies as so methodologically flawed that they yielded no information whatsoever (Bednar & Kaul, 1978, 1979, 1994; Fuhriman & Burlingame, 1994; Kaul & Bednar, 1986). Those studies that did use valid methods, however, generally weighed in favor of group-level interventions.

Group methods also earn relatively high marks in meta-analytic reviews of various types of therapies. Gary Burlingame and his colleagues, after statistically combining the results of hundreds of experimental, quasi-experimental, and correlational studies, concluded that group methods are effective treatments for a wide variety of psychological problems (Burlingame, Fuhriman, & Mosier, 2003; Burlingame & Krogel, 2005; Fuhriman & Burlingame, 1994; Kösters et al., 2006; McRoberts, Burlingame, & Hoag, 1998). Group methods have also been found to be effective (1) when used to treat children and adolescents (Hoag & Burlingame, 1997), (2) when used for the primary prevention of health problems in children (Kulic, Horne, & Dagley, 2004), and (3) with incarcerated individuals, particularly when cognitive–behavioral methods are paired with homework assignments to be completed after the sessions (Morgan & Flora, 2002). A comprehensive review of support groups also suggested that individuals gain positive outcomes through membership in such groups, relative to individuals in control conditions (Barlow et al., 2000).

Individuals who have participated in group therapy—the consumers of group-based treatments—also give group approaches relatively high marks. One study, conducted by *Consumer Reports*, asked respondents to rate a variety of treatments. All psychological methods, including group interventions, were rated positively. AA received particularly positive evaluations in this study (Seligman, 1995, 1996; see also Christensen &

Jacobson, 1994). In sum, the "accumulated evidence indicates that group treatments have been more effective than no treatment, than placebo or nonspecific treatments, or than other recognized psychological treatments, at least under some circumstances" (Bednar & Kaul, 1994, p. 632).

These positive conclusions, however, require some qualification. First, the changes brought about by group experiences are often more perceptual than behavioral. Second, in some cases, groups can do more harm than good for participants. Third, all groups are not created equal; some may be more effective in promoting change than others. These issues are examined next.

### Perceptions versus Behaviors

Richard Bednar and Theodore Kaul (1979), after culling the studies of change that were methodologically flawed, concluded that most studies had reported changes only on self-report data, but not on behavioral data. Reviews of experiential groups, for example, generally found stronger evidence of perceptual changes than of behavioral changes (Bates & Goodman, 1986; Budman et al., 1984; Ware, Barr, & Boone, 1982). One review, for instance, identified 26 controlled studies of personal growth groups that (1) used both pretest and posttest measures, (2) met for at least 10 hours, and (3) had a long-term follow-up (at least one month after termination). Summarizing these methodologically superior studies, the reviewers concluded that group treatments did result in enduring positive changes, particularly at the self-report level (Berman & Zimpfer, 1980). These and other findings suggest that groups are most useful in promoting changes in the "ability to manage feelings, directionality of motivation, attitudes towards the self, attitudes towards others, and interdependence," but that behavior is more resistant to change (Gibb, 1970, p. 2114; Shaw, 1981).

### Evidence of Negative Effects

Not everyone who joined the group following the bus accident remained in the group. Four individuals, after the first session, did not return to the group. Several members attended the sessions during the return trip only sporadically. One person, when later asked about the experience, said it did not help at all (Turner, 2000).

Bednar and Kaul noted that groups can fail in two distinct ways. First, a participant may decide to leave the group before he or she has benefited in any way; such an individual is usually labeled a **premature termination**, or *dropout* (Holmes, 1983). A **casualty**, in contrast, is significantly harmed by the group experience. A casualty might, for example, attempt suicide as a result of the group experience, require individual therapy to correct harm caused by the group, or report continued deteriorations in adjustment over the course of the group experience. The number of casualties reported in studies has ranged from a low of none among 94 participants in a human relations training lab followed up after five months (Smith, 1975, 1980) to a high of 8% of the participants in a study of 17 encounter groups (Lieberman et al., 1973). A relatively high casualty rate (18%) was obtained in one study of 50 married couples who participated in marathon encounter groups, but this rate was inflated by the problems the couples were experiencing before entering the group (Doherty, Lester, & Leigh, 1986). No evidence is available concerning the rate of casualties in support groups, but statistics maintained by the NTL indicate that 25 individuals who participated in the program prior to 1974 experienced a severe psychological reaction (Back, 1974). This number represented less than 0.2% of the participants.

Bednar and Kaul (1978) noted that most premature terminations result from failed expectations about the purposes of the group or from an inadequate match between the group member's goals and the leader's methods. Casualties, in contrast, can most often be traced to a

---

**premature termination** The withdrawal of a participant from a change-promoting group that occurs before the individual has reached his or her therapeutic goals.
**casualty** An individual whose psychological well-being declines rather than improves as a result of his or her experiences in a change-promoting group.

particularly negative event in the group. In one study, for example, an individual sought psychiatric treatment immediately after the group attacked her for being overweight:

> She stated that the group was an extremely destructive one for her. The group operated by everybody "ganging up on one another, thirteen to one, and bulldozing them until they were left on the ground panting." She was bitterly attacked by the group and finally dropped out after an attack on her in which she was labeled "a fat Italian mama with a big shiny nose." She was also told that she probably had "a hell of a time getting any man to look at her." (Lieberman et al., 1973, p. 189)

Given these potential problems, group therapists, trainers, facilitators, and members themselves are urged to use care when interacting in their groups. Casualties can be minimized by limiting conflict during sessions and by making certain that the group atmosphere is supportive, nonevaluative, and nonthreatening (Mitchell & Mitchell, 1984; Scheuble et al., 1987).

## Types of Groups and Effectiveness

Change-promoting groups conform to no single set of procedures: Some groups are leader centered (psychoanalytic or Gestalt groups), whereas others are group focused (encounter groups and T-groups); and the group's activities can range from the highly structured (interpersonal learning groups) to the wholly unstructured (encounter groups). In some groups, the members themselves are responsible for running the meeting, whereas in other situations, the facilitator runs the session (structured groups). Group practitioners also vary greatly in their orientations and techniques: Some focus on emotions with Gestalt exercises, others concentrate on the here and now of the group's interpersonal processes, and still others train members to perform certain behaviors through videotaped feedback, behavioral rehearsal, and systematic reinforcement.

Given this diversity of purposes and procedures, one might expect some types of groups to emerge as more effective than others. Yet differences in treatment effectiveness are relatively rare. Morton Lieberman, Irvin Yalom, and Matthew Miles (1973), for example, investigated the overall impact of a 12-week experiential group on members' adjustment. They began by assigning 206 Stanford University students to 1 of 18 therapy groups representing ten different theoretical orientations. Trained observers coded the groups' interactions, with particular attention to leadership style. Before, during, immediately after, and six months following the participation, they administered a battery of items assessing group members' self-esteem, attitudes, self-satisfaction, values, satisfaction with friendships, and so on. Measures were also completed by the comembers, the leaders, and by group members' acquaintances.

Somewhat unexpectedly, the project discovered that no one theoretical approach had a monopoly on effectiveness. For example, two separate Gestalt groups with different leaders were included in the design, but the members of these two groups evidenced widely discrepant gains. One of the Gestalt groups ranked among the most successful in stimulating participant growth, but the other Gestalt group yielded fewer benefits than all of the other groups.

A number of factors could account for this apparent equivalence of therapies (Stiles, Shapiro, & Elliott, 1986). First, the various group therapies may be differentially effective, but researchers' measures may not be sensitive enough to detect these variations. Second, a group's effectiveness may depend as much on who is in the group and who leads the group as on the methods used. The question is not "Is Therapy X more effective than Therapy Y?" but, "What type of group run by which therapist is effective for this individual with this type of problem?" (Paul, 1967). Third, although group interventions are based on widely divergent theoretical assumptions, these assumptions may not lead to differences in practice. The leader of a Gestalt group and the leader of a psychodynamic group, for example, may explain their goals and methods in very different theoretical terms, but they may nonetheless rely on identical methods in their groups. Fourth, as the concept of therapeutic factors suggests, despite their heterogeneity in purposes and procedures, therapeutic groups have certain characteristics in common, and these common aspects of groups and their dynamics may account for their therapeutic effects.

### The Value of Groups

Groups are not all benefit with no cost. Groups can demand great investments of time and energy from their members. Although groups provide social support, they are also a source of considerable stress for their members. Groups, too, can socialize members in ways that are not healthy and set social identity processes in motion that increase conflict between groups (Forsyth & Elliott, 2000).

The checkered impact of groups, however, in no way detracts from their significance in shaping mental health. Groups help their members define and confirm their values, beliefs, and identities. When individuals are beset by problems and uncertainties, groups offer reassurance, security, support, and assistance. Groups are places where people can learn new social skills and discover things about themselves and others. Groups, too, can produce changes in members when other approaches have failed. Both researchers and mental health professionals who understand groups recognize their healing power, for groups help their members change for the better (Lewin, 1951, p. 228).

## SUMMARY IN OUTLINE

*What are some of the ways that groups are used to help their members change?*

1. Individuals often turn to groups for help in achieving personal and therapeutic change. As *Lewin's law of change* states, "It is usually easier to change individuals formed into a group than to change any one of them separately."
2. Most change-oriented groups focus either on therapeutic adjustment (*psychotherapy groups*), interpersonal and emotional growth (*interpersonal learning groups*), or overcoming addictions or other life stresses (*support groups*).
3. Group psychotherapy sessions, conducted by a mental health professional, focus on psychological problems.
   - In *group psychoanalysis*, the therapist helps members to gain insight into their problems by offering interpretations and working through *transference* effects. Such therapies use a variety of analytic methods drawn from Freud's approach to treatment, including dream interpretation.
   - *Gestalt group therapy*, developed by Perls, makes use of experiments, techniques, and extensive role-playing methods to stimulate emotional growth.
   - *Psychodrama*, developed by Moreno, also uses role play and physical activities.
   - In *interpersonal group psychotherapy*, the leader takes advantage of the group's dynamics to help members learn about how they influence others and how others influence them. This method was developed by Yalom.
   - In *cognitive–behavioral therapy groups*, the therapist uses principles derived from learning theory to encourage specific behaviors while extinguishing others. This approach makes use of behavioral methods, including behavioral contracts, modeling, behavior rehearsal, and feedback.
4. Interpersonal learning groups involve attempts to help relatively well-adjusted individuals improve their self-understanding and relationships with others.

- In *training groups*, or *T-groups*, members are encouraged to actively confront and resolve interpersonal issues through unstructured discussions.
- In growth groups, such as *sensitivity training groups* or *encounter groups*, individuals are urged to disclose personal aspects of themselves to others and to provide other members with positive feedback.
- In *structured learning groups*, members take part in planned exercises that focus on a specific interpersonal problem or skill. Most of these interventions involve a learning cycle that begins with an orienting overview and then moves from experience to discussion to analysis to application.

5. Support groups often form spontaneously when people combine their energies and efforts in an attempt to cope with or overcome a common problem. These groups tend to be problem-specific, highly interpersonal, communal, autonomous, and perspective-based.
   - Many support groups, such as Alcoholics Anonymous (AA), emphasize inspirational testimonials, mutual help, shared similarities, collective encouragement, and changing the member's social networks.
   - Studies of online support groups for problems ranging from cancer to sexual abuse to psychological disorders have suggested that these groups provide many of the same resources to members as do face-to-face support groups.

*How do groups promote change?*

1. A number of *therapeutic factors* operate in groups to promote change.
2. Groups, by providing opportunities to engage in social comparison and mutual support, convince members of the universality of their problems and give them hope.
3. Because groups include multiple individuals, rather than just a single therapist/helper and a single client, they can make use of the sources of interpersonal learning described in Bandura's *social learning theory*.
   - Groups facilitate vicarious learning (modeling of behaviors), interpersonal feedback, and guidance (direct instruction).
   - *Coleadership* (two leaders are present at all sessions) provides more opportunities for social learning and feedback. Group facilitators, like all group leaders, vary considerably along the directive–nondirective dimension.
4. Cohesive groups offer individuals the opportunity to help others and to be helped by them, and they serve as buffers against stress. Therapeutic groups, like all groups, generally become more cohesive over time.
5. Groups become more intimate as members reveal private information about themselves (*self-disclosure*). When group members vent strong emotions, the resulting *catharsis* may reduce their stress.
6. Group members also benefit from the increased self-confidence produced by helping others and by gaining insight about their personal qualities from other group members.
7. Many stress management crisis interventions implemented following community disasters and crises make use of group-level therapeutic coping processes, including social comparison, social support, social learning, and mutual help.

*How effective are groups in bringing about change?*

1. Most group approaches are effective methods for helping individuals change their thoughts, emotions, and actions. However,
   - Changes fostered by group experiences are often more perceptual than behavioral.

- Participation in groups can also lead to a number of negative consequences, although not every *premature termination* from a group is necessarily a psychological *casualty*.

2. Group methods, despite their diversity, tend to be equally effective. This general but non-specific effectiveness may reflect the operation of common therapeutic factors across most therapeutic groups.

## FOR MORE INFORMATION

*Chapter Case: The Bus Group*

- "Group Treatment of Trauma Survivors Following a Fatal Bus Accident: Integrating Theory and Practice," by Andrew L. Turner (2000), details the methods used to help college students recover from a tragic bus accident that occurred during a semester abroad program.

*Group Approaches to Change*

- *The Theory and Practice of Group Psychotherapy* (5th ed.), by Irvin D. Yalom with Molyn Leszcz (2005), describes with cases, theory, and syntheses of available research Yalom's basic principles of interpersonal group therapy, which stress the therapeutic factors common to all group approaches to change.
- "Groups as Change Agents" by Donelson R. Forsyth and John G. Corazzini (2000), provides a general overview of group approaches to treatment.
- *Psychological Effects of Catastrophic Disasters: Group Approaches to Treatment*, by Leon A. Schein, Henry I. Spitz, Gary M. Burlingame, and Philip R. Muskin, with Shannon Vargo (2006), is a comprehensive compendium of group-based methods of dealing with traumatic events.
- "Self-Help Groups," by Leon H. Levy (2000), reviews a number of forms of self-help groups, and thoroughly reviews the empirical literature pertaining to their effectiveness.

*Group Effectiveness*

- "Small-Group Treatment: Evidence for Effectiveness and Mechanisms of Change," by Gary Burlingame, K. Roy MacKenzie, and Berhard Strauss (2004), is a cutting-edge synthesis of research studies that have investigated the nature and efficacy of group psychotherapy empirically.

### Media Resources

Visit the Group Dynamics companion website at www.cengage.com/psychology/forsyth to access online resources for your book, including quizzes, flash cards, web links, and more!

# 17

# Crowds and Collective Behavior

## CHAPTER OVERVIEW

The science of group dynamics is based on one core assumption: People act collectively. Much of this collective action occurs in relatively small groups, but people sometimes join larger collectives, including crowds, mobs, audiences, fads, crazes, and social movements. For well over a century, most theorists and researchers have assumed that crowds are unique social aggregations, but collectives are, at their core, groups.

- What is collective behavior?
- What theories explain collective behavior?
- How different are collectives from other types of groups?

## CHAPTER OUTLINE

### The Who Concert Stampede: A Crowd Gone Mad?

The crowd, nearly 8000 strong, was waiting to get into Cincinnati's Riverfront Coliseum to hear a concert by the '70s rock band The Who. Many fans had festival seating, which meant that they were not assigned specific seats on the arena floor. So, in order to get a spot near the stage, fans had come to the venue early so they could enter as soon as the doors opened. But logistical problems delayed the staff from opening the doors, so by late afternoon thousands of people were massed outside the building in a tightly packed throng. When pranksters pushed against people standing at the periphery of the crowd, the shove passed through the group like a ripple through water (see Figure 17.1).

The doors opened at 7:30, and the crowd surged forward. A crowd of 8000 people is loud, but above the din, the concertgoers could hear the band warming up. As those on the periphery pushed forward, people near the doors were packed together tighter and tighter. The ticket takers worked as fast as they could, but too few doors were opened to handle the large collective. The back of the group moved faster than the front, and the flow jammed near the clogged doors. People were literally swept off their feet by the surge and some slipped to the concrete floor. Those around them tried to pull them back to their feet, but the overcrowded mass of people pushed on toward open doors and the music. As the rear of the crowd continued to push forward the crowd swept past those who had fallen, and they were trampled underfoot.

Eleven people died that night, killed by the surge of a crowd of people. Most suffocated, caught so long in the press of the crowd that they could not breathe. Many of those who survived were bruised and battered; their "bodies were marked with multiple contusions, bruises" and "hemorrhages" ("The Who," 1979, p. A-19).

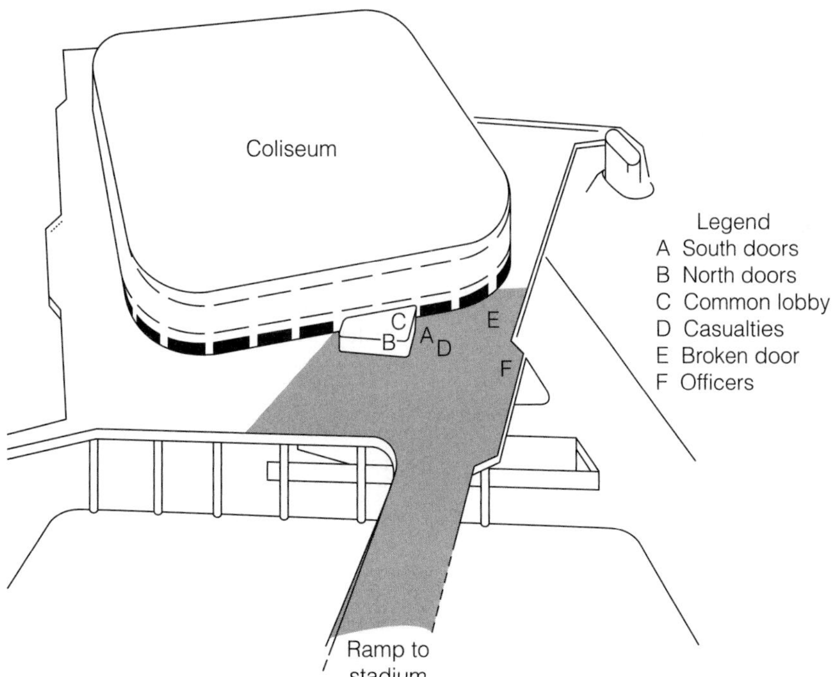


**FIGURE 17.1** Diagram of Cincinnati's Riverfront Coliseum and surrounding plaza, with area of densest occupancy shaded and referenced locations marked.

SOURCE: "Panic at 'The Who Concert Stampede': An Empirical Assessment," by N. R. Johnson. Reprinted from *Social Problems*, 34, 1987, by permission. 

This tragedy is a grim example of **collective behavior**—the actions of a large group of people who are responding in a similar way to an event or situation. Earlier chapters focused on smaller groups—cliques, work squads, juries, sports teams, corporate boards, crews, and bands of explorers. But individuals also—sometimes unwittingly and sometimes purposely—can become members of much larger aggregates. Some collectives, like the concertgoers at the Who concert, form when people are concentrated in a specific location. Others, however, occur when widely dispersed individuals engage in markedly similar actions, as when all the individuals in a community, city, or country begin to adopt a fad or fashion style. In most cases, collectives do not behave in odd, atypical ways. Each day, thousands upon thousands of collectives form and disband around the world, and in nearly all cases, these collectives help rather than hurt their members. But collectives are, at their core, groups, and like any other group, they can go wrong.

This chapter's analysis of collectives is a mixture of description, explanation, and rectification. It begins by first describing the wide variety of collectives, for they can range from the accidental convergences of unrelated individuals to groups with faithful followers who remain members for many years. The chapter then considers both classic and contemporary theoretical analyses of collective behavior, beginning with the provocative arguments presented by Gustave Le Bon (1895/1960) in his book *The Crowd* and ending with new theories that strive to rectify common misconceptions about these extraordinary forms of human association.

---

**collective behavior**The actions of a group of people who are responding in a similar way to an event or situation, including people who all occupy the same location (a *crowd*), as well as mass phenomena in which individuals are dispersed across a wide area (*collective movements*).

## THE NATURE OF COLLECTIVES

In 1943, Mrs. Mullane, a contestant on a radio program, was told to collect pennies as a service to the nation's war effort. The announcer then suggested that listeners should send Mrs. Mullane a penny, and gave her address on the air. Within weeks, she received more than 200,000 letters and well over 300,000 pennies. On Halloween night in 1938, Orson Welles broadcast the radio program *The War of the Worlds*. In some parts of the country people panicked, thinking the dramatization was a real news broadcast and that Martian invaders were attacking Earth. In 1978, only 8% of households in the United States had microwave ovens. This percentage increased slowly until 1985, when the percentage jumped from 34% to 61%. On the afternoon of October 27, 2005, a confrontation between police and youths in Paris, France, resulted in the tragic accidental deaths of two young men. The incident triggered a series of riots; each night wandering mobs set hundreds of cars on fire. The final number burned: over 8,000. Recently an Internet prank known as "rickrolling" spread across message boards, forums, and websites until eventually moving offline. When a viewer clicked on a link that promised content on a particular topic he or she was instead taken to a site that showed a video of British singer Rick Astley performing the 1987 song "Never Gonna Give You Up." Self-appointed "rickrollers" took to playing the song loudly in public places to disrupt events. On the ninth day of the month of hajj, at noon, more than two million people gather on the Plain of Arafat in Saudi Arabia, the site of the prophet Mohammad's farewell sermon—arguably the largest gathering of people to assemble in one place at any time in history. In 2008, a Wal-Mart employee died when he was trampled by a large crowd of shoppers on the biggest shopping day of the holiday season in the United States—"Black Friday."

The science of group dynamics is based on one core assumption—that people act collectively.

Much of this collective action occurs in relatively small groups, and the field of group dynamics (and this book) has concentrated on such groups. But as these historical examples reveal, people also join very large groups, and the impact of these groups on their members can be large as well.

## What Is a Collective?

A *collective*, as noted in Chapter 1, is a relatively large group of people who display similarities in actions and outlook. Families, clubs, juries, a work crew, and teams are not collectives, for they are too small, too structured, and their membership too well-defined and stable. **Collectives**, as Table 17.1 indicates, are larger and more diffuse in character: A crowd forming around a street magician doing a trick, an audience at a play, a line of people (a *queue*) waiting their turn to enter a theater, a mob of Parisians setting fire to a parked car, and a panicked group trying to escape danger are all examples of collectives. The list of such groups would also include people who, even though they are not collocated, nonetheless respond to something in a similar way. Individuals on the Internet in a large simulated world (such as Second Life) or people responding to the same television or radio program (say, by voting for their favorite contestant on *American Idol*) could also be considered a collective.

The diversity of collectives is so great that no single classification scheme is sufficient to categorize their many forms. They tend to be large, but some collectives are huge—as when millions of individuals respond similarly to some fashion craze. In some cases, all the members of a collective are together in one place, and so they "can monitor each other by being visible to or within earshot of one another" (Snow & Oliver, 1995, p. 572). Some collectives, in contrast, involve individuals who are dispersed across great distances. All collectives, however, are distinguished by their members' "common or concerted" form of behavior or reaction (McPhail, 1991, p. 159). Members of a crowd, for example, may move in the same direction or perform the same general types of behaviors. Members of collective movements, although not interacting in face-to-face settings, act in similar ways to achieve a common purpose—they are moving in the same direction, even though they are dispersed.

Collectives also vary in their duration and cohesion. Although some collectives are concocted, planned groups that are created for a specific purpose, in most cases they are emergent groups that

**TABLE 17.1 Various Types of Collectives**

| Type | Defining Characteristics |
|---|---|
| Crowd | A temporary gathering of individuals who share a common focus of interest |
| Audience | Spectators at an exhibition, performance, or event |
| Queue | A waiting line or file of individuals |
| Mob | An acting crowd, often aggressive in character |
| Riot | A large, less localized and less organized mob |
| Panic | A threatened crowd, either seeking escape from danger or competing for a scarce commodity |
| Mass delusion and rumor | The spontaneous outbreak of atypical thoughts, feelings, or actions in a group or aggregate, including psychogenic illness, common hallucinations, and bizarre actions |
| Trends (fads, crazes, fashions) | An abrupt but short-lived change in the opinions, behaviors, life-style, or dress of a large number of widely dispersed individuals |
| Social movement | A deliberate, organized attempt to achieve a change or resist a change in a social system |

---

**collective** A relatively large aggregation or group of individuals who display similarities in actions and outlook.

result from the press of circumstances or through self-organizing dynamics (Arrow et al., 2000). They tend to be open groups, for they have no standards for defining membership and do not adopt operational strategies. In consequence, the relationships between members are more superficial and impersonal than those that link members of smaller groups. If a typical group is two or more individuals who are connected to one another by interpersonal relationships, a typical collective is a large number of individuals who are connected by similarity in action and outlook rather than by close, intimate relationships. Collectives, too, are by reputation more unconventional than other groups. They tend to exist outside of traditional forms of social structures and institutions, and as a result, their members sometimes engage in atypical, unruly, unconventional, or even aberrant behaviors (Turner, R., 2001).

## Crowds

The throng of concertgoers massed outside the Who show was a **crowd**—a group of individuals sharing a common focus and concentrated in a single location. Individuals who are sitting on benches in a park or walking along a city block occupy a common location, but they do not become a crowd unless something happens—a fire, a car collision, or a mugging, for example—to create a common focus of attention (Milgram & Toch, 1969). Shoppers in a mall are just individuals, until a woman spanks her small child when he cries too loudly. Suddenly, the hundred pairs of eyes of an instantly formed crowd focus on the woman, who hurries out the door. The most common types of crowds are street crowds, queues, mobs, and panics.

**Street Crowds** Crowds tend to spring up, unexpectedly and spontaneously; a group of otherwise unrelated individuals who, while going about their own personal business, end up in the same general vicinity and share a common experience (see Focus 17.1). Variously labeled *street crowds*, *public crowds*, or *gatherings*, these crowds form in public or semi-public places, and are made up of people who are strangers to one another—except for the clusters of intact groups that they enfold. At the Who concert, for example, groups of friends waited together for the concert to begin, and these subgroups remained intact until the fatal crush at the entrance doors.

Although such crowds are often short-lived, even these fleeting collectives possess a rudimentary social structure. Their boundaries are relatively permeable at the edges of the crowd, where individuals are allowed to enter and exit freely, but permeability diminishes as one moves nearer the center of the crowd. Also, roles, status hierarchies, and other group structures may not be very evident in such crowds, but close probing usually reveals some underlying structure. For example, they usually take on one of two distinctive shapes—*arcs* (half-circles with all members facing some focal point) and *rings* (full circles). The focal point is known as a *crowd crystal*—one or more individuals who, by drawing attention to themselves or some event, prompt others to join them (Canetti, 1962). Evidence also indicates that those who occupy central positions in crowds are likely to be more actively involved in the experience than those who are content to remain on the fringes (Milgram & Toch, 1969).

Consistencies in action parallel these consistencies in structure. Clark McPhail and his colleagues, after observing all kinds of public gatherings, identified a number of elementary behaviors common to such groups (McPhail, 1991, 2006; Tucker, Schweingruber & McPhail, 1999). Their listing includes:

- *Movement*: Actions taken in common by group members, such as clustering, queueing, surging, marching, jogging, and running.
- *Positioning*: The stance assumed by members in the space, including sitting, standing, jumping, bowing, and kneeling.

---

**crowd** A gathering of individuals, usually in a public place, who are present in the same general vicinity and share a common focus.

## Focus 17.1 How Do You Trigger Crowd Formation?

*We are often told that the dullness of the country drives the people to the towns. But that statement inverts the truth. It is the crowd in the towns, the vast human herd, that exerts a baneful attraction on those outside it.*

—William McDougall (1908, p. 303)

A crowd can spring into existence in a moment, when otherwise unrelated individuals suddenly become entwined in a discernable, if fleeting, collective. One moment the street corner or walkway contains only individuals going about their personal activities, and the next moment a crowd crystallizes as these individuals join together to form a group.

Stanley Milgram and his colleagues examined this process by creating, experimentally, crowds on a street in New York City. On two winter afternoons in 1968 they attempted to trigger the formation of crowds by having confederates stop in the middle of the sidewalk and stare, in rapt attention, at the sixth floor of a nearby building. They would remain in place as passersby flowed around them, and the researchers recorded—from that very same window of the nearby building—how many stopped. They selected a busy street for their study, for an average of 50 people passed by during any given observation period. And they varied the number of people who planted the seed for the group. In some conditions just one person stood staring up, but other conditions included as many as 15 confederates.

How many would be drawn by the "baneful attraction" of the crowd and how many would resist? Milgram and his associates discovered that size mattered when it came to triggering the formation of a stationary crowd. When they counted the number of people who actually stopped walking and stood with the group, taking up the collective stare, they discovered that more and more people joined in as the stimulus crowd of confederates grew larger. Only 4% of the passersby joined a single starer, but 40% stopped in their tracks and joined the large crowd—swelling the group in size from 15 to about 35 people (see Figure 17.2). However, if a less stringent criterion for a crowd was used —people needed only to share the same focus of attention—then even a single individual was capable of influencing 42% of the passersby to look up. The crowd of 15 influenced even more—86% (Milgram, Bickman, & Berkowitz, 1969). The crowds may have grown larger still, but for two factors. First, the confederates dispersed in different directions after one minute, and their departure signaled the crowd's end. Second, the holding power of the crowd would have been greater if there was actually something to observe. With nothing to hold their shared focus, these groups disappeared as soon as the attentional bonds that held their group together faded away.

This study of street crowds confirms the power of groups. Even strangers, passing by each other on the streets of a large and anonymous city, influenced each other, as each person imitated the actions of the other (Cialdini, 2005). Milgram and his colleagues note, however, that those who joined their crowds were not necessarily sheep following the crowd, for there is a logical basis for joining in such crowds: "all other things being equal, the larger the crowd the more likely its members are attending to a matter of interest" (1969, pp. 81–82).

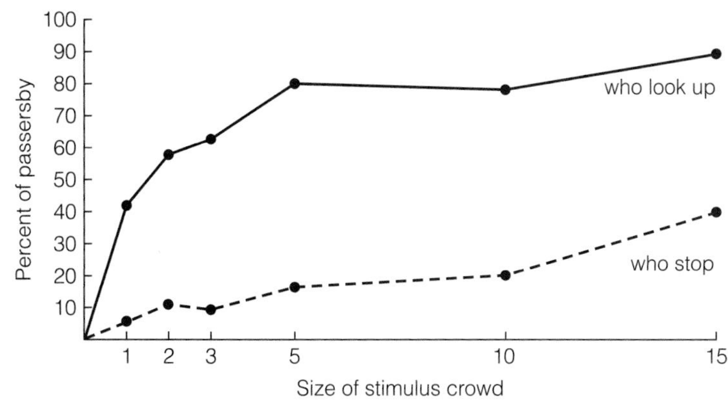


**FIGURE 17.2** The mean percentage of people who looked up or stopped when they passed a single person or a group of 2, 3, 5, 10, or 15 people looking up at a building.

SOURCE: From "Note on the Drawing Power of Crowds of Different Size," by S. Milgram, L. Bickman, & L. Berkowitz, *Journal of Personality and Social Psychology, 13*, 1969. Copyright 1969 by the American Psychological Association.

- *Manipulation*: Alternation of objects in the setting, such as throwing or moving objects.
- *Gesticulation*: Gesturing, such as saluting and signaling (e.g., the raised middle finger, power fist).
- *Verbalization*: Communicating through language forms, such as chanting, singing, praying, reciting, or pledging.
- *Vocalization*: Communicating with paralinguistic sounds, such as ooh-ing and ahh-ing, cheering, booing, whistling, laughing, or wailing.
- *Orientation*: Moving into a particular formation within the space, such as clustering, arcing, ringing, gazing, facing, or vigiling.

**Audiences** A crowd that deliberately gathers in a particular area to observe some event or activity is called an **audience** (or *conventional crowd*). Unlike a crowd that forms spontaneously when some event creates a shared focus, individuals join audiences deliberately, and they are bound more tightly by social conventions that dictate their location and movements (Blumer, 1946). They enter the focal area via aisles or pathways and occupy locations that are determined by seating arrangements or by custom. While observing, they may perform a variety of behaviors, including clapping, cheering, shouting, or questioning, but these actions are usually in accord with the norms of the particular setting. Moreover, when the event or performance has ended, the audience disperses in an orderly fashion (Hollingworth, 1935).

**Queues** A **queue**—a group of persons awaiting their turn—is a unique type of crowd. *Queue* comes from the French word for a braid of hair and so pays etymological homage to the queue's most common shape—a relatively straight line. But some settings, such as theme parks, lobbies, and registration offices, shape the queue into a zigzag pattern through the use of stanchions and ropes. Other establishments create dispersed queues by assigning queuers a number and then summoning them through a beeper or announcement when it is their turn. Queues can also be segmented into subgroups that are permitted to enter together, as when passengers board a plane in groups based on seat assignment. Some queues, too, are not at all linear, as when those waiting to board a bus (or to enter a crowded concert venue) move in a relatively unregulated way toward the entryway.

Like the common crowd, the queue includes strangers who will probably never meet again. But like the members of an audience, those in a queue have joined deliberately to achieve a particular goal, and thus, as members of the collective, they are bound by certain norms of behavior (Mann, 1969, 1970). Queues are an interference, for they prevent people from immediately achieving their goal of acquiring tickets, services, or other commodities, but they also protect people from late-arriving competitors for these commodities. As Milgram and his colleagues noted,

> As in the case of most social arrangements, people defer to the restraints of the form, but they are also its beneficiary. The queue thus constitutes a classic illustration of how individuals create social order, on the basis of a rudimentary principle of equity, in a situation that could otherwise degenerate into chaos. (Milgram et al., 1986, p. 683)

But what prevents the queue from breaking down into a disorderly crowd? Milgram noted that in addition to environmental supports, such as ushers and ropes, queues are also protected by norms of civility and justice. People in many cultures implicitly recognize the basic fairness of the principle "first come, first served" (or "first in, first out,") which the queue protects (Zhou & Soman, 2008). When members join the queue, they accept its rules, and even though the group will disband

---

**audience** A gathering of onlookers who observe some performance, event, or activity; audiences tend to be conventional in behavior, and they disperse when the event they are watching concludes.

**queue** A line, file, or set of people who are waiting for some service, commodity, or opportunity.

as soon as the event begins, members conform to its norms and enforce them as needed (Miller, 2001).

Milgram studied queues by having both male and female accomplices break into 129 lines waiting outside ticket offices and the like in New York City. Working either alone or in pairs, the accomplices would simply say, "Excuse me, I'd like to get in here," and then insert themselves in the line. In an attempt to determine who would be most likely to enforce the norm, Milgram also included either one or two passive confederates in some of the queues he studied. These individuals, who were planted in the line in advance, stood directly behind the point of intrusion (Milgram et al., 1986).

Objections occurred in nearly half of the lines studied. In a few cases (10.1%), queuers used physical action, such as a tap on the shoulder or a push. In 21.7% of the lines, the reaction was verbal, such as "No way! The line's back there. We've all been waiting and have trains to catch," or "Excuse me, it's a line." In another 14.7% of the lines, queuers used dirty looks, staring, and hostile gestures to object to the intrusion nonverbally. Objections were also more prevalent when two persons broke into the line rather than one, and they were least prevalent when two confederates separated the intruders from the other queuers. Overall, 73.3% of the complaints came from people standing behind the point of intrusion rather than from people standing in front of the intrusion. Other investigators found that queue-breakers encountered less hostility when they appeared to be joining someone they knew and when they only broke in near the very end of the line (Schmitt, Dubé, & Leclerc, 1992). These findings suggest that self-interest, as well as the normative force of the queue's rules, mediated reactions to the queue-breakers' actions.

**Mobs** When a gathering of people—a crowd, an audience, or even a queue—becomes emotionally charged, the collective can become a **mob**. Mobs tend to form when some event, such as a crime, a catastrophe, or a controversial action, evokes the same kind of affect and action in a substantial number of people. The hallmark of the mob is its emotion (Lofland, 1981). Early accounts of mobs argued that individuals in mobs were so overwhelmed by their emotions that they could no longer control their actions. Unless the situation is diffused, the mob becomes volatile, unpredictable, and capable of violent action. Mobs, as their name implies, are often highly *mobile*, with members moving together from one location to another, massing in a single location, or just milling about in unpatterned ways (Hughes, 2003).

Mobs, even though they stimulate their members' emotions, are not necessarily irrational, nor are they necessarily violent. When sports fans celebrate a victory, when partiers parade New Orleans streets during Mardi Gras, or when patriots celebrate the end of a conflict, the members of a mob share positive emotions—joy, jubilation, and exhilaration—in a carnival-like atmosphere (Vider, 2004). Their aggressive counterparts, however, tend to be more common—or at least they receive more attention in the media (Milgram & Toch, 1969). *Lynch mobs* terrorized Black men in the southern United States until recently. The first documented lynch mob occurred in the United States in 1882, but by 1950, lynch mobs had killed thousands. Virtually all the victims were Black, and many of the killings were savagely brutal (Mullen, 1986; Tolnay & Beck, 1996). *Hooligans* are a specific type of violent sports fans—particularly of football (soccer)—in Europe. These mobs of fans, often intoxicated, mill about in the streets and pubs around the stadiums, fighting with fans who support the opposing team (Dunning, Murphy, & Williams, 1986; Oyserman & Saltz, 1993). The abuse of low-status group members by groups of bullies, which is sometimes termed *mobbing*, is a regular occurrence in both school and work settings (Schuster, 1996; Whitney & Smith, 1993).

---

**mob** A disorderly, emotionally charged crowd; mobs tend to form when some event, such as a crime, a catastrophe, or a controversial action, evokes the same kind of affect and action in a substantial number of people.

**Riots** can be construed as mobs on a grander scale. They often begin when a relatively peaceful crowd is transformed by a negative experience into a violent mob. For example, on the final night of the 1999 Woodstock music festival, an anti-violence group named PAX asked the audience to light candles as an expression of unity. A small group of concertgoers instead used the candles to burn down the outdoor venue. MTV news correspondent Kurt Loder described the incident as "the history of human terrestrial evolution recounted in reverse" (quoted in Vider, 2004, p. 114). In other cases, riots are an expression of unrest and protest in the general population. In 1921, for example, Whites in Tulsa, Oklahoma, attacked the highly successful Black business community of Greenwood. Hundreds were killed, and 35 city blocks of Black-owned businesses were destroyed. In the 1960s, riots diffused throughout many large American cities due, in part, to intergroup competition and racial tensions (Myers, 1997). In 1980 and 1992, residents of Liberty City, Florida, and Los Angeles, California, rioted when police officers charged with brutality were found not guilty. Riots are also sometimes motivated by the desire to loot and steal rather than by group-level processes. For example, in 1969, when the police force of Montreal went on strike for 17 hours, riots broke out all over the city. As expected, professional crimes skyrocketed, but the noncriminal population also ran amok. A heterogeneous crowd, including impoverished, wealthy, and middle-class people rampaged along the central business corridor, looting and vandalizing (Clark, 1969).

**Panics** Some mobs are charged with a different set of emotions than anger; they are fearful, anxious, and frightened. These mobs have *panicked*, for they are either fleeing from an aversive situation (*escape panics*) or seeking out a limited resource that they fear will run out (*acquisitive panics*). Escaping mobs occur when crowds of people are overtaken by some catastrophe, such as a fire, flood, or earthquake, and they must escape en masse from the dangerous situation. Many groups exit such situations calmly, but if the situation is seen as very dangerous, and the escape routes are limited, a crowd can become a panicked mob (Strauss, 1944). Members, fearing personal harm or injury, struggle to escape both from the situation and from the crowd itself:

> The individual breaks away and wants to escape from it because the crowd, as a whole, is endangered. But because he is still stuck in it, he must attack it. . . . The more fiercely each man "fights for his life," the clearer it becomes he is fighting against all the others who hem him in. They stand there like chairs, balustrades, closed doors, but different from these in that they are alive and hostile. (Canetti, 1962, pp. 26–27)

Panics often result in a staggering loss of life. In 1903, for example, a panic at Chicago's Iroquois Theater killed nearly 600 people. When a small fire broke out backstage, the management tried to calm the audience. But when the house lights when out and the fire was visible behind the stage, the crowd stampeded for the exits. Some were burned, and others died by jumping from the fire escapes to the pavement, but many more were killed as fleeing patrons trampled them. One observer described the panic this way:

> In places on the stairways, particularly where a turn caused a jam, bodies were piled seven or eight feet deep. Firemen and police confronted a sickening task in disentangling them. An occasional living person was found in the heaps, but most of these were terribly injured. The heel prints on the dead faces mutely testified to the cruel fact that human animals stricken in terror are as mad and ruthless as stampeding cattle. Many bodies had the clothes

---

**riot** A large and often widely dispersed crowd whose wanton and unrestrained behavior violates rules of civil and legal authority (e.g., harassment, looting, destruction of property, assault, violence).

torn from them, and some had the flesh trodden from their bones. (Foy & Harlow, 1928/1956)

Experimental simulations of panicked crowds suggest that individuals who must take turns exiting from a dangerous situation are most likely to panic when they believe that the time available to escape is very limited and when they are very fearful of the consequences of a failure to escape (Kelley et al., 1965; Mintz, 1951). Larger groups, even if given more time to effect their escape, are also more likely to panic than smaller ones (Chertkoff, Kushigian, & McCool, 1996). If a large group can be split up into smaller groups that are led separately to exits, the time taken to exit is reduced, but groups usually are unable to effect this level of control over their movements during a panic (Sugiman & Misumi, 1988).

The group waiting for the Who concert was initially a queue—a disorganized queue, but a queue nonetheless. But when the doors opened, the queue became a surging crowd, and then a panic. Although the news media described the crowd as a drug-crazed stampede bent on storming into the concert, police interviews with survivors indicated that the crowd members in the center of the crush were trying to flee from the dangerous overcrowding rather than to get into the concert. Also, some individuals in the crowd were clearly fighting to get out of the danger, but some were Good Samaritans who helped others to safety (Johnson, 1987).

Many municipalities and promoters, to prevent a repeat of the Who concert tragedy, have banned general admission seating: all tickets are for specific seats within the venue. However, in places where general admission seating is permitted, norms often develop to create queues to prevent crowding. Before shows by the band U2 in the United States, for example, fans holding general admission tickets arrive at the venue hours (or even days) before the doors open. They organize their wait, however, in a fairly elaborate normative system, in which each person's order in the line is recorded by self-appointed "line Nazis." Line breaking is not tolerated, although friends are permitted to hold places for late-arriving friends, provided that others nearby in the line are fully informed about the later arrival of additional queue members. In general, more committed fans are more adamant about maintaining the queue's norms (Helweg-Larsen & LoManaco, 2008). Other steps that can be taken to protect people when in crowds in public places are discussed in Focus 17.2.

## Collective Movements

Not all collective phenomena transpire at close distances. In some cases, individuals who are physically dispersed may act and react in similar and often atypical ways. Such curious phenomena are variously termed **collective movements**, *mass movements*, or *dispersed collective behavior*, although this terminology is by no means formalized or universally recognized (Genevie, 1978; Smelser, 1962). But like crowds, collective phenomena come in many varieties, including rumors, trends, and social movements (see Figure 17.3).

**Rumors and Mass Delusions** In 1954, rumors that windshields were being damaged by nuclear fallout began circulating in the Seattle area. The rumors escalated into a mild form of mass hysteria as reporters devoted much attention to the issue, residents jammed police telephone lines reporting damage, and civic groups demanded government intervention. Subsequent investigation revealed that no damage at all had occurred (Medalia & Larsen, 1958).

*Rumors* provide people with a means of exchanging information about threatening situations and, in many cases, have a calming effect on groups and communities. In some cases, however, rumors can instigate more negative reactions to uncertainty, and play a part in triggering riots and panics. Future rioters, for example, often mill about for hours swapping stories about injustices before taking any aggressive action. Panics and crazes, too, are often sustained by rumors, particularly when the mass

---

**collective movement** A large aggregation of individuals, widely dispersed across space and time, who strive to attain common goals, interests, or aspirations.

### Focus 17.2 What Can Be Done to Make Crowds Safer?

*The mob has no judgment, no discretion, no direction, no discrimination, no consistency.*

—Cicero

A dozen people were killed when a police raid triggered a panic in a crowded club in Mexico City, Mexico. When thousands of pilgrims massed on a narrow road to the Chamunda Devi temple in India, the crowd suddenly stampeded and 147 people were killed and scores injured. In China, at least three shoppers died during a rush on sale items at a superstore located in Beijing. When a rumor raced through a huge gathering of Shiite Muslims in Baghdad that a suicide bomber was in their midst, the crowd panicked and pushed forward across a narrow bridge with concrete barriers for security. Nearly 1,000 people were killed.

The primary cause of such tragedies is that the number of people present is too great for the space available, resulting in partial entrapment. Once constrained, if some event causes the group to feel threatened, then the members may try to move more quickly than they can, given the available space. The group then becomes uncoordinated, as portions of the crowd begin to move more slowly than other portions. Those caught in the jam lose their footing, fall, and then are trampled by the rest of the crowd as it passes over them.

Researchers have studied this breakdown in how group members move together in an attempt to identify ways to prevent tragedies due to overcrowding. In many cases, the work is being conducted by physicists and engineers, who approach the study of crowds by considering them to be flow systems of movement that obey the same laws that fluids and gasses do. Their basic model of pedestrian movement assumes that these self-organizing systems are stable, so long as volume does not reach critical levels. Once the volume surpasses this threshold for safety, then the system becomes chaotic and unpredictable—and a stampede may occur.

Dirk *Helbing* and his colleagues (2007), for example, have examined the causes of stampedes that occur, nearly every year, at the Jamarat Bridge during hajj. The investigators, to determine the source of the danger, conducted extensive analyses of the tapes taken from videocameras that recorded a deadly stampede in 2006. They discovered that, in most cases, the large group moved slowly, but inconsistently, through the crowded space. Some portions of the group moved more quickly than others, and density varied significantly across the entire crowd. Moreover, just as in engineering studies of traffic jams, they also noted the tendency for the groups to move in stop-and-go waves: Portions of the crowd would move forward more quickly than seemed prudent, given the congestion, and would then have to stop quickly when those in front of them were moving slower. Groups could tolerate these waves unless density became high, but density did reach very high levels at certain times—as great as 10 people per square meter. When such levels occurred, the group transitioned into what *Helbing* calls the "turbulence phase," in which individuals were no longer moving in the same direction. Turbulence, the researchers discovered, caused people to lose their footing, and if they fell the densely packed crowd unintentionally moved over them, killing or injuring them (Helbing, Johansson, & Al-Abideen, 2007; Johansson et al., 2008).

These findings suggest one certain solution: Control the number of people entering the area by constricting the size of the entry points so that they are smaller than the size of the exits. Cross-flows within the crowd should also be minimized, if possible, by creating lanes within the space—similar to lanes on a highway. The researchers also recommend installing "pressure relief valves": structures that can be opened should the densities become too great. These recommendations are being applied in the renovation of the Jamarat Bridge, which includes emergency exit ramps leading down from the sides of the bridge.

media perpetuate hearsay in news reports and announcements (Allport & Postman, 1947; Milgram & Toch, 1969). A recent epidemic of *koro* (a rare delusion characterized by the fear that one's sex organs will disappear) that swept through the Han region of China, for example, was traced to exposure to rumors about the fictitious malady (Cheng, 1997). Similarly, the riot that occurred at the 1999 Woodstock music festival was preceded by a day of rumors circulating through the crowd about what the final night of the concert would bring (Vider, 2004).

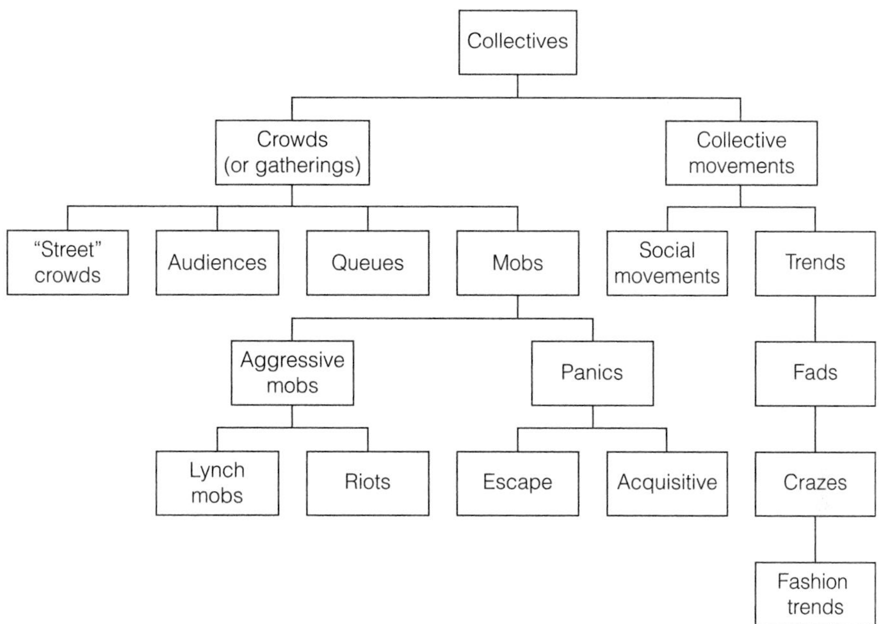


**FIGURE 17.3** A classification of collectives.

Ralph Rosnow (1980) argued that two conditions tend to influence the spread of rumor—the degree of *anxiety* that individuals are experiencing and their *uncertainty* about the true nature of the situation. He argued that just as individuals often affiliate with others in threatening situations, "ambiguous or chaotic" situations tend to generate rumors. By passing rumors, individuals convey information (albeit false) about the situation. Rumors also reduce anxiety by providing, in most cases, reassuring reinterpretations of the ambiguous event (Walker & Berkerle, 1987). After the Three Mile Island nuclear power plant accident, for example, rumors circulated so rampantly that a rumor control center had to be opened to supply more accurate information. Rosnow, after studying this incident, maintained that even though many of the rumors were preposterous, they gave people a sense of security in a time of great anxiety (Rosnow & Kimmel, 1979; Rosnow, Yost, & Esposito, 1986).

Rumors also provide the basis for **mass delusion**—the spontaneous outbreak of atypical thoughts, feelings, or actions in a group or aggregation, including psychogenic illness, common hallucinations, and bizarre actions (Pennebaker, 1982; Phoon, 1982). Such episodes are uncommon, but they have occurred regularly throughout the modern era. For example, the *Werther syndrome* is named for Johann Wolfgang von Goethe's (1749–1832) novel *Die Leiden des Jungen Werthers* (The Sorrows of Young Werther), which triggered a fashion fad (many young men of the time imitated the eccentric style of dress of the book's hero, Werther) but also led to cluster suicides—many readers also killed themselves in the same way as

**mass delusion** The spontaneous outbreak of atypical thoughts, feelings, or actions in a group or aggregation, including psychogenic illness, common hallucinations, and bizarre actions.

Werther did. *Choreomania* is the term used to describe the compulsive dancing crazes of the late Middle Ages. *Tulipmania* caused financial ruin for many who speculated in the bulb market in Holland. In the 1600s, the price of tulip bulbs skyrocketed in the Netherlands, and trading for the precious bulbs was frenzied. Many traders lost their life savings when the price of bulbs plummeted in 1637. *Biting mania* was a 15th-century epidemic of mass delusion, which began when a German nun developed a compulsive urge to bite her associates, who in turn bit others, until the mania spread to convents throughout Germany, Holland, and Italy (see Bartholomew & Goode, 2000, for a review).

In some cases, unexplained epidemics of illnesses are thought to have been cases of **psychogenic illness** rather than organic illness. For example, in June 1962, workers at a garment factory began complaining of nausea, pain, disorientation, and muscular weakness; some actually collapsed at their jobs or lost consciousness. Rumors spread rapidly that the illness was caused by "some kind of insect" that had infested one of the shipments of cloth from overseas, and the owners began making efforts to eradicate the bug. No bug was ever discovered, however, and experts eventually concluded that the "June Bug incident" had been caused by mass delusion (Kerckhoff & Back, 1968; Kerckhoff, Back, & Miller, 1965).

Researchers can never definitively determine which cases of widespread illness are socially produced rather than biologically produced, but one study of work groups identified 23 separate cases that involved large numbers of individuals afflicted with "physical symptoms . . . in the absence of an identifiable pathogen" (Colligan & Murphy, 1982, p. 35). More than 1200 people were affected by these outbreaks, with most reporting symptoms that included headaches, nausea, dizziness, and weakness. Many were women working in relatively repetitive, routinized jobs, and the illness often spread through friendship networks. Similarly, studies of pupils in school often conclude that many epidemics, such as outbreaks of fainting or nausea, are caused by hysterical contagion (Bartholomew, 1997; Bartholomew & Sirois, 1996; Lee et al., 1996). Some experts believe that many of the illnesses and medical complaints that are blamed on the presence of irritants in office buildings and schools—the so-called *sick building syndrome*—are actually psychogenic illnesses (Murphy, 2006).

How can group-level delusions be controlled? Organizational experts suggest that as soon as the possibility of a physical cause is eliminated, workers should be told that their problems are more psychological than physical. A second means of limiting the spread of such delusions involves altering the setting. The outbreaks often occur when employees have been told to increase their productivity, or when they have been working overtime. Poor labor–management relations have also been implicated, as have negative environmental factors, such as noise, poor lighting, and exposure to dust, foul odors, or chemicals (Colligan, Pennebaker, & Murphy, 1982). Larger outbreaks of rumors and hysteria that sweep across whole regions and countries can be countered by providing citizens with clear, accurate information from trusted sources.

**Trends** In 1929, as the United States plunged into the Great Depression, people had little time or money to spend playing golf. But several entrepreneurs set up "miniature golf courses" in cities, and the idea took hold of the nation with a vengeance. Miniature golf spread over the entire country, and some people were predicting that the game would replace all other sports as the country's favorite form of recreation. The craze died out within six months (LaPiere, 1938).

**Trends** are changes in attitudes, actions, and behaviors that influence large segments of a population,

---

**psychogenic illness** A set of symptoms of illness in a group of persons when there is no evidence of an organic basis for the illness and no identifiable environmental cause.

**trend** The general direction in which the attitudes, interests, and actions of a large segment of a population change over time, including fashion trends, fads, and crazes.

such as whole communities or regions. Many of these changes are relatively pedestrian ones; shifts in the use of the Internet, for example, illustrate the diffusion of a technological innovation across the world. Others, in contrast, are more capricious and unpredictable. A *fad*, for example, is an unexpected, short-lived change in the opinions, behaviors, or lifestyles of a large number of widely dispersed individuals. Fads such as the Hula Hoop, Live Strong bracelets, and Mood rings are remarkable both because they influence so many people so rapidly and because they disappear without leaving any lasting impact on society. *Crazes* are similar to fads in most respects, except that they are just a bit more irrational, expensive, or widespread. Streaking (running naked) on college campuses, the widespread use of cocaine in the 1980s, and playing hacky sack all qualify as crazes. Finally, fads that pertain to styles of dress or manners are generally termed *fashion trends*. Clamdiggers gave way to hip-huggers, which were supplanted by bellbottoms, which lost out to blue jeans, which gave way to khaki. Ties and lapels expand and contract, women's hemlines move up and down, and last season's color takes a backseat to this season's shade (Ragone, 1981).

**Social Movements** In 1096, thousands upon thousands of Europeans, urged on by Pope Urban II, marched to Jerusalem to "wrest that land from the wicked race." In 1789, large bands of French citizens fought government forces and eventually overthrew the government. In 1955, Dr. Martin Luther King, Jr., and a dozen other ministers founded the Montgomery Improvement Association, which succeeded in dismantling the segregated bus system in Montgomery, Alabama. In 1971, a group of protesters, calling themselves Greenpeace, organized a campaign to prevent environmental degradation. Greenpeace now claims 2.9 million supporters (contributors) and is involved in 40 countries across Europe, the Americas, Asia, and the Pacific.

A **social movement** is a deliberate, relatively organized attempt to achieve a change or resist a change in a social system. Social movements, like other forms of collective behavior, often arise spontaneously in response to some problem, such as unfair government policies, societal ills, or threats to personal values. They are, in a sense, very large support groups, seeking to improve the lives of both members and nonmembers (de la Roche, 1996). Social movements are not short-lived, however. Over time, social movements tend to gain new members, set goals, and develop leadership structures, until eventually they change from spontaneous gatherings of people into *social movement organizations*, or *SMOs*. SMOs have all the structural characteristics of any organization, including clearly defined goals, rational planning, and bureaucratic leadership structures (see van Zomeren, Postmes, & Spears, 2008, for a detailed review).

Social movements, like crowds, vary in their longevity and their goals (Appelbaum & Chambliss, 1995; Cameron, 1966). *Reformist movements* seek to improve existing institutions, often through civil disobedience and demonstrations. The U.S. civil rights movement, for example, sought to change existing laws that gave unfair power to Whites, but the movement did not challenge the basic democratic principles of the country. *Revolutionary movements*, in contrast, seek more sweeping changes in existing social institutions. The revolts in France in the late 1700s, for example, were revolutionary movements, for the protesters sought to overthrow the monarchy and replace it with a democracy. *Reactionary movements*, instead of trying to achieve change, seek to resist it or even to reinstate extinct social systems. The Ku Klux Klan is one such movement, as are many militia groups and groups that argue against alternative lifestyles. *Communitarian movements* strive to create more ideal living conditions than currently exist in modern society, often by withdrawing from contact with nonmembers. The communes of the 1960s were communitarian movements, as are such radical

---

**social movement** A collective movement making a deliberate, organized attempt to achieve a change or resist a change in a social system.

religious groups as Heaven's Gate, the Branch Davidians, the People's Temple, and the Solar Temple.

## COLLECTIVE DYNAMICS

Scholars have pondered and debated the vagaries of collectives for centuries, seeking to specify the factors that can transform individuals so thoroughly and so unexpectedly. Although many answers have been offered, this section narrows the analysis by focusing on five theoretical explanations that have stood the test of time and study. Each theory focuses on a different aspect of collective behavior, including motivational mechanisms, normative interpretations, and identity and its loss. Each one is selective in its focus, but taken together they provide considerable insight into a wide array of collective phenomena.

### Le Bon's Crowd Psychology: Contagion

Gustave Le Bon published his classic analysis of mobs and movements, *The Crowd*, in 1895. Le Bon was fascinated by large groups, but he also feared their tendency to erupt into violence. Perhaps because of these biases, he concluded that a crowd of people could, in certain instances, become a unified entity that acted as if guided by a single collective mind. Le Bon wrote,

> Whoever be the individuals that compose it, however like or unlike be their mode of life, their occupations, their character, or their intelligence, the fact that they have been transformed into a crowd puts them in possession of a sort of collective mind which makes them feel, think, and act in a manner quite different from that in which each individual of them would feel, think, and act were he in a state of isolation. (1895/1960, p. 27)

Le Bon believed that no matter what the individual qualities of the people in the group, the crowd would transform them, changing them from rational, thoughtful individuals into impulsive, unreasonable, and extreme followers. Once people fall under the "law of the mental unity of crowds" (1895/1960, p. 24), they act as the collective mind dictates.

Le Bon was a physician, so he viewed the collective mind as a kind of disease that infected one part of the group and then spread throughout the rest of the crowd (see Focus 17.3). After observing many crowds firsthand, Le Bon concluded that emotions and behaviors could be transmitted from one person to another just as germs can be passed along, and he believed that this process of **contagion** accounted for the tendency of group members to behave in very similar ways (Wheeler, 1966).

Many of Le Bon's speculations have been discredited, but he was right about one thing: Contagion is common in groups. People unconsciously mimic each other during everyday social interaction—if one person stands with her arms crossed over her chest, before long several of the others in the group will also cross their arms (Chartrand & Bargh, 1999). One person laughing in an audience will stimulate laughter in others. Question and answer sessions after a lecture usually begin very slowly, but they soon snowball as more and more questioners begin raising their hands. Individuals' emotions tend to converge over time when they interact frequently in groups (Anderson, Keltner, & Oliver, 2003). Mimicry of others is so basic a process that researchers believe that so-called *mirror neurons* are active when others' actions are observed, and that these neurons play a role in producing the identical behavior in the observer (Semin, 2007). Mimicry explains why members of collectives act as if they are guided by a single mind: As one person imitates the next, the collective begins to act in a uniform manner.

---

**contagion** The spread of behaviors, attitudes, and affect through crowds and other types of social aggregations from one member to another.

**Focus 17.3 Are Social Trends Infectious?**

*In a crowd every sentiment and act is contagious.*
—Le Bon (1895/1960, p. 50)

Society changes gradually over time as new ideas, behaviors, and innovations pass from one person and group to another in waves. But in the cases of fads, crazes, and other fast-moving trends, diffusion spreads rapidly across large segments of society. In 1978, few people owned microwave ovens. By 1990, nearly everyone did. The compact disc was a novelty for several years, until it suddenly and almost completely replaced vinyl records. Sales of Hush Puppy shoes jumped from 30,000 pairs to 430,000 pairs in one year.

Malcolm Gladwell's (2000) *tipping point theory* suggests that fast-moving trends are flu-like, spreading like contagious diseases through social groups. Gladwell drew the concept of a tipping point from studies of rapid changes in residential composition that occurred in predominantly White neighborhoods in the 1980s. These neighborhoods changed little when a few Black families moved in. But when the number of Black families reached a certain value—the *tipping point*—a large proportion of the prejudiced White residents moved out, and the neighborhood resegregated. Unlike most social changes, which are gradual and ubiquitous, this "White flight" was an abrupt, threshold-crossing process.

An illness, such as the flu, passes from one person to another, and individuals who interact with large numbers of people when their flu is in its communicable stage will infect far more people than will a person who stays at home. Similarly, Gladwell noted that certain types of individuals play prominent roles in the generation of social change. They are the people with large social networks (*connectors*), the individuals who are opinion authorities (*mavens*), and those who are able to persuade others to change their minds (*salespeople*). Relative to most people, these influential individuals can push an idea much more rapidly to many more people. Connectors, for example, have been identified as one source of the rapid shift in popularity of new musical groups. When investigators asked fans of a new musical group how many other people they told about the band, they discovered that most fans told only a few other people. But a small number of the fans—the connectors—told many more of their friends about the group, including one individual who claimed to have spread the message to more than 150 people (Reifman, Lee, & Apparala, 2004). Advertisers now target such influential persons, in the belief that if they win them over as customers, the rest of their network will follow (Keller & Berry, 2003).

Le Bon believed that such contagion processes reflected the heightened suggestibility of crowd members, but other processes may be at work as well. Because many crowd settings are ambiguous, social comparison processes may prompt members to rely heavily on other members' reactions when they interpret the situation (Singer et al., 1982). Contagion may also arise in crowds through imitation, social facilitation, or conformity (Chapman, 1973; Freedman & Perlick, 1979; Nosanchuk & Lightstone, 1974; Tarde, 1903).

Herbert Blumer combined these various processes when he argued that contagion involves circular reactions rather than interpretive reactions (Blumer, 1946, 1951, 1957). During interpretive interactions, group members carefully reflect on the meaning of others' behavior and try to formulate valid interpretations before making any kind of comment or embarking on a line of action. During circular reactions, however, the group's members fail to examine the meaning of others' actions cautiously and carefully and, therefore, tend to misunderstand the situation. When they act on the basis of such misunderstandings, the others in the group also begin to interpret the situation incorrectly, and a circular process is thus initiated that eventually culminates in full-blown behavioral contagion.

### Who Joins In: Convergence

Many explanations of collective behavior, rather than considering the processes that transform a wide variety of people so that they all act similarly, suggest that the members of the collective may have been similar to one another from the very start—that it was their similarities that prompted them to join the collective in the first place.

**Convergence theory** assumes that individuals who join rallies, riots, movements, crusades, and the like all possess particular personal characteristics that influence their group-seeking tendencies. Such aggregations are not haphazard gatherings of dissimilar strangers; rather, they represent the convergence of people with compatible needs, desires, motivations, and emotions. By joining in the group, the individual makes possible the satisfaction of these needs, and the crowd situation serves as a trigger for the spontaneous release of previously controlled behaviors. As Eric Hoffer (1951) wrote, "All movements, however different in doctrine and aspiration, draw their early adherents from the same types of humanity; they all appeal to the same types of mind" (p. 9).

But what "types of mind" are likely to join a crowd or movement? Are crowd members "joiners"? Are people who seek out membership in collective movements different, in terms of their personalities and values, than people who do not join such groups? Early conceptions of crowds, which portrayed their members as less intelligent, more easily influenced, more impulsive, and more violent, have not received consistent empirical support (Martin, 1920; Meerloo, 1950). Participants in mobs—particularly in connection with sports—tend to be younger men who have engaged in aggressive crowd activities in the past (Arms & Russell, 1997; Russell & Arms, 1998). People who join radical religious groups are usually teenagers or young adults, and although they tend to be more idealistic and open to new experiences, and higher in psychological dependency, they show no signs of psychological disturbance (Bromley, 1985; Levine, 1984; Walsh, Russell, & Wells, 1995).

Convergence theory, with its emphasis on the distinctive characteristics of the individuals who seek out membership in a collective, explains why only some people take part in social movements. Most people recognize the need to take action to make needed changes in society—to protect the environment, to reduce discrimination and prejudice, or to influence policy makers, for example. However, only some individuals within society become involved in social movements, raising the question of what sets these individuals apart from others (Snow & Oliver, 1995).

In a recent meta-analysis of this question, researchers identified three particularly important predictors of engagement in a social movement: a sense of injustice; efficacy; and social identity (van Zomeren, Postmes, & Spears, 2008). First, people who feel that principles of fairness and justice are violated by the status quo are more likely to take part in social movements. Collectives are often composed of those who are impoverished, persecuted, or endangered, but it is more the perceived unfairness of the deprivation that determines involvement in a collective rather than the deprivation itself. **Relative deprivation** is therefore more motivating than actual deprivation: those who join social movements tend to be people who have higher expectations but who have not succeeded in realizing these expectations.

Second, people who join social movements tend to be higher in a sense of *efficacy*—they believe that through their personal involvement, they can make a difference (Snow & Oliver, 1995). Self-confidence, achievement orientation, need for autonomy, dominance, self-acceptance, and maturity are all positively correlated with social activism (Werner, 1978). Individuals who have a history of taking part in collectives tend to jump at the chance to join new ones (Corning & Myers, 2002), but those who have a history of avoiding conflict are less likely to join (Ulbig & Funk, 1999).

---

**convergence theory** An explanation of collective behavior assuming that individuals with similar needs, values, or goals tend to converge to form a single group.

**relative deprivation** The psychological state that occurs when individuals feel that their personal attainments (*egoistic* deprivation) or their group's attainments (*fraternalistic* deprivation) are below their expectations.

Third, as social identity would suggest, the more an individual identifies with the group and its purposes, then the more likely he or she will devote time and energy to increasing its outcomes (Simon & Klandermans, 2001). As social identity theory explains, individuals do not think of themselves only in terms of their individual qualities, but also those that are based on their membership in groups. Because of this close connection between the self and the group, people react negatively if they feel that their own group does not enjoy the same level of prosperity as other groups. This group-level sense of deprivation, which is termed *fraternal deprivation*, tends to be even more motivating than individual-level, or *egoistic deprivation* (Runcimann, 1966). Individuals who are active in revolutionary social movements, such as the national separatist movements in Quebec and Ireland, are more likely to be dissatisfied with their group's outcomes than with their own personal outcomes (Abrams, 1990; Guimond & Dubé-Simard, 1983).

### Loss of Identity: Deindividuation

Philip Zimbardo's (1969, 2007) theory of **deindividuation**, unlike convergence theory, maintains that a collective can be so powerful that it can, under the right set of circumstances, transform nearly anyone, no matter what their personal characteristics. Stressing the power of the group situation, the theory assumes that people *escape* normative regulation in mobs and crowds. This theory suggests that in some cases people can become so deeply submerged in their group that they feel as though they no longer stand out as individuals, and this feeling can create a "reduction of inner restraints" (Festinger, Pepitone, & Newcomb, 1952).

Zimbardo's theory is an input–process–output model, for it identifies factors that cause deindividuation (inputs), the process of deindividuation itself, and the consequences of deindividuation (outputs). The inputs include situational factors, such as degree of anonymity and the size of the group, as well as more psychological factors: sense of responsibility, degree of arousal, and altered states of consciousness due to the use of drugs or alcohol. These factors, if present to a sufficient degree and intensity, may cause the members of the collective to become deindividuated, which is a state of altered awareness characterized by minimal self-awareness and regulation. Once in this state, individuals become more irrational, emotional, and impulsive, and so are more likely to perform aggressive, violent actions (Zimbardo, 1969, 1975, 1977a).

**Anonymity** Deindividuation theory suggests that collectives weaken the power of norms to restrain people's actions. Most people follow the norms of a given situation, both because they have internalized these standards but also because they fear public ridicule or legal sanction should they violate them. But when shielded from scrutiny by the anonymity of a crowd, people may engage in behavior that they would never consider undertaking as isolated, and highly identifiable, individuals. The 10% to 20% reduction in crime in the United Kingdom in recent years has been attributed, in part, to the proliferation of closed circuit television, which increases the identifiability of people when in public (Welsh & Farrington, 2004).

Any factor that augments the anonymizing effects of collectives further increases the likelihood of untoward group behavior. Crowds and mobs that form at night, under the cover of darkness, tend to be more unruly and aggressive than daylight crowds (e.g., Mann, 1981). According to anthropological evidence, warriors in 92.3% (12 out of 13) of the most highly aggressive cultures—ones known to practice headhunting and to torture captives—disguised themselves prior to battle, whereas only 30% (3 out of 10) of the low-aggression cultures featured similar rituals (Watson, 1973). Even groups assembled in classroom and laboratory settings behave more inappropriately when their members are anonymous: They use obscene language, break conventional norms governing conversation, express

---

**deindividuation** An experiential state caused by a number of input factors, such as group membership and anonymity, that is characterized by the loss of self-awareness, altered experiencing, and atypical behavior.

themselves in extreme ways, criticize one another, and perform embarrassing behaviors (Cannavale, Scarr, & Pepitone, 1970; Lindskold & Finch, 1982; Mathes & Guest, 1976; Singer, Brush, Lublin, 1965).

Zimbardo confirmed anonymity's impact experimentally by comparing the aggressiveness of anonymous groups to ones whose members were identifiable. Under an elaborate pretense, he asked all-female groups to give 20 electric shocks to two women. *Anonymous* women wore large lab coats (size 44) and hoods over their heads, and they were not permitted to use their names. Women who were *identifiable* were greeted by name and wore large name tags, and the experimenter emphasized their uniqueness and individuality. Although identifiability was unrelated to the number of shocks given (the average was 17 of 20), the unidentifiable participants held their switches down nearly twice as long as the identifiable participants (0.90 seconds versus 0.47 seconds).

Zimbardo's decision to dress his participants in hoods—the garb of lynch mobs and other criminals—may have exaggerated the relationship between anonymity and aggression. His participants might have responded to the experimenter's orders to deliver the shock differently if prosocial cues rather than antisocial cues had been present in the setting. Researchers verified this tendency, giving the White women who acted as participants costumes to wear under the guise of masking individual characteristics. In the *prosocial cues condition*, the experimenter explained that "I was fortunate the recovery room let me borrow these nurses' gowns." But in the *antisocial cues condition*, the experimenter mentioned that the costumes resembled Ku Klux Klan outfits: "I'm not much of a seamstress; this thing came out looking kind of Ku Klux Klannish" (Johnson & Downing, 1979, p. 1534). Anonymity *polarized* the groups, making them more prosocial or more antisocial depending on the valence of the situational cues.

Anonymity also polarized responses of participants who were sitting in a totally darkened room. All the participants in this study were escorted to and from the room and were assured that the other participants would not be told their identities. The individuals in the dark room reported feeling aroused, but in no case did the anonymous (and possibly deindividuated) group members exhibit hostility, aggressiveness, or violence. Rather, nearly all became more intimate and supportive. In the words of one participant, a "group of us sat closely together, touching, feeling a sense of friendship and loss as a group member left. I left with a feeling that it had been fun and nice" (Gergen, Gergen, & Barton, 1973, p. 129). Apparently, the situation helped people express feelings that they would have otherwise kept hidden, but these feelings were those of affection rather than aggression (see Figure 17.4).

**Responsibility** As Le Bon argued many years ago, the crowd is "anonymous, and in consequence irresponsible" (1895/1960, p. 30). This *diffusion of responsibility* has been verified in dozens of studies of people who faced various emergencies alone or in a group (see Chapter 7). Members of groups may also experience a reduction in responsibility if an authority demands compliance (Milgram, 1974) or if they do not recognize the connections between their personal actions and their final consequences. Some groups actually take steps to ensure the diffusion of responsibility, as when murderers pass around their weapons from hand to hand so that responsibility for the crime is distributed through the entire group rather than concentrated in the one person who pulls the trigger or wields the knife (Zimbardo, 1969, 2007).

**Group Membership** Deindividuation is a group-level process—individuals may feel unrecognizable or uncertain as to their identity, but only groups create the sense of anonymity and diffusion of responsibility that generates deindividuation. Edward Diener and his associates tested this assumption in an ingenious study of Halloween trick-or-treating (Diener et al., 1976). Their participants were 1352 children from the Seattle area who visited one of the 27 experimental homes scattered throughout the city. Observers hidden behind decorative panels recorded the number of extra candy bars and money (pennies and nickels) taken by the trick-or-treaters

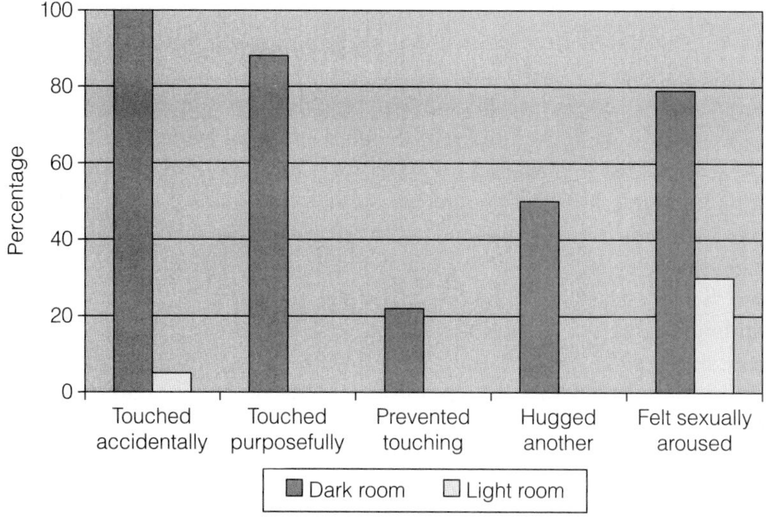


**FIGURE 17.4** The reactions reported by participants in the dark room or the light room.

SOURCE: From data presented in "Deviance in the Dark" by K. J. Gergen, M. M. Gergen, & W. H. Barton. Reprinted with permission from *Psychology Today* magazine. Copyright © 1973 (Sussex Publishers, Inc.).

who were told to take one candy bar each. The children came to the house alone or in small groups (exceedingly large groups were not included in the study, nor were groups that included an adult). An experimenter manipulated anonymity by asking some children to give their names and addresses. As expected, the children took more money and candy in groups than alone and when they were anonymous rather than identified. The effects of anonymity on solitary children were not very pronounced. However, in the group conditions, the impact of anonymity was enhanced (see Figure 17.5). These findings, which have been supported by other investigations, suggest that the term *deindividuation* is used most appropriately in reference to people who perform atypical behavior while they are members of a group (Cannavale, Scarr, & Pepitone, 1970; Mathes & Guest, 1976; Mathes & Kahn, 1975).

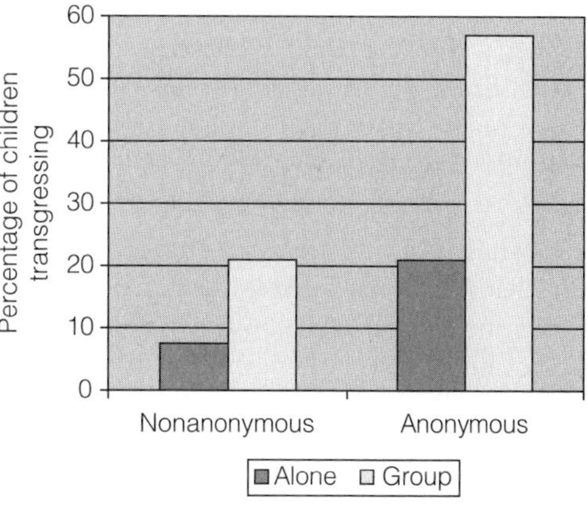


**FIGURE 17.5** The combined effects of anonymity and group membership on counternormative behavior.

SOURCE: From data from "Effects of deindividuating variables on stealing by Halloween trick-or-treaters," by E. Diener, S. C. Fraser, A. L. Beaman, & R. T. Kelem, *Journal of Personality and Social Psychology, 33*, 1976. Copyright 1976 by the American Psychological Association. Reprinted by permission.

**Group Size** Are larger groups more likely to act in unusual ways? Leon Mann discovered that people are more likely to respond to religious messages when they are part of a larger rather than a smaller group (Newton & Mann, 1980). At the end of many religious meetings, audience members are invited to become "inquirers" by coming forward and declaring their dedication to Christ. In 57 religious meetings, the correlation between crowd size and the proportion of people who moved down to the stage to become inquirers was .43. On Sundays, the correlation rose to .78. Larger lynch mobs are also more violent than smaller ones.

A review of historical records of 60 such groups reveals that they ranged in size from 4 to 15,000, but that larger mobs were more likely to attack more victims (Mullen, 1986).

**Arousal** Zimbardo listed a number of other variables that stimulate deindividuated action, including altered temporal perspective, sensory overload, heightened involvement, lack of situational structure, and use of drugs. Many of these factors, he suggested, function by both arousing and distracting group members. Zimbardo even suggested that certain rituals, such as war dances and group singing, are actually designed to arouse participants and enable them to be deindividuated when the fighting starts: "Among cannibals, like the Cenis or certain Maori and Nigerian tribes, the activity of ritual bonfire dance which precedes eating the flesh of another human being is always more prolonged and intense when the victim is to be eaten alive or uncooked" (1969, p. 257). Aroused individuals, as deindividuation theory suggests, tend to respond more aggressively, particularly when in a group (Goldstein, 2002).

**Self-Awareness** Zimbardo's deindividuation theory posits that situational variables, such as anonymity and membership in a group, can in some cases combine to induce psychological changes in group members. Deindividuated people, Zimbardo predicted, should feel very little self-awareness, and this minimization of self-scrutiny is the most immediate cause of the atypical behaviors seen in collectives.

Diener (1979, 1980) tested this hypothesis by making use of an Asch-type experimental situation. He created eight-person groups, but he included in each group six accomplices trained to facilitate or inhibit the development of deindividuation. In the *self-aware condition*, the confederates seemed restless and fidgety. Everyone wore name tags as they worked on tasks designed to heighten self-awareness, such as providing personal responses to questions, sharing their opinions on topics, and disclosing personal information about themselves. In the *non-self-aware condition*, Diener shifted the participants' focus of attention outward by having them perform a series of mildly distracting tasks. The problems were not difficult, but they required a good deal of concentration and creativity. In the *deindividuation condition*, Diener tried to foster feelings of group cohesiveness, unanimity, and anonymity by treating the members as interchangeable and by putting the groups through a variety of arousing activities.

When Diener asked the participants to describe how they felt during the study, he identified the two clusters, or factors, shown in Table 17.2. The first factor, *loss of self-awareness*, encompasses a lack of self-consciousness, little planning of action, high group unity, and uninhibited action. The second dimension, *altered experiencing*, is also consistent with the deindividuation theory in that it ties together a number of related processes, such as "unusual" experiences, altered perceptions, and a loss of individual identity. When Diener compared the responses of participants in the three conditions of his experiment, he discovered that (1) deindividuated

**TABLE 17.2 Characteristics of Factors That Combine to Create a State of Deindividuation**

| Factor | Typical Characteristics |
|---|---|
| **Loss of self-awareness** | Minimal self-consciousness<br>Lack of conscious planning as behavior becomes spontaneous<br>Lack of concern for what others think of one<br>Subjective feeling that time is passing quickly<br>Liking for the group and feelings of group unity<br>Uninhibited speech<br>Performing uninhibited tasks |
| **Altered experiencing** | Unusual experiences, such as hallucinations<br>Altered states of consciousness<br>Subjective loss of individual identity<br>Feelings of anonymity<br>Liking for the group and feelings of group unity |

SOURCE: "Deindividuation, Self-Awareness, and Disinhibition," by E. Diener, *Journal of Personality and Social Psychology, 37*, 1160–1171. 

participants displayed a greater loss of self-awareness than both the non-self-aware and the self-aware participants and (2) deindividuated participants reported more extreme altered experiencing than the self-aware participants.

Steven Prentice-Dunn and Ronald W. Rogers (1982) extended these findings by leading the members of four-man groups to believe that they were going to deliver electric shocks to another person. Half of the participants were led through a series of experiences that focused their attention on the situation, whereas the others were frequently reminded to pay attention to their personal feelings. Moreover, some participants were told that their actions would be carefully monitored, whereas others were led to believe that their actions were not going to be linked to them personally. The results of the study supported Diener's two-factor model of deindividuation on three counts. First, the participants who were prompted to focus on the situation were lower in private self-awareness, and they tended to behave more aggressively. Second, analysis of the participants' questionnaire responses revealed the two components emphasized by Diener: low self-awareness and altered experiencing. Third, using a statistical procedure known as path analysis, Prentice-Dunn and Rogers found that both of these components mediated the relationship between the variables they manipulated and the participants' aggressive response (Prentice-Dunn & Rogers, 1980, 1982, 1983; Prentice-Dunn & Spivey, 1986; Rogers & Prentice-Dunn, 1981).

### Emergent Norm Theory

Zimbardo's theory of deindividuation suggests that members of collectives are more likely to act in extreme and unusual ways, and researchers have confirmed the relationship between such factors as anonymity and increasing group size on negative behaviors. However, when Tom Postmes and Russell Spears (1998) conducted a meta-analysis of 60 studies that examined the theory, they found little support for the assumption that these factors trigger psychological changes, or that these changes mediate the relationship between situational factors and aberrant actions. In fact, their analysis suggested that these factors *decrease* the variability of people's actions in collectives. Crowd members are not rule breakers, they concluded, but rather conformists who are following the example set by others in the group.

This analysis is consistent with Ralph Turner and Lewis Killian's **emergent norm theory** (Turner, 1964; Turner & Killian, 1972). Turner and Killian rejected one of the fundamental assumptions of most collective behavior theories—that crowds are extremely homogeneous—and concluded that the mental unity of crowds is primarily an illusion. Crowds, mobs, and other collectives only seem to be unanimous in their emotions and actions because the members all adhere to norms that are relevant in the given situation. Granted, these *emergent norms* may be unique and sharply contrary to more general societal standards, but as they emerge in the group situation, they exert a powerful influence on behavior.

Turner and Killian based their analysis on Sherif's (1936) classic analysis of the gradual alignment of action in groups. As noted in Chapter 6, norms emerge gradually in ambiguous situations as members align their actions. Individuals do not actively try to conform to the judgments of others, but instead use the group consensus when making their own behavioral choices. In most cases, the group's norms are consistent with more general social norms pertaining to work, family, relations, and civility. In other cases, however, norms emerge in groups that are odd, atypical, or unexpected.

A normative approach partly explains the unusual behavior of some crowds that form near buildings where a person is threatening to commit suicide by leaping to his or her death. In some cases these crowds transform from relatively passive audiences into **baiting crowds** whose members urge

---

**emergent norm theory** An explanation of collective behavior suggesting that the uniformity in behavior often observed in collectives is caused by members' conformity to unique normative standards that develop spontaneously in those groups.

**baiting crowd** A gathering of people in a public location whose members torment, tease, or goad others.

the jumper to take his or her life. When Mann studied members of such crowds, he was unable to identify any similarities in personality or demographic characteristics (as convergence theory would suggest). He did note, however, that baiting became more likely as crowd size increased. Mann suggested that larger crowds are more likely to include at least one person who introduces the baiting norm into the group. "In a large crowd at least one stupid or sadistic person will be found who is prepared to cry 'Jump!' and thereby provide a model for suggestible others to follow" (Mann, 1981, p. 707). Mann reported evidence of conformity to the baiting norm in crowds that not only encouraged the victim to "end it all" but also jeered and booed as rescuers attempted to intervene.

Emergent norm theory, in contrast to other analyses of crowds and collectives, argues that collectives are not out of control or normless. Rather, their behavior is socially structured, but by an unusual, temporary norm rather than by more traditional social standards. For example, some cults, such as Heaven's Gate, condone mass suicide. Adolescent peer cliques pressure members to take drugs and commit illegal acts (Corsaro & Eder, 1995; Giordano, 2002). Groups of women, such as sororities, can develop norms that promote unhealthy actions such as binge eating and purging (Crandall, 1988). Urban gangs accept norms that emphasize toughness, physical strength, and the use of drugs (Coughlin & Venkatesh, 2003; Jankowski, 1991). Groups of hooligans at British soccer matches consider violence a normal part of the event, and mass media sustain this view (Dunning, Murphy, & Williams, 1986; Ward, 2002). Although these actions—when viewed from a more objective perspective—may seem out of control and very strange, for the group members they are literally "normal."

## Collectives and Social Identity

Social identity theory, like emergent norm theory, also takes issue with one of deindividuation theory's core assumptions. Deindividuation suggests that people in collectives experience a loss of identity, but social identity suggests that another aspect of their identity—their collective, social identity—is actually augmented in collectives. The act of joining a social movement, for instance, can be one of self-definition (Polletta & Jasper, 2001). For example, the alcoholic who joins Alcoholics Anonymous proclaims, "I am an alcoholic," just as the man who joins Promise Keepers lays public claim to his religiosity and masculinity (Melucci, 1989). Collectives are also intergroup settings, so when individuals join them, their personal and social identities change (Reicher & Levine, 1994; Reicher, Spears, & Postmes, 1995; Waddington, 2008).

**Social Identity and Intergroup Conflict** Mobs, riots, and gangs are often intergroup phenomena. Riots in inner cities, for example, usually occur when inner-city residents contend against another group: the police (Goldberg, 1968). Violence during athletic competitions often occurs when the fans of one team attack, en masse, the fans or players of another team (Leonard, 1980). Protests on college campuses pit students against the university administration (Lipset & Wolin, 1965). Inner-city gangs vie for turf against other gangs (Sanders, 1994). Militia groups rise up to confront civil and judicial authorities (Flynn & Gerhardt, 1989). Lynch mobs were crowds of Whites with high solidarity who attacked Blacks (de la Roche, 2002). A lone collective is a rarity, for in most cases, collectives emerge in opposition to other collectives.

Collectives, as intergroup phenomena, provide members with an enlarged view of the self, based not just on individual qualities but also on collectivistic qualities. Such collectives do not lead to deindividuation but to a depersonalized sense of self that reflects group-level qualities rather than individual ones. The presence of an outgroup increases the salience of the collective identity, and members begin to perceive themselves and the situation in ways that reflect the ingroup–outgroup bias: Other members of the ingroup are viewed positively, as are their actions, whereas outgroup members and their actions are denigrated (see Chapter 14).

Stephen Reicher's (1984, 1987, 1996, 2001) analyses of participants in riots are consistent with social identity theory. For example, one riot occurred when members of the National Union of Students organized a demonstration in London. The leaders of the group planned to march to the Houses of Parliament, and as police blocked their path, conflict erupted. As the tension between the groups escalated, the students became more unified. When one member of the group was arrested by the police, students attacked the police unit as a group. They also felt that the police were behaving violently and that they themselves only responded in self-defense. As one student put it, "To some extent there was a feeling of there was the students and there was the police and you knew which side you were on so you had to be up in the front with students, you know. And there was a lot of crowd empathy" (quoted in Reicher, 1996, p. 126).

**Individuation** A paradox permeates the analysis of individuality and collectives. On the one hand, many theorists assume that submersion in a group results in the attainment of power and an escape from societal inhibitions; hence, group members seek and try to maintain the experience of deindividuation. On the other hand, many psychologists believe that people can enjoy psychological well-being only when they are able to establish and maintain their own unique identities: "A firm sense of one's own autonomous identity is required in order that one may be related as one human being to another. Otherwise, any and every relationship threatens the individual with loss of identity" (Laing, 1960, p. 44; see, too, Dipboye, 1977; Fromm, 1965; Maslow, 1968).

An *identity affirmation* approach to collective behavior suggests that group members who feel "lost" in a group will try to reestablish their individual identities. People in large crowds, for example, may act oddly to regain a sense of individuality, not because they feel anonymous. Individuals who take part in riots may do so not to protest their group's unfair treatment, but to reaffirm their individual identities. As one resident of the riot-torn community of Watts (in Los Angeles) explained, "I don't believe in burning, stealing, or killing, but I can see why the boys did what they did. They just wanted to be noticed, to let the world know the seriousness of their state of life" (Milgram & Toch, 1969, p. 576). Similarly, members of large groups, such as industrial workers, students in large classrooms, people working in bureaucratic organizations, and employees in companies with high turnover rates, may perform atypical actions just to stand apart from the crowd.

Christina Maslach (1972) examined this *individuation* process by making two people in a four-person group feel individuated; she referred to them by name, made more personal comments to them, and maintained a significant amount of eye contact. She made the other two feel deindividuated by avoiding close contact with them and addressing them impersonally. When these individuals were later given the opportunity to engage in a free-response group discussion and to complete some questionnaires, the deindividuated participants evidenced various identity-seeking reactions. Some attempted to make themselves seem as different as possible from the other group members by giving more unusual answers to the questions, making longer comments, joining in the discussion more frequently, and attempting to capture the attention of the experimenter. Other participants seemed to redefine their identities by revealing more intimate details of their personalities and beliefs through longer and more unusual self-descriptions.

## COLLECTIVES ARE GROUPS

All groups are intriguing, but groups that undertake extreme actions under the exhortation of exotic, charismatic leaders—cults, mobs, crowds, and the like—fascinate both layperson and researcher. Although groups are so commonplace that they often go unnoticed and unscrutinized, atypical groups invite speculation and inquiry. But are such groups mad? Do human beings lose their rationality when they are immersed in mobs?

### The Myth of the Madding Crowd

For well over a century, most theorists and researchers have assumed that crowds are unique social aggregations, a "perversion of human potential" (Zimbardo, 1969, p. 237) where impulse and chaos replace reason and order. Le Bon argued that crowds develop a collective mind that leaves individual members unable to think for themselves. Convergence theories assume that atypical groups are staffed by atypical people. Groups often develop odd, unusual norms, and members may forget who they are when they sink too deeply into their groups. This belief in the "madness of crowds" is so deeply ingrained in our conception of collectives that some individuals who commit violent crimes in groups face reduced sentences. Deindividuated and driven to conform to their group's norms, they are not held personally responsible for their actions (Colman, 1991).

Yet collectives are, at their core, groups, and so the processes that shape group behaviors also shape collective behaviors. Many contemporary theorists, rather than assuming that collectives are atypical groups that require special theories that include novel or even mysterious processes, argue that the "madding crowd" is more myth than reality. Collective behavior is not bizarre, but instead a rational attempt by a number of individuals to seek change through united action. These groups form, change, and disband following the same patterns that govern other groups, and the internal structures and processes of a collective and a group are more similar than they are different.

Clark McPhail (1991) elaborated this viewpoint in his book *The Myth of the Madding Crowd*. McPhail maintained that early theorists were too biased by their preconceived belief that crowds are crazed. McPhail himself carried out extensive field studies of actual collective movements over a 10-year period so that he could determine firsthand what such groups do. His conclusions were threefold:

> First, individuals are not driven mad by crowds; they do not lose cognitive control! Second, individuals are not compelled to participate by some madness-in-common, or any other sovereign psychological attribute, cognitive style, or predisposition that distinguishes them from nonparticipants. Third, the majority of behaviors in which members of these crowds engaged are neither mutually inclusive nor extraordinary, let alone mad. (McPhail, 1991, p. xxii)

A hundred years of theory and research that have pushed the "crowd-as-mad" position is a stalwart legacy that cannot be easily dismissed. Yet the available evidence favors the view that the crowd is a group. When scholars have reviewed some of the famous examples of crowd delusions, such as dancing mania and the supposed panic during the *War of the Worlds* broadcast, they have discovered that these events were sensationalized (Bartholomew & Goode, 2000). Le Bon's (1895/1960) crowd psychology made dire predictions about crowds and mobs, but his analysis was driven more by his prejudices than the facts (Bendersky, 2007). The media and laypersons are quick to call crowds irrational and mad, but the data do not support this conjecture. McPhail (1991), for example, concluded that violence is very rare in crowds. In most cases, individuals in the crowd are committed to particular goals, and like any performing group, they do their share of the work to increase the group's chances for success. Moreover, when violence does occur, it takes the form of intergroup conflict rather than mindless savagery. Even the group at the Who concert did not behave badly. Many experts condemned the crowd, calling it a stampede, but when Cincinnati sociologist Norris Johnson (1987) looked more closely at the evidence, he concluded that the crowd did not stampede or engage in selfish, destructive behavior. Indeed, the amount of helping shown by the people in the crowd exceeded what we would normally expect to find among a group of bystanders.

The crowd-as-mad and the crowd-as-group views must be reconciled in a more complete understanding of collective behavior. Crowds do, on occasion, perpetrate great wrongs—wrongs that seem more malevolent than any one individual's capacity for evil. Yet people in crowds usually act in ways that are unremarkable. Crowds are groups, and collective dynamics are for the most part the same as small group dynamics. Hence, the next time you hear of a crowd behaving oddly, do not dismiss its actions as one more illustration of a group gone wrong.

### Studying Groups and Collectives

In this book, we have examined many different groups—a band of outcasts from the art community that generated a cohesive movement that redefined the world of art; a sports team that survived against all odds when their plane crashed in the Andes; a cohesive hockey team that outperformed a superior opponent; a jury reaching a verdict by carefully reviewing its mission and the evidence it was given; a group led by a powerful authority figure who manipulated the members through deceit and subterfuge; teams that worked to make products and decisions, including military and political experts who planned an ill-fated invasion; groups that had to deal with conflict within their ranks and conflict with other groups; a heroic group trying to return to Earth after circling the Moon; and a group of people who made use of the restorative, curative impact of a group to gain self-understanding and improve their well-being. In this final chapter we have turned to examine crowds, mobs, and social movements.

These analyses have illuminated many of a group's most basic processes—how groups take in and reject members; evolve over time; organize their members in hierarchies of authority; perform tasks, both effectively and ineffectively; make plans and decisions; and succor their members and regulate behavior in context. But these analyses have also revealed that groups, like large collectives, are often misunderstood and mismanaged. It is ironic that whereas scientists have studied aspects of the physical world for centuries, only in the last hundred years have they turned their attention to human experiences, and human groups in particular. Yet the theories and studies of group dynamics we have examined here repeatedly confirm the important role that groups play in all aspects of social life. Human beings are in many ways individuals who are seeking their personal, private objectives, yet they are also members of larger social units that may be seeking collective outcomes. As social creatures, embedded in a rich network of mutual, collective, and reciprocal relationships, individuals cannot be understood fully without considering the social groups to which they belong.

Fortunately, the field of group dynamics offers the means of reducing our ignorance of this fundamental aspect of the human condition. Stanley Milgram and Hans Toch, writing 35 years ago, asked this question: If we "do not take up the job of understanding riots, panics, and social movements, who will?" (1969, p. 590). Their question applies, with equal force, to the study of groups in general. If we do not take up the job of understanding groups, who will?

## SUMMARY IN OUTLINE

*What is collective behavior?*

1. The term *collective behavior* has many interpretations, but in general, it describes instances in which a relatively large group of people respond in a similar way to an event or situation. *Collectives* differ from other types of groups in terms of:
   - Size: Collectives tend to be large rather than small.
   - Proximity: In some cases, members of a collective are together in one place (e.g., crowds), but other collectives involve individuals who are dispersed across great distances (e.g., social movements).
   - Duration: Collectives sometimes, but not always, form and disband rapidly.

- Conventionality: Members sometimes engage in atypical, unconventional, or even aberrant behaviors.
- Relationships between members: Collectives are often weak associations of individuals rather than cohesive groups.

2. *Crowds* include common crowds, such as street crowds or public gatherings, audiences, queues, and mobs (aggressive mobs and panics).
   - Street crowds, although unstable and short-lived, display consistent structures and behavioral tendencies. McPhail has documented the types of behaviors common in such groups and Milgram has studied how they form.
   - *Audiences* and *queues* are more normatively regulated than crowds. Milgram's studies of line breaking suggest that queue members are both group- and self-motivated.
   - *Mobs* include both positive and negative types of crowds, such as hooligans, *riots*, and lynch mobs.
   - Panics occur when crowds seek to escape a situation or when fearful a valued resource will run out (acquisitive panics).
   - Studies of very large crowds, such as those conducted by *Helbing* at the Jamarat Bridge, have identified the factors that contribute to injury in such crowds and ways to reduce the danger.
3. Individuals need not be concentrated in a single location to display convergence in action, for such *collective movements* as rumors, *trends* (fads, crazes, fashion trends), *mass delusions*, *psychogenic illness*, and *social movements* can influence widely dispersed individuals.
   - Rosnow suggests that anxiety and uncertainty are key triggers for rumor transmission.
   - Researchers have identified four types of social movements: reformist, revolutionary, reactionary, and communitarian.

*What theories explain collective behavior?*

1. Le Bon maintained that crowds are governed by a collective mind and that *contagion* causes crowd members to experience similar thoughts and emotions.
   - People tend to imitate each other, thereby increasing the likelihood that their actions will become unified and coordinated.
   - Gladwell's tipping point theory suggests that fast-moving trends can spread like contagious diseases through social groups.
2. *Convergence theories* propose that the individuals who join groups often possess similar needs and personal characteristics.
   - Involvement in social movements is related to individuals' sense of injustice, efficacy, and identity.
   - Studies of *relative deprivation*, for example, suggest that people whose attainments fall below their expectations are more likely to join social movements.
3. Zimbardo's deindividuation theory traces collective phenomena back to *deindividuation*, which can be broken down into three components—inputs, internal changes, and behavioral outcomes. Inputs, or causes, of deindividuation include feelings of anonymity, reduced responsibility (diffusion of responsibility), membership in large groups, and a heightened state of physiological arousal.
   - Zimbardo's study of aggression in hooded college students, Diener's study of Halloween trick-or-treaters, and Mann's studies of religious groups, all support the basic model.
   - Diener's work, as well as that of Prentice-Dunn and Rogers, suggests that the deindividuated state has two basic

components—reduced self-awareness (minimal self-consciousness, etc.) and altered experiencing (disturbances in concentration and judgment, etc.).

4. A meta-analysis conducted by Postmes and Spears (1998) suggests that individuals in collectives are more, rather than less, likely to act in ways that are consistent with the group's norms. These findings support Turner and Killian's *emergent norm theory*, which posits that crowds often develop unique standards for behavior and that these atypical norms exert a powerful influence on behavior. The *baiting crowd*, for example, forms when a group of onlookers collectively urges someone to injure him- or herself.
5. Social identity theory suggests that much of the behavior of individuals in collectives can be explained by basic identity mechanisms.
   - As Reicher notes, collective behavior is often intergroup behavior, and so individuals maximize their individual sense of worth by identifying with the ingroup.
   - Work by Maslach and others indicates that collective behavior in some cases represents an attempt to reestablish a sense of individuality.

*How different are collectives from other types of groups?*

1. Recent analyses of crowds and collectives have questioned the "crowd-as-mad" assumption. Collectives differ from more routine groups in degree rather than in kind.
2. Collectives, like groups in general, are often misunderstood and mismanaged, but the field of group dynamics offers a means of dispelling this ignorance.

## FOR MORE INFORMATION

*Chapter Case: The Who Concert*

- "Panic at 'The Who Concert Stampede': An Empirical Assessment," by Norris R. Johnson (1987), provides considerable background information and theoretical analysis of the crowd that pushed through the doors at Cincinnati's Riverfront Coliseum in 1979.

*Crowds and Collectives*

- "Collective Behavior: Crowds and Social Movements," by Stanley Milgram and Hans Toch (1969), though written 40 years ago, still offers fundamental insights into collective behavior.
- *Collective Behavior*, by Ralph Turner (2001), is a succinct yet comprehensive overview of the key theories of "those forms of social behavior in which the usual conventions cease to guide social action and people collectively transcend, bypass, or subvert established institutional patterns and structures" (p. 348).
- "The Human Choice: Individuation, Reason, and Order Versus Deindividuation, Impulse, and Chaos," by Phillip G. Zimbardo (1969), is a wide-ranging analysis of the causes and consequences of the loss of identity that sometimes occurs in groups.
- "Toward an Integrative Social Identity Model of Collective Action: A Quantitative Research Synthesis of Three Socio-Psychological Perspectives," by Martijn van Zomeren, Tom Postmes, and Russell Spears (2008), provides a scholarly review of the vast literature on social movements, as well as results from their meta-analysis of the impact of injustice, efficacy, and identity on social participation.

*Collectives as Groups*

- *The Myth of the Madding Crowd*, by Clark McPhail (1991), expertly synthesizes prior theoretical work on crowds with McPhail's field studies of actual crowds to dispel many absurd myths about crowds and replace them with data-based propositions.

- "Rethinking Crowd Violence: Self-Categorization Theory and the Woodstock 1999 Riot," by Stephen Vider (2004), is a conceptually rich case study of a riot that occurred, ironically, during a music festival celebrating the peace movement of the 1960s.

## Media Resources

Visit the Group Dynamics companion website at www.cengage.com/psychology/forsyth to access online resources for your book, including quizzes, flash cards, web links, and more!

# References


Aarts, H., & Dijksterhuis, A. (2003). The silence of the library: Environment, situational norm, and social behavior. *Journal of Personality and Social Psychology, 84,* 18–28.

Aarts, H., Dijksterhuis, A., & Custers, R. (2003). Automatic normative behavior in environments: The moderating role of conformity in activating situational norms. *Social Cognition, 21,* 447–464.

Abele, A. E. (2003). The dynamics of masculine-agentic and feminine-communal traits: Findings from a prospective study. *Journal of Personality and Social Psychology, 85,* 768–776.

Abrams, D. (1990). *Political identity: Relative deprivation, social identity, and the case of Scottish nationalism.* London: Economic and Social Research Council.

Abrams, D., & Hogg, M. A. (2001). Collective identity: Group membership and self-conception. In M. A. Hogg & R. S. Tindale (Eds.), *Blackwell handbook of social psychology: Group processes* (pp. 425–460). Malden, MA: Blackwell.

Abrams, D., Hogg, M. A., Hinkle, S., & Often, S. (2005). The social identity perspective on small groups. In M. S. Poole & A. B. Hollingshead (Eds.), *Theories of small groups: Interdisciplinary perspectives* (pp. 99–137). Thousand Oaks, CA: Sage.

Abrams, D., Hogg, M. A., & Marques, J. M. (2005). A social psychological framework for understanding social inclusion and exclusion. In D. Abrams, M. A. Hogg, & J. M. Marques (Eds.), *The social psychology of inclusion and exclusion* (pp. 1–23). New York: Psychology Press.

Abrams, D., Hopthrow, T., Hulbert, L., & Frings, D. (2006). "Groupdrink"? The effect of alcohol on risk attraction among groups versus individuals. *Journal of Studies on Alcohol, 67,* 628–636.

Adams, R. B. (1998). Inciting sociological thought by studying the Deadhead community: Engaging publics in dialogue. *Social Forces, 77,* 1–25.

Adler, P. A., & Adler, P. (1995). Dynamics of inclusion and exclusion in preadolescent cliques. *Social Psychology Quarterly, 58,* 145–162.

Agazarian, Y. M. (2001). *A systems-centered approach to inpatient group psychotherapy.* Philadelphia: Jessica Kingsley.

Aiello, J. R. (1987). Human spatial behavior. In D. Stokols & I. Altman (Eds.), *Handbook of environmental psychology* (Vol. 1, pp. 389–504). New York: Wiley.

Aiello, J. R., & Douthitt, E. A. (2001). Social facilitation: From Triplett to electronic performance monitoring. *Group Dynamics: Theory, Research, and Practice, 5,* 163–180.

Aiello, J. R., & Kolb, K. J. (1995). Electronic performance monitoring and social context: Impact on productivity and stress. *Journal of Applied Psychology, 80,* 339–353.

Albright, L., Kenny, D. A., & Malloy, T. E. (1988). Consensus in personality judgments at zero acquaintance. *Journal of Personality and Social Psychology, 55,* 387–395.

Alge, B. J. (2001). Effects of computer surveillance on perceptions of privacy and procedural justice. *Journal of Applied Psychology, 86,* 797–804.

Alicke, M. D., Braun, J. C., Glor, J. E., Klotz, M. L., Magee, J., Sederholm, H., & Siegel, R. (1992). Complaining behavior in social interaction. *Personality and Social Psychology Bulletin,18,* 286–295.

Allen, K. M., Blascovich, J., & Mendes, W. B. (2002). Cardiovascular reactivity in the presence of pets, friends, and spouses: The truth about cats and dogs. *Psychosomatic Medicine, 64,* 727–739.

Allen, K. M., Blascovich, J., Tomaka, J., & Kelsey, R. M. (1991). Presence of human friends and pet dogs as moderators of autonomic responses to stress in women. *Journal of Personality and Social Psychology, 61,* 582–589.

Allen, N. J., & Hecht, T. D. (2004). The 'romance of teams': Toward an understanding of its psychological underpinnings and implications. *Journal of Occupational and Organizational Psychology, 77,* 439–461.

Allen, V. L. (1975). Social support for nonconformity. *Advances in Experimental Social Psychology, 8,* 2–43.

Allison, G., & Zelikow, P. (1999). *Essence of decision: Explaining the Cuban Missile Crisis* (2nd ed.). New York: Longman.

Allison, S. T., McQueen, L. R., & Schaerfl, L. M. (1992). Social decision making processes and the equal partitionment of shared resources. *Journal of Experimental Social Psychology, 28,* 23–42.

Allison, S. T., & Messick, D. M. (1985a). Effects of experience on performance in a replenishable resource trap. *Journal of Personality and Social Psychology, 49,* 943–948.

Allison, S. T., & Messick, D. M. (1985b). The group attribution error. *Journal of Experimental Social Psychology, 21,* 563–579.

Allison, S. T., & Messick, D. M. (1990). Social decision heuristics in the use of shared resources. *Journal of Behavioral Decision Making, 3,* 195–204.

Allison, S. T., Worth, L. T., & King, M. C. (1990). Group decisions as social inference heuristics. *Journal of Personality and Social Psychology, 58,* 801–811.

Allmendinger, J., Hackman, J. R., & Lehman, E. V. (1996). Life and work in symphony orchestras. *Musical Quarterly, 80,* 194–219.

Allport, F. H. (1920). The influence of the group upon association and thought. *Journal of Experimental Psychology, 3,* 159–182.

Allport, F. H. (1924). *Social psychology.* Boston: Houghton Mifflin.

Allport, F. H. (1934). The J-curve hypothesis of conforming behavior. *Journal of Social Psychology, 5,* 141–183.

Allport, F. H. (1961). The contemporary appraisal of an old problem. *Contemporary Psychology, 6,* 195–197.

Allport, F. H. (1962). A structuronomic conception of behavior: Individual and collective. I. Structural theory and the master problem of social psychology. *Journal of Abnormal and Social Psychology, 64,* 3–30.

Allport, F. H., & Lepkin, M. (1943). Building war morale with news-headlines. *Public Opinion Quarterly, 7,* 211–221.

Allport, G. W. (1954). *The nature of prejudice.* New York: Addison-Wesley.

Allport, G. W., & Postman, L. J. (1947). *The psychology of rumor.* New York: Henry Holt.

Altemeyer, B. (1988). *Enemies of freedom: Understanding right-wing authoritarianism.* San Francisco: Jossey-Bass.

Alterman, E. (2004). *When presidents lie: A history of official deception and its consequences.* New York: Viking.

Altman, I. (1973). An ecological approach to the functioning of socially isolated groups. In J. E. Rasmussen (Ed.), *Man in isolation and confinement* (pp. 241–269). Chicago: Aldine.

Altman, I. (1975). *The environment and social behavior.* Pacific Grove, CA: Brooks/Cole.

Altman, I. (1977). Research on environment and behavior: A personal statement of strategy. In D. Stokols (Ed.), *Perspectives on environment and behavior* (pp. 303–324). New York: Plenum Press.

Altman, I., & Chemers, M. M. (1980). *Culture and environment.* Pacific Grove, CA: Brooks/Cole.

Altman, I., & Churchman, A. S. (Eds.). (1994). *Human behavior and the environment: Advances in theory and research: Place attachment* (Vol. 12 ). New York: Plenum Press.

Altman, I., & Haythorn, W. W. (1967). The ecology of isolated groups. *Behavioral Science, 12,* 169–182.

Altman, I., & Taylor, D. A. (1973). *Social penetration: The development of interpersonal relationships.* New York: Holt, Rinehart & Winston.

Altman, I., Taylor, D. A., & Wheeler, L. (1971). Ecological aspects of group behavior in social isolation. *Journal of Applied Social Psychology, 1,* 76–100.

Amegashie, J. A., & Runkel, M. (2007). Sabotaging potential rivals. *Social Choice and Welfare, 28,* 143–162.

Ames, D. R., & Flynn, F. J. (2007). What breaks a leader: The curvilinear relation between assertiveness and leadership. *Journal of Personality and Social Psychology, 92,* 307–324.

Amichai-Hamburger, Y. (Ed.). (2005). *The social net: Understanding human behavior in cyberspace.* Oxford: Oxford University Press.

Amir, Y. (1969). Contact hypothesis in ethnic relations. *Psychological Bulletin, 71,* 319–342.

Andersen, S. M. (1984). Self-knowledge and social inference: II. The diagnosticity of cognitive/affective and behavioral data. *Journal of Personality and Social Psychology, 46,* 294–307.

Anderson, C., & Galinsky, A. D. (2006). Power, optimism, and risk-taking. *European Journal of Social Psychology, 36,* 511–536.

Anderson, C., John, O. P., Keltner, D., & Kring, A. M. (2001). Who attains social status? Effects of personality and physical attractiveness in social groups. *Journal of Personality and Social Psychology, 81,* 116–132.

Anderson, C., Keltner, D., & Oliver, J. (2003). Emotional convergence between people over time. *Journal of Personality and Social Psychology, 84,* 1054–1068.

Anderson, C. A., & Bushman, B. J. (1997). External validity of "trivial" experiments: The case of laboratory aggression. *Review of General Psychology, 1,* 19–41.

Anderson, C. M., & Martin, M. M. (1995). The effects of communication motives, interaction involvement, and loneliness on satisfaction: A model of small groups. *Small Group Research, 26,* 118–137.

Anderson, L. R. (1978). Groups would do better without humans. *Personality and Social Psychology Bulletin, 4,* 557–558.

Anderson, N., De Dreu, C. K. W., & Nijstad, B. A. (2004). The routinization of innovation research: A constructively critical review of the state-of-the-science. *Journal of Organizational Behavior, 25,* 147–173.

Andersson, J., Hitch, G., & Meudell, P. (2006). Effects of the timing and identity of retrieval cues in individual recall: An attempt to mimic cross-cueing in collaborative recall. *Memory, 14,* 94–103.

Annett, J., & Stanton, N. (2001). Team work—a problem for ergonomics? *Ergonomics, 43,* 1045–1051.

*Apodoca v. Oregon*, 406 U.S. 404 (1972).

Appelbaum, R. P., & Chambliss, W. J. (1995). *Sociology.* New York: HarperCollins.

Applebaum, E., & Blatt, R. (1994). *The new American workplace.* Ithaca, NY: ILR.

Ardry, R. (1970). *The territorial imperative: A personal inquiry into the animal origins of property and nations.* New York: Atheneum.

Argyle, M., & Dean, J. (1965). Eye-contact, distance, and affiliation. *Sociometry, 28,* 289–304.

Arkes, H. R. (1993). Some practical judgment and decision-making research. In N. J. Castellan, Jr. (Ed.), *Individual and group decision making: Current issues* (pp. 3–18). Mahwah, NJ: Erlbaum.

Arkes, H. R., & Blumer, C. (1985). The psychology of sunk cost. *Organizational Behavior and Human Decision Processes, 35,* 124–140.

Arkin, R. M., & Burger, J. M. (1980). Effects of unit relation tendencies on interpersonal attraction. *Social Psychology Quarterly, 43,* 380–391.

Arms, R. L., & Russell, G. W. (1997). Impulsivity, fight history, and camaraderie as predictors of a willingness to escalate a disturbance. *Current Psychology: Developmental, Learning, Personality, Social, 15,* 279–285.

Arnardottir, A. A. (2002). *Leadership style in colead psychotherapy groups, assessed from leaders', co-leaders', and group members' perspective.* Unpublished doctoral dissertation. Richmond: Virginia Commonwealth University.

Arnold, D. W., & Greenberg, C. I. (1980). Deviate rejection within differentially manned groups. *Social Psychology Quarterly, 43,* 419–424.

Aronson, E. (2000). *Nobody left to hate: Teaching compassion after Columbine.* New York: Henry Holt.

Aronson, E., & Mills, J. (1959). The effects of severity of initiation on liking for a group. *Journal of Abnormal and Social Psychology, 59,* 177–181.

Aronson, E., & Patnoe, S. (1997). *Cooperation in the classroom: The jigsaw method.* New York: Longman.

Aronson, E., Stephan, C., Sikes, J., Blaney, N., & Snapp, M. (1978). *The jigsaw classroom.* Thousand Oaks, CA: Sage.

Arriaga, X. B., & Agnew, C. R. (2001). Being committed: Affective, cognitive, and conative components of relationship commitment. *Personality and Social Psychology Bulletin, 27,* 1190–1203.

Arrow, H. (1997). Stability, bistability, and instability in small group influence patterns. *Journal of Personality and Social Psychology, 72,* 75–85.

Arrow, H., Henry, K. B., Poole, M. S., Wheelan, S., & Moreland, R. (2005). Traces, trajectories, and timing: The temporal perspective on groups. In M. S. Poole & A. B. Hollingshead (Eds.), *Theories of small groups: Interdisciplinary perspectives* (pp. 313–367). Thousand Oaks, CA: Sage.

Arrow, H., & McGrath, J. E. (1995). Membership dynamics in groups at work: A theoretical framework. *Research in Organizational Behavior, 17,* 373–411.

Arrow, H., McGrath, J. E., & Berdahl, J. L. (2000). *Small groups as complex systems: Formation, coordination, development, and adaptation.* Thousand Oaks, CA: Sage.

Arterberry, M. E., Cain, K. M., & Chopko, S. A. (2007). Collaborative problem solving in five-year-old children: Evidence of social facilitation and social loafing. *Educational Psychology, 27,* 577–596.

Asch, S. E. (1952). *Social psychology.* Upper Saddle River, NJ: Prentice-Hall.

Asch, S. E. (1955). Opinions and social pressures. *Scientific American, 193,* 31–35.

Asch, S. E. (1957). An experimental investigation of group influence. In *Symposium on preventive and social psychiatry.* Washington, DC: U.S. Government Printing Office.

Asch, S. E. (2003). Effects of group pressure upon the modification and distortion of judgments. In L. W. Porter, H. L. Angle, & R. W. Allen (Eds.), *Organizational influence processes* (pp. 295–303). Armonk, NY: M. E. Sharpe. (Original work published in 1963)

Asendorpf, J. B., & Meier, G. H. (1993). Personality effects on children's speech in everyday life: Sociability-mediated exposure and shyness-mediated reactivity in social situations. *Journal of Personality and Social Psychology, 64,* 1072–1083.

Asendorpf, J. B., & Wilpers, S. (1998). Personality effects on social relationships. *Journal of Personality and Social Psychology, 74,* 1531–1544.

Ashburn-Nardo, L., Voils, C. I., & Monteith, M. J. (2001). Implicit associations as the seeds of intergroup bias: How easily do they take root? *Journal of Personality and Social Psychology, 81,* 789–799.

Asher, S. R., & Paquette, J. A. (2003). Loneliness and peer relations in childhood. *Current Directions in Psychological Science, 12,* 75–78.

Ashmore, R. D., Deaux, K., & McLaughlin-Volpe, T. (2004). An organizing framework for collective identity: Articulation and significance of multidimensionality. *Psychological Bulletin, 130,* 80–114.

Augustine, A. A., & Hemenover, S. H. (2008). Extraversion and the consequences of social interaction on affect repair. *Personality and Individual Differences, 44,* 1151–1161.

Averill, J. R. (1983). Studies on anger and aggression: Implications for theories of emotion. *American Psychologist, 38,* 1145–1160.

Avolio, B. J. (2004). Transformational and transactional leadership. In G. R. Goethals, G. J. Sorenson, & J. M. Burns (Eds.), *The encyclopedia of leadership* (pp. 1558–1566). Thousand Oaks, CA: Sage.

Avolio, B. J., & Bass, B. M. (1995). Individual consideration viewed at multiple levels of analysis: A multi-level framework for examining the diffusion of transformational leadership. *Leadership Quarterly, 6,* 199–218.

Avolio, B. J., & Locke, E. E. (2002). Contrasting different philosophies of leader motivation: Altruism versus egoism. *Leadership Quarterly, 13,* 169–191.

Avolio, B. J., Walumbwa, F. O., & Weber, T. J. (2009). Leadership: Current theories, research, and future directions. *Annual Review of Psychology, 60,* 421–449.

Axelrod, R. (1984). *The evolution of cooperation.* New York: Basic Books.

Axelrod, R., & Hamilton, W. D. (1981). The evolution of cooperation. *Science, 211,* 1390–1396.

Axsom, D. (1989). Cognitive dissonance and behavior change in psychotherapy. *Journal of Experimental Social Psychology, 25,* 234–252.

Axtell, J. (1998). *The pleasures of academe.* Lincoln, NB: University of Nebraska Press.

Ayman, R., Chemers, M. M., & Fiedler, F. (2007). The contingency model of leadership effectiveness: Its levels of analysis. In R. P. Vecchio (Ed.), *Leadership: Understanding the dynamics of power and influence in organizations* (2nd ed., pp. 335–360). University of Notre Dame Press: Notre Dame.

Azuma, H. (1984). Secondary control as a heterogeneous category. *American Psychologist, 39,* 970–971.

Back, K. W. (1951). Influence through social communication. *Journal of Abnormal and Social Psychology, 46,* 9–23.

Back, K. W. (1973). *Beyond words: The story of sensitivity training and the encounter movement.* Baltimore: Penguin.

Back, K. W. (1974). Intervention techniques: Small groups. *Annual Review of Psychology, 25,* 367–387.

Bakeman, R. (2000). Behavioral observation and coding. In H. T. Reis & C. M. Judd (Eds.), *Handbook of research methods in social and personality psychology* (pp. 138–159). New York: Cambridge University Press.

Bales, R. F. (1950). *Interaction process analysis: A method for the study of small groups.* Reading, MA: Addison-Wesley.

Bales, R. F. (1953). The equilibrium problem in small groups. In T. Parsons, R. F. Bales, & E. A. Shils (Eds.), *Working papers in the theory of action* (pp. 111–161). New York: Free Press.

Bales, R. F. (1955). How people interact in conferences. *Scientific American, 192,* 31–35.

Bales, R. F. (1958). Task roles and social roles in problem-solving groups. In E. E. Maccoby, T. M. Newcomb, & E. L. Hartley (Eds.), *Readings in social psychology* (pp. 437–447). New York: Holt, Rinehart & Winston.

Bales, R. F. (1965). The equilibrium problem in small groups. In A. P. Hare, E. F. Borgatta, & R. F. Bales (Eds.), *Small groups: Studies in social interaction* (Revised ed., pp. 444–483). New York: Knopf.

Bales, R. F. (1970). *Personality and interpersonal behavior.* New York: Holt, Rinehart & Winston.

Bales, R. F. (1980). *SYMLOG case study kit.* New York: Free Press.

Bales, R. F. (1999). *Social interaction systems: Theory and measurement.* New Brunswick, NJ: Transaction.

Bales, R. F., & Cohen, S. P. with Williamson, S. A. (1979). *SYMLOG: A system for the multiple level observation of groups.* New York: Free Press.

Bales, R. F., & Hare, A. P. (1965). Diagnostic use of the interaction profile. *Journal of Social Psychology, 67,* 239–258.

Bales, R. F., & Slater, P. E. (1955). Role differentiation in small decision-making groups. In T. Parsons and R. F. Bales (Eds.), *Family, socialization, and interaction process* (pp. 259–306). New York: Free Press.

Bales, R. F., & Strodtbeck, F. L. (1951). Phases in group problem solving. *Journal of Abnormal and Social Psychology, 46,* 485–495.

Baltes, B. B., Dickson, M. W., Sherman, M. P., Bauer, C. C., & LaGanke, J. (2002). Computer-mediated communication and group decision making: A meta-analysis. *Organizational Behavior and Human Decision Processes, 87,* 156–179.

Bandura, A. (1977). *Social-learning theory.* Upper Saddle River, NJ: Prentice Hall.

Bandura, A. (1986). *Social foundations of thought and action: A social cognitive theory.* Upper Saddle River, NJ: Prentice Hall.

Bandura, A. (1997). *Self-efficacy: The exercise of control.* New York: Freeman.

Bandura, A. (1999). Moral disengagement in the perpetration of inhumanities. *Personality and Social Psychology Review, 3,* 193–209.

Bandura, A., Underwood, B., & Fromson, M. E. (1975). Disinhibition of aggression through diffusion of responsibility and dehumanization of victims. *Journal of Research in Personality, 9,* 253–269.

Barabási, A. (2003). *Linked: How everything is connected to eveerthing else and what it means for business, science, and everyday life.* New York: Plume.

Bargal, D. (2008). Action research: A paradigm for achieving social change. *Small Group Research, 39,* 17–27.

Barge, J. K. (2002). Enlarging the meaning of group deliberation: From discussion to dialogue. In L. R. Frey (Ed.), *New directions in group communication* (pp. 159–177). Thousand Oaks, CA: Sage.

Bargh, J. A., & McKenna, K. Y. A. (2004). The Internet and social life. *Annual Review of Psychology, 55,* 573–590.

Barker, R. G. (1968). *Ecological psychology.* Stanford, CA: Stanford University Press.

Barker, R. G. (1987). Prospecting in ecological psychology: Oskaloosa revisited. In D. Stokols & I. Altman (Eds.), *Handbook of environmental psychology* (Vol. 2, pp. 1413–1432). New York: Wiley.

Barker, R. G. (1990). Recollections of the Midwest Psychological Field Station. *Environment and Behavior, 22,* 503–513.

Barker, R. G., & Associates. (1978). *Habitats, environments, and human behavior: Studies in ecological psychology and eco-behavioral sciences from the Midwest Psychological Field Station, 1947–1972.* San Francisco: Jossey-Bass.

Barlow, S. H., Burlingame, G. M., & Fuhriman, A. (2000). Therapeutic applications of groups: From Pratt's "thought control classes" to modern group psychotherapy. *Group Dynamics: Theory, Research, and Practice, 4,* 115–134.

Barlow, S. H., Burlingame, G. M., Nebeker, R. S., & Anderson, E. (2000). Meta-analysis of medical self-help groups. *International Journal of Group Psychotherapy, 50,* 53–69.

Barnett, L. A. (2006). Flying high or crashing down: Girls' accounts of trying out for cheerleading and dance. *Journal of Adolescent Research, 21,* 514–541.

Baron, R. A., & Bell, P. A. (1975). Aggression and heat: Mediating effects of prior provocation and exposure to an aggressive model. *Journal of Personality and Social Psychology, 31,* 825–832.

Baron, R. A., & Bell, P. A. (1976). Aggression and heat: The influence of ambient temperature, negative affect, and a cooling drink on physical aggression. *Journal of Personality and Social Psychology, 33,* 245–255.

Baron, R. S. (1986). Distraction-conflict theory: Progress and problems. *Advances in Experimental Social Psychology, 19,* 1–40.

Baron, R. S. (2000). Arousal, capacity, and intense indoctrination. *Personality and Social Psychology Review, 4,* 238–254.

Baron, R. S. (2005). So right it's wrong: Groupthink and the ubiquitous nature of polarized group decision making. *Advances in Experimental Social Psychology, 37,* 219–253.

Baron, R. S., Kerr, N. L., & Miller, N. (1992). *Group process, group decision, group action.* Pacific Grove, CA: Brooks/Cole.

Baron, R. S., Vandello, J. A., & Brunsman, B. (1996). The forgotten variable in conformity research: Impact of task importance on social influence. *Journal of Personality and Social Psychology, 71,* 915–927.

Barsade, S. G., Ward, A. J., Turner, J. D. F., & Sonnenfeld, J. A. (2000). To your heart's content: A model of affective diversity in top management teams. *Administrative Science Quarterly, 45,* 802–836.

Bar-Tal, D. (2000). *Shared beliefs in a society: Social psychological analysis.* Thousand Oaks, CA: Sage.

Bar-Tal, D. (2007). Sociopsychological foundations of intractable conflicts. *American Behavioral Scientist, 50,* 1430–1453.

Bartels, L. (May, 2001). No looking back. *Rocky Mountain News.* Retrieved January 3, 2004, from http://www.rockymountainnews.com.

Bartholomew, R. E. (1997). Mass hysteria. *British Journal of Psychiatry, 170,* 387–388.

Bartholomew, R. E., & Goode, E. (2000). Mass delusions and hysterias: Highlights from the past millennium. *Skeptical Inquirer, 24,* 20–28.

Bartholomew, R. E., & Sirois, F. (1996). Epidemic hysteria in schools: An international and historical overview. *Educational Studies, 22,* 285–311.

Bartis, S., Szymanski, K., & Harkins, S. G. (1988). Evaluation and performance: A two-edged knife. *Personality and Social Psychology Bulletin, 14,* 242–251.

Bartlem, C. S., & Locke, E. A. (1981). The Coch and French study: A critique and reinterpretation. *Human Relations, 34,* 555–566.

Bartone, P. T., & Adler, A. B. (1999). Cohesion over time in a peacekeeping medical task force. *Military Psychology, 11,* 85–107.

Basden, B. H., Basden, D. R., Bryner, S., & Thomas, R. L. (1997). A comparison of group and individual remembering: Does collaboration disrupt retrieval strategies? *Journal of Experimental Psychology: Learning, Memory and Cognition, 23,* 1176–1189.

Basow, S. A., Foran, K. A., & Bookwala, J. (2007). Body objectification, social pressure, and disordered eating behavior in college women: The role of sorority membership. *Psychology of Women Quarterly, 31,* 394–400.

Bass, B. M. (1990). *Bass and Stogdill's handbook of leadership: Theory, research, and managerial applications* (3rd ed.). New York: Free Press.

Bass, B. M. (1997). Does the transactional–transformational leadership paradigm transcend organizational and national boundaries? *American Psychologist, 52,* 130–139.

Bass, B. M., & Ryterband, E. C. (1979). *Organizational psychology* (2nd ed.). Boston: Allyn & Bacon.

Batchelor, J. P., & Goethals, G. R. (1972). Spatial arrangements in freely formed groups. *Sociometry, 35,* 270–279.

Bates, B., & Goodman, A. (1986). The effectiveness of encounter groups: Implications of research for counselling practice. *British Journal of Guidance and Counselling, 14,* 240–251.

Baum, A., & Davis, G. E. (1980). Reducing the stress of high-density living: An architectural intervention. *Journal of Personality and Social Psychology, 38,* 471–481.

Baum, A., Davis, G. E., & Valins, S. (1979). Generating behavioral data for the design process. In J. R. Aiello & A. Baum (Eds.), *Residential crowding and design* (pp. 175–196). New York: Plenum.

Baum, A., Harpin, R. E., & Valins, S. (1976). The role of group phenomena in the experience of crowding. In S. Saegert (Ed.), *Crowding in real environments.* Thousand Oaks, CA: Sage.

Baum, A., Singer, J., & Baum, C. (1982). Stress and the environment. *Journal of Social Issues, 37,* 4–35.

Baum, A., & Valins, S. (1977). *Architecture and social behavior: Psychological studies of social density.* Mahwah, NJ: Erlbaum.

Baumeister, R. F. (1984). Choking under pressure: Self-consciousness and paradoxical effects of incentives on skillful performance. *Journal of Personality and Social Psychology, 46,* 610–620.

Baumeister, R. F. (1985). The championship choke. *Psychology Today, 19,* 48–52.

Baumeister, R. F. (1995). Disputing the effects of championship pressures and home audiences. *Journal of Personality and Social Psychology, 68,* 644–648.

Baumeister, R. F., Brewer, L. E., Tice, D. M., & Twenge, J. M. (2007). Thwarting the need to belong: Understanding the interpersonal and inner effects of social exclusion. *Social and Personality Psychology Compass, 1,* 506–520.

Baumeister, R. F., Chesner, S. P., Senders, P. S., & Tice, D. M. (1988). Who's in charge here? Group leaders do lend help in emergencies. *Personality and Social Psychology Bulletin, 14,* 17–22.

Baumeister, R. F., & Leary, M. R. (1995). The need to belong: Desire for interpersonal attachments as a fundamental human motivation. *Psychological Bulletin, 117,* 497–529.

Baumeister, R. F., & Showers, C. J. (1986). A review of paradoxical performance effects: Choking under pressure in sports and mental tests. *European Journal of Social Psychology, 16,* 361–383.

Baumeister, R. F., & Sommer, K. L. (1997). What do men want? Gender differences and two spheres of belongingness. *Psychological Bulletin, 122,* 38–44.

Bavelas, A. (1948). A mathematical model for group structures. *Applied Anthropology, 7,* 16–30.

Bavelas, A. (1950). Communication patterns in task-oriented groups. *Journal of the Acoustical Society of America, 22,* 725–730.

Bavelas, A., & Barrett, D. (1951). An experimental approach to organization communication. *Personnel, 27,* 367–371.

Bayazit, M., & Mannix, E. A. (2003). Should I stay or should I go? Predicting team members' intent to remain in the team. *Small Group Research, 34,* 290–321.

Beach, S. R. H., & Tesser, A. (2000). Self-evaluation maintenance and evolution: Some speculative notes. In J. Suls & L. Wheeler (Eds.), *Handbook of social comparison: Theory and research* (pp. 123–140). New York: Kluwer Academic.

Beach, S. R. H., Tesser, A., Fincham, F. D., Jones, D. J., Johnson, D., & Whitaker, D. J. (1998). Pleasure and pain in doing well, together: An investigation of performance-related affect in close relationships. *Journal of Personality and Social Psychology, 74,* 923–938.

Beal, D. J., Cohen, R. R., Burke, M. J., & McLendon, C. L. (2003). Cohesion and performance in groups: A meta-analytic clarification of construct relations. *Journal of Applied Psychology, 88,* 989–1004.

Beaman, A. L., Cole, C. M., Preston, M., Klentz, B., & Steblay, N. M. (1983). Fifteen years of foot-in-the door research: A meta-analysis. *Personality and Social Psychology Bulletin, 9,* 181–196.

Beaton, E. A., Schmidt, L. A., Schulkin, J., Antony, M. M., Swinson, R. P., & Hall, G. B. (2008). Different neural responses to stranger and personally familiar faces in shy and bold adults. *Behavioral Neuroscience, 122,* 704–709.

Beauchamp, M. R., Bray, S. R., Eys, M. A., & Carron, A. V. (2002). Role ambiguity, role efficacy, and role performance: Multidimensional and mediational relationships within interdependent sport teams. *Group Dynamics: Theory, Research, and Practice, 6,* 229–242.

Bechtel, R. B. (2002). On to Mars! In R. B. Bechtel & A. Churchman (Eds.), *Handbook of environmental psychology* (pp. 676–685). New York: Wiley.

Bechtel, R. B., & Churchman, A. (Eds.). (2002). *Handbook of environmental psychology.* New York: Wiley.

Becker, F. (2004). *Offices that work: Balancing cost, flexibility, and communication.* San Francisco: Jossey-Bass.

Bedeian, A. G., & Day, D. V. (2004). Can chameleons lead? *Leadership Quarterly, 15,* 687–718.

Bedeian, A. G., & Hunt, J. G. (2006). Academic amnesia and vestigial assumptions of our forefathers. *Leadership Quarterly, 17,* 190–205.

Bednar, R. L., & Kaul, T. (1978). Experiential group research: Current perspectives. In S. L. Garfield & A. E. Bergin (Eds.), *Handbook of psychotherapy and behavior change* (2nd ed., pp. 769–815). New York: Wiley.

Bednar, R. L., & Kaul, T. (1979). Experiential group research: What never happened. *Journal of Applied Behavioral Science, 15,* 311–319.

Bednar, R. L., & Kaul, T. (1994). Experiential group research: Can the canon fire? In S. L. Garfield and A. E. Bergin (Eds.), *Handbook of psychotherapy and behavior change* (4th ed., pp. 631–663). New York: Wiley.

Behfar, K. J., Peterson, R. S., Mannix, E. A., & Trochim, W. M. K. (2008). The critical role of conflict resolution in teams: A close look at the links between conflict type, conflict management strategies, and team outcomes. *Journal of Applied Psychology, 93,* 170–188.

Bell, P. A. (1992). In defense of the negative affect escape model of heat and aggression. *Psychological Bulletin, 111,* 342–346.

Bell, P. A., Green, T. C., Fisher, J. D., & Baum, A., (2001). *Environmental psychology.* (5th ed.). Orlando: Harcourt.

Bell, S. T. (2007). Deep-level composition variables as predictors of team performance: A meta-analysis. *Journal of Applied Psychology, 92,* 595–615.

Bellah, R. N., Madsen, R., Sullivan, W. M., Swidler, A., & Tipton, S. M. (1985). *Habits of the heart: Individualism and commitment in American life.* New York: Harper & Row.

Bem, D. J. (1972). Self-perception theory. *Advances in Experimental Social Psychology, 6,* 2–62.

Bem, S. L. (1982). Gender schema theory and self-schema theory compared: A comment on Markus, Crane, Bernstein, and Siladi's "Self-schemas and gender." *Journal of Personality and Social Psychology, 43,* 1192–1194.

Bem, S. L. (1985). Androgyny and gender schema theory: A conceptual and empirical integration. *Nebraska Symposium on Motivation, 32,* 179–226.

Bendersky, J. W. (2007). "Panic": The impact of Le Bon's crowd psychology on U.S. military thought. *Journal of the History of the Behavioral Sciences, 43,* 257–283.

Benford, R. D. (1992). Social movements. In E. F. Borgatta & M. L. Borgatta (Eds.), *Encyclopedia of sociology* (Vol. 4, pp. 1880–1887). New York: MacMillan.

Benjamin, L. T., Jr., & Crouse, E. M. (2002). The American Psychological Association's response to *Brown v. Board of Education:* The case of Kenneth B. Clark. *American Psychologist, 57,* 38–50.

Benne, K. D., & Sheats, P. (1948). Functional roles of group members. *Journal of Social Issues, 4,* 41–49.

Bennett, H. S. (1980). *On becoming a rock musician.* Amherst: University of Massachusetts Press.

Bennett, M., & Sani, F. (2008). Children's subjective identification with social groups: A self-stereotyping approach. *Developmental Science, 11,* 69–75.

Bennis, W., & Biederman, P. W. (1997). *Organizing genius: The secrets of creative collaboration.* Reading, MA: Addison-Wesley.

Bennis, W. G. (1975). *Where have all the leaders gone?* Washington, DC: Federal Executive Institute.

Bennis, W. G., & Shepard, H. A. (1956). A theory of group development. *Human Relations, 9,* 415–437.

Berdahl, J. L., & Anderson, C. (2005). Men, women, and leadership centralization in groups over time. *Group Dynamics: Theory, Research, and Practice, 9,* 45–57.

Berdahl, J. L., & Henry, K. (2005). Contemporary issues in group research. In S. A. Wheelan (Ed.), *Handbook of group research and practice* (pp. 19–37). Thousand Oaks, CA: Sage.

Berdahl, J. L., & Martorana, P. (2006). Effects of power on emotion and expression during a controversial group discussion. *European Journal of Social Psychology, 36,* 497–509.

Berger, J., Ridgeway, C. L., & Zelditch, M. (2002). Construction of status and referential structures. *Sociological Theory, 20,* 157–179.

Berger, R. E. (1981). *Heart rate, arousal, and the "mere presence" hypothesis of social facilitation.* Unpublished doctoral dissertation, Virginia Commonwealth University, Richmond, VA.

Berger, S. M., Carli, L. L., Garcia, R., & Brady, J. J., Jr. (1982). Audience effects in anticipatory learning: A comparison of drive and practice-inhibitionanalyses. *Journal of Personality and Social Psychology, 42,* 478–486.

Berger, S. M., Hampton, K. L., Carli, L. L., Grandmaison, P. S., Sadow, J. S., Donath, C. H., & Herschlag, L. R. (1981). Audience-induced inhibition of overt practice during learning. *Journal of Personality and Social Psychology, 40,* 479–491.

Bergman, T. J., Beehner, J. C., Cheney, D. L., & Sayfarth, R. M. (2003). Hierarchical classification by rank and kinship in baboons. *Science, 302,* 1234–1236.

Berkowitz, L. (1954). Group standards, cohesiveness, and productivity. *Human Relations, 7,* 509–519.

Berkowitz, L., & Lundy, R. M. (1957). Personality charactersitics related to susceptibility to influence by peers or authority figures. *Journal of Personality, 25,* 306–316.

Berman, J. J., & Zimpfer, D. G. (1980). Growth groups: Do the outcomes really last? *Review of Educational Research, 50,* 505–524.

Berns, G. S., Chappelow, J., Zink, C. F., Pagnoni, G., Martin-Skurski, M. E., & Richards, J. (2005). Neurobiological correlates of social conformity and independence during mental rotation. *Biological Psychiatry, 58,* 245–253.

Bernthal, P. R., & Insko, C. A. (1993). Cohesiveness without groupthink: The interactive effects of social and task cohesion. *Group and Organizational Management, 18,* 66–87.

Betancourt, H., & Blair, I. (1992). A cognition (attribution)-emotion model of violence in conflict situations. *Personality and Social Psychology Bulletin, 18,* 343–350.

Bettencourt, B. A., Brewer, M. B., Croak, M. R., & Miller, N. (1992). Cooperation and the reduction of intergroup bias: The role of reward structure and social orientation. *Journal of Experimental Social Psychology, 28,* 301–309.

Bettencourt, B. A., & Sheldon, K. (2001). Social roles as mechanism for psychological need satisfaction within social groups. *Journal of Personality and Social Psychology, 81,* 1131–1143.

Biddle, B. J. (2001). Role theory. In E. F. Borgatta & R. J. V. Montgomery (Eds.), *Encyclopedia of sociology* (2nd ed., Vol. 4, pp. 2415–2420). New York: Macmillan Reference.

Biernat, M., Crandall, C. S., Young, L. V., Kobrynowicz, D., & Halpin, S. M. (1998). All that you can be: Stereotyping of self and others in a military context. *Journal of Personality and Social Psychology, 75,* 301–317.

Biernat, M., & Kobrynowicz, D. (1997). Gender- and race-based standards of competence: Lower minimum standards but higher ability standards for devalued groups. *Journal of Personality and Social Psychology, 72,* 544–557.

Biernat, M., Vescio, T. K., & Green, M. L. (1996). Selective self-stereotyping. *Journal of Personality and Social Psychology, 71,* 1194–1209.

Birnbaum, M. L., & Cicchetti, A. (2005). A model for working with the group life cycle in each group session across the life span of the group. *Groupwork, 15,* 23–43.

Bischoff, I. (2007). Institutional choice versus communication in social dilemmas—an experimental approach. *Journal of Economic Behavior & Organization, 62,* 20–36.

Blader, S., & Tyler, T. R. (2003). What constitutes fairness in work settings? A four-component model of procedural justice. *Human Resource Management Review, 12,* 107–126.

Blake, R. R., & McCanse, A. A. (1991). *Leadership dilemmas—Grid solutions.* Houston, TX: Gulf.

Blake, R. R., & Mouton, J. S. (1964). *The managerial grid.* Houston, TX: Gulf.

Blake, R. R., & Mouton, J. S. (1982). How to choose a leadership style. *Training and Development Journal, 36,* 39–46.

Blake, R. R., & Mouton, J. S. (1984). *Solving costly organizational conflicts: Achieving intergroup trust, cooperation, and teamwork.* San Francisco: Jossey-Bass.

Blake, R. R., & Mouton, J. S. (1985). Presidential (Grid) styles. *Training and Development Journal, 39,* 30–34.

Blake, R. R., & Mouton, J. S. (1986). From theory to practice in interface problem solving. In S. Worchel & W. G. Austin (Eds.), *Psychology of intergroup relations* (2nd ed., pp. 67–87). Chicago: Nelson-Hall.

Blanchard, F. A., Adelman, L., & Cook, S. W. (1975). Effect of group success and failure upon interpersonal attraction in cooperating interracial groups. *Journal of Personality and Social Psychology, 31,* 1020–1030.

Blanchard, K., & Johnson, S. (1981). *The one minute manager.* New York: Berkley.

Blanchard, K., Zigarmi, D., & Nelson, R. (1993). Situational leadership after 25 years: A retrospective. *Journal of Leadership Studies, 1,* 22–36.

Blascovich, J., Ginsburg, G. P., & Howe, R. C. (1975). Blackjack and the risky shift, II: Monetary stakes. *Journal of Experimental Social Psychology, 11,* 224–232.

Blascovich, J., Ginsburg, G. P., & Howe, R. C. (1976). Blackjack, choice shifts in the field. *Sociometry, 39,* 274–276.

Blascovich, J., Loomis, J., Beall, A. C., Swinth, K. R., Hoyt, C. L., & Bailenson, J. N. (2002). Immersive virtual environment technology as a methodological tool for social psychology. *Psychological Inquiry, 13,* 103–124.

Blascovich, J., Mendes, W. B., Hunter, S. B., & Salomon, K. (1999). Social "facilitation" as challenge and threat. *Journal of Personality and Social Psychology, 77,* 68–77.

Blascovich, J., Nash, R. F., & Ginsburg, G. P. (1978). Heart rate and competitive decision making. *Personality and Social Psychology Bulletin, 4,* 115–118.

Blass, T. (1991). Understanding behavior in the Milgram obedience experiment: The role of personality, situations, and their interactions. *Journal of Personality and Social Psychology, 60,* 398–413.

Blass, T. (1995). Right-wing authoritarianism and role as predictors of attributions about obedience to authority. *Personality and Individual Differences, 19,* 99–100.

Blass, T. (1996). Attribution of responsibility and trust in the Milgram obedience experiment. *Journal of Applied Social Psychology, 26,* 1529–1535.

Blass, T. (2000a). The Milgram paradigm after 35 years: Some things we now know about obedience to authority. In T. Blass (Ed.). *Obedience to authority: Current perspectives on the Milgram paradigm* (pp. 35–59). Mahwah, NJ: Erlbaum.

Blass, T. (Ed.). (2000b). *Obedience to authority: Current perspectives on the Milgram paradigm.* Mahwah, NJ: Erlbaum.

Blass, T. (2004). *The man who shocked the world: The life and legacy of Stanley Milgram.* New York: Basic Books.

Bliese, P. D., & Halverson, R. R. (1996). Individual and nomothetic models of job stress: An examination of work hours, cohesion, and well-being. *Journal of Applied Social Psychology, 26,* 1171–1189.

Blumer, H. (1946). Collective behavior. In A. M. Lee (Ed.), *New outline of the principles of sociology* (pp. 166–222). New York: Barnes & Noble.

Blumer, H. (1951). Collective behavior. In A. M. Lee (Ed.), *Principles of sociology* (pp. 167–224). New York: Barnes & Noble.

Blumer, H. (1957). Collective behavior. In J. B. Gittler (Ed.), *Review of sociology: Analysis of a decade* (pp. 127–158). New York: Wiley.

Blumer, H. (1964). Collective behavior. In J. Gould & W. L. Kolb (Eds.), *Dictionary of the social sciences* (pp. 100–101). New York: Free Press.

Bó, P. D. (2005). Cooperation under the shadow of the future: Experimental evidence from infinitely repeated games. *American Economic Review, 95,* 1591–1604.

Bogardus, E. S. (1954). Group behavior and groupality. *Sociology and Social Research, 38,* 401–403.

Bohrnstedt, G. W., & Fisher, G. A. (1986). The effects of recalled childhood and adolescent relationships compared to current role performances on young adults' affective functioning. *Social Psychology Quarterly, 49,* 19–32.

Boldry, J. G., Gaertner, L., & Quinn, J. (2007). Measuring the measures: A meta-analytic investigation of the measures of outgroup homogeneity. *Group Processes & Intergroup Relations, 10,* 157–178.

Bollen, K. A., & Hoyle, R. H. (1990). Perceived cohesion: A conceptual and empirical examination. *Social Forces, 69,* 479–504.

Bonacich, P. (1987). Communication networks and collective action. *Social Networks, 9,* 389–396.

Bonanno, G. A., Galea, S., Bucciarelli, A., & Vlahov, D. (2007). What predicts psychological resilience after disaster? The role of demographics, resources, and life stress. *Journal of Consulting and Clinical Psychology, 75,* 671–682.

Bond, C. F., Atoum, A. O., & VanLeeuwen, M. D. (1996). Social impairment of complex learning in the wake of public embarrassment. *Basic and Applied Social Psychology, 18,* 31–44.

Bond, C. F., & Titus, L. J. (1983). Social facilitation: A meta-analysis of 241 studies. *Psychological Bulletin, 94,* 265–292.

Bond, J., Kaskutas, L. A., & Weisner, C. (2003). The persistent influence of social networks and Alcoholics Anonymous on abstinence. *Quarterly Journal of Studies on Alcohol, 64,* 579–588.

Bond, M. H. (2002). Reclaiming the individual from Hofstede's ecological analysis—A 20-year odyssey: Comment on Oyserman et al. (2002). *Psychological Bulletin, 128,* 73–77.

Bond, R. (2005). Group size and conformity. *Group Processes & Intergroup Relations, 8,* 331–354.

Bond, R., & Smith, P. B. (1996). Culture and conformity: A meta-analysis of studies using Asch's (1952b, 1956) line judgment task. *Psychological Bulletin, 119,* 111–137.

Bonikowski, B., & McPherson, M. (2006). The sociology of voluntary associations. In C. D. Bryant & D. L. Peck (Eds.), *21st Century Sociology: A reference handbook* (Vol 1, pp. 197–207). Thousand Oaks, CA: Sage.

Bonito, J. A., & Hollingshead, A. B. (1997). Participation in small groups. *Communication Yearbook, 20,* 227–261.

Bonner, B. L., & Baumann, M. R. (2008). Informational intra-group influence: The effects of time pressure and group size. *European Journal of Social Psychology, 38,* 46–66.

Bonney, M. E. (1947). Popular and unpopular children: A sociometric study. *Sociometry Monographs, No. 99,* A80.

Bonta, B. D. (1997). Cooperation and competition in peaceful societies. *Psychological Bulletin, 121,* 299–320.

Boone, C., Van Olffen, W., Van Witteloostuijn, A., & De Brabander, B. (2004). The genesis of top management team diversity: Selective turnover among top management team in Dutch newspaper publishing, 1970–94. *Academy of Management Journal, 47,* 633–656.

Booth, A. (1972). Sex and social participation. *American Sociological Review, 37,* 183–193.

Borah, L. A., Jr. (1963). The effects of threat in bargaining: Critical and experimental analysis. *Journal of Abnormal and Social Psychology, 66,* 37–44.

Borgatta, E. F., & Bales, R. F. (1953). Task and accumulation of experience as factors in the interaction of small groups. *Sociometry, 16,* 239–252.

Borgatta, E. F., Couch, A. S., & Bales, R. F. (1954). Some findings relevant to the great man theory of leadership. *American Sociological Review, 19,* 755–759.

Borgatti, S. P. (2002a). A statistical method for comparing aggregate data across a priori groups. *Field Methods, 14,* 88–107.

Borgatti, S. P. (2002b). *Netdraw: Graphic visualization software.* Boston, MA: Analytic Technologies.

Borgatti, S. P. (2005). Centrality and network flow. *Social Networks, 27,* 55–71.

Bormann, E. G. (1975). *Discussion and group methods: Theory and practices* (2nd ed.). New York: Harper & Row.

Bornstein, G. (2003). Intergroup conflict: Individual, group, and collective interests. *Personality and Social Psychology Review, 7,* 129–145.

Bornstein, G., Budescu, D., & Zamir, S. (1997). Cooperation in intergroup, *N*-person, and two-person games of chicken. *Journal of Conflict Resolution, 41,* 384–406.

Bornstein, R. F. (1989). Exposure and affect: Overview and meta-analysis of research, 1968–1987. *Psychological Bulletin, 106,* 265–289.

Bornstein, R. F. (1992). The dependent personality: Developmental, social, and clinical perspectives. *Psychological Bulletin, 112,* 3–23.

Bouchard, T. J. (1972). A comparison of two group brainstorming procedures. *Journal of Applied Psychology, 56,* 418–421.

Bourgeois, K. S., & Leary, M. R. (2001). Coping with rejection: Derogating those who choose us last. *Motivation and Emotion, 25,* 101–111.

Bourgeois, P., & Hess, U. (2008). The impact of social context on mimicry. *Biological Psychology, 77,* 343–352.

Bowers, C. A., Pharmer, J. A., & Salas, E. (2000). When member homogeneity is needed in work teams: A meta-analysis. *Small Group Research, 31,* 305–327.

Bowers, C. A., Weaver, J. L., & Morgan, B. B., Jr. (1996). Moderating the performance effects of stressors. In J. E. Driskell & E. Salas (Eds.), *Stress and human performance* (pp. 163–192). Mahwah, NJ: Erlbaum.

Bowers, D. G., & Seashore, S. E. (1966). Predicting organizational effectiveness with a four-factor theory of leadership. *Administrative Science Quarterly, 11,* 238–263.

Bowlby, J. (1980). *Attachment and loss* (Vol. 1). London: Hogarth.

Bowling, N. A., Beehr, T. A., Johnson, A. L., Semmer, N. K., Hendricks, E. A., & Webster, H. A. (2004). Explaining potential antecedents of workplace social support: Reciprocity or attractiveness? *Journal of Occupational Health Psychology, 9,* 339–350.

Bradley, P. H. (1978). Power, status, and upward communication in small decision-making groups. *Communication Monographs, 45,* 33–43.

Bradshaw, S. D. (1998). I'll go if you will: Do shy persons utilize social surrogates? *Journal of Social and Personal Relationships, 15,* 651–669.

Bramel, D., & Friend, R. (1981). Hawthorne, the myth of the docile worker, and class bias in psychology. *American Psychologist, 36,* 867–878.

Brandes, U., Kenis, P., Raab, J., Schneider, V., & Wagner, D. (1999). Explorations into the visualization of policy networks. *Journal of Theoretical Politics, 11,* 75–106.

Branscombe, N. R. (1998). Thinking about one's gender group's privileges or disadvantages: Consequences for well-being in women and men. *British Journal of Social Psychology, 37,* 167–184.

Branscombe, N. R., Spears, R., Ellemers, N., & Doosje, B. (2002). Intragroup and intergroup evaluation effects on group behavior. *Personality and Social Psychology Bulletin, 28,* 744–753.

Brauer, M., Judd, C. M., & Gliner, M. D. (1995). The effects of repeated expressions on attitude polarization during group discussions. *Journal of Personality and Social Psychology, 68,* 1014–1029.

Bray, R. M., Johnson, D., & Chilstrom, J. T., Jr. (1982). Social influence by group members with minority opinions: A comparison of Hollander & Moscovici. *Journal of Personality and Social Psychology, 43,* 78–88.

Brechner, K. C. (1977). An experimental analysis of social traps. *Journal of Experimental Social Psychology, 13,* 552–564.

Brehm, J. W. (1976). Responses to loss of freedom: A theory of psychological reactance. In J. W. Thibaut, J. T. Spence, & R. C. Carson (Eds.), *Contemporary topics in social psychology* (pp. 51–78). Morristown, NJ: General Learning Press.

Brehm, J. W., & Sensenig, J. (1966). Social influence as a function of attempted and implied usurpation of choice. *Journal of Personality and Social Psychology, 4,* 703–707.

Brehm, S. S., & Brehm, J. W. (1981). *Psychological reactance: A theory of freedom and control.* New York: Academic Press.

Brennan, K. A., Clark, C. L., & Shaver, P. R. (1998). Self-report measurement of adult attachment: An integrative overview. In J. A. Simpson & W. S. Rholes (Eds.), *Attachment theory and close relationships* (pp. 46–76). New York: Guilford.

Brenner, O. C., & Vinacke, W. E. (1979). Accommodative and exploitative behavior of males versus females and managers versus nonmanagers as measured by the Test of Strategy. *Social Psychology Quarterly, 42,* 289–293.

Brewer, M. B. (1979). In-group bias in the minimal intergroup situation: A cognitive-motivational analysis. *Psychological Bulletin, 86,* 307–324.

Brewer, M. B. (2000). Reducing prejudice through cross-categorization: Effects of multiple social identities. In S. Oskamp (Ed.), *Reducing prejudice and discrimination* (pp. 165–183). Mahwah, NJ: Erlbaum.

Brewer, M. B. (2007). The social psychology of intergroup relations: Social categorization, ingroup bias, and outgroup prejudice. In A. W. Kruglanski & E. T. Higgins (Eds.), *Social psychology: Handbook of basic principles* (2nd ed., pp. 695–715). New York: Guilford.

Brewer, M. B., & Brown, R. J. (1998). Intergroup relations. In D. T. Gilbert, S. T. Fiske, & G. Lindzey (Eds.), *The handbook of social psychology* (4th ed., Vol. 2, pp. 554–594). New York: McGraw-Hill.

Brewer, M. B., & Campbell, D. T. (1976). *Ethnocentrism and intergroup attitudes: East African evidence.* New York: Halsted Press.

Brewer, M. B., & Chen, Y. (2007). Where (who) are collectives in collectivism? toward conceptual clarification of individualism and collectivism. *Psychological Review, 114,* 133–151.

Brewer, M. B., & Gardner, W. (1996). Who is this "We"? Levels of collective identity and self representations. *Journal of Personality and Social Psychology, 71,* 83–93.

Brewer, M. B., & Kramer, R. M. (1986). Choice behavior in social dilemmas: Effects of social identity, group size, and decision framing. *Journal of Personality and Social Psychology, 50,* 543–549.

Brewer, M. B., Manzi, J. M., & Shaw, J. S. (1993). In-group identification as a function of depersonalization, distinctiveness, and status. *Psychological Science, 4,* 88–92.

Brewer, M. B., & Miller, N. (1984). Beyond the contact hypothesis: Theoretical perspectives on desegregation. In N. Miller & M. Brewer (Eds.), *Groups in contact: The psychology of desegregation* (pp. 281–302). New York: Academic Press.

Brewer, M. B., & Pickett, C. L. (2002). The social self and group identification: Inclusion and distinctiveness motives in interpersonal and collective identities. In J. P. Forgas & K. D. Williams (Eds.), *The social self: Cognitive, interpersonal, and intergroup perspectives* (pp. 255–272). New York: Psychology Press.

Brickner, M. A., Harkins, S. G., & Ostrom, T. M. (1986). Effects of personal involvement: Thought-provoking implications for social loafing. *Journal of Personality and Social Psychology, 51,* 763–770.

Brief, A. P., Schuler, R. S., & Van Sell, M. (1981). *Managing job stress.* Boston: Little, Brown.

Brief, A. P., & Weiss, H. M. (2002). Organizational behavior: Affect in the workplace. *Annual Review of Psychology, 53,* 279–307.

Brinthaupt, T. M., Moreland, R. L., & Levine, J. M. (1991). Sources of optimism among prospective group members. *Personality and Social Psychology Bulletin, 17,* 36–43.

Brockner, J. (1995). How to stop throwing good money after bad: Using theory to guide practice. In D. A. Schroeder (Ed.), *Social dilemmas: Perspectives on individuals and groups* (pp. 163–182). Westport, CT: Praeger.

Brockner, J., & Rubin, J. Z. (1985). *The social psychology of conflict escalation and entrapment.* New York: Springer Verlag.

Brockner, J., & Wiesenfeld, B. M. (1996). An integrative framework for explaining reactions to decisions: Interactive effects of outcomes and procedures. *Psychological Bulletin, 120,* 189–208.

Brodbeck, F. C., Kerschreiter, R., Mojzisch, A., Frey, D., & Schulz-Hardt, S. (2002). The dissemination of critical, unshared information in decision-making groups: The effects of prediscussion dissent. *European Journal of Social Psychology, 32,* 35–56.

Bromley, D. G. (1985). Cult facts and fiction. *VCU Magazine, 14,* 10–15.

Bronzaft, A. L. (2002). Noise pollution: A hazard to physical and mental well-being. In R. B. Bechtel & A. Churchman (Eds.), *Handbook of environmental psychology* (pp. 499–510). New York: Wiley.

Brooks, G. R. (1996). Treatment for therapy-resistant men. In M. P. Andronico (Ed.), *Men in groups: Insights, interventions, and psychoeducational work* (pp. 7–19). Washington, DC: American Psychological Association.

Brosnan, S. F., & de Waal, F. B. M. (2003). Monkeys reject unequal pay. *Nature, 425,* 297–299.

Broverman, I. K., Vogel, S. R., Broverman, D. M., Clarkson, F. E., & Rosenkrantz, P. S. (1972). Sex-role stereotypes: A current appraisal. *Journal of Social Issues, 28,* 59–78.

Brown, B. B. (1987). Territoriality. In D. Stokols & I. Altman (Eds.), *Handbook of environmental psychology* (Vol. 1, pp. 505–531). New York: Wiley.

Brown, B. B., & Lohr, N. (1987). Peer group affiliation and adolescent self-esteem: An integration of ego-identity and symbolic-interaction theories. *Journal of Personality and Social Psychology, 52,* 47–55.

Brown, D. E. 1991. *Human universals.* New York: McGraw-Hill.

Brown, J. D., & Dutton, K. A. (1995). The thrill of victory, the complexity of defeat: Self-esteem and people's emotional reactions to success and failure. *Journal of Personality and Social Psychology, 68,* 712–722.

Brown, L. H., Silvia, P. J., Myin-Germeys, I., & Kwapil, T. R. (2007). When the need to belong goes wrong: The expression of social anhedonia and social anxiety in daily life. *Psychological Science, 18,* 778–782.

Brown, R. (1974). Further comment on the risky shift. *American Psychologist, 29,* 468–470.

Brown, R., Condor, S., Matthews, A., Wade, G., & Williams, J. A. (1986). Explaining intergroup differentiation in an industrial organization. *Journal of Occupational Psychology, 59,* 273–286.

Brown, R., & Hewstone, M. (2005). An integrative theory of intergroup contact. *Advances in Experimental Social Psychology, 37,* 255–343.

Brown, R., Maras, P., Masser, B., Vivian, J., & Hewstone, M. (2001). Life on the ocean wave: Testing some intergroup hypotheses in a naturalistic setting. *Group Processes & Intergroup Relations, 4,* 81–97.

Brown, R., & Zagefka, H. (2005). Ingroup affiliations and prejudice. In J. F. Dovidio, P. Glick, & L. A. Rudman (Eds.), *On the nature of prejudice: Fifty years after Allport* (pp. 54–70). Malden, MA: Blackwell.

Brown, T. M., & Miller, C. E. (2000). Communication networks in task-performing groups: Effects of task complexity, time pressure, and interpersonal dominance. *Small Group Research, 31,* 131–157.

Brown, V., & Paulus, P. B. (1996). A simple dynamic model of social factors in group brainstorming. *Small Group Research, 27,* 91–114.

Browning, L. (1978). A grounded organizational communication theory derived from qualitative data. *Communication Monographs, 45,* 93–109.

Brownstein, A. L. (2003). Biased predecision processing. *Psychological Bulletin, 129,* 545–568.

Budman, S. H., Demby, A., Feldstein, M., & Gold, M. (1984). The effects of time-limited group psychotherapy: A controlled study. *International Journal of Group Psychotherapy, 34,* 587–603.

Bugental, D. B., & Lewis, J. C. (1999). The paradoxical misuse of power by those who see themselves as powerless: How does it happen? *Journal of Social Issues, 55,* 51–64.

Bukowski, W. M., Newcomb, A. F., & Hartup, W. W. (Eds.). (1996). *The company they keep: Friendships in childhood and adolescence.* New York: Cambridge University Press.

Bunderson, J. S. (2003). Recognizing and utilizing expertise in work groups: A status characteristics perspective. *Administrative Science Quarterly, 48,* 557–591.

Burke, M. J., & Day, R. R. (1986). A cumulative study of the effectiveness of managerial training. *Journal of Applied Psychology, 71,* 232–245.

Burke, P. J. (1967). The development of task and social-emotional role differentiation. *Sociometry, 30,* 379–392.

Burkley, M., & Blanton, H. (2008). Endorsing a negative in-group stereotype as a self-protective strategy: Sacrificing the group to save the self. *Journal of Experimental Social Psychology, 44,* 37–49.

Burlingame, G. M., Fuhriman, A., & Johnson, J. E. (2001). Cohesion in group psychotherapy. *Psychotherapy: Theory, Research, Practice, Training, 38,* 373–379.

Burlingame, G. M., Fuhriman, A., & Mosier, J. (2003). The differential effectiveness of group psychotherapy: A meta-analytic perspective. *Group Dynamics: Theory, Research, and Practice, 7,* 3–12.

Burlingame, G. M., & Krogel, J. (2005). Relative efficacy of individual versus group psychotherapy. *International Journal of Group Psychotherapy, 55,* 607–611.

Burlingame, G. M., MacKenzie, K. R., & Strauss, B. (2004). Small group treatment: Evidence for effectiveness and mechanisms of change. In M. J. Lambert (Ed.), *Bergin & Garfield's handbook of psychotherapy and behavior change* (5th ed., pp. 647–696). New York: Wiley & Sons.

Burnette, J. L., & Forsyth, D. R. (2008). "I didn't do it": Responsibility biases in open and closed groups. *Group Dynamics: Theory, Research, and Practice, 12,* 210–222.

Burney, C. (1961). *Solitary confinement* (2nd ed). New York: St. Martin's Press.

Burnham, T., McCabe, K., & Smith, V. L. (2000). Friend-or-foe intentionality priming in an extensive form trust game, *Journal of Economic Behavior & Organization, 43,* 57–73.

Burns, J. M. (1978). *Leadership.* New York: Harper.

Burns, J. M. (2003). *Transforming leadership: The pursuit of happiness.* New York: Atlantic Monthly Press.

Burnstein, E., & Vinokur, A. (1973). Testing two classes of theories about group-induced shifts in individual choice. *Journal of Experimental Social Psychology, 9,* 123–137.

Burnstein, E., & Vinokur, A. (1977). Persuasive arguments and social comparison as determinants of attitude polarization. *Journal of Experimental Social Psychology, 13,* 315–332.

Burnstein, E., & Worchel, P. (1962). Arbitrariness of frustration and its consequences for aggression in a social situation. *Journal of Personality, 30,* 528–540.

Bushe, G. R., & Coetzer, G. H. (2007). Group development and team effectiveness: Using cognitive representations to measure group development and predict task performance and group viability. *Journal of Applied Behavioral Science, 43,* 184–212.

Butkovic, A., & Bratko, D. (2007). Family study of manipulation tactics. *Personality and Individual Differences, 43,* 791–801.

Butler, D., & Geis, F. L. (1990). Nonverbal affect responses to male and female leaders: Implications for leadership evaluations. *Journal of Personality and Social Psychology, 58,* 48–59.

Butler, T., & Fuhriman, A. (1983). Level of functioning and length of time in treatment variables influencing patients' therapeutic experience in group psychotherapy. *International Journal of Group Psychotherapy, 33,* 489–505.

Buton, F., Fontayne, P., Heuzé, J., Bosselut, G., & Raimbault, N. (2007). The QAG-a: An analog version of the Questionnaire sur l'Ambiance du Groupe for measuring the dynamic nature of group cohesion. *Small Group Research, 38,* 235–264.

Buunk, A. P., & Gibbons, F. X. (2007). Social comparison: The end of a theory and the emergence of a field. *Organizational Behavior and Human Decision Processes, 102,* 3–21.

Buunk, B. P., & Hoorens, V. (1992). Social support and stress: The role of social comparison and social exchange processes. *British Journal of Clinical Psychology, 31,* 445–457.

Buunk, B. P., Nauta, A., & Molleman, E. (2005). In search of the true group animal: The effects of affiliation orientation and social comparison orientation upon group satisfaction. *European Journal of Personality, 19,* 69–81.

Buunk, B. P., Oldersma, F. L., & De Dreu, C. K. (2001). Enhancing satisfaction through downward comparison: The role of relational discontent and individual differences in social comparison orientation. *Journal of Experimental Social Psychology, 37,* 452–467.

Buys, C. J. (1978a). Humans would do better without groups. *Personality and Social Psychology Bulletin, 4,* 123–125.

Buys, C. J. (1978b). On humans would do better without groups: A final note. *Personality and Social Psychology Bulletin, 4,* 568.

Byrne, D. (1961). Anxiety and the experimental arousal of affiliation need. *Journal of Abnormal and Social Psychology, 63,* 660–662.

Byrne, D. (1971). *The attraction paradigm.* New York: Academic Press.

Byrne, Z. S., & LeMay, E. (2006). Different media for organizational communication: Perceptions of quality and satisfaction. *Journal of Business and Psychology, 21,* 149–173.

Cacioppo, J. T., Hawkley, L. C., & Bernston, G. G. (2003). The anatomy of loneliness. *Current Directions in Psychological Science, 12,* 71–74.

Cadinu, M. R., & Cerchioni, M. (2001). Compensatory biases after ingroup threat: 'yeah, but we have a good personality.' *European Journal of Social Psychology, 31,* 353–367.

Cahill, S., Fine, G. A., & Grant, L. (1995). Dimensions of qualitative research. In K. S. Cook, G. A. Fine, & J. S. House (Eds.), *Sociological perspectives on social psychology* (pp. 605–628). Boston: Allyn & Bacon.

Caldwell, D. F., & Burger, J. M. (1997). Personality and social influence strategies in the workplace. *Personality and Social Psychology Bulletin, 23,* 1003–1012.

Callaway, M. R., Marriott, R. G., & Esser, J. K. (1985). Effects of dominance on group decision making: Toward a stress-reduction explanation of groupthink. *Journal of Personality and Social Psychology, 49,* 949–952.

Camacho, L. M., & Paulus, P. B. (1995). The role of social anxiousness in group brainstorming. *Journal of Personality and Social Psychology, 68,* 1071–1080.

Cameron, J. E. (1999). Social identity and the pursuit of possible selves: Implications for the psychological well-being of university students. *Group Dynamics: Theory, Research, and Practice, 3,* 179–189.

Cameron, W. B. (1966). *Modern social movements: A sociological outline.* New York: Random House.

Campbell, D. T. (1958a). Common fate, similarity, and other indices of the status of aggregates of persons as social entities. *Behavioral Science, 3,* 14–25.

Campbell, D. T. (1958b). Systematic error on the part of human links in communication systems. *Information and Control, 1,* 334–369.

Campbell, D. T. (1965). Ethnocentric and other altruistic motives. *Nebraska Symposium on Motivation, 13,* 283–311.

Campbell, L., Simpson, J. A., Stewart, M., & Manning, J. G. (2002). The formation of status hierarchies in leaderless groups: The role of male waist-to-hip ratio. *Human Nature, 13,* 345–362.

Campbell, T. (2005). The cognitive neuroscience of auditory distraction. *Trends in Cognitive Sciences, 9,* 3–5.

Canetti, E. (1962). *Crowds and power.* London: Gollancz.

Cannavale, F. J., Scarr, H. A., & Pepitone, A. (1970). Deindividuation in the small group: Further evidence. *Journal of Personality and Social Psychology, 16,* 141–147.

Cannon, M. D., & Edmondson, A. C. (2005). Failing to learn and learning to fail (intelligently): How great organizations put failure to work to innovate and improve. *Long Range Planning: International Journal of Strategic Management, 38,* 299–319.

Cannon-Bowers, J. A., Tannenbaum, S. I., Salas, E., & Volpe, C. E. (1995). Defining team competencies and establishing team training requirements. In R. Guzzo, E. Salas, & Associates (Eds.), *Team effectiveness and decision making in organizations* (pp. 333–380). San Francisco: Jossey-Bass.

Caporael, L. R. (2007). Evolutionary theory for social and cultural psychology. In A. W. Kruglanski & E. T. Higgins (Eds.), *Social psychology: Handbook of basic principles* (2nd ed., pp. 3–18). New York: Guilford.

Caporael, L., Wilson, D. S., Hemelrijk, C., & Sheldon, K. M. (2005). Small groups from an evolutionary perspective. In M. S. Poole & A. B. Hollingshead (Eds.), *Theories of small groups: Interdisciplinary perspectives* (pp. 369–396). Thousand Oaks, CA: Sage.

Carew, D. K., Parisi-Carew, E., & Blanchard, K. H. (1986). Group development and situational leadership: A model for managing groups. *Training and Development Journal, 40,* 46–50.

Carless, S. A., & De Paola, C. (2000). The measurement of cohesion in work teams. *Small Group Research, 31,* 71–88.

Carli, L. L. (1989). Gender differences in interaction style and influence. *Journal of Personality and Social Psychology, 56,* 565–576.

Carli, L. L. (1999). Gender, interpersonal power, and social influence. *Journal of Social Issues, 55,* 81–99.

Carli, L. L. (2001). Gender and social influence. *Journal of Social Issues, 57,* 725–741.

Carli, L. L., LaFleur, S. J., & Loeber, C. C. (1995). Nonverbal behavior, gender, and influence. *Journal of Personality and Social Psychology, 68,* 1030–1041.

Carlopio, J. R. (1996). Construct validity of a physical work environment satisfaction questionnaire. *Journal of Occupational Health Psychology, 1,* 330–344.

Carlyle, T. (1841). *On heroes, hero-worship, and the heroic.* London: Fraser.

Carnaghi, A., Maass, A., Gresta, S., Bianchi, M., Cadinu, M., & Arcuri, L. (2008). Nomina sunt omina: On the inductive potential of nouns and adjectives in person perception. *Journal of Personality and Social Psychology, 94,* 839–859.

Carneiro, R. L. (1970). A theory of the origin of the state. *Science, 169,* 239–249.

Carnevale, P. J. D. (1986a). Mediating disputes and decisions in organizations. *Research on Negotiation in Organizations, 1,* 251–269.

Carnevale, P. J. D. (1986b). Strategic choice in mediation. *Negotiation Journal, 2,* 41–56.

Carnevale, P. J., & Pruitt, D. G. (1992). Negotiation and mediation. *Annual Review of Psychology, 43,* 531–582.

Carpenter, C. R. (1958). Territoriality: A review of concepts and problems. In A. Roe & G. G. Simpson (Eds.), *Behavior and evolution* (pp. 224–250). New Haven: Yale University Press.

Carrere, S., & Evans, G. W. (1994). Life in an isolated and confined environment: A qualitative study of the role of the designed environment. *Environment and Behavior, 26,* 707–741.

Carron, A. V. (1982). Cohesiveness in sports groups: Interpretations and considerations. *Journal of Sport Psychology, 4,* 123–128.

Carron, A. V., Colman, M. M., Wheeler, J., & Stevens, D. (2002). Cohesion and performance in sport: A meta analysis. *Journal of Sport and Exercise Psychology, 24,* 168–188.

Carson, P. P., Carson, K. D., & Roe, C. W. (1993). Social power bases: A meta-analytic examination of interrelationships and outcomes. *Journal of Applied Social Psychology, 23,* 1150–1169.

Carson, R. C. (1969). *Interaction concepts of personality.* Chicago: Aldine.

Cartwright, D. (1951). Achieving change in people: Some applications of group dynamics theory. *Human Relations, 4,* 381–392.

Cartwright, D. (1959). A field theoretical conception of power. In D. Cartwright (Ed.), *Studies in social power.* Ann Arbor, MI: Institute for Social Research.

Cartwright, D., & Harary, F. (1956). Structural balance: A generalization of Heider's theory. *Psychological Review, 63,* 277–293.

Cartwright, D., & Harary, F. (1970). Ambivalence and indifference in generalizations of structural balance. *Behavioral Science, 14,* 497–513.

Cartwright, D., & Zander, A. (Eds.). (1968). *Group dynamics: Research and theory* (3rd ed.). New York: Harper & Row.

Caruso, E., Epley, N., & Bazerman, M. H. (2006). The costs and benefits of undoing egocentric responsibility assessments in groups. *Journal of Personality and Social Psychology, 91,* 857–871.

Carvalho, E. R., & Brito, V. C. A. (1995). Sociometric intervention in family therapy: A case study. *Journal of Group Psychotherapy, Psychodrama & Sociometry, 47,* 147–164.

Cascio, W. F. (1995). Whither industrial and organizational psychology in a changing world of work? *American Psychologist, 50,* 928–939.

Casey-Campbell, M., & Martens, M. L. (2008). Sticking it all together: A critical assessment of the group cohesion-performance literature. *International Journal of Management Reviews, 10,* published online, DOI: 10.1111/j.1468-2370.2008.00239.x.

Castano, E., Yzerbyt, V., & Bourguignon, D. (2003). We are one and I like it: The impact of ingroup entitativity on ingroup identification. *European Journal of Social Psychology, 33,* 735–754.

Castore, C. H., & Murnighan, J. K. (1978). Determinants of support for group decisions. *Organizational Behavior and Human Performance, 22,* 75–92.

Cattell, R. B. (1948). Concepts and methods in the measurement of group syntality. *Psychological Review, 55,* 48–63.

Ceci, S. J., Williams, W. M., & Mueller-Johnson, K. (2006). Is tenure justified? An experimental study of faculty beliefs about tenure, promotion, and academic freedom. *Behavioral and Brain Sciences, 29,* 553–569.

Cecil, J. S., Hans, V. P., & Wiggins, E. C. (1991). Citizen comprehension of difficult issues: Lessons from civil jury trials. *American University Law Review, 40,* 727–774.

Chagnon, N. A. (1997). *Yanomamö* (5th ed.). Fort Worth, TX: Harcourt Brace.

Chamley, C. P. (2004). *Rational herds: Economic models of social learning.* Cambridge: Cambridge University Press.

Chan, J., To, H., & Chan, E. (2006). Reconsidering social cohesion: Developing a definition and analytical framework for empirical research. *Social Indicators Research, 75,* 273–302.

Chang, A., & Bordia, P. (2001). A multidimensional approach to the group cohesion–group performance relationship. *Small Group Research, 32,* 379–405.

Chansler, P. A., Swamidass, P. M., & Cammann, C. (2003). Self-managing work teams: An empirical study of group cohesiveness in "natural work groups" at a Harley-Davidson Motor Company plant. *Small Group Research, 34,* 101–120.

Chaplin, W. F., Phillips, J. B., Brown, J. D., Clanton, N. R., & Stein, J. L. (2000). Handshaking, gender, personality, and first impressions. *Journal of Personality and Social Psychology, 79,* 110–117.

Chapman, A. J. (1973). Funniness of jokes, canned laughter, and recall performance. *Sociometry, 36,* 569–578.

Chartrand, T. L., & Bargh, J. A. (1999). The chameleon effect: The perception–behavior link and social interaction. *Journal of Personality and Social Psychology, 76,* 893–910.

Chatman, J. A., & Spataro, S. E. (2005). Using self-categorization theory to understand relational demography-based variations in people's responsiveness to organizational culture. *Academy of Management Journal, 48,* 321–331.

Cheavens, J. S., Feldman, D. B., Gum, A., Michael, S. T., & Snyder, C. R. (2006). Hope therapy in a community sample: A pilot investigation. *Social Indicators Research, 77,* 61–78.

Cheek, J. M., & Buss, A. H. (1981). Shyness and sociability. *Journal of Personality and Social Psychology, 41,* 330–339.

Chemers, M. M. (1997). *An integrative theory of leadership.* Mahwah, NJ: Erlbaum.

Chemers, M. M. (2000). Leadership research and theory: A functional integration. *Group Dynamics: Theory, Research, and Practice, 4,* 27–43.

Chen, F. F., & West, S. G. (2008). Measuring individualism and collectivism: The importance of considering differential components, reference groups, and measurement invariance. *Journal of Research in Personality, 42,* 259–294.

Chen, S., Lee-Chai, A. Y., & Bargh, J. A. (2001). Relationship orientation as a moderator of the effects of social power. *Journal of Personality and Social Psychology, 80,* 173–187.

Chen, S., Shechter, D., & Chaiken, S. (1996). Getting at the truth or getting along: Accuracy- versus impression-motivated heuristic and systematic processing. *Journal of Personality and Social Psychology, 71,* 262–275.

Chen, Z., Lawson, R. B., Gordon, L. R., & McIntosh, B. (1996). Groupthink: Deciding with the leader and the devil. *Psychological Record, 46,* 581–590.

Cheng, S. (1997). Epidemic genital retraction syndrome: Environmental and personal risk factors in southern China. *Journal of Psychology and Human Sexuality, 9,* 57–70.

Chertkoff, J. M., Kushigian, R. H., & McCool, M. A., Jr. (1996). Interdependent exiting: The effects of group size, time limit, and gender on the coordination of exiting. *Journal of Environmental Psychology, 16,* 109–121.

Cherulnik, P., & Wilderman, S. (1986). Symbols of status in urban neighborhoods. *Environment and Behavior, 18,* 604–622.

Cheyne, J. A., & Efran, M. G. (1972). The effect of spatial and interpersonal variables on the invasion of group controlled territories. *Sociometry, 35,* 477–487.

Chirot, D., & McCauley, C. (2006). *Why not kill them all.* Princeton, NJ: Princeton University Press.

Chiu, C., Hong, Y., & Dweck, C. S. (1997). Lay dispositionism and implicit theories of personality. *Journal of Personality and Social Psychology, 73,* 19–30.

Christakis, N. A., & Fowler, J. H. (2007). The spread of obesity in a large social network over 32 years. *New England Journal of Medicine, 357,* 370–379.

Christensen, A., & Jacobson, N. S. (1994). Who (or what) can do psychotherapy: The status and challenge of nonprofessional therapies. *Psychological Science, 5,* 8–12.

Christensen, P. N., & Kashy, D. A. (1998). Perceptions of and by lonely people in initial social interaction. *Personality and Social Psychology Bulletin, 24,* 322–329.

Cialdini, R. B. (2005). Basic social influence is underestimated. *Psychological Inquiry, 16,* 158–161.

Cialdini, R. B. (2009). *Influence: Science and practice* (6th ed.). Boston: Allyn and Bacon.

Cialdini, R. B., Borden, R., Thorne, A., Walker, M., Freeman, S., & Sloane, L. R. (1976). Basking in reflected glory: Three (football) field studies. *Journal of Personality and Social Psychology, 34,* 366–375.

Cialdini, R. B., & Goldstein, N. J. (2004). Social influence: Compliance and conformity. *Annual Review of Psychology, 55,* 591–621.

Cialdini, R. B., Kallgren, C. A., & Reno, R. R. (1991). A focus theory of normative conduct: A theoretical refinement and reevaluation of the role of norms in human behavior. *Advances in Experimental Social Psychology, 24,* 201–234.

Cialdini, R. B., Reno, R. R., & Kallgren, C. A. (1990). A focus theory of normative conduct: Recycling the concept of norms to reduce littering in public places. *Journal of Personality and Social Psychology, 58,* 1015–1026.

Cialdini, R. B., Wosinska, W., Barrett, D. W., Butner, J., & Gornik-Durose, M. (1999). Compliance with a request in two cultures: The differential influence of social proof and commitment/consistency on collectivists and individualists. *Personality and Social Psychology Bulletin, 25,* 1242–1253.

Cianni, M., & Romberger, B. (1995). Interactions with senior managers: Perceived differences by race/ethnicity and by gender. *Sex Roles, 32,* 353–373.

Cini, M. A., Moreland, R. L., & Levine, J. M. (1993). Group staffing levels and responses to prospective and new group members. *Journal of Personality and Social Psychology, 65,* 723–734.

Clack, B., Dixon, J., & Tredoux, C. (2005). Eating Together Apart: Patterns of Segregation in a Multiethnic Cafeteria. *Journal of Community & Applied Social Psychology, 15,* 1–16.

Claiborn, C. D., Goodyear, R. K., & Horner, P. A. (2001). Feedback. *Psychotherapy: Theory, Research, Practice, Training, 38,* 401–405.

Clapp, J. D., Holmes, M. R., Reed, M. B., Shillington, A. M., Freisthler, B., & Lange, J. E. (2007). Measuring college students' alcohol consumption in natural drinking environments: Field methodologies for bars and parties. *Evaluation Review, 31,* 469–489.

Clapp, J. D., Min, J. W., Shillington, A. M., Reed, M. B., & Croff, J. K. (2008). Person and environment predictors of blood alcohol concentrations: A multi-level study of college parties. *Alcoholism: Clinical and Experimental Research, 32,* 100–107.

Clark, G. (1969, November). What happens when the police strike? *New York Times Magazine*, p. 45.

Clark, K. B. (1971). The pathos of power. *American Psychologist, 26,* 1047–1057.

Clark, M. S., Oullette, R., Powell, M. C., & Milberg, S. (1987). Recipient's mood, relationship type, and helping. *Journal of Personality and Social Psychology, 53,* 94–103.

Clark, N. K., Stephenson, G. M., & Kniveton, B. (1990). Social remembering: Quantitative aspects of individual and collaborative remembering by police officers and students. *British Journal of Psychology, 81,* 73–94.

Clark, R. D. (1990). Minority influence: The role of argument refutation on the majority position and social support for the minority position. *European Journal of Social Psychology, 20,* 489–497.

Clark, R. D. (1999). Effect of number of majority defectors on minority influence. *Group Dynamics: Theory, Research, and Practice, 3,* 303–312.

Clark, R. D. (2001). Effects of majority defection and multiple minority sources on minority influence. *Group Dynamics: Theory, Research, and Practice, 5,* 57–62.

Clark, R. D., & Sechrest, L. B. (1976). The mandate phenomenon. *Journal of Personality and Social Psychology, 34,* 1057–1061.

Clark, R. D., & Word, L. E. (1972). Why don't bystanders help? Because of ambiguity? *Journal of Personality and Social Psychology, 24,* 392–400.

Clark, R. D., & Word, L. E. (1974). Where is the apathetic bystander? Situational characteristics of the emergency. *Journal of Personality and Social Psychology, 29,* 279–287.

Clark, S. (1998). International competition and the treatment of minorities: Seventeenth-century cases and general propositions. *American Journal of Sociology, 103,* 1267–1308.

Clayton, D. A. (1978). Socially facilitated behavior. *The Quarterly Review of Biology, 53,* 373–392.

Clement, R. W., & Krueger, J. (1998). Liking persons versus liking groups: A dual-process hypothesis. *European Journal of Social Psychology, 28,* 457–469.

Clendenen, V. I., Herman, C. P., & Polivy, J. (1994). Social facilitation of eating among friends and strangers. *Appetite, 23,* 1–13.

CNN (2005). Profiles of U2 and The Dave Matthews Band. Retrieved June 2, 2008, from CNN.com, http://transcripts.cnn.com/TRANSCRIPTS/0505/14/pitn.01.html.

Coch, L., & French, J. R. P., Jr. (1948). Overcoming resistance to change. *Human Relations, 1,* 512–532.

Cohen, F., Ogilvie, D. M., Solomon, S., Greenberg, J., & Pyszczynski, T. (2005). American roulette: The effect of reminders of death on support for George W. Bush in the 2004 presidential election. *Analyses of Social Issues and Public Policy, 5,* 177–187.

Cohen, F., Solomon, S., Maxfield, M., Pyszczynski, T., & Greenberg, J. (2004). Fatal attraction: The effects of mortality salience on evaluations of charismatic, task-oriented, and relationship-oriented leaders. *Psychological Science, 15,* 846–851.

Cohen, L. L., & Swim, J. K. (1995). The differential impact of gender ratios on women and men: Tokenism, self-confidence, and expectations. *Personality and Social Psychology Bulletin, 21,* 876–884.

Cohen, S., & Weinstein, N. (1981). Nonauditory effects of noise on behavior and health. *Journal of Social Issues, 37,* 36–70.

Cohen, S. G., & Bailey, D. E. (1997). What makes teams work: Group effectiveness research from the shop floor to the executive suite. *Journal of Management, 23,* 239–290.

Coleman, P. T. (2000). Intractable conflict. In M. Deutsch & P. T. Coleman (Eds.), *The handbook of conflict resolution: Theory and practice* (pp. 428–450). San Francisco: Jossey-Bass.

Colligan, M. J., & Murphy, L. R. (1982). A review of mass psychogenic illness in work settings. In M. J. Colligan, J. W. Pennebaker, & L. R. Murphy (Eds.), *Mass psychogenic illness: A social psychological analysis* (pp. 33–52). Mahwah, NJ: Erlbaum.

Colligan, M. J., Pennebaker, J. W., & Murphy, L. R. (Eds.). (1982). *Mass psychogenic illness: A social psychological analysis*. Mahwah, NJ: Erlbaum.

Collins, B. E., & Guetzkow, H. (1964). *A social psychology of group processes for decision-making*. New York: Wiley.

Collins, R. (2004). *Interaction ritual chains*. Princeton, NJ: Princeton University Press.

Collins, R. L. (2000). Among the better ones: Upward assimilation in social comparison. In J. Suls & L. Wheeler (Eds.), *Handbook of social comparison: Theory and research* (pp. 159–171). New York: Kluwer Academic.

Colman, A. M. (1991). Crowd psychology in South African murder trials. *American Psychologist, 46,* 1071–1079.

Colquitt, J. A., & Greenberg, J. (2003). Organizational justice: A fair assessment of the state of the literature. In J. Greenberg (Ed.), *Organizational behavior: The state of the science* (2nd ed., pp. 165–209). Mahwah, NJ: Erlbaum.

Conroy, J., & Sundstrom, E. (1977). Territorial dominance in a dyadic conversation as a function of similarity of opinion. *Journal of Personality and Social Psychology, 35,* 570–576.

Cook, K. S., Cheshire, C., & Gerbasi, A. (2006). Power, dependence, and social exchange. In P. J. Burke (Ed.), *Contemporary social psychological theories* (pp. 194–216). Stanford, CA: Stanford University Press.

Cook, S. W. (1985). Experimenting on social issues: The case of school desegregation. *American Psychologist, 40,* 452–460.

Cooley, C. H. (1902). *Human nature and the social order*. New York: Scribner.

Cooley, C. H. (1909). *Social organization*. New York: Scribner.

Cooper, H. M. (1979). Statistically combining independent studies: A meta-analysis of sex differences in conformity research. *Journal of Personality and Social Psychology, 37,* 131–146.

Coovert, M., & Burke, J. (2005). Leadership and decision making. In Y. Amichai-Hamburger (Ed.), *The social net: Understanding human behavior in cyberspace* (pp. 219–246). Oxford: Oxford University Press.

Cordery, J. (2004). Another case of the emperor's new clothes? *Journal of Occupational and Organizational Psychology, 77,* 481–484.

Corey, M., & Corey, G. (1992). *Groups: Process and practice* (4th ed.). Pacific Grove, CA: Brooks/Cole.

Corning, A. F., & Myers, D. J. (2002). Individual orientation toward engagement in social action. *Political Psychology, 23,* 703–729.

Corsaro, W. A., & Eder, D. (1995). Development and socialization of children and adolescents. In K. S. Cook, G. A. Fine, & J. S. House (Eds.), *Sociological perspectives on social psychology* (pp. 421–451). Needham Heights, MA: Allyn and Bacon.

Coser, L. A. (1956). *The functions of social conflict*. New York: Free Press.

Costa, P. T., & McCrae, R. R. (1988). Personality in adulthood: A six-year longitudinal study of self-reports and spouse ratings on the NEO personality inventory. *Journal of Personality and Social Psychology, 54,* 853–863.

Costa, P. T., Terracciano, A., & McCrae, R. R. (2001). Gender differences in personality traits across cultures: Robust and surprising findings. *Journal of Personality and Social Psychology, 81,* 322–331.

Costanzo, P. R. (1970). Conformity development as a function of self-blame. *Journal of Personality and Social Psychology, 14,* 366–374.

Costanzo, P. R., & Shaw, M. E. (1966). Conformity as a function of age level. *Child Development, 37,* 967–975.

Cotton, J. L. (1993). *Employee involvement*. Thousand Oaks, CA: Sage.

Cottrell, N. B. (1972). Social facilitation. In C. G. McClintock (Ed.), *Experimental social psychology* (pp. 185–236). New York: Holt, Rinehart & Winston.

Coughlin, B. C., & Venkatesh, S. A. (2003). The urban street gang after 1970. *Annual Review of Sociology, 29,* 41–64.

Courneya, K. S., & Carron, A. V. (1991). Effects of travel and length of home stand/road trip on the home advantage. *Journal of Sport and Exercise Psychology, 13,* 42–49.

Cousins, S. D. (1989). Culture and self-perception in Japan and the United States. *Journal of Personality and Social Psychology, 56,* 124–131.

Covey, S. R. (2004). *The 8th habit: From effectiveness to greatness.* New York: Free Press.

Cozzolino, P. J., & Snyder, M. (2008). Good times, bad times: How personal disadvantage moderates the relationship between social dominance and efforts to win. *Personality and Social Psychology Bulletin, 34,* 1420–1433.

Crandall, C. S. (1988). Social contagion of binge eating. *Journal of Personality and Social Psychology, 55,* 588–598.

Crano, W. D., & Seyranian, V. (2007). Majority and minority influence. *Social and Personality Psychology Compass, 1,* 572–589.

Crawford, M. T., Sherman, S. J., & Hamilton, D. L. (2002). Perceived entitativity, stereotype formation, and the interchangeability of group members. *Journal of Personality and Social Psychology, 83,* 1076–1094.

Cress, U. (2005). Ambivalent effect of member portraits in virtual groups. *Journal of Computer Assisted Learning, 21,* 281–291.

Crisp, R. J., & Hewstone, M. (2007). Multiple social categorization. *Advances in Experimental Social Psychology, 39,* 163–254.

Crocker, J., & Luhtanen, R. (1990). Collective self-esteem and ingroup bias. *Journal of Personality and Social Psychology, 58,* 60–67.

Crocker, J., Luhtanen, R., Blaine, B., & Broadnax, S. (1994). Collective self-esteem and psychological well-being among White, Black, and Asian college students. *Personality and Social Psychology Bulletin, 20,* 503–513.

Crocker, J., & Major, B. (1989). Social stigma and self-esteem: The self-protective properties of stigma. *Psychological Review, 96,* 608–630.

Crocker, J., & McGraw, K. M. (1984). What's good for the goose is not good for the gander: Solo status as an obstacle to occupational achievement for males and females. *American Behavioral Scientist, 27,* 357–369.

Cross, S. E., Bacon, P. L., & Morris, M. L. (2000). The relational–interdependent self-construal and relationships. *Journal of Personality and Social Psychology, 78,* 791–808.

Cross, S. E., & Madson, L. (1997). Models of the self: Self-construals and gender. *Psychological Bulletin, 122,* 5–37.

Crouch, E. C., Bloch, S., & Wanlass, J. (1994). Therapeutic factors: Interpersonal and intrapersonal mechanisms. In A. Fuhriman & G. M. Burlingame (Eds.), *Handbook of group psychotherapy* (pp. 269–315). New York: Wiley.

Crutchfield, R. S. (1955). Conformity and character. *American Psychologist, 10,* 191–198.

Csoka, L. S., & Bons, P. M. (1978). Manipulating the situation to fit the leader's style—Two validation studies of Leader Match. *Journal of Applied Psychology, 63,* 295–300.

Cuddy, A. J. C., Fiske, S. T., & Glick, P. (2007). The BIAS map: Behaviors from intergroup affect and stereotypes. *Journal of Personality and Social Psychology, 92,* 631–648.

Cuddy, A. J. C., Fiske, S. T., & Glick, P. (2008). Warmth and competence as universal dimensions of social perception: The stereotype content model and the BIAS map. *Advances In Experimental Social Psychology, 40,* 61–149.

Cullum, J., & Harton, H. C. (2007). Cultural evolution: Interpersonal influence, issue importance, and the development of shared attitudes in college residence halls. *Personality and Social Psychology Bulletin, 33,* 1327–1339.

Curhan, J. R., Neale, M. A., & Ross, L. (2004). Dynamic valuation: Preference changes in the context of face-to-face negotiation. *Journal of Experimental Social Psychology, 40,* 142–151.

Curtis, J. E., Baer, D. E., & Grabb, E. G. (2001). Nations of joiners: Explaining voluntary association membership in democratic societies. *American Sociological Review, 66,* 783–805.

Dabbs, J. M., Jr., & Ruback, R. B. (1987). Dimensions of group process: Amount and structure of vocal interaction. *Advances in Experimental Social Psychology, 20,* 123–169.

Dahl, R. A. (1957). The concept of power. *Behavioral Science, 2,* 201–215.

Dale, R. (1952). *Planning and developing the company organization structure.* New York: American Management Association.

Dane, F. C., & Wrightsman, L. S. (1982). Effects of defendants' and victims' characteristics on jurors' verdicts. In N. L. Kerr & R. M. Bray (Eds.), *Psychology of the courtroom* (pp. 83–115). New York: Academic Press.

Dansereau, F., Graen, G. B., & Haga, W. (1975). A vertical dyad linkage approach to leadership in formal organizations. *Organizational Behavior and Human Performance, 13,* 46–78.

Darley, J. G., Gross, N., & Martin, W. E. (1951). Studies of group behavior: Stability, change, and interrelations of psychometric and sociometric variables. *Journal of Abnormal and Social Psychology, 46,* 565–576.

Darley, J. M. (1992). Social organization for the production of evil. *Psychological Inquiry, 3,* 199–218.

Darley, J. M. (1995). Constructive and destructive obedience: A taxonomy of principal–agent relationships. *Journal of Social Issues, 51,* 125–154.

Darley, J. M., & Latané, B. (1968). Bystander intervention in emergencies: Diffusion of responsibility. *Journal of Personality and Social Psychology, 8,* 377–383.

Davidson-Shivers, G. V., Morris, S. B., & Sriwongkol, T. (2003). Gender differences: Are they diminished in online discussions? *International Journal on E-Learning, 2,* 29–36.

Davies, D. R., Burlingame, G. M., & Layne, C. M. (2006). Integrating small-group process principles into trauma-focused group psychotherapy: What should a group trauma therapist know? In L. A. Schein, H. I. Spitz, G. M. Burlingame, & P. R. Muskin (Eds.), with S. Vargo, *Psychological effects of catastrophic disasters: Group approaches to treatment* (pp. 385–423). New York: Haworth Press.

Davis, J. A., & Smith, T. W. (2007). *General social surveys (1972–2006).* [machine-readable data file]. Chicago: National Opinion Research Center & Storrs, CT: The Roper Center for Public Opinion Research. Available at http://www.norc.uchicago.edu.

Davis, J. H. (1973). Group decision and social interaction: A theory of social decision schemes. *Psychological Review, 80,* 97–125.

Davis, J. H., Bray, R. M., & Holt, R. W. (1977). The empirical study of decision processes in juries: A critical review. In J. L. Tapp & F. J. Levine (Eds.), *Law, justice, and the individual in society* (pp. 326–361). New York: Holt, Rinehart & Winston.

Davis, J. H., Kameda, T., & Stasson, M. (1992). Group risk taking: Selected topics. In J. F. Yates (Ed.), *Risk-taking behavior* (pp. 163–199). Chichester: Wiley.

Davis, J. H., Kerr, N. L., Atkin, R. S., Holt, R., & Meek, D. (1975). The decision processes of 6- and 12-person mock juries assigned unanimous and two-thirds majority rules. *Journal of Personality and Social Psychology, 32,* 1–14.

Davis, J. H., Stasson, M., Ono, K., & Zimmerman, S. (1988). Effects of straw polls on group decision making: Sequential voting pattern, timing, and local majorities. *Journal of Personality and Social Psychology, 55,* 918–926.

Davis, J. R. (1982). *Street gangs: Youth, biker, and prison groups.* Dubuque, IA: Kendall/Hunt.

Davison, K. P., Pennebaker, J. W., & Dickerson, S. S. (2000). Who talks? The social psychology of illness support groups. *American Psychologist, 55,* 205–217.

Dawes, R. M. (1988). *Rational choice in an uncertain world.* San Diego: Harcourt Brace Jovanovich.

de Castro, J. M., Bellisle, F., Feunekes, G. L. J., Dalix, A. M., & de Graaf, C. (1997). Culture and meal patterns: A comparison of the food intake of free-living Americans, Dutch, and French students. *Nutrition Research, 17,* 807–829.

De Dreu, C. K. W. (1997). Productive conflict: The importance of conflict management and conflict issue. In C. K. W. De Dreu & E. Van de Vliert (Eds.), *Using conflict in organizations* (pp. 9–22). Thousand Oaks, CA: Sage.

De Dreu, C. K. W. (2003). Time pressure and closing of the mind in negotiation. *Organizational Behavior and Human Decision Processes, 91,* 280–295.

De Dreu, C. K. W., Beersma, B., Steinel, W., & Van Kleef, G. A. (2007). The psychology of negotiation: Principles and basic processes. In A. W. Kruglanski & E. T. Higgins (Eds.), *Social psychology: Handbook of basic principles* (2nd ed., pp. 608–629). New York: Guilford.

De Dreu, C. K. W., Nauta, A., & Van de Vliert, E. (1995). Self-serving evaluations of conflict behavior and escalation of the dispute. *Journal of Applied Social Psychology, 25,* 2049–2066.

De Dreu, C. K. W., & Van Vianen, A. E. M. (2001). Responses to relationship conflict and team effectiveness. *Journal of Organizational Behavior, 22,* 309–328.

De Dreu, C. K. W., & Weingart, L. R. (2003). Task versus relationship conflict, team performance, and team member satisfaction: A meta-analysis. *Journal of Applied Psychology, 88,* 741–749.

De Dreu, C. K. W., Weingart, L. R., & Kwon, S. (2000). Influence of social motives on integrative negotiation: A meta-analytic review and test of two theories. *Journal of Personality and Social Psychology, 78,* 889–905.

De Grada, E., Kruglanski, A. W., Mannetti, L., & Pierro, A. (1999). Motivated cognition and group interaction: Need for closure affects the contents and processes of collective negotiations. *Journal of Experimental Social Psychology, 35,* 346–365.

de la Roche, R. S. (2002). Why is collective violence collective? *Sociological Theory, 19,* 126–144.

de Tocqueville, A. (1969). *Democracy in America* (G. Lawrence, Trans.). New York: Doubleday. (Original work published in 1831)

de Waal, F. B. M. (2000). Primates—a natural heritage of conflict resolution. *Science, 289,* 586–590.

de Waal, F. B. M. (2006). *Primates and philosophers: How morality evolved.* Princeton, NJ: Princeton University Press.

Dean, L. M., Willis, F. N., & Hewitt, J. (1975). Initial interaction distance among individuals equal and unequal in military rank. *Journal of Personality and Social Psychology, 32,* 294–299.

Deci, E. L., Nezlek, J., & Sheinman, L. (1981). Characteristics of the rewarder and intrinsic motivation of the rewardee. *Journal of Personality and Social Psychology, 40,* 1–10.

Decker, S. H., & Van Winkle, B. (1996). *Life in the gang: Family, friends, and violence.* New York: Cambridge University Press.

Delbecq, A. L., & Van de Ven, A. H. (1971). A group process model for problem identification and program planning. *Journal of Applied Behavioral Science, 7,* 466–492.

DeLucia-Waack, J. L., & Kalodner, C. R. (2005). Contemporary issues in group practice. In S. A. Wheelan (Ed.), *The handbook of group research and practice* (pp. 65–84). Thousand Oaks, CA: Sage.

DeMatteo, J. S., Eby, L. T., & Sundstrom, E. (1998). Team-based rewards: Current empirical evidence and directions for future research. *Research in Organizational Behavior, 20,* 141–183.

Den Hartog, D. N., House, R. J., Hanges, P. J., Ruiz-Quintanilla, S. A., Dorfman, P. W., & Associates (1999). Culture specific and cross-culturally generalizable implicit leadership theories: Are attributes of charismatic/transformational leadership universally endorsed? *Leadership Quarterly, 10,* 219–256.

Denrell, J., & Le Mens, G. (2007). Interdependent sampling and social influence. *Psychological Review, 114,* 398–422.

Denson, T. F., Lickel, B., Curtis, M., Stenstrom, D. M., & Ames, D. R. (2006). The roles of entitativity and essentiality in judgments of collective responsibility. *Group Processes & Intergroup Relations, 9,* 43–61.

Denvir, B. (1993). *The chronicle of impressionism.* New York: Little, Brown.

DeRosa, D. M., Smith, C. L., & Hantula, D. A. (2007). The medium matters: Mining the long-promised merit of group interaction in creative idea generation tasks in a meta-analysis of the electronic group brainstorming literature. *Computers in Human Behavior, 23,* 1549–1581.

Deutsch, M. (1949a). An experimental study of the effects of cooperation and competition upon group process. *Human Relations, 2,* 199–231.

Deutsch, M. (1949b). A theory of cooperation and competition. *Human Relations, 2,* 129–152.

Deutsch, M. (1969). Socially relevant science: Reflections on some studies of interpersonal conflict. *American Psychologist, 24,* 1076–1092.

Deutsch, M. (1973). *The resolution of conflict: Constructive and destructive processes.* New Haven, CT: Yale University Press.

Deutsch, M. (1980). Fifty years of conflict. In L. Festinger (Ed.), *Retrospections on social psychology* (pp. 46–77). New York: Oxford University Press.

Deutsch, M., & Coleman, P. T. (Eds.). (2000). *The handbook of conflict resolution: Theory and practice.* San Francisco: Jossey-Bass.

Deutsch, M., & Gerard, H. B. (1955). A study of normative and informational social influences upon individual judgment. *Journal of Abnormal and Social Psychology, 51,* 629–636.

Deutsch, M., & Krauss, R. M. (1960). The effect of threat upon interpersonal bargaining. *Journal of Abnormal and Social Psychology, 61,* 181–189.

Deutsch, M., & Lewicki, R. J. (1970). "Locking in" effects during a game of Chicken. *Journal of Conflict Resolution, 14,* 367–378.

Devine, D. J. (2002). A review and integration of classification systems relevant to teams in organizations. *Group Dynamics: Theory, Research, and Practice, 6,* 291–310.

Devine, D. J., Clayton, L. D., Dunford, B. B., Seying, R., & Pryce, J. (2001). Jury decision making: 45 years of empirical research on deliberating groups. *Psychology, Public Policy, & Law, 7,* 622–727.

Devine, D. J., Clayton, L. D., Philips, J. L., Dunford, B. B., & Melner, S. B. (1999). Teams in organizations: Prevalence, characteristics, and effectiveness. *Small Group Research, 30,* 678–711.

Devine, D. J., & Philips, J. L. (2001). Do smarter teams do better: A meta-analysis of cognitive ability and team performance. *Small Group Research, 32,* 507–532.

Devine, P. G. (1989). Stereotypes and prejudice: Their automatic and controlled components. *Journal of Personality and Social Psychology, 56,* 5–18.

Devine, P. G. (2005). Breaking the prejudice habit: Allport's "inner conflict" revisited. In J. F. Dovidio, P. Glick & L. A. Rudman (Eds.), *On the nature of prejudice: Fifty years after Allport* (pp. 327–342). Malden, MA: Blackwell.

DeWall, C. N., & Baumeister, R. F. (2006). Alone but feeling no pain: Effects of social exclusion on physical pain tolerance and pain threshold, affective forecasting, and interpersonal empathy. *Journal of Personality and Social Psychology, 91,* 1–15.

DeYoung, C. G., Peterson, J. B., & Higgins, D. M. (2002). Higher-order factors of the Big Five predict conformity: Are there neuroses of health? *Personality and Individual Differences, 33,* 533–552.

Di Salvo, V. S., Nikkel, E., & Monroe, C. (1989). Theory and practice: A field investigation and identification of group members' perceptions of problems facing natural work groups. *Small Group Behavior, 20,* 551–567.

Diehl, M., & Stroebe, W. (1987). Productivity loss in brainstorming groups: Toward the solution of a riddle. *Journal of Personality and Social Psychology, 53,* 497–509.

Diehl, M., & Stroebe, W. (1991). Productivity loss in idea-generating groups: Tracking down the blocking effect. *Journal of Personality and Social Psychology, 61,* 392–403.

Diener, E. (1979). Deindividuation, self-awareness, and disinhibition. *Journal of Personality and Social Psychology, 37,* 1160–1171.

Diener, E. (1980). Deindividuation: The absence of self-awareness and self-regulation in group members. In P. B. Paulus (Ed.), *Psychology of group influence* (pp. 209–242). Mahwah, NJ: Erlbaum.

Diener, E., Fraser, S. C., Beaman, A. L., & Kelem, R. T. (1976). Effects of deindividuating variables on stealing by Halloween trick-or-treaters. *Journal of Personality and Social Psychology, 33,* 178–183.

Dienesch, R. M., & Liden, R. C. (1986). Leader/member exchange model of leadership: A critique and further development. *Academy of Management Review, 11,* 618–634.

Dies, R. R. (1994). Therapist variables in group psychotherapy research. In A. Fuhriman & G. M. Burlingame (Eds.), *Handbook of group psychotherapy* (pp. 114–154). New York: Wiley.

Dietz-Uhler, B., & Murrell, A. (1998). Effects of social identity and threat on self-esteem and group attributions. *Group Dynamics: Theory, Research, and Practice, 2,* 24–35.

Dijke, M. V., & Poppe, M. (2004). Social comparison of power: Interpersonal versus intergroup effects. *Group Dynamics: Theory, Research, and Practice, 8,* 13–26.

Dillard, J. P. (1991). The current status of research on sequential-request compliance techniques. *Personality and Social Psychology Bulletin, 17,* 283–288.

Dillard, J. P., & Fitzpatrick, M. A. (1985). Compliance-gaining in marital interaction. *Personality and Social Psychology Bulletin, 11,* 419–433.

Dion, K. L. (2000). Group cohesion: From "field of forces" to multidimensional construct. *Group Dynamics: Theory, Research, and Practice, 4,* 7–26.

Dionne, S. D., Yammarino, F. J., Howell, J. P., & Villa, J. (2005). Theoretical letters: Substitutes for leadership, or not. *Leadership Quarterly, 16,* 169–193.

Dipboye, R. L. (1977). Alternative approaches to deindividuation. *Psychological Bulletin, 84,* 1057–1075.

Dishion, T. J., & Dodge, K. A. (2005). Peer contagion in interventions for children and adolescents: Moving towards an understanding of the ecology and dynamics of change. *Journal of Abnormal Child Psychology, 33,* 395–400.

Dobbins, G. H., & Platz, S. J. (1986). Sex differences in leadership: How real are they? *Academy of Management Review, 11,* 118–127.

Doherty, W. J., Lester, M. E., & Leigh, G. K. (1986). Marriage encounter weekends: Couples who win and couples who lose. *Journal of Marital and Family Therapy, 12,* 49–61.

Doise, W. (1969). Intergroup relations and polarization of individual and collective judgments. *Journal of Personality and Social Psychology, 12,* 136–143.

Dolinski, D., Nawrat, M., & Rudak, I. (2001). Dialogue involvement as a social influence technique. *Personality and Social Psychology Bulletin, 27,* 1395–1406.

Doll, B., Murphy, P., & Song, S. Y. (2003). The relationship between children's self-reported recess problems, and peer acceptance and friendships. *Journal of School Psychology, 41,* 113–130.

Dollar, N. J., & Merrigan, G. M. (2002). Ethnographic practices in group communication research. In L. R. Frey (Ed.), *New directions in group communication* (pp. 59–78). Thousand Oaks, CA: Sage.

Dollinger, S. J., Preston, L. A., O'Brien, S. P., & DiLalla, D. L. (1996). Individuality and relatedness of the self: An autophotographic study. *Journal of Personality and Social Psychology, 71,* 1268–1278.

Dooley, D., & Catalano, R. (1984). The epidemiology of economic stress. *American Journal of Community Psychology, 12,* 387–409.

Doosje, B. J., & Branscombe, N. R. (2003). Attributions for the negative historical actions of a group. *European Journal of Social Psychology, 33,* 235–248.

Doosje, B., Ellemers, N., & Spears, R. (1999). Commitment and intergroup behavior. In N. Ellemers R. Spears, & B. Doosje (Eds.), *Social identity: Context, commitment, content* (pp. 84–106). Oxford: Blackwell Science.

Doreian, P. (1986). Measuring relative standing in small groups and bounded social networks. *Social Psychology Quarterly, 49,* 247–259.

Dorfman, P. W., Hanges, P. J., & Brodbeck, F. C. (2004). Leadership and cultural variation: The identification of culturally endorsed leadership profiles. In R. J. House, P. J. Hanges, M. Javidan, P. W. Dorfman, & V. Gupta (Eds.), *Culture, leadership, and organizations: The GLOBE study of 62 societies* (pp. 669–719). Thousand Oaks, CA: Sage.

Douthitt, E. A., & Aiello, J. R. (2001). The role of participation and control in the effects of computer monitoring on fairness perceptions, task satisfaction, and performance. *Journal of Applied Psychology, 86,* 867–874.

Dovidio, J. F., Brown, C. E., Heltman, K., Ellyson, S. L., & Keating, C. F. (1988). Power displays between women and men in discussions of gender-linked tasks: A multichannel study. *Journal of Personality and Social Psychology, 55,* 580–587.

Dovidio, J. F., Gaertner, S. L., Esses, V. M., & Brewer, M. B. (2003). Social conflict, harmony, and integration. In T. Millon, M. J. Lerner, & I. B. Weiner (Eds.), *Handbook of psychology: Personality and social psychology* (Vol. 5, pp. 485–506). New York: Wiley.

Dovidio, J. F., Gaertner, S. L., Nier, J. A., Kawakami, K., & Hodson, G. (2004). Contemporary racial bias: When good people do bad things. In A. G. Miller (Ed.), *The social psychology of good and evil* (pp. 141–167). New York: Guilford.

Dovidio, J. F., Glick, P., & Rudman, L. A. (Eds.). (2005). *On the nature of prejudice: Fifty years after Allport.* Malden, MA: Blackwell.

Driskell, J. E., Goodwin, G. F., Salas, E., & O'Shea, P. G. (2006). What makes a good team player? Personality and team effectiveness. *Group Dynamics: Theory, Research, and Practice, 10,* 249–271.

Driskell, J. E., & Mullen, B. (1990). Status, expectations, and behavior: A meta-analytic review and test of theory. *Personality and Social Psychology Bulletin, 16,* 541–553.

Driskell, J. E., Radtke, P. H., & Salas, E. (2003). Virtual teams: Effects of technological mediation on team performance. *Group Dynamics: Theory, Research, and Practice, 7,* 297–323.

Driskell, J. E., & Salas, E. (1992). Can you study real teams in contrived settings? The value of small group research to understanding teams. In R. W. Swezey & E. Salas (Eds.), *Teams: Their training and performance* (pp. 101–124). Norwood, NJ: Ablex.

Driskell, J. E., & Salas, E. (2005). The effect of content and demeanor on reactions to dominance behavior. *Group Dynamics: Theory, Research, and Practice, 9,* 3–14.

Dryer, D. C., & Horowitz, L. M. (1997). When do opposites attract? Interpersonal complementarity versus similarity. *Journal of Personality and Social Psychology, 72,* 592–603.

Dubrovsky, V. J., Kiesler, S., & Sethna, B. N. (1991). The equalization phenomenon: Status effects in computer-mediated and face-to-face decision-making groups. *Human-Computer Interaction, 6,* 119–146.

Ducheneaut, N., Yee, N., Nickell, E., & Moore, R. (2006). "Alone together?" Exploring the social dynamics of massively multiplayer online games. *CHI Proceedings: Games and Performance.* Montreal: ACM.

Duckitt, J. (2006). Differential effects of right wing authoritarianism and social dominance orientation on outgroup attitudes and their mediation by threat from and competitiveness to outgroups. *Personality and Social Psychology Bulletin, 32,* 684–696.

Duckitt, J., & Mphuthing, T. (1998). Group identification and intergroup attitudes: A longitudinal analysis in South Africa. *Journal of Personality and Social Psychology, 74,* 80–85.

Duffy, F. (1997). *The new office.* London: Conran Octopus.

Dugo, J. M., & Beck, A. P. (1997). Significance and complexity of early phases in the development of the co-therapy relationship. *Group Dynamics: Theory, Research, and Practice, 1,* 294–305.

Dugosh, K. L., Paulus, P. B., Roland, E. J., & Yang, H. (2000). Cognitive stimulation in brainstorming. *Journal of Personality and Social Psychology, 79,* 722–735.

Dunning, E. G., Murphy, P. J., & Williams, J. M. (1986). Spectator violence at football matches: Towards a sociological explanation. *British Journal of Sociology, 37,* 221–244.

Dupue, R. L. (2007). A theoretical profile of Seung Hui Cho: From the perspective of a forensic behavioral scientist. In Virginia Tech Review Panel, *Mass shootings at Virginia Tech: Report of the review panel.* Retrieved June 15, 2007, from http://www.governor.virginia.gov.

Durand, D. E. (1977). Power as a function of office space and physiognomy: Two studies of influence. *Psychological Reports, 40,* 755–760.

Durkheim, É. (1965). *The elementary forms of religious life.* New York: Free Press. (Original work published in 1912)

Durkheim, É. (1966). *Suicide.* New York: Free Press. (Original work published in 1897)

Durkheim, É. (1973). *Emile Durkheim on morality and society.* Chicago: University of Chicago Press. (Original work published in 1900)

Dvir, T., Eden, D., Avolio, B. J., & Shamir, B. (2002). Impact of transformational leadership on follower development and performance: A field experiment. *Academy of Management Journal, 45,* 735–744.

Eagly, A. H. (1987). *Sex differences in social behavior: A social-role interpretation.* Mahwah, NJ: Erlbaum.

Eagly, A. H., & Carli, L. L. (1981). Sex of researchers and sex-typed communications as determinants of sex differences in influenceability: A meta-analysis of social influence studies. *Psychological Bulletin, 90,* 1–20.

Eagly, A. H., & Carli, L. L. (2007). *Through the labyrinth: The truth about how women become leaders.* Boston: Harvard Business School Press.

Eagly, A. H., Johannesen-Schmidt, M. C., & van Engen, M. L. (2003). Transformational, transactional, and laissez-faire leadership styles: A meta-analysis comparing women and men. *Psychological Bulletin, 129,* 569–591.

Eagly, A. H., & Johnson, B. T. (1990). Gender and leadership style: A meta-analysis. *Psychological Bulletin, 108,* 233–256.

Eagly, A. H., & Karau, S. J. (2002). Role congruity theory of prejudice toward female leaders. *Psychological Review, 109,* 573–598.

Eagly, A. H., Karau, S., & Makhijani, M. (1995). Gender and the effectiveness of leaders: A meta-analysis. *Journal of Personality and Social Psychology, 117,* 125–145.

Eagly, A. H., Makhijani, M. G., & Klonsky, B. G. (1992). Gender and the evaluation of leaders: A meta-analysis, *Psychological Bulletin, 111,* 3–22.

Eagly, A. H., Wood, W., & Fishbaugh, L. (1981). Sex differences in conformity: Surveillance by the group as a determinant of male nonconformity. *Journal of Personality and Social Psychology, 40,* 384–394.

Eaton, J. W. (1947). Experiments in testing for leadership. *American Journal of Sociology, 52,* 523–535.

Ebbesen, E. B., Kjos, G. L., & Konecni, V. J. (1976). Spatial ecology: Its effects on the choice of friends and enemies. *Journal of Experimental Social Psychology, 12,* 505–518.

Edelstein, M. R. (2002). Contamination: The invisible built environment. In R. B. Bechtel & A. Churchman (Eds.), *Handbook of environmental psychology* (pp. 559–588). New York: Wiley.

Edmondson, A., Bohmer, R., & Pisano, G. (2001). Speeding up team learning. *Harvard Business Review, 79*(9), 125–132.

Edney, J. J. (1975). Territoriality and control: A field experiment. *Journal of Personality and Social Psychology, 31,* 1108–1115.

Edney, J. J. (1976). Human territories: Comment on functional properties. *Environment and Behavior, 8,* 31–48.

Edney, J. J., & Grundmann, M. J. (1979). Friendship, group size, and boundary size: Small group spaces. *Small Group Behavior, 10,* 124–135.

Edney, J. J., & Jordan-Edney, N. L. (1974). Territorial spacing on a beach. *Sociometry, 37,* 92–104.

Ehrhart, M. G., & Naumann, S. E. (2004). Organizational citizenship behavior in work groups: A group norms approach. *Journal of Applied Psychology, 89,* 960–974.

Eisenberger, N. I., Lieberman, M. D., & Williams, K. D. (2003). Does rejection hurt? An fMRI study of social exclusion. *Science, 302,* 290–292.

Eisenberger, R., Lynch, P., Aselage, J., & Rohdieck, S. (2004). Who takes the most revenge? Individual differences in negative reciprocity norm endorsement. *Personality and Social Psychology Bulletin, 30,* 789–799.

Elder, G. H., & Clipp, E. C. (1988). Wartime losses and social bonding: Influences across 40 years in men's lives. *Psychiatry: Journal for the Study of Interpersonal Processes, 51,* 177–198.

Eldredge, N., & Gould, S. J. (1972). Punctuated equilibria: An alternative to phyletic gradualism. In T. M. Schopf (Ed.), *Models in palaeobiology* (pp. 82–115). New York: Freeman.

Ellemers, N., Spears, R., & Doosje, B. (1997). Sticking together or falling apart: In-group identification as a psychological determinant of group commitment versus individual mobility. *Journal of Personality and Social Psychology, 72,* 617–626.

Ellemers, N., Spears, R., & Doosje, B. (2002). Self and social identity. *Annual Review of Psychology, 53,* 161–186.

Ellis, A. P. J., Hollenbeck, J. R., Ilgen, D. R., Porter, C. O. L. H., West, B. J., & Moon, H. (2003). Team learning: Collectively connecting the dots. *Journal of Applied Psychology, 88,* 821–835.

Ellsworth, P. C., & Reifman, A. (2000). Juror comprehension and public policy: Perceived problems and proposed solutions. *Psychology, Public Policy, & Law, 6,* 788–821.

Elms, A. C. (1995). Obedience in retrospect. *Journal of Social Issues, 51,* 21–31.

Emans, B. J. M., Munduate, L., Klaver, E., & Van de Vliert, E. (2003). Constructive consequences of leaders' forcing influence styles. *Applied Psychology: An International Review, 52,* 36–54.

Emerson, R. M. (1962). Power-dependence relations. *American Sociological Review, 27,* 31–40.

Emler, N., & Cook, T. (2001). Moral integrity in leadership: Why it matters and why it may be difficult to achieve. In B. W. Roberts & R. Hogan (Eds.), *Personality psychology in the workplace* (pp. 277–298). Washington, DC: American Psychological Association.

Emmelkamp, P. M. G. (2004). Behavior therapy with adults. In M. J. Lambert (Ed.), *Bergin & Garfield's handbook of psychotherapy and behavior change* (5th ed., pp. 393–446). New York: Wiley & Sons.

Emrich, C. G. (1999). Context effects in leadership perception. *Personality and Social Psychology Bulletin, 25,* 991–1006.

End, C. M., Dietz-Uhler, B., Harrick, E. A., & Jacquemotte, L. (2002). Identifying with winners: A reexamination of sport fans' tendency to BIRG. *Journal of Applied Social Psychology, 32,* 1017–1030.

Epitropaki, O., & Martin, R. (2004). Implicit leadership theories in applied settings: Factor structure, generalizability, and stability over time. *Journal of Applied Psychology, 89,* 293–310.

Epley, N., & Gilovich, T. (1999). Just going along: Nonconscious priming and conformity to social pressure. *Journal of Experimental Social Psychology, 35,* 578–589.

Esser, A. H. (1968). Dominance hierarchy and clinical course of psychiatrically hospitalized boys. *Child Development, 39,* 147–157.

Esser, A. H. (1973). Cottage Fourteen: Dominance and territoriality in a group of institutionalized boys. *Small Group Behavior, 4,* 131–146.

Esser, A. H., Chamberlain, A. S., Chapple, E. D., & Kline, N. S. (1965). Territoriality of patients on a research ward. In J. Wortis (Ed.), *Recent advances in biological psychiatry* (Vol. 3, pp. 37–44). New York: Plenum.

Esser, J. K. (1998). Alive and well after 25 years: A review of groupthink research. *Organizational Behavior and Human Decision Processes, 73,* 116–141.

Esses, V. M., Jackson, L. M., Dovidio, J. F., & Hodson, G. (2005). Instrumental relations among groups: Group competition, conflict, and prejudice. In J. F. Dovidio, P. Glick & L. A. Rudman (Eds.), *On the nature of prejudice: Fifty years after Allport* (pp. 227–243). Malden, MA: Blackwell.

Ettin, M. F. (1992). *Foundations and applications of group psychotherapy: A sphere of influence.* Boston: Allyn & Bacon.

Etzioni, A. (1968). A model of significant research. *International Journal of Psychiatry, 6,* 278–280.

Evans, G. W. (1979). Behavioral and physiological consequences of crowding in humans. *Journal of Applied Social Psychology, 9,* 27–46.

Evans, G. W., & Cohen, S. (1987). Environmental stress. In D. Stokols & I. Altman (Eds.), *Handbook of environmental psychology* (Vol. 1, pp. 571–610). New York: Wiley.

Evans, G. W., & Howard, R. B. (1973). Personal space. *Psychological Bulletin, 80,* 334–344.

Evans, G. W., & Lepore, S. J. (1992). Conceptual and analytic issues in crowding research. *Journal of Environmental Psychology, 12,* 163–173.

Evans, G. W., Lepore, S. J., & Allen, K. M. (2000). Cross-cultural differences in tolerance for crowding: Fact or fiction? *Journal of Personality and Social Psychology, 79,* 204–210.

Evans, G. W., Palsane, M. N., Lepore, S. J., & Martin, J. (1989). Residential density and psychological health: The mediating effects of social support. *Journal of Personality and Social Psychology, 57,* 994–999.

Evans, G. W., & Stecker, R. (2004). Motivational consequences of environmental stress. *Journal of Environmental Psychology, 24,* 143–165.

Evans, G. W., & Wener, R. E. (2007). Crowding and personal space invasion on the train: Please don't make me sit in the middle. *Journal of Environmental Psychology, 27,* 90–94.

Evans, N. J., & Jarvis, P. A. (1986). The Group Attitude Scale: A measure of attraction to group. *Small Group Behavior, 17,* 203–216.

Eysenck, H. (1990). Biological dimensions of personality. In L. A. Pervin (Ed.), *Handbook of personality: Theory and research* (pp. 244–276). New York: Guilford.

Falbo, T. (1977). The multidimensional scaling of power strategies. *Journal of Personality and Social Psychology, 35,* 537–548.

Falbo, T., & Peplau, L. A. (1980). Power strategies in intimate relationships. *Journal of Personality and Social Psychology, 38,* 618–628.

Falk, A., & Fischbacher, U. (2006). A theory of reciprocity. *Games and Economic Behavior, 54,* 293–315.

Falloon, I. R. H., Lindley, P., McDonald, R., & Marks, I. M. (1977). Social skills training of outpatient groups: A controlled study of rehearsal and homework. *British Journal of Psychiatry, 131,* 599–609.

Fanon, F. (1963). *The wretched of the earth.* New York: Grove.

Farbstein, J., & Kantrowitz, M. (1978). *People in places: Experiencing, using, and changing the built environment.* Upper Saddle River, NJ: Prentice Hall.

Farrell, M. P. (1982). Artists' circles and the development of artists. *Small Group Behavior, 13,* 451–474.

Farrell, M. P. (2001). *Collaborative circles: Friendship dynamics & creative work.* University of Chicago Press: Chicago.

Feeley, T. H. (2000). Testing a communication network model of employee turnover based on centrality. *Journal of Applied Communication Research, 28,* 262–277.

Feigenson, N. (2000). *Legal blame: How jurors think and talk about accidents.* Washington, DC: American Psychological Association.

Feld, S. L. (1982). Social structural determinants of similarity among associates. *American Sociological Review, 47,* 797–801.

Feldman, S. (2003). Enforcing social conformity: A theory of authoritarianism. *Political Psychology, 24,* 41–74.

Ferencik, B. M. (1992). The helping process in group therapy: A review and discussion. *Group, 16,* 113–124.

Ferguson, T. J., & Rule, B. G. (1983). An attributional analysis of anger and aggression. In R. G. Geen & E. I. Donnerstein (Eds.), *Aggression: Theoretical and empirical reviews* (Vol. 1). New York: Academic Press.

Ferris, G. R., & Rowland, K. M. (1983). Social facilitation effects on behavioral and perceptual task performance measures: Implications for work behavior. *Group and Organization Studies, 8,* 421–438.

Festinger, L. (1950). Informal social communication. *Psychological Review, 57,* 271–282.

Festinger, L. (1954). A theory of social comparison processes. *Human Relations, 7,* 117–140.

Festinger, L. (1957). *A theory of cognitive dissonance.* Stanford, CA: Stanford University Press.

Festinger, L. (1983). *The human legacy.* New York: Columbia University Press.

Festinger, L., Pepitone, A., & Newcomb, T. (1952). Some consequences of deindividuation in a group. *Journal of Abnormal and Social Psychology, 47,* 382–389.

Festinger, L., Riecken, H. W., & Schachter, S. (1956). *When prophecy fails.* Minneapolis: University of Minnesota Press.

Festinger, L., Schachter, S., & Back, K. (1950). *Social pressures in informal groups.* New York: Harper.

Festinger, L., & Thibaut, J. (1951). Interpersonal communication in small groups. *Journal of Abnormal and Social Psychology, 46,* 92–99.

Fiedler, F. E. (1955). The influence of leader–keyman relations on combat crew effectiveness. *Journal of Abnormal and Social Psychology, 51,* 227–235.

Fiedler, F. E. (1964). A contingency model of leadership effectiveness. *Advances in Experimental Social Psychology, 1,* 150–190.

Fiedler, F. E. (1967). *A theory of leadership effectiveness.* New York: McGraw-Hill.

Fiedler, F. E. (1971). *Leadership.* Morristown, NJ: General Learning Press.

Fiedler, F. E. (1978). The contingency model and the dynamics of the leadership process. *Advances in Experimental Social Psychology, 12,* 59–112.

Fiedler, F. E. (1981). Leadership effectiveness. *American Behavioral Scientist, 24,* 619–632.

Fiedler, F. E. (1986). The contribution of cognitive resources to leadership performance. *Journal of Applied Social Psychology, 16,* 532–548.

Fiedler, F. E. (1993). The leadership situation and the black box in contingency theories. In M. M. Chemers & R. Ayman (Eds.), *Leadership theory and research: Perspectives and directions* (pp. 1–28). San Diego: Academic Press.

Fiedler, F. E. (1996). Research on leadership selection and training: One view of the future. *Administrative Science Quarterly, 41,* 241–250.

Fiedler, F. E., Chemers, M. M., & Mahar, L. (1976). *Improving leadership effectiveness: The Leader Match concept.* New York: Wiley.

Filkins, J. W., Smith, C. M., & Tindale, R. S. (1998). An evaluation of the biasing effects of death qualification: A meta-analytic/computer simulation approach. In R. S. Tindale, L. Heath, J. Edwards, E. J. Posavac, F. B. Bryant, Y. Suarez-Balcazar, E. Henderson-King, & J. Myers (Eds.), *Theory and research on small groups* (pp. 153–175). New York: Plenum Press.

Fincham, F. D., & Bradbury, T. N. (1992). Assessing attributions in marriage: The Relationship Attribution Measure. *Journal of Personality and Social Psychology, 62,* 457–468.

Fincham, F. D., & Bradbury, T. N. (1993). Marital satisfaction, depression, and attributions: A longitudinal analysis. *Journal of Personality and Social Psychology, 64,* 442–452.

Fine, G. A. (1979). Small groups and culture creation. *American Sociological Review, 44,* 733–745.

Fine, G. A. (1987). *With the boys: Little League baseball and preadolescent culture.* Chicago: University of Chicago Press.

Fine, G. A., & Holyfield, L. (1996). Secrecy, trust, and dangerous leisure: Generating group cohesion in voluntary organizations. *Social Psychology Quarterly, 59,* 22–38.

Finlay, F., Hitch, G., & Meudell, P. R. (2000). Mutual inhibition in collaborative recall: Evidence for a retrieval-based account. *Journal of Experimental Psychology: Learning, Memory, & Cognition, 26,* 1556–1567.

Finn, J. D., Pannozzo, G. M., & Achilles, C. M. (2003). The "why's" of class size: Student behavior in small classes. *Review of Educational Research, 73,* 321–368.

Fischer, R., Smith, P. B., Richey, B., Ferreira, M. C., Assmar, E. M. L., Maes, J., & Stumpf, S. (2007). How do organizations allocate rewards?: The predictive validity of national values, economic and organizational factors across six nations. *Journal of Cross-Cultural Psychology, 38,* 3–18.

Fisher, B. A. (1980). *Small group decision making* (2nd ed.). New York: McGraw-Hill.

Fisher, J. D., & Byrne, D. (1975). Too close for comfort: Sex differences in response to invasions of personal space. *Journal of Personality and Social Psychology, 32,* 15–21.

Fisher, R. (1983). Negotiating power. *American Behavioral Science, 27,* 149–166.

Fisher, R., & Ury, W. (with B. Patton, Ed.). (1981). *Getting to YES: Negotiating agreement without giving in.* Boston: Houghton Mifflin.

Fisher, W. A., & Fisher, J. D. (1993). A general social psychological model for changing AIDS risk behavior. In J. B. Pryor & G. D. Reeder (Eds.), *The social psychology of HIV infection* (pp. 127–153). Mahwah, NJ: Erlbaum.

Fiske, A. P. (1992). The four elementary forms of sociality: Framework for a unified theory of social relations. *Psychological Review, 99,* 689–723.

Fiske, A. P. (2002). Using individualism and collectivism to compare cultures—A critique of the validity and measurement of the constructs: Comment on Oyserman et al. (2002). *Psychological Bulletin, 128,* 78–88.

Fiske, S. T. (1993). Controlling other people: The impact of power on stereotyping. *American Psychologist, 48,* 621–628.

Fiske, S. T. (2004). What's in a category? Responsibility, intent, and the avoidability of bias against outgroups. In A. G. Miller (Ed.), *The social psychology of good and evil* (pp. 127–140). New York: Guilford.

Fiske, S. T., & Berdahl, J. (2007). Social power. In A. W. Kruglanski & E. T. Higgins (Eds.), *Social psychology: Handbook of basic principles* (2nd ed., pp. 678–692). New York: Guilford.

Fiske, S. T., Harris, L. T., & Cuddy, A. J. C. (2004). Why ordinary people torture enemy prisoners. *Science, 306,* 1482–1483.

Fiske, S. T., & Yamamoto, M. (2005). Coping with rejection: Core social motives across cultures. In K. D. Williams, J. P. Forgas, & W. von Hippel (Eds.), *The social outcast: Ostracism, social exclusion, rejection, and bullying* (pp. 185–198). New York: Psychology Press.

Fleeson, W., Malanos, A. B., & Achille, N. M. (2002). An intraindividual process approach to the relationship between extraversion and positive affect: Is acting extraverted as "good" as being extraverted? *Journal of Personality and Social Psychology, 83,* 1409–1422.

Fleishman, E. A. (1953). The description of supervisory behavior. *Journal of Applied Psychology, 37,* 1–6.

Flores, P. J. (1997). *Group psychotherapy with addicted populations: An integration of twelve step and psychodynamic theory.* Binghamton, NY: Haworth Press.

Flowers, M. L. (1977). A laboratory test of some implications of Janis' groupthink hypothesis. *Journal of Personality and Social Psychology, 35,* 888–896.

Flynn, K., & Gerhardt, G. (1989). *The silent brotherhood: Inside America's racist underground.* New York: Penguin.

Foddy, M., & Smithson, M. (1996). Relative ability, paths of relevance, and influence in task-oriented groups. *Social Psychology Quarterly, 59,* 140–153.

Fodor, E. M. (1984). The power motive and reactivity to power stresses. *Journal of Personality and Social Psychology, 47,* 853–859.

Fodor, E. M. (1985). The power motive, group conflict, and physiological arousal. *Journal of Personality and Social Psychology, 49,* 1408–1415.

Fodor, E. M., & Riordan, J. M. (1995). Leader power motive and group conflict as influences on leader behavior and group member self-affect. *Journal of Research in Personality, 29,* 418–431.

Fodor, E. M., & Smith, T. (1982). The power motive as an influence on group decision making. *Journal of Personality and Social Psychology, 42,* 178–185.

Fodor, E. M., Wick, D. P., & Hartsen, K. M. (2006). The power motive and affective response to assertiveness. *Journal of Research in Personality, 40,* 598–610.

Foer, F. (2004). *How soccer explains the world.* New York: HarperCollins.

Fogg, B. J. (2003). *Persuasive technology: Using computers to change what we think and do.* New York: Morgan Kaufmann.

Folk, G. E., Jr. (1974). *Textbook of environmental physiology.* Philadelphia: Lea & Febiger.

Forgas, J. P. (1998). On feeling good and getting your way: Mood effects on negotiator cognition and bargaining strategies. *Journal of Personality and Social Psychology, 74,* 565–577.

Forsyth, D. R., Berger, R. E., & Mitchell, T. (1981). The effects of self-serving vs. other-serving claims of responsibility on attraction and attribution in groups. *Social Psychology Quarterly, 44,* 59–64.

Forsyth, D. R., & Burnette, J. L. (2005). The history of group research. In S. A. Wheelan (Ed.), *The handbook of group research and practice* (pp. 3–18). Thousand Oaks, CA: Sage.

Forsyth, D. R., & Corazzini, J. G. (2000). Groups as change agents. In C. R. Snyder & R. E. Ingram (Eds.), *Handbook of psychological change: Psychotherapy processes and practices for the 21st century* (pp. 309–336). New York: Wiley.

Forsyth, D. R., & Elliott, T. R. (1999). Group dynamics and psychological well-being: The impact of groups on adjustment and dysfunction. In R. Kowalski & M. R. Leary (Eds.), *The social psychology of emotional and behavioral problems: Interfaces of social and clinical psychology* (pp. 339–361). Washington, DC: American Psychological Association.

Forsyth, D. R., Heiney, M. M., & Wright, S. S. (1997). Biases in appraisals of women leaders. *Group Dynamics: Theory, Research, and Practice, 1,* 98–103.

Forsyth, D. R., & Nye, J. L. (2008). Seeing and being a leader: The perceptual, cognitive, and interpersonal roots of conferred influence. In C. L. Hoyt, G. R. Goethals, & D. R. Forsyth (Eds.), *Leadership at the crossroads: Leadership and psychology* (Vol. 1, pp. 116–131). Westport, CT: Praeger.

Forsyth, D. R., Schlenker, B. R., Leary, M. R., & McCown, N. E. (1985). Self-presentational determinants of sex differences in leadership behavior. *Small Group Behavior, 16,* 197–210.

Forsyth, D. R., Zyzniewski, L. E., & Giammanco, C. A. (2002). Responsibility diffusion in cooperative collectives. *Personality and Social Psychology Bulletin, 28,* 54–65.

Fortin, M., & Fellenz, M. R. (2008). Hypocrisies of fairness: Towards a more reflexive ethical base in organizational justice research and practice. *Journal of Business Ethics, 78,* 415–433.

Foschi, M. (1996). Double standards in the evaluation of men and women. *Social Psychology Quarterly, 59,* 237–254.

Foschi, M., Warriner, G. K., & Hart, S. D. (1985). Standards, expectations, and interpersonal influence. *Social Psychology Quarterly, 48,* 108–117.

Foss, R. D. (1981). Structural effects in simulated jury decision making. *Journal of Personality and Social Psychology, 40,* 1055–1062.

Foti, R. J., & Hauenstein, N. M. A. (2007). Pattern and variable approaches in leadership emergence and effectiveness. *Journal of Applied Psychology, 92,* 347–355.

Foti, R. J., & Lord, R. G. (1987). Prototypes and scripts: The effects of alternative methods of processing information on rating accuracy. *Organizational Behavior and Human Decision Processes, 39,* 318–340.

Foushee, H. C. (1984). Dyads and triads at 35,000 feet: Factors affecting group process and aircrew performance. *American Psychologist, 39,* 886–893.

Foy, D. W., & Schrock, D. A. (2006). Future directions. In L. A. Schein, H. I. Spitz, G. M. Burlingame, & P. R. Muskin (Eds.), with S. Vargo, *Psychological effects of catastrophic disasters: Group approaches to treatment* (pp. 879–903). New York: Haworth Press.

Foy, E., & Harlow, A. F. (1956). *Clowning through life.* New York: Dutton. (Original work published in 1928)

Frable, D. E. S., Platt, L., & Hoey, S. (1998). Concealable stigmas and positive self-perceptions: Feeling better around similar others. *Journal of Personality and Social Psychology, 74,* 909–922.

Frager, R. (1970). Conformity and anticonformity in Japan. *Journal of Personality and Social Psychology, 15,* 203–210.

Fraine, G., Smith, S. G., Zinkiewicz, L., Chapman, R., & Sheehan, M. (2007). At home on the road? Can drivers' relationships with their cars be associated with territoriality? *Journal of Environmental Psychology, 27,* 204–214.

Francis, L. J. (1998). Self-esteem as a function of personality and gender among 8-11 year olds: Is Coopersmith's index fair? *Personality and Individual Differences, 25,* 159–165.

Francis, R. C. (2004). *Why men won't ask for directions: The seduction of sociobiology.* Princeton, NJ: Princeton University Press.

Franke, R. H., & Kaul, J. D. (1978). The Hawthorne experiments: First statistical interpretation. *American Sociological Review, 43,* 623–643.

Franklin, M. E., Jaycox, L. H., & Foa, E. B. (1999). Social skills training. In M. Hersen & A. S. Bellack (Eds.), *Handbook of comparative interventions for adult disorders* (2nd ed., pp. 317–339). New York: Wiley.

Freedman, J. L. (1975). *Crowding and behavior.* San Francisco: Freeman.

Freedman, J. L. (1979). Reconciling apparent differences between responses of humans and other animals to crowding. *Psychological Review, 86,* 80–85.

Freedman, J. L., & Fraser, S. C. (1966). Compliance without pressure: The foot-in-the-door technique. *Journal of Personality and Social Psychology, 4,* 195–202.

Freedman, J. L., & Perlick, D. (1979). Crowding, contagion, and laughter. *Journal of Experimental Social Psychology, 15,* 295–303.

Freeman, K. A. (1996). Attitudes toward work in project groups as predictors of academic performance. *Small Group Research, 27,* 265–282.

Freeman, L. C. (1979). Centrality in social networks: I. Conceptual clarification. *Social Networks, 1,* 215–239.

Freeman, L. C. (2004). *The development of social network analysis: A study in the sociology of science.* Vancouver, British Columbia: Empirical Press.

French, J. R. P., Jr. (1941). The disruption and cohesion of groups. *Journal of Abnormal and Social Psychology, 36,* 361–377.

French, J. R. P., Jr., & Raven, B. (1959). The bases of social power. In D. Cartwright (Ed.), *Studies in social power.* Ann Arbor, MI: Institute for Social Research.

Freud, S. (1922). *Group psychology and the analysis of the ego* ( J. Strachey, Trans.). London: Hogarth Press and the Institute of Psycho-Analysis.

Frey, L. R. (Ed.). (2003). *Group communication in context: Studies of bona fide groups* (2nd ed.). Mahwah, NJ: Erlbaum.

Friedkin, N. E. (1999). Choice shift and group polarization. *American Sociological Review, 64,* 856–875.

Friedkin, N. E. (2004). Social cohesion. *Annual Review of Sociology, 30,* 409–425.

Friedland, N. (1976). Social influence via threats. *Journal of Experimental Social Psychology, 12,* 552–563.

Friedman, R. (2008). Dreamtelling as a request for containment: Three uses of dreams in group therapy. *International Journal of Group Psychotherapy, 58,* 327–344.

Friedman, S. D., & Saul, K. (1991). A leader's wake: Organization member reactions to CEO succession. *Journal of Management, 17,* 619–642.

Frings, D., Hopthrow, T., Abrams, D., Hulbert, L., & Gutierrez, R. (2008). Groupdrink: The effects of alcohol and group process on vigilance errors. *Group Dynamics: Theory, Research, and Practice, 12,* 179–190.

Froman, L. A., Jr., & Cohen, M. D. (1969). Threats and bargaining efficiency. *Behavioral Science, 14,* 147–153.

Fromm, E. (1965). *Escape from freedom.* New York: Holt, Rinehart & Winston.

Fu, P. P., Peng, T. K., Kennedy, J. C., & Yukl, G. (2004). Examining the preferences of influence tactics in Chinese societies: A comparison of Chinese managers in Hong Kong, Taiwan and mainland China. *Organizational Dynamics, 33,* 32–46.

Fuegen, K., & Biernat, M. (2002). Reexamining the effects of solo status for women and men. *Personality and Social Psychology Bulletin, 28,* 913–925.

Fuhriman, A., & Burlingame, G. M. (1994). Group psychotherapy: Research and practice. In A. Fuhriman & G. M. Burlingame (Eds.), *Handbook of group psychotherapy: An empirical and clinical synthesis* (pp. 3–40). New York: Wiley.

Gabarro, J. J. (1987). The development of working relationships. In J. W. Lorsch (Ed.), *Handbook of organizational behavior* (pp. 172–189). Upper Saddle River, NJ: Prentice Hall.

Gabriel, S., & Gardner, W. L. (1999). Are there "his" and "her" types of interdependence? The implications of gender differences in collective versus relational interdependence for affect, behavior, and cognition. *Journal of Personality and Social Psychology, 77,* 642–655.

Gaertner, L., & Sedikides, C. (2005). A hierarchy within: On the motivational and emotional primacy of the individual self. In M. D. Alicke, D. A. Dunning, & J. I. Krueger (Eds.), *The self in social judgment* (pp. 213–239). New York: Psychology Press.

Gaertner, L., Sedikides, C., Vevea, J. L., & Iuzzini, J. (2002). The "I," the "we," and the "when": A meta-analysis of motivational primacy in self-definition. *Journal of Personality and Social Psychology, 83,* 574–591.

Gaertner, S. L., & Dovidio, J. F. (2000). *Reducing intergroup bias: The common ingroup identity model.* Philadelphia: Psychology Press.

Gaertner, S. L., Dovidio, J. F., Banker, B. S., Houlette, M., Johnson, K. M., & McGlynn, E. A. (2000). Reducing intergroup conflict: From superordinate goals to decategorization, recategorization, and mutual differentiation. *Group Dynamics: Theory, Research, and Practice, 4,* 98–114.

Gaertner, S. L., Dovidio, J. F., Nier, J. A., Ward, C. M., & Banker, B. S. (1999). Across cultural divides: The value of a superordinate identity. In D. A. Prentice & D. T. Miller (Eds.), *Cultural divides: Understanding and overcoming group conflict* (pp. 173–212). New York: Russell Sage Foundation.

Gaertner, S. L., Dovidio, J. F., Rust, M. C., Nier, J. A., Banker, B. S., Ward, C. M., Mottola, G. R., & Houlette, M. (1999). Reducing intergroup bias: Elements of intergroup cooperation. *Journal of Personality and Social Psychology, 76,* 388–402.

Gailliot, M. T., & Baumeister, R. F. (2007). Self-esteem, belongingness, and worldview validation: Does belongingness exert a unique influence upon self-esteem? *Journal of Research in Personality, 41,* 327–345.

Gaines, S. O., Jr., Marelich, W. D., Bledsoe, K. L., Steers, W. N., Henderson, M. C., Granrose, C. S., Barájas, L., Hicks, D., Lyde, M., Takahashi, Y., Yum, N., Ríos, D. I., García, B. F., Farris, K. R., & Page, M. S. (1997). Links between race/ethnicity and cultural values as mediated by racial/ethnic identity and moderated by gender. *Journal of Personality and Social Psychology, 72,* 1460–1476.

Gaines, S. O., Jr., & Reed, E. S. (1995). Prejudice: From Allport to DuBois. *American Psychologist, 50,* 96–103.

Gajendran, R. S., & Harrison, D. A. (2007). The good, the bad, and the unknown about telecommuting: Meta-analysis of psychological mediators and individual consequences. *Journal of Applied Psychology, 92,* 1524–1541.

Galinsky, A. D., Gruenfeld, D. H., & Magee, J. C. (2003). From power to action. *Journal of Personality and Social Psychology, 85,* 453–466.

Galinsky, A. D., Jordan, J., & Sivanathan, N. (2008). Harnessing power to capture leadership. In C. L. Hoyt, G. R. Goethals, & D. R. Forsyth (Eds.), *Leadership at the Crossroads: Leadership and psychology* (Vol. 1, pp. 283–299). Westport, CT: Praeger.

Galinsky, A. D., Ku, G., & Wang, C. S. (2005). Perspective-taking and self–other overlap: Fostering social bonds and facilitating social coordination. *Group Processes & Intergroup Relations, 8,* 109–124.

Galinsky, A. D., Magee, J. C., Inesi, M. E., & Gruenfeld, D. H. (2006). Power and perspectives not taken. *Psychological Science, 17,* 1068–1074.

Gallo, P. S., Jr. (1966). Effects of increased incentives upon the use of threat in bargaining. *Journal of Personality and Social Psychology, 4,* 14–20.

Gammage, K. L., Carron, A. V., & Estabrooks, P. A. (2001). Team cohesion and individual productivity: The influence of the norm for productivity and the identifiability of individual effort. *Small Group Research, 32,* 3–18.

Gannon, T. M. (1966). Emergence of the "defensive" group norm. *Federal Probation, 30,* 44–47.

Garcia, S. M., Weaver, K., Moskowitz, G. B., & Darley, J. M. (2002). Crowded minds: The implicit bystander effect. *Journal of Personality and Social Psychology, 83,* 843–853.

Gardham, K., & Brown, R. (2001). Two forms of intergroup discrimination with positive and negative outcomes: Explaining the positive–negative asymmetry effect. *British Journal of Social Psychology, 40,* 23–34.

Gardner, H., with Laskin, E. (1995). *Leading minds: An anatomy of leadership*. New York: Basic Books.

Gardner, J. W. (1965). *The antileadership vaccine*. Annual Report of the Carnegie Corporation. New York: Carnegie Corporation.

Gardner, W. L., & Knowles, M. L. (2008). Love makes you real: Favorite television characters are perceived as "real" in a social facilitation paradigm. *Social Cognition, 26,* 156–168.

Gardner, W. L., Pickett, C. L., & Brewer, M. B. (2000). Social exclusion and selective memory: How the need to belong influences memory for social events. *Personality and Social Psychology Bulletin, 26,* 486–496.

Gardner, W. L., Pickett, C. L., Jefferis, V., & Knowles, M. (2005). On the outside looking in: Loneliness and social monitoring. *Personality and Social Psychology Bulletin, 31,* 1549–1560.

Gawronski, B., Walther, E., & Blank, H. (2005). Cognitive consistency and the formation of interpersonal attitudes: Cognitive balance affects the encoding of social information. *Journal of Experimental Social Psychology, 41,* 618–626.

Gazda, G. M., & Brooks, D. K. (1985). The development of the social/life skills training movement. *Journal of Group Psychotherapy, Psychodrama, and Sociometry, 38,* 1–10.

Gecas, V., & Burke, P. J. (1995). Self and identity. In K. S. Cook, G. A. Fine, & J. S. House (Eds.), *Sociological perspectives on social psychology* (pp. 41–67). Boston: Allyn & Bacon.

Geffner, R., Braverman, M., Galasso, J., & Marsh, J. (Eds.). (2004). *Aggression in organizations: Violence, abuse, and harassment at work and in schools.* Binghamton, NY: Haworth.

Gelfand, M. J., Leslie, L. M., & Keller, K. (2008). On the etiology of organizational conflict cultures. *Research in Organizational Behavior, 28,* 137–166.

Gemmill, G. (1986). The mythology of the leader role in small groups. *Small Group Behavior, 17,* 41–50.

Genevie, L. E. (Ed.). (1978). *Collective behavior and social movements*. Itasca, IL: Peacock.

George, J. M. (1995). Leader positive mood and group performance: The case of customer service. *Journal of Applied Social Psychology, 25,* 778–794.

George, J. M., & Brief, A. P. (1992). Feeling good/doing good: A conceptual analysis of the mood at work/organizational spontaneity relationship. *Psychological Bulletin, 112,* 310–329.

Georgesen, J. C., Harris, M. J. (1998). Why's my boss always holding me down? A meta-analysis of power effects on performance evaluations. *Personality and Social Psychology Review, 2,* 184–195.

Gerard, H. B. (1953). The effect of different dimensions of disagreement on the communication process in small groups. *Human Relations, 6,* 249–271.

Gerard, H. B. (1964). Conformity and commitment to the group. *Journal of Abnormal and Social Psychology, 68,* 209–211.

Gerard, H. B. (1983). School desegregation: The social science role. *American Psychologist, 38,* 869–877.

Gerard, H. B., & Mathewson, G. C. (1966). The effects of severity of initiation on liking for a group: A replication. *Journal of Experimental Social Psychology, 2,* 278–287.

Gerard, H. B., & Orive, R. (1987). The dynamics of opinion formation. *Advances in Experimental Social Psychology, 20,* 171–202.

Gergen, K. J., Gergen, M. M., & Barton, W. H. (1973). Deviance in the dark. *Psychology Today, 10,* 129–130.

Gersick, C. J. G. (1989). Marking time: Predictable transitions in task groups. *Academy of Management Journal, 32,* 274–309.

Gerstner, C. R., & Day, D. V. (1997). Meta-analytic review of leader-member exchange theory: Correlates and construct issues. *Journal of Applied Psychology, 82,* 827–844.

Giannetti, C. C., & Sagarese, M. (2001). *Cliques*. New York: Broadway Books.

Gibb, C. A. (1969). Leadership. In G. Lindzey & E. Aronson (Eds.), *The handbook of social psychology* (Vol. 4, 2nd ed., pp. 205–282). Reading, MA: Addison-Wesley.

Gibb, J. R. (1970). Effects of human relations training. In A. E. Bergin & S. L. Garfield (Eds.), *Handbook of psychotherapy and behavior change*. New York: Wiley.

Gibbons, D., & Olk, P. M. (2003). Individual and structural origins of friendship and social position among professionals. *Journal of Personality and Social Psychology, 84,* 340–351.

Gibbons, F. X., & Buunk, B. P. (1999). Individual differences in social comparison: Development of a scale of social comparison orientation. *Journal of Personality and Social Psychology, 76,* 129–142.

Gibson, D. R. (2003). Participation shifts: Order and differentiation in group conversation. *Social Forces, 81,* 1335–1380.

Gibson, L. L., Mathieu, J. E., Shalley, C. E., & Ruddy, T. M. (2005). Creativity and standardization: Complementary or conflicting drivers of team effectiveness. *Academy of Management Journal, 48,* 521–531.

Gieryn, T. F. (2000). A space for place in sociology. *Annual Review of Sociology, 26,* 463–496.

Giesen, M., & McClaren, H. A. (1976). Discussion, distance, and sex: Changes in impressions and attraction during small group interaction. *Sociometry, 39,* 60–70.

Gigone, D., & Hastie, R. (1997). Proper analysis of the accuracy of group judgments. *Psychological Bulletin, 121,* 149–167.

Gilbert, S. J. (1981). Another look at the Milgram obedience studies: The role of the graduated series of shocks. *Personality and Social Psychology Bulletin, 7,* 690–695.

Gilboa, S., Shirom, A., Fried, Y., & Cooper, C. (2008). A meta-analysis of work demand stressors and job performance: Examining main and moderating effects. *Personnel Psychology, 61,* 227–271.

Gilchrist, J. C. (1952). The formation of social groups under conditions of success and failure. *Journal of Abnormal and Social Psychology, 47,* 174–187.

Giles, H., & Wadleigh, P. M. (1999). Accommodating nonverbally. In L. K. Guerrero, J. A. DeVito, & M. L. Hecht (Eds.), *The nonverbal communication reader: Classic and contemporary readings* (2nd. ed., pp. 425–436). Prospect Heights, IL: Waveland Press.

Gill, D. L. (1984). Individual and group performance in sport. In J. M. Silva & R. S. Weinberg (Eds.), *Psychological foundations of sport* (pp. 315–328). Champaign, IL: Human Kinetics.

Gillies, R. M. (2007). Cooperative learning: Integrating theory and practice. Thousand Oaks, CA: Sage.

Ginnett, R. C. (1993). Crews as groups: Their formation and their leadership. In E. L. Wiener, B. G. Kanki, & R. L. Helmreich (Eds.), *Cockpit resource management* (pp. 71–98). San Diego: Academic Press.

Giordano, P. C. (2003). Relationships in adolescence. *Annual Review of Sociology, 29,* 257–281.

Gladwell, M. (2000). *The tipping point: How little things can make a big difference.* Boston: Little, Brown.

Glaser, D. (1964). *The effectiveness of a prison and parole system.* Indianapolis: Bobbs-Merrill.

Glass, D. C., Singer, J. E., & Pennebaker, J. W. (1977). Behavioral and physiological effects of uncontrollable environmental events. In D. Stokols (Ed.), *Perspectives on environment and behavior* (pp. 131–151). New York: Plenum Press.

Gleitman, H., Rozin, P., & Sabini, J. (1997). Solomon E. Asch (1907–1996). *American Psychologist, 52,* 984–985.

Glick, J. C., & Staley, K. (2007). Inflicted traumatic brain injury: Advances in evaluation and collaborative diagnosis. *Pediatric Neurosurgery, 43,* 436–441.

Glick, P. (2005). Choice of scapegoats. In J. F. Dovidio, P. Glick, & L. A. Rudman (Eds.), *On the nature of prejudice: Fifty years after Allport* (pp. 244–261). Malden, MA: Blackwell.

Gockel, C., Kerr, N. L., Seok, D., & Harris, D. W. (2008). Indispensability and group identification as sources of task motivation. *Journal of Experimental Social Psychology, 44,* 1316–1321.

Godfrey, D. K., Jones, E. E., & Lord, C. G. (1986). Self-promotion is not ingratiating. *Journal of Personality and Social Psychology, 50,* 106–115.

Godwin, R.(Ed.). (2000). *Apollo 13: The NASA mission reports.* Burlington, Ontario: Apogee.

Goethals, G. R. (2005). Presidential leadership. *Annual Review of Psychology, 56,* 545–570.

Goethals, G. R., Sorenson, G. J., & Burns, J. M. (Eds.). (2004). *Encyclopedia of leadership.* Thousand Oaks, CA: Sage.

Goethals, G. R., & Zanna, M. P. (1979). The role of social comparison in choice shifts. *Journal of Personality and Social Psychology, 37,* 1469–1476.

Goetsch, G. G., & McFarland, D. D. (1980). Models of the distribution of acts in small discussion groups. *Social Psychology Quarterly, 43,* 173–183.

Goffman, E. (1959). *The presentation of self in everyday life.* Garden City, NY: Doubleday.

Goldberg, L. (1968). Ghetto riots and others: The faces of civil disorder in 1967. *Journal of Peace Research, 2,* 116–132.

Goldhammer, J. (1996). *Under the influence: The destructive effects of group dynamics.* Amherst, NY: Prometheus Books.

Golding, W. (1954). *Lord of the flies.* New York: Putnam.

Goldman, M., & Fraas, L. A. (1965). The effects of leader selection on group performance. *Sociometry, 28,* 82–88.

Goldstein, A. P. (2002). *The psychology of group aggression.* New York: Wiley.

Goleman, D., Boyatzis, R., & McKee, A. (2002). *Primal leadership: Learning to lead with emotional intelligence.* Boston: Harvard Business School Press.

Goodacre, D. M. (1953). Group characteristics of good and poor performing combat units. *Sociometry, 16,* 168–178.

Goodman, G., & Jacobs, M. K. (1994). The self-help, mutual-support group. In A. Fuhriman & G. M. Burlingame (Eds.), *Handbook of group psychotherapy* (pp. 489–526). New York: Wiley.

Goodwin, D. K. (2005). *Team of rivals: The political genius of Abraham Lincoln.* New York: Simon & Schuster.

Gordijn, E. H., De Vries, N. K., & De Dreu, C. K. W. (2002). Minority influence on focal and related attitudes: Change in size, attributions and information processing. *Personality and Social Psychology Bulletin, 28,* 1315–1326.

Gore, J. S., & Cross, S. E. (2006). Pursuing goals for us: Relationally autonomous reasons in long-term goal pursuit. *Journal of Personality and Social Psychology, 90,* 848–861.

Goulding, R. L., & Goulding, M. M. (1979). *Changing lives through redecision therapy.* New York: Brunner/Mazel.

Gouldner, A. W. (1960). The norm of reciprocity: A preliminary statement. *American Sociological Review, 25,* 161–178.

Gouran, D. S., & Hirokawa, R. Y. (1996). Functional theory and communication in decision-making and problem-solving groups: An expanded view. In R. Y. Hirokawa & M. S. Poole (Eds.), *Communication and group decision making* (2nd ed., pp. 55–80). Thousand Oaks, CA: Sage.

Graeff, C. L. (1997). Evolution of situational leadership theory: A critical review. *Leadership Quarterly, 8,* 153–170.

Graen, G. B., & Uhl-Bien, M. (1991). The transformation of professionals into self-managing and partially self-designing contributors: Toward a theory of leadership making. *Journal of Management Systems, 3,* 33–48.

Graen, G. B., & Uhl-Bien, M. (1995). Relationship-based approach to leadership: Development of leader–member exchange (LMX) theory of leadership over 25 years: Applying a multi-level multi-domain perspective. *Leadership Quarterly, 6,* 219–247.

Granovetter, M. S. (1973). The strength of weak ties. *American Journal of Sociology, 78,* 1360–1380.

Graziano, W. G., Hair, E. C., & Finch, J. F. (1997). Competitiveness mediates the link between personality and group performance. *Journal of Personality and Social Psychology, 73,* 1394–1408.

Graziano, W. G., Jensen-Campbell, L. A., & Hair, E. C. (1996). Perceiving interpersonal conflict and reacting to it: The case for agreeableness. *Journal of Personality and Social Psychology, 70,* 820–835.

Green, L. R., Richardson, D. S., Lago, T., & Schatten-Jones, E. C. (2001). Network correlates of social and emotional loneliness in young and older adults. *Personality and Social Psychology Bulletin, 27,* 281–288.

Green, R. B., & Mack, J. (1978). Would groups do better without social psychologists? *Personality and Social Psychology Bulletin, 4,* 561–563.

Greenberg, C. I., & Firestone, I. J. (1977). Compensatory responses to crowding: Effects of personal space intrusion and privacy reduction. *Journal of Personality and Social Psychology, 35,* 637–644.

Greenberg, J. (1996). "Forgive me, I'm new": Three experimental demonstrations of the effects of attempts to excuse poor performance. *Organizational Behavior and Human Decision Processes, 66,* 165–178.

Greenberg, J., Solomon, S., & Pyszczynski, T. (1997). Terror management theory of self-esteem and cultural worldviews: Empirical assessments and conceptual refinements. *Advances in Experimental Social Psychology, 29,* 61–139.

Greenwald, A. G., McGhee, D. E., & Schwartz, J. L. K. (2008). Measuring individual differences in implicit cognition: The implicit association test. In R. H. Fazio, & R. E. Petty (Eds.), *Attitudes: Their structure, function, and consequences* (pp. 109–131). New York: Psychology Press.

Greenwood, J. D. (2004). *The disappearance of the social in American social psychology*. New York: Cambridge University Press.

Greer, D. L. (1983). Spectator booing and the home advantage: A study of social influence in the basketball arena. *Social Psychology Quarterly, 46,* 252–261.

Greitemeyer, T., & Schulz-Hardt, S. (2003). Preference-consistent evaluation of information in the hidden profile paradigm: Beyond group-level explanations for the dominance of shared information in group decisions. *Journal of Personality and Social Psychology, 84,* 322–339.

Greitemeyer, T., Schulz-Hardt, S., Brodbeck, F. C., & Frey, D. (2006). Information sampling and group decision making: The effects of an advocacy decision procedure and task experience. *Journal of Experimental Psychology: Applied, 12,* 31–42.

Greve, D. W. (1993). Gestalt group psychotherapy. In H. I. Kaplan & M. J. Sadock (Eds.), *Comprehensive group psychotherapy* (3rd ed., pp. 228–235). Baltimore: Williams & Wilkins.

Griffin, J. (1983). *Homer on life and death.* New York: Oxford University Press.

Griffitt, W. (1970). Environmental effects on interpersonal affective behavior: Ambient effective temperature and attraction. *Journal of Personality and Social Psychology, 15,* 240–244.

Griffitt, W., & Veitch, R. (1971). Hot and crowded: Influence of population density and temperature on interpersonal affective behavior. *Journal of Personality and Social Psychology, 17,* 92–98.

Griskevicius, V., Goldstein, N. J., Mortensen, C. R., Cialdini, R. B., & Kenrick, D. T. (2006). Going along versus going alone: When fundamental motives facilitate strategic (non)conformity. *Journal of Personality and Social Psychology, 91,* 281–294.

Grose, M. (2003). *Why first-borns rule the world and last-borns want to change it.* New York: Random House.

Guastello, S. J. (2007). Non-linear dynamics and leadership emergence. *Leadership Quarterly, 18,* 357–369.

Guerin, B., & Innes, J. M. (1982). Social facilitation and social monitoring: A new look at Zajonc's mere presence hypothesis. *British Journal of Social Psychology, 21,* 7–18.

Guetzkow, H., & Gyr, J. (1954). An analysis of conflict in decision-making groups. *Human Relations, 7,* 367–382.

Guimond, A., & Dubé-Simard, L. (1983). Relative deprivation theory and the Quebec nationalist movement: The cognitive–emotion distinction and the personal–group deprivation issue. *Journal of Personality and Social Psychology, 44,* 526–535.

Guinote, A. (2007). Power affects basic cognition: Increased attentional inhibition and flexibility. *Journal of Experimental Social Psychology, 43,* 685–697.

Guinote, A. (2008). Power and affordances: When the situation has more power over powerful than powerless individuals. *Journal of Personality and Social Psychology, 95,* 237–252.

Guinote, A., Brown, M., & Fiske, S. T. (2006). Minority status decreases sense of control and increases interpretive processing. *Social Cognition, 24,* 169–186.

Guinote, A., Judd, C. M., & Brauer, M. (2002). Effects of power on perceived and objective group variability: Evidence that more powerful groups are more variable. *Journal of Personality and Social Psychology, 82,* 708–721.

Gullahorn, J. T. (1952). Distance and friendship as factors in the gross interaction matrix. *Sociometry, 15,* 123–134.

Gully, S. M., Devine, D. J., & Whitney, D. J. (1995). A meta-analysis of cohesion and performance: Effects of level of analysis and task interdependence. *Small Group Research, 26,* 497–520.

Gump, P. V. (1990). A short history of the Midwest Psychological Field Station. *Environment and Behavior, 22,* 436–457.

Gunderson, E. K. E. (1973). Individual behavior in confined or isolated groups. In J. E. Rasmussen (Ed.), *Man in isolation and confinement* (pp. 145–164). Chicago: Aldine.

Gurr, T. R. (1970). *Why men rebel.* Princeton, NJ: Princeton University Press.

Gustafson, D. H., Shukla, R. M., Delbecq, A. L., & Walster, G. W. (1973). A comparative study of differences in subjective likelihood estimates made by individuals, interacting groups, Delphi groups, and nominal groups. *Organizational Behavior and Human Performance, 9,* 280–291.

Guthman, E. (1971). *We band of brothers.* New York: Harper & Row.

Haas, D. F., & Deseran, F. A. (1981). Trust and symbolic exchange. *Social Psychology Quarterly, 44,* 3–13.

Haber, G. M. (1980). Territorial invasion in the classroom: Invadee response. *Environment and Behavior, 12,* 17–31.

Haber, G. M. (1982). Spatial relations between dominants and marginals. *Social Psychology Quarterly, 45,* 219–228.

Hackman, J. R. (1986). The psychology of self-management in organizations. In M. S. Pallak & R. O. Perloff (Eds.), *Psychology and work: Productivity, change, and employment* (pp. 89–136). Washington, DC: American Psychological Association.

Hackman, J. R. (Ed.). (1990). *Groups that work (and those that don't).* San Francisco: Jossey-Bass.

Hackman, J. R. (1992). Group influences on individuals in organizations. In M. D. Dunnette & L. M. Hough (Eds.), *Handbook of industrial and organizational psychology* (2nd ed., Vol. 3, pp. 199–267). Palo Alto, CA: Consulting Psychologists Press.

Hackman, J. R. (2002). *Leading teams: Setting the stage for greater performances.* New York: Harvard Business School Press.

Hackman, J. R. (2003). Learning more by crossing levels: Evidence from airplanes, hospitals, and orchestras. *Journal of Organizational Behavior, 24,* 905–922.

Hackman, J. R., Brousseau, K. R., & Weiss, J. A. (1976). The interaction of task design and group performance strategies in determining group effectiveness. *Organizational Behavior and Human Performance, 16,* 350–365.

Hackman, J. R., & Morris, C. G. (1975). Group tasks, group interaction process, and group performance effectiveness: A review and proposed integration. *Advances in Experimental Social Psychology, 8,* 47–99.

Haines, V. Y., & Taggar, S. (2006). Antecedents of team reward attitude. *Group Dynamics: Theory, Research, and Practice, 10,* 194–205.

Hains, S. C., Hogg, M. A., & Duck, J. M. (1997). Self-categorization and leadership: Effects of group prototypicality and leader stereotypicality. *Personality and Social Psychology Bulletin, 23,* 1087–1099.

Hall, E. T. (1966). *The hidden dimension.* New York: Doubleday.

Hall, J. A. (2006). Nonverbal behavior, status, and gender: How do we understand their relations? *Psychology of Women Quarterly, 30,* 384–391.

Hall, J. A., Coats, E. J., & LeBeau, L. S. (2005). Nonverbal behavior and the vertical dimension of social relations: A meta-analysis. *Psychological Bulletin, 131,* 898–924.

Hallinan, M. T. (1981). Recent advances in sociometry. In S. R. Asher & J. M. Gottman (Eds.), *The development of children's friendships* (pp. 91–115). New York: Cambridge University Press.

Halperin, E. (2008). Group-based hatred in intractable conflict in Israel. *Journal of Conflict Resolution, 52,* 713–736.

Halpin, A. W., & Winer, B. J. (1952). *The leadership behavior of the airplane commander.* Columbus, OH: Ohio State University Research Foundation.

*Ham v. S. Carolina*, 409 U.S. 524 (1973).

Hamaguchi, E. (1985). A contextual model of the Japanese: Toward a methodological innovation in Japanese studies. *Journal of Japanese Studies, 11,* 289–321.

Hamilton, D. L., & Sherman, S. J. (1989). Illusory correlations: Implications for stereotype theory and research. In D. Bar-Tal, C. F. Graumann, A. W. Kruglanski, & W. Stroebe (Eds.), *Stereotyping and prejudice: Changing conceptions* (pp. 59–82). New York: Springer-Verlag.

Hamilton, V. L., & Sanders, J. (1995). Crimes of obedience and conformity in the workplace: Surveys of Americans, Russians, and Japanese. *Journal of Social Issues, 51,* 67–88.

Hamilton, V. L., & Sanders, J. (1999). The second face of evil: Wrongdoing in and by the corporation. *Personality and Social Psychology Review, 3,* 222–233.

Haney, C., Banks, C., & Zimbardo, P. (1973). Interpersonal dynamics in a simulated prison.

*International Journal of Criminology and Psychology, 1,* 69–97.

Hans, V. P., Hannaford-Agor, P. L., Mott, N. L., & Munsterman, G. T. (2003). The hung jury: The American jury's insights and contemporary understanding. *Criminal Law Bulletin, 39,* 33–50.

Hans, V. P., & Vidmar, N. (1982). Jury selection. In N. L. Kerr & R. M. Bray (Eds.), *Psychology of the courtroom* (pp. 39–82). New York: Academic Press.

Hans, V. P., & Vidmar, N. (1991). The American jury at twenty-five years. *Law and Social Inquiry, 16,* 323–351.

Hansen, W. B., & Altman, I. (1976). Decorating personal places: A descriptive analysis. *Environment and Behavior, 8,* 491–504.

Hardin, G. (1968). The tragedy of the commons. *Science, 162,* 1243–1248.

Harding, J., Proshansky, H., Kutner, B., & Chein, I. (1969). Prejudice and ethnic relations. In G. Lindzey & E. Aronson (Eds.), *The handbook of social psychology* (2nd ed., Vol. 5, pp. 1–76). Reading, MA: Addison-Wesley.

Hardy, C., & Latané, B. (1986). Social loafing on a cheering task. *Social Science, 71(2-3),*165–172.

Hare, A. P. (1967). Small group development in the relay assembly testroom. *Sociological Inquiry, 37,* 169–182.

Hare, A. P. (1976). *Handbook of small group research* (2nd ed.). New York: Free Press.

Hare, A. P. (1982). *Creativity in small groups.* Thousand Oaks, CA: Sage.

Hare, A. P. (1985). The significance of SYMLOG in the study of group dynamics. *International Journal of Small Group Research, 1,* 38–50.

Hare, A. P. (2003). Roles, relationships, and groups in organizations: Some conclusions and recommendations. *Small Group Research, 34,* 123–154.

Hare, A. P. (2005). Analysis of social interaction systems. In A. P. Hare, E. Sjøvold, H. G. Baker, & J. Powers (Eds.), *Analysis of social interaction systems: SYMLOG research and applications* (pp. 1–14). Lanham, MD: University Press of America.

Hare, A. P., & Bales, R. F. (1963). Seating position and small group interaction. *Sociometry, 26,* 480–486.

Hare, A. P., Borgatta, E. F., & Bales, R. F. (1965). Preface to the revised edition. In A. P. Hare, E. F. Borgatta, & R. F. Bales (Eds.), *Small groups: Studies in social interaction* (Revised ed., pp. *v–ix*). New York: Knopf.

Hare, A. P., & Hare, J. R. (1996). *J. L. Moreno.* Thousand Oaks, CA: Sage.

Hare, A. P., & Naveh, D. (1986). Conformity and creativity: Camp David, 1978. *Small Group Behavior, 17,* 243–268.

Hare, A. P., Sjøvold, E., Baker, H. G., & Powers, J. (Eds.). (2005). *Analysis of social interaction systems: SYMLOG research and applications.* Lanham, MD: University Press of America.

Hare, S. E., & Hare, A. P. (2005). Role repertoires of members in an effective small group: A simulation. In A. P. Hare, E. Sjøvold, H. G. Baker, & J. Powers (Eds.), *Analysis of social interaction systems: SYMLOG research and applications* (pp. 273–298). Lanham, MD: University Press of America.

Harinck, F. (2004). Persuasive arguments and beating around the bush in negotiations. *Group Processes & Intergroup Relations, 7,* 5–18.

Harkins, S. G., & Jackson, J. M. (1985). The role of evaluation in eliminating social loafing. *Personality and Social Psychology Bulletin, 11,* 457–465.

Harkins, S. G., Latané, B., & Williams, K. (1980). Social loafing: Allocating effort or taking it easy. *Journal of Experimental Social Psychology, 16,* 457–465.

Harkins, S. G., & Szymanski, K. (1987). Social loafing and social facilitation: New wine in old bottles. In C. Hendrick (Ed.), *Review of Personality and Social Psychology: Group Process and Intergroup Relations* (Vol. 9, pp. 167–188). Thousand Oaks, CA: Sage.

Harkins, S. G., & Szymanski, K. (1988). Social loafing and self-evaluation with an objective standard. *Journal of Experimental Social Psychology, 24,* 354–365.

Harkins, S. G., & Szymanski, K. (1989). Social loafing and group evaluation. *Journal of Personality and Social Psychology, 56,* 934–941.

Harlow, H. F. (1932). Social facilitation of feeding in the albino rat. *Journal of Genetic Psychology, 41,* 211–221.

Harlow, H. F., & Harlow, M. K. (1966). Learning to love. *American Scientist, 54,* 244–272.

Harlow, R. E., & Cantor, N. (1995). To whom do people turn when things go poorly? Task orientation and functional social contacts. *Journal of Personality and Social Psychology, 69,* 329–340.

Harlow, R. E., & Cantor, N. (1996). Still participating after all these years: A study of life task participation in later life. *Journal of Personality and Social Psychology, 71,* 1235–1249.

Harms, P. D., Roberts, B. W., & Wood, D. (2007). Who shall lead? An integrative personality approach to the study of the antecedents of status in informal social organizations. *Journal of Research in Personality, 41,* 689–699.

Harris, C. B., Paterson, H. M., & Kemp, R. I. (2008). Collaborative recall and collective memory: What happens when we remember together? *Memory, 16,* 213–230.

Harris, J. R. (1995). Where is the child's environment? A group socialization theory of development. *Psychological Review, 102,* 458–489.

Harris, L. T., & Fiske, S. T. (2006). Dehumanizing the lowest of the low: Neuroimaging responses to extreme out-groups. *Psychological Science, 17,* 847–853.

Harrison, A. A., Clearwater, Y. A., & McKay, C. P. (Eds.). (1991). *From Antarctica to outer space: Life in isolation and confinement.* New York: Springer-Verlag.

Harrison, A. A., & Connors, M. M. (1984). Groups in exotic environments. *Advances in Experimental Social Psychology, 18,* 50–87.

Harrison, D. A., & Klein, K. J. (2007). What's the difference? Diversity constructs as separation, variety, or disparity in organizations. *Academy of Management Review, 32,* 1199–1228.

Harrison, D. A., Price, K. H., Gavin, J. H., & Florey, A. T. (2002). Time, teams, and task performance: Changing effects of surface- and deep-level diversity on group functioning. *Academy of Management Journal, 45,* 1029–1045.

Harrod, W. J. (1980). Expectations from unequal rewards. *Social Psychology Quarterly, 43,* 126–130.

Hart, J. W., Bridgett, D. J., & Karau, S. J. (2001). Coworker ability and effort as determinants of individual effort on a collective task. *Group Dynamics: Theory, Research, and Practice, 5,* 181–190.

Härtel, C. E. J., & Härtel, G. F. (1997). SHAPE-assisted intuitive decision making and problem solving: Information-processing-based training for conditions of cognitive busyness. *Group Dynamics: Theory, Research, and Practice, 1,* 187–199.

Harton, H. C., & Bullock, M. (2007). Dynamic social impact: A theory of the origins and evolution of culture. *Social and Personality Psychology Compass, 1,* 521–540.

Harton, H. C., Green, L. R., Jackson, C., & Latané, B. (1998). Demonstrating dynamic social impact: Consolidation, clustering, correlation, and (sometimes) the correct answer. *Teaching of Psychology, 25,* 31–35.

Harvey, J. B. (1988). The Abilene paradox and other meditations on management. New York: Wiley.

Haslam, N. (2006). Dehumanization: An integrative review. *Personality and Social Psychology Review, 10,* 252–264.

Haslam, N., Rothschild, L., & Ernst, D. (2002). Are essentialist beliefs associated with prejudice? *British Journal of Social Psychology, 41,* 87–100.

Haslam, S. A. (2004). Psychology in organizations: The social identity approach (2nd ed.).Thousand Oaks, CA: Sage.

Haslam, S. A., & Oakes, P. J. (1995). How context-independent is the outgroup homogeneity effect? A response to Bartsch and Judd. *European Journal of Social Psychology, 12,* 469–475.

Haslam, S. A., & Reicher, S. (2006). Stressing the group: Social identity and the unfolding dynamics of responses to stress. *Journal of Applied Psychology, 91,* 1037–1052.

Haslam, S. A., Ryan, M. K., Postmes, T., Spears, R., Jetten, J., & Webley, P. (2006). Sticking to our guns: Social identity as a basis for the maintenance of commitment to faltering organizational projects. *Journal of Organizational Behavior, 27,* 607–628.

Hastie, R., & Kameda, T. (2005). The robust beauty of majority rules in group decisions. *Psychological Review, 112,* 494–508.

Hastie, R., Penrod, S. D., & Pennington, N. (1983). *Inside the jury.* Boston, MA: Harvard University Press.

Hastorf, A. H., & Cantril, H. (1954). They saw a game. *Journal of Abnormal and Social Psychology, 49,* 129–134.

Hayduk, L. A. (1978). Personal space: An evaluative and orienting overview. *Psychological Bulletin, 85,* 117–134.

Hazan, C., & Shaver, P. (1987). Romantic love conceptualized as an attachment process. *Journal of Personality and Social Psychology, 52,* 511–524.

Healey, A. N., Undre, S., & Vincent, C. A. (2006). Defining the technical skills of teamwork in surgery. *Quality & Safety in Health Care, 15,* 231–234.

Hearne, G. (1957). Leadership and the spatial factor in small groups. *Journal of Abnormal and Social Psychology, 54,* 269–272.

Hechter, M., & Op, K. (Eds.). (2001). *Social norms.* New York: Russell Sage Foundation.

Heffron, M. H. (1972). The naval ship as an urban design problem. *Naval Engineers Journal, 12,* 49–64.

Heider, F. (1958). *The psychology of interpersonal relations.* New York: Wiley.

Heilman, M. E., Block, C. J., & Martell, R. F. (1995). Sex stereotypes: Do they influence perceptions of managers? *Journal of Social Behavior and Personality, 10,* 237–252.

Heinicke, C. M., & Bales, R. F. (1953). Developmental trends in the structure of small groups. *Sociometry, 16,* 7–38.

Helbing, D., Johansson, A., & Al-Abideen, H. Z. (2007). *Crowd turbulence: The physics of crowd disasters.* Paper presented at the Fifth International Conference on Nonlinear Mechanics (ICNM-V), Shanghai.

Heller, J. F., Groff, B. D., & Solomon, S. H. (1977). Toward an understanding of crowding: The role of physical interaction. *Journal of Personality and Social Psychology, 35,* 183–190.

Helmreich, R. L. (1974). Evaluation of environments: Behavioral observations in an undersea habitat. In J. Lang, C. Burnette, W. Moleski, & D. Vachon (Eds.), *Designing for human behavior.* Stroudsburg, PA: Dowden, Hutchinson, & Ross.

Helmreich, R. L., & Foushee, H. C. (1993). Why crew resource management? Empirical and theoretical bases of human factors training in aviation. In E. L. Wiener, B. G. Kanki, & R. L. Helmreich (Eds.), *Cockpit resource management* (pp. 3–45). San Diego: Academic Press.

Helweg-Larsen, M., & LoMonaco, B. L. (2008). Queuing among U2 fans: Reactions to social norm violations. *Journal of Applied Social Psychology, 38,* 2378–2393.

Hembroff, L. A. (1982). Resolving status inconsistency: An expectation states theory and test. *Social Forces, 61,* 183–205.

Hembroff, L. A., & Myers, D. E. (1984). Status characteristics: Degrees of task relevance and decision process. *Social Psychology Quarterly, 47,* 337–346.

Hemphill, J. K. (1950). Relations between the size of the group and the behavior of "superior" leaders. *Journal of Social Psychology, 32,* 11–22.

Henchy, T., & Glass, D. C. (1968). Evaluation apprehension and the social facilitation of dominant and subordinate responses. *Journal of Personality and Social Psychology, 10,* 446–454.

Henderson, W. D. (1985). *Cohesion, the human element in combat: Leadership and societal influence in the armies of the Soviet Union, the United States, North Vietnam, and Israel.* Washington, DC: National Defense University Press.

Henley, N. M. (1995). Body politics revisited: What do we know today? In P. J. Kalbfleisch, & M. J. Cody (Eds.), *Gender, power, and communication in human relationships* (pp. 27–61). Mahwah, NJ: Erlbaum.

Henningsen, D. D., & Henningsen, M. L. M. (2003). Examining social influence in information-sharing contexts. *Small Group Research, 34,* 391–412.

Henningsen, D. D., & Henningsen, M. L. M. (2007). Do groups know what they don't know? Dealing with missing information in decision-making groups. *Communication Research, 34,* 507–525.

Henningsen, D. D., Henningsen, M. L. M., Eden, J., & Cruz, M. G. (2006). Examining the symptoms of groupthink and retrospective sensemaking. *Small Group Research, 37,* 36–64.

Henrich, J., Boyd, R., Bowles, S., Camerer, C., Fehr, E., Gintis, H., & McElreath, R. (2004). Overview and synthesis. In J. Henrich, R. Boyd, S. Bowles, C. Camerer, E. Fehr, & H. Gintis (Eds.), *Foundations of human sociality: Economic experiments and ethnographic evidence from fifteen small-scale societies* (pp. 8–54). New York: Oxford University Press.

Henry, K. B., Arrow, H., & Carini, B. (1999). A tripartite model of group identification: Theory and measurement. *Small Group Research, 30,* 558–581.

Heppner, P. P., Kivlighan, D. M., Burnett, J. W., Berry, T. R., Goedinghaus, M., Doxsee, D. J., Hendricks, F. M., Krull, L. A., Wright, G. E., Bellatin, A. M., Durham, R. J., Tharp, A., Kim, H., Brossart, D. F., Wang, L., Witty, T. E., Kinder, M. H., Hertel, J. B., & Wallace, D. L. (1994). Dimensions that characterize supervisor interventions delivered in the context of live supervision of practicum counselors. *Journal of Counseling Psychology, 41,* 227–235.

Hepworth, J. T., & West, S. G. (1988). Lynchings and the economy: A time-series reanalysis of Hovland and Sears (1940). *Journal of Personality and Social Psychology, 55,* 239–247.

Herek, G. M., Janis, I. L., & Huth, P. (1987). Decision-making during international crises: Is quality of process related to outcome? *Journal of Conflict Resolution, 31,* 203–226.

Herek, G. M., Janis, I. L., & Huth, P. (1989). Quality of U.S. decision making during the Cuban missile crisis: Major errors in Welch's reassessment. *Journal of Conflict Resolution, 33,* 446–459.

Herman, C. P., Roth, D. A., & Polivy, J. (2003). Effects of the presence of others on food intake: A normative interpretation. *Psychological Bulletin, 129,* 873–886.

Hernández, B., Carmen Hidalgo, M., Salazar-Laplace, M. E., & Hess, S. (2007). Place attachment and place identity in natives and non-natives. *Journal of Environmental Psychology, 27,* 310–319.

Hersey, P. (1985). A letter to the author of "Don't be misled by LEAD." *Journal of Applied Behavioral Sciences, 21,* 152–153.

Hersey, P., & Blanchard, K. H. (1976). Leader effectiveness and adaptability description (LEAD). In J. W. Pfeiffer & J. E. Jones (Eds.), *The 1976 annual handbook for group facilitators* (Vol. 5, pp. 133–142). La Jolla, CA: University Associates.

Hersey, P., & Blanchard, K. H. (1982). *Management of organizational behavior* (4th ed.).Upper Saddle River, NJ: Prentice Hall.

Hersey, P., Blanchard, K. H., & Johnson, D. E. (2001). *Management of organizational behavior: Leading human resources* (8th ed.).Upper Saddle River, NJ: Prentice Hall.

Herzog, T. R., & Chernick, K. K. (2000). Tranquility and danger in urban and natural settings. *Journal of Environmental Psychology, 20,* 29–39.

Hewstone, M. (1990). The "ultimate attribution error"? A review of the literature on intergroup causal attribution. *European Journal of Social Psychology, 20,* 311–335.

Hewstone, M., Rubin, M., & Willis, H. (2002). Intergroup bias. *Annual Review of Psychology, 53,* 575–604.

Highhouse, S. (2002). A history of the T-group and its early applications in management development. *Group Dynamics: Theory, Research, and Practice, 6,* 277–290.

Hill, C. A. (1991). Seeking emotional support: The influence of affiliative need and partner warmth. *Journal of Personality and Social Psychology, 60,* 112–121.

Hill, C. E., Helms, J. E., Tichenor, V., Spiegel, S. B., O'Grady, K. E., & Perry, E. S. (1988). Effects of therapist response modes in brief psychotherapy. *Journal of Counseling Psychology, 35,* 222–233.

Hill, W. F., & Gruner, L. (1973). A study of development in open and closed groups. *Small Group Behavior, 4,* 355–381.

Hinkle, S., & Schopler, J. (1986). Bias in the evaluation of in-group and out-group performance. In S. Worchel & W. G. Austin (Eds.), *Psychology of intergroup relations* (2nd ed., pp. 196–212). Chicago: Nelson-Hall.

Hinrichs, K. T. (2007). Follower propensity to commit crimes of obedience: The role of leadership beliefs. *Journal of Leadership & Organizational Studies, 14,* 69–76.

Hinsz, V. B. (1995). Goal setting by groups performing an additive task: A comparison with individual goal setting. *Journal of Applied Social Psychology, 25,* 965–990.

Hinsz, V. B. (2005). The influences of social aspects of competition in goal-setting situations. *Current Psychology: Developmental, Learning, Personality, Social, 24,* 258–273.

Hinsz, V. B., Tindale, R. S., & Vollrath, D. A. (1997). The emerging conceptualization of groups as information processors. *Psychological Bulletin, 121,* 43–64.

Hirokawa, R. Y. (1980). A comparative analysis of communication patterns within effective and ineffective decision-making groups. *Communication Monographs, 47,* 312–321.

Hirst, W., & Manier, D. (2008). Towards a psychology of collective memory. *Memory, 16,* 183–200.

Hirt, E. R., Zillmann, D., Erickson, G. A., & Kennedy, C. (1992). Costs and benefits of allegiance: Changes in fans' self-ascribed competencies after team victory versus defeat. *Journal of Personality and Social Psychology, 63,* 724–738.

Hoag, M. J., & Burlingame, G. M. (1997). Evaluating the effectiveness of child and adolescent group treatment: A meta-analytic review. *Journal of Clinical Child Psychology, 26,* 234–246.

Hodges, B. H., & Geyer, A. L. (2006). A nonconformist account of the Asch experiments: Values, pragmatics, and moral dilemmas. *Personality and Social Psychology Review, 10,* 2–19.

Hodgkinson, G. P., & Healey, M. P. (2008). Cognition in organizations. *Annual Review of Psychology, 59,* 387–417.

Hodson, G., & Sorrentino, R. M. (1997). Groupthink and uncertainty orientation: Personality differences in reactivity to the group situation. *Group Dynamics: Theory, Research, and Practice, 1,* 144–155.

Hoffer, E. (1951). *The true believer.* New York: Harper & Row.

Hoffman, J. R., & Rogelberg, S. G. (2001). All together now? College students' preferred project group grading procedures. *Group Dynamics: Theory, Research, and Practice, 5,* 33–40.

Hofstede, G. (1980). *Culture's consequences: International differences in work-related values.* Thousand Oaks, CA: Sage.

Hogan, R. (2005). In defense of personality measurement: New wine for old whiners. *Human Performance, 18,* 331–341.

Hogan, R., & Kaiser, R. B. (2005). What we know about leadership. *Review of General Psychology, 9,* 169–180.

Hogg, M. A. (1992). *The social psychology of group cohesiveness: From attraction to social identity.* New York: New York University Press.

Hogg, M. A. (2001). Social categorization, depersonalization, and group behavior. In M. A. Hogg & R. S. Tindale (Eds.), *Blackwell handbook of social psychology: Group processes* (pp. 56–85). Malden, MA: Blackwell.

Hogg, M. A. (2004). Identity in modern society: A social psychological perspective. *European Psychologist, 9,* 284–285.

Hogg, M. A. (2005). The social identity perspective. In S. Wheelan (Ed.), *The handbook of group research and practice* (pp. 133–157). Thousand Oaks, CA: Sage.

Hogg, M. A. (2007). Social psychology of leadership. In A. W. Kruglanski & E. T. Higgins (Eds.), *Social psychology: Handbook of basic principles* (2nd ed., pp. 716–733). New York: Guilford.

Hogg, M. A. (2008). Social identity theory of leadership. In C. L. Hoyt, G. R. Goethals, & D. R. Forsyth (Eds.), *Leadership at the crossroads: Leadership and psychology* (Vol. 1, pp. 62–77). Westport, CT: Praeger.

Hogg, M. A., & Abrams, D. (1999). Social identity and social cognition: Historical background and current trends. In D. Abrams & M. A. Hogg (Eds.), *Social identity and social cognition* (pp. 1–25). Malden, MA: Blackwell.

Hogg, M. A., Sherman, D. K., Dierselhuis, J., Maitner, A. T., & Moffitt, G. (2007). Uncertainty, entitativity, and group identification. *Journal of Experimental Social Psychology, 43,* 135–142.

Hogg, M. A., & Turner, J. C. (1987). Intergroup behaviour, self-stereotyping and the salience of social categories. *British Journal of Social Psychology, 26,* 325–340.

Hogg, M. A., Turner, J. C., & David, B. (1990). Polarized norms and social frames of references: A test of the self-categorization theory of group polarization. *Basic and Applied Social Psychology, 11,* 77–100.

Hollander, E. P. (1965). Validity of peer nominations in predicting a distance performance criterion. *Journal of Applied Psychology, 49,* 434–438.

Hollander, E. P. (1971). *Principles and methods of social psychology* (2nd ed.). New York: Oxford University Press.

Hollander, E. P. (2006). Influence processes in leadership–followership: Inclusion and the idiosyncrasy credit model. In D. A. Hantula (Ed.), *Advances in social & organizational psychology: A tribute to Ralph Rosnow* (pp. 293–312). Mahwah, NJ: Erlbaum.

Hollander, E. P., & Offermann, L. R. (1990). Power and leadership in organizations: Relationships in transition. *American Psychologist, 45,* 179–189.

Hollingshead, A. B. (2001a). Cognitive interdependence and convergent expectations in transactive memory.

*Journal of Personality and Social Psychology, 81,* 1080–1089.

Hollingshead, A. B. (2001b). Communication technologies, the Internet, and group research. In M. A. Hogg & R. S. Tindale (Eds.), *Blackwell handbook of social psychology: Group processes* (pp. 557–573). Malden, MA: Blackwell.

Hollingshead, A. B., Wittenbaum, G. M., Paulus, P. B., Hirokawa, R. Y., Ancona, D. G., Peterson, R. S., Jehn, K. A., & Yoon, K. (2005). A look at groups from the functional perspective. In M. S. Poole & A. B. Hollingshead (Eds.), *Theories of small groups: Interdisciplinary perspectives* (pp. 21–62). Thousand Oaks, CA: Sage.

Hollingworth, H. L. (1935). *The psychology of the audience.* New York: American Books.

Hollon, S. D., & Beck, A. T. (2004). Cognitive and cognitive behavioral therapies. In M. J. Lambert (Ed.), *Bergin & Garfield's handbook of psychotherapy and behavior change* (5th ed., pp. 447–492). New York: Wiley & Sons.

Holmes, P. (1983). "Dropping out" from an adolescent therapeutic group: A study of factors in the patients and their parents which may influence this process. *Journal of Adolescence, 6,* 333–346.

Homans, G. C. (1950). *The human group.* New York: Harcourt, Brace & World.

Homans, G. C. (1967). *The nature of social science.* New York: Harcourt, Brace & World.

Honeywell-Johnson, J. A., & Dickinson, A. M. (1999). Small group incentives: A review of the literature. *Journal of Organizational Behavior Management, 19,* 89–120.

Hooijberg, R., & DiTomaso, N. (1996). Leadership in and of demographically diverse organizations. *Leadership Quarterly, 7,* 1–19.

Hooper, D. T., & Martin, R. (2008). Beyond personal Leader–Member Exchange (LMX) quality: The effects of perceived LMX variability on employee reactions. *The Leadership Quarterly, 19,* 20–30.

Hopthrow, T., Abrams, D., Frings, D., & Hulbert, L. G. (2007). Groupdrink: The effects of alcohol on intergroup competitiveness. *Psychology of Addictive Behaviors, 21,* 272–276.

Horne, A. M., Jolliff, D. L., & Roth, E. W. (1996). Men mentoring men in groups. In M. P. Andronico (Ed.), *Men in groups: Insights, interventions, and psychoeducational work* (pp. 97–112). Washington, DC: American Psychological Association.

Horne, A. M., Stoddard, J. L., & Bell, C. D. (2007). Group approaches to reducing aggression and bullying in school. *Group Dynamics: Theory, Research, and Practice, 11,* 262–271.

Horowitz, I. A., & Kirkpatrick, L. C. (1996). A concept in search of a definition: The effects of reasonable doubt instructions on certainty of guilt standards and jury verdicts. *Law and Human Behavior, 20,* 655–670.

Horwitz, S. K., & Horwitz, I. B. (2007). The effects of team diversity on team outcomes: A meta-analytic review of team demography. *Journal of Management, 33,* 987–1015.

Houle, C. O. (1989). *Governing boards: Their nature and nurture.* San Francisco: Jossey-Bass.

House, R. J., & Javidan, M. (2004). Overview of GLOBE. In R. J. House, P. J. Hanges, M. Javidan, P. W. Dorfman, & V. Gupta (Eds.), *Culture, leadership, and organizations: The GLOBE study of 62 societies* (pp. 9–28). Thousand Oaks, CA: Sage.

House, R. L., & Baetz, M. L. (1979). Leadership: Some empirical generalizations and new research directions. *Research in Organizational Behavior, 1,* 341–423.

Houston, T. K., Cooper, L. A., & Ford, D. E. (2002). Internet support groups for depression: A 1-year prospective cohort study. *American Journal of Psychiatry, 159,* 2062–2068.

Hovland, C., & Sears, R. (1940). Minor studies of aggression: VI. Correlation of lynchings with economic indices. *Journal of Psychology, 9,* 301–310.

Howard, J. A., Blumstein, P., & Schwartz, P. (1986). Sex, power, and influence tactics in intimate relationships. *Journal of Personality and Social Psychology, 51,* 102–109.

Howard, J. W., & Rothbart, M. (1980). Social categorization and memory for in-group and out-group behavior. *Journal of Personality and Social Psychology, 38,* 301–310.

Howells, L. T., & Becker, S. W. (1962). Seating arrangement and leadership emergence. *Journal of Abnormal and Social Psychology, 64,* 148–150.

Hoyle, R. H. (2005). Design and analysis of experimental research on groups. In S. A. Wheelan (Ed.), *The handbook of group research and practice* (pp. 223–239). Thousand Oaks, CA: Sage.

Hoyle, R. H., & Crawford, A. M. (1994). Use of individual-level data to investigate group phenomena: Issues and strategies. *Small Group Research, 25,* 464–485.

Hoyle R. H., Pinkley R. L., & Insko C. A. (1989). Perceptions of behavior: Evidence of differing expectations for interpersonal and intergroup interactions. *Personality and Social Psychology Bulletin, 15,* 365–376.

Hoyt, C. L. (2007). Women and leadership. In P. G. Northouse, *Leadership: Theory and practice* (4th ed., pp. 265–299). Thousand Oaks, CA: Sage.

Hoyt, C. L., & Blascovich, J. (2003). Transformational and transactional leadership in virtual and physical environments. *Small Group Research, 6,* 678–715.

Hoyt, C. L., & Blascovich, J. (2007). Leadership efficacy and women leaders' responses to stereotype activation. *Group Processes & Intergroup Relations, 10,* 595–616.

Hoyt, C. L., & Chemers, M. M. (2008). Social stigma and leadership: A long climb up a slippery ladder. In C. L. Hoyt, G. R. Goethals, & D. R. Forsyth (Eds.), *Leadership at the crossroads: Leadership and psychology* (Vol. 1, pp. 165–180). Westport, CT: Praeger.

Hoyt, C. L., Goethals, G. R., & Forsyth, D. R. (Eds.). (2008). *Leadership at the crossroads: Leadership and psychology* (Vol. 1). Westport, CT: Praeger.

Hoyt, C. L., Simon, S., & Reid, L. (in press). The effect of mortality salience on leader preference based on gender. *Leadership Quarterly.*

Hubbard, J. A., Dodge, K. A., Cillessen, A. H. N., Coie, J. D., & Schwartz, D. (2001). The dyadic nature of social information processing in boys' reactive and proactive aggression. *Journal of Personality and Social Psychology, 80,* 268–280.

Hughes, R. L. (2003). The flow of human crowds. *Annual Review of Fluid Mechanics, 35,* 169–182.

Huguet, P., Galvaing, M. P., Monteil, J. M., & Dumas, F. (1999). Social presence effects in the Stroop task: Further evidence for an attentional view of social facilitation. *Journal of Personality and Social Psychology, 77,* 1011–1025.

Humphreys, L. (1975). *Tearoom trade* (enlarged ed.). Hawthorne, NY: Aldine.

Hurley, J. R. (1997). Interpersonal theory and measures of outcome and emotional climate in 111 personal development groups. *Group Dynamics: Theory, Research, and Practice, 1,* 86–97.

Hyman, H. (1942). The psychology of status. *Archives of Psychology, 38* (269).

Hyman, H. M., & Tarrant, C. M. (1975). Aspects of American trial jury history. In R. J. Simon (Ed.), *The jury system in America.* Thousand Oaks, CA: Sage.

Iacoboni, M., Liberman, M. D., Knowlton, B. J., Molnar-Szakas, I., Moritz, M., Throop, C. J., Fiske, A. P. (2004). Watching social interactions produces dorsomedial prefrontal and medial parietal BOLD fMRI signal increases compared to a resting baseline. *NeuroImage, 21,* 1167–1173.

Iannaccone, L. R. (1994). Why strict churches are strong. *American Journal of Sociology, 99,* 1180–1211.

Ickes, W., & Turner, M. (1983). On the social advantages of having an older, opposite-sex sibling: Birth order influence in mixed-sex dyads. *Journal of Personality and Social Psychology, 45,* 210–222.

Ilgen, D. R., Hollenbeck, J. R., Johnson, M., & Jundt, D. (2005). Teams in organizations: From input-process-output models to IMOI models. *Annual Review of Psychology, 56,* 517–543.

Ilgen, D. R., Mitchell, T. R., & Fredrickson, J. W. (1981). Poor performances: Supervisors' and subordinates' responses. *Organizational Behavior and Human Performance, 27,* 386–410.

Ilies, R., Morgeson, F. P., & Nahrgang, J. D. (2005). Authentic leadership and eudaemonic well-being: Understanding leader–follower outcomes. *Leadership Quarterly, 16,* 373–394.

Ilies, R., Nahrgang, J. D., & Morgeson, F. P. (2007). Leader–member exchange and citizenship behaviors: A meta-analysis. *Journal of Applied Psychology, 92,* 269–277.

IMDb (Internet Movie Database). (2008). *Reginald Rose.* Retrieved Sept. 3, 2008, from IMDb website, http://www.imdb.com.

Indik, B. P. (1965). Organization size and member participation: Some empirical tests of alternate explanations. *Human Relations, 15,* 339–350.

Ingram, R. E., Hayes, A., & Scott, W. (2000). Empirically supported treatments: A critical analysis. In C. R. Snyder & R. E. Ingram (Eds.). *Handbook of psychological change: Psychotherapy processes & practices for the 21st century* (pp. 40–60). New York: Wiley.

Insko, C. A., Gilmore, R., Drenan, S., Lipsitz, A., Moehle, D., & Thibaut, J. (1983). Trade versus expropriation in open groups: A comparison of two types of social power. *Journal of Personality and Social Psychology, 44,* 977–999.

Insko, C. A., Pinkley, R. L., Hoyle, R. H., Dalton, B., Hong, G., Slim, R., Landry, P., Holton, B., Ruffin, P. F., & Thibaut, J. (1987). Individual–group discontinuity: The role of intergroup contact. *Journal of Experimental Social Psychology, 23,* 250–267.

Insko, C. A., & Schopler, J. (1972). *Experimental social psychology.* New York: Academic Press.

Insko, C. A., Schopler, J., Drigotas, S. M., Graetz, K., Kennedy, J., Cox, C., & Bornstein, G., (1993). The role of communication in interindividual–intergroup discontinuity. *Journal of Conflict Resolution, 37,* 108–138.

Insko, C. A., Schopler, J., Graetz, K. A., Drigotas, S. M., Currey, K. P., Smith, S. L., Brazil, D., & Bornstein, G. (1994). Interindividual–intergroup discontinuity in the Prisoner's Dilemma Game. *Journal of Conflict Resolution, 38,* 87–116.

Insko, C. A., Schopler, J., Hoyle, R. H., Dardis, G. J., & Graetz, K. A. (1990). Individual–group discontinuity as a function of fear and greed. *Journal of Personality and Social Psychology, 58,* 68–79.

Inkso, C. A., Thibaut, J. W., Moehle, D., Wilson, M., Diamond, W. D., Gilmore, R., Solomon, M. R., & Lipsitz, A. (1980). Social evolution and the emergence of leadership. *Journal of Personality and Social Psychology, 39,* 431–448.

Instone, D., Major, B., & Bunker, B. B. (1983). Gender, self confidence, and social influence strategies: An organizational simulation. *Journal of Personality and Social Psychology, 44,* 322–333.

Ip, G. W., Chiu, C., & Wan, C. (2006). Birds of a feather and birds flocking together: Physical versus behavioral cues may lead to trait- versus goal-based group perception. *Journal of Personality and Social Psychology, 90,* 368–381.

Isenberg, D. J. (1986). Group polarization: A critical review and meta-analysis. *Journal of Personality and Social Psychology, 50,* 1141–1151.

Isenberg, D. J., & Ennis, J. G. (1981). Perceiving group members: A comparison of derived and imposed dimensions. *Journal of Personality and Social Psychology, 41,* 293–305.

Islam, G., & Zyphur, M. J. (2005). Power, voice, and hierarchy: Exploring the antecedents of speaking up in groups. *Group Dynamics: Theory, Research, and Practice, 9,* 93–103.

Iverson, M. A. (1964). Personality impressions of punitive stimulus persons of differential status. *Journal of Abnormal and Social Psychology, 68,* 617–626.

Jablin, F. M. (1979). Superior–subordinate communication: The state of the art. *Psychological Bulletin, 86,* 1201–1222.

Jackson, D., Engstrom, E., & Emmers-Sommer, T. (2007). Think leader, think male and female: Sex vs. seating arrangement as leadership cues. *Sex Roles, 57,* 713–723.

Jackson, J. M. (1987). Social impact theory: A social forces model of influence. In B. Mullen & G. R. Goethals (Eds.), *Theories of group behavior* (pp. 112–124). New York: Springer-Verlag.

Jackson, J. M., & Latané, B. (1981). All alone in front of all those people: Stage fright as a function of number and type of co-performances and audience. *Journal of Personality and Social Psychology, 40,* 73–85.

Jackson, S. E. (1992). Team composition in organizational settings: Issues in managing an increasingly diverse workforce. In S. Worchel, S. Wood, & J. A. Simpson (Eds.), *Group process and productivity* (pp. 138–172). Thousand Oaks, CA: Sage.

Jacobs, A. (1974). The use of feedback in groups. In A. Jacobs & W. W. Spradlin (Eds.), *Group as an agent of change.* New York: Behavioral Publications.

Jacobs, D., & O'Brien, R. M. (1998). The determinants of deadly force: A structural analysis of police violence. *American Journal of Sociology, 103,* 837–862.

Jacobs, M. K., & Goodman, G. (1989). Psychology and self-help groups: Predictions on a partnership. *American Psychologist, 44,* 536–545.

Jacobs, R. C., & Campbell, D. T. (1961). The perpetuation of an arbitrary tradition through several generations of a laboratory microculture. *Journal of Abnormal and Social Psychology, 62,* 649–658.

Jahoda, G. (2007). *A history of social psychology: From the eighteenth-century enlightenment to the Second World War.* Cambridge: Cambridge University Press.

James, J. (1951). A preliminary study of the size determinant in small group interaction. *American Sociological Review, 16,* 474–477.

James, R. (1959). Status and competency of jurors. *American Journal of Sociology, 64,* 563–570.

Janicik, G. A., & Bartel, C. A. (2003). Talking about time: Effects of temporal planning and time awareness norms on group coordination and performance. *Group Dynamics: Theory, Research, and Practice, 7,* 122–134.

Janis, I. L. (1972). *Victims of groupthink.* Boston: Houghton Mifflin.

Janis, I. L. (1982). *Groupthink: Psychological studies of policy decisions and fiascos* (2nd ed.). Boston: Houghton Mifflin.

Janis, I. L. (1983). Groupthink. In H. H. Blumberg, A. P. Hare, V. Kent, & M. F. Davis (Eds.), *Small groups and social interaction* (Vol. 2, pp. 39–46). New York: Wiley.

Janis, I. L. (1985). International crisis management in the nuclear age. *Applied Social Psychology Annual, 6,* 63–86.

Janis, I. L. (1989). *Crucial decisions: Leadership in policy making and crisis management.* New York: Free Press.

Janis, I. L., & Mann, L. (1977). *Decision making: A psychological analysis of conflict, choice, and commitment.* New York: Free Press.

Jankowski, M. S. (1991). *Islands in the street: Gangs and American urban society.* Berkeley: University of California Press.

Jarboe, S. C., & Witteman, H. R. (1996). Intragroup conflict management in task-oriented groups: The influence of problem sources and problem analyses. *Small Group Research, 27,* 316–338.

Jehn, K. A. (1995). A multimethod examination of the benefits and detriments of intragroup conflict. *Administrative Science Quarterly, 40,* 256–282.

Jehn, K. A. (1997). Affective and cognitive conflict in work groups: Increasing performance through value-based intragroup conflict. In C. K. W. De Dreu & E. Van de Vliert (Eds.), *Using conflict in organizations* (pp. 87–100). Thousand Oaks, CA: Sage.

Jehn, K. A., & Bendersky, C. (2003). Intragroup conflict in organizations: A contingency perspective on the conflict–outcome relationship. In R. M. Kramer & B. M. Staw (Eds.), *Research in organizational behavior* (Vol. 25, pp. 187–242). Oxford: Elsevier Science.

Jehn, K. A., & Mannix, E. A. (2001). The dynamic nature of conflict: A longitudinal study of intragroup conflict and group performance. *Academy of Management Journal, 44,* 238–251.

Jehn, K. A., & Shah, P. P. (1997). Interpersonal relationships and task performance: An examination of mediating processes in friendship and acquaintance groups. *Journal of Personality and Social Psychology, 72,* 775–790.

Jetten, J., Branscombe, N. R., Spears, R., & McKimmie, B. (2003). Predicting the paths of peripherals: The interaction of identification and future possibilities. *Personality and Social Psychology Bulletin, 29,* 130–140.

Jetten, J., Hornsey, M. J., & Adarves-Yorno, I. (2006). When group members admit to being conformist: The role of relative intragroup status in conformity self-reports. *Personality and Social Psychology Bulletin, 32,* 162–173.

Jimerson, J. B. (1999). "Who has next?" The symbolic, rational, and methodical use of norms in pickup basketball. *Social Psychology Quarterly, 62,* 136–156.

Johansson, A., Helbing, D., Al-Abideen, H. Z., & Al-Bosta, S. (2008). From crowd dynamics to crowd safety: A video-based analysis. *Advances in Complex Systems, 11,* 497–527.

Johnson, F. (1988). Encounter group therapy. In S. Long (Ed.), *Six group therapies* (pp. 115–158). New York: Plenum Press.

Johnson, N. R. (1987). Panic at "The Who concert stampede": An empirical assessment. *Social Problems, 34,* 362–373.

Johnson, R. D., & Downing, L. L. (1979). Deindividuation and valence of cues: Effects on prosocial and antisocial behavior. *Journal of Personality and Social Psychology, 37,* 1532–1538.

Joiner, T. E., Jr., Hollar, D., & Van Orden, K. (2006). On Buckeyes, Gators, Super Bowl Sunday, and the Miracle on Ice: "Pulling together" is associated with lower suicide rates. *Journal of Social & Clinical Psychology, 25,* 179–195.

Jones, E. E., & Kelly, J. R. (2007). Contributions to a group discussion and perceptions of leadership: Does quantity always count more than quality? *Group Dynamics: Theory, Research, and Practice, 11,* 15–30.

Jones, E. S., Gallois, C., Callan, V. J., & Barker, M. (1995). Language and power in an academic context: The effects of status, ethnicity, and sex. *Journal of Language & Social Psychology, 14,* 434–461.

Jones, M. B. (1974). Regressing group on individual effectiveness. *Organizational Behavior and Human Decision Processes, 11,* 426–451.

Jones, W. H., & Carver, M. D. (1991). Adjustment and coping implications of loneliness. In C. R. Snyder & D. R. Forsyth (Eds.), *Handbook of social and clinical psychology: The health perspective* (pp. 395–415). New York: Pergamon.

Jorgenson, D. O., & Dukes, F. O. (1976). Deindividuation as a function of density and group membership. *Journal of Personality and Social Psychology, 34,* 24–29.

Jourard, S. (1971). *Self-disclosure: An experimental analysis of the transparent self.* New York: Wiley.

Judge, T. A., Bono, J. E., Ilies, R., & Gerhardt, M. W. (2002). Personality and leadership: A qualitative and quantitative review. *Journal of Applied Psychology, 87,* 765–780.

Judge, T. A., & Cable, D. M. (1997). Applicant personality, organizational culture, and organization attraction. *Personnel Psychology, 50,* 359–394.

Judge, T. A., & Piccolo, R. F. (2004). Transformational and transactional leadership: A meta-analytic test of their relative validity. *Journal of Applied Psychology, 89,* 755–768.

Jung, C. G. (1924). *Psychological types, or the psychology of individuation* (H. G. Baynes, Trans.). New York: Harcourt, Brace & World.

Jung, D., Wu, A., & Chow, C. W. (2008). Towards understanding the direct and indirect effects of CEOs' transformational leadership on firm innovation. *The Leadership Quarterly, 19,* 582–594.

Kagan, J., Snidman, N., & Arcus, D. M. (1992). Initial reactions to unfamiliarity. *Current Directions in Psychological Science, 1,* 171–174.

Kahn, A., Hottes, J., & Davis, W. L. (1971). Cooperation and optimal responding in the Prisoner's Dilemma Game: Effects of sex and physical attractiveness. *Journal of Personality and Social Psychology, 17,* 267–279.

Kahn, R. (1973). *The boys of summer.* New York: HarperCollins.

Kahn, R. L., Wolfe, D. M., Quinn, R. P., Snoek, J. D., & Rosenthal, R. A. (1964). *Organizational stress: Studies in role conflict and ambiguity.* New York: Wiley.

Kaiser, R. B., Hogan, R., & Craig, S. B. (2008). Leadership and the fate of organizations. *American Psychologist, 63,* 96–110.

Kalven, H., Jr., & Zeisel, H. (1966). *The American jury.* Boston: Little, Brown.

Kamarck, T. W., Manuck, S. B., & Jennings, J. R. (1990). Social support reduces cardiovascular reactivity to psychological challenge: A laboratory model. *Psychosomatic Medicine, 52,* 42–58.

Kameda, T. (1994). Group decision making and social sharedness. *Japanese Psychological Review, 37,* 367–385.

Kameda, T. (1996). Procedural influence in consensus formation: Evaluating group decision making from a social choice perspective. In E. Witte & J. Davis (Eds.), *Understanding group behavior: Consensual action by small groups* (Vol. 1, pp. 137–161). Mahwah, NJ: Erlbaum.

Kameda, T., Stasson, M. F., Davis, J. H., Parks, C. D., & Zimmerman, S. K. (1992). Social dilemmas, subgroups, and motivation loss in task-oriented groups: In search of an "optimal" team size in division of work. *Social Psychology Quarterly, 55,* 47–56.

Kameda, T., & Sugimori, S. (1995). Procedural influence in two-step group decision making: Power of local majorities in consensus formation. *Journal of Personality and Social Psychology, 69,* 865–876.

Kameda, T., Takezawa, M., & Hastie, R. (2005). Where do social norms come from? The example of communal sharing. *Current Directions in Psychological Science, 14,* 331–334.

Kameda, T., Takezawa, M., Tindale, R. S., & Smith, C. M. (2002). Social sharing and risk reduction: Exploring a computational algorithm for the psychology of windfall gains. *Evolution and Human Behavior, 23,* 11–33.

Kameda, T., & Tamura, R. (2007). "To eat or not to be eaten?" Collective risk-monitoring in groups. *Journal of Experimental Social Psychology, 43,* 168–179.

Kameda, T., & Tindale, R. S. (2006). Groups as adaptive devices: Human docility and group aggregation mechanisms in evolutionary context. In M. Schaller, J. A. Simpson, & D. T. Kenrick (Eds.), *Evolution and social psychology* (pp. 317–341). Madison, WI: Psychosocial Press.

Kanagawa, C., Cross, S. E., & Markus, H. R. (2001). "Who am I?" The cultural psychology of the conceptual self. *Personality and Social Psychology Bulletin, 27,* 90–103.

Kanas, N. (1999). Group therapy with schizophrenic and bipolar patients. In V. L. Schermer & M. Pines (Eds.), *Group psychotherapy of the psychoses: Concepts, interventions and contexts* (pp. 129–147). London: Jessica Kingsley.

Kandel, D. B. (1978). Similarity in real-life adolescent friendship pairs. *Journal of Personality and Social Psychology, 36,* 306–312.

Kanter, R. M. (1977). Some effects of proportions on group life: Skewed sex ratios and responses to token women. *American Journal of Sociology, 82,* 465–490.

Kanzer, M. (1983). Freud: The first psychoanalytic group leader. In H. I. Kaplan & B. J. Sadock (Eds.), *Comprehensive group psychotherapy* (2nd ed., pp. 8–14). Baltimore: Williams & Wilkins.

Kaplan, M. F. (1982). Cognitive processes in the individual juror. In N. L. Kerr & R. M. Bray (Eds.), *Psychology of the courtroom* (pp. 197–220). New York: Academic Press.

Kaplan, M. F., & Miller, C. E. (1987). Group decision making and normative versus informational influence: Effects of type of issue and assigned decision rule. *Journal of Personality and Social Psychology, 53,* 306–313.

Kaplan, R. E. (1979). The conspicuous absence of evidence that process consultation enhances task performance. *Journal of Applied Behavioral Science, 15,* 346–360.

Kaplowitz, S. A. (1978). Towards a systematic theory of power attribution. *Social Psychology, 41,* 131–148.

Karau, S. J., & Williams, K. D. (1993). Social loafing: A meta-analytic review and theoretical integration. *Journal of Personality and Social Psychology, 65,* 681–706.

Karau, S. J., & Williams, K. D. (2001). Understanding individual motivation in groups: The collective effort model. In M. E. Turner (Ed.), *Groups at work: Theory and research* (pp. 113–141). Mahwah, NJ: Erlbaum.

Kashima, Y., Yamaguchi, S., Kim, U., Choi, S., Gelfand, M. J., & Yuki, M. (1995). Culture, gender, and self: A perspective from individualism–collectivism research. *Journal of Personality and Social Psychology, 69,* 925–937.

Kaskutas, L. A., Ammon, L., Delucchi, K., Room, R., Bond, J., & Weisner, C. (2005). Alcoholics Anonymous careers: Patterns of AA involvement five years after treatment entry. *Alcoholism: Clinical and Experimental Research, 29,* 1983–1990.

Katz, A. H. (1993). *Self-help in America: A social movement perspective.* New York: Twayne.

Katz, D., & Kahn, R. L. (1978). *The social psychology of organizations* (2nd ed.). New York: Wiley.

Katz, N., Lazer, D., Arrow, H., & Contractor, N. (2005). The network perspective on small groups: Theory and research. In M. S. Poole & A. B. Hollingshead (Eds.), *Theories of small groups: Interdisciplinary perspectives* (pp. 277–312). Thousand Oaks, CA: Sage.

Katz, R. (1977). The influence of group conflict on leadership effectiveness. *Organizational Behavior and Human Performance, 20,* 265–286.

Katz, R., & Tushman, M. (1979). Communication patterns, project performance, and task characteristics: An empirical evaluation and integration in an R & D setting. *Organization Behavior and Group Performance, 23,* 139–162.

Katzenbach, J. R., & Smith, D. K. (2001). *The discipline of teams.* New York: John Wiley & Sons.

Kaul, T. J., & Bednar, R. L. (1986). Experiential group research: Results, questions, and suggestions. In S. L. Garfield & A. E. Bergin (Eds.), *Handbook of psychotherapy and behavior change* (3rd ed., pp. 671–714). New York: Wiley.

Kayes, D. C. (2006). *Destructive goal pursuit: The Mount Everest disaster.* New York: Palgrave-Macmillan Press.

Keinan, G., & Koren, M. (2002). Teaming up type as and bs: The effects of group composition on performance and satisfaction. *Applied Psychology: An International Review, 51,* 425–445.

Keller, E., & Berry, J. (2003). *The influentials: One American in ten tells the other nine how to vote, where to eat, and what to buy.* New York: Free Press.

Kelley, H. H. (1952). Two functions of reference groups. In G. E. Swanson, T. M. Newcomb, & E. L. Hartley (Eds.), *Readings in social psychology* (2nd ed., pp. 410–414). New York: Holt.

Kelley, H. H. (1979). *Personal relationships: Their structures and processes.* Mahwah, NJ: Erlbaum.

Kelley, H. H., Contry, J. C., Dahlke, A. E., & Hill, A. H. (1965). Collective behavior in a simulated panic situation. *Journal of Experimental Social Psychology, 1,* 20–54.

Kelley, H. H., & Stahelski, A. J. (1970a). Errors in perceptions of intentions in a mixed-motive game. *Journal of Experimental Social Psychology, 6,* 379–400.

Kelley, H. H., & Stahelski, A. J. (1970b). Social interaction basis of cooperators' and competitors' beliefs about others. *Journal of Personality and Social Psychology, 16,* 66–91.

Kelley, H. H., & Stahelski, A. J. (1970c). The inference of intentions from moves in the Prisoner's Dilemma Game. *Journal of Experimental Social Psychology, 6,* 401–419.

Kelley, H. H., & Thibaut, J. W. (1978). *Interpersonal relations: A theory of interdependence.* New York: Wiley.

Kelley, R. E. (2004). Followership. In G. R. Goethals, G. J. Sorenson, & J. M. Burns (Eds.), *The encyclopedia of leadership* (pp. 504–513). Thousand Oaks CA: Sage.

Kelley, R. E. (1988). In praise of followers. *Harvard Business Review. 66(6),* 142–148.

Kelly, J. R. (2001). Mood and emotion in groups. In M. A. Hogg & R. S. Tindale (Eds.), *Blackwell handbook of social psychology: Group processes* (pp. 164–181). Malden, MA: Blackwell.

Kelly, J. R. (2004). Mood and emotion in groups. In M. B. Brewer & M. Hewstone (Eds.), *Emotion and motivation* (pp. 95–112). Malden, MA: Blackwell.

Kelly, J. R., Futoran, G. C., & McGrath, J. E. (1990). Capacity and capability: Seven studies of entrainment of task performance rates. *Small Group Research, 21,* 283–314.

Kelly, J. R., & Karau, S. J. (1993). Entrainment of creativity in small groups. *Small Group Research, 24,* 179–198.

Kelly, J. R., & Karau, S. J. (1999). Group decision making: The effects of initial preferences and time pressure. *Personality and Social Psychology Bulletin, 25,* 1342–1354.

Kelly, J. R., & Loving, T. J. (2004). Time pressure and group performance: Exploring underlying processes in the attentional focus model. *Journal of Experimental Social Psychology, 40,* 185–198.

Kelman, H. C. (1958). Compliance, identification, and internalization: Three processes of attitude change. *Journal of Conflict Resolution, 2,* 51–60.

Kelman, H. C. (1961). Processes of opinion change. *Public Opinion Quarterly, 25,* 57–78.

Kelman, H. C. (1992). Informal mediation by the scholar/practitioner. In J. Bercovitch & J. Rubin (Eds.), *Mediation in international relations: Multiple approaches to conflict management* (pp. 64–96). New York: St. Martin's Press.

Kelman, H. C. (2006). Interests, relationships, identities: Three central issues for individuals and groups in negotiating their social environment. *Annual Review of Psychology, 57,* 1–26.

Kelman, H. C., & Hamilton, V. L. (1989). *Crimes of obedience: Toward a social psychology of authority and responsibility.* New Haven, CT: Yale University Press.

Keltner, D., Gruenfeld, D. H., & Anderson, C. (2003). Power, approach, and inhibition. *Psychological Review, 110,* 265–284.

Keltner, D., Van Kleef, G. A., Chen, S., & Kraus, M. W. (2008). A reciprocal influence model of social power: Emerging principles and lines of inquiry. *Advances in Experimental Social Psychology, 40,* 151–192.

Kemery, E. R., Bedeian, A. G., Mossholder, K. W., & Touliatos, J. (1985). Outcomes of role stress: A multisample constructive replication. *Academy of Management Review, 28,* 363–375.

Kennedy, R. F. (1969). *Thirteen days.* New York: Norton.

Kenney, R. A., Schwartz-Kenney, B. M., & Blascovich, J. (1996). Implicit leadership theories: Defining leaders described as worthy of influence. *Personality and Social Psychology Bulletin, 22,* 1128–1143.

Kenny, D. A., Kieffer, S. C., Smith, J. A., Ceplenski, P., & Kulo, J. (1996). Circumscribed accuracy among well-acquainted individuals. *Journal of Experimental Social Psychology, 32,* 1–12.

Kent, S. (1991). Partitioning space: Cross-cultural factors influencing domestic spatial segmentation. *Environment and Behavior, 23,* 438–473.

Kenworthy, J. B., Hewstone, M., Levine, J. M., Martin, R., & Willis, H. (2008). The phenomenology of minority–majority status: Effects on innovation in argument generation. *European Journal of Social Psychology, 38,* 624–636.

Kenworthy, J. B., Popan, J. R., Moerhl, T. G., Holovics, M. A., Jones, J. R., & Diamon, S. (2008). *Antecedents, correlates, and consequences of social identity strength: A meta-analytic review*. Presented at the Annual Meeting of the Society of Personality and Social Psychology, Albequerque, NM.

Kenworthy, J. B., Turner, R. N., Hewstone, M., & Voci, A. (2005). Intergroup contact: When does it work, and why? In J. F. Dovidio, P. Glick & L. A. Rudman (Eds.), *On the nature of prejudice: Fifty years after Allport* (pp. 278–292). Malden, MA: Blackwell.

Kerckhoff, A. C., & Back, K. W. (1968). *The June Bug: A study of hysterical contagion*. New York: Appleton-Century-Crofts.

Kerckhoff, A. C., Back, K. W., & Miller, N. (1965). Sociometric patterns in hysterical contagion. *Sociometry, 28,* 2–15.

Kerckhoff, A. C., & Davis, K. E. (1962). Value consensus and need complementarity in mate selection. *American Sociological Review, 27,* 295–303.

Kerr, N. L., Aronoff, J., & Messé, L. A. (2000). Methods of small group research. In H. T. Reis & C. M. Judd (Eds.), *Handbook of research methods in social and personality psychology* (pp. 160–189). New York: Cambridge University Press.

Kerr, N. L., Atkin, R. S., Stasser, G., Meek, D., Holt, R. W., & Davis, J. H. (1976). Guilt beyond a reasonable doubt: Effect of concept definition and assigned decision rule on the judgments of mock jurors. *Journal of Personality and Social Psychology, 34,* 282–294.

Kerr, N. L., & Bruun, S. E. (1981). Ringelmann revisited: Alternative explanations for the social loafing effect. *Personality and Social Psychology Bulletin, 7,* 224–231.

Kerr, N. L., & Bruun, S. E. (1983). Dispensability of member effort and group motivation losses: Free-rider effects. *Journal of Personality and Social Psychology, 44,* 78–94.

Kerr, N. L., & Huang, J. Y. (1986). Jury verdicts: How much difference does one juror make? *Personality and Social Psychology Bulletin, 12,* 325–343.

Kerr, N. L., & MacCoun, R. J. (1985). The effects of jury size and polling method on the process and product of jury deliberation. *Journal of Personality and Social Psychology, 48,* 349–363.

Kerr, N. L., MacCoun, R. J., & Kramer, G. P. (1996a). Bias in judgment: Comparing individuals and groups. *Psychological Review, 103,* 687–719.

Kerr, N. L., MacCoun, R. J., & Kramer, G. P. (1996b). "When are *N* heads better (or worse) than one?" Biased judgment in individuals and groups. In E. H. Witte & J. H. Davis (Eds.), *Understanding group behavior: Consensual action by small groups* (Vol. 1, pp. 105–136). Mahwah, NJ: Erlbaum.

Kerr, N. L., Messé, L. A., Seok, D., Sambolec, E. J., Lount, R. B., & Park, E. S. (2007). Psychological mechanisms underlying the Köhler motivation gain. *Personality and Social Psychology Bulletin, 33,* 828–841.

Kerr, N. L., & Tindale, R. S. (2004). Group performance and decision making. *Annual Review of Psychology, 55,* 623–655.

Kerr, S., & Jermier, J. M. (1978). Substitutes for leadership: Their meaning and measurement. *Organizational Behavior and Human Performance, 22,* 375–403.

Kerr, S., Schriesheim, C. A., Murphy, C. J., & Stogdill, R. M. (1974). Toward a contingency theory of leadership based upon the consideration and initiating structure literature. *Organizational Behavior and Human Performance, 12,* 62–82.

Keshet, S., Kark, R., Pomerantz-Zorin, L., Koslowsky, M., & Schwarzwald, J. (2006). Gender, status and the use of power strategies. *European Journal of Social Psychology, 36,* 105–117.

Kessler, T., & Cohrs, J. C. (2008). The evolution of authoritarian processes: Fostering cooperation in large-scale groups. *Group Dynamics: Theory, Research, and Practice, 12,* 73–84.

Kessler, T., & Mummendey, A. (2001). Is there any scapegoat around? Determinants of intergroup conflicts at different categorization levels. *Journal of Personality and Social Psychology, 81,* 1090–1102.

Kiesler, C. A., & Corbin, L. H. (1965). Commitment, attraction, and conformity. *Journal of Personality and Social Psychology, 2,* 890–895.

Kiesler, C. A., Zanna, M., & Desalvo, J. (1966). Deviation and conformity: Opinion change as a function of commitment, attraction, and presence of a deviate. *Journal of Personality and Social Psychology, 3,* 458–467.

Kiesler, D. J. (1991). Interpersonal methods of assessment and diagnosis. In C. R. Snyder & D. R. Forsyth (Eds.), *Handbook of social and clinical psychology: The health perspective* (pp. 438–468). New York: Pergamon Press.

Kiesler, S., & Cummings, J. N. (2002). What do we know about proximity and distance in work groups? A legacy of research. In P. Hinds & S. Kiesler (Eds.), *Distributed work* (pp. 57–80). Cambridge, MA: MIT Press.

Kilham, W., & Mann, L. (1974). Level of destructive obedience as a function of transmitter and executant roles in the Milgram obedience paradigm. *Journal of Personality and Social Psychology, 29,* 696–702.

Kilmartin, C. T. (1994). *The masculine self.* New York: Macmillan.

Kim, H., & Markus, H. R. (1999). Deviance or uniqueness, harmony or conformity? A cultural analysis. *Journal of Personality and Social Psychology, 77,* 785–800.

Kim, K., & Bonk, C. J. (2002). Cross-cultural comparisons of online collaboration. *Journal of Computer-Mediated Communication, 8*(1). Retrieved October 12, 2008, from http://jcmc.indiana.edu/vol8/issue1/kimandbonk.html.

Kim, Y., Jung, J., Cohen, E. L., & Ball-Rokeach, S. J. (2004). Internet connectedness before and after September 11, 2001. *New Media & Society, 6,* 611–631.

King, G. A., & Sorrentino, R. M. (1983). Psychological dimensions of goal-oriented interpersonal situations. *Journal of Personality and Social Psychology, 44,* 140–162.

King, L. A. (2004). Measures and meaning: The use of qualitative data in social and personality psychology. In C. Sansone, C. C. Morf, & A. T. Panter (Eds.), *The Sage handbook of methods in social psychology* (pp. 173–194). Thousand Oaks, CA: Sage.

Kipnis, D. (1974). *The powerholders.* Chicago: University of Chicago Press.

Kipnis, D. (1984). The use of power in organizations and in interpersonal settings. *Applied Social Psychology Annual, 5,* 179–210.

Kipnis, D., Castell, P. J., Gergen, M., & Mauch, D. (1976). Metamorphic effects of power. *Journal of Applied Psychology, 61,* 127–135.

Kipnis, D., Schmidt, S. M., Swaffin-Smith, C., & Wilkinson, I. (1984). Patterns of managerial influence: Shotgun managers, tacticians, and bystanders. *Organizational Dynamics, 12,* 58–67.

Kipper, D. A. (2006). The canon of spontaneity–creativity revisited: The effect of empirical findings. *Journal of Group Psychotherapy, Psychodrama & Sociometry, 59,* 117–125.

Kipper, D. A., & Ritchie, T. D. (2003). The effectiveness of psychodramatic techniques: A meta-analysis. *Group Dynamics: Theory, Research, and Practice, 7,* 13–25.

Kirkpatrick, L. A., & Shaver, P. (1988). Fear and affiliation reconsidered from a stress and coping perspective: The importance of cognitive clarity and fear reduction. *Journal of Social & Clinical Psychology, 7,* 214–233.

Kitayama, S. (2002). Culture and basic psychological theory—Toward a system view of culture: Comment on Oyserman et al. (2002). *Psychological Bulletin, 128,* 89–96.

Kivlighan, D. M., Jr. (1985). Feedback in group psychotherapy: Review and implications. *Small Group Behavior, 16,* 373–386.

Kivlighan, D. M., Jr. (1997). Leader behavior and therapeutic gain: An application of situational leadership theory. *Group Dynamics: Theory, Research, and Practice, 1,* 32–38.

Kivlighan, D. M., Jr., McGovern, T. V., & Corazzini, J. G. (1984). Effects of content and timing of structuring interventions on group therapy process and outcome. *Journal of Counseling Psychology, 31,* 363–370.

Kivlighan, D. M., Jr., & Mullison, D. (1988). Participants' perception of therapeutic factors in group counseling: The role of interpersonal style and stage of group development. *Small Group Behavior, 19,* 452–468.

Kivlighan, D. M., Jr., Multon, K. D., & Brossart, D. F. (1996). Helpful impacts in group counseling: Development of a multidimensional rating system. *Journal of Counseling Psychology, 43,* 347–355.

Kivlighan, D. M., Jr., & Tarrant, J. M. (2001). Does group climate mediate the group leadership–group member outcome relationship? A test of Yalom's hypotheses about leadership priorities. *Group Dynamics: Theory, Research, and Practice, 5,* 220–234.

Kiyonari, T., & Barclay, P. (2008). Cooperation in social dilemmas: Free riding may be thwarted by second-order reward rather than by punishment. *Journal of Personality and Social Psychology, 95,* 826–842.

Klauer, K. C., Herfordt, J., & Voss, A. (2008). Social presence effects on the Stroop task: Boundary conditions and an alternative account. *Journal of Experimental Social Psychology, 44,* 469–476.

Kleinpenning, G., & Hagendoorn, L. (1993). Forms of racism and the cumulative dimension of ethnic attitudes. *Social Psychology Quarterly, 56,* 21–36.

Klimoski, R., & Mohammed, S. (1994). Team mental model: Construct or metaphor? *Journal of Management, 20,* 403–437.

Klocke, U. (2007). How to improve decision making in small groups: Effects of dissent and training interventions. *Small Group Research, 38,* 437–468.

Knight, G. P., & Dubro, A. F. (1984). Cooperative, competitive, and individualistic social values: An individualized regression and clustering approach. *Journal of Personality and Social Psychology, 46,* 98–105.

Knowles, E. S. (1973). Boundaries around group interaction: The effect of group size and member status on boundary permeability. *Journal of Personality and Social Psychology, 26,* 327–331.

Knowles, E. S., & Bassett, R. L. (1976). Groups and crowds as social entities: The effects of activity, size, and member similarity on nonmembers. *Journal of Personality and Social Psychology, 34,* 837–845.

Knowles, E. S., & Condon, C. A. (1999). Why people say "yes": A dual-process theory of acquiescence. *Journal of Personality and Social Psychology, 77,* 379–386.

Knowles, E. S., Kreuser, B., Haas, S., Hyde, M., & Schuchart, G. E. (1976). Group size and the extension of social space boundaries. *Journal of Personality and Social Psychology, 33,* 647–654.

Köhler, O. (1926). Kraftleistungen bei Einzel- und Gruppenarbeit. *Industrielle Psychotechnik, 3,* 274–282.

Kolb, D. M., & Williams, J. (2003). *Everyday negotiation: Navigating the hidden agendas in bargaining.* San Francisco: Jossey-Bass.

Kollock, P. (1998). Social dilemmas: The anatomy of cooperation. *Annual Review of Sociology, 24,* 183–214.

Komorita, S. S., Hilty, J. A., & Parks, C. D. (1991). Reciprocity and cooperation in social dilemmas. *Journal of Conflict Resolution, 35,* 494–518.

Komorita, S. S., & Parks, C. D. (1994). *Social dilemmas.* Dubuque, IA: Brown & Benchmark.

Komorita, S. S., Parks, C. D., & Hulbert, L. G. (1992). Reciprocity and the induction of cooperation in social dilemmas. *Journal of Personality and Social Psychology, 62,* 607–617.

Kopp, W. (2003). *One day, all children . . . The unlikely triumph of Teach for America and what I learned along the way.* New York: Public Affairs.

Korda, M. (1975). *Power! How to get it, how to use it.* New York: Ballantine.

Kösters, M., Burlingame, G. M., Nachtigall, C., & Strauss, B. (2006). A meta-analytic review of the effectiveness of inpatient group psychotherapy. *Group Dynamics: Theory, Research, and Practice, 10,* 146–163.

Kotter, J. P. (1990). *A force for change: How leadership differs from management.* New York: Free Press.

Kounin, J. S. (1970). *Discipline and group management in classrooms.* New York: Holt, Rinehart & Winston.

Kounin, J. S., & Gump, P. V. (1958). The ripple effect in discipline. *Elementary School Journal, 59,* 158–162.

Kowalski, R. M. (1996). Complaints and complaining: Functions, antecedents, and consequences. *Psychological Bulletin, 119,* 179–196.

Kowert, P. A. (2002). *Groupthink or deadlock: When do leaders learn from their advisors?* Albany, NY: State University of New York Press.

Kozlowski, S. W. J., & Bell, B. S. (2003). Work groups and teams in organizations. In W. C. Borman, D. R. Ilgen, R. J. Klimoski, & I. B. Weiner (Eds.), *Handbook of psychology: Industrial and organizational psychology* (Vol. 12, pp. 333–376). New York: Wiley.

Kozlowski, S. W. J., Gully, S. M., Nason, E. R., & Smith, E. M. (1999). Developing adaptive teams: A theory of compilation and performance across levels and time. In D. R. Ilgen & E. D. Pulakos (Eds.), *The changing nature of work performance: Implications for staffing, personnel actions, and development* (pp. 240–292). San Francisco: Jossey-Bass.

Kozlowski, S. W. J., & Ilgen, D. R. (2006). Enhancing the effectiveness of work groups and teams. *Psychological Science in the Public Interest, 7,* 77–124.

Krackhardt, D. (2003). *KrackPlot: A social network visualization program.* Retrieved August 23, 2004, from Carnegie Mellon University website, http://www.andrew.cmu.edu/user/krack/krackplot/krackindex.html.

Krackhardt, D., & Porter, L. W. (1986). The snowball effect: Turnover embedded in communication networks. *Journal of Applied Psychology, 71,* 50–55.

Krakauer, J. (1997). *Into thin air.* New York: Random House.

Kramer, R. M. (1998). Paranoid cognition in social systems: Thinking and acting in the shadow of doubt. *Personality and Social Psychology Review, 2,* 251–275.

Kramer, R. M. (2004). The "dark side" of social context: The role of intergroup paranoia in intergroup negotiations. In M. J. Gelfand & J. M. Brett (Eds.), *The handbook of negotiation and culture* (pp. 219–237). Stanford, CA: Stanford University Press.

Kramer, R. M. (2006). The great intimidators. *Harvard Business Review, 84,* 88–96.

Kramer, R. M. (2008). Presidential leadership and group folly: Reappraising the role of groupthink in the Bay of Pigs decisions. In C. L. Hoyt, G. R. Goethals, & D. R. Forsyth (Eds.), *Leadership at the crossroads: Leadership and psychology* (Vol. 1, pp. 230–249). Westport, CT: Praeger.

Kraus, L. A., Davis, M. H., Bazzini, D. G., Church, M., & Kirchman, C. M. (1993). Personal and social influences on loneliness: The mediating effect of social provisions. *Social Psychology Quarterly, 56,* 37–53.

Krause, C. A. (1978). *Guyana massacre: The eyewitness account.* New York: Berkley.

Krause, D. E. (2006). Power and influence in the context of organizational innovation: Empirical findings. In C. A. Schriesheim & L. L. Neider (Eds.), *Power and influence in organizations: New empirical and theoretical perspectives* (pp. 21–58). Greenwich, CT: Information Age Publishing.

Krause, D. E., & Kearney, E. (2006). The use of power bases in different contexts: Arguments for a context-specific perspective. In C. A. Schriesheim & L. L. Neider (Eds.), *Power and influence in organizations: New empirical and theoretical perspectives* (pp. 59–86). Greenwich, CT: Information Age Publishing.

Krause, N. (2006). Church-based social support and change in health over time. *Review of Religious Research, 48,* 125–140.

Krause, N., & Wulff, K. M. (2005). Church-based social ties, a sense of belonging in a congregation, and physical health status. *International Journal for the Psychology of Religion, 15,* 73–93.

Krauss, R. M., & Morsella, E. (2000). Communication and conflict. In M. Deutsch & P. T. Coleman (Eds.), *The handbook of conflict resolution: Theory and practice* (pp. 131–143). San Francisco: Jossey-Bass.

Kraut, R. E., Rice, R. E., Cool, C., & Fish, R. S. (1998). Varieties of social influence: The role of utility and norms in the success of a new communication medium. *Organization Science, 9,* 437–453.

Kravitz, D. A., Cohen, J. L., Martin, B., Sweeney, J., McCarty, J., Elliott, E., & Goldstein, P. (1978). Humans would do better without other humans. *Personality and Social Psychology Bulletin, 4,* 559–560.

Kravitz, D. A., & Martin, B. (1986). Ringelmann rediscovered: The original article. *Journal of Personality and Social Psychology, 50,* 936–941.

Kreager, D. (2004). Strangers in the halls: Isolation and delinquency in school networks. *Social Forces, 83,* 351–390.

Kressel, K. (2000). Mediation. In M. Deutsch & P. T. Coleman (Eds.), *The handbook of conflict resolution: Theory and practice* (pp. 522–545). San Francisco: Jossey-Bass.

Kristnamurti, J. (1969). *Freedom from the known.* London: Gollancz.

Kristof-Brown, A., Barrick, M. R., & Stevens, C. K. (2005). When opposites attract: A multi-sample demonstration of complementary person–team fit on extraversion. *Journal of Personality, 73,* 935–958.

Krueger, J. (2000). The projective perception of the social world: A building block of social comparison processes. In J. Suls & L. Wheeler (Eds.), *Handbook of social comparison: Theory and research* (pp. 323–351). New York: Kluwer Academic.

Krueger, J., & Clement, R. W. (1997). Estimates of social consensus by majorities and minorities: The case for social projection. *Personality and Social Psychology Review, 1,* 299–312.

Kruglanski, A. W., Pierro, A., Mannetti, L., & De Grada, E. (2006). Groups as epistemic providers: Need for closure and the unfolding of group-centrism. *Psychological Review, 113,* 84–100.

Kruglanski, A. W., Shah, J. Y., Pierro, A., & Mannetti, L. (2002). When similarity breeds content: Need for closure and the allure of homogeneous and self-resembling groups. *Journal of Personality and Social Psychology, 83,* 648–662.

Kruglanski, A. W., & Webster, D. M. (1991). Group members' reactions to opinion deviates and conformists at varying degrees of proximity to decision deadline and of environmental noise. *Journal of Personality and Social Psychology, 61,* 212–225.

Kuhn, T. S. (1970). *The structure of scientific revolutions* (2nd ed., enlarged). Chicago: University of Chicago Press.

Kulic, K. R., Horne, A. M., & Dagley, J. C. (2004). A comprehensive review of prevention groups for children and adolescents. *Group Dynamics: Theory, Research, and Practice, 8,* 139–151.

Kulik, J. A., & Mahler, H. I. M. (1989). Stress and affiliation in a hospital setting: Preoperative roommate preference. *Personality and Social Psychology Bulletin, 15,* 183–193.

Kulik, J. A., & Mahler, H. I. M. (2000). Social comparison, affliation, and emotional contagion under threat. In J. Suls & L. Wheeler (Eds.), *Handbook of social comparison: Theory and research* (pp. 295–320). New York: Kluwer Academic.

Kulik, J. A., Mahler, H. I. M., & Moore, P. J. (1996). Social comparison and affiliation under threat: Effects on recovery from major surgery. *Journal of Personality and Social Psychology, 71,* 967–979.

Kuntsche, E., Knibbe, R., Gmel, G., & Engels, R. (2005). Why do young people drink? A review of drinking motives. *Clinical Psychology Review, 25,* 841–861.

Kurland, N. B., & Pelled, L. H. (2000). Passing the word: Toward a model of gossip and power in the workplace. *Academy of Management Review, 25,* 428–438.

Kushnir, T. (1984). Social psychological factors associated with the dissolution of dyadic business partnerships. *Journal of Social Psychology, 122,* 181–188.

Kuypers, B. C., Davies, D., & Glaser, K. H. (1986). Developmental arrestations in self-analytic groups. *Small Group Behavior, 17,* 269–302.

Kwan, V. S. Y., Bond, M. H., Boucher, H. C., Maslach, C., & Gan, Y. (2002). The construct of individuation: More complex in collectivist than in individualist cultures. *Personality and Social Psychology Bulletin, 28,* 300–310.

LaBarge, E., Von Dras, D., & Wingbermuehle, C. (1998). An analysis of themes and feelings from a support group for people with Alzheimer's disease. *Psychotherapy: Theory, Research, Practice, Training, 35,* 537–544.

Lacoursiere, R. B. (1980). *The life cycle of groups.* New York: Human Sciences Press.

Ladbury, J. L., & Hinsz, V. B. (2005). *Individual meta-knowledge of group decision processes: Evidence for over-estimation of majority influence.* Presented at the Annual Meeting of the Society of Personality and Social Psychology, New Orleans, LA.

Laing, R. D. (1960). *The divided self.* London: Tavistock.

Lakin, M. (1972). Experiential groups: The uses of interpersonal encounter, psychotherapy groups, and sensitivity training. Morristown, NJ: General Learning Press.

Lal Goel, M. (1980). Conventional political participation. In D. H. Smith, J. Macaulay, & Associates (Eds.), *Participation in social and political activities: A comprehensive analysis of political involvement, expressive leisure time, and helping behavior* (pp. 108–132). San Francisco: Jossey-Bass.

Lalonde, R. N. (1992). The dynamics of group differentiation in the face of defeat. *Personality and Social Psychology Bulletin, 18,* 336–342.

Lam, S. K., & Schaubroeck, J. (2000). Improving group decisions by better pooling information: A comparative advantage of group decision support systems. *Journal of Applied Psychology, 85,* 565–573.

Lambert, A. J., Cronen, S., Chasteen, A. L., & Lickel, B. (1996). Private vs. public expressions of racial prejudice. *Journal of Experimental Social Psychology, 32,* 437–459.

Lambert, A. J., Payne, B. K., Jacoby, L. L., Shaffer, L. M., Chasteen, A. L., & Khan, S. R. (2003). Stereotypes as dominant responses: On the "social facilitation" of prejudice in anticipated public contexts.

*Journal of Personality and Social Psychology, 84,* 277–295.

Lamm, H., & Myers, D. G. (1978). Group-induced polarization of attitudes and behavior. *Advances in Experimental Social Psychology, 11,* 145–195.

Lammers, J., Galinsky, A. D., Gordijn, E. H., & Otten, S. (2008). Illegitimacy moderates the effects of power on approach. *Psychological Science, 19,* 558–564.

Landau, J. (1995). The relationship of race and gender to managers' ratings of promotion potential. *Journal of Organizational Behavior, 16,* 391–401.

Landau, M. J., Johns, M., Greenberg, J., Pyszczynski, T., Martens, A., Goldenberg, J. L., & Solomon, S. (2004). A function of form: Terror management and structuring the social world. *Journal of Personality and Social Psychology, 87,* 190–210.

Langfred, C. W. (1998). Is group cohesiveness a double-edged sword? An investigation of the effects of cohesiveness on performance. *Small Group Research, 29,* 124–143.

Langner, C. A., & Keltner, D. (2008). Social power and emotional experience: Actor and partner effects within dyadic interactions. *Journal of Experimental Social Psychology, 44,* 848–856.

Langs, R. J. (1973). *The technique of psychoanalytic psychotherapy.* New York: J. Aronson.

Lanzetta, J. T., & Roby, T. B. (1960). The relationship between certain group process variables and group problem-solving efficiency. *Journal of Social Psychology, 52,* 135–148.

LaPiere, R. (1938). *Collective behavior.* New York: McGraw-Hill.

Larsen, K. S. (1982). Cultural conditions and conformity: The Asch effect. *Bulletin of the British Psychological Society, 35,* 347.

Larson, J. R., & Christensen, C. (1993). Groups as problem solving units: Toward a new meaning of social cognition. *British Journal of Social Psychology, 32,* 5–30.

Larson, J. R., Christensen, C., Abbott, A. S., & Franz, T. M. (1996). Diagnosing groups: Charting the flow of information in medical decision-making teams. *Journal of Personality and Social Psychology, 71,* 315–330.

Larson, J. R., Foster-Fishman, P. G., & Keys, C. B. (1994). The discussion of shared and unshared information in decision-making groups. *Journal of Personality and Social Psychology, 67,* 446–461.

Latané, B. (1981). The psychology of social impact. *American Psychologist, 36,* 343–356.

Latané, B. (1996). Strength from weakness: The fate of opinion minorities in spatially distributed groups. In E. Witte & J. Davis (Eds.), *Understanding group behavior: Consensual action by small groups* (Vol. 1, pp. 193–219). Mahwah, NJ: Erlbaum.

Latané, B. (1997). Dynamic social impact: The societal consequences of human interaction. In C. McGarty & A. Haslam (Eds.), *The message of social psychology: Perspectives on mind and society* (pp. 200–220). Malden, MA: Blackwell.

Latané, B., & Bourgeois, M. J. (1996). Experimental evidence for dynamic social impact: The emergence of subcultures in electronic groups. *Journal of Communication, 46,* 35–47.

Latané, B., & Bourgeois, M. J. (2001). Dynamic social impact and the consolidation, clustering, correlation, and continuing diversity of culture. In M. A. Hogg & R. S. Tindale (Eds.), *Blackwell handbook of social psychology: Group processes* (pp. 235–258). Malden, MA: Blackwell.

Latané, B., & Darley, J. M. (1970). *The unresponsive bystander: Why doesn't he help?* New York: Appleton-Century-Crofts.

Latané, B., & Nida, S. A. (1981). Ten years of research on group size and helping. *Psychological Bulletin, 89,* 308–324.

Latané, B., Williams, K., & Harkins, S. (1979). Many hands make light the work: The causes and consequences of social loafing. *Journal of Personality and Social Psychology, 37,* 822–832.

Latané, B., & Wolf, S. (1981). The social impact of majorities and minorities. *Psychological Review, 88,* 438–453.

Latham, G. P., & Baldes, J. J. (1975). The "practical significance" of Locke's theory of goal settings. *Journal of Applied Psychology, 60,* 122–124.

Latham, G. P., & Locke, E. A. (2007). New developments in and directions for goal-setting research. *European Psychologist, 12,* 290–300.

LaTour, S. (1978). Determinants of participant and observer satisfaction with adversary and inquisitorial modes of adjudication. *Journal of Personality and Social Psychology, 36,* 1531–1545.

LaTour, S., Houlden, P., Walker, L., & Thibaut, J. (1976). Some determinants of preference for modes of conflict resolution. *Journal of Conflict Resolution, 20,* 319–356.

Lau, D. C., & Murnighan, J. K. (1998). Demographic diversity and faultlines: The compositional dynamics of organizational groups. *Academy of Management Review, 23,* 325–340.

Laughlin, P. R. (1980). Social combination processes of cooperative problem solving groups on verbal intellective tasks. In M. Fishbein (Ed.), *Progress in social psychology* (pp. 127–155). Mahwah, NJ: Erlbaum.

Laughlin, P. R., Bonner, B. L., & Miner, A. G. (2002). Groups perform better than the best individuals on letters-to-numbers problems. *Organizational Behavior and Human Decision Processes, 88,* 605–620.

Laughlin, P. R., & Hollingshead, A. B. (1995). A theory of collective induction. *Organizational Behavior and Human Decision Processes, 61,* 94–107.

Laughlin, P. R., Zander, M. L., Knievel, E. M., & Tan, T. K. (2003). Groups perform better than the best individuals on letters-to-numbers problems: Informative equations and effective strategies. *Journal of Personality and Social Psychology, 85,* 684–694.

Lawler, E. E., & Mohrman, S. A. (1985). Quality circles after the fad. *Harvard Business Review, 85,* 64–71.

Lawler, E. J. (1975). An experimental study of factors affecting the mobilization of revolutionary coalitions. *Sociometry, 38,* 163–179.

Lawler, E. J., Ford, R. S., & Blegen, M. A. (1988). Coercive capability in conflict: A test of bilateral deterrence versus conflict spiral theory. *Social Psychology Quarterly, 51,* 93–107.

Lawler, E. J., & Thompson, M. E. (1978). Impact of a leader's responsibility for inequity on subordinate revolts. *Social Psychology Quarterly, 41,* 264–268.

Lawler, E. J., & Thompson, M. E. (1979). Subordinate response to a leader's cooptation strategy as a function of type of coalition power. *Representative Research in Social Psychology, 9,* 69–80.

Lawler, E. J., & Yoon, J. (1996). Commitment in exchange relations: Test of a theory of relational cohesion. *American Sociological Review, 61,* 89–108.

Lawrence, R. J. (2002). Healthy residential environments. In R. B. Bechtel & A. Churchman (Eds.), *Handbook of environmental psychology* (pp. 394–412). New York: Wiley.

Layne, C. M., Pynoos, R. S., Saltzman, W. R., Arslanagic, B., Black, M., Savjak, N., Popovic, T., Durakovic, E., Mušic, M., Campara, N., Djapo, N., & Houston, R. (2001). Trauma/grief-focused group psychotherapy: School-based postwar intervention with traumatized Bosnian adolescents. *Group Dynamics: Theory, Research, and Practice, 5,* 277–290.

Lazarsfeld, P. F., & Merton, R. K. (1954). Friendship as a social process: A substantive and methodological analysis. In M. Berger, T. Abel, & C. H. Page (Eds.), *Freedom and control in modern society* (pp. 18–66). New York: Van Nostrand.

Lazonder, A. W. (2005). Do two heads search better than one? Effects of student collaboration on web search behavior and search outcomes. *British Journal of Educational Technology, 36,* 465–475.

Le Bon, G. (1960). *The crowd: A study of the popular mind [La psychologie des foules].* New York: Viking Press. (Original work published in 1895)

Leach, C. W., Spears, R., Branscombe, N. R., & Doosje, B. (2003). Malicious pleasure: Schadenfreude at the suffering of another group. *Journal of Personality and Social Psychology, 84,* 932–943.

Leach, C. W., van Zomeren, M., Zebel, S., Vliek, M. L. W., Pennekamp, S. F., Doosje, B., Ouwerkerk, J. W., & Spears, R. (2008). Group-level self-definition and self-investment: A hierarchical (multicomponent) model of in-group identification. *Journal of Personality and Social Psychology, 95,* 144–165.

Leaper, C., & Ayres, M. M. (2007). A meta-analytic review of gender variations in adults' language use: Talkativeness, affiliative speech, and assertive speech. *Personality and Social Psychology Review, 11,* 328–363.

Leary, M. R. (1983). *Understanding social anxiety.* Thousand Oaks, CA: Sage.

Leary, M. R. (1990). Responses to social exclusion: Social anxiety, jealousy, loneliness, depression, and low self-esteem. *Journal of Social & Clinical Psychology, 9,* 221–229.

Leary, M. R. (2001). Shyness and the self: Attentional, motivational, and cognitive self-processes in social anxiety and inhibition. In W. R. Crozier & L. E. Alden (Eds.), *International handbook of social anxiety: Concepts, research and interventions relating to the self and shyness* (pp. 217–234). New York: Wiley.

Leary, M. R. (2007). Motivational and emotional aspects of the self. *Annual Review of Psychology, 58,* 317–344.

Leary, M. R., & Baumeister, R. F. (2000). The nature and function of self-esteem: Sociometer theory. *Advances in Experimental Social Psychology, 32,* 1–62.

Leary, M. R., & Forsyth, D. R. (1987). Attributions of responsibility for collective endeavors. *Review of Personality and Social Psychology, 8,* 167–188.

Leary, M. R., & Kowalski, R. M. (1995). *Social anxiety.* New York: Guilford.

Leary, M. R., Kowalski, R. M., Smith, L., & Phillips, S. (2003). Teasing, rejection, and violence: Case studies of the school shootings. *Aggressive Behavior, 29,* 202–214.

Leary, M. R., Rogers, P. A., Canfield, R. W., & Coe, C. (1986). Boredom in interpersonal encounters: Antecedents and social implications. *Journal of Personality and Social Psychology, 51,* 968–975.

Leary, M. R., Tambor, E. S., Terdal, S. K., & Downs, D. L. (1995). Self-esteem as an interpersonal monitor: The sociometer hypothesis. *Journal of Personality and Social Psychology, 68,* 518–530.

Leary, M. R., Twenge, J. M., & Quinlivan, E. (2006). Interpersonal rejection as a determinant of anger and aggression. *Personality and Social Psychology Review, 10,* 111–132.

Leary, M. R., Wheeler, D. S., & Jenkins, T. B. (1986). Aspects of identity and behavioral preferences: Studies of occupational and recreational choice. *Social Psychology Quarterly, 49,* 11–18.

Leather, P., Beale, D., & Sullivan, L. (2003). Noise, psychosocial stress and their interaction in the workplace. *Journal of Environmental Psychology, 23,* 213–222.

Leavitt, H. J. (1951). Some effects of certain communication patterns on group performance. *Journal of Abnormal and Social Psychology, 46,* 38–50.

Lee, E., & Nass, C. (2002). Experimental tests of normative group influence and representation effects in computer-mediated communication: When interacting via computers differs from interacting with computers. *Human Communication Research, 28,* 349–381.

Lee, M. T., & Ofshe, R. (1981). The impact of behavioral style and status characteristics on social influence: A test of two competing theories. *Social Psychology Quarterly, 44,* 73–82.

Lee, P. W. H., Leung, P. W. L., Fung, A. S. M., & Low, L. C. K. (1996). An episode of syncope attacks in adolescent schoolgirls: Investigations, intervention and outcome. *British Journal of Medical Psychology, 69,* 247–257.

Lee, R. M., Dean, B. L., & Jung, K. (2008). Social connectedness, extraversion, and subjective well-being: Testing a mediation model. *Personality and Individual Differences, 45,* 414–419.

Leffler, A., Gillespie, D. L., & Conaty, J. C. (1982). The effects of status differentiation on nonverbal behavior. *Social Psychology Quarterly, 45,* 153–161.

Leichtentritt, J., & Shechtman, Z. (1998). Therapist, trainee, and child verbal response modes in child group therapy. *Group Dynamics: Theory, Research, and Practice, 2,* 36–47.

Lencioni, P. (2004). *Death by meeting: A leadership fable… about solving the most painful problem in business.* San Francisco: Jossey Bass.

Leon, G. R. (1991). Individual and group process characteristics of polar expedition teams. *Environment and Behavior, 23,* 723–748.

Leonard, W. M., II. (1980). *A sociological perspective on sport.* Minneapolis: Burgess.

LePine, J. A. (2003). Team adaptation and postchange performance: Effects of team composition in terms of members' cognitive ability and personality. *Journal of Applied Psychology, 88,* 27–39.

LePine, J. A., Piccolo, R. F., Jackson, C. L., Mathieu, J. E., & Saul, J. R. (2008). A meta-analysis of teamwork processes: Tests of a multidimensional model and relationships with team effectiveness criteria. *Personnel Psychology, 61,* 273–307.

Lepore, S. J., Evans, G. W., & Schneider, M. L. (1991). Dynamic role of social support in the link between chronic stress and psychological distress. *Journal of Personality and Social Psychology, 61,* 899–909.

Leung, A. S. M. (2008). Matching ethical work climate to in-role and extra-role behaviors in a collectivist work setting. *Journal of Business Ethics, 79,* 43–55.

Leung, K. (1997). Negotiation and reward allocations across cultures. In P. C. Earley & M. Erez (Eds.),

*New perspectives on international industrial/organizational psychology* (pp. 640–675). San Francisco: The New Lexington Press/Jossey-Bass.

Levesque, M. J. (1997). Meta-accuracy among acquainted individuals: A social relations analysis of interpersonal perception and metaperception. *Journal of Personality and Social Psychology, 72,* 66–74.

Levin, H. M. (2006). Worker democracy and worker productivity. *Social Justice Research, 19,* 109–121.

Levine, D. I., & D'Andrea Tyson, L. (1990). Participation, productivity, and the firm's environment. In A. S. Blinder (Ed.), *Paying for productivity* (pp. 183–237). Washington, DC: Brookings Institute.

Levine, J. M. (1980). Reaction to opinion deviance in small groups. In P. B. Paulus (Ed.), *Psychology of group influence* (pp. 375–429). Mahwah, NJ: Erlbaum.

Levine, J. M., & Kerr, N. L. (2007). Inclusion and exclusion: Implications for group processes. In A. W. Kruglanski & E. T. Higgins (Eds.), *Social psychology: Handbook of basic principles* (2nd ed., pp. 759–784). New York: Guilford.

Levine, J. M., & Moreland, R. L. (1995). Group processes. In A. Tesser (Ed.), *Advanced social psychology* (pp. 419–465). New York: McGraw-Hill.

Levine, J. M., Moreland, R. L., & Choi, H. (2001). Group socialization and newcomer innovation. In M. A. Hogg & R. S. Tindale (Eds.), *Blackwell handbook of social psychology: Group processes* (pp. 86–106). Malden, MA: Blackwell.

Levine, J. M., & Russo, E. M. (1987). Majority and minority influence. *Review of Personality and Social Psychology, 8,* 13–54.

Levine, J. M., & Thompson, L. (1996). Conflict in groups. In E. T. Higgins & A. W. Kruglanski (Eds.), *Social psychology: Handbook of basic principles* (pp. 745–776). New York: Guilford.

Levine, S. V. (1984). Radical departures. *Psychology Today, 18(8),* 21–27.

Levy, L. H. (2000). Self-help groups. In J. Rappaport & E. Seidman (Eds.), *Handbook of community psychology* (pp. 591–613). Dordrecht, Netherlands: Kluwer Academic.

Lewicki, R. J., Saunders, D. M., & Barry, B. (2006). *Negotiation* (5th ed.).New York: McGraw-Hill/Irwin.

Lewin, K. (1943). Forces behind food habits and methods of change. *Bulletin of the National Research Council, 108,* 35–65.

Lewin, K. (1948). *Resolving social conflicts: Selected papers on group dynamics.* New York: Harper.

Lewin, K. (1951). *Field theory in social science.* New York: Harper.

Lewin, K., Lippitt, R., & White, R. (1939). Patterns of aggressive behavior in experimentally created "social climates." *Journal of Social Psychology, 10,* 271–299.

Ley, D., & Cybriwsky, R. (1974). Urban graffiti as territorial markers. *Annals of the Association of American Geographers, 64,* 491–505.

Leyens, J., & Corneille, O. (1999). Asch's social psychology: Not as social as you may think. *Personality and Social Psychology Review, 3,* 345–357.

Leyens, J., Cortes, B., Demoulin, S., Dovidio, J. F., Fiske, S. T., Gaunt, R., Paladino, M., Rodriguez-Perez, A., Rodriguez-Torres, R., & Vaes, J. (2003). Emotional prejudice, essentialism, and nationalism: The 2002 Tajfel Lecture. *European Journal of Social Psychology, 33,* 703–717.

Lickel, B., Hamilton, D. L., & Sherman, S. J. (2001). Elements of a lay theory of groups: Types of groups, relationship styles, and the perception of group entitativity. *Personality and Social Psychology Review, 5,* 129–140.

Lickel, B., Hamilton, D. L., Wieczorkowska, G., Lewis, A., Sherman, S. J., & Uhles, A. N. (2000). Varieties of groups and the perception of group entitativity. *Journal of Personality and Social Psychology, 78,* 223–246.

Liden, R. C., Erdogan, B., Wayne, S. J., & Sparrowe, R. T. (2006). Leader–member exchange, differentiation, and task interdependence: implications for individual and group performance. *Journal of Organizational Behavior, 27,* 723–746.

Liden, R. C., Wayne, S. J., Jaworski, R. A., & Bennett, N. (2004). Social loafing: A field investigation. *Journal of Management, 30,* 285–304.

Lieberman, M. A. (1993). Self-help groups. In H. I. Kaplan & M. J. Sadock (Eds.), *Comprehensive group psychotherapy* (3rd ed., pp. 292–304). Baltimore: Williams & Wilkins.

Lieberman, M. A. (1994). Growth groups in the 1980s: Mental health implications. In A. Fuhriman & G. M. Burlingame (Eds.), *Handbook of group psychotherapy* (pp. 527–558). New York: Wiley.

Lieberman, M. A., & Golant, M. (2002). Leader behaviors as perceived by cancer patients in professionally directed support groups and outcomes. *Group Dynamics: Theory, Research, and Practice, 6,* 267–276.

Lieberman, M. A., Yalom, I., & Miles, M. (1973). *Encounter groups: First facts.* New York: Basic Books.

Likert, R. (1967). *The human organization.* New York: McGraw-Hill.

Lindblom, C. E. (1965). *The intelligence of democracy.* New York: Free Press.

Lindeman, M. (1997). Ingroup bias, self-enhancement and group identification. *European Journal of Social Psychology, 27,* 337–355.

Lindskold, S. (1978). Trust development, the GRIT proposal, and the effects of conciliatory acts on conflict and cooperation. *Psychological Bulletin, 85,* 772–793.

Lindskold, S., Albert, K. P., Baer, R., & Moore, W. C. (1976). Territorial boundaries of interacting groups and passive audiences. *Sociometry, 39,* 71–76.

Lindskold, S., & Finch, M. L. (1982). Anonymity and the resolution of conflicting pressures from the experimenter and from peers. *Journal of Psychology, 112,* 79–86.

Linville, P. W., & Fischer, G. W. (1998). Group variability and covariation: Effects on intergroup judgment and behavior. In C. Sedikides, J. Schopler, & C. A. Insko (Eds.), *Intergroup cognition and intergroup behavior* (pp. 123–150). Mahwah, NJ: Erlbaum.

Linzmayer, O. W. (2004). Apple confidential 2.0: The definitive history of the world's most colorful company. New York: No Starch Press.

Lipman-Blumen, J. (2005). *The allure of toxic leaders: Why we follow destructive bosses and corrupt politicians—and how we can survive them.* Oxford: Oxford University Press.

Lippmann, W. (1922). *Public opinion.* New York: Harcourt & Brace.

Lipset, S. M., & Wolin, S. S. (1965). *The Berkeley student revolt.* Garden City, NY: Anchor.

Lischetzke, T., & Eid, M. (2006). Why extraverts are happier than introverts: The role of mood regulation. *Journal of Personality, 74,* 1127–1162.

List, J. A. (2006). Friend or foe? A natural experiment of the prisoner's dilemma. *Review of Economics and Statistics, 88,* 463–471.

Littlepage, G. E. (1991). Effects of group size and task characteristics on group performance: A test of Steiner's model. *Personality and Social Psychology Bulletin, 17,* 449–456.

Littlepage, G. E., Hollingshead, A. B., Drake, L. R., & Littlepage, A. M. (2008). Transactive memory and performance in work groups: Specificity, communication, ability differences, and work allocation. *Group Dynamics: Theory, Research, and Practice, 12,* 223–241.

Littlepage, G. E., & Karau, S. J. (1997). Utility and limitations of the SHAPE-assisted intuitive decision-making procedure. *Group Dynamics: Theory, Research, and Practice, 1,* 200–207.

Littlepage, G. E., & Mueller, A. L. (1997). Recognition and utilization of expertise in problem-solving groups: Expert characteristics and behavior. *Group Dynamics: Theory, Research, and Practice, 1,* 324–328.

Littlepage, G. E., Nixon, C. T., & Gibson, C. R. (1992). Influence strategies used in meetings. *Journal of Social Behavior & Personality, 7,* 529–538.

Littlepage, G. E., Robison, W., & Reddington, K. (1997). Effects of task experience and group experience on group performance, member ability, and recognition of expertise. *Organizational Behavior and Human Decision Processes, 69,* 133–147.

Littlepage, G. E., Schmidt, G. W., Whisler, E. W., & Frost, A. G. (1995). An input-process-output analysis of influence and performance in problem-solving groups. *Journal of Personality and Social Psychology, 69,* 877–889.

Littlepage, G. E., & Silbiger, H. (1992). Recognition of expertise in decision-making groups: Effects of group size and participation patterns. *Small Group Research, 23,* 344–355.

Liu, J. H., & Latané, B. (1998). Extremitization of attitudes: Does thought- and discussion-induced polarization cumulate? *Basic and Applied Social Psychology, 20,* 103–110.

Locke, E. A., Tirnauer, D., Roberson, Q., Goldman, B., Latham, M. E., & Weldon, E. (2001). *The importance of the individual in an age of groupism.* In M. E. Turner (Ed.), *Groups at work: Theory and research* (pp. 501–528). Mahwah, NJ: Erlbaum.

Lockwood, P., & Kunda, Z. (1997). Superstars and me: Predicting the impact of role models on the self. *Journal of Personality and Social Psychology, 73,* 91–103.

Lodewijkx, H. F. M., & Syroit, J. E. M. M. (1997). Severity of initiation revisited: Does severity of initiation increase attractiveness in real groups? *European Journal of Social Psychology, 27,* 275–300.

Lofland, J. (1981). Collective behavior: The elementary forms. In M. Rosenberg & R. H. Turner (Eds.), *Social psychology* (pp. 411–446). New York: Basic Books.

Lois, J. (2003). *Heroic efforts: The emotional culture of search and rescue volunteers.* New York: New York University Press.

Long, C. R., Seburn, M., Averill, J. R., & More, T. A. (2003). Solitude experiences: Varieties, settings, and individual differences. *Personality and Social Psychology Bulletin, 29,* 578–583.

Longley, J., & Pruitt, D. G. (1980). Groupthink: A critique of Janis's theory. In L. Wheeler (Ed.), *Review of personality and social psychology* (Vol. 1). Thousand Oaks, CA: Sage.

Lopes, P. N., & Salovey, P. (2008). Emotional intelligence and leadership: Implications for leader development. In C. L. Hoyt, G. R. Goethals, & D. R. Forsyth (Eds.), *Leadership at the crossroads: Leadership and psychology* (Vol. 1, pp. 78–98). Westport, CT: Praeger.

Lord, R. G. (1977). Functional leadership behavior: Measurement and relation to social power and leadership perceptions. *Administrative Science Quarterly, 22,* 114–133.

Lord, R. G. (1985). An information processing approach to social perceptions, leadership, and behavioral measurement in organizations. *Research in Organizational Behavior, 7,* 87–128.

Lord, R. G., De Vader, C. L., & Alliger, G. M. (1986). A meta-analysis of the relation between personality traits and leadership perceptions: An application of validity generalization procedures. *Journal of Applied Psychology, 71,* 402–410.

Lord, R. G., Foti, R. J., & De Vader, C. L. (1984). A test of leadership categorization theory: Internal structure, information processing, and leadership perceptions. *Organization Behavior and Human Performance, 34,* 343–378.

Lord, R. G., & Maher, K. J. (1991). Leadership and information processing: Linking perceptions and performance. Boston: Unwin Hyman.

Lorge, I., Fox, D., Davitz, J., & Brenner, M. (1958). A survey of studies contrasting quality of group performance and individual performance, 1920–1957. *Psychological Bulletin, 55,* 337–372.

Lott, A. J., & Lott, B. E. (1965). Group cohesiveness as interpersonal attraction: A review of relationships with antecedent and consequent variables. *Psychological Bulletin, 64,* 259–309.

Lovaglia, M. J., & Houser, J. A. (1996). Emotional reactions and status in groups. *American Sociological Review, 61,* 867–883.

Lovell, J., & Kluger, J. (1994). *Lost moon: The perilous journey of Apollo 13.* New York: Houghton Mifflin.

Lowry, P. B., Roberts, T. L., Romano, N. C., Jr., Cheney, P. D., & Hightower, R. T. (2006). The impact of group size and social presence on small-group communication: Does computer-mediated communication make a difference? *Small Group Research, 37,* 631–661.

Lucas, R. E. (2008). Personality and subjective well-being. In M. Eid & R. J. Larsen (Eds.), *The science of subjective well-being* (pp. 171–194). New York: Guilford.

Lucas, R. E., & Diener, E. (2001). Understanding extraverts' enjoyment of social situations: The importance of pleasantness. *Journal of Personality and Social Psychology, 81,* 343–356.

Lucas, R. E., Diener, E., Grob, A., Suh, E. M., & Shao, L. (2000). Cross-cultural evidence for the fundamental features of extraversion. *Journal of Personality and Social Psychology, 79,* 452–468.

Lucas, R. E., & Fujita, F. (2000). Factors influencing the relation between extraversion and pleasant affect. *Journal of Personality and Social Psychology, 79,* 1039–1056.

Luce, R. D., & Raiffa, H. (1957). *Games and decisions.* New York: Wiley.

Lueder, D. C. (1985). Don't be misled by LEAD. *Journal of Applied Behavioral Science, 21,* 143–151.

Luft, J. (1984). *Groups process: An introduction to group dynamics* (3rd ed.). Palo Alto, CA: Mayfield.

Luhtanen, R., & Crocker, J. (1992). A collective self-esteem scale: Self-evaluation of one's social identity. *Personality and Social Psychology Bulletin, 18,* 302–318.

Lukes, S. (1973). *Individualism.* New York: Harper & Row.

Lukes, S. (2005). *Power: A radical view* (2nd ed.).New York: Palgrave.

Luong, A., & Rogelberg, S. G. (2005). Meetings and more meetings: The relationship between meeting load and the daily well-being of employees. *Group Dynamics: Theory, Research, and Practice, 9,* 58–67.

Luria, S. M. (1990). More about psychology and the military. *American Psychologist, 45,* 296–297.

Lutsky, N. (1995). When is "obedience" obedience? Conceptual and historical commentary. *Journal of Social Issues, 51,* 55–65.

Lyman, S. M., & Scott, M. B. (1967). Territoriality: A neglected sociological dimension. *Social Problems, 15,* 236–249.

Maass, A. (1999). Linguistic intergroup bias: Stereotype perpetuation through language. *Advances in Experimental Social Psychology, 31,* 79–121.

Maass, A., West, S. G., & Cialdini, R. B. (1987). Minority influence and conversion. *Review of Personality and Social Psychology, 8,* 55–79.

Maassen, G. H., Akkermans, W., & van der Linden, J. L. (1996). Two-dimensional sociometric status determination with rating scales. *Small Group Research, 27,* 56–78.

Maccoby, E. E. (2002). Gender and group process: A developmental perspective. *Current Directions in Psychological Science, 11,* 54–58.

MacCracken, M. J., & Stadulis, R. E. (1985). Social facilitation of young children's dynamic balance performance. *Journal of Sport Psychology, 7,* 150–165.

MacDonald, G., & Leary, M. R. (2005). Why does social exclusion hurt? The relationship between social and physical pain. *Psychological Bulletin, 131,* 202–223.

MacIver, R. M., & Page, C. H. (1937). *Society: An introductory analysis.* New York: Rinehart and Co.

MacKenzie, K. R. (1994). Group development. In A. Fuhriman & G. M. Burlingame (Eds.), *Handbook of group psychotherapy* (pp. 223–268). New York: Wiley.

MacKenzie, K. R. (1997). Clinical application of group development ideas. *Group Dynamics: Theory, Research, and Practice, 1,* 275–287.

Mackie, D. (1987). Systematic and nonsystematic processing of majority and minority persuasive communications. *Journal of Personality and Social Psychology, 53,* 41–52.

Mackie, D. M., & Queller, S. (2000). The impact of group membership on persuasion: Revisiting "who says what to whom with what effect?" In D. J. Terry & M. A. Hogg (Eds.), *Attitudes, behavior, and social context: The role of norms and group membership* (pp. 135–155). Mahwah, NJ: Erlbaum.

Mackie, M. (1980). The impact of sex stereotypes upon adult self imagery. *Social Psychology Quarterly, 43,* 121–125.

MacKinnon, C. A. (2003). The social origin of sexual harassment. In M. Silberman (Ed.), *Violence and society: A reader* (pp. 251–258). Upper Saddle River, NJ: Prentice Hall.

MacNair-Semands, R. R. (2002). Predicting attendance and expectations for group therapy. *Group Dynamics: Theory, Research, and Practice, 6,* 219–228.

MacNair-Semands, R. R., & Lese, K. P. (2000). Interpersonal problems and the perception of therapeutic factors in group therapy. *Small Group Research, 31,* 158–174.

MacNeil, M. K., & Sherif, M. (1976). Norm change over subject generations as a function of arbitrariness of prescribed norm. *Journal of Personality and Social Psychology, 34,* 762–773.

Macy, B. A., & Izumi, H. (1993). Organizational change, design, and work innovation: A meta-analysis of 131 North American field studies—1961–1991. *Research in Organizational Change and Development, 7,* 235–313.

Mael, F. A., & Ashforth, B. E. (2001). Identification in work, war, sports, and religion: Contrasting the benefits and risks. *Journal for the Theory of Social Behaviour, 31,* 197–222.

Magee, J. C., Galinsky, A. D., & Gruenfeld, D. H. (2007). Power, propensity to negotiate, and moving first in competitive interactions. *Personality and Social Psychology Bulletin, 33,* 200–212.

Mai-Dalton, R. R. (1993). Managing cultural diversity on the individual, group, and organizational levels. In M. M. Chemers & R. Ayman (Eds.), *Leadership theory and research: Perspectives and directions* (pp. 189–215). San Diego: Academic Press.

Maier, N. R. F., & Solem, A. R. (1952). The contribution of a discussion leader to the quality of group thinking: The effective use of minority opinions. *Human Relations, 5,* 277–288.

Maio, G. R., & Haddock, G. (2007). Attitude change. In A. W. Kruglanski & E. T. Higgins (Eds.), *Social psychology: Handbook of basic principles* (2nd ed., pp. 565–586). New York: Guilford.

Major, D. A., Kozlowski, S. W. J., Chao, G. T., & Gardner, P. D. (1995). A longitudinal investigation of newcomer expectations, early socialization outcomes, and the moderating effects of role development factors. *Journal of Applied Psychology, 80,* 418–431.

Maki, J. E., Thorngate, W. B., & McClintock, C. G. (1979). Prediction and perception of social motives. *Journal of Personality and Social Psychology, 37,* 203–220.

Malloy, T. E., & Janowski, C. L. (1992). Perceptions and metaperceptions of leadership: Components, accuracy, and dispositional correlates. *Personality and Social Psychology Bulletin, 18,* 700–708.

Maner, J. K., DeWall, C. N., Baumeister, R. F., & Schaller, M. (2007). Does social exclusion motivate interpersonal reconnection? Resolving the "porcupine problem." *Journal of Personality and Social Psychology, 92,* 42–55.

Maney, K. (2005). Tech titans wish we wouldn't quote them on this baloney. *USA Today*. Retrieved November 27, 2008, from http://www.usatoday.com/tech/columnist/kevinmaney/2005-07-05-famous-quotes_x.htm.

Manis, M., Cornell, S. D., & Moore, J. C. (1974). Transmission of attitude-relevant information through a communication chain. *Journal of Personality and Social Psychology, 30,* 81–94.

Mann, F. C. (1965). Toward an understanding of the leadership role in formal organizations. In R. Dubin, G. C. Homans, F. C. Mann, & D. C. Miller (Eds.), *Leadership and productivity.* San Francisco: Chandler.

Mann, J. H. (1959). A review of the relationships between personality and performance in small groups. *Psychological Bulletin, 56,* 241–270.

Mann, L. (1969). Queue culture. The waiting line as a social system. *American Journal of Sociology, 75,* 340–354.

Mann, L. (1970). The psychology of waiting lines. *American Scientist, 58,* 390–398.

Mann, L. (1981). The baiting crowd in episodes of threatened suicide. *Journal of Personality and Social Psychology, 41,* 703–709.

Mann, L. (1986). Cross-cultural studies of rules for determining majority and minority decision rights. *Australian Journal of Psychology, 38,* 319.

Mann, L. (1988). Cultural influence on group processes. In M. H. Bond (Ed.), *The cross-cultural challenge to social psychology* (pp. 182–195). Thousand Oaks, CA: Sage.

Mannix, E. A. (1993). Organizations as resource dilemmas: The effects of power balance on coalition formation in small groups. *Organizational Behavior and Human Decision Processes, 55,* 1–22.

Mannix, E., & Neale, M. A. (2005). What differences make a difference? The promise and reality of diverse teams in organizations. *Psychological Science in the Public Interest, 6,* 31–55.

Mantell, D. M., & Panzarella, R. (1976). Obedience and responsibility. *British Journal of Social & Clinical Psychology, 15,* 239–245.

Maoz, I., & McCauley, C. (2008). Threat, dehumanization, and support for retaliatory aggressive policies in asymmetric conflict. *Journal of Conflict Resolution, 52,* 93–116.

Marcus, D. K. (1998). Studying group dynamics with the social relations model. *Group Dynamics: Theory, Research, and Practice, 2,* 230–240.

Marcus, D. K., & Wilson, J. R. (1996). Interpersonal perception of social anxiety: A social relations analysis. *Journal of Social & Clinical Psychology, 15,* 471–487.

Markovsky, B., Smith, L. F., & Berger, J. (1984). Do status interventions persist? *American Sociological Review, 49,* 373–382.

Marks, M. E., Mathieu, J. E., & Zaccaro, S. J. (2001). A temporally based framework and taxonomy of team processes. *Academy of Management Review, 26,* 356–376.

Markus, H. (1978). The effect of mere presence on social facilitation: An unobtrusive test. *Journal of Experimental Social Psychology, 14,* 389–397.

Markus, H. R., Kitayma, S., & Heiman, R. J. (1996). Culture and "basic" psychological principles. In E. T. Higgins & A. W. Kruglanski (Eds.), *Social psychology: Handbook of basic principles* (pp. 857–913). New York: Guilford.

Marmarosh, C. L., & Corazzini, J. G. (1997). Putting the group in your pocket: Using collective identity to enhance personal and collective self-esteem. *Group Dynamics: Theory, Research, and Practice, 1,* 65–74.

Marmarosh, C. L., Holtz, A., & Schottenbauer, M. (2005). Group cohesiveness, group-derived collective self-esteem,group-derived hope, and the well-being of group therapy members. *Group Dynamics: Theory, Research, and Practice, 9,* 32–44.

Marsh, C. (2000). A science museum exhibit on Milgram's obedience research: History, description, and visitors' reactions. In T. Blass (Ed.), *Obedience to authority: Current perspectives on the Milgram paradigm* (pp. 145–159). Mahwah, NJ: Erlbaum.

Marsh, P., & Morris, D. (1988). *Tribes.* Layton, UT: Gibbs Smith.

Martens, R., Landers, D. M., & Loy, J. (1972). *Sports cohesiveness questionnaire.* Reston, VA: American Association of Health, Physical Education, and Recreation.

Martin, E. D. (1920). *The behavior of crowds.* New York: Harper.

Martin, R., & Hewstone, M. (2008). Majority versus minority influence, message processing and attitude change: The Source–Context–Elaboration Model. *Advances in Experimental Social Psychology, 40,* 237–326.

Martins, L. L., Gilson, L. L., & Maynard, M. T. (2004). Virtual teams: What do we know and where do we go from here? *Journal of Management, 30,* 805–835.

Marx, K., & Engels, F. (1947). *The German ideology.* New York: International Publishers.

Maslach, C. (1972). Social and personal bases of individuation. *Proceedings of the 80th Annual Convention of the American Psychological Association, 7,* 213–214.

Maslach, C., Santee, R. T., & Wade, C. (1987). Individuation, gender role, and dissent: Personality mediators of situational forces. *Journal of Personality and Social Psychology, 53,* 1088–1093.

Maslach, C., Stapp, J., & Santee, R. T. (1985). Individuation: Conceptual analysis and assessment. *Journal of Personality and Social Psychology, 49,* 729–738.

Maslow, A. H. (1968). *Toward a psychology of being.* New York: Van Nostrand Reinhold.

Maslow, A. H. (1970). *Motivation and personality.* New York: Harper & Row.

Mason, C. M., & Griffin, M. A. (2002). Group task satisfaction: Applying the construct of job satisfaction to groups. *Small Group Research, 33,* 271–312.

Mathes, E. W., & Guest, T. A. (1976). Anonymity and group antisocial behavior. *Journal of Social Psychology. 100,* 257–262.

Mathes, E. W., & Kahn, A. (1975). Diffusion of responsibility and extreme behavior. *Journal of Personality and Social Psychology, 5,* 881–886.

Mathews, E., Canon, L. K., & Alexander, K. R. (1974). The influence of level of empathy and ambient noise on body buffer zone. *Personality and Social Psychology Bulletin, 1,* 367–369.

Mathieu, J., Maynard, M. T., Rapp, T., & Gilson, L. (2008). Team effectiveness 1997–2007: A review of recent advancements and a glimpse into the future. *Journal of Management, 34,* 410–476.

Matthews, M. D., Eid, J., Kelly, D., Bailey, J. K. S., & Peterson, C. (2006). Character strengths and virtues of developing military leaders: An international comparison. *Military Psychology, 18*(Suppl.), 257–268.

Matz, D. C., & Wood, W. (2005). Cognitive dissonance in groups: The consequences of disagreement. *Journal of Personality and Social Psychology, 88,* 22–37.

Matz, D. C., Hofstedt, P. M., & Wood, W. (2008). Extraversion as a moderator of the cognitive dissonance associated with disagreement. *Personality and Individual Differences, 45,* 401–405.

Mausner, B. (1954). The effect of one partner's success in a relevant task on the interaction of observer pairs. *Journal of Abnormal and Social Psychology, 49,* 557–560.

Mayer, J. D., Salovey, P., & Caruso, D. R. (2008). Emotional intelligence: New ability or eclectic traits? *American Psychologist, 63,* 503–517.

Mayo, E. (1945). *The social problems of an industrial civilization.* Boston, MA: Harvard University Press.

Mazur, A. (2005). *Biosociology of dominance and deference.* Lanham: Rowman & Littlefield.

McAdams, D. P. (1982). Experiences of intimacy and power: Relationships between social motives and autobiographical memory. *Journal of Personality and Social Psychology, 42,* 292–301.

McAdams, D. P. (1995). What do we know when we know a person? *Journal of Personality, 63,* 365–396.

McAdams, D. P., & Constantian, C. A. (1983). Intimacy and affiliation motives in daily living: An experience sampling analysis. *Journal of Personality and Social Psychology, 45,* 851–861.

McAdams, D. P., Healy, S., & Krause, S. (1984). Social motives and patterns of friendship. *Journal of Personality and Social Psychology, 47,* 828–838.

McBurney, D. H., Levine, J. M., & Cavanaugh, P. H. (1977). Psychophysical and social ratings of human body odor. *Personality and Social Psychology Bulletin, 3,* 135–138.

McCammon, S. L., & Long, T. E. (1993). A post-tornado support group: Survivors and professionals in concert. *Journal of Social Behavior and Personality, 8,* 131–148.

McClelland, D. C. (1975). *Power: The inner experience.* New York: Irvington.

McClelland, D. C. (1985). How motives, skills, and values determine what people do. *American Psychologist, 40,* 812–825.

McClelland, D. C., & Boyatzis, R. E. (1982). Leadership motive pattern and long-term success in management. *Journal of Applied Psychology, 67,* 737–743.

McClintock, C. G., Stech, F. J., & Keil, L. J. (1983). The influence of communication on bargaining. In P. B. Paulus (Ed.), *Basic group processes* (pp. 205–233). New York: Springer-Verlag.

McCoy, J. M. (2002). Work environments. In R. B. Bechtel & A. Churchman (Eds.), *Handbook of environmental psychology* (pp. 443–460). New York: Wiley.

McCrae, R. R. (1996). Social consequences of experiential openness. *Psychological Bulletin, 120,* 323–337.

McCrae, R. R., & Costa, P. T., Jr. (1986). A five-factor theory of personality. In L. A. Pervin & O. P. John (Eds.), *Handbook of personality: Theory and research* (2nd ed.). New York: Guilford.

McDougall, W. (1908). *An introduction to social psychology.* London: Methuen.

McGillicuddy, N. B., Pruitt, D. G., & Syna, H. (1984). Perceptions of firmness and strength in negotiation. *Personality and Social Psychology Bulletin, 10,* 402–409.

McGrath, J. E. (1984). *Groups: Interaction and performance.* Upper Saddle River, NJ: Prentice Hall.

McGrath, J. E., & Altermatt, T. W. (2001). Observation and analysis of group interaction over time: Some methodological and strategic choices. In M. A. Hogg & R. S. Tindale (Eds.), *Blackwell handbook of social psychology: Group processes* (pp. 525–556). Malden, MA: Blackwell.

McGraw, K. M., & Bloomfield, J. (1987). Social influence on group moral decisions: The interactive effects of moral reasoning and sex role orientation. *Journal of Personality and Social Psychology, 53,* 1080–1087.

McGregor, D. (1960). *The human side of enterprise.* New York: McGraw-Hill.

McGregor, I., Nail, P. R., Marigold, D. C., & Kang, S. (2005). Defensive pride and consensus: Strength in imaginary numbers. *Journal of Personality and Social Psychology, 89,* 978–996.

McGrew, J. F., Bilotta, J. G., & Deeney, J. M. (1999). Software team formation and decay: Extending the standard model for small groups. *Small Group Research, 30,* 209–234.

McGuire, G. M. (2007). Intimate work: A typology of the social support that workers provide to their network members. *Work and Occupations, 34,* 125–147.

McGuire, J. P., & Leak, G. K. (1980). Prediction of self-disclosure from objective personality assessment techniques. *Journal of Clinical Psychology, 36,* 201–204.

McGuire, W. J., & McGuire, C. V. (1988). Content and process in the experience of self. *Advances in Experimental Social Psychology, 21,* 97–144.

McKenna, K. Y. A. (2008). Influences on the nature and functioning of online groups. In A. Barak (Ed.), *Psychological aspects of cyberspace: Theory, research, applications* (pp. 228–242). New York: Cambridge University Press.

McKenna, K. Y. A., & Green, A. S. (2002). Virtual group dynamics. *Group Dynamics: Theory, Research, and Practice, 6,* 116–127.

McKenna, K. Y. A., & Seidman, G. (2005). You, me and we: Self, identity and interpersonal processes in electronic groups. In Y. A. Hamburger (Ed.), *The social net: The social psychology of the Internet* (pp. 191–217). Oxford: Oxford Press.

McLeod, P. L., Lobel, S. A., & Cox, T. H. (1996). Ethnic diversity and creativity in small groups. *Small Group Research, 27,* 248–264.

McMorris, L. E., Gottlieb, N. H., & Sneden, G. G. (2005). Developmental stages in public health partnerships: A practical perspective. *Health Promotion Practice, 6,* 219–226.

McNally, R. J., Bryant, R. A., & Ehlers, A. (2003). Does early psychological intervention promote recovery from posttraumatic stress? *Psychological Science in the Public Interest, 4,* 45–79.

McNeill, W. H. (1995). *Keeping together in time: Dance and drill in human history.* Boston: Harvard University Press.

McNiel, J. M., & Fleeson, W. (2006). The causal effects of extraversion on positive affect and neuroticism on negative affect: Manipulating state extraversion and state neuroticism in an experimental approach. *Journal of Research in Personality, 40,* 529–550.

McPhail, C. (1991). *The myth of the madding crowd.* Hawthorne, NY: Aldine de Gruyter.

McPhail, C. (2006). The crowd and collective behavior: Bringing symbolic interaction back in. *Symbolic Interaction, 29,* 433–464.

McPherson, M., & Smith-Lovin, L. (2002). Cohesion and membership duration: Linking groups, relations and individuals in an ecology of affiliation. In S. R. Thye & E. J. Lawler (Eds.), *Group cohesion, trust and solidarity* (pp. 1–36). New York: Elsevier Science/JAI Press.

McPherson, M., Smith-Lovin, L., & Cook, J. M. (2001). Birds of a feather: Homophily in social networks. *Annual Review of Sociology, 27,* 415–444.

McRoberts, C., Burlingame, G. M., & Hoag, M. J. (1998). Comparative efficacy of individual and group psychotherapy: A meta-analytic perspective. *Group Dynamics: Theory, Research, and Practice, 2,* 101–117.

Mead, M. (1935). *Sex and temperament.* Oxford: Morrow.

Medalia, N. Z., & Larsen, O. N. (1958). Diffusion and belief in a collective delusion: The Seattle windshield pitting epidemic. *American Sociological Review, 23,* 180–186.

Meerloo, J. A. (1950). *Patterns of panic.* New York: International Universities Press.

Meeus, W. H. J., & Raaijmakers, Q. A. W. (1995). Obedience in modern society: The Utrecht studies. *Journal of Social Issues, 51,* 155–175.

Megargee, E. I. (1969). Influence of sex roles on the manifestation of leadership. *Journal of Applied Psychology, 53,* 377–382.

Mehrabian, A., & Diamond, S. G. (1971). Effects of furniture arrangement, props, and personality on social interaction. *Journal of Personality and Social Psychology, 20,* 18–30.

Meier, B. P., & Hinsz, V. B. (2004). A comparison of human aggression committed by groups and individuals: An interindividual–intergroup discontinuity. *Journal of Experimental Social Psychology, 40,* 551–559.

Meier, B. P., Hinsz, V. B., & Heimerdinger, S. R. (2008). A framework for explaining aggression involving groups. *Social and Personality Psychology Compass, 2,* 298–312.

Meindl, J. R., Ehrlich, S. B., & Dukerich, J. M. (1985). The romance of leadership and the evaluation of organizational performance. *Academy of Management Journal, 30,* 90–109.

Meindl, J. R., Pastor, J. C., & Mayo, M. (2004). The romance of leadership. In G. R. Goethals, G. J. Sorenson, & J. M. Burns (Eds.), *The encyclopedia of leadership* (pp. 1347–1351). Thousand Oaks, CA: Sage.

Melamed, B. G., & Wills, T. A. (2000). Comment on Turner (2000). *Group Dynamics: Theory, Research, and Practice, 4,* 150–156.

Melucci, A. (1989). *Nomads of the present: Social movements and individual needs in contemporary society* (J. Keanne & P. Mier, Eds.). Philadelphia: Temple University Press.

Merritt, A. C., & Helmreich, R. L. (1996). Human factors on the flight deck: The influence of national culture. *Journal of Cross-Cultural Psychology, 27,* 5–24.

Merton, R. K. (1976). *Sociological ambivalence and other essays.* New York: Free Press.

Messick, D. M. (1999). Dirty secrets: Strategic uses of ignorance and uncertainty. In L. L. Thompson,

J. M. Levine, & D. M. Messick (Eds.), *Shared cognition in organizations: The management of knowledge* (pp. 71–87). Mahwah, NJ: Erlbaum.

Messick, D. M. (2005). On the psychological exchange between leaders and followers. In D. M. Messick & R. M. Kramer (Eds.), *The psychology of leadership: New perspectives and research* (pp. 81–96). Mahwah, NJ: Erlbaum.

Messick, D. M., & Brewer, M. B. (1983). Solving social dilemmas: A review. In L. Wheeler & P. Shaver (Eds.), *Review of Personality and Social Psychology* (Vol. 4, pp. 11–44). Thousand Oaks, CA: Sage.

Meudell, P. R., Hitch, G. J., & Kirby, P. (1992). Are two heads better than one? Experimental investigations of the social facilitation of memory. *Applied Cognitive Psychology, 6,* 525–543.

Meumann, E. (1904). Haus- und Schularbeit: Experimente an Kindern der Volkschule. *Die Deutsche Schule, 8,* 278–303, 337–359, 416–431.

Michaels, J. W., Blommel, J. M., Brocato, R. M., Linkous, R. A., & Rowe, J. S. (1982). Social facilitation and inhibition in a natural setting. *Replications in Social Psychology, 2,* 21–24.

Michaelsen, L. K., Watson, W. E., & Black, R. H. (1989). A realistic test of individual versus group consensus decision making. *Journal of Applied Psychology, 74,* 834–839.

Michels, R. (1959). *Political parties: A sociological study of the oligarchical tendencies of modern democracy.* New York: Dover. (Original work published in 1915)

Michener, H. A., & Burt, M. R. (1975). Use of social influence under varying conditions of legitimacy. *Journal of Personality and Social Psychology, 32,* 398–407.

Michener, H. A., & Lawler, E. J. (1975). The endorsement of formal leaders: An integrative model. *Journal of Personality and Social Psychology, 31,* 216–223.

Middlemist, R. D., Knowles, E. S., & Matter, C. F. (1976). Personal space invasions in the lavatory: Suggestive evidence for arousal. *Journal of Personality and Social Psychology, 33,* 541–546.

Mikolic, J. M., Parker, J. C., & Pruitt, D. G. (1997). Escalation in response to persistent annoyance: Groups versus individuals and gender effects. *Journal of Personality and Social Psychology, 72,* 151–163.

Milanovich, D. M., Driskell, J. E., Stout, R. J., & Salas, E. (1998). Status and cockpit dynamics: A review and empirical study. *Group Dynamics: Theory, Research, and Practice, 2,* 155–167.

Milgram, S. (1963). Behavioral study of obedience. *Journal of Abnormal and Social Psychology, 67,* 371–378.

Milgram, S. (1974). *Obedience to authority.* New York: Harper & Row.

Milgram, S. (1992). *The individual in a social world: Essays and experiments* (2nd ed.). New York: McGraw-Hill.

Milgram, S., Bickman, L., & Berkowitz, L. (1969). Note on the drawing power of crowds of different size. *Journal of Personality and Social Psychology, 13,* 79–82.

Milgram, S., Liberty, H. J., Toledo, R., & Wackenhut, J. (1986). Response to intrusion into waiting lines. *Journal of Personality and Social Psychology, 51,* 683–689.

Milgram, S., & Toch, H. (1969). Collective behavior: Crowds and social movements. In G. Lindzey & E. Aronson (Eds.), *The handbook of social psychology* (Vol. 4, 2nd ed., pp. 507–610). Reading, MA: Addison-Wesley.

Miller, A. G. (2004). What can the Milgram obedience experiments tell us about the Holocaust? Generalizing from the social psychology laboratory. In A. G. Miller (Ed.), *The social psychology of good and evil* (pp. 193–239). New York: Guilford.

Miller, D. T. (2001). Disrespect and the experience of injustice. *Annual Review of Psychology, 52,* 527–553.

Miller, D. T., & Holmes, J. G. (1975). The role of situational restrictiveness on self-fulfilling prophecies: A theoretical and empirical extension of Kelley and Stahelski's triangle hypothesis. *Journal of Personality and Social Psychology, 31,* 661–673.

Miller, D. T., & McFarland, C. (1991). When social comparison goes awry: The case of pluralistic ignorance. In J. Suls and T. A. Wills (Eds.), *Social comparison: Contemporary theory and research* (pp. 287–313). Mahwah, NJ: Erlbaum.

Miller, D. T., & Prentice, D. A. (1996). The construction of social norms and standards. In E. T. Higgins & A. W. Kruglanski (Eds.), *Social psychology: Handbook of basic principles* (pp. 799–829). New York: Guilford.

Miller, G. A., Galanter, E., & Pribram, K. H. (1960). *Plans and the structure of behavior.* New York: Holt.

Miller, J. G. (2002). Bringing culture to basic psychological theory—Beyond individualism and collectivism: Comment on Oyserman et al. (2002). *Psychological Bulletin, 128,* 97–109.

Miller, J. K., & Gergen, K. J. (1998). Life on the line: The therapeutic potentials of computer-mediated conversation. *Journal of Marital and Family Therapy, 24,* 189–202.

Miller, J. L., Schmidt, L. A., Vaillancourt, T., McDougall, P., & Laliberte, M. (2006). Neuroticism and introversion: A risky combination for disordered eating among a non-clinical sample of undergraduate women. *Eating Behaviors, 7,* 69–78.

Miller, K. I., & Monge, P. R. (1986). Participation, satisfaction, and productivity: A meta-analytic review. *Academy of Management Journal, 29,* 727–753.

Miller, N., & Davidson-Podgorny, G. (1987). Theoretical models of intergroup relations and the use of cooperative teams as an intervention for desegregated settings. In C. Hendrick (Ed.), *Review of Personality and Social Psychology: Group Process* (Vol. 9, pp. 41–67). Thousand Oaks, CA: Sage.

Miller, R. S., Perlman, D., & Brehm, S. S. (2007). *Intimate relationships* (4th ed.). Boston: McGraw-Hill.

Mills, J., Clark, M. S., Ford, T. E., & Johnson, M. (2004). Measurement of communal strength. *Personal Relationships, 11,* 213–230.

Mills, T. M. (1979). Changing paradigms for studying human groups. *Journal of Applied Behavioral Science, 15,* 407–423.

Minami, H., & Tanaka, K. (1995). Social and environmental psychology: Transaction between physical space and group-dynamic processes. *Environment and Behavior, 27,* 43–55.

Miner, J. B. (1978). Twenty years of research on role-motivation theory of managerial effectiveness. *Personnel Psychology, 31,* 739–760.

Mintz, A. (1951). Non-adaptive group behavior. *Journal of Abnormal and Social Psychology, 46,* 150–159.

Mintzberg, H. (1973). *The nature of managerial work.* New York: Harper & Row.

Mischel, W., & DeSmet, A. L. (2000). Self-regulation in the service of conflict resolution. In M. Deutsch & P. T. Coleman (Eds.), *The handbook of conflict resolution: Theory and practice* (pp. 256–275). San Francisco: Jossey-Bass.

Misumi, J. (1995). The development in Japan of the performance–maintenance (PM) theory of leadership. *Journal of Social Issues, 51,* 213–228.

Mitchell, J. T., & Everly, G. S., Jr., (2006). Critical incident stress management in terrorist events and disasters. In L. A. Schein, H. I. Spitz, G. M. Burlingame, & P. R. Muskin (Eds.), with S. Vargo, *Psychological effects of catastrophic disasters: Group approaches to treatment* (pp. 425–480). New York: Haworth Press.

Mitchell, R. C., & Mitchell, R. R. (1984). Constructive management of conflict in groups. *Journal for Specialists in Group Work, 9,* 137–144.

Mixon, D. (1977). Why pretend to deceive? *Personality and Social Psychology Bulletin, 3,* 647–653.

Mobley, W. H., Griffeth, R. W., Hand, H. H., & Meglino, B. M. (1979). Review and conceptual analysis of employee turnover process. *Psychological Bulletin, 86,* 493–522.

Modigliani, A., & Rochat, F. (1995). The role of interaction sequences and the timing of resistance in shaping obedience and defiance to authority. *Journal of Social Issues, 51,* 107–123.

Moehrle, M. G. (2005). What is TRIZ? From conceptual basics to a framework for research. *Creativity and Innovation Management, 14,* 3–13.

Moemeka, A. A. (1998). Communalism as a fundamental dimension of culture. *Journal of Communication, 48,* 118–141.

Molm, L. D. (1986). Gender, power, and legitimation: A test of three theories. *American Journal of Sociology, 91,* 1156–1186.

Molm, L. D. (1994). Is punishment effective? Coercive strategies in social exchange. *Social Psychology Quarterly, 57,* 75–94.

Molm, L. D. (1997). Risk and power use: Constraints on the use of coercion in exchange. *American Sociological Review, 62,* 113–133.

Montoya, R. M., & Insko, C. A. (2008). Toward a more complete understanding of the reciprocity of liking effect. *European Journal of Social Psychology, 38,* 477–498.

Moore, J. (1991). *Going down in the barrio: Homeboys and homegirls in change.* Philadelphia: Temple University Press.

Moos, R. H., Insel, P. M., & Humphrey, B. (1974). *Preliminary manual for Family Environment Scale, Work Environment Scale, and Group Environment Scale.* Palo Alto, CA: Consulting Psychologists Press.

Moreland, R. L. (1985). Social categorization and the assimilation of "new" group members. *Journal of Personality and Social Psychology, 48,* 1173–1190.

Moreland, R. L. (1987). The formation of small groups. *Review of Personality and Social Psychology, 8,* 80–110.

Moreland, R. L., Argote, L., & Krishnan, R. (1996). Socially shared cognition at work: Transactive memory and group performance. In J. L. Nye & A. M. Brower (Eds.), *What's social about social cognition? Research on socially shared cognitions in small groups* (pp. 57–84). Thousand Oaks, CA: Sage.

Moreland, R. L., & Levine, J. M. (1982). Socialization in small groups: Temporal changes in individual–group relations. *Advances in Experimental Social Psychology, 15,* 137–192.

Moreland, R. L., & Levine, J. M. (2002). Socialization and trust in work groups. *Group Processes & Intergroup Relations, 5,* 185–201.

Moreland, R. L., Levine, J. M, & Cini, M. A. (1993). Group socialization: The role of commitment. In M. Hogg & D. Abrams (Eds.), *Group motivation: Social psychological perspectives* (pp. 105–129). London: Harvester Wheatsheaf.

Moreland, R. L., Levine, J. M., & Wingert, M. L. (1996). Creating the ideal group: Composition effects at work. In E. H. Witte & J. H. Davis (Eds.), *Understanding group behavior: Small group processes and interpersonal relations* (Vol. 2, pp. 11–35). Mahwah, NJ: Erlbaum.

Moreno, J. L. (1934). *Who shall survive? A new approach to the problem of human interrelations.* Washington, DC: Nervous and Mental Disease Publishing Co.

Moreno, J. L. (1953). How Kurt Lewin's "research center for group dynamics" started. *Sociometry, 16,* 101–104.

Morgan, R. D., & Flora, D. B. (2002). Group psychotherapy with incarcerated offenders: A research synthesis. *Group Dynamics: Theory, Research, and Practice, 6,* 203–218.

Morgeson, F. P., Reider, M. H., & Campion, M. A. (2005). Selecting individuals in team settings: The importance of social skills, personality characteristics, and teamwork knowledge. *Personnel Psychology, 58,* 583–611.

Morran, K. D., Stockton, R., Cline, R. J., & Teed, C. (1998). Facilitating feedback exchange in groups: Leader interventions. *Journal for Specialists in Group Work, 23,* 257–268.

Morrill, C. (1995). *The executive way.* Chicago: University of Chicago Press.

Morris, W. N., Worchel, S., Bois, J. L., Pearson, J. A., Rountree, C. A., Samaha, G. M., Wachtler, J., & Wright, S. L. (1976). Collective coping with stress: Group reactions to fear, anxiety, and ambiguity. *Journal of Personality and Social Psychology, 33,* 674–679.

Moscovici, S. (1976). *Social influence and social change.* New York: Academic Press.

Moscovici, S. (1980). Toward a theory of conversion behavior. *Advances in Experimental Social Psychology, 13,* 209–239.

Moscovici, S. (1985). Social influence and conformity. In G. Lindzey & E. Aronson (Eds.), *Handbook of social psychology* (Vol. 2, pp. 397–412). New York: Random House.

Moscovici, S. (1994). Three concepts: Minority, conflict, and behavioral styles. In S. Moscovici, A. Mucchi-Faina, & A. Maass (Eds.), *Minority influence* (pp. 233–251). Chicago: Nelson-Hall.

Moscovici, S., Lage, E., & Naffrechoux, M. (1969). Influence of a consistent minority on the responses of a majority in a color perception task. *Sociometry, 12,* 365–380.

Moscovici, S., & Personnaz, B. (1980). Studies in social influence: V. Minority influence and conversion behavior in a perceptual task. *Journal of Experimental Social Psychology, 16,* 270–282.

Moscovici, S., & Zavalloni, M. (1969). The group as a polarizer of attitudes. *Journal of Personality and Social Psychology, 12,* 125–135.

Moser, G., & Uzzell, D. L. (2003). Environmental psychology. In T. Millon, M. J. Lerner, & I. B. Weiner (Eds.), *Handbook of psychology: Personality and social psychology* (Vol. 5, pp. 419–445). New York: Wiley.

Moskowitz, G. B., & Chaiken, S. (2001). Mediators of minority social influence: Cognitive processing mechanisms revealed through a persuasion paradigm. In C. K. W. De Dreu & N. K. De Vries

(Eds.), *Group consensus and minority influence: Implications for innovation* (pp. 60–90). Malden, MA: Blackwell.

Mowat, F. (1977). *Ordeal by ice: The search for the Northwest Passage*. Toronto: McClelland & Steward.

Mowday, R. T., & Sutton, R. I. (1993). Organizational behavior: Linking individuals and groups to organizational contexts. *Annual Review of Psychology, 44,* 195–229.

Moxnes, P. (1999). Understanding roles: A psychodynamic model for role differentiation in groups. *Group Dynamics: Theory, Research, and Practice, 3,* 99–113.

Mudrack, P. E. (1989). Defining group cohesiveness: A legacy of confusion? *Small Group Behavior, 20,* 37–49.

Mudrack, P. E., & Farrell, G. M. (1995). An examination of functional role behavior and its consequences for individuals in group settings. *Small Group Behavior, 26,* 542–571.

Mullen, B. (1986). Atrocity as a function of lynch mob composition: A self-attention perspective. *Personality and Social Psychology Bulletin, 12,* 187–197.

Mullen, B. (1987). Self-attention theory: The effects of group composition on the individual. In B. Mullen & G. R. Goethals (Eds.), *Theories of group behavior* (pp. 125–146). New York: Springer-Verlag.

Mullen, B., Anthony, T., Salas, E., & Driskell, J. E. (1994). Group cohesiveness and quality of decision making: An integration of tests of the groupthink hypothesis. *Small Group Research, 25,* 189–204.

Mullen, B., & Baumeister, R. F. (1987). Group effects on self-attention and performance: Social loafing, social facilitation, and social impairment. *Review of Personality and Social Psychology, 9,* 189–206.

Mullen, B., & Copper, C. (1994). The relation between group cohesiveness and performance: An integration. *Psychological Bulletin, 115,* 210–227.

Mullen, B., Johnson, C., & Salas, E. (1991). Productivity loss in brainstorming groups: A meta-analytic review. *Basic and Applied Social Psychology, 12,* 3–23.

Mullen, B., Rozell, D., & Johnson, C. (1996). The phenomenology of being in a group: Complexity approaches to operationalizing cognitive representation. In J. L. Nye & A. M. Brower (Eds.), *What's social about social cognition?* (pp. 205–229). Thousand Oaks, CA: Sage.

Muller, D., & Butera, F. (2007). The focusing effect of self-evaluation threat in coaction and social comparison. *Journal of Personality and Social Psychology, 93,* 194–211.

Murnighan, J. K. (1986). Organizational coalitions: Structural contingencies and the formation process. *Research on Negotiation in Organizations, 1,* 155–174.

Murnighan, J. K., & Conlon, D. E. (1991). The dynamics of intense work groups: A study of British string quartets. *Administrative Science Quarterly, 36,* 165–186.

Murphy, M. (2006). *Sick building syndrome and the problem of uncertainty*. Durham, NC: Duke University Press.

Murphy, S. A., & Keating, J. P. (1995). Psychological assessment of postdisaster class action and personal injury litigants: A case study. *Journal of Traumatic Stress, 8,* 473–482.

Murphy-Berman, V., & Berman, J. (1978). Importance of choice and sex invasions of personal space. *Personality and Social Psychology Bulletin, 4,* 424–428.

Myers, A. E. (1962). Team competition, success, and the adjustment of group members. *Journal of Abnormal and Social Psychology, 65,* 325–332.

Myers, D. G. (1978). The polarizing effects of social comparison. *Journal of Experimental Social Psychology, 14,* 554–563.

Myers, D. G. (1982). Polarizing effects of social interaction. In H. Brandstätter, J. H. Davis, & G. Stocker-Kreichgauer (Eds.), *Group decision making* (pp. 125–161). New York: Academic Press.

Myers, D. G. (2002). *Social psychology*. New York: McGraw-Hill.

Myers, D. G., & Bishop, G. D. (1970). Discussion effects on racial attitudes. *Science, 169,* 778–789.

Myers, D. G., & Lamm, H. (1976). The group polarization phenomenon. *Psychological Bulletin, 83,* 602–627.

Myers, D. J. (1997). Racial rioting in the 1960s: An event history analysis of local conditions. *American Sociological Review, 62,* 94–112.

Nagasundaram, M., & Dennis, A. R. (1993). When a group is not a group: The cognitive foundation of group idea generation. *Small Group Research, 24,* 463–489.

Nail, P. R., MacDonald, G., & Levy, D. A. (2000). Proposal of a four-dimensional model of social response. *Psychological Bulletin, 126,* 454–470.

National Transportation Safety Board. (1994). *A review of flightcrew-involved, major accidents of U.S. air carriers, 1978 through 1990* (Safety Study NTSB/SS-94/01). Washington, DC: NTSB.

Nemeth, C. J. (1986). Differential contributions of majority and minority influence. *Psychological Review, 93,* 23–32.

Nemeth, C. J., Endicott, J., & Wachtler, J. (1976). From the '50s to the '70s: Women in jury deliberations. *Sociometry, 39,* 293–304.

Nemeth, C., J.,Mayseless, O., Sherman, J., & Brown, Y. (1990). Exposure to dissent and recall of information. *Journal of Personality and Social Psychology, 58,* 429–437.

Nemeth, C. J., & Wachtler, J. (1974). Creating the perceptions of consistency and confidence: A necessary condition for minority influence. *Sociometry, 37,* 529–540.

Newcomb, T. M. (1943). *Personality and social change.* New York: Dryden.

Newcomb, T. M. (1960). Varieties of interpersonal attraction. In D. Cartwright & A. Zander (Eds.), *Group dynamics: Research and theory* (2nd ed., pp. 104–119). Evanston, IL: Row, Peterson.

Newcomb, T. M. (1961). *The acquaintance process.* New York: Holt, Rinehart & Winston.

Newcomb, T. M. (1963). Stabilities underlying changes in interpersonal attraction. *Journal of Abnormal and Social Psychology, 66,* 376–386.

Newcomb, T. M. (1979). Reciprocity of interpersonal attraction: A nonconfirmation of a plausible hypothesis. *Social Psychology Quarterly, 42,* 299–306.

Newcomb, T. M. (1981). Heiderian balance as a group phenomenon. *Journal of Personality and Social Psychology, 40,* 862–867.

Newcomb, T. M., Koenig, K., Flacks, R., & Warwick, D. (1967). *Persistence and change: Bennington College and its students after 25 years.* New York: Wiley.

Newman, K. S., Fox, C., Harding, D. J., Mehta, J., & Roth, W. (2004). *Rampage: The social roots of school shootings.* Basic Books: New York.

Newman, O. (1972). *Defensible space.* New York: Macmillan.

Newsom, J. T., Mahan, T. L., Rook, K. S., & Krause, N. (2008). Stable negative social exchanges and health. *Health Psychology, 27,* 78–86.

Newton, J. W., & Mann, L. (1980). Crowd size as a factor in the persuasion process: A study of religious crusade meetings. *Journal of Personality and Social Psychology, 39,* 874–883.

Nicholls, J. R. (1985). A new approach to situational leadership. *Leadership and Organization Development Journal, 6,* 2–7.

Nielsen, J. M. (1990). *Sex and gender in society: Perspectives on stratification.* Prospect Heights, IL: Waveland Press.

Nielsen, M. E., & Miller, C. E. (1997). The transmission of norms regarding group decision rules. *Personality and Social Psychology Bulletin, 23,* 516–525.

Nier, J. A., Gaertner, S. L., Dovidio, J. F., Banker, B. S., Ward, C. M., & Rust, M. C. (2001). Changing interracial evaluations and behavior: The effects of a common group identity. *Group Processes & Intergroup Relations, 4,* 299–316.

Nieva, V. F., Fleishman, E. A., & Rieck, A. M. (1978). *Team dimensions: Their identity, their measurement, and their relationships.* Technical report. Washington, DC: ARRO.

Nijstad, B. A., & Stroebe, W. (2006). How the group affects the mind: A cognitive model of idea generation in groups. *Personality and Social Psychology Review, 10,* 186–213.

Nijstad, B. A., Stroebe, W., & Lodewijkx, H. F. M. (2006). The illusion of group productivity: A reduction of failures explanation. *European Journal of Social Psychology, 36,* 31–48.

Nisbett, R. E., & Cohen, D. (1996). *Culture of honor: The psychology of violence in the south.* Boulder, CO: Westview.

Nisbett, R. E., & Storms, M. D. (1974). Cognitive and social determinants of food intake. H. London & R. E. Nisbett (Eds.), *Thought and feeling: Cognitive alteration of feeling states* (pp. 190–208). Chicago: Aldine.

Nixon, H. L. (1979). *The small group.* Englewood Cliffs, NJ: Prentice Hall.

Noel, J. G., Wann, D. L., & Branscombe, N. R. (1995). Peripheral ingroup membership status and public negativity toward outgroups. *Journal of Personality and Social Psychology, 68,* 127–137.

Nord, W. R. (1969). Social exchange theory: An integrative approach to social conformity. *Psychological Bulletin, 71,* 174–208.

Norris, F. H., & Murrell, S. A. (1990). Social support, life events, and stress as modifiers of adjustment to bereavement by older adults. *Psychology and Aging, 5,* 429–436.

Northouse, P. G. (2007). *Leadership: Theory and practice* (4th ed.).Thousand Oaks, CA: Sage.

Norton, M. I., Frost, J. H., & Ariely, D. (2007). Less is more: The lure of ambiguity, or why familiarity breeds contempt. *Journal of Personality and Social Psychology, 92,* 97–105.

Nosanchuk, T. A., & Lightstone, J. (1974). Canned laughter and public and private conformity. *Journal of Personality and Social Psychology, 29,* 153–156.

Nosek, B. A., Greenwald, A. G., & Banaji, M. R. (2007). The implicit association test at age 7: A methodological and conceptual review. In J. A. Bargh (Ed.), *Social psychology and the unconscious: The automaticity of higher mental processes* (pp. 265–292). New York: Psychology Press.

Nowak, A., Vallacher, R. R, & Miller, M. E. (2003). Social influence and group dynamics. In T. Millon, M. J. Lerner, & I. B. Weiner (Eds.), *Handbook of psychology: Social psychology* (Vol. 5, pp. 383–418). New York: Wiley.

Nunamaker, J. F., Jr., Briggs, R. O., Mittleman, D. D., Vogel, D. R., & Balthazard, P. A. (1997). Lessons from a dozen years of group systems research: A discussion of lab and field findings. *Journal of Management Information Systems, 13,* 163–207.

Nutt, P. C. (2002). *Why decisions fail: Avoiding the blunders and traps that lead to debacles.* San Francisco: Berrett-Koehler.

Nuwer, H. (1999). *Wrongs of passage: Fraternities, sororities, hazing, and binge drinking.* Indianapolis: Indiana University Press.

Nyquist, L. V., & Spence, J. T. (1986). Effects of dispositional dominance and sex role expectations on leadership behaviors. *Journal of Personality and Social Psychology, 50,* 87–93.

Oberholzer-Gee, F., Waldfogel, J., & White, M. W. (2003). *Social learning and coordination in high-states games: Evidence from Friend or Foe.* NBER Working Paper No. W9805. Retrieved November 7, 2008, from SSRN: http://ssrn.com/abstract=420319.

O'Connell, P., Pepler, D., & Craig, W. (1999). Peer involvement in bullying: Insights and challenges for intervention. *Journal of Adolescence, 22,* 437–452.

O'Connor, B. P., & Dyce, J. (1997). Interpersonal rigidity, hostility, and complementarity in musical bands. *Journal of Personality and Social Psychology, 72,* 362–372.

OED Online (1989). Teams. Retrieved December 6, 2008, from the *Oxford English Dictionary,* http://dictionary.oed.com.

Ogrodniczuk, J. S., & Piper, W. E. (2003). The effect of group climate on outcome in two forms of short-term group therapy. *Group Dynamics: Theory, Research, and Practice, 7,* 64–76.

Ohbuchi, K., Chiba, S., & Fukushima, O. (1996). Mitigation of interpersonal conflicts: Politeness and time pressure. *Personality and Social Psychology Bulletin, 22,* 1035–1042.

Oishi, S., Lun, J., & Sherman, G. D. (2007). Residential mobility, self-concept, and positive affect in social interactions. *Journal of Personality and Social Psychology, 93,* 131–141.

Oldmeadow, J. (2007). Status generalization in context: The moderating role of groups. *Journal of Experimental Social Psychology, 43,* 273–279.

Oliver, L. W., Harman, J., Hoover, E., Hayes, S. M., & Pandhi, N. A. (1999). A quantitative integration of the military cohesion literature. *Military Psychology, 11,* 57–83.

Olson, R., Verley, J., Santos, L., & Salas, C. (2004). What we teach students about the Hawthorne studies: A review of content within a sample of introductory I-O and OB textbooks. *The Industrial-Organizational Psychologist, 41,* 23–39.

Olweus, D. (1997). Tackling peer victimization with a school-based intervention program. In D. P. Fry & K. Björkqvist (Eds.), *Cultural variation in conflict resolution: Alternatives to violence* (pp. 215–231). Mahwah, NJ: Erlbaum.

Olweus, D. (2000). Bullying. In A. E. Kazdin (Ed.), *Encyclopedia of psychology* (Vol. 1, pp. 487–489).

Washington, DC: American Psychological Association.

Opotow, S. (2000). Aggression and violence. In M. Deutsch & P. T. Coleman (Eds.), *The handbook of conflict resolution: Theory and practice* (pp. 403–427). San Francisco: Jossey-Bass.

Ormont, L. R. (1984). The leader's role in dealing with aggression in groups. *International Journal of Group Psychotherapy, 34,* 553–572.

Orne, M. T., & Holland, C. H. (1968). On the ecological validity of laboratory deceptions. *International Journal of Psychiatry, 6,* 282–293.

Örtqvist, D., & Wincent, J. (2006). Prominent consequences of role stress: A meta-analytic review. *International Journal of Stress Management, 13,* 399–422.

Osborn, A. F. (1957). *Applied imagination.* New York: Scribner.

Osgood, D. W., Wilson, J. K., O'Malley, P. M., Bachman, J. G., & Johnson, L. D. (1996). Routine activities and individual deviant behavior. *American Sociological Review, 61,* 635–655.

Oskamp, S., & Hartry, A. (1968). A factor-analytic study of the double standard in attitudes toward U.S. and Russian actions. *Behavioral Science, 13,* 178–188.

Overbeck, J. R., & Park, B. (2001). When power does not corrupt: Superior individuation processes among powerful perceivers. *Journal of Personality and Social Psychology, 81,* 549–565.

Oyserman, D. (2007). Social identity and self-regulation. In A. W. Kruglanski & E. T. Higgins (Eds.), *Social psychology: Handbook of basic principles* (2nd ed., pp. 432–453). New York: Guilford.

Oyserman, D., Coon, H. M., & Kemmelmeier, M. (2002). Rethinking individualism and collectivism: Evaluation of theoretical assumptions and meta-analyses. *Psychological Bulletin, 128,* 3–72.

Oyserman, D., & Lee, S. W. S. (2008). Does culture influence what and how we think? Effects of priming individualism and collectivism. *Psychological Bulletin, 134,* 311–342.

Oyserman, D., & Saltz, E. (1993). Competence, delinquency, and attempts to attain possible selves. *Journal of Personality and Social Psychology, 65,* 360–374.

Pace, J. L., & Hemmings, A. (2007). Understanding authority in classrooms: A review of theory, ideology, and research. *Review of Educational Research, 77,* 3–27.

Packer, D. J. (2008). Identifying systematic disobedience in Milgram's obedience experiments: A meta-analytic review. *Perspectives on Psychological Science, 3,* 301–304.

Page, R. C., Weiss, J. F., & Lietaer, G. (2002). Humanistic group psychotherapy. In D. J. Cain & J. Seeman (Eds.), *Humanistic psychotherapies: Handbook of research and practice* (pp. 339–368). Washington, DC: American Psychological Association.

Page-Gould, E., Mendoza-Denton, R., & Tropp, L. R. (2008). With a little help from my cross-group friend: Reducing anxiety in intergroup contexts through cross-group friendship. *Journal of Personality and Social Psychology, 95,* 1080–1094.

Palinkas, L. A. (1991). Effects of physical and social environments on the health and well-being of Antarctic winter-over personnel. *Environment and Behavior, 23,* 782–799.

Palmer, G. J. (1962). Task ability and effective leadership. *Psychological Reports, 10,* 863–866.

Paluck, E. L., & Green, D. P. (2009). Prejudice reduction: What do we know? A critical look at evidence from the field and the laboratory. *Annual Review of Psychology, 60,* 339–367.

Paris, C. R., Salas, E., & Cannon-Bowers, J. A. (1999). Human performance in multi-operator systems. In P. A. Hancock (Ed.), *Human performance and ergonomics* (2nd ed., pp. 329–386). San Diego: Academic Press.

Parker, K. C. (1988). Speaking turns in small group interaction: A context-sensitive event sequence model. *Journal of Personality and Social Psychology, 54,* 965–971.

Parkinson, C. N. (1957). *Parkinson's law and other studies in administration.* Boston: Houghton Mifflin.

Parks, C. D., & Komorita, S. S. (1997). Reciprocal strategies for large groups. *Personality and Social Psychology Review, 1,* 314–322.

Parks, M. R. (2007). *Personal relationships and personal networks.* Mahwah, NJ: Erlbaum.

Parks, S. D. (2005). *Leadership can be taught: A bold approach for a complex world.* Boston: Harvard Business School Press.

Parkum, K. H., & Parkum, V. C. (1980). Citizen participation in community planning and decision making. In D. H. Smith, J. Macaulay, & Associates (Eds.), *Participation in social and political activities: A comprehensive analysis of political involvement, expressive leisure time, and helping behavior* (pp. 153–167). San Francisco: Jossey-Bass.

Parrado, N., with Rause, V. (2006). *Miracle in the Andes.* New York: Crown.

Parsons, H. M. (1976). Work environments. In I. Altman & J. Wohlwill (Eds.), *Human behavior and environment* (Vol. 1, pp. 163–209). New York: Plenum Press.

Parsons, T., Bales, R. F., & Shils, E. (Eds.). (1953). *Working papers in the theory of action.* New York: Free Press.

Paskevich, D. M., Brawley, L. R., Dorsch, K. D., & Widmeyer, W. N. (1999). Relationship between collective efficacy and team cohesion: Conceptual and measurement issues. *Group Dynamics: Theory, Research, and Practice, 3,* 210–222.

Patel, K. A., & Schlundt, D. G. (2001). Impact of moods and social context on eating behavior. *Appetite, 36,* 111–118.

Patterson, M. L. (1975). Personal space—Time to burst the bubble? *Man–Environment Systems, 5,* 67.

Patterson, M. L. (1991). A functional approach to nonverbal exchange. In R. S. Feldman & B. Rimé (Eds.), *Fundamentals of nonverbal behavior* (pp. 458–495). New York: Cambridge University Press.

Patterson, M. L. (1996). Social behavior and social cognition: A parallel process approach. In J. L. Nye & A. M. Brower (Eds.), *What's social about social cognition? Research on socially shared cognitions in small groups* (pp. 87–105). Thousand Oaks, CA: Sage.

Patterson, M. L., Kelley, C. E., Kondracki, B. A., & Wulf, L. J. (1979). Effects of seating arrangement on small group behavior. *Social Psychology Quarterly, 42,* 180–185.

Patterson, M. L., Roth, C. P., & Schenk, C. (1979). Seating arrangement, activity, and sex differences in small group crowding. *Personality and Social Psychology Bulletin, 5,* 100–103.

Patterson, M. L., & Sechrest, L. B. (1970). Interpersonal distance and impression formation. *Journal of Personality, 38,* 161–166.

Paul, G. L. (1967). Strategy of outcome research in psychotherapy. *Journal of Consulting Psychology, 31,* 109–118.

Paulus, P. B., Annis, A. B., Seta, J. J., Schkade, J. K., & Matthews, R. W. (1976). Density does affect task performance. *Journal of Personality and Social Psychology, 34,* 248–353.

Paulus, P. B., & Brown, V. R. (2007). Toward more creative and innovative group idea generation: A cognitive-social-motivational perspective of brainstorming. *Social and Personality Psychology Compass, 1,* 248–265.

Paulus, P. B., Dzindolet, M. T., Poletes, G., & Camacho, L. M. (1993). Perception of performance in group brainstorming: The illusion of group productivity. *Personality and Social Psychology Bulletin, 19,* 78–89.

Paulus, P. B., Nakui, T., Putman, V. L., & Brown, V. R. (2006). Effects of task instructions and brief breaks on brainstorming. *Group Dynamics: Theory, Research, and Practice, 10,* 206–219.

Pavelshak, M. A., Moreland, R. L., & Levine, J. M. (1986). Effects of prior group memberships on subsequent reconnaissance activities. *Journal of Personality and Social Psychology, 50,* 56–66.

Paxton, P., & Moody, J. (2003). Structure and sentiment: Explaining emotional attachment to group. *Social Psychology Quarterly, 66,* 34–47.

Pearce, C. L., & Conger, J. A. (Eds.). (2003). *Shared leadership: Reframing the hows and whys of leadership.* Thousand Oaks, CA: Sage.

Pearce, C. L., Conger, J. A., & Locke, E. A. (2008). Shared leadership theory. *The Leadership Quarterly, 19,* 622–628.

Pearsall, M. J., & Ellis, A. P. J. (2006). The effects of critical team member assertiveness on team performance and satisfaction. *Journal of Management, 32,* 575–594.

Pedersen, D. M. (1999). Model for types of privacy by privacy functions. *Journal of Environmental Psychology, 19,* 397–405.

Peeters, M. A. G., Van Tuijl, H. F. J. M., Rutte, C. G., Reymen, I. M. M. J. (2006). Personality and team performance: A meta-analysis. *European Journal of Personality, 20,* 377–396.

Pelled, L. H., Eisenhardt, K. M., & Xin, K. R. (1999). Exploring the black box: An analysis of work group diversity, conflict, and performance. *Administrative Science Quarterly, 44,* 1–28.

Pelletier, L. G., & Vallerand, R. J. (1996). Supervisors' beliefs and subordinates' intrinsic motivation: A behavioral confirmation analysis. *Journal of Personality and Social Psychology, 71,* 331–340.

Pelz, D. C. (1956). Some social factors related to performance in a research organization. *Administrative Science Quarterly, 1,* 310–325.

Pelz, D. C. (1967). Creative tensions in the research and development climate. *Science, 157,* 160–165.

Pemberton, M. B., Insko, C. A., & Schopler, J. (1996). Memory for and experience of differential competitive behavior of individuals and groups. *Journal of Personality and Social Psychology, 71,* 953–966.

Pemberton, M. B., & Sedikides, C. (2001). When do individuals help close others improve? The role of information diagnosticity. *Journal of Personality and Social Psychology, 81,* 234–246.

Pennebaker, J. W. (1982). Social and perceptual factors affecting symptom reporting and mass psychogenic illness. In M. J. Colligan, J. W. Pennebaker, & L. R. Murphy (Eds.), *Mass psychogenic illness: A social psychological analysis* (pp. 139–153). Mahwah, NJ: Erlbaum.

Pennebaker, J. W. (1997). *Opening up: The healing power of expressing emotions* (rev. ed.).New York: Guilford.

Pennington, N., & Hastie, R. (1986). Evidence evaluation in complex decision-making. *Journal of Personality and Social Psychology, 51,* 242–258.

Pennington, N., & Hastie, R. (1992). Explaining the evidence: Tests of the Story Model for juror decision making. *Journal of Personality and Social Psychology, 62,* 189–206.

Pepitone, A., & Reichling, G. (1955). Group cohesiveness and the expression of hostility. *Human Relations, 8,* 327–337.

Pepitone, A., & Wilpinski, C. (1960). Some consequences of experimental rejection. *Journal of Abnormal and Social Psychology, 60,* 359–364.

Pérez, J. A., & Mungy, G. (1996). The conflict elaboration theory of social influence. In E. Witte & J. Davis (Eds.), *Understanding group behavior: Small group processes and interpersonal relations* (Vol. 2, pp. 191–210). Mahwah, NJ: Erlbaum.

Perls, F. (1969). *Gestalt therapy verbatim.* Lafayette, CA: Real People Press.

Perls, F., Hefferline, R., & Goodman, P. (1951). *Gestalt therapy: Excitement and growth in the human personality.* New York: Julian Press.

Perrin, S., & Spencer, C. P. (1980). The Asch effect—A child of its time? *Bulletin of the British Psychological Society, 32,* 405–406.

Perrin, S., & Spencer, C. P. (1981). Independence or conformity in the Asch experiment as a reflection of cultural and situational factors. *British Journal of Social Psychology, 20,* 205–210.

Peters, D. (2006). Tenure is fine, but rank is sublime. *Behavioral and Brain Sciences, 29,* 583.

Peters, W. (1987). *A class divided: Then and now.* New York: Yale University Press.

Peterson, R. S. (1997). A directive leadership style in group decision making can be both virtue and vice: Evidence from elite and experimental groups. *Journal of Personality and Social Psychology 72,* 1107–1121.

Peterson, R. S., & Behfar, K. J. (2003). The dynamic relationship between performance feedback, trust, and conflict in groups: A longitudinal study. *Organizational Behavior and Human Decision Processes, 92,* 102–112.

Peterson, R. S., & Nemeth, C. J. (1996). Focus versus flexibility: Majority and minority influence can both improve performance. *Personality and Social Psychology Bulletin, 22,* 14–23.

Peterson, R. S., Owens, P. D., Tetlock, P. E., Fan, E. T., & Martorana, P. (1998). Group dynamics in top management teams: Groupthink, vigilance, and alternative models of organizational failure and success. *Organizational Behavior and Human Decision Processes, 73,* 272–305.

Petrie, T. A., & Greenleaf, C. A. (2007). Eating disorders in sport: From theory to research to intervention. In G. Tenenbaum & R. C. Eklund (Eds.), *Handbook of sport psychology* (3rd ed., pp. 352–378). Hoboken: John Wiley & Sons Inc.

Pettigrew, T. F. (1997). Generalized intergroup contact effects on prejudice. *Personality and Social Psychology Bulletin, 23,* 173–185.

Pettigrew, T. F. (2001). The ultimate attribution error: Extending Allport's cognitive analysis of prejudice. In M. A. Hogg & D. Abrams (Eds.), *Intergroup relations: Essential readings* (pp. 162–173). Philadelphia: Psychology Press.

Pettigrew, T. F., & Tropp, L. R. (2000). Does intergroup contact reduce prejudice: Recent meta-analytic findings. In S. Oskamp (Ed.), *Reducing prejudice and discrimination* (pp. 93–114). Mahwah, NJ: Erlbaum.

Pettigrew, T. F., & Tropp, L. R. (2006). A meta-analytic test of intergroup contact theory. *Journal of Personality and Social Psychology, 90,* 751–783.

Phillips, K. W. (2003). The effects of categorically based expectations on minority influence: The importance of congruence. *Personality and Social Psychology Bulletin, 29,* 3–13.

Phinney, J. S., & Ong, A. D. (2007). Conceptualization and measurement of ethnic identity: Current status and future directions. *Journal of Counseling Psychology, 54,* 271–281.

Phoon, W. H. (1982). Outbreaks of mass hysteria at workplaces in Singapore: Some patterns and modes of presentation. In M. J. Colligan, J. W. Pennebaker, & L. R. Murphy (Eds.), *Mass psychogenic illness: A social psychological analysis* (pp. 21–31). Mahwah, NJ: Erlbaum.

Pickett, C. L. (2001). The effects of entitativity beliefs on implicit comparisons between group members. *Personality and Social Psychology Bulletin, 27,* 515–525.

Pierro, A., Cicero, L., & Raven, B. H. (2008). Motivated compliance with bases of social power. *Journal of Applied Social Psychology, 38,* 1921–1944.

Pillutla, M. M., & Murnighan, J. K. (1996). Unfairness, anger, and spite: Emotional rejections of ultimatum offers. *Organizational Behavior and Human Decision Processes, 68,* 208–224.

Pinter, B., Insko, C. A., Wildschut, T., Kirchner, J. L., Montoya, R. M., & Wolf, S. T. (2007). Reduction of interindividual–intergroup discontinuity: The role of leader accountability and proneness to guilt. *Journal of Personality and Social Psychology, 93,* 250–265.

Pisano, G. P., Bohmer, R. M. J., & Edmondson, A. C. (2001). Organizational differences in rates of learning: Evidence from the adoption of minimally invasive cardiac surgery. *Management Science, 47,* 752–768.

Pittard-Payne, B. (1980). Nonassociational religious participation. In D. H. Smith, J. Macaulay, & Associates (Eds.), *Participation in social and political activities: A comprehensive analysis of political involvement, expressive leisure time, and helping behavior* (pp. 214–243). San Francisco: Jossey-Bass.

Pittman, T. S., & Zeigler, K. R. (2007). Basic human needs. In A. W. Kruglanski & E. T. Higgins (Eds.), *Social psychology: Handbook of basic principles* (2nd ed., pp. 473–489). New York: Guilford.

Platania, J., & Moran, G. P. (2001). Social facilitation as a function of mere presence of others. *Journal of Social Psychology, 141,* 190–197.

Platow, M. J., Durante, M., Williams, N., Garrett, M., Walshe, J., Cincotta, S., Lianos, G., & Barutchu, A. (1999). The contribution of sport fan social identity to the production of prosocial behavior. *Group Dynamics: Theory, Research, and Practice, 3,* 161–169.

Plous, S. (1993). *The psychology of judgment and decision making.* New York: McGraw-Hill.

Polletta, F., & Jasper, J. M. (2001). Collective identity and social movements. *Annual Review of Sociology, 27,* 283–305.

Polley, R. B. (1989). On the dimensionality of interpersonal behavior: A reply to Lustig. *Small Group Behavior, 20,* 270–278.

Polzer, J. T. (1996). Intergroup negotiations: The effects of negotiating teams. *Journal of Conflict Resolution, 40,* 678–698.

Polzer, J. T., Kramer, R. M., & Neale, M. A. (1997). Positive illusions about oneself and one's group. *Small Group Research, 28,* 243–266.

Poole, M. S., & Hollingshead, A. B. (Eds.). (2005). *Theories of small groups: Interdisciplinary perspectives.* Thousand Oaks, CA: Sage.

Poppe, E. (2001). Effects of changes in GNP and perceived group characteristics on national and ethnic stereotypes in Central and Eastern Europe. *Journal of Applied Social Psychology, 31,* 1689–1708.

Porter, N., Geis, F. L., Cooper, E., & Newman, E. (1985). Androgyny and leadership in mixed-sex groups. *Journal of Personality and Social Psychology, 49,* 808–823.

Postmes, T., & Spears, R. (1998). Deindividuation and antinormative behavior: A meta-analysis. *Psychological Bulletin, 123,* 238–259.

Postmes, T., Spears, R., & Cihangir, S. (2001). Quality of decision making and group norms. *Journal of Personality and Social Psychology, 80,* 918–930.

Postmes, T., Spears, R., & Lea, M. (2000). The formation of group norms in computer-mediated communication. *Human Communication Research, 26,* 341–371.

Poundstone, W. (1992). *Prisoner's dilemma.* New York: Doubleday.

Prapavessis, H., & Carron, A. V. (1997). Sacrifice, cohesion, and conformity to norms in sport teams. *Group Dynamics: Theory, Research, and Practice, 1,* 231–240.

Pratt, J. H. (1922). The principle of class treatment and their application to various chronic diseases. *Hospital Social Services, 6,* 401–417.

Prentice, D. A. (2007). Pluralistic ignorance. In R. F. Baumeister & K. D. Vohs (Eds.), *Encyclopedia of social psychology* (pp. 673–674). Thousand Oaks, CA: Sage.

Prentice, D. A., & Miller, D. T. (1993). Pluralistic ignorance and alcohol use on campus: Some consequences of misperceiving the social norm. *Journal of Personality and Social Psychology, 64,* 243–254.

Prentice, D. A., & Miller, D. T. (2007). Psychological essentialism of human categories. *Current Directions in Psychological Science, 16,* 202–206.

Prentice-Dunn, S., & Rogers, R. W. (1980). Effects of deindividuating situation cues and aggressive models on subjective deindividuation and aggression. *Journal of Personality and Social Psychology, 39,* 104–113.

Prentice-Dunn, S., & Rogers, R. W. (1982). Effects of public and private self-awareness on deindividuation and aggression. *Journal of Personality and Social Psychology, 43,* 503–513.

Prentice-Dunn, S., & Rogers, R. W. (1983). Deindividuation and aggression. In R. G. Geen & E. I. Donnerstein (Eds.), *Aggression: Theoretical and empirical reviews* (Vol. 1). New York: Academic Press.

Prentice-Dunn, S., & Spivey, R. W. (1986). Extreme deindividuation in the laboratory: Its magnitude and subjective components. *Personality and Social Psychology Bulletin, 12,* 206–215.

Prislin, R., Brewer, M., & Wilson, D. J. (2002). Changing majority and minority positions within a group versus an aggregate. *Personality and Social Psychology Bulletin, 28,* 640–647.

Prislin, R., Limbert, W. M., & Bauer, E. (2000). From majority to minority and vice versa: The asymmetrical effects of losing and gaining majority position within a group. *Journal of Personality and Social Psychology, 79,* 385–397.

Pritchard, R. D., Harrell, M. M., DiazGranados, D., & Guzman, M. J. (2008). The productivity measurement and enhancement system: A meta-analysis. *Journal of Applied Psychology, 93,* 540–567.

Propp, K. M. (1999). Collective information processing in groups. In L. Frey, D. S. Gouran, & M. S. Poole (Eds.), *The handbook of group communication: Theory and research* (pp. 225–250). Thousand Oaks, CA: Sage.

Pruitt, D. G. (1971). Choice shifts in group discussion: An introductory review. *Journal of Personality and Social Psychology, 20,* 339–360.

Pruitt, D. G. (1983). Strategic choice in negotiation. *American Behavioral Science, 27,* 167–194.

Pruitt, D. G. (1998). Social conflict. In D. T. Gilbert, S. T. Fiske, & G. Lindzey (Eds.), *The handbook of social psychology* (4th ed., Vol. 2, 470–503). New York: McGraw-Hill.

Pruitt, D. G., & Kim, S. H. (2004). *Social conflict: Escalation, stalemate, and settlement* (3rd ed.). New York: McGraw-Hill.

Pruitt, D. G., & Rubin, J. Z. (1986). *Social conflict: Escalation, stalemate, and settlement.* New York: Random House.

Putnam, R. D. (1995). Bowling alone: America's declining social capital. *Journal of Democracy, 6,* 65–78.

Putnam, R. D. (2000). *Bowling alone: The collapse and revival of American community.* New York: Simon & Schuster.

Quattrone, G. A., & Jones, E. E. (1980). The perception of variability within in-groups and out-groups: Implications for the law of small numbers. *Journal of Personality and Social Psychology, 38,* 141–152.

Quinn, A., & Schlenker, B. R. (2002). Can accountability produce independence? Goals as determinants of the impact of accountability on conformity. *Personality and Social Psychology Bulletin, 28,* 472–483.

Rabbie, J. (1963). Differential preference for companionship under stress. *Journal of Abnormal and Social Psychology, 67,* 643–648.

Radloff, R., & Helmreich, R. (1968). *Groups under stress: Psychological research in SEALAB II.* New York: Irvington.

Ragone, G. (1981). Fashion, "crazes," and collective behavior. *Communications, 7,* 249–268.

Raiffa, H. (1983). Mediation of conflicts. *American Behavioral Science, 27,* 195–210.

Ranie, L., & Kalsnes, B. (2001, October 10). *The commons of the tragedy: How the internet was used by millions after the terror attacks to grieve, console, share news, and debate the country's response.* Retrieved July 17, 2004, from the Pew Internet and American Life Project website, http://www.pewtrusts.com/pdf/vf_pew_internet_attack_aftermath.pdf.

Rantilla, A. K. (2000). Collective task responsibility allocation: Revisiting the group-serving bias. *Small Group Research, 31,* 739–766.

Raphael, B., & Wooding, S. (2006). Group intervention for the prevention and treatment of acute initial stress reactions in civilians. In L. A. Schein, H. I. Spitz, G. M. Burlingame, & P. R. Muskin (Eds.), with S. Vargo, *Psychological effects of catastrophic disasters: Group approaches to treatment* (pp. 481–503). New York: Haworth Press.

Ratner, R. K., & Miller, D. T. (2001). The norm of self-interest and its effects on social action. *Journal of Personality and Social Psychology, 81,* 5–16.

Raven, B. H. (1965). Social influence and power. In I. D. Steiner & M. Fishbein (Eds.), *Current studies in social psychology* (pp. 371–382). New York: Holt, Rinehart & Winston.

Raven, B. H. (1992). A power/interaction model of interpersonal influence: French and Raven thirty years later. *Journal of Social Behavior and Personality, 7,* 217–244.

Raven, B. H., Schwarzwald, J., & Koslowsky, M. (1998). Conceptualizing and measuring a power/interaction model of interpersonal influence. *Journal of Applied Social Psychology, 28,* 307–332.

Rawlinson, J. W. (2000). Does psychodrama work? A review of the literature. *British Journal of Psychodrama and Sociometry, 15,* 67–101.

Read, K. E. (1986). *Return to the high valley: Coming full circle.* Berkeley, CA: University of California Press.

Read, P. P. (1974). *Alive.* New York: Avon.

Redl, F. (1942). Group emotion and leaders. *Psychiatry, 5,* 573–596.

Reeder, K., Macfadyen, L., Roche, J., & Chase, M. (2004). Negotiating cultures in cyberspace: Participation patterns and problematics. *Language Learning & Technology, 8,* 88–105.

Rees, C. R., & Segal, M. W. (1984). Role differentiation in groups: The relationship between instrumental and expressive leadership. *Small Group Behavior, 15,* 109–123.

Reicher, S. D. (1984). The St. Pauls riot: An explanation of the limits of crowd action in terms of a social identity model. *European Journal of Social Psychology, 14,* 1–21.

Reicher, S. D. (1987). Crowd behavior as social action. In J. C. Turner, M. A. Hogg, P. J. Oakes, S. D. Reicher, & M. S. Wetherell (Eds.), *Rediscovering the social group: A self-categorization theory* (pp. 171–202). Oxford, UK: Blackwell.

Reicher, S. D. (1996). "The Battle of Westminster": Developing the social identity model of crowd behavior in order to explain the initiation and development of collective conflict. *European Journal of Social Psychology, 26,* 115–134.

Reicher, S. D. (2001). The psychology of crowd dynamics. In M. A. Hogg & R. S. Tindale (Eds.), *Blackwell handbook of social psychology: Group processes* (pp. 182–208). Malden, MA: Blackwell.

Reicher, S. D., Haslam, S. A., & Hopkins, N. (2005). Social identity and the dynamics of leadership: Leaders and followers as collaborative agents in the transformation of social reality. *The Leadership Quarterly, 16,* 547–568.

Reicher, S. D., Haslam, S. A., & Rath, R. (2008). Making a virtue of evil: A five-step social identity model of the development of collective hate. *Social and Personality Psychology Compass, 2,* 1313–1344.

Reicher, S. D., & Levine, M. (1994). Deindividuation, power relations between groups and the expression of social identity: The effects of visibility to the out-group. *British Journal of Social Psychology, 33,* 145–163.

Reicher, S. D., Spears, R., & Postmes, T. (1995). A social identity model of deindividuated phenomena. In W. Stroebe & M. Hewstone (Eds.), *European review of social psychology* (Vol. 6, pp. 161–198). Chichester, UK: Wiley.

Reichl, A. J. (1997). Ingroup favoritism and outgroup favoritism in low status minimal groups: Differential responses to status-related and status-unrelated measures. *European Journal of Social Psychology, 27,* 617–633.

Reifman, A., Lee, L., & Apparala, M. (2004). *Spreading popularity of two musical artists: A "tipping point" study.* Poster presented at the Annual Meeting of the Society for Personality and Social Psychology, Austin, TX.

Reimer, T., Reimer, A., & Hinsz, V. B. (2008). *Presenting decision tasks in meetings as old versus new business instigates different group processes in the hidden-profile paradigm.* Unpublished manuscript. Berlin, Germany: Max Planck Institute for Human Development.

Remland, M. S., Jones, T. S., & Brinkman, H. (1995). Interpersonal distance, body orientation, and touch: Effects of culture, gender, and age. *Journal of Social Psychology, 135,* 281–297.

Rempel, J. K., Holmes, J. G., & Zanna, M. P. (1985). Trust in close relationships. *Journal of Personality and Social Psychology, 49,* 95–112.

Renkema, L. J., Stapel, D. A., & Van Yperen, N. W. (2008). Go with the flow: Conforming to others in the face of existential threat. *European Journal of Social Psychology, 38,* 747–756.

Reno, R. R., Cialdini, R. B., & Kallgren, C. A. (1993). The transsituational influence of social norms. *Journal of Personality and Social Psychology, 64,* 104–112.

Rentsch, J. R., & Steel, R. P. (1998). Testing the durability of job characteristics as predictors of absenteeism over a six-year period. *Personnel Psychology, 51,* 165–190.

Reston, J., Jr. (2000). *Our father who art in hell.* Lincoln, NE: iUniverse.

Rhee, E., Uleman, J. S., Lee, H. K., & Roman, R. J. (1995). Spontaneous self-descriptions and ethnic identities in individualistic and collectivistic cultures. *Journal of Personality and Social Psychology, 69,* 142–152.

Rheingold, H. (2002). *Smart mobs: The next social revolution.* New York: Basic Books.

Rice, O. K. (1978). *The Hatfields and the McCoys.* Lexington, KY: University Press of Kentucky.

Rice, R. W. (1979). Reliability and validity of the LPC Scale: A reply. *Academy of Management Review, 4,* 291–294.

Rice, R. W., Instone, D., & Adams, J. (1984). Leader sex, leader success, and leadership process: Two field studies. *Journal of Applied Psychology, 69,* 12–31.

Richard, F. D., Bond, C. F., Jr., & Stokes-Zoota, J. J. (2003). One hundred years of social psychology quantitatively described. *Review of General Psychology, 7,* 331–363.

Ridgeway, C. L. (1982). Status in groups: The importance of motivation. *American Sociological Review, 47,* 76–88.

Ridgeway, C. L. (1983). *The dynamics of small groups.* New York: St. Martin's Press.

Ridgeway, C. L. (2001). Social status and group structure. In M. A. Hogg & R. S. Tindale (Eds.), *Blackwell handbook of social psychology: Group processes* (pp. 352–375). Malden, MA: Blackwell.

Ridgeway, C. L., & Balkwell, J. W. (1997). Group processes and the diffusion of status beliefs. *Social Psychology Quarterly, 60,* 14–31.

Riess, M. (1982). Seating preferences as impression management: A literature review and theoretical integration. *Communication, 11,* 85–113.

Riess, M., & Rosenfeld, P. (1980). Seating preferences as nonverbal communication: A self-presentational analysis. *Journal of Applied Communications Research, 8,* 22–30.

Rimal, R. N., & Real, K. (2005). How behaviors are influenced by perceived norms: A test of the theory of normative social behavior. *Communication Research, 32,* 389–414.

Ringelmann, M. (1913). Research on animate sources of power: The work of man. *Annales de l'Institut National Agronomique, 2e serié—tome XII,* 1–40.

Riordan, C., & Riggiero, J. (1980). Producing equal-status interracial interaction: A replication. *Social Psychology Quarterly, 43,* 131–136.

Rivera, A. N., & Tedeschi, J. T. (1976). Public versus private reactions to positive inequity. *Journal of Personality and Social Psychology, 34,* 895–900.

Robak, R. W. (2001). Self-definition in psychotherapy: Is it time to revisit self-perception theory? *North American Journal of Psychology, 3,* 529–534.

Robbins, A. (2004). *Pledged: The secret life of sororities.* New York: Hyperion.

Robert, H. M. (1971). *Robert's rules of order* (Rev. ed.). New York: Morrow. (Original work published in 1915)

Roccas, S., Sagiv, L., Schwartz, S., Halevy, N., & Eidelson, R. (2008). Toward a unifying model of identification with groups: Integrating theoretical perspectives. *Personality and Social Psychology Review, 12,* 280–306.

Rodin, J., & Baum, A. (1978). Crowding and helplessness: Potential consequences of density and loss of control. In A. Baum & Y. Epstein (Eds.), *Human responses to crowding*. Mahwah, NJ: Erlbaum.

Rodin, J., Solomon, S. K., & Metcalf, J. (1978). Role of control in mediating perceptions of density. *Journal of Personality and Social Psychology, 36,* 988–999.

Roethlisberger, F. J., & Dickson, W. J. (1939). *Management and the worker.* Boston, MA: Harvard University Press.

Rofé, Y. (1984). Stress and affiliation: A utility theory. *Psychological Review, 91,* 235–250.

Rogelberg, S. G., Leach, D. J., Warr, P. B., & Burnfield, J. L. (2006). "Not another meeting!" Are meeting time demands related to employee well-being? *Journal of Applied Psychology, 91,* 83–96.

Rogelberg, S. G., & O'Connor, M. S. (1998). Extending the stepladder technique: An examination of self-paced stepladder groups. *Group Dynamics: Theory, Research, and Practice, 2,* 82–91.

Rogelberg, S. G., & Rumery, S. M. (1996). Gender diversity, team decision quality, time on task, and interpersonal cohesion. *Small Group Research, 27,* 79–90.

Rogers, C. (1970). *Encounter groups.* New York: Harper & Row.

Rogers, R. W., & Prentice-Dunn, S. (1981). Deindividuation and anger-mediated interracial aggression: Unmasking regressive racism. *Journal of Personality and Social Psychology, 41,* 63–73.

Rom, E., & Mikulincer, M. (2003). Attachment theory and group processes: The association between attachment style and group-related representations, goals, memories, and functioning. *Journal of Personality and Social Psychology, 84,* 1220–1235.

Roos, P. D. (1968). Jurisdiction: An ecological concept. *Human Relations, 21,* 75–84.

Rose, R., & Sergel, S. L. (1958). *Twelve angry men: A play in three acts.* New York: The Dramatic Publishing Co.

Rosenbaum, M. E. (1986). The repulsion hypothesis: On the nondevelopment of relationships. *Journal of Personality and Social Psychology, 51,* 1156–1166.

Rosenbloom, T., Shahar, A., Perlman, A., Estreich, D., & Kirzner, E. (2007). Success on a practical driver's license test with and without the presence of another testee. *Accident Analysis & Prevention, 39,* 1296–1301.

Rosenthal, S. A., & Pittinsky, T. L. (2006). Narcissistic leadership. *Leadership Quarterly, 17,* 617–633.

Roseth, C. J., Johnson, D. W., & Johnson, R. T. (2008). Promoting early adolescents' achievement and peer relationships: The effects of cooperative, competitive, and individualistic goal structures. *Psychological Bulletin, 134,* 223–246.

Rosnow, R. L. (1980). Psychology of rumor reconsidered. *Psychological Bulletin, 87,* 578–591.

Rosnow, R. L., & Kimmel, A. J. (1979). Lives of a rumor. *Psychology Today, 13,* 88–92.

Rosnow, R. L., Yost, J. H., & Esposito, J. L. (1986). Belief in rumor and likelihood of rumor transmission. *Language and Communication, 6,* 189–194.

Ross, L. (1977). The intuitive psychologist and his shortcomings: Distortions in the attribution process. *Advances in Experimental Social Psychology, 10,* 173–220.

Ross, L., Bierbrauer, G., & Hoffman, S. (1976). The role of attribution processes in conformity and dissent: Revisiting the Asch situation. *American Psychologist, 31,* 148–157.

Ross, L., & Ward, A. (1995). Psychological barriers to dispute resolution. *Advances in Experimental Social Psychology, 27,* 255–304.

Ross, M., & Holmberg, D. (1992). Are wives' memories for events in relationships more vivid than their husbands' memories? *Journal of Social & Personal Relationships, 9,* 585–604.

Ross, M., & Sicoly, E. (1979). Egocentric biases in availability and attribution. *Journal of Personality and Social Psychology, 37,* 322–336.

Ross, T. M., Jones, E. C., & Adams, S. (2008). Can team effectiveness be predicted? *Team Performance Management, 14,* 248–268.

Ross, W. H., Brantmeier, C., & Ciriacks, T. (2002). The impact of hybrid dispute-resolution procedures on constituent fairness judgments. *Journal of Applied Social Psychology, 32,* 1151–1188.

Ross, W. H., & Conlon, D. E. (2000). Hybrid forms of dispute resolution: Theoretical implications of combining mediation and arbitration. *Academy of Management Review, 25,* 416–427.

Rost, J. (2008). Followership: An outmoded concept. In R. E. Riggio, I. Chaleff & J. Lipman-Blumen (Eds.), *The art of followership: How great followers create great leaders and organizations* (pp. 53–64). San Francisco: Jossey-Bass.

Roth, B. E. (1993). Freud: The group psychologist and group leader. In H. I. Kaplan & M. J. Sadock (Eds.), *Comprehensive group psychotherapy* (3rd. ed., pp. 10–21). Baltimore: Williams & Wilkins.

Rothbart, M., Sriram, N., & Davis-Stitt, C. (1996). The retrieval of typical and atypical category members. *Journal of Experimental Social Psychology, 32,* 309–336.

Rothgerber, H. (1997). External intergroup threat as an antecedent to perceptions in in-group and out-group homogeneity. *Journal of Personality and Social Psychology, 73,* 1206–1212.

Rothgerber, H., & Worchel, S. (1997). The view from below: Intergroup relations from the perspective of the disadvantaged group. *Journal of Personality and Social Psychology, 73,* 1191–1205.

Rotton, J., & Cohn, E. G. (2002). Climate, weather, and crime. In R. B. Bechtel & A. Churchman (Eds.), *Handbook of environmental psychology* (pp. 481–498). New York: Wiley.

Rouhana, N. N., & Bar-Tal, D. (1998). Psychological dynamics of intractable ethnonational conflicts: The Israeli-Palestinian case. *American Psychologist, 53,* 761–770.

Rouhana, N. N., & Kelman, H. C. (1994). Promoting joint thinking in international conflicts: An Israeli-Palestinian continuing workshop. *Journal of Social Issues, 50,* 157–178.

Rousseau, J. (1968). *A discourse on inequality.* New York: Penguin Books.

Rowe, G., & Wright, G. (1999). The Delphi technique as a forecasting tool: Issues and analysis. *International Journal of Forecasting, 15,* 353–375.

Roy, D. F. (1973). "Banana time"—Job satisfaction and informal interaction. In W. G. Bennis, D. E. Berlew, E. H. Schein, & F. I. Steele (Eds.), *Interpersonal dynamics* (pp. 403–417). Homewood, IL: Dorsey. (Original work published in 1960.)

Roy, M. C., Gauvin, S., & Limayem, M. (1996). Electronic group brainstorming: The role of feedback and productivity. *Small Group Research, 27,* 214–247.

Rozin, P., Lowery, L., Imada, S., & Haidt, J. (1999). The CAD triad hypothesis: A mapping between three moral emotions (contempt, anger, disgust) and three moral codes (community, autonomy, divinity). *Journal of Personality and Social Psychology, 76,* 574–586.

Ruback, R. B., Dabbs, J. M., Jr., & Hopper, C. H. (1984). The process of brainstorming: An analysis with individual and group vocal parameters. *Journal of Personality and Social Psychology, 47,* 558–567.

Rubin, J. Z. (1980). Experimental research on third-party intervention in conflict: Toward some generalizations. *Psychological Bulletin, 87,* 379–391.

Rubin, J. Z. (1986). Third parties within organizations: A responsive commentary. *Research on Negotiation in Organizations, 1,* 271–283.

Rubin, J. Z. (1994). Models of conflict management. *Journal of Social Issues, 50*(1), 33–46.

Rubin, J. Z., & Brown, B. R. (1975). *The social psychology of bargaining and negotiation.* New York: Academic Press.

Rubin, R. B. (1985). The validity of the Communication Competency Assessment Instrument. *Communication Monographs, 52,* 173–185.

Rubonis, A. V., & Bickman, L. (1991). Psychological impairment in the wake of disaster: The disaster–psychopathology relationship. *Psychological Bulletin, 109,* 384–399.

Rudman, L. A., & Glick, P. (2001). Prescriptive gender stereotypes and backlash toward agentic women. *Journal of Social Issues, 57,* 743–762.

Runcimann, W. G. (1966). *Relative deprivation and social justice.* London: Routledge & Kegan Paul.

Rusbult, C. E., & Van Lange, P. A. M. (2003). Interdependence, interaction and relationships. *Annual Review of Psychology, 54,* 351–375.

Ruscher, J. B., & Hammer, E. D. (2006). The development of shared stereotypic impressions in conversation: An emerging model, methods, and extensions to cross-group settings. *Journal of Language and Social Psychology, 25,* 221–243.

Russell, B. (1938). *Power.* London: Allen & Unwyn.

Russell, G. W., & Arms, R. L. (1998). Toward a social psychological profile of would-be rioters. *Aggressive Behavior, 24,* 219–226.

Russell, J. A. (2003). Core affect and the psychological construction of emotion. *Psychological Review, 110,* 145–172.

Russell, J. A., & Snodgrass, J. (1987). Emotion and the environment. In D. Stokols & I. Altman (Eds.), *Handbook of environmental psychology* (pp. 245–280). New York: Wiley.

Rydell, R. J., Hugenberg, K., Ray, D., & Mackie, D. M. (2007). Implicit theories about groups and stereotyping: The role of group entitativity. *Personality and Social Psychology Bulletin, 33,* 549–558.

Rydell, R. J., & McConnell, A. R. (2005). Perceptions of entitativity and attitude change. *Personality and Social Psychology Bulletin, 31,* 99–110.

Ryen, A. H., & Kahn, A. (1975). The effects of intergroup orientation on group attitudes and proxemic behavior: A test of two models. *Journal of Personality and Social Psychology, 31,* 302–310.

Sabini, J., Garvey, B., & Hall, A. L. (2001). Shame and embarrassment revisited. *Personality and Social Psychology Review, 27,* 104–117.

Sacerdote, B., & Marmaros, D. (2005). *How do friendships form?* National Bureau of Economic Research, Working Paper Series. Retrieved July 31, 2008, from http://www.nber.org/papers/w11530.

Sadler, M. S., & Judd, C. M. (2001). Overcoming dependent data: A guide to the analysis of group data. In M. A. Hogg & R. S. Tindale (Eds.), *Blackwell handbook of social psychology: Group processes* (pp. 497–524). Malden, MA: Blackwell.

Sadler, P., & Woody, E. (2003). Is who you are who you're talking to? Interpersonal style and complementarity in mixed-sex interactions. *Journal of Personality and Social Psychology, 84,* 80–95.

Sagar, H. A., & Schofield, J. W. (1980). Racial and behavioral cues in black and white children's perceptions of ambiguously aggressive acts. *Journal of Personality and Social Psychology, 39,* 590–598.

Saks, M. J. (1977). *Jury verdicts.* Lexington, MA: Heath.

Saks, M. J., & Hastie, R. (1978). *Social psychology in court.* New York: Van Nostrand Reinhold.

Saks, M. J., & Marti, M. W. (1997). A meta-analysis of the effects of jury size. *Law and Human Behavior, 21,* 451–467.

Salas, E., Nichols, D. R., & Driskell, J. E. (2007). Testing three team training strategies in intact teams: A meta-analysis. *Small Group Research, 38,* 471–488.

Sampson, E. E., & Brandon, A. C. (1964). The effects of role and opinion deviation on small group behavior. *Sociometry, 27,* 261–281.

Samuelson, C. D., & Allison, S. T. (1994). Cognitive factors affecting the use of social decision heuristics in resource-sharing tasks. *Organizational Behavior and Human Decision Processes, 58,* 1–27.

Samuelson, C. D., & Messick, D. M. (1995). When do people want to change the rules for allocating shared resources? In D. A. Schroeder (Ed.), *Social dilemmas: Perspectives on individuals and groups* (pp. 144–162). Westport, CT: Praeger.

Sandal, G. M., Vaernes, R., Bergan, T., Warncke, M., & Ursin, H. (1996). Psychological reactions during polar expeditions and isolation in hyperbaric chambers. *Aviation, Space, and Environmental Medicine, 67,* 227–234.

Sanders, G. S. (1981). Driven by distraction: An integrative review of social facilitation theory and research. *Journal of Experimental Social Psychology, 17,* 227–251.

Sanders, G. S., & Baron, R. S. (1977). Is social comparison irrelevant for producing choice shifts? *Journal of Experimental Social Psychology, 13,* 303–314.

Sanders, G. S., Baron, R. S., & Moore, D. L. (1978). Distraction and social comparison as mediators of social facilitation effects. *Journal of Experimental Social Psychology, 14,* 291–303.

Sanders, W. B. (1994). *Gangbangs and drive-bys: Grounded culture and juvenile gang violence.* New York: Aldine de Gruyter.

Sani, F., Bowe, M., & Herrera, M. (2008). Perceived collective continuity and social well-being: Exploring the connections. *European Journal of Social Psychology, 38,* 365–374.

Sanna, L. J. (1992). Self-efficacy theory: Implications for social facilitation and social loafing. *Journal of Personality and Social Psychology, 62,* 774–786.

Sanna, L. J., & Parks, C. D. (1997). Group research trends in social and organizational psychology: Whatever happened to intragroup research? *Psychological Science, 8,* 261–267.

Sanna, L. J., Parks, C. D., Chang, E. C., & Carter, S. E. (2005). The hourglass is half full or half empty: Temporal framing and the group planning fallacy. *Group Dynamics: Theory, Research, and Practice, 9,* 173–188.

Sapp, S. G., Harrod, W. J., & Zhao, L. (1996). Leadership emergence in task groups with egalitarian gender-role expectations. *Sex Roles, 34,* 65–83.

Sarbin, T. R., & Allen, V. L. (1968). Increasing participation in a natural group setting: A preliminary report. *Psychological Record, 18,* 1–7.

Sattler, D. N., & Kerr, N. L. (1991). Might versus morality explored: Motivational and cognitive bases for social motives. *Journal of Personality and Social Psychology, 60,* 756–765.

Savitsky, K. (2007). Egocentrism. In R. F. Baumeister & K. D. Vohs (Eds.), *Encyclopedia of social psychology* (p. 278). Thousand Oaks, CA: Sage.

Savitsky, K., Van Boven, L., Epley, N., & Wight, W. (2005). The unpacking effect in responsibility allocations for group tasks. *Journal of Experimental Social Psychology, 41,* 447–457.

Sawyer, K. (2007). *Group genius: The creative power of collaboration.* New York: Basic Books.

Sayette, M. A., Kirchner, T. R., Moreland, R. L., Levine, J. M., & Travis, T. (2004). Effects of alcohol on risk-seeking behavior: A group-level analysis. *Psychology of Addictive Behaviors, 18,* 190–193.

Scandura, T. A., & Lankau, M. J. (1996). Developing diverse leaders: A leader–member exchange approach. *Leadership Quarterly, 7,* 243–263.

Schachter, S. (1951). Deviation, rejection, and communication. *Journal of Abnormal and Social Psychology, 46,* 190–207.

Schachter, S. (1959). *The psychology of affiliation.* Stanford, CA: Stanford University Press.

Schachter, S., Ellertson, N., McBride, D., & Gregory, D. (1951). An experimental study of cohesiveness and productivity. *Human Relations, 4,* 229–238.

Schauer, A. H., Seymour, W. R., & Geen, R. G. (1985). Effects of observation and evaluation on anxiety in beginning counselors: A social facilitation analysis. *Journal of Counseling and Development, 63,* 279–285.

Schein, E. H. (1961). *Coercive persuasion.* New York: Norton.

Schein, L. A., Spitz, H. I., Burlingame, G. M., & Muskin, P. R. (Eds.), with S. Vargo (2006). *Psychological effects of catastrophic disasters: Group approaches to treatment.* New York: Haworth Press.

Schein, V. (2007). Women in management: Reflections and projections. *Women in Management Review, 22,* 6–8.

Scheuble, K. J., Dixon, K. N., Levy, A. B., & Kagan-Moore, L. (1987). Premature termination: A risk in eating disorder groups. *Group, 11,* 85–93.

Schlenker, B. R. (1975). Liking for a group following an initiation: Impression management or dissonance reduction? *Sociometry, 38,* 99–118.

Schlenker, B. R., Phillips, S. T., Boniecki, K. A., & Schlenker, D. R. (1995a). Championship pressures: Choking or triumphing in one's own territory. *Journal of Personality and Social Psychology, 68,* 632–643.

Schlenker, B. R., Phillips, S. T., Boniecki, K. A., & Schlenker, D. R. (1995b). Where is the home choke? *Journal of Personality and Social Psychology, 68,* 649–652.

Schlenker, B. R., Pontari, B. A., & Christopher, A. N. (2001). Excuses and character: Personal and social implications of excuses. *Personality and Social Psychology Review, 5,* 15–32.

Schlesinger, A. M., Jr. (1965). *A thousand days.* Boston: Houghton Mifflin.

Schmid Mast, M. S. (2002). Female dominance hierarchies: Are they any different from males'? *Personality and Social Psychology Bulletin, 28,* 29–39.

Schmidt, D. E., & Keating, J. P. (1979). Human crowding and personal control: An integration of the research. *Psychological Bulletin, 86,* 680–700.

Schmidt, N., & Sermat, V. (1983). Measuring loneliness in different relationships. *Journal of Personality and Social Psychology, 44,* 1038–1047.

Schmitt, B. H., Dubé, L., & Leclerc, F. (1992). Intrusions into waiting lines: Does the queue constitute a social system? *Journal of Personality and Social Psychology, 63,* 806–815.

Schmitt, B. H., Gilovich, T., Goore, N., & Joseph, L. (1986). Mere presence and social facilitation: One more time. *Journal of Experimental Social Psychology, 22,* 242–248.

Schmitt, D. R. (1981). Performance under cooperation or competition. *American Behavioral Scientist, 24,* 649–679.

Schneebaum, T. (1969). *Keep the river on your right.* New York: Grove Press.

Schneider, D. J. (2004). *The psychology of stereotyping.* New York: Guilford.

Schneider, J., & Cook, K. (1995). Status inconsistency and gender: Combining revisited. Special issue: Extending interaction theory. *Small Group Research, 26,* 372–399.

Schofield, J. W. (1978). School desegregation and intergroup relations. In D. Bar-Tal & L. Saxe (Eds.), *The social psychology of education.* Washington, DC: Halstead.

Schofield, J. W., & Sagar, H. A. (1977). Peer interaction patterns in an integrated middle school. *Sociometry, 40,* 130–138.

Schofield, J. W., & Whitley, B. E., Jr. (1983). Peer nomination vs. rating scale measurement of children's peer preferences. *Social Psychology Quarterly, 46,* 242–251.

Scholten, L., van Knippenberg, D., Nijstad, B. A., & De Dreu, C. K. W. (2007). Motivated information processing and group decision-making: Effects of process accountability on information processing and decision quality. *Journal of Experimental Social Psychology, 43,* 539–552.

Schopler, J., & Insko, C. A. (1992). The discontinuity effect in interpersonal and intergroup relations: Generality and mediation. In W. Stroebe & M. Hewstone (Eds.), *European Review of Social Psychology* (Vol. 3, pp. 121–151). Chichester, England: Wiley.

Schopler, J., Insko, C. A., Drigotas, S. M., Wieselquist, J., Pemberton, M., & Cox, C. (1995). The role of identifiability in the reduction of interindividual–intergroup discontinuity. *Journal of Experimental Social Psychology, 31,* 553–574.

Schriesheim, C. A., Castro, S. L., & Cogliser, C. C. (1999). Leader–member exchange (LMX) research: A comprehensive review of theory, measurement, and data-analytic practices. *The Leadership Quarterly, 10,* 63–113.

Schriesheim, C. A., & Eisenbach, R. J. (1995). An exploratory and confirmatory factor-analytic investigation of item wording effects on the obtained factor structures of survey questionnaire measures. *Journal of Management, 21,* 1177–1193.

Schriesheim, C. A., Hinkin, T. R., & Podsakoff, P. M. (1991). Can ipsative and single-item measures produce erroneous results in field studies of French and Raven's (1959) five bases of power? An empirical investigation. *Journal of Applied Psychology, 76,* 106–114.

Schroeder, H. W. (2007). Place experience, gestalt, and the human–nature relationship. *Journal of Environmental Psychology, 27,* 293–309.

Schubert, M. A., & Borkman, T. J. (1991). An organizational typology for self-help groups. *American Journal of Community Psychology, 19,* 769–787.

Schultz, P. W., Shriver, C., Tabanico, J. J., & Khazian, A. M. (2004). Implicit connections with nature. *Journal of Environmental Psychology, 24,* 31–42.

Schulz-Hardt, S., Frey, D., Luethgens, C., & Moscovici, S. (2000). Biased information search in group decision making. *Journal of Personality and Social Psychology, 78,* 655–669.

Schulz-Hardt, S., Jochims, M., & Frey, D. (2002). Productive conflict in group decision making: Genuine and contrived dissent as strategies to counteract biased information seeking. *Organizational Behavior and Human Decision Processes, 88,* 563–586.

Schuster, B. (1996). Mobbing, bullying, and peer rejection. *Psychological Science Agenda, 9,* 12–13.

Schuster, M. A., Stein, B. D., Jaycox, L. H., Collins, R. L., Marshall, G. N., Elliott, M. N., Zhou, A. J., Kanouse, D. E., Morrison, J. L., & Berry, S. H. (2001). A national survey of stress reactions after the September 11, 2001, terrorist attacks. *New England Journal of Medicine, 345,* 1507–1512.

Schutz, W. C. (1958). *FIRO: A three-dimensional theory of interpersonal behavior.* New York: Rinehart.

Schutz, W. C. (1992). Beyond FIRO-B. Three new theory-driven measures—Element B: behavior, Element F: feelings, Element S: self. *Psychological Reports, 70,* 915–937.

Schwartz, B., & Barsky, S. F. (1977). The home advantage. *Social Forces, 55,* 641–661.

Schwartz, S. H. (1994). Are there universal aspects in the structure and contents of human values? *Journal of Social Issues, 50,* 19–45.

Schwartz, S. H. (2007). Universalism values and the inclusiveness of our moral universe. *Journal of Cross-Cultural Psychology, 38,* 711–728.

Schwartz, S. H., & Gottlieb, A. (1976). Bystander reactions to a violent theft: Crime in Jerusalem. *Journal of Personality and Social Psychology, 34,* 1188–1199.

Schwarzwald, J., Amir, Y., & Crain, R. L. (1992). Long-term effects of school desegregation experiences on interpersonal relations in the Israeli Defense Forces. *Personality and Social Psychology Bulletin, 18,* 357–368.

Schweitzer, M. E., & Kerr, J. L. (2000). Bargaining under the influence: The role of alcohol in negotiations. *The Academy of Management Executive, 14,* 47–57.

Sculley, J. (with J. A. Byme). (1987). *Odyssey: Pepsi to Apple … A journey of adventure, ideas, and the future.* New York: Harper & Row.

Seal, D. W., Bogart, L. M., & Ehrhardt, A. A. (1998). Small group dynamics: The utility of focus group discussion as a research method. *Group Dynamics: Theory, Research, and Practice, 2,* 253–267.

Seashore, S. E. (1954). *Group cohesiveness in the industrial work group.* Ann Arbor, MI: Institute for Social Research.

Seashore, S. E., & Bowers, D. G. (1970). Durability of organizational change. *American Psychologist, 25,* 227–233.

Sedgwick, J. (1982). *Night vision.* New York: Simon & Schuster.

Sedikides, C., Gaertner, L., & Toguchi, Y. (2003). Pancultural self-enhancement. *Journal of Personality and Social Psychology, 84,* 60–79.

Seeman, A. A., & Hellman, P. (1975). *Chief!* New York: Avon.

Seers, A., Keller, T., & Wilkerson, J. M. (2003). Can team members share leadership? Foundations in research and theory. In C. L. Pearce & J. A. Conger (Eds.), *Shared leadership: Reframing the hows and whys of leadership* (pp. 77–102). Thousand Oaks, CA: Sage.

Seers, A., & Woodruff, S. (1997). Temporal pacing in task forces: Group development or deadline pressure? *Journal of Management, 23,* 169–187.

Segal, H. A. (1954). Initial psychiatric findings of recently repatriated prisoners of war. *American Journal of Psychiatry, 111,* 358–363.

Segal, M. W. (1974). Alphabet and attraction: An unobtrusive measure of the effect of propinquity in a field setting. *Journal of Personality and Social Psychology, 30,* 654–657.

Sekaquaptewa, D., & Thompson, M. (2002). The differential effects of solo status on members of high- and low-status groups. *Personality and Social Psychology Bulletin, 28,* 694–707.

Sekaquaptewa, D., & Thompson, M. (2003). Solo status, stereotype threat, and performance expectancies: Their effects on women's performance. *Journal of Experimental Social Psychology, 39,* 68–74.

Seligman, M. E. P. (1995). The effectiveness of psychotherapy: The Consumer Reports study. *American Psychologist, 50,* 965–974.

Seligman, M. E. P. (1996). Science as an ally of practice. *American Psychologist, 51,* 1072–1079.

Sell, J. (1997). Gender, strategies, and contributions to public goods. *Social Psychology Quarterly, 60,* 252–265.

Sell, J., Lovaglia, M. J., Mannix, E. A., Samuelson, C. D., & Wilson, R. K. (2004). Investigating conflict, power, and status within and among groups. *Small Group Research, 35,* 44–72.

Semin, G. R. (2007). Grounding communication: Synchrony. In A. W. Kruglanski & E. T. Higgins (Eds.), *Social psychology: Handbook of basic principles* (2nd ed., pp. 630–649). New York: Guilford.

Semin, G. R., & Rubini, M. (1990). Unfolding the concept of person by verbal abuse. *European Journal of Social Psychology, 20,* 463–474.

Service, E. R. (1975). *Origins of the state and civilization.* New York: Norton.

Sessa, V. I., & London, M. (2008). Group learning: An introduction. In V. I. Sessa & M. London (Eds.), *Work group learning: Understanding, improving and assessing how groups learn in organizations* (pp. 3–13). New York: Taylor & Francis Group/Erlbaum.

Seta, C. E., & Seta, J. J. (1995). When audience presence is enjoyable: The influences of audience awareness of prior success on performance and task interest. *Basic and Applied Social Psychology, 16,* 95–108.

Seta, J. J., Crisson, J. E., Seta, C. E., & Wang, M. A. (1989). Task performance and perceptions of anxiety: Averaging and summation in an evaluative setting. *Journal of Personality and Social Psychology, 56,* 387–396.

Seta, J. J., Seta, C. E., & Donaldson, S. (1991). The impact of comparison processes on coactors' frustration and willingness to expend effort. *Personality and Social Psychology Bulletin, 17,* 560–568.

Seta, J. J., Seta, C. E., & McElroy, T. (2006). Better than better-than-average (or not): Elevated and depressed self-evaluations following unfavorable social comparisons. *Self and Identity, 5,* 51–72.

Sexton, J. B., & Helmreich, R. L. (2000). Analyzing cockpit communications: The links between language, performance, error, and workload. *Human Performance in Extreme Environments, 5,* 63–68.

Shackelford, S., Wood, W., & Worchel, S. (1996). Behavioral styles and the influence of women in mixed-sex groups. *Social Psychology Quarterly, 59,* 284–293.

Shales, T., & Miller, J. A. (2002). *Live from New York: An uncensored history of Saturday Night Live.* New York: Little, Brown.

Shaver, P., & Buhrmester, D. (1983). Loneliness, sex-role orientation, and group life: A social needs perspective. In P. B. Paulus (Ed.), *Basic group processes* (pp. 259–288). New York: Springer-Verlag.

Shaver, P., Schwartz, J., Kirson, D., & O'Connor, C. (1987). Emotion knowledge: Further exploration of a prototype approach. *Journal of Personality and Social Psychology, 52,* 1061–1086.

Shaw, M. E. (1964). Communication networks. *Advances in Experimental Social Psychology, 1,* 111–147.

Shaw, M. E. (1978). Communication networks fourteen years later. In L. Berkowitz (Ed.), *Group processes.* New York: Academic Press.

Shaw, M. E. (1981). *Group dynamics: The psychology of small group behavior* (3rd ed.). New York: McGraw-Hill.

Shaw, M. E., & Shaw, L. M. (1962). Some effects of sociometric grouping upon learning in a second grade classroom. *Journal of Social Psychology, 57,* 453–458.

Shaw, Marjorie E. (1932). A comparison of individuals and small groups in the rational solution of complex problems. *American Journal of Psychology, 44,* 491–504.

Sheatsley, P. B., & Feldman, J. J. (1964). The assassination of President Kennedy: A preliminary report on public attitudes and behavior. *Public Opinion Quarterly, 28,* 189–215.

Shebilske, W. L., Jordon, J. A., Goettl, B. P., & Paulus, L. E. (1998). Observation versus hands-on practice of complex skills in dyadic, triadic, and tetradic training-teams. *Human Factors, 40,* 525–540.

Shechtman, Z. (1994). The effect of group psychotherapy on close same-gender friendships among boys and girls. *Sex Roles, 30,* 829–834.

Shelly, R. K., Troyer, L., Munroe, P. T., & Burger, T. (1999). Social structure and the duration of social acts. *Social Psychology Quarterly, 62,* 83–95.

Sheppard, B. H. (1983). Managers as inquisitors: Some lessons from the law. In H. Bazerman & R. J. Lewicki (Eds.), *Negotiating in organizations* (pp. 193–213). Thousand Oaks, CA: Sage.

Shepperd, J. A. (1993). Productive loss in performance groups: A motivational analysis. *Psychological Bulletin, 113,* 67–81.

Shepperd, J. A. (1995). Remedying motivation and productivity loss in collective settings. *Current Directions in Psychological Science, 5,* 131–133.

Shepperd, J. A., & Wright, R. A. (1989). Individual contributions to a collective effort: An incentive analysis. *Personality and Social Psychology Bulletin, 15,* 141–149.

Sheridan, C. L., & King, R. G., Jr. (1972). Obedience to authority with an authentic victim. *Proceedings of the 80th Annual Convention of the American Psychological Association, 7,* 165–166.

Sherif, M. (1936). *The psychology of social norms.* New York: Harper & Row.

Sherif, M. (1966). *In common predicament: Social psychology of intergroup conflict and cooperation.* Boston: Houghton Mifflin.

Sherif, M., Harvey, O. J., White, B. J., Hood, W. R., & Sherif, C. W. (1961). *Intergroup conflict and cooperation. The Robbers Cave Experiment.* Norman, OK: Institute of Group Relations.

Sherif, M., & Sherif, C. W. (1953). *Groups in harmony and tension.* New York: Harper & Row.

Sherif, M., & Sherif, C. W. (1956). *An outline of social psychology* (rev. ed.). New York: Harper & Row.

Sherif, M., White, B. J., & Harvey, O. J. (1955). Status in experimentally produced groups. *American Journal of Sociology, 60,* 370–379.

Sherrod, D. R., & Cohen, S. (1979). Density, personal control, and design. In J. R. Aiello & A. Baum (Eds.), *Residential crowding and design* (pp. 217–227). New York: Plenum.

Shipper, F., & Davy, J. (2002). A model and investigation of managerial skills, employees' attitudes, and managerial performance. *Leadership Quarterly, 13,* 95–120.

Short, J. F., Jr. (Ed). (1968). *Gang delinquency and delinquent subcultures.* New York: Harper & Row.

Shure, G. H., & Meeker, J. R. (1967). A personality/attitude scale for use in experimental bargaining studies. *Journal of Psychology, 65,* 233–252.

Shure, G. H., Rogers, M. S., Larsen, I. M., & Tassone, J. (1962). Group planning and task effectiveness. *Sociometry, 25,* 263–282.

Sias, P. M., Krone, K. J., & Jablin, F. M. (2002). An ecological systems perspective on workplace relationships. In M. L. Knapp & J. A. Daly (Eds.), *Handbook of interpersonal communication* (3rd ed., pp. 615–642). Thousand Oaks, CA: Sage.

Sidanius, J., Haley, H., Molina, L., & Pratto, F. (2007). Vladimir's choice and the distribution of social resources: A group dominance perspective. *Group Processes & Intergroup Relations, 10,* 257–265.

Sidanius, J., & Pratto, F. (1999). *Social dominance: An intergroup theory of social hierarchy and oppression.* New York: Cambridge University Press.

Siebold, G. L. (2007). The essence of military group cohesion. *Armed Forces & Society, 33,* 286–295.

Sigall, H., Mucchi-Faina, A., & Mosso, C. (2006). Minority influence is facilitated when the communication employs linguistic abstractness. *Group Processes & Intergroup Relations, 9,* 443–451.

Silver, W. S., & Bufanio, K. A. (1996). The impact of group efficacy and group goals on group task performance. *Small Group Research, 27,* 347–349.

Simmel, G. (1902). The number of members as determining the sociological form of the group. *American Journal of Sociology, 8,* 1–46, 158–196.

Simmel, G. (1950). *The sociology of Georg Simmel* (K. H. Wolff, Trans.). New York: Free Press.

Simmel, G. (1955). *Conflict.* New York: Free Press.

Simon, B., Glässner-Bayerl, B., & Stratenwerth, I. (1991). Stereotyping and self-stereotyping in a natural intergroup context: The case of heterosexual and homosexual men. *Social Psychology Quarterly, 54,* 252–266.

Simon, B., & Hamilton, D. L. (1994). Self-stereotyping and social context: The effects of relative ingroup size and ingroup status. *Journal of Personality and Social Psychology, 66,* 699–711.

Simon, B., & Klandermans, B. (2001). Politicized collective identity: A social-psychological analysis. *American Psychologist, 56,* 319–331.

Simon, B., Pantaleo, G., & Mummendey, A. (1995). Unique individual or interchangeable group member? The accentuation of intragroup differences versus similarities as an indicator of the individual self versus the collective self. *Journal of Personality and Social Psychology, 69,* 106–119.

Simon, R. J. (1980). *The jury: Its role in American society.* Lexington, MA: Heath.

Simonson, I., & Nowlis, S. M. (2000). The role of explanations and need for uniqueness in consumer decision making: Unconventional choices based on reasons. *Journal of Consumer Research, 27,* 49–68.

Simonton, D. K. (1985). Intelligence and personal influence in groups: Four nonlinear models. *Psychological Review, 92,* 532–547.

Simpson, B. (2003). Sex, fear, and greed: A social dilemma analysis of gender and cooperation. *Social Forces, 82,* 35–52.

Simpson, J. A. (2007). Psychological foundations of trust. *Current Directions in Psychological Science, 16,* 264–268.

Singer, E. (1990). Reference groups and social evaluations. In M. Rosenberg & R. H. Turner (Eds.), *Social psychology: Sociological perspectives* (pp. 66–93). New Brunswick, NJ: Transaction Publishers.

Singer, J. E., Baum, C. S.Baum, A., & Thew, B. D. (1982). Mass psychogenic illness: The case for social comparison. In M. J. Colligan, J. W. Pennebaker, & L. R. Murphy (Eds.), *Mass psychogenic illness: A social psychological analysis* (pp. 155–169). Mahwah, NJ: Erlbaum.

Singer, J. E., Brush, C. A., & Lublin, S. C. (1965). Some aspects of deindividuation: Identification and conformity. *Journal of Experimental Social Psychology, 1,* 356–378.

Skinner, B. F. (1953). *Science and human behavior.* New York: Macmillan.

Skinner, B. F. (1971). *Beyond freedom and dignity*. New York: Knopf.

Skitka, L. J., Winquist, J., & Hutchinson, S. (2003). Are outcome fairness and outcome favorability distinguishable psychological constructs? A meta-analytic review. *Social Justice Research, 16,* 309–341.

Skyrms, B. (2004). *The stag hunt and the evolution of social structure*. New York: Cambridge University Press.

Slavson, S. R. (1950). Group psychotherapy. *Scientific American, 183,* 42–45.

Smart, R. (1965). Social-group membership, leadership, and birth order. *Journal of Social Psychology, 67,* 221–225.

Smeesters, D., Warlop, L., Van Avermaet, E., Corneille, O., & Yzerbyt, V. (2003). Do not prime hawks with doves: The interplay of construct activation and consistency of social value orientation on cooperative behavior. *Journal of Personality and Social Psychology, 84,* 972–987.

Smelser, N. J. (1962). *Theory of collective behavior*. New York: Free Press.

Smith, C. M. (2008). Adding minority status to a source of conflict: An examination of influence processes and product quality in dyads. *European Journal of Social Psychology, 38,* 75–83.

Smith, D. H. (1980). Participation in outdoor recreation and sports. In D. H. Smith, J. Macaulay, & Associates (Eds.), *Participation in social and political activities: A comprehensive analysis of political involvement, expressive leisure time, and helping behavior* (pp. 177–201). San Francisco: Jossey-Bass.

Smith, D. H. (2000). *Grassroots organizations*. Thousand Oaks, CA: Sage.

Smith, E. R., & Mackie, D. M. (2005). Aggression, hatred, and other emotions. In J. F. Dovidio, P. Glick & L. A. Rudman (Eds.), *On the nature of prejudice: Fifty years after Allport* (pp. 361–376). Malden, MA: Blackwell.

Smith, E. R., Murphy, J., & Coats, S. (1999). Attachment to groups: Theory and management. *Journal of Personality and Social Psychology, 77,* 94–110.

Smith, E. R., Seger, C. R., & Mackie, D. M. (2007). Can emotions be truly group level? Evidence regarding four conceptual criteria. *Journal of Personality and Social Psychology, 93,* 431–446.

Smith, J. A., & Foti, R. J. (1998). A pattern approach to the study of leader emergence. *Leadership Quarterly, 9,* 147–160.

Smith, K. P., & Christakis, N. A. (2008). Social networks and health. *Annual Review of Sociology, 34,* 405–429.

Smith, M. B. (1972). Is experimental social psychology advancing? *Journal of Experimental Social Psychology, 8,* 86–96.

Smith, P. B. (1975). Controlled studies of the outcome of sensitivity training. *Psychological Bulletin, 82,* 597–622.

Smith, P. B. (1980). The outcome of sensitivity training and encounter. In P. B. Smith (Ed.), *Small groups and personal change* (pp. 25–55). New York: Methuen.

Smith, P. B., & Bond, M. H. (1993). *Social psychology across cultures: Analysis and perspectives*. Boston: Allyn & Bacon.

Smith, P. K., Jostmann, N. B., Galinsky, A. D., & van Dijk, W. W. (2008). Lacking power impairs executive functions. *Psychological Science, 19,* 441–447.

Smith, P. K., & Trope, Y. (2006). You focus on the forest when you're in charge of the trees: Power priming and abstract information processing. *Journal of Personality and Social Psychology, 90,* 578–596.

Smith, R. H. (2000). Assimilative and contrastive emotional reactions to upward and downward social comparisons. In J. Suls & L. Wheeler (Eds.), *Handbook of social comparison: Theory and research* (pp. 173–200). New York: Kluwer Academic.

Smoke, W. H., & Zajonc, R. B. (1962). On the reliability of group judgments and decisions. In J. H. Criswell, H. Solomon, & P. Suppes (Eds.), *Mathematical methods in small group processes*. Stanford, CA: Stanford University Press.

Sniezek, J. A. (1992). Groups under uncertainty: An examination of confidence in group decision making. *Organizational Behavior and Human Decision Processes, 52,* 124–155.

Snow, D. A., & Oliver, P. E. (1995). Social movements and collective behavior: Social psychological dimensions and considerations. In K. S. Cook, G. A. Fine, & J. S. House (Eds.), *Sociological perspectives on social psychology* (pp. 571–599). Needham Heights, MA: Allyn and Bacon.

Snyder, C. R., & Fromkin, H. L. (1980). *Uniqueness: The human pursuit of difference*. New York: Plenum Press.

Snyder, C. R., Higgins, R. L., & Stucky, R. J. (1983). *Excuses: Masquerades in search of grace.* New York: Wiley.

Sommer, R. (1959). Studies in personal space. *Sociometry, 22,* 247–260.

Sommer, R. (1967). Small group ecology. *Psychological Bulletin, 67,* 145–152.

Sommer, R. (1969). *Personal space.* Englewood Cliffs, NJ: Prentice Hall.

Sorrels, J. P., & Kelley, J. (1984). Conformity by omission. *Personality and Social Psychology Bulletin, 10,* 302–305.

Sorrentino, R. M., & Boutillier, R. G. (1975). The effect of quantity and quality of verbal interaction on ratings of leadership ability. *Journal of Experimental Social Psychology, 11,* 403–411.

Sorrentino, R. M., & Field, N. (1986). Emergent leadership over time: The functional value of positive motivation. *Journal of Personality and Social Psychology, 50,* 1091–1099.

Spears, R., Lea, M., & Postmes, T. (2007). CMC and social identity. In A. N. Joinson, K. Y. A. McKenna, T. Postmes, & U.-D. Reips (Eds.), *The Oxford handbook of internet psychology* (pp. 253–269). Oxford: Oxford University Press.

Spears, R., Postmes, T., Lea, M., & Wolbert, A. (2002). When are net effects gross products? The power of influence and the influence of power in computer-mediated communication. *Journal of Social Issues, 58,* 91–107.

Spencer, H. (1897). *The principles of sociology.* New York: Appleton.

Spencer, R. W., & Huston, J. H. (1993). Rational forecasts: On confirming ambiguity as the mother of conformity. *Journal of Economic Psychology, 14,* 697–709.

Spencer Stuart. (2004). The 2004 Spencer Stuart route to the top: Our survey of Fortune 700 CEOs provides a snapshot of today's CEOs and the major trends emerging. Retrieved June 29, 2004, from http://www.spencerstuart.com.

Spitzberg, B. H., & Cupach, W. R. (2002). Interpersonal skills. In M. L. Knapp & J. A. Daly (Eds.), *Handbook of interpersonal communication* (3rd ed., pp. 564–611). Thousand Oaks, CA: Sage.

Spoor, J. R., & Kelly, J. R. (2004). The evolutionary significance of affect in groups: Communication and group bonding. *Group Processes & Intergroup Relations, 7,* 398–412.

Squire, S. (1983). *The slender balance.* New York: Pinnacle.

Srivastava, S., & Beer, J. S. (2005). How self-evaluations relate to being liked by others: Integrating sociometer and attachment perspectives. *Journal of Personality and Social Psychology, 89,* 966–977.

St. John, W. (2004). *Rammer Jammer Yellow Hammer: A journey into the heart of fan mania.* New York: Crown.

Stager, S. F., Chassin, L., & Young, R. D. (1983). Determinants of self-esteem among labeled adolescents. *Social Psychology Quarterly, 46,* 3–10.

Stangor, C., Jonas, K., Stroebe, W., & Hewstone, M. (1996). Influence of student exchange on national stereotypes, attitudes, and perceived group variability. *European Journal of Social Psychology, 26,* 663–675.

Stark, E. M., Shaw, J. D., & Duffy, M. K. (2007). Preference for group work, winning orientation, and social loafing behavior in groups. *Group & Organization Management, 32,* 699–723.

Stasser, G. (1992). Pooling of unshared information during group discussions. In S. Worchel, W. Wood, & J. A. Simpson (Eds.), *Group process and productivity* (pp. 48–67). Thousand Oaks, CA: Sage.

Stasser, G., & Dietz-Uhler, B. (2001). Collective choice, judgment, and problem solving. In M. A. Hogg & R. S. Tindale (Eds.), *Blackwell handbook of social psychology: Group processes* (pp. 31–55). Malden, MA: Blackwell.

Stasser, G., Kerr, N. L., & Bray, R. M. (1982). The social psychology of jury deliberations: Structure, process, and product. In N. L. Kerr & R. M. Bray (Eds.), *Psychology of the courtroom* (pp. 221–256). New York: Academic Press.

Stasser, G., & Stewart, D. (1992). Discovery of hidden profiles by decision-making groups: Solving a problem versus making a judgment. *Journal of Personality and Social Psychology, 63,* 426–434.

Stasser, G., & Titus, W. (1987). Effects of information load and percentage of shared information on the dissemination of unshared information during group discussion. *Journal of Personality and Social Psychology, 53,* 81–93.

Stasson, M. F., & Bradshaw, S. D. (1995). Explanations of individual–group performance differences: What sort of "bonus" can be gained through group interaction? *Small Group Research, 26,* 296–308.

Stasson, M. F., Kameda, T., & Davis, J. H. (1997). A model of agenda influences on group decisions. *Group Dynamics: Theory, Research, and Practice, 1,* 316–323.

Staub, E. (1989). *The roots of evil: The origins of genocide and other group violence.* New York: Cambridge University Press.

Staub, E. (1990). Moral exclusion, personal goal theory, and extreme destructiveness. *Journal of Social Issues, 46,* 47–64.

Staub, E. (2004). Basic human needs, altruism, and aggression. In A. G. Miller (Ed.), *The social psychology of good and evil* (pp. 51–84). New York: Guilford.

Staudacher, C. (1994). *Time to grieve.* San Francisco: HarperCollins.

Staw, B. M., & Ross, J. (1987). Behavior in escalation situations: Antecedents, prototypes, and solutions. *Research in Organizational Behavior, 9,* 39–78.

Steele, C. M., & Aronson, J. (1995). Stereotype threat and the intellectual test performance of African Americans. *Journal of Personality and Social Psychology, 69,* 797–811.

Stein, R. T., & Heller, T. (1979). An empirical analysis of the correlations between leadership status and participation rates reported in the literature. *Journal of Personality and Social Psychology, 37,* 1993–2002.

Steinel, W., & De Dreu, C. K. (2004). Social motives and strategic misrepresentation in social decision making. *Journal of Personality and Social Psychology, 86,* 419–434.

Steiner, I. D. (1972). *Group process and productivity.* New York: Academic Press.

Steiner, I. D. (1974). Whatever happened to the group in social psychology? *Journal of Experimental Social Psychology, 10,* 94–108.

Steiner, I. D. (1983). What ever happened to the touted revival of the group? In H. Blumberg, A. Hare, V. Kent, & M. Davies (Eds.), *Small groups and social interaction* (Vol. 2, pp. 539–547). New York: Wiley.

Steiner, I. D. (1986). Paradigms and groups. *Advances in Experimental Social Psychology, 19,* 251–289.

Steinzor, B. (1950). The spatial factor in face to face discussion groups. *Journal of Abnormal and Social Psychology, 45,* 552–555.

Stempfle, J., Hübner, O., & Badke-Schaub, P. (2001). A functional theory of task role distribution in work groups. *Group Processes & Intergroup Relations, 4,* 138–159.

Stephan, F. F., & Mischler, E. G. (1952). The distribution of participation in small groups: An exponential approximation. *American Sociological Review, 17,* 598–608.

Stephan, W. G. (1987). The contact hypothesis in intergroup relations. In C. Hendrick (Ed.), *Review of personality and social psychology: Group process* (Vol. 9, pp. 13–40). Thousand Oaks, CA: Sage.

Stephan, W. G., & Rosenfield, D. (1982). Racial and ethnic stereotypes. In A. G. Miller (Ed.), *In the eye of the beholder: Contemporary issues in stereotyping.* New York: Praeger.

Stephan, W. G., & Stephan, C. W. (2005). Intergroup relations program evaluation. In J. F. Dovidio, P. Glick & L. A. Rudman (Eds.), *On the nature of prejudice: Fifty years after Allport* (pp. 431–446). Malden, MA: Blackwell.

Stern, E. K. (1997). Probing the plausibility of newgroup syndrome: Kennedy and the Bay of Pigs. In P. 't Hart, E. K. Stern, & B. Sundelius (Eds.), *Beyond groupthink: Political group dynamics and foreign policy-making* (pp. 153–189). Ann Arbor: University of Michigan Press.

Sternberg, R. J. (2003). A duplex theory of hate: Development and application to terrorism, massacres, and genocide. *Review of General Psychology, 7,* 299–328.

Sternberg, R. J., & Dobson, D. M. (1987). Resolving interpersonal conflicts: An analysis of stylistic consistency. *Journal of Personality and Social Psychology, 52,* 794–812.

Stets, J. E. (1997). Status and identity in marital interaction. *Social Psychology Quarterly, 60,* 185–217.

Stevens, M. J., & Campion, M. A. (1994). The knowledge, skill, and ability requirements for teamwork: Implications for human resource management. *Journal of Management, 20,* 503–530.

Stevens, M. J., & Campion, M. A. (1999). Staffing work teams: Development and validation of a selection test for teamwork settings. *Journal of Management, 25,* 207–228.

Stevenson, W. B., Pearce, J. L., & Porter, L. W. (1985). The concept of "coalition" in organization theory and research. *Academy of Management Journal, 10,* 256–268.

Stevenson, R. J., & Repacholi, B. M. (2003). Age-related changes in children's hedonic response to male body odor. *Developmental Psychology, 39,* 670–679.

Stewart, D. D., & Stasser, G. (1998). The sampling of critical, unshared information in decision-making groups: The role of an informed minority. *European Journal of Social Psychology, 28,* 95–113.

Stewart, G. L. (2006). A meta-analytic review of relationships between team design features and team performance. *Journal of Management, 32,* 29–55.

Stewart, G. L., & Manz, C. C. (1995). Leadership for self-managing work teams: A typology and integrative model. *Human Relations, 48,* 747–770.

Stewart, P. A., & Moore, J. C. (1992). Wage disparities and performance expectations. *Social Psychology Quarterly, 55,* 78–85.

Stice, E., Marti, C. N., Spoor, S., Presnell, K., & Shaw, H. (2008). Dissonance and healthy weight eating disorder prevention programs: Long-term effects from a randomized efficacy trial. *Journal of Consulting and Clinical Psychology, 76,* 329–340.

Stiles, W. B., Lyall, L. M., Knight, D. P., Ickes, W., Waung, M., Hall, C. L., & Primeau, B. E. (1997). Gender differences in verbal presumptuousness and attentiveness. *Personality and Social Psychology Bulletin, 23,* 759–772.

Stiles, W. B., Shapiro, D. A., & Elliott, R. (1986). "Are all psychotherapies equivalent?" *American Psychologist, 41,* 165–180.

Stinson, D. A., Logel, C., Zanna, M. P., Holmes, J. G., Cameron, J. J., Wood, J. V., Spencer, S. J., (2008). The cost of lower self-esteem: Testing a self- and social-bonds model of health. *Journal of Personality and Social Psychology, 94,* 412–428.

Stogdill, R. M. (1948). Personal factors associated with leadership. *Journal of Psychology, 23,* 35–71.

Stogdill, R. M. (1974). *Handbook of leadership.* New York: Free Press.

Stokes, J. P. (1983). Components of group cohesion: Intermember attraction, instrumental value, and risk taking. *Small Group Behavior, 14,* 163–173.

Stokes, J. P. (1985). The relation of social network and individual difference variables to loneliness. *Journal of Personality and Social Psychology, 48,* 981–990.

Stokols, D. (1972). On the distinction between density and crowding: Some implications for future research. *Psychological Review, 79,* 275–278.

Stokols, D. (1978). In defense of the crowding construct. In A. Baum, J. E. Singer, & S. Valins (Eds.), *Advances in environmental psychology* (Vol. 1, pp. 111–130). Mahwah, NJ: Erlbaum.

Stokols, D., & Altman, I. (Eds.). (1987). *Handbook of environmental psychology* (Vols. 1 & 2). New York: Wiley.

Stolte, J. F., Fine, G. A., & Cook, K. S. (2001). Sociological miniaturism: Seeing the big through the small in social psychology. *Annual Review of Sociology, 27,* 387–413.

Stoner, J. A. F. (1961). *A comparison of individual and group decisions involving risk.* Unpublished master's thesis, Massachusetts Institute of Technology.

Stoner, J. A. (1968). Risky and cautious shifts in group decisions: The influence of widely held values. *Journal of Experimental Social Psychology, 4,* 442–459.

Stones, C. R. (1982). A community of Jesus people in South Africa. *Small Group Behavior, 13,* 264–272.

Stoop, J. R. (1932). Is the judgment of the group better than that of the average member of the group? *Journal of Experimental Psychology, 15,* 550–562.

Storms, M. D., & Thomas, G. C. (1977). Reactions to physical closeness. *Journal of Personality and Social Psychology, 35,* 319–328.

Storr, A. (1988). *Solitude: A return to the self.* New York: Free Press.

Stratham, A. (1987). The gender model revisited: Differences in the management styles of men and women. *Sex Roles, 16,* 409–429.

Straus, S. G. (1997). Technology, group process, and group outcomes: Testing the connections in computer-mediated and face-to-face groups. *Human–Computer Interaction, 12,* 227–266.

Strauss, A., & Corbin, J. (1998). *Basics of qualitative research: Techniques and procedures for developing grounded theory* (2nd ed.). Thousand Oaks, CA: Sage.

Strauss, A. L. (1944). The literature on panic. *Journal of Abnormal and Social Psychology, 39,* 317–328.

Strauss, B. (2002). Social facilitation in motor tasks: A review of research and theory. *Psychology of Sport & Exercise, 3,* 237–256.

Streufert, S., & Streufert, S. C. (1986). The development of international conflict. In S. Worchel & W. G. Austin (Eds.), *Psychology of intergroup relations* (2nd ed., pp. 134–152). Chicago: Nelson-Hall.

Strickland, L. H., Barefoot, J. C., & Hockenstein, P. (1976). Monitoring behavior in the surveillance and trust paradigm. *Representative Research in Social Psychology, 7,* 51–57.

Strodtbeck, F. L., & Hook, L. H. (1961). The social dimensions of a twelve-man jury table. *Sociometry, 24,* 397–415.

Strodtbeck, F. L., James, R. M., & Hawkins, C. (1957). Social status in jury deliberations. *American Sociological Review, 22,* 713–719.

Strodtbeck, F. L., & Lipinski, R. M. (1985). Becoming first among equals: Moral considerations in jury foreman selection. *Journal of Personality and Social Psychology, 49,* 927–936.

Strodtbeck, F. L., & Mann, R. D. (1956). Sex role differentiation in jury deliberations. *Sociometry, 19,* 3–11.

Stroebe, M. S. (1994). The broken heart phenomenon: An examination of the mortality of bereavement. *Journal of Community and Applied Social Psychology, 4,* 47–61.

Stroebe, W., Diehl, M., & Abakoumkin, G. (1992). The illusion of group effectivity. *Personality and Social Psychology Bulletin, 18,* 643–650.

Stroebe, W., Stroebe, M. S., Abakoumkin, G., & Schut, H. (1996). The role of loneliness and social support in adjustment to loss: A test of attachment versus stress theory. *Journal of Personality and Social Psychology, 70,* 1241–1249.

Strong, S. R., Hills, H. I., Kilmartin, C. T., DeVries, H., Lanier, K., Nelson, B. N., Strickland, D., & Meyer, C. W. (1988). The dynamic relations among interpersonal behaviors: A test of complementarity and anticomplementarity. *Journal of Personality and Social Psychology, 54,* 798–810.

Strube, M. J. (2005). What did Triplett really find? A contemporary analysis of the first experiment in social psychology. *The American Journal of Psychology, 118,* 271–286.

Stryker, S., & Burke, P. J. (2000). The past, present, and future of an identity theory. *Social Psychology Quarterly, 63,* 284–297.

Stuster, J. (1996). *Bold endeavors: Lessons from polar and space exploration.* Annapolis, MD: Naval Institute Press.

Suedfeld, P. (1987). Extreme and unusual environments. In D. Stokols & I. Altman (Eds.), *Handbook of environmental psychology* (Vol. 1, pp. 863–887). New York: Wiley.

Suedfeld, P. (1997). The social psychology of "invictus": Conceptual and methodological approaches to indomitability. In C. McGarty & S. A. Haslam (Eds.), *The message of social psychology: Perspectives on mind in society* (pp. 329–341). Malden, MA: Blackwell.

Suedfeld, P., & Steel, G. D. (2000). The environmental psychology of capsule habitats. *Annual Review of Psychology, 51,* 227–253.

Sugiman, T., & Misumi, J. (1988). Development of a new evacuation method for emergencies: Control of collective behavior by emergent small groups. *Journal of Applied Psychology, 73,* 3–10.

Sugisawa, H., Liang, J., Liu, X. (1994). Social networks, social support, and mortality among older people in Japan. *Journals of Gerontology, 49,* S3–S13.

Suh, E. J., Moskowitz, D. S., Fournier, M. A., & Zuroff, D. C. (2004). Gender and relationships: Influences on agentic and communal behaviors. *Personal Relationships, 11,* 41–59.

Sulloway, F. J. (1996). *Born to rebel: Birth order, family dynamics, and creative lives.* New York: Pantheon Books.

Suls, J., Martin, R., & David, J. P. (1998). Person–environment fit and its limits: Agreeableness, neuroticism, and emotional reactivity to interpersonal conflict. *Personality and Social Psychology Bulletin, 24,* 88–98.

Suls, J., & Wheeler, L. (Eds.). (2000). *Handbook of social comparison: Theory and research.* New York: Kluwer Academic.

Sumner, W. G. (1906). *Folkways.* New York: Ginn.

Sundstrom, E. (1987). Work environments: Offices and factories. In D. Stokols & I. Altman (Eds.), *Handbook of environmental psychology* (Vol. 1, pp. 733–782). New York: Wiley.

Sundstrom, E., & Altman, I. (1974). Field study of dominance and territorial behavior. *Journal of Personality and Social Psychology, 30,* 115–125.

Sundstrom, E., Bell, P. A., Busby, P. L., & Asmus, C. (1996). Environmental psychology: 1989–1994. *Annual Review of Psychology, 47,* 485–512.

Sundstrom, E., McIntyre, M., Halfhill, T., & Richards, H. (2000). Work groups: From the Hawthorne studies to work teams of the 1990s and beyond. *Group Dynamics: Theory, Research, and Practice, 4,* 44–67.

Sunstein, C. R. (2002). The law of group polarization. *The Journal of Political Philosophy, 10,* 175–195.

Sunwolf. (2002). Getting to "GroupAha!": Provoking creative processes in task groups. In L. R. Frey (Ed.), *New directions in group communication* (pp. 203–217). Thousand Oaks, CA: Sage.

Surowiecki, J. (2004). *The wisdom of crowds: Why the many are smarter than the few and how collective wisdom shapes business, economies, societies, and nations.* New York: Random House.

Sussman, S., Pokhrel, P., Ashmore, R. D., & Brown, B. B. (2007). Adolescent peer group identification and characteristics: A review of the literature. *Addictive Behaviors, 32,* 1602–1627.

't Hart, P. (1998). Preventing groupthink revisited: Evaluating and reforming groups in government. *Organizational Behavior and Human Decision Processes, 73,* 306–326.

Tajfel, H. (1972). Some developments in European social psychology. *European Journal of Social Psychology, 2,* 307–321.

Tajfel, H. (1981). *Human groups and social categories.* Cambridge: Cambridge University Press.

Tajfel, H., & Turner, J. C. (1979). An integrative theory of intergroup conflict. In W. G. Austin & S. Worchel (Eds.), *Psychology of intergroup relations* (pp. 33–47). Monterey, CA: Brooks/Cole.

Tajfel, H., & Turner, J. C. (1986). The social identity theory of intergroup behavior. In S. Worchel & W. G. Austin (Eds.), *Psychology of intergroup relations* (2nd ed., pp. 7–24). Chicago: Nelson-Hall.

Takeda, M. B., Helms, M. M., & Romanova, N. (2006). Hair color stereotyping and CEO selection in the United Kingdom. *Journal of Human Behavior in the Social Environment, 13,* 85–99.

Tal-Or, N. (2008). Communicative behaviors of outperformers and their perception by the outperformed people. *Human Communication Research, 34,* 234–262.

Tang, J. (1997). The Model Minority thesis revisited: (Counter) evidence from the science and engineering fields. *Journal of Applied Behavioral Science, 33,* 291–314.

Tang, T. L., & Butler, E. A. (1997). Attributions of quality circles' problem-solving failure: Differences among management, supporting staff, and quality circle members. *Public Personnel Management, 26,* 203–225.

Tanis, M. (2007). Online social support groups. In A. N. Joinson, K. Y. A. McKenna, T. Postmes, & U. Reips (Eds.), *The Oxford handbook of internet psychology* (pp. 139–153). New York: Oxford.

Tanis, M., & Postmes, T. (2005). Short communication: A social identity approach to trust: Interpersonal perception, group membership and trusting behaviour. *European Journal of Social Psychology, 35,* 413–424.

Tarde, G. (1903). *The laws of imitation.* New York: Holt.

Tarnow, E. (2000). Self-destructive obedience in the airplane cockpit and the concept of obedience optimization. In T. Blass (Ed.), *Obedience to authority: Current perspectives on the Milgram paradigm* (pp. 111–123). Mahwah, NJ: Erlbaum.

Tata, J., Anthony, T., Hung-yu, L., Newman, B., Tang, S., Millson, M., & Sivakumar, K. (1996). Proportionate group size and rejection of the deviate: A meta-analytic integration. *Journal of Social Behavior and Personality, 11,* 739–752.

Tate, D. F., & Zabinski, M. F. (2004). Computer and Internet applications for psychological treatment: Update for clinicians. *Journal of Clinical Psychology, 60,* 209–220.

Taylor, F. W. (1923). *The principles of scientific management.* New York: Harper.

Taylor, H. F. (1970). *Balance in small groups.* New York: Van Nostrand Reinhold.

Taylor, R. B., & Lanni, J. C. (1981). Territorial dominance: The influence of the resident advantage in triadic decision making. *Journal of Personality and Social Psychology, 41,* 909–915.

Taylor, S. E. (2006). Tend and befriend: Behavioral bases of affiliation under stress. *Current Directions in Psychological Science, 15,* 273–277.

Taylor, S. E. (2007). Social support. In H. S. Friedman & R. C. Silver (Eds.), *Foundations of health psychology* (pp. 145–171). New York: Oxford University Press.

Taylor, S. E., Klein, L. C., Lewis, B. P., Gruenewald, T. L., Gurung, R. A. R., & Updegraff, J. A. (2000). Biobehavioral responses to stress in females: Tend-and-befriend, not fight-or-flight. *Psychological Review, 107,* 411–429.

Taylor, S. E., & Lobel, M. (1989). Social comparison activity under threat: Downward evaluation and upward contacts. *Psychological Review, 96,* 569–575.

Teger, A. (1980). *Too much invested to quit.* New York: Pergamon.

Ten Velden, F. S., Beersma, B., & De Dreu, C. K. W. (2007). Majority and minority influence in group negotiation: The moderating effects of social motivation and decision rules. *Journal of Applied Psychology, 92,* 259–268.

Tennen, H., McKee, T. E., & Affleck, G. (2000). Social comparison processes in health and illness. In J. Suls & L. Wheeler (Eds.), *Handbook of social comparison: Theory and research* (pp. 443–483). New York: Kluwer Academic/Plenum.

Teppner, B. J. (2006). What do managers do when subordinates just say, "No"? An analysis of incidents involving refusal to perform downward requests. In C. A. Schriesheim & L. L. Neider (Eds.), *Power and influence in organizations: New empirical and theoretical perspectives* (pp. 1–20). Greenwich, CT: Information Age Publishing.

Terry, D. J., & Callan, V. J. (1998). In-group bias in response to an organizational merger. *Group Dynamics: Theory, Research, and Practice, 2,* 67–81.

Tesser, A. (1988). Toward a self-evaluation maintenance model of social behavior. *Advances in Experimental Social Psychology, 21,* 181–227.

Tesser, A. (1991). Emotion in social comparison and reflection processes. In J. Suls & T. A. Wills (Eds.), *Social comparison: Contemporary theory and research* (pp. 117–148). Mahwah, NJ: Erlbaum.

Tesser, A., Campbell, J., & Smith, M. (1984). Friendship choice and performance: Self-evaluation maintenance in children. *Journal of Personality and Social Psychology, 46,* 561–574.

Tetlock, P. E. (1979). Identifying victims of groupthink from public statements of decision makers. *Journal of Personality and Social Psychology, 37,* 1314–1324.

Tetlock, P. E., Peterson, R. S., McGuire, C., Chang, S., & Feld, P. (1992). Assessing political group dynamics: A test of the groupthink model. *Journal of Personality and Social Psychology, 63,* 403–425.

"The Who," the what, but why? (1979, December 5). *Richmond News Leader*, p. A19.

Thibaut, J. W., & Kelley, H. H. (1959). *The social psychology of groups.* New York: Wiley.

Thoits, P. A. (1992). Identity structures and psychological well-being: Gender and marital status comparisons. *Social Psychology Quarterly, 55,* 236–256.

Thomas, K. W. (1992). Conflict and negotiation processes in organizations. In M. D. Dunnette & L. M. Hough (Eds.), *Handbook of industrial and organizational psychology* (2nd ed., Vol. 3, pp. 651–717). Palo Alto, CA: Consulting Psychologists Press.

Thomas, W. I., & Thomas, D. S. (1928). *The child in America: Behavior problems and programs.* New York: Knopf.

Thomas-Hunt, M. C., & Phillips, K. W. (2004). When what you know is not enough: Expertise and gender dynamics in task groups. *Personality and Social Psychology Bulletin, 30,* 1585–1598.

Thompson, L. (1991). Information exchange in negotiation. *Journal of Experimental Social Psychology, 27,* 161–179.

Thompson, L., & Nadler, J. (2000). Judgmental biases in conflict resolution and how to overcome them. In M. Deutsch & P. T. Coleman (Eds.), *The handbook of conflict resolution: Theory and practice* (pp. 213–235). San Francisco: Jossey-Bass.

Thompson, L. L., Mannix, E. A., & Bazerman, M. H. (1988). Group negotiation: Effects of decision rule, agenda, and aspiration. *Journal of Personality and Social Psychology, 54,* 86–95.

Thoreau, H. D. (1962). *Walden and other writings.* New York: Bantam.

Thorne, B. (1993). *Gender play.* New Brunswick, NJ: Rutgers University Press.

Thrasher, F. M. (1927). *The gang.* Chicago: University of Chicago Press.

Thurlow, C., Lengel, L., & Tomic, A. (2004). *Computer mediated communication: Social interaction and the Internet.* Thousand Oaks, CA: Sage.

Thye, S. R. (2000). A status value theory of power in exchange relations. *American Sociological Review, 65,* 407–432.

Thye, S. R., Yoon, J., & Lawler, E. J. (2002). The theory of relational cohesion: Review of a research program. In S. R. Thye & E. J. Lawler (Eds.), *Group cohesion, trust and solidarity* (pp. 139–166). New York: Elsevier Science/JAI Press.

Tiedens, L. Z. (2001). Anger and advancement versus sadness and subjugation: The effect of negative emotion expressions on social status conferral. *Journal of Personality and Social Psychology, 80,* 86–94.

Tiedens, L. Z., Ellsworth, P. C., & Mesquita, B. (2000). Stereotypes about sentiments and status: Emotional expectations for high- and low-status group members. *Personality and Social Psychology Bulletin, 26,* 560–574.

Tiedens, L. Z., & Fragale, A. R. (2003). Power moves: Complementarity in dominant and submissive nonverbal behavior. *Journal of Personality and Social Psychology, 84,* 558–568.

Tiedens, L. Z., Unzueta, M. M., & Young, M. J. (2007). An unconscious desire for hierarchy? The motivated perception of dominance complementarity in task partners. *Journal of Personality and Social Psychology, 93,* 402–414.

Tiger, L., & Fox, R. (1998). *The imperial animal.* New Brunswick, NJ: Transaction.

Tindale, R. S., Meisenhelder, H. M., Dykema-Engblade, A. A., & Hogg, M. A. (2001). Shared cognitions in small groups. In M. A. Hogg & R. S. Tindale (Eds.), *Blackwell handbook of social psychology: Group processes* (pp. 1–30). Oxford, UK: Blackwell.

Tindale, R. S., Stawiski, S., & Jacobs, E. (2008). Shared cognition and group learning. In V. I. Sessa & M. London (Eds.), *Work group learning: Understanding, improving and assessing how groups learn in organizations* (pp. 73–90). New York: Taylor & Francis Group/ Erlbaum.

Tjosvold, D. (1995). Cooperation theory, constructive controversy, and effectiveness: Learning from crisis. In R. A. Guzzo, E. Salas, & Associates, *Team effectiveness and decision making in organizations* (pp. 79–112). San Francisco: Jossey-Bass.

Tjosvold, D., Johnson, D. W., Johnson, R. T., & Sun, H. (2006). Competitive motives and strategies: Understanding constructive competition. *Group Dynamics: Theory, Research, and Practice, 10,* 87–99.

Tobin, K. (2008). *Gangs: An individual–group perspective.* Upper Saddle River, NJ: Prentice-Hall.

Toennies, F. (1963). *Community and society [Gemeinscheaft and Gesellschaft].* New York: Harper & Row. (Original work published in 1887)

Tolnay, S. E., & Beck, E. M. (1996). Vicarious violence: Spatial effects on southern lynchings, 1890–1919. *American Journal of Sociology, 102,* 788–815.

Tolstoy, L. (1952). *War and peace.* Chicago: Encyclopedia Britannica. (Original work published in 1887)

Tong, E. M. W., Tan, C. R. M., Latheef, N. A., Selamat, M. F. B., & Tan, D. K. B. (2008). Conformity: Moods matter. *European Journal of Social Psychology, 38,* 601–611.

Toobin, J. (2007). *The nine: Inside the secret world of the Supreme Court.* New York: Doubleday.

Torrance, E. P. (1954). The behavior of small groups under the stress conditions of "survival." *American Sociological Review, 19,* 751–755.

Tracey, T. J., Ryan, J. M., & Jaschik-Herman, B. (2001). Complementarity of interpersonal circumplex traits. *Personality and Social Psychology Bulletin, 27,* 786–797.

Travis, L. E. (1928). The influence of the group upon the stutterer's speed in free association. *Journal of Abnormal and Social Psychology, 23,* 45–51.

Treadwell, T., Lavertue, N., Kumar, V. K., & Veeraraghavan, V. (2001). The group cohesion scale-revised: Reliability and validity. *International Journal of Action Methods: Psychodrama, Skill Training, and Role Playing, 54,* 3–12.

Triandis, H. C. (1995). *Individualism and collectivism.* Boulder, CO: Westview Press.

Triandis, H. C. (1996). The psychological measurement of cultural syndromes. *American Psychologist, 51,* 407–415.

Triandis, H. C., Carnevale, P. J., Gelfand, M., Robert, C., Wasti, A., Probst, T. M., Kashima, E. S., Dragonas, T., Chan, D., Chen, X. P., Kim, U.,

Kim, K., De Dreu, C., Van de Vliert, E., Iwao, S., Ohbuchi, K., & Schmitz, P. (2001). Culture, personality, and deception in intercultural management negotiations. *International Journal of Cross-Cultural Management, 1,* 73–90.

Triandis, H. C., McCusker, C., & Hui, C. H. (1990). Multimethod probes of individualism and collectivism. *Journal of Personality and Social Psychology, 59,* 1006–1013.

Triandis, H. C., & Suh, E. M. (2002). Cultural influences on personality. *Annual Review of Psychology, 53,* 133–160.

Triplett, N. (1898). The dynamogenic factors in pacemaking and competition. *American Journal of Psychology, 9,* 507–533.

Tsui, A. S. (1984). A role-set analysis of managerial reputation. *Organizational Behavior and Human Performance, 34,* 64–96.

Tsui, A. S., Egan, T. D., & O'Reilly, C. A. (1992). Being different: Relational demography and organizational attachment. *Administrative Science Quarterly, 37,* 549–579.

Tubre, T. C., & Collins, J. M. (2000). Jackson and Schuler (1985) revisited: A meta-analysis of the relationships between role ambiguity, role conflict, and job performance. *Journal of Management, 26,* 155–169.

Tucker, C. W., Schweingruber, D., & McPhail, C. (1999). Simulating arcs and rings in gatherings. *International Journal of Human–Computer Studies, 50,* 581–588.

Tuckman, B. W. (1965). Developmental sequences in small groups. *Psychological Bulletin, 63,* 384–399.

Tuckman, B. W., & Jensen, M. A. C. (1977). Stages of small group development revisited. *Group and Organizational Studies, 2,* 419–427.

Turner, A. L. (2000). Group treatment of trauma survivors following a fatal bus accident: Integrating theory and practice. *Group Dynamics: Theory, Research, and Practice, 4,* 139–149.

Turner, J. C. (1984). Social identification and psychological group formation. In H. Tajfel (Ed.), *The social dimension* (Vol. 2, pp. 518–540). Cambridge: Cambridge University Press.

Turner, J. C. (1991). *Social influence.* Belmont, CA: Wadsworth/Cengage.

Turner, J. C. (1999). Some current issues in research on social identity and self-categorization theories. In N. Ellemers, R. Spears, & B. Doosje (Eds.), *Social identity* (pp. 6–34). Oxford, UK: Blackwell.

Turner, J. C., Hogg, M. A., Oakes, P. J., Reicher, S. D., & Wetherell, M. S. (1987). *Rediscovering the social group: A self-categorization theory.* Malden, MA: Blackwell.

Turner, M. E. (Ed.). (2001). *Groups at work: Theory and research.* Mahwah, NJ: Erlbaum.

Turner, M. E., & Pratkanis, A. R. (1998a). A social identity maintenance model of groupthink. *Organizational Behavior and Human Decision Processes, 73*(2–3), 210–235.

Turner, M. E., & Pratkanis, A. R. (1998b). Twenty-five years of groupthink theory and research: Lessons from the evaluation of a theory. *Organizational Behavior and Human Decision Processes, 73*(2–3), 105–115.

Turner, R. (2001). Collective behavior. In E. F. Borgatta & R. J. V. Montgomery (Eds.), *Encyclopedia of sociology* (2nd ed., Vol. 1, pp. 348–354). New York: Macmillan Reference.

Turner, R. H. (1964). Collective behavior. In R. E. L. Faris (Ed.), *Handbook of modern sociology.* Chicago: Rand McNally.

Turner, R. H., & Colomy, P. (1988). Role differentiation: Orienting principles. *Advances in Group Processes, 5,* 1–27.

Turner, R. H., & Killian, L. M. (1972). *Collective behavior* (2nd ed.).Englewood Cliffs, NJ: Prentice Hall.

Twenge, J. M. (2001). Changes in women's assertiveness in response to status and roles: A cross-temporal meta-analysis, 1931–1993. *Journal of Personality and Social Psychology, 81,* 133–145.

Twenge, J. M. (2006). *Generation me : Why today's young Americans are more confident, assertive, entitled—and more miserable than ever before.* New York: Free Press.

Twenge, J. M., Baumeister, R. F., DeWall, C. N., Ciarocco, N. J., & Bartels, J. M. (2007). Social exclusion decreases prosocial behavior. *Journal of Personality and Social Psychology, 92,* 56–66.

Twenge, J. M., Baumeister, R. F., Tice, D. M., & Stucke, T. S. (2001). If you can't join them, beat them: Effects of social exclusion on aggressive behavior. *Journal of Personality and Social Psychology, 81,* 1058–1069.

Twenge, J. M., Catanese, K. R., & Baumeister, R. F. (2002). Social exclusion causes self-defeating behavior. *Journal of Personality and Social Psychology, 83,* 606–615.

Twenge, J. M., & Crocker, J. (2002). Race and self-esteem:Meta-analyses comparing Whites, Blacks, Hispanics, Asians, and American Indians and comment on Gray-Little and Hafdahl (2000). *Psychological Bulletin, 128,* 371–408.

Tyler, T. R. (2005). Introduction: Legitimating ideologies. *Social Justice Research, 18,* 211–215.

Tyler, T. R., & Blader, S. L. (2003). The group engagement model: Procedural justice, social identity, and cooperative behavior. *Personality and Social Psychology Review, 7,* 349–361.

Uchino, B. N. (2004). *Social support and physical health: Understanding the health consequences of relationships.* New Haven: Yale University Press.

Uglow, J. S. (2002). *Lunar men: Five friends whose curiosity changed the world.* New York: Farrar, Straus, Giroux.

Ulbig, S. G., & Funk, C. L. (1999). Conflict avoidance and political participation. *Political Behavior, 21,* 265–282.

Urban, L. M., & Miller, N. (1998). A theoretical analysis of crossed categorization effects: A meta-analysis. *Journal of Personality and Social Psychology, 74,* 894–908.

Uris, A. (1978). *Executive dissent: How to say no and win.* New York: AMACOM.

U.S. Senate Select Committee on Intelligence (2004). *Report of the Select Committee on Intelligence on the U.S. intelligence community's prewar intelligence assessments on Iraq together with additional views.* Retrieved November 11, 2008, from http://intelligence.senate.gov/108301.pdf.

Utman, C. H. (1997). Performance effects of motivational state: A meta-analysis. *Personality and Social Psychology Review, 1,* 170–182.

Utz, S., & Sassenberg, K. (2002). Distributive justice in common-bond and common-identity groups. *Group Processes & Intergroup Relations, 5,* 151–162.

Uziel, L. (2007). Individual differences in the social facilitation effect: A review and meta-analysis. *Journal of Research in Personality, 41,* 579–601.

Vaillancourt, T., Hymel, S., & McDougall, P. (2003). Bullying is power: Implications for school-based intervention strategies. *Journal of Applied School Psychology, 19,* 157–176.

Vallacher, R. R., & Nowak, A. (2007). Dynamical social psychology: Finding order in the flow of human experience. In A. W. Kruglanski & E. T. Higgins (Eds.), *Social psychology: Handbook of basic principles* (2nd ed., pp. 734–758). New York: Guilford.

Van de Vliert, E., & Euwema, M. C. (1994). Agreeableness and activeness as components of conflict behaviors. *Journal of Personality and Social Psychology, 66,* 674–687.

Van de Vliert, E., & Janssen, O. (2001). Description, explanation, and prescription of intragroup conflict behaviors. In M. E. Turner (Ed.), *Groups at work: Theory and research* (pp. 267–297). Mahwah, NJ: Erlbaum.

van den Bos, K., Wilke, H., & Lind, E. A. (1998). When do we need procedural fairness? The role of trust in authority. *Journal of Personality and Social Psychology, 75,* 1449–1458.

Van Dijke, M., & Poppe, M. (2006). Striving for personal power as a basis for social power dynamics. *European Journal of Social Psychology, 36,* 537–556.

van Engen, M. L. (2001). *Gender and leadership: A contextual perspective.* Unpublished doctoral dissertation. Tilburg, Netherlands: Tilburg University.

Van Hiel, A., & Franssen, V. (2003). Information acquisition bias during the preparation of group discussion: A comparison of prospective minority and majority members. *Small Group Research, 34,* 557–574.

Van Kleef, G. A., & De Dreu, C. K. W. (2002). Social value orientation and impression formation: A test of two competing hypotheses about information search in negotiation. *International Journal of Conflict Management, 13,* 59–77.

Van Kleef, G. A., De Dreu, C. K. W., & Manstead, A. S. (2004). The interpersonal effects of anger and happiness in negotiations. *Journal of Personality and Social Psychology, 86,* 57–76.

van Knippenberg, D., De Dreu, C. K. W., & Homan, A. C. (2004). Work group diversity and group performance: An integrative model and research agenda. *Journal of Applied Psychology, 89,* 1008–1022.

van Knippenberg, D., & Schippers, M. C. (2007). Work group diversity. *Annual Review of Psychology, 58,* 515–541.

Van Lange, P. A. M., De Bruin, E. M. N., Otten, W., & Joireman, J. A. (1997). Development of prosocial, individualistic, and competitive orientations: Theory and preliminary evidence. *Journal of Personality and Social Psychology, 73,* 733–746.

Van Lange, P. A. M., De Cremer, D., Van Dijk, E., & Van Vugt, M. (2007). Self-interest and beyond: Basic principles of social interaction. In A. W. Kruglanski & E. T. Higgins (Eds.), *Social psychology: Handbook of basic principles* (2nd ed., pp. 540–561). New York: Guilford.

Van Lange, P. A. M., Ouwerkerk, J. W., & Tazelaar, M. J. (2002). How to overcome the detrimental effects of noise in social interaction: The benefits of generosity. *Journal of Personality and Social Psychology, 82,* 768–780.

van Oostrum, J., & Rabbie, J. M. (1995). Intergroup competition and cooperation within autocratic and democratic management regimes. *Small Group Research, 26,* 269–295.

Van Overwalle, F., & Heylighen, F. (2006). Talking nets: A multiagent connectionist approach to communication and trust between individuals. *Psychological Review, 113,* 606–627.

Van Raalte, J. L., Cornelius, A. E., Linder, D. E., & Brewer, B. W. (2007). The relationship between hazing and team cohesion. *Journal of Sport Behavior, 30,* 491–507.

Van Swol, L. M. (2008). Performance and process in collective and individual memory: The role of social decision schemes and memory bias in collective memory. *Memory, 16,* 274–287.

Van Vugt, M. (2006). Evolutionary origins of leadership and followership. *Personality and Social Psychology Review, 10,* 354–371.

Van Vugt, M., De Cremer, D., & Janssen, D. P. (2007). Gender differences in cooperation and competition: The male-warrior hypothesis. *Psychological Science, 18,* 19–23.

Van Vugt, M., & Hart, C. M. (2004). Social identity as social glue: The origins of group loyalty. *Journal of Personality and Social Psychology, 86,* 585–598.

Van Vugt, M., Hogan, R., & Kaiser, R. B. (2008). Leadership, followership, and evolution: Some lessons from the past. *American Psychologist, 63,* 182–196.

Van Zelst, R. H. (1952). Sociometrically selected work teams increase production. *Personnel Psychology, 5,* 175–185.

van Zomeren, M., Postmes, T., & Spears, R. (2008). Toward an integrative social identity model of collective action: A quantitative research synthesis of three socio-psychological perspectives. *Psychological Bulletin, 134,* 504–535.

Vandello, J. A., & Cohen, D. (1999). Patterns of individualism and collectivism across the United States. *Journal of Personality and Social Psychology, 77,* 279–292.

Vandello, J. A., & Cohen, D. (2003). Male honor and female fidelity: Implicit cultural scripts that perpetuate domestic violence. *Journal of Personality and Social Psychology, 84,* 997–1010.

Vandello, J. A., & Cohen, D. (2004). When believing is seeing: Sustaining norms of violence in cultures of honor. In M. Schaller & C. S. Crandall (Eds.), *The psychological foundations of culture* (pp. 281–304). Mahwah, NJ: Erlbaum.

Vandello, J. A., Cohen, D., & Ransom, S. (2008). U.S. southern and northern differences in perceptions of norms about aggression: Mechanisms for the perpetuation of a culture of honor. *Journal of Cross-Cultural Psychology, 39,* 162–177.

Varela, J. A. (1971). *Psychological solutions to social problems.* New York: Academic Press.

Varvel, S. J., He, Y., Shannon, J. K., Tager, D., Bledman, R. A., Chaichanasakul, A., Mendoza, M., & Mallinckrodt, B. (2007). Multidimensional, threshold effects of social support in firefighters: Is more support invariably better? *Journal of Counseling Psychology, 54,* 458–465.

Vecchio, R. P. (1987). Situational leadership theory: An examination of a prescriptive theory. *Journal of Applied Psychology, 72,* 444–451.

Vecchio, R. P., & Boatwright, K. J. (2002). Preferences for idealized styles of supervision. *Leadership Quarterly, 13,* 327–342.

Veitch, J. A. (1990). Office noise and illumination effects on reading comprehension. *Journal of Environmental Psychology, 10,* 209–217.

Veitch, J. A., Charles, K. E., Farley, K. M. J., & Newsham, G. R. (2007). A model of satisfaction with open-plan office conditions: COPE field findings. *Journal of Environmental Psychology, 27,* 177–189.

Vela-McConnell, J. A. (1999). *Who is my neighbor? Social affinity in a modern world*. Albany, NY: State University of New York Press.

Venkatesh, B., & Goyal, S. (1998). Learning from neighbours. *Review of Economic Studies, 65,* 595–621.

Venkatesh, S. (2008). *Gang leader for a day*. New York: Penguin.

Venkatesh, S. (2008). *Gang leader for a day: A rogue sociologist takes to the streets*. New York: Penguin Press.

Vertue, F. M. (2003). From adaptive emotion to dysfunction: An attachment perspective on social anxiety disorder. *Personality and Social Psychology Review, 7,* 170–191.

Vider, S. (2004). Rethinking crowd violence: Self-categorization theory and the Woodstock 1999 riot. *Journal for the Theory of Social Behaviour, 34,* 141–166.

Vidmar, N., & Hans, V. P. (2007). *American juries: The verdict*. Amherst, NY: Prometheus Books.

Vinokur, A., & Burnstein, E. (1974). The effects of partially shared persuasive arguments on group-induced shifts: A group-problem-solving approach. *Journal of Personality and Social Psychology, 29,* 305–315.

Vinokur, A., & Burnstein, E. (1978). Depolarization of attitudes in groups. *Journal of Personality and Social Psychology, 36,* 872–885.

Vinokur, A., Burnstein, E., Sechrest, L., & Wortman, P. M. (1985). Group decision making by experts: Field study of panels evaluating medical technologies. *Journal of Personality and Social Psychology, 49,* 70–84.

Vinsel, A., Brown, B. B., Altman, I., & Foss, C. (1980). Privacy regulation, territorial displays, and effectiveness of individual functioning. *Journal of Personality and Social Psychology, 39,* 1104–1115.

Vroom, V. H. (2003). Educating managers in decision making and leadership. *Management Decision, 10,* 968–978.

Vroom, V. H., & Jago, A. G. (1988). *The new leadership: Managing participation in organizations*. Upper Saddle River, NJ: Prentice Hall.

Vroom, V. H., & Jago, A. G. (2007). The role of the situation in leadership. *American Psychologist, 62,* 17–24.

Vroom, V. H., & Mann, F. C. (1960). Leader authoritarianism and employee attitudes. *Personnel Psychology, 13,* 125–140.

Vroom, V. H., & Yetton, P. W. (1973). *Leadership and decision making*. Pittsburgh, PA: University of Pittsburgh Press.

Waddington, D. (2008). The madness of the mob? Explaining the "irrationality" and destructiveness of crowd violence. *Sociology Compass, 2,* 675–687.

Wagner, D. G. (1995). Gender differences in reward preference: A status-based account. *Small Group Research, 26,* 353–371.

Wagner, D. G., & Berger, J. (2002). Expectation states theory: An evolving research program. In J. Berger & M. Zelditch (Eds.), *New directions in contemporary sociological theory* (pp. 41–76). Lanham, MD: Rowman & Littlefield.

Walker, C. J., & Berkerle, C. A. (1987). The effect of state anxiety on rumor transmission. *Journal of Social Behavior and Personality, 2,* 353–360.

Walker, H. A., Ilardi, B. C., McMahon, A. M., & Fennell, M. L. (1996). Gender, interaction, and leadership. *Social Psychology Quarterly, 59,* 255–272.

Wall, V. D., Jr., & Nolan, L. L. (1987). Small group conflict: A look at equity, satisfaction, and styles of conflict management. *Small Group Behavior, 18,* 188–211.

Wallach, M. A., Kogan, N., & Bem, D. J. (1962). Group influence on individual risk taking. *Journal of Abnormal and Social Psychology, 65,* 75–86.

Wallenius, M. A. (2004). The interaction of noise stress and personal project stress on subjective health. *Journal of Environmental Psychology, 24,* 167–177.

Walsh, D. (2003). *Classroom sociometrics*. Retrieved August 23, 2004 from Walsh's classroom sociometrics website, http://www.classroomsociometrics.com.

Walsh, Y., Russell, R. J. H., & Wells, P. A. (1995). The personality of ex-cult members. *Personality and Individual Differences, 19,* 339–344.

Walther, E., Bless, H., Strack, F., Rackstraw, P., Wagner, D., & Werth, L. (2002). Conformity effects in memory as a function of group size, dissenters and uncertainty. *Applied Cognitive Psychology, 16,* 793–810.

Wang, A. Y., Newlin, M. H., & Tucker, T. L. (2001). A discourse analysis of online classroom chats: Predictors of cyber-student performance. *Teaching of Psychology, 28,* 222–226.

Wann, D. L. (2006). Understanding the positive social psychological benefits of sport team identification: The team identification–social psychological health model. *Group Dynamics: Theory, Research, and Practice, 10,* 272–296.

Wann, D. L., Dolan, T. J., McGeorge, K. K., & Allison, J. A. (1994). Relationships between spectator identification and spectators' perceptions of influence, spectators' emotions, and competition outcome. *Journal of Sport and Exercise Psychology, 16,* 347–364.

Ward, R. E., Jr. (2002). Fan violence: Social problem or moral panic? *Aggression and Violent Behavior, 7,* 453–475.

Ware, R., Barr, J. E., & Boone, M. (1982). Subjective changes in small group processes: An experimental investigation. *Small Group Behavior, 13,* 395–401.

Warner HBO (Production Company). (2001). *Do you believe in miracles? The story of the 1980 U.S. Hockey Team [Videotape].* New York: HBO Studios.

Warr, M. (2002). *Companions in crime: The social aspects of criminal conduct.* New York: Cambridge University Press.

Wasserman, S., & Faust, K. (1994). *Social network analysis: Methods and applications.* New York: Cambridge University Press.

Watson, C., & Hoffman, L. R. (1996). Managers as negotiators: A test of power versus gender as predictors of feelings, behavior, and outcomes. *Leadership Quarterly, 7,* 63–85.

Watson, D., & Clark, L. A. (1997). Extraversion and its positive emotional core. In R. Hogan & J. A. Johnson (Eds.), *Handbook of personality psychology* (pp. 767–793). San Diego: Academic Press.

Watson, R. I., Jr. (1973). Investigation into deindividuation using a cross-cultural survey technique. *Journal of Personality and Social Psychology, 25,* 342–345.

Watson, W. E., Kumar, K., & Michaelsen, L. K. (1993). Cultural diversity's impact on interaction process and performance: Comparing homogeneous and diverse task groups. *Academy of Management Journal, 36,* 590–602.

Webb, N. M., Troper, J. D., & Fall, R. (1995). Constructive activity and learning in collaborative small groups. *Journal of Educational Psychology, 87,* 406–423.

Weber, B., & Hertel, G. (2007). Motivation gains of inferior group members: A meta-analytical review. *Journal of Personality and Social Psychology, 93,* 973–993.

Weber, J. M., & Messick, D. M. (2004). Conflicting interests in social life: Understanding social dilemma dynamics. In M. J. Gelfand & J. M. Brett (Eds.), *The handbook of negotiation and culture* (pp. 374–394). Stanford, CA: Stanford University Press.

Weber, M. (1946). The sociology of charismatic authority. In H. H. Gert & C. W. Mills (Trans. & Eds.), *From Max Weber: Essay in sociology* (pp. 245–252). New York: Oxford University Press. (Original work published in 1921)

Webster, M., Jr., & Driskell, J. E., Jr. (1983). Processes of status generalization. In H. H. Blumberg, A. P. Hare, V. Kent, & M. F. Davies (Eds.), *Small groups and social interaction* (Vol. 1, pp. 57–67). New York: Wiley.

Wech, B. A., Mossholder, K. W., Steel, R. P., & Bennett, N. (1998). Does work group cohesiveness affect individuals' performance and organizational commitment? A cross-level examination. *Small Group Research, 29,* 472–494.

Wegge, J., & Haslam, S. A. (2005). Improving work motivation and performance in brainstorming groups: The effects of three group goal-setting strategies. *European Journal of Work and Organizational Psychology, 14,* 400–430.

Wegner, D. M. (1987). Transactive memory: A contemporary analysis of the group mind. In B. Mullen & G. R. Goethals (Eds.), *Theories of group behavior* (pp. 185–208). New York: Springer Verlag.

Wegner, D. M., Giuliano, T., & Hertel, P. T. (1985). Cognitive interdependence in close relationships. In W. Ickes (Ed.), *Compatible and incompatible relationships* (pp. 253–276). New York: Springer Verlag.

Weigold, M. F., & Schlenker, B. R. (1991). Accountability and risk taking. *Personality and Social Psychology Bulletin, 17,* 25–29.

Weingart, L. R. (1992). Impact of group goals, task component complexity, effort, and planning on group performance. *Journal of Applied Psychology, 77,* 682–693.

Weingart, L. R. (1997). How did they do that? The ways and means of studying group process. *Research in Organizational Behavior, 19,* 189–239.

Weingart, L. R., & Olekalns, M. (2004). Communication processes in negotiation: Frequencies, sequences, and phases. In M. J. Gelfand & J. M. Brett (Eds.), *The handbook of negotiation and culture* (pp. 143–157). Stanford, CA: Stanford University Press.

Weingart, L. R., & Weldon, E. (1991). Processes that mediate the relationship between a group goal and group member performance. *Human Performance, 4,* 33–54.

Welch, D. A. (1989). Crisis decision making reconsidered. *Journal of Conflict Resolution, 33,* 430–445.

Weldon, E., Jehn, K. A., & Pradhan, P. (1991). Processes that mediate the relationship between a group goal and improved group performance. *Journal of Personality and Social Psychology, 61,* 555–569.

Weldon, E., & Weingart, L. R. (1993). Group goals and group performance. *British Journal of Social Psychology, 32,* 307–334.

Weldon, M. S., & Bellinger, K. D. (1997). Collective memory: Collaborative and individual processes in remembering. *Journal of Experimental Psychology: Learning, Memory, and Cognition, 23,* 1160–1175.

Weldon, M. S., Blair, C., & Huebsch, D. (2000). Group remembering: Does social loafing underlie collaborative inhibition? *Journal of Experimental Psychology: Learning, Memory, & Cognition, 26,* 1568–1577.

Welsh, B. C., & Farrington, D. P. (2004). Surveillance for crime prevention in public space: Results and policy choices in Britain and America. *Criminology & Public Policy, 3,* 497–526.

Werner, C. M., Brown, B. B., & Altman, I. (2002). Transactionally oriented research: Examples and strategies. In R. Bechtel & A. Churchman (Eds.), *Handbook of environmental psychology* (pp. 203–221). New York: Wiley.

Werner, P. (1978). Personality and attitude-activism correspondence. *Journal of Personality and Social Psychology, 36,* 1375–1390.

West, S. G., Gunn, S. P., & Chernicky, P. (1975). Ubiquitous Watergate: An attributional analysis. *Journal of Personality and Social Psychology, 23,* 55–65.

Weybrew, B. B. (1963). Psychological problems of prolonged marine submergence. In J. N. Burns, R. Chambers, & E. Hendler (Eds.), *Unusual environments and human behavior.* New York: Macmillan.

Wheelan, S. A. (1994). *Group process: A developmental perspective.* Boston: Allyn & Bacon.

Wheelan, S. A. (Ed.). (2005). *The handbook of group research and practice.* Thousand Oaks, CA: Sage.

Wheelan, S. A., Davidson, B., & Tilin, F. (2003). Group development across time: Reality or illusion? *Small Group Research, 34,* 223–245.

Wheelan, S. A., & McKeage, R. L. (1993). Developmental patterns in small and large groups. *Small Group Research, 24,* 60–83.

Wheeler, D. D., & Janis, I. L. (1980). *A practical guide for making decisions.* New York: Free Press.

Wheeler, L. (1966). Toward a theory of behavioral contagion. *Psychological Review, 73,* 179–192.

Wheeler, L., & Miyake, K. (1992). Social comparison in everyday life. *Journal of Personality and Social Psychology, 62,* 760–773.

White, R. K. (1965). Images in the context of international conflict. In H. Kelman (Ed.), *International behavior: A social-psychological analysis.* New York: Holt, Rinehart & Winston.

White, R. K. (1966). Misperception and the Vietnam war. *Journal of Social Issues, 22,* 1–156.

White, R. K. (1969). Three not-so-obvious contributions of psychology to peace. *Journal of Social Issues, 25,* 23–29.

White, R. K. (1977). Misperception in the Arab–Israeli conflict. *Journal of Social Issues, 33,* 190–221.

White, R. K. (1990). Democracy in the research team. In S. A. Wheelan, E. Pepitone, & V. Abt (Eds.), *Advances in field theory* (pp. 19–26). Thousand Oaks, CA: Sage.

White, R. K. (1998). American acts of force: Results and misperceptions. *Peace and Conflict: Journal of Peace Psychology, 4,* 93–128.

White, R. K., & Lippitt, R. (1960). *Autocracy and democracy.* New York: Harper & Row.

White, R. K., & Lippitt, R. (1968). Leader behavior and member reaction in three "social climates." In D. Cartwright & A. Zander (Eds.), *Group dynamics: Research and theory* (3rd ed., pp. 318–335). New York: Harper & Row.

Whitley, B. E., Jr. (1999). Right-wing authoritarianism, social dominance orientation, and prejudice. *Journal of Personality and Social Psychology, 77,* 126–134.

Whitney, I., & Smith, P. K. (1993). A survey of the nature and extent of bullying in junior/middle and secondary schools. *Educational Research, 35,* 3–25.

Whitney, K., Sagrestano, L. M., & Maslach, C. (1994). Establishing the social impact of individuation. *Journal of Personality and Social Psychology, 66,* 1140–1153.

Whittal, M. L., & McLean, P. D. (2002). Group cognitive behavioral therapy for obsessive compulsive disorder. In R. O. Frost & G. Steketee (Eds.), *Cognitive approaches to obsessions and compulsions: Theory, assessment, and treatment* (pp. 417–433). Amsterdam: Pergamon/Elsevier Science.

Whyte, W. F. (1943). *Street corner society*. Chicago: University of Chicago Press.

Whyte, W. F. (1955). *Street corner society* (2nd ed.). Chicago: University of Chicago Press.

Whyte, W. F., Greenwood, D. J., & Lazes, P. (1991). Participatory action research: Through practice to science in social research. In W. F. Whyte (Ed.), *Participatory action research* (pp. 19–55). Thousand Oaks, CA: Sage.

Wicker, A. W. (1979). *An introduction to ecological psychology*. Pacific Grove, CA: Brooks/Cole.

Wicker, A. W. (1987). Behavior settings reconsidered: Temporal stages, resources, internal dynamics, context. In D. Stokols & I. Altman (Eds.), *Handbook of environmental psychology* (Vol. 1, pp. 613–653). New York: Wiley.

Wicker, A. W. (2002). Ecological psychology: Historical contexts, current conception, prospective directions. In R. Bechtel & A. Churchman (Eds.), *Handbook of environmental psychology* (pp. 114–126). New York: Wiley.

Wicker, A. W., & August, R. A. (1995). How far should we generalize? The case of a workload model. *Psychological Science, 6,* 39–44.

Wicker, A. W., Kirmeyer, S. L., Hanson, L., & Alexander, D. (1976). Effects of manning levels on subjective experiences, performance, and verbal interaction in groups. *Organizational Behavior and Human Performance, 17,* 251–274.

Widmeyer, W. N. (1990). Group composition in sport. *International Journal of Sport Psychology, 21,* 264–285.

Widmeyer, W. N., Brawley, L. R., & Carron, A. V. (1992). Group dynamics in sports. In T. S. Horn (Ed.), *Advances in sport psychology* (pp. 163–180). Champaign, IL: Human Kinetics Publishers.

Wilder, D. A. (1977). Perception of groups, size of opposition, and social influence. *Journal of Experimental Social Psychology, 13,* 253–268.

Wilder, D. A. (1986). Social categorization: Implications for creation and reduction of intergroup bias. *Advances in Experimental Social Psychology, 19,* 293–355.

Wilder, D. A., Simon, A. F., & Faith, M. (1996). Enhancing the impact of counterstereotypic information: Dispositional attributions for deviance. *Journal of Personality and Social Psychology, 71,* 276–287.

Wilder, D. A., & Thompson, J. E. (1980). Intergroup contact with independent manipulations of in-group and out-group interaction. *Journal of Personality and Social Psychology, 38,* 589–603.

Wildschut, T., Pinter, B., Vevea, J. L., Insko, C. A., & Schopler, J. (2003). Beyond the group mind: A quantitative review of the interindividual–intergroup discontinuity effect. *Psychological Bulletin, 129,* 698–722.

Wilke, H. A. M. (1996). Status congruence in small groups. In E. Witte & J. H. Davis (Eds.), *Understanding group behavior: Small group processes and interpersonal relations* (Vol. 2, pp. 67–91). Mahwah, NJ: Erlbaum.

*Williams v. Florida*, 399 U.S. 78 (1970).

Williams, J. E., & Best, D. L. (1990). *Measuring sex stereotypes: A multination study*. Thousand Oaks, CA: Sage.

Williams, K. D. (2007). Ostracism. *Annual Review of Psychology, 58,* 425–452.

Williams, K. D., Cheung, C. K. T., & Choi, W. (2000). Cyberostracism: Effects of being ignored over the Internet. *Journal of Personality and Social Psychology, 79,* 748–762.

Williams, K. D., Govan, C. L., Croker, V., Tynan, D., Cruickshank, M., & Lam, A. (2002). Investigations into differences between social- and cyber-ostracism.

*Group Dynamics: Theory, Research, and Practice, 6,* 65–77.

Williams, K. D., Harkins, S., & Latané, B. (1981). Identifiability as a deterrent to social loafing: Two cheering experiments. *Journal of Personality and Social Psychology, 40,* 303–311.

Williams, K. D., & Karau, S. J. (1991). Social loafing and social compensation: The effects of expectations of co-worker performance. *Journal of Personality and Social Psychology, 61,* 570–581.

Williams, K. D., & Sommer, K. L. (1997). Social ostracism by coworkers: Does rejection lead to loafing or compensation? *Personality and Social Psychology Bulletin, 23,* 693–706.

Williams, K. Y., & O'Reilly, C. A. (1998). Demography and diversity in organizations: A review of 40 years of research. *Research in Organizational Behavior, 20,* 77–140.

Willis, F. N. (1966). Initial speaking distance as a function of the speakers' relationship. *Psychonomic Science, 5,* 221–222.

Wills, T. A. (1991). Social comparison processes in coping and health. In C. R. Snyder & D. R. Forsyth (Eds.), *Handbook of social and clinical psychology: The health perspective* (pp. 376–394). Elmsford, NY: Pergamon.

Wills, T. A., & DePaulo, B. M. (1991). Interpersonal analysis of the help-seeking process. In C. R. Snyder & D. R. Forsyth (Eds.), *Handbook of social and clinical psychology: The health perspective* (pp. 350–375). New York: Pergamon Press.

Wills, T. A., & Filer, M. (2000). Social networks and social support. In A. Baum & T. Revenson (Eds.), *Handbook of health psychology* (pp. 209–232). Mahwah, NJ: Erlbaum.

Wilmot, W. W., & Hocker, J. L. (2007). *Interpersonal conflict* (7th ed.). Boston: McGraw-Hill.

Wilson, M. S., & Liu, J. H. (2003). Social dominance orientation and gender: The moderating role of gender identity. *British Journal of Social Psychology, 42,* 187–198.

Wilson, S. R. (1992). Face and facework in negotiation. In L. L. Putnam & M. E. Roloff (Eds.), *Communication and negotiation* (pp. 176–205). Thousand Oaks, CA: Sage.

Winch, R. F. (1958). *Mate-selection: A study of complementary needs.* New York: Harper.

Winquist, J. R., & Larson, J. R., Jr. (1998). Information pooling: When it impacts group decision making. *Journal of Personality and Social Psychology, 74,* 371–377.

Winter, D. G. (1973). *The power motive.* New York: Free Press.

Winthrop, R. C. (1667). Life and letters of JohnWinthrop. Boston: Tichnor & Fields. (Original work published in 1630)

Wiseman, R. (2002). *Queen bees and wannabes: Helping your daughter survive cliques, gossip, boyfriends, and other realities of adolescence.* New York: Crown.

Wiseman, R. L., & Schenck-Hamlin, W. (1981). A multidimensional scaling validation of an inductively derived set of compliance-gaining strategies. *Communication Monographs, 48,* 251–270.

Wisman, A., & Koole, S. L. (2003). Hiding in the crowd: Can mortality salience promote affiliation with others who oppose one's worldviews? *Journal of Personality and Social Psychology, 84,* 511–526.

Witte, E. H. (1989). Köhler rediscovered: The anti-Ringelmann effect. *European Journal of Social Psychology, 19,* 147–154.

Witteman, H. (1991). Group member satisfaction: A conflict-related account. *Small Group Research, 22,* 24–58.

Wittenbaum, G. M. (1998). Information sampling in decision-making groups: The impact of members' task-relevant status. *Small Group Research, 29,* 57–84.

Wittenbaum, G. M., Hollingshead, A. B., & Botero, I. C. (2004). From cooperative to motivated information sharing in groups: Moving beyond the hidden profile paradigm. *Communication Monographs, 71,* 286–310.

Wittenbaum, G. M., Hollingshead, A. B., Paulus, P. B., Hirokawa, R. Y., Ancona, D. G., Peterson, R. S., Jehn, K. A., & Yoon, K. (2004). The functional perspective as a lens for understanding groups. *Small Group Research, 35,* 17–43.

Wittenbaum, G. M., Hubbell, A. P., & Zuckerman, C. (1999). Mutual enhancement: Toward an understanding of the collective preference for shared information. *Journal of Personality and Social Psychology, 77,* 967–978.

Wittenbaum, G. M., & Moreland, R. L. (2008). Small group research in social psychology: Topics and trends over time. *Social and Personality Psychology Compass, 2,* 187–203.

Wittenbaum, G. M., Stasser, G., & Merry, C. J. (1996). Tacit coordination in anticipation of small group task completion. *Journal of Experimental Social Psychology, 32,* 129–152.

Wolf, S. (1987). Majority and minority influence: A social impact analysis. In M. P. Zanna, J. M. Olson, & C. P. Herman (Eds.), *Social influence: The Ontario Symposium* (Vol. 5, pp. 207–235). Mahwah, NJ: Erlbaum.

Wolf, S. T., Insko, C. A., Kirchner, J. L., & Wildschut, T. (2008). Interindividual–intergroup discontinuity in the domain of correspondent outcomes: The roles of relativistic concern, perceived categorization, and the doctrine of mutual assured destruction. *Journal of Personality and Social Psychology, 94,* 479–494.

Wood, A. M., Linley, P. A., Maltby, J., Baliousis, M., & Joseph, S. (2008). The authentic personality: A theoretical and empirical conceptualization and the development of the authenticity scale. *Journal of Counseling Psychology, 55,* 385–399.

Wood, J. (1996). What is social comparison and how should we study it? *Personality and Social Psychology Bulletin, 22,* 520–537.

Wood, W. (1987). A meta-analytic review of sex differences in group performance. *Psychological Bulletin, 102,* 53–71.

Wood, W., Lundgren, S., Ouellette, J. A., Busceme, S., & Blackstone, T. (1994). Minority influence: A meta-analytic review of social influence processes. *Psychological Bulletin, 115,* 323–345.

Wood, W., Polek, D., & Aiken, C. (1985). Sex differences in group task performance. *Journal of Personality and Social Psychology, 48,* 63–71.

Worchel, S. (1986). The role of cooperation in reducing intergroup conflict. In S. Worchel & W. G. Austin (Eds.), *Psychology of intergroup relations* (2nd ed., pp. 288–304). Chicago: Nelson-Hall.

Worchel, S., & Brehm, J. W. (1971). Direct and implied social restoration of freedom. *Journal of Personality and Social Psychology, 18,* 294–304.

Worchel, S., & Teddlie, C. (1976). The experience of crowding: A two-factor theory. *Journal of Personality and Social Psychology, 34,* 30–40.

Worchel, S., & Yohai, S. (1979). The role of attribution in the experience of crowding. *Journal of Experimental Social Psychology, 15,* 91–104.

Worringham, C. J., & Messick, D. M. (1983). Social facilitation of running: An unobtrusive study. *Journal of Social Psychology, 121,* 23–29.

Worthington, E. L., Jr.,Hight, T. L., Ripley, J. S., Perrone, K. M., Kurusu, T. A., & Jones, D. R. (1997). Strategic hope-focused relationship-enrichment counseling with individual couples. *Journal of Counseling Psychology, 44,* 381–389.

Wright, S. C., Aron, A., McLaughlin-Volpe, T., & Ropp, S. A. (1997). The extended contact effect: Knowledge of cross-group friendships and prejudice. *Journal of Personality and Social Psychology, 73,* 73–90.

Wright, S. C., Aron, A., & Tropp, L. R. (2002). Including others (and groups) in the self: Self-expansion and intergroup relations. In J. P. Forgas & K. D. Williams (Eds.), *The social self: Cognitive, interpersonal and intergroup perspectives* (pp. 343–363). Philadelphia: Psychology Press.

Wright, S. S., & Forsyth, D. R. (1997). Group membership and collective identity: Consequences for self-esteem. *Journal of Social & Clinical Psychology, 16,* 43–56.

Wrightsman, L. S., Nietzel, M. T., & Fortune, W. H. (1998). *Psychology and the legal system* (4th ed.). Pacific Grove, CA: Brooks/Cole.

Wu, J. Z., & Axelrod, R. (1995). How to cope with noise in the iterated prisoner's dilemma. *Journal of Conflict Resolution, 39,* 183–189.

Wundt, W. (1916). *Elements of folk psychology.* Oxford: MacMillan.

Wyden, P. H. (1979). *Bay of Pigs: The untold story.* New York: Simon & Schuster.

Yablonsky, L. (1959). The delinquent gang as a near group. *Social Problems, 7,* 108–117.

Yablonsky, L. (1962). *The violent gang*. New York: Macmillan.

Yalom, I. D. with Leszcz, M. (2005). *The theory and practice of group psychotherapy* (5th ed.). New York: Basic Books.

Yamagishi, K. (1994). Social dilemmas. In K. S. Cook, G. A. Fine, & J. S. House (Eds.), *Sociological perspectives on social psychology* (pp. 311–334). Boston: Allyn & Bacon.

Yammarino, F. J., & Bass, B. M. (1990). Long-term forecasting of transformational leadership and its effects among naval officers: Some preliminary findings. In K. E. Clark & M. B. Clark (Eds.), *Measure of leadership* (pp. 151–169). West Orange, NJ: Leadership Library of America.

Yammarino, F. J., & Dansereau, F. (2008). Multi-level nature of and multi-level approaches to leadership. *Leadership Quarterly, 19,* 135–141.

Yammarino, F. J., Dionne, S. D., Chun, J. U., & Dansereau, F. (2005). Leadership and levels of analysis: A state-of-the-science review. *Leadership Quarterly, 16,* 879–919.

Yang, J., & Mossholder, K. W. (2004). Decoupling task and relationship conflict: The role of intragroup emotional processing. *Journal of Organizational Behavior, 25,* 589–605.

Yang, K., & Bond, M. H. (1990). Exploring implicit personality theories with indigenous or imported constructs: The Chinese case. *Journal of Personality and Social Psychology, 58,* 1087–1095.

Yao, R. (1987). *An introduction to Fundamentalists Anonymous*. New York: Fundamentalists Anonymous.

Yin, R. K. (2009). *Case study research: Design and methods* (4th ed.). Thousand Oaks, CA: Sage.

York, E., & Cornwell, B. (2006). Status on trial: Social characteristics and influence in the jury room. *Social Forces, 85,* 455–477.

Youngreen, R., & Moore, C. D. (2008). The effects of status violations on hierarchy and influence in groups. *Small Group Research*, published online, DOI:10.1177/1046496408320120.

Youngs, G. A., Jr. (1986). Patterns of threat and punishment reciprocity in a conflict setting. *Journal of Personality and Social Psychology, 51,* 541–546.

Yukelson, D., Weinberg, R., & Jackson, A. (1984). A multidimensional group cohesion instrument for intercollegiate basketball teams. *Journal of Sport Psychology, 6,* 103–117.

Yukl, G. (2006). *Leadership in organizations*. Upper Saddle River, NJ: Prentice Hall.

Yukl, G., Kim, H., & Falbe, C. (1996). Antecedents of influence outcomes. *Journal of Applied Psychology, 81,* 309–317.

Yukl, G., & Michel, J. W. (2006). Proactive influence tactics and leader member exchange. In C. A. Schriesheim & L. L. Neider (Eds.), *Power and influence in organizations: New empirical and theoretical perspectives* (pp. 87–104). Greenwich, CT: Information Age Publishing.

Yzerbyt, V., Judd, C. M., & Corneille, O. (Eds.). (2004). *The psychology of group perception: Perceived variability, entitativity, and essentialism*. New York: Psychology Press.

Zaccaro, S. J. (2007). Trait-based perspectives of leadership. *American Psychologist, 62,* 6–16.

Zaccaro, S. J., & Banks, D. J. (2001). Leadership, vision, and organizational effectiveness. In S. J. Zaccaro & R. J. Klimoski (Eds.), *The nature of organizational leadership: Understanding the performance imperatives confronting today's leaders* (pp. 181–218). San Francisco: Jossey-Bass.

Zaccaro, S. J., Blair, V., Peterson, C., & Zazanis, M. (1995). Collective efficacy. In J. E. Maddux (Ed.), *Self-efficacy, adaptation, and adjustment: Theory, research, and application* (pp. 305–328). New York: Plenum.

Zaccaro, S. J., Foti, R. J., & Kenny, D. A. (1991). Self-monitoring and trait-based variance in leadership: An investigation of leader flexibility across multiple group situations. *Journal of Applied Psychology, 76,* 308–315.

Zaccaro, S. J., Gualtieri, J., & Minionis, D. (1995). Task cohesion as a facilitator of team decision making under temporal urgency. *Military Psychology, 7,* 77–93.

Zaccaro, S. J., Gulick, L. M., & Khare, V. P. (2008). Personality and leadership. In C. L. Hoyt, G. R. Goethals, & D. R. Forsyth (Eds.), *Leadership at the crossroads: Leadership and psychology* (Vol. 1, pp. 14–29). Westport, CT: Praeger.

Zajonc, R. B. (1965). Social facilitation. *Science, 149,* 269–274.

Zajonc, R. B. (1980). Compresence. In P. B. Paulus (Ed.), *Psychology of group influence* (pp. 35–60). Mahwah, NJ: Erlbaum.

Zajonc, R. B., Heingartner, A., & Herman, E. M. (1969). Social enhancement and impairment of performance in the cockroach. *Journal of Personality and Social Psychology, 13,* 83–92.

Zamarripa, P. O., & Krueger, D. L. (1983). Implicit contracts regulating small group leadership. *Small Group Behavior, 14,* 187–210.

Zander, A. (1985). *The purposes of groups and organizations.* San Francisco: Jossey-Bass.

Zander, A., Stotland, E., & Wolfe, D. (1960). Unity of group, identification with group, and self-esteem of members. *Journal of Personality, 28,* 463–478.

Zelditch, M. (2001). Processes of legitimation: Recent developments and new directions. *Social Psychology Quarterly, 64,* 4–17.

Zhou, J., & George, J. M. (2001). When job dissatisfaction leads to creativity: Encouraging the expression of voice. *Academy of Management Journal, 44,* 682–696.

Zhou, R., & Soman, D. (2008). Consumers' waiting in queues: The role of first-order and second-order justice. *Psychology and Marketing, 25,* 262–279.

Ziller, R. C. (1965). Toward a theory of open and closed groups. *Psychological Bulletin, 64,* 164–182.

Zimbardo, P. G. (1969). The human choice: Individuation, reason, and order versus deindividuation, impulse, and chaos. *Nebraska Symposium on Motivation, 17,* 237–307.

Zimbardo, P. G. (1975). Transforming experimental research into advocacy for social change. In M. Deutsch & H. A. Hornstein (Eds.), *Applying social psychology* (pp. 33–66). Mahwah, NJ: Erlbaum.

Zimbardo, P. G. (1977). *Psychology and life.* Glenview, IL: Scott, Foresman.

Zimbardo, P. G. (2004). A situationist perspective on the psychology of evil: Understanding how good people are transformed into perpetrators. In A. G. Miller (Ed.), *The social psychology of good and evil* (pp. 21–50). New York: Guilford.

Zimbardo, P. G. (2007). *The Lucifer effect.* New York: Random House.

Zimbardo, P. G., Butler, L. D., & Wolfe, V. A. (2003). Cooperative college examinations: More gain, less pain when students share information and grades. *Journal of Experimental Education, 71,* 101–125.

Zimbardo, P. G., Maslach, C., & Haney, C. (2000). Reflections on the Stanford Prison Experiment: Genesis, transformations, consequences. In T. Blass (Ed.), *Obedience to authority: Current perspectives on the Milgram paradigm.* Mahwah, NJ: Erlbaum.

Zubek, J. P. (1973). Behavioral and physiological effects of prolonged sensory and perceptual deprivation: A review. In J. E. Rasmussen (Ed.), *Man in isolation and confinement* (pp. 9–83). Chicago: Aldine.

Zuber, J. A., Crott, H. W., & Werner, J. (1992). Choice shift and group polarization: An analysis of the status of arguments and social decision schemes. *Journal of Personality and Social Psychology, 62,* 50–61.

Zuckerman, E. W., & Jost, J. T. (2001). What makes you think you're so popular? Self-evaluation maintenance and the subjective side of the "friendship paradox." *Social Psychology Quarterly, 64,* 207–223.

Zurcher, L. A., Jr. (1969). Stages of development in poverty program neighborhood action committees. *Journal of Applied Behavioral Science, 15,* 223–258.

Zyphur, M. J., & Islam, G. (2006). *Toward understanding the existence of groups: The relationship between climate strength and entitativity.* IBMEC Working Paper (WPE–12-2006). Retrieved December 15, 2008, from http://www.ibmecsp.edu.br.

Zyphur, M. J., Kaplan, S. A., & Christian, M. S. (2008). Assumptions of cross-level measurement and structural invariance in the analysis of multilevel data: Problems and solutions. *Group Dynamics: Theory, Research, and Practice, 12,* 127–140.

# Author Index

# Subject Index

Page numbers for definitions are in boldface.